THE NEW INTERPRETER'S® BIBLE

IN TWELVE VOLUMES

Volume Seven

EDITORIAL BOARD

THE NEW INTERPRETER'S® BIBLE

GENERAL ARTICLES
&
INTRODUCTION, COMMENTARY, & REFLECTIONS
FOR EACH BOOK OF THE BIBLE
INCLUDING
THE APOCRYPHAL / DEUTEROCANONICAL BOOKS
IN
TWELVE VOLUMES

VOLUME
VII

ABINGDON PRESS
Nashville

THE NEW INTERPRETER'S® BIBLE
VOLUME VII

Copyright © 1996 by Abingdon Press

This book is printed on recycled, acid-free paper.

Library of Congress Cataloging-in-Publication Data

The New Interpreter's Bible: general articles & introduction,
    commentary, & reflections for each book of the Bible, including the
Apocryphal/Deuterocanonical books.
        p. cm.
    Full texts and critical notes of the New International Version and
the New Revised Standard Version of the Bible in parallel columns.
    Includes bibliographical references.
    ISBN 0-687-27820-1 (v. 7: alk. paper)
        1. Bible—Commentaries. 2. Abingdon Press. I. Bible. English.
New International. 1994. II. Bible. English. New Revised
Standard. 1994.
BS491.2.N484 1994
220.7'7—dc20
                                                                                                        94-21092
                                                                                                        CIP

The Hebraica® and Graeca® fonts used to print this work are available from Linguist's Software, Inc., PO Box 580, Edmonds, WA 98020-0580 tel (206) 775-1130.

PUBLICATION STAFF
President and Publisher: Neil M. Alexander
Managing Editor: Michael E. Lawrence
Project Director: Jack A. Keller, Jr.
Assistant Editor: Eli D. Fisher, Jr.
Production Editor: Linda S. Allen
Designer: J. S. Laughbaum
Copy Processing Manager: Sylvia S. Marlow
Composition Specialist: Kathy M. Harding
Publishing Systems Analyst: Glenn R. Hinton
Prepress Manager: William E. Gentry
Prepress Systems Technicians: Thomas E. Mullins
                                            J. Calvin Buckner
Director of Production Processes: James E. Leath
Scheduling: Laurene M. Brazzell
            Tracey D. Seay
Print Procurement Coordinator: David M. Sanders

96 97 98 99 00 01 02 03 04 05—10 9 8 7 6 5 4 3 2 1

MANUFACTURED IN THE UNITED STATES OF AMERICA

CONSULTANTS

NEIL M. ALEXANDER
President and Publisher
The United Methodist Publishing House
Nashville, Tennessee

OWEN F. CAMPION
Associate Publisher
Our Sunday Visitor
Huntington, Indiana

MINERVA G. CARCAÑO
Minister-in-Charge
South Valley Cooperative Ministry
Albuquerque, New Mexico

V. L. DAUGHTERY, JR.
Pastor
Park Avenue United Methodist Church
Valdosta, Georgia

SHARON NEUFER EMSWILER
Pastor
First United Methodist Church
Rock Island, Illinois

JUAN G. FELICIANO VALERA
Pastor
Iglesia Metodista "Juan Wesley"
Arecibo, Puerto Rico

CELIA BREWER MARSHALL
Lecturer
University of North Carolina at Charlotte
Charlotte, North Carolina

NANCY C. MILLER-HERRON
Attorney and clergy member of the
Tennessee Conference
The United Methodist Church
Dresden, Tennessee

ROBERT C. SCHNASE
Pastor
First United Methodist Church
McAllen, Texas

BILL SHERMAN
Pastor
Woodmont Baptist Church
Nashville, Tennessee

RODNEY T. SMOTHERS
Pastor
Central United Methodist Church
Atlanta, Georgia

WILLIAM D. WATLEY
Pastor
St. James African Methodist Episcopal Church
Newark, New Jersey

TALLULAH FISHER WILLIAMS
Pastor
Trinity United Methodist Church
Mt. Prospect, Illinois

SUK-CHONG YU
Pastor
San Francisco Korean United Methodist Church
San Francisco, California

CONTRIBUTORS

ELIZABETH ACHTEMEIER
Adjunct Professor of Bible and Homiletics
Union Theological Seminary in Virginia
Richmond, Virginia
(Presbyterian Church [U.S.A.])
Joel

LESLIE C. ALLEN
Professor of Old Testament
Fuller Theological Seminary
Pasadena, California
(Baptist)
1 & 2 Chronicles

GARY A. ANDERSON
Associate Professor of Religious Studies
University of Virginia
Charlottesville, Virginia
(The Roman Catholic Church)
Introduction to Israelite Religion

DAVID L. BARTLETT
Lantz Professor of Preaching and
Communication
The Divinity School
Yale University
New Haven, Connecticut
(American Baptist Churches in the U.S.A.)
1 Peter

ROBERT A. BENNETT, PH.D.
Cambridge, Massachusetts
(The Episcopal Church)
Zephaniah

ADELE BERLIN
Robert H. Smith Professor of Hebrew Bible
Associate Provost for Faculty Affairs
University of Maryland
College Park, Maryland
Introduction to Hebrew Poetry

BRUCE C. BIRCH
Professor of Old Testament
Wesley Theological Seminary
Washington, DC
(The United Methodist Church)
1 & 2 Samuel

PHYLLIS A. BIRD
Associate Professor of Old Testament
Interpretation
Garrett-Evangelical Theological Seminary
Evanston, Illinois
(The United Methodist Church)
The Authority of the Bible

C. CLIFTON BLACK
Associate Professor of New Testament
Perkins School of Theology
Southern Methodist University
Dallas, Texas
(The United Methodist Church)
1, 2, & 3 John

JOSEPH BLENKINSOPP
John A. O'Brien Professor of Biblical Studies
Department of Theology
University of Notre Dame
Notre Dame, Indiana
(The Roman Catholic Church)
Introduction to the Pentateuch

M. EUGENE BORING
I. Wylie and Elizabeth M. Briscoe Professor of
New Testament
Brite Divinity School
Texas Christian University
Fort Worth, Texas
(Christian Church [Disciples of Christ])
Matthew

WALTER BRUEGGEMANN
William Marcellus McPheeters Professor of Old Testament
Columbia Theological Seminary
Decatur, Georgia
(United Church of Christ)
Exodus

DAVID G. BUTTRICK
Professor of Homiletics and Liturgics
The Divinity School
Vanderbilt University
Nashville, Tennessee
(United Church of Christ)
The Use of the Bible in Preaching

RONALD E. CLEMENTS
Samuel Davidson Professor of Old Testament
King's College
University of London
London, England
(Baptist Union of Great Britain and Ireland)
Deuteronomy

RICHARD J. CLIFFORD
Professor of Old Testament
Weston School of Theology
Cambridge, Massachusetts
(The Roman Catholic Church)
Introduction to Wisdom Literature

JOHN J. COLLINS
Professor of Hebrew Bible
The Divinity School
University of Chicago
Chicago, Illinois
(The Roman Catholic Church)
Introduction to Early Jewish Religion

ROBERT B. COOTE
Professor of Old Testament
San Francisco Theological Seminary
San Anselmo, California
(Presbyterian Church [U.S.A.])
Joshua

FRED B. CRADDOCK
Bandy Distinguished Professor of Preaching and New Testament, Emeritus
Candler School of Theology
Emory University
Atlanta, Georgia
(Christian Church [Disciples of Christ])
Hebrews

TONI CRAVEN
Professor of Hebrew Bible
Brite Divinity School
Texas Christian University
Fort Worth, Texas
(The Roman Catholic Church)
Introduction to Narrative Literature

JAMES L. CRENSHAW
Robert L. Flowers Professor of Old Testament
The Divinity School
Duke University
Durham, North Carolina
(Baptist)
Sirach

KEITH R. CRIM
Pastor
New Concord Presbyterian Church
Concord, Virginia
(Presbyterian Church [U.S.A.])
Modern English Versions of the Bible

R. ALAN CULPEPPER
Dean
The School of Theology
Mercer University
Atlanta, Georgia
(Southern Baptist Convention)
Luke

KATHERYN PFISTERER DARR
Associate Professor of Hebrew Bible
The School of Theology
Boston University
Boston, Massachusetts
(The United Methodist Church)
Ezekiel

ROBERT DORAN
Professor of Religion
Amherst College
Amherst, Massachusetts
1 & 2 Maccabees

THOMAS B. DOZEMAN
Professor of Old Testament
United Theological Seminary
Dayton, Ohio
(Presbyterian Church [U.S.A.])
Numbers

JAMES D. G. DUNN
Lightfoot Professor of Divinity
Department of Theology
University of Durham
Durham, England
(The Methodist Church [Great Britain])
1 & 2 Timothy; Titus

ELDON JAY EPP
Harkness Professor of Biblical Literature
and Chairman of the Department of Religion
Case Western Reserve University
Cleveland, Ohio
(The Episcopal Church)
Ancient Texts and Versions of the New Testament

KATHLEEN ROBERTSON FARMER
Professor of Old Testament
United Theological Seminary
Dayton, Ohio
(The United Methodist Church)
Ruth

CAIN HOPE FELDER
Professor of New Testament Language
and Literature
The School of Divinity
Howard University
Washington, DC
(The United Methodist Church)
Philemon

TERENCE E. FRETHEIM
Professor of Old Testament
Luther Seminary
Saint Paul, Minnesota
(Evangelical Lutheran Church in America)
Genesis

FRANCISCO O. GARCÍA-TRETO
Professor of Religion and Chair of the
Department of Religion
Trinity University
San Antonio, Texas
(Presbyterian Church [U.S.A.])
Nahum

CATHERINE GUNSALUS GONZÁLEZ
Professor of Church History
Columbia Theological Seminary
Decatur, Georgia
(Presbyterian Church [U.S.A.])
The Use of the Bible in Hymns, Liturgy, and Education

JUSTO L. GONZÁLEZ
Adjunct Professor of Church History
Columbia Theological Seminary
Decatur, Georgia
(The United Methodist Church)
How the Bible Has Been Interpreted in Christian Tradition

DONALD E. GOWAN
Robert Cleveland Holland Professor of Old
Testament
Pittsburgh Theological Seminary
Pittsburgh, Pennsylvania
(Presbyterian Church [U.S.A.])
Amos

JUDITH MARIE GUNDRY-VOLF
Assistant Professor of New Testament
Fuller Theological Seminary
Pasadena, California
(Presbyterian Church [U.S.A.])
Ephesians

DANIEL J. HARRINGTON
Professor of New Testament
Weston School of Theology
Cambridge, Massachusetts
(The Roman Catholic Church)
Introduction to the Canon

RICHARD B. HAYS
Associate Professor of New Testament
The Divinity School
Duke University
Durham, North Carolina
(The United Methodist Church)
Galatians

THEODORE HIEBERT
Professor of Old Testament
McCormick Theological
Seminary
Chicago, Illinois
(Mennonite Church)
Habakkuk

CARL R. HOLLADAY
Professor of New Testament
Candler School of Theology
Emory University
Atlanta, Georgia
Contemporary Methods of Reading the Bible

MORNA D. HOOKER
Lady Margaret's Professor of Divinity
The Divinity School
University of Cambridge
Cambridge, England
(The Methodist Church [Great Britain])
Philippians

DAVID C. HOPKINS
Professor of Old Testament
Wesley Theological Seminary
Washington, DC
(United Church of Christ)
Life in Ancient Palestine

DENISE DOMBKOWSKI HOPKINS
Professor of Old Testament
Wesley Theological Seminary
Washington, DC
(United Church of Christ)
Judith

LUKE T. JOHNSON
Robert W. Woodruff Professor of New
Testament and Christian Origins
Candler School of Theology
Emory University
Atlanta, Georgia
(The Roman Catholic Church)
James

WALTER C. KAISER, JR.
Colman Mockler Distinguished Professor
of Old Testament
Gordon-Conwell Theological Seminary
South Hamilton, Massachusetts
(The Evangelical Free Church of America)
Leviticus

LEANDER E. KECK
Winkley Professor of Biblical Theology
The Divinity School
Yale University
New Haven, Connecticut
(Christian Church [Disciples of Christ])
Introduction to The New Interpreter's Bible

CHAN-HIE KIM
Professor of New Testament and Director of
Korean Studies
The School of Theology at Claremont
Claremont, California
(The United Methodist Church)
Reading the Bible as Asian Americans

RALPH W. KLEIN
Dean and Christ Seminary-Seminex Professor of
Old Testament
Lutheran School of Theology at Chicago
Chicago, Illinois
(Evangelical Lutheran Church in America)
Ezra; Nehemiah

MICHAEL KOLARCIK
Assistant Professor
Regis College
Toronto, Ontario
Canada
(The Roman Catholic Church)
Book of Wisdom

WILLIAM L. LANE
Paul T. Walls Professor of Wesleyan
and Biblical Studies
Department of Religion
Seattle Pacific University
Seattle, Washington
(Free Methodist Church of North America)
2 Corinthians

ANDREW T. LINCOLN
Department of Biblical Studies
University of Sheffield
Sheffield, England
(The Church of England)
Colossians

J. CLINTON MCCANN, JR.
Evangelical Associate Professor of
Biblical Interpretation
Eden Theological Seminary
St. Louis, Missouri
(Presbyterian Church [U.S.A.])
Psalms

ABRAHAM J. MALHERBE
Buckingham Professor of New Testament
Criticism and Interpretation, Emeritus
The Divinity School
Yale University
New Haven, Connecticut
(Church of Christ)
*The Cultural Context of the New Testament:
The Greco-Roman World*

W. E<small>UGENE</small> M<small>ARCH</small>
Dean and Arnold Black Rhodes Professor
of Old Testament
Louisville Presbyterian Theological Seminary
Louisville, Kentucky
(Presbyterian Church [U.S.A.])
Haggai

J<small>AMES</small> E<small>ARL</small> M<small>ASSEY</small>
Dean Emeritus and
Distinguished Professor-at-Large
The School of Theology
Anderson University
Preacher-in-Residence, Park Place Church
Anderson, Indiana
(Church of God [Anderson, Ind.])
*Reading the Bible from Particular Social
Locations: An Introduction;
Reading the Bible as African Americans*

J. M<small>AXWELL</small> M<small>ILLER</small>
Professor of Old Testament
Candler School of Theology
Emory University
Atlanta, Georgia
(The United Methodist Church)
Introduction to the History of Ancient Israel

P<small>ATRICK</small> D. M<small>ILLER</small>
Charles T. Haley Professor of Old Testament
Theology
Princeton Theological Seminary
Princeton, New Jersey
(Presbyterian Church [U.S.A.])
Jeremiah

F<small>REDERICK</small> J. M<small>URPHY</small>
Professor
Department of Religious Studies
College of the Holy Cross
Worcester, Massachusetts
(The Roman Catholic Church)
Introduction to Apocalyptic Literature

C<small>AROL</small> A. N<small>EWSOM</small>
Associate Professor of Old Testament
Candler School of Theology
Emory University
Atlanta, Georgia
(The Episcopal Church)
Job

G<small>EORGE</small> W. E. N<small>ICKELSBURG</small>
Professor of Christian Origins and Early Judaism
School of Religion
University of Iowa
Iowa City, Iowa
(Evangelical Lutheran Church in America)
*The Jewish Context of the New
Testament*

I<small>RENE</small> N<small>OWELL</small>
Associate Professor of Religious Studies
Benedictine College
Atchison, Kansas
(The Roman Catholic Church)
Tobit

K<small>ATHLEEN</small> M. O'C<small>ONNOR</small>
Professor of Old Testament Language,
Literature, and Exegesis
Columbia Theological Seminary
Decatur, Georgia
(The Roman Catholic Church)
Lamentations

G<small>AIL</small> R. O'D<small>AY</small>
Almar H. Shatford Associate Professor of Homiletics
Candler School of Theology
Emory University
Atlanta, Georgia
(United Church of Christ)
John

B<small>EN</small> C. O<small>LLENBURGER</small>
Professor of Biblical Theology
Associated Mennonite Biblical Seminary
Elkhart, Indiana
(Mennonite Church)
Zechariah

D<small>ENNIS</small> T. O<small>LSON</small>
Assistant Professor of Old Testament
Princeton Theological Seminary
Princeton, New Jersey
(Evangelical Lutheran Church in America)
Judges

C<small>AROLYN</small> O<small>SIEK</small>
Professor of New Testament
Department of Biblical Languages
and Literature
Catholic Theological Union
Chicago, Illinois
(The Roman Catholic Church)
Reading the Bible as Women

SAMUEL PAGÁN
President
Evangelical Seminary of Puerto Rico
San Juan, Puerto Rico
(Christian Church [Disciples of Christ])
Obadiah

SIMON B. PARKER
Associate Professor of Hebrew Bible and
Harrell F. Beck Scholar in Hebrew Scripture
The School of Theology
Boston University
Boston, Massachusetts
(The United Methodist Church)
*The Ancient Near Eastern Literary
Background of the Old Testament*

PHEME PERKINS
Professor of New Testament
Boston College
Chestnut Hill, Massachusetts
(The Roman Catholic Church)
Mark

DAVID L. PETERSEN
Professor of Old Testament
The Iliff School of Theology
Denver, Colorado
(Presbyterian Church [U.S.A.])
Introduction to Prophetic Literature

CHRISTOPHER C. ROWLAND
Dean Ireland's Professor of the Exegesis
of Holy Scripture
The Queen's College
Oxford, England
(The Church of England)
Revelation

ANTHONY J. SALDARINI
Professor of Biblical Studies
Boston College
Chestnut Hill, Massachusetts
(The Roman Catholic Church)
Baruch; Letter of Jeremiah

J. PAUL SAMPLEY
Professor of New Testament and
Christian Origins
The School of Theology and The Graduate Division
Boston University
Boston, Massachusetts
(The United Methodist Church)
1 Corinthians

JUDITH E. SANDERSON
Assistant Professor of Hebrew Bible
Department of Theology and Religious Studies
Seattle University
Seattle, Washington
*Ancient Texts and Versions of the Old
Testament*

EILEEN M. SCHULLER, O.S.U.
Professor
Department of Religious Studies
McMaster University
Hamilton, Ontario
Canada
(The Roman Catholic Church)
Malachi

FERNANDO F. SEGOVIA
Associate Professor of New Testament
and Early Christianity
The Divinity School
Vanderbilt University
Nashville, Tennessee
(The Roman Catholic Church)
Reading the Bible as Hispanic Americans

CHRISTOPHER R. SEITZ
Associate Professor of Old Testament
The Divinity School
Yale University
New Haven, Connecticut
(The Episcopal Church)
Isaiah 40–66

CHOON-LEONG SEOW
Associate Professor of Old Testament
Princeton Theological Seminary
Princeton, New Jersey
(Presbyterian Church [U.S.A.])
1 & 2 Kings

MICHAEL A. SIGNER
Abrams Professor of Jewish Thought and
Culture
Department of Theology
University of Notre Dame
Notre Dame, Indiana
*How the Bible Has Been Interpreted in
Jewish Tradition*

MOISÉS SILVA
Professor of New Testament
Westminster Theological Seminary
Philadelphia, Pennsylvania
(The Orthodox Presbyterian Church)
*Contemporary Theories of Biblical
Interpretation*

DANIEL J. SIMUNDSON
Professor of Old Testament
Luther Seminary
Saint Paul, Minnesota
(Evangelical Lutheran Church in America)
Micah

ABRAHAM SMITH
Assistant Professor of New Testament
and Christian Origins
The School of Theology
Boston University
Boston, Massachusetts
(The National Baptist Convention, USA, Inc.)
1 & 2 Thessalonians

DANIEL L. SMITH-CHRISTOPHER
Associate Professor of Theological Studies
Department of Theology
Loyola Marymount University
Los Angeles, California
(The Society of Friends [Quaker])
*Daniel; Bel and the Dragon; Prayer of
Azariah; Susannah*

MARION L. SOARDS
Professor of New Testament Studies
Louisville Presbyterian Theological Seminary
Louisville, Kentucky
(Presbyterian Church [U.S.A.])
Acts

ROBERT C. TANNEHILL
Academic Dean and Harold B. Williams
Professor of Biblical Studies
Methodist Theological School in Ohio
Delaware, Ohio
(The United Methodist Church)
The Gospels and Narrative Literature

GEORGE E. TINKER
Associate Professor of Cross-Cultural Ministries
The Iliff School of Theology
Denver, Colorado
(Evangelical Lutheran Church in America)
Reading the Bible as Native Americans

W. SIBLEY TOWNER
The Reverend Archibald McFadyen Professor of
Biblical Interpretation
Union Theological Seminary in Virginia
Richmond, Virginia
(Presbyterian Church [U.S.A.])
Ecclesiastes

PHYLLIS TRIBLE
Baldwin Professor of Sacred Literature
Union Theological Seminary
New York, New York
Jonah

GENE M. TUCKER
Professor of Old Testament, Emeritus
Candler School of Theology
Emory University
Atlanta, Georgia
(The United Methodist Church)
Isaiah 1–39

CHRISTOPHER M. TUCKETT
Rylands Professor of Biblical Criticism
and Exegesis
Faculty of Theology
University of Manchester
Manchester, England
(The Church of England)
Jesus and the Gospels

RAYMOND C. VAN LEEUWEN
Professor of Religion and Theology
Eastern College
Saint Davids, Pennsylvania
(Christian Reformed Church in North America)
Proverbs

ROBERT W. WALL
Professor of Biblical Studies
Department of Religion
Seattle Pacific University
Seattle, Washington
(Free Methodist Church of North America)
Introduction to Epistolary Literature

DUANE F. WATSON
Associate Professor of New Testament Studies
Department of Religion and Philosophy
Malone College
Canton, Ohio
(The United Methodist Church)
2 Peter; Jude

RENITA J. WEEMS
Associate Professor of Hebrew Bible
The Divinity School
Vanderbilt University
Nashville, Tennessee
(African Methodist Episcopal Church)
Song of Songs

SIDNIE A. WHITE
Assistant Professor of Religion
Department of Religion
Albright College
Reading, Pennsylvania
(The Episcopal Church)
Esther; Additions to Esther

VINCENT L. WIMBUSH
Professor of New Testament and
Christian Origins
Union Theological Seminary
New York, New York
(Progressive National Baptist Convention, Inc.)
*The Ecclesiastical Context of the New
Testament*

N. THOMAS WRIGHT
Lecturer in New Testament Studies
Fellow, Tutor, and Chaplain
Worcester College
Oxford, England
(The Church of England)
Romans

GALE A. YEE
Associate Professor of Old Testament
Department of Theology
University of Saint Thomas
Saint Paul, Minnesota
(The Roman Catholic Church)
Hosea

FEATURES OF
THE NEW INTERPRETER'S® BIBLE

The general aim of *The New Interpreter's Bible* is to bring the best in contemporary biblical scholarship into the service of the church to enhance preaching, teaching, and study of the Scriptures. To accomplish that general aim, the design of *The New Interpreter's Bible* has been shaped by two controlling principles: (1) form serves function, and (2) maximize ease of use.

General articles provide the reader with concise, up-to-date, balanced introductions and assessments of selected topics. In most cases, a brief bibliography points the way to further exploration of a topic. Many of the general articles are placed in volumes 1 and 8, at the beginning of the coverage of the Old and New Testaments, respectively. Others have been inserted in those volumes where the reader will encounter the corresponding type of literature (e.g., "Introduction to Prophetic Literature" appears in Volume 6 alongside several of the prophetic books).

Coverage of each biblical book begins with an "Introduction" that acquaints the reader with the essential historical, sociocultural, literary, and theological issues necessary to understand the biblical book. A short bibliography and an outline of the biblical book are found at the end of each Introduction. The introductory sections are the only material in *The New Interpreter's Bible* printed in a single wide-column format.

The biblical text is divided into coherent and manageable primary units, which are located within larger sections of Scripture. At the opening discussion of any large section of Scripture, readers will often find material identified as "Overview," which includes remarks applicable to the large section of text. The primary unit of text may be as short as a few verses or as long as a chapter or more. This is the point at which the biblical text itself is reprinted in *The New Interpreter's Bible*. Dealing with Scripture in terms of these primary units allows discussion of important issues that are overlooked in a verse-by-verse treatment. Each scriptural unit is identified by text citation and a short title.

The full texts and critical notes of the New International Version and the New Revised Standard Version of the Bible are presented in parallel columns for quick reference. (For the Apocryphal/Deuterocanonical works, the NIV is replaced by The New American Bible.) Since every translation is to some extent an interpretation as well, the inclusion of these widely known and influential modern translations provides an easy comparison that in many cases will lead to a better understanding of a passage. Biblical passages are set in a two-column format and placed in green tint-blocks to make it easy to recognize them at a glance. The NAB, NIV, and NRSV material is clearly identified on each page on which the text appears.

Immediately following each biblical text is a section marked "Commentary," which provides an exegetical analysis informed by linguistic, text-critical, historical-critical, literary, social-scientific, and theological methods. The Commentary serves as a reliable, judicious guide through the text, pointing out the critical problems as well as key interpretive issues.

The exegetical approach is "text-centered." That is, the commentators focus primarily on the text in its final form rather than on (a) a meticulous rehearsal of problems of scholarship associated with a text, (b) a thorough reconstruction of the pre-history of the text, or (c) an exhaustive rehearsal of the text's interpretive history. Of course, some attention to scholarly problems, to the pre-history of a text, and to historic interpretations that have shaped streams of tradition is important in particular cases precisely in order to illumine the several levels of meaning in the final form of the text. But the *primary* focus is on the canonical text itself. Moreover, the Commentary not only describes pertinent aspects of the text, but also teaches the reader what to look for in the text so as to develop the reader's own capacity to analyze and interpret the text.

Commentary material runs serially for a few paragraphs or a few pages, depending on what is required by the biblical passage under discussion.

Commentary material is set in a two-column format. Occasional subheads appear in a bold green font. The next level of subdivisions appears as bold black fonts and a third level as black italic fonts. Footnotes are placed at the bottom of the column in which the superscripts appear.

Key words in Hebrew, Aramaic, or Greek are printed in the original-language font, accompanied by a transliteration and a translation or explanation.

Immediately following the Commentary, in most cases, is the section called "Reflections." A detailed exposition growing directly out of the discussion and issues dealt with in the Commentary, the Reflections are geared specifically toward helping those who interpret Scripture in the life of the church by providing "handles" for grasping the significance of Scripture for faith and life today. Recognizing that the text has the capacity to shape the life of the Christian community, this section presents multiple possibilities for preaching and teaching in light of each biblical text. That is, instead of providing the preacher or teacher full illustrations, poems, outlines, and the like, the Reflections offer *several* trajectories of possible interpretation that connect with the situation of the contemporary listeners. Recognizing the power of Scripture to speak anew to diverse situations, not all of the suggested trajectories could be appropriated on any one occasion. Preachers and teachers want some specificity about the implications of the text, but not so much specificity that the work is done for them. The ideas in the Reflections are meant to stimulate the thought of preachers and teachers, not to replace it.

Three-quarter width columns distinguish Reflections materials from biblical text and Commentary.

Occasional excursuses have been inserted in some volumes to address topics of special importance that are best treated apart from the flow of Commentary and Reflections on specific passages. Set in three-quarter width columns, excursuses are identified graphically by a green color bar that runs down the outside margin of the page.

Occasional maps, charts, and illustrations appear throughout the volumes at points where they are most likely to be immediately useful to the reader.

CONTENTS

VOLUME VII

CONTENTS

INTRODUCTION TO APOCALYPTIC LITERATURE

FREDERICK J. MURPHY

The terms *apocalypticism, apocalypse,* and *apocalyptic* are widely used within biblical scholarship, and they also appear in more popular settings—literature, film, and the news media, for example. The words derive from the Greek ἀποκάλυψις (*apokalypsis*), which means "revelation." Modern use of these words to describe a certain kind of literature and a specific worldview is due to the book of Revelation, which begins, "The revelation [*apokalypsis*] of Jesus Christ." The book of Revelation is often called the Apocalypse, and the title "Revelation" is simply a translation of that term. Beginning in the nineteenth century, scholars perceived similarities of form and content between Revelation and other ancient Jewish and Christian works, so they began to call such works "apocalypses" by analogy. Other ancient works written after Revelation explicitly call themselves apocalypses, but none before. Nonetheless, many Jewish works written before Revelation share its literary genre.

Until the 1970s, the word *apocalyptic* was used as a noun, denoting a rather amorphous entity made up of certain texts, a specific kind of imagery, vision reports, a variety of worldviews, and particular social groups. A wide range of Jewish and Christian texts, many of them not apocalypses, were used in this construction of "apocalyptic." The resulting construct was then used to interpret specific texts, persons, and events. Ideas like "apocalyptic move-ment" emerged, implying that there was a single movement that could be called apocalyptic in which the various expressions of the phenomenon were included. The problem with this approach is that the theoretical "apocalyptic" that results does not always fit the apocalypses. There is tremendous variation in apocalypses with respect to form and content, beliefs, expectations, historical circumstances, political positions, and so on. Nothing like a single apocalyptic movement ever existed. A basic worldview is common to all apocalypses, but it is common in the Hellenistic world even outside apocalypses, leaving room for a wide spectrum of particular apocalyptic theologies and ideologies.

Greater precision is attained through distinguishing between apocalypse as a literary genre, apocalypticism as a worldview, and "apocalyptic" as an adjective applied in the first instance to apocalypses and in a derivative way to texts and ideas that have much in common with apocalypses. What is apocalyptic is first of all what one finds in apocalypses. Anything else is apocalyptic by comparison. Further, it is no longer assumed that a given text necessarily represents a historical community or movement, rather than the point of view of an individual or of a small group fairly indistinguishable from society as a whole. The basics of the apocalyptic worldview were widespread enough in the Hellenistic world that apocalypses do not necessarily imply a sectarian group that produced and preserved them. The judgment about whether a sect stands behind a given apocalypse must be made anew for each text.

The book of Daniel in the Hebrew Bible and the book of Revelation in the New Testament are the only biblical examples of apocalypses. But apocalyptic influence in the Bible is far broader than that fact suggests. A number of prophetic texts written during and after the Babylonian exile share features of content and form with the apocalypses, so they are sometimes called "proto-apocalyptic." Apocalyptic influence is also evident throughout most of the New Testament. Of course, the Bible presents only aspects of ancient Judaism and Christianity, thus it is part of the task of biblical scholars to look beyond the canon to situate the biblical texts within their original contexts. In this connection, it is noteworthy that a substantial proportion of Jewish literature written between 300 BCE and 200 CE is either in the form of apocalypses or displays apocalyptic features. Likewise, apocalypses and apocalyptic thought played a prominent role in early Christianity. This article concentrates on the period between 300 BCE and 200 CE. References to and analyses of specific apocalypses are illustrative rather than exhaustive.

THE APOCALYPTIC GENRE

The first step in discussing apocalyptic literature is to decide which texts are apocalypses. In the late 1970s, a group of scholars examined all documents considered apocalypses and constructed a definition that fits all of them and distinguishes them from other sorts of ancient literature.[1] All apocalypses are narratives, stories describing the disclosure of otherwise inaccessible secrets to a human seer by a heavenly being. The disclosures are usually through visions. (The term *seer* literally means "see-er," one who sees visions.) Often the visions themselves are enigmatic and must be interpreted by a heavenly being, usually an angel. There are two main kinds of apocalyptic narratives. In the first, the seer travels to the heavenly realm or to parts of the cosmos usually inaccessible to human beings. The second type contains no otherworldly journey. This type often incorporates a review of history, culminating in an eschatological crisis and resolution, such as a conflict between the forces of good and evil, resulting in evil's defeat. That review is frequently in the form of fictive "prediction" of history (actually, the past of the real author) by the pseudonymous seer, a device known as *vaticinia ex eventu,* "prophecies after the event." At the end of such reviews is genuine prediction of things to happen in the author's future. A Jewish apocalypse from the end of the first century CE, the *Apocalypse of Abraham,* contains both an otherworldly journey and a review of history, but such a combination is unusual.

Apocalyptic revelation has temporal and spatial dimensions. The spatial aspect deals with the supernatural world, often conceived of as being above or below this world. It sometimes involves a heaven divided into levels, and it discloses the activities of supernatural beings, such as angels and demons. The natural and supernatural realms are closely interrelated. Decisions made in the supernatural realm or events that transpire there affect and sometimes determine what happens on earth. Conversely, earthly events can have repercussions in the supernatural world. True understanding of historical events and concrete earthly circumstances requires knowledge of the heavenly world not generally available. The temporal aspect of apocalyptic revelation concerns eschatological judgment. That judgment can involve cosmic catastrophe and public judgment of all humanity, a scenario that conforms to what is popularly termed apocalyptic, but it might involve only individual judgment after death. The element common to all apocalypses is postmortem rewards and punishments, an idea that enters Judaism through the medium of apocalypticism, since it does not occur elsewhere in the Hebrew Bible. Israel's religion as presented in the Hebrew Bible is focused on this life. After death, good and bad alike descend into Sheol and live a shadowy existence that bears little resemblance to later concepts of heaven and hell. Daniel is the only biblical book in which transcendence of death through resurrection is clearly attested, and it is the last-written book to be included in the Hebrew Bible (c. 165 BCE). Even before Daniel, transcendence of death is expressed in the *Book of the Watchers,* a Jewish apocalypse from the third century BCE, now preserved as *1 Enoch* 1–36. Resurrection becomes a regular feature of apocalyptic scenarios of the eschaton. The future life is often conceived of as taking place in the supernatural realm. In Daniel 12 and *2 Baruch* 51, for example, the righteous join the stars. In other

1. See John J. Collins, ed., *Apocalypse: The Morphology of a Genre,* Semeia 14 (Missoula, Mont.: Scholars Press, 1979).

instances, there is a new heaven and a new earth in which the saved live. In Revelation 21–22, the new Jerusalem descends to earth, and God and Christ live on the new earth with the righteous.

All Jewish apocalypses and many Christian ones are pseudonymous. The seer is an ancient hero, such as Enoch, Abraham, Moses, Baruch, or Ezra. Such attributions enhance the authority of the works. The specific choice of seer is often appropriate. Three Jewish apocalypses were written as responses to the destruction of the Jerusalem Temple by the Romans in 70 CE. *Second Baruch* is attributed to a writer who lived through the earlier destruction of the Temple by the Babylonians in 587 BCE. Fourth Ezra is credited to the scribe who brought the Torah back to Israel after the Babylonian exile, and the work ends with Ezra reconstituting the Torah, which was burned in the destruction, by dictating it to scribes (4 Ezra 14). The *Apocalypse of Abraham* takes the vision experienced by Abraham in Genesis 15 as the occasion of a sweeping view of world history that puts the destruction of the Temple into perspective. A large number of apocalypses were assigned to Enoch. At least five such apocalypses are now preserved in a collection called *1 Enoch,* preserved in Ethiopic, in Aramaic fragments from Qumran, in several Greek fragments, and in one Latin fragment. Enoch appears in Gen 5:24 as one who walked with God—i.e., as righteous. It is stated enigmatically that "God took him," a phrase later interpreted as God's taking him to heaven. Enoch thus became an appropriate figure to whom heavenly revelations could be given. In *1 Enoch* 14, he makes a trip to the heavenly throne room, and in chapters 17–36 he tours parts of the cosmos not accessible to other humans.

Although apocalypses are often permeated by scriptural language, images, and patterns, they do not try to convince their readers through exegesis of Scripture. Nor is rational persuasion their technique. Rather, the authority of an apocalypse comes from the seer's direct reception of revelation. In effect, the author claims divine authority for the content of the apocalypse. Apocalypses are the more compelling in that they do not merely relay information, but allow their readers to accompany the seer through the process of revelation by describing that process in detail. So, for example, the readers experience Enoch's awe as he enters the heavenly sanctuary (*1 Enoch* 14), Daniel's terror as he sees mysterious beasts arising from the sea and a powerful

angel descending from heaven (Daniel 7; 10), John's wonder as he sees the great harlot dressed in crimson and purple and riding on the seven-headed, ten-horned beast (Revelation 17). Through such means, apocalypses do more than convey information or demand specific behavior. They also contain a powerful emotional element that cannot be translated into other terms. They allow the reader to experience the supernatural world that affects this one and to see firsthand the coming eschatological judgment. Through that experience they can put their own circumstances into perspective. Through historical apocalypses, readers can contemplate history as a whole and understand their place in it. Apocalypses concerned with politics can allow readers to perceive their struggles with evil rulers as part of a larger struggle between good and evil forces. They derive hope from the knowledge that as in the mythological combat between the most high God and forces inimical to divine order, good will be victorious.

Discussions of apocalyptic genre have been complicated by the fact that apocalypses are sometimes found embedded in other genres, that they frequently incorporate other genres, and that apocalyptic elements can be found in a variety of texts. Two other genres show particular affinities with apocalypses: testaments and oracle collections. Testaments are last words of major figures before their deaths. The form was popular in the period under consideration. A common element in testaments is prediction of the future. Such predictions often include eschatological scenarios and so are suited for apocalyptic predictions. There are many such passages in the *Testaments of the Twelve Patriarchs,* and one of the texts in that collection, the *Testament of Levi,* contains a short apocalypse in chapters 2–5. In the *Testament of Moses,* Moses predicts the course of Israel's history, culminating in the appearance of God's kingdom (chap. 10). Satan is destroyed, and God comes as the divine warrior to put an end to idols and to vindicate Israel.

The prophetic books in the Hebrew Bible are for the most part oracle collections. Their relevance for the apocalypses will be examined below. Another oracle collection that is very significant for the study of Jewish apocalyptic literature is the *Sibylline Oracles.* The notion of a woman prophet (sibyl) who utters prophecies of a political nature was taken over by the Jews from their environment in the Hellenistic period. Sibylline collections also figured largely in Greek and Roman settings. The *Sibylline Oracles* in standard editions are Jewish (books 3–5 and 11–14) and Christian (only books 6 and 7 were originally Christian; the others adapt Jewish works). Although the form of revelation is quite different from that found in apocalypses, they contain political prophecy that resembles what is found in many historical apocalypses. They employ mythological elements; criticize the present state of affairs, particularly Roman rulers; and predict future disaster.

WORLDVIEW

The form and content of apocalypses imply a basic worldview common to all of them. There is a supernatural world that is closely related to this one, and there is an eschatological judgment for humans and often for supernatural beings as well. This basic foundation allows for a wide variety of theologies, messages, and social ideologies.

Most past scholarship on apocalypticism has been dominated by Christian concerns. Since eschatology and messianism are so important to early Christian thought, those aspects of apocalypses, both Jewish and Christian, have often attracted attention disproportionate to their actual importance in apocalyptic literature. That imbalance is now being addressed by studies that do greater justice to the noneschatological and nonmessianic nature of many of the revelations in particular apocalypses. The heavenly journey apocalypses in particular show an interest in a wide range of topics—cosmology, meteorology, astronomy, astrology, calendar, angelology, etc.—in addition to eschatology. Many of the topics addressed by such apocalypses do not receive much attention in the Hebrew Bible. Such apocalypses may not conform to what is popularly thought of as apocalyptic, because they do not always contain cosmic upheavals or eschatological sufferings. But they share with the historical apocalypses interest in the supernatural world, a world that is crucial for understanding this one, and belief in rewards and punishments after death.

Apocalypses frequently display some degree of dualism. A distinction is drawn between this world and the supernatural realm and between life before and life after death. Some apocalypses go beyond these dualisms to see a cosmic dualism consisting of an opposition between supernatural forces of good and evil. This is not a thoroughgoing dualism, pos-

iting an evil entity equal to God. Rather, it opposes lesser forces, such as Michael against Satan (Revelation 12), Michael against Belial,[2] Gabriel and Michael against the heavenly patrons of Persia and Greece (Daniel 10; cf. Jesus against Satan in the Gospel of Mark). God is always supreme. The degree of cosmic dualism varies across the apocalypses, and so it cannot be taken as a universal characteristic of them.

Social dualism is also frequent in apocalypses and is correlated with cosmic dualism when present. Humanity is divided into good and evil, the elect and the rest, those who are being saved and those who are perishing (see 1 Cor 1:18). There is a final struggle between good and evil, which usually involves supernatural powers. The nature of human participation in that struggle varies. In Daniel, it is God who destroys Judaism's enemy, the Seleucid king Antiochus IV Epiphanes, and the heavenly patrons of various nations clash with Gabriel and Michael. In Revelation, Christians participate in the battle against Satan and Rome only through their witness to Christ and their refusal to accommodate themselves to Hellenistic culture and to the imperial cult. Christ has already defeated Satan in his death and resurrection. Satan has been ejected from heaven by Michael and the good angels (Revelation 12) and now wages war against Christians on earth. The final military victory is fought between Christ and his heavenly armies on the one side and Satan and his allies on the other.

All apocalypses involve eschatology, but some forms of apocalypticism have a strong eschatological focus. The conflict between good and evil will be resolved through victory for the forces of good. That victory is conceptualized in many ways. It may be renewal of the earth, where life will be lived as it should be, in union with God and without evil of any sort, or it may be a future heavenly existence for humans.

THE ORIGINS OF APOCALYPTICISM

The origins of apocalypses and apocalypticism have been a major preoccupation of scholars. The main debate has been between those who consider apocalypses to be a natural development of elements already existent within Judaism and those who see

2. See 1QM 17.

apocalypticism as a foreign entity, imported from the Gentile world. The most widely accepted position today is that apocalypses resulted from a complex interplay of foreign and domestic elements. The debate over whether apocalypticism is authentically Jewish can be misleading. Israel was always to some degree open to outside influences. Israelite and Jewish religion was full of elements adapted from its environment. The Hellenistic age saw a particularly fertile interaction of different cultures and national and ethnic heritages, and Judaism shared in that interaction. Writers of Jewish apocalypses responded to the new conditions and circumstances of the Hellenistic and Roman periods, and they used both domestic and foreign elements to do so.

The Hebrew Bible furnishes much raw material for apocalypticism. The idea that God communicates in mysterious dreams or visions that require inspired interpretation is found in the story of Joseph in Egypt (Genesis 40–41) as well as in the books of Zechariah and Ezekiel. That God controls human events from the heavenly court is clear in the story of the prophet Micaiah ben Imlah, who is granted a view of God deciding to send a lying spirit into Ahab's prophets so as to mislead him (1 Kings 22). The apocalyptic picture of a warrior God who intervenes in history to defeat evil has its roots in the notion of the divine warrior, a common biblical idea.

Efforts to find the origins of Jewish apocalypticism in Israel's proverbial and speculative wisdom tradition have not won many supporters, but the exilic and post-exilic prophets are a particularly fruitful source of comparison. Zechariah attests to the vision-reaction-interpretation pattern common in apocalypses. Ezekiel contains extended metaphors, such as the prostitute of chapter 16, which Revelation uses in chapter 17 (see also the oracles against Babylon in Jeremiah 50–51). Ezekiel's vision in chapters 40–48 of the restored Jerusalem inspired later apocalyptic visions. The visions of the heavenly throne room found in texts such as *1 Enoch* 14, Daniel 7, and Revelation 4–5 find counterparts in the earlier visions of Isaiah 6 and Ezekiel 1. Beyond formal similarities there are also similarities of content. Although prophetic texts never contain the idea of postmortem rewards and punishments, they do provide elements that were used in apocalyptic eschatological scenarios. A good example is Isaiah 24–27, often called the Isaiah Apocalypse, although it is not written in the form of an apocalypse. Isaiah

24:21-23 speaks of punishment of the heavenly host and earthly kings who are shut up in prison until a final punishment. This is like the scheme found in the *Book of the Watchers* (see also Revelation 20). Isaiah 26:19 calls for the rising of those who dwell in the dust, an apparent reference to resurrection. This may be simply a metaphor, as is the revivification of dry bones in Ezekiel 37, but it at least hints at the later apocalyptic idea of resurrection. Zechariah 14 and Ezekiel 38–39 speak of a great eschatological battle, and those texts inspired later versions of the final battle between forces for and against God.

Apocalypses differ from prophetic texts in their combination of heavy use of techniques like vision-reaction-interpretation and heavenly journeys, intense interest in the supernatural world, and eschatology that includes transcendence of death. Each of these elements was common in the Hellenistic world, as were pseudepigraphy, periodization of history, and *ex eventu* prophecy.

Scholars have noted phenomena in Persian, Egyptian, and Mesopotamian texts that correspond to features of Jewish apocalypses. Persian sources contain evidence of resurrection, postmortem judgment, division of history into periods, eschatological tumult, dualistic conflict between the forces of good and evil, and the ascent of the soul. Although the Persian sources are difficult to date, it is likely that many of these ideas go back at least to the Hellenistic period, if not before. Egyptian sources provide examples of political prophecy, as do Mesopotamian texts. Mesopotamia also furnishes examples of *ex eventu* prophecy combined with authentic prediction, as is found in Daniel 11. Daniel 8 betrays the influence of Mesopotamian astrology.

It is difficult to know precisely how these influences fed into Israel's traditions so as to emerge in apocalypses. It is possible that Jews in the eastern diaspora were the first to incorporate such features into their works and worldview. The seer of the two earliest extant Jewish apocalypses, the *Book of the Watchers* and the *Astronomical Book* (*1 Enoch* 72–82), is Enoch. The figure of Enoch originates in Gen 5:18-24, but it has been developed according to the model of the Enmeduranki, who was the seventh of the kings on the Sumerian king list. Enmeduranki founded an association of Babylonian diviners. The book of Daniel shows various Eastern influences, and the stories in the first six chapters of the book are set in the royal courts of Babylonia, Media, and Persia. Those stories may have originally existed independently of the book of Daniel and have come from the eastern diaspora. But given the fluid interchange of ideas, symbolism, and traditions that marked the Hellenistic age in general and the amount of Hellenistic influence that occurred even among Palestinian Jews, it is unwise to draw too sharp a distinction between the Jews in the diaspora and those who remained in the homeland. Both groups were influenced by their Hellenistic environment, thus both can be called Hellenistic Jews, although perhaps to different degrees and in different ways.

Apocalypses make creative use of mythology. Indeed, they are more heavily mythological than is the Hebrew Bible itself. Although the Hebrew Bible contains mythological elements, they are often historicized. They are not related as full myths, but are used to comment on or to embellish Israel's history. Nonetheless, some parts of the Hebrew Bible, the book of Psalms and Second Isaiah, for example, do attest to a certain vitality of mythology in Israel. Apocalypses tap into the deep wellsprings of ancient Near Eastern mythology. In doing so, they render fuller versions of some myths that are used more sparingly in the Hebrew Bible. For example, Gen 6:1-4 briefly recounts the descent of angels to have intercourse with human women, resulting in offspring who were giants. The story is mentioned, but not developed. A much fuller version of this story appears in the *Book of the Watchers,* where the watchers' development of their plan, their descent, and its consequences are related in much more detail. The angels' descent becomes the explanation for the existence of evil in the world. Another example of a more developed mythology concerns the punishment of humans and supernatural figures mentioned in passing in Isa 24:21-23. They "will be gathered together like prisoners in a pit" and "shut up in a prison" (Isa 24:22 NRSV) until the time of their punishment. This pattern is found in much greater detail in the *Book of the Watchers,* and it may have influenced the story of the binding, releasing, and defeat of Satan in Revelation 20. A last example involves the combat myth, the notion that there once was a great battle between supernatural figures that determined the subsequent course of the universe. One finds that myth in various forms throughout the ancient Near East. It serves as a model for Revelation 12 and Dan 8:10.

The proximate sources for the mythological traditions found in Jewish and Christian apocalypses are something of an open question. The cult may well have preserved mythological elements that are not entirely clear through our extant texts. Israel may also have passed down such elements in its general culture or adopted them from its environment at different stages of its history. Since Jews lived in the Hellenistic world, which was characterized by a fertile interaction of cultures, their literature may have received many elements from that interaction. In any case, scholarship will not grasp the meaning of apocalypses merely by tracing the origin of their individual traditions. Apocalypses must be read as whole units and as creative responses to the new conditions of the Hellenistic world.

Another open question is to what extent apocalypses attest to actual visions experienced by their authors. There is not enough evidence to decide the answer to this question definitively. The descriptions of preparations to receive revelations found in some apocalypses suggest genuine techniques to induce visions. Some scholars have pointed to the scribal nature of apocalypses and their heavy use of tradition to argue against this position, but apocalypses may be the results of learned elaboration of an original experience rather than a simple description of what actually happened to the seer. Some scholars have attempted to develop criteria by which it might be decided which apocalyptic passages represent real visions and which are stylized accounts, but no set of criteria has won general approval. What is clear is that the authors of apocalypses expected their claims to visionary experience to be taken seriously and to affect their audiences profoundly.

Apocalypses have often been considered crisis literature, composed during times of oppression or even persecution. Two crises in the Second Temple period led to the production of apocalypses. When Antiochus IV Epiphanes, the Seleucid king, tried to outlaw Judaism in 167 BCE, one result was the Maccabean revolt, and another was the writing of apocalypses. Daniel dates to this time, as does a small apocalypse embedded in the collection called *1 Enoch:* the *Animal Apocalypse* (*1 Enoch* 85–90). The *Apocalypse of Weeks* (*1 Enoch* 93:1-10; 91:12-17) probably dates from about the same time. The

Animal Apocalypse clearly supports the militant resistance of the Maccabees and sees it as the culmination of history, leading to the messianic era. But Daniel takes a more quietistic stand. Humans are not expected to take up arms, a fact that makes it seem unlikely that the author had much enthusiasm for the revolt. Daniel 11:34 may refer to the Maccabees as "a little help" (NRSV), judging them to be ultimately irrelevant to the solution of the problem. The real solution will be provided by God's direct intervention. The differing stands taken by these contemporary apocalypses show that the apocalyptic worldview does not imply any special political ideology. Another crisis that led to the writing of apocalypses was the Roman destruction of Jerusalem and its Temple in 70 CE. Shortly afterward, four apocalypses appeared: 4 Ezra, *2 Baruch,* the *Apocalypse of Abraham,* and probably *3 Baruch.*

Although many apocalypses clearly arise from circumstances of crisis, that is not so clear for others. No public crisis is obvious in the *Similitudes of Enoch (1 Enoch* 37–71), the *Testament of Abraham, 2 Enoch,* or the *Apocalypse of Zephaniah,* for example. Of course, what constitutes a crisis may be in the eye of the beholder. What might look like a period of prosperity and peace from the viewpoint of the well-to-do can appear as a time of oppression and suffering to those at the bottom of the social hierarchy. Even those who are not poor or obviously oppressed might see a crisis in the fact that a foreign power rules their land. Recent research on Revelation and its social and political setting agrees that there was no large-scale persecution of Christianity in the late first century under Emperor Domitian, when Revelation was written. Opposition to Christianity, where it existed at all, was probably local and resulted not in Christians' being thrown to the beasts, but in informal social and economic sanctions on a small scale. The function of Revelation may have been less to comfort Christians at the onset of a major persecution than to warn them of the demonic nature of the Roman Empire so as to discourage the accommodation to Hellenistic and Roman culture that the author observed going on around him.

Although a crisis setting is not provable or even probable for many apocalypses, they all express, at least implicitly, a dissatisfaction with the temporal world. The impulse to explore the supernatural world and to look beyond death is due at least in part to a perception that all is not as it should be on earth. The wrong king may be on the throne, a foreign power may occupy the land, there may be laxity in ordering society according to God's will.

APOCALYPTIC DISCOURSE

The way that apocalypses make meaning is foreign to most modern people. Scholars have often dealt with the strangeness of apocalypticism by reducing it to more understandable terms. At times, apocalypses have been treated as encoded forms of exhortation, timeless truths, or descriptions of historical situations. At other times, they have been treated as sources from which to extract bits of information about topics of interest, such as messianism and eschatology. These approaches to understanding apocalypses are not without some justification. Apocalypses do make references to historical events and circumstances, and they sometimes express truths that speak to ages other than their own, and they can be used to supply information about messianic and eschatological beliefs. But to appreciate apocalypses for what they are, one must read them on their own terms.

Apocalyptic discourse has been called poetic and even mythopoetic. Apocalypses project experience onto a cosmic screen, using all the resources at their disposal, including elements from their own religious traditions as well as from their broader environment. The result is imaginative literature, which uses symbolic language to evoke aspects of reality that are beyond our powers of literal description. They allow their readers to see their own situations from the perspectives of the supernatural world and from the vantage point of life after death. This change of perspective allows a different consciousness to emerge, thereby changing experience itself. Human experience is found to be connected to larger, even cosmic realities. One's own historical period or personal life is viewed within a broad vista and can thereby be ordered correctly. This does not just make experience more tolerable; it actually changes experience, since experience is inseparable from perception. To change perception is to change the world.

A consideration of the use of mythology displayed in apocalypses can produce insight into the ways in which they make meaning. Ancient Near Eastern myths were stories about supernatural figures. Those stories shed light on human life, its institutions, hopes, fears, and struggles. Myths incorporate patterns that correspond to deeply held convictions, profound emotions, and basic attitudes toward life. To tap into this sort of discourse is to access the power of such stories and the images and symbols they contain. For many people, the beasts from the sea and the Son of Man coming on the clouds in Daniel 7 are still potent symbols of the victory of good over evil. The same is true of the battle between Christ and Satan depicted in Revelation and in the Gospels. If the strength of such symbols can still be felt today, the effect they had in ancient Mediterranean and Near Eastern cultures where they originated can be imagined as well.

Because apocalypses project human experience onto a broad screen, temporally and spatially, they have something to say not just to the particular circumstances in which they were written, but also to other times and situations. The history of interpretation of the two canonical apocalypses, Daniel and Revelation, bears eloquent testimony to the adaptability of apocalypses. Daniel itself was crucial to the writing of parts of the Enochic literature, and it was also important to Revelation and 4 Ezra, for example. Revelation supported the hopes of the early Christians who expected a thousand-year period of blessedness, was interpreted as a description of Christian life between Christ's resurrection and the parousia (by Augustine and many others), served as a map of church history, and has been seen by some contemporary Christians as the key to current events and a disclosure of the future. A solid understanding of the genre, the worldview, and the original historical circumstances of apocalypses can enable today's believers to benefit from their spiritual insights and strange beauty without being misled by simplistic and sometimes dangerous interpretations.

THE CANONICAL APOCALYPSES: DANIEL AND REVELATION

The two biblical apocalypses, Daniel and Revelation, are similar in many respects. Each responds to a specific crisis—Daniel to the persecution of the Jews by Antiochus IV Epiphanes in the second century BCE, Revelation to what the author perceives as an impending persecution of true Christians by the Roman Empire in the first century CE. Each document provides typically apocalyptic solutions to its crisis. In each case a revelation is granted to a human seer in which the seer has visions of the supernatural world—visions at least partially explained by an angelic interpreter. The visions reveal that the supernatural world determines the natural world and human history. It is disclosed that the earthly adversary of God's people will be defeated through divine intervention, and the righteous will live in union with God forever after. Each text anticipates resurrection. Each attempts to persuade readers of its viewpoint. Because Daniel and Revelation supply insights into the heavenly world and into God's own decisions, the points of view that each book advocates receive divine sanction and attain the status of divine revelation.

Daniel and Revelation receive detailed analysis elsewhere in *The New Interpreter's Bible* volumes. This article looks at only a few selected passages that illustrate how the works are apocalyptic.

Daniel. This book falls into two parts. Chapters 1–6 are a prologue to the apocalypse proper, which occupies chapters 7–12. Chapters 1–6 are set in the royal courts of the Babylonian, Median, and Persian empires, where Daniel distinguishes himself both as a champion of Jewish piety and as a divinely inspired interpreter of dreams and signs. This portrait of Daniel makes him an ideal mediator of heavenly secrets. This is true particularly because Daniel credits God with his dream interpretations and does not attribute them to his own talents or efforts (2:28, 30). In chapters 7–12, Daniel has his own visions in the night, interpreted for him by an angel. His vision in chapter 7 contains the essential elements of the other dreams. He sees a succession of four beasts rising out of the sea. In the ancient Near East and in Israel, the sea represented the powers of chaos, a cosmic force opposed to God and to God's order. The beasts' origin in the sea reveals their nature as opponents of God. They are both like and unlike earthly animals. Because the beasts are in some ways similar to earthly creatures, the readers can get some idea of the strength and fearful qualities of these beasts. Since as a whole they correspond to no earthly creature but are a bizarre combination of known beasts, they assume an otherworldly and awful aspect. They are suitable, therefore, to represent powers that are both this-worldly and cosmic.

Later in the vision, Daniel learns that the beasts represent four kings (7:17), but in 7:23-24 it is clear that the fourth beast is also a kingdom and that its horns are individual kings. The fluidity of the imagery here should be a warning not to insist on a rigid, one-to-one correspondence between elements of the visions and the natural or supernatural realities to which they refer (see also Revelation 17). Such correspondences do occur, but the visions are mytho-poetic, so their full import always exceeds such simple references. The fourth beast differs from those that precede it in its destructiveness. Then a horn arises on the fourth beast that supplants three other horns and begins to speak arrogantly. Commentators agree that the arrogant horn is Antiochus IV Epiphanes, whose rise to power was at the expense of other royal pretenders and whose persecution of Judaism was arrogant in the extreme, since by it he opposed God.

After the vision of the four beasts, the focus suddenly shifts to God's heavenly court, where God, the Ancient of Days, sits on a throne. As the court sits in judgment, books are opened. Abruptly, the focus leaves the heavenly court and is back on the fourth beast, who is slain. After some words about the fate of the other beasts, the scene again jumps to heaven, where one like a "son of man" comes on the clouds and is presented before God and receives kingship. The rest of the chapter indicates that just as the one like a son of man and the holy ones receive the kingdom in heaven, so also their people, Israel, receive sovereignty on earth. The holy ones are angels, and the one like a son of man is a prominent angel, probably Michael, Israel's heavenly patron (see Dan 10:21).

Daniel 8–11 covers much the same material as Daniel 7, but there is more detail concerning the Seleucids, especially Antiochus IV Epiphanes. In chapter 10, the mode of revelation shifts from vision and interpretation to direct instruction of Daniel by an angel, probably Gabriel. The angel tells Daniel that an angelic war is being waged in which he is fighting against a series of "princes" representing earthly empires (10:13, 20-21; 11:1). Gabriel has only Michael, Israel's heavenly patron (10:21), as an ally. The angel's words assume that each nation has its own patron angel and that conflicts between earthly nations reflect struggles between their supernatural patrons. This notion builds on ancient Near Eastern mythology as glimpsed in Psalms 82; 89:5-7; Deut 32:8-9, and serves apocalyptic purposes by emphasizing the close connection between entities and events in the natural and supernatural realms. In Daniel 12, Israel's protector, Michael, appears,

and there is turmoil such as has never been seen in the world's history. There is a resurrection that does not seem to include all of humanity, but only certain select good and evil persons, and some of the elect "shine . . . like the stars" (Dan 12:3 NRSV) forever. Daniel is then told to seal up his book until the end.

This brief review of Daniel 7–12 highlights several elements typical of apocalypses. Daniel, a human seer, is granted visions mediated by an angel. He is allowed to see the supernatural world, even heaven itself, and to know of the divine decree for the eschatological defeat of Israel's enemy, Antiochus. Daniel thus learns the truth behind the historical events in the time of the actual author. True interpretation of events depends on divine revelation. Daniel does not come to this understanding through his own talents or insight. His understanding comes through the unveiling of heavenly mysteries.

In addition to features that Daniel shares with all apocalypses, there are a number of ways in which it fits the subgenre of historical apocalypses. There is a review of events that are actually in the real author's past, such as the rise of the Babylonian, Median, Persian, and Greek empires in the form of *ex eventu* prophecy, made possible by the attribution of the work to the ancient seer. When the review reaches Antiochus's persecution, in the real author's present, it shifts to genuine prediction. In fact, the prediction of Antiochus's death in chapter 11 is historically inaccurate in a number of ways. The review builds confidence in the real prediction contained in the text by showing how Daniel accurately foretells the rest of history. It also implies God's control of history. Since there are four beasts, history is periodized, another way of saying that it is controlled by God. History is seen as a whole, under the rubric of divine sovereignty and purpose. History leads to the ultimate goal of the defeat of God's (and so God's people's) enemies and the establishment of God's authority over a harmonious cosmos and a faithful people.

There is a complex and intimate connection between the natural and the supernatural worlds, illustrated especially well by Daniel 7. The scene undergoes several sudden and unexplained shifts between the earthly and the supernatural realms. The implication is that there is a close connection between decisions made in heaven and events in human history. The text does not say that explicitly;

it demonstrates it graphically. Because Antiochus is judged in the heavenly court, he dies on earth. The earthly realm can also affect the heavenly, as when Antiochus's persecution is portrayed as an attack on heaven and the angels (Dan 8:10-12, 23-25). The lack of literary transition between the heavenly and the earthly parts of the vision reinforces the impression that the two realms are mutually dependent.

Revelation. The book of Revelation is a Christian work written in western Asia Minor at the end of the first century CE, when Roman Emperor Domitian was on the throne. In Revelation's environment, religious devotion to the goddess Roma and to past and present emperors as gods was an expression of loyalty to Rome. The author viewed the imperial cult as symbolic of Christian accommodation to Hellenistic culture. Such accommodation violated the Christian obligation to render worship to God alone. The letters in Revelation 2–3 bear witness to the extent to which some Christians were at home in Hellenistic and Roman culture, but Revelation's author was convinced that the empire that seduced some Christians and threatened others drew its power from Satan and would soon be defeated by God. Indeed, Satan had already been defeated in heaven by Michael and his angels. Satan's dominion on earth was visible in the oppression of the Christian churches, but his ultimate defeat was inevitable.

In Revelation 4, the seer John ascends to the heavenly throne room, where he sees God and the heavenly court. In God's hand is a sealed scroll containing the eschatological events. There is lamentation in heaven that no one is worthy to open the scroll because until the scroll is opened, the eschatological events cannot take place. In chapter 5, a slain lamb appears, representing the crucified and risen Christ. He takes the scroll from God, and the heavenly host sings a hymn that reveals that he is able to take the scroll and open it because of his death. Here we have the traditional Christian notion that the death and resurrection of Christ set in motion the events of the end time. As in Paul's letters, something eschatological has already happened—Satan's defeat through the death of Christ—and something is still to happen—Satan's ultimate defeat at the hands of Christ at the end of time. The conviction that the end time has already been inaugurated in the death and resurrection of Christ is the major point of difference between Jewish and Christian apocalypticism.

As the seals of the scroll are broken, the events of the end time unfold. The point is that God has a plan for the eschatological events—a plan set in motion by the Christ event. The rest of Revelation reinforces the idea that all of the final events on earth are initiated in heaven and implemented by angels. Eschatological judgment is evident throughout the book. In chapter 19, Christ emerges as the heavenly warrior at the head of his army. He defeats the first beast (the Roman Empire and its emperors) and the second beast (leaders of the imperial cult), and he throws them into the lake of fire. Final judgment comes in chapter 20, where the dragon (Satan) is thrown into the fiery lake. Then the righteous live forever in God's and Christ's presence in the new Jerusalem, now descended onto earth.

Revelation never explicitly quotes Scripture, but it is permeated by biblical allusions and patterns. The use of Isaiah, Ezekiel, Jeremiah, Joel, and Daniel is particularly evident. But events in Revelation are never said to fulfill biblical prophecy. As with other apocalypses, Revelation draws its authority not from biblical proof but from the seer's visions. What he sees divulges what is happening in heaven itself, and this special knowledge grounds the entire book. The use of biblical allusions gives Revelation deep roots in Israel's sacred traditions and taps into their power. Revelation contextualizes its own revelations in the vast sweep of God's previous actions and revelations, but its authority remains steadily grounded in the seer's experience.

Although Daniel is a historical apocalypse and Revelation belongs to the otherworldly journey variety, these books are quite similar in form and content. Indeed, the definition of *apocalypticism* employed by many is dependent on the worldview shared by Daniel and Revelation. Eschatology plays a dominant role in both works, as it does in many definitions of *apocalypticism*. Both works expect public upheaval and eschatological woes. Both look forward to resurrection. Both see heavenly events, including conflict between supernatural beings, reflected on earth. Both symbolize evil powers in bizarre beasts coming from the sea (four in Daniel 7, one in Revelation 13). Both see society in somewhat dualistic terms, although both leave room for movement from the category of those who will perish to those who will be saved. Both refer to the Son of Man, a heavenly figure who plays a role in the eschatological events. Given the fact that Daniel and Revelation are the canonical examples of apocalypses, it is not surprising that the elements they share in common have assumed importance in the definition of *apocalypticism* that is in some cases out of proportion to the presence of these elements in apocalypses in general. Nonetheless, the basic elements of the apocalyptic genre and of its implied worldview are, indeed, shared with all other apocalypses from this period.

THE EARLIEST APOCALYPSES

The earliest extant apocalypses are embedded in *1 Enoch.* They are the *Book of the Watchers* (*1 Enoch* 1–36) and the *Astronomical Book* (*1 Enoch* 72–82). They both date from the third century BCE, and both involve otherworldly journeys. The *Book of the Watchers* is in three parts. The first part (chaps. 1–5) serves to introduce the *Book of the Watchers* in particular and the whole of *1 Enoch* in general. It describes the coming of the divine warrior in eschatological judgment. God comes to judge because humans have not followed the example of the cosmos in its obedience to divine commands. The second part (chaps. 6–16) concerns the introduction of evil into the world through the activity of angels, called "watchers," a name that may come from their original function as heavenly guards (see also Dan 4:13, 17, 23). Two strands of tradition are discernible here. One concerns intercourse between angels and human women, a tradition similar to but more fully developed than the fragmentary narrative in Gen 6:1-4. The other tradition concentrates on illicit revelation of heavenly secrets to humans by angels. Both strands see catastrophic consequences, including violence, following from these violations. The earth cries to heaven for relief, and the good angels bring the case before God, who decrees punishment. The sinful watchers enlist Enoch to intercede for them, but he is told of God's irrevocable sentence and is brought to the heavenly sanctuary (chap. 14). In chapters 17–36, Enoch tours the universe. Most of what he sees concerns eschatological judgment. For example, he sees the place of torment prepared for the sinful watchers and the chambers in which human souls await final judgment. Finally, he sees the preparations that have been made for the restoration of Jerusalem, in which the righteous will live.

The precise historical circumstances that led to the writing of the *Book of the Watchers* are unclear. Two suggestions are the suffering caused by the wars between successors of Alexander the Great and dissatisfaction caused by the laxity toward Torah of the Jerusalem priesthood. What is clear is that the author of the book is unhappy with present circumstances and sees their cause as the people's deviance from God's original plans for the cosmos. The solution is typically apocalyptic—sentence is passed in the supernatural world, evidence for which Enoch receives both directly from God and indirectly through his tour of the universe. Eschatological judgment is inevitable.

The *Astronomical Book* is an excellent example of how closely human history is interrelated with the cosmos. Most of the book is a somewhat dry review of astronomical laws. It takes the form of a tour of the cosmos by Enoch, guided by the angel Uriel. Enoch learns that because of human sinfulness, the universe is disrupted (chap. 80). Crops will not grow properly, rain is withheld, and the orbits of the heavenly bodies are disturbed. The book is presently integrated into *1 Enoch,* so it is not in its original form, but Enoch's tour of heaven assumes some sort of ascent as described in *1 Enoch* 14. In chapter 81, Enoch reads heavenly tablets that reveal the course of human history, and he is sent back to earth to write down what he has seen and to warn of eschatological judgment.

LATE APOCALYPSES

Four Jewish apocalypses were written in reaction to the destruction of Jerusalem in 70 CE: 4 Ezra, *2 Baruch,* the *Apocalypse of Abraham,* and *3 Baruch.* The book of 4 Ezra is now preserved as 2 Esdras 3–14; 2 Esdras 1–2 and 15–16 are Christian additions to the Jewish work, and 2:42-48 is itself a little apocalypse. Set in the time of the destruction of Solomon's Temple by the Babylonians in 587 BCE, 4 Ezra was really written after the destruction six and a half centuries later. It consists of seven sections. In the first three, Ezra argues with the angel Uriel and challenges the justice of a God who allows Israel to be punished at the hands of unrighteous Gentiles. Uriel offers Ezra an apocalyptic solution. The angel first stresses the inaccessibility of the heavenly information that is necessary to understand earthly events. Humans can no more achieve such understanding on their own than they can weigh fire, measure wind, or recall days that are past (4 Ezra 4:5). Nonetheless, God can choose to reveal such information, and that is precisely what happens as Uriel speaks to Ezra. Uriel says that God made two worlds, and it is only in the world to come that the righteous will receive their just reward and the wicked their punishment. Ezra protests that there are so few righteous people that the angel's words provide little comfort.

In the fourth section of the book, Ezra receives a vision of a woman weeping, whom he tries to distract by telling her of Zion's destruction. She is then transformed into a marvelous city, and the angel tells Ezra that she is Zion restored. From this point on, Ezra's attitude changes. He accepts God's judgments as expressed by the angel. Then follow two visions predicting the victory of the forces of good over the powers of evil. In the first vision, an eagle represents Rome. It is reproached and defeated by a lion, representing the Messiah. In the second vision, "something like the figure of a man" arises from the sea (a probable allusion to Daniel 7), does battle with the nations at Zion, and emerges victorious. In the last section of the book, Ezra preserves the Torah, which had been burned in the destruction. Under inspiration, he dictates it to scribes. The twenty-four books of the Torah are meant for the public. Ezra also dictates seventy other books that are to be revealed only to the elect, and those books appear to be held in even higher esteem than the Torah itself, "for in them is the spring of understanding, the fountain of wisdom, and the river of knowledge" (14:47). It would appear that these other books are apocalyptic revelations, necessary for true understanding.

An interesting aspect of 4 Ezra is that it polemicizes against the notion, common in other apocalypses, that anyone could possibly ascend to heaven (see John 3:13). It does so to emphasize human beings' inability to understand heavenly realities on their own, an understanding that is necessary to comprehend earthly happenings. Nonetheless, Uriel does reveal those heavenly secrets to Ezra.

A perennial problem of interpreting 4 Ezra is the question of why Ezra changes his attitude during the course of the book. In the first three visions and during part of the fourth, Ezra complains about God's ways, questions the angel sharply, and seems dissatisfied with the angel's answers. Even if, as some interpreters claim, Ezra does show some

movement in his position in the first half of the book, there is still a remarkable change in his attitude after the fourth vision. Once he sees the woman transformed into the restored Zion, he accepts God's ways and the angel's answers. A plausible solution to this quandary is that Ezra's religious experience—his encounter with the grieving woman and her transformation into restored Zion—is necessary for him to transcend his sorrowful circumstances and accept the apocalyptic solution offered to him. The angel and the seer may represent two aspects of the real author, a person so anguished by the destruction of Jerusalem that he was torn between acceptance of God's ways and rebellion against them. It was only the author's own religious experience, perhaps the very visions described in this book, that led him to accept and to espouse the solution the book provides. Writing the book allowed the author to impart his experiences to others and lead them through the same process he had undergone. This explanation suggests that a real religious experience, perhaps an authentic vision or set of visions, underlies this apocalypse and perhaps others as well.

Another response to the destruction of the Second Temple in 70 CE is *2 Baruch,* which is also set in the time of the destruction of the previous Temple by the Babylonians in the sixth century BCE. This work stresses the foundational importance of the Torah for the continued existence of Israel, emphasizes the temporary nature of this world, and anticipates an eschatological judgment in which Israel's enemies will be punished and the righteous will be elevated to the positions of the stars. It thereby relativizes the loss of the Temple and helps to provide for Israel's survival without a sacrificial cult.

The *Apocalypse of Abraham* develops Abraham's vision in Genesis 15 into a full-blown apocalypse. The idea that Abraham received more extensive revelation than is narrated in Genesis 15 is also found in *2 Baruch* 4. The apocalypse is in two parts. Chapters 1–8 tell of Abraham's discovery of the falseness of idolatry and his rejection of it. In chapters 9–32, Abraham makes a heavenly journey assisted by the angel Yaoel. This twofold structure recalls that of Daniel, where the stories about Daniel in chapters 1–6 prepare for the apocalypse proper in chapters 7–12. During the cosmic journey, Abraham views the whole of human history. This section of the apocalypse has been adapted by Christians, but most of the material is Jewish. The review of history leads to eschatological judgment. As with the other apocalypses, the key to understanding human history lies in the supernatural world and is able to be known only through direct revelation.

The book of *3 Baruch* is a Jewish apocalypse dating from the early second century CE. It describes Baruch's ascent through five levels of heaven. Baruch never enters the presence of God. There is a door in the fifth heaven through which the archangel Michael goes to bring the prayers of the faithful to God, but Baruch never passes through that door. Thus the apocalypse may envisage the more common scheme of seven heavens, even though Baruch sees only five. This apocalypse contains no cosmic upheavals, political turmoil, or public eschatology. Baruch observes the places of reward and punishment in heaven reserved for those who have died. Therefore, this apocalypse offers an example of personalized eschatology.

THE *SIMILITUDES OF ENOCH*

The *Similitudes of Enoch* has survived as part of the Ethiopic form of the collection called *1 Enoch* (chaps. 37–71). It is the only one of the five books in that collection not preserved at Qumran. (The Qumran fragments do contain part of another Enochic book called the *Book of the Giants,* not present in the Ethiopic manuscript.) The *Similitudes* is a fascinating document both as a witness to Jewish belief and thought and as a parallel to Christian notions. Because it is not attested in the Aramaic fragments at Qumran and because of its similarity to Christian ideas, some scholars have sought to date it quite late, perhaps in the third century CE. Scholarly opinion now tends strongly to a first century CE date.

The *Similitudes of Enoch* is an otherworldly journey apocalypse. Enoch is caught up to the heavenly throne room and is given revelations that make him understand the way the world is and the inevitability of eschatological judgment. The most common designation for God in this book is "Lord of the Spirits," which appears to be an adaptation of the biblical "Lord of Hosts." The change to "Spirits" indicates the view, common in apocalypticism, that an unseen world of spiritual beings determines what happens in this world. When Enoch first views God in heaven, he also sees another figure, called the "Elect One of righteousness" (*1 Enoch* 39). In

chapter 46, the dependence of the *Similitudes* on Daniel 7 for its vision of heaven becomes clear. God is called one with a "head of days" who has a head "white like wool," recalling Dan 7:9, where God is called the Ancient of Days who wears white and has hair like pure wool. With God in *1 Enoch* 46 is one whose "face was like the appearance of a son of man." Elsewhere in the *Similitudes* this mysterious figure is called the Righteous One, the Elect One, and the Messiah. The adjectives *righteous* and *elect* are also applied to faithful humans on earth, who recognize the authority of the Lord of Spirits. Just as the one like a son of man is hidden in heaven, known only to Enoch and to those to whom he reveals him, so also the righteous are hidden on earth, to be recognized only at the eschatological judgment (*1 Enoch* 38:1). The ultimate fate of the righteous will be to live with the one like a son of man forever (*1 Enoch* 62:14). In the *Similitudes,* the relation of the one like a son of man to the elect on earth is analogous to the relation between the one like a son of man and Israel in Daniel 7. In each case, the figure like a son of man is the heavenly patron of the faithful.

Contrasted with the righteous are the sinners. They are portrayed as the powerful and wealthy of the earth, those persons who trust in their own power and riches. They do not acknowledge the Lord of Spirits, nor do they admit that their status is due to the Lord. Therefore, the one like a son of man will judge them. He will sit on a throne to judge them (*1 Enoch* 62:1-12), and he will lift them from their own thrones (*1 Enoch* 46:4-8). Their acknowledgment of the Lord's authority and their pleas for mercy at the final judgment will go unheeded. They will be punished, together with the angels who disobeyed God (*1 Enoch* 67). Eschatological judgment is sure, and it will result in a reversal of fortune between those who are now wealthy, powerful, and arrogant and those who are now righteous and persecuted. This reversal is fairly common in Jewish and Christian eschatological thought of this period (e.g., the *Epistle of Enoch* [*1 Enoch* 91–104]; Matt 19:30; 20:16; Luke 1:46-55; 1 Cor 1:20-25; Revelation), and it is especially powerful in apocalyptic settings. For apocalypses, the certainty of reversal rests on divine revelation and involves rewards and punishments even after death. The *Similitudes* contain the idea that a certain number of righteous people must shed their blood before the eschatological judgment can take place (*1 Enoch* 47:3-4). According to 4 Ezra 4:36 and *2 Bar* 23:4-5; 48:46, the number of humans to be created is fixed, and must be completed before the end can come. Revelation 6:11 adapts that idea to its own purposes by making it a certain number of martyrs that must be fulfilled. The *Similitudes* is close to Revelation here. All such schemes imply that history is determined by God in advance.

Enoch emphasizes the uniqueness of his revelation. He says, "Till the present day such wisdom has never been given by the Lord of Spirits as I have received" (*1 Enoch* 37:4). Chapter 42 claims that when personified Wisdom was sent out by God to find a dwelling place among humans, she had to return to heaven because she could find no such place. This contrasts with Sirach 24, where Wisdom finds a home in Zion and is equated with the Torah. The *Similitudes* claim that true wisdom can be found only in heaven, in the presence of the Lord of Spirits and the one like a son of man. Enoch must go there to find it. While there, he sees the founts of wisdom and reads the heavenly books (see Dan 7:10; Rev 3:5; 20:12). At the end of the apocalypse, Enoch is permanently exalted to heaven after having conveyed his revelations to humans (*1 Enoch* 70). In what is probably a later ending, he is identified with the son of man (*1 Enoch* 71:14).

The *Similitudes of Enoch* is certainly an apocalyptic text, with its otherworldly journey, its disclosure of secrets that explain this world and the next, and its anticipation of postmortem rewards and punishments. Its final judgment is public and involves a strong critique of the powerful and wealthy people of the earth. It is especially interesting for students of early Christianity because of the enigmatic figure of the one like a son of man, the Righteous One and the Elect One, who is to judge the world at the end and with whom the righteous will live forever. The similarities between this figure and the Christ of some early Christian documents have led to theories of Christian dependence on the *Similitudes* and, conversely, to suggestions that the *Similitudes* depend on Christian ideas. Dependence in either direction has never been convincingly argued. It is of great interest, however, that such a mediating figure is attested to in a Jewish document of the first century CE, because it helps to provide a context for early Christian concepts of Christ.

QUMRAN AND CHRISTIANITY AS APOCALYPTIC MOVEMENTS

If discussions of apocalypses and apocalypticism are rife with debates and disagreements, the difficulties increase when the topic is actual apocalyptic groups. Some scholars insist that a group can be considered apocalyptic only if it produces apocalypses. Others opt for a wider definition, considering those groups apocalyptic whose worldview is like that found in the apocalypses. In most cases, this means the particular worldview especially characteristic of historical apocalypses, including public eschatology. A good deal of discussion of this issue centers on two collections of documents: the Dead Sea Scrolls and the New Testament.

Qumran. The Dead Sea Scrolls are a collection of manuscripts, some fairly well preserved and others in fragmentary form, that were found in caves in the Judean desert in a series of discoveries beginning in 1947. They are commonly thought to have been the library of a community that inhabited a settlement nearby, whose ruins are called Qumran. The scrolls fall into three basic categories: biblical manuscripts, texts written by members of the community, and other texts that are neither biblical nor written by the sect. This is a somewhat simplified typology, since the community may have had a complex history involving several groups over time with varying relationships to one another and to the authorities at Jerusalem. To date there is no clear evidence that the sect living at Qumran produced any apocalypses. However, they seem to have had a high regard for Daniel and *1 Enoch,* both of which are found in multiple copies among the scrolls. They also possessed the book of *Jubilees,* a work of mixed genres with apocalyptic features, written in the second century BCE.

Although the matter is disputed among scholars, most still consider the community at Qumran to have been an apocalyptic community. Its members were intensely interested in the supernatural world, explaining events in Israel's history and in the history of the sect itself in terms of that other world. They saw their own time as part of what they called the "Age of Wrath," an age dominated by Belial and the human and supernatural beings under his sway. They expected a great eschatological battle to be conducted in a preordained way, which would result in the victory of the forces of good over the powers of evil. The Qumran community thought itself to be allied with the good angels, chief of whom was Michael, who would fight alongside members of the community—the sons of light—against Satan and his supernatural allies and human allies—the sons of darkness. It considered that it had such knowledge through divine mysteries revealed to the Teacher of Righteousness, a key figure in the origins of the community. Because of the revelations made to the Teacher, the community knew the correct interpretation of Torah and therefore was able to please God and able to interpret the prophetic literature accurately. The people at Qumran saw history as culminating in themselves and interpreted the prophets and several psalms as predicting the community's own history.

Parallels between the Qumran community and early Christianity are plentiful and have been explored in depth. Each interpreted Scripture eschatologically and saw it as pointing to itself. Just as the Teacher of Righteousness unlocked the mysteries of Scripture for his followers, so also did Jesus for his own. Each had an authoritative interpretation of Torah that contradicted that of the ruling authorities. Each expected an eschatological resolution to the problems of this sinful world.

The Synoptic Gospels. Revelation is the only apocalypse in the New Testament, but apocalyptic influence is strong throughout the rest of the New Testament as well. The synoptic Gospels have strong apocalyptic attributes. In each of them, Jesus delivers what is usually referred to as an apocalyptic discourse (Mark 13; Matthew 24–25; Luke 21), in which he predicts eschatological sufferings to be endured by his followers, followed by the return of the Son of Man to rescue the elect. Matthew repeatedly refers to the close of the age, and as part of his apocalyptic discourse he has Jesus tell of the last judgment for all humans, followed by eternal rewards and punishments (Matt 25:31-46; see also Matt 13:24-30, 36-43). Matthew associates Jesus' death and resurrection with other eschatological events (Matt 27:51-55). Whether Jesus himself thought in apocalyptic terms is highly debated. No one claims that Jesus wrote apocalypses. Many think that since he began his career as a follower of John the Baptist, an eschatological prophet, and since the New Testament documents present him in an apocalyptic light, Jesus himself probably thought in such terms. Others see the apocalyptic characteristic in the New Testament portrait of Jesus as a later development by the church, and they see Jesus as being similar to a wisdom teacher, a sort of countercultural figure who could be compared to other such teachers and philosophers in the ancient world.

Paul. The apostle Paul is often characterized as having an apocalyptic worldview. He traces his call to a "revelation" (*apokalypsis*; Gal 1:12). He claims to have made a heavenly journey and to have received other visions and revelations (2 Cor 12:1-7). He divides humanity into those being saved and those perishing (1 Cor 1:18). He thinks that his work is being hindered by Satan (1 Thess 2:18). He expects this world to pass away soon (1 Cor 7:26, 31; Rom 13:11). He even presents brief eschatological scenarios. In 1 Thess 4:13-18, he expects Christ to return with a trumpet blast, at which time the faithful dead will rise and be caught up together with the living believers into the clouds, to be with Christ forever. Paul insists, however, that the exact time of the end is unknowable (1 Thess 5:1-11). In 1 Cor 15:20-28, he says that Christ is the firstfruits of the dead. At the end of time, all of the righteous will rise, and then Christ will hand over the kingdom to God, having conquered "every ruler and every authority and power" (1 Cor 15:24 NRSV) and all his enemies. That these enemies are supernatural is supported by the fact that the last enemy to be overcome is death (1 Cor 15:26). In 1 Cor 15:50-57, Paul divulges an eschatological "mystery" about the transformation of the faithful at the end, and in Rom 11:25-32 he shares another "mystery" concerning the inclusion of the Jews among the saved at the end time. In Rom 8:18-25, Paul claims that the entire creation waits for the eschaton and the revelation of the righteous.

CONCLUSION

Apocalypticism played a far greater role in early Judaism and early Christianity than is attested by the presence of only two apocalypses in the Bible. The Jewish and Christian apocalypses written between 300 BCE and 200 CE constitute a substantial body of literature. Consideration of other genres that display features, imagery, patterns, and views typical of apocalypses leads to examination of a still larger body of texts. Discussions of apocalypses and apocalypticism are central to conversations about Second Temple Judaism, earliest Christianity, and the historical Jesus. They have helped to situate various forms of Judaism within both the sweep of Israel's history and culture and the larger Hellenistic world. They have also shed light on Christianity's Jewish roots and on its relation to its Hellenistic environment. Studies of apocalypticism and of individual apocalypses will continue to contribute to biblical studies and to modern assessments of the two ancient religions for some time to come.

BIBLIOGRAPHY

Charlesworth, James H., ed. *The Old Testament Pseudepigrapha*. 2 vols. Garden City, N.Y.: Doubleday, 1983–1985.

Collins, John J., ed. *Apocalypse: The Morphology of a Genre*. Semeia 14. Missoula, Mont.: Scholars Press, 1979.

———. *The Apocalyptic Imagination: An Introduction to the Jewish Matrix of Christianity*. New York: Crossroad, 1984.

Collins, John J., and James H. Charlesworth, eds. *Mysteries and Revelations: Apocalyptic Studies Since the Uppsala Coloquium*. Sheffield: JSOT, 1991.

Hanson, Paul D. *The Dawn of Apocalyptic: The Historical and Sociological Roots of Jewish Apocalyptic Eschatology*. Rev. ed. Philadelphia: Fortress, 1979; orig. ed. 1975.

Hellholm, David. *Apocalypticism in the Mediterranean World and the Near East: Proceedings of the International Colloquium on Apocalypticism, Uppsala, August 12-17, 1979*. Tübingen: Mohr, 1983.

Rowland, Christopher. *The Open Heaven: A Study of Apocalyptic in Judaism and Christianity*. New York: Crossroad, 1982.

Stone, Michael. "Apocalyptic Literature." In *Jewish Writings of the Second Temple Period*. Edited by Michael Stone. Philadelphia: Fortress, 1984.

THE BOOK OF DANIEL

INTRODUCTION, COMMENTARY, AND REFLECTIONS
BY
DANIEL L. SMITH-CHRISTOPHER

THE BOOK OF
DANIEL

INTRODUCTION

The book of Daniel is arguably the most unusual book of the Hebrew Bible. Certainly part of its notoriety can be attributed to the textual and literary problems that have perplexed scholars for generations. But, as we will have occasion to point out in the commentary that follows, some moderns would suggest that Daniel is also a notoriously dangerous book that has fueled religious speculation as well as contributing to social unrest and even revolution. In order to appreciate reading a biblical book of such multifaceted interest, one needs to place Daniel in some literary, historical, and—perhaps just as important—sociological and political context.

LITERARY CONTEXT: THE COURT STORIES (DANIEL 1–6) AND THE APOCALYPTIC VISIONS (DANIEL 7–12)

The book of Daniel comes to us in two different, although related, Semitic languages. Chapters 1:1–2:4*a* and 8–12 are written in Hebrew, while chaps. 2:4*b*-7 are written in Aramaic, the *lingua franca* of the ancient Near East, especially in Mesopotamia, in the late Babylonian, Persian, and early Hellenistic periods (before Aramaic was replaced by Greek). There have been some attempts to relate these language changes in the book to stages in the composition of the book (suggesting, e.g., chaps. 2–7 as an original and early version of the text, before chaps. 1; 8–12 were added), but such theories have never achieved a general consensus in textual studies of the book. One of the main reasons for the difficulty is that the language differences do *not* coincide with the literary changes between chaps. 1–6 and 7–12.

Daniel 1–6. It is obvious to any reader of the book of Daniel that the first six chapters differ dramatically from the last six chapters. The first half of the book consists of six stories that have been called, variously, "diaspora novellas/stories,"[1] "court stories,"[2] and even divided more specifically into "contest" stories (chaps. 2; 4–5) and "conflict" stories (chaps. 3; 6).[3] These first stories in the book are usually assumed to have derived from the life of the Jewish eastern diaspora after the time of the exile in 587/586, but usually are assigned to the Persian (539–333 BCE) or Hellenistic (333–63 BCE) periods rather than to the Babylonian period (597–539 BCE).[4] Although some of the court details seem, at first sight, to be impressive, most scholars argue that the Daniel stories as well as the stories of his friends Hananiah, Mishael, and Azariah are fictional accounts that represent the folklore of the diaspora communities. Furthermore, these details are something that a healthy imagination could create, drawing from the gossip and speculation of the surrounding peoples under Persian occupation. There was similar speculation about the pomp and circumstance of the Persian court among the Greeks as well.[5]

Recent attention to the stories in chaps. 1–6 has also emphasized their literary character as stories that recommend a "lifestyle for the Diaspora."[6] Most literary analysis of these stories, however, has tended to overlook their potent sociopolitical power as stories of resistance to cultural and spiritual assimilation of a minority by a dominant foreign power.[7] From this perspective, these stories take on a more ominous shade than from the perspective of purely folkloristic analysis.

Related to these questions is that of who actually wrote these stories. It is often suggested that these stories derived from an upper class of the Eastern diaspora community simply because only a member of the upper classes could aspire to service in the emperor's court. It is further assumed that these stories reflect a somewhat benign view of the foreign emperor and, therefore, are certainly much older than the assumed setting for the second half of the book of Daniel, which is much darker and more pessimistic about worldly powers, because of the persecution of the Palestinian Jewish communities under Antiochus IV Epiphanes, the reigning Seleucid Hellenistic ruler between 167 and 164 BCE.

It will be the perspective of this commentary, however, that the authors of Daniel 1–6 did *not* aspire actually to work for the foreign emperor. Rather, the emperor's court served as an ideal setting for a political and religious folklore that speaks of surviving and flourishing

---

1. A. Meinhold, "Die Diasporanovelle: Eine Alttestamentliche Gattung" (Ph.D. diss., University of Greifswald, 1969).

2. L. Wills, *The Jew in the Court of the Foreign King* (Minneapolis: Fortress, 1990); S. Niditch and R. Doran, "The Success Story of the Wise Courtier: A Formal Approach," *JBL* 96 (1977) 179-93.

3. W. L. Humphreys, "A Life-Style for Diaspora: A Study of the Tales of Esther and Daniel," *JBL* 93 (1973) 211-23; John J. Collins, *The Apocalyptic Visions of the Book of Daniel* (Missoula, Mont.: Scholars Press, 1977) and Collins, *Daniel,* Hermeneia (Minneapolis: Fortress, 1993).

4. Collins dates the "traditions," rather than the texts as we have them, to the late Persian period. The Aramaic of the book of Daniel is older than the Aramaic of the Dead Sea Scrolls. This suggests that the tales should be dated early in the Hellenistic era, which began in 333 BCE with the conquests of Alexander the Great.

5. J. M. Cook, *The Persian Empire* (New York: Schocken, 1983) 132-33.

6. The classic study is Humphreys, "A Life-Style for Diaspora: A Study of the Tales of Esther and Daniel," 211-23.

7. A notable exception is D. N. Fewell, *Circle of Sovereignty: A Story of Stories in Daniel 1–6* (Sheffield: Almond, 1988).

in a foreign land, in a hostile environment. It effectively communicates as well the powerful images of lowly Jewish exiles standing with faith and courage before the very throne of the occupying (and militarily superior) emperor, overcoming his military and political power through the power of God. The perspective of the book of Daniel toward foreign conquerors, even in the first six chapters, is not nearly so benign as is often thought; in fact, it is openly hostile to their authority. This hostile challenge to authority provides one of the major unifying factors of Daniel as a whole, and is not merely an aspect of the latter half of the book.[8] This hostility requires a creative theology of confrontation as an essential aspect of the modern use of the book.

Court story narratives are not, of course, unique to Daniel. Besides the obvious similarities with Esther and the Joseph tales of Genesis (the striking similarities among these three texts were systematically noted as early as 1895) and even Ezra and Nehemiah (Nehemiah is a courtier), we should note the story of Zerubbabel in 1 Esdras. The discovery of the Dead Sea Scrolls and their publication since 1948 has provided other court stories of Jewish courtiers that resemble Daniel in some interesting details. The most dramatic example of such a story is the *Prayer of Nabonidus,* which many scholars believe is a more ancient form of a Daniel legend, even though Daniel is not explicitly mentioned in the fragments that have been found. The fragment reads as follows (with gaps and difficulties indicated by brackets):

1 Words of the prayer which Nabonidus, king of the la[nd of Baby]lon, [the great] king, pra[yed when we were afflicted]
2 by an evil inflammation, by the decree of God the All-Highest, in Teiman. [I Nabonidus] was afflicted [with an evil inflammation]
3 for seven years and was banished far from [men until I prayed to God the All Highest]
4 and an exorcist pardoned my sin. He was a Jewish [man] of the [exiles, and he said to me:]
5 Proclaim and write to the glory, exa[ltation and honor] of the name of Go[d the All-Highest. And I wrote as follows; When]
6 I was afflicted with an evil inflammation and I stayed in Teiman [by the decree of the all Highest God, I]
7 prayed for seven years [to all] Gods of silver and gold, [bronze, of iron]
8 of wood, of stone, of clay, for [I thought] they were Gods.[9]

This fragment contains a number of interesting details that relate to the study of Daniel. First, and most important, it specifically names and, therefore, connects Nabonidus, last king of Babylon, to the Daniel traditions. It is often assumed that the images of Nebuchadnezzar in many of the Daniel stories seem better suited to the historical Nabonidus (who was the historical father of Belshazzar of Daniel chap. 5), and this fragment would seem

8. Note the perspective of D. Berrigan in his series on Daniel, "Till the End of Empire," in *The Other Side* (July-August 1990) 8-14; (September October 1990) 8-17; (November-December 1990) 36-42.
9. 4QPrNab. Translation from F. García-Martínez, *Qumran and Apocalyptic: Studies on the Aramaic Texts from Qumran* (Leiden: Brill, 1992) 119-20.

to confirm that suspicion. That Nebuchadnezzar was eventually substituted is not hard to understand, given that he was, after all, the conqueror of Jerusalem and responsible for the destruction of the Temple—and thus a more powerful symbol of Babylonian rule than was Nabonidus. Second, however, this fragment suggests that many Daniel stories may have circulated among the Jewish people in a kind of Daniel "folklore cycle" and that our present book of Daniel contains only a selection from that folklore tradition. Finally, there are some interesting specifics in this fragment, such as the list of materials in lines 7-8 that resembles lists in the book of Daniel and the story line that the Babylonian king had to learn that God is the true god, and not one of the gods of gold and silver. Although the historicity of many of the biblical and nonbiblical accounts must be doubted, given what we know from other sources, the theology of these stories (and the visions) is not significant for their time alone, but remains significant for modern Christians who seek to construct a biblically informed theology for contemporary living.

Daniel 7–12. The last six chapters of Daniel are the most important example of apocalyptic literature in the Hebrew Bible. A considerable amount of scholarly research has gone into the definition and description of apocalyptic literature, of which we have many examples outside the canon of the Old and the New Testaments.[10] Clearly, apocalyptic was an important style of theological writing for at least 500 years, during the Hellenistic and Roman periods (roughly 333 BCE–200 CE, although it may extend back into the Persian period, if some Persian influences are accepted).[11] We have both Jewish and Christian examples of this type of literature. Apocalyptic is most generally defined as literature that deals with the revelation and understanding of mysteries, but there have been attempts to be even more specific and comprehensive. For example, Collins has proposed the following definition:

> "Apocalypse" is a genre of revelatory literature with a narrative framework, in which a revelation is mediated by an otherworldly being to a human recipient, disclosing a transcendent reality which is both temporal, insofar as it envisages eschatological salvation, and spatial insofar as it involves another, supernatural world.

An apocalypse is intended to interpret present earthly circumstances in the light of the supernatural world and of the future, and to influence both the understanding and the behavior of the audience by means of divine authority.[12]

The advantage of such a definition is not that it is finally complete, but that it gives students and scholars at least some kind of common language in their analysis of actual texts. The point is not to exclude certain texts from consideration (as if to create some

---

10. See the article in this volume by Frederick J. Murphy, "Introduction to Apocalyptic Literature," 1-16.

11. On Persian influences, see esp. A. Hultgård, "The Bahman Yasht: A Persian Perspective," in *Mysteries and Revelations: Apocalyptic Studies Since the Uppsala Colloquium,* ed. John J. Collins and J. H. Charlesworth (Sheffield: JSOT, 1991).

12. John J. Collins, "Genre, Ideology, and Social movements in Jewish Apocalypticism," in Collins and Charlesworth, *Mysteries and Revelations,* 19.

kind of informal canon of "real" apocalyptic texts) but to facilitate our understanding of any particular text in all its unique originality as well as formal resemblances to other texts. Daniel, for example, has clear resemblances to books like *1 Enoch,* but they were not issued from some sort of theological or literary mold, and assumptions about their similarity can be hazardous.

Equally hazardous is the attempt to generalize about a sociological context for apocalyptic literature as a whole. Reid, for example, used a sophisticated sociological outline in order to compare *1 Enoch* and Daniel, and he concluded that they have quite different source communities.[13] Other scholars, however, are content to generalize that apocalyptic literature seems to come from "disenfranchised" communities, without being more specific.[14] It is not necessary, however, to suggest that an entire genre has the same sociological setting in every specific case (attractive as such a conclusion may be!). The sociological setting of Daniel must also be determined on the basis of internal evidence as well as the genre of the stories and visions. That the authors of Daniel are hostile to foreign conquerors and to ancient Near Eastern empire building is clear from *what* the book says, and not only from *how* it is said. Furthermore, the social context of the exile itself and the realities of occupation from then on should alert the reader to certain attitudes that are revealed in Daniel. For this reason it is important to review the basic historical background before discussing the meaning of that background for a reading of the book of Daniel.

HISTORICAL BACKGROUND OF DANIEL: THE CONTEXT OF EMPIRE

The independent Jewish kingdom was short lived in the ancient Near East. Allowing for a 200-year period of decentralized tribal existence (roughly 1200–1000 BCE), the united kingdom existed under the Davidic monarchy from 1020 to 922 BCE, with the northern breakaway kingdom lasting until the Assyrian conquest of 722 BCE. The southern state of Judah continued until the Babylonian conquests began in 597 BCE and was completely overrun when Jerusalem was devastated in 587/586 BCE, the beginning of the Babylonian exile. Both the northern and the southern kingdoms ended tragically (but not atypically for the ancient Near East) in military conquest and deportation of a sizable segment of the populace—taken, it appears, from the institutional leadership of royal, military, and religious sectors. We know more about the Babylonian exiles than we do about the Assyrian captives because this community survived the ordeal. With the brief exception of the Hasmonean client state (which, given the realities of Hellenistic and Roman power, is not much of an exception), there was never again a military-royalist state of the ancient Hebrews in Palestine.

Around 539 BCE, Cyrus the Persian conquered Babylon and soon thereafter began

---

13. S. B. Reid, *Enoch and Daniel,* Bibal Monograph Series (Berkeley: Bibal, 1989).

14. G. W. F. Nickelsburg, "Social Aspects of Palestinian Jewish Apocalypticism," in D. Hellholm, ed., *Apocalypticism in the Mediterranean World and the Near East* (Tübingen: Mohr, 1983) 641-54; see also, in the same volume, E. P. Sanders, "The Genre of Palestinian Jewish Apocalypses," 447-59. Note recent disagreements in Stephen L. Cook, *Prophecy and Apocalypticism: The Postexilic Social Setting* (Minneapolis: Fortress, 1995).

allowing parties of Jews to return to Palestine (Ezra 1–6). This action is often interpreted as a freedom policy on the part of the Persians. But it must be kept in mind that these missions back to Palestine had particular Persian goals in mind—particularly the shoring up of the western flank of the Persian Empire when the Greeks became a troublesome presence in the Mediterranean rim.

The Persian period ended with the conquests of Alexander the Great in 333 BCE. After Alexander's death in 323 BCE in Babylon, his massive empire was divided among his generals. After a period of internal warfare, lines were drawn in the Near East between the eastern portion of the empire, based in Syria and Mesopotamia, and Egypt to the west. The Ptolemies ruled Egypt, which included Palestine until 198 BCE, when the Seleucids (Antiochus III), who ruled the eastern section of the empire, annexed Palestine to their region. Alexander's conquests brought an intensification of Hellenistic influence on life, but as Morton Smith has recently pointed out, western influence on Palestine is documented from the Philistine involvement in the early monarchy, and only intensifies in the Babylonian, Persian, and post-Alexandrian historical eras.[15] Following Alexander's death, and until Seleucid rule in 198 BCE, the Ptolemaic rule of Egypt was economically rigid, although most scholars doubt that there was any severe persecution when compared to the Seleucid period that followed. Newsome noted that, according to the Zenon Papyri from the Ptolemaic period, the Jews were "considered little more than serfs in that economic pyramid which placed the Greeks and Macedonians at the top."[16]

The era of Hellenistic rule that is of greatest interest for the study of the book of Daniel is the reign of Antiochus IV Epiphanes (175–164 BCE). Antiochus's father, Antiochus III, had already managed to expel the Ptolemies from Palestine by 200 BCE, and at first the Jewish residents welcomed him as a liberator (especially from Ptolemaic taxation!). Already during the years of Seleucus IV Philopater (187–175 BCE), the immediate successor of Antiochus III, the Jewish community was fractured into rival parties. A certain Simon denounced Onias III, at that time the high priest, and suggested that the high priest should not have such control of the great wealth of the temple treasury. Simon and his allies were pro-Seleucid, while Onias and Hyrcanus (the head of one of the aristocratic families named Tobias) were pro-Ptolemaic. When Onias traveled to Antioch-on-Orantes to appeal to the king, the new successor to the throne, Antiochus IV, imprisoned him. Jason, brother of Onias, paid a large sum of money to Antiochus IV, who promptly made Jason the high priest. Jason was at the head of the move to modernize and Hellenize Jewish life, and he became a significant ally to Antiochus IV's efforts to rule the unruly Jews.

Matters took an even more complex turn when Simon's brother Menelaus, the old rival of Onias, outbid Jason for the office of high priest. So the situation involved two rival Hellenizing factions among the Jewish aristocracy and a third anti-Hellenistic party of Jews, led by the religious resistance known as the Hasidim (the "pious ones," although some

15. M. Smith, "Hellenization," in M. Stone and D. Satran, eds., *Emerging Judaism* (Minneapolis: Fortress, 1989) 111-12.

16. J. D. Newsome, *Greeks, Romans, Jews* (Philadelphia: Trinity Press International, 1992) 37.

have suggested the translation "the committed ones"); there were many other factions among the anti-Hellenistic parties as well. These events took a serious turn for the worse at the end of Antiochus IV's campaigns in Egypt. Antiochus IV managed to destroy the Egyptian army of Ptolemy VI Philometer (180–145 BCE) in 168 BCE. But instead of allowing Antiochus IV to consolidate power even over Egypt, Rome intervened to halt Antiochus IV's advance. Roman intervention is symbolized in the person of Popilius, who forced a humiliated Antiochus to withdraw his forces when they met at Eleusis. Back in Jerusalem, Jason had imprisoned Menelaus after hearing that Antiochus IV had been killed in battle. But the word that Jason had acted on was false, and when Antiochus assessed the situation in Jerusalem, it appeared to be open revolt against his authority, initiated perhaps by those who thought Antiochus was in a weakened position, even if not actually dead. Antiochus IV's response to the disarray in Jerusalem was violent. Not only were many Jews killed or sold into slavery, but also the Temple was violated; eventually certain aspects of Jewish traditional practice were banned as contributing factors to what Antiochus IV perceived as disloyalty. For some scholars, persecution of religiously motivated resisters to Antiochus's Hellenization policies under Jewish leaders like Jason makes sense—even in the context of otherwise tolerant policies that normally allowed diverse religious expressions: "If the revolt was led by Hasidim, for whom the commandments of the Torah were of the utmost sanctity, and if devotion to the Mosaic Law was the watchword of the uprising, then that Law had to be extirpated if the rebellion was to be put down."[17]

These political policies toward the rebellious Jews resulted in an intensification of intracommunal hostility as well as hostility toward the rulers. Antiochus IV's indulgences of rival priests who sought the office of high priest created internal struggles in the Jewish community that are now recognized as important to the strife of 167–164 BCE as were Antiochus IV's own policies. The emperor's endorsement of the move to make the Temple a home for an altar (rather than, most scholars think, an actual image) for Baal Shamem/Zeus Olympios as well as the strengthening of the Greek garrison (the Akra) and the building of such Hellenistic institutions as a gymnasium as a part of the process of Hellenizing the Jews all resulted in violent factionalism in the Jewish community. Part of Antiochus's policies clearly involved the strengthening of the military presence in Jerusalem—the garrison with whom the later Maccabees would have to contend for control of the city. One result of this action was the open Maccabean revolt (along with Josephus, 1 Maccabees is the most reliable source for this period). But the book of Daniel represents other forms of political and religious resistance during this same time. To summarize, scholars have discussed the outbreak of the resistance and the resultant repression of the Jews in different ways. Was it mainly the result of rival factions among the aristocratic Jewish families? Tcherikover, for one, has pointed out that we must not minimize the temptations that Hellenistic wealth and control offered to those members of local aristocracies who could successfully become part of the ruling elite.[18] Was it mainly the

17. V. Tcherikover, *Hellenistic Civilization and the Jews* (New York: Atheneum, 1970) 198.
18. Ibid., 202-3.

result of tensions between Ptolemaic and Seleucid sympathizers? Or was it a symptom of the larger conflict between the Seleucid and the Ptolemaic rulers of the Near East? How much of a role can we attribute to the desire for religious freedom among the Jews themselves, as portrayed in such pious documents as the books of the Maccabees? History, we know, is seldom so simple as a choice among opposing factors—all were clearly elements contributing to this period of severe disturbance, violence, and, for some, horrendous persecution. The precise causes are less significant to us than is the context of uncertainty and instability facing the average person, who then reflected on the words of the apocalyptic dreamers and speakers.

While Daniel 7–12 are usually dated to the time of greatest conflict under Antiochus IV Epiphanes (i.e., between 167, when the Temple was desecrated with the pagan altar, and 164 BCE, when the rule of Antiochus IV ended), it is important to keep in mind that one of the main reasons why so much attention is focused on this episode is because of the existence of 1 Maccabees. This can easily give the impression that Jewish life under the Ptolemies and the Seleucids was otherwise peaceful or without major incident, and therefore any language of resistance or unrest that we find in Daniel must also be from the time of Antiochus IV. This would be a false impression.

Morton Smith recently calculated that in the period between Alexander's conquest in 333 BCE, and the Roman takeover of Palestinian affairs around 63 BCE under Pompey, some 200 military campaigns were fought in or around Palestine and that "this military history alone shows that no part of the country can have escaped Greek influence."[19] Thus military conquest, the taking of slaves and the temptations of mercenary service (it appears that some Jews welcomed military opportunities), and Greek settlement would have taken their toll on Jewish traditional life throughout the period from the exile to the Roman occupation of Palestine. The background of Daniel must include the social and political realities of exile and occupation throughout this period, and not only during any specific crisis. Late Hebrew thought, the Bible itself as a document, and both Rabbinic Judaism and Christianity were all formed under one or another system of political domination or occupation. This social and political reality will help to inform our reading of the book of Daniel.

It is common for many biblical scholars of the twentieth century to deal with the exile in a most peculiar manner: as an event that may have begun tragically, but resulted in an exilic existence that "must not have been that bad" under the Babylonians. This situation then improved even more, it is thought, under the benevolent rule of the Persians from the time of Cyrus's conquest of Babylon in 539 BCE until the coming of Alexander the Great in 333 BCE. While the Hellenistic rule that followed Alexander was not exactly political independence, the Hellenistic rulers over Palestine—the Ptolemies first and then after 198 BCE the Seleucids—must not have been so bad with the one exception of Antiochus IV Epiphanes' severe persecution of the Jews. Greek influence allowed for a

19. Smith, "Hellenization," 111-12.

blossoming of Jewish "philosophy" and the translation of the Septuagint (the Greek version of the Hebrew Bible).

There are a number of severe historical and sociological problems with the (admittedly somewhat exaggerated) summary of this dominant paradigm for understanding the exile and the post-exilic developments within Jewish society. The main problem with this perspective is the lack of sensitivity to, and awareness of, the realities of living in exile and under military occupation. Although we have understood for some time that the exile must have had a dramatic impact on the ancient Jewish communities, we are only recently confronting the wider sociological and political, not to mention psychological, impact of these experiences, largely because we are only recently hearing from modern "exiles," minorities who insist that their stories of disenfranchisement be heard. Even more recently, some of these voices are taking up the scholarly study of the Bible, maintaining their unique perspectives as racial or cultural minorities in a variety of political circumstances.[20] By listening to modern exiles, minorities whose stories reflect the powerlessness of captivity of various kinds, we become far more alive to the meaning of the stories of the Bible—especially stories that reflect the realities of captivity and subordination. Furthermore, these voices are being heard against a new awareness of the historical realities of Persian and Hellenistic imperial politics.

The influence of Hellenism is already under severe reassessment, led by important older works such as S. K. Eddy's *The King Is Dead*[21] and Peter Green, who states that the "civilizing and missionary aspects [of Hellenistic conquests] have been greatly exaggerated, not least by modern historians anxious to find some moral justification for aggressive imperialism."[22] Such a reassessment, however, must also extend to the widespread notion of Persian "benevolence" as well. In a recent popular commentary on Ezra and Nehemiah, Holmgren reflects this general perspective in a most interesting manner. In his comment on Neh 9:36-37, a text that contains one of the most significant and explicit complaints against the Persians, Holmgren recognizes that this passage indicates a measure of resentment and unrest, but then continues at some length to maintain the general assumption about Jewish attitudes to Persian rule:

> To be "almost free" is never enough; if you are a slave, "almost free" means that you are still a slave. Under Persian rule the Jews were "almost free." Jews did not despise this "almost free" existence, however, because under benevolent monarchs the Jews were free to return to the land and there to rebuild the temple and the city of Jerusalem. The writings of both Ezra and Nehemiah portray the Persian rulers as cooperative and fair . . . toward the Jewish community.[23]

20. See the volume of essays, *Voices from the Margin: Interpreting the Bible in the Third World,* ed. R. S. Sugirtharajah (New York: Orbis, 1991) and Daniel Smith-Christopher, ed., *Text and Experience: Papers on Cultural Exegesis from the 1992 Casassa Conference* (Sheffield: Sheffield University Press, 1996).

21. S. K. Eddy, *The King Is Dead: Studies in the Near Eastern Resistance to Hellenism 334–31 bc* (Lincoln: University of Nebraska Press, 1961).

22. P. Green, "Greek Gifts?" *History Today* (June 1990) 27-34.

23. F. C. Holmgren, *Israel Alive Again* (Grand Rapids: Eerdmans, 1987) 134-35.

Thus the idea of Persian benevolence has become an almost unquestionable doctrine of research on the exilic and post-exilic periods of the Bible, and is obviously relevant to the study of the book of Daniel. Such a positive view is typically considered a reliable collective memory of the Jews in the diaspora. So Collins writes that "the benevolence of the king is assumed" in the court tales,[24] and Wills, in an otherwise very interesting study, further presumes the positive view of the foreign rulers.[25] Blenkinsopp, commenting on Ezra and Nehemiah, also notes "the theme of the benevolence of the Persian kings."[26] Indeed, such a positive view is often used as an argument for dating the Daniel materials in an era other than that of the hated Antiochus Epiphanes IV, because it is hard to accept stories of a benign foreign ruler in that time. It is the argument of this commentary that such an assumption about the benign rulers of either Babylon or Persia overlooks many of the significant symbols of domination that are indicated in the stories themselves— threats of death from the king, fear of the king's rage, name changing as a sign of subordination, symbolic warfare in the visions, etc. Thus that assumption fails to appreciate fully the themes of resistance and opposition that are major aspects of these stories. In short, one need not find calls to open and violent revolution in order to recognize calls to resistance, even if it is nonviolent resistance. It is true that some passages from the Bible would seem to support such assumptions, perhaps most powerfully in the enthusiastic bestowal of the title "Messiah" on Cyrus in Isa 45:1 or the clearly more sympathetic portrayal of Darius in Daniel 6 (but see the commentary below).

Finally, because Jewish names turn up among the Murashu Documents (an archive of business affairs from the Persian period, discovered in the ancient city of Nippur), many scholars have concluded that life must have been profitable for some of the community members. Zadok's studies, however, note that very few Jewish names turn up as officials or members of the upper echelons of society. Nehemiah, he argued, was a clear exception to the rule.[27] While there is nothing in the Elephantine correspondence[28] of Jewish soldiers under Persian mercenary employment in Egypt to suggest resentment, it must not be overlooked that it was a military colony in the service of the Persians, opposed to a hostile local Egyptian populace. What might a new view of Persian imperial policy do for a reading of the book of Daniel?

The "positive attitude" notion is based on very few biblical sources that have nevertheless been allowed to dominate the interpretation of all Persian period biblical literature and

24. John J. Collins, *Daniel,* FOTL (Grand Rapids: Eerdmans, 1984) 72.

25. L. Wills, *The Jew in the Court of the Foreign King* (Minneapolis: Fortress, 1990). This view is maintained in recent commentaries, such as that of André Lacocque, *The Book of Daniel,* trans. D. Pellauer (Atlanta: John Knox, 1979) 113; N. Porteous, *Daniel: A Commentary,* OTL (Philadelphia: Westminster, 1965) 90; and O. Plöger, *Daniel,* KAT (Leipzig: Gütersloh, 1965) 98.

26. J. Blenkinsopp, *Ezra–Nehemiah* (London: SCM, 1988) 160.

27. R. Zadok, *The Jews in Babylonia During the Chaldean and Achaemenid Periods* (Haifa: University of Haifa, 1979) 86-90.

28. Part of a group of papyrus documents and fragments written in Aramaic in the fifth century BCE, originating at Elephantine, an island in the Nile opposite Aswan (ancient Syrene); they were discovered during the nineteenth and twentieth centuries CE.

the Jewish experience of Achaemenid rule. This has led scholars to overlook important sociological and sociopsychological factors in biblical and nonbiblical literature that are crucial for a modern assessment of the historical and ideological understanding of the Persian period.

In a recent analysis, Root contrasts the Persians' own self-image and propaganda as portrayed in official artwork with actual practice: "The world was at peace on the walls of Persepolis as it never was in actuality. While news of the Persian sack of Miletus was striking terror in the Athenian soul, artisans from near and far were carving dreams in stone for Darius."[29] In her important reassessment of the implications of the famous Cyrus Cylinder, Amelie Kuhrt also warns against allowing "a blatant piece of Persian propaganda" to convince modern historians of the benevolence of Cyrus.[30] Finally, in a recent forum in which the historical image of Cyrus was examined again, Van der Spek also takes issue with the older view on the basis of the historical sources, concluding that "Cyrus and the other Persian kings ruled their empire in a way which was quite common in antiquity. . . . Cyrus introduced no new policy toward subdued nations, but acted in conformity with firmly established traditions, sometimes favorable, sometimes cruel. Under his responsibility temples were destroyed, Ecbatana was plundered, after the battle of Opis Cyrus 'carried off the plunder (and) slaughtered the people.' "[31]

This historical reconsideration is beginning to have an impact on biblical analysis. For example, Jenner considers the Cyrus decree recorded in Ezra 1 to be a falsification by Darius, who needed to legitimate a strong western flank, and the Jewish Temple would certainly serve his purposes. Furthermore, that Cyrus is called "Messiah" should not be overread, since, Jenner suggests, the meaning attached to such a title could have been much cooler than many modern interpreters assume, since "Cyrus, being in a position of dependency and obedience to JHWH, was no more than a useful tool in the service of Jerusalem."[32] This conclusion will have an important impact on a reading of Daniel.

The most important recent voice along these lines is that of Kenneth Hoglund.[33] Hoglund argues convincingly for a reassessment of the role of such Jewish representatives of the Persians as Ezra and Nehemiah, but especially the military leader Nehemiah. Nehemiah, declares Hoglund, was a Persian official (courtier?) whose task was more military than spiritual and who was concerned with the further imposition of Persian control over Palestine, not with any supposed free expression of local religion by the Jewish residents there. The Persians built a series of garrisons that represented strong military control of

29. M. C. Root, *The King and Kingship in Achaemenid Art: Essays on the Creation of an Iconography of Empire*, vol. 9 of Acta Iranica, Textes et Memoires (Leiden: Brill, 1979) 311.

30. A. Kuhrt, "The Cyrus Cylinder and Achaemenid Imperial Policy," *JSOT* 25 (1983) 94-95.

31. R. J. van der Spek, "Did Cyrus the Great Introduce a New Policy Towards Subdued Nations? Cyrus in Assyrian Perspective," *Persica* 10 (1982) 278-79, 281-82.

32. K. D. Jenner, "The Old Testament and Its Appreciation of Cyrus," *Persica* 10 (1982) 284.

33. K. G. Hoglund, *Achaemenid Imperial Administration in Syria-Palestine and the Missions of Ezra and Nehemiah*, SBLDS 125 (Atlanta: Scholars Press, 1992). See also Kuhrt, "The Cyrus Cylinder and Achaemenid Imperial Policy," 83-97; R. J. van der Spek, "Did Cyrus the Great Introduce a New Policy Towards Subdued Nations?" *Persica* 10 (1982) 278-83.

their western flank; thus any Jewish "returns to the land" under the Persians must be seen now as part of this strategic plan and not as the result of enlightened Persian rulership. In short, as Hoglund summarizes, "the appearance of these garrisons in the mid-fifth century is the indelible fingerprint of the hand of the Achaemenid empire tightening its grip on local affairs in the Levant."[34]

How do such historical realities about both Persian and Hellenistic policies influence interpretation of Daniel? Perhaps they simply alert the reader to look for the realities of political occupation and to learn how to see those realities, by reading Daniel in new ways. Given the sociopolitical context of empire in the latter half of the first millennium, the era of world empire, a full understanding of such post-exilic books as Daniel (not to mention Ezra–Nehemiah, Malachi, Esther, and many others) requires an understanding of the meaning and the impact of the exile and the kind of captivity it represented. It also requires that portions of the Bible be read "in the shadows," in order to fully comprehend their meaning and significance to a subordinated minority population. For minorities throughout the world, certain conversations must take place in the shadows, away from the "king's ear"—informers or guards. These conversations include stories, jokes, or tales told in whispers. Where a minority feels subordinated by either tradition or law, these stories can become a creative world of resistance in which heroes are drawn from among their own people, standing against the dominant majority culture.[35]

RETHINKING THE CONDITIONS OF CONQUEST AND EXILE

The exile was an experience of military defeat, deportation, and oppression in a new and strange land, which ended the days of independence for ancient Israel. At the hands of Nebuchadnezzar, Jerusalem, its Temple, and much of the environs were devastated (2 Kings 25). As was their policy, the Babylonians exiled large sections of the conquered population. Josephus, in his review of the history of the prisoners of war taken to Babylon, spoke of their being bound and chained. Whether this report can be taken as historically reliable and how far it is reconstruction on the basis of Josephus's time period is unclear, but note the language about fetters in Jer 40:1 (cf. Nah 3:10). As recounted in 2 Kings 25 and Jeremiah 52, only the poorest of the land were left to be "vinedressers and plowmen."

We know that under imperial rule subject populations and conquered territories were treated as sources of resources and labor; scholars sum this up graphically as a huge military and administrative apparatus designed to secure a constant flow of goods from the periphery to the center. Biblical traditions of proclamation against Babylon lead the reader to believe that Babylonian policies were severe; the oracles in Jeremiah, for example, threaten punishment of Babylon for its severity (Jer 50:15-16, 29; 51:20-22) and idolatry (50:2, 36; 51:44). But clearly the most crushing reality of Babylonian policy was the deportation itself, the disruption of life and the constant reminder of being a conquered people.

---

34. Hoglund, "Achaemeid Imperial Administration," 433.
35. See D. Smith, *The Religion of the Landless* (New York: Meyer-Stone, 1989).

As for the actual number of people exiled, the evidence is unclear. Second Kings 24:14 states that there were 10,000 captives, but 2 Kgs 24:26 lists 7,000 "men of valor" and 1,000 craftsmen. Jeremiah claims that in all 4,600 persons were taken to Babylonia, listing them by year as follows in Nebuchadnezzar's seventh year, 3,023 Jews; in his eighteenth year, 832; and in the twenty-third year, 745 (Jer 52:28-30).

The usual means of calculating the number of exiles is to multiply a "typical family" unit (four to five members of an immediate family) by the number 4,600—who are assumed to have been only men—which results in approximately 20,000-25,000. However, if only "important" men were counted (heads of households, etc.), then the total figure could easily be much higher.

It is often strongly asserted in studies of the Babylonian exile that the exiles were *not* slaves, although at least one important building inscription has Nebuchadnezzar bragging that he "imposed the brick basket" on exiles taken from the western reaches of his empire, most certainly including Palestine.[36] We have noted, even under the rule of the supposedly tolerant Persians, that Ezra mentions in his prayer to God that "we are slaves" (Ezra 9:9 NRSV; cf. Neh 9:36).[37] But do we really know what we are talking about when we say that the exiles were (or were not) slaves? For North Americans, the image of slavery is indelibly marked by African American slavery in the early United States. But that is not the only form slavery has taken throughout history. In his book *Slavery and Social Death*,[38] Orlando Patterson analyzes the structure of slave societies using data from over forty different slave systems from all over the world and in different times. Common to all is the significance of *symbolic* institutions, what Patterson calls "the symbolic whips of slavery . . . woven from many areas of culture." These symbols include forceable name changes, hair or clothing changes, body markers, and anything that symbolized the death of one's identity at birth by means of a "rebirth" to a new identity given by the dominant authorities. Patterson notes that in different slave systems, a slave may be forced to change his or her name or "eat" the old identity through a food ceremony. Hence, according to Patterson's analysis, slavery is, in essence, the removal of one's identity and a social death. Therefore, the reconstruction and resistance of an ethnic group can be seen as a potential response to just such a threat of social death. One of the ways we see Jewish resistance to the symbols of powerlessness in the exile and afterward is in the telling of stories of Jewish courage in the face of tremendous foreign power. The tales of the book of Daniel are stories and writings of this kind.

Once we consider the significance of the symbols of domination, we are better prepared to note their significance in the Bible. For example, name changing is a common symbol used by foreign rulers in the Bible. Even though the stories of Daniel and his friends come

---

36. F. H. Weissbach, *Das Hauptheiligtum des Marduk in Babylon* (Leipzig, 1938) 47. See also S. Langdon, *Building Inscriptions of the Neo-Babylonian Empire* (Paris, 1905) 59, 149.

37. It has been suggested that this refers to the fact that all Persian citizens routinely referred to themselves as slaves of the emperor. But is this what Ezra and Nehemiah were referring to? In the context, it can hardly be read as merely an equivalent term to "citizen." J. M. Cook, *The Persian Empire* (New York: Schocken, 1983) 132.

38. Orlando Patterson, *Slavery and Social Death* (Cambridge, Mass.: Harvard University Press, 1982).

from a late era in their final form, the symbol of name changing is an important factor in their association with the Babylonians and may not be an incidental detail. Furthermore, Nebuchadnezzar also changed the name of Zedekiah, when he placed him on the throne of Judah in Jehoiachin's absence (2 Kgs 24:17). That biblical writers mention these policies seems to reflect an awareness of the symbols of power that the exiles had to live with and struggle against.

Clearly, one element of recognizing these symbols is to note the constant reminders of foreign imperial power over the Jews. Indeed, so often is this context of empire noted in Ezra–Nehemiah, Daniel, and Esther that we may overlook its significance. For example, simply to pay attention to the frequency of the word *decree* in these works is revealing. The vast majority of occurrences of this term in the Bible are commands of foreign emperors dealing with the Jewish minority. The terms translated into English as "decree" in these books have been borrowed from political and administrative vocabulary of Imperial Aramaic or Persian, the official languages of the time. This is hardly surprising, since minorities would learn quickly such words as "police," "papers," "command," "authorized," and "order."

Such terms signal that the Jewish community was trapped by the competing claims to authority made by the local non-Jewish officials and the Persian court ("Who gave you a decree to build this house?" [Ezra 5:3]). They depended on Persian benevolence and support and had to appeal to the Persian court for permission at every turn. The biblical books from this period exhibit a heightened consciousness of a people not in control of their own lives: "I, Darius, make a decree," "You are permitted to go to Jerusalem," "I decree that any of the people . . . may go with you," "the unchangeable law of the Persians." Once again, the exile's legacy casts its shadow—the shadow of the guard tower—whether real or symbolic. Read in the shadows, Daniel becomes a revolutionary book of resistance, albeit nonviolent resistance.

Finally, one of the reasons why the revolutionary nature of the call to resistance in Daniel is not noted more frequently is the tendency among many modern historians to regard only violent forms of resistance as evidence of any kind of resistance activity. If violence is not present, then the literature is deemed unrealistic or fantasy. Yet, 1 Maccabees is seldom criticized as being either, even though it proposes to celebrate the preposterous notion of a military confrontation between a divided Jewish community and a vastly superior force. It would appear that if we do not have texts that explicitly state that the people did not like the conditions under which they lived and that thus they would fight for independence, then some scholars conclude that conditions must not have been so bad. It is hard to avoid the conclusion that more than historical evidence is implicated in such viewpoints. Yet this perspective overlooks the subtleties of spiritual, social, and political resistance, which are not always obvious to those who simply equate violence with resistance. In short, the Maccabean uprising was not the only form of Jewish social resistance to world empire in the Persian and Hellenistic era. A reading of Daniel "in the shadows of empire" greatly facilitates this historical conclusion.

POSTSCRIPT ON READING THE REFLECTIONS IN THIS COMMENTARY

It is somewhat dangerous to ask a Quaker to write a commentary on Daniel. Quaker associations with this book are long and interesting—and not a little controversial. Indeed, there is no other Hebrew biblical book that is more a Quaker's book than Daniel. Quakerism arose, after all, in the throes of the English civil war. The founder of Quakerism, George Fox, was himself offered an officership in Cromwell's anti-Royalist forces. It was not an unusual offer, as there were certainly other (and similarly minded) Christian radicals who believed that dethroning and then beheading the king and fighting for a much wider participation in national affairs, including in some cases the extreme notion of the vote for all persons, was a fulfillment of the book of Daniel. Some of these radicals called themselves "The Fifth Monarchy Men," a term inspired directly from the sequence of four empires named in Daniel 2 and 7. Many of Cromwell's more theologically extreme soldiers, including many Fifth Monarchists, swelled the ranks of Quakerism in its first generation.

Daniel has engendered more bizarre speculations than those of the seventeenth-century Puritan revolutionaries, of course, and part of its continued appeal is precisely the sense of crisis out of which the book arose, which then seems to speak to the frequent recurrence of crises in human society over the centuries. In short, people who sense that the world is not right are drawn to a book that shares their conviction. One of the ways in which we will read Daniel "in the shadows" is to read two authors along the way: Franz Fanon and Albert Memmi. Fanon was an Algerian psychologist who wrote about the Algerian resistance to French colonialism. His work written in 1961, *The Wretched of the Earth,* remains a classic statement of the colonized perspective.[39] Already in 1957, however, the Tunisian Jewish author Albert Memmi had written *The Colonizer and the Colonized* with a similar interest in analyzing the impact of colonization on native peoples.[40] Both works will help us to understand important aspects of reading Daniel as a book that reflects the domination of the Jewish people by Babylonians, Persians, and Greeks. The situations, so different and so far apart historically, are not exactly the same, of course, but Fanon and Memmi provide provocative suggestions for helping us to rethink the implications of social context in a reading of Daniel. We may also draw on the experiences of minority peoples, drawing especially on Native American comments.[41]

The danger inherent in the book of Daniel is clear from the fact that Josephus found himself attempting to tone down the rhetoric, lest it offend his Roman readers. In short,

---

39. F. Fanon, *The Wretched of the Earth* (New York: Grove, 1963).
40. A. Memmi, *The Colonizer and the Colonized* (Boston: Beacon, 1965).
41. During the time I spent in research for this commentary, I was able to sit with Lakota Christians and Traditionalists on the Rosebud Reservation in South Dakota and read chapters from the book of Daniel with them. Some of the comments in the following commentary reflect that research. These interviews form part of an upcoming study on cultural influences on the reading of the Bible.

Daniel directs its severe judgment toward human rulers, and a serious assumption of the work is that the people of faith will inevitably find themselves in opposition to the state and its accompanying forms of political loyalties and idolatrous patriotism. Albert Memmi summarized the position of anyone who would begin to be sympathetic to those who suffer under present political circumstances, which in his context meant the colonized of North Africa. He wrote that a European in North Africa who begins to have sympathy and then to identify with the colonized is to choose "treason" against the values of the powerful.[42] Such a position will generate a reaction: "Wonder has been expressed at the vehemence of colonizers against any among them who put colonization in jeopardy. It is clear that such a colonizer is nothing but a traitor. He challenges their very existence."[43] The book of Daniel calls people of faith to just such a treason against the rule of the powerful, a treason based on loyalty to the rule of God.

Such thoughts should immediately bring pause to any modern pastor who would attempt to preach or teach on Daniel—you are venturing into subversive territory. There is no message of facile patriotism, of "good citizenship," or of merely personal, pietistic faith in Daniel. Thus there can be no such thing as a non-political reading of Daniel, if it is to be true to the living spirit of Scripture and to the suffering of those who wrote it under the inspiration of a God who first delivered slaves from Pharaoh.

Reading Daniel in some contexts raises disturbing questions. How can a book meant to encourage the faith of a politically subordinated people be made meaningful for those of us in a dominant culture, such as European Americans, European Canadians, or European Australians? In short, do we read Daniel as modern "Babylonians," "Persians" and "Greeks," or as their captive peoples?

The frequency with which I draw on the experiences or comments of historically subordinated peoples in this commentary is not intended to be an exercise in collective guilt. The intention is not only to highlight the possible similarities in experience between the writers of Daniel and modern conquered or colonized peoples, but to suggest further that if the Christian faith is to be one that challenges the modern world, then it must accept a certain alienation from the dominant culture and its religious traditions of dominance.

To read the book of Daniel in one hand while holding Fanon or modern Native American works in the other is to suggest that biblical faith will of necessity find significant social and spiritual parallels with the life of alienated peoples. This is because Christians know that they live in Babylon and not in the kingdom of God. To come to that realization means embracing a theology of Christ against culture, particularly where that culture is based on the products of military conquest and economic abuse of conquered peoples.

---

42. Memmi, *The Colonizer and the Colonized,* 22.
43. Ibid., 21.

BIBLIOGRAPHY

Commentaries:

Bentzen, Aage. *Daniel.* HAT 19. Tübingen: Mohr, 1952. A brief critical commentary that is now somewhat dated.

Collins, John J. *Daniel.* Hermeneia. Minneapolis: Fortress, 1993. This is clearly the new standard-bearer for thorough reading of Daniel. Essential for serious study.

Goldingay, John. *Daniel.* WBC 30. Dallas: Word, 1988. A thorough and helpful work, particularly valuable for its attention to cross-references throughout the Bible.

Hartman, Louis F., and Alexander A. DeLella. *The Book of Daniel.* AB 23. Garden City, N.Y.: Doubleday, 1978. Helpful, but dated, entry in the Anchor Bible series.

Koch, Klaus. *Das Buch Daniel.* Darmstadt: Wissenschaftliche Buchgesellschaft, 1980. Particularly attentive to Jewish tradition.

Lacocque, André. *The Book of Daniel.* Translated by D. Pellauer. Atlanta: John Knox, 1979. An erudite literary masterpiece.

Montgomery, James A. *A Critical and Exegetical Commentary on the Book of Daniel.* ICC. Edinburgh: T. & T. Clark, 1927. An older, but still valuable, contribution.

Porteous, Norman W. *Daniel: A Commentary.* OTL. Philadelphia: Westminster, 1965. Translated from the German original, this is a helpful, brief survey of issues.

Towner, W. Sibley. *Daniel.* Interpretation. Atlanta: John Knox, 1984. Good for preaching and adult education.

Background Information:

Collins, John J. *The Apocalyptic Vision of the Book of Daniel.* Missoula, Mont.: Scholars Press, 1977.

Fewell, Danna Nolan. *Circle of Sovereignty: Plotting Politics in the Book of Daniel.* Nashville: Abingdon, 1991. An excellent literary analysis, sensitive to political issues.

Ginsberg, Harold. "The Oldest Interpretation of the Suffering Servant." *VT* 3 (1953). The classic article that further defends the nonviolence of Daniel.

Hellholm, David, ed. *Apocalypticism in the Mediterranean World and the Near East: Proceedings of the International Colloquium on Apocalypticism.* Tübingen: Mohr-Siebeck, 1983. Excellent collection of scholarly background articles.

Kippenberg, Hans G. *Religions und Klassenbildung im antiken Judaä: Eine Religions-soziologie Studie zum Verhältnes von Tradition und gesellschaftlicher Entwicklung.* Vandenhoeck und Ruprecht: Göttingen, 1982. Controversial work that argues for class conflict in the post-exilic society.

Kvanvig, Helge S. *The Roots of Apocalyptic: The Mesopotamian Background of the Enoch Figure and of the Son of Man.* Neukirchen-Vluyn: Neukirchener Verlag, 1988. Important for analysis of apocalyptic literature.

Otzen, Benedikt. *Judaism in Antiquity: Political Development and Religious Currents from Alexander to Hadrian.* Sheffield: JSOT, 1990. Very good survey of historical background.

Rowland, Christopher. *The Open Heaven: A Study of Apocalyptic in Judaism and Early Christianity.* London: SPCK, 1982. A unique and important theory about apocalyptic literature.

Smith, Daniel. *The Religion of the Landless: The Sociology of the Babylonian Exile.* New York: Meyer-Stone, 1989. A more detailed elaboration of some of the sociological assumptions of this commentary.

Tcherikover, Victor. *Hellenistic Civilization and the Jews.* Atheneum: New York, 1970. The classic survey of the Hellenistic period.

VanderKam, James C. *Enoch and the Growth of an Apocalyptic Tradition.* CBQMS 16. Washington, D.C.: Catholic Biblical Association, 1984. A very important study for Daniel/Enoch comparisons.

Weinberg, Joel. *The Citizen Temple Community.* Sheffield: JSOT, 1992. An important and unique argument with regard to the nature of the post-exilic socioeconomic community setting.

OUTLINE OF DANIEL

I. Daniel 1:1–6:28, The Court Stories

    A. 1:1-21, The Cuisine of Resistance

    B. 2:1-49, Speaking Truth to Power: Daniel and Nebuchadnezzar's Dream

    C. 3:1-30, Political Atheism and Radical Faith

    D. 4:1-37, The True Throne and False Thrones

    E. 5:1-31, The Humiliation of the Conquered: Belshazzar's Feast

    F. 6:1-28, In Defiance of Death: Daniel in the Lion Pit

II. Daniel 7:1–12:13, The Apocalyptic Visions

    A. 7:1-28, Visions of Change

    B. 8:1-27, The Ram and the Goat

    C. 9:1-27, Textual Interpretation and Angelic Revolution

    D. 10:1–12:13, The Final Vision

DANIEL 1:1–6:28

THE COURT STORIES

DANIEL 1:1-21, THE CUISINE OF RESISTANCE

NIV

1 In the third year of the reign of Jehoiakim king of Judah, Nebuchadnezzar king of Babylon came to Jerusalem and besieged it. [2]And the Lord delivered Jehoiakim king of Judah into his hand, along with some of the articles from the temple of God. These he carried off to the temple of his god in Babylonia[a] and put in the treasure house of his god.

[3]Then the king ordered Ashpenaz, chief of his court officials, to bring in some of the Israelites from the royal family and the nobility— [4]young men without any physical defect, handsome, showing aptitude for every kind of learning, well informed, quick to understand, and qualified to serve in the king's palace. He was to teach them the language and literature of the Babylonians.[b] [5]The king assigned them a daily amount of food and wine from the king's table. They were to be trained for three years, and after that they were to enter the king's service.

[6]Among these were some from Judah: Daniel, Hananiah, Mishael and Azariah. [7]The chief official gave them new names: to Daniel, the name Belteshazzar; to Hananiah, Shadrach; to Mishael, Meshach; and to Azariah, Abednego.

[8]But Daniel resolved not to defile himself with the royal food and wine, and he asked the chief official for permission not to defile himself this way. [9]Now God had caused the official to show favor and sympathy to Daniel, [10]but the official told Daniel, "I am afraid of my lord the king, who has assigned your[c] food and drink. Why should he see you looking worse than the other young men your age? The king would then have my head because of you."

[a]2 Hebrew *Shinar*   [b]4 Or *Chaldeans*   [c]10 The Hebrew for *your* and *you* in this verse is plural.

NRSV

1 In the third year of the reign of King Jehoiakim of Judah, King Nebuchadnezzar of Babylon came to Jerusalem and besieged it. [2]The Lord let King Jehoiakim of Judah fall into his power, as well as some of the vessels of the house of God. These he brought to the land of Shinar,[a] and placed the vessels in the treasury of his gods.

[3]Then the king commanded his palace master Ashpenaz to bring some of the Israelites of the royal family and of the nobility, [4]young men without physical defect and handsome, versed in every branch of wisdom, endowed with knowledge and insight, and competent to serve in the king's palace; they were to be taught the literature and language of the Chaldeans. [5]The king assigned them a daily portion of the royal rations of food and wine. They were to be educated for three years, so that at the end of that time they could be stationed in the king's court. [6]Among them were Daniel, Hananiah, Mishael, and Azariah, from the tribe of Judah. [7]The palace master gave them other names: Daniel he called Belteshazzar, Hananiah he called Shadrach, Mishael he called Meshach, and Azariah he called Abednego.

[8]But Daniel resolved that he would not defile himself with the royal rations of food and wine; so he asked the palace master to allow him not to defile himself. [9]Now God allowed Daniel to receive favor and compassion from the palace master. [10]The palace master said to Daniel, "I am afraid of my lord the king; he has appointed your food and your drink. If he should see you in poorer condition than the other young men of your own age, you would endanger my head with the king." [11]Then Daniel asked the guard whom

[a] Gk Theodotion: Heb adds *to the house of his own gods*

NIV

¹¹Daniel then said to the guard whom the chief official had appointed over Daniel, Hananiah, Mishael and Azariah, ¹²"Please test your servants for ten days: Give us nothing but vegetables to eat and water to drink. ¹³Then compare our appearance with that of the young men who eat the royal food, and treat your servants in accordance with what you see." ¹⁴So he agreed to this and tested them for ten days.

¹⁵At the end of the ten days they looked healthier and better nourished than any of the young men who ate the royal food. ¹⁶So the guard took away their choice food and the wine they were to drink and gave them vegetables instead.

¹⁷To these four young men God gave knowledge and understanding of all kinds of literature and learning. And Daniel could understand visions and dreams of all kinds.

¹⁸At the end of the time set by the king to bring them in, the chief official presented them to Nebuchadnezzar. ¹⁹The king talked with them, and he found none equal to Daniel, Hananiah, Mishael and Azariah; so they entered the king's service. ²⁰In every matter of wisdom and understanding about which the king questioned them, he found them ten times better than all the magicians and enchanters in his whole kingdom. ²¹And Daniel remained there until the first year of King Cyrus.

NRSV

the palace master had appointed over Daniel, Hananiah, Mishael, and Azariah: ¹²"Please test your servants for ten days. Let us be given vegetables to eat and water to drink. ¹³You can then compare our appearance with the appearance of the young men who eat the royal rations, and deal with your servants according to what you observe." ¹⁴So he agreed to this proposal and tested them for ten days. ¹⁵At the end of ten days it was observed that they appeared better and fatter than all the young men who had been eating the royal rations. ¹⁶So the guard continued to withdraw their royal rations and the wine they were to drink, and gave them vegetables. ¹⁷To these four young men God gave knowledge and skill in every aspect of literature and wisdom; Daniel also had insight into all visions and dreams.

18At the end of the time that the king had set for them to be brought in, the palace master brought them into the presence of Nebuchadnezzar, ¹⁹and the king spoke with them. And among them all, no one was found to compare with Daniel, Hananiah, Mishael, and Azariah; therefore they were stationed in the king's court. ²⁰In every matter of wisdom and understanding concerning which the king inquired of them, he found them ten times better than all the magicians and enchanters in his whole kingdom. ²¹And Daniel continued there until the first year of King Cyrus.

COMMENTARY

1:1-2, The Ideological and Political Significance of the Setting. The first two verses of the first chapter serve notice to the reader that the context of these stories is of paramount importance to the writers and editors of the book of Daniel. These verses introduce the book as a whole and not merely the first story, reminding the reader of the context of dominance from which these stories derive their life and power. The bare facts are that Nebuchadnezzar conquered Jerusalem, captured King Jehoiachin (son of Jehoiakim, who died while Jerusalem was under seige), and took captive not only the king

but the temple implements as well. These implements were placed, significantly, in the "treasury of his gods" (v. 2). This is an important note, since we know that the Babylonians were highly aware of the propaganda value of placing captured religious symbols "under" the Babylonian gods in the Babylonian imperial shrines, thus symbolizing the captivity of conquered gods as well as people. Since the Jews did not have an image of their God, the Babylonians used their temple vessels instead. Note that these materials were not merely melted down (see chap. 5), but kept intact so as to serve as symbols of the Jews' subordinate position in relation to Babylonian imperial and religious power.[44]

It has long been noted that the historical details of vv. 1-2 cannot be accepted literally, although attempts have been made to suggest that the author is drawing on a combination of Jer 25:1, 11 and 2 Chr 36:6 in order to arrive at his ideas about a campaign during Jehoiakim's reign[45] as well as conforming to Jeremiah's prediction of a seventy-year exile. It seems conclusive, however, that Nebuchadnezzar did not campaign in Palestine before his success at Carchemish in 605 BCE. Surely it is much more sensible to assume that a folktale is interested not in chronological details, but in the power of the context of exile.[46] Much more interesting, however, is the reference to "Shinar," a name for Babylon that recalls the story of the tower of Babel in Genesis 11 and associates Babylon with the hubris evident in that tale.[47]

Therefore, the introduction serves notice to readers, ancient and modern, that these important facts of life serve as the essential background to the proper appreciation of the stories and the visions of the book of Daniel. As we will see, reminders of the exilic status of the characters in Daniel run through the twelve chapters like a political litany.

1:3-7, The Selection of Jewish Exiles for Training. The first story in the book of Daniel focuses on the treatment of the exiles from the perspective of the Babylonian conquerors. The king requests that members of the captured peoples be selected (specifically from the leadership of the Jewish people) for specialized training in Babylonian language and culture. Note that the assessment of their competence to serve in the king's palace is made before they have been trained, implying that they have something to offer the king's court, and that, therefore, their knowledge of Jewish language and culture is what the king is particularly interested in. For what other reason could they be useful than for maximizing the efficiency of Babylonian rule? If they are actually drawn from the royal families or from the priestly families, as Lacocque has suggested, noting that the ones chosen were "without blemish,"[48] then the Babylonians' interest in them would surely be even greater.

The four Jewish men chosen are to be issued rations of royal food and wine during their three-year course of study. (Many scholars have noted that three years of study is mentioned in Persian sources as the time required for training in knowledge of religious matters.)

Significantly, the four Jewish exiles are carefully introduced with their Jewish names, before it is noted that their names have been changed to Babylonian names. There does not appear to be any particular importance attached to the non-Israelite names, and scholars do not agree on the precise meanings. Roughly, Daniel is renamed "Belteshazzar," or "Protect the king's life"; Azariah's new name becomes "Abednego," "Servant of Nabu"; Hananiah is renamed "Shadrach," or "Shining" (from Persian?); and Mishael becomes Meschach from the Persian religious name "Mithra." Name changing is, of course, a prominent biblical sign of dependent status, thus Abram to Abraham in covenant with God (Gen 17:5); Jehoiakim is renamed by Pharaoh (2 Kgs 23:34); and Zedekiah is renamed by Nebuchadnezzar (2 Kgs 24:17). The practice became common in late biblical literature. While it is true that many observant Jews in the Hellenistic period took on non-Jewish names (Philo), and even earlier there is evidence of names like "Zerubbabel," the issue here is not whether the names are non-Israelite, but that it is done by a power that assumes the authority to make such a change.[49]

1:8-21, Resistance to Partaking of the King's Food and Wine. The planned assimilation of the four Jewish representatives of the exile

---

44. The Persians were especially attuned to the significance of symbols that are directed to mass consumption. See M. C. Root, *The King and Kingship in Achaemenid Art: Essays on the Creation of an Iconography of Empire*, vol. 9 of Acta Iranica, Textes et Memoires (Leiden: Brill, 1979). Note also N. Porteous, *Daniel: A Commentary*, OTL (Philadelphia: Westminster, 1965) 26-27; and John Goldingay, *Daniel*, WBC 30 (Dallas: Word, 1988) 15-17.

45. André Lacocque, *The Book of Daniel*, trans. D. Pellauer (Atlanta: John Knox, 1979) 25.

46. John J. Collins, *Daniel*, Hermeneia (Minneapolis: Fortress, 1993) 132. Collins is rather critical of attempts to mesh the dates in Daniel with some configuration of dates drawn from Chronicles, Jeremiah, or elsewhere.

47. After Lacocque, *The Book of Daniel*, 25. The association of exile, Nebuchadnezzar, and the tower of Babel is explicit in the enigmatic Dead Sea Scroll fragments designated 4QpsDan a, b, and c in F. García-Martínez, *Qumran and Apocalyptic, Studies on the Aramaic Texts from Qumran* (Leiden: Brill, 1992) 127-61; but also published as 4Q243-245 in R. Eisenman and M. Wise, *The Dead Sea Scrolls Uncovered* (Shaftsbury: Element, 1992) 64-67.

48. Lacocque, *The Book of Daniel*, 27.

49. Thus, I would respectfully take issue with Goldingay, Collins, and Porteous. On this matter, Lacocque is much more alive to the impact of forced name changes. See Lacocque, *The Book of Daniel*, 29.

community runs into a brick wall. Daniel (Why not the others? Does this imply a division among the Jews on these issues of resistance?) firmly states his refusal to accept the king's offer of food and wine, stating that he would be "polluted" (גאל *gāʾal*) by them. This powerful term is highly suggestive for the exilic and post-exilic experience. Ezra the priest would also strongly assert the necessity of maintaining "purity" in the conditions of subordination in the post-exilic community, and we know that the priests involved themselves diligently in the codification of levitical purity law during the exile. Furthermore, purity concerns that even exceeded the specific demands of the priestly purity laws are not unusual in the late biblical and Hellenistic periods (e.g., Tob 1:10-11; Jdt 12:1-4; 2 Maccabees 6–7; *Jub.* 22:16; and Josephus *The Life of Flavius Josephus* 3.14). As Mary Douglas has shown, worries about the purity of the body are symbolic reflections of concerns for the integrity of the social group, and purity laws serve as effective barriers to assimilation. The assertion of purity concerns during the exile served as an important spiritual and social bulwark against the dangers of disappearing as a people, and Daniel 1 obviously maintains this important theological motif.[50]

50. Mary Douglas, *Purity and Danger* (London: Routledge and Kegan Paul, 1966).

Scholars have debated the reasons for Daniel's resistance of the rations. Of course, Daniel does accept the "vegetables" (זרעים *zērōʿîm*; lit., "pulses" or "seeds") from the royal supply, so the likelihood that he wanted to avoid any Babylonian food that had been dedicated to pagan deities seems not to be the issue. The consumption of wine is clearly not forbidden in levitical purity laws. But as Goldingay has noted, meat and wine are not only the foods of festivity (Isa 22:13), which may need to be avoided when the attitude of exiles ought to be mourning for the destruction of Jerusalem, but they are also the foods of the wealthy rather than the peasants. The issue is dependence on royal largess and wealth—wealth that was not incidentally stolen from the livelihood of the nations conquered by the Babylonian Empire.[51] This point deserves concentrated attention in the following excursus.

51. Goldingay's discussion of this matter is very helpful. See his *Daniel,* 18-19. See also D. Berrigan, who states: "They must know, these favored ones, that the princely diet offered them is the fruit of murder and oppression" ("Till the End of Empire," *The Other Side* [July-August 1990] 11).

❖   ❖   ❖   ❖

EXCURSUS: FOOD AND POWER

A full appreciation of this story also requires that one keep in mind the prominence of food as a symbol of privilege and wealth and foreign overindulgence. Lacocque notes that Daniel 1 illustrates "the custom in ancient royal courts of introducing important prisoners to the national diet."[52] But if the modern reader is alerted to the significance of food in the context of post-exilic conditions, Daniel 1 takes on added significance.

Throughout biblical history, control of food, especially large amounts of it, is symbolic of power. This can best be summarized in a discussion of feasting and the taxation of foodstuffs (in-kind taxation). This discussion obviously anticipates some of the symbolism of Belshazzar's feast in chap. 5 as well.

A banquet suggests the celebration of a joyful occasion, such as the weaning of Isaac in Gen 21:8, Pharaoh's birthday in Gen 40:22, and Samson's wedding in Judg 14:10. Such feasts were to be occasions for rejoicing and were contrasted with occasions for mourning in Eccl 7:2 and Jer 16:8. But it is clear that feasting is also a symbol of power. In 1 Kgs 3:15, Solomon declares a joyous feast after his "conversation" with God. Job and his sons feast as a symbol of their good fortune (Job 1:4), and the "messianic banquet" in Isaiah 25 carries this theme

52. Lacocque, *The Book of Daniel,* 28.

of celebration into eschatological expectation. The exiled King Jehoiachin "put aside his prison clothes. Every day of his life he dined regularly in the king's presence" (2 Kgs 25:29-30 NRSV).

Improper or impious revelries, by the same token, are seen as symbolic of wealthy excess and oppressive power and are condemned by the prophets Isaiah (Isa 5:8-14) and Amos (Amos 4:1-3). This prophetic condemnation of misplaced revelry is also connected to feasting as a symbol of foreign excess and privilege. Royal largess is thus a motif in the banquets of Pharaoh in Gen 40:20, a portion of the Genesis material that is probably post-exilic.[53] The post-exilic author thus used these banquets to symbolize further the power of the pharaoh.

Over 40 percent of all the occurrences of the word "banquet" (משתה *mišteh*) are in the book of Esther alone. Indeed, banquets appear so frequently in Esther as to suggest a framework for the story as a whole, each feast marking a major step from humble origins to crisis and finally to victory:

A the king's feast (rise of Esther among exiles) 1:3, 5; 2:18
   B Esther's feast (threat to Esther and Jews) 5:5, 8, 12, 14; 6:14
A' the Jews' feast (victory of Esther and Jews) 8:17; 9:17-18

In her analysis of the book of Esther, Berg elaborates on the centrality of banqueting in the story as a whole: "Esther's author constructed a tale whose beginning, middle, and conclusion center upon the motif of feasting. In addition, each of these banquet pairs recalls the others, simultaneously paralleling and contrasting with them."[54]

Finally, in the late book of Judith, the time of Judith's triumph is at the feast of Holofernes (Jdt 12:10) a reversal of fortune precisely at the time of the foreign king's display of power and extravagance. And within the same book is the assertion that Judith maintained purity from Gentile food!

These examples reveal banqueting to be a potent biblical symbol of power, that moves from a positive symbol of prosperity in the pre-exilic texts and stories to a predominantly negative symbol of foreign oppression in the prophetic and post-exilic contexts, when the oppressors would have feasted on utensils taken from Jewish tables to satisfy their appetite for materials and money.

This final point clearly derives from the fact that taxation of the supply of food was already a source of consternation in the deuteronomic "anti-king" text: "He will take the best of your fields, your vineyards and your olive groves and give them to his officials. He will tithe your crops and vineyards to provide for his courtiers and his officials. . . . He will tithe your flocks, and you yourselves will become his slaves" (1 Sam 8:14-17 NJB).

Taxes were usually paid in kind, the value of such payments being accounted for in monetary equivalents. It is clear that, from at least the deuteronomic period, taxation in kind was a symbol of royal privilege and power. As Hoglund points out, in the Persian and Hellenistic empires, the economics of the imperial systems was rooted in a "tributary mode of production." The rural countryside, the source of such supplies, was heavily taxed in order to maintain tribute to the imperial coffers, feeding the bureaucracy of the imperial program.[55]

Malachi 1:8 undoubtedly refers to in-kind taxation imposed on the Jews by their governors. That taxation of the means of subsistence was common among the governors of the area of Judea between the exile and the mission of Nehemiah is clear both from the complaints

---

53. The post-exilic dating of portions of the Joseph story was suspected by German scholars as early as the 1890s, but has been impressively argued in detail by D. Redford, *A Study of the Biblical Story of Joseph* (Leiden: Brill, 1970).

54. S. Berg, *The Book of Esther,* SBLDS 44 (Atlanta: Scholars Press, 1979) 35.

55. K. G. Hoglund, *Achaemenid Imperial Administraion in Syria-Palestine and the Missions of Ezra and Nehemiah,* SBLDS 125 (Atlanta: Scholars Press, 1992) 9, 11.

of the people in Nehemiah's time about the crippling level of taxation (Neh 5:1-5) and from Nehemiah's own assurances that he intends to lighten their burden (Neh 5:14-16). Further-more, and most important, in the prayer/poem in Nehemiah 9, foreign control over food materials was clearly understood as a potent symbol of foreign domination and of God's punishment:

> Here we are, slaves to this day—slaves in the land that you gave to our ancestors to enjoy its fruit and its good gifts. Its rich yield goes to the kings whom you have set over us because of our sins; they have power also over our bodies and over our livestock at their pleasure, and we are in great distress. (Neh 9:36-37 NRSV)

Resistance to food in Daniel 1, therefore, and the clear condemnation of Belshazzar, pictured in drunken revelry in chap. 5, clearly relate to symbolic awareness of the meaning of controlling food stores as a key to controlling lives. In short, I agree with Davies' assertion that Daniel 1 is "a symbolic denial of the king's implicit claim to be sole provider,"[56] but when this observation is set within the context of the politicization of food as symbol, Daniel 1 (and chap. 5) is read with more appreciation of the theme of resistance.[57]

56. P. Davies, *Daniel* (Sheffield: JSOT, 1989) 91.

57. My argument here is in contrast to the view that fasting is an ascetic practice. See, e.g., D. Satran, "Daniel: Seer, Philosopher, Holy Man," in G. Nickelsburg and John J. Collins, eds., *Ideal Figures in Ancient Judaism* (Chico, Calif.: Scholars Press, 1980) 33-48.

❖   ❖   ❖   ❖

1:9-10. Verse 9, which asserts that Daniel received protection from God, is an important answer to an obvious question: Why wasn't this upstart captive cut down where he stood for such blatant insubordination? Anyone who might think that this is assuming too much about Babylonian attitudes is clearly forgetting the reminders of vv. 1-2, let alone the destructive anger of the emper-ors discussed in the entire book!

One answer is that the king was not present, but only the official called Ashpenaz (the name probably derives from the Persian for "Innkeeper," or keeper of the court). Many commentators have noted the sympathy of Ashpenaz toward Daniel and its significance for the continued idea about a positive view of foreigners in Daniel 1–6. But Ashpenaz is not so powerful that he does not have to fear for his life if called before the emperor (v. 10). The friendship between Daniel and Ash-penaz, therefore, is the solidarity of the oppressed, both of whom serve the imperial will under threat of death; and this solidarity crosses ethnic lines, as Ashpenaz obviously admires Daniel's courage. This is hardly a sign of positive attitudes toward Babylonians!

Another answer is that Daniel received God's חסד (*ḥesed*). The NRSV's implication that this *ḥesed*—favor and compassion—came from the

palace master is misleading. God influenced events in Daniel's favor by giving Daniel *ḥesed*. The term is typically translated as "steadfast love," but because of Katherine Doob Sakenfeld's de-tailed work, we understand the full implications of *ḥesed* as "deliverance or protection as a respon-sible keeping of faith with another with whom one is in a relationship."[58] Although *ḥesed* appears often in the context of praise for the building or rebuilding of the Temple in the psalms (Psalms 100; 106; 107; 118; 136; cf. 1 Chronicles 34; 41; 2 Chr 5:13; 7:3, 6; Ezra 3:11), note that *ḥesed* is the particular power of God to deliver Israel from its enemies (see Psalm 143). In Jer 33:11, the restoration after exile is clearly the intended result of God's *ḥesed*: "For I will restore the fortunes of the land" (NRSV). Finally, the shout of praise for God's *ḥesed* is associated with the miraculous defeat of enemies in 2 Chr 20:21, which is associated (by the act of fasting) with Ezra 8:21-23 (God's deliverance from enemies).[59]

So in v. 9 God makes Daniel the object of *ḥesed* and mercy before Ashpenaz. *Ḥesed* is

58. K. Sakenfeld, *The Meaning of Ḥesed in the Hebrew Bible: A New Inquiry* (Missoula, Mont.: Scholars Press, 1978) 233.

59. My full study on fasting and its military associations in Daniel can be found as "Hebrew Satyagraha: The Politics of Biblical Fasting in the Post-Exilic Period (Sixth to Second Century BCE)," *Food and Foodways: An Interdisciplinary Journal* 5 (1993) 269-92.

closely associated with "mercy" (see Neh 1:11, in which Nehemiah requests mercy before "this man," the emperor; cf. Psalm 106). Sakenfeld's concluding statement on the use of *hesed* in the psalms is that the term is "predominantly associated with deliverance rather than any special blessing."[60] Sakenfeld suggests that *hesed* as "delivering power" reaches its height in a series of texts in which it parallels "strength." Prominent among these texts is Exod 15:13:

You led in your *hesed*
The people whom you redeemed
You guided in your strength
to your holy encampment.[61]

Hesed and mercy, especially in the context of late biblical theology, are given to those Jews who appear before the Babylonian and Persian monarchs, which forces us to conclude that the passage assumes the necessity for God's delivering action against a presumed enemy. Praise was directed to God's delivering power, not to the Babylonian or Persian monarch's (or an assistant's) good intentions.

1:11-17. These verses summarize the "contest" of this story. The Jewish captives are to be tested and compared to the "young men" (Babylonians? Other captives/non-Babylonians with fewer scruples?) for ten days. The folkloric nature of the story is obvious in the selection of the number ten, although one might have expected a number like seven or forty.

In any case, physical appearance, rather than knowledge or wisdom, is the deciding factor in choosing these young men; however, their wisdom is mentioned (v. 17) as an additional aspect of their superior performance. The last section of v. 17*b*, which mentions Daniel's insights into visions and dreams, is clearly a foreshadowing of the stories to come, further suggesting that this story was a late addition to the series that evolved into the present book of Daniel. Knowledge and wisdom, however, become the crucial factors in the following verses, when the four Jewish men stand before the king.

1:18-20. The story ends with the young men appearing before the king. Standing before the king is a common motif in biblical literature. It is interesting to note the frequency with which the narrators of stories set in the exilic period (and later) emphasize the significance of standing before the foreign king. In vv. 3 and 18, the appearances before the king are the frame scenes for the story as a whole. Daniel and his friends stood before the king for the first time when introduced with their challenge and again when they are rewarded for their success.[62] In other biblical stories, Esther and Mordecai (who stands rather than bows before Haman), as well as Ezra and Nehemiah, had their turn to stand before the king. The scene is dramatic and crucial. Rarely do these figures stand before some lower official, which would more likely have been the case historically.[63] Incidentally, this is among the most significant indications of the folkloric setting of these stories.

That these scenes are unique is clearer when they are compared to the mention of bowing or doing obeisance, which is more common in the deuteronomic historian (1 Sam 24:8; 28:4; 2 Sam 1:2; 9:6, 8; 14:4, 22, 33). Scholars have noted that the Persian courts especially captured the imagination of the Greeks and certainly seemed a dramatic setting for the Jewish diaspora tales as well.[64] But it was a dreaded fascination, and the wise, according to Proverbs, would avoid such appearances before powerful rulers, unless specifically called upon:

Do not put yourself forward in
  the king's presence
  or stand in the place of the great;
for it is better to be told, "Come
  up here,"
  than to be put lower in the
  presence of a noble. (Prov 25:6-7 NRSV)

---

60. Sakenfeld, *The Meaning of Hesed in the Hebrew Bible,* 218. See also K. D. Sakenfeld's more recent summary statement of her work on hesed in the Bible: *Faithfulness in Action: Loyalty in Biblical Perspective* (Minneapolis: Fortress, 1985).

61. Sakenfeld, *The Meaning of Hesed in the Hebrew Bible,* 212.

62. Also note that in Dan 2:2, Nebuchadnezzar's advisers come to his presence and stand before the king prior to the introduction of the Jewish resisters. These resisters will stand rather than bow before the image of the king. Similarly, in Dan 10:11-12 Daniel is to stand before God's messenger.

63. There are some "standing before the king" scenes in the deuteronomic historian (note 1 Kgs 1:28, in which Bathsheba is called to stand before the king; 1 Kgs 3:16, where two prostitutes stand before the king; and 1 Kgs 18:15, where Elijah points out that he stands before God [rather than merely the king?]); see also 1 Kgs 17:1; 2 Kgs 3:14.

In the narratives, it is more typical to mention that someone was "before" the king (no mention of standing) or simply going to the king, with no court scene mentioned at all.

64. "In Asia Minor, Mesopotamia, and Israel, the power of the centralized court evidently captured the imagination of the masses. . . . The gracious gifts to be received or the terrible punishments to be inflicted here were greater than anywhere else" (L. Wills, *The Jew in the Court of the Foreign King* [Minneapolis: Fortress, 1990] 19-20).

Similarly, both Ezra and Nehemiah include significant appearances before the king. In the Nehemiah text, the relationship of Nehemiah to the king should not distract one from the language of fear. In Neh 2:2, Nehemiah is "very much afraid." Fear of the authorities and their opposition appears in Neh 4:14. Ashpenaz states that he is afraid of the king (v. 10). Like Daniel, Nehemiah is granted mercy before "this man."[65] This term "mercy" is found also in 1 Kgs 8:50; 2 Chr 30:9; and Ps 106:46, all cases of God's assurance before intimidating power.

The implication is that the court of Nebuchadnezzar is a setting of awe and majesty. The king's questions, clearly intended to be a test, are also common features of many of the biblical and post-biblical Jewish writings (note the abundant questioning in the Letter of Aristeas and Zerubbabel's clever solving of problems posed by the king in 2 Esdras). The king's interrogation of the four Jews results in the conclusion that the Jewish exiles are "ten times better" (note the repetition of the theme of multiples of ten from vv. 12-17) than all the magicians and enchanters throughout the kingdom, and not merely the others who were in training. That Babylon was known as a center for magic and enchanters is a theme the Bible will elsewhere affirm, and this passes into Jewish lore from the time of the exile onward, even to the "wise men" tradition of the New Testament Gospels. "Chaldean" (כשׂדים *kaśdîm*) is a term used throughout Daniel to refer to an astrologer as one of the royal court officials, rather than the general term for an ethnic Babylonian.[66]

1:21. The final verse notes that Daniel began his work during the reign of King Nebuchadnezzar and remained in his position until the first year of King Cyrus. This information can be somewhat confusing—even if one has already stated doubts about the historicity of any of these stories. The editor of the material clearly wants to connect Daniel to the fate of the exiles, from the time of the conquest by Nebuchadnezzar (586/587 BCE) to the beginning of the reign of Cyrus as liberator of Babylon (539 BCE). While this is not impossible during a usual life span (roughly fifty years in royal service added to the age of the young Daniel—Thirteen? Sixteen?—when he was taken into Babylonian service), we must also contend with the fact that the stories have Daniel still active in the court of Darius, who is surely based on the Persian ruler who succeeded Cambyses, as well. The reign of the historical Darius began after considerable turmoil around 522 BCE! The Darius in Daniel, however, was supposed to have been a Mede who ruled *before* the time of Cyrus.

Goldingay notes that chap. 1 begins with Nebuchadnezzar and ends with Cyrus, suggesting a thematic structure that parallels the beginning and the end of the exile, by beginning with the capture of the Jews and ending with Daniel's "victory" over the Babylonians.[67] But as Knibb has shown, Daniel as a whole does not imagine that the exile has ended; rather extends it to seventy weeks of years, or 490 years—far beyond Jeremiah's predicted seventy years (Jer 25:1, 29)![68] Indeed, the book of Daniel does not presume an end to exile at all; thus any reading and theological understanding must begin with the realities of exilic existence. The book comes to us from the midst of resistance, and not from a sense that the danger has passed.

---

65. Blenkinsopp wonders whether the use of "this man" is a slightly pejorative term. See J. Blenkinsopp, *Ezra–Nehemiah,* OTL (London: SCM, 1988). Kellerman, however, compares it to other uses of courtroom language where one imagines a gesture toward the person being accused. See U. Kellerman, *Nehemia,* BZAW (Berlin: Kaiser, 1967) 85-86.
66. See Herodotus *The History* 1:181-183.

67. John Goldingay, *Daniel,* WBC 30 (Dallas: Word, 1988) 12.
68. M. Knibb, "The Exile in the Literature of the Intertestamental Period," *The Heythrop Journal* 17 (1976) 253-72.

REFLECTIONS

Christian faith inevitably calls us to active nonconformity with the world, even in the manner in which we daily live our lives—the food we choose to consume, and the clothing we choose to wear. The message of Daniel 1 is a powerful reminder for us to search within ourselves for those aspects of "the king's food and wine" that we ought to resist for the sake of the gospel message. For the writer of Daniel, food was merely one symbol among many others of the resistance to total domination and total assimilation to the culture and ways of dominant powers. So, too, is the Christian life a life of resistance—to the enticements of financial power and control over the destiny of others—such as powerful nations over the developing world—and to the enticements of luxury that come from the abuse of underpaid laborers in struggling societies. For Christians from dominant cultures in North America, Australia, and Europe, a man like Ashpenaz, rather than Daniel, may provide a more apt role model of resistance. Ashpenaz emerges from the power elite to have sympathy for those who suffer and resist. But like Ashpenaz, the faithful among the elite must be aware that their faith borders on treason; hence identification with, let alone sympathy for, the "exiled" peoples may have its cost.[69]

Therefore, the first question one needs to ask in a consideration of a theology of Daniel 1 (and in many ways the book as a whole) is, What is the food and wine that the modern emperors are offering us? The key here is that these enticements can be disguised as necessities, like food! So much of contemporary advertising and marketing is directed toward changing people's habits, to entice them to buy products that will become necessities, that they simply "can't live without." North American consumers especially are not used to asking serious questions about their consumption habits—not only whether it is too much, but also whether it is consumption that supports a living wage and a safe environment for workers. The market entices us to ignore such matters, but we are not to be enticed by the king's food and wine.

John Woolman, the great American Quaker traveling minister of the eighteenth century, asked a powerful question that is relevant to all modern Christian resisters. Woolman himself refused to wear certain articles of clothing that were either dyed or made by means of slave labor. In his essay "A Plea for the Poor," Woolman asks life-style questions: "May we look upon our treasures, the furniture of our houses, and the garments in which we array ourselves—and ask whether the seeds of war have any nourishment in these our possessions or not."

A call to faithful resistance may require modern Christians to think through whole new approaches to living our lives so that we no longer defile ourselves with the food and wine of kings and their militias, and begin to work with those exiled peoples whom these kings and their militias intended to control.

69. See A. Memmi, *The Colonizer and the Colonized* (Boston: Beacon, 1965). See also Introduction.

DANIEL 2:1-49, SPEAKING TRUTH TO POWER: DANIEL AND NEBUCHADNEZZAR'S DREAM

NIV

2 In the second year of his reign, Nebuchadnezzar had dreams; his mind was troubled and he could not sleep. [2]So the king summoned the magicians, enchanters, sorcerers and astrologers[a] to tell him what he had dreamed. When they came in and stood before the king, [3]he said to them, "I have had a dream that troubles me and I want to know what it means.[b]"

[4]Then the astrologers answered the king in

a2 Or *Chaldeans;* also in verses 4, 5 and 10   b3 Or *was*

NRSV

2 In the second year of Nebuchadnezzar's reign, Nebuchadnezzar dreamed such dreams that his spirit was troubled and his sleep left him. [2]So the king commanded that the magicians, the enchanters, the sorcerers, and the Chaldeans be summoned to tell the king his dreams. When they came in and stood before the king, [3]he said to them, "I have had such a dream that my spirit is troubled by the desire to understand it." [4]The Chaldeans said to the king (in Aramaic),[a]

a The text from this point to the end of chapter 7 is in Aramaic

NIV

Aramaic,^a "O king, live forever! Tell your servants the dream, and we will interpret it."

⁵The king replied to the astrologers, "This is what I have firmly decided: If you do not tell me what my dream was and interpret it, I will have you cut into pieces and your houses turned into piles of rubble. ⁶But if you tell me the dream and explain it, you will receive from me gifts and rewards and great honor. So tell me the dream and interpret it for me."

⁷Once more they replied, "Let the king tell his servants the dream, and we will interpret it."

⁸Then the king answered, "I am certain that you are trying to gain time, because you realize that this is what I have firmly decided: ⁹If you do not tell me the dream, there is just one penalty for you. You have conspired to tell me misleading and wicked things, hoping the situation will change. So then, tell me the dream, and I will know that you can interpret it for me."

¹⁰The astrologers answered the king, "There is not a man on earth who can do what the king asks! No king, however great and mighty, has ever asked such a thing of any magician or enchanter or astrologer. ¹¹What the king asks is too difficult. No one can reveal it to the king except the gods, and they do not live among men."

¹²This made the king so angry and furious that he ordered the execution of all the wise men of Babylon. ¹³So the decree was issued to put the wise men to death, and men were sent to look for Daniel and his friends to put them to death.

¹⁴When Arioch, the commander of the king's guard, had gone out to put to death the wise men of Babylon, Daniel spoke to him with wisdom and tact. ¹⁵He asked the king's officer, "Why did the king issue such a harsh decree?" Arioch then explained the matter to Daniel. ¹⁶At this, Daniel went in to the king and asked for time, so that he might interpret the dream for him.

¹⁷Then Daniel returned to his house and explained the matter to his friends Hananiah, Mishael and Azariah. ¹⁸He urged them to plead for mercy from the God of heaven concerning this mystery, so that he and his friends might not be executed with the rest of the wise men of Babylon. ¹⁹During the night the mystery was revealed

^a4 The text from here through chapter 7 is in Aramaic.

NRSV

"O king, live forever! Tell your servants the dream, and we will reveal the interpretation." ⁵The king answered the Chaldeans, "This is a public decree: if you do not tell me both the dream and its interpretation, you shall be torn limb from limb, and your houses shall be laid in ruins. ⁶But if you do tell me the dream and its interpretation, you shall receive from me gifts and rewards and great honor. Therefore tell me the dream and its interpretation." ⁷They answered a second time, "Let the king first tell his servants the dream, then we can give its interpretation." ⁸The king answered, "I know with certainty that you are trying to gain time, because you see I have firmly decreed: ⁹if you do not tell me the dream, there is but one verdict for you. You have agreed to speak lying and misleading words to me until things take a turn. Therefore, tell me the dream, and I shall know that you can give me its interpretation." ¹⁰The Chaldeans answered the king, "There is no one on earth who can reveal what the king demands! In fact no king, however great and powerful, has ever asked such a thing of any magician or enchanter or Chaldean. ¹¹The thing that the king is asking is too difficult, and no one can reveal it to the king except the gods, whose dwelling is not with mortals."

12Because of this the king flew into a violent rage and commanded that all the wise men of Babylon be destroyed. ¹³The decree was issued, and the wise men were about to be executed; and they looked for Daniel and his companions, to execute them. ¹⁴Then Daniel responded with prudence and discretion to Arioch, the king's chief executioner, who had gone out to execute the wise men of Babylon; ¹⁵he asked Arioch, the royal official, "Why is the decree of the king so urgent?" Arioch then explained the matter to Daniel. ¹⁶So Daniel went in and requested that the king give him time and he would tell the king the interpretation.

17Then Daniel went to his home and informed his companions, Hananiah, Mishael, and Azariah, ¹⁸and told them to seek mercy from the God of heaven concerning this mystery, so that Daniel and his companions with the rest of the wise men of Babylon might not perish. ¹⁹Then the mystery

NIV

to Daniel in a vision. Then Daniel praised the God of heaven [20]and said:

"Praise be to the name of God for ever and ever;
 wisdom and power are his.
[21]He changes times and seasons;
 he sets up kings and deposes them.
He gives wisdom to the wise
 and knowledge to the discerning.
[22]He reveals deep and hidden things;
 he knows what lies in darkness,
 and light dwells with him.
[23]I thank and praise you, O God of my fathers:
 You have given me wisdom and power,
you have made known to me what we asked of you,
 you have made known to us the dream of the king."

[24]Then Daniel went to Arioch, whom the king had appointed to execute the wise men of Babylon, and said to him, "Do not execute the wise men of Babylon. Take me to the king, and I will interpret his dream for him."

[25]Arioch took Daniel to the king at once and said, "I have found a man among the exiles from Judah who can tell the king what his dream means."

[26]The king asked Daniel (also called Belteshazzar), "Are you able to tell me what I saw in my dream and interpret it?"

[27]Daniel replied, "No wise man, enchanter, magician or diviner can explain to the king the mystery he has asked about, [28]but there is a God in heaven who reveals mysteries. He has shown King Nebuchadnezzar what will happen in days to come. Your dream and the visions that passed through your mind as you lay on your bed are these:

[29]"As you were lying there, O king, your mind turned to things to come, and the revealer of mysteries showed you what is going to happen. [30]As for me, this mystery has been revealed to me, not because I have greater wisdom than other living men, but so that you, O king, may know the interpretation and that you may understand what went through your mind.

[31]"You looked, O king, and there before you stood a large statue—an enormous, dazzling statue, awesome in appearance. [32]The head of the

NRSV

was revealed to Daniel in a vision of the night, and Daniel blessed the God of heaven.
[20] Daniel said:

"Blessed be the name of God from age to age,
 for wisdom and power are his.
[21] He changes times and seasons,
 deposes kings and sets up kings;
he gives wisdom to the wise
 and knowledge to those who have understanding.
[22] He reveals deep and hidden things;
 he knows what is in the darkness,
 and light dwells with him.
[23] To you, O God of my ancestors,
 I give thanks and praise,
for you have given me wisdom and power,
 and have now revealed to me what we asked of you,
 for you have revealed to us what the king ordered."

[24]Therefore Daniel went to Arioch, whom the king had appointed to destroy the wise men of Babylon, and said to him, "Do not destroy the wise men of Babylon; bring me in before the king, and I will give the king the interpretation."

[25]Then Arioch quickly brought Daniel before the king and said to him: "I have found among the exiles from Judah a man who can tell the king the interpretation." [26]The king said to Daniel, whose name was Belteshazzar, "Are you able to tell me the dream that I have seen and its interpretation?" [27]Daniel answered the king, "No wise men, enchanters, magicians, or diviners can show to the king the mystery that the king is asking, [28]but there is a God in heaven who reveals mysteries, and he has disclosed to King Nebuchadnezzar what will happen at the end of days. Your dream and the visions of your head as you lay in bed were these: [29]To you, O king, as you lay in bed, came thoughts of what would be hereafter, and the revealer of mysteries disclosed to you what is to be. [30]But as for me, this mystery has not been revealed to me because of any wisdom that I have more than any other living being, but in order that the interpretation may be known to the king and that you may understand the thoughts of your mind.

[31]"You were looking, O king, and lo! there was a great statue. This statue was huge, its brilliance extraordinary; it was standing before

NIV

statue was made of pure gold, its chest and arms of silver, its belly and thighs of bronze, [33]its legs of iron, its feet partly of iron and partly of baked clay. [34]While you were watching, a rock was cut out, but not by human hands. It struck the statue on its feet of iron and clay and smashed them. [35]Then the iron, the clay, the bronze, the silver and the gold were broken to pieces at the same time and became like chaff on a threshing floor in the summer. The wind swept them away without leaving a trace. But the rock that struck the statue became a huge mountain and filled the whole earth.

[36]"This was the dream, and now we will interpret it to the king. [37]You, O king, are the king of kings. The God of heaven has given you dominion and power and might and glory; [38]in your hands he has placed mankind and the beasts of the field and the birds of the air. Wherever they live, he has made you ruler over them all. You are that head of gold.

[39]"After you, another kingdom will rise, inferior to yours. Next, a third kingdom, one of bronze, will rule over the whole earth. [40]Finally, there will be a fourth kingdom, strong as iron—for iron breaks and smashes everything—and as iron breaks things to pieces, so it will crush and break all the others. [41]Just as you saw that the feet and toes were partly of baked clay and partly of iron, so this will be a divided kingdom; yet it will have some of the strength of iron in it, even as you saw iron mixed with clay. [42]As the toes were partly iron and partly clay, so this kingdom will be partly strong and partly brittle. [43]And just as you saw the iron mixed with baked clay, so the people will be a mixture and will not remain united, any more than iron mixes with clay.

[44]"In the time of those kings, the God of heaven will set up a kingdom that will never be destroyed, nor will it be left to another people. It will crush all those kingdoms and bring them to an end, but it will itself endure forever. [45]This is the meaning of the vision of the rock cut out of a mountain, but not by human hands—a rock that broke the iron, the bronze, the clay, the silver and the gold to pieces.

"The great God has shown the king what will

NRSV

you, and its appearance was frightening. [32]The head of that statue was of fine gold, its chest and arms of silver, its middle and thighs of bronze, [33]its legs of iron, its feet partly of iron and partly of clay. [34]As you looked on, a stone was cut out, not by human hands, and it struck the statue on its feet of iron and clay and broke them in pieces. [35]Then the iron, the clay, the bronze, the silver, and the gold, were all broken in pieces and became like the chaff of the summer threshing floors; and the wind carried them away, so that not a trace of them could be found. But the stone that struck the statue became a great mountain and filled the whole earth.

[36]"This was the dream; now we will tell the king its interpretation. [37]You, O king, the king of kings—to whom the God of heaven has given the kingdom, the power, the might, and the glory, [38]into whose hand he has given human beings, wherever they live, the wild animals of the field, and the birds of the air, and whom he has established as ruler over them all—you are the head of gold. [39]After you shall arise another kingdom inferior to yours, and yet a third kingdom of bronze, which shall rule over the whole earth. [40]And there shall be a fourth kingdom, strong as iron; just as iron crushes and smashes everything,[a] it shall crush and shatter all these. [41]As you saw the feet and toes partly of potter's clay and partly of iron, it shall be a divided kingdom; but some of the strength of iron shall be in it, as you saw the iron mixed with the clay. [42]As the toes of the feet were part iron and part clay, so the kingdom shall be partly strong and partly brittle. [43]As you saw the iron mixed with clay, so will they mix with one another in marriage,[b] but they will not hold together, just as iron does not mix with clay. [44]And in the days of those kings the God of heaven will set up a kingdom that shall never be destroyed, nor shall this kingdom be left to another people. It shall crush all these kingdoms and bring them to an end, and it shall stand forever; [45]just as you saw that a stone was cut from the mountain not by hands, and that it crushed the iron, the bronze, the clay, the silver, and the gold. The great God has informed the king what shall

[a] Gk Theodotion Syr Vg: Aram adds *and like iron that crushes*
[b] Aram *by human seed*

NIV

take place in the future. The dream is true and the interpretation is trustworthy."

⁴⁶Then King Nebuchadnezzar fell prostrate before Daniel and paid him honor and ordered that an offering and incense be presented to him. ⁴⁷The king said to Daniel, "Surely your God is the God of gods and the Lord of kings and a revealer of mysteries, for you were able to reveal this mystery."

⁴⁸Then the king placed Daniel in a high position and lavished many gifts on him. He made him ruler over the entire province of Babylon and placed him in charge of all its wise men. ⁴⁹Moreover, at Daniel's request the king appointed Shadrach, Meshach and Abednego administrators over the province of Babylon, while Daniel himself remained at the royal court.

NRSV

be hereafter. The dream is certain, and its interpretation trustworthy."

46Then King Nebuchadnezzar fell on his face, worshiped Daniel, and commanded that a grain offering and incense be offered to him. ⁴⁷The king said to Daniel, "Truly, your God is God of gods and Lord of kings and a revealer of mysteries, for you have been able to reveal this mystery!" ⁴⁸Then the king promoted Daniel, gave him many great gifts, and made him ruler over the whole province of Babylon and chief prefect over all the wise men of Babylon. ⁴⁹Daniel made a request of the king, and he appointed Shadrach, Meshach, and Abednego over the affairs of the province of Babylon. But Daniel remained at the king's court

COMMENTARY

2:1a, Chronological Note. Like chap. 1, chap. 2 begins with a somewhat perplexing chronological note that defies modern attempts to treat it seriously. In this case, the "second year of Nebuchadnezzar" would place the story before the year 600 BCE and before the time of the preceding story. Despite many attempts to deal with these chronological indicators in any historical sense, it is best to treat them as further evidence that these stories once circulated independently of one another and that the editor of the collection that now comprises Daniel 1–6 chose to leave some of the enigmatic chronological notes alone, rather than straighten them out. However, as Daniel is apparently reintroduced to the Babylonian monarch in chap. 2, simply rearranging the dates will not do either. Rather than doubt the sophistication (or the attentiveness) of the editor, perhaps the reader is meant to see that the book of Daniel is, after all, to be taken as a collection of stories that were never originally intended to be told together in a single sitting.[70]

2:1b-6, The Troubled Emperor in His Court. 2:1b. The emperor cannot sleep. He is

troubled—not by the thousands of people he has forceably displaced or the thousands he has massacred on the battlefield or the wealth he has pillaged from the surrounding nations. He is troubled by his dreams, which is perhaps a way of saying that these issues *do* trouble the monarch. As Lacocque has trenchantly commented, the emperor has good reason to be troubled! His dreams announce to him that his powerful regime teeters on a foundation of clay: "Underlying the empires is an insatiable will to destruction; this is why they contain within themselves the seed of their destruction."[71]

The notion that an emperor's dreams conveyed important messages was widely held. Indeed, the dreams of emperors and kings were carefully noted in one of the earliest formalized works of dream interpretation, Artemidorus's *Oneiro-critica*.[72] A. L. Oppenheim, in his classic study of dream interpretation in ancient Near Eastern thought, points out that dreams were believed to have evil powers over the dreamer, and one of the reasons why ancient peoples were so anxious to have the dreams interpreted was not only to

70. Collins, typically, does an impressive job of analyzing the various opinions about these chronological notes. See John J. Collins, *Daniel,* Hermeneia (Minneapolis: Fortress, 1993) 154-56.

71. André Lacocque, *The Book of Daniel,* trans. D. Pellauer (Atlanta: John Knox, 1979) 48.

72. See Artemidorus, *The Interpretation of Dreams,* trans. Robert White (New York: Noyes, 1975) 17.

know what they meant, but also to use that knowledge to conduct appropriate rituals to do away with the evil powers that produced the dream.[73] What is more critical to our consideration here is that the power of dreams must also have been known to the Jewish author of this dream story, which is attributed to Nebuchadnezzar. The reader need not be so enchanted by the story as to forget that it is a Jewish diaspora composition about the Babylonian emperor, and not a court document from Babylonian sources. Thus the reader needs to be attentive to what this dream suggests about the Jewish attitude to the Babylonian monarch and his successors, and particularly whether the symbols in the dream refer to succeeding Babylonian monarchs (as some scholars suggest) or to succeeding empires (as the majority of modern scholars hold).

When we are introduced to Nebuchadnezzar as a monarch who is unable to sleep because his "spirit is troubled," it is inevitable that we recall Pharaoh's troubling dreams in Gen 41:8 and his response of calling in his advisers; this is only one of many parallels (sometimes quite strikingly similar) between the Daniel stories and the Joseph stories (cf. Esther). These parallels were systematically noted as early as 1895[74] and ever since have been a common feature of scholarship.[75]

But most important is the fact the last Neo-Babylonian monarch, Nabonidus, was famous for his inscriptions dealing with his dreams. In his dreams, Nabonidus was instructed to restore the statue of the god Sin in Harran, and he was even reassured in his dreams by appearances of Nebuchadnezzar himself. On the basis of this widely known aspect of Nabonidus, and the fact that we have a Dead Sea Scroll fragment of another Daniel-like story that specifically mentions Nabonidus, many scholars believe that he was the actual ruler upon whom many of the Daniel stories were based, and that the name naturally changed over time to the more well-known and infamous conquerer of Jerusalem.[76] In short, we need not insist that Daniel 2 presupposed Genesis 41, but could equally suggest similar circumstances of authorship for both texts in the same era.[77]

2:2. The list of advisers, "magicians, enchanters, sorcerers, and Chaldeans" is interesting. The term translated "magicians" (חרטמים *ḥarṭummîm*), likely an Egyptian loan word (because it was borrowed from the Joseph stories?), is the same term that is used in the Joseph story in Genesis 41 and in the story of the Egyptian magicians who were able to match Moses' tricks before Pharaoh in Exodus (7:11, 22; 8:3, 14-15; 9:11). Oppenheim, again, strongly suggests that dream interpretation was a serious science in Egypt, while it was of minimal interest in Mesopotamia.[78] "Enchanters" (אשפים *'aššāpîm*), on the other hand, is not a widely used term, although already encountered in Dan 1:20. "Sorcerers" (מכשפים *mĕkaššĕpîm*), also used in Exodus (7:11), is a term with much darker connotations, especially in prophetic literature. Sorcery is mentioned as a sin in the same breath with condemnation of the oppression of the poor. Prophetic interests clearly associate both with the religious influence of Canaanite culture and society (see Jer 27:9, addressed to the surrounding nations of Edom, Moab, Tyre, Sidon, and Ammon; Mic 5:11; Nah 3:4, with reference to Assyria; Mal 3:5). To round out this list with "Chaldeans" is somewhat surprising, although the term has come to mean "astrologer" in most of Daniel (see Commentary on 1:18-20), as in classical Greek literature, long after the specific national association was lost.

Finally, an interesting geographical spread is represented in this list through the inclusion of the wise professionals from Egypt to Babylon (and

---

73. A. L. Oppenheim, *The Interpretation of Dreams in the Ancient Near East* (Philadelphia: American Philosophical Society, 1956) 219.

74. In a series of articles by the German scholar L. A. Rosenthal, beginning with "Die Josephsgeschichte mit den Büchern Ester und Daniel verglichen," *ZAW* 15 (1895) 278-84.

75. Although all scholars recognize the parallels, Lacocque goes a bit far in saying that "all agree" that Daniel 2 is a midrash of Genesis 41. See Lacocque, *The Book of Daniel,* 43-44.

76. C. J. Gadd takes this notion further. On the basis of an inscription discovered in 1956 that mentions foreign troops in Nabonidus's military, Gadd surmises that some of the Daniel stories may well have originated among Nabonidus's Jewish troops. That Nabonidus mentions oases that are later referred to by Islamic sources as having Jewish populations lends even further weight to Gadd's suggestions. See his article "The Harran Inscriptions of Nabonidus," *Anatolian Studies* 8 (1958) 35-92, esp. 85. The *Prayer of Nabonidus* has by now inspired a great deal of comment, the most recent comprehensive treatment being F. Garcia-Martinez, *Qumran and Apocalyptic.*

77. This view is defended convincingly by Redford, *A Study of the Biblical Story of Joseph,* VTSup20 (Leiden: E. J. Brill, 1970). Goldingay is typically interesting with his suggestion that, just as the Joseph stories pre-figure the exodus, so also the Daniel stories elicit hope for a new exodus. See John Goldingay, *Daniel,* WBC 30 (Dallas: Word, 1988) 43.

78. Oppenheim, *The Interpretation of Dreams in the Ancient Near East,* 200, 243.

by association of the terms used, also Canaan). Is the intention, then, to portray the court of Nebuchadnezzar as being composed of an international assembly of advisers and religious practitioners from around the ancient Near East? Oppenheim notes that the Assyrian monarch Esarhaddon mentions Egyptian magicians among his prisoners of war.[79] Thus we are once again alerted to the reach of the empire and its unmistakable power as the context for the full appreciation of this story.

If this cosmopolitan emphasis is intended, then Daniel and his friends, whose wisdom is not of the world (2:30), are set up against the best of the world's advisers. Daniel is facing not merely his Babylonian opposition in the king, but also the power and prestige that the Babylonian monarch is able to draw upon throughout the empire. The theme, as many scholars have pointed out, is that the wisdom of the world will prove impotent before knowledge of the true God.

2:3-4. When Nebuchadnezzar makes his request, it is the Chaldeans who reply, speaking Aramaic. From this point until the end of chap. 7, the book of Daniel switches to Aramaic (see Introduction). The opening greeting of the Chaldeans, "Live forever!" (which is used throughout Daniel) is here a particularly clever irony, given the fact that the dream will soon reveal that Nebuchadnezzar will certainly not live forever, and neither will his regime.

2:5. After the Chaldeans have made their perfectly reasonable request to hear the dream so that they might comment on it, Nebuchadnezzar's surprising reply sets up the crisis and the task for Daniel and his Jewish compatriots. Nebuchadnezzar makes a "decree," a "firm matter" (the term is a Persian loan word, borrowed from the official terminology of the Persian Empire). To punctuate this "firm decree," a threat of death and destruction comes before any possibility of reward. The threat, to "be torn limb from limb" if they do not tell him "the dream and its interpretation," is a legal phrase[80] that has been translated variously as "you be cut in pieces" (Lacocque) or "you will be dismembered" (Collins). But if the language is difficult, the point is frighteningly clear. The Baby-

lonian monarch is portrayed as affirming his unchangeable commands and decrees, which are backed up by the authority that all imperial power must ultimately appeal to: brute force, which is not merely lethal, but *spectacularly* lethal. Furthermore, their houses will be destroyed. In short, it is to be public punishment, which totalitarian regimes both past and present are always particularly fond of, since such spectacles are useful in keeping a restive population in check with examples of what might befall them if they attempt to resist. One thinks immediately of the ancient Roman tradition of hanging political prisoners on crosses as a public humiliation.

2:6. These punishments are then contrasted with rewards. Among those things that the king offers in possible reward is "honor." Daniel will later inform the king that this honor is, in fact, a gift from Daniel's God (v. 37), and not inherent in the king's office. We are intended to see in Nebuchadnezzar the arrogance of power: "See how I can punish, or reward, at my pleasure!"

2:7-16. Some scholars have suggested that Nebuchadnezzar's offer of a reward attempts to show a certain fairness or even-handedness. But these rewards are hardly meant to portray the king as even-handed, as is clarified by the fact that the conversation with the Chaldeans takes a more serious turn in vv. 7-12, where the advisers' inability to do as the king (unreasonably) asks drives him into a rage. This rage is noted by Collins as a "stock motif" of court tales (see Esth 1:12; 7:7; Dan 3:13, 19; 3 Macc 3:1; 5:1), but contributes to a sense that power is in the hands of a foolish human being, dangerously susceptible to unrealistic demands.

The king's rage then leads him to decree the destruction of *all* of his advisory department, including Daniel and his companions, who must have been promoted to this position, although that is not stated explicitly in chaps. 1–2. Yet, this is complicated by the fact that Arioch will introduce Daniel as an apparent stranger in v. 25, which is probably the way the original story read, particularly given its resemblance to the *Prayer of Nabonidus* at this point (see Introduction). Perhaps the original Daniel tales always presumed a court setting, and chap. 1, which purports to tell the story of how Daniel and his friends originally

79. Ibid., 238.
80. F. Rosenthal, *A Grammar of Biblical Aramaic* (Wiesbaden: Harrassowitz, 1983) 59.

arrived in the court, is a later development of the legends.

When Daniel, through the king's official Arioch, requests that he be given time to present an interpretation of the king's dreams, Daniel is challenging both the king and his decree before he has assurance from God as to the nature of the dream. In the face of danger to his life, Daniel does not hesitate to assume that God would prefer matters were otherwise. Note that the Chaldean (and other) advisers had earlier angered the king by attempting to gain time—so thought Nebuchadnezzar (v. 8). This is important, as God is praised by Daniel in v. 21 as "one who changes times," in the same context as "deposes kings and sets up kings" (2:21 NRSV). The implication is that God is above the royal authority and is able to change what the world's authorities declare to be unchangeable.

There is a somewhat surprising implication in v. 16 that Daniel simply burst in on the king. Apparently unable to believe that Daniel could have had such easy access to the king, some of the ancient texts add that Daniel sent Arioch to petition the king on his behalf.[81]

2:17-23, The Prayer of Appeal and Praise. One of the crucial centers of this chapter is certainly the prayer for aid and response of praise in these verses. This section follows a well-established pattern of post-exilic literature in which the Jewish people appeal to God in the face of apparently overwhelming odds. The pattern is usually: (1) clarification of the threat; (2) gathering of the community to appeal to God (often associated with fasting), typically for "steadfast love" and "mercy" as aspects of deliverance; (3) songs of praise, rehearsing God's majestic existence and God's mighty power to deliver the people in times of need. This pattern will be fully explicated in the Commentary on chap. 9, but suffice it here to note that it is not merely an insignificant detail that Daniel proceeds to return to his compatriots and gather them together for prayer. Scholars often mention that the three friends are noted here merely to set up chap. 3, but this gathering is crucial for what follows; Daniel is mustering spiritual power for warfare. Note that Ezra also calls on the protection of God

by first gathering his community, declaring a fast, and proclaiming God's ability to deliver them (Ezra 8:21-22, 31*b*).

Seen in this post-exilic context of corporate prayers of deliverance, the song of praise in vv. 20-23 is interesting in many respects. The name "God of heaven" (אלה שמיא *'ĕlāh šĕmayyā'*, v. 19) is a standard post-exilic term, appearing in Ezra–Nehemiah as well. The blessing of God's name from age to age recalls Isaiah 47, and also recalls the "name theology" of Deuteronomy, particularly when the Temple is discussed as the place where God's name dwells. That wisdom and power belong to God is rehearsed already in Jeremiah 10 and 51. Notably, many of the other biblical contexts where these same motifs are found are hymns directed against foreign powers, and thus fit this hymn of political praise in Daniel 2.

God's power is rehearsed as being over and above the apparent power of the kings of this world. If God can change the times and seasons, God can certainly change whatever the Babylonian monarch declares unchangeable. That God not only places but also unseats kings is a theme found in other Daniel material (cf. the dramatic anti-Roman polemic by Mary in Luke 1:47-55). Further, the expression "knows what is in the darkness" (v. 22) is very similar to Job 12:9, 22. Note, moreover, the highly political context of Job 12:22-25, which discusses God's ability to unseat or otherwise strip of authority kings, counselors, priests, and judges. Job 12 thus contains "reversal of fortune" motifs:[82]

He makes nations great, then
    destroys them;
  he enlarges nations, then leads
    them away. (Job 12:23 NRSV)

The prayer concludes with a reference to the "God of my ancestors" (אלה אבהתי *'ĕlāh 'ăbāhātî*) before praising God's blessing on Daniel. It is instructive to note the increase in popularity of this term in the late biblical literature. Although "God of ancestors" is found four times in Exodus and eleven times throughout the deuteronomic historian, it is used twenty-six times in Chronicles and becomes prominent in prayers of the post-exilic literature of the Hellenistic period as well. The

81. E.g., Theodotion and the Syriac text; See N. Porteous, *Daniel: A Commentary,* OTL (Philadelphia: Westminster, 1965) 41.

82. D. J. Clines, *Job 1–20,* WBC 17 (Dallas: Word, 1989).

context for the use of the phrase "God of our ancestors" is interesting, particularly in the following:

Ezra 7:27—standing before the Persian king
Tob 8:5—prayer for safety in times of trouble
Jdt 10:8—prayer for Judith's success against the Assyrian king
3 Macc 7:16—the survival of defilement by foreigners
1 Esdr 9:8—breakup of mixed marriages
Prayer of Azariah—survival in the fiery furnace

To refer to God as a "God of my ancestors," then, is clearly a defining term that is relevant outside the homeland. The term becomes particularly relevant, therefore, when religious matters pit Jewish faith (based on the experience of this God from the ancestors) against the challenges of foreign powers or religious temptations. To assert anything about "the God of my/our ancestors" is to say something equally about that particular God, and the identity of the person using the terminology.

2:24-30, Daniel Before Nebuchadnezzar. As has been noted, the appearance or "audience" before the emperor is an important scene for virtually all of the stories that deal with the foreign court. To stand before the king was a setting of danger and threat. Daniel, therefore, speaks with courage in requesting an audience. His status is clearly established by Arioch: Daniel is from "among the exiles" (v. 25). The Hebrew terms (בני גלות *běnê gālût*) behind this phrase may be significant. The phrase "sons of exile" was a significant indicator of community identity in Ezra, and it may also serve that function here, rather than simply being a conventional way to speak of the Jewish population in the eastern diaspora.[83]

The conversation with Nebuchadnezzar establishes Daniel's credentials to speak before the king. It is a tense moment, and Daniel speaks with disarming respect, given that he knows that he is about to tell the king that his regime will not last.

Daniel first dissociates himself from the world's wisdom by pointing out the failure of the "wise men, enchanters, magicians, or diviners" (v. 27;

perhaps he diplomatically leaves out Chaldeans). In contrast to the king's powerlessness to call on the wisdom traditions from the far reaches of his empire, there is a God who is able to reveal mysteries. Daniel insists that the point of his appearing before the king is not to prove his own status or wisdom, but so that the king will know of the existence of this God (cf. Genesis 41). Daniel clarifies that the matter is between God and the king. Daniel is only the messenger of God's pronouncement to the foreign king. The theme of God's reigning over "mysteries" is also developed in the Dead Sea Scroll texts, as many scholars have noted.

2:31-35, The Statue. Daniel begins his interpretation of the dream by describing the great statue the king was looking at in the dream, which "was standing before you" (v. 31). The words "you looked, and *behold!*" appear in many dream/vision reports of prophets, beginning with Amos 4:7; 7:2; and Jeremiah through Zech 1:8; 8:3, etc. In short, it was an apparition that demanded the attention of the king by its imposing presence. It was not to be ignored—indeed, it was frightening. Was this merely one aspect of its appearance? Or was it frightening because it was clear even before Daniel's detailed explanation that the various metals that comprise the statue suggested instability?[84]

Oppenheim notes the frequency of large apparitions, like statues, in ancient dream reports. He suggests that this may be partially explained by the ancient practice of seeking dreams at the feet of idols, a form of what the Greeks called incubation (intentionally seeking answers in dreams by sleeping in a shrine). But the size of the images has other suggestions as well. Porteous is on the right track when he notes the monumental scale of Mesopotamian statuary,[85] a form of propagandist art intended as massive public displays of the size, permanence, and strength of a regime (typically depicted as a powerful animal—a lion or a bull). One thinks of the role of the triumphal arch in imperial Roman architecture or a siege-minded Pentagon (see Reflections).

The statue is made of several different metals,

---

83. The term appears in the Dead Sea Scroll fragments of the Pseudo-Daniel material as well. See R. Eisenman and M. Wise, *The Dead Sea Scrolls Uncovered* (Shaftsbury: Element, 1992) 66-67.

84. See J. H. Charlesworth, "Folk Traditions in Jewish Apocalyptic Literature," in *Mysteries and Revelations: Apocalyptic Studies Since the Uppsala Colloquium*, ed. J. J. Collins and J. H. Charlesworth (Sheffield: JSOT, 1991) 91-113.

85. N. Porteous, *Daniel*, OTL (Philadelphia: Westminster, 1965) 45.

each declining in value, from gold, to silver, to bronze, and then finishing with a mixture of iron and clay. Such a calculation of value is interestingly mentioned in 2 Esdr 7:55-57:

"Say to [the earth], 'You produce gold and silver and bronze, and also iron, and lead and clay; but silver is more abundant than gold, and bronze than silver, and iron than bronze, and lead than iron, and clay than lead.' Judge therefore which things are precious and desirable, those that are abundant or those that are rare?" (NRSV)

But what do the metals mean? There is precedent outside the Bible for the use of metals to represent successive empires. Hesiod (700 BCE?) dealt with a succession of four empires represented as metals of declining value. Collins, among others, considers Persian comparisons, also suggesting successive empires, to be even clearer and closer to Nebuchadnezzar's dream.[86]

However, the obsession with gold and silver, yet a further indication of the typical monetary concerns of empire, is interesting in this context. Goldingay surely goes too far in suggesting that the head, being gold, represents "the world power in originally positive terms, impressive and deserving of admiration in its God-given might."[87] After all, gold, silver, and bronze were the metals taken from the Temple (2 Kgs 24:13ff.) when Nebuchadnezzar sacked Jerusalem.[88] That a Jewish author would portray Nebuchadnezzar as dreaming of his regime as golden would hardly bring forth admiration; rather it would be the bitter realization of where at least some of the empire's gold had come from. Gold and silver are the means of trade, accumulation, and wealth. Of course, the essential question is, To whom is gold and silver of more value than iron and clay? To the common person, iron and clay are the materials of daily living and useful materials, whether they be plows or bowls. Who possesses gold but the powerful (cf. Job 3:15)? Gold and silver have their main value as monetary units, or decoration

for religious idols or temple vessels. In the later prophetic material, Isaiah mentions gold and silver in the context of decorations for Babylonian/pagan idols (Isa 31:7; 40:9). Silver, especially, was the preferred medium of taxation since the time of Darius, which forced many Jews into poverty when they were forced to trade their agricultural produce for the coin of state (see Nehemiah 5).[89] In short, in the context of the exile, the head of gold was hardly a sign of admiration, but a sign of a Near Eastern empire's insatiable drive to horde precious metals.

The focus of interest in Nebuchadnezzar's dream, however, is the stone—not to be associated with any human achievement—that destroys the entire statue. Surely the careful dissociation with humanity rules out an association with Cyrus as the destroyer of the Babylonian regime. Interestingly, Artemidorus notes that dreams of the destruction of cult statues are inauspicious for all people who dream them[90] (although Nebuchadnezzar's dream does not necessarily suggest a religious significance to his statue). The stone, then, is the key (see Reflections).

2:36-45, Daniel Interprets the Dream. 2:36-38. The interpretation begins with Daniel's reiteration of where the source of true power is to be located. This is a bold statement, even for a religious folktale. The one who claimed power and authority from the Babylonian gods is actually given authority only by the permission of the God of Daniel and his friends. Nebuchadnezzar is allowed to have "power, might, and glory." This is a familiar refrain in late biblical literature; 1 Chr 29:11-12 rehearses similar sentiments: "Riches and honor come from you, and you rule over all. In your hand are power and might" (author's trans.; note also 2 Chr 20:6; Jdt 9:14; 3 Macc 6:12; Tob 13:6.) Similar suggestions can be noted in New Testament thought. In John 19:10, Jesus tells Pilate that any authority Pilate might have is given from God, and Paul shares similar sentiments in Romans 13. All of these references can be read in either of two mutually exclusive ways. Either they are an affirmation of authority as granted by God, or they are a challenge to human authority in itself, pointing out that authority is

---

86. John J. Collins, *Daniel*, Hermeneia (Minneapolis: Fortress, 1993) 162-63. Goldingay isn't quite convinced, suggesting that the sequence may well be Babylonian rulers within the Babylonian regime itself; after all, Nebuchadnezzar himself is the head of gold, not Babylon generally. If this is so, then the rock could be read as Cyrus rather than as a direct heavenly intervention. See Goldingay, *Daniel*, 49-50.
87. Goldingay, *Daniel*, 50.
88. This association was already made in later Jewish legend. See Ginzberg, *Legends of the Jews* (New York: Jewish Publication Society, 1910–1938) 4:328.

89. See H. Kippenberg, *Religion und Klassenbildung im antiken Judäa* (Göttingen: Vandenhoeck und Ruprecht, 1982).
90. Artemidorus, *The Interpretation of Dreams*, trans. Robert White (New York: Noyes, 1975) 112.

really only in God. The dominant line in Christian circles has been a conservative affirmation of worldly authority as somehow delegated from God. However, a challenge to human pretensions is far more in keeping with the spirit of these passages, both in Daniel and in the New Testament. To suggest that God has ultimate control is to affirm the weakness and the merely utilitarian nature of human authority, which can just as easily be passed to another at God's whim. It is as if worldly power is *not* the central concern!

That Nebuchadnezzar rules over beasts and birds and, according to the LXX, "fish of the sea" has raised interesting speculation among commentators. Does Nebuchadnezzar echo Adam's rule over God's creation? Or does he merely follow the ways of other Mesopotamian rulers, who maintained animals and who were often pictured hunting, suggesting their power even over the animal kingdom?

2:39-45. The king is given to understand that his regime will not be the final power on earth. Indeed, there will be many to come. The kingdoms decline in significance from gold to bronze and then to iron mixed with clay. An interesting amount of attention is given to the statue's feet— the mixing of iron and clay. The incompatibility of iron and clay is an intriguing theme, noted in other late biblical passages. Wisdom 7:9 suggests that clay is worthless compared to silver, and Wis 15:8-10 suggests that idols are made of worthless clay. Consider Sir 13:2-3:

Do not lift a weight too heavy for you,
    or associate with one mightier and richer than you.
How can the clay pot associate with the iron kettle?
    The pot will strike against it and be smashed.
A rich person does wrong, and even adds insults;
    a poor person suffers wrong, and must add apologies.
    (NRSV)

In this passage, we see both the use of the iron/clay contrast and its use as a metaphor. Scholars have suggested that the mixing of iron and clay represents the attempts of the Ptolemaic and Seleucid rulers to cement ties with marriages—Antiochus III to Berenice in 252 or Ptolemy Epiphanes to Cleopatra in 193/194 (also suggested in Dan 11:6, 17). In any case, the amount of attention given to the interpretation of the feet and the mixed iron and clay suggests that this is the era of greatest interest to the writers.

As this is almost universally taken to be a reference to the Hellenistic period, we can conclude that the interpretation—perhaps even the dream itself—was a composition of the Hellenistic period.

But as indicated above, the real interest is focused on the mountain of God as the true, everlasting kingdom and thus on the imminent expectation of the end of the Hellenistic regimes over the Jewish people. The use of a mountain to symbolize God's rule is familiar from the great prophecy of world peace in Isaiah 2, where God's rule from the mountain will allow nations (including Israel) to beat their swords and spears into farming tools.

Many scholars have noted that Josephus did not go into much detail about this rock turned mountain, because it might offend his Roman readers.[91] If this is true, then how deeply revealing is Josephus's silence! He is correct, because the mountain of God will end the reign of terror perpetuated by humans. When Goldingay, commenting on v. 44, suggests that God's kingdom also includes "the capacity to crush and shatter [which] is not wicked in itself,"[92] he neglects the important aspect of the stone—precisely that it was not cut by human hands. God's everlasting kingdom will be peaceful (Isaiah 2), and if it involves arresting evil, it will be a striking followed by healing of those who are stricken (Isa 19:22-25). When humans try to cut the stone, even if they do so in God's name, the result is inevitably violent destruction with no healing.

The dream attributed to Nebuchadnezzar by the Jewish author of Daniel 2 is a dream of destruction of world terror and power in the name of God's rule over humanity. It is, furthermore, a striking reminder that God achieves this destruction through means unavailable to human beings. The belief in the destruction of Babylonian, Median, Persian, and Greek rule is a powerful pronouncement to the listener that God will bring these reigns of terror to an end. All forms of inhumanity are destined to end, and it is this destiny that the faithful are invited to know and to act upon by means of an insight into the future of God's plan.

91. Collins, *Daniel*, Hermeneia, 171.
92. Goldingay, *Daniel*, 59.

2:46-49. Transformation of the King and Promotion of the Jews. The reaction of the king is somewhat curious. It is affirmed that his regime will not last, and yet he is deeply impressed with Daniel and praises Daniel's God. These are two themes in vv. 46-49 that will recur in the Daniel stories (parts of which are seen in the Joseph and Esther stories as well)—namely, the conversion of the foreign monarch (or at least the impressive affirmation of God by the king) and the attribution of a kingdom's impressive achievements to its Jewish administrators.

The transformation of the king is an important issue. The idea that the Daniel stories have a benign or positive view of the foreign rulers is usually not alive to the fact that the monarch changes in the end. It is a *changed* monarch who is affirmed, not the image that we have had throughout the story before his change. Before the change, the reader is presented with an image of a power-mad ruler who makes commands he thinks are permanent and decrees the massacre of many people. To say that the Daniel stories affirm all aspects of the royal figures is to ignore the significance of the transformation of Nebuchadnezzar, or if not the conversion the significance of his realization of the power of God. In a sense, the monarch finally learns what Daniel has been affirming throughout the story: that God exists and that God has ultimate power over all aspects of life. This is not to say, of course, that such a change in the king transforms his nature completely. Another element of these stories is precisely the element of reversal of fortune, and often the enemies of the Jews are killed rather than the Jews who were earlier threatened (see the book of Esther for the best example of this).

REFLECTIONS

Two themes are particularly interesting in chap. 2: the image of stones and the significance of the dreams of the disenfranchised.

1. *Uncut Stones and Moving the Unmovable Stone.* God's stone, which turns into a mountain, reminds us of the frequency of the use of stones and rocks in the Bible as symbols of strength and power. In Daniel, the stone is in the hand of God against human authority, but in the New Testament, the stone is in the hand of human authority against God. The contrast is instructive. God's stone in Daniel reminds us of another particular stone that attempted to prevent the founding of God's kingdom. It was a stone of death, sealed with the official insignias of Roman power. In a dramatic act of civil disobedience against the power of the state, God (no human hand!) rolled away this stone to free God's chosen founder of the new kingdom, and at the same time deny worldly powers to stop God's reign. This stone, too, was destined to crush human power. Is there a sense that Daniel calls us to be stones in the hand of God, rather than in the hands of human authority?

The image of uncut stones, suggesting no human involvement, has interesting associations in rabbinic tradition as well. According to the laws of Moses, the stones used to make altars for sacrifice are not to be "cut" (Deut 27:6). This idea is a point of departure for a rabbinic commentary:

> *For if thou lift up thy sword upon it (Ex. 20:25).* In this connection R. Simon b. Eleazar used to say, "The altar is made to prolong the years of man and iron is made to shorten the years of man. It is not right for that which shortens life to be lifted up against that which prolongs life."

R. Yohanan b. Zakkai says, "Behold it says: *Thou shalt build . . . of whole stones (Deut. 27:6).* They are to be stones that establish peace.

"Now, by using the method of *qal vahomer,* you reason: The stones for the altar do not see nor hear nor speak. Yet because they serve to establish peace between Israel and their Father in heaven, the Holy One, blessed be He, said, *Thou shalt lift up no iron tool upon them (v. 5).* How much the more then should he who establishes peace between man and his fellow-man, between husband and wife, between city and city, between nation and nation, between family and family, between government and government, be protected so that no harm should come to him."[93]

In Daniel 2, the stone "not cut by human hands" teaches us that God is directly involved in the matter of political sovereignty over the symbol of world power: the statue. Daniel 2 suggests that God will bring an end to oppression, but the stone is not cut using tools. God's stone is effective without human involvement, rather like Rabbi Yohanan ben Zakkai's call for the faithful to be God's peaceful altar stones who do not touch the weapons of war.

Note further that the stone, being uncut, has not been mined, like silver and gold. The stone does not have the same value placed on precious metals by humans. A stone cannot be used to pay taxes or to make idols glisten in the sunlight. But this stone is in the hand of God, and its destruction of the human pretense to power is total. God will not rule as humans rule, through the hording of the symbols of labor and achievement, much less by violence. God rules through peaceful altar stones, but God may also hurl them at human pretenses!

2. *The Dreams of the Disenfranchised.* Is there any significance to the kind of dreams attributed to Babylonian rulers in Daniel 2–6? To speculate on this, one must keep in mind that these dreams are compositions of Jewish authors, attributed to the emperor. Do the oppressed dream about particular themes, or do their dreams feature unique images? If an answer could be established, we might have some general themes to compare to dream content in the Bible, keeping in mind the important cultural and historical contexts involved.

It would help us to understand Daniel and Joseph, for example, if psychologists were to notice a difference in dream content between lower and upper classes of society. However, it is significant to note that there are virtually no studies in contemporary psychology, let alone in ancient dream materials, of whether poor or disenfranchised people dream in the same way that the privileged do. Some psychological researchers have admitted that one of the reasons why there are so few studies of such an interesting social question is the fact that private psychotherapy, a source for much data on dream interpretation, is expensive for the patients involved. Still, a few studies of "ethnic" dreams can give us some ideas of how to settle this issue.[94]

Renaldo Maduro wrote of the prominence of "journey dreams" among modern Mexican Americans who search for their identities because they are often rejected in modern American society.[95] Do dreams, then, provide compensation for being powerless or disenfranchised (as a Jungian might suggest)? On the other hand, a Freudian approach would also emphasize family and sexual dynamics: "Faced with painful, humiliating exigencies that generate feelings of powerlessness and rage the individual welcomes an alternative view of reality, namely the illusion that his enemies will be destroyed and that he will be reborn in a mystical reunion with mother."[96]

The hints provided by such views suggest that dream life is certainly influenced by the sociopolitical realities of waking life. Fanon, in his work as a psychiatrist during the Algerian resistance to French rule, regarded the dreams of the colonized as attempts to gain power by imaging alternative realities:

---

93. *Mekhilta of R. Ishmael,* J. Z. Lauterback, ed. (Philadelphia: Jewish Publication Society, 1933–35) 2:290.

94. Precisely such a theoretical association between the dreams of pre-industralized societies and those of lower classes in industrialized societies was suggested by Vittorio Lanternari, "Dreams as Charismatic Significants: Their Bearing on the Rise of New Religious Movements," in A. Bharati, ed., *The Realm of the Extra-Human: Ideas and Actions* (The Hague/Paris: Mouton, 1976).

95. R. Maduro, "Journey Dreams in Latino Group Psychotherapy," *Psychotherapy: Theory, Research and Practice* 13 (1976) 148-55; M. Kramer, "Dream Translation: An Approach to Understanding Dreams," in *New Directions in Dream Interpretation,* ed. G. Delaney (New York: SUNY Press, 1993); M. Ullman, "Dreams, the Dreamer, and Society," in ibid., 11-40.

96. M. Ostrow, "Archetypes of Apocalypse in Dreams and Fantasies, and in Religious Scripture," *American Imago* 43 (1986) 307-34.

The dreams of the native are always of muscular prowess; his dreams are of action and of aggression. I dream that I am jumping, swimming, running, climbing, I dream that I burst out laughing, that I span a river in one stride, or that I am followed by a flood of motorcars which never catch up to me. During the period of colonization, the native never stops achieving his freedom from nine in the evening until six in the morning.[97]

Roger Bastide's work on the dreams of African Brazilians lends further weight to Fanon's observations, and it adds helpful nuances. Bastide's interviews suggested that the very poor in the slums dreamed only of fulfilling immediate needs—winning lotteries, eating in abundance. It was the more educated Brazilians of African descent, those who began to understand political dynamics and the economic impact of racism, who dreamed of conquest, destruction of European Brazilians and their homes, and reversal of fortune.[98]

On the basis of these suggestions, can we hazard some observations about the book of Daniel, and chap. 2 in particular? The dreams attributed to Nebuchadnezzar are obviously images of an alternative reality—one in which God reverses present conditions. We see how the dreams of the disenfranchised, whether based on actual experiences or on literary products of daytime thought, reveal further elements of a theology composed "in the shadows of empire." Dreams are beyond the control of even a world emperor. As Fanon suggests, dreams reveal uncontrolled worlds of the subordinate person where he or she can, at last, move freely. Bastide's work, however, suggests that the dreamers in the book of Daniel clearly understand the source of their suppression. Their dreams grow from their understanding. But dreams are not in and of themselves revolutionary.

The dreams of the people can be dangerous for those in power. In the first half of the twentieth century, European surrealist artists and philosophers were involved in a movement based on an appropriation of "dream forms," most famously depicted in the bizarre dreamscapes by surrealist painters like Dali. The political message of surrealism, however, is similar to the understanding of the dreams in Daniel. Andre Breton wrote in the *Surrealist Manifesto:* "The dream alone entrusts to man all his rights to freedom." But surrealism runs the risk of staying in dreamland. The question for the modern Christian who reads Daniel as a basis for faith and practice is whether these dreams of an end to human exploitation can be liberated from dreamland to break into reality. In short, can dreams become strategies?

97. F. Fanon, *The Wretched of the Earth* (New York: Grove, 1963) 52.
98. R. Bastide, "Reve de noirs," *Psyche: revue internationale des sciences de l'homme et de psychanalyse* 49 (1950) 802-11.

DANIEL 3:1-30, POLITICAL ATHEISM AND RADICAL FAITH

NIV	NRSV
3 King Nebuchadnezzar made an image of gold, ninety feet high and nine feet[a] wide, and set it up on the plain of Dura in the province of Babylon. ²He then summoned the satraps, prefects, governors, advisers, treasurers, judges, magistrates and all the other provincial officials to come to the dedication of the image he had set	**3** King Nebuchadnezzar made a golden statue whose height was sixty cubits and whose width was six cubits; he set it up on the plain of Dura in the province of Babylon. ²Then King Nebuchadnezzar sent for the satraps, the prefects, and the governors, the counselors, the treasurers, the justices, the magistrates, and all the officials of the provinces, to assemble and come to the dedication of the statue that King Neb-

a1 Aramaic sixty cubits high and six cubits wide (about 27 meters high and 2.7 meters wide)

NIV

up. ³So the satraps, prefects, governors, advisers, treasurers, judges, magistrates and all the other provincial officials assembled for the dedication of the image that King Nebuchadnezzar had set up, and they stood before it.

⁴Then the herald loudly proclaimed, "This is what you are commanded to do, O peoples, nations and men of every language: ⁵As soon as you hear the sound of the horn, flute, zither, lyre, harp, pipes and all kinds of music, you must fall down and worship the image of gold that King Nebuchadnezzar has set up. ⁶Whoever does not fall down and worship will immediately be thrown into a blazing furnace."

⁷Therefore, as soon as they heard the sound of the horn, flute, zither, lyre, harp and all kinds of music, all the peoples, nations and men of every language fell down and worshiped the image of gold that King Nebuchadnezzar had set up.

⁸At this time some astrologers^a came forward and denounced the Jews. ⁹They said to King Nebuchadnezzar, "O king, live forever! ¹⁰You have issued a decree, O king, that everyone who hears the sound of the horn, flute, zither, lyre, harp, pipes and all kinds of music must fall down and worship the image of gold, ¹¹and that whoever does not fall down and worship will be thrown into a blazing furnace. ¹²But there are some Jews whom you have set over the affairs of the province of Babylon—Shadrach, Meshach and Abednego—who pay no attention to you, O king. They neither serve your gods nor worship the image of gold you have set up."

¹³Furious with rage, Nebuchadnezzar summoned Shadrach, Meshach and Abednego. So these men were brought before the king, ¹⁴and Nebuchadnezzar said to them, "Is it true, Shadrach, Meshach and Abednego, that you do not serve my gods or worship the image of gold I have set up? ¹⁵Now when you hear the sound of the horn, flute, zither, lyre, harp, pipes and all kinds of music, if you are ready to fall down and worship the image I made, very good. But if you do not worship it, you will be thrown immediately into a blazing furnace. Then what god will be able to rescue you from my hand?"

¹⁶Shadrach, Meshach and Abednego replied to

NRSV

uchadnezzar had set up. ³So the satraps, the prefects, and the governors, the counselors, the treasurers, the justices, the magistrates, and all the officials of the provinces, assembled for the dedication of the statue that King Nebuchadnezzar had set up. When they were standing before the statue that Nebuchadnezzar had set up, ⁴the herald proclaimed aloud, "You are commanded, O peoples, nations, and languages, ⁵that when you hear the sound of the horn, pipe, lyre, trigon, harp, drum, and entire musical ensemble, you are to fall down and worship the golden statue that King Nebuchadnezzar has set up. ⁶Whoever does not fall down and worship shall immediately be thrown into a furnace of blazing fire." ⁷Therefore, as soon as all the peoples heard the sound of the horn, pipe, lyre, trigon, harp, drum, and entire musical ensemble, all the peoples, nations, and languages fell down and worshiped the golden statue that King Nebuchadnezzar had set up.

8Accordingly, at this time certain Chaldeans came forward and denounced the Jews. ⁹They said to King Nebuchadnezzar, "O king, live forever! ¹⁰You, O king, have made a decree, that everyone who hears the sound of the horn, pipe, lyre, trigon, harp, drum, and entire musical ensemble, shall fall down and worship the golden statue, ¹¹and whoever does not fall down and worship shall be thrown into a furnace of blazing fire. ¹²There are certain Jews whom you have appointed over the affairs of the province of Babylon: Shadrach, Meshach, and Abednego. These pay no heed to you, O king. They do not serve your gods and they do not worship the golden statue that you have set up."

13Then Nebuchadnezzar in furious rage commanded that Shadrach, Meshach, and Abednego be brought in; so they brought those men before the king. ¹⁴Nebuchadnezzar said to them, "Is it true, O Shadrach, Meshach, and Abednego, that you do not serve my gods and you do not worship the golden statue that I have set up? ¹⁵Now if you are ready when you hear the sound of the horn, pipe, lyre, trigon, harp, drum, and entire musical ensemble to fall down and worship the statue that I have made, well and good.^a But if you do not worship, you shall immediately be

---

^a8 Or *Chaldeans*

^a Aram lacks *well and good*

NIV

the king, "O Nebuchadnezzar, we do not need to defend ourselves before you in this matter. [17]If we are thrown into the blazing furnace, the God we serve is able to save us from it, and he will rescue us from your hand, O king. [18]But even if he does not, we want you to know, O king, that we will not serve your gods or worship the image of gold you have set up."

[19]Then Nebuchadnezzar was furious with Shadrach, Meshach and Abednego, and his attitude toward them changed. He ordered the furnace heated seven times hotter than usual [20]and commanded some of the strongest soldiers in his army to tie up Shadrach, Meshach and Abednego and throw them into the blazing furnace. [21]So these men, wearing their robes, trousers, turbans and other clothes, were bound and thrown into the blazing furnace. [22]The king's command was so urgent and the furnace so hot that the flames of the fire killed the soldiers who took up Shadrach, Meshach and Abednego, [23]and these three men, firmly tied, fell into the blazing furnace.

[24]Then King Nebuchadnezzar leaped to his feet in amazement and asked his advisers, "Weren't there three men that we tied up and threw into the fire?"

They replied, "Certainly, O king."

[25]He said, "Look! I see four men walking around in the fire, unbound and unharmed, and the fourth looks like a son of the gods."

[26]Nebuchadnezzar then approached the opening of the blazing furnace and shouted, "Shadrach, Meshach and Abednego, servants of the Most High God, come out! Come here!"

So Shadrach, Meshach and Abednego came out of the fire, [27]and the satraps, prefects, governors and royal advisers crowded around them. They saw that the fire had not harmed their bodies, nor was a hair of their heads singed; their robes were not scorched, and there was no smell of fire on them.

[28]Then Nebuchadnezzar said, "Praise be to the God of Shadrach, Meshach and Abednego, who has sent his angel and rescued his servants! They trusted in him and defied the king's command and were willing to give up their lives rather than serve or worship any god except their own God. [29]Therefore I decree that the people of any nation

NRSV

thrown into a furnace of blazing fire, and who is the god that will deliver you out of my hands?"

[16]Shadrach, Meshach, and Abednego answered the king, "O Nebuchadnezzar, we have no need to present a defense to you in this matter. [17]If our God whom we serve is able to deliver us from the furnace of blazing fire and out of your hand, O king, let him deliver us.[a] [18]But if not, be it known to you, O king, that we will not serve your gods and we will not worship the golden statue that you have set up."

[19]Then Nebuchadnezzar was so filled with rage against Shadrach, Meshach, and Abednego that his face was distorted. He ordered the furnace heated up seven times more than was customary, [20]and ordered some of the strongest guards in his army to bind Shadrach, Meshach, and Abednego and to throw them into the furnace of blazing fire. [21]So the men were bound, still wearing their tunics,[b] their trousers,[b] their hats, and their other garments, and they were thrown into the furnace of blazing fire. [22]Because the king's command was urgent and the furnace was so overheated, the raging flames killed the men who lifted Shadrach, Meshach, and Abednego. [23]But the three men, Shadrach, Meshach, and Abednego, fell down, bound, into the furnace of blazing fire.

[24]Then King Nebuchadnezzar was astonished and rose up quickly. He said to his counselors, "Was it not three men that we threw bound into the fire?" They answered the king, "True, O king." [25]He replied, "But I see four men unbound, walking in the middle of the fire, and they are not hurt; and the fourth has the appearance of a god."[c] [26]Nebuchadnezzar then approached the door of the furnace of blazing fire and said, "Shadrach, Meshach, and Abednego, servants of the Most High God, come out! Come here!" So Shadrach, Meshach, and Abednego came out from the fire. [27]And the satraps, the prefects, the governors, and the king's counselors gathered together and saw that the fire had not had any power over the bodies of those men; the hair of their heads was not singed, their tunics[b] were not harmed, and not even the smell of fire came from them. [28]Nebuchadnezzar said, "Blessed be the

a Or If our God whom we serve is able to deliver us, he will deliver us from the furnace of blazing fire and out of your hand, O king. b Meaning of Aram word uncertain c Aram a son of the gods

NIV	NRSV
or language who say anything against the God of Shadrach, Meshach and Abednego be cut into pieces and their houses be turned into piles of rubble, for no other god can save in this way." 30Then the king promoted Shadrach, Meshach and Abednego in the province of Babylon.	God of Shadrach, Meshach, and Abednego, who has sent his angel and delivered his servants who trusted in him. They disobeyed the king's command and yielded up their bodies rather than serve and worship any god except their own God. 29Therefore I make a decree: Any people, nation, or language that utters blasphemy against the God of Shadrach, Meshach, and Abednego shall be torn limb from limb, and their houses laid in ruins; for there is no other god who is able to deliver in this way." 30Then the king promoted Shadrach, Meshach, and Abednego in the province of Babylon.

COMMENTARY

3:1, The Statue. This chapter begins abruptly with the construction of a statue. The dimensions of this statue are certainly odd; the height is ten times greater than the width, giving the impression that it is a pole-like structure. Montgomery suggests that we should understand that it is a stele (that is, a tower of stone, like an obelisk) with a carving of a figure or covered with inscriptions. We are not told that the statue is of Nebuchadnezzar himself, but the text certainly allows this impression, particularly noting that the statue in chap. 2 is in the form of a human being. Hippolytus of Rome (c. 220 CE) suggested that Nebuchadnezzar actually sought to build the image that he saw in the previous dream, being overly impressed with his reign's being represented by gold.

This statue, then, is made of gold, the substance of highest commercial value. In his recent work, Dutch theologian Ton Veerkamp speaks powerfully of the use of gold and its meaning, as well as the location of "Dura." Veerkamp believes that the present form of Daniel 3 took its redactional shape in the Seleucid period, and thus writes that the statue portrayed in Daniel 3 is "a golden monstrosity. . . . Medium of exchange, deposit of value, measure of worth—gold was the gravitational center of the Hellenistic economy. The King of Kings made an image of it—he established the economy and made from it a cult object—he made a fetish of gold. The Empire establishes Gold as a god of the whole world—that is the meaning of what is here described here."[99]

Basing his analysis on his proposal that "Dura" (which can mean "plain") is in fact the famous Dura-Europos (270 miles northwest of Babylon), Veerkamp notes that although this Dura was not significant in the Babylonian period, it was a place of significant activity for Antiochus III and Antiochus IV, because it was located along important trade routes and was the site of a temple to Zeus. Veerkamp supposes that the writer unites the crisis of the Jews under Nebuchadnezzar with the height of Seleucid power, the latter's rule being one in which gold reigned; but a Seleucid era insertion of the reference to Dura would have this impact just as effectively. Other scholars, however, are more cautious about the reference to Dura, noting that the term is used for many locations. The Greek historian Herodotus also goes to some length to describe what he had heard about the amount of gold in the religious shrines of the Babylonians, including statues and tables for sacrifice.[100] Finally, Brown has noted that already in the fifth century BCE, gold was becoming the "primary circulating source of value."[101]

99. My own translation of T. Veerkamp, *Autonomie und Egalität* (Berlin: Alektor-Verlag, 1992) 243-44.
100. Herodotus *The History* 1:183.
101. J. P. Brown, "Proverb-Book, Gold Economy, Alphabet," *JBL* 100 (1981) 177.

Lacocque draws attention to the Greek versions, which insert a date for this event as the eighteenth year of Nebuchadnezzar—in other words, the year of his conquest of Jerusalem. Thus the statue went up in the year the Temple came down—false worship as opposed to true worship.[102]

Although not always using of gold, Mesopotamian regimes certainly built monstrous images; this is clear to any visitor to the British Museum, where Nineveh's massive winged bulls are on display and to this day communicate very powerfully the message they were originally meant to convey: the power of an empire. Collins, on the other hand, suggests that a memory of Nabonidus's construction and restoration of the statue of Sin, the moon god, at Harran (which apparently infuriated the priesthood of Marduk in Babylon) may be behind the motif of the Babylonian monarch's erecting the statue.

Is the construction of the statue an act of pride? Does the story suggest that the Babylonian monarch wanted to be divinized? If so, is there any historical precedent for this? Judith 3:8 records a legend that Nebuchadnezzar certainly did want to be looked upon as a god, and the grandiose claims of the Mesopotamian rulers could easily give this impression, even if it is not technically accurate. Whether Nebuchadnezzar ever erected such a statue is totally beside the point. The point was that he could—he could amass that much gold; he could assemble the leaders; he could demand obedience and threaten horrible punishment—and this is the plausibility (that is, a political plausibility) that the stories of Daniel are based on.

3:2-7, The Command of Obedience. 3:2. As if to remove any doubt of what the gold is to symbolize, there follows a gathering of all the highest officials of the government—the representatives of Babylonian power and prestige—called by Nebuchadnezzar to announce his cult of gold. The book communicates the great size of the court, Persian as well as Babylonian, and the various levels of administration by its use of lists of various types of officials. Note also, however, that the Jewish writers are familiar with the terminology of governance. Rosenthal notes that the first few terms are borrowed from Mesopotamian (Akkadian) languages, while most of the others are from Persian terms, such as the words translated in the NRSV as "counselors," "treasurers," "law officials," "magistrates/police chiefs," and the general category of "all who rule/have authority."[103] The presence of treasurers is, of course, particularly interesting for the origin of Nebuchadnezzar's "image of gold." In his attempt to suggest a date, Collins proposes that the use of Persian names requires a long enough period of time for the language of the Persians to sink in to the Jewish population,[104] but all minority peoples learn the vocabulary of authority very quickly (see Introduction).

3:3a. This verse repeats the list, in response to Nebuchadnezzar's command. This frequent repetition of orders, usually repeated word for word, gives the impression that all the minions of the Babylonian emperor obey his whim to the letter. This is what he wanted, and this is exactly what happened.

3:3b-4. The herald cries in a loud voice, a term also used in association with the military; thus it is a commanding voice. The address is directed to the "peoples, nations, and languages." The vastness of the territories under imperial control is suggested here. Empires of the ancient Near East frequently claimed to control massive numbers of the peoples in the known world. The Assyrian monarch Sennacherib wrote: "Sennacherib, the great king, king of the universe, king of Assyria, king of the four quarters. . . ."[105] Nebuchadnezzar II, in one of the Wadi-Brisa inscriptions, claims to have made Babylon "foremost among all the countries and every human habitation,"[106] while in the so-called Cyrus Cylinder, Cyrus claims, "I am Cyrus, king of the world, great king, legitimate king, king of Babylon, king of Sumer and Akkad, king of the four rims of the earth."[107] Such is the rhetoric of power, perhaps reaching a zenith in Roman rhetoric of Roman rule: "Cities now gleam in splendor and beauty, and the whole earth is arrayed like a paradise."[108]

102. André Lacocque, *The Book of Daniel,* trans. D. Pellauer (Atlanta: John Knox, 1979) 56.

103. F. Rosenthal, *A Grammar of Biblical Aramaic* (Wiesbaden: Otto Harrassowitz, 1983).

104. John J. Collins, *Daniel,* Hermeneia (Minneapolis: Fortress, 1993).

105. D. D. Luckenbill, *The Annals of Sennacherib* (Chicago: University of Chicago Press, 1924) 23. I an indebted to Dr. Millard Lind for reminding me of other examples of this, including the Assyrian cases.

106. *Ancient Near Eastern Texts Relating to the Old Testament* (*ANET*), ed. James B. Pritchard (Princeton, N.J.: Princeton University Press, 1969) 307.

107. Ibid., 316.

108. Aelius Aristides *Eulogy of Rome* 103.

3:5. Scholarly comment on the musical instruments is interesting because of the presence of at least one Greek term, συμφωνία (*symphōnia* [סומפניה *sûmpōnyâ*]; NIV, "pipes"; NRSV, "drum"), usually taken to be some primitive form of bagpipe. But Lacocque's comments on the instruments are also interesting. "The flute" (NIV, NRSV, "pipe" [משרוקיתא *mašrôqîtā'*]) was a simple peasant's instrument (Judg 5:16), while the "lyre" (NRSV, NIV, "zither" [קיתרוס *qayṭĕrôs*]) would be made of precious metal or ivory and would be an aristocrat's instrument.[109] Both the *sambyka* (NRSV, "trigon"; NIV, "lyre" [סבכא *sabbĕkā'*]) and the *symphonia* have bad reputations with the Greeks, the former repudiated by Plato and the latter an instrument that inspired Antiochus IV to dance in what was seen as a shameful public spectacle. It may be that the instruments themselves, and the social class associated with them, suggest a kind of universal demand on all peoples (poor and wealthy) to be obedient to the king.

3:6. Punishment by fire is not entirely unknown, as seen in Jeremiah 29. As Collins notes, punishment by fire became the "eschatological punishment par excellence in the post-exilic prophecy and apocalyptic literature."[110] (Note the destruction of the beast in Revelation as well as in Daniel 7.)

3:7. The peoples are to "fall down" (נפל *nĕpal*, a position of submission) and "do honor" (סגד *sĕgad*; the NRSV translates this as "worship," but this will be somewhat problematic, as noted below) when they hear the music. As earlier in the story, the repetition fits exactly, and the people respond as they are commanded. As Nebuchadnezzar wants it, so shall he have it—except for one slight problem: Jewish resistance breaks out again.

3:8-12, The Denunciation of the Jews. Here, the story begins to get interesting. The setting is the presence of the king. The Chaldeans (the use of this term for Babylonians is perhaps intended to be ethnically specific, rather than to refer to court astrologers) accuse the Jews of disobedience and insolence before the king. The literal phrase used for "accusation" (אכלו קרציהון *'ăkalû qarṣêhôn*) is rather interesting: "they ate bits off," which is an Akkadian idiom meaning "to accuse." The Chaldeans remind the king of the decree he has made, repeating all that was stated before with one interesting exception: The Jews also "do not worship your gods." This was not, of course, part of Nebuchadnezzar's original decree about the statue, but it adds to the sense that the Jews are guilty because they are foreigners—merely conquered exiles—who were trusted by the king (as in Esther). The king's rage is perhaps to be understood to have arisen not only from the disobedience of the command to fall before the statue, but also from the fact that the judgment of the king is brought into question for having appointed these four Jews to positions of importance in the first place. Thus betrayal is added to insubordination.

The motif of the evil counselors vs. the Jewish court officials runs through many of these stories and suggests some ethnic tensions between the tellers, and hearers, of these stories and the surrounding peoples. In his analysis of the Daniel stories, Meinhold was particularly alert to this sociopsychological aspect of the stories.[111]

Interestingly, the term translated "worship" (of your gods [פלח *pĕlaḥ*]) is different from that used for "worship" (of the statue [סגד *sĕgid*]) in v. 5. The latter term can be read as "honor"—that is, that the statue was to be honored. When Nebuchadnezzar fell before Daniel in 2:46, he honored Daniel, but did not worship him in the same sense that the Jews did not worship the gods of Nebuchadnezzar.

It seems odd that the king does not know that these Jews will not worship the Babylonian gods, irrespective of their attitude toward the golden statue. This is further indication of the isolation of these stories from one another at some point before they were joined together. The stubborn refusal to compromise their faith is reintroduced in story after story. It seems that almost each time, the king needs to learn something about these Jews, including those aspects that were introduced already in a previous story. That Daniel and his friends Hananiah, Mishael, and Azariah worshiped the Hebrew God should hardly have been news to Nebuchadnezzar. In any case, as a result

---

109. Lacocque, *The Book of Daniel*, 57.
110. Collins, *Daniel*, Hermeneia, 185.
111. A. Meinhold, "Die Diasporanovelle: Eine Alttestamentliche Gattung" (Ph.D. diss., University of Greifswald, 1969) 170.

of the accusation, the Jews will be brought before the king.

3:13-18, The Appearance Before the King and Jewish Defiance. 3:13-14. The king, once again in a "furious rage," summons the insubordinate Jewish exiles. As with many of the Daniel stories, the turning point occurs in the presence of, or before the king. The setting of these crucial scenes is obvious given the power and majesty of the emperor. To actually stand before this ruler who commands such authority and wealth is an awesome fate. Thus in v. 14 the question is put to the young Jewish men, and now regards two accusations: "You do not worship my gods . . . and . . . honor my statue?" (cf. Bel and the Dragon in the Commentary on the Additions to Daniel, 185-94).

3:15. Nebuchadnezzar offers the Jews one last chance; thus this verse is full of the folkloric repetition of lists that is typical of Daniel. What is interesting is the final phrase, which has been translated variously as "and who is the god that will deliver you out of my hands" (NRSV) and "who ever is the god who could rescue you from my power?"[112] Nebuchadnezzar's rule and authority are such that only a god can deliver the accused Jews. The Babylonian ruler is a man of great arrogance. Porteous writes, "We see here the worldly power absolutely confident that there is no limit to its authority."[113]

3:16-18. The reaction of the accused Jews is to declare their independence from royal authority. Their response in v. 17 is a statement of faith, proclaiming the existence of the God who can deliver them—indeed, there is one with greater authority than Nebuchadnezzar. Such is their faith. But their belief has consequences. Verse 18 is a statement of the resulting action: If their God does not deliver them, still they "will not worship the golden statue." They boldly express civil disobedience to the law of the king.

Verse 18 contains one of the most powerful statements in the entire book of Daniel, with consequences reaching far beyond this little story: "But if not. . . ." They profess that their God is able to deliver them, but even if not, they will not obey the king's commands. This is a statement of faith against the appearance of defeat. The most infuriating aspect of radical faith is its adamant refusal to be impressed with the obvious—namely, the subordinated status and powerlessness of the Jews before the mighty emperor—and their steadfast adherence to an alternative reality: God reigns. Nebuchadnezzar's response is hardly unexpected in the face of this open defiance in the name of faith.

3:19-27, The Salvation of the Jews. The strength of those who overpower the Jews in order to cast them into the furnace is impressive. Again, the specific vocabulary used for this action suggests a military association. The garment terminology ("robes, trousers, turbans and other clothes") has caused some difficulty, but the Aramaic has an almost rhythmic, rhyming quality to it, reminding one of a phrase like the English "lock, stock, and barrel." In any case, taking care to point out that they are wearing clothes when they are placed in the furnace will allow the later observation that their garments do not even smell of smoke, let alone look burnt.

A key to this description of their impending execution is the binding. Binding is the symbol of police authority *par excellence.* In his analysis of symbols of power carried by each Roman soldier, Wengst noted that handcuffs "stand for the maintenance of the new situation brought about by force of arms."[114] In Daniel 3, the act of binding the young Jewish men is repeated (1) when the three are cast into the furnace; (2) when the king asks if his order has been fulfilled, including the binding (v. 24); and (3) when Nebuchadnezzar sees the men walking, unbound (v. 25). Furthermore, as in 2:15, the king's decree is punctuated by his hysterical rage, without regard for clear thought. The death of those who would kill the Jewish exiles recalls similar reversals of fortune, such as one finds in the book of Esther, but the motif may be used here to convey the absurdity of the king's rage, which results in the senseless loss of his own officials who were killed by the flames when they threw the three Jews into the furnace.[115]

---

112. John Goldingay, *Daniel,* WBC 30 (Dallas: Word, 1988) 64.
113. N. Porteous, *Daniel: A Commentary,* OTL (Philadelphia: Westminster, 1965) 59.

114. This observation was based on Josephus's inventory of what the typical Roman soldier carried. See K. Wengst, *Pax Romana and the Peace of Jesus Christ* (London: SCM, 1987) 27.
115. The Septuagint inserts The Song of the Three, or The Prayer of Azariah, at this point in Daniel. That text will be dealt with in this volume in the separate commentary on the Additions to Daniel, 158-70.

Verse 24 introduces another of the most interesting aspects of the story. The "fourth person" whom the king sees inside the furnace has given rise to considerable scholarly debate. The Aramaic reads literally "son of god." Was this intended to be a reference to an angel? Perhaps the reference is to a special presence of God with the three young men? The Aramaic word בר-אלהין (*bar 'ĕlāhîn*) is typically taken to refer to a member of the "sons of god," who are collectively known as the "host of heaven" (Gen 6:2; 1 Kgs 22:19; Job 1:6; 38:7; Ps 148:2). There is also frequent mention of the presence of a court of heaven in the Ugaritic/Canaanite materials.[116] Goldingay suggests that Old Testament promises of heavenly aides to protect God's people become concrete here (cf. Pss 34:8; 91:11).[117] Collins relates the fourth person to the "Angel/Messenger of Yahweh" who protects Israel in Exod 14:19 and who guides Israel (Exod 23:20), helps Elijah (1 Kgs 19:7), and destroys the Assyrian army (2 Kgs 19:35; Isa 37:36).[118] This seems particularly suggestive in the light of the appearances of Michael as the protector of the Israelite people during the exilic experience (Daniel 7; 10–12).

What is further interesting is that the presence of the fourth figure and the survival of the three young men in the fiery furnace brings forth a statement of faith by Nebuchadnezzar, who calls them, "servants of the Most High God" (v. 26). The phrase "Most High God" (עבדוהי די-אלהא *'ăbdôhî dî-'ĕlāhā*) is a form of reference used for the God of the Jews in many exilic and post-exilic writings.

Many scholars have suggested an interesting resemblance to the near burning of Croesus by Cyrus, who wanted to know if gods would come to Croesus's rescue.[119] But fire imagery has other associations with the exilic experience in the Bible. Isaiah 48:10 refers to the exile itself as a "refining fire," and many scholars have pointed to the imagery of Isa 43:2 as obviously related to this story: "When you walk through fire you shall not be burned,/ and the flame shall not consume you" (NRSV).[120] If this Isaiah passage was in the mind of the storyteller, the implication that the exile (which is compared by Isaiah to the exodus) was like a fiery threat ought once again to give pause to those who argue that the exile was "not that bad."

3:28-30, Glorification of the Jews, Promotion, and Proclamation. 3:28. Nebuchadnezzar not only honors the trust of the Jews, but also emphasizes that his decree has been successfully disobeyed. This theme of changing the supposedly unchangeable decree of the king is noted throughout Daniel (Dan 2:9; 3:19; 5:6, 9; 6:18; 7:7; note also the theme in Ezra 2:21; 6:9, 11, 16; 7:25). The defiance that appears to be obvious—in other words, the political "atheism" of the Jews in their refusal to bow to the symbols of Babylonian power—is a key point to the teller of the stories. Those who hear these stories learn to see a new reality that is informed by the "Most High God."

3:29-30. Now the proclamation is made throughout the many lands under Babylonian rule that God's signs and wonders are great and mighty. More important, God's kingdom and the sovereignty of God are everlasting. In the face of the mistaken power of Babylon, even Nebuchadnezzar is made to recognize his limitations before this God. But the humbling of the mighty emperor was instigated by the civil disobedience of three who lived by another reality, because they served another sovereign.

116. Lacocque, *The Book of Daniel,* 61.
117. Goldingay, *Daniel,* 68.
118. Collins, *Daniel,* Hermeneia, 191.
119. Herodotus *The History* 1:86.

120. Many scholars go so far as to suggest that Daniel 3 was inspired by the Isaiah passage. I agree, however, with those who suggest that this is too sweeping a statement for a much richer tradition in Daniel 3.

REFLECTIONS

1. Fanon reminds the reader of Daniel of the power and impact of symbols of colonialism and imposition of foreign culture: "The colonial world is a world where the settler makes history and is conscious of making it . . . a world of statues: the statue of the general who carried out the conquest, the statue of the engineer who built the bridge. . . . The first thing the native learns is to stay in his place, and not to go beyond certain limits."[121]

Memmi echoes this observation: "The few statues which decorate the city represent (with incredible scorn for the colonized who pass them every day) the great deeds of colonization. The buildings are patterned after the colonizer's own favorite designs; the same is true of the street names, which recall the faraway provinces from which he came. . . . Traditions and acquirements, habits and conquests, deeds and acts of previous generations are thus bequeathed and recorded in history."[122] Memmi insists that there is a certain inevitability to such displays in the mind of the conqueror, because "he loves the most flashy symbols, the most striking demonstrations of the power of his country. He attends all the military parades and he desires and obtains frequent and elaborate ones; he contributes his part by dressing up carefully and ostentatiously. He admires the army and its strength, reverses uniforms and covets decorations . . . this corresponds to a deep necessity . . . to impress the colonized is just as important as to reassure oneself."[123]

It is possible, in the light of what Fanon and Memmi reveal, to look on the ruins of ancient Babylon with a new eye—an eye to the impact that such sights would have had on those whose suffering formed the very bricks of this ancient wonder of the world. Yet, Fanon writes that the *inward* life of the colonized person is quite different: "He is overpowered but not tamed; he is treated as an inferior but he is not convinced of his inferiority . . . the settler pits brute force against the weight of numbers. He is an exhibitionist. His preoccupation with security makes him remind the native out loud that he alone is master. The settler keeps alive in the native an anger which he deprives of outlet."[124]

In Daniel 3, the statue as a symbol of power communicates the power of this story, but Daniel 3 itself communicates the inward conviction that the Jewish population is *not* powerless or without recourse. As is often the case with the Bible, the reader must turn to the world of subordinated peoples, minorities, the displaced and threatened, to learn how to ask socially appropriate questions of a book that reflects an exiled or politically occupied people.

Nebuchadnezzar's statue stands for political and economic power. As such, it only weakens the message of Daniel 3 to reduce it to merely a pious lesson about idolatry or the fall of the proud, as if to relate it to any proud person of any station in life. Daniel 3 is about a particular kind of pride that comes from a system that derives its prestige and power from the suffering of others; in short, it is the unique pride of the wealthy and the powerful. Who else can erect golden monuments? Along this same line, it is perhaps somewhat dangerous to see in chap. 3 any sympathetic portrayal of Nebuchadnezzar (who is portrayed, in the words of Fanon, as both an "exhibitionist" of power and the raging executioner).[125] To suggest that chap. 3 has a sympathetic portrayal of the emperor at the end is merely to point out that in the end the monarch's power is humbled, defeated because of the statue's powerlessness over the Jews; and thus the monarch is transformed. There is no sympathy with tyranny in Daniel 3; there is only the possibility of change.

2. Is Daniel 3 a martyr legend? Porteous suggests that martyr legends can indeed result in the last-minute salvation of the heroes as well as their death,[126] but Collins prefers to suggest that Daniel 3 is an emergent form of a martyr legend that will be fully developed in a test like 2 Maccabees 7.[127] In any case, a martyr legend is intended to promote action—to embolden faith—and in the case of Daniel 3, to call people to active, nonviolent resistance to the symbols of worldly power and its religious expressions. In short, it is a call to political atheism.

121. F. Fanon, *The Wretched of the Earth* (New York: Grove, 1963) 51-52.
122. A. Memmi, *The Colonizer and the Colonized* (Boston: Beacon, 1965) 104.
123. Ibid., 59.
124. Fanon, *The Wretched of the Earth,* 53.
125. Ibid.
126. Porteous, *Daniel.*
127. Collins, *Daniel,* Hermeneia, 55.

In his recent history of Christianity, W. H. C. Frend often refers to the Roman charge of "atheism" directed against the Christians because of their refusal to recognize the Roman state gods.[128] Concomitant to this, of course, was their refusal of military service both because of Jesus' commands to love enemies and because of the pagan worship required of those who took the Roman commands. As he stood before the authorities who demanded to know the reason for his insubordination in refusing to bear arms, it is reported that the Roman centurion Marcellus, a Christian convert, replied, "I am a soldier of Jesus Christ, the eternal king. From now on I cease to serve your emperors and I despise the worship of your gods of wood and stone . . . it is not fitting that a Christian, who fights for Christ his Lord, should be a soldier according to the brutalities of this world." The annals of the radical reformation traditions— Quaker, Mennonite, and Church of the Brethren—are filled with such encounters "before the king," standing in the courts of states. The early Brethren leader John Naas of Nordheim, for example, in the eighteenth century stood before the king of Prussia and refused to bear arms because he was already enlisted in the army of Christ. Likewise, George Fox refused Oliver Cromwell's offer of an officership in his army.

Christian faith involves the refusal to bow before the golden statues of Nebuchadnezzar. But what is critical in the modern era is the realization that in our time Nebuchadnezzar is now perfectly capable of building his statues with the face of Jesus—evil appears as an angel of light. (E.g., a U.S. nuclear submarine capable of dozens of Hiroshimas was named *Corpus Christi,* "the body of Christ"!) For Americans who believe that they live in a "Christian" country, it is far too easy to accept political or economic policies that involve bowing to golden statues in the name of national interests. The bombing of Baghdad during the Persian Gulf War resulted in thousands of civilian deaths and continued to wreak havoc for the poor of that society years after the cease-fire through the destruction of a vital infrastructure for distribution of medical supplies, food, water, and other essentials of peaceful existence. Yet, the bombing was accompanied by a political rhetoric of "faith and patriotism" that played as sweetly on international television as did Nebuchadnezzar's orchestra. But the Christian is called to resistance, and to "atheism" in the face of *all* false gods. If chapter 1 was a call to resist the enticements of the king's food and wine, chap. 3 is just as clearly a call not to lose heart before the sight of the monumental self-importance of the conquering regime, both then and now. Modern Christians ought to refuse all attempts to serenade violence and exploitation with the tunes of patriotism. It is precisely the responsibility of Christians to point out the falsehoods of using Christian symbolism and language to defend exploitation and military brutality. The beginning of that task, however, is for us to refuse to be moved by the music of national interest. Mishael, Azariah, and Hananiah, then, are Hebrew apostles of a radical faith that is, at the same time, a political atheism.

3. Sovereignty is a central issue in the book of Daniel. In 3:27, once again the king gathers many of his officers, who share his astonishment that the fire has no sovereignty over the three men. The king's punishment failed. Not even the fire, let alone the king, can rule over them. Traditional Christian suggestions that there is a reference here to a "resurrection motif" may not be theologically acceptable in modern historical-critical discussion, but read as a comparison to the sociopolitical circumstances of first-century Roman Palestine, such comments are near the mark, particularly if Jesus' resurrection is seen as a defiant reversal of the Roman authorities' attempt to impose their will on the subordinated minority Jewish population of first-century Palestine.

---

128. W. H. C. Frend, *The Rise of Christianity* (Philadelphia: Fortress, 1984) 148, 181-82, 234-35.

DANIEL 4:1-37, THE TRUE THRONE
AND FALSE THRONES

NIV

4 King Nebuchadnezzar,

To the peoples, nations and men of every language, who live in all the world:

May you prosper greatly!

[2]It is my pleasure to tell you about the miraculous signs and wonders that the Most High God has performed for me.

[3]How great are his signs,
  how mighty his wonders!
His kingdom is an eternal kingdom;
  his dominion endures from
    generation to generation.

[4]I, Nebuchadnezzar, was at home in my palace, contented and prosperous. [5]I had a dream that made me afraid. As I was lying in my bed, the images and visions that passed through my mind terrified me. [6]So I commanded that all the wise men of Babylon be brought before me to interpret the dream for me. [7]When the magicians, enchanters, astrologers[a] and diviners came, I told them the dream, but they could not interpret it for me. [8]Finally, Daniel came into my presence and I told him the dream. (He is called Belteshazzar, after the name of my god, and the spirit of the holy gods is in him.)

[9]I said, "Belteshazzar, chief of the magicians, I know that the spirit of the holy gods is in you, and no mystery is too difficult for you. Here is my dream; interpret it for me. [10]These are the visions I saw while lying in my bed: I looked, and there before me stood a tree in the middle of the land. Its height was enormous. [11]The tree grew large and strong and its top touched the sky; it was visible to the ends of the earth. [12]Its leaves were beautiful, its fruit abundant, and on it was food for all. Under it the beasts of the field found shelter, and the birds of the air lived in its branches; from it every creature was fed.

[13]"In the visions I saw while lying in my bed, I looked, and there before me was a messenger,[b]

a7 Or Chaldeans   b13 Or watchman; also in verses 17 and 23

NRSV

4[a] King Nebuchadnezzar to all peoples, nations, and languages that live throughout the earth: May you have abundant prosperity! [2]The signs and wonders that the Most High God has worked for me I am pleased to recount.

[3] How great are his signs,
  how mighty his wonders!
His kingdom is an everlasting kingdom,
  and his sovereignty is from generation to
    generation.

[4][b]I, Nebuchadnezzar, was living at ease in my home and prospering in my palace. [5]I saw a dream that frightened me; my fantasies in bed and the visions of my head terrified me. [6]So I made a decree that all the wise men of Babylon should be brought before me, in order that they might tell me the interpretation of the dream. [7]Then the magicians, the enchanters, the Chaldeans, and the diviners came in, and I told them the dream, but they could not tell me its interpretation. [8]At last Daniel came in before me—he who was named Belteshazzar after the name of my god, and who is endowed with a spirit of the holy gods[c]—and I told him the dream: [9]"O Belteshazzar, chief of the magicians, I know that you are endowed with a spirit of the holy gods[c] and that no mystery is too difficult for you. Hear[d] the dream that I saw; tell me its interpretation.

[10][e] Upon my bed this is what I saw;
    there was a tree at the center of the earth,
    and its height was great.
[11] The tree grew great and strong,
    its top reached to heaven,
    and it was visible to the ends of the whole
      earth.
[12] Its foliage was beautiful,
    its fruit abundant,
    and it provided food for all.
  The animals of the field found shade under it,
    the birds of the air nested in its branches,
    and from it all living beings were fed.

a Ch 3.31 in Aram   b Ch 4.1 in Aram   c Or a holy, divine spirit
d Theodotion: Aram The visions of   e Theodotion Syr Compare
Gk: Aram adds The visions of my head

NIV

a holy one, coming down from heaven. [14]He called in a loud voice: 'Cut down the tree and trim off its branches; strip off its leaves and scatter its fruit. Let the animals flee from under it and the birds from its branches. [15]But let the stump and its roots, bound with iron and bronze, remain in the ground, in the grass of the field.

"'Let him be drenched with the dew of heaven, and let him live with the animals among the plants of the earth. [16]Let his mind be changed from that of a man and let him be given the mind of an animal, till seven times[a] pass by for him.

[17]"'The decision is announced by messengers, the holy ones declare the verdict, so that the living may know that the Most High is sovereign over the kingdoms of men and gives them to anyone he wishes and sets over them the lowliest of men.'

[18]"This is the dream that I, King Nebuchadnezzar, had. Now, Belteshazzar, tell me what it means, for none of the wise men in my kingdom can interpret it for me. But you can, because the spirit of the holy gods is in you."

[19]Then Daniel (also called Belteshazzar) was greatly perplexed for a time, and his thoughts terrified him. So the king said, "Belteshazzar, do not let the dream or its meaning alarm you."

Belteshazzar answered, "My lord, if only the dream applied to your enemies and its meaning to your adversaries! [20]The tree you saw, which grew large and strong, with its top touching the sky, visible to the whole earth, [21]with beautiful leaves and abundant fruit, providing food for all, giving shelter to the beasts of the field, and having nesting places in its branches for the birds of the air— [22]you, O king, are that tree! You have become great and strong; your greatness has grown until it reaches the sky, and your dominion extends to distant parts of the earth.

[23]"You, O king, saw a messenger, a holy one, coming down from heaven and saying, 'Cut down the tree and destroy it, but leave the stump, bound with iron and bronze, in

[a]16 Or years; also in verses 23, 25 and 32

NRSV

[13]I continued looking, in the visions of my head as I lay in bed, and there was a holy watcher, coming down from heaven. [14]He cried aloud and said:

'Cut down the tree and chop off its branches,
    strip off its foliage and scatter its fruit.
Let the animals flee from beneath it
    and the birds from its branches.
[15] But leave its stump and roots in the ground,
    with a band of iron and bronze,
    in the tender grass of the field.
Let him be bathed with the dew of heaven,
    and let his lot be with the animals of the field
    in the grass of the earth.
[16] Let his mind be changed from that of a human,
    and let the mind of an animal be given to him.
And let seven times pass over him.
[17] The sentence is rendered by decree of the watchers,
    the decision is given by order of the holy ones,
in order that all who live may know
    that the Most High is sovereign over the kingdom of mortals;
he gives it to whom he will
    and sets over it the lowliest of human beings.'

[18]This is the dream that I, King Nebuchadnezzar, saw. Now you, Belteshazzar, declare the interpretation, since all the wise men of my kingdom are unable to tell me the interpretation. You are able, however, for you are endowed with a spirit of the holy gods."[a]

19Then Daniel, who was called Belteshazzar, was severely distressed for a while. His thoughts terrified him. The king said, "Belteshazzar, do not let the dream or the interpretation terrify you." Belteshazzar answered, "My lord, may the dream be for those who hate you, and its interpretation for your enemies! [20]The tree that you saw, which grew great and strong, so that its top reached to heaven and was visible to the end of the whole earth, [21]whose foliage was beautiful and its fruit abundant, and which provided food for all, under

[a]Or a holy, divine spirit

NIV

the grass of the field, while its roots remain in the ground. Let him be drenched with the dew of heaven; let him live like the wild animals, until seven times pass by for him.'

24"This is the interpretation, O king, and this is the decree the Most High has issued against my lord the king: 25You will be driven away from people and will live with the wild animals; you will eat grass like cattle and be drenched with the dew of heaven. Seven times will pass by for you until you acknowledge that the Most High is sovereign over the kingdoms of men and gives them to anyone he wishes. 26The command to leave the stump of the tree with its roots means that your kingdom will be restored to you when you acknowledge that Heaven rules. 27Therefore, O king, be pleased to accept my advice: Renounce your sins by doing what is right, and your wickedness by being kind to the oppressed. It may be that then your prosperity will continue."

28All this happened to King Nebuchadnezzar. 29Twelve months later, as the king was walking on the roof of the royal palace of Babylon, 30he said, "Is not this the great Babylon I have built as the royal residence, by my mighty power and for the glory of my majesty?"

31The words were still on his lips when a voice came from heaven, "This is what is decreed for you, King Nebuchadnezzar: Your royal authority has been taken from you. 32You will be driven away from people and will live with the wild animals; you will eat grass like cattle. Seven times will pass by for you until you acknowledge that the Most High is sovereign over the kingdoms of men and gives them to anyone he wishes."

33Immediately what had been said about Nebuchadnezzar was fulfilled. He was driven away from people and ate grass like cattle. His body was drenched with the dew of heaven until his hair grew like the feathers of an eagle and his nails like the claws of a bird.

34At the end of that time, I, Nebuchadnezzar, raised my eyes toward heaven, and my sanity was restored. Then I praised the Most

NRSV

which animals of the field lived, and in whose branches the birds of the air had nests— 22it is you, O king! You have grown great and strong. Your greatness has increased and reaches to heaven, and your sovereignty to the ends of the earth. 23And whereas the king saw a holy watcher coming down from heaven and saying, 'Cut down the tree and destroy it, but leave its stump and roots in the ground, with a band of iron and bronze, in the grass of the field; and let him be bathed with the dew of heaven, and let his lot be with the animals of the field, until seven times pass over him'— 24this is the interpretation, O king, and it is a decree of the Most High that has come upon my lord the king: 25You shall be driven away from human society, and your dwelling shall be with the wild animals. You shall be made to eat grass like oxen, you shall be bathed with the dew of heaven, and seven times shall pass over you, until you have learned that the Most High has sovereignty over the kingdom of mortals, and gives it to whom he will. 26As it was commanded to leave the stump and roots of the tree, your kingdom shall be re-established for you from the time that you learn that Heaven is sovereign. 27Therefore, O king, may my counsel be acceptable to you: atone for[a] your sins with righteousness, and your iniquities with mercy to the oppressed, so that your prosperity may be prolonged."

28All this came upon King Nebuchadnezzar. 29At the end of twelve months he was walking on the roof of the royal palace of Babylon, 30and the king said, "Is this not magnificent Babylon, which I have built as a royal capital by my mighty power and for my glorious majesty?" 31While the words were still in the king's mouth, a voice came from heaven: "O King Nebuchadnezzar, to you it is declared: The kingdom has departed from you! 32You shall be driven away from human society, and your dwelling shall be with the animals of the field. You shall be made to eat grass like oxen, and seven times shall pass over you, until you have learned that the Most High has sovereignty over the kingdom of mortals and gives it to whom he will." 33Immediately the sentence was fulfilled against Nebuchadnezzar. He was driven away

a Aram *break off*

NIV

High; I honored and glorified him who lives forever.

His dominion is an eternal dominion;
    his kingdom endures from generation to
        generation.
35All the peoples of the earth
    are regarded as nothing.
He does as he pleases
    with the powers of heaven
    and the peoples of the earth.
No one can hold back his hand
    or say to him: "What have you done?"

36At the same time that my sanity was restored, my honor and splendor were returned to me for the glory of my kingdom. My advisers and nobles sought me out, and I was restored to my throne and became even greater than before. 37Now I, Nebuchadnezzar, praise and exalt and glorify the King of heaven, because everything he does is right and all his ways are just. And those who walk in pride he is able to humble.

NRSV

from human society, ate grass like oxen, and his body was bathed with the dew of heaven, until his hair grew as long as eagles' feathers and his nails became like birds' claws.

34When that period was over, I, Nebuchadnezzar, lifted my eyes to heaven, and my reason returned to me.

I blessed the Most High,
    and praised and honored the one who lives
        forever.
For his sovereignty is an everlasting
        sovereignty,
    and his kingdom endures from generation
        to generation.
35 All the inhabitants of the earth are accounted
        as nothing,
    and he does what he wills with the host of
        heaven
    and the inhabitants of the earth.
There is no one who can stay his hand
    or say to him, "What are you doing?"
36At that time my reason returned to me; and my majesty and splendor were restored to me for the glory of my kingdom. My counselors and my lords sought me out, I was re-established over my kingdom, and still more greatness was added to me. 37Now I, Nebuchadnezzar, praise and extol and honor the King of heaven,
    for all his works are truth,
        and his ways are justice;
    and he is able to bring low
        those who walk in pride.

COMMENTARY

Chapter 4 is particularly interesting because of two elements. It includes a wealth of potential influences from traditions attested in Greek and Mesopotamian sources (the arrogance of Nebuchadnezzar, the madness and/or absence of the Babylonian ruler in Babylon, dwelling with beasts, etc.) And it reflects a wealth of Jewish sources that are obviously relevant to understanding the chapter.

The nonbiblical sources include a story in Eusebius, attributed to Megasthenes (300 BCE?): *Concerning the Assyrians.* In brief, the story portrays Nebuchadnezzar, in a fit of madness or possession, climbing to his roof and predicting the coming of a Persian mule that will enslave the Babylonians. Nebuchadnezzar wishes that this mule would join the wild beasts in the desert and leave him alone. There are intriguing parallels as well as significant differences between this tale and Daniel 4. The significance of this tale, however, is that it may point to certain collective memories of Nebuchadnezzar or Nabonidus that the author of Daniel 4 draws on—e.g., Nebuchadnezzar's odd behavior, the fear of his reign's coming to an end, and the location "on the roof."

A second series of sources surrounds Nabonidus, who left Babylon for a sojourn in the desert, spending time in Teima, an oasis village. Many ancient texts give negative portrayals of him, which most scholars presume to have been written by angry Babylonian religious leaders who resented both the king's absence and his apparent neglect of the Marduk cult in Babylon.[129]

That the historical Nabonidus, rather than Nebuchadnezzar, may be the source of the portrayal of the monarch in Daniel 4 is a view that received a major piece of corroborating evidence with the publication of the Dead Sea Scroll fragment entitled *Prayer of Nabonidus* (see Introduction), which parallels Daniel 4 in many ways and specifically names Nabonidus.

Finally, there are fascinating differences between the Greek and the Aramaic versions of the chapter. The two versions are quite distinct, although clearly covering the same ground. In the Greek, Nebuchadnezzar narrates his dream, and then Daniel interprets it. What is particularly interesting in the Greek, however, is a much stronger confession of faith/conversion by Nebuchadnezzar:

From now on I will serve him. From fear of him trembling has seized me, and I praise all his holy ones. For the gods of the nations do not have in themselves power to turn over the kingdom of a king to another king, to kill and make alive and to do signs and great and terrible wonders, and to change very great things, as the God of heaven has done in my case. . . . Every day of my reign I will offer sacrifices to the Most High for my life, for a pleasing odor to the Lord, and I will do what is pleasing before him.[130]

This is an important addition, suggesting that the themes of the transformation of Nebuchadnezzar, already suggested in the Aramaic version of the Masoretic Text, were enlarged and made stronger in the Hellenistic period, which is a tendency we also see in the Greek additions to Daniel, especially Bel and the Dragon (see commentary on Additions to Daniel).

4:1-3, Confessional Introduction. Chapter 4 begins with a standard Aramaic letter form,

including the wish for *shalom* ("peace") and the clear identification of the sender. The concern to publish the proclamation in "all languages" is reflected in Darius's famous Behistun Inscription, which still survives on the cliff face on which it was carved. The inscription is written in three different languages, and it describes Darius's rise to power as the third Persian monarch.[131] Chapter 4, then, begins with Nebuchadnezzar speaking in the first person in praise of the Jewish God, and the chapter also ends with his praise of the Jewish God. It is worth noting that dream reports, as well as epistles, are typically cast in the first person.

The key term in the confessional introduction, and the focus of Daniel 4, is the issue that has been raised already in previous stories: sovereignty or political power. The issue of the nature of political authority was obviously a critical one for the exiles and the exiles in the diaspora, who constantly encountered the claims of total sovereignty by their foreign rulers. The Aramaic term that is usually translated "sovereignty" (שָׁלְטָן *šāltān*) can be found running through the text of Daniel again and again in chaps. 1–6 and is particularly prominent in the first vision of chap. 7 (see Dan 2:38-39; 3:27, 33; 4:19, 31; 5:7, 16; 6:25; 7:6, 12, 14, 26-27; cf. Ezra 4:20; 7:24).

4:4-9, Nebuchadnezzar Calls His Counselors. 4:4-6. The setting of Nebuchadnezzar's experience is important. He was in his palace, and was "prospering/flourishing." Goldingay provides a very helpful description of the Babylonian setting and Nebuchadnezzar's vantage point over Babylon and its wonders from the palace.[132] The Old Greek text also dates this story to Nebuchadnezzar's eighteenth year, which would, as in the previous chapter, be the year of Nebuchadnezzar's conquest of Jerusalem and the destruction of the Temple. In any case, things were going well for the king—or so he thought. But just as he was enjoying his success, the king has a dream that frightens him, and so he decrees that the "wise of Babylon" be brought in.

4:7. The listing of those who are brought in includes magicians (using an Egyptian term), enchanters (Persian), Chaldeans (here "astrologers"),

129. "Verse Account of Nabonidus," in *Ancient Near Eastern Texts Relating to the Old Testament* (*ANET*), ed. James B. Pritchard (Princeton, N.J.: Princeton University Press, 1969) 312-15.

130. J. J. Collins, *Daniel,* Hermeneia (Minneapolis: Fortress, 1993) 213.

131. J. M. Cook, *The Persian Empire* (New York: Schocken, 1983) 12-13, 19.

132. John Goldingay, *Daniel,* WBC 30 (Dallas: Word, 1988) 89-90.

and exorcists. The term for "exorcist" is unique to this story, and is the same word used to describe the Jew who heals Nabonidus's illness in 4QPrNab (see Introduction). Again, as expected, all of these advisers to the king fail him.

4:8-9. It would be interesting to know why Daniel is delayed in his arrival, but as many scholars have suggested, it certainly serves to build the drama for his entrance. In any case, the delay serves the function of giving Nebuchadnezzar time to realize that he will not be able to get his answers from anyone else in his regime. Notably, Daniel's slave name is repeated by Nebuchadnezzar, "Belteshazzar after the name of my god" (v. 8). Are we to believe, then, that Nebuchadnezzar does not know Daniel's given name? Nebuchadnezzar knows him well enough to say that he is one who is "endowed with a spirit of the holy gods." Nebuchadnezzar appears to lack understanding about where the source of Daniel's great wisdom is to be found. Goldingay notes that this title is not used for the Jewish God elsewhere.[133] This is perhaps the main hint in chap. 4 that once again we are dealing with the separate story that was eventually joined to the series that appears in the book. In v. 9, Nebuchadnezzar realizes his dependence on Daniel and openly attests to Daniel's wisdom and his ability to interpret dreams and mysteries.

4:10-18, The Description of Nebuchadnezzar's Dream. 4:10-11. Nebuchadnezzar then describes the dream to Daniel. In the dream he saw a tree of "great height," like the statue in chap. 2 (note the prevalence of things that are great, tall, mighty, awesome in these dreams). Many scholars suggest that this tree is a reference to the widely held notion of the "cosmic tree" that stretches to the heavens in many different ancient mythologies (and perhaps related also to the tree of life portrayed by sacred poles in the Jerusalem Temple; see 2 Kgs 17:10; 18:4; 23:14), which may be the source of the tree imagery in Ezekiel 31, where Pharaoh is described as a great tree. There are many nonbiblical references similar to this, such as Herodotus's description of the dream of Astyages the Mede in which a vine grows from the womb of his daughter and stretches across the earth (a reference to the birth of Cyrus, the conquerer of the Medes).[134] Note

also the portrayal of Babylon as a tree in the Dead Sea Scroll fragments.[135] In v. 11 the emphasis on the height of the tree—reaching into the heavens—is reminiscent of the tower of Babel story in Genesis 11 (as was the reference to Shinar in Daniel 2). The idea that this tree is "visible to the ends of the earth" is another comment on the megalomania of the emperor.

4:12. The tree's foliage was beautiful, but the issue here is the control of provisions. Twice, the fact is repeated that the tree fed all humanity and then all living things. In this initial description, the impression is given that animals found shade under the tree and that birds lived in it by choice. However, when the imagery changes, another perspective is revealed.

4:13. This verse introduces the concept of a "watchful one" or "watcher." This nomenclature for a representative of heaven is especially prominent in *1 Enoch*. Goldingay associates the watchmen with God's court, but others have also made reference to the Persian officials known as the "King's Eyes," who regularly informed the emperor of matters throughout his empire. It is possible, then, that these watchmen are God's informants, in contradistinction to the Persian secret service. The empire that spies on others is now itself being spied upon by the regime of God! For exiles and foreign immigrants, such an image would be potent, since fear of betrayal to the authorities would be a daily reality. That these informants are themselves matched by even greater watchmen of God would be an interesting source of satisfaction for the exilic hearers of such stories.[136]

4:14. The result of the visit of the heavenly messenger is the near total destruction of the tree. The animals are told to flee. Have they been released? It is hard not to equate them with the captive peoples of Babylon and Persia. For the Persians, especially, the self-delusion that the people dwelt among them peacefully and by their

---

133. Ibid., 80.
134. Herodotus *The History* 1:108.

135. See 4Q547 in R. Eisenman and M. Wise, *The Dead Sea Scrolls Uncovered* (Shaftsbury: Element, 1992) 71-73. It is worth noting in passing that the Dead Sea Scroll fragments 4Q 234-245 include Daniel, Belshazzar, Nebuchadnezzar, the seventy-year period of exile, and the tower of Babel traditions among the historical references cited. See ibid., 64-68; F. García-Martínez, *Qumran and Apocalyptic, Studies on the Aramaic Texts from Qumran* (Leiden: Brill, 1992) 137-45.
136. For an argument that the "King's Eye" may have existed only in Greek (and apparently Hebrew!) imagination, note Steven Hirsch, *The Friendship of the Barbarians* (Hanover: University Press of New England, 1985) 101-31.

---

choice was, as already noted, a common notion. For a later period, historians also note the cynicism of the Roman writers who spoke of a "peace of Rome" (*Pax Romana*). This peace referred to a time of opulence that disregarded the suffering at the frontiers of the empire, even though the suffering of the conquered peoples at the perimeters of the empire made such comforts possible for the elite of Rome.

In the presence of Daniel, the heavenly visitor attacks the central political administration directly by cutting down the great tree. "Let the animals flee" (the jussive form in Aramaic)[137] suggests that the animals are finally released from captivity by the destruction of the tree.

4:15-16. Attempts to explain the significance of the binding of the tree are difficult. Was Nebuchadnezzar to be bound in some fashion? Another difficulty here is that the binding imagery gives way to the animal imagery, which provides the main theme of the dream. The problem derives from the mixing of the images of beasts and trees. Does the tree eat grass? Is the animal bound? Are we perhaps to see that a limitation has been placed on the expansion of this "tree" into the lives of countless thousands in the ancient Near East? Certainly this would agree with what is stated later in v. 27. Many scholars have suspected that two original themes (trees and animals) have been artifically and awkwardly joined at this point, bringing about the confusion. The Greek versions make this shackling of Nebuchadnezzar much clearer.[138] The "mind" (Aramaic, "heart" [לבב *lēbab*], which is the seat of thought in ancient Semitic psychology) of Nebuchadnezzar is changed to that of an animal, and he must act accordingly, living among the beasts of the field.[139] Attempts to see in this some form of recognizable mental illness (e.g., lycanthropy) push the sense of the story beyond the more common motifs of reversal of fortune and the bringing down of the proud. Finally, the reversal of fortune will last for "seven times" (avoiding the specific "years").

---

137. I. Jerusalmi, *The Aramaic Sections of Ezra and Daniel* (Cincinnati: Hebrew Union College, 1972) 99.

138. Collins, *Daniel*, Hermeneia, 227.

139. There is a possible influence from the Gilgamesh Epic here, in which Enkidu also "ranges over the hills . . . with the beasts [he feeds on grass]" (*ANET,* 74). But as M. Lind has suggested, Enkidu rises from animal to ruler, whereas Nebuchadnezzar goes in the opposite direction, until he is restored.

4:17-18. It is now time for a decree by the angel, and not by the emperor. The question of who can give decrees with true authority is answered here. Throughout the book of Daniel the answer is consistent: God alone. The entire point is dramatically summed up in the phrase "in order that all who live may know/ that the Most High is sovereign/ over the kingdom of mortals." "All who live," not merely Nebuchadnezzar himself, will recognize God's sovereignty. The ruler is to be humbled in the sight of all who have suffered at his hands as well as those who believed him to be invincible.

4:19-27, Daniel Delivers the Interpretation. 4:19. At the end of the description of the dream, Nebuchadnezzar is curious, apparently without a clue as to the consequences of what he has seen. In direct contrast to this, Daniel is apparently already fully cognizant of the implications of what he has just heard. The terror of his thoughts is reminiscent of his reactions to other dreams that he experiences (2:25; 3:24; 4:2, 16; 5:6, 9-10; 6:20; 7:15, 28). But Daniel's terror is also the realization of truth and of the fact that this truth will now be spoken against power. In short, it is the terror of the prophet (Jeremiah noted threats against him by quoting his enemies: "Let us destroy the tree with its fruit" (Jer 11:19 NRSV; see also Jer 20:7-18). Daniel's initial expression does not mask the truth of what he is about to say against the power of the king. Scholars often read far too much into Daniel's reply to the king, as if Daniel is terribly sympathetic to Nebuchadnezzar. As Oppenheim's study reveals, however, actions must be taken or words spoken to counteract the evil of a dream, and this phrase may simply be Daniel's version of his obligatory ritual of neutralizing the evil.[140] But the truth of the dream is not a mere "curse" that can be averted, and to this, Daniel proceeds.

4:20-24. Most of Daniel's interpretation of Nebuchadnezzar's dream is repeated from the description given to Daniel by the king in the first place. The tree is, not unexpectedly, identified as the king himself. If the tree is to be cut down, then its grand expanse into the lives of other people will be curtailed. In v. 24, Daniel interprets the decree from the "Most High." The continued

---

140. A. L. Oppenheim, *The Interpretation of Dreams in the Ancient Near East* (Philadelphia: American Philosophical Society, 1956) 218-20.

image of the king in heaven versus the king on earth goes with the contrast between the apparent unchangeability of the decrees on earth and their only apparent power, as opposed to the decrees issued from God.

4:25-26. The king will be driven from human society. As the king has done to thousands of subjects, so he will be cast out from human society and will be forced to live among the wild animals. The punishment is to give the king a lesson—"until he has learned" who has true control over the kingdom of humans. It is significant that the kingdom of Nebuchadnezzar will be returned only when he realizes that he does not really have a kingdom; his reign is only by permit from the One who truly reigns over all living beings on the earth. The issue here is sovereignty. In reference to this exile, Lacocque writes that "there is a sort of visceral fear of animality in the book of Daniel"[141] (cf. Nebuchadnezzar's curse to the lions of chap. 6 and the beasts of chap. 7).

4:27. As a result of his exile among the animals, the king is to "tear away" or "break off" (פרק *pĕraq*) his sins, like the branches of a tree (v. 11). But lest we be ill informed as to the nature of Nebuchadnezzar's abuse of power and what it has meant, it is made clear by one of the demands of restitution: "mercy to the oppressed." The Aramaic term meaning "poor" or "oppressed" (ענין *ănāyin*) is related to the more common Hebrew term עני (*ānî*), which is often found in characteristic prophetic passages about the treatment of the poor (Isa 29:19; 32:7; Amos 2:7; 8:4). Collins notes that later Jewish commentaries relate this treatment to the actual treatment of the Jewish exiles to whom mercy should be extended.[142] Lacocque, also, refers to "the organic ties established by the Law and Prophets between the poor and oppressed, on the one hand, and the community of Israel on the other."[143] In short, the Babylonian emperor must no longer behave like a Babylonian emperor; he must no longer act like the destroyer of Jerusalem and the tyrannical mover of whole populations like pieces on a chess board. The branches of this oppressive tree must be torn away. The animal imagery is similar. To

be exiled among the animals is to become *like those who found shade and food from the tree,* but who were able to flee when the tree was destroyed (v. 14). In short, Nebuchadnezzar must identify with the victims of his own rule.

We can follow this association of pride and the treatment of the lowly elsewhere in the Bible. Note, for example, how many of the themes of Daniel 4 are picked up in Psalm 79, about the destruction of Jerusalem: Ps 79:1—the nations who ruined God's temple and destroyed Jerusalem; 79:2—servants of God given as food to birds and wild animals; 79:8—the "low state" of those who are defeated; 79:11—the groans of the prisoners should be heard by God; 79:12—a sevenfold return on the taunts of the neighbors against Jerusalem; 79:13—the remembrance of God "from generation to generation." All of this serves as a reminder that the identification with his victims and the recognition of God's sovereignty are crucial aspects of what Nebuchadnezzar must learn from his exile among the animals (that is, among the conquered).

4:28-33, The Dream Fulfilled. Verses 28-29 are masterful irony. After having read Daniel's interpretation, we are not told how Nebuchadnezzar reacted to it. We are only shown that he continues in his arrogant claims to be sovereign over all the earth. He is pictured as surveying the vastness of his empire and attributing to himself "power," "might," and "glorious majesty/great honor"—all of which are traits attributed to God in 2:37.

A key phrase occurs in v. 32*b*: "until you have learned that the Most High has sovereignty over the kingdom of mortals and gives it to whom he will." God has the ability to give power to whomever God pleases (note that "doing as one pleases" is a frequent indication of political power in the book of Daniel). The emphasis here is not on Nebuchadnezzar's being for a time the one chosen, but on the tenuous nature of being God's chosen ruler. As the kings of Israel and Judah were to learn (and often fail to learn), God's sovereignty is partially guaranteed by the fact that someone else can be chosen at any time. The threat of recall is real and instantaneous!

In the classic Hebraic sense of reversal of fortune, Nebuchadnezzar's fate befalls him "while the words were still in the king's mouth" (v. 31)—at the moment that the king attributes his

141. André Lacocque, *The Book of Daniel,* trans. D. Pellauer (Atlanta: John Knox, 1979) 86.

142. Collins, *Daniel,* Hermeneia, 230.

143. Lacocque, *The Book of Daniel,* 84.

power to himself and to what he has built. Nebuchadnezzar's fate is described in precisely the language of Daniel's interpretation (vv. 32-33).

4:34-37, Nebuchadnezzar's Confession. At the beginning of v. 34, Nebuchadnezzar's narration in the first person resumes. The "confession" in vv. 34-35 is the longest such confession in the stories in Daniel, and it includes several important themes: (1) that God's sovereignty lasts forever, "from generation to generation." This involves a reversal of Nebuchadnezzar's statement in 4:3; (2) that

God's control extends to all the earth (similar to the extension of the branches of a tree, the image used earlier of Nebuchadnezzar's reign); (3) no one has the power or the ability to question God.

The final verse of chapter 4 reaffirms God's ability to bring down the proud. This repeats a theme found in wisdom literature (see Prov 11:2; 16:18; 29:23; see also James 4:6) but is also powerfully found in late prophetic passages (Isa 2:11, 17; 13:11; Ezek 16:49, 56, where pride is associated with mistreatment of the poor specifically).

REFLECTIONS

Two different, but related, theological issues arise from contemporary reflection on Daniel 4: (1) the significance of rulers on earth acting by God's permission and (2) the significance of Nebuchadnezzar's exile and confession.

1. *Rulers on Earth.* The words of another arrogant world authority ring from the past: " 'Do you refuse to speak to me? Do you not know that I have power to release you and power to crucify you?' Jesus answered him, "You would have no power over me unless it had been given you from above' " (John 19:10-11 NRSV).

Beginning with St. Augustine's apologia excusing Christians so that they might wield the power of Rome's thundering legions without guilt, it is amazing how many attempts there have been in Christian history to reverse totally the point of saying that authorities act only as proxies under God. To say that the emperor rules only by God's allowance is *not* an invitation to a total surrender to the state and is hardly to be taken as approval of the power and strength of the state. It is precisely the opposite. To say that God truly reigns is to make human authority tentative, temporary, and always liable to being disregarded in favor of the higher authority. In the Bible it is the *prophet* who wields the symbol of office—the horn of oil—and not the king!

The book of Daniel asks us, What does it mean to say that God rules? How can we speak of the rule of God in a way that is not merely a pious platitude—a platitude that masks more mundane political commitments? The key, according to Daniel 4, is genuine transformation, not pious rhetoric. Nebuchadnezzar actually claimed to be meek and just, as did many of the Mesopotamian rulers in their public inscriptions and official party propaganda. In the annual new year festival, the Babylonian monarch was slapped in the face by a priest as a reminder that he rules in Marduk's place only. Yet this hardly tempered his passion for conquests. From the perspective of the exiles, such rhetoric would have had a hollow ring, as does any modern reference to a land of the free when spoken in the context of domestic or global poverty. Fanon, in his context of French occupation of Algeria, accused Christianity itself of being such a hollow, self-justifying ideology: "The church in the colonies is the white people's church, the foreigner's church. She does not call the native to God's ways but to the ways of the white man, of the master, of the oppressor. And as we know, in this matter, many are called but few chosen."[144]

The book of Daniel suggests that the mere fact that Christians may find themselves under the rule of an oppressive state (whether overt or more subtle), does not mean that they need bow to its authority. Note the interesting paradox in the words of 1 Pet 2:16 (NRSV): "As

144. F. Fanon, *The Wretched of the Earth* (New York: Grove, 1963) 42.

servants of God, live as free people"! The modern state is a reality with which Christians must work for more just and peaceful structures in our lives—not to preserve the sanctity of the state, but to uphold justice and peace as the way of the Christian in the world. Because God reigns, the state is merely a tool—sometimes to be used, sometimes to be prophetically condemned, but never to be baptized. In their involvement in the government of the state, whether it be political office or civil service or some other role, Christians should maintain a sense of the tentativeness of the state's role as a tool of God.

2. *Nebuchadnezzar's Exile and Lesson.* We have had occasion in the commentary to question the scholarly opinion that these stories show a positive attitude of the Jews toward the foreign king. These scholars support their claim by pointing to the confessions of honor or even the belief that the king is made to speak once he has learned his many lessons at the hands of the Jewish exiles. This notion of the confessions of the ruler in Daniel is worth further thought. When we are introduced to Nebuchadnezzar in chapter 4, we recognize the proud and domineering emperor of the Babylonian empire—a regime built on the extortion and pillage of both people and resources throughout the ancient Near East. But this man undergoes a transformation through being forced to endure what he has inflicted upon others. Further- more, restitution is demanded from him for his sins, especially his treatment of the dispossessed. In Daniel, it is a humbled and transformed emperor who finally confesses that God's "works are truth," and God's "ways are justice" (Dan 4:37 NRSV).

In short, Daniel does not teach that it is impossible for foreign emperors to be righteous and God-fearing. In order to be so, however, they must not be a "tree" whose military "branches" invade other peoples, nor can they continue to oppress the weak. The book of Daniel teaches that, of course, it is possible for a political leader to be righteous, but he or she must be totally transformed from conventional perspectives and practices and be one who knows the true God. Similarly, it is not the view of Daniel (or Jonah, or Isaiah 19) that a Babylonian or Assyrian is by virtue of race barred from the kingdom of God. But conversion means much more than inward, pious assent to the rule of God. It means no longer being Assyrian or Babylonian in a profound sense. These powers may still rule, but not in the traditional sense. Is it even possible to have a state with such a transformed monarch who is now unwilling to oppress and ruthlessly exercise the power of the state? To even ask this question is evidence that the force of these stories in Daniel is being heard.

In the radical reformation traditions of Christianity (Quakerism, Mennonites, Church of the Brethren, among others), there is a long-standing debate about the possibility of Christian righteousness within the secular political systems of world states. The most radical rejection of this possibility is the nonconformity of such groups as the Amish, whose conception of the church is that it is a social reality in the world, but an entity entirely apart from the world. Such Christian communities would refuse almost any participation in a system that is apart from the church. The Quaker tradition, while aware of the import of these ethical questions, has always taken a more hopeful, and at times utilitarian, approach to this issue. Quakerism is utilitarian in that it accepts the present realities, even if less than ideal, but remains hopeful that God's transforming justice can at least influence partially any system of humanity. Therefore, lobbying, prophetically advocating, and perhaps even running for office within any governmental system may result in a bit more light in the world, even if it is never bright sunshine! A respectful eye on our more radical Christian brothers and sisters is necessary to maintain a clearheaded approach about the reality of the demands of God's justice, which must never be compromised for political expediency. The book of Daniel teaches that transformation is possible, but the very fact that we are dealing with fictional accounts of transformed emperors (which were ironic twists in the stories and must surely have raised a smile among those Jews who first repeated them to one another) makes one wonder whether the possibility for conscientious Christians to "rule" is an ethically viable choice. Perhaps the answer is that when we reach the point at which we find that such participation in the kingdoms of the world involves impossible compromise, Christians become, with Daniel, Hananiah, Mishael, and Azariah, a part of the prophetic resistance.

DANIEL 5:1-31, THE HUMILIATION OF THE CONQUERED: BELSHAZZAR'S FEAST

NIV

5 King Belshazzar gave a great banquet for a thousand of his nobles and drank wine with them. [2]While Belshazzar was drinking his wine, he gave orders to bring in the gold and silver goblets that Nebuchadnezzar his father[a] had taken from the temple in Jerusalem, so that the king and his nobles, his wives and his concubines might drink from them. [3]So they brought in the gold goblets that had been taken from the temple of God in Jerusalem, and the king and his nobles, his wives and his concubines drank from them. [4]As they drank the wine, they praised the gods of gold and silver, of bronze, iron, wood and stone.

[5]Suddenly the fingers of a human hand appeared and wrote on the plaster of the wall, near the lampstand in the royal palace. The king watched the hand as it wrote. [6]His face turned pale and he was so frightened that his knees knocked together and his legs gave way.

[7]The king called out for the enchanters, astrologers[b] and diviners to be brought and said to these wise men of Babylon, "Whoever reads this writing and tells me what it means will be clothed in purple and have a gold chain placed around his neck, and he will be made the third highest ruler in the kingdom."

[8]Then all the king's wise men came in, but they could not read the writing or tell the king what it meant. [9]So King Belshazzar became even more terrified and his face grew more pale. His nobles were baffled.

[10]The queen,[c] hearing the voices of the king and his nobles, came into the banquet hall. "O king, live forever!" she said. "Don't be alarmed! Don't look so pale! [11]There is a man in your kingdom who has the spirit of the holy gods

NRSV

5 King Belshazzar made a great festival for a thousand of his lords, and he was drinking wine in the presence of the thousand.

2Under the influence of the wine, Belshazzar commanded that they bring in the vessels of gold and silver that his father Nebuchadnezzar had taken out of the temple in Jerusalem, so that the king and his lords, his wives, and his concubines might drink from them. [3]So they brought in the vessels of gold and silver[a] that had been taken out of the temple, the house of God in Jerusalem, and the king and his lords, his wives, and his concubines drank from them. [4]They drank the wine and praised the gods of gold and silver, bronze, iron, wood, and stone.

5Immediately the fingers of a human hand appeared and began writing on the plaster of the wall of the royal palace, next to the lampstand. The king was watching the hand as it wrote. [6]Then the king's face turned pale, and his thoughts terrified him. His limbs gave way, and his knees knocked together. [7]The king cried aloud to bring in the enchanters, the Chaldeans, and the diviners; and the king said to the wise men of Babylon, "Whoever can read this writing and tell me its interpretation shall be clothed in purple, have a chain of gold around his neck, and rank third in the kingdom." [8]Then all the king's wise men came in, but they could not read the writing or tell the king the interpretation. [9]Then King Belshazzar became greatly terrified and his face turned pale, and his lords were perplexed.

10The queen, when she heard the discussion of the king and his lords, came into the banqueting hall. The queen said, "O king, live forever! Do not let your thoughts terrify you or your face grow pale. [11]There is a man in your kingdom who is endowed with a spirit of the holy gods.[b] In the

a2 Or *ancestor;* or *predecessor;* also in verses 11, 13 and 18   b7 Or *Chaldeans;* also in verse 11   c10 Or *queen mother*

a Theodotion Vg: Aram lacks *and silver*   b Or *a holy, divine spirit*

NIV

in him. In the time of your father he was found to have insight and intelligence and wisdom like that of the gods. King Nebuchadnezzar your father—your father the king, I say—appointed him chief of the magicians, enchanters, astrologers and diviners. [12]This man Daniel, whom the king called Belteshazzar, was found to have a keen mind and knowledge and understanding, and also the ability to interpret dreams, explain riddles and solve difficult problems. Call for Daniel, and he will tell you what the writing means."

[13]So Daniel was brought before the king, and the king said to him, "Are you Daniel, one of the exiles my father the king brought from Judah? [14]I have heard that the spirit of the gods is in you and that you have insight, intelligence and outstanding wisdom. [15]The wise men and enchanters were brought before me to read this writing and tell me what it means, but they could not explain it. [16]Now I have heard that you are able to give interpretations and to solve difficult problems. If you can read this writing and tell me what it means, you will be clothed in purple and have a gold chain placed around your neck, and you will be made the third highest ruler in the kingdom."

[17]Then Daniel answered the king, "You may keep your gifts for yourself and give your rewards to someone else. Nevertheless, I will read the writing for the king and tell him what it means.

[18]"O king, the Most High God gave your father Nebuchadnezzar sovereignty and greatness and glory and splendor. [19]Because of the high position he gave him, all the peoples and nations and men of every language dreaded and feared him. Those the king wanted to put to death, he put to death; those he wanted to spare, he spared; those he wanted to promote, he promoted; and those he wanted to humble, he humbled. [20]But when his heart became arrogant and hardened with pride, he was deposed from his royal throne and stripped of his glory. [21]He was driven away from people and given the mind of an animal; he lived with the wild donkeys and ate grass like cattle; and his body was drenched with the dew of heaven, until he acknowledged that the Most High God is sovereign over the kingdoms of men and sets over them anyone he wishes.

NRSV

days of your father he was found to have enlightenment, understanding, and wisdom like the wisdom of the gods. Your father, King Nebuchadnezzar, made him chief of the magicians, enchanters, Chaldeans, and diviners,[a] [12]because an excellent spirit, knowledge, and understanding to interpret dreams, explain riddles, and solve problems were found in this Daniel, whom the king named Belteshazzar. Now let Daniel be called, and he will give the interpretation."

13Then Daniel was brought in before the king. The king said to Daniel, "So you are Daniel, one of the exiles of Judah, whom my father the king brought from Judah? [14]I have heard of you that a spirit of the gods[b] is in you, and that enlightenment, understanding, and excellent wisdom are found in you. [15]Now the wise men, the enchanters, have been brought in before me to read this writing and tell me its interpretation, but they were not able to give the interpretation of the matter. [16]But I have heard that you can give interpretations and solve problems. Now if you are able to read the writing and tell me its interpretation, you shall be clothed in purple, have a chain of gold around your neck, and rank third in the kingdom."

17Then Daniel answered in the presence of the king, "Let your gifts be for yourself, or give your rewards to someone else! Nevertheless I will read the writing to the king and let him know the interpretation. [18]O king, the Most High God gave your father Nebuchadnezzar kingship, greatness, glory, and majesty. [19]And because of the greatness that he gave him, all peoples, nations, and languages trembled and feared before him. He killed those he wanted to kill, kept alive those he wanted to keep alive, honored those he wanted to honor, and degraded those he wanted to degrade. [20]But when his heart was lifted up and his spirit was hardened so that he acted proudly, he was deposed from his kingly throne, and his glory was stripped from him. [21]He was driven from human society, and his mind was made like that of an animal. His dwelling was with the wild asses, he was fed grass like oxen, and his body was bathed with the dew of heaven, until he

[a] Aram adds *the king your father*   [b] Or *a divine spirit*

NIV

22"But you his son,[a] O Belshazzar, have not humbled yourself, though you knew all this. 23Instead, you have set yourself up against the Lord of heaven. You had the goblets from his temple brought to you, and you and your nobles, your wives and your concubines drank wine from them. You praised the gods of silver and gold, of bronze, iron, wood and stone, which cannot see or hear or understand. But you did not honor the God who holds in his hand your life and all your ways. 24Therefore he sent the hand that wrote the inscription.

25"This is the inscription that was written:

MENE, MENE, TEKEL, PARSIN[b]

26"This is what these words mean:

Mene[c]: God has numbered the days of your reign and brought it to an end.
27Tekel[d]: You have been weighed on the scales and found wanting.
28Peres[e]: Your kingdom is divided and given to the Medes and Persians."

29Then at Belshazzar's command, Daniel was clothed in purple, a gold chain was placed around his neck, and he was proclaimed the third highest ruler in the kingdom.

30That very night Belshazzar, king of the Babylonians,[f] was slain, 31and Darius the Mede took over the kingdom, at the age of sixty-two.

a22 Or descendant; or successor   b25 Aramaic UPARSIN (that is, AND PARSIN)   c26 Mene can mean numbered or mina (a unit of money).   d27 Tekel can mean weighed or shekel.   e28 Peres (the singular of Parsin) can mean divided or Persia or a half mina or a half shekel.   f30 Or Chaldeans

NRSV

learned that the Most High God has sovereignty over the kingdom of mortals, and sets over it whomever he will. 22And you, Belshazzar his son, have not humbled your heart, even though you knew all this! 23You have exalted yourself against the Lord of heaven! The vessels of his temple have been brought in before you, and you and your lords, your wives and your concubines have been drinking wine from them. You have praised the gods of silver and gold, of bronze, iron, wood, and stone, which do not see or hear or know; but the God in whose power is your very breath, and to whom belong all your ways, you have not honored.

24"So from his presence the hand was sent and this writing was inscribed. 25And this is the writing that was inscribed: MENE, MENE, TEKEL, and PARSIN. 26This is the interpretation of the matter: MENE, God has numbered the days of[a] your kingdom and brought it to an end; 27TEKEL, you have been weighed on the scales and found wanting; 28PERES,[b] your kingdom is divided and given to the Medes and Persians."

29Then Belshazzar gave the command, and Daniel was clothed in purple, a chain of gold was put around his neck, and a proclamation was made concerning him that he should rank third in the kingdom.

30That very night Belshazzar, the Chaldean king, was killed. 31And Darius the Mede received the kingdom, being about sixty-two years old.

a Aram lacks the days of   b The singular of Parsin   c Ch 6.1 in Aram

COMMENTARY

5:1-4, The Revelry of the Powerful. Although there are problems with the historical aspects of this story, we are now certain of the existence of Bel-shar-usur (Belshazzar). He was the son of Nabonidus, and not Nebuchadnezzar, as v. 2 claims. Nabonidus left Babylon for a time and lived in the oasis of Teima, leaving his son in charge of Babylon.[145] It is noted in the Baby-

145. "The Nabonidus Chronicle" in Ancient Near Eastern Texts Relating to the Old Testament (ANET), ed. James B. Pritchard (Princeton, N.J.: Princeton University Press, 1969) 305-7.

lonian cuneiform sources that the new year festival was not observed during Nabonidus's absence, which most scholars take to mean that Belshazzar was not recognized as king. It was from Nabonidus that Cyrus seized control of Babylon in 539 BCE.

Chapter 5, like the previous chapters, begins somewhat abruptly, with Belshazzar and his great feast. Note once again the emphasis on the epic setting and number (e.g., "a thousand of his lords," "drinking in front of the thousands") and on the excesses of drunkenness. We certainly do have evidence that Persian kings would occasionally conduct massive banquets,[146] but what is particularly interesting is the fact that this chapter portrays this night as Belshazzar's last—the night of the conquest of Babylon by the Persians. This story may be based on oral traditions about the fall of Babylon, since similar ideas about revelry on the eve of the fall of Babylon are found in both Xenophon and Herodotus.[147] Furthermore, the ease with which the Persians conquered Babylon was taken by the Cyrus Cylinder to be an indication of the blessings of the god Marduk on the Persian conquest.[148]

Describing King Belshazzar as being under the influence of alcohol, (the Aramaic reads "in the taste of the wine"), chapter 5 continues the theme of excess and abuse. We are reminded of the exile by the gold and silver vessels taken from the Jerusalem Temple by Nebuchadnezzar. This is an important point. The Babylonian policy was to commandeer the religious icons or statues of the gods of the conquered people. In the case of the Jews, since no image of their God could be found in the Temple, the ritual vessels were taken instead. Nebuchadnezzar is often noted as the one who took the temple vessels (Ezra 5:14; 6:5). Therefore, the vessels serve as a symbol of the subordinate status of the Jews throughout their exile. They are captives in the same sense that the people are captive. The gold and silver vessels once again highlight the hunger for valuables that symbolizes the appetite for power of conquering empires.[149]

Feasting was typically used in biblical narratives, especially post-exilic writings, to portray the abuse of power and privilege by the wealthy, and especially foreign monarchs. Taxes were paid in kind, and such great feasts would be resented just as much as the waste of tax money to fund government programs! As has been noted, in Esther and Judith feasts or banquets serve as the setting for Jewish victory over foreign power, much in the same way that a royal banquet serves as the backdrop for God's punishment of Babylon in this chapter.

Verses 2-3 repeat the list of people—including "concubines," apparently a pejorative term in Aramaic—who join in defiling the holy implements. People of decidedly unholy reputations despoil these implements. As if to add to the shame of the event, the revelry also includes idolatry and the offering of libations to the gods. Verse 4 lists the materials from which the various Babylonian idols were made, which serves to tie this chapter to the themes of idolatry in other chapters. In v. 4, is it to be understood that these gods were, in fact, statues and idols taken from other conquered peoples? More likely, it is the biblical manner of speaking of foreign images of gods by emphasizing that they are *merely* gold, silver, bronze, etc. The list of elements in v. 4 repeats the elements of the statue in chapter 2, with the one exception of wood.[150] Most scholars have assumed that what is involved here is some sort of libation offered to the gods. Lacocque notes that the Persian custom was to offer such libations after the meal was completed.[151]

5:5-9, The Hand of Judgment. The text clearly emphasizes the abuse of the temple implements, because judgment begins immediately after this abuse is described. There is no waiting, no delay. The message ("writing on the wall") is delivered *during* the revelry. Furthermore, there is a strong emphasis on the public display of the appearance of the fingers of a human hand writing on the wall and the reaction of the king. Repeating a theme that readers are by now familiar with, the writer notes that the countenance of the king falls and that his thoughts "terrified" or "appalled" him (v. 6; cf. 2:29-30; 4:16; 5:6, 10; 7:28; see also Ps 69:24; Isa 21:3; Ezek 21:11; Nah 2:11). Lacocque seems to imply that the king was the only one who saw the apparition,[152] but this is not clear from the text. The writing obviously is seen by others, however, since the various court magicians are not able to interpret it. Collins notes that the strange appearance of the hand is similar to the strange appearance of the fourth person in the fiery furnace of chapter 3.[153] Finally, there is an emphasis on the strength of the king's

146. N. Porteus, *Daniel,* OTL (Philadelphia: Westminster, 1965) 78.
147. Xenophon *Cyropedia* VII.5.15-16; Herodotus *History* 1:191.
148. *ANET,* 315-36.
149. It is interesting that Collins has noted other extra-biblical sources for a Persian preference for gold cups. See John J. Collins, *Daniel,* Hermeneia (Minneapolis: Fortress, 1993) 245.

150. Interestingly, a similar sequence is noted in 4QPrNab.
151. André Lacocque, *The Book of Daniel,* trans. D. Pellauer (Atlanta: John Knox, 1979) 94.
152. Ibid., 95.
153. Collins, *Daniel,* Hermeneia, 246.

voice as he calls for "the enchanters, the Chaldeans, and the diviners."

The king sets the challenge and offers the reward, following the contest pattern. It is interesting that a promotion in authority is included among the rewards (the wearing of purple and the promotion to third in authority/sovereignty), which relates this story to the fate of Daniel and his friends in the previous stories; it signals as well the separation of this story from the previous stories. The offering of a purple robe (a sign of authority) and a gold chain is a custom Daniel's audience would have been familiar with. A purple robe was given to Mordecai (Esth 8:15), and a gold chain was presented to Joseph (Gen 41:42). Both items were commonly given as gifts in the Persian period.[154] However, there is some scholarly debate as to the exact nature of the "third position" that is offered as a reward.[155]

These counselors, following the set pattern of the Daniel stories, are not able to interpret the meaning of the event. Belshazzar remains terrified, and the counselors are perplexed.

5:10-12, The Queen Mother's Introduction. Once again, Daniel is reintroduced to the Babylonian ruler—this time by the queen mother herself! The term used here for the king's mother, מלכה (*malkâ*), has been taken to mean "queen mother" by nearly all commentators, who cite not only her extensive knowledge of previous Babylonian administrations but also the important theme of the power of the queen mother in ancient Near Eastern literary traditions.[156] Furthermore, there is a series of intriguing legends about the power of Nebuchadnezzar's wife in Herodotus.[157] She was credited with great wisdom, with the building of Babylon's outer fortifications (where she had herself buried in the wall over one of the entrance gates), and with a humorous cleverness that appears to have impressed Herodotus. It is possible that such legends about this unusual woman were drawn upon for local color in the Belshazzar story.

The queen mother has not appeared in any of the Daniel stories until now, and her introduction

here suggests that Daniel's potential promotion to "third" means that he would rank third in authority, after the king and the queen mother. Whether the queen mother actually had such authority is an interesting historical question, but it is somewhat irrelevant to the point of the story as here presented. Goldingay notes that the queen mother's function in the story is not unlike that of Arioch, who earlier served to introduce Daniel. Daniel's attributes are listed in the queen's speech: He is endowed with a spirit of the holy god(s) (i.e., "excellent spirit"?), enlightened (cf. 2:22), knowledgeable/understanding, wise, experienced (Nebuchadnezzar made him chief of his magicians, enchanters, Chaldeans, and diviners, noting the words of 4:4 exactly; cf. the list in 2:27), able to interpret dreams, explain riddles, and solve problems (figuratively, "untie knots"). The only aspersion cast upon Daniel by the queen mother is the mention of the changing of his name, suggesting a changed status for this Daniel and perhaps reminding Belshazzar of Daniel's exile status.

5:13-16, Daniel Before the King: The Challenge. The all-important scene, "standing before the king," appears next, with Daniel being questioned. After all of his impressive qualifications have been listed by the queen mother, it is Daniel's status as an exile and a conquered foreigner that Belshazzar mentions first, which presumes a conversation much more in keeping with 2:25, where Arioch introduces Daniel as being one from "among the exiles."[158]

The king begins his interrogation of Daniel with a reminder of his station as a prisoner of war before repeating what he has heard about Daniel's abilities. The king then rehearses the fact that nobody else has been able to interpret the handwriting, and then finishes with a restatement of the rewards for the one who can.

5:17-23, Daniel Before the King: The Judgment. Like Nathan before David, Daniel immediately declares his independence from the power and fearsomeness of Belshazzar. Goldingay notes that there is no salutation, such as "O King, Live Forever!"[159] The brash reply, "Keep your

---

154. Herodotus *The History* 3:20; Xenophon *Cyropedia* 2.4.6.

155. Lacocque cites the *Testament of Joseph* 13:5, which refers to "Third after Pharaoh," but this is clearly influenced by the Daniel traditions. See Lacocque, *The Book of Daniel*, 92.

156. Collins, *Daniel*, Hermeneia, 248.

157. Herodotus *The History* 1:185-186.

158. Again, a similar introduction that mentions the status of the individual is noted in 4QPrNab. It is clearly an important detail for these traditions.

159. John Goldingay, *Daniel*, WBC 30 (Dallas: Word, 1988) 110.

---

gifts, or give them away," signals an attitude on Daniel's part that is considerably more antagonistic than was the case in any of the previous stories (and is particularly interesting, since Daniel appears to accept the gifts at the end of the story).

There are some suggestions that this entire section may not be original to the story. It does not appear in the Old Greek versions of the story. Without it, there is no contradiction with Daniel's acceptance of the gifts at the end. But its presence here signals a serious turn in the polemics directed against authorities, and it further suggests to us how these stories were earlier interpreted in a more negative light than modern readers interpret them. Collins notes that in the Roman era Josephus softened the tone of Daniel here, as he also tried to soften the impact of the "stone uncut by human hands" as God's destruction of human governmental authority in chapter 2.[160]

In any case, Daniel's story of Nebuchadnezzar in vv. 18-21 is very much in the prophetic style. Daniel begins with a story, a true-life parable, much in the same way that Nathan told a story standing before David (2 Samuel 12). Most of this section repeats the previous chapter, except for an interesting assessment of the power of Nebuchadnezzar: Those whom he wanted to kill were killed; those whom he wanted to smite (or spare) were struck down (or spared; the Aramaic (מחא *maḥē*') is somewhat ambiguous, so both possibilities need to be noted here); those whom he wanted to honor were honored; and those whom he wanted to make low were dishonored. No description of the capricious nature of the head of a Near Eastern empire could be more telling. The ruler claims for himself what are actually God's prerogatives: the ability to give or take life, death, and prosperity. This passage has an intriguing similarity to Job 5:11-16, where these attributes are assigned to God (cf. 1 Sam 2:7; Ps 75:8; Sir 7:11); but it can be further pointed out that included in Job's rehearsal are the powers of God to "[save] the needy . . . / from the hand of the mighty,/ So the poor have hope,/ and injustice shuts its mouth" (Job 5:15-16 NRSV). God is able to give life; Nebuchadnezzar can only kill or refrain from killing. The irony of this description of power by Daniel is the fact that Nebuchadnezzar

thought he had this ability, but in reality he did not. As did his friends in chapter 2, Daniel stands as the political atheist of radical faith.

Nebuchadnezzar's faulty impression of his power is in stark contrast to the statement that such power is God's alone in the world, as reaffirmed in v. 21. After Daniel's parable, and once again like Nathan (2 Sam 12:7), the judgment falls on the one being addressed: "You, Belshazzar" (v. 22).

"Humbling of the heart" is synonymous with the treatment of the conquered, the "lowly," as noted in v. 27. The mistreatment of the temple vessels is read as an object lesson of Belshazzar's treatment of people. Like Nebuchadnezzar's exile with the animals, Belshazzar is tainted with the injustices of the Babylonian regime.

The accusation about worshiping idols of gold, silver, bronze, wood, iron, and stone is in stark contrast to the lack of honor for the true God, in whose power, says Daniel, is "your breath" and who controls "your ways." Typically eloquent, Lacocque writes, "Whether a Jew serves the government or not, history has a sense and it moves toward its omega, even though men untiringly repeat their choice for nonsense."[161]

5:24-28, The Interpretation of the Writing on the Wall. As one would expect, the meaning of the symbolic terms "mene, mene, tekel, and parsin" has been debated extensively. First, it is important to indicate that the Old Greek version of this text has only three terms, and most scholars believe that a second "mene" was added in order to conform to the "four kingdom" motif that becomes a central aspect of the book of Daniel as a whole, when all the parts have been joined. Porteous takes these words to be an indication of declining value and thus a representation of the value of the kings of Babylon.[162] Finally, Brown has suggested that the words have been borrowed from a money changer's rhyme, heard in the marketplaces of international trade from the fifth century BCE. In its present form, suggests Brown, the message reads as an epitaph for the fall of the Seleucid Empire, attributing the empire's fall to its political and financial policies; but it is possibly derived from an older critique of

160. Collins, *Daniel,* Hermeneia, 249.

161. Lacocque, *The Book of Daniel,* 101.
162. Porteous, *Daniel,* 82.

Babylon, which "merited the critique more than the Seleucids."[163]

Lacocque reads "Babylonians, Belshazzar, Medes" for the original sequence of three, with a fourth entity added later to change the representation to Babylonians, Medes, Persians, and Greeks. This suggestion assumes that Darius "the Mede" is also represented. There is no evidence of a historical "Darius the Mede"; thus the importance of inserting a Median presence into the Daniel stories is usually attributed to the need to fulfill the prophecy that the Medes would precede the Persians.

Goldingay helpfully summarizes many of the different approaches, but he prefers to avoid the notion that this is a judgment on the empire. To him, it is simply "a judgment on one man's sin."[164] Surely this is an unnecessary avoidance of the powerful political critique that is typical of Daniel from beginning to end. Collins believes that the original sequence was one of straight declining value: Mina, Parsin, Tekel (as in the preface to the chapter in Old Greek) and that these words represent the only three Babylonian kings mentioned in the Daniel traditions (including 4QPrNab): Nebuchadnezzar, Nabonidus, and Belshazzar.[165] "Parsin" was subsequently moved to accommodate the wordplay on "Persians."

Whatever these words may represent in terms of a sequence of empires, all scholars agree that they are essentially monetary terms, denoting coins and weights. In fine biblical fashion, the obsessions of the empire (power and monetary gain, tribute payments and accounting) become the symbolic basis for judgment. The judgment

takes place not so much in the courtroom as in the bank lobby! The place of judgment and the language used are significant. "Mene" is related to the term for "count," and "Tekel" is related to "weigh." "Peres" is an Akkadian loan word meaning "half-mina," but it is taken also to mean "divide." Thus the king has been counted and weighed in the balances (audited?), and has been judged at a deficit. In short, the interpretation of these words offered by Daniel 5 sounds like the activities of a countinghouse—weighing, counting, and dividing. This chapter, then, parallels the theme of chapter 4: Just as Nebuchadnezzar suffered the same fate he subjected the exiles to, so also Belshazzar will be audited in the midst of his wasteful, demeaning opulence.

5:29-31, Fulfillment of the Prophecy. As noted, Daniel appears to accept the gifts and rewards that he earlier refused. However, if Daniel had not been rewarded, even if the message he delivered was one of serious judgment, then this story would have diverged from the folkloric form of the tale. Either Daniel's refusal of gifts in v. 17 was part of a later, and politically significant, redaction or the constraints of the story form require that the story end in the traditional manner.

That the Babylonians were conquered by the Persians remains one aspect of historical recollection that is valid in the story of Belshazzar; however, the details appear to have been muddled in the oral retellings of the story before it was finally put to writing. The concluding verse (v. 30) presents the contrast and the reversal of fortune: Daniel is clothed in purple, Belshazzar dies, and the kingdom passes to the Medes ("Darius") and finally, at the end of chapter 6, to Cyrus the Persian.

163. J. P. Brown, "Proverb-Book, Gold Economy, Alphabet," *JBL* 100 (1981) 187.
164. Goldingay, *Daniel,* 111.
165. Collins, *Daniel,* Hermeneia, 251.

REFLECTIONS

What is the nature of the "sin" of Belshazzar? Attention in this story focuses on the banquet (a theme also of chap. 1) and on the desecration of the temple vessels. Here we have a significant theme of the abuse of conquered people's culture and values. We see in Daniel 5 one of the most insidious elements of imperial power and oppression: the destruction of faith and identity, the attack on a culture as well as a people. The intoxication of power releases the ruler from maintaining any further pretenses: "We are the conquerors; we are the superior culture. Let us parade their treasures and mock the defeated." Pacific native peoples bitterly recall the desecration of native holy sites by Captain Cook, and today's Cheyenne recount another "Belshazzar's Feast"—the parade of body parts of slain Cheyenne through downtown Denver following the 1864 Sand Creek Massacre, led by the Rev. Col. Chivington of the U.S. Cavalry.[166] Defeat and destruction are never enough for the powerful; they must also glorify themselves with acts of unspeakable humiliation of the defeated. A society based on injustice must find ways to sustain its existence; it must appear to be more civilized, more advanced, more cultured than those conquered, who must, therefore, be portrayed as bloodthirsty, disrespectful of the land, heathen. Humiliating the conquered, then, helps to sustain the myth of superiority.

In 1990, the Congress of the United States finally ended a centuries-long "Belshazzar's feast" by passing the Native American Graves Protection and Repatriation Act. Indigenous peoples across North America have long demanded that their sacred objects be returned to them. For modern Christians, Daniel 5 is a call to understand the humiliation of defeated cultures and peoples, and perhaps to work toward reconciliation and restitution so that finally ours can be a society that appreciates and celebrates the diverse traditions that enrich our life.

Finally, Daniel 5 is a call to modern Christians to involve themselves in prophetic delivery of God's judgment on the gluttony of the hundreds of "Belshazzar's feasts" that have victimized so many people over the centuries. Perhaps it needs to be said that for many Christians who have been born to the privileges afforded by the dominant culture, such a prophetic task begins by excusing ourselves from Belshazzar's table!

---

166. See G. Obeyesekeve, *The Apotheosis of Captain Cook: European Mythmaking in the Pacific* (Princeton: Princeton University Press, 1992). The story of the Sand Creek Massacre was recounted to me by the Rev. Lawrence Hart, a Cheyenne chief of the Southern Cheyenne, Oklahoma. See also Stan Hoig. *The Sand Creek Massacre* (Norman: University of Oklahoma Press, 1961).

DANIEL 6:1-28, IN DEFIANCE OF DEATH: DANIEL IN THE LION PIT

NIV

6 It pleased Darius to appoint 120 satraps to rule throughout the kingdom, [2]with three administrators over them, one of whom was Daniel. The satraps were made accountable to them so that the king might not suffer loss. [3]Now Daniel so distinguished himself among the administrators and the satraps by his exceptional qualities that the king planned to set him over the whole kingdom. [4]At this, the administrators and the satraps tried to find grounds for charges against Daniel in his conduct of government affairs, but they were unable to do so. They could find no corruption in him, because he was trustworthy and neither corrupt nor negligent. [5]Finally these men said, "We will never find any basis for charges against this man Daniel unless it has something to do with the law of his God."

[6]So the administrators and the satraps went as a group to the king and said: "O King Darius, live

NRSV

6 It pleased Darius to set over the kingdom one hundred twenty satraps, stationed throughout the whole kingdom, [2]and over them three presidents, including Daniel; to these the satraps gave account, so that the king might suffer no loss. [3]Soon Daniel distinguished himself above all the other presidents and satraps because an excellent spirit was in him, and the king planned to appoint him over the whole kingdom. [4]So the presidents and the satraps tried to find grounds for complaint against Daniel in connection with the kingdom. But they could find no grounds for complaint or any corruption, because he was faithful, and no negligence or corruption could be found in him. [5]The men said, "We shall not find any ground for complaint against this Daniel unless we find it in connection with the law of his God."

6So the presidents and satraps conspired and came to the king and said to him, "O King Darius,

NIV

forever! [7]The royal administrators, prefects, satraps, advisers and governors have all agreed that the king should issue an edict and enforce the decree that anyone who prays to any god or man during the next thirty days, except to you, O king, shall be thrown into the lions' den. [8]Now, O king, issue the decree and put it in writing so that it cannot be altered—in accordance with the laws of the Medes and Persians, which cannot be repealed." [9]So King Darius put the decree in writing.

[10]Now when Daniel learned that the decree had been published, he went home to his upstairs room where the windows opened toward Jerusalem. Three times a day he got down on his knees and prayed, giving thanks to his God, just as he had done before. [11]Then these men went as a group and found Daniel praying and asking God for help. [12]So they went to the king and spoke to him about his royal decree: "Did you not publish a decree that during the next thirty days anyone who prays to any god or man except to you, O king, would be thrown into the lions' den?"

The king answered, "The decree stands—in accordance with the laws of the Medes and Persians, which cannot be repealed."

[13]Then they said to the king, "Daniel, who is one of the exiles from Judah, pays no attention to you, O king, or to the decree you put in writing. He still prays three times a day." [14]When the king heard this, he was greatly distressed; he was determined to rescue Daniel and made every effort until sundown to save him.

[15]Then the men went as a group to the king and said to him, "Remember, O king, that according to the law of the Medes and Persians no decree or edict that the king issues can be changed."

[16]So the king gave the order, and they brought Daniel and threw him into the lions' den. The king said to Daniel, "May your God, whom you serve continually, rescue you!"

[17]A stone was brought and placed over the mouth of the den, and the king sealed it with his own signet ring and with the rings of his nobles, so that Daniel's situation might not be changed. [18]Then the king returned to his palace and spent the night without eating and without any entertainment being brought to him. And he could not sleep.

[19]At the first light of dawn, the king got up and

NRSV

live forever! [7]All the presidents of the kingdom, the prefects and the satraps, the counselors and the governors are agreed that the king should establish an ordinance and enforce an interdict, that whoever prays to anyone, divine or human, for thirty days, except to you, O king, shall be thrown into a den of lions. [8]Now, O king, establish the interdict and sign the document, so that it cannot be changed, according to the law of the Medes and the Persians, which cannot be revoked." [9]Therefore King Darius signed the document and interdict.

10Although Daniel knew that the document had been signed, he continued to go to his house, which had windows in its upper room open toward Jerusalem, and to get down on his knees three times a day to pray to his God and praise him, just as he had done previously. [11]The conspirators came and found Daniel praying and seeking mercy before his God. [12]Then they approached the king and said concerning the interdict, "O king! Did you not sign an interdict, that anyone who prays to anyone, divine or human, within thirty days except to you, O king, shall be thrown into a den of lions?" The king answered, "The thing stands fast, according to the law of the Medes and Persians, which cannot be revoked." [13]Then they responded to the king, "Daniel, one of the exiles from Judah, pays no attention to you, O king, or to the interdict you have signed, but he is saying his prayers three times a day."

14When the king heard the charge, he was very much distressed. He was determined to save Daniel, and until the sun went down he made every effort to rescue him. [15]Then the conspirators came to the king and said to him, "Know, O king, that it is a law of the Medes and Persians that no interdict or ordinance that the king establishes can be changed."

16Then the king gave the command, and Daniel was brought and thrown into the den of lions. The king said to Daniel, "May your God, whom you faithfully serve, deliver you!" [17]A stone was brought and laid on the mouth of the den, and the king sealed it with his own signet and with the signet of his lords, so that nothing might be changed concerning Daniel. [18]Then the king went to his palace and spent the night fasting; no food was brought to him, and sleep fled from him.

19Then, at break of day, the king got up and

NIV

hurried to the lions' den. 20When he came near the den, he called to Daniel in an anguished voice, "Daniel, servant of the living God, has your God, whom you serve continually, been able to rescue you from the lions?"

21Daniel answered, "O king, live forever! 22My God sent his angel, and he shut the mouths of the lions. They have not hurt me, because I was found innocent in his sight. Nor have I ever done any wrong before you, O king."

23The king was overjoyed and gave orders to lift Daniel out of the den. And when Daniel was lifted from the den, no wound was found on him, because he had trusted in his God.

24At the king's command, the men who had falsely accused Daniel were brought in and thrown into the lions' den, along with their wives and children. And before they reached the floor of the den, the lions overpowered them and crushed all their bones.

25Then King Darius wrote to all the peoples, nations and men of every language throughout the land:

"May you prosper greatly!

26"I issue a decree that in every part of my kingdom people must fear and reverence the God of Daniel.

"For he is the living God
  and he endures forever;
his kingdom will not be destroyed,
  his dominion will never end.
27He rescues and he saves;
  he performs signs and wonders
  in the heavens and on the earth.
He has rescued Daniel
  from the power of the lions."

28So Daniel prospered during the reign of Darius and the reign of Cyrusᵃ the Persian.

a28 Or Darius, that is, the reign of Cyrus

NRSV

hurried to the den of lions. 20When he came near the den where Daniel was, he cried out anxiously to Daniel, "O Daniel, servant of the living God, has your God whom you faithfully serve been able to deliver you from the lions?" 21Daniel then said to the king, "O king, live forever! 22My God sent his angel and shut the lions' mouths so that they would not hurt me, because I was found blameless before him; and also before you, O king, I have done no wrong." 23Then the king was exceedingly glad and commanded that Daniel be taken up out of the den. So Daniel was taken up out of the den, and no kind of harm was found on him, because he had trusted in his God. 24The king gave a command, and those who had accused Daniel were brought and thrown into the den of lions—they, their children, and their wives. Before they reached the bottom of the den the lions overpowered them and broke all their bones in pieces.

25Then King Darius wrote to all peoples and nations of every language throughout the whole world: "May you have abundant prosperity! 26I make a decree, that in all my royal dominion people should tremble and fear before the God of Daniel:

For he is the living God,
  enduring forever.
His kingdom shall never be destroyed,
  and his dominion has no end.
27 He delivers and rescues,
  he works signs and wonders in heaven and
    on earth;
  for he has saved Daniel
    from the power of the lions."
28So this Daniel prospered during the reign of Darius and the reign of Cyrus the Persian.

COMMENTARY

6:1-3, Prologue and "Darius the Mede." Many essays have been written on the subject of Darius the Mede. Historically, Darius I Hystaspis (522–486 BCE) certainly was a notable figure, having seized the throne of Persia after political

instability in the empire. He was also notable as a great organizer, and the discussion of satrapies in this chapter is a vague but accurate recollection of the fact that the third Persian ruler after Cyrus certainly did divide the Achaemenid territories into administrative units called satrapies. But in no other document has there been a reference to any Median connection. It is typically thought, then, that the Median association is influenced more by the desire to have a Median presence before Persia, in order that earlier biblical prophecy be seen to unfold correctly. But the historical figure alluded to in Daniel 6 must be Darius I, the usurper of the Persian throne after the death of Cambyses. Once again, however, it is undoubtedly fruitless to try to force the folklore of Daniel to fit what we know of the actual circumstances of Persian history. That Darius I was chosen as the historical model for this otherwise fictional character is undoubtedly due to the length of the historical Darius's reign, but also perhaps because of the influence of this same ruler's important role as the defender of the Jewish reconstruction work under Zerubbabel (Ezra 6). Furthermore, the intra-court intrigue may reflect some of the administrative tensions that led to Darius's rise to power,[167] although scholars point out that this is an essential aspect of the folklore form. Other Persian rulers are mentioned in the Greek versions of Daniel, adding to the general confusion.

Verses 2-3 mention 120 satrapies[168] and over them three *sarkin,* a Persian term meaning "chief ministers" (NIV, "administrators"; NRSV, "presidents") Daniel was appointed one of these *sarkin.* What is interesting by its absence is a story of Daniel's rise in this Median (Persian?) court. We find him assigned there at the outset of this story, without explanation of how he attained that status. Thus the form of this story is much closer to a restoration than to a rags-to-riches story, more typical of the previous chapters.

Daniel is said to have an "excellent spirit" (cf. 5:12, missing the usual, "spirit of the god" form). The story as a whole gives one the impression that excellence of spirit must have to do with trustworthiness or loyalty, as opposed to an endowment of the gods.

6:4-9, The Conspiracy Against Daniel Is Launched. The other two *sarkin,* presumably Persians, conspire with the heads of the satraps against Daniel, thus indicating a sense of tension between the Jewish exiles and the Persian nationals. There has been some scholarly debate as to the possible ethnic overtones of the tension. Lacocque resists the effort to see no anti-Semitism in this story, stating that "the sacred cause is to prevent an alien from assisting in the dismemberment of the empire . . . the Jew is always an alien body in the illusory constructions of the nations."[169] But it is unnecessary to avoid the implication of ethnic tensions in this story, hence the perception of ethnic tensions among the tellers and the hearers of the Daniel stories. These stories certainly include such elements of ethnic and religious tensions in them. Chapter 6 is much more in line with chap. 3, as each story presents the Jewish heroes as facing evil conspirators who seek their defeat, rather than simply solving a riddle or a problem that baffles the other advisers to the king. However, the stories of the Jewish courtiers' success seem essential to a full appreciation of the resentment of the Jewish courtiers in the first place. Apart from the "rise to success" stories, the restoration stories would not have nearly the power and dramatic impact they possess.

The story of Darius has been the prime case for those scholars who have emphasized the benign nature of the representation of the kings in Daniel 1–6. These scholars use this characterization to further the general assumption that the situation of the Jews who told and heard these stories must not have been so terrible. But let us not be hasty about Darius's benevolence. Even Darius "the Mede" is a king who maintains lions to dispose of his enemies, and he will sacrifice a loyal adviser for the sake of the letter of the law, even his own law, as the sovereign principle of the empire. When compared to chap. 3, where the king ruled as absolute monarch, chap. 6 introduces the "rule of law," but it is still the king's own law.

The Aramaic term הרגשו (*hargišû*), used to describe the group of conspirators who approach the king (v. 6) has engendered considerable discussion. Did they "come in a throng" in a raucous mass gathering? The eighteenth-century Quaker Bible translator Anthony Purver rendered it: "they crowded in to the king," which captures the image suggested by the term, which includes the satraps as well as the two other Persian officials.[170] The last phrase in this verse, the basis of their

167. Lacocque, *The Book of Daniel,* 110.
168. Esth 1:1 mentions 127 satrapies; Herodotus (*The History* 3:89) suggests only 20 and Josephus claims 320 (*Antiquities of the Jews* 11.33:127)!

169. Lacocque, *The Book of Daniel,* 111.
170. Collins, *Daniel,* Hermeneia, 265-66.

proposed accusation against Daniel, raises an issue that has not arisen yet in the entire book: the matter of the law of the Jews. The mention of the "law" of God was not mentioned even in chap. 3, where one might have expected it. (That the Persian authorities were aware of the religious importance of the law of the Jews is noted in Ezra 7:12, 14, 21, 25-26 and will become an issue in Daniel 7.) A reference to the Jewishness of Daniel by specifically mentioning the laws/traditions of the Jews lends weight to arguments for the significance of ethnic tensions as an important part of the traditions in Daniel.

In contrast to the previous chapters that mention the religious worship practiced by the Jews, Daniel will now be accused because he follows the ethical requirements of his religion. Interestingly enough, the fact that Daniel prays regularly to his God is certainly not a matter of the law. Daniel prays three times daily toward Jerusalem, but this is nowhere mandated in the Torah as we now have it. Does this represent a diaspora innovation? Praying three times a day (morning, noon, and evening) is found in later rabbinic tradition, and certainly it influenced early Christianity; but there is no evidence that it was already in practice this early. Praying toward the Temple is mentioned in 1 Kings 8, itself an early exilic-deuteronomic passage.

The notion that the Persian people should not pray to anyone other than the king is a fanciful aspect of the story that may have more relevance in the Hellenistic era than in the memories of the Persian exile. The historical Darius, especially, carefully attributed his success to Ahura Mazda, the Zoroastrian deity (some scholars suggest that Cyrus was Zoroastrian). But this aspect of the story is clearly a folklore element. The king signs the law and establishes an "edict." The Aramaic term, אסר ('ĕsār), which is related to the terms for "binding" and for "prison," suggests that what is established here is Persian law and the punishment for violation of that law. The symbolic weight of the state stands behind this new enactment. Daniel 6 repeats the concept of the unchangeable laws of the emperor, which is repeated in Ezra 6:11-12 as well. Lacocque noted that Diodorus of Sicily also made reference to the unchangeable laws of the Persians.[171] We have learned from chap. 2, however, that God changes what humans consider unchangeable (Dan 2:21).

171. Lacocque, *The Book of Daniel.*

❖   ❖   ❖   ❖

EXCURSUS: IMPRISONMENT AND EXILE

It appears to be the advisers' idea that Daniel be thrown to the lions. This deserves careful consideration, since the lions' den may well be an example of an interesting motif of punishment and imprisonment within the Daniel tradition.

It is interesting to note how often the motif of imprisonment occurs in exilic texts, like the book of Daniel. Because imprisonment or confinement is a potent symbol for the exile in other biblical texts, this aspect of Daniel more than any other may help us to understand the circumstances of the writers of these stories.

There are a number of terms in the OT that translators render as "prison," but the most common term for "prisoners" is from the verb "to tie," "to bind," or "to imprison" (אסר 'āsar), which is frequently used in the late Joseph stories (Gen 39:20; 40:3, 5). It appears also in Isa 42:7; 49:9; 61:1; and Ps 146:7-8 (cf. Ps 107:10); it is interesting to note that in Isa 49:9 and Ps 146:7c-8a, the combination of release from prison, with "opening eyes" or "sight to the blind" is common (cf. Zech 9:12). A "Surpu Hymn" (incantation to Marduk of Babylon) contains the same association:

"[beginning 'It rests with you, Marduk . . .']
31 to set free the prisoner, to show (him) daylight
32 him who has been taken captive, to rescue him
33 him whose city is distant, whose road is far away

34 let him go safely to his city
35 to return the prisoner of war and the captive to his people

———

73 may the sick get well, the fallen get up
74 the fettered go free, the captive go free
75 the prisoner see the light (of day)."[172]

The "Verse Account of Nabonidus" celebrates the end of his reign with the following passage:

[to the inhabitants of] Babylon, a joyful heart is given,
[like prisoners] when the prisons are opened
[Liberty is restored] to those who were surrounded by oppression.[173]

Here, too, imprisonment is equated with conquest. What do we know about imprisonment in the Ancient Near East? In an important article exploring the subject, San Nicolo states, "A prison-punishment in the formal sense is essentially unknown in Near Eastern jurisprudence."[174]

The most common term for "prison" in the OT is an Akkadian loan word, בית כלא (*bêt kele*'), which relates to the use of the verb "to restrain," "to hold back" (cf. Gen 23:6; Num 11:28; 1 Sam 25:33; Pss 88:9; 119:101; Jer 32:2-3; and in reference to exiles, Isa 43:6). The term is found in the deuteronomic historian (1 Kgs 22:27; 2 Kgs 17:4), in direct reference to the Assyrians and to Jehoiachin's internment and release (2 Kgs 25:27). One of the most interesting passages is Jeremiah 37, especially vv. 4, 15-16, where three different terms for "prison" are used. Of particular interest is the fact that the recurring phrase about a pit "where there is no water" occurs in three passages, the first in Genesis 37, the second in Jer 38:6, and the third, in direct reference to exiles, in Zech 9:11. The image of the pit is associated with death in Psalm 88, and in Jer 41:7-9 Gedaliah and his followers are thrown into the pit after their murder. Lamentations 3:53, 55 compares the catastrophe of exile to being thrown into a pit from which the people call on God's name. This has obvious relevance to Daniel in the lion pit.

The vast majority of instances of the use of the term for prisons and imprisonment are cases of unjust imprisonment of the righteous, whether individual prophets or an entire community. Furthermore, most examples, apart from the imprisonment of prophets, are cases of people being detained in foreign prisons. Indeed, it appears that the judicial system of Israel and Judah did not include prisons. They are never mentioned in the legal corpus of the Pentateuch, and (with the exception of 2 Sam 20:3, which is obviously not much of an exception), prisons are mentioned only toward the end of the monarchical era, in Jeremiah 37–38, where Jeremiah is confined by Zedekiah, Nebuchadnezzar's puppet ruler in Jerusalem. But Jeremiah's imprisonment fits the theme of unjust confinement/punishment. Most hero types of the exilic period (Joseph, Jehoiachin, Jeremiah, Daniel, and the Suffering Servant of Isaiah) suffer imprisonment innocently and are eventually delivered.

So, if imprisonment was not a typical form of punishment in Israelite practice, then one may conclude that the images in the biblical material and in other Near Eastern texts more likely refer to punishment or confinement, especially confinement as a result of superior military power. The obvious social significance of the Daniel stories as hero stories leads one to conclude that confinement became an established symbol for the exiles who reflected on their fate in Babylon. The metaphor of imprisonment, whether intended to be confinement or punishment or execution, and references to places of imprisonment do not grow more plentiful during the exilic period by pure chance, especially in view of its foreignness to the Israelite judicial system.

172. Erica Reiner, *Surpu: A Collection of Sumerian and Akkadian Incantations* (Graz: Archiv fur Orient Forschung, 1958) 25.
173. *ANET,* 306.
174. M. San Nicolo, "Eine Kleine Gefängnismeuterei in Eanna zur Zeit des Kambyses," *Münchener Beiträge zur Papyrusforschung und Antiken Rechtsgeschichte* (1945) 2.

The experience of exile was compared to being in prison, and liberation was seen as release from that prison, the "opening of eyes of the imprisoned." Thus the diaspora hero types, whether king, courtier, or collective remnant, had to overcome this social reality. This is the context from which we must understand the wider sociopolitical importance of the theme of the lions' den in the book of Daniel. Daniel's emerging from the lions' den unharmed was a source of hope for surviving the exile itself.

The diaspora hero stories were maintained by a people who compared their social existence to imprisonment, and it is only within the context of this symbolism that the function of these stories as resistance literature makes sense. It is not surprising, therefore, that prison (and the various terms that are used) was a favorite metaphor for the exile experience:

> I have kept you and given you
> as a covenant to the people,
> to establish the land,
> to apportion the desolate heritages;
> saying to the prisoners, "Come out,"
> to those who are in darkness, "Show yourselves."
> (Isa 49:8-9 NRSV)

> The Spirit of the Lord God is upon me,
> because the Lord has anointed me;
> he has sent me to bring good news to the oppressed,
> to bind up the brokenhearted,
> to proclaim liberty to the captives,
> and release to the prisoners.
> (Isa 61:1 NRSV)

The lions' den experience, then, is to be read as both folktale and a symbol of the exile itself.

❖   ❖   ❖   ❖

6:10-11, Daniel's Civil Disobedience. The focus of these two verses is on two facts: (1) Daniel knows that the law has been signed, and (2) Daniel breaks the law by praying as he always had done before. What is not clear is the meaning of his opening the windows. Had Daniel always opened the windows, or was it an act of civil disobedience? Side issues need not detain us here, such as the implication of his having an upper room (a sign of wealth or prestige?).[175]

Interesting questions arise when one examines the text of Dan 6:10[11], particularly with regard to the presumption that Daniel actually threw open his windows in defiance of Darius's law. The text clearly means to suggest that Daniel disobeys the king's decree. But is he found out

or has Daniel openly violated the law? The Aramaic reads in the passive—that is, the windows "were opened," implying that they always were that way. The Theodotian text of the Septuagint reflects the Aramaic passive construction, using a passive participle form. The passive form suggests that, although Daniel was defying the law, he was not intending to defy it in any way that was innovative or different from his routine. However, the Old Greek text reads in the active voice, with Daniel actually throwing open his windows before he prays. The Vulgate also reflects this reading, which is rendered in the Douay as: "Now when Daniel knew . . . that the law was made, he went into his house and, opening the windows in his upper chamber toward Jerusalem, he knelt down three times a day."

The Ethiopic texts (4th century?)[176] echo this

---

175. See John Goldingay, *Daniel*, WBC 30 (Dallas: Word, 1988). Behrman cites 2 Kgs 13:17 as a comparison of Daniel's opening of the windows. See Georg Behrman, *Das Buch Daniel* (Göttingen: Vandenhoeck und Ruprecht, 1894) 40.

176. Ernst Würthwein, *The Text of the Old Testament* (Grand Rapids: Eerdmans, 1979) 98.

construction, rather than the Theodotion/MT passive voice.[177] Clearly, the active voice tends to emphasize Daniel's prayers as an act of open or public defiance more than does the passive, although the theme of defiance is not thereby totally absent even in the Theodotion/MT reading.

It is interesting that earlier commentators did not see any sense of defiance in Daniel's actions.[178] Montgomery commented on the rituals of the passage (e.g., prayer toward Jerusalem) and summarized that the story was written for the encouragement of the community. That Daniel was praying for mercy, seeking favor from the Lord, suggests that he knew what the implications of his actions would be. Seeking mercy is the usual response of Jewish diaspora communities when confronted with potential tragedy (see chap. 2). Although it is strange that fasting is not mentioned here, given the argument about Jewish fasting in exile (see Commentary on 9:3-19; Excursus "On Fasting, Communal Prayer, and Heavenly Warfare," 123-26) perhaps this is because Darius himself is depicted as fasting.

The story, in short, represents an act of civil disobedience on Daniel's part, whether that disobedience was public or whether he was spied upon to discover him defying the king's decree. The mention of open windows, however, mitigates against the idea that he was spied upon. Daniel was openly declaring his disobedience by keeping open, or even throwing open, his windows.

6:12-15, The Conspiracy Comes to Fruition.
The counselors repeat (note the continued use of repetition throughout the Daniel stories) the decree that the king had ordered, almost to entrap the king by means of his answer that the law cannot be changed. Daniel is then charged in words that echo his status and the status of the Jews throughout the book of Daniel: "Daniel, one of the exiles from Judah." Daniel, the foreigner, the defeated, the mere Jew is accused before the king. As in chap. 3, the mixed implication is clear: The foreigner whom the king had trusted has betrayed him by defying his order.[179]

Yet, Darius is troubled by the scenario. Here we have perhaps the most significant piece of evidence for those scholars who argue for the benign image of the foreign rulers in the book of Daniel. Darius "set his mind to deliver Daniel" (author's trans.) and made efforts to release him—presumably trying to determine a legally acceptable way to set Daniel free. As indicated, it is certainly true that the portrayal of the Persians in the Bible is occasionally, but not universally, positive. We will see in Daniel 7–12, however, that the image of the Persians, along with the Greeks and the Babylonians, is painted in significantly darker colors.

6:16-18, Daniel Is Punished.
The all-important throne-room scene is presumably in the background of the story, because of the nature of Daniel's civil disobedience. But what is there to try and to determine? There does not need to be a trial to determine the guilt of the accused, because he clearly confesses. Both the king and Daniel know that he is guilty, and he is thus immediately sentenced to his fate.

Contrast the sympathetic statement of Darius, "May your God, whom you faithfully serve, deliver you!" (v. 16) with the arrogant statement of Nebuchadnezzar in 3:15: "Who is the god that will deliver you out of my hands?" (NRSV). Once again, Darius is portrayed somewhat sympathetically; yet he carries out the act of state, Daniel's destruction by lions, which will serve as an example to other would-be dissidents. The hope—indeed, the calculation—is that word will spread quickly among the masses about the fate of any who disobey the will of the state. Note the sealing of the stone with the signs of state, including not only that of Darius, but of the counselors as well (including the conspirators?). For Christian readers, this is reminiscent of Matt 27:62, in which the rock used to seal Jesus' tomb includes the official insignia of the emperor. In both the cases of Daniel and Jesus, life was ensured by God in defiance of the empire. Goldingay also draws attention to the similar delivery of Peter from prison in Acts 12.[180]

The lion imagery has raised interesting suggestions from scholars. In Ps 91:13, lions are symbolic of chaos (see also Pss 22:14; 57:5) and are also noted in 1 Kgs 13:23-26 and Ezek 19:2-9.

177. O. Löfgren, *Die Äthiopische Übersetzung des Propheten Daniel* (Paris: Librarie Orientaliste Paul Geuthner, 1927) 127.

178. Behrman, *Das Buch Daniel*, 1894; R. H. Charles, *A Critical and Exegetical Commentary on the Book of Daniel* (Clarendon: Oxford, 1929).

179. On this point, see Goldingay, *The Book of Daniel*, 132.

180. See ibid.

The older idea that Daniel in the lion pit was somehow representative of an ancient myth of a descent into the underworld is not widely held today, although it is clear that resurrection themes were attributed to this story in both Jewish and Christian traditions.[181] My view on this matter has already been suggested: The lions' den is a metaphor of the exile.

The fasting of Darius may be seen not only as a symptom of his being upset by Daniel's fate, but also in the context of a miraculous delivery from death. There is a sense in which Darius is almost interceding for Daniel by fasting. Darius was not brought any "food" (NRSV) or "entertainment" (NIV); some scholars have suggested that "entertainment" may have implied concubines[182] (note that sexual abstinence is sometimes associated with fasting as a part of military preparation, so Uriah, in the David and Bathsheba affair, protests that he must not eat or drink while his comrades are in battle [2 Sam 11:11]).

6:19-24, The Miraculous Delivery and Reversal of Fortune. Darius goes in haste to the lion pit to check on the fate of Daniel. Presumably a minimum period of time needed to pass before the legal status of Daniel would be changed. Darius cries in a painful voice, "O Daniel, servant of the living God"; a foreign ruler's addressing the God of the Jews as "Most High" is not unusual, but this particular form of address is somewhat unusual.

Daniel begins his answer with respect for the king—a detail that further emphasizes his innocence, which he then proceeds to verify. He has done no "hurtful thing" before God or before the king. Verse 24 notes that Daniel was totally unharmed, an emphasis similar to the lack of smoke on the clothes of the three men thrown into the furnace in chap. 3. Goldingay notes that Daniel's calm contrasts nicely with the king's agitation.[183]

The episode is completed with a reversal of fortune: Those who had unjustly accused the innocent are sentenced to the same punishment, their families along with them. This troublesome detail is not made easier by the reference to punishment for false witness in Deut 19:16-19.

But this excess in the reversal of fortune is not altogether unusual in the diaspora stories; the ending of the book of Esther is a particularly good example. There is a sense here of the thoroughness of the miraculous acts of God. One can only note that one of the certain effects of oppressive, evil actions is the suffering of the innocent. Are we to applaud the deaths of the innocent in this passage, or, as at the traditional Passover seder, do we set aside a moment to remember the death of innocent Egyptians in the liberation of Israel?

6:25-28, The Restoration of Daniel. The end of the story relates the restoration and elevation of Daniel the hero. This is complete with a powerful confession of faith as decreed by Darius. But this statement goes much further than simply honoring the Jewish God; now Darius appears to be almost a convert to Judaism! God is the living God, and God's kingdom and sovereignty endure forever. What is interesting here is the note about deliverance and rescue as attributes of God. This is the faith response, the doctrinal response if you will, to the parable/story itself. The creator God also delivers and rescues, while the emperors of the world only kill or refrain from killing!

The final verse only adds to modern scholars' misery in trying to date the Daniel stories, as it appears that Cyrus follows Darius. That one historical person's life could span these various reigns, from Nebuchadnezzar to Cyrus, gives further evidence for the folkloric nature of these stories.

In the New Testament (Heb 11:33-34) both Daniel 3 and 6 are referred to in one sentence, anticipating modern scholarly discussion on the similarities between the two chapters. Goldingay suggests a systematic comparison:

Introduction	6:2-9	3:1-7
First Part	10-19	8-23
Second	20-25	24-27
Conclusion	26-29	28-33[184]

Other scholars have made observations about further similarities, as well as pointing out the significant differences between the two stories.

Goldingay notes that there are details in chap.

181. André Lacocque, *The Book of Daniel,* trans. D. Pellauer (Atlanta: John Knox, 1979) 113.

182. John J. Collins, *Daniel,* Hermeneia (Minneapolis: Fortress, 1993) 270.

183. Goldingay, *Daniel,* 133.

184. Lacocque, *The Book of Daniel.*

6 that associate it with either the Babylonian (lions in captivity, Jewish faith under pressure) or Greek periods (divinization of kings), but that the story fits most easily into the Persian period (bureaucratic organization, satrapies, Jews in respected positions, strict law of the Persians, and the dropping of Daniel's Babylonian name).[185] Collins, on the other hand, wants to date it at a time late enough for confusion to occur on the details of the Persian rulers, but before the time of Antiochus IV Epiphanes. The portrayal of Darius hardly fits a symbolic representation of Antiochus, since Darius comes out so positively and sympathetically

in this story.[186] The story certainly suggests ethnic tensions and serious threats to life from the power of the state (unjust and arbitrary power at that, because Daniel was innocent!). Finally, we must face the story from the perspective of the hearers of Daniel 6. The court of Darius is a kangaroo court, the kind of justice system that is always suspect in the eyes of the subordinated sections of society. Daniel was innocent; yet Persian law threw him to the lions quite legally and properly. Only among the conquerors are there the reactions of indignation, as if such atrocities are unusual; but the conquered peoples know better.

185. Goldingay, *The Book of Daniel*, 123.

186. Collins, *Daniel*, Hermeneia, 273.

REFLECTIONS

Two issues seem of particular importance when reflecting on Daniel 6: (1) the meaning of nonviolent resistance and (2) the violence of reactions to injustice. Let us begin by reflecting on the fact that Daniel 6 evokes great passion. The story of Daniel facing the lions is one of the most well-known of all biblical tales, frequently portrayed in artistic renderings in children's Bibles. But it is hardly the stuff of children's stories when its full political and theological intentions are realized. Note, for example, John Calvin's strong language in his commentary on Daniel 6: "Earthly princes deprive themselves of all authority when they rise up against God, yea, they are unworthy to be counted amongst the company of men. We ought rather to spit in their faces than to obey them when they . . . spoil God of his right."[187]

1. *Daniel 6 and Nonviolent Resistance: Gandhi and Daniel's Prayer.* Mahatma Gandhi made interesting comments, between 1909 and 1937, on the book of Daniel in his work in both South Africa and India. Gandhi stated that he had "found much consolation in reading the book of the prophet Daniel in the Bible" and declared Daniel to be "one of the greatest passive resisters that ever lived." Gandhi appears to have been particularly intrigued with chap. 6, the story of Daniel in the lions' den, vv. 10-11 especially. In his earliest article referring to Daniel, Gandhi suggested that Daniel was a model of resistance to South African "pass laws" for Indian South Africans. It is interesting to see how Gandhi used the Daniel theme when he stated that the Indians should "sit with their doors flung wide open and tell those gentlemen [South African authorities] that whatever laws they passed were not for them unless those laws were from God."[188]

Clearly, Gandhi assumed that Daniel had actually flung open the windows in flagrant disregard of Darius's decree against prayers to any god but the king: "When Daniel disregarded the laws of the Medes and Persians which offended his conscience, and meekly suffered the punishment for his disobedience, he offered satyagraha in its purest form."[189] Particularly when dealing with Western audiences, Gandhi returned to his Daniel interpretation, again emphasizing the opening of the windows. Furthermore, however, Gandhi also stressed the idea that

187. John Calvin, Commentary on Daniel 6, quoted in C. Hill, *The English Bible and the Seventeenth Century Revolution* (London: Penguin, 1993) 59.

188. M. K. Gandhi, *Gandhi's Complete Writings*, (Bombay: Indian Government) Vol. IX, 541 from *Indian Opinion*, London, Nov. 12, 1909, "Speech at Farewell Meeting." See also Vol. LXXXIV, 1946, "Talk with Missionaries," where Gandhi referred to Daniel's open windows so that all could see him praying, from *Harijan*, 28-4-1946.

189. M. K. Gandhi, *Writings of Gandhi*, Volume XVII, "Congress Report on the Punjab Disorders" (March 25, 1920) 152.

Daniel was otherwise portrayed as a model citizen: "It must be remembered, that neither Daniel nor Socrates . . . had any ill will towards their persecutors. Daniel and Socrates are regarded as having been model citizens of the states to which they belonged."[190]

Gandhi's comments suggest a number of possibilities for understanding Daniel 6 and, by implication, the other stories as well. Clearly, a story can have differing circumstances, depending on where one is reading it. From a South African prison, Daniel 6 made perfect sense to one engaged in nonviolent resistance to unjust laws. Here, perhaps, we have an important clue to reordering our own reading of the text in the modern era. Stories of resistance were written by a diaspora community who faced such trials often enough to identify with the fate of the heroes in these stories.

The lions' den, then, serves as a metaphor of both unjust punishment and imprisonment. There is clearly more than initially meets the eye in the early church's use of Daniel 6 (and chap. 3) as resurrection stories. Resurrection itself is a direct threat to imperial power. Putting it bluntly, if the imperial armies cannot keep their executed prisoners dead, where now is their power?

2. *The Violence of the Reaction to Injustice.* One of the main motifs of "reversal of fortune" stories in the Bible, and Daniel especially, is the punishment of those who seek the death of Jewish heroes. Sometimes this theme of the "discomfiture of the Egyptians" reaches disturbing proportions, as it does in Daniel 6, where the entire families of the evil advisers are cast into the lions' den. While such aspects of these stories are disturbing, it is important not to overlook the psychology of the dispossessed—and especially their anger. Fanon writes:

> The settlers' town is a well-fed town, an easygoing town; its belly is always full of good things. The settlers' town is a town of white people, of foreigners.
>
> The town belonging to the colonized people, or at least the native town, the Negro village, the medina, the reservation, is a place of ill fame, peopled by men of evil repute . . . the native town is a crouching village, a town on its knees, a town wallowing in the mire. It is a town of niggers and dirty Arabs. The look that the native turns on the settler's town is a look of lust, a look of envy; it expresses his dreams of possession—all manner of possession: to sit at the settlers' table, to sleep in the settlers' bed, with his wife if possible. The colonized man is an envious man. And this the settler knows very well; when their glances meet he ascertains bitterly, always on the defensive, "They want to take our place." It is true, for there is no native who does not dream at least once a day of setting himself up in the settlers' place.[191]

The punishment of the innocent is definitely an offensive theme in many of the biblical stories, and it is equally offensive in the words of Fanon. But is this element of these stories to be attributed to the anger of the suffering? I would argue that these stories in Daniel often reflect the physical and spiritual crises brought about by the conquerors and rulers in the ancient Near East from 587 through the Hellenistic despots of the second century BCE. It is precisely the angry details that open a historical window onto the emotions of occupied Palestine and diaspora Judaism. It is not the people of God in their finest moment, but it is the reality of social conditions. Their ability eventually to embrace nonviolence and even to welcome the foreigner is all the more amazing—and all the more a witness to the involvement of revelation!

Members of the dominant culture in all times often delude themselves into expecting great praise and thanks for having paid attention to those who suffer injustice. Instead they often find anger and resentment from these suffering people. For many, this initial response is enough to send them back to their comfortable homes behind locked doors in separate neighborhoods. Such expressions of anger are all too often turned against people as evidence of their "irresponsibility" or "unwillingness to compromise." But surely we must patiently listen to the

190. M. Gandhi, *Writings,* Vol. XVII, 152.
191. F. Fanon, *The Wretched of the Earth* (New York: Grove, 1963) 39.

anger of those people who are hurting, in the hope of eventually earning the trust and friendship of people who have so much to teach us. Furthermore, is it not true that even Christians are tempted by such emotional failures of conscience? Are we no less members of the body of Christ despite our occasional failures of moral courage?

Let us be cautious here. This is not an excuse or a plea for understanding the violence of the oppressed. There is no such thing as "righteous" violence, as if brutal actions are somehow transformed by calling them aspects of the struggle for justice. Such manipulation is as offensive in progressive circles as are the more nationalistic versions of justification of violence by using patriotic terms. Both sides only succeed in justifying violence. Christians are correct to reject all such reprehensible special pleading. Our call is to understand anger and to accept it as a reality in people's lives, precisely because our nonviolent action must be based on the realities of human life and not on fantasy worlds.

The popular media bombard the world with the false virtue of vengeance and "paybacks." Thus it is a constant struggle against popular wisdom to maintain the witness that vengeance is not the way of God. It is particularly disturbing when Christians, in false attempts to identify with the sufferers, somehow suspend their convictions of peace and nonviolence and find ways to justify the violence of those who have suffered, saying, "There is no peace without justice." But understanding anger is not an invitation to suspend commitment to the way of peace. Rather, it is an invitation to prophetic endurance of anger while not compromising the gospel of nonviolence. Ultimately, there is no justice without peace.

THE APOCALYPTIC VISIONS

DANIEL 7:1-28, VISIONS OF CHANGE

NIV

7 In the first year of Belshazzar king of Babylon, Daniel had a dream, and visions passed through his mind as he was lying on his bed. He wrote down the substance of his dream.

[2] Daniel said: "In my vision at night I looked, and there before me were the four winds of heaven churning up the great sea. [3] Four great beasts, each different from the others, came up out of the sea.

[4] "The first was like a lion, and it had the wings of an eagle. I watched until its wings were torn off and it was lifted from the ground so that it stood on two feet like a man, and the heart of a man was given to it.

[5] "And there before me was a second beast, which looked like a bear. It was raised up on one of its sides, and it had three ribs in its mouth between its teeth. It was told, 'Get up and eat your fill of flesh!'

[6] "After that, I looked, and there before me was another beast, one that looked like a leopard. And on its back it had four wings like those of a bird. This beast had four heads, and it was given authority to rule.

[7] "After that, in my vision at night I looked, and there before me was a fourth beast—terrifying and frightening and very powerful. It had large iron teeth; it crushed and devoured its victims and trampled underfoot whatever was left. It was different from all the former beasts, and it had ten horns.

[8] "While I was thinking about the horns, there before me was another horn, a little one, which came up among them; and three of the first horns were uprooted before it. This horn had eyes like the eyes of a man and a mouth that spoke boastfully.

NRSV

7 In the first year of King Belshazzar of Babylon, Daniel had a dream and visions of his head as he lay in bed. Then he wrote down the dream:[a] [2]I,[b] Daniel, saw in my vision by night the four winds of heaven stirring up the great sea, [3]and four great beasts came up out of the sea, different from one another. [4]The first was like a lion and had eagles' wings. Then, as I watched, its wings were plucked off, and it was lifted up from the ground and made to stand on two feet like a human being; and a human mind was given to it. [5]Another beast appeared, a second one, that looked like a bear. It was raised up on one side, had three tusks[c] in its mouth among its teeth and was told, "Arise, devour many bodies!" [6]After this, as I watched, another appeared, like a leopard. The beast had four wings of a bird on its back and four heads; and dominion was given to it. [7]After this I saw in the visions by night a fourth beast, terrifying and dreadful and exceedingly strong. It had great iron teeth and was devouring, breaking in pieces, and stamping what was left with its feet. It was different from all the beasts that preceded it, and it had ten horns. [8]I was considering the horns, when another horn appeared, a little one coming up among them; to make room for it, three of the earlier horns were plucked up by the roots. There were eyes like human eyes in this horn, and a mouth speaking arrogantly.

[9] As I watched,

> thrones were set in place,
>> and an Ancient One[d] took his throne,
> his clothing was white as snow,

---

[a] Q Ms Theodotion: MT adds *the beginning of the words; he said*
[b] Theodotion: Aram *Daniel answered and said, "I*   [c] Or *ribs*
[d] Aram *an Ancient of Days*

NIV

9"As I looked,

"thrones were set in place,
and the Ancient of Days took his seat.
His clothing was as white as snow;
the hair of his head was white like wool.
His throne was flaming with fire,
and its wheels were all ablaze.
10A river of fire was flowing,
coming out from before him.
Thousands upon thousands attended him;
ten thousand times ten thousand stood before
him.
The court was seated,
and the books were opened.

11"Then I continued to watch because of the boastful words the horn was speaking. I kept looking until the beast was slain and its body destroyed and thrown into the blazing fire. 12(The other beasts had been stripped of their authority, but were allowed to live for a period of time.)

13"In my vision at night I looked, and there before me was one like a son of man, coming with the clouds of heaven. He approached the Ancient of Days and was led into his presence. 14He was given authority, glory and sovereign power; all peoples, nations and men of every language worshiped him. His dominion is an everlasting dominion that will not pass away, and his kingdom is one that will never be destroyed.

15"I, Daniel, was troubled in spirit, and the visions that passed through my mind disturbed me. 16I approached one of those standing there and asked him the true meaning of all this.

"So he told me and gave me the interpretation of these things: 17'The four great beasts are four kingdoms that will rise from the earth. 18But the saints of the Most High will receive the kingdom and will possess it forever—yes, for ever and ever.'

19"Then I wanted to know the true meaning of the fourth beast, which was different from all the others and most terrifying, with its iron teeth and bronze claws—the beast that crushed and devoured its victims and trampled underfoot whatever was left. 20I also wanted to know about the ten horns on its head and about the other horn that came up, before which three of them fell—the horn that looked more imposing than

NRSV

and the hair of his head like pure wool;
his throne was fiery flames,
and its wheels were burning fire.
10 A stream of fire issued
and flowed out from his presence.
A thousand thousands served him,
and ten thousand times ten thousand stood
attending him.
The court sat in judgment,
and the books were opened.

11I watched then because of the noise of the arrogant words that the horn was speaking. And as I watched, the beast was put to death, and its body destroyed and given over to be burned with fire. 12As for the rest of the beasts, their dominion was taken away, but their lives were prolonged for a season and a time. 13As I watched in the night visions,

I saw one like a human being[a]
coming with the clouds of heaven.
And he came to the Ancient One[b]
and was presented before him.
14 To him was given dominion
and glory and kingship,
that all peoples, nations, and languages
should serve him.
His dominion is an everlasting dominion
that shall not pass away,
and his kingship is one
that shall never be destroyed.

15As for me, Daniel, my spirit was troubled within me,[c] and the visions of my head terrified me. 16I approached one of the attendants to ask him the truth concerning all this. So he said that he would disclose to me the interpretation of the matter: 17"As for these four great beasts, four kings shall arise out of the earth. 18But the holy ones of the Most High shall receive the kingdom and possess the kingdom forever—forever and ever."

19Then I desired to know the truth concerning the fourth beast, which was different from all the rest, exceedingly terrifying, with its teeth of iron and claws of bronze, and which devoured and broke in pieces, and stamped what was left with its feet; 20and concerning the ten horns that were on its head, and concerning the other horn, which

a Aram one like a son of man   b Aram the Ancient of Days
c Aram troubled in its sheath

NIV

the others and that had eyes and a mouth that spoke boastfully. [21]As I watched, this horn was waging war against the saints and defeating them, [22]until the Ancient of Days came and pronounced judgment in favor of the saints of the Most High, and the time came when they possessed the kingdom.

[23]"He gave me this explanation: 'The fourth beast is a fourth kingdom that will appear on earth. It will be different from all the other kingdoms and will devour the whole earth, trampling it down and crushing it. [24]The ten horns are ten kings who will come from this kingdom. After them another king will arise, different from the earlier ones; he will subdue three kings. [25]He will speak against the Most High and oppress his saints and try to change the set times and the laws. The saints will be handed over to him for a time, times and half a time.[a]

[26]" 'But the court will sit, and his power will be taken away and completely destroyed forever. [27]Then the sovereignty, power and greatness of the kingdoms under the whole heaven will be handed over to the saints, the people of the Most High. His kingdom will be an everlasting kingdom, and all rulers will worship and obey him.'

[28]"This is the end of the matter. I, Daniel, was deeply troubled by my thoughts, and my face turned pale, but I kept the matter to myself."

[a]25 Or *for a year, two years and half a year*

NRSV

came up and to make room for which three of them fell out—the horn that had eyes and a mouth that spoke arrogantly, and that seemed greater than the others. [21]As I looked, this horn made war with the holy ones and was prevailing over them, [22]until the Ancient One[a] came; then judgment was given for the holy ones of the Most High, and the time arrived when the holy ones gained possession of the kingdom.

23This is what he said: "As for the fourth beast,
there shall be a fourth kingdom on earth
   that shall be different from all the other
      kingdoms;
it shall devour the whole earth,
   and trample it down, and break it to pieces.
[24] As for the ten horns,
out of this kingdom ten kings shall arise,
   and another shall arise after them.
This one shall be different from the former
      ones,
   and shall put down three kings.
[25] He shall speak words against the Most High,
   shall wear out the holy ones of the Most
      High,
   and shall attempt to change the sacred
      seasons and the law;
and they shall be given into his power
   for a time, two times,[b] and half a time.
[26] Then the court shall sit in judgment,
   and his dominion shall be taken away,
   to be consumed and totally destroyed.
[27] The kingship and dominion
   and the greatness of the kingdoms under the
      whole heaven
   shall be given to the people of the holy ones
      of the Most High;
their kingdom shall be an everlasting kingdom,
   and all dominions shall serve and obey
      them."

28Here the account ends. As for me, Daniel, my thoughts greatly terrified me, and my face turned pale; but I kept the matter in my mind.

[a] Aram *the Ancient of Days*   [b] Aram *a time, times*

COMMENTARY

Chapter 7 begins a new genre in the book of Daniel. Instead of the king's dreams, now we focus on the dreams, thoughts, and visions of Daniel himself. This chapter has been called "the veritable center of the book"[192] and the "heart" of Daniel.[193] These evaluations derive mainly from the fact that the book has so many connections with the stories in chaps. 1–6 (issues of sovereignty and dominion, negative evaluations of empires, and most especially the sequence of four kingdoms in chap. 2) that it serves almost as a capstone—as if the stories were leading up to this chapter. The fact that chap. 7 was written in Aramaic also gives this interesting impression. Lenglet pointed out a plausible chiastic symmetry to chaps. 2–7:

A chap. 2, vision of four empires
  B chap. 3, faithfulness of the Jews and their rescue
    C chap. 4, judgment on empire (Nebuchadnezzar)
    C′ chap. 5, judgment on empire (Belshazzar)
  B′ chap. 6, faithfulness of a Jew and his rescue
A′ chap. 7, vision of four empires.[194]

The relationships among these chapters have led many scholars to suggest that chaps. 2–7 were, in fact, originally a separate document (which included, of course, the older stories that became chaps. 2–6), to which chaps. 1 and 8–12 were added at a later time. When they were added is a tricky question. Most scholars assign chap. 7 in its present form to 167 BCE, just before Antiochus IV desecrated the Temple, since this event would surely have been alluded to in this chapter, if it had happened by the time this section was written. (It is referred to later in Daniel 10–12.)

On the other hand, chap. 7 has obvious literary connections to 8–12. It is the first of the clearly apocalyptic chapters of the book of Daniel, and while there are references to earlier phrases and terms, there is no story narrative in chap. 7 that would relate it to the older diaspora stories in chaps. 1–6.

There has always been considerable scholarly debate as to the origins of Daniel 7. Was there an earlier vision that did not mention Antiochus so specifically? If so, then, with many scholars, I might suggest that the references to the "little horn" (referring to Antiochus IV) may have been added at the time chapter 7 took its present shape—i.e., 167 BCE. However, there are many scholars who defend the unity of this chapter, considering vv. 21-22 as the only possible candidates for later additions, if any.

In any case, it will be clear from this analysis that chap. 7 certainly turns the theological/ideological direction of the book as a whole in a dramatic, and darker, direction. The images here are those of struggle and warfare between the forces of evil and chaos against the heavens, the "holy ones," and by implication the Jewish tellers and hearers of the story. Even those scholars who see the kings negatively in chaps. 1–6 also see a change in chap. 7, where the attitude is decidedly angry and alarmed. The hope for a change in the foreign rulers has been abandoned; the empires are revealed for what they always have been: beasts who rose out of chaos and evil.

7:1, In the Time of Belshazzar. The first vision is associated with the time of Belshazzar. This is an interesting move, because it associates this vision with the most negative portrayal of a foreign ruler thus far. We are to understand that this dream (a night dream is clearly implied here because Daniel is lying in bed) is occasioned by the kind of negative political rule that was typified by the story of Belshazzar. This is a significant point. Dreams of deliverance, then, are associated with adverse political rule.

The terminology used for Daniel's dream, "visions of his head," is precisely that used for Nebuchadnezzar earlier. It is interesting that the assumption here is that Daniel is an important interpreter not only of others' dreams, but of his own as well (through the aid of an angelic assistant).

7:2-8, The Rise of the Beasts. 7:2. The

192. Lacocque, *The Book of Daniel.*
193. N. Porteous, *Daniel,* OTL (Philadelphia: Westminster, 1965) 95.
194. A. Lenglet, "La structure litteraire de Daniel 2-7," *Biblica* 53 (1972) 169-90.

narrative shifts to first person, as Daniel describes his dream. The "four winds of heaven" (ארבע רוחי שמיא 'arba' rûḥê šĕmayyā') relate closely to imagery found in *1 Enoch,* where four "angels" of heaven represent the winds from the four directions. In Daniel 7, these winds are "stirring the sea" (מגיחן לימא mĕgîḥān lĕyammā'). The Greek suggests "attacked" (προσβάλλω *prosballō*), and the implication is even greater that what this sentence describes is spiritual/mythical warfare between the winds of heaven and the sea. The winds of heaven were part of God's weapons, or tools, in the creation (Job 26:12-13; Ps 89:9-11). This is an echo of the ancient Semitic myth of the storm god (Baal in Canaanite mythology, Marduk in the Babylonian version; the stories are essentially parallel) at battle with the god of the sea (Yam, Canaanite; Tiamat, Babylonian; the sea god was frequently associated with or identified with monsters or dragons from the deep), the latter representing the powers of chaos that must be controlled by the god of the storm. Marduk, for example, uses the four winds as weapons in his struggle against Tiamat.[195] This myth, with its many suggestive echoes in the Bible, is often used creatively to refer to historical struggles of the Israelite people, in which God is a major participant. The most dramatic example of this is Isa 51:8-11 (NRSV), the significant portion of which is:

Was it not you who cut Rahab in pieces,
   who pierced the dragon?
Was it not you who dried up the sea,
   the waters of the great deep;
who made the depths of the sea a way,
   for the redeemed to cross over?

Here the ancient myth is brilliantly used to represent the crossing of the Reed Sea; the ancient Semitic myth becomes historicized as Yahweh's doing battle with the Reed Sea, which the Hebrew slaves then crossed in the exodus. Goldingay points out that "great sea" is *always* used to refer to the Mediterranean Sea—that is, the actual place—rather than a primordial, mythical sea.[196]

Such aspects of realism add to the power of the message.

Therefore, 7:2 sets the scene for what follows. Many scholars have suggested that this is the first event in the series that follows, implying that the four winds of heaven are actually the catalyst that brings forth the beasts from the deep and that God initiates that action. But this is not what is intended here. Verse 2 sets the scene of battle, and the following verses then describe what occurs during that battle. God is at war with the sea, not bringing forth the beasts. There is no suggestion here, then, that the beasts rise at God's request.

7:3. During the battle, four great beasts rise from the sea. The sea is the enemy, chaos, the realm of Leviathan (Lotan, Rahab, Tunannu, etc.). And so the beasts, which will be interpreted as world powers, are associated with the forces of chaos in the world and at odds with the powers of heaven. As the rest of the chapter will represent battle and judgment images, it is clear that these beasts arise one by one to do battle. Theologically, the battle is between good and evil. Note that the kingdoms of this world are associated with powers of the sea, with evil. This is a long-standing, though typically neglected, element of biblical tradition that carries through into the New Testament, where Jesus is tempted by Satan, who is assumed to have control of the kingdoms of the earth (Matt 4:8-10). Von Rad suggested that the four beasts mean "all the world," referring to Zechariah 1.[197] Certainly we see such animal symbolism in Pss 68:31; 74:13; 87:4; Isa 27:1; Ezek 29:3, 32; and *1 Enoch* 85–90. The most dramatic parallel to this section, however, is Hos 13:6*b*-9, which lists the same animals in succession (though not in the same order):

they were satisfied, and their heart was proud;
   therefore they forgot me,
So I will become like a lion to them,
   like a leopard I will lurk beside the way.
I will fall upon them like a bear
   robbed of her cubs,
   and will tear open the covering of their heart
there I will devour like a lion,
   as a wild animal would mangle them.
I will destroy you, O Israel;
   who can help you? (NRSV)

195. André Lacocque, *The Book of Daniel,* trans. D. Pellauer (Atlanta: John Knox, 1979) 138; see also the "Akkadian Creation Story" (Enuma Elish), in *Ancient Near Eastern Texts Relating to the Old Testament* (*ANET*), ed. James B. Pritchard (Princeton, N.J.: Princeton University Press, 1969) 60-72.

196. John Goldingay, *Daniel,* WBC 30 (Dallas: Word, 1988) 160.

197. G. von Rad, *The Message of the Prophets* (New York: Harper & Row, 1962) 278n. 2.

Note that the final animal is undefined, as is the fourth beast in Daniel 7 (although in parallel with lion). What is perhaps most interesting in this passage is the fact that these animals are seen as a threat to the northern agricultural and herding society. All, then, are predators, animals of the hunt that become useful as images of God's making war on Israel. But the images in Daniel 7 are *more* than lions, bears, and leopards. The images are mixed, therefore violating the clear categories enumerated in levitical law and further suggesting that they are "unclean."

7:4. The first beast conveys the image of a lion. Lions are frequently used in modern iconography as symbols of courage and strength (particularly by the British), even in children's stories; but it is rare to have such a favorable image of a lion in the Bible, in which they are usually seen as wild threats to civilized life and horrific menaces (Amos 3:12). Although many scholars see this lion image in Daniel as finally a positive representation of Nebuchadnezzar ("a human mind given to it"), this is not likely to be what is intended. That this beast is transformed into a human may signify that this represents human beings—Babylonians at that. In other words, the lion suggests that this first "government" or "ruler" is the personification of the powerful threat represented by lions. If such a positive or specific reference to Nebuchadnezzar's insanity is intended here (cf. chap. 4), then it is appropriate to point out that his fearsomeness and his "wings" (often a symbol of the swiftness of conquest) must be removed before he can have a human mind. Once again, a transformation of the ruler is a way of conquering the enemy!

7:5. The second beast, also associated with threats to human life from wild animals, is a bear. It is portrayed as already devouring; as the Aramaic suggests, it has "ribs" between its teeth, already starting to fulfill the command, "Arise, devour many bodies!" *Who* tells the bear to devour many bodies? Goldingay and others presume that this is God's command,[198] implying that the destructiveness of the empires is also under God's direction—dare I say blessing! But God never speaks in this vision. Contrast the images of Antiochus IV, the "little horn," who speaks too much

198. Goldingay, *Daniel,* 160-65.

(vv. 8, 11). The voice here is the antagonistic Chaos, in battle against the forces of heaven.

7:6. The third beast, represented as a leopard, is seen as having great ability because of its numerous wings and heads. Do these four wings and four heads somehow represent the four Persian kings (Darius, Cyrus, Xerxes, Artaxerxes) mentioned in Scripture? Or do they represent the four corners of the earth? The term "sovereignty" (שלטן *šālṭān*; NIV, "authority"; NRSV, "dominion") is used often in Daniel, and here is given to the leopard. Of all the beasts, this one alone may be a neutral image, in contrast to the first two—since "dominion" was given to Darius as well. But this interpretation must not be stretched too far; the leopard is hardly benign!

7:7-8. The last beast is not given an earthly association, but is described in strong language: "fearsome," "terrible," "very strong." It has great iron teeth, devouring its victims and trampling all else under its feet. Some scholars have suggested that the beast in mind may well be an elephant, "breaking in pieces, and stamping what was left with its feet." Greeks brought the war elephant from the east, and they are mentioned in 1 Macc 1:17; 3:34; and 6:28-47. Note especially 3 Maccabees, a first-century document that describes the threat to faithful Jews by Ptolemy, who ordered them to be trampled by elephants "equipped with horrible implements" (3 Macc 5:45). Whatever kind of beast this may be, its power is purely destructive. The context suggests that this beast differs from the previous three because of the magnitude of its destructive force. Despite its strength, its ten horns are soon overpowered by the force of one who comes later, who speaks arrogantly.

As can be imagined, there has been considerable debate about the meaning of the ten horns and the later three horns. The little horn certainly is meant to represent Antiochus IV, but who are the three who are "plucked up by the roots"? The most likely suggestion is that there were three men in line for the throne upon the death of Antiochus III: Seleucus IV Philopater and his sons, Demetrius and Antiochus. We know that Antiochus IV killed his young nephew Antiochus, but it is not clear whether he can be implicated in the deaths of the other two except indirectly. The variety of options increases dramatically when one tries to figure out who the "ten horns" might refer to. Alexander and six of the Seleucids who followed (so Collins)?[199] Or is "ten" simply to be reckoned as "many"? Does it matter? It is hard to avoid an image of diaspora Jews (even in Palestine) as, in fact, a minority quite disengaged from the powers of the empire and who, in fact, see it taking place over their heads. The frequent change of rulers might then be a basis for cynicism—at which point the ten horns crowding together on an animal become a dark-humored, satirical comment on the constant intrigue in the Hellenistic courts.

Finally, there arises a horn with eyes and a mouth speaking arrogantly—Antiochus IV (for the immodest speech of Antiochus, see 1 Macc 1:24-25; 2 Macc 5:17). Later Christian groups would interpret Rome as the final and great beast, an understandable confusion, given Christian suffering under Roman imperial rule. In 2 Esdr 12:10-12, there is a conscious change to Rome as the last beast, which seems to presume the earlier series of Hellenistic empires. It is clear, however, that Antiochus IV was the original reference, and the earliest interpretation of this passage[200] strongly supports the importance of seeing the beast as a metaphor for Antiochus IV.

The elasticity of these symbols is what lends Daniel one of its enduring points of interest for later generations who were able to fill in the blanks with whatever powers they were opposing at the time (e.g., Rome, England's Charles I during the civil war, George III during the American Revolution, Louis XVI during the French Revolution, etc.; see Reflections below). It seems hardly surprising, then, that there is considerable debate on who the four beasts were meant to signify.

7:9-14, The Heavenly Judgment. As Daniel is trying to understand these events, the battle shifts to the heavenly arena, where an interesting description of God's actions takes place. We are "standing before" another king in another throne room (v. 9). As Daniel watches, "thrones" are set in place. Why is "thrones" plural? Is a heavenly council suggested? Is there a throne for the "one like a son of man" introduced later?[201] What is clear is that we are in the

realm of political sovereignty once again—except that this throne room is the one with true authority. The description of the "Ancient of Days" (NIV; "Ancient One," NRSV) is fanciful and impressive, suggesting an old man with great authority (the white robes and white hair are also noted in *1 Enoch* 14:20, resembling descriptions of El, the father/king figure in Canaanite imagery), surrounded by miraculous signs of power, like light and fire. While Canaanite mythology is clearly a part of the resources available to the visionary writer of Daniel, other biblical images certainly verify that these ideas were already well known in Hebrew circles. Consider, especially, portions of the "enthronement of God as king" theme in Psalm 97:1-3 (NRSV):

The LORD is king! Let the earth rejoice;
  let the many coastlands be glad!
Clouds and thick darkness are all around him;
  righteousness and justice are the foundation
    of his throne
Fire goes before him,
  and consumes his adversaries on every side.

As if to magnify the power of this ruler in Daniel 7, "a thousand thousands" attend him (v. 10), much more than the mere thousand that attended Belshazzar in the earlier story. As the "court" is in session, there follows a startlingly brief dispatch of the beasts (vv. 11-12). The worst one, the beast with the horn that speaks arrogantly, is immediately burned in judgment. The speed of this judgment contrasts with our modern fascination for the battle itself. Surely there must be struggle, a matching of power and force until finally good wins over evil. Not so in biblical apocalypticism. Almost as soon as the Ancient of Days arrives, the judgment is settled. Note also Revelation, where the supposedly "great battle" is so easily missed as to be made insignificant. There, too, the beast is dispatched to a fiery destruction (Rev 19:19-21).

The others, made powerless, are allowed to live "for a season and a time" (v. 12). The implication that dominion has been taken from the remaining beasts, although they have been allowed to live for a while, is important. Many scholars have wondered whether this is an indication that when the Hellenistic Empire is destroyed, the former kingdoms would live once again as independent states. But this can hardly be the meaning of this

199. John J. Collins, *Daniel,* Hermeneia (Minneapolis: Fortress, 1993) 299.
200. See Sibylline Oracles 3:388-400.
201. Collins notes the idea of thrones of judgment in Matt 19:28. See Collins, *Daniel,* Hermeneia, 301.

text. Each beast symbolizes an empire, and each one's dominion is removed. The emphasis, then, is on the delay of destruction, even after the beasts are left powerless. That the powers of this earth exist but are already defeated is an important aspect of political atheism and radical faith. What this means is that the apocalyptic writer no longer believes in the power of the empires, but points instead to an alternative reality.

The rationale for rendering the empires powerless, instead of obliterating them, is because authority is given to the mysterious one who is now introduced, the "one like a human being" (vv. 13-14), literally, "son of man" (בר אנשׁ *bar 'ĕnāš*), which is taken to mean "human being," thus "someone who looks like a human being." Given Jesus' use of the "son of man" image, this spectacular entrance at precisely this moment in the vision of Daniel 7 has brought forth torrents of scholarly debate as to the origin and meaning of the term. That the New Testament writers drew on this image of a powerful authority under God is clear. But one must not allow the later Christian use of the term to affect one's understanding of what is meant in the context of the vision of Daniel 7.[202]

Irrespective of the precise origin or meaning of the "son of man" figure, the important aspect of this figure is that he is a heavenly representative, appointed by the source of heavenly authority, the Ancient of Days. Some scholars have pointed out that God "appears on clouds" in Deut 33:26 and Ps 104:3, but in Canaanite mythology, Baal appears on clouds as well. Since Baal is lesser than El, this suggests a closer parallel to Daniel 7.

Some scholars have suggested that the "one like a son of man" is a priestly figure,[203] but this association has not been widely accepted in the most recent commentaries. Attention is focused on the fact that this person has supernatural attributes—he is one who "looks like" a human being, as the other beasts "look like" lions, bears, etc. Also, this person comes from heaven, ruling out an earthly figure. Finally, this person has authority and is part of the preceding judgment/

battle scene. As Collins and Goldingay both conclude, the candidate best suited for the identification as "one like a son of man" in Daniel 7 is the angel Michael, who will do battle on Israel's behalf in later visions (Dan 10:13, 21), and is, of course, a supernatural figure. Michael is well known in the New Testament as well, appearing in Matt 16:27; 25:31; and Revelation 12. Furthermore, in the Dead Sea Scrolls Michael is named as one whose "kingdom will be raised up" when the other kingdoms are destroyed.[204]

But there are further implications, if this identification is accepted. Michael is an angelic representation of the people of Israel. Michael's going to battle, then, is a symbolic representation of the struggles of the people of Israel, much in the same way that God was pictured as fighting when Israel was at war (Exodus 15).

Thus, through this viceroy, heaven is claiming its right to rule. The terms used in reference to the authority of the son of man figure are significant in their direct contrast to the assumed power of the Babylonians and Persians in the previous stories. In other stories in Daniel, these attributes were ultimately assigned to God: sovereignty, 2:20-23; honor/glory, 4:17; kingship, 4:34-37; over all peoples, nations, and languages, 6:25; 3:4, 7, 29; 4:1; 5:19; he shall be served, 3:28; his authority will last forever.

7:15-18, The Summary of the Vision. Daniel is greatly distressed by these visions, presumably because of his own confusion on the matter. He asks one of the attendants for an explanation. It is typical of such apocalyptic visions that there is a conversation between a heavenly mediator and the seer. So Daniel seeks out an interpreter. In reply, he is given a simple summary of the entire vision: The worldly powers will arise ("kingdoms from the earth"; note the interpretation of the earlier image of the beasts coming from the sea), but God will conquer them all and God's kingdom will be everlasting. The conflict and its results are certain. Daniel, however, is more curious about the fourth beast; the writer focuses attention on the beast that undoubtedly has the most importance for the hearers and readers of this visionary experience: the beast with which they are currently contending.

---

202. Jesus is not being "predicted" or "announced" in Daniel 7. Rather, Daniel 7 is among many of the Hebrew images in the OT that the NT, and Jesus himself, draws upon in order to compose a biblically informed picture of Jesus as the Messiah.

203. Lacocque, *The Book of Daniel.*

204. 1QM 17:5-8.

7:19-28, The Elaboration of the Fourth Beast. 7:19-20. In typical fashion for Daniel, these verses repeat precisely what we have read already in vv. 7-8. The new elements that follow, therefore, are of greatest interest—namely, the war with the "holy ones."

7:21-22. Like "one like a son of man," the precise referent of the "holy ones" (קדישׁין *qaddîsîn*) has engendered considerable comment. Here, however, the conclusions of recent scholars are on somewhat more solid ground, given the wider evidence of the Dead Sea Scrolls as well as the wider extra-biblical Jewish literature that can be drawn upon.

It would seem, at first glance, that the holy ones might be a name given to the faithful Jews of the community, but it is much more common for this image to refer to supernatural beings (see Deut 33:2; Job 5:1; 15:15; Ps 89:6, 8; Zech 14:5; see also Dan 4:14, compared with "watchers"; 4:20; 8:13) and thus in line with the earlier image of Michael. Both Lacocque and Collins, however, refer to the fact that angels are mixed with real people in combat themes in the Dead Sea documents (esp. the "War Scroll").[205] Goldingay suggests that the holy ones may be either supernatural or a symbol of Israel. It is important to point out that the fate of the holy ones is certainly intended to reflect the fate of the Jewish people themselves, much in the same way that Michael does. Therefore, we should understand the close association between the holy ones and the people of Israel suffering under Hellenistic domination. Furthermore, these holy ones are associated with "the Most High," which is the term diaspora Jews often used for God and, in turn, was used by non-Jews in reference to the Jewish God. Furthermore, to these holy ones some authority is given within the everlasting kingdom that is inaugurated by the Ancient of Days.

Whoever the holy ones are assumed to be, they are suffering near defeat. Surely this is the moment of greatest relevance for the reader—and strongly suggests that the writer identified strongly with the holy ones and felt powerfully their near defeat. The war is specifically against the "arrogant horn" of the final beast.

7:23-25. The beast is described in more detail in these verses, before a repetition of the heavenly court that defeats the beast finally in vv. 26-27. The attributes of the beast are worldwide dominion, destructive power,[206] division of leadership within the empire, and the eventual success of one of the leaders within the empire.

Although most scholars consider this last beast to be the Hellenistic Empire inaugurated by Alexander, it is interesting to note that some of the beast's attributes are reminiscent of images associated with Cyrus in Isa 41:25b: "He shall trample on rulers as on mortar, as the putter treads clay." One is cautious about reading such descriptions positively!

Furthermore, this final leader is also described as: different from the former ones (more powerful?); one who will make war with the holy ones and nearly win; someone who will attempt to change "sacred seasons and law" (undoubtedly a reference to attempts by Antiochus IV to change the religious observances of the Jewish people); one who will rule for only a time, and one who will be the last to rule. It will be his power that is given to the holy ones. As Porteous writes: "It is a sobering reflection that it was this empire, for all that it mediated to the ancient peoples of East the achievements of Greek culture, that could appear, in the eyes of a member of a subject people, to be the worst of all tyrannies."[207] Yet, this view of oppressive power is precisely what one finds in v. 23, where the beast is said to be "devouring," "trampling," and "breaking."

7:26-27. In the end, the holy ones will rule in God's everlasting kingdom, and all nations will serve and obey them. The final sense of a rule of the holy ones echoes some of the reversal of fortune motif that is found not only throughout the book of Daniel to this point, but also in such important passages as Isa 19:16-25. Thus to the holy ones will be given "kingship," "dominion," "the greatness of the kingdoms." However, one should not be too quick to assume that this is

205. Lacocque, *The Book of Daniel*, 131; Collins, *Daniel*, Hermeneia, 314-15. They are opposed, among others, by V. S. Poythress, "The Holy Ones of the Most High in Daniel VII," *VT* 26 (1976) 208-13.

206. Note the use of the same term "crush" in the eschatological fragment 4Q246, Col 2, Line 3, "shooting stars who crush people, and nation (will crush) nation." See R. Eisenman and M. Wise, *The Dead Sea Scrolls Uncovered* (Shaftsbury: Element, 1992) 68-70.

207. N. Porteous, *Daniel*, OTL (Philadelphia: Westminster, 1965) 113.

merely a reversal of fortune motif that presumes that the former slaves will be the masters of the rest of the world. While it is true that some biblical passages have a more vengeful tone (including Daniel 2 and 6), it is also true that in other passages the rule of the holy ones, or God's final rule, will be one of peace and worldwide healing. Isaiah speaks of Assyrians and Egyptians worshiping together (Isa 19:23-25) and then sharing equally with the Israelites in the blessings of God (Isaiah 2; Zech 9:10, where dominion from sea to sea means that God will "command peace to the nations" [NRSV]).

7:28. Finally, Daniel remains alarmed and concerned about what he has seen. His reaction is interesting, given the somewhat positive nature of what he has seen. Are we to presume that the experience of seeing such a vision of holiness and power itself, though positive, gives rise to fearful awe? That such a vision would be, at the very least, exhausting is hardly surprising.

REFLECTIONS

It is easy for scholars, who are used to categorizing apocalyptic texts according to such characteristics as visions, dreams, and otherworldly visits to overlook the significance of the vision/dream as a medium of communication for the subordinated people of Palestine in the Hellenistic period. It was a powerful medium of communication that encouraged the people by drawing on a reservoir of possibilities beyond current realities. It is the nature of faith to look beyond the powers of this world to ask not only about the meaning of these powers, but also about their ultimate reality. Dreams are the beginning of the release from oppression. Dreams are images of what could be, what may be, and, most dramatically, what will be!

In a widely read and influential study of biblical apocalyptic literature, Paul Hanson articulated a view of biblical apocalyptic that represents it as the literature of those who suffered so severely that they began to lose their moorings in reality. Apocalyptic is disengaged from the realities of this world, as the earlier prophets were not. In such a view, dreams and visions are signs of sociopsychological breakdown, and thus apocalyptic is the literature of desperation: "When separated from the realism, the vision leads to a retreat into the world of ecstasy and dreams and to an abdication of the social responsibility of translating the vision of the divine order into the realm of everyday earthly concerns."[208]

Apocalyptic, according to such a view, is often a "flight into the timeless repose of myth."[209] One only hopes that God will miraculously, and irrationally, intervene to halt the suffering and the horror. Perhaps apocalyptic, then, is passive, waiting, and resigned, thus allowing the oppression to continue. It is a small step to see apocalyptic as a slave religion, what Karl Marx described as an opiate to salve the wounds of political dominance rather than actually engaging in resistance or other action to change matters. But in Marx himself we see the beginnings of the great flaw in this assessment of apocalypticism. Marx, after all, propounded a view of revolution that was supposedly scientific, and thus inevitable. There would inevitably be a struggle between the workers and the owners of the means of production—the great class war. However, this inevitability hardly resulted in the workers of the world sitting back and desperately waiting for scientific certainties to come to pass. Yet, can anyone now dispute the fact that Marx's descriptions of a stateless society were as "timeless a flight into myth" as was Daniel 7–12? I would argue that apocalyptic consciousness, like Marx's scientific inevitabilities, need not result in a resigned invitation for God to intervene unilaterally in reality.

Fanon speaks of the "updating" of national myths and legends in the process of resistance to the colonizer by bringing "conflicts up to date and modernizing the kinds of struggle which

208. P. Hanson, *The Dawn of Apocalyptic* (Minneapolis: Fortress, 1986) 30.
209. Ibid., 134.

the stories evoke, together with the names of heroes and the types of weapons."[210] Such is the power, for example, of rethinking the appearance of the angel Michael in the social circumstances of the book of Daniel.

As a result of the westward movement of European American settlers, Native American societies experienced horrible convulsions of change, violence, deportation, unknown disease, and desperation. In such circumstances and across tribal lines many prophet-like figures arose who delivered messages based on visions. One thinks of the famous Ghost Dance religion across many tribal lines, or the Handsome Lake religion among the Seneca/Iroquois, or the Indian Shaker church from northwest Indian John Slocum's visions. In many cases, these visions imagined the intervention of supernatural forces to drive away the European settlers and restore the old ways of tribal life. The results of these visions were varied—sometimes revolutionary violence (the Ghost Dance alone was expressed in various ways among different Native American nations), sometimes a new cultural adjustment in tribal traditions that allowed the people to survive and flourish even under grim circumstances. But the result was not passivity or withdrawal—the result of the vision was a new approach to reality, a new opening of a way forward for the people.

Native American philosopher Vine Deloria writes of this function of reasserting traditions and visions:

> We might therefore expect American Indians to discern out of the chaos of their shattered lives, the same kind of message and mission that inspired the Hebrew prophets. Indians would, in this situation, begin to develop a new interpretation of their religious tradition with a universal application. They would further begin to seek out areas in which they could communicate with sympathetic people in larger society, and put their own house in order. A process of intense commitment to certain social goals might then emerge in which the traditional values of pre-contact days would be seen as religious principles having a universal application. Most important, Indians would begin to probe deeper into their own past and view their remembered history as a primordial covenant.[211]

Such transformation of apocalyptic into action can also be illustrated in the Radical Reformation traditions (esp. Quakers and Mennonites), which have deep roots in European apocalyptic traditions. Many of the early Quakers were involved with a revolutionary group supporting Oliver Cromwell's seventeenth-century English new model army, a group that called itself The Fifth Monarchy Men. The Fifth Monarchists derived their name directly from Daniel 2 and 7, and they believed that in removing Charles I and asserting the power of parliament controlled by the faithful, they were bringing about the coming rule of "holy ones": the fifth empire of the "one like a son of man." Their reading of the Bible's apocalyptic visions hardly engendered passivity; yet the books of Daniel and Revelation were read with a consuming passion and were debated with great zeal around the campfires of the Roundhead forces who faced the royalist armies. Vavasor Powell (1617–1670), a Fifth Monarchist leader, noted Dan 4:17 (similar to chap. 7) in reference to the lower classes ruling instead of the monarchy. Another Fifth Monarchist sermon, commenting on the assassinations of France's Henri III and Henri IV, noted that "such princes might read their destiny in . . . Daniel 11:20."[212]

The struggle for peace and justice that is traditional in Mennonite and Quaker traditions draws part of its fire from a visionary openness to what may be possible, even if modern representatives of these traditions are embarrassed in polite theological company by their historical roots in such apocalyptic events as Thomas Müntzer's rebellion or George Fox's dreams and visions. Frank Borchardt makes the interesting observation that "there is no sense

210. F. Fanon, *The Wretched of the Earth* (New York: Grove, 1963) 240.
211. V. Deloria, Jr., "Out of Chaos," *Parabola* 10 (1985) 3-11.
212. C. Hill, *The English Bible and the Seventeenth-Century Revolution,* 76, 96.

in mocking Doomsday speculation for its countless failures to predict the end of the world accurately. The system does not continue to seize the minds of great numbers of people on account of its failures. It must succeed somewhere. It must conform to experience sufficiently to survive as a system, indeed to flourish. *It does so in its evaluation of the present.*"[213]

Historians and sociologists, such as Norman Cohn[214] and Guenther Lewy,[215] frequently point to the violent destructiveness engendered by such visions (ignoring, however, that violence is not inevitably a result), and therefore attempt to point out the great danger in tolerating, much less encouraging, such forms of antinomian religious expressions. It remains for historians following the lead of Christopher Hill to maintain a persistent reminder that such treasured values as full democracy, equality of women, economic justice and opportunity, self-determination, and freedom of religion and speech often find their most stalwart, consistent, and self-sacrificing proponents among these apocalyptic visionaries. In short, history itself witnesses that suggestions of passivity or withdrawal from society in biblical apocalyptic are hardly inevitable or unbiased conclusions, or even sociologically compelling. The dreamers of apocalyptic visions can be visionaries of a new order of equality, democracy, or world peace.

Visionary religion has always been dangerous and uncontrolled for any institutional status quo. Visionary religion draws deep from the hopes and passions of people, especially in dire and despairing conditions. Visionary religion speaks to the failure of established attitudes and traditions, and it opens the way to new possibilities. It accomplishes this by prying open the sealed doors of tradition and imagining possibilities beyond the realities dictated by world powers. Apocalyptic visions can lead to hope—and hopes have the potential of giving birth to *plans.* For Christians, to live with a constant sense of the advent of Christ is not an irresponsible disengagement from the world but a life-style *within* the world that is built on the vision of God's true kingship and dominion. It is to live as if the sentence on the beasts has already been carried out, despite the fact that their lives appear to be "prolonged for a season and a time."

213. F. Borchardt, *Doomsday Speculation as a Strategy of Persuasion: A Study of Apocalypticism as Rhetoric* (Atlanta: Mellon, 1987) 114, italics added.
214. N. Cohn, *The Pursuit of the Millennium* (New York: Oxford University Press, 1970).
215. G. Lewy, *Religion and Revolution* (New York: Oxford University Press, 1974).

DANIEL 8:1-27, THE RAM AND THE GOAT

NIV	NRSV
8 In the third year of King Belshazzar's reign, I, Daniel, had a vision, after the one that had already appeared to me. ²In my vision I saw myself in the citadel of Susa in the province of Elam; in the vision I was beside the Ulai Canal. ³I looked up, and there before me was a ram with two horns, standing beside the canal, and the horns were long. One of the horns was longer than the other but grew up later. ⁴I watched the ram as he charged toward the west and the north and the south. No animal could stand against him, and none could rescue from his power. He did as he pleased and became great.	**8** In the third year of the reign of King Belshazzar a vision appeared to me, Daniel, after the one that had appeared to me at first. ²In the vision I was looking and saw myself in Susa the capital, in the province of Elam,[a] and I was by the river Ulai.[b] ³I looked up and saw a ram standing beside the river.[c] It had two horns. Both horns were long, but one was longer than the other, and the longer one came up second. ⁴I saw the ram charging westward and northward and southward. All beasts were powerless to with-

a Gk Theodotion: MT Q Ms repeat *in the vision I was looking*
b Or *the Ulai Gate*   *c* Or *gate*

NIV

[5]As I was thinking about this, suddenly a goat with a prominent horn between his eyes came from the west, crossing the whole earth without touching the ground. [6]He came toward the two-horned ram I had seen standing beside the canal and charged at him in great rage. [7]I saw him attack the ram furiously, striking the ram and shattering his two horns. The ram was powerless to stand against him; the goat knocked him to the ground and trampled on him, and none could rescue the ram from his power. [8]The goat became very great, but at the height of his power his large horn was broken off, and in its place four prominent horns grew up toward the four winds of heaven.

[9]Out of one of them came another horn, which started small but grew in power to the south and to the east and toward the Beautiful Land. [10]It grew until it reached the host of the heavens, and it threw some of the starry host down to the earth and trampled on them. [11]It set itself up to be as great as the Prince of the host; it took away the daily sacrifice from him, and the place of his sanctuary was brought low. [12]Because of rebellion, the host ⌊of the saints⌋[a] and the daily sacrifice were given over to it. It prospered in everything it did, and truth was thrown to the ground.

[13]Then I heard a holy one speaking, and another holy one said to him, "How long will it take for the vision to be fulfilled—the vision concerning the daily sacrifice, the rebellion that causes desolation, and the surrender of the sanctuary and of the host that will be trampled underfoot?"

[14]He said to me, "It will take 2,300 evenings and mornings; then the sanctuary will be reconsecrated."

[15]While I, Daniel, was watching the vision and trying to understand it, there before me stood one who looked like a man. [16]And I heard a man's voice from the Ulai calling, "Gabriel, tell this man the meaning of the vision."

[17]As he came near the place where I was standing, I was terrified and fell prostrate. "Son of man," he said to me, "understand that the vision concerns the time of the end."

[18]While he was speaking to me, I was in a deep

[a]12 Or rebellion, the armies

NRSV

stand it, and no one could rescue from its power; it did as it pleased and became strong.

[5]As I was watching, a male goat appeared from the west, coming across the face of the whole earth without touching the ground. The goat had a horn[a] between its eyes. [6]It came toward the ram with the two horns that I had seen standing beside the river,[b] and it ran at it with savage force. [7]I saw it approaching the ram. It was enraged against it and struck the ram, breaking its two horns. The ram did not have power to withstand it; it threw the ram down to the ground and trampled upon it, and there was no one who could rescue the ram from its power. [8]Then the male goat grew exceedingly great; but at the height of its power, the great horn was broken, and in its place there came up four prominent horns toward the four winds of heaven.

[9]Out of one of them came another[c] horn, a little one, which grew exceedingly great toward the south, toward the east, and toward the beautiful land. [10]It grew as high as the host of heaven. It threw down to the earth some of the host and some of the stars, and trampled on them. [11]Even against the prince of the host it acted arrogantly; it took the regular burnt offering away from him and overthrew the place of his sanctuary. [12]Because of wickedness, the host was given over to it together with the regular burnt offering;[d] it cast truth to the ground, and kept prospering in what it did. [13]Then I heard a holy one speaking, and another holy one said to the one that spoke, "For how long is this vision concerning the regular burnt offering, the transgression that makes desolate, and the giving over of the sanctuary and host to be trampled?"[d] [14]And he answered him,[e] "For two thousand three hundred evenings and mornings; then the sanctuary shall be restored to its rightful state."

[15]When I, Daniel, had seen the vision, I tried to understand it. Then someone appeared standing before me, having the appearance of a man, [16]and I heard a human voice by the Ulai, calling, "Gabriel, help this man understand the vision." [17]So he came near where I stood; and when he came, I became frightened and fell prostrate. But

[a] Theodotion: Gk one horn; Heb a horn of vision   [b] Or gate
[c] Cn Compare 7.8: Heb one   [d] Meaning of Heb uncertain
[e] Gk Theodotion Syr Vg: Heb me

NIV

sleep, with my face to the ground. Then he touched me and raised me to my feet.

[19]He said: "I am going to tell you what will happen later in the time of wrath, because the vision concerns the appointed time of the end.[a] [20]The two-horned ram that you saw represents the kings of Media and Persia. [21]The shaggy goat is the king of Greece, and the large horn between his eyes is the first king. [22]The four horns that replaced the one that was broken off represent four kingdoms that will emerge from his nation but will not have the same power.

[23]"In the latter part of their reign, when rebels have become completely wicked, a stern-faced king, a master of intrigue, will arise. [24]He will become very strong, but not by his own power. He will cause astounding devastation and will succeed in whatever he does. He will destroy the mighty men and the holy people. [25]He will cause deceit to prosper, and he will consider himself superior. When they feel secure, he will destroy many and take his stand against the Prince of princes. Yet he will be destroyed, but not by human power.

[26]"The vision of the evenings and mornings that has been given you is true, but seal up the vision, for it concerns the distant future."

[27]I, Daniel, was exhausted and lay ill for several days. Then I got up and went about the king's business. I was appalled by the vision; it was beyond understanding.

[a]19 Or *because the end will be at the appointed time*

NRSV

he said to me, "Understand, O mortal,[a] that the vision is for the time of the end."

18As he was speaking to me, I fell into a trance, face to the ground; then he touched me and set me on my feet. [19]He said, "Listen, and I will tell you what will take place later in the period of wrath; for it refers to the appointed time of the end. [20]As for the ram that you saw with the two horns, these are the kings of Media and Persia. [21]The male goat[b] is the king of Greece, and the great horn between its eyes is the first king. [22]As for the horn that was broken, in place of which four others arose, four kingdoms shall arise from his[c] nation, but not with his power.

[23] At the end of their rule,
    when the transgressions have reached their
        full measure,
a king of bold countenance shall arise,
    skilled in intrigue.
[24] He shall grow strong in power,[d]
    shall cause fearful destruction,
    and shall succeed in what he does.
He shall destroy the powerful
    and the people of the holy ones.
[25] By his cunning
    he shall make deceit prosper under his hand,
    and in his own mind he shall be great.
Without warning he shall destroy many
    and shall even rise up against the Prince of
        princes.
But he shall be broken, and not by human
    hands.

[26]The vision of the evenings and the mornings that has been told is true. As for you, seal up the vision, for it refers to many days from now."

27So I, Daniel, was overcome and lay sick for some days; then I arose and went about the king's business. But I was dismayed by the vision and did not understand it.

[a] Heb *son of man*   [b] Or *shaggy male goat*   [c] Gk Theodotion Vg: Heb *the*   [d] Theodotion and one Gk Ms: Heb repeats (from 8.22) *but not with his power*

COMMENTARY

With chapter 8 the book of Daniel returns to the Hebrew language. With the change of lan-

guage comes another set of observations that scholars have noted, such as the fact that from chap. 8 to chap. 12 we have visions, and not dreams. Some have suggested that chaps. 8–12 were added to the Aramaic original (chaps. 2–7) at a much later time. However this may be, it is important to note that chap. 8 has many parallels to chap. 7 as well as occasional references to chaps. 1–6. Porteous, for one, wonders whether one important difference is that chap. 7 was based on a genuine ecstatic vision, while chap. 8 (and the following chapters, for that matter) seem much more contrived and planned.[216] Goldingay, however, notes that there are considerably more scriptural allusions in chap. 8 than in chap. 7, and he suggests that the visionary style "adds mystery" to the discussion in chap. 8 and those following.[217] What is certainly clear is that the visions of chaps. 8–12 are much more transparent in their presentation of contemporary events, as will be clear in the commentary that follows on these chapters.

8:1-2, The Setting of Belshazzar's Reign and Daniel's Transportation to Susa. The editor is interested in relating this vision to the events during the reign of Belshazzar. He is a transitional figure, as seen from the fact that v. 2 moves to Susa, the capital of Persia, in the province of Elam, beside the River Ulai. Most commentators note a resemblance to the visions of transportation experienced by Ezekiel, and reckon that this is a vision of Daniel's being transported to the great city ("walled/fortified city") of the Persian Empire. Elam is modern Khuzistan, and the Ulai is a canal that is mentioned in extra-biblical sources. Except for the notion that Daniel is "carried" from the kingdom of the Babylonians to that of the Persians in his dream, there seems little significance to the specific location of the vision.

Furthermore, there may be significance to the note about Daniel's standing "by the river Ulai" (some commentators assume the Hebrew to actually read "the Ulai gate" here, but on analogies presented below, "river" seems best; "Ulai" [אולי 'ûlāy] is literally "perhaps"). It is interesting to note how often a visionary stands on a riverbank in the setting for a vision. Ezra gathers exiles "by the river Ahava" (Ezra 8:15, 21; called "Thera" in 1 Esdr 8:14); Ezekiel experiences his first vision "by the River Chebar" (Ezek 1:1), where he was with other exiles; and Pharaoh's dream takes place on the banks of the Nile (Gen 41:1). This is perhaps only to be attributed to the fact that riverbanks (or canals) are logical locations for settlements, or perhaps for geographical locations to be mentioned in a text, but the frequency of the use of such settings is worthy of note, particularly in the visionary section of Daniel (see chap. 12). Was there a diaspora tradition of gathering on a riverbank for certain ceremonies or services of penitence/remembrance? Or were canals a frequent setting because they were places of labor for the exiles? After all, canals in Mesopotamia—the agricultural lifeblood of the people—required massive human effort to maintain them so that they would not silt up and become blocked.[218] But such speculation ought not to go too far.

8:3-8, The Vision of the Ram and the Goat. The source of the images for this vision is debated among scholars. For example, art historians have noted that the Persians used the ram motif in architecture, as decorations on columns, for instance. In ancient astrological speculation (a form of wisdom that was of obvious interest to some of the Jewish apocalyptic writers as much as to the ancient Greeks, Persians, and Egyptians, etc.), the ram is the symbol of Aries, the sign under which the Persians were located, and Capricorn the goat is Syria (thus the Seleucid inheritors of their section of Alexander's empire). Collins, however, objects to this source for the images, noting that the events described in the vision refer to Alexander's empire *before* the battles of Issus in 333 BCE and Ipsus in 301 BCE, when the four generals took charge of the former united Hellenistic Empire were confirmed: Ptolemy (Egypt); Seleucus (Babylon/Syria); Lysimachus (Asia Minor); and Cassander (Macedonia-Greece).[219] In short, the ram must be Persia and the goat the Hellenistic Empire, united still under Alexander, who is the single "great horn" (v. 8). Whatever the source, a further curiosity is the move in this vision from wild beasts to apparently tamer beasts, even domestic livestock (goats certainly), which are depicted in battle.

216. N. Porteous, *Daniel*, OTL (Philadelphia: Westminster, 1965) 119.
217. John Goldingay, *Daniel*, WBC 30 (Dallas: Word, 1988) 201-2.
218. D. Smith, *The Religion of the Landless* (New York: Meyer-Stone, 1989) 116-20.
219. John J. Collins, *Daniel*, Hermeneia (Minneapolis: Fortress, 1993) 330.

The second horn of the ram is undoubtedly Cyrus, who defeated the Medes (the other horn). The ram struck in three directions, but most manuscripts omit the mention of east. Is this because the Persian Empire *was* the east as far as biblical writers were concerned? Was it because the Persians' eastern campaigns (into northern India) were of little interest to the biblical writers? Collins points out that east is included in two important early sources, Papyri 967 and a Dead Sea Scroll fragment,[220] and therefore should be reestablished in this passage to complete the balance of the "four corners" of the earth—a standard ancient manner of speaking of all the world.

It was stated that all beasts were powerless, beasts here representing nations, as noted in the Commentary on chapter 7. The interesting phrase that this verse uses for political and military power, that the ruler "does as he pleases," is a stock phrase found in both the Hebrew and the Aramaic sections of Daniel and is used to refer to rulers' having power to act of their will. Note its use in late biblical texts in reference to the emperors in Esth 1:8; 9:5; Dan 11:3, 16, 36; and Neh 9:24, 37. The phrase further seems to paint a picture of the arbitrary whim of political power from the perspective of the subordinated minorities and controlled populations.

The goat comes from the west with one "horn of vision" or "horn between its eyes" (v. 5). The goat symbolizes the Macedonian Greek juggernaut, with its great horn: Alexander the Great. The use of horns to symbolize rulers (see Commentary on chap. 7) is not uncommon outside the book of Daniel as well (Ps 132:17; Jer 48:25; Mic 4:13). The horn of a wild beast is its destructive power (and with these particular animals, the only real weapon). The fact that this goat moved without touching the ground, combined with references to these animals' having wings in chap. 7, serves to suggest the speed with which the Greek war machine moved.

It is interesting that Daniel would emphasize the "bitterness" of the battle—an Eastern diaspora perspective on battles that have passed into Western history as the great formative battles of the Greeks against the Persians. The Greek victories over the forces of the Eastern world in the ancient Near East would have permanent impact on the development of both Near Eastern and western European civilizations, and the classical Greek writers would provide symbols and themes of warfare for European nations that attempted to create empires in the nineteenth and twentieth centuries. Green notes with irony that the supposed "civilizing and missionary aspect" of the Greek conquests has been "greatly exaggerated, not least by modern historians anxious to find some moral justification for aggressive imperialism."[221] But there is no admiration for the bravery or *esprit de corps* of conquest in Hebrew Scriptures—no celebration of military culture, pride, and bravado—only the humble recognition that God, and not their own power, delivered them. Daniel's visions present the cold facts of empire: destruction and bitterness. The image of trampling the enemy is used throughout the Hebrew Bible as a powerful expression of overwhelming military conquest and defeat, almost suggesting the impunity of Cyrus (Isa 41:25; see also Mic 7:8, where a lion tramples its enemies, but note 2 Kgs 9:33 for the death of Jezebel; Isa 1:12 for the trampling of courts; and Ezek 34:17-22 for the images of goats and rams against the sheep of Israel). The preferred metaphorical self-image of the Jewish nation is the lamb—others are the beasts of prey or destruction.

No one can rescue the ram (v. 7), as no one could rescue anyone *from* the ram in v. 4. Great events are going on under the visionary eye of Daniel—or over the heads of the exiles, for whom sitting and watching was the only viable option. One thinks of ordinary people throughout the Third World, for whom warfare, politics, and government are matters of different-colored jets fighting overhead and land mines to watch out for while harvesting their crops.

The kingdom of Alexander is divided among his four generals after he is "broken" (v. 8). The use of the phrase "toward the four winds of heaven" probably suggests the helter-skelter notion of the pieces of the empire flying in different directions; but it may foreshadow another battle, keeping the imagery of 7:2, between the horns and the weapons of God. It is interesting that all the successor generals, then, are seen as antago-

220. Ibid., 329-30.

221. P. Green, "Greek Gifts?" *History Today* (June 1990) 27.

112

nistic to God. This would have interesting implications for understanding Jewish attitudes to life under the Ptolemies even before the Seleucid nightmare began. All of this initial vision of the ram and goat is background to what follows, and the focus of interest is on Antiochus IV Epiphanes.

8:9-14, Earthly and Spiritual Battle with Antiochus IV Epiphanes. 8:9. Another horn/leader grows toward the south and the east and toward "the beautiful land." The Hebrew term (צבי *ṣĕbî*) can also be translated as "gazelle," standard iconography in modern Israel to represent the land. "Zvi" may refer to Zion and Jerusalem more specifically in Jer 3:19; Ezek 20:6, 15; Dan 11:16, 41; and *1 Enoch* 89:40.

8:10-11. In v. 10, the horn grows toward and does battle with "the host of heaven" or "the armies" of heaven. Here is an interesting association of the host/armies of heaven and stars, and this has resulted in yet another debate in modern scholarship on Daniel and the metaphorical imagery of the book. The belief that stars were actual beings is suggested in a variety of places in the Bible, usually associated with Canaanite/pagan belief (see 2 Kgs 23:5; Jer 19:13; Zeph 1:5). Isaiah 24:21 animates stars, and Isa 5:9-11 uses Canaanite images such as the battle between God and the sea. (For stars personified and doing battle, see Judg 5:20 and Pr Azar 1:41; see also Commentary on the Additions to Daniel.) The most commonly cited instance of the use of star imagery is Isaiah 14, an important discussion of God's warfare against Babylon, which includes the depiction of Babylon as a fallen star who attempts to raise his throne above the "stars of God." The importance here is the fact that celestial imagery is used for God's dealings with foreign nations. Goldingay notes that in 169 BCE, Antiochus had coins minted that pictured a star over his head.[222] Collins also points to the Canaanite myth of the morning star 'Attar doing battle against Baal[223] as a possible source for star imagery. The intention, clearly, is to focus on the battles as cosmic and not merely worldly.

Irrespective of the specific celestial images involved, the notion of spiritual warfare between the powers of the world and the hosts of heaven is implicit in this chapter and will carry on throughout Daniel's visions. Note that "trampling" (רמס *rāmas*) is one of the verbs used to describe conquest. The identity of "the prince of the host" who is challenged (v. 11) is certainly open to question. Porteous believes that it must be God.[224] The military associations of the term suggest an association with the angelic warrior Michael, the one like a son of man "coming with the clouds of heaven" (7:13 NRSV), who will be reintroduced as a prince in chaps. 11-12. In v. 11, however, the Temple offerings and the sanctuary are associated with this prince, creating problems for an easy identification with Michael. Thus most commentators suggest that the "prince of the host" in v. 11 can only refer to God. The "regular burnt offering" refers to the daily sacrifices discussed, and mandated, in the Mosaic laws (Exod 29:38-42; Numbers 28-29) and mentioned in Ezra 3:5; Neh 10:34; and Ezek 46:1-5.

It is important to remember that this interest in the temple cult must be seen in the context of the exile, in which priestly leadership became the dominant form of Jewish leadership, stepping into the vacuum left by the removal of the kingship. This interest is clearly seen in the development of the high priest figure in the visions of Zechariah—Joshua the priest standing equal to the Davidic Zerubbabel—and Ezra the priest, who is intentionally contrasted with Nehemiah, the royal military leader.[225]

In short, spiritual warfare on earth is an attack on the ritual observances of the people, e.g., the offering and the temple sanctuary, which represent their unique life and identity in the absence of other, more secular symbols of royalty and administration. One is hard pressed to suggest alternative realities among the Jewish people that are open to attack by foreign authorities other than the Temple and its observances. If Michael, as the angelic prince of the Israelite people, is being attacked on earth, what else can this battle involve but the Temple as the symbol of the

---

222. Goldingay, *Daniel,* 210.
223. Collins, *Daniel,* Hermeneia, 332.

224. Porteous, *Daniel,* 125. Collins and Goldingay concur, the latter noting that this assigns too much authority to Michael, even though Gen 21:22 and 1 Sam 12:9 have a similar title for an army general. Lacocque, on the other hand, following his strong association of Daniel's vision with the Jerusalem Temple, believes that the specific term שר (*śar*) can also be used for priests in 1 Chr 24:5 or Ezra 8:24. The term is somewhat generic, however, and must be weighted according to the accompanying clarification. Its usual association is military, supporting a stronger association with Michael.
225. This is discussed in T. Eskenazi, *In a Time of Prose* (Atlanta: Scholars Press, 1988).

people? Furthermore, in vv. 13-14, the trampling includes both the sanctuary and the "hosts," suggesting a possible identification with or close association between the priesthood of the sanctuary and the hosts of heaven.

8:12. This verse suggests the partial victory of Antiochus IV against the hosts of heaven and, by implication, against those earthly Jews who are associated spiritually with the hosts of heaven. This temporary setback in the spiritual battle is referred to elsewhere as well (7:25). It can hardly be otherwise, since the original hearers of these visions would have known that their present situation looked grim. The precise translation of this verse has vexed scholars for some time. Collins suggests the reading, "A host was given over together with the daily offering, in the course of transgression. It cast truth to the ground and it acted successfully."[226] The difficulties of a precise translation (and whether changes must be made in the Hebrew), however, do not make substantial changes in how this verse is understood.

8:13. The author now summarizes one of the main points of this entire chapter: "How long?" Porteous compares this agonized question to the initial chapter of Zechariah,[227] and Collins notes that this question is a regular feature of penitential literature in the Bible and even in ancient Near Eastern literature more generally.[228] The interesting concept in v. 13 is the "abomination that makes desolate" (NIV, "rebellion that causes desolation"; NRSV, "transgression that makes desolate"). Most scholars now accept the notion that this phrase in Hebrew is a play on the title "Baal Shamem—'Lord of Heaven'—who was identified with 'Olympian Zeus,' "[229] and thus is associated with an image that Antiochus IV is said to have erected within the Temple in Jerusalem, rebuilding the altar (and thus defiling it) in order to offer sacrifice to this god (see 1 Macc 4:38-39).

8:14. The answer to the question of how long is answered. That it is answered is perhaps more important than the answer. The *raison d'être* of apocalyptic literature is that it attempts to answer the agonized question, "How long?" and thus

begins to offer comfort to those suffering under the heels of an oppressive and tyrannical regime (see Reflections). Despite this key element, the number of "evenings and mornings" left of their suffering is interesting. It is assumed that the 2,300 evenings and mornings refer to the daily sacrifices (twice a day) and thus would be 1,150 days. This is short of the three and a half years between 167 and 164 BCE, the time from the desecration of the Temple to its rededication, but Collins wonders whether it is shorter precisely because the vision comes after the desecration, and thus time had already begun to pass.[230] Goldingay, on the other hand, suggests that no specific length of time was intended, and perhaps we are to understand simply a "fixed, significant period."[231] This is closer to the perspective of this commentary, which points to the limitation to suffering that a number (any number) would imply.

8:15-17, Gabriel Appears to Daniel.
8:15-16. There is a break here, as Daniel tries to understand what he has seen (note also the continued mention of the River Ulai as the location for this visionary experience). Whatever literary function these breaks perform (usually a change of scene or subject) they occur regularly in Daniel. Note the break between the actual events of Nebuchadnezzar's dream in chap. 2 and the interpretation, as well as the break in the vision in 7:15-16. With the break in v. 15, the scene shifts to a vision of "someone" with the "appearance of a man." This is another angelic figure who will introduce Daniel to Gabriel. Here we have the first occasion in the Bible in which an angelic figure is named; later, the reader will encounter Michael again, who was unnamed in the earlier material.

8:17. Daniel falls to the ground before the vision of Gabriel. Note that Daniel takes this extreme action only before the representatives of God. Daniel will say the obligatory "O king, live forever," but there is no mention that he ever bowed or was subservient "before the king" in earlier chapters. Daniel's actions might also be a physical reaction to the apparition itself, as if Daniel is simply overcome.

Daniel is told that his vision is for "the time of

226. Collins, *Daniel,* Hermeneia, 326.
227. Porteous, *Daniel,* 126.
228. Collins, *Daniel,* Hermeneia, 334-35.
229. Goldingay, *Daniel,* 212.

230. Collins, *Daniel,* Hermeneia, 336.
231. Goldingay, *Daniel,* 213.

the end." This is an important theme in these visions. Apocalyptic derives its power from the fact that both the writer and the reader believe that they are, in fact, living in the end time. "The time of the end," for them, begins now. Apocalyptic writing, it must be remembered, remains a popular literature precisely because of the frequently recurring sense in history that "ours *must be* the last age."

8:18-22, Gabriel Begins to Interpret the Vision. 8:18. The impact of these experiences on Daniel is once again mentioned. The NIV renders the Hebrew more accurately as "deep sleep" (רדם *rādam*; the same term is used for the sleep imposed on Adam in Gen 2:21 before the divine surgery to make Eve), rather than the NRSV's "trance," providing us with interesting details about physiological effect of visionary experiences for the ancient writer. Such visions are clearly exhausting, and the visionary often requires assistance and strengthening by the angelic figure or the one to whom he is speaking.

Furthermore, the weakness of the people is an important theme, and the visionary experiences strengthen them in their struggle to maintain faith and identity in the face of defeat and subordination. Gabriel's response is to touch Daniel and raise him to his feet. Lacocque, interestingly, notes the importance of the theme of the healing touch of the heavenly one, or even of an authority figure (see Ezra 1:1, 5; Isa 6:7; Jer 1:9; Dan 9:21; 10:10, 16, 18; 4 Esdr 5:4; *1 Enoch*; Rev 1:17; it is used often in the Gospels as the touch of Jesus).[232]

8:19. The "period of wrath/indignation" is reminiscent of the notion of the "wrath of God" as judgment (Pss 38:3; 69:24; 102:10; Isa 10:5, 25; 26:20). This day of anger is also a day of judgment, and eventually salvation (Isa 30:27; Ezek 22:31). However, this period of wrath is equated with the "period of the time of the end." The idea that the end is a span of time rather than a single point at which all things end is emphasized by many scholars. Collins notes that the term often used for "end" (אחרי *'aḥărê*) was used by the writers of the Dead Sea Scroll materials to signify a span of years.[233] Goldingay, moreover, wants to detach the time of the end, the period of wrath, from the notion that it is the time of "God's punishment." The "wrath" here, in short, may be the furor of the foreign nations; thus the end would be the end of the tyranny of world empires.

232. André Lacocque, *The Book of Daniel,* trans. D. Pellauer (Atlanta: John Knox, 1979) 171.
233. Collins, *Daniel,* Hermeneia, 338.

❖　　❖　　❖　　❖

EXCURSUS: THE "PERIOD OF WRATH" AND MODERN THEOLOGY

Commentaries on the book of Daniel frequently lapse into decidedly modern theological issues when interpreting the reference "the period of wrath." The issue is clear: Moderns wish to avoid the simplistic idea that ancient Jews always believed that their suffering was punishment from God. Thus many wish to read this "period of wrath" as the tyranny of foreign nations against the Jews. Although the sins and cruelty of the foreign nations are clearly what is discussed in 8:23, but there is strong biblical precedent for considering the exilic events as God's punishment and, therefore, for considering the suffering of the Jews in exile as a period of wrath. Indeed, that was at the root of the entire deuteronomic theology of exile, so a precedent for such thinking was clearly in the tradition. Deuteronomic theology involved the notion that "we brought this upon ourselves by rejecting God and God's prophets," rather than attributing power to the foreign gods and armies. There seems to be an element of this in Daniel's confession in chapter 9. The modern reader wishes to guard against the simplistic notion that horrible experiences are God's punishment—and even the biblical witness (especially in Deutero-Isaiah) pointed in more creative directions for interpreting the suffering of exile ("the refiner's fire," Jonah's message of exile as "preparation for our world mission," etc.). But in our caution to prevent a serious theological mistake of portraying God as an angry scorekeeper of sins, we must not overlook the fact that attributing the exile to God was at least one way for biblical writers to deny victory to foreign armies and gods. Early deuteronomic theologies of God's judgment did imply that it would be impious to resist those foreign rulers who carried out the judgment (e.g., Jeremiah 27–29).

One might see deuteronomic theology leading to a kind of fatalism—in other words, "Do not resist the conquerors, because that is your punishment." Such fatalism is totally foreign to Daniel. Even Jeremiah, after all, advised survival *and* resistance in his letter to exiles in Jeremiah 29, and Second Isaiah clearly amended deuteronomic theology by insisting that Jerusalem had "paid double" for its sins. The resistance shown in the Daniel tradition is clearly post-deuteronomic; yet it is informed by the deuteronomic tendency (seen especially in the editorial line of 1 Samuel 8) to lay particular blame on Israelite experiments with militant nationalism (what George Mendenhall called a return to Canaanite polity)[234] and kingship, so that new forms of social existence must be considered in the light of the previous failures. The political theology of Daniel, in short, learned from previous mistakes, while not necessarily denying that mistakes were made (see Commentary on Susanna 52).

Finally, it is surely a mistake to try to pretend—as moderns constantly try to do—that we live in a world in which mistakes do not have consequences, whether errors in personal choice, misguided national policies, or worldwide environmental negligence. Forgiveness, after all, does not always involve avoiding consequences.

234. See G. Mendenhall, *The Tenth Generation* (Baltimore: Johns Hopkins University Press, 1973).

❖   ❖   ❖   ❖

8:20-22. The interpretation of Daniel's vision is significant in that political realities are now explicitly identified. Daniel's interpretations of dreams in chaps. 2 and 5 were somewhat vague apart from the specific identification of Nebuchadnezzar, but in the visions of chaps. 8–12, there is no doubt about the identity of those involved. The ram with two horns is the eastern empire, uniting the Medes and the Persians under Cyrus, and the goat is the king of Greece, Alexander the Great. The four horns are the kingdoms that follow, the four regions of the divided Alexandrian empire.

8:23-25, Antiochus IV Rises and Falls.
8:23. This verse equals in intensity any judgment made against the powers of the nations throughout the book of Daniel. Their careers are "transgressions reaching a full measure." Porteous notes that God recognizes the pagan nations' tendency to overstep their authority as God's tools.[235] But one can be much bolder and state that Daniel portrays this transgression to be the very nature of world empires, and not merely a tendency.

From the midst of these four kingdoms will arise one who is "skilled in intrigue." This is undoubtedly a reference to Antiochus IV, who created internal division in the Palestinian Jewish community by aligning himself with certain factions of the people. This division is the reason why this figure is so often associated with intrigue and deceit. His attempts to propagandize the Jewish people by selectively choosing allies and rewarding them is an ancient form of a public relations campaign. One of the results of these policies was the breakup of the Jewish community into factions that remained active into the first century CE.

8:24. Antiochus will grow strong. The Hebrew inserts "but not with his power," which is omitted from English translations on the basis of Greek witnesses; it does not seem to add much here. In this verse, we see once again the notion that Antiochus IV will succeed for a time. The "powerful"/"mighty" that Antiochus destroys is typically taken to refer to the other claimants to the throne who are put out of the way by Antiochus IV.[236] But also in this verse, we have another

235. Porteous, *Daniel,* 128.

236. Collins, *Daniel,* Hermeneia, 340-41.

reference to a group of people/angels that causes some controversy. In the Aramaic section, a group was called the "holy ones," and this is often taken to mean celestial or angelic beings. The phrase in Hebrew is literally "people of the holy ones" (עם־קדשׁים *'am-qĕdōšîm*), and suggests actual persons in league with the angelic forces. However, if angels are intended here, this would be another build up to a confrontation with God, as noted in the vision itself.

8:25. The arrogance of this figure is also used often as a reference to Antiochus IV, and his arrogance builds to a desire to do battle with even the "Prince of princes." This is undoubtedly yet another reference to the angelic Michael, who is often referred to in this manner; but it certainly also could be a reference to God. The enigmatic expression "he shall be broken, and not by human hands" recalls God's action of finally destroying the world empires in Daniel 2 (the stone "not cut by human hand"). The image of the prince, then, seems to fit a battle against Michael, after which God intervenes, finally and thoroughly—from "offstage" as it were—breaking Antiochus IV without human hands. God is not often portrayed as taking active part in Daniel's visions, but is a presiding, commanding presence whose will is carried out by secondary figures. The angelic warriors act, and stones and other things move, but not God.

This lack of human agency in the defeat of Antiochus IV is taken by Collins to be a further reference to the largely nonviolent character of Daniel. "It is apparent from this verse that Daniel does not base his hopes on the success of the armed rebellion of the Maccabees."[237]

8:26-27, The Conclusion and Sealing. Because this vision is for the "end times," Daniel is instructed to seal the vision—that is, to keep it to himself (or to his group?). This aspect of sealing and secrecy is typically understood to be a reference to the fact that this material supposedly remained secret from the time of Daniel (i.e., the end of the Babylonian Empire) until the time of Antiochus IV. We should not presume, however, that this sealing implies that the writers and the readers of this material were, in the first case, a secret sect.[238]

Once again, the impact of the vision on Daniel is repeated, this time mentioning the mental impact it makes on Daniel. He goes about the king's business, knowing that the king's power has already been taken away—the die is cast. Daniel's response to the apocalyptic assurance of the end is not to radically alter his responsibilities, but to know that God is ultimately in control.

237. Ibid., 341. See the excursus on Daniel and nonviolence in chap. 11.

238. See Collins, *The Apocalyptic Vision of the Book of Daniel,* 210-18, who points to their very public responsibilities as teachers of wisdom in chaps. 10–12.

REFLECTIONS

Two major themes of Daniel 8 are worthy of reflection. The first is the use of metaphorical imagery to speak of political realities. The second is the notion of a limitation to the present reality.

1. *Imagery and Political Realities.* Rams and goats are spoken of in Daniel 8—animals that fight by knocking horned heads together. The names of rulers—although clearly alluded to—are not used. Instead, the reader is confronted with the simple reality of military-political entities. In today's conventions we use respectfully the names of generals and presidents as the chief actors of history, or we personify the enemy as one man, one woman, as if the destruction of warfare is aimed only at a single individual. But in the book of Daniel, the vision is concerned not with individuals but with the power realities—kingdoms and rulers who "do as they please." There is nothing to honor their imperial designs with respectability, and no cult of the hero. Tyrants and dictators portray themselves as benign paternal figures. Thus one will see an Iraqi dictator holding a child, a Soviet premier listening to the songs of young pioneers, a president playing with his dogs—all while their armies wreak havoc on the lives of other human beings around the world. The book of Daniel portrays world leaders in a different light: They are feuding animals. Berrigan writes: "There is no such thing as a purely earthbound war . . . war on earth is above all a spiritual reality. Whether in ancient Persia or in today's Persian Gulf, war is always and everywhere a demonic assault on God."[239]

The goat, not entirely coincidentally, is particularly ruthless. As this image of the Hellenists is often at odds with popular portrayals of the Greeks as one of the pillars of Western civilization, some comment on the goat is in order. Peter Green, in a short piece ironically entitled "Greek Gifts?" points out that Aristotle considered foreigners as "barbarians" hardly worthy of education. The Greek ideal was to cash in on conquests, not to spread civilization. Hellenistic treatment of Egyptians under the Ptolemies, for example, is recorded with frequent references to Egyptians who complain of mistreatment because of their race and nationality. Certainly, the Greeks influenced art and architecture wherever they went; but the peoples they conquered did not learn Greek culture in schools or by joining Greek societies. Indeed, Hellenism spread among two well-defined categories of persons: local aristocrats who were sent west to be educated, rather like the education of selected Indians in England during British imperial rule, and intelligent collaborators who comprised, at best, merely 2.5 percent of the ruling elite, compared to the otherwise imposing entirety of Greeks on foreign soil. These persons were hired as interpreters, tax collectors, accountants: "the prime motive in such cases was clearly, social and professional ambition."[240] It is interesting to note, then, that with either of these classes of people, one can hardly imagine a less compatible picture of "courtiers" than the ones presented in the early chapters of Daniel (but even here, recall, we are supposed to be reading about the visions of the courtier Daniel). Indeed, one wonders whether the Daniel tales were partly intended to satirize those Jews who served in the foreign militia, those who bowed to every statue and statute that was passed, no matter how compromising it may have been to Jewish faith and authenticity. In such a case, the Daniel stories were written about *ideal* Jewish courtiers in contrast to real ones.

2. *How Long?* Finally, there is the agonized question in chapter 8: "How long?" The second major theme of this chapter is that the time of wrath is limited and thus the people's suffering is limited as well. This is surely one of the most powerful appeals of apocalyptic literature and apocalyptic movements. Theologically, it is one of the most important messages of the book of Daniel for a modern world. It is the promise of the gospel that darkness will not last forever, that innocence will not be crushed forever, that justice will be had. Surely this is the most important function of "last judgment" scenes, such as the division of the sheep from the goats in Matthew 25 or most powerfully the Lazarus legend in Luke 16:19-31. Judgment scenes clearly are an important coexistent theme with reversal of fortune motifs in these materials.

239. D. Berrigan, "A Frightful Vision," *The Other Side* (September-October 1990) 37.
240. P. Green, "Greek Gifts?" *History Today* (June 1990) 29.

DANIEL 9:1-27, TEXTUAL INTERPRETATION AND ANGELIC REVOLUTION

NIV

9 In the first year of Darius son of Xerxes[a] (a Mede by descent), who was made ruler over the Babylonian[b] kingdom— ²in the first year

a1 Hebrew *Ahasuerus*   b1 Or *Chaldean*

NRSV

9 In the first year of Darius son of Ahasuerus, by birth a Mede, who became king over the realm of the Chaldeans— ²in the first year of his reign, I, Daniel, perceived in the books the number of years that, according to the word of

NIV

of his reign, I, Daniel, understood from the Scriptures, according to the word of the LORD given to Jeremiah the prophet, that the desolation of Jerusalem would last seventy years. ³So I turned to the Lord God and pleaded with him in prayer and petition, in fasting, and in sackcloth and ashes.

⁴I prayed to the LORD my God and confessed:

"O Lord, the great and awesome God, who keeps his covenant of love with all who love him and obey his commands, ⁵we have sinned and done wrong. We have been wicked and have rebelled; we have turned away from your commands and laws. ⁶We have not listened to your servants the prophets, who spoke in your name to our kings, our princes and our fathers, and to all the people of the land.

⁷"Lord, you are righteous, but this day we are covered with shame—the men of Judah and people of Jerusalem and all Israel, both near and far, in all the countries where you have scattered us because of our unfaithfulness to you. ⁸O LORD, we and our kings, our princes and our fathers are covered with shame because we have sinned against you. ⁹The Lord our God is merciful and forgiving, even though we have rebelled against him; ¹⁰we have not obeyed the LORD our God or kept the laws he gave us through his servants the prophets. ¹¹All Israel has transgressed your law and turned away, refusing to obey you.

"Therefore the curses and sworn judgments written in the Law of Moses, the servant of God, have been poured out on us, because we have sinned against you. ¹²You have fulfilled the words spoken against us and against our rulers by bringing upon us great disaster. Under the whole heaven nothing has ever been done like what has been done to Jerusalem. ¹³Just as it is written in the Law of Moses, all this disaster has come upon us, yet we have not sought the favor of the LORD our God by turning from our sins and giving attention to your truth. ¹⁴The LORD did not hesitate to bring the disaster upon us, for the LORD our God is righteous in everything he does; yet we have not obeyed him.

¹⁵"Now, O Lord our God, who brought your people out of Egypt with a mighty hand and who made for yourself a name that en-

NRSV

the LORD to the prophet Jeremiah, must be fulfilled for the devastation of Jerusalem, namely, seventy years.

3Then I turned to the Lord God, to seek an answer by prayer and supplication with fasting and sackcloth and ashes. ⁴I prayed to the LORD my God and made confession, saying,

"Ah, Lord, great and awesome God, keeping covenant and steadfast love with those who love you and keep your commandments, ⁵we have sinned and done wrong, acted wickedly and rebelled, turning aside from your commandments and ordinances. ⁶We have not listened to your servants the prophets, who spoke in your name to our kings, our princes, and our ancestors, and to all the people of the land.

7"Righteousness is on your side, O Lord, but open shame, as at this day, falls on us, the people of Judah, the inhabitants of Jerusalem, and all Israel, those who are near and those who are far away, in all the lands to which you have driven them, because of the treachery that they have committed against you. ⁸Open shame, O LORD, falls on us, our kings, our officials, and our ancestors, because we have sinned against you. ⁹To the Lord our God belong mercy and forgiveness, for we have rebelled against him, ¹⁰and have not obeyed the voice of the LORD our God by following his laws, which he set before us by his servants the prophets.

11"All Israel has transgressed your law and turned aside, refusing to obey your voice. So the curse and the oath written in the law of Moses, the servant of God, have been poured out upon us, because we have sinned against you. ¹²He has confirmed his words, which he spoke against us and against our rulers, by bringing upon us a calamity so great that what has been done against Jerusalem has never before been done under the whole heaven. ¹³Just as it is written in the law of Moses, all this calamity has come upon us. We did not entreat the favor of the LORD our God, turning from our iniquities and reflecting on his*ᵃ* fidelity. ¹⁴So the LORD kept watch over this calamity until he brought it upon us. Indeed, the LORD our God is right in all that he has done; for we have disobeyed his voice.

ᵃ Heb *your*

NIV

dures to this day, we have sinned, we have done wrong. [16]O Lord, in keeping with all your righteous acts, turn away your anger and your wrath from Jerusalem, your city, your holy hill. Our sins and the iniquities of our fathers have made Jerusalem and your people an object of scorn to all those around us.

[17]"Now, our God, hear the prayers and petitions of your servant. For your sake, O Lord, look with favor on your desolate sanctuary. [18]Give ear, O God, and hear; open your eyes and see the desolation of the city that bears your Name. We do not make requests of you because we are righteous, but because of your great mercy. [19]O Lord, listen! O Lord, forgive! O Lord, hear and act! For your sake, O my God, do not delay, because your city and your people bear your Name."

[20]While I was speaking and praying, confessing my sin and the sin of my people Israel and making my request to the LORD my God for his holy hill— [21]while I was still in prayer, Gabriel, the man I had seen in the earlier vision, came to me in swift flight about the time of the evening sacrifice. [22]He instructed me and said to me, "Daniel, I have now come to give you insight and understanding. [23]As soon as you began to pray, an answer was given, which I have come to tell you, for you are highly esteemed. Therefore, consider the message and understand the vision:

[24]"Seventy 'sevens'[a] are decreed for your people and your holy city to finish[b] transgression, to put an end to sin, to atone for wickedness, to bring in everlasting righteousness, to seal up vision and prophecy and to anoint the most holy.[c]

[25]"Know and understand this: From the issuing of the decree[d] to restore and rebuild Jerusalem until the Anointed One,[e] the ruler, comes, there will be seven 'sevens,' and sixty-two 'sevens.' It will be rebuilt with streets and a trench, but in times of trouble. [26]After the sixty-two 'sevens,' the Anointed One will be cut off and will have nothing.[f] The people of the ruler who will come will destroy the city and the sanctuary. The end will come like a flood: War will continue until the end, and desolations have been decreed. [27]He will confirm a covenant with many for one 'seven.'[g] In the middle of the 'seven'[g] he will put

a24 Or 'weeks'; also in verses 25 and 26   b24 Or restrain   c24 Or Most Holy Place; or most holy One   d25 Or word   e25 Or an anointed one; also in verse 26   f26 Or off and will have no one; or off, but not for himself   g27 Or 'week'

NRSV

[15]"And now, O Lord our God, who brought your people out of the land of Egypt with a mighty hand and made your name renowned even to this day—we have sinned, we have done wickedly. [16]O Lord, in view of all your righteous acts, let your anger and wrath, we pray, turn away from your city Jerusalem, your holy mountain; because of our sins and the iniquities of our ancestors, Jerusalem and your people have become a disgrace among all our neighbors. [17]Now therefore, O our God, listen to the prayer of your servant and to his supplication, and for your own sake, Lord,[a] let your face shine upon your desolated sanctuary. [18]Incline your ear, O my God, and hear. Open your eyes and look at our desolation and the city that bears your name. We do not present our supplication before you on the ground of our righteousness, but on the ground of your great mercies. [19]O Lord, hear; O Lord, forgive; O Lord, listen and act and do not delay! For your own sake, O my God, because your city and your people bear your name!"

[20]While I was speaking, and was praying and confessing my sin and the sin of my people Israel, and presenting my supplication before the LORD my God on behalf of the holy mountain of my God— [21]while I was speaking in prayer, the man Gabriel, whom I had seen before in a vision, came to me in swift flight at the time of the evening sacrifice. [22]He came[b] and said to me, "Daniel, I have now come out to give you wisdom and understanding. [23]At the beginning of your supplications a word went out, and I have come to declare it, for you are greatly beloved. So consider the word and understand the vision:

[24]"Seventy weeks are decreed for your people and your holy city: to finish the transgression, to put an end to sin, and to atone for iniquity, to bring in everlasting righteousness, to seal both vision and prophet, and to anoint a most holy place.[c] [25]Know therefore and understand: from the time that the word went out to restore and rebuild Jerusalem until the time of an anointed prince, there shall be seven weeks; and for sixty-two weeks it shall be built again with streets and moat, but in a troubled time. [26]After the sixty-two

a Theodotion Vg Compare Syr: Heb for the Lord's sake   b Gk Syr: Heb He made to understand   c Or thing or one

NIV

an end to sacrifice and offering. And on a wing ⌊of the temple⌋ he will set up an abomination that causes desolation, until the end that is decreed is poured out on him.*ᵃ"ᵇ*

a27 Or it   b27 Or And one who causes desolation will come upon the pinnacle of the abominable ⌊temple⌋, until the end that is decreed is poured out on the desolated ⌊city⌋

NRSV

weeks, an anointed one shall be cut off and shall have nothing, and the troops of the prince who is to come shall destroy the city and the sanctuary. Its*ᵃ* end shall come with a flood, and to the end there shall be war. Desolations are decreed. [27]He shall make a strong covenant with many for one week, and for half of the week he shall make sacrifice and offering cease; and in their place*ᵇ* shall be an abomination that desolates, until the decreed end is poured out upon the desolator."

a Or His   b Cn: Meaning of Heb uncertain

COMMENTARY

9:1, Chronological Setting. Daniel 9 is set in the first year of Darius, who is identified here as the son of Ahasuerus (usually taken to be Xerxes, who actually reigned after Darius). Clearly, we are again dealing with the book of Daniel's own idiosyncratic chronology, which has Darius "the Mede" following Belshazzar, who reigned during the time of Daniel's visions in chaps. 7–8. Whether important or not, this Darius is mentioned in a favorable light in a number of places in the book of Daniel.

9:2, Daniel and His Liberation Exegesis of "the Books." Daniel is engaged in study of "the books," here making reference to the prophet Jeremiah. It is impossible to say how early some of the writings that eventually became the Hebrew Bible (Old Testament) were used for study and reflection. It is interesting, however, that mention should be made of Jeremiah in this passage. As one of the prophets who made numerous references to the exile, Jeremiah's legacy was clearly of continued interest; witness the number of apocryphal texts that base themselves on some aspect of Jeremiah's, or his scribal associate Baruch's, life. What is clear from this reference in Daniel is the importance of Jeremiah's prophecies about the length of the exile. Jeremiah had predicted that the exile would last seventy years (Jer 25:11-12; 29:10-14). The dates we can be certain of are as follows: The initial surrender of King Jehoiachin and the fall and destruction of Jerusalem occurred in 597 BCE, and the massive deportation of Jewish residents by Nebuchadnez-

zar took place in 587/586 BCE. Cyrus the Persian conquered Babylon in 539 BCE, and Jewish groups began to return to Palestine, although under Persian control and auspices (see Ezra–Nehemiah, usually dated between 460 and 440 BCE). The Temple was probably rebuilt sometime between 520 and 515 BCE. No matter how you calculate it, Jeremiah was wrong, but his use of "seventy years" had become a tradition by Daniel's time. Diaspora Jews must have contemplated the meaning of such numbers, suggesting other interpretive possibilities. What, then, was the meaning of the "seventy years"? The book of Daniel extends the concept of exile by referring to seventy *weeks* of years—i.e., 490 years. Jeremiah's seventy years, however, was probably not intended to be a precise number in the first place, and may simply have meant an entire lifetime, so that Jeremiah was telling the exiles that *they,* undoubtedly, would never see Palestine again, even if their children would. But because the exile did not end, and a new David was not on the throne, and also because the foreign nations remained in power, later Jewish scholars, mystics, and seers returned to contemplating the possible meanings of Jeremiah's promised end of exile. And this is the question that Daniel is pondering. The significance of the letter in Jeremiah 29, with its appeal for nonviolence,[241]

---

241. I have elsewhere tried to argue that the letter to exiles in Jeremiah 29 was not simply a call to obey Babylon, but involved a strategy of resistance and survival as well. See D. Smith, "Jeremiah as Prophet of Nonviolence" *JSOT* 43 (1989) 95-107.

may also be important in the context of Daniel's call to nonviolent resistance to despotism.

Finally, it is important to note that a belief in the *continuous exile* is sociologically significant for the mind-set of the writers of the later sections of Daniel in the Hellenistic period. This is why texts like Jeremiah—which discuss exile and its end, after a necessary period of subordination to foreign power—were so important. The circumstances of subordination and suffering under Antiochus IV Epiphanes were considered part of the entire exile experience that had begun with the Babylonian conquest centuries before. In short, Daniel is engaging in a "liberation exegesis" of Jeremiah in the context of exile.

9:3-19, The Diaspora Prayer for Forgiveness and Deliverance. These verses include a standardized form of prayer or confession and request for deliverance, which can be compared to other texts with similar emphases and content. Before considering the meaning of this prayer, it is interesting to point out that there is considerable debate over whether this prayer was a late addition to the text. The debate focuses on the propriety of such a prayer in the context of the rest of the chapter.

Porteous and Lacocque note that v. 21 follows v. 2 quite comfortably, and vv. 3 and 20 look like "seams" written in to accommodate the addition of the prayer in vv. 4-19.[242] Lacocque even ventures to suggest that vv. 1-3 and 21-27 were written between 166 and 164 BCE, before the rededication of the Temple by Judas Maccabeus. Furthermore, as Goldingay and Collins note, the Hebrew of the prayer is much more regular and free of Aramaic influences.[243] Finally, many scholars have wondered why a prayer of confession would follow Daniel's seeking of illumination in the context of v. 2. Both Goldingay and Collins,

however, while noting these arguments, go on to suggest good reasons why this prayer, even if very traditional and perhaps even pre-existing the book of Daniel in its present form, was added by the author of the rest of chap. 9. In addition the prayer uses vocabulary similar to the rest of chap. 9 (such as "poured out"/"poured" [נתך *nātak*] in vv. 11 and 27; the mention of Jerusalem only in these two places in the entire book of Daniel; the use of "sin" [חטאת *ḥaṭṭāʾt*] in vv. 20, 24, and throughout the prayer).

The author of chap. 9 (and much of the later parts of Daniel) included the prayer at this point for good reasons, but not simply because it is a traditional prayer of lament and penitence (influenced by deuteronomistic theology) about the exile's being punishment for Israel's (and especially the kings') sins. The key to the inclusion of this prayer is precisely the relationship between the supposedly "different" parts of the chapter as a whole—that is, the relationship between the prayer and the appearance of the angelic figure Gabriel. In short, Gabriel responds to the prayer. Why would an angelic warrior respond to the prayer of a human being? The answer is in the nature of fasting as an essential aspect of communal prayers for deliverance. These prayers are part of an exilic tradition of calling God to spiritual warfare.

Prayers directed toward God, accompanied by fasting, were clearly a major element of diaspora life and passed into Scripture. Many of these prayers have similar themes, mention similar issues, and are accompanied by similar ritual acts—namely, fasting and often the wearing of sackcloth, traditional garb representing emotional distress.

What is important to note about these prayers for national forgiveness, usually prayed by an individual on behalf of the people as a whole, is that they are usually resorted to in times of great danger or distress.

242. N. Porteous, *Daniel,* OTL (Philadelphia: Westminster, 1965) 135; André Lacocque, *The Book of Daniel,* trans. D. Pellauer (Atlanta: John Knox, 1979) 178.

243. John Goldingay, *Daniel,* WBC 30 (Dallas: Word, 1988) 236-37; Collins, 347.

❖   ❖   ❖   ❖

EXCURSUS: ON FASTING, COMMUNAL PRAYER, AND HEAVENLY WARFARE

Among the theological developments that characterize post-exilic Israel, one notes a significant idealization of God's ability to deliver miraculously the community that trusts in God. Two aspects of this idealization are the role of communal fasting as a means of inviting God's intervention or protection and a highly stylized prayer of confession and salvation.

Fasting is often used in late biblical literature in combination with another term that is usually translated "to humble oneself" (להתענות lĕhit'annôt; see Dan 10:12). Although many instances of fasting in ancient Israelite practice are related to mourning for the dead or to the observance of acts of piety (Gen 50:10; 2 Sam 3:35 // 1 Chr 10:12; 2 Sam 1:12; Jdt 16:24), there is also some evidence of fasting at a time of natural disaster (Jer 49:28-33; Joel 2:1-5).[244] Finally, fasting is associated with preparation for revelation. Moses ate no bread and drank no water before the theophany in Exod 34:28, and similarly it is implied that Elijah fasted for forty days and nights in 1 Kgs 19:8. The association of fasting with revelations and visions, such as that found in Daniel, whose fasting was rewarded with wisdom, is a recurrent theme in Jewish piety in the intertestamental and early common eras. Fasting as preparation for theophany may have become more explicit as contact with Hellenism became more pronounced; but in any case, passages like the following increased in frequency: "Therefore go away, and sanctify yourself for seven days, and do not eat bread and do not drink water and after this time come to this place and I shall reveal Myself to you" (2 Bar 20:5-6a; similar passages can be found in 2 Bar 12:5; 21:1-3; Apocalypse of Elijah (1st–4th cent. CE) 1:21; the Greek Apocalypse of Ezra (2nd–9th cent. CE); Testament of Isaac (2nd cent. CE).

But why fast in some of these dangerous circumstances? Was fasting considered to be a special way of calling on God to take action? Both von Rad and Schwally, in their early and influential works on the concept of divine warfare, suggested that fasting was a part of the preparations for warfare in monarchical Israel. Von Rad stated that "the army stood . . . under strict sacral ordinances, they underwent a strict asceticism, the camp was to be ritually pure."[245] Schwally specifically mentioned fasting, and he compared Israelite military fasting to similar practices observed in the late nineteenth-century Native American ethnographic literature.[246] But there is only indirect support in other ancient Near Eastern texts for the practice of fasting before war.[247] Brongers, for example, denies that fasting was a preparatory rite for warfare, stating that "there is in the Old Testament not the slightest evidence of fasting before the battle."[248] Brongers may be correct with regard to pre-exilic texts. Even those texts that do associate fasting with military activity may be explained on other grounds, such as rites of penitence or mourning. In Judg 20:26, for example, a fast is part of the preparations of the sons of Israel before they face the recalcitrant tribe of

---

244. A. Malamat, "A New Record of Nebuchadnezzar's Palestinian Campaigns," *Israel Exploration Journal* 6 (1956) 246-56; W. Holladay, *Jeremiah* (Minneapolis: Fortress, 1989) 256.

245. G. Von Rad, *Der Heilige Krieg im alten Israel* (Zürich, 1951) 81.

246. F. Schwally, *Semitische Kriegsaltertümer* (Leipzig, 1901) 50-51. See also J. Blemensohn, "The Fast Among North American Indians," *American Anthropologist* 35 (1933) 451-69.

247. The evidence in Near Eastern materials does not appear to establish whether fasting was a part of preparations for war. This does not necessarily mean that it could not have been a uniquely Hebrew practice, but it raises doubts about the pre-exilic period. See S. M. Kang, *Divine War in the Old Testament and in the Ancient Near East* (Berlin: de Gruyter, 1989).

248. H. A. Brongers, "Fasting in Israel in Biblical and Post-Biblical Times," *Oudtestamentische Studien* 20 (1977), 7.

Benjamin. Was this a case of mourning for the dead or a plea to God to help them? In 1 Samuel 7 there is a gathering at Mizpah to cry out to God, but was the fast an act of penitence or part of the preparations to face a Philistine threat? Not only are these cases ambiguous with regard to the question of military fasting, but virtually all commentators agree that these passages show post-exilic redactional activity as well, suggesting that the association of fasting may have been added later.[249]

But in post-exilic texts, as we have seen, fasting clearly becomes part of preparations for a crisis or even a military encounter. This is mentioned in 1 Macc 3:46, along with the wearing of sackcloth and other mourning practices, when the Maccabean forces gather at Mizpah. Note that the fasting comes after they have assembled for battle, thus the fast was part of the preparation (1 Macc 3:44; see also 2 Macc 13:12). This fasting rite in the Maccabean source was influenced by a uniquely post-exilic theology that allowed for a fast to call for God's miraculous assistance in warfare. No historical basis can be established for the practice of fasting before battles in the First Temple period. I suspect that it did not exist. I would argue that there was a unique post-exilic concept of calling on God to engage in spiritual warfare against the foreign enemy, either unilaterally, as in Daniel, or in assistance of human soldiers, as in Maccabees, and that fasting and/or wearing sackcloth and asking for forgiveness were seen as essential aspects of facing a crisis and calling on God to act on the community's behalf.

There is clear evidence of an increase of days for fasting in the post-exilic period, as mentioned in Zech 7:5 (NRSV): "When you fasted and lamented in the fifth month and in the seventh, for these seventy years, was it for me that you fasted?" Milgrom, for one, does not believe that there were any specific and regular fast days before the exile.[250] If he is correct, then such rites of fasting and prayers for deliverance were a diaspora innovation that became an established aspect of late Jewish piety, especially on those occasions when a great adversary or challenge was about to be faced.

A number of examples of such resorts to fasting can be cited, beginning with Ezra 8:21-23, 31b (NRSV):

> Then I proclaimed a fast there, at the river Ahava, that we might deny ourselves before our God, to seek from him a safe journey for ourselves, our children, and all our possessions. For I was ashamed to ask the king for a band of soldiers and cavalry to protect us against the enemy on our way, since we had told the king that the hand of our God is gracious to all who seek him, but his power and his wrath are against all who forsake him. So we fasted and petitioned our God for this, and he listened to our entreaty . . . the hand of our God was upon us and he delivered us from the hand of the enemy and from ambushes along the way.

Jehoshaphat calls a communal fast to "come to seek help from the LORD" (2 Chr 20:4 NRSV), because the people felt powerless against this "great multitude." Although we are not told the content of the prayers, they are mentioned as an earnest part of the preparation.

Similarly, in the book of Esther all the main elements are present in chapter 4, where Esther prepares to face the Persian monarch on behalf of her people. Here, too, there is a tendency (1) to elaborate on Esther's and the Jews' pious preparations through (2) a gathering of "all" the Jews in reply to Esther's request and (3) prayers clearly rehearsing the power of God to deliver them: "You are LORD of all, and there is no one who can resist you, LORD" (Esth C, 4 NAB). Furthermore, there is the (4) emphasis on Esther's relative powerlessness in facing the king (she is convinced that she may die [Esth 4:16]) and (5) specific mention of the communal fast for Esther.

The association of a communal fast with a request for God to deliver those who cannot help themselves toward deliverance from enemies can also be seen in the Aramaic Papyri from

---

249. See B. Birch, *The Rise of the Israelite Monarchy* (Missoula, Mont.: Scholars Press, 1976) 64-70; J. Blenkinsopp, "Jonathan's Sacrilege 1 Sam 14, 1-16: A Study in Literary History," *CBQ* 26 (1964) 423-49.

250. J. Milgrom, "Fasting," *Encyclopedia Judaica* (Jerusalem: Qetar 1971) 1191.

Elephantine. Specifically, there is the letter requesting assistance to rebuild the Jewish religious center. In this letter, fasting and praying are associated with the punishment of the Egyptian enemies:

> And when this had been done [to us], we with our wives and our children were wearing sackcloth and fasting and praying to Yahweh the Lord of Heaven who let us gloat over that Vidranga. The [dogs] removed the fetter from his feet and all goods which he had acquired were lost. And all persons who sought evil for that Temple, all [of them] were killed and we gazed upon them.[251]

The emphasis is clearly on the powerlessness of the Jewish settlement to act for itself, on communal participation in the fast, and on the relationship between their fasting and the destruction of their enemies. In short, it is a further case of what we have already noted in biblical passages.

Finally, fasting is enjoined in the *Testament of Joseph.* In this work, Joseph fasts continually to ask God to assist him in resisting the advances of Potiphar's wife, which clearly had little to do with penitence. In the summary of the work, fasting was recommended as a form of requesting God's assistance that was considered to be especially effective: "You see, my children, how great are the things that patience and prayer with fasting accomplish."[252]

The very phrase "to call on God" is frequently associated with prayers and fasting, and sometimes in the context of warfare or a response to a perceived crisis (see esp. 2 Chr 15:4: "in their distress they turned to Yahweh, God of Israel, and sought him, and he let them find him" (author's trans.); note also Jer 29:13: "When you search for me, you will find me"; and Pss 40:16; 70:5). Calling on God is used in combination with fasting in the post-exilic period (see 1 Chr 16:11; 2 Chr 20:3-4; Dan 9:3; Jonah 3:5; cf. these references to 2 Chr 11:16, where many nations are seeking/calling God; see also Jer 50:4, "weeping as they seek the LORD their God" [NRSV]; Zech 8:21-22).

In sum, communal fasts to call on divine assistance are clearly an aspect of post-exilic theology. Communal fasting was an act of spiritual warfare that was either requested to assist with or to contrast with human military assistance. Since military action was impossible for a people dominated by foreign powers, the theology of God's assistance to the powerless is a notable development. The presence of such passages as the following one from Baruch suggests that the association of penitence (is fasting presumed here by the wearing of sackcloth?) as a prelude to calling on God's miraculous deliverance was maintained in the late Hellenistic period as well:

> I have taken off the robe of peace
>   and put on sackcloth for my supplication;
> I will cry to the Everlasting all my days.
>
> Take courage, my children, cry to God,
>   and he will deliver you from the power and hand of the enemy.
> (Bar 4:20-21 NRSV)

Such a practice finds its clear ideological context within other post-exilic and even late Hellenistic ideas that were expressed powerfully as late as in the book of Judith: "Your strength does not depend on numbers, nor your might on the powerful. But you are the God of the lowly, helper of the oppressed, upholder of the weak, protector of the forsaken, savior of those without hope" (Jdt 9:11 NRSV).[253]

---

251. A. Cowley, *Aramaic Papyri of the Fifth Century B.C.* (Oxford: Clarendon, 1923) 112-14; see also B. Porten and A. Yardeni, *Textbook of Aramaic Documents from Ancient Egypt* (Jerusalem: Hebrew University Press, 1986) 71.
252. "The Testament of Joseph," in J. H. Charlesworth, ed., *The Old Testament Pseudepigrapha,* 2 vols. (New York: Doubleday, 1983) 1:820-21.
253. Such a theology may well be behind such suggestive and controversial New Testament passages as Mark 9:29.

But *how* is God expected to act on the Jewish community's behalf? Logically, either by miraculous intervention directly or by assisting and empowering a human militia. In the book of Daniel, human military action is rejected, but calling on the angelic hosts of heaven certainly was not. The politics of angelic assistance in circumstances of social or political subordination provides the key to understanding the rise of such concepts in post-exilic Israel. This interpretation of fasting is in contrast to tendencies to see fasting only in the context of asceticism, which is not a major element in exilic/post-exilic Hebrew tradition. It is critical to point out that in post-exilic texts fasting is always associated with a communal call on God to act when the odds seem overwhelming. Fasting was not merely a rite used to ask for forgiveness, but was an act of spiritual warfare that was presumed to have material results—to invite the direct intervention of God.[254]

254. For further development of this theme, see "Hebrew Satyagraha: The Politics of Biblical Fasting in the Post-Exilic Period," *Food and Foodways* 5 (1993) 269-92.

❖   ❖   ❖   ❖

As a result of this analysis, we can now turn to the prayer of confession and deliverance in Daniel 9 and compare it to three other prayers of this type, which do not necessarily include the aspect of fasting but do include the standard review of Israelite history that is typical of these confessional prayers. Not all confessional prayers were a communal fast, but the prayers are highly stylized whenever we find them (see 1 Kings 8; Ezra 9; Baruch 1–3. These prayers are separated by a considerable span of time (1 Kings 8 probably from the deuteronomic historian just before, or just after, the exilic events began [c. 600–595 BCE; Baruch, second century BCE; and Ezra, c. 450 BCE]), each exemplifying the maintenance of tradition.[255] The purpose of this comparison is to see the traditional elements in the prayer in Daniel within the context of post-exilic prayers of deliverance.

Obviously, there are a number of important themes in these exilic prayers of deliverance. The prayers convey a profound sense of the history of the relationship between God and God's people. As a part of this history, there is an acknowledgment that the human community has often failed to uphold its part of the relationship. Significantly, then, the affirmation of the law of God is implied in the acceptance of God's "righteous" anger and rejection of the people. It is for the sake of this law, the expression of God in human society, that the prayers plead for God's continued involvement with the Jewish community. Thus,

255. These texts can be compared to the Prayer of Azariah (see Commentary on Additions to Daniel) and 1QS 1.22–2.1.

although Jerusalem and national questions are not absent in these prayers, they are decidedly secondary to the overall affirmation of God's law—the ideology of ethical monotheism, despite human failing. It is also important to note that in the context of these prayers, the Mosaic covenant, which involves human responsibility, is pre-eminent over the Abrahamic and Davidic covenants, which consist of direct promises of God without human responsibility. Human failure does *not* lead to an assessment or renegotiation of God's law as unrealistic or antiquated. Rather, the prayer affirms the continued human aspiration to follow God's law and the relationship that this implies.

9:20-23, The Angelic Hosts Respond to the Call. In response to the prayer, Daniel receives a visit from an angelic figure: Gabriel. What is interesting about this appearance is that it is not clear that Daniel is having a vision. Daniel has seen Gabriel before in a vision, and that is why Daniel now recognizes him. Is this ambiguity part of a reticence to distinguish between reality and visions? In any case, Gabriel is usually associated with messages and will later explain more to Daniel.

Gabriel declares that he has appeared in direct response to Daniel's prayers. Thus the story serves to verify the importance of prayer as an active engagement with powers relevant to the political and the spiritual condition of the Jewish people. Gabriel has come to explain the realities of power in the world. It is frequently noted that Gabriel says that he was "dispatched" at the beginning of Daniel's prayer, and not at the end. This is often taken to mean that Gabriel's explanations are *not* in answer to Daniel's prayer, but rather provide an

Figure 1: A Selection of Exilic Prayers of Confession and Deliverance

(1) We have sinned, committed iniquity, wickedness, rebellion
Ezra 9:6-7   1 Kings 8:47   Baruch 2:12   Daniel 9:5*a*, 9

(2) Turning from the commandments and from justice/ordinances*
Ezra 9:10   1 Kings 8:58   Baruch 1:18   Daniel 9:5*b*, 10

(3) Not listening to "your servants the prophets"**
Ezra 9:11   Baruch 1:21   Daniel 9:6, 10

(4) All Israel is guilty
Ezra 9:7   1 Kings 8:46   Baruch 1:15   Daniel 9:7*a*, 11

(5) We are driven into foreign lands, as you threatened[+]
Ezra 9:9   1 Kings 8:46   Baruch 2:1-2*a*   Daniel 9:7*b*, [12-13]

(6) Mention of Moses, the "servant of God"
Ezra 9:11ff.   1 Kings 8:53   Baruch 2:20   Daniel 9:13

(7) God is correct in what God has done[++]
Ezra 9:13   Baruch 1:15   Daniel 9:14

At this point, the prayers usually turn on the phrase "and now," and go from a review of Israel's confession of guilt, to the request for deliverance:

(1) Remember that you brought us from Egypt
                    1 Kings 8:51   Baruch 2:11   Daniel 9:15

(2) Please turn aside your righteous anger
Ezra 9:15   Baruch 2:13   Daniel 9:16

(3) Preserve Jerusalem and the Temple (Holy Mountain)
Ezra 9:9?   1 Kings 8:44*b*   Baruch 2:26   Daniel 9:16

(4) We are a disgrace amongst the neighbors (obviously not appropriate to Solomon's prayer)
Ezra 9:7   Baruch 3:8   Daniel 9:16

(5) Listen, for your sake
Ezra 9:14   1 Kings 8:28   Baruch 3:2   Daniel 9:17, 19

(6) Look on our situation (open eyes, ears, etc.)
                    1 Kings 8:29*a*   Baruch 3:4-5   Daniel 9:18

(7) Forgive us
Ezra 9:14   1 Kings 8:30   Daniel 9:19

(8) Act for *your name's sake,* and your people, and your city
Ezra 9:14   1 Kings 8:29*a*   Baruch 2:15   Daniel 9:19

---

* See Deut 17:11, 17, 20.
** This is a particular theme in Jer 26:5; 29:19; 35:15; 44:4-5.
+ See Jer 16:15; 23:3; 32:37.
++ God is "right" in *all* ways that God deals with Israel. See John Goldingay, *Daniel,* WBC 30 (Dallas: Word, 1988) 243.

answer to Daniel's situation. But surely this comment that Gabriel was sent after Daniel began praying is an emphasis on God's quick response to prayer, and not a comment on the irrelevance of the rest of the prayer (see Isa 65:24; cf. Matt 6:8).

9:24-27, Gabriel's Explanation of the "Seventy Weeks." It is interesting that Gabriel refers to "your" people and "your" city (rather than "the" holy city), which somewhat distances him from this matter. Perhaps this is to be attributed to the fact that Gabriel is not, according to vv. 11-12, the protector of Israel; that is the job of the one identified as Michael. Gabriel, then, is only the messenger.

The interpretation of the "seventy weeks" has, as can be imagined, been a conundrum of the book of Daniel. It appears to be a description of the total amount of time from the beginning of the exile to the end of political subjugation and the restoration of Jewish religious, if not also political, independence. "Seventy weeks" (of years, thus 490 years) refers to the time to put an end to sin, atone for iniquity, bring in righteousness, seal the prophet and his vision, and anoint a most holy place. God reaffirms the relationship with Israel. But what does this time refer to precisely? Scholars have often referred to the fact that Jeremiah's prophecy was not only associated with 2 Chr 36:18-21 and Leviticus 25–26 so that "seventy weeks" takes on a sabbatical-year association, but also the fact that groups of 70 and 490 became a standard form of referring to periods of history in other apocalyptic works, pre-eminently in *1 Enoch* and *Jubilees.* Such a standardization, then, ought to warn against the idea that these numbers can be matched to actual events.

Some scholars suggest that the first "seven weeks" refers to the time from the destruction of the Temple (586 BCE), to the anointing of another high priest (presumably Joshua, from the book of Zechariah). The book of Daniel never mentions this precise date and is otherwise hardly known for its chronological exactitude. Whatever the beginning point is understood to be, the longer period of sixty-two weeks refers to the period of exile, which extends down to the time of specific interest to the writer of this passage—near the time of Antiochus IV Epiphanes (c. 165 BCE). This period ends with an "anointed one's" being cut off. Is this the murder of Onias III, the high priest who was deposed by Jason and then murdered by Jews in league with Antiochus IV's Hellenization campaigns?

The rest of v. 26 describes the activities of Antiochus, which seem to have cosmic significance ("flood," "war," "desolations"), reminding us of the descriptions of cataclysmic events in other apocalyptic works, especially the book of Revelation.

Verse 27 levels three accusations about the end events. First, Antiochus will make a covenant— presumably the covenant with apostate Jews, mentioned in 1 Macc 1:11. Second, Antiochus will attempt to change the sacrificial observances and rituals of the Temple, and third, in the place of the proper observances there will be an "abomination of desolation." This last element most likely refers to the erection of a pagan altar over the Jewish one, in order to make sacrifices to Zeus Olympus rather than the placing of a statue in the Temple.[256]

In apocalyptic literature, the final dispatch of evil powers is often portrayed as a brief, matter-of-fact end (as in Revelation). Accordingly, the end of the evil rule in Daniel's vision is brief and quick, without detail. This is perhaps for two reasons: It has not taken place as yet, and it is only a promised reality for the future.

256. See Josephus *Antiquities of the Jews* 12.5.4.

REFLECTIONS

Daniel 9 suggests two important theological notions: the important relationship of confession and action, and taking first steps.

1. *Confession and Action.* In Christian faith and practice there ought to be an integral connection between confession and action—whether that action be directed to mission, to social justice, to peacemaking, or to consciousness raising. Confession involves the grave awareness that alone we are incapable of anything beyond self-interest and self-promotion. Action that is attempted apart from confession of weakness or failure is either unsuccessful or, even worse, successful by means of using, diminishing, or hurting others. Thus confession is prayer that prepares us not only to listen to God, but also to listen to each other (which is what George Fox called "answering that of God" in each person). Our confessions to others are acknowledgments that we need each other as well as our realization that we need God.

The prayer of confession in Daniel 9 is typically communal in nature (note the first-person plural that dominates throughout).

Action, then, must arise from confession as much as from preparation. This is the reason why the Society of Friends (Quakers) insist that "business meetings" are actually meetings for worship, for the conduct of business, and that such monthly, quarterly, or yearly meetings begin with silent waiting on the Spirit of Christ, as does each Sunday morning worship. The ideal, when kept in mind, is to seek God's will in mutual discernment, and not merely a human consensus. The emphasis on Christ as "our Present Teacher" is the basis for our practice as well as for our faith; for a Quaker reader of Daniel 9, there is no difficulty with the fact that Daniel's prayer of confession and request for deliverance result in the receiving of instruction. The beginning of action is realization—not only the realization of what we cannot do on our own, but also the further realization of what is possible under the leading of God's Spirit. The angelic hosts have engaged the battle before us; we rise from silent listening to God and to each other in order to join the battle.

2. *Taking First Steps in Discipleship.* In Gabriel's reassuring words about the seventy weeks, Daniel learns that the present grim realities will indeed have their predetermined end. To be Christian in the modern world involves two seemingly contradictory notions, two "realities": The ruler of this world will often appear victorious, but the final battle has already been determined—and won. Evil (an entity often not clearly perceived) and its consequences of suffering (all too clearly perceived) will run its course and be struck down. We must not be paralyzed by the enormity of the opponent.

From the message of Daniel (and for Christians Revelation as well), the readers suffering under Hellenistic and then Roman oppression learn to trust that evil and suffering have a predetermined end. This is a powerful doctrine that obviously holds out hope in darkest hours. Despair visits us when the first reality overshadows the second. But we are called to be "adventists" in the radical sense of those who live under the ethics of expectation. Such an ethic will clearly express itself, as the Mennonite statement reads, "in active nonconformity to the world as it is." Nonconformity is the way we begin to take steps in the grim realities of world conflict, the growing population of poor and homeless people, and the distracting escapism of modern Western entertainment industries. We have a most unusual description of such an active nonconformity in the early Christian document the Epistle to Diognetus:

> The difference between Christians and the rest of mankind is not a matter of nationality, or language, or customs . . . they pass their lives in whatever township—Greek or foreign—each man's lot has determined; and conform to ordinary local usage in their clothing, diet, and other habits . . . nevertheless, the organization of their community does exhibit some features that are remarkable, and even surprising. For instance, though they are residents at home in their own countries, their behavior there is more like that of sojourners; they take their full part as citizens, but they also submit to anything and everything as if they were aliens. For them, any foreign country is a motherland, and any motherland is a foreign country . . . though destiny has placed them here in the flesh, they do not live after the flesh, their days are passed on the earth but their citizenship is above in the heavens . . . they show love to all men—and all men persecute them.[257]

To begin to wonder how we as Christians ought to express this nonconformity is the beginning of an ethic of expectation, a radical "adventism" as presumed by the writer of Daniel. How do we live with an expectation that is not yet fully realized? That is Daniel's question—and it is our own. It involves the courage to take first steps in faith. On this theme, an American Quaker legend lights the path. Joseph Hoag was a Vermont Quaker traveling in Knoxville, Tennessee, during Andrew Jackson's campaigns of the War of 1812, before the climactic Battle of New Orleans. Hoag, stopping for a rest at a local inn, had an interesting confrontation with

257. Epistle to Diognetus sections 5-6.

one of Jackson's officers, who wanted to know why Quakers refused to fight. On hearing of Hoag's nonviolent principles, the officer said that, although he too would prefer to live in peace, he would be able to lay down his rifle only when everyone else laid down his armaments as well. Hoag's response has passed into Quaker folklore: "So, then, thou hast a mind to be one of the last men in the world to be good. I have a mind to be one of the first and set the rest an example."

DANIEL 10:1–12:13, THE FINAL VISION

NIV

10 In the third year of Cyrus king of Persia, a revelation was given to Daniel (who was called Belteshazzar). Its message was true and it concerned a great war.[a] The understanding of the message came to him in a vision.

²At that time I, Daniel, mourned for three weeks. ³I ate no choice food; no meat or wine touched my lips; and I used no lotions at all until the three weeks were over.

⁴On the twenty-fourth day of the first month, as I was standing on the bank of the great river, the Tigris, ⁵I looked up and there before me was a man dressed in linen, with a belt of the finest gold around his waist. ⁶His body was like chrysolite, his face like lightning, his eyes like flaming torches, his arms and legs like the gleam of burnished bronze, and his voice like the sound of a multitude.

⁷I, Daniel, was the only one who saw the vision; the men with me did not see it, but such terror overwhelmed them that they fled and hid themselves. ⁸So I was left alone, gazing at this great vision; I had no strength left, my face turned deathly pale and I was helpless. ⁹Then I heard him speaking, and as I listened to him, I fell into a deep sleep, my face to the ground.

¹⁰A hand touched me and set me trembling on my hands and knees. ¹¹He said, "Daniel, you who are highly esteemed, consider carefully the words I am about to speak to you, and stand up, for I have now been sent to you." And when he said this to me, I stood up trembling.

¹²Then he continued, "Do not be afraid, Daniel. Since the first day that you set your mind to gain understanding and to humble yourself before your God, your words were heard, and I have come in response to them. ¹³But the prince of the

[a]1 Or true and burdensome

NRSV

10 In the third year of King Cyrus of Persia a word was revealed to Daniel, who was named Belteshazzar. The word was true, and it concerned a great conflict. He understood the word, having received understanding in the vision.

2At that time I, Daniel, had been mourning for three weeks. ³I had eaten no rich food, no meat or wine had entered my mouth, and I had not anointed myself at all, for the full three weeks. ⁴On the twenty-fourth day of the first month, as I was standing on the bank of the great river (that is, the Tigris), ⁵I looked up and saw a man clothed in linen, with a belt of gold from Uphaz around his waist. ⁶His body was like beryl, his face like lightning, his eyes like flaming torches, his arms and legs like the gleam of burnished bronze, and the sound of his words like the roar of a multitude. ⁷I, Daniel, alone saw the vision; the people who were with me did not see the vision, though a great trembling fell upon them, and they fled and hid themselves. ⁸So I was left alone to see this great vision. My strength left me, and my complexion grew deathly pale, and I retained no strength. ⁹Then I heard the sound of his words; and when I heard the sound of his words, I fell into a trance, face to the ground.

10But then a hand touched me and roused me to my hands and knees. ¹¹He said to me, "Daniel, greatly beloved, pay attention to the words that I am going to speak to you. Stand on your feet, for I have now been sent to you." So while he was speaking this word to me, I stood up trembling. ¹²He said to me, "Do not fear, Daniel, for from the first day that you set your mind to gain understanding and to humble yourself before your God, your words have been heard, and I have come because of your words. ¹³But the prince of the kingdom of Persia opposed me twenty-one

NIV

Persian kingdom resisted me twenty-one days. Then Michael, one of the chief princes, came to help me, because I was detained there with the king of Persia. [14]Now I have come to explain to you what will happen to your people in the future, for the vision concerns a time yet to come."

[15]While he was saying this to me, I bowed with my face toward the ground and was speechless. [16]Then one who looked like a man[a] touched my lips, and I opened my mouth and began to speak. I said to the one standing before me, "I am overcome with anguish because of the vision, my lord, and I am helpless. [17]How can I, your servant, talk with you, my lord? My strength is gone and I can hardly breathe."

[18]Again the one who looked like a man touched me and gave me strength. [19]"Do not be afraid, O man highly esteemed," he said. "Peace! Be strong now; be strong."

When he spoke to me, I was strengthened and said, "Speak, my lord, since you have given me strength."

[20]So he said, "Do you know why I have come to you? Soon I will return to fight against the prince of Persia, and when I go, the prince of Greece will come; [21]but first I will tell you what is written in the Book of Truth. (No one supports me against them except Michael, your prince.

11 [1]And in the first year of Darius the Mede, I took my stand to support and protect him.)

[2]"Now then, I tell you the truth: Three more kings will appear in Persia, and then a fourth, who will be far richer than all the others. When he has gained power by his wealth, he will stir up everyone against the kingdom of Greece. [3]Then a mighty king will appear, who will rule with great power and do as he pleases. [4]After he has appeared, his empire will be broken up and parceled out toward the four winds of heaven. It will not go to his descendants, nor will it have the power he exercised, because his empire will be uprooted and given to others.

[5]"The king of the South will become strong, but one of his commanders will become even stronger than he and will rule his own kingdom

a16 Most manuscripts of the Masoretic Text; one manuscript of the Masoretic Text, Dead Sea Scrolls and Septuagint *Then something that looked like a man's hand*

NRSV

days. So Michael, one of the chief princes, came to help me, and I left him there with the prince of the kingdom of Persia,[a] [14]and have come to help you understand what is to happen to your people at the end of days. For there is a further vision for those days."

[15]While he was speaking these words to me, I turned my face toward the ground and was speechless. [16]Then one in human form touched my lips, and I opened my mouth to speak, and said to the one who stood before me, "My lord, because of the vision such pains have come upon me that I retain no strength. [17]How can my lord's servant talk with my lord? For I am shaking,[b] no strength remains in me, and no breath is left in me."

[18]Again one in human form touched me and strengthened me. [19]He said, "Do not fear, greatly beloved, you are safe. Be strong and courageous!" When he spoke to me, I was strengthened and said, "Let my lord speak, for you have strengthened me." [20]Then he said, "Do you know why I have come to you? Now I must return to fight against the prince of Persia, and when I am through with him, the prince of Greece will come. [21]But I am to tell you what is inscribed in the book of truth. There is no one with me who contends against these princes except Michael, your prince.

11 [1]As for me, in the first year of Darius the Mede, I stood up to support and strengthen him.

[2]"Now I will announce the truth to you. Three more kings shall arise in Persia. The fourth shall be far richer than all of them, and when he has become strong through his riches, he shall stir up all against the kingdom of Greece. [3]Then a warrior king shall arise, who shall rule with great dominion and take action as he pleases. [4]And while still rising in power, his kingdom shall be broken and divided toward the four winds of heaven, but not to his posterity, nor according to the dominion with which he ruled; for his kingdom shall be uprooted and go to others besides these.

[5]"Then the king of the south shall grow strong, but one of his officers shall grow stronger than

a Gk Theodotion: Heb *I was left there with the kings of Persia*
b Gk: Heb *from now*

NIV

with great power. [6]After some years, they will become allies. The daughter of the king of the South will go to the king of the North to make an alliance, but she will not retain her power, and he and his power[a] will not last. In those days she will be handed over, together with her royal escort and her father[b] and the one who supported her.

[7]"One from her family line will arise to take her place. He will attack the forces of the king of the North and enter his fortress; he will fight against them and be victorious. [8]He will also seize their gods, their metal images and their valuable articles of silver and gold and carry them off to Egypt. For some years he will leave the king of the North alone. [9]Then the king of the North will invade the realm of the king of the South but will retreat to his own country. [10]His sons will prepare for war and assemble a great army, which will sweep on like an irresistible flood and carry the battle as far as his fortress.

[11]"Then the king of the South will march out in a rage and fight against the king of the North, who will raise a large army, but it will be defeated. [12]When the army is carried off, the king of the South will be filled with pride and will slaughter many thousands, yet he will not remain triumphant. [13]For the king of the North will muster another army, larger than the first; and after several years, he will advance with a huge army fully equipped.

[14]"In those times many will rise against the king of the South. The violent men among your own people will rebel in fulfillment of the vision, but without success. [15]Then the king of the North will come and build up siege ramps and will capture a fortified city. The forces of the South will be powerless to resist; even their best troops will not have the strength to stand. [16]The invader will do as he pleases; no one will be able to stand against him. He will establish himself in the Beautiful Land and will have the power to destroy it. [17]He will determine to come with the might of his entire kingdom and will make an alliance with the king of the South. And he will give him a daughter in marriage in order to overthrow the kingdom, but his plans[c] will not succeed or help

[a]6 Or *offspring*   [b]6 Or *child* (see Vulgate and Syriac)   [c]17 Or *but she*

NRSV

he and shall rule a realm greater than his own realm. [6]After some years they shall make an alliance, and the daughter of the king of the south shall come to the king of the north to ratify the agreement. But she shall not retain her power, and his offspring shall not endure. She shall be given up, she and her attendants and her child and the one who supported her.

"In those times [7]a branch from her roots shall rise up in his place. He shall come against the army and enter the fortress of the king of the north, and he shall take action against them and prevail. [8]Even their gods, with their idols and with their precious vessels of silver and gold, he shall carry off to Egypt as spoils of war. For some years he shall refrain from attacking the king of the north; [9]then the latter shall invade the realm of the king of the south, but will return to his own land.

[10]"His sons shall wage war and assemble a multitude of great forces, which shall advance like a flood and pass through, and again shall carry the war as far as his fortress. [11]Moved with rage, the king of the south shall go out and do battle against the king of the north, who shall muster a great multitude, which shall, however, be defeated by his enemy. [12]When the multitude has been carried off, his heart shall be exalted, and he shall overthrow tens of thousands, but he shall not prevail. [13]For the king of the north shall again raise a multitude, larger than the former, and after some years[a] he shall advance with a great army and abundant supplies.

[14]"In those times many shall rise against the king of the south. The lawless among your own people shall lift themselves up in order to fulfill the vision, but they shall fail. [15]Then the king of the north shall come and throw up siegeworks, and take a well-fortified city. And the forces of the south shall not stand, not even his picked troops, for there shall be no strength to resist. [16]But he who comes against him shall take the actions he pleases, and no one shall withstand him. He shall take a position in the beautiful land, and all of it shall be in his power. [17]He shall set his mind to come with the strength of his whole kingdom, and he shall bring terms of peace[b] and perform them. In order to destroy the kingdom,[c]

[a] Heb *and at the end of the times years*   [b] Gk: Heb *kingdom, and upright ones with him*   [c] Heb *it*

NIV

him. [18]Then he will turn his attention to the coastlands and will take many of them, but a commander will put an end to his insolence and will turn his insolence back upon him. [19]After this, he will turn back toward the fortresses of his own country but will stumble and fall, to be seen no more.

[20]"His successor will send out a tax collector to maintain the royal splendor. In a few years, however, he will be destroyed, yet not in anger or in battle.

[21]"He will be succeeded by a contemptible person who has not been given the honor of royalty. He will invade the kingdom when its people feel secure, and he will seize it through intrigue. [22]Then an overwhelming army will be swept away before him; both it and a prince of the covenant will be destroyed. [23]After coming to an agreement with him, he will act deceitfully, and with only a few people he will rise to power. [24]When the richest provinces feel secure, he will invade them and will achieve what neither his fathers nor his forefathers did. He will distribute plunder, loot and wealth among his followers. He will plot the overthrow of fortresses—but only for a time.

[25]"With a large army he will stir up his strength and courage against the king of the South. The king of the South will wage war with a large and very powerful army, but he will not be able to stand because of the plots devised against him. [26]Those who eat from the king's provisions will try to destroy him; his army will be swept away, and many will fall in battle. [27]The two kings, with their hearts bent on evil, will sit at the same table and lie to each other, but to no avail, because an end will still come at the appointed time. [28]The king of the North will return to his own country with great wealth, but his heart will be set against the holy covenant. He will take action against it and then return to his own country.

[29]"At the appointed time he will invade the South again, but this time the outcome will be different from what it was before. [30]Ships of the western coastlands[a] will oppose him, and he will lose heart. Then he will turn back and vent his fury against the holy covenant. He will return

a30 Hebrew of Kittim

NRSV

he shall give him a woman in marriage; but it shall not succeed or be to his advantage. [18]Afterward he shall turn to the coastlands, and shall capture many. But a commander shall put an end to his insolence; indeed,[a] he shall turn his insolence back upon him. [19]Then he shall turn back toward the fortresses of his own land, but he shall stumble and fall, and shall not be found.

[20]"Then shall arise in his place one who shall send an official for the glory of the kingdom; but within a few days he shall be broken, though not in anger or in battle. [21]In his place shall arise a contemptible person on whom royal majesty had not been conferred; he shall come in without warning and obtain the kingdom through intrigue. [22]Armies shall be utterly swept away and broken before him, and the prince of the covenant as well. [23]And after an alliance is made with him, he shall act deceitfully and become strong with a small party. [24]Without warning he shall come into the richest parts[b] of the province and do what none of his predecessors had ever done, lavishing plunder, spoil, and wealth on them. He shall devise plans against strongholds, but only for a time. [25]He shall stir up his power and determination against the king of the south with a great army, and the king of the south shall wage war with a much greater and stronger army. But he shall not succeed, for plots shall be devised against him [26]by those who eat of the royal rations. They shall break him, his army shall be swept away, and many shall fall slain. [27]The two kings, their minds bent on evil, shall sit at one table and exchange lies. But it shall not succeed, for there remains an end at the time appointed. [28]He shall return to his land with great wealth, but his heart shall be set against the holy covenant. He shall work his will, and return to his own land.

[29]"At the time appointed he shall return and come into the south, but this time it shall not be as it was before. [30]For ships of Kittim shall come against him, and he shall lose heart and withdraw. He shall be enraged and take action against the holy covenant. He shall turn back and pay heed to those who forsake the holy covenant. [31]Forces sent by him shall occupy and profane the temple and fortress. They shall abolish the regular burnt

a Meaning of Heb uncertain   b Or among the richest men

NIV

and show favor to those who forsake the holy covenant.

[31]"His armed forces will rise up to desecrate the temple fortress and will abolish the daily sacrifice. Then they will set up the abomination that causes desolation. [32]With flattery he will corrupt those who have violated the covenant, but the people who know their God will firmly resist him.

[33]"Those who are wise will instruct many, though for a time they will fall by the sword or be burned or captured or plundered. [34]When they fall, they will receive a little help, and many who are not sincere will join them. [35]Some of the wise will stumble, so that they may be refined, purified and made spotless until the time of the end, for it will still come at the appointed time.

[36]"The king will do as he pleases. He will exalt and magnify himself above every god and will say unheard-of things against the God of gods. He will be successful until the time of wrath is completed, for what has been determined must take place. [37]He will show no regard for the gods of his fathers or for the one desired by women, nor will he regard any god, but will exalt himself above them all. [38]Instead of them, he will honor a god of fortresses; a god unknown to his fathers he will honor with gold and silver, with precious stones and costly gifts. [39]He will attack the mightiest fortresses with the help of a foreign god and will greatly honor those who acknowledge him. He will make them rulers over many people and will distribute the land at a price.[a]

[40]"At the time of the end the king of the South will engage him in battle, and the king of the North will storm out against him with chariots and cavalry and a great fleet of ships. He will invade many countries and sweep through them like a flood. [41]He will also invade the Beautiful Land. Many countries will fall, but Edom, Moab and the leaders of Ammon will be delivered from his hand. [42]He will extend his power over many countries; Egypt will not escape. [43]He will gain control of the treasures of gold and silver and all the riches of Egypt, with the Libyans and Nubians in submission. [44]But reports from the east and the north will alarm him, and he will set out in a great rage to destroy and annihilate many. [45]He

[a]39 Or land for a reward

NRSV

offering and set up the abomination that makes desolate. [32]He shall seduce with intrigue those who violate the covenant; but the people who are loyal to their God shall stand firm and take action. [33]The wise among the people shall give understanding to many; for some days, however, they shall fall by sword and flame, and suffer captivity and plunder. [34]When they fall victim, they shall receive a little help, and many shall join them insincerely. [35]Some of the wise shall fall, so that they may be refined, purified, and cleansed,[a] until the time of the end, for there is still an interval until the time appointed.

[36]"The king shall act as he pleases. He shall exalt himself and consider himself greater than any god, and shall speak horrendous things against the God of gods. He shall prosper until the period of wrath is completed, for what is determined shall be done. [37]He shall pay no respect to the gods of his ancestors, or to the one beloved by women; he shall pay no respect to any other god, for he shall consider himself greater than all. [38]He shall honor the god of fortresses instead of these; a god whom his ancestors did not know he shall honor with gold and silver, with precious stones and costly gifts. [39]He shall deal with the strongest fortresses by the help of a foreign god. Those who acknowledge him he shall make more wealthy, and shall appoint them as rulers over many, and shall distribute the land for a price.

[40]"At the time of the end the king of the south shall attack him. But the king of the north shall rush upon him like a whirlwind, with chariots and horsemen, and with many ships. He shall advance against countries and pass through like a flood. [41]He shall come into the beautiful land, and tens of thousands shall fall victim, but Edom and Moab and the main part of the Ammonites shall escape from his power. [42]He shall stretch out his hand against the countries, and the land of Egypt shall not escape. [43]He shall become ruler of the treasures of gold and of silver, and all the riches of Egypt; and the Libyans and the Ethiopians[b] shall follow in his train. [44]But reports from the east and the north shall alarm him, and he shall go out with great fury to bring ruin and complete destruction to many. [45]He shall pitch his palatial tents between the sea and the beautiful holy

[a] Heb made them white   [b] Or Nubians; Heb Cushites

NIV

will pitch his royal tents between the seas at[a] the beautiful holy mountain. Yet he will come to his end, and no one will help him.

12 "At that time Michael, the great prince who protects your people, will arise. There will be a time of distress such as has not happened from the beginning of nations until then. But at that time your people—everyone whose name is found written in the book—will be delivered. [2]Multitudes who sleep in the dust of the earth will awake: some to everlasting life, others to shame and everlasting contempt. [3]Those who are wise[b] will shine like the brightness of the heavens, and those who lead many to righteousness, like the stars for ever and ever. [4]But you, Daniel, close up and seal the words of the scroll until the time of the end. Many will go here and there to increase knowledge."

[5]Then I, Daniel, looked, and there before me stood two others, one on this bank of the river and one on the opposite bank. [6]One of them said to the man clothed in linen, who was above the waters of the river, "How long will it be before these astonishing things are fulfilled?"

[7]The man clothed in linen, who was above the waters of the river, lifted his right hand and his left hand toward heaven, and I heard him swear by him who lives forever, saying, "It will be for a time, times and half a time.[c] When the power of the holy people has been finally broken, all these things will be completed."

[8]I heard, but I did not understand. So I asked, "My lord, what will the outcome of all this be?"

[9]He replied, "Go your way, Daniel, because the words are closed up and sealed until the time of the end. [10]Many will be purified, made spotless and refined, but the wicked will continue to be wicked. None of the wicked will understand, but those who are wise will understand.

[11]"From the time that the daily sacrifice is abolished and the abomination that causes desolation is set up, there will be 1,290 days. [12]Blessed is the one who waits for and reaches the end of the 1,335 days.

[13]"As for you, go your way till the end. You will rest, and then at the end of the days you will rise to receive your allotted inheritance."

a45 Or the sea and   b3 Or who impart wisdom   c7 Or a year, two years and half a year

NRSV

mountain. Yet he shall come to his end, with no one to help him.

12 "At that time Michael, the great prince, the protector of your people, shall arise. There shall be a time of anguish, such as has never occurred since nations first came into existence. But at that time your people shall be delivered, everyone who is found written in the book. [2]Many of those who sleep in the dust of the earth[a] shall awake, some to everlasting life, and some to shame and everlasting contempt. [3]Those who are wise shall shine like the brightness of the sky,[b] and those who lead many to righteousness, like the stars forever and ever. [4]But you, Daniel, keep the words secret and the book sealed until the time of the end. Many shall be running back and forth, and evil[c] shall increase."

5Then I, Daniel, looked, and two others appeared, one standing on this bank of the stream and one on the other. [6]One of them said to the man clothed in linen, who was upstream, "How long shall it be until the end of these wonders?" [7]The man clothed in linen, who was upstream, raised his right hand and his left hand toward heaven. And I heard him swear by the one who lives forever that it would be for a time, two times, and half a time,[d] and that when the shattering of the power of the holy people comes to an end, all these things would be accomplished. [8]I heard but could not understand; so I said, "My lord, what shall be the outcome of these things?" [9]He said, "Go your way, Daniel, for the words are to remain secret and sealed until the time of the end. [10]Many shall be purified, cleansed, and refined, but the wicked shall continue to act wickedly. None of the wicked shall understand, but those who are wise shall understand. [11]From the time that the regular burnt offering is taken away and the abomination that desolates is set up, there shall be one thousand two hundred ninety days. [12]Happy are those who persevere and attain the thousand three hundred thirty-five days. [13]But you, go your way,[e] and rest; you shall rise for your reward at the end of the days."

a Or the land of dust   b Or dome   c Cn Compare Gk: Heb knowledge   d Heb a time, times, and a half   e Gk Theodotion: Heb adds to the end

COMMENTARY

Daniel 10–12 as a whole comprise the finale to the book, a single visionary experience, although amended by a secondary vision in chap. 12, which itself has a few additional amendments at the end. In fact, chap. 10 is actually a long introduction to the detailed vision of conflict that is elaborated in chap. 11 and part of chap. 12. This involves Daniel's preparations, his response to the visions, and the strengthening of the visionary by the heavenly messenger so that he can see and understand what he is about to experience. Lacocque outlines the vision simply and helpfully as prologue, 10:1–11:2*a*; revelation, 11:2*b*–12:4; and epilogue, 12:5-13.[258]

10:1. Chapter 10 begins in the third year of the reign of Cyrus. Once again, attempts to be precise about historical details defy us. But there are a number of particularly interesting aspects to this opening verse. First, Daniel's captive name, "Belteshazzar," is used here, despite the fact that the name was not used in the story of Darius in chap. 6, suggesting that, for the author of chaps. 7–12, the Persians do not necessarily have such a positive image, which will be confirmed. The "word," in any case, concerns "a great conflict/battle."

What is unusual about this introduction is the mention of a "word" coming to Daniel. This is the first occasion for a spoken message in place of a vision; yet as the chapter continues, it is clear that this message is not just an audio message. Is this a fragment of something else? We can only assume that "word" is to be taken as inclusive of the entire experience that follows. What is emphasized, however, is the auditory nature of the visionary experience.

10:2-6. Daniel is "mourning," which is clearly, and frequently, associated with fasting. (That mourning is associated with fasting as an aspect of diaspora faith and practice can be noted in Ezra 10:6; Neh 8:9; Esth 4:3; 9:22; for the significance of fasting, see Commentary on Daniel 9.) In this chapter, however, the mourning fast lasts an unusually long time. Physiological studies have proved that fasting or other forms of extreme dietary practices begin to take a physical and psycho-

logical toll within a few days. What is interesting about the time mentioned in these verses is that the time is the twenty-fourth day of the first month of the year; therefore, Daniel is mourning/fasting through Passover, the traditional Jewish celebration of release from captivity. Is this intended to express Daniel's lack of freedom by having him mourn during a time of celebration? If so, Daniel does not mention this significance, but the chronological note in v. 4 hardly allows this detail to pass unnoticed. Finally, we must note that the third year of Cyrus, according to v. 1, would place this event after the first mission of Jews back to Palestine under Sheshbezzar (see Ezra 1). This, too, is passed over by the author of Daniel.

Once again, the reference to Daniel's standing on the bank of the River Tigris (many scholars want to amend this to read "Euphrates") is an aspect of the fasting/mourning activity of Daniel. Daniel has a visionary experience (v. 5), similar at first glance to the image in Nebuchadnezzar's dream (chap. 2). The description of the person who appears to Daniel, however, is considerably different and resembles the descriptions of heavenly envoys in Ezek 9:2-3, 11; 10:2, 6-7:

(a) clothed in linen (Lev 6:10; 16:4—typically associated with priesthood, and thus probably to be understood as a sign of holiness, rather than implying a closer association with the Temple)
(b) belt of gold of Uphaz (Jer 10:9; should be Ophir? 1 Kgs 9:28)
(c) body like beryl (yellow jasper? One of the stones on high priest's breastplate: Exod 28:20; Ezek 28:13)
(d) face like a "vision of lightning" (lightning was in the arsenal of the storm god in the Semitic myth of the storm god vs. the sea god)
(e) eyes like torches of fire
(f) arms and legs like bronze
(g) sounds of words like the sounds of a crowd

As to the identity of the figure, the most obvious suggestion is that it is Gabriel, who will appear later in the vision. The main problem with this identification is that Daniel's reaction seems so different from the other times Gabriel appeared to him. But it is not so different from 8:15-18.[259]

---

258. André Lacocque, *The Book of Daniel,* trans. D. Pellauer (Atlanta: John Knox, 1979) 201.

259. Collins further suggests that Daniel 9 is a rough draft for the great vision and allows the identification of the figure as Daniel. See John J. Collins, *Daniel,* Hermeneia (Minneapolis: Fortress, 1993) 204.

It is instructive to compare this vision with Nebuchadnezzar's dream in chap. 2. First, Nebuchadnezzar saw in his dream a faceless statue, describing only the head. Daniel's vision notes not only the dress (because linen is associated with purity and the priesthood, the linen is thus of interest), but also the details of the face and the eyes; most important, Daniel's image speaks. In short, this image lives in a way that Nebuchadnezzar's vision of his kingdom does not. The latter was a lifeless idol.

10:7. Here we have an interesting admission that only Daniel saw these images.[260] We might expect, in a more fantastic description, the idea that many people saw this vision. This lends a certain credibility to those who argue that the basis for some elements of these reports may be actual experiences of Jewish visionaries.[261] What the people did share was a sense of presence and foreboding, which lends authenticity to the report about Daniel's experience, although why the author would choose this device, rather than simply having others see the vision, in order to authenticate the experience is suggestive. This fact alone tends to emphasize the importance of Daniel, whose stature has clearly grown more important in chaps. 7–12 (but see Commentary on 10:11).

The description of Daniel's "trembling" appears very similar to the kind of group religio/psychological experiences of modern charismatic movements (Pentecostal movements, Quakers, Russian Molokons) and Native American spiritual movements, like the Ghost Dance and the Maru cult of the Pomo people of central California.[262] This sign was clearly seen as evidence of a spiritual event, a sense of presence.

10:8-10. The impact of these experiences on Daniel is frequently described in chaps. 7–12. Not only does he seem exhausted and overcome emotionally and physically, but he also feels alone and is without strength. But three times he is lifted up and strengthened for the task of understanding what is to come (vv. 10, 16, 18). In this case, it

is the roaring sound of the words that overcomes Daniel, but he is raised to his feet to receive the messenger.

10:11. Daniel is called one who is "greatly beloved" (איש־חמדות 'îš-ḥămûdôt), and surely these are intended to be comforting words. This phrase may well be the indication of why Daniel would become such a significant figure in Jewish religious folklore. He is no longer a mere Jew who can live and pray like all the others. Now he steps out from the crowd as having a special relationship with God.

10:12. This verse begins with a call to arms: "Fear not!" (cf. Deuteronomy 20, the laws of "Yahweh War"). Daniel has looked to God for strength, and receives the call to arms, and is honored for humbling himself before God. (For the significance of this act, see Excursus "On Fasting, Communal Prayer, and Heavenly Warfare," 123-26.) God answers Daniel because of his "words" and his sincerity in seeking knowledge. Notice as well that Gabriel refers to the "first day that you set your mind to gain understanding." This is a theme of chap. 9, where Daniel's prayer begins to be answered even before he finishes praying (9:23).

10:13. This verse refers once again to the notion, apparently widespread in some circles of Jewish apocalyptic writing, that the various nations have spiritual counterparts, as Israel has the angel Michael (see Deut 29:26; 32:8-9; see also Ecclus 17:17; *Jub* 15:31-32). The sources of this notion have been debated by scholars, many of whom see its roots in the idea of a heavenly council of celestial beings, perhaps a Jewish attempt to deal with the complexity of gods among the various foreign powers. Such a reaction would seem natural in the Hellenistic period especially, when knowledge of many different peoples and their religious traditions was becoming common throughout the empire. Whatever the source of the idea, its function within Daniel is of particular interest—a heavenly version of the conflicts on earth between the foreign nations and the Jewish people. In this context, the specific mention of a conflict between Michael and Gabriel and the Persian Empire is further evidence that we must not rush to a positive evaluation of the Persian rulers. Keep in mind that the setting of this vision is within the reign of Cyrus, and although this is

260. Collins compares this detail with Acts 9:7, where only Paul sees the vision.

261. One of the most recent proponents of the idea that some apocalyptic reports may come from actual psychological phenomena is Michael Stone, "Apocalyptic: Vision or Hallucination?" *Milla wa-Milla* 14 (1974) 47-56.

262. Blenkinsopp suggests that such a group of ancient "trembler/quakers" can be found in Ezra 9:4; 10:3, 9; and Isaiah 2; 5. See J. Blenkinsopp, *Ezra–Nehemiah* (London: SCM, 1988) 178.

clearly a fictional account from the perspective of the second century BCE, the combination of this chronological note and the image of struggles with Persia need not be the result of hazy and inaccurate memories of "how good it was" under the Persians. The implication is clearly negative here.

The Persians were, of course, as capable of cruelty as was any other ancient empire, despite their somewhat undeserved reputation for enlightenment.[263] In addition to the discussion in the Introduction, one needs to recall that Cambyses killed over 2,000 people in the siege of Memphis. Darius's destruction of Miletus resulted in most of the males being murdered, and the women and children being led in chains to Susa.[264] Xerxes savagely crushed the Egyptian revolt, confiscating temple lands and increasing the tax burden and upkeep of garrisons, conditions that led to the revolt in the first place. When Xerxes died, both Egyptian and Babylonian sources claimed that his death was due to vengeance over injustices.[265] The biblical witness in Daniel, then, seems more in keeping with these reports than does the idea of Persian benevolence encountered in Ezra–Nehemiah (although even there Ezra mentions in his prayers that the Jews under the Persians are "slaves in our own land" [Neh 9:36]; cf. Ezra 9:8-9).

10:14-19. Gabriel explains to Daniel what is to happen "at the end of days." Throughout this work, various terms are used to describe the events at the end, but it is clear that the "end" is a series of events, rather than one single period of time. Gabriel's announcement of what Daniel is to see once again brings a reaction from Daniel—humility, weakness, and trembling. But the strengthening of the "beloved Daniel" continues, and he is able to carry on. The specific mention of Gabriel's touching his lips is a clear association with Isaiah 6, the call of Isaiah to be a prophet. These call narratives, like Isaiah 6 and Jeremiah 1 (cf. the call of Gideon in Judges 6) seem to be modeled on the call of Moses (Exodus 3) at the burning bush: the initial approach of God, the resistance of the one being called, the reassurance of God to the one called, and then

the commission/message. The similarity of this pattern to Daniel's call in the vision is an interesting connection with the prophetic tradition, especially with calls like those of Isaiah and Ezekiel. Like Moses, Daniel protests that he cannot speak, and this brings the final touch from Gabriel that prepares Daniel for what he is about to see. When compared to other prophets, Daniel seems to need more reassurance than most, but this serves to heighten the drama of what he is about to witness. Finally, the relationship between Daniel and the heavenly messengers is also emphasized in this interaction.

The final verse of this call narrative once again repeats the admonition for Daniel not to fear, but to have strength and take courage. Daniel now announces that he is ready to listen. He is, in a sense, prepared for spiritual battle.

10:20–11:2a, The Angelic Battle with the Powers. The theme of struggle against the Persians is repeated in this short identification of who is involved in the actual events that Daniel and his readers perceive. Since the vision was announced in the time of Cyrus, it is logical that Gabriel begins by informing him that the battle against the "powers of the world" has already begun with the struggle against the Persian "prince," after which the battle will shift to a new power, the Greek "prince." The term "prince" (שַׂר *śar*) is used to refer to the celestial beings set over the nations, as Michael is over Israel (here, however, Michael is joined in battle by Gabriel). Heidt, on the other hand, suggests that the term *śar* should be read as the slightly altared "demons" (the change involves a very slight difference in the Hebrew between שָׂרִים [*śārîm*] and שֵׁדִים [*śēdîm*]), which would then relate to Paul's use in 1 Cor 10:20, quoting Deut 32:17 and Ps 106:37.[266]

Note how the Jewish writer of the final vision in chaps. 10–12 takes little comfort in the change of powers from Persian to Greek. There is no consideration here that one world power's policies are better than another's. This is the clear perspective of sufferers throughout history, who may hear the promises of the new regime to "love justice" and "liberate the people at long last"; but the Jewish writer knows that the reality is the struggle against the powers of the world. For the writer

263. Daniel L. Smith-Christopher, "Resistance in a 'Culture of Permission,'" in *Truth's Bright Embrace,* ed. F. S. A. Roberts (Newberg, Ore.: George Fox University Press, 1996) 15-38.

264. See Herodotus *The History* 6.22.

265. M. Dandamaev, *A Political History of the Achaemenid Empire* (Leiden: Brill, 1989) 75, 165, 182, 234.

266. W. G. Heidt, *Angelology of the Old Testament* (Washington, D.C.: Catholic University of America Press, 1949).

of Daniel, the rhetoric of the world powers is empty. The writer, then, is not among those who see an opportunity in this change of rulers. Hengel writes:

Interest in Hellenistic civilization . . . remained predominantly limited to the well-to-do aristocracy of Jerusalem. Intensive economic exploitation and the social unconcernedness of the new masters and their imitators, who were concerned purely with economics, only served to exacerbate the situation of the lower strata of the population.[267]

Combined with the fact that even under the Seleucid rulers estimates are that merely 2.5 percent of the ruling aristocracy and royal appointments were non-Hellenist natives of the conquered lands,[268] we then begin to understand how the writer of Daniel sees world politics as a matter of spiritual warfare.

The "book of truth" is not the same, apparently, as the book of names of Dan 12:1. While the image of these various books is somewhat difficult to unravel, it is significant that we are dealing with the image of books at all; we are clearly in the realm of a literate writer and readership. The use of various books, however, recalls the kind of scribal work that a courtier might do within a foreign court. Like many scholars and students, Daniel is surrounded by, and even dreams about, books!

Finally, in 11:1, it is important to understand the referents. In the first year of Darius, Gabriel stood up to support Michael in his struggle, and was not on the side of Darius the ruler. The support is required because, in 10:21 it was emphasized that Michael stood alone in the battle while Gabriel was with Daniel to explain matters.

11:2b. This passage is quite explicit about the nations being referred to (Persia and Greece), but the names of the particular rulers remain a problem. The three additional kings mentioned are identified as Persian. As Darius is supposed to be Median, the most likely identifications of these Persian kings are Cyrus (560–530 BCE), Xerxes (486–465 BCE), and Artaxerxes (465–424 BCE), since these three are mentioned elsewhere in the Old Testament. Other suggestions have been

made as well. If there is an emphasis on attacks on the Greeks, the most likely candidate for the final Persian ruler is Xerxes. But if Xerxes is in mind here, that would mean a long jump to the time of Alexander. Darius III Codomannus (336–330 BCE) was the final Persian ruler before Alexander the Great. It is difficult to count Darius I (522–486 BCE) among the Persian kings in this passage, when this reference in Daniel is usually taken to refer to the Median ruler just before Cyrus, rather than the historical Darius, who claimed the Persian throne after the death of Cambyses (530–522 BCE). What is clear from this passage, however, is the awareness that a succession of Persian kings ruled before the coming of Alexander. The final Persian ruler seems to stand for Persian rulers in general, gathering wealth that leads to megalomania and attacks on other kingdoms.

11:3. The warrior who arises is clearly Alexander the Great. His conquests allow him to do as he pleases, which is the expression of arrogant power that the book of Daniel has used previously.

11:4. This verse essentially repeats elements of the initial dream in chap. 8, which recalled the ram and the goat. Here, Alexander's sudden death in Babylon is recalled, and his empire is divided among his four generals. The use of the phrase "four winds of heaven" is probably not to be taken as a specific reference to the four generals who inherited Alexander's empire (after considerable jockeying for position in the years immediately following Alexander's death). Rather, it is a reference to the four geographical directions, a sense that the empire will be dramatically divided in different directions—a virtual explosion. The two generals that we are most interested in, once the dust has settled in the ancient Near East, are Seleucus, who reigned over much of the former Babylonian/Persian territories, and Ptolemy, who reigned over an expanded Egyptian territory that included Palestine.

11:5-39. These verses deal with the complex history in the relations between the Ptolemies and the Seleucids and the eventual rise to power of Antiochus IV Epiphanes, the Seleucid ruler who reigned over one of the most significant crises in Jewish life since the Babylonian exile. Scholars often comment that we have in these verses a

---

267. M. Hengel, *Judaism and Hellenism* (Philadelphia: Fortress, 1974) 56.
268. F. W. Walbank, *The Hellenistic World* (Cambridge, Mass.: Harvard University Press, 1981) 65.

strikingly accurate portrayal of the events between 301 and 175 BCE. A survey of these verses, therefore, will include historical comments, the likely referents of the enigmatic discussion of the kings of the north and of the south, who are, respectively, the Seleucids and the Ptolemies.

11:5. The king of the south, Ptolemy I Soter (323–283 BCE) reigned in Egypt. The former Alexanderian general Seleucus sought refuge under Ptolemy in his conflict with Antigonus. In 312 BCE, Ptolemy and Seleucus, as allies, soundly defeated Demetrius's son Antigonus at Gaza. After this, Seleucus then moved toward gaining control of the largest portion of Alexander's old regime, the eastern Persian sector, which Seleucus began to rule from Seleucia, near Babylon, in 305 BCE. Syria-Palestine, however, remained under the control of Ptolemy. Ironically, Palestine would become a bone of contention precisely as it had been in earlier centuries, and for precisely the same reason: its strategic location as the land bridge between the two great cultural centers of the ancient Near East, Egypt and Mesopotamia. The history of these two regimes in this period is fraught with complications and intrigue, and some patience is required to understand, even in a general way, the shifting tides in foreign policy. In 281 BCE, Seleucus acquired Asia Minor, and there were conflicts between Antiochus I and Ptolemy II in 280 and 274–271 BCE, and war between Antiochus II and Ptolemy II between 260 and 253 BCE.

11:6. The "alliance" mentioned in this verse is the marriage of Antiochus II Theos (261–246 BCE), a Seleucid, to Berenice, the daughter of Ptolemy II in 252 BCE. This was an attempt to stop the constant conflicts between the two regimes. Antiochus II, however, divorced his first wife, Laodice, in order to seal the political truce with Ptolemy through marriage to Berenice. Antiochus II and Laodice had already produced two sons, Seleucus and Antiochus. When Antiochus eventually left Berenice to reunite with Laodice, however, Laodice sought revenge by poisoning Antiochus II and having Berenice and her sons murdered. This paved the way for Seleucus II Callinicus (the son of Laodice) to assume the throne in Babylon.

11:7-8. The brother of the murdered Berenice became Ptolemy III Euergetes. He attacked the Seleucid realm (in reprisal of the murder of Berenice and her sons) and advanced as far as Babylon. His campaign succeeded in capturing many of the images of gods kept in Babylon, including some important Egyptian idols that were first taken by Cambyses, the Persian ruler, over 250 years earlier. What is notable here is the plunder of warfare, the taking of gods, idols, silver and gold (v. 8). We are once again reminded of the true motivation of military ideology despite all claims to patriotic fervor (or vengeance for the honor of Berenice)—namely, commerce.

11:9-13. Antiochus III the Great (223–187 BCE), one of the two sons of Seleucus II Callinicus, was able to recapture much of the western territories of his empire between 221 and 217 BCE, capturing Seleucia and eventually gaining control of the strategic ports of Tyre and Ptolemais. Verses 10-11 refer to the great battle of Raphia, which was part of Antiochus III's campaign to expand his territory. The battle took place in 217 BCE, and Greek sources tell us that Antiochus III brought 62,000 infantry, 6,000 cavalry, and 102 war elephants, matched against 70,000 infantry, 5,000 cavalry, and 73 elephants of Ptolemy IV. Even though Ptolemy IV was victorious, he settled for peace with Antiochus III (the reference to "being defeated" with regard to Antiochus III). This is undoubtedly the meaning of the reference to "return to his own land" (v. 9). At the same time, there may be a vague memory of a visit of Ptolemy IV to Jerusalem in the enigmatic work entitled 3 Maccabees, a pseudepigraphal work.

Ptolemy IV's army, interestingly, was composed now of a mix of Hellenistic soldiers and a large percentage of native Egyptians. These Egyptians were given a taste of power in this military campaign, and soon the Ptolemies were engaged in putting down revolutionary activity at home, as the Egyptians rose in rebellion in various locations. Despite his "exalted heart," then, Ptolemy would face the forces of Antiochus III again (v. 13).

The peace made between Ptolemy IV and Antiochus III after Antiochus's defeat at Raphia was not a sagacious move for the Egyptian monarch, and it gave time for Antiochus III to consolidate his regime. In 203 BCE, Ptolemy IV died, leaving a six-year-old son to assume power as Ptolemy V. Egypt was actually ruled by the regent Agathocles, who was ruthless and whose oppressive regency led to further revolts within the Egyptian populace. During this time (212–205 BCE), Antiochus was successful in the eastern regions of his empire, and soon he was able to create an alliance with Philip V of Macedonia, in order to attack Ptolemy once again.

11:14. The expressions "sons of the violent ones" of "your own people" appear in a very negative context in Ezek 7:22, referring to the violent sons of righteous people (the righteous are not held morally responsible for their children's actions), and in Jeremiah's reference to the "den of robbers," or "violent ones." Such allusions strongly imply a negative evaluation of those who are portrayed with this term. Was this an indication of Jewish involvement in the earlier insurrections against Ptolemy V? Most scholars consider it to be a reference to the rivalry between the Tobiad family (who sought the leadership of the Temple, the main position of authority in the Judean Jewish communities) and the family of Onias III, the high priest who clearly had Egyptian sympathies. These "lawless" people are identified either as the renegade Oniads who joined with the rival Tobiad faction,[269] or as a pro-Ptolemaic party who "fail/stumble" when General Scopas finally loses Jerusalem.[270]

General Scopas was a Ptolemaic military governor who retook Judea before finally losing it again to Antiochus III in 198 BCE. The "lawless" among the Jews may well have been inspired by a rival visionary faction, similar to the visionary circle responsible for, and responsive to, the visions of Daniel. But this other group (and their vision) is clearly rejected by the writer of Daniel. Many scholars suggest that this is another indication of the nonviolent ethos of Daniel, since the assumption is that the rival vision was acted upon violently and that it ultimately failed. Perhaps this visionary faction was inspired by some attempt to revive a messianic speculation among the Egyptian Jewish community.

11:15-16. The "well-fortified city" (v. 15) is Sidon, where Scopas retreated after the fall of Jerusalem. At first, Antiochus III received a warm welcome from the Jewish residents of Jerusalem, to which he responded by promising tax relief and support for the temple treasury. It is possible that Jews assisted in the siege against Scopas at Sidon. The result of these events is that Antiochus III takes possession of Jerusalem and Judea, the "beautiful land" (v. 16).

11:17. Antiochus III's growing power led to a series of moves intended to further extend his influence into Egypt. He gave his daughter, Cleopatra (the first of this name), to be married to Ptolemy V. But if his intention was to use his daughter in a plot against the Egyptian regime, the plan failed badly, because Cleopatra was loyal to her new husband, and an alliance was created between Ptolemy V, Cleopatra, and Rome. Even though the opening years of his reign proved dismal, Ptolemy V proved an able monarch.

11:18-19. When Antiochus III moved west to Greece, "his face to the coastlands,"[271] he was defeated in 191 BCE by the Romans at the pass of Thermopylae, and again at Magnesia in Asia Minor in 190 BCE. As a result, Antiochis III was charged with massive tribute payments to Rome (15,000 talents of silver and all possessions west of Taurus) and was ordered to cease his interests in Egyptian land. Furthermore, one of his sons, Antiochus IV, was taken to Rome as a hostage against further advances. Antiochus III began to rob temples within his domain in order to raise the massive tribute payments, and it was while engaged in the robbery of a temple of Bel at Elymais (in a distant area of Elam) that he was assassinated in 187 BCE. Seleucus IV succeeded him, cursed with his father's massive tribute debts.

11:20. A tribute/tax collector, undoubtedly Heliodorus, arrived in Palestine in order to raise the necessary tribute funds. Seleucus IV, however, was killed in a plot involving Heliodorus. This reference to the tax collector in Jewish territories is a most interesting point, a memory of the kind of contact Jews had with the officials of the realm as opposed to the fictional contact of the courtier stories in Daniel 1–6. Such contact with officials like tax collectors represents the most likely historical reality for most of the Jewish people, who were, after all, merely sources of revenue rather than exalted workers in the emperor's palace.

11:21. This verse arrives at the focus of sus-

---

269. See John Goldingay, *Daniel*, WBC 30 (Dallas: Word, 1988).
270. See Josephus *Antiquities of the Jews* 12.3.

271. John J. Collins, *Daniel*, Hermeneia (Minneapolis: Fortress, 1993) 365.

tained attention in the great vision: the rise of Antiochus IV Epiphanes (175–163 BCE). The book of Daniel's emphasis on the nature of Antiochus IV is that he is deceitful and works in "quiet." Psalm 12 warns of deceit as false propaganda:

They utter lies to each other
 with flattering lips and a double heart they speak.
May the LORD cut off all flattering lips,
 the tongue that makes great boasts. (Ps 12:2-3 NRSV)

This deceitfulness leads to the despoiling of the poor, according to Ps 12:5, "Because the poor are despoiled, because the needy groan, I will now rise up, says the Lord." Isaiah 30:9-11 equates deceit with faithlessness among the people:

For they are a rebellious people,
 faithless children,
children who will not hear
 the instruction of the LORD;
who says to the seers, "Do not see";
 and to the prophets, "Do not prophesy to us
  what is right;
speak to us smooth things,
 prophesy illusions,
leave the way turn aside from the path,
 let us hear no more about the Holy One of Israel."
  (NRSV)

The rise to power of Antiochus IV is surrounded by intrigue. He is at least implicated in the death of Seleucus IV, but most certainly was responsible for the death of rivals to power, such as the son of Seleucus IV, who ruled for a time as co-regent with Antiochus IV.

11:22-23. Antiochus IV will be victorious in his battles for consolidation of power. But he will be deeply involved in lining up supporters from within the Jewish community as well. In the description of his destructive acts is a reference to the fall of a "prince of the covenant." This may be a reference to the same figure in 9:26, who is a (false?) leader from among the Jewish people. However, most scholars consider it to refer to the removal of Onias III as high priest. Antiochus IV is able to win the support of the new high priest, Jason, and of the Tobiad family, of whom Jason is a member. The Tobiads were descendants of Ammonites who married into power with the foreign regime; one of their descendants, Joseph, would become a well-known and influential tax collector in the Ptolemaic regime (221–198 BCE). Those in alliance with the Tobiads may well be the "small party" noted in v. 23, referring to an alliance with some of the Jewish people that created factions and dissensions.

11:24. In quiet, Antiochus comes into the land and lavishes on a "small party" plunder, spoil, and wealth. "Plunder" (בזה *bizzâ*) is found in many late sources (see 2 Chr 14:13; Ezra 9:7; Esth 9:10, 15-16). In its usage in this verse, the term refers to things taken from conquered peoples after a battle, usually in punishment for evil done by or to the Jewish nation. "Spoil" (שלל *šālāl*) is a term used in Josh 7:21 to refer to the goods taken by Achan, which caused so much grief for the early Jewish nation. "Wealth" does not necessarily have a military association, although it is used as such in Genesis 14. Ordinarily, it is used to refer to goods taken on journeys, as in Ezra 1:4, 6 and 8:21. The point here is that this wealth is the spoils of war, and it is given to the "small party" of Jews who align themselves with the Hellenizing portion of the leadership. Thus there appears to be strong condemnation of those who would accept these things, obtained through the wars of the deceitful ruler Antiochus IV.

11:25-27. The history of Antiochus's designs against Egypt is, once again, somewhat complex. When Ptolemy V died in 181 BCE, his young son became Ptolemy VI Philometor. Antiochus IV's sister, Cleopatra, was regent during the youth of Ptolemy Philometor. She died in 176 BCE, leaving the leadership in the hands of the ambitious and scheming courtiers Eulaeus and Lenaeus. They incited political unrest against Antiochus IV, prompting him to invade Egyptian territory. Those who plot against the northern ruler are these two who "eat of the royal food" (v. 26, author's trans.). The term translated "royal food" is a Persian loan word (the same term appears in Daniel 1 in reference to the food served to Daniel and the others).

Antiochus and Ptolemy attempt to make peace (v. 27). They "sit at one table and exchange lies," an eloquent evaluation by the writer of the sincerity of these peace negotiations—but also closely tied to the notion that these negotiations were intended, according to the writer, to avert what has already been determined by God. This treaty will fail.

11:28. The reference to the holy covenant may mean that Antiochus IV will continue his assault on the traditional Jewish parties of Palestine who are represented in the editor/writer of this material. It could also mean that he will not observe the "holy covenant"—e.g., treaty—formed in the previous verses. Most scholars, however, believe that a "holy covenant" must mean that Antiochus IV directed an assault on the Temple, as suggested in 1 Macc 1:20. This is the beginning, then, of the serious oppression of the Jews in Judea.

11:29-30. Antiochus invades Egypt once again. "Kittim" is taken to be a reference to Rome, to those forces who come from the western areas of the Mediterranean Sea. They are represented by the term "ships of Kittim" (although the Hebrew phrase כתים ציים [*ṣiyyîm kittîm*] could be read "beasts of Kittim," which may carry on some of the symbolism of chaps. 7–8; for *ṣiyyîm* as "beast," see Isa 13:21; 23:13; 34:14; Jer 50:39). Rome certainly did come to the aid of the co-regents Ptolemy Philometor and Ptolemy Euergetes, and demanded that Antiochus withdraw. Collins points to the humiliation of Antiochus, the "day of Eleusis," noted in a variety of classical sources.[272] The text suggests, however, that the result of this humiliation is that Antiochus unleashes considerable anger toward the Jewish people and their religion (cf. Ptolemy's rage toward the Jews in 3 Maccabees). There is a reference here to apostate Jews, "those who forsake" the covenant. This is to be noted also in Ezra 8, where God's wrath is against "those who forsake the covenant."

11:31-35, Persecutions and Divisions Among the Jews. *11:31.* Here we have the clearest references to the events during the reign of Antiochus IV Epiphanes. Although there is some doubt as to who is really responsible for the attack on the Jewish cult in Jerusalem, the book of Daniel clearly lays the blame on the deceitful Antiochus, as well as those who went along with him.

Recent scholarship has emphasized that Antiochus's policies toward the Jews arose partly from his own imperial ambitions and were partly in support of Hellenizing elements within the Jewish population that called for modernization in the first place and the competition between Jason and Menelaus for the position of high priest, each offering money for the privilege. Certainly financial rewards were possible for those who entered

more fully into the world economy created by Hellenistic conquests. It would certainly also be tempting for some Jews to abandon their religious scruples about treatment of the poor and advance toward the more luxurious and uncaring attitudes of the Greek elite.

The resulting policies, agreed on by the Jewish innovators and Antiochus's imperial support, include the occupation and profaning of the Temple, the abolishing of the burnt sacrifice, and the setting up of the "desolating abomination." It is very probable that one of Antiochus's actions was to garrison troops in Jerusalem, which necessitated the creation of a citadel to quarter the Greek troops.[273] It was placed near the temple mount. The Temple, then, would be transformed to serve the religious symbolism of the occupying troops. The Hebrew terms typically translated in English as "abomination that desolates" (שקוץ משמם *haššiqqûṣ měšômēm*) are often seen as a play on words with the name of the god to whom the new altar was dedicated: Baal Shamem. This god was honored throughout northern Syria and Phoenicia, and was typically seen as the equivalent of Zeus Olympios; both terms translate roughly as "God Most High." What actually was placed in the Temple is disputed. While it is tempting to insist that a statue or image of the god was set up on the altar in the Jerusalem Temple (especially noting the prominence of images in Daniel 2–3), it is likely that a new altar was built over the existing one, thus desecrating it, in order to be used for Baal Shamem.

11:32. This verse creates a clear distinction between the Jews who have become "friends" of the king and those who remain loyal to God. An important strategy of the Hellenistic rulers was to make allies of the most powerful members of conquered peoples by purchasing their loyalty. The ones who do remain loyal to God, interestingly, not only will stand firm, but also will "take action." Certainly these are the people with whom the writers and readers of Daniel identified, which will become more evident in the verse that follows.

11:33. The righteous are described in Hebrew as "the wise ones" (משכילים *maśkîlîm*) who will teach "the many" (רבים *rabbîm*).[274] The "action"

---

272. Collins, *Daniel,* Hermeneia, 384 and n. 134. For classical sources, see Polybius 29.27; Diodorus Siculus 31.2.

273. M. Smith, "Hellenization," in M. Stone and D. Satran, eds., *Emerging Judaism* (Minneapolis: Fortress, 1989).
274. For this latter group, "the many," Collins reads "the common people," although this is interpretation as much as translation. See Collins, *Daniel,* Hermeneia, 367.

taken by these wise ones is education; they are the leaders of the resistance, advising others to resist. The persecution of the wise ones includes death by "sword and flame" and "captivity and plunder." The sword represents policing power. The flame certainly recalls the form of capital punishment noted in Daniel 3, but it is also possibly a reference to the destruction of dwellings. Captivity is likely a reference to the current status of the Jewish population, or perhaps even to slavery, since prisons were not a significant institution at this time. Plunder most likely is the massive taxation that the Jewish people suffered under a succession of regimes.

11:34. This verse has incited a heated debate among commentators, since Collins had already focused attention on it in his early work on Daniel.[275] The meaning and implications of "little help" are pursued in the Excursus "Daniel and Nonviolence."

275. John J. Collins, *The Apocalyptic Visions of the Book of Daniel* (Missoula, Mont.: Scholars Press, 1977).

❖   ❖   ❖   ❖

EXCURSUS: DANIEL AND NONVIOLENCE

The context for virtually all of the stories of Daniel 1–6 is that of nonviolent resistance to foreign political authority. The success of the Jewish courtiers in the foreign court comes from their spiritual strength and their courage, and not from their weaponry. Indeed, the defeat of Nebuchadnezzar by the "stone" that was formed by no human hand was a significant further indication of this spirit of resistance without arms (see Commentary on 2:39-45).

Many scholars believe that Dan 11:34 clearly reveals the writer of Daniel's attitude toward the violent Maccabean resistance, which was gaining ground at the same time as the events described in Daniel 7–12. The Maccabean resistance is described in Dan 11:34 as "little help." Despite some scholarly protest that little help is still at least *some* help (and is not necessarily a negative judgment) this "little help" is in the context of "those who join insincerely," and thus both groups are to be seen negatively. In other words, 11:34 compares the "little help" to another useless category: those who join the wise ones without full sincerity.

This passage is written, therefore, in the same spirit as other passages that display a contemptuous attitude toward the "violent ones" (see 11:14). These texts are further evidence of the nonviolent orientation of Daniel's visionary attitude to foreign power. The book of Daniel *does* call for resistance, but nonviolent resistance. Lebram agrees: "The principles of the pious man of the Apocalypse consist in the rejection of all violence, particularly of the implementation of the kingdom of God by force."[276] Goldingay, on the other hand, dismisses such a notion on the basis that most scholars assume this vision to be set *before* the Maccabean resistance was finally successful in liberating Jerusalem.[277] Presumably, then, the visionary behind Daniel would have abandoned such pacifistic notions when he saw how violence was so effective. Goldingay's assumption here that effectiveness was the measure of faithfulness can be criticized not only on political and philosophical grounds,[278] but also on textual grounds. Collins, for instance, cites other examples of the more nonviolent orientation in post-exilic, Hellenistic literature, such as the stories of Taxo in the *Testament of Moses.*[279] One can further cite the patient resistance of faith exemplified by Joseph in the *Testament of the Twelve Patriarchs:* "And if anyone wishes to do you harm, you should pray for him, along with doing good, and you will

276. J. Lebram, "The Piety of Apocalyptic," in D. Hellholm, *Apocalypticism in the Mediterranean World* (Tübingen: Mohr, 1983) 138.

277. Goldingay, *Daniel,* 303.

278. Goldingay's criticism of reading nonviolence in Daniel clearly involves the extra-textual assumptions that nonviolence is not an effective means of resistance, that violence is obviously the more effective means of achieving liberation, and that it is a very modern idea for some to try to "read back" into ancient sources. All points, it needs hardly be said, are at the very least debatable.

279. See also J. Licht, "Taxo, or the Apcalyptic Doctrine of Vengeance," *JJS* 12 (1961) 95-103.

be rescued by the Lord from every evil."[280] Certainly, if Ginsberg was correct that the scriptural model for the "wise ones" in Daniel 11 was the suffering servant of Isa 52:13–53:12, there is even further support for this notion.[281] Ginsberg had argued that the very term "the wise," used in Daniel, is taken from Isa 52:13, "My servant will act wisely," and that the notion of the "wise" in Daniel who make many understand their cause, and cause many people to act righteously, was borrowed from the descriptions of the suffering servant in Second Isaiah. That at least some Hellenistic Jews were advocating a nonviolent approach is clear. Later Pharisaic aversion to killing is widely documented for the time of early rabbinic Judaism,[282] contemporary to the early nonviolence of Jesus and Christianity, particularly noted in the nonviolent teachings of Rabbi Yochanon Ben Zakkai.[283]

It could be argued that in the context of exile, *only* nonviolent resistance is possible. While this would suggest that Daniel's call to nonviolent resistance is not necessarily a principled rejection of all violence (a kind of ancient Hebrew pacifism), the book still insists at the very least that nonviolent resistance is effective and is based on spiritual values of allegiance to the sovereignty of God. Further, the book of Daniel never suggests that its recommended forms of resistance are only interim ethics until a time when Jews will once again be a world power. If anything, this interim period will end with the coming of the reign of God.

In the light of this, how to defeat one's enemies is a serious question in late post-exilic literature. Conquest was always an option—as in the Maccabean movement. But transformation (if not full conversion) was another option; Jonah provides an example, as does Isaiah 19 and particularly Isaiah 2 (nations' "learning the ways of God," and, therefore, not learning war anymore, which is accompanied by a universal destruction of weapons), and perhaps less certainly the story of Ruth. The message of Daniel 1–6, however, is certainly that enemies are conquered by transformation of character and behavior.

Confusion with anemic, liberal notions of pacifism is a serious exegetical block to appreciating fully the models of nonviolence in apocalyptic texts like Daniel 7–12, which presume the concept of spiritual warfare. The writers of these texts are not passive, nor are they averse to using militant language (the latter being a particular difficulty for modern interpreters). Modern Christian pacifists may be embarrassed by the militant language of Jesus and Paul (calling on "legions of angels," "bringing swords," comparing faith to swords, armor, shields, etc.), but the use of such imagery indicates the writer's seriousness and the intensity of the resistance called for. Such imagery is also, inevitably, an ironic rejection of actual swords in favor of the more powerful spiritual ones. But "spiritual weapons" are to be wielded in a real world. The call to the "wise" in Daniel is clearly a call to a form of resistance that is not so removed from worldly realities that it does not engender material, political consequences, such as the reply of the enemies' "sword and flame . . . captivity and plunder" (Dan 11:33 NRSV).

Although Hellenistic texts may not have a fully developed condemnation of violent resistance similar to the later teachings of Jesus, it is clear that their calls for resistance apart from violence provide an important step in this direction. Lest we dismiss even the possibility that the writers of Daniel maintained a principled rejection of violence, we need to remind ourselves that other post-exilic writers were beginning to envision an era without warfare

---

280. Test. Joseph 18:2, in J. H. Charlesworth, ed., *Old Testament Pseudepigrapha* (Garden City, N.Y.: Doubleday, 1983) 823. See also Walter Harrelson, "Patient Love in the Testament of Joseph," *Perspectives in Religious Studies* 4 (1977) 4-13.

281. H. L. Ginsberg, "The Oldest Interpretation of the Suffering Servant," *VT* 3 (1953) 400-404. For Zerbe this is the most convincing argument in the otherwise highly skeptical review of the entire question of Daniel and nonviolence. G. Zerbe, " 'Pacifism' and 'Passive Resistance' in Apocalyptic Writings: A Critical Evaluation," in J. H. Charlesworth and C. A. Evans, *The Pseudepigrapha and Early Biblical Interpretation* (Sheffield: JSOT, 1993) 65-95.

282. See L. Finkelstein, *The Pharisees* (Philadelphia: Jewish Publication Society, 1940) 286-91.

283. Emphasized most clearly in J. Neusner, *A Life of Rabban Yohanan Ben Zakkai* (Leiden: E. J. Brill, 1962), and *Development of a Legend: Studies on the Traditions Concerning Rabban Yohanan Ben Zakkai* (Leiden: E. J. Brill, 1970). See also S. Schwarzschild, "Shalom," *Confrontation* (1981) 166-76.

or domination of others, such as the post-exilic visions of Isa 2:2-4 and 19:22-25. See also *1 Enoch* 52:7-9, a work not otherwise noted for irenic tendencies, which also looks to an era when the breastplate will no longer be worn and iron, used to make weapons, will be taken away by God. We know from the study of visions that such hopes for the future cannot easily be dismissed, since the content of such utopian visions can reflect expressions of contemporary ethical beliefs.

Given all the theological/ethical possibilities raised by post-exilic discussions of foreigners, enemies, transformation, future peaceful disarmament, and resistance in foreign lands, to read Dan 11:34 as a further condemnation of the Maccabean "option" is hardly stretching historical credibility.[284]

284. See Daniel L. Smith-Christopher, "Between Ezra and Isaiah: Exclusion, Transformation, and Inclusion of the 'Foreigners' in Post-Exilic Biblical Theology," in M. Brett, ed., *Ethnicity and the Bible* (Leiden: E. J. Brill, 1996) 117-42.

❖   ❖   ❖   ❖

11:35. For the wise, and for those who listen to them, martyrdom is a reality. The persecution of the wise makes them "refined," "purified," and cleansed ("to whiten"). This portrayal of the faithful is common in the exilic community.

Smelting and refining are often used in the literal sense of the production of metals, especially concerning the creation of idols (see Isa 40:19; 41:7; 46:6). But when used figuratively, these words can mean to "test" someone (see Ps 17:3); the figurative use of smelting as a test is explicit in Jer 6:29: "In vain the refining goes on, for the wicked are not removed" (see also Jer 9:6: "I will now refine and test them, for what else can I do with my sinful people?"). The trials of exile and conquest are often seen as God's testing of the people, as in Zech 13:9: "I will put this third into the fire, /refine them as one refines silver . . . and I will answer them. I will say, 'They are my people' " (NRSV); and Isa 48:10: "I have refined you . . . I have tested you in the furnace of adversity" (NRSV). The adversity of the "wise," therefore, is part of their particular selection by God.

11:36-39, The Impieties of the Greek Ruler. *11:36.* In this section, we find some interesting comments about the religious attitudes of Antiochus IV. The king will act as he pleases, and this hubris includes the claim to near divinity. Associating themselves with cults of emperor worship was typical for Hellenistic rulers, so it was hardly unique of Antiochus IV. The title "Epiphanes," "God manifest"), taken by Antiochus IV, may represent a perceived attitude on his part, and it would have been particularly offensive to the Jews. It is all the more offensive because of Antiochus's intrusion into the internal affairs of the Jewish religion—his intrigue in creating divisions within the Jewish community by buying and selling the high priesthood. The reference to the "God of gods" is an unusual reference to the Jewish God, but is the only possible implication in this verse. On the other hand, the "period of wrath" may refer to God's wrath; it is used elsewhere in the book of Daniel to refer to the wrath of the foreign powers.

11:37. What is particularly interesting about this passage is the comment on Hellenistic religious practices by a Jewish observer. That Antiochus IV did not respect the gods of his ancestors is here apparently meant to be a criticism, indicating the level of sophistication of the writer of the visions. The writer lives in an obviously cosmopolitan world, in which the diversities of religious expressions hold some fascination for him. One can hardly imagine an earlier Jewish writer commenting on whether a particular practitioner of Canaanite ritual was "orthodox" or "heretical" in their Canaanite practice. Here, the implication points to impiety—even in Antiochus's own context and on his terms!

The expression "the one beloved by women" is probably a reference to a cult of Tammuz. Tammuz was an ancient Near Eastern deity particularly revered in a female cult (see Ezek 8:14, where Jewish women are implicated as having participated in this cult).

Antiochus's impieties toward his own traditional religious ways are paralleled, or perhaps pre-eminently represented, in his attacks on the God of gods as well as on the gods of his ancestors. This could be mistaken for monolatry—the worship of one god, without rejecting the idea that other gods may also exist—but the intention is to paint a picture of general impiety and disrespect.

11:38. The god that the visionary of Daniel 10–12 associates with Antiochus IV carries the interesting title "God of fortresses." The fortress refers, undoubtedly, to the citadel established in Jerusalem for the quartering of troops. It was associated with the abomination of desolation in the Temple. Collins has a particularly interesting discussion of this term, calling it "a derisive title, based on its association with the hated Akra, the garrison established by Antiochus in the City of David."[285] In other words, Antiochus associates religion with power based on the military, and he showers on this new form of religious expression the spoils of such power: gold and silver and precious stones. The passage implies a derision of the "loyalty" that money can buy from Antiochus's officials, who are rewarded handsomely. The writer paints a compelling picture of corruption at high levels because of economic gain. Walbank notes the spread of money after Alexander's campaigns in the east—and especially the fact that control of a city was the goal of this purchased loyalty.[286] Green points out that those natives who "went Greek" to seek acceptance were clearly motivated by "social and professional ambition."[287] The garrison is the prime symbol, then, of Antiochus's "reforms" and the ambitions of his Jewish compatriots. Hengel writes that the spirit of Greece was first encountered in the East not by the achievements of philosophy or art, but by its "perfected, superior technique of war."[288] A "god of the fortress" would be a bitter term for a false form of piety that is enforced by the sword rather than by conviction.

11:39. This verse further explicates the ambitious motivation of those who align themselves with power. Hengel points out that apostates were typically given the land dispossessed from the conquered peoples, who were seen as a threat to the state, and that these lands were often worked by semi-slaves (cf. 1 Macc 9:23ff.).[289] The worries of the exiles that they would lose their land (Ezek 11:14-18; 33:23-27) in the Babylonian exile suggests that this was a long-standing practice and a sensitive intra-communal issue throughout the period of foreign rule.

11:40-45, The End of Antiochus. Verse 40 begins the section that goes beyond prophecy that is based on known events. Here we are dealing with speculative material, most of which did not "come pass," as here predicted. In v. 40, Antiochus IV is represented as overextending himself in a campaign against the south—Egypt. But there is no further record of Antiochus IV in Egypt; in fact, he died in the east during a campaign. In this new battle, great emphasis is placed on the amount of technology thrown into the fray—cavalry, chariots, and ships. Antiochus is described almost in the terms of a new Alexander—passing through nations "like a flood." The implication is that this is a time of building power. In v. 41, he brings his war machine into Judea once again, and many thousands of people are killed. A note on the wide extent of the battle includes those who will be spared: the Edomites, the Moabites, and some from the Ammonites. Presumably, they are spared because these three archaic nations once again conspire with the aggressor against the Jewish people. In v. 42, Antiochus's reach extends even into Egypt. Note here that Egypt is named explicitly and that there are references to far-flung peoples of Libya and Ethiopia ("Cush"). The riches of war and command are emphasized: gold and silver and the apparent loyalty of nations. When he finally overextends himself (v. 44), he meets his end; typical of apocalyptic battles, it is brief, quick, and anticlimactic. He will die alone, despite having conquered so many nations. There is no one to help him—the ignoble end of a ravenous emperor. Alexander seems a fitting model here as well.

This section reads as a massive buildup that parallels in an interesting way the buildup in chap. 8, which resulted in attacks against the very stars of heaven. And then it is over. The buildup to a final end is a form familiar in the book of Revelation as well. In short, vv. 40-45 follow apoca-

285. Collins, *Daniel,* Hermeneia, 388.
286. F. W. Walbank, *The Hellenistic World* (Cambridge, Mass.: Harvard University Press, 1982) 65 160-61.
287. P. Green, "Greek Gifts?" *History Today* (June 1990) 29.
288. M. Hengel, *Judaism and Hellenism* (Philadelphia: Fortress, 1974) 12.

289. Ibid.

lyptic style, rather than historical events, toward a final crisis.

12:1-13, The Angels and the Nations at War. Chapter 12 consists of two main sections: A final note on the great vision of chaps. 10–12 (12:1-4) and an additional vision of the two figures on the riverbank, which seems to act as an epilogue to the book as a whole (12:5-13).

12:1-4. *12:1.* We are now reintroduced to Michael, whom the writer left in battle with the Persian and Greek forces (10:21–11:1). Michael is said to "arise," or perhaps to "stand" in the sense of standing before a judicial hearing, which seems warranted by the judgment that follows. Michael is called on because there is to be a time of great distress for the people as a whole, and Michael is meant to be a comforting presence. But most important, the time of great anguish is to be seen as the time of the deliverance of Israel. The obvious relevence of this idea to those who suffer stands without further comment.

Those who are "found written in the book" will survive. The concept of names written in a book for future judgment is a well-known biblical theme (see Ps 69:28; Isa 4:3; Mal 3:16-18) that is carried into the New Testament book of Revelation.

12:2. Historically and theologically, this verse is one of the most important in the entire book of Daniel because of its direct reference to resurrection. Many scholars have speculated that it is because of this reference that Daniel as a work was included in the Hebrew Bible canon by the rabbis in the first centuries of the common era, who affirmed the belief in resurrection as much as did Jesus of Nazareth. But at the same time, a sense of judgment and punishment is also evident here, giving rise to the notion of a final separation, or critical judgment, the good and the evil in the final days (cf. Matt 25:31-46, where the imagery of sheep and goats was clearly influenced by apocalyptic language).

Daniel's reference to resurrection is reminiscent of Isa 26:19: "O dwellers in the dust, awake and sing for joy!" (NRSV). It seems similar also to ideas about reanimation in Ezekiel 37. But it is further emphasized in Dan 12:2 that not all will rise in resurrection. Those who do will look forward to "everlasting life"—a notion that has passed into both rabbinic and Christian theological specula-

tion. As many scholars have shown, this verse in Daniel is the only clear reference to the idea of resurrection and everlasting life (and punishment) throughout the Hebrew Bible. It is also found in roughly contemporary sections of *1 Enoch,* but like the idea of angels, is still a fluid notion that takes different forms in different contexts.[290]

12:3. This verse contains an affirmation of the wise, who were praised for their loyalty to God in 11:31-34, with an emphasis on the brightness of their glory. Light and images of light have served as the main symbol of righteousness throughout the book of Daniel, and this reward awaits those who are rightous. That the "righteous of the people" are equated with stars is once again a reference to a belief in stars as physical beings (see Commentary on 8:10-11).

12:4. The great vision concludes with an emphasis on Daniel's keeping secret what he has seen and understood. That secrecy must be maintained is emphasized because evil will increase (translating as "evil" [הרעת *hārā'ōt*] rather than "knowledge" [הדעת *haddā'at*], two words that look very similar in the Hebrew text). Knowledge is power; thus knowledge of these events would be a comfort to those who seek to be strong in their faith and not "run back and forth." There is an emphasis as well on the avoidance of confusion, which is what is sought through knowledge provided by the wise.

12:5-13, The Epilogue to Daniel: The Two Figures on the Riverside. *12:5.* This verse begins as an addition to the previous vision. Daniel is seeing something more, even after he has been asked to seal and keep secret what he has seen in v. 4. The location of this latter vision is clearly stated, once again, as taking place on a riverbank. The two figures stand on opposite banks of the river.

12:6. The first figure wants to know the same thing that Daniel (and, undoubtedly, the writer of this epilogue) wants to know—namely, the time when these things will come to pass. Note the reference again to linen, the garment of holiness as noted above in reference to the appearance of Gabriel (see Commentary on chap. 10). This one "clothed in linen" thus is a symbol of holiness, and may well represent the heavenly messenger,

---

290. Matt 25:31-46 is a development along the lines pursued by Paul's interesting speculations about the nature of the resurrection body.

while the other is a figure like Daniel himself, or is Daniel himself, which is how the Greek version reads (note that it is Daniel who asks the follow-up question in v. 8). If this is a conversation between two angelic figures, then it suggests that these angels are concerned about the events that have been described. The giving of information associates Gabriel even more with this figure clothed in linen.

12:7. The answer given by the messenger angel (Gabriel?) is interesting: The end time will be "a time, and a time, and a half time," which is a repetition of 7:25. Both passages seem somewhat reminiscent of the words written on the wall for Belshazzar: "MENE, MENE, AND PARSIN" (but not including "TEKEL," which makes this comparison far from exact).

There is a reference to the "shattering of the power of the holy people," once again a collective reference to the entire period of suffering that has been seen in chaps. 10–12. On this, Collins suggests the reading "at the end of the power of the shatterer of the holy people."[291] Either version refers to the same reality, however: the end of the persecution by Antiochus IV.

12:8-9. The narrative returns to the first person, and now it is clearly Daniel who is speaking to the one clothed in linen. Daniel appears to request more information—a precise time (v. 8). It is interesting that the answer is not direct. Rather, Daniel is told to go his way (v. 9). In Hebrew, the two words "closed" (סתמים *sĕtumîm*) and "sealed" (חתמים *ḥătumîm*) rhyme and are written very similarly, and the thought is a stock phrase about apocalyptic secrecy.

12:10. This verse refers to a difference between the righteous and the wicked, repeating elements from chap. 11. The wise "understand" and will know that they are to act as teachers of wisdom during the crisis period. Note that in Matt 24:37-44, Jesus' emphasis on the "final events" includes an "exhortation to watchfulness" precisely because the exact times are unknown. The warning that such events are close but not precisely known is an important technique in apocalyptic litera-ture—with the accompanying emphasis on watch-fulness and faithfulness.

12:11-13. One figure is given in v. 11, 1,290 days, as the time of the end. But then v. 12 has a second figure: 1,335 days. The significance of the two figures is impossible to determine. How-ever, one thing is clear: This section was written by a later editor who continued to wonder when the vision of Daniel would actually be fulfilled. The message in vv. 11-12 is, then, essentially, "It may be at this time, but the faithful will remain strong even if the time continues." The final word in v. 13 is that Daniel should not worry, for his reward is certain in resurrection. The reader is to presume that his or her obedience to the advice of this book will result in a reward, not only for Daniel, but for the reader as well.

Most commentators read the end of chap. 12 as an indication of what happens to millennialist groups that risk making precise predictions about the coming of supernatural events. Certainly there have been many Christian and Jewish sects that have attempted such predictions. But it is inter-esting that many of these groups were not devas-tated when the designated time came and went—there are various theological ways that groups can explain away their error. Christianity as a whole had to deal with the delay of the return of Christ. But the summons to watchful-ness in the light of this delay in Daniel is not a call to irresponsibility because of expectations of imminent changes. It is, rather, a call to faithful-ness knowing that the end is predetermined, even if postponed.

The writer of the book of Daniel, it is true, tried to make precise predictions. But the very fact that we still have this work, and that it is still read with great reverence, is testimony not only to the elasticity of the numbers involved, but also to the fact that the sociology of the book, its attitude of apocalypticism, continues to speak to the condition of peoples in crisis. It is the accuracy of this aspect of the book, and not the numbers themselves, that offers the great comfort of the book of Daniel. Here, at last, is discussion of realities that are suffered by minorities or by people who are forcibly subordinated, discrimi-nated against, or displaced.

291. Collins, *Daniel,* Hermeneia, 369.

REFLECTIONS

The great vision raises a host of important theological issues: resurrection, faith in persecution, the realism or lack of realism in apocalyptic thought. Any of these could be pursued to great benefit. However, the issue of the rise and prominence of angels in this vision, presaged by chaps. 7–9 and even hinted at in chaps. 1–6 (the fourth person in the furnace of Nebuchadnezzar, Daniel's salvation from the lions), may be a provocative entry into a discussion of other interesting issues for modern speculation, especially the subject of spiritual warfare.

Numerous scholarly studies reveal a lively interest in the subject of angels—in the Bible, in the intertestamental period, and in early Christianity. We need not rehearse the many insights provided by these studies on "angelology," most of which consist of amassing the evidence in biblical, Qumran, and non-canonical material.[292] Suffice it to say that there seems to be no coherent "doctrine" of angels such that we can see a detailed consistency in all the texts in which angels appear.

Although an "intermediary" figure is suggested as early as the "angel of the LORD" in Genesis 16 (cf. the angel of the Passover in Exodus), this appears to be an early form of a "presence of God" (note the interplay of references to an intermediary, and then to God, in Genesis 16, Hagar in the wilderness). Rowland, among others, sees a kind of evolution toward an increasingly personified figure—from Genesis 16 to Ezekiel, and thence to Daniel—until writers could speak of angels by name and rank in the late exilic period.[293]

What is perplexing is the question of why angels should become such a focus of attention. As the circumstances of the exilic life-style continue, there is an angelic population explosion in some of the Jewish writings. Just as significant, there is a complex bureaucracy of angels as well. The two most frequent metaphors are clearly court and military. Angels are messengers and courtiers, on the one hand, and military officers, on the other; they attend to matters of state in the kingdom of God, and they fight this kingdom's battles. Some angels are involved in a betrayal of the court and intrigue (the "fall" of some angels in *1 Enoch*). All of this strongly suggests that the guiding metaphor for angelic elaboration in Jewish Hellenistic (and perhaps late Persian) literature is precisely the realities of world empire, under whose boots the Jews lived. As the legions of Nebuchadnezzar, Cyrus, and Alexander marched across the ancient Near East, angelic legions marched from the Jewish apocalypticists' theological speculations. And just as legends about the emperor became more and more spectacular and removed from common experience, so also God somewhat retreats behind the layers of angelic bureaucracy. In Daniel, certainly, the angels are far more active than is the omniscient, omnipotent power represented as the Ancient of Days, about whom we have only impressive descriptions of power and thrones. This leads to a possible conclusion that God becomes the ultimate conquerer whose throne outshines and overpowers all the thrones of the earth, but about whom we know as little as we do about the emperor himself, to whom God is contrasted.

Stated in this way, we see an obvious reason why Daniel 1–6 is connected to Daniel 7–12. Emphasizing court tales vs. apocalyptic has overdrawn the contrast between the two halves of the book when, in fact, both halves deal with God's court vs. human courts. God as sovereign is an idea intended to challenge the idea of the emperor as sovereign. Daniel the visionary in chaps. 7–12 is also a courtier of the true king; the tales in chaps. 1–6 serve only to highlight the difference in loyalties between one who lives in one court, serving one king, while actually being obedient to the other king, his God.

292. Some recent studies include S. Olyan, *A Thousand Thousands Serve Him* (Tübingen: J. C. B. Mohr, 1993); W. Heidt, *Angelology of the Old Testament* (Washington, D.C.: Catholic University Press, 1949); M. J. Davidson, *Angels at Qumran* (Sheffield: JSOT, 1992); C. Newsom, "Angels," *ABD*, 6 vols. (New York: Doubleday, 1992) 1:248-53; M. Mach, *Entwicklungsstaudien des jüdischen Engeiglaubens in vorrabbinischer Zeit* (Tübingen: Mohr, 1992).

293. Christopher Rowland, *The Open Heavens* (London: SPCK, 1982) 78-123.

This is not to deny that chaps. 7–12 certainly make the opposition to earthly rulers more obvious than do the stories in chaps. 1–6. The resistance in the first half of the book of Daniel stops short of actually pulling princes down from their thrones. One could argue that, in a profound sense, these rulers step down of their own accord, accepting a transformed basis for rulership and a new ethic of ruling in the light of their insights into the true sovereignty of God. But if the stories ended with a military conquest of the enemy, their effectiveness would have been seriously limited for those who knew that violent revolution was pointless. The power of the calls to resistance in Daniel is precisely the subversive call to resist *even under the present circumstances.*

If Daniel 1–6 is about previous loyalties, then the entire book of Daniel is a call to arms for spiritual warfare, or a training manual for serving in God's "court" while living in the human world. The weapons of war and the training for service both involve the same thing: knowledge of the truth. That is why the wise are warriors—their weapon is knowledge. In chaps. 7–12 (esp. chaps. 10–12), we see the offensive weapon of the faithful: truth (or "instruction," 11:35). Truth is a weapon far more powerful than a sword, which is why it is so often *called* a sword in both the Hebrew Bible and the New Testament (the prophets "slay with the sword": Job 5:15; Isa 49:2; Jer 25:16; Amos 4:10; "the sword, which is the word of God," Eph 6:17; Rev 1:16; 2:12).

Violence masquerades as action. Guns make people believe that they are doing something. But violence always covers truth, attempts to hide it or destroy it. Consider all the machinery of the former Soviet Union, dedicated to keeping words from its citizenry or the careful control of the news media by the United States during the Persian Gulf War. Further, in so many of the revolutionary struggles brought about by swords instead of truth, the swords are then soon turned on their own citizens when these revolutionaries are in power. Yet, all the millions spent on armaments cannot hide the truth forever. Dictators fear *knowledge* most of all.

"The wise will take action . . . and instruct the many." The beginning of action is knowledge. *The Pedagogy of the Oppressed,* by Paolo Freire is the early classic of Latin American thought that fed directly into liberation theology's emphasis on conscientization.[294] Conscientization— education to make one conscious of the realities of one's social and spiritual condition—is the process of encouraging an emerging awareness of the mechanics of economic and social realities—in Daniel's case, spiritual realities. The importance of this basic truth should prevent anyone from the false criticism that Daniel advocates passive or resigned nonaction rather than a Maccabean, active engagement by means of violence. Daniel calls for war, but not warfare like that of the nations. To take Daniel seriously as a basis for contemporary theology, we must be prepared for a call to arms, for we are called to nothing less than spiritual warfare with material realities; what the early Quakers called "The Lamb's War" (borrowing the image from the other biblical apocalyptic work, Revelation). Daniel's final vision is a description of the powers of this world and the struggles of the "covenanted people" within the orbit of these powers.

"Speaking truth to power" is a recent Quaker ideal that is the equivalent of Daniel's imagery of Michael's taking up the sword of truth against the foreign powers. Speaking truth is not mere advocacy as opposed to action. Speaking truth *is* action because truth empowers, inspires, and guides. If God is our emperor and Christ is our victorious general, then no earthly power will command our total loyalty again. Truth, if taught, will not be defeated. The most revolutionary act under Antiochus IV, according to Daniel, was for one to *be* a Jew and to teach others to be a Jew. The most revolutionary act in the modern world is first of all to be a woman or a man of faith—to reject violence, to reject the abuse of the weak, and to embrace the gospel of life and teach it to others. The revolution of truth must arise from education

---

294. Paolo Freire, *The Pedagogy of the Oppressed* (New York: Herder & Herder, 1970).

and conviction by the truth, and never by coercion. Coercion always demands empty exercises in false discipline and obedience to idols, because both are necessary to the rule of the armed few. How can a democracy emerge from a militaristic, hierarchical, disciplined culture of unquestioned obedience to superiors? Truth rules by the power of the many. It is inherently democratic, because its power derives from the convictions of the masses, and not from the forced obedience of the masses. It is, in short, war by angelic power—a lamb's war. It is the way of Daniel the wise. It is a way of saying: "Michael has conquered—let us teach of his victory!"

THE ADDITIONS TO DANIEL

INTRODUCTION, COMMENTARY, AND REFLECTIONS
BY
DANIEL L. SMITH-CHRISTOPHER

THE ADDITIONS TO
DANIEL

INTRODUCTION

THE GREEK TRANSLATION OF THE OLD TESTAMENT

The importance of the Greek translations of the Old Testament for biblical and textual research is hard to exaggerate. Indeed, Ernst Wurthwein states that the Septuagint is so significant that "apart from it both Christendom and Western Culture would be inconceivable."[1] But how these Greek versions were produced is a controversial subject in scholarly debate.

According to the Letter of Aristeas, which scholars date from about the second century BCE into the first century CE, Ptolemy II Philadelphus commissioned the translation of the Jewish Scriptures to be a part of his great library at Alexandria. The text was miraculously translated by seventy-two elders in precisely seventy-two days, thus it was named "Septuagint." The translation was read and proved to be without error by the Jewish community itself. The story gives us the impression that there was one book that was considered "the" Greek version of the Old Testament. But scholarly views of the origin of the Septuagint suggest that the production was considerably more complex than a single event or version, and furthermore had much more to do with the need of Jews in the diaspora for a version of the Bible in their newly adopted language, Greek. The need for a Greek version of the Hebrew Bible sometime after Alexander's conquests of the ancient Near East, therefore, is a measure of cultural change and social transformation in the Jewish community.

1. E. Wurthwein, *The Text of the Old Testament,* trans. E. F. Rhoades (Grand Rapids: Eerdmans, 1979) 57.

Scholarly study of the Greek versions of Daniel focuses on two older Greek versions of the book of Daniel: the Old Greek or LXX version and the "Theodotion" version. Moore points out that in the story of Susanna, the differences between the LXX and the Theodotion versions are the greatest, while in the Song of the Three the differences are not very significant.[2] Bel and the Dragon occupies a middle position.

Although the entire Theodotion Old Testament is usually dated to the second century CE, the book of Daniel itself presents special problems. Since the Theodotion version of Daniel is cited in the New Testament, the book of Daniel that became a part of the later Theodotion version must itself be older. This Theodotion version of Daniel, however, became the accepted version for the Christian church, over the Old Greek version. In this commentary, I will use the Theodotion text and occasionally draw attention to differing readings in the LXX.

When these Greek translations were produced, many of the books of the Hebrew Bible were expanded with material that may or may not go back to a Hebrew or Aramaic original. Although, in the case of the additions to Daniel, many scholars argue that these stories do go back to Semitic originals, no evidence of a Semitic language version of these stories has been found as yet.

Writing as a Protestant scholar, I regard it a pity that Protestants generally have little exposure to the Greek additions to Daniel because of Luther's insistence on the Hebrew text as the acceptable canon of the Old Testament, as opposed to the traditional Christian use of the Greek canon of the Old Testament, which included these Deutero-canonical works. Apart from any theological issues of what constituted the canon (which is a doctrinal issue that quite properly has little bearing on scholarly and historical study of texts), these additions are fascinating indicators of concerns and issues in the Jewish community in the late Hellenistic period. A study of the additional Greek material about figures like Jeremiah, Daniel, Esther, and Joseph reveals further concerns with themes of intercultural contact, political occupation and exile, and the traditions of facing foreign power with faith in God's redeeming power. Such issues were on the minds of Jews in Hellenistic and Roman occupied Near Eastern territories from the second century BCE into the common era. We will see in these additions to Daniel that many of the themes of the canonical book of Daniel—sovereignty, resistance, and idolatry, for example—are developed and expanded upon. This also means that a key to understanding these additions, as much as the canonical stories of Daniel, is the experience of disenfranchisement and loss of self-determination that exile, as well as political occupation in one's own homeland, involves.

(See the annotated bibliography for the Hebrew book of Daniel.)

2. C. A. Moore, *Daniel, Esther, and Jeremiah: The Additions,* AB 44 (Garden City, N.Y.: Doubleday, 1977) 16.

OUTLINE OF THE ADDITIONS TO DANIEL

I. The Prayer of Azariah and the Song of the Three Jews, verses 1-68

    A. Verses 1-22, The Prayer of Azariah
    B. Verses 23-27, The Angelic Liberation from the Fire
    C. Verses 28-68, The Song of the Three Jews

II. Susanna, verses 1-64

III. Bel and the Dragon, verses 1-42

    A. Verses 1-22, The Story of Bel
    B. Verses 23-42, The Story of the Dragon

THE PRAYER OF AZARIAH AND THE SONG OF THE THREE JEWS

VERSES 1-68

OVERVIEW

Tradition assigns this addition to the name of one of Daniel's three companions, Azariah. But the other two, Hananiah and Mashael, are present in the second part of the text, the Psalm of Praise, because it is an extension of chap. 3, located between vv. 23-24 of the Hebrew/Aramaic text. Notably, their Jewish names rather than their Babylonian slave names are highlighted, further emphasizing that early tradition certainly did not miss the significance of the names, even if most modern commentators attach little importance to it.

Moore divides this section along the following lines: vv. 1-22, prayer; vv. 23-28, prose; vv. 29-34, ode; vv. 35-68, psalm.[3] However, Moore himself notes that not many scholars make a clear distinction between the ode and the psalm. There is little linguistic basis for such a differentiation. But the three general sections—prayer, prose, and psalm—are helpful divisions for a reading of this text.

3. Moore, *Daniel, Esther, and Jeremiah*, 41-43.

VERSES 1-22, THE PRAYER OF AZARIAH

NAB	NRSV

[24] They walked about in the flames, singing to God and blessing the Lord. [25] In the fire Azariah stood up and prayed aloud:
 [26] "Blessed are you, and praiseworthy,
    O Lord, the God of our fathers,
    and glorious forever is your name.
 [27] For you are just in all you have done;
    all your deeds are faultless, all your ways right,
    and all your judgments proper.
 [28] You have executed proper judgments
    in all that you have brought upon us
    and upon Jerusalem, the holy city of our
       fathers.
    By a proper judgment you have done all this
    because of our sins;
	(Additions to Daniel, inserted between 3.23 and 3.24)
	    [1]They[a] walked around in the midst of the flames, singing hymns to God and blessing the Lord. [2]Then Azariah stood still in the fire and prayed aloud:
	 [3] "Blessed are you, O Lord, God of our
	       ancestors, and worthy of praise;
	    and glorious is your name forever!
	 [4] For you are just in all you have done;
	    all your works are true and your ways right,
	    and all your judgments are true.
	 [5] You have executed true judgments in all you
	       have brought upon us
	    and upon Jerusalem, the holy city of our
	       ancestors;

Verse numbering of the NAB is taken from the Greek text of Daniel, which includes these verses as part of a longer section between verses 3:23 and 3:24 of the corresponding Hebrew text.
  3, 24-90. According to Th; not in MT.

[a] That is, Hananiah, Mishael, and Azariah (Dan 2.17), the original names of Shadrach, Meshach, and Abednego (Dan 1.6-7)

29 For we have sinned and transgressed
by departing from you,
and we have done every kind of evil.
30 Your commandments we have not heeded or
observed,
nor have we done as you ordered us for our
good.
31 Therefore all you have brought upon us,
all you have done to us,
you have done by a proper judgment.
32 You have handed us over to our enemies,
lawless and hateful rebels;
to an unjust king, the worst in all the world.
33 Now we cannot open our mouths;
we, your servants, who revere you,
have become a shame and a reproach.
34 For your name's sake, do not deliver us up
forever,
or make void your covenant.
35 Do not take away your mercy from us,
for the sake of Abraham, your beloved,
Isaac your servant, and Israel your holy one,
36 To whom you promised to multiply their
offspring
like the stars of heaven,
or the sand on the shore of the sea.
37 For we are reduced, O Lord, beyond any other
nation,
brought low everywhere in the world this
day
because of our sins.
38 We have in our day no prince, prophet, or
leader,
no holocaust, sacrifice, oblation, or incense,
no place to offer first fruits, to find favor
with you.
39 But with contrite heart and humble spirit
let us be received;
40 As though it were holocausts of rams and
bullocks,
or thousands of fat lambs,
So let our sacrifice be in your presence today
as we follow you unreservedly;
for those who trust in you cannot be put to
shame.
41 And now we follow you with our whole heart,
we fear you and we pray to you.
42 Do not let us be put to shame,

by a true judgment you have brought all this
upon us because of our sins.
6 For we have sinned and broken your law in
turning away from you;
in all matters we have sinned grievously.
7 We have not obeyed your commandments,
we have not kept them or done what you
have commanded us for our own
good.
8 So all that you have brought upon us,
and all that you have done to us,
you have done by a true judgment.
9 You have handed us over to our enemies,
lawless and hateful rebels,
and to an unjust king, the most wicked in
all the world.
10 And now we cannot open our mouths;
we, your servants who worship you, have
become a shame and a reproach.
11 For your name's sake do not give us up
forever,
and do not annul your covenant.
12 Do not withdraw your mercy from us,
for the sake of Abraham your beloved
and for the sake of your servant Isaac
and Israel your holy one,
13 to whom you promised
to multiply their descendants like the stars
of heaven
and like the sand on the shore of the sea.
14 For we, O Lord, have become fewer than any
other nation,
and are brought low this day in all the world
because of our sins.
15 In our day we have no ruler, or prophet, or leader,
no burnt offering, or sacrifice, or oblation,
or incense,
no place to make an offering before you and
to find mercy.
16 Yet with a contrite heart and a humble spirit
may we be accepted,
17 as though it were with burnt offerings of rams
and bulls,
or with tens of thousands of fat lambs;
such may our sacrifice be in your sight
today,
and may we unreservedly follow you,[a]

a Meaning of Gk uncertain

NAB

but deal with us in your kindness and great mercy.

43 Deliver us by your wonders,
and bring glory to your name, O Lord:

44 Let all those be routed
who inflict evils on your servants;
Let them be shamed and powerless,
and their strength broken;

45 Let them know that you alone are the Lord God,
glorious over the whole world."

NRSV

for no shame will come to those who trust in you.

18 And now with all our heart we follow you;
we fear you and seek your presence.

19 Do not put us to shame,
but deal with us in your patience
and in your abundant mercy.

20 Deliver us in accordance with your marvelous works,
and bring glory to your name, O Lord.

21 Let all who do harm to your servants be put to shame;
let them be disgraced and deprived of all power,
and let their strength be broken.

22 Let them know that you alone are the Lord God,
glorious over the whole world."

COMMENTARY

Verses 1-2, Facing the Threat with Singing. The first section, the Prayer of Azariah (or The Three), is a prayer of confession and forgiveness, very much on the same model as Daniel 9. See the Commentary on Daniel 9 for extensive comparisons, but suffice it to say that here we find many of the same themes that were obviously typical of this form of penitential prayer of communal confession. What is significant here is the context of mortal danger that once again accompanies such prayers of confession. The obvious intention of such prayers was to call on the power of God's deliverance.

Part of the context is the importance of the danger itself. Twice, in vv. 1-2, it is emphasized that Azariah stood "in the midst of" the flames. It is not the case that there was no danger; they actually faced a true threat, and thus the earlier comments recorded in Daniel 3 that they would not bow down to Nebuchadnezzar's statue "even if God does *not* deliver them" ought to be fresh in mind.

The text records that the three "sang hymns" while in the furnace. The very term "hymn" comes from the Greek, and the call to sing to the Lord is often found in circumstances of great celebration (see Judg 16:24, where the Philistines sing to their gods; see also 1 Chr 16:9; 2 Chr

23:13; Jdt 15:13; 16:13). Such celebration is found elsewhere besides this instance in the fiery furnace. Note the striking similarity to Acts 16, where Paul and Silas sing hymns in prison (see below). The obvious theme is one of remembering God's liberating power, even in the midst of apparent defeat.

Verses 3-22, The Penitential Prayer in the Furnace. Although the Theodition text has only Azariah praying, in the LXX tradition, all three men pray. This is a minor point, however, since it is clear that it is meant to be a communal prayer in any case. Moore finds this prayer "glaringly inappropriate"[4] because these three are praying a prayer of confession, even though they are being punished precisely for their obedience to God. However, as indicated in the Commentary on Daniel 9, this formulaic confession is appropriate as a preparation for calling on God's deliverance. Thus it is no more out of place than moderns who begin a prayer of request with a word of repentance and was clearly the set form in any case. Moore's criticism takes the setting of a story a bit too literally. The story is meant to teach—i.e., when in trouble, pray in this fashion.

4. Ibid., 40, 60.

Verses 3:8. Many of the phrases found in this confessional prayer are worthy of comment. For example, the phrase "God of *our* ancestors," found in vv. 3 and 29, is significant (note the late occurences of the first-person plural form in 1 Kings 8; Ezra 7:27; Dan 2:23; 1 Esdr 1:50; 4:60; Tob 8:5). The phrase is particularly significant in late biblical use. The second-person form "your ancestors" is more common in the deuteronomic materials. But the change to first person as the more typical form may not be an insignificant detail, given its prominent setting in prayers of confession, which emphasize the sins of "our" fathers as well. The speaker, then, is included in these prayers, and the reader/hearer of the story is equally drawn in. (Note also that Jerusalem is called the holy city of "our" ancestors in v. 5. Similarly, the phrase "ways of truth" [v. 4] is notable in Dan 4:37; 1 Esdr 4:40; Tob 3:2.)

Furthermore, the legal language of God as judge appears in the use of the expression "true judgments" in vv. 5 and 8. However, the term carries significant implications for God's assurance of social justice for the oppressed as well (cf. Zech 7:9-10: "Thus says the Lord of hosts: Render true judgments, show kindness and mercy to one another; do not oppress the widow, the orphan, the alien, or the poor; and do not devise evil in your hearts against one another"; Zech 8:16 adds, significantly, that true judgments "make peace").

The NRSV translation of v. 7 unfortunately misses an interesting progression in responding to the law. The first phrase contains the Greek term for "listening" (rendered in the NRSV as "obeyed"), which can be compared to Dan 7:28, where it is often translated "kept in mind." But if the term is read more as "heard," then we have the interesting progression:

> Your commandments, we have not heard
> we have not considered
> we have not obeyed[5]

Verse 9. The circumstances of exile and political oppression come to mind powerfully in this verse. The suggestion is that the Jews face "enemies" and the "wicked," virtually embodied in a king who is called "unjust" and "the most wicked

in the world." The same term for "wicked" (πονηρός *ponēros*) is used as a noun to refer to Satan in the New Testament (Matt 13:19). Forms of the same term occur in powerful pieces of sage advice in Sir: "Never trust your enemy, for like corrosion in copper, so is his *wickedness*" (12:10); "The knowledge of *wickedness* is not wisdom" (19:22); and, provocatively, "There is a cleverness that is *detestable*!" (19:23).

Verse 10. This verse laments the condition of "shame and reproach." Once again, the writer has used terms that often appear together in wisdom literature. Note Prov 19:26, which refers to "children who cause shame and bring reproach," and Sir 6:1, "a bad name incurs shame and reproach." The emphasis here, as is also found in some deuteronomic phrases, is on the public nature of Jewish life in a cosmopolitan world. They are very aware that their status as members of a defeated nation presents a challenge to the credibility of their faith claims. Clearly, the call to sing hymns in prison is either a bold belief that this prison does not represent ultimate realities, or it is a very public display of hopelessness that borders on insanity. Much of the post-exilic materials display a very keen awareness of the fact that for a people living under occupation, every aspect of life is circumspect, including the exercise of faith. The faith of occupied people is a faith that is daily examined by the eyes and ears of their oppressors, and thus the fear of shame and reproach is quite real.[6] It is important to note the awareness of others' watching and controlling, which is an aspect of political occupation as well as other similar situations of what Erving Goffman called "institutions of total control":

Total institutions disrupt or defile precisely those actions that in civil society have the role of attesting to the actor and those in his presence that he has some command over his world—that he is a person with "adult" self-determination, autonomy, and freedom of action.[7]

Verse 11. This sense of being in the midst of foreigners who are watching is also clear in the deuteronomic phrase in v. 11: "for your name's sake." The danger is that the people's circum-

---

5. C. A. Moore, *Daniel, Esther, and Jeremiah: The Additions* (Garden City, N.Y.: Doubleday, 1977) 57, compares Deut 4:1; 5:1; 6:3; 7:12.

6. Note the studies of Japanese Americans who were sent to concentration camps in the United States during World War II. See Daniel Smith, *The Religion of the Landless: The Sociology of the Babylonian Exile* (New York: Meyer-Stone, 1989) 71-73.

7. E. Goffman, *Asylums* (Aldine: Chicago, 1961) 43.

stances will be such that the covenant with God will appear to be annulled (v. 11*b*; cf. the deuteronomic fear of abrogating the covenant in Deut 31:16, 20; Judg 2:1; 1 Kgs 15:19; and in the prophetic literature in Isa 24:5; Jer 11:10; 14:21; Zech 11:10, 14).

Verses 12-14. The contingency of the covenant, alluded to in v. 11, is then compared to the unilateral promise to Abraham referred to in vv. 12-13. Note the reference to the "stars of heaven," clearly referring to God's promise to Abraham in Gen 15:5. Here we see the significance of the constant emphasis on "our ancestors," for they represent both the consistency of God's saving action in the past and the promise of God's saving presence in the future.

The reality of the present state of the people, however, is that they are *not* as numerous as the stars in the heavens or the sands on the shore. The threat is that they will diminish. Verse 14 refers to their being fewer than any other nation; the same worry is expressed in Bar 2:34, where the discussion is once again in the context of mentioning the promise to the patriarchs. The advice to encourage marriage and procreation was advised in the letter to the exiles in Jer 29:6, where Jeremiah commands: "Do not decrease!" Finally, note the importance of the hymn of praise in 1 Chr 16:19-22*a,* where the issue of being few in number is directly associated with the conditions of the post-exilic community:

When they were few in number,
    of little account, and strangers in the land,
wandering from nation to nation,
    from one kingdom to another people,
he allowed no one to oppress them;
    he rebuked kings on their account,
saying, "Do not touch my anointed ones." (NRSV)

Verses 15-18. The list of offices that are missing among the people in v. 15 is an interesting reference to the lack of complete independence in post-exilic, occupied Palestine. The first two terms, "ruler" (ἄρχων *archōn*) and "prophet" (προφήτης *prophētēs*), are clear in the Greek, but the third term (ἡγούμενος *hēgoumenos*), translated simply as "leader" in the NRSV, is indeed an ambiguous word that often is used to translate quite different terms in Hebrew that delineate distinct and fairly specific levels of authority, whether political or military ("governor," "officer," etc.). But the generality of having

no such leaders seems appropriate here—in essence a representation of not being master of one's own fate. Moore, however, protests that part of this is not accurate for a setting in the exile, since prophets like Ezekiel were active.[8] He argues, therefore, for a later historical setting for this writing, presumably when prophecy really was considered to have ended.[9]

That the Jews are not able to offer sacrifice is an interesting reference to the exilic period specifically, despite the fact that this work was clearly written during the time of the Second Temple (515 BCE?–70 CE). But the inability to offer sacrifice sets up an important mention of a "humble spirit and a contrite heart" (v. 16), which is deemed superior to temple sacrifice. Indeed, references to humbleness of spirit and contrition of heart are often seen in contexts of severe doubt about the efficacy of the sacrificial system:

For you have no delight in sacrifice;
    if I were to give a burnt offering, you would not be
        pleased.
The sacrifice acceptable to God is a broken spirit;
    a broken and contrite heart, O God, you will not
        despise. (Ps 51:16-17 NRSV)

I dwell in the high and holy place,
    and also with those who are contrite and humble in
        spirit,
to revive the spirit of the humble,
    and to revive the heart of the contrite. (Isa 57:15 NRSV)

But this is the one to whom I will look,
    to the humble and contrite in spirit,
    who trembles at my word. (Isa 66:2 NRSV)

The final passage quoted, Isa 66:2, is perhaps most noted for its rejection of a narrow definition not only of the efficacy of sacrifice, but also of *who* is acceptable to God, and it suggests that foreigners will be added to the number of the people of God. Thus humble contrition becomes almost the very definition of faith.

Trust in contrition and humbleness is thus contrasted with outward expressions of religious observance. When it is said that no shame will come to those who trust in God (v. 17*b*), we are

---

8. Moore, *Daniel, Esther, and Jeremiah,* 58.
9. This is, of course, a relative statement. Some Jewish groups, including Christianity and then second-century CE Christian sects, believed that prophecy never ceased.

reminded of Ezra's faith in God when he rejected a military guard offered by the king, so as to avoid the shame of appearing faithless (Ezra 8:22).

Verses 19-22. In vv. 19-20, shame is contrasted with God's very public deliverance of the people. Once again, we are reminded of the public and, therefore, confessional and apologetic nature of shame and trust for Israelites under political occupation. The constant reference to mercy

(ἐλέους *eleoys*; חסד *ḥesed*) is a reminder that God's mercy was often seen as God's liberating power against the overwhelming enemies of God's people.

Those who watch, assess, judge, and evaluate the occupied peoples (vv. 21-22) are referred to most powerfully in the final sentence, "Let them know . . ." with a reference to God's power to bring about the end of "their" power. (See Reflections at vv. 28-68).

VERSES 23-27, THE ANGELIC LIBERATION FROM THE FIRE

NAB	NRSV
[46] Now the king's men who had thrown them in continued to stoke the furnace with brimstone, pitch, tow, and faggots. [47] The flames rose forty-nine cubits above the furnace, [48] and spread out, burning the Chaldeans nearby. [49] But the angel of the Lord went down into the furnace with Azariah and his companions, drove the fiery flames out of the furnace, [50] and made the inside of the furnace as though a dew-laden breeze were blowing through it. The fire in no way touched them or caused them pain or harm.	[23]Now the king's servants who threw them in kept stoking the furnace with naphtha, pitch, tow, and brushwood. [24]And the flames poured out above the furnace forty-nine cubits, [25]and spread out and burned those Chaldeans who were caught near the furnace. [26]But the angel of the Lord came down into the furnace to be with Azariah and his companions, and drove the fiery flame out of the furnace, [27]and made the inside of the furnace as though a moist wind were whistling through it. The fire did not touch them at all and caused them no pain or distress.

COMMENTARY

Similar to Daniel 7–12, immediately following the penitential prayer an angelic messenger appears, representing God's assistance to humble servants. This passage takes its cue from an expansion of the Aramaic text in Daniel 3:22. Moore notes that many scholars have considered this prose section about angelic liberation to belong to the original Semitic version of Daniel 3, since there appears to be a gap between verses 23 and 24 of that chapter.[10] Further, the prayer should be set before the deliverance. But note that in the Theodotion version of these events, the early death of the officers who threw the three into the fire is omitted, only to be mentioned here; therefore, no

contradiction is evident. This prose section provides further details missing from the canonical version.

In typical fashion for Daniel, a list is provided to emphasize the way that the fire was made even hotter—so hot that it burned those who forced the Jews into the flames.[11] Thus verses 23-25 serve as further clarification of the brief summary statement made in the Hebrew text.

Verses 26-27. The one who had the appearance of a "son of the gods" in the Aramaic text (Dan 3:25) and who caused Nebuchadnezzar such alarm is here explicitly identified as an angelic

10. Moore, *Daniel, Esther, and Jeremiah.*

11. There is evidence that the historical Nebuchadnezzar used fire as a form of punishment and execution. See ibid., 62; C. Kuhl, *Die drei Männer im Feure,* BZAW 55 (1940).

messenger of God. The agent of God's deliverance is the "angel of the Lord," or "messenger of the Lord" as seen in such important passages as Genesis 16 (saving Hagar in the wilderness), Exod 3:2 (the presence in the burning bush in the call of Moses), Exod 14:19 (the protective presence of God with the people in the wilderness), and, in a more secular setting, in 2 Sam 2:5 (messengers sent by David). Thus, while this passage is typical of late post-exilic and apocalyptic literature in its detailed interest in angelic couriers of God's will, it is certainly also in line with much older textual representations of God's deliverance of the weak.

The text further explains exactly how the three Jews were spared by God. The heat of the flame was transformed by a "wind of dew" or "moist wind" that blew through the furnace. The term "dew" (δρόσος *drosos*) is used in a number of places throughout Scripture where it is related to

God's saving grace. In the context of God's healing of rebellious Israel, Hos 14:5 has God saying, "I shall be like the dew to Israel." Micah 5:7 states that the remnant of Jacob "shall be like dew from the Lord." When God sows peace, the "skies shall give their dew" (Zech 8:12). Finally, and perhaps most powerfully, note Isa 26:19 (NRSV):

Your dead shall live, their corpses shall rise.
  O dwellers in the dust, awake and sing for joy!
For your dew is a radiant dew,
  and the earth will give birth to those long dead.

So it is not merely that a "dew" from heaven contrasts markedly with the flames, but that this dew is frequently associated with God's grace and power in comforting God's people (see also Sir 18:16; 43:22).[12] (See Reflections at vv. 28-68.)

12. See also the discussion of rain as justice in Moshe Weinfeld, *Social Justice in Ancient Israel and in the Ancient Near East* (Minneapolis: Fortress, 1995) 53.

VERSES 28-68, THE SONG OF THE THREE JEWS

NAB	NRSV
[51] Then these three in the furnace with one voice sang, glorifying and blessing God:	[28] Then the three with one voice praised and glorified and blessed God in the furnace:
[52] "Blessed are you, O Lord, the God of our fathers,	[29] "Blessed are you, O Lord, God of our ancestors,
praiseworthy and exalted above all forever;	and to be praised and highly exalted forever;
And blessed is your holy and glorious name,	[30] And blessed is your glorious, holy name,
praiseworthy and exalted above all for all ages.	and to be highly praised and highly exalted forever.
[53] Blessed are you in the temple of your holy glory,	[31] Blessed are you in the temple of your holy glory,
praiseworthy and glorious above all forever.	and to be extolled and highly glorified forever.
[54] Blessed are you on the throne of your kingdom,	[32] Blessed are you who look into the depths from your throne on the cherubim,
praiseworthy and exalted above all forever.	and to be praised and highly exalted forever.
[55] Blessed are you who look into the depths from your throne upon the cherubim,	[33] Blessed are you on the throne of your kingdom,
praiseworthy and exalted above all forever.	and to be extolled and highly exalted forever.
[56] Blessed are you in the firmament of heaven,	[34] Blessed are you in the firmament of heaven,
praiseworthy and glorious forever.	and to be sung and glorified forever.
[57] Bless the Lord, all you works of the Lord,	
praise and exalt him above all forever.	[35] "Bless the Lord, all you works of the Lord;

3,54f: Trsp *eulogēmenos ei 'o epiblepōn abyssous, kathēmenos epi cheroubein* with *eulogēmenos ei epi thronou tēs basileias sou:* so LXX.

NAB

58 Angels of the Lord, bless the Lord,
    praise and exalt him above all forever.
59 You heavens, bless the Lord,
    praise and exalt him above all forever.
60 All you waters above the heavens, bless the
        Lord,
    praise and exalt him above all forever.
61 All you hosts of the Lord, bless the Lord;
    praise and exalt him above all forever.
62 Sun and moon, bless the Lord;
    praise and exalt him above all forever.
63 Stars of heaven, bless the Lord;
    praise and exalt him above all forever.
64 Every shower and dew, bless the Lord;
    praise and exalt him above all forever.
65 All you winds, bless the Lord;
    praise and exalt him above all forever.
66 Fire and heat, bless the Lord;
    praise and exalt him above all forever.
67 [Cold and chill, bless the Lord;
    praise and exalt him above all forever.
68 Dew and rain, bless the Lord;
    praise and exalt him above all forever.]
69 Frost and chill, bless the Lord;
    praise and exalt him above all forever.
70 Ice and snow, bless the Lord;
    praise and exalt him above all forever.
71 Nights and days, bless the Lord;
    praise and exalt him above all forever.
72 Light and darkness, bless the Lord;
    praise and exalt him above all forever.
73 Lightnings and clouds, bless the Lord;
    praise and exalt him above all forever.
74 Let the earth bless the Lord,
    praise and exalt him above all forever.
75 Mountains and hills, bless the Lord;
    praise and exalt him above all forever.
76 Everything growing from the earth, bless the
        Lord;
    praise and exalt him above all forever.
77 You springs, bless the Lord;
    praise and exalt him above all forever.
78 Seas and rivers, bless the Lord;
    praise and exalt him above all forever.

3, 67-72: Order of verses as in LXX.
3, 67: Variant of v 69; not in Th.
3, 68: Variant of v. 64; not in Th.
3, 69: (eulogeite,) pagoi kai psychos: so LXX.
3, 77f: Trsp v 77 with v 78: so LXX.

NRSV

    sing praise to him and highly exalt him
        forever.
36 Bless the Lord, you heavens;
    sing praise to him and highly exalt him
        forever.
37 Bless the Lord, you angels of the Lord;
    sing praise to him and highly exalt him
        forever.
38 Bless the Lord, all you waters above the
        heavens;
    sing praise to him and highly exalt him
        forever.
39 Bless the Lord, all you powers of the Lord;
    sing praise to him and highly exalt him
        forever.
40 Bless the Lord, sun and moon;
    sing praise to him and highly exalt him
        forever.
41 Bless the Lord, stars of heaven;
    sing praise to him and highly exalt him
        forever.
42 "Bless the Lord, all rain and dew;
    sing praise to him and highly exalt him
        forever.
43 Bless the Lord, all you winds;
    sing praise to him and highly exalt him
        forever.
44 Bless the Lord, fire and heat;
    sing praise to him and highly exalt him
        forever.
45 Bless the Lord, winter cold and summer
        heat;
    sing praise to him and highly exalt him
        forever.
46 Bless the Lord, dews and falling snow;
    sing praise to him and highly exalt him
        forever.
47 Bless the Lord, nights and days;
    sing praise to him and highly exalt him
        forever.
48 Bless the Lord, light and darkness;
    sing praise to him and highly exalt him
        forever.
49 Bless the Lord, ice and cold;
    sing praise to him and highly exalt him
        forever.
50 Bless the Lord, frosts and snows;

NAB

⁷⁹ You dolphins and all water creatures, bless the Lord;
    praise and exalt him above all forever.
⁸⁰ All you birds of the air, bless the Lord;
    praise and exalt him above all forever.
⁸¹ All you beasts, wild and tame, bless the Lord;
    praise and exalt him above all forever.
⁸² You sons of men, bless the Lord;
    praise and exalt him above all forever.
⁸³ O Israel, bless the Lord;
    praise and exalt him above all forever.
⁸⁴ Priests of the Lord, bless the Lord;
    praise and exalt him above all forever.
⁸⁵ Servants of the Lord, bless the Lord;
    praise and exalt him above all forever.
⁸⁶ Spirits and souls of the just, bless the Lord;
    praise and exalt him above all forever.
⁸⁷ Holy men of humble heart, bless the Lord;
    praise and exalt him above all forever.
⁸⁸ Hananiah, Azariah, Mishael, bless the Lord;
    praise and exalt him above all forever.
For he has delivered us from the nether world,
    and saved us from the power of death;
He has freed us from the raging flame
    and delivered us from the fire.
⁸⁹ Give thanks to the Lord, for he is good,
    for his mercy endures forever.
⁹⁰ Bless the God of gods, all you who fear the Lord;
    praise him and give him thanks,
    because his mercy endures forever."
Hearing them sing, and astonished at seeing them alive,

3, 84: (*eulogeite, iereis*) *Kyriou,* (*ton Kyrion*): so Th^MSS.
3, 85: (*eulogeite, douloi*) *Kyriou,* (*ton Kyrion*): so Th^MSS.
3, 90: *Kai egeneto en tō akousai ton basilea ymnountōn autōn kai estōs etheōrei autous zōntas:* so LXX.

NRSV

sing praise to him and highly exalt him forever.
⁵¹ Bless the Lord, lightnings and clouds;
    sing praise to him and highly exalt him forever.

⁵² "Let the earth bless the Lord;
    let it sing praise to him and highly exalt him forever.
⁵³ Bless the Lord, mountains and hills;
    sing praise to him and highly exalt him forever.
⁵⁴ Bless the Lord, all that grows in the ground;
    sing praise to him and highly exalt him forever.
⁵⁵ Bless the Lord, seas and rivers;
    sing praise to him and highly exalt him forever.
⁵⁶ Bless the Lord, you springs;
    sing praise to him and highly exalt him forever.
⁵⁷ Bless the Lord, you whales and all that swim in the waters;
    sing praise to him and highly exalt him forever.
⁵⁸ Bless the Lord, all birds of the air;
    sing praise to him and highly exalt him forever.
⁵⁹ Bless the Lord, all wild animals and cattle;
    sing praise to him and highly exalt him forever.

⁶⁰ "Bless the Lord, all people on earth;
    sing praise to him and highly exalt him forever.
⁶¹ Bless the Lord, O Israel;
    sing praise to him and highly exalt him forever.
⁶² Bless the Lord, you priests of the Lord;
    sing praise to him and highly exalt him forever.
⁶³ Bless the Lord, you servants of the Lord;
    sing praise to him and highly exalt him forever.
⁶⁴ Bless the Lord, spirits and souls of the righteous;
    sing praise to him and highly exalt him forever.

NRSV

⁶⁵ Bless the Lord, you who are holy and humble
in heart;
sing praise to him and highly exalt him
forever.

⁶⁶ "Bless the Lord, Hananiah, Azariah, and
Mishael;
sing praise to him and highly exalt him
forever.
For he has rescued us from Hades and saved
us from the power[a] of death,
and delivered us from the midst of the
burning fiery furnace;
from the midst of the fire he has delivered
us.
⁶⁷ Give thanks to the Lord, for he is good,
for his mercy endures forever.
⁶⁸ All who worship the Lord, bless the God of
gods,
sing praise to him and give thanks to him,
for his mercy endures forever."

a Gk *hand*

COMMENTARY

In contrast to the first section, which singles out Azariah specifically and highlights his leadership of the three (in the Theodotion text), the psalm in vv. 30-65 emphasizes the equal participation of the three, who praise with "one voice." Significantly, the opening praise (v. 29) is to the God of "our" ancestors (see above).

These praises, which typically are accompanied by the refrain "praise to him and exalt him forever," are divided into rough subject areas in terms of their specific content:

vv. 30-34, blessings of God as Ruler/Enthroned
vv. 35-41, blessings from the "works of the Lord"[13]
vv. 42-51, blessings from astronomical/meteorological creations
vv. 52-59, blessings from the earth and geological creations
vv. 60-65, blessings from selected leaders (e.g., priests)

Verses 30-34, God Enthroned. The first set of blessings emphasizes God, God's Temple, and

the glory of God's enthroned place over against those who rule in the world. This is in keeping with an important general emphasis in the Hebrew text of Daniel, where the oppressive rulers of the world are contrasted with the true and liberating rulership of God. It is the hope of the rule of God that gives hope to those who suffer from human rulers.

Verse 32 specifically mentions the "cherubim." Collins notes that the cherubim are hybrid winged creatures who often have been pictured as upholding or serving the throne of God, protecting God's holy garden (Genesis 3), or bearing God up in epiphanies (1 Chr 13:6).[14] Note that wind and cherubim are related in Ps 18:10; winds are often listed among the arsenal of God as divine warrior (clearly alluding to comparisons with Baal, the Canaanite storm god).

Verses 35-41, Works of the Lord. Included in this clearly differentiated list, interestingly, are

13. Moore suggests "Highest Heavens," and then "Things *from* Heavens."

14. John J. Collins, *Daniel,* Hermeneia (Minneapolis: Fortress, 1993) 206

heavens, angels, waters, and powers (cf. Psalm 148, where powers are seen in the context of the "host of heaven"), the sun/moon, and the stars of heaven. Indeed, as Collins notes, Psalm 148 is a very similar list of aspects of God's control over heavenly bodies, including angels.[15]

Verses 42-51, Astronomical Phenomena. It is not difficult to see in this list a reference to the ancient comparisons between the God of the Bible, Yahweh, and the ascendant god of the Canaanites, Baal. The Canaanite storm god and thus the "rider of the clouds," Baal ruled over meteorological phenomena such as this list represents, particularly those that begin and end the list, winds and lightning (cf. Psalm 29, which many scholars consider to be an ancient hymn to Baal, simply converted for Israelite use through changing the referent names of the god).

Verses 52-59, From the Earth and Geological Creations. This series emphasizes God as creator. It was often noted in Hebrew texts that God's qualifications to challenge the reality of idols is precisely God's authority as Creator of all creation, an authority that gives God power over the gods represented by idols of mere wood and stone (Isaiah 18–19 celebrates the creator: "The Lord . . . who formed the earth and made it." The recognition of the true God is then contrasted to the making of idols in Isaiah 20–22).[16]

Verses 60-65, Blessings from Leaders. What is notable by their absence from this list of the people of Israel is military or royal figures. Indeed, the series presents what Joel Weinberg calls the "Citizen-Temple-Community," an ethnopolitical enclave of occupied Palestine in which

authority is vested in the Temple and temple personnel: people and priests.[17] Furthermore, once again the "humble in heart" are honored (Isa 57:15; 66:2; Sir 35:21; cf. Matt 11:29) among the people of God.

Verses 66-68, The Conclusion. In v. 66, the Jewish names of the prisoners of Babylonian imperialism are used, in contrast to their slave names. To be rescued from "Hades" is an interesting thematic association with the rescue from the fiery furnace—a comparison that can be seen in other texts as well. The chiastic form of v. 66*b* reads as follows:

```
A   He delivered us
  B   from the midst of the burning furnace
  B′  from the midst of the flame
A′  He delivered us
```

The deliverance is celebrated, as we would expect, in the context of God's delivering power, God's "steadfast love," translated often as "mercy"—a mercy that will "endure forever."

Mercy is often called for in the context of overwhelming fear of an enemy. Thus, given the context of the fiery furnace, to emphasize the themes of mercy, of God's creator authority over idolatry, and of God's rulership over the powers of this world is to place this material firmly in the context of political occupation and possibly a context of persecution. The very fact that this particular episode, is the context for an extension of the tradition in Greek suggests that *persecution* is the preferred context for this hymn and that it remained an important context for later editors and readers in the Hellenistic period.

---

15. Ibid., 206; see also Moore, *Daniel, Esther, and Jeremiah,* 75.

16. J. Blenkinsopp has noted the increase in references to God as *creator* in the post-exilic period. See his *Ezra–Nehemiah,* OTL (London: SCM, 1988).

17. See J. Weinberg, *The Citizen Temple Community,* trans. D. Smith-Christopher (Sheffield: JSOT, 1992).

REFLECTIONS

This passage represents a significant development of the exilic theme and particularly the theme of persecution by foreigners. The theme of resistance, represented in Daniel 3 of the Hebrew text, is lengthened here. Thus the focus shifts from Nebuchadnezzar's mad megalomania to the successful resistance of the Jews. However, both themes must be held together for a full appreciation of what is accomplished by the editor, who skillfully placed this section into the earlier text. The presence of this tradition is ample proof of the significance of this theme of persecution and endurance for late (post 150 BCE?) occupied Palestine. The placement of a passage can often reveal what was on the redactor's mind in expanding the text.

God as Creator—that is, not God as a specific national deity, but the one God of all people—is celebrated as the one who controls ultimate authority over claims by human rulers to be universal rulers of the "four corners of the earth." Only God as Creator ultimately trumps the claims of rulership of Cyrus, Alexander, Nebuchadnezzar, or Tiglath-pileser III. God as Creator (and thus the emphasis on the God of "our" ancestors) becomes a universalist polemic for God's ultimate authority. This subversive theology of God's control contains great power in an age when empires extended throughout the known world. In short, naming the true God is a call to resist the false powers of the world.

For the Jews of occupied Palestine, as well as in the diaspora, resistance was fired by an appeal to the God not merely of a nation that once existed, but of all creation. Albert Memmi writes that the colonizer must always show strength as in "flashy symbols, the most striking demonstrations of the power of his country," which include "all military parades." Memmi says that it is a "deep necessity of colonial life; to impress the colonized is just as important as to reassure oneself."[18] But in the face of this, Memmi writes about the reinvestment of religion with new political meaning, particularly in Muslim countries:

> Now, the young intellectual who had broken with religions, internally at least, and ate during Ramadan, begins to fast with ostentation. He who considered the rites as inevitable family drudgery, reintroduces them into his social life, gives them a place in his conception of the world. To use them better, he reexplains the forgotten messages and adapts them to present-day needs. He then discovers that religion is not simply an attempt to communicate with the invisible, but also an extraordinary place of communion for the whole group. The colonized, his leaders and intellectuals, his traditionalists and liberals, all classes of society, can meet there, reinforce their bonds, verify and re-create their unity.[19]

Fanon writes that the native is "treated as an inferior but he is not convinced of his inferiority."[20] Memmi agrees: "In order for that legitimacy to be complete, it is not enough for the colonized to be a slave, he must also accept his role."[21] It is in the flame of religious resistance that we can see the beginnings of the fires of revolt. Just as Mary sang of the defeat of Roman occupation with the birth of the Messiah in the Gospel of Luke ("He has brought down the powerful from their thrones"), so also sang Paul and Silas, in the book of Acts, serenading their jailers with songs about the greatness of their liberator, who was once again about to send a "messenger" to liberate the chosen ones. Singing to the jailers, like singing in the flames of Nebuchadnezzar's furnace, represents a powerful refusal to be bowed by the power of the state, which is always preeminently represented in its power to do violence to those who disobey.

A similar theme occurs in the *Testament of Joseph* 8:5 (second century BCE). After Joseph resists the temptation to commit adultery, he is falsely accused and thrown into prison:

> When I was in fetters, the Egyptian woman was overtaken with grief. She came and heard the report how I gave thanks to the Lord and sang praise in the house of darkness, and how I rejoiced with cheerful voice, glorifying my God, because through her trumped up charge I was set free from this Egyptian woman.[22]

This example of ancient Jewish resistance raises an important question for Christians today: If the power of violence merely brings forth songs from the defiant, where then, is their power? The Jews of exile and occupation faced their more powerful conquerors with cries to God and

---

18. A. Memmi, *The Colonizer and the Colonized* (Boston: Beacon, 1965) 59.
19. Ibid., 132-33.
20. F. Fanon, *The Wretched of the Earth* (New York: Grove, 1963) 53.
21. Memmi, *The Colonizer and the Colonized,* 89.
22. *Testament of Joseph,* in 821, OTP, Charlesworth, Vol. 1; see also 495; E. Haenchen, *The Acts of the Apostles* (Philadelphia: Westminster, 1971); Conzelman also quotes Epictetus 2.6.26: "and then we shall be emulating Socrates when we are able to write paeans in prison" (*Acts of the Apostles,* H. Conzelman, Hermeneia [Philadelphia: Fortress, 1987] 132).

songs of God's mastery over all creation. Would the cries of today's oppressed peoples in the slums of Cairo, the refugee camps of Lebanon and Jordan and Ethiopia, the poor sections of multiple cities sound any different to Babylonian, Persian, Greek, or Roman ears?

Christendom long ago sold itself to the modern nation-state and would not think of challenging the power and authority of that rule with radically alternative values or alternative ways of living. But Westerners can hardly believe that they still hear the defiant call, "God is great!" in the face of the West's overwhelming military might. Perhaps in reading about Hananiah, Mishael, Azariah, Joseph, and Paul and Silas, we should remember that there was once a faith that burned brightly in Christian hearts and souls as they confronted Roman power with a persistent faith that declared, "Jesus is Lord!"

VERSES 1-64

NAB

13 [1] In Babylon there lived a man named Joakim, [2] who married a very beautiful and God-fearing woman, Susanna, the daughter of Hilkiah; [3] her pious parents had trained their daughter according to the law of Moses. [4] Joakim was very rich; he had a garden near his house, and the Jews had recourse to him often because he was the most respected of them all.

[5] That year, two elders of the people were appointed judges, of whom the Lord said, "Wickedness has come out of Babylon: from the elders who were to govern the people as judges." [6] These men, to whom all brought their cases, frequented the house of Joakim. [7] When the people left at noon, Susanna used to enter her husband's garden for a walk. [8] When the old men saw her enter every day for her walk, they began to lust for her. [9] They suppressed their consciences; they would not allow their eyes to look to heaven, and did not keep in mind just judgments. [10] Though both were enamored of her, they did not tell each other their trouble, [11] for they were ashamed to reveal their lustful desire to have her. [12] Day by day they watched eagerly for her. [13] One day they said to each other, "Let us be off for home, it is time for lunch." So they went out and parted; [14] but both turned back, and when they met again, they asked each other the reason. They admitted their lust, and then they agreed to look for an occasion when they could meet her alone.

[15] One day, while they were waiting for the right moment, she entered the garden as usual, with two maids only. She decided to bathe, for the weather was warm. [16] Nobody else was there except the two elders, who had hidden themselves and were watching her. [17] "Bring me oil and soap," she said to the maids, "and shut the garden doors while I bathe." [18] They did as she

Verse numbering of the NAB is taken from the Greek text of Daniel, which includes these verses as part of a longer section after chapter 12 for Susanna of the corresponding Hebrew text.

NRSV

(Chapter 13 of the Greek version of Daniel)

[1] There was a man living in Babylon whose name was Joakim. [2] He married the daughter of Hilkiah, named Susanna, a very beautiful woman and one who feared the Lord. [3] Her parents were righteous, and had trained their daughter according to the law of Moses. [4] Joakim was very rich, and had a fine garden adjoining his house; the Jews used to come to him because he was the most honored of them all.

[5] That year two elders from the people were appointed as judges. Concerning them the Lord had said: "Wickedness came forth from Babylon, from elders who were judges, who were supposed to govern the people." [6] These men were frequently at Joakim's house, and all who had a case to be tried came to them there.

[7] When the people left at noon, Susanna would go into her husband's garden to walk. [8] Every day the two elders used to see her, going in and walking about, and they began to lust for her. [9] They suppressed their consciences and turned away their eyes from looking to Heaven or remembering their duty to administer justice. [10] Both were overwhelmed with passion for her, but they did not tell each other of their distress, [11] for they were ashamed to disclose their lustful desire to seduce her. [12] Day after day they watched eagerly to see her.

[13] One day they said to each other, "Let us go home, for it is time for lunch." So they both left and parted from each other. [14] But turning back, they met again; and when each pressed the other for the reason, they confessed their lust. Then together they arranged for a time when they could find her alone.

[15] Once, while they were watching for an opportune day, she went in as before with only two maids, and wished to bathe in the garden, for it was a hot day. [16] No one was there except the two elders, who had hidden themselves and were watching her. [17] She said to her maids, "Bring me

NAB

said; they shut the garden doors and left by the side gate to fetch what she had ordered, unaware that the elders were hidden inside.

19 As soon as the maids had left, the two old men got up and hurried to her. 20 "Look," they said, "the garden doors are shut, and no one can see us; give in to our desire, and lie with us. 21 If you refuse, we will testify against you that you dismissed your maids because a young man was here with you."

22 "I am completely trapped," Susanna groaned. "If I yield, it will be my death; if I refuse, I cannot escape your power. 23 Yet it is better for me to fall into your power without guilt than to sin before the Lord." 24 Then Susanna shrieked, and the old men also shouted at her, 25 as one of them ran to open the garden doors. 26 When the people in the house heard the cries from the garden, they rushed in by the side gate to see what had happened to her. 27 At the accusations by the old men, the servants felt very much ashamed, for never had any such thing been said about Susanna.

28 When the people came to her husband Joakim the next day, the two wicked elders also came, fully determined to put Susanna to death. Before all the people they ordered: 29 "Send for Susanna, the daughter of Hilkiah, the wife of Joakim." When she was sent for, 30 she came with her parents, children and all her relatives. 31 Susanna, very delicate and beautiful, 32 was veiled; but those wicked men ordered her to uncover her face so as to sate themselves with her beauty. 33 All her relatives and the onlookers were weeping.

34 In the midst of the people the two elders rose up and laid their hands on her head. 35 Through her tears she looked up to heaven, for she trusted in the Lord wholeheartedly. 36 The elders made this accusation: "As we were walking in the garden alone, this woman entered with two girls and shut the doors of the garden, dismissing the girls. 37 A young man, who was hidden there, came and lay with her. 38 When we, in a corner of the garden, saw this crime, we ran toward them. 39 We saw them lying together, but the man we could not hold, because he was stronger than we; he opened the doors and ran off. 40 Then we seized this one and asked who the young man

NRSV

olive oil and ointments, and shut the garden doors so that I can bathe." 18They did as she told them: they shut the doors of the garden and went out by the side doors to bring what they had been commanded; they did not see the elders, because they were hiding.

19When the maids had gone out, the two elders got up and ran to her. 20They said, "Look, the garden doors are shut, and no one can see us. We are burning with desire for you; so give your consent, and lie with us. 21If you refuse, we will testify against you that a young man was with you, and this was why you sent your maids away."

22Susanna groaned and said, "I am completely trapped. For if I do this, it will mean death for me; if I do not, I cannot escape your hands. 23I choose not to do it; I will fall into your hands, rather than sin in the sight of the Lord."

24Then Susanna cried out with a loud voice, and the two elders shouted against her. 25And one of them ran and opened the garden doors. 26When the people in the house heard the shouting in the garden, they rushed in at the side door to see what had happened to her. 27And when the elders told their story, the servants felt very much ashamed, for nothing like this had ever been said about Susanna.

28The next day, when the people gathered at the house of her husband Joakim, the two elders came, full of their wicked plot to have Susanna put to death. In the presence of the people they said, 29"Send for Susanna daughter of Hilkiah, the wife of Joakim." 30So they sent for her. And she came with her parents, her children, and all her relatives.

31Now Susanna was a woman of great refinement and beautiful in appearance. 32As she was veiled, the scoundrels ordered her to be unveiled, so that they might feast their eyes on her beauty. 33Those who were with her and all who saw her were weeping.

34Then the two elders stood up before the people and laid their hands on her head. 35Through her tears she looked up toward Heaven, for her heart trusted in the Lord. 36The elders said, "While we were walking in the garden alone, this woman came in with two maids,

NAB

was, [41] but she refused to tell us. We testify to this." The assembly believed them, since they were elders and judges of the people, and they condemned her to death.

[42] But Susanna cried aloud: "O eternal God, you know what is hidden and are aware of all things before they come to be: [43] you know that they have testified falsely against me. Here I am about to die, though I have done none of the things with which these wicked men have charged me."

[44] The Lord heard her prayer. [45] As she was being led to execution, God stirred up the holy spirit of a young boy named Daniel, [46] and he cried aloud: "I will have no part in the death of this woman." [47] All the people turned and asked him, "What is this you are saying?" [48] He stood in their midst and continued, "Are you such fools, O Israelites! To condemn a woman of Israel without examination and without clear evidence? [49] Return to court, for they have testified falsely against her."

[50] Then all the people returned in haste. To Daniel the elders said, "Come, sit with us and inform us, since God has given you the prestige of old age." [51] But he replied, "Separate these two far from one another that I may examine them."

[52] After they were separated one from the other, he called one of them and said: "How you have grown evil with age! Now have your past sins come to term: [53] passing unjust sentences, condemning the innocent, and freeing the guilty, although the Lord says, "The innocent and the just you shall not put to death.' [54] Now, then, if you were a witness, tell me under what tree you saw them together." [55] "Under a mastic tree," he answered. "Your fine lie has cost you your head," said Daniel; "for the angel of God shall receive the sentence from him and split you in two." [56] Putting him to one side, he ordered the other one to be brought. "Offspring of Canaan, not of Judah," Daniel said to him, "beauty has seduced you, lust has subverted your conscience. [57] This is how you acted with the daughters of Israel, and in their fear they yielded to you; but a daughter of Judah did not tolerate your wickedness. [58] Now then, tell me under what tree you surprised them together." [59] "Under an oak," he said. "Your fine

NRSV

shut the garden doors, and dismissed the maids. [37] Then a young man, who was hiding there, came to her and lay with her. [38] We were in a corner of the garden, and when we saw this wickedness we ran to them. [39] Although we saw them embracing, we could not hold the man, because he was stronger than we, and he opened the doors and got away. [40] We did, however, seize this woman and asked who the young man was, [41] but she would not tell us. These things we testify."

Because they were elders of the people and judges, the assembly believed them and condemned her to death.

[42] Then Susanna cried out with a loud voice, and said, "O eternal God, you know what is secret and are aware of all things before they come to be; [43] you know that these men have given false evidence against me. And now I am to die, though I have done none of the wicked things that they have charged against me!"

[44] The Lord heard her cry. [45] Just as she was being led off to execution, God stirred up the holy spirit of a young lad named Daniel, [46] and he shouted with a loud voice, "I want no part in shedding this woman's blood!"

[47] All the people turned to him and asked, "What is this you are saying?" [48] Taking his stand among them he said, "Are you such fools, O Israelites, as to condemn a daughter of Israel without examination and without learning the facts? [49] Return to court, for these men have given false evidence against her."

[50] So all the people hurried back. And the rest of the[a] elders said to him, "Come, sit among us and inform us, for God has given you the standing of an elder." [51] Daniel said to them, "Separate them far from each other, and I will examine them."

[52] When they were separated from each other, he summoned one of them and said to him, "You old relic of wicked days, your sins have now come home, which you have committed in the past, [53] pronouncing unjust judgments, condemning the innocent and acquitting the guilty, though the Lord said, 'You shall not put an innocent and righteous person to death.' [54] Now then, if you really saw this woman, tell me this: Under what

a Gk lacks rest of the

NAB

lie has cost you also your head," said Daniel; "for the angel of God waits with a sword to cut you in two so as to make an end of you both."

60 The whole assembly cried aloud, blessing God who saves those that hope in him. 61 They rose up against the two elders, for by their own words Daniel had convicted them of perjury. According to the law of Moses, they inflicted on them the penalty they had plotted to impose on their neighbor: 62 they put them to death. Thus was innocent blood spared that day.

63 Hilkiah and his wife praised God for their daughter Susanna, as did Joakim her husband and all her relatives, because she was found innocent of any shameful deed. 64 And from that day onward Daniel was greatly esteemed by the people.

NRSV

tree did you see them being intimate with each other?" He answered, "Under a mastic tree."[a] 55And Daniel said, "Very well! This lie has cost you your head, for the angel of God has received the sentence from God and will immediately cut[a] you in two."

56Then, putting him to one side, he ordered them to bring the other. And he said to him, "You offspring of Canaan and not of Judah, beauty has beguiled you and lust has perverted your heart. 57This is how you have been treating the daughters of Israel, and they were intimate with you through fear; but a daughter of Judah would not tolerate your wickedness. 58Now then, tell me: Under what tree did you catch them being intimate with each other?" He answered, "Under an evergreen oak."[b] 59Daniel said to him, "Very well! This lie has cost you also your head, for the angel of God is waiting with his sword to split[b] you in two, so as to destroy you both."

60Then the whole assembly raised a great shout and blessed God, who saves those who hope in him. 61And they took action against the two elders, because out of their own mouths Daniel had convicted them of bearing false witness; they did to them as they had wickedly planned to do to their neighbor. 62Acting in accordance with the law of Moses, they put them to death. Thus innocent blood was spared that day.

63Hilkiah and his wife praised God for their daughter Susanna, and so did her husband Joakim and all her relatives, because she was found innocent of a shameful deed. 64And from that day onward Daniel had a great reputation among the people.

[a] The Greek words for *mastic tree* and *cut* are similar, thus forming an ironic wordplay   [b] The Greek words for *evergreen oak* and *split* are similar, thus forming an ironic wordplay

COMMENTARY

The story of Susanna stands in some of the Greek versions as the first of the Daniel stories, before the Hebrew Daniel 1, but after chapter 12 in others. The motivation to place the story before the Daniel 1 was undoubtedly be- cause Daniel is portrayed as a very young man (who is wise beyond his years) in this story.

There are significant differences between the style of the story of Susanna and the Hebrew/Aramaic stories in Daniel 1–6 (the non-miraculous form of deliverance, the internal Jewish matters, among others). Further, Susanna differs from the other two additional works included in the Greek canon of the book of Daniel mainly because of its focus on the subjects of women, sexual abuse, and internal corruption in the Jewish community.

It is often suggested that even though the story of Susanna is considered the most sophisticated and well developed of the three additions to Daniel (the Song of the Three, for example, seems a hodgepodge of literary styles; Bel and the Dragon are clearly two separate stories), it was rejected by those rabbis who determined the canon because the court procedure was improper[23] and because the authority of elders is seriously questioned (especially in the LXX version). It can be argued, however, that there are important reasons why it is significant that Susanna appears in the Daniel collection. First, it presents a female model of courage in a community that needs all of its resources and in which all persons share the threat of political exile and occupation. Second, Susanna includes a significant criticism of internal communal corruption, similar to that found in Ezra and Nehemiah, where it is also directed against corrupt or corruptible leaders of the community. Furthermore, the story of Susanna gives us an interesting episode in the life of the young Daniel, the legendary hero.

Many theories have been suggested for the origin of the story. These include that it was a midrash on the evil prophets mentioned in Jeremiah 29; a late polemic between Pharisees and Sadducees on court procedure; and a folk tale that exhibits well-known themes in folklore, such as the wisdom of the elders overturned by a child.[24] No single view, however, has commanded wide agreement. While Susanna is a tale that has clear similarities with the themes of Daniel 1–6, there is nothing within the story that allows a clear date or even a sociopolitical context for the Jewish community that treasured and maintained this story as a part of its religious lore.

The story of Susanna affords us the opportunity to raise questions that have not previously arisen in the study of the book of Daniel—most important, the issue of women's rights and place in society. Indeed, besides Susanna there is only one other significant woman in the entire Daniel corpus: the queen mother, who makes her appearance in Daniel 5. There seems little evidence that Susanna was written with any aspect of the queen mother in mind as the "other woman" of the Daniel tradition. But was Susanna written with Daniel even in mind? Some scholars wonder whether Daniel originally had a role at all in an earlier form of the Susanna legend—perhaps references to him being added only when the story was made a part of the Daniel tradition at about the time of its translation into Greek (c. 100 BCE).

However, this account of life in the exilic community from a woman's perspective gives us the opportunity to consider a Jewish woman as doubly a symbol of resistance—both to the oppression of exile and to male domination within the Jewish community—and as a model of the kind of spiritual tenacity necessary for faithful resistance in circumstances of exile or occupation. It seems hard to deny that Susanna as a woman within Jewish society is meant to mirror the Jew in foreign society. She is called to resist oppression within that society as the Jews were generally called to resist oppression from outside. Her resistance, her ability to speak truth to power, is honored in this story, as well as the young Daniel's clever courtroom technique in defending her.

Mieke Bal has asserted that there is a "dominant reading" of biblical texts and interpretative strategies that is "a monolithically misogynist view of those biblical stories wherein female characters play a role, and a denial of the importance of women in the Bible as a whole."[25] Part of this dominant reading, according to Bal, is to dismiss certain aspects of texts and stories that seem to be "meaningless details," particularly where women are concerned. But attention to such details may have the effect of inverting previous perspectives. Such an analysis of the Susanna story, for example, has been provided by both Bal and Glancy, who focus important attention on Susanna as a woman whose actions are interpreted according to her "appearance" to the "male

23. This issue is pursued helpfully in C. A. Moore, *Daniel, Esther, and Jeremiah: The Additions* (Garden City, N.Y.: Doubleday, 1977) 87.

24. These and other suggestions are explained in more detail, with references to the technical literature, in the works of both Collins and Moore.

25. M. Bal, *Lethal Love: Feminist Literary Readings of Biblical Love Stories* (Bloomington: Indiana University Press, 1987) 2.

gaze."[26] Another way that one can become attuned to such details is through a survey of the literature on violence against women. This commentary will have occasion to relate the study of Susanna to feminist and other sociological studies of rape and violence against women.[27]

Glancy notes that Susanna is largely the passive victim and the crime that stands "behind" the story is violation of possessions and honor of men—in this case Joakim the husband. Brownmiller argues that male possession laws are the foundation for most modern rape laws in Western society in that rape "was first and foremost a violation of male rights of possession, based on male requirements of virginity, chastity, and consent to private access as the female bargain in the marriage contract."[28]

Similarly, then, Glancy notes the intriguing symmetry between Susanna, the "violated wife," and Joakim's privileged garden:

What is at stake in the story is not Susanna's physical well-being as she is threatened with rape and death but the honor of Joachim's household. When garden and wife are closed against intruders, Joachim's honor is secure. When the garden is open to intruders, or if the wife is open to a young lover, the entire household is ashamed, its honor lost.[29]

Glancy is surely correct in her insistence that modern readers often go along with the assumption of the story that the crime is attempted seduction rather than attempted rape—mainly because the modern reader is also beguiled by Susanna's reputed beauty. Seduction seems, from such a reading, "natural" or "normal." As Glancy puts it, the narrative of Susanna "relies on a code that represents femininity in terms of 'to-be-looked-at-ness.' "[30] Is it an overstatement to call what happens to Susanna rape? The elders, as we

shall see, do not physically force themselves upon her. But the difficulty with calling their actions "seduction" is that this term does not adequately express the unequal power dynamics between Susanna and two respected (male) leaders of the community. While their confrontation may not have involved physical contact, in a real way it was overpowering to Susanna and would be referred to in modern terms as sexual harassment with important power dynamics involved. Brownmiller comments:

All rape is an exercise in power, but some rapists have an edge that is more than physical. They operate within an institutionalized setting that works to their advantage and in which a victim has little chance to redress her grievance.[31]

Given these dynamics, it is important to proceed with an assumption that we are dealing with what ought to be interpreted as attempted rape.

Glancy's analysis also alerts us to the significance of "seeing," "gazing," and "staring" in this story. The reader is invited to imagine the beauty of the bathing Susanna, for example, and thus to relate to the gaze of the hidden elders, who "burn with lust." Significantly, Daniel catches the deceit of the elders precisely on what they have done, and not on what they have seen. The focused attention of the criminal elders on Susanna is so intent on the attempted rape of her that they give no thought to anything else.

Finally, there is the curious reversal of roles for the figure of Daniel. Susannah is celebrated in this story as the persecuted Jew—persecuted by fellow Jews no less than by the Babylonians—and it is Daniel who assumes the role of the God-sent savior. Indeed, one would have to say that Daniel assumes the role of the angelic messenger—the God-sent salvation in virtually all the other Daniel stories. All of these details will be discussed at more length in the following analysis.

Verses 1-4, Introduction and Setting Among the Babylonian Exiles. The first character to whom the reader is introduced in this story is Joakim, the husband of Susanna.[32] He is among the exiles in Babylon, but is apparently

26. J. Glancy, "The Accused: Susanna and Her Readers," *JSOT* 58 (1993) 103-16.

27. For this study, I have consulted P. B. Bart and E. G. Moran, eds., *Violence Against Women* (London: Sage, 1993) esp. three essays therein: "Put Up and Shut Up: Workplace Sexual Assaults," Beth E. Schneider, 57-72; " 'Riding the Bull at Gilley's': Convicted Rapists Describe the Rewards of Rape," Diana Scully and Joseph Marolla, 26-46; "The Imperishable Virginity of Saint Maria Goretti," Kathleen Young, 105-13. See also Susan Brownmiller, *Against Our Will: Men, Women, and Rape* (New York: Simon and Schuster, 1975); L. Baron and M. A. Straus, *Four Theories of Rape in American Society* (New Haven: Yale University Press, 1989); L. Ellis, *Theories of Rape: Inquiries into the Causes of Sexual Aggression* (London: Hemisphere, 1989); and J. R. and H. Schwendinger, *Rape and Inequality* (London: Sage, 1983).

28. Brownmiller, *Against Our Will*, 377.

29. Glancy, "The Accused," 107.

30. Ibid., 112.

31. Brownmiller, *Against Our Will*, 256.

32. Glancy notes that it is significant that the male is introduced first, even though he is virtually absent from most of the story. See Glancy, "The Accused," 107.

rather well situated. The text describes him as rich, possessing a home with a fine garden. That Joakim is described as having married Susanna and built his fine home while in exile may well be a nod in the direction of Jeremiah's advice in his letter to exiles that they marry and build houses (and plant gardens) so that their numbers will not decrease while in exile (see Jeremiah 29).

We know from the book of Ezekiel (chaps. 14 and 20) that elders met in Ezekiel's home for important gatherings, much as the writer of Susanna reports the elders' meeting in the home of Joakim. While this detail may be dependent on sources such as Ezekiel, there is reason to believe that it was a significant memory of the sociological circumstances of the Babylonian exiles. This form of limited self-governance in exile is an important indicator that not only were the exiles able to maintain a familiar form of governance, but also that they settled in large enough groups to make this a viable social form.[33]

The Greek term used for Joakim's garden (παράδεισος *paradeisos*) is a Persian loan word from which we also get the English word "paradise" (see 2 Chr 33.20, Neh 2.8). There is another term that generally refers to a small garden (a vegetable garden? see Neh 3:16, 26). When this term is used together with the Greek term for a "paradise" (Eccl 2:5; Sir 24:30-31), it gives the reader the impression that the "paradise," in contrast to the smaller garden, is a large area kept in a somewhat natural state of beauty. Note that the Garden of Eden is called a "paradise."

It is significant that Susanna is described as being both beautiful and God fearing. Is the reader meant to understand that these attributes go together or that they are traits that somehow balance each other? Is feminine beauty a potential danger in a male-oriented reading of these verses? It is not unusual for matriarchs of Israel to be described as beautiful (the description of Sarah [Gen 12:14] and Rachel [Gen 29:17] use the same Greek terms; see also 1 Sam 25:3; 2 Sam 11:2; Ezek 16:13; Jdt 8:7). This very beauty, however, is taken almost inevitably as a foreshadowing of trouble (see Tob 3:14-15; 6:12). In her work on rape and violence against women, Susan Brownmiller notes the frequency with which rape cases are reported in the media with a comment about the "beauty" of the victim:

> The murder of a beautiful young woman is no more regrettable, no greater tragedy, than the murder of a plain one, except in a culture that values beauty in women above other qualities. By putting greater store in the murder of a beauty, beauty acquires the seeds of its own destruction . . . thus the myth that rape is a crime of passion touched off by female beauty is given great credence, and women are influenced to believe that to be raped, and even murdered, is a testament to beauty.[34]

In contrast to, or in connection with, this beauty, Susanna "fears the Lord."

The phrase used to describe Susanna as one who "feared the Lord" brings this text into an interesting relation with Sirach. The importance of "fear of the Lord" is repeated frequently in Sirach (Sir 1:13-14; 2:7-9; 6:16; 10:19-20; 21:6; 32:16; 34:14, 16), suggesting a possible relationship between the writer of Susanna and the wisdom tradition in late post-exilic Israel. Susanna, in short, practiced the way of the wise. Many readers, however, regard Sirach as blatantly misogynist (see Sir 25:16-26; 26:5-12; 42:9-14), so one must carefully note the contrasting positive view of a woman in Susanna. In short, one can make too much of wisdom connections (as has occurred frequently since such a suggestion was originally made by von Rad).[35] Furthermore, it is noted that Susanna's parents raised her in the knowledge of the law of Moses. This mention of the law of Moses is rather unique (and not present in the LXX version), but here in Susanna it serves as one piece of an important frame; the parents will be mentioned again in v. 62.

Verses 5-6, Introduction to the Corrupt Elders. Two elders are singled out and are introduced as being newly appointed judges. Verse 5 also features an unknown prophetic saying that is often related to Jer 23:14-15 and to the accusation against false elders in Jer 29:21-23.

The Greek term used here for "wickedness" (ἀνομία *anomia*) is used to translate a variety of Hebrew words that are rendered in English

---

33. For a full discussion of the import of this detail, see Daniel Smith, *The Religion of the Landless: The Sociology of the Babylonian Exile* (New York: Meyer-Stone, 1989).

34. Brownmiller, *Against Our Will*, 341.

35. G. von Rad, *Wisdom in Israel* (Nashville: Abingdon, 1972).

variously as "sin," "transgression," and "iniquity." Judgment is expressed against elders in Isa 3:14 and 9:15, and such leaders of the people were certainly vilified by Ezra (Ezra 10:14). The internal issues of wickedness suggest that Susanna was written in the Hellenistic era at a time when internal factions among the Jewish people began to tear apart the community and divide it into mutually antagonistic parties (a situation well established by the beginning of the New Testament era). It is this internal emphasis that gives Susanna its unique context in the rest of the book of Daniel.

Verses 7-12, The Lust of the Elders. Susanna takes daily walks in Joakim's garden—a detail that is essential to the development of the story. As she walks, she is seen by the two elders, who seeing her "desire" her (the term ἐπιθυμία [epithymia] is used for "covet" in Exod 20:17 LXX). The term epithymia runs throughout the story (vv. 8, 11, 14, 20, 56) and is a significant term that appears in wisdom tradition as well. According to Sirach, one is to "desire" wisdom and avoid the cheap lust of foolishness (Sir 16:1; 24:19). Consider also the wisdom context of the advice offered in 4 Maccabees:

Self-control, then, is dominance over the desires [epithymia]. Some desires are mental, others are physical, and reason obviously rules over both. (4 Macc 1:31-32 NRSV)

And why is it amazing that the desires of the mind for the enjoyment of beauty are rendered powerless? It is for this reason, certainly, that the temperate Joseph is praised, because by mental effort he overcame sexual desire. (4 Macc 2:1-2 NRSV)

Verse 9 contains an interesting interrelation of phrases and ideas. The elders do three things: (1) suppress their consciences; (2) turn away their eyes from heaven; and (3) forget their duty to administer justice. The term used in the first phrase, "suppressed" or "perverted," is common in wisdom literature (see Prov 6:14; 10:9; 11:20; Sir 19:25; 22:23). Perversion of judgment is also known in prophetic literature (see Isa 59:8; Mic 3:9; Hab 1:4).

The phrase "to look into heaven" is not common in the Bible, but similar ideas certainly occur. The book of Isaiah contains a call to vigilance for God's near deliverance (Isa 51:6) and describes Hezekiah as being weary from "looking into heaven" (Isa 38:14). Similarly Daniel "looked up" from fasting when he turned to God (Dan 10:5).

Isaiah 33:15 suggests that people who survive God's judgment are those who "shut their eyes from looking on evil." Presumably, then, the phrase is a way to talk about trusting in God, and turning away from heaven is seen as the equivalent of the other two phrases in the verse. Moore notes, incidentally, that "heaven" could also be a replacement for "God" as is the case in the New Testament use of "kingdom of heaven" instead of "kingdom of God."[36] In general, the context reminds the reader of prophetic condemnation of the leaders of the Jewish community.

Verse 12 brilliantly establishes the importance of the "gaze," a dark sense of watching, in this story. The specific term used here is also used in Ps 37:12, where it is translated into English as: "The wicked plot against [or "watch for opportunities against"] the righteous, and gnash their teeth at them" (NRSV). Note that the wicked also "watched" Daniel to accuse him in Dan 6:12. In the story of Susanna, this gaze is intensified.

Verses 13-14, The Plot Is Set. When, in v. 13, the two elders discover each other heading back to look once again upon the beauty of Susanna, these false judges ply their trade on each other! They "examine" each other with the acumen of lawyers and discover the truth about themselves. They agree to keep each other's secret, and thus the second act of secrecy appears in the story (the first being the unnoticed watching of Susanna by these same elders, a watching that led to their taking their eyes off heaven). Throughout the story, secrecy is contrasted with openness, as the lustful gaze is contrasted with "seeing" in the sense of knowing the truth. The elders, however, now work in collusion. Brownmiller comments on modern cases:

When men rape in pairs or in gangs, the sheer physical advantage of their position is clear-cut and unquestionable. No simple conquest of man over woman, group rape is the conquest of Men over Women. It is within the phenomenon of group rape, stripped of the possibility of equal combat, that the male ideology of rape is most strongly evident. Numerical odds are proof of brutal intention. They are proof, too, of male bonding . . . and proof of a desire to humiliate the victim beyond the act of rape through the process of anonymous mass assault.[37]

36. C. A. Moore, *Daniel, Esther, and Jeremiah: The Additions*, AB 44 (Garden City, N.Y.: Doubleday, 1977) 96.
37. Brownmiller, *Against Our Will*, 187.

Verses 15-27, The Main Events of the Story. The main events of the story must begin with the elders' secret entrance into the garden (a third act of secrecy). The writer does not specify when and how these men enter the garden, only that they are there when Susanna prepares to bathe. With the mention of Susanna's bath, the reader is reminded of David's walk on the roof of his palace and his lust for Bathsheba as he gazed on her bathing (2 Samuel 11). Like Susanna as well, Bathsheba is described as beautiful. Collins cites a number of other cases in Jewish tradition of men who are filled with desire when watching women bathe.[38] The LXX does not include the bath scene at all, however, but instead related that the elders desire her merely from watching her on her occasional walks in the garden.

Unlike David, whose position and power did not necessitate hiding, the elders watch Susanna in secret. Since the elders are in hiding, the maids who attend Susanna do not see them, and so the maids innocently shut the doors of the garden, leaving only the two elders and Susanna in the garden without further witnesses. At the moment the doors are shut the elders become like David. They now have the power of the male over the female, of an elder over a young person, and of judges within the community.

In vv. 19-21, the elders speak as if Susanna can freely choose whether to comply with their desires—but she is not free. It is, rather, an act of coercion. Moore points out that the LXX is much stronger in the insistence of the elders and their initial approach to Susanna—suggesting rape.[39] If Susanna is unwilling to have sexual intercourse with each of them, then the judges will use their powerful weapon of false accusation—the word of a trusted official over a mere woman. False accusation by the powerful was the same weapon used against Daniel (Dan 6:25). It is worth pausing to reflect on the fact that false accusation is a threat *only* when there is an unequal distribution of power. Susanna's word is not equivalent to the word of the two male judges. Moreover, there are two of them to dispute Susanna's accu-

sations—two is the required number of witnesses for a capital case (Deuteronomy 19).

In vv. 22-23, Susanna knows that she is threatened with being given over "into the hand" of her oppressor. Daniel, too, suffered the threat of being "in the hand" of his oppressor (Dan 3:15; cf. Deut 7:24; 32:39; 2 Kgs 18:29-30, 33-35; Jer 21:12; Dan 11:41; Mic 4:10).

When faced with such overwhelming power over her, Susanna responds with the cry of the oppressed, "with a loud voice" (v. 24; see also vv. 42 and 60). Susanna thereby also fulfills Deut 22:24, which states that if a woman is threatened with rape within the city (that is, where she could be heard) she must call out; otherwise, she is suspected of complicity.[40] The same Greek term used here is used of the Jews crying out from the oppression of Pharaoh (Exod 2:23; 14:10 LXX), and it is the same "weapon" used by Hagar in the wilderness, when she cries out to God (Gen 21:16), who delivers her. Similarly, the Jews cry out for mercy from the king in 3 Macc 5:51. This is not to suggest, however, that this outcry is a special or unique term, but the recurrence of the theme is hardly coincidental. To call out with a loud voice occurs in other important contexts as well. In Num 20:16, the call of the people in slavery is answered by God's "sending an angel" (an obviously intriguing passage in the context of angelic deliverance in the Daniel tradition); and in Deut 26:7, the call is directed to the "God of our ancestors," a term noted in the Song of the Three (see also Jdt 4:9, 12; 5:12; Ezek 11:13, where Ezekiel pleads with God not to bring an end to the people).

But as Susanna cries out to God, the elders cry out to the other Jews. The elders make their accusation at this point in Theodotion, but in the LXX, they do not make their accusation public until the tribunal has been gathered. She has presented her fate to the only power that she now has: the delivering power of truth and, ultimately, of God. So Susanna joins Daniel and Mishael and Hananiah and Azariah, among many others, in becoming a model of piety and trustfulness in the context of exile and apparent defeat.

In response to Susanna's cries, the people in the house come to "see." But they do not see;

---

38. John J. Collins, *Daniel,* Hermeneia (Minneapolis: Fortress, 1993) 431.

39. Moore, *Daniel, Esther, and Jeremiah,* 97.

40. Collins, *Daniel,* Hermeneia, 431.

they only know what the elders tell them. Curiously, it is not said that Susanna tries to tell another version of the events at this point in the story. She is calm before her accusers. The elders' version of the story is believed instantly; Susanna's youth and femininity (and beauty?) disqualify her immediately in the face of the older male judges. Even the servants are ashamed of her.

Verses 28-33, The Humiliation of the Oppressed. It is only at this point in the story that we hear of Susanna's children. When summoned to appear before the judges, Susanna comes with her parents, husband, and children. Although in the Theodotion text the husband is not mentioned specifically (Did he refuse to risk humiliation?), he is noted in the LXX version. Furthermore, as Collins points out, it is significant that they gather back at the house of Joakim—that is, the scene of the crime—so that they can all see the trees about which Daniel will soon question the "witnesses."[41] Why is the family included at this point? Is it because it is precisely the integrity of the family that is at issue here? In circumstances of exile and occupation and colonization, family takes on heightened importance. Memmi, for one, does not necessarily celebrate this fact, suggesting that the family becomes the only place where self-governing authority is still possible.[42] But we know that the familial structure was economically important too. Hence the tremendous importance given to the crisis of intermarriage in Ezra–Nehemiah.[43]

In the Septuagint version of the book of Susanna, she is stripped before her accusers. The intention of the translators was probably to convey that she was stripped naked, at least to the waist. (Being stripped for adultery is attested in Ezek 16:37-39; Hos 2:3, 10.) But there may be more going on here; Susanna has not even been adequately tried before this condemning act of stripping her is called for. The elders desire that Susanna be unveiled, so that they might "look" at her again. No reason is given for the order that Susanna be unveiled. Is her beauty supposed to

be taken as further evidence against her by the court that has been called into session? Are we readers invited to be sympathetic to the elders' lust because of her reputed beauty? Why do they demand this humiliation of her? The Greek terms used here are correctly rendered in English as "feast the eyes" (NRSV). The same complex term is used in Ps 78:29 in reference to being satiated, filled. The Old Greek adds the element of the elders' lust in looking at her. Thus Susanna is not merely overpowered; she is to be humiliated (note the discussion of the humiliation of the defeated in the Commentary on Daniel 5).

Verses 34-41, The Denunciation of Susanna. Verse 34 relates that the elders, rising to tell their stories, lay their hands on Susanna's head. Is this a way of identifying the guilt of the accused? In Lev 3:2, 8, 13 and 4:4, 11, 15, the officiating priest lays his hand on the sacrificial offering, an action intended to transfer punishment of guilt.[44] If this is true, then once again her guilt is presumed in their first act, before they even begin to tell their version of the events.

For the significance of "looking into heaven," see Commentary on v. 9. Here, Susanna's looking to heaven means trusting in the Lord. To trust in the Lord is an important post-exilic expression for faithfulness. God, according to Nebuchadnezzar, delivered servants who "trusted in him" (Dan 3:28) since no harm came to Daniel in the lions' den "because he had trusted in God" (Dan 6:23). Sirach teaches the reader to "consider the generations of old and see: has anyone trusted in the Lord and been disappointed?" (Sir 2:10 NRSV; see also 11:21; 32:24; see also the trust in God noted in 2 Macc 8:18; 3 Macc 2:4; 4 Macc 7:21). In the post-exilic context, trusting in the Lord is clearly a concept related to the power of God to deliver in circumstances of overwhelming threat. Once again, the writer uses terminology that equates Susanna's plight with the most serious of threats to Jews by foreigners in the book of Daniel and elsewhere.

The accusation brought against Susanna in vv. 36-41*a* is adultery. The elders, so they claim, saw her lying with a young man, who escaped when the elders presented themselves to the young

---

41. Collins, *Daniel*, Hermeneia, 431.

42. A. Memmi, *The Colonizer and the Colonized* (Boston: Beacon, 1965) 98-99.

43. See Daniel Smith-Christopher, "The Mixed Marriage Crisis in Ezra 9–10 and Nehemiah 13: A Study of the Sociology of Post-Exilic Judean Community," in Eskenazi and Richards, eds., *Second Temple Studies 2* (Sheffield: JSOT, 1994) 243-65.

44. Collins adds references to scapegoating in Lev 8:14, 18, 22; Exod 29:10, 15, 19, and especially Lev 24:14. See Collins, *Daniel*, Hermeneia, 432.

couple in the course of sexual intimacy. The Greek terms used here make the sexual nature of this accusation clear (see Gen 19:5; 39:10; and Jdt 12:16). In the Theodotion version, the alleged young man was too strong for the elders to restrain him, while in the LXX the young man escapes in disguise. In the Theodotion version, the elders claim to be overpowered, but in reality it is Susanna who is overpowered by the elders' story. The judges are believed, and Susanna is convicted. The reader is invited to experience indignation at this injustice and to side with, if not identify with, the female against the authority of the male elders.

Verses 42-51, Susanna's Cry and Daniel's Arrival. Once again, Susanna is portrayed as the oppressed "crying out" to God. This is obviously an important theme in the story and, as the commentary has indicated, throughout the Bible—especially in the post-exilic period. But what is of further interest here is precisely what Susanna cries out. The phrase "O eternal God" is not widely attested in the Bible (Gen 21:33; Isa 26:4; 40:28), but it is found rather extensively in the book of Daniel (Dan 3:33 [v. 100 of The Song of the Three]; 4:31 [Theodotion]; 7:14, 27; 9:24; 12:2). It appears to be the case that this is yet another of the ways of referring to God ("the living God," "God of heaven," etc.) that became popular in the period of exile and occupation.

A second interesting phrase in this prayer is the reference to God as the "knower of secrets" or the "one who knows things hidden" (author's trans.). This aspect of God is of obvious importance in a story where evil and corruption have been associated with persons, ideas, and thoughts that are hidden. Truth will be a revelation in the sense that it will be released from its captivity at the hands of the powerful. Susanna knows their deceit, of course, and now finally protests her innocence (v. 43). Susanna, once again, is similar to Daniel (see Daniel 6).

Verse 44 is deceptively short, but politically powerful: "The Lord heard her cry." Compare the hearing of God in stories of two other women of Jewish history and lore: Hagar (Gen 21:12, 17) and Judith (Jdt 4:13; 8:17). In v. 45, God's action

is to stir up trouble for human leaders once again—God's resistance to human oppression and incompetence. Daniel, now in the role usually expected of an angelic messenger, is "stirred" by the Spirit of God (see Judg 5:12; Isa 51:9, 17; 52:1; Dan 7:4; 11:25; 12:2; 2 Macc 13:4).

Daniel calls out, in prophetic tones, that he will not be a party to the shedding of innocent blood (cf. Jer 7:6 as a classic example of this phrase in prophetic literature; it is used extensively as an image of killing the innocent, especially God's chosen messengers). Daniel describes the people as "fools." Jeremiah, too, condemned his listeners as fools (Jer 5:21), and the image of the fool runs through Sirach as the antithesis to the godly, the pious, and the wise: "The mind of fools is in their mouth/ but the mouth of the wise is in their mind" (Sir 21:26; see also Sir 4:27; 8:17; 16:23; 21:14).

Daniel calls on the judges to judge properly. The witnesses have not been thoroughly examined. This is necessary in Jewish law,[45] but is the reader to presume from the story that Daniel is reacting to the improper conduct of the trial or to some knowledge he possesses of the events that he has not yet revealed? Should the reader assume that Daniel was clever enough to sense something wrong about the elders' story or that such knowledge comes with being "stirred" by God? Whatever the reason for Daniel's coming to Susanna's defense, the other elders recognize in him a wisdom beyond his years.[46] Daniel is invited to come and to finally reveal what has been hidden from everyone but Susanna, the two corrupt judges, and Daniel himself.

Verses 52-59, The Examination of the Judges and the Truth Revealed. Daniel separates the two false judges, intending to examine each of them in turn. He requests that each judge be brought to him separately. What is interesting is that Daniel greets each of them with hostility.

---

45. See *m. 'Abot* 1.9, in which a similar case of examining witnesses is given in regard to the first-century CE rabbinic teacher Rabbi Yochanan ben Zakkai. There, however, the emphasis is on the rabbi's aversion to killing. Both the story about Susanna and the rabbinic case are similar to the illustration in the Gospel of John of the woman caught in adultery and Jesus' dismissal of the "witnesses" and those who would stone her. See J. Neusner, *A Life of Yohanan Ben Zakkai Ca. 1–80* CE (Leiden: Brill, 1970); and *Development of a Legend: Studies on the Traditions Concerning Yohanan Ben Zakkai* (Leiden: Brill, 1970) 51-53.

46. Collins quotes just such a tradition. See John J. Collins, *Daniel*, Hermeneia (Minneapolis: Fortress, 1993) 433.

The first is called "an old relic of wicked days."[47] (Since the "day of adversity" is noted in Isa 50:9; 51:6; Jer 16:19; and Amos 6:3, one may wonder whether "the evil days" that are referred to here are the days leading up to the exile. After all, it was a central tenet of deuteronomistic theology that the exile was brought on by the sins of the people, and the leaders particularly.) Daniel delivers a searing condemnation of the generation of the exile in words similar to those of Jeremiah or Isaiah. In v. 53, Daniel lists the sins of leaders in a manner that is highly stylized in prophetic speech (see Isa 5:23; 29:21; Jer 7:6; 19:4; 22:3, 17) but is also noteworthy in wisdom literature (Prov 17:15; 24:24).

Verse 54 leaves no doubt that sexual impropriety/adultery is the accusation here (cf. the situation in Judith 12 that uses some of the same Greek terminology). Daniel's asking the elder about what kind of tree under which this alleged sin took place allows for a clever wordplay in Greek. The type of tree the elder names is called σχῖνος (schinos; NAB and NRSV, "mastic"), and Daniel follows this up with a condemnation that calls for the false witness "to be cut in two", or σχίζω (schizō, v. 55). Moore, interestingly, suggests that we maintain the wordplay even in English and, therefore, supplies "clove tree" and "cleave" in the first instance, and "yew" and "hew" in the second instance.[48] It is also noteworthy that an angel appears as an agent of judgment in Daniel's condemnation of the lying elder.[49]

Verse 56 mirrors the preceding questioning, this time of the second elder. Once again, Daniel meets the false witness with hostility, and once again the specific vocabulary of abuse is noteworthy: Daniel calls him a "son of Canaan" (NAB and NRSV, "offspring of Canaan"). Both Ezra 9:1 and Neh 9:8 use "Canaanite" as a term of derision, referring to the peoples traditionally conquered by Joshua at the Israelites' entry into the land; by Ezra's time, the term had long since ceased to be an accurate description of an actual, contemporary cultural/religious group.[50] It is possible that Ezek 16:3 is intended to be a similar slur in the context of delivering a judgment. However, the use of "Canaan" as the name for the people who dwelled in Palestine before the Israelite settlement was common in the late Hellenistic literature (see Judith 5; Bar 3:22; 1 Macc 9:37). Its use here, strikingly, seems to be intended as an ethnic slur. Again, in this accusation, lust is given the blame for leading the judge into sin. The wisdom associations of this idea have already been noted (it plays a role in the beginning of the story, v. 14, and at the end, v. 56), but note also that "corruption" also turns up at the beginning and ending (vv. 9 and 56). There is a circular sense of "just rewards" in the story of Susanna; the lying, lustful elders are condemned for what they gave themselves up to in the beginning.

The contrast between the daughters of Israel and the daughters of Judah is quite interesting, although somewhat obscure. Are we to see in Daniel's statement a reference to the well-known northern propensity to mix with Canaanite religious ideas on a scale supposedly not tolerated in the southern kingdom before the exile? Collins doubts this, because Susanna herself is called an Israelite earlier, and he suggests that perhaps the later Samaritan split is what is referred to here.[51] This would be a post-exilic religious development in the Jewish community. The precise nature of the Samaritan split, however, is still quite controversial,[52] so this must remain an enigmatic reference in the story.

When questioned about the kind of tree under which they witnessed Susanna's "adultery" taking place, the second elder answers, "Under an evergreen oak" (v. 58). The reader is struck by the difference in the testimony of the elders and joins the surrounding community, as if sitting in a modern courtroom, when they all come to know the truth of the matter. The second elder, too, is condemned by Daniel to face the executing angel of God, who stands ready with sword in hand.

Verses 60-64, Reaction and Conclusion. The people cry out, but this time in jubilation.

47. Moore translates this phrase as "aged in evil days" or "You who have grown old in wickedness," but I argue that "old relic *of* wicked days" makes more sense, especially in the light of Daniel's second appeal to history in the examination of the other elder.

48. C. A. Moore, *Daniel, Esther, and Jeremiah: The Additions* (Garden City, N.Y.: Doubleday, 1977) 106-7.

49. Collins, *Daniel*, Hermeneia, 434, notes Isa 37:36 and Ezekiel 9 for the theme of the avenging angel.

50. See Daniel Smith, "Mixed Marriage," in *Second Temple Studies*, vol. 2 (Sheffield: JSOT, 1993) 60-65.

51. Collins, *Daniel*, Hermeneia, 434.

52. See references to the Samaritan debate in Daniel Smith, *The Religion of the Landless: The Sociology of the Babylonian Exile* (New York: Meyer-Stone, 1989).

God is celebrated as the one who saves those who hope in God (see Pss 33:18; 42:5, 11; 69:6; Sir 34:13; 49:10; 2 Macc 2:18; 7:20; 9:20; 4 Macc 17:4). Verses 61-62 participate in the role-reversal that is typical of the Daniel stories—the guilty are condemned, and the innocent are vindicated.

Five verses seems a lot of text to dedicate to the happy ending of this story, but the passage serves to justify the conclusion that putting the world right and vindicating the innocent are extremely important aspects of the story. This is an idealistic ending—the restoration of the community under the law of Moses. And it is precisely these last five verses that represent the vision and the hope of the writer of the story of Susanna.

The LXX has a rather nice thought at the end:

On account of this, the youths are the beloved of Jacob, in their singlemindedness. Let us also watch out for capable young sons, for youths will be pious, and there will be in them a spirit of knowledge and understanding for ever and ever.[53]

Given Susanna's courage, obviously we should amend this quotation to read that we should watch out for capable sons and daughters! Collins suggests that this ending has the tendency to focus the story on youth vs. elders, rather than Theodotion's emphasis on the courage of Susanna. But we should note that the general themes of innocence, guilt, and truth are all seen as significant in the conclusion of the story. This should not distract the reader from the central elements of the story as a whole—that is, the oppression of the powerless by the powerful.

53. Collins, *Daniel*, Hermeneia, 424.

REFLECTIONS

Germaine Greer has suggested two categories of rape: "grand rape" and "petit rape." The former is what we ordinarily associate with forcible rape. The latter, however, is a form of rape in which "the seducer in fact has some disproportionately unfair advantage over the woman. He need not threaten her, but it is his superior power which induces her to acquiesce against her will."[54] Clearly, the difference between seduction and rape is not so clear, especially in a case like that of Susanna.

Only when one reads literature on rape does one begin to realize how complicit one becomes in Susanna's abuse by "understanding" (read: excusing) the near rape of her as just a symptom of the social circumstances of exile. Such a view diminishes Susanna's suffering and marginalizes her as a possession of her husband and as a temptress (only because she is beautiful). But it is only when we understand the story about rape, when we confront the sobering impact of using the term itself, that the story actually unfolds with all its power as a part of the Daniel corpus about resistance.

Susanna is approached by two men who try to exert their influence, power, and authority over her. The distribution of power and choice is clearly weighted in favor of these elders. She must either give herself to them or face death as a falsely accused adulteress. Susanna's courage, her turning to God in the face of overwhelming danger, is, therefore, the equivalent to Hananiah, Mishael, and Azariah standing before Nebuchadnezzar and refusing his command to bow down and pray to him.

The story of Susanna invites us to consider injustice within as well as outside of our religious life. Thus the context of exile is almost an ironic twist—as if to say to the reader, "The Babylonians aren't the *only* sources of injustice here." Finally, we must remember that the story is not only about the sin of the elders, but also about the corruptibility and foolishness of the entire exiled community. The elders are not the only fools identified by the young

54. Quoted by L. C. Curran, "Rape and Rape Victims in Metamorphoses," in *Women in the Ancient World,* J. Peradotto and J. P. Sullivan, eds. (Albany: SUNY Press, 1984) 263-86.

Daniel. The community in the story of Susanna is ready to judge her without a trial, and she is marched through a kangaroo court. The community, too, is showing signs of internal corruption and lack of fortitude. Daniel calls for solidarity as well as wisdom when he labels them fools for condemning "a daughter of Israel without examination and without learning the facts" (v. 48 NRSV). Note, further, the enigmatic saying "This is how you have been treating the daughters of Israel, and they were intimate with you through fear; but a daughter of Judah would not tolerate your wickedness" (v. 57 NRSV). It has been speculated that this verse refers to conditions before the exile, or perhaps to the Samaritan split (i.e., Samaritans=north/Israelites). In at least one significant passage, "daughters" is a metaphor for the people as a whole. In Ezekiel 23, the northern kingdom, called Oholah (Samaria), and the southern kingdom, called Oholibah (Jerusalem), are condemned for having committed "adultery" with Assyria, Babylonia, and Egypt. If Daniel intends a similar metaphor, then the "daughters" are the people as a whole, corrupted by the "foreigners," implied in his calling the corrupt elders "Canaanite" (v. 56). Susanna's treatment, then, is severely condemned by Daniel in terms that suggest that the elder's behavior is equivalent to idolatrous behavior of the people as a whole in previous eras.

It is clear that Susanna goes through all the steps of the otherwise oppressed *male* Jews in the Daniel tradition: confrontation with an overpowering threat, calling out to God, angelic/miraculous delivery, and punishment of the accusers. Reflection on this detail calls on us to face a most uncomfortable reality in the modern church: We can become so wrapped up in the faith and justice issues of the world that we fail to address the insidious presence of injustice within our own fellowship.

The continued second-class status of women within some churches, and particularly the continued refusal of some faith traditions to accept a woman's call to equal leadership in ministry, is simply an acceptance of the world's judgment of women, and it makes a mockery of the church's claim to seek justice and the full expression of the kingdom of God within our world.[55] Those who would continue such suppression and oppression, even in the church, ought to keep in mind that the story of Susanna emphasizes that "the Lord heard her cry"!

---

55. The world's judgment of women is only too clear. Between 1960 and 1987, the reported cases of rape in the United States increased 440%. See L. Baron and M. A. Straus, *Four Theories of Rape* (New York: Hemisphere, 1989).

BEL AND THE DRAGON

VERSES 1-42

OVERVIEW

This chapter consists of two stories that are only loosely related. There is considerable scholarly debate as to whether these stories originally belonged together or were artificially joined when they were made a part of the Daniel tradition.[56] Moore ingeniously suggests that just as the Susanna story represents Daniel as a precocious and wise youth, so also the stories of Bel and the Dragon—taking place during the Persian rule—represent the old and wise Daniel still true to his faith.[57] Certainly both stories deal with idolatry, although in one case the idol is fashioned by human hands and in the other case it is a living animal. Both parts obviously deal with the theme of idolatry in exile, already a major concern in Second Isaiah and in the Hebrew/Aramaic stories of

Daniel 1–6. Finally, some scholars have suggested that Daniel brings these contests upon himself.[58] But let us not forget the ominous words of the king, which begin the episode of Bel and the Dragon: "Why do you not worship Bel?" (v. 4). From the lips of a man who can dispatch death in seconds, the implied threat is obvious. However, there is another clear difference between the stories of this chapter and Daniel 1–6, with which they otherwise have much in common. The Jewish courtier Daniel is much bolder now; he not only wisely advises the king, but also laughs at the king's mistakes. Indeed, one of the most important details of this story is precisely that Daniel has developed a dangerous sense of humor.

56. Moore, *Daniel, Esther, and Jeremiah,* 146-47.
57. Ibid., 9.

58. L. Wills, *The Jew in the Court of the Foreign King* (Minneapolis: Fortress, 1990) 134.

VERSES 1-22, THE STORY OF BEL

NAB

14 [1] After King Astyages was laid with his fathers, Cyrus the Persian succeeded to his kingdom. [2] Daniel was the king's favorite and was held in higher esteem than any of the friends of the king. [3] The Babylonians had an idol called Bel, and every day they provided for it six barrels of fine flour, forty sheep, and six measures of wine. [4] The king worshiped it and went every day to adore it; but Daniel adored only his God. [5] When the king asked him, "Why do you not adore Bel?" Daniel replied, "Because I worship not idols made with hands, but only the living God who made

Verse numbering of the NAB is taken from the Greek text of Daniel, which includes these verses as part of a longer section after chapter 12 for Bel and the Dragon.

NRSV

1When King Astyages was laid to rest with his ancestors, Cyrus the Persian succeeded to his kingdom. [2]Daniel was a companion of the king, and was the most honored of all his Friends.

3Now the Babylonians had an idol called Bel, and every day they provided for it twelve bushels of choice flour and forty sheep and six measures[a] of wine. [4]The king revered it and went every day to worship it. But Daniel worshiped his own God.

So the king said to him, "Why do you not worship Bel?" [5]He answered, "Because I do not revere idols made with hands, but the living God, who created heaven and earth and has dominion over all living creatures."

[a] A little more than fifty gallons

NAB

heaven and earth and has dominion over all mankind." 6 Then the king continued, "You do not think Bel is a living god? Do you not see how much he eats and drinks every day?" 7 Daniel began to laugh. "Do not be deceived, O king," he said; "it is only clay inside and bronze outside; it has never taken any food or drink." 8 Enraged, the king called his priests and said to them, "Unless you tell me who it is that consumes these provisions, you shall die. 9 But if you can show that Bel consumes them, Daniel shall die for blaspheming Bel." Daniel said to the king, "Let it be as you say!" 10 There were seventy priests of Bel, besides their wives and children.

When the king went with Daniel into the temple of Bel, 11 the priests of Bel said, "See, we are going to leave. Do you, O king, set out the food and prepare the wine; then shut the door and seal it with your ring. 12 If you do not find that Bel has eaten it all when you return in the morning, we are to die; otherwise Daniel shall die for his lies against us." 13 They were not perturbed, because under the table they had made a secret entrance through which they always came in to consume the food. 14 After they departed the king set the food before Bel, while Daniel ordered his servants to bring some ashes, which they scattered through the whole temple; the king alone was present. Then they went outside, sealed the closed door with the king's ring, and departed. 15 The priests entered that night as usual, with their wives and children, and they ate and drank everything.

16 Early the next morning, the king came with Daniel. 17 "Are the seals unbroken, Daniel?" he asked. And Daniel answered, "They are unbroken, O king." 18 As soon as he had opened the door, the king looked at the table and cried aloud, "Great you are, O Bel; there is no trickery in you." 19 But Daniel laughed and kept the king from entering. "Look at the floor," he said; "whose footprints are these?" 20 "I see the footprints of men, women, and children!" said the king. 21 The angry king arrested the priests, their wives, and their children. They showed him the secret door by which they used to enter to consume what was on the table. 22 He put them to death, and handed Bel over to Daniel, who destroyed it and its temple.

NRSV

6The king said to him, "Do you not think that Bel is a living god? Do you not see how much he eats and drinks every day?" 7And Daniel laughed, and said, "Do not be deceived, O king, for this thing is only clay inside and bronze outside, and it never ate or drank anything."

8Then the king was angry and called the priests of Bel[a] and said to them, "If you do not tell me who is eating these provisions, you shall die. 9But if you prove that Bel is eating them, Daniel shall die, because he has spoken blasphemy against Bel." Daniel said to the king, "Let it be done as you have said."

10Now there were seventy priests of Bel, besides their wives and children. So the king went with Daniel into the temple of Bel. 11The priests of Bel said, "See, we are now going outside; you yourself, O king, set out the food and prepare the wine, and shut the door and seal it with your signet. 12When you return in the morning, if you do not find that Bel has eaten it all, we will die; otherwise Daniel will, who is telling lies about us." 13They were unconcerned, for beneath the table they had made a hidden entrance, through which they used to go in regularly and consume the provisions. 14After they had gone out, the king set out the food for Bel. Then Daniel ordered his servants to bring ashes, and they scattered them throughout the whole temple in the presence of the king alone. Then they went out, shut the door and sealed it with the king's signet, and departed. 15During the night the priests came as usual, with their wives and children, and they ate and drank everything.

16Early in the morning the king rose and came, and Daniel with him. 17The king said, "Are the seals unbroken, Daniel?" He answered, "They are unbroken, O king." 18As soon as the doors were opened, the king looked at the table, and shouted in a loud voice, "You are great, O Bel, and in you there is no deceit at all!"

19But Daniel laughed and restrained the king from going in. "Look at the floor," he said, "and notice whose footprints these are." 20The king said, "I see the footprints of men and women and children."

21Then the king was enraged, and he arrested

a Gk his priests

NRSV

the priests and their wives and children. They showed him the secret doors through which they used to enter to consume what was on the table. ²²Therefore the king put them to death, and gave Bel over to Daniel, who destroyed it and its temple.

COMMENTARY

Verses 1-2, Introduction and Setting. In the LXX version of this story, Daniel is curiously identified as a priest, and there is an early mention of the prophet Habakkuk, who will play an important part in the second story about the "dragon." Moore wonders whether this mention of a priestly Daniel suggests that these stories were originally about another Daniel.[59] That is possible, but may simply be a detail that developed when these stories circulated separately.

The stories in Bel and the Dragon are identified with the Persian period in the Theodotion text, although the subjects are Babylonian ("Bel" is an epithet for "Marduk," the great national god of the Babylonians). It is possible that the chronological identification with the period of Cyrus is intended to establish Daniel as one of the trusted leaders of the empire ("friend of the king"), rather like Daniel's fame in Daniel 6. Once again, we see that the Greek stories that have become a part of the Daniel tradition take most of their clues from the sixth of the Aramaic/Hebrew stories, where the ruler is identified as Darius "the Mede" (who, nevertheless, is most likely modeled on the historical Darius, third ruler of the Persian Empire after Cyrus). What is curious, however, is that Cyrus is not mentioned by name throughout the rest of the story, creating suspicion that the opening lines were added later. In the story, the ruler is identified only as "the king" (in the LXX, Cyrus is not mentioned at all), and the reader may have questions about a story that has Cyrus worshiping a Babylonian idol.

In the writings of Herodotus, King Astyages (v. 1) dreams of his daughter giving "birth" to the destruction of his Median regime; in fact, Cyrus

the Great is the grandson of Astyages, and he did defeat the Median Empire in his early moves toward the consolidation of power in the Persian Empire. This is the only mention of King Astyages in the Daniel tradition—clearly intended to make up for the mistake of placing Darius before Cyrus in Daniel 6.

Verses 3-4a, The Worship of the Idol. The idol Bel is introduced here. The idol is "fed" from the king's holdings every day and is honored each day by the king. Moore notes that the specific amounts fed to the idol are not so important as the intention to indicate "large amounts."[60] Furthermore, we know from Herodotus that a table, presumably for human food, was indeed present in certain Babylonian shrines.[61] Is it only a coincidence that once again the issue of food is at the heart of a Daniel story (cf. Daniel 1)?

It is written that the king traveled every day to "do honor" to the idol. Incidentally, we know that Cyrus claimed (in the Cyrus Cylinder) as part of his imperial propaganda for Babylonian consumption that he revered Marduk, and he further claimed that Marduk made his conquest of Babylon possible.[62] Since the identification of this king as "Cyrus" plays a rather insignificant role, however, little importance need be assigned to this coincidence. The term used for "doing honor," one of many used for acts of worship or reverence (typically translated as "doing reverence" or "homage" by kissing the hand or by prostration), is not only common in the Daniel stories (see Dan 3:5-7, 11-12, 14-15, 18, 27-28) but is also used of proper worship in the book of Psalms (Pss 22:27; 29:2; 45:12; 66:4; 72:11; 81:9) and in

---

59. Moore, *Daniel, Esther, and Jeremiah*, 133.

60. Ibid., 134.
61. Herodotus *The History* 1:181.
62. *ANET*, 315-16.

Isaiah (Isa 2:8, 20; 27:13; 37:38; 44:15, 17, 19; 45:14; 46:6; 49:7, 23; 66:23). Such acts, therefore, include the implication of recognizing a higher authority as well as a spiritual authority. The term runs through the story of Bel like a major theme.

Verses 4b-9, The King Establishes the Contest: Bel vs. Yahweh. The king's questioning of Daniel's refusal to honor Bel sets the stage for the coming challenge—and certainly implies a threat. Daniel must respond; it is not a matter of choice, as some commentators have suggested. This is similar to the opening sequences of the Hebrew/Aramaic Daniel traditions: Daniel does not stop praying to his God (Daniel 6), and Azariah, Mishael, and Hananiah do not bow to Nebuchadnezzar's statue (Daniel 3). The contrast between Bel and Yahweh sets the parameters for the challenge that follows, which is reminiscent of Elijah's challenge to the priests of Baal on Mt. Carmel.

Daniel contrasts the idol with the living God. The Greek term for "idol" (χειροποίητος *cheiropoiētos*) is an interesting, complex term composed of "made" (ποιέω *poieō*) and "hand" (χείρ *cheir*), thus "handmade god" (cf. Lev 26:1, 30, "carved image"; Judg 8:18; Isa 2:18; 10:11; 16:12; 19:1; 21:9; 31:7; 46:6; Wis 14:8). In contrast, the "living God" (cf. 3 Macc 6:28) is the God whom Daniel worships. "Living God" is also an interesting term, where one might have expected a more specific title that identifies this God with the Jews. At this point in Jewish tradition, however, the writer is asking his audience to take a somewhat more philosophical position. It is no longer a question of "your" god vs. "our" God, but the living God vs. mere idols; and thus Daniel's use of the phrase "living God" is not merely an alternative to the king's chosen object of reverence, but a direct challenge: the living God as opposed to your foolishness.

In v. 6, the king responds to Daniel's challenge instantly with a reasoned argument: If Bel does not live, how then does Daniel explain Bel's appetite? Daniel's reply entails what is perhaps the most shocking aspect of the entire Bel tradition, and a detail that dramatically sets this story apart from the rest of the Daniel tradition, yet

binds it inextricably to that tradition: Daniel *laughs.*

How is Daniel's laughter to be understood? Moore suggests that Daniel must have felt quite secure to mock the king in this way,[63] but there is much more to this laughter than mere security within the context of the story line. It is important to note that laughter in the Hebrew Bible is usually an act of derision and mockery (only a few exceptions to this can be noted, such as Gen 21:6; Eccl 2:2; 3:4). Abraham and Sarah laugh from incredulity bordering on irony (Gen 17:17; 18:12-13, 15). In Job, laughter is a sign of scorn or mockery, particularly as the result of reversal of fortune (Job 8:21; 17:6; 22:19; cf. Ps 80:6; Jer 20:8; 48:26, 39; Lam 1:7; 3:14; Ezek 23:32; Amos 7:9). The theme of laughter as reversal is clear, for example, in Ps 52:6-7:

> The righteous will see, and fear,
>   and will laugh at the evildoer, saying,
> "See the one who would not take
>   refuge in God,
> but trusted in abundant riches,
>   and sought refuge in wealth!" (NRSV)

In wisdom literature, laughter from mirth is discouraged (Eccl 7:4, 6; Sir 19:30; 27:13) as in Sir 21:20:

> A fool raises his voice when he laughs,
>   but the wise smile quietly. (NRSV)

As we approach the later Hellenistic period materials, the theme of laughter as scorn increases. Wisdom 5:3 speaks eloquently of the oppressors who once mocked the poor and righteous in laughter, while in Jdt 12:12, the Assyrian men fear that Judith will laugh at them if they do not sexually use her, and in 4 Macc 5:28, the martyr story of Eleazar has him saying to his persecutors, "You shall have no such occasion to laugh at me" (NRSV). Finally, social reversal is implicit in Jesus' dramatic remark in the Gospel of Luke: "Woe to you who are laughing now,/ for you will mourn and weep" (Luke 6:25*b* NRSV). When this is all taken into consideration, Daniel's laughter becomes an interesting advance in the entire corpus of Daniel stories. By the time of the writing of the story of Bel, the quiet confidence of Daniel,

63. Moore, *Daniel, Esther, and Jeremiah,* 136.

Hananiah, Azariah, and Mishael that God would deliver them had become the mocking laughter of the revolutionary reversal of fortune that is a central aspect of apocalyptic political doctrine.

Daniel warns the king not to be deceived. That the leaders of Israel deceived the Jews is a central aspect of the theology of Isaiah (e.g., Isa 3:12; 9:15) and Ezekiel (e.g., Ezek 8:17; 13:10), but openness to deception is considered a form of foolishness in the late wisdom tradition as well (e.g., Sir 3:24; 9:7-8; 15:12; 16:23). The idol is made of "clay and bronze," two materials that the reader of the book of Daniel is familiar with in association with handmade gods in Daniel 1–6, although one might have expected the more precious silver and gold at this point. His advising the king not to be deceived once again associates Daniel with wisdom.

In v. 8, the king's response is anger. The allusion to the anger of Nebuchadnezzar in Daniel 3 (see also Dan 9:16; 11:44) is the warning that a serious challenge is about to be set: If Bel is no god, then the priests will die; but if Bel is genuine, then Daniel will die for blasphemy. Collins notes the "cavalier introduction of the death penalty" in this story, but in any context of exile and occupation the threat of death is a constant reality.[64] Given this element, it seems strange that some scholars would continue to argue that these stories are "less negative" toward the king than are the stories of Daniel 1–6.[65]

Verses 10-17, The Contest Is Carried Out. Verse 10 clarifies that Daniel is alone, pitted against a large number of the priests of Bel. This adds drama to the story, of course, but sociologically it represents Daniel as a minority facing the majority Babylonian culture. Both aspects are important. (Note also the possible allusion to Elijah facing the priests of Baal in 1 Kings 18.) But the inclusion of the wives and children is a comment on the corruption of the entire pagan society. It is ambiguous, when the time arrives, whether the entire families are also punished when Bel is revealed to be false.

The priests invite the king to view the contest, indeed, to participate himself, by overseeing the placement of the food in the idol's temple. The king is then invited to seal the door with his symbol of authority. (In the LXX, the priests as well as the king are invited to seal the opening.) We are reminded of another chamber that was sealed with the sign of the occupying ruler in Matt 27:66. The priests, then, invite the king to participate in their deception. This invitation further increases their risk, of course, but the priests are confident in the king's presence because of what they know is hidden—picking up a theme from the Susanna tradition of the hidden vs. the revealed. Daniel reveals truth; his opponents hide the truth.

After the king, then Daniel is invited to oversee the preparations. But Daniel takes one further precaution. Although the reader is not led to believe that Daniel knows about the secret entrance, he does know that the removal of the food must involve the priests' gaining access to it in some fashion. The spreading of ashes is meant, therefore, to detect *any* entrance into the chamber in the vicinity of the food. The Greek text clarifies that the priests of Bel did not observe Daniel's placing of the ashes on the floor; only the king witnessed this action, and thus the king is privy to Daniel's plan from the beginning.

The king rises early in the morning. The particular time reference may not necessarily be important, although rising early was a sign of intentionality, a measure of the importance of an act (cf. Moses with Pharaoh Exod 8:20; 9:13). Sirach advises to seek wisdom "from early morning" (Sir 4:14; 6:36; and to seek God early, Sir 32:14; 39:5). The slow development of the story masterfully builds tension before the moment of revelation. It appears at first that Daniel is defeated. (Note that in the LXX Daniel challenges the priests to also verify that the seals have not been broken. The LXX at this point seems to enjoy heightening the extent of the irony.)

Verses 18-19, The Royal Fool and the Laughing Jew. Verses 18-19 must be read together. The king commits a foolish act by saying in a "loud voice": "You are great, O Bel, and in you there is no deceit at all!" He proclaims that his previous actions were correct before he even gives time to a full consideration of the facts. Now the king is portrayed as not only gullible, but

---

64. Collins, *Daniel,* Hermeneia, 413.
65. L. Wills, *The Jew in the Court of the Foreign King* (Minneapolis: Fortress, 1990) 133-34.

foolish and hasty as well. The trap is set for Daniel to spring.

In response to the king's claim to power, to truth, and to religious wisdom, Daniel laughs and tells the king to look at the footprints in the ashes. In the LXX, Daniel laughs "heartily," increasing the level of mockery. The king is invited to "look [imperative] and know." The priests' faith is based on deception, but Daniel's faith is based on what is open and can be seen.

Verses 20-22, Daniel Reveals the Truth. When he realizes the truth about the priests' deception, once again he is enraged. He orders not only the priests but also their wives and children arrested. When the priests reveal the truth about their secret entrance, the king has them put to death (One wonders whether they expected some form of clemency for this act of revelation.) In the LXX, however, Daniel reveals the hidden door—which presumes that he knew what was going to happen all along—and the king is taken to the houses of the priests, where the food is found. Although it is left somewhat vague whether the wives and children are also killed, it would not be totally unexpected, given their mention throughout the rest of the story. Once again, although moderns may be disturbed at this aspect of the punishment, it is not an unusual element of reversal in Hebrew lore. This detail also serves to mag-

nify the megalomania of the king; his anger is so irrational that he will even kill children (cf. Dan 3:13; 8:6, 19; 9:16, 26). Perhaps we should view these events—fictional though they may be—with the same sadness of heart that, during the Passover seder, accompanies the spilling of drops of wine in remembrance of those Egyptians whose death was a part of liberation from Egyptian slavery.

Daniel, rather than participate in the killing of persons, destroys the idol and its house. This is an interesting contrast of Daniel's religious action and the king's murderous decree (note the number of executions in the book of Daniel: 2:13, 24; 3:23; 4:34; 6:34; 11:44). It is possible that Daniel's actions allude to Jer 51:44: "I will punish Bel in Babylon." (Bel is also mentioned in Isa 46:1 and in the apocryphal Letter of Jeremiah, which is largely concerned with idolatry as well.)

Many scholars have noted that the temple of Bel/Marduk was actually destroyed by the Persian ruler Xerxes I (486–465 BCE), and that occurrence must have been in the background of the events described in this story. One can hardly miss the significance of placing a Jew at the center of the destruction of the temple of Marduk—the very religious symbol of power for the conquering Babylonians.

VERSES 23-42, THE STORY OF THE DRAGON

NAB	NRSV
[23] There was a great dragon which the Babylonians worshiped. [24] "Look!" said the king to Daniel, "you cannot deny that this is a living god, so adore it." [25] But Daniel answered, "I adore the Lord, my God, for he is the living God. [26] Give me permission, O king, and I will kill this dragon without sword or club." "I give you permission," the king said. [27] Then Daniel took some pitch, fat, and hair; these he boiled together and made into cakes. He but them into the mouth of the dragon, and when the dragon ate them, he burst asunder. "This," he said, "is what you worshiped."	[23]Now in that place[a] there was a great dragon, which the Babylonians revered. [24]The king said to Daniel, "You cannot deny that this is a living god; so worship him." [25]Daniel said, "I worship the Lord my God, for he is the living God. [26]But give me permission, O king, and I will kill the dragon without sword or club." The king said, "I give you permission." [27]Then Daniel took pitch, fat, and hair, and boiled them together and made cakes, which he fed to the dragon. The dragon ate them, and burst
	[a] Other ancient authorities lack *in that place*

NAB

28 When the Babylonians heard this, they were angry and turned against the king. "The king has become a Jew," they said; "he has destroyed Bel, killed the dragon, and put the priests to death." 29 They went to the king and demanded: "Hand Daniel over to us, or we will kill you and your family." 30 When he saw himself threatened with violence, the king was forced to hand Daniel over to them. 31 They threw Daniel into a lions' den, where he remained six days. 32 In the den were seven lions, and two carcasses and two sheep had been given to them daily. But now they were given nothing, so that they would devour Daniel.

33 In Judea there was a prophet, Habakkuk; he mixed some bread in a bowl with the stew he had boiled, and was going to bring it to the reapers in the field, 34 when an angel of the Lord told him, "Take the lunch you have to Daniel in the lions' den at Babylon." 35 But Habakkuk answered, "Babylon, sir, I have never seen, and I do not know the den!" 36 The angel of the Lord seized him by the crown of his head and carried him by the hair; with the speed of the wind, he set him down in Babylon above the den. 37 "Daniel, Daniel," cried Habakkuk, "take the lunch God has sent you." 38 "You have remembered me, O God," said Daniel; "you have not forsaken those who love you." 39 While Daniel began to eat, the angel of the Lord at once brought Habakkuk back to his own place.

40 On the seventh day the king came to mourn for Daniel. As he came to the den and looked in, there was Daniel, sitting there! 41 The king cried aloud, "You are great, O Lord, the God of Daniel, and there is no other besides you!" 42 Daniel he took out, but those who had tried to destroy him he threw into the den, and they were devoured in a moment before his eyes.

NRSV

open. Then Daniel said, "See what you have been worshiping!"

28When the Babylonians heard about it, they were very indignant and conspired against the king, saying, "The king has become a Jew; he has destroyed Bel, and killed the dragon, and slaughtered the priests." 29Going to the king, they said, "Hand Daniel over to us, or else we will kill you and your household." 30The king saw that they were pressing him hard, and under compulsion he handed Daniel over to them.

31They threw Daniel into the lions' den, and he was there for six days. 32There were seven lions in the den, and every day they had been given two human bodies and two sheep; but now they were given nothing, so that they would devour Daniel.

33Now the prophet Habakkuk was in Judea; he had made a stew and had broken bread into a bowl, and was going into the field to take it to the reapers. 34But the angel of the Lord said to Habakkuk, "Take the food that you have to Babylon, to Daniel, in the lions' den." 35Habakkuk said, "Sir, I have never seen Babylon, and I know nothing about the den." 36Then the angel of the Lord took him by the crown of his head and carried him by his hair; with the speed of the wind[a] he set him down in Babylon, right over the den.

37Then Habakkuk shouted, "Daniel, Daniel! Take the food that God has sent you." 38Daniel said, "You have remembered me, O God, and have not forsaken those who love you." 39So Daniel got up and ate. And the angel of God immediately returned Habakkuk to his own place.

40On the seventh day the king came to mourn for Daniel. When he came to the den he looked in, and there sat Daniel! 41The king shouted with a loud voice, "You are great, O Lord, the God of Daniel, and there is no other besides you!" 42Then he pulled Daniel[b] out, and threw into the den those who had attempted his destruction, and they were instantly eaten before his eyes.

a Or by the power of his spirit   b Gk him

COMMENTARY

Verses 23-42 bear an interesting relation to Daniel 6, as each places Daniel in the lions' den as punishment for his religious faith. However, the story of the dragon has some curious elements to it, not the least of which is the strange involvement of a prophet traditionally named Habakkuk.

Verse 23, The Setting and the "Dragon." The term used for "dragon" is a Greek term (δράκων *drakōn*) that translates the Hebrew for "serpent" (תנין *tannîn*), more specifically for "snake." In the Moses story, the connotation is clearly a snake (Exod 7:9-10, 12; Deut 32:33). But the term is also used to refer to the echoes of the ancient Canaanite belief about Yam (Job 7:12), the god of the sea, represented as a coiling serpent, and "Leviathan" (Job 9:13; 26:12; Pss 74:13-14; 104:26; 148:7; Isaiah 27; Amos 9:3). Many scholars have speculated about snake worship (zoolatry) as an aspect of Babylonian worship, but despite some interesting archaeological fragments, the case remains unconvincing. Since living snakes were certainly an aspect of Egyptian religious practice, some scholars have suggested that the origin of this story is in the Egyptian Jewish diaspora.[66]

Other scholars have suggested that the snake/dragon story is a midrash (a story that develops, or expands upon, an earlier short text) on Jer 51:34, 44:

"King Nebuchadnezzar of Babylon has devoured me,
 he has crushed me;
he has made me an empty vessel,
 he has swallowed me like a monster;
he has filled his belly with my delicacies,
 he has spewed me out.
.   .   .   .
I will punish Bel in Babylon,
 and make him disgorge what he has swallowed.
The nations shall no longer stream to him;
 the wall of Babylon has fallen." (NRSV)[67]

66. Collins's discussion is helpful. See Collins, *Daniel,* Hermeneia, 414.

67. The text from Jeremiah, incidentally, is also often seen as the basis for the Jonah story, particularly for those scholars who see in the Jonah story elements of an allegory of the exile. Many scholars dismiss the allegorical interpretation of Jonah as a reference to the Babylonian exile simply because the entire story cannot be matched up point by point with the experience of the exile. But this is wooden thinking. Certainly there is more to Jonah than merely an allegorical analogy of the exile, but that does not cancel its allegorical aspects.

Ezekiel 29:3 LXX calls Pharaoh the "great dragon" (see also Ezek 32:2). Given this association of the "dragon" to the exile, one can see that, like Jeremiah and Ezekiel, the story of the dragon runs in close association with the tradition of Jonah in making references to the exilic experience. I would argue that there is a thematic connection between these texts, rather than interpreting the dragon story in the Daniel tradition as a specific development of the scriptural tradition of Jeremiah 51. If, for example, Jonah's "dragon" is an allegory of Babylon's "swallowing" of the Jewish community, then Daniel's destruction of the dragon is at least as compelling for its listeners as was his destruction of Bel and the sanctuary of Babylonian power.

Verses 24-26, The Challenge and the Contest. The king challenges Daniel—a clear reference to the story of Bel, which precedes this episode. The dragon, unlike the god Bel, however, is a living animal and not merely a handmade idol, lending credence to the notion that this story is based on the keeping of sacred animals as symbols of deities.

Daniel's response to the king's challenge to him to worship the dragon is to focus not on the aspect of its being a living creature, but on who is actually sovereign, on who is "Lord," and—ultimately—on who is powerful. Thus Daniel presents a counterchallenge to the king. Daniel proposes to kill the dragon without using the weapons of worldly power—without "sword or club." Daniel will prove the truth without the world's tools, for it is inherently blasphemous to suggest that truth can be derived from weapons.

Verse 27, The Killing of the Serpent. The particular formula that Daniel mixes—that is, fat, hair, and pitch—does not appear to have particular significance. Although unpleasant even to the modern reader, this mixture hardly appears lethal. But perhaps that is just the point. Those commentators who have suggested that Daniel must have slipped something lethal into the mixture may well be missing a significant detail that Daniel succeeds precisely without lethal weapons. Some scholars have argued that the original Aramaic source for this story must have contained a reference to a wind that brought about the death of the dragon. The idea is that this wind is related to the story of Marduk's destruction of Tiamat in the Babylonian creation story in the *Enuma Elish,* where Marduk uses wind to burst the belly of the sea monster Tiamat. Others suggest that Daniel knew of the explosive nature of the mixture. Moore rehearses some of the traditional ways that this concoction has been amended to include lethal elements like nails, combs, and hatchets.[68] The result, in any case, is that when the serpent eats the cakes that Daniel makes from this mixture, the dragon bursts open. And with this Daniel demonstrates to the king that no true god could have been defeated so easily. This quick dispatch of the serpent becomes the opening sequence to the central theme of the story of the dragon: the Babylonians' attempt to avenge the destruction of Bel.

Verses 28-32, Daniel Thrown to the Lions. Verse 28 contains a startling concept. The Babylonians are angry because of Daniel's influence on the king, and to express their frustration they use a surprising phrase: "The king has become a Jew." By the time of the Hellenistic period, it is not inconceivable in Jewish thought that a foreigner might "become" a Jew—presumably referring to a convert. Collins objects that even this fact does not necessarily refer to conversion in the modern sense.[69] But can we even know what "conversion" meant in that period? A clear transformation of character and religious observance is suggested by the vocabulary of the passage. The degrees of transformation in the foreign king make an interesting study in the Daniel tradition, including the statements made by Nebuchadnezzar and Darius in Daniel 1–6.[70] The foreign monarchs often proclaim that they are impressed by the God of the Jews, and they even acknowledge this God's impressive achievements. But does this suggest conversion or transformation? I would argue that the oft-noted positive view of kings in Daniel 1–6 is only a positive view of transformed and humbled kings. Here in Bel and the Dragon, we have moved beyond simply a change of behavior in favor of the

Jews. The reader must keep in mind that the story does not so much suggest that the king did, in fact, convert, but merely that the Babylonians accuse him of having done so. This accusatory context lends credence to reading this phrase as an actual conversion precisely because it would be considered so shocking.

Daniel, the Jewish exile, has revealed the religious foundation of the Babylonians to be based on fraud, so now the Babylonians seek to kill him. They force the king to hand Daniel over to them. Similar to Daniel's laughter in the story of Bel, the story of the dragon reveals some conceptual developments from the Hebrew/Aramaic Daniel stories. The Babylonian advisers do not even bother with a ruse to trick the king as they did in Daniel 3 and 6. Here, they resort to the only basis of their power in the first place: the threat of violence. They demand that either Daniel be handed over to them, or they will revolt against the king. Given what we know of the constant threat of revolt and rebellion in the Achaemenid and Hellenistic eras, such threats would have clear meaning.

The text suggests that Daniel was in the lions' den for six days, and then proceeds to exaggerate the danger by pointing out that the lions had not been fed their daily rations of two humans and two sheep. Surely this detail is intended to increase the horror of the threat to Daniel, so as to further magnify the miracle of his deliverance.

Verses 33-39, The Intervention of Habakkuk. The intervention of the prophet Habakkuk is one of the strangest aspects of all of the Daniel traditions. The writer tells us that Habakkuk, at home in Judea, had prepared bread and stew for the reapers when an angel appeared to tell him to take it instead to Daniel in Babylonia.[71] It is curious why Habakkuk should have been chosen. His time of prophecy was at the beginning of the Babylonian era—apparently prior to 598 BCE—and includes a message of doom for Jerusalem, facing the ravenous conquests of the Babylonians. However, there is a strong polemic against idolatry in Hab 2:18-19 that may well have recommended this prophet to the writer of this tale:

68. Moore, *Daniel, Esther, and Jeremiah,* 142-44.

69. Collins, *Daniel,* Hermeneia, 415

70. See Daniel L. Smith-Christopher, "Between Ezra and Israel: Exclusion, Transformation, and Inclusion of the 'Foreigner' in Post-Exilic Biblical Theology," in *Ethnicity and the Bible,* ed. M. Brett (Leiden: E. J. Brill, 1996).

71. Collins points out other OT texts that report instances of spiritual "travel," especially comparing the reference here in v. 36 with the travels of Elijah, Elisha, and Ezekiel, who was also transported by an angel holding his hair (Ezek 8:3). See Collins, *Daniel,* Hermeneia, 416.

What use is an idol
  once its maker has shaped it—
  a cast image, a teacher of lies?
For its maker trusts in what has been made,
  though the product is only an

    idol that cannot speak!
Alas for you who say to the wood, "Wake up!"
  to silent stone, "Rouse yourself!"
  Can it teach?
See, it is gold and silver plated,
  and there is no breath in it at all. (NRSV)

There is a strong theme of punishment for the Babylonian conquerors in Habakkuk as well—although arguably not unique to the prophetic corpus.

An angel of God brings Habakkuk to Babylon and into the presence of Daniel. Habakkuk's feeding of Daniel (reminiscent of God's care for Elijah in his exile) is seen as God's answer to Daniel's prayer for aid, for Daniel responds with thanksgiving in terms that are familiar to the Daniel tradition: "You have remembered me, O God, and have not forsaken those who love you" (v. 38; cf. Ezra 8, where the fasting Jews are protected by God).

Verses 40-42, The Reversal. The king, like Darius in Daniel 6, comes to mourn Daniel. Darius was less certain of Daniel's death than is the king of the dragon story, but the result is similar. When the king learns that Daniel lives, he shouts "with a loud voice" (similar to the shouts earlier, "You are great, O Bel" [v. 18 NRSV]). What the king shouts is a statement of existence: There is no God but the God of Daniel. This is in keeping with the transformation (perhaps conversion) implied in the earlier accusation of the Babylonians (v. 28).

The story is complete with the expected reversal of fortune; those who sought to destroy Daniel are themselves destroyed. What is missing is any indication of a reward for Daniel—a curious omission, given its frequent mention in the other stories.

REFLECTIONS

1. Stories like Bel and the Dragon presume the contact between cultures—the arguments over the validity of one religious belief over another. These are, therefore, diaspora issues as well as issues of political occupation, and part of their profundity is precisely the power of those who hold such false beliefs and the apparent lack of worldly power held by the Jews, who nevertheless prove the beliefs of the dominant power to be false. The suggestion is clear: If the oppressors' religious beliefs are false, then their power must be limited as well. Mockery is a powerful weapon for those living in the shadows. The laughing Daniel is an important symbol of resistance.[72]

2. The Babylonians in the stories of Bel and the Dragon are portrayed as idolatrous, and their persistence, their faith, is made "real" by superior force. The two go hand in hand, for the only way for idols to be portrayed to "live" is by force of arms. Thus Daniel overcomes them with wit and wisdom, and not with swords and clubs. Truth is hidden by violence, but it is revealed by the subversive teaching of the wise, and especially by the stories of clever Jews who are able to defeat the powerful with the weapon of cleverness and wisdom.

72. See the role of humor in slave religion in A. Raboteau, *Slave Religion* (New York: Oxford University Press, 1978) 290-95.

THE BOOK OF HOSEA

INTRODUCTION, COMMENTARY, AND REFLECTIONS
BY
GALE A. YEE

THE BOOK OF
HOSEA

INTRODUCTION

THE BOOK

The play *The Marriage of Hosea,* published in 1929 under the pseudonym Izachak, carries the subtitle "A Passion Play." In describing the work as a *passion* play, the anonymous twentieth-century author understood the ancient prophetic book of Hosea very well. The multivalent word *passion* captures the incendiary relations existing among the characters of the book. It typifies the feverish lust of a wife chasing after her various lovers. As profound suffering, passion describes the torment her husband experiences because of her infidelity. It also embodies the violent anger with which the husband lashes out against his wife to punish her and bring her to her senses. Finally, it embraces the ardor between the couple as they reconcile and commit themselves to each other again.

Structure and Theological Themes. The prophetic book of Hosea is indeed a passionate work. Its vivid metaphor of marriage for the covenant between God and Israel usually comes to mind when one thinks of this book. Hosea is the first biblical work to employ such an image to describe the God/Israel relationship. Although a major one, however, marriage is not the only covenantal metaphor for Hosea. The book's structure evinces another important image of the special God/Israel relationship and another kind of "passion" as well.

The book is divided into three sections, each highlighting a particular metaphor for the covenant between God and Israel. Hosea 1–3 concentrates on the husband/wife metaphor. The tragic marriage of Hosea to his promiscuous wife, Gomer, and the births of their three children (chap. 1) parallel Yahweh's tumultuous union with the faithless wife, Israel (chap. 2). Hosea represents Israel's worship of illicit gods figuratively as adultery, punishable by death if God so chooses. God's eventual reconciliation with "his wife," Israel, provides a model for Hosea's own reunion with Gomer (chap. 3).

Chapters 4–11, the second and largest section, contain the bulk of Hosea's oracles against Israelite politics and cult. Chapter 11, which summarizes and concludes this section, takes up the parent/child metaphor for the God/Israel relationship. God becomes the loving, caring parent, while Israel in its transgression of the covenant is the rebellious son. The passion of the mother/father God exhibits itself in the parent's compassionate refusal to kill the intractable child, even though the laws of the land would sanction death.

In the third and final section, chaps. 12–14, the prophet interweaves both the husband/wife metaphor and the rebellious son metaphor. The unwise son is threatened with destruction, unless he repents of his accumulated guilt (Hosea 13). The repentant wife returns to her husband and to the land from whence she was banished (Hosea 12). Symbolizing the wife and her reunion with the husband, the land that had formerly been devastated by the husband blossoms forth into a fruitful, luxurious plantation (Hosea 14).

The first and final verses of the work are structurally significant. Hosea 1:1 contextualizes the tradition of Hosea during a particular time in the history of the Israelite people. Hosea 14:9 concludes the book with a word of wisdom, enjoining the reader to heed God's Word inscribed therein.

Hosea 3, 11, and 14 also have structural importance. These chapters conclude the three major sections of the work. Each presents a story about the God/Israel relationship through the metaphor either of the husband/wife (Hosea 3; 14) or of the parent/child (Hosea 11). Each highlights the themes of human repentance/return (the Hebrew word שוב [šûb] encompasses both meanings) and divine forgiveness and mercy. Each chapter also unfolds a journey motif that occurs at two levels: the wife's/son's spiritual journey back to the husband/parent and the physical journey back to the homeland from exile.

In addition to the themes of repentance/return and journey home, each major section of the work is characterized by a movement from barrenness to fertility. In Hosea 2 the land that was ravaged and laid waste (2:3, 12) participates cosmically in the bounty that flows from the rebetrothal of husband and wife. The wife/Israel is figuratively sown in the land (2:18-23). In the 4–11 complex, the symbolic barrenness of the people is reflected in the destitution of the cosmos (see Commentary on 4:3). Nevertheless, three hope passages (5:15–6:3; 10:12; 11:10-11) articulate a movement from barrenness to fertility. Hosea 1–3 concludes with the wife/Israel sown in the land. Hosea 14:5-8 manifests the wonderful results of the sowing by depicting the wife/Israel breaking forth as a lush and flourishing land.

Authorship. Over a hundred years of scholarship on the prophetic books reveal that not every saying or oracle in the work comes directly from the prophet himself.[1] A prophetic book is the literary result of a long traditioning process, encompassing not only the lifetime of the prophet but also centuries following his death. Successive generations who inherit the prophet's sayings reinterpret them for their own particular time, putting a distinctive stamp upon the different literary phases of the book.

Earlier biblical scholarship tended to value what it saw as the *ipsissima verba,* or the "authentic words," of the prophet.[2] Evidence of later editorial activity was regarded as secondary, not only chronologically, but also in theological importance. Recent critical studies, however, recognize the significance of later stages of the work: those of the collectors and redactors.[3] In their collection, arrangement, and commentary on the prophetic tradition they inherit, these later editors are responsible for the biblical work as we have it today.

Hence, the authorship of the book of Hosea is a complex matter that is still disputed. Many scholars insist that most of the book originated with the prophet Hosea.[4] Others think that redactional activity was more extensive than previously thought.[5] Relevant for the oracles of this eighth-century BCE prophet are three major interpretive stages that can be detected in the book of Hosea: an eighth–seventh-century BCE collection of the prophet's oracles; a seventh-century BCE deuteronomistic redaction during the time of the Judean king Josiah; and a sixth-century BCE deuteronomistic redaction during the Babylonian exile (587–539 BCE). Whether one thinks that Hosea's original oracles were particularly influential for these later interpretive periods or whether one maintains that redactors expanded Hosea's original oracles during these later times with their own theologies, it is clear that these stages were critical in the book's formation.

Since the focus of *The New Interpreter's Bible* is the final canonical text itself, we must reckon very seriously with the later interpretive stages as well as the prophet's earlier oracles. Although not all of the sayings can be credited to the prophet Hosea, from a scriptural vantage point they *now* belong fully to him and his book. Acceptance of every stage in the formation of a prophetic book recognizes that God's word, spoken by the prophet in a specific historical context, was not limited to that context. Later eras appropriated Hosea's words as *tradition* that spoke in some way to their own circumstances, often expanding upon or even modifying them. The content of the original message was not dissipated when its initial context was past.

1. I am assuming with good reason that the prophet and the collectors and redactors of his tradition are male.
2. The classic example was that of T. H. Robinson, *Prophecy and the Prophets in Ancient Israel* (London: Gerald Duckworth, 1923) 52-58. On Hosea in particular, see his commentary, *Die zwölf kleinen Propheten,* HAT 14 (Tübingen: J. C. B. Mohr, 1938) 1-2. For a review of the literature, see Graham I. Davies, *Hosea* (Sheffield: JSOT, 1993) 94-96.
3. See Grace I. Emmerson, *Hosea: An Israelite Prophet in Judean Perspective* (Sheffield: JSOT, 1984); Gale A. Yee, *Composition and Tradition in the Book of Hosea: A Redaction Critical Investigation,* SBLDS 102 (Atlanta: Scholars Press, 1987) 27-46; and Martti Nissinen, *Prophetie, Redaktion und Fortschreibung im Hoseabuch* (Kevelaer: Neukirchen-Vluyn, 1991).
4. For example, Francis I. Andersen and David Noel Freedman, *Hosea,* AB 24 (Garden City, N.Y.: Doubleday, 1980) 59.
5. See Yee, *Composition and Tradition,* 1-25, for a review of the literature.

THE HISTORICAL CONTEXTS OF THE BOOK

The Period of the Eighth-Century BCE Prophet. Social Turmoil. Very little is known about the northern prophet Hosea. The superscription to his book, which was added later by a redactor (see Commentary on 1:1), identifies Hosea as the son of Beeri, about whom nothing more can be said. The superscription situates Hosea between 750 and 724 BCE—i.e., between the last years of Jeroboam II (786–746 BCE) and three years before the fall of Israel to the Assyrians in 721 BCE. If the superscription is correct, Hosea prophesied during a politically turbulent period after the peaceful rule of Jeroboam II (cf. 2 Kgs 14:23–17:41). The monarchy was plagued by a number of assassinations. Of the six kings to ascend the throne, all but one died violently. Corruption at court and partisan intrigue were rampant (Hos 6:8-10; 7:1-7). The northern kingdom not only contended with the western encroachment of the Assyrian king Tiglath-pileser III, but also clashed with its southern rival, Judah, during the Syro-Ephraimite war (735–733 BCE). Israel's foreign policy was often unpredictable. The nation curried favor with international powers, such as Egypt and Assyria, who competed with each other in the political arena (Hos 7:8-15; 12:1).

The nation was rife with economic abuses. The social inequities between rich and poor that were very much apparent during the time of Jeroboam II became exacerbated after his death. The war with Judah and heavy tribute to Assyria (Hos 8:10; 10:6) depleted economic resources. The richer classes intensified their exploitation of the peasants in order to pay these debts. Many resorted to fraud and cheating (Hos 12:7-8).

Cultic Turmoil. The book of Hosea is perhaps best known for its condemnation of Israel's cult. One gets the impression from reading this book (as well as many other books in the Hebrew Bible) that worship of Yahweh had become infected with the Canaanite religion of the land the Israelites had conquered. The wife/Israel is accused of chasing after her lovers, the *baals* (2:7-8, 13). In Canaanite mythology, Baal was the storm god responsible for life-giving rains. In an arid climate like Israel's, such rains were a matter of life and death. The fertility rituals grounded in this mythology supposedly involved orgiastic sex with temple prostitutes.

Recent scholarship calls into question this notion of Canaanite infiltration of a pure Yahwism.[6] Monotheism, belief in a single God to the exclusion of any other, was not always practiced in Israel. The monotheistic theology represented in the book of Hosea eventually became normative for Israel. In their formative stages, however, Israel's diverse religious beliefs and practices were influenced by those of other cultures.

Particularly important for understanding Hosea is recognizing that the religion of the ancient Israelites had a strong heritage in Canaanite religion. Although Yahweh was its primary God, early Israelite religion included the worship of several other deities. Veneration of the Canaanite deities El, Baal, and perhaps even the goddess

6. Mark S. Smith, *The Early History of God: Yahweh and the Other Deities in Ancient Israel* (San Francisco: Harper & Row, 1990) 145-60.

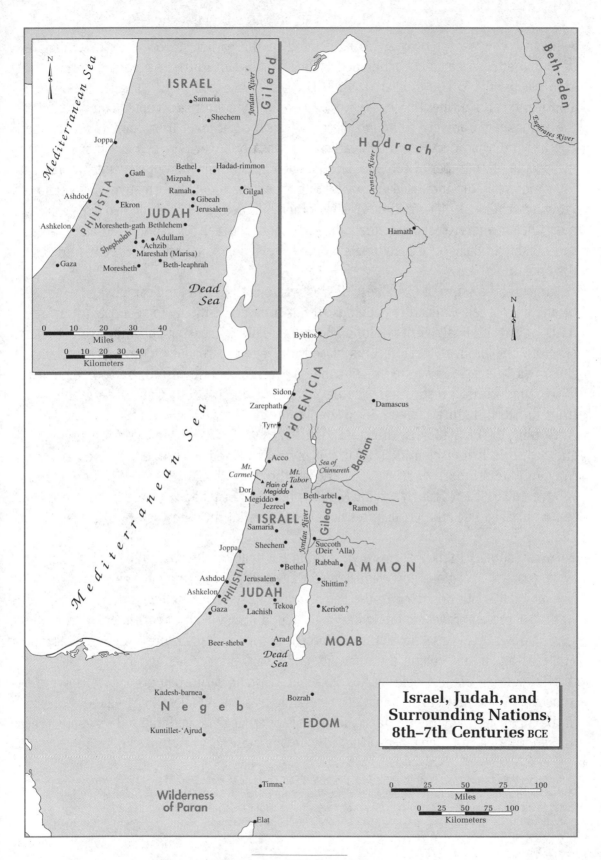

Inset map

N

Mediterranean Sea

ISRAEL

• Samaria

• Shechem

Jordan River

Gilead

Joppa •

Bethel •   • Hadad-rimmon

Gath •   Mizpah •

PHILISTIA   Ramah •   • Gilgal

Ashdod •   Ekron •   Gibeah •

JUDAH   • Jerusalem

Ashkelon •   Moresheth-gath Bethlehem •

Shephelah   • Adullam

• Achzib

• Mareshah (Marisa)

Gaza •   Moresheth •   • Beth-leaphrah

Dead Sea

Miles
0 10 20 30 40

Kilometers
0 10 20 30 40

Main map

Beth-eden

Euphrates River

Hadrach

Orontes River

• Hamath

Mediterranean Sea

Byblos •

PHOENICIA

Sidon •   • Damascus

Zarephath •

Tyre •

Acco •   Bashan

Mt. Carmel   Sea of Chinnereth

Dor •   Mt. Tabor   Plain of Megiddo

Megiddo •   • Beth-arbel

Jezreel •   • Ramoth

ISRAEL   Gilead

Samaria •   Jordan River

Joppa •   Shechem •   Succoth (Deir ʿAlla)

Ashdod •   • Bethel   • Rabbah   AMMON

Ashkelon •   Jerusalem •

PHILISTIA   JUDAH   • Shittim?

Gaza •   • Tekoa   • Kerioth?

Lachish •

Beer-sheba •   • Arad   MOAB

Dead Sea

Kadesh-barnea •   Bozrah •

N e g e b

Kuntillet-ʿAjrud •   EDOM

Israel, Judah, and Surrounding Nations, 8th–7th Centuries BCE

Wilderness of Paran

• Timnaʿ

• Elat

Miles
0 25 50 75 100

Kilometers
0 25 50 75 100

Asherah,[7] was accepted or at least tolerated in the earlier stages of Israel's religious development. What stand condemned as Baal worship in Hosea—e.g., cultic rites on the high places (4:13; 10:8), pillars (3:4; 10:1-2), divining rods (4:12), images (4:17; 8:4; 14:8), and calf figurines (8:5-6; 10:5; 13:2)—were for centuries accepted components of the worship of Yahweh. Although these had been taken over from foreign cults, their appropriation had occurred much earlier and was no longer regarded as syncretistic by the people.[8] A number of complex factors, such as centralization of the cult, the rise of the monarchy, the increased use of writing that disseminated normative views, and a growing religious self-definition vis-à-vis other cultures, eventually led to an evolving monotheism and a rejection of much, though not all, of Israel's Canaanite heritage. Hence, the worship of Baal, once a legitimate part of Israelite religion, now stands condemned by the book of Hosea.

Although worship of Canaanite deities was most likely a long-established practice in ancient Israel, Canaanite religious rituals are very difficult to reconstruct on the basis of the biblical witness alone. Because of its increasing polemic against that religion, the biblical text presents biased and even distorted pictures of Canaanite rites. One alleged Canaanite practice that is specifically relevant to the book of Hosea is so-called cultic prostitution. We have learned much about Canaanite mythology from the Ras Shamra tablets, discovered some fifty years ago on the coast of Syria. According to these tablets, the storm god Baal was killed by Mot, god of barrenness and death. In its prescientific milieu, this myth explained the hot, dry period between May and September, when no rains fell on the land. Baal's sister-lover, the goddess Anat, came to the rescue by slaying Mot and bringing Baal back to life. Their passionate sexual intercourse, the Canaanites believed, initiated the rainy season that began in October.

Many scholars think that this mythic drama of death and renewed life was rehearsed every year in a religious new year festival that took place in the fall,[9] even though the festival itself is not described in the Ras Shamra tablets. Supposedly, part of this festival was a "sacred marriage" imitating Baal and Anat, during which Canaanite men, from the king on down, had ritual sex with cultic prostitutes in order to ensure fertility in the land. The religious intent behind these fertility cults was very serious, indeed—nothing less than the survival of the people in a hostile climate. Human nature being of a piece, however, some worshipers may have frequented these cultic prostitutes for less than religious reasons. In the minds of many interpreters, such rituals often degenerated into full-scale orgies at the sanctuaries and high places. Allegedly, it was these services that so offended Hosea

7. Cf. Saul M. Olyan, *Asherah and the Cult of Yahweh in Israel,* SBLMS 34 (Atlanta: Scholars Press, 1988).

8. Rainer Albertz, *A History of Israelite Religion in the Old Testament Period,* vol. 1: *From the Beginnings to the End of the Monarchy,* trans. John Bowden (Louisville: Westminster/John Knox, 1994) 172-75. Analogously, one would hardly think today that Christmas trees or Easter eggs represent a tainting of a pure Christian celebration of these events, even though trees and eggs were originally part of non-Christian religious rites.

9. For example, James L. Mays, *Hosea,* OTL (Philadelphia: Westminster, 1969) 25-26.

(4:11-19; 9:1-3). Some critics even suggest that Hosea's wife, Gomer, like other Israelite women (see 4:14), was a cultic prostitute.[10]

Nevertheless, a number of scholars have questioned the phenomenon of cultic prostitution, not only in Canaan, but also in the rest of the ancient Near East.[11] No substantive textual or archaeological evidence verifies that such a class of prostitutes ever existed or that such sexual rites were ever performed. Although used by some to support the existence of cultic prostitution, the testimonies of certain ancient authors like the Greek writers Herodotus and Strabo are actually quite unreliable, because they were written at a far later date and are markedly tendentious. Although in the prophet's mind certain rituals involved sexual intercourse, it would be a mistake to accept this assertion at face value. The biblical text is simply too polemical, revealing more about the prophetic mind that leveled the accusation than about actual observances in the cult.

Thus far I have assumed that condemnations of Israel's cult originated with the eighth-century BCE prophet Hosea. If worship of Baal, along with rituals on the high places, pillars, calves, etc., had long been part and parcel of Israelite religion, then Hosea should not be considered a religious reformer, hearkening the Israelites back to "old time religion," the uncontaminated worship of Yahweh alone. Instead, Hosea would actually be a religious innovator, a spokesperson for a developing monotheistic theology.[12] His new theological ideas would influence the later deuteronomistic writers, for whom belief in the one God Yahweh was normative. Another possibility exists, however. It could be that censure of the "baalization" of the Israelite cult in the book of Hosea originated in the later deuteronomistic redaction of the book (see below).[13]

The Period of the Collector. In 721 BCE the prophet Hosea's predictions came true. The northern kingdom of Israel was destroyed by the Assyrians under Sargon II. Upper-class Israelites were exiled to other parts of the Assyrian Empire, while the poorer classes endured Assyrian occupation of the land. The lucky ones escaped to Judah in the south. Scholars think that Hosea's oracles survived the destruction because refugees brought them to Judah, where they were collected and preserved.[14]

10. Ibid., 3, and those cited in H. H. Rowley, "The Marriage of Hosea," in *Men of God* (London: Nelson, 1963) 76-77. Providing a feminist twist to the sacred prostitution argument, H. Balz-Cochois, "Gomer oder die Macht der Astarte: Versuch einer feministischen Interpretation von Hos 1-4," *EvT* 42 (1982) 37-65, thinks that such cultic sexual service was part of a larger cult of the goddess practiced by Israelite women.

11. Cf. Robert A. Oden, Jr., "Religious Identity and the Sacred Prostitution Accusation," in *The Bible Without Theology: The Theological Tradition and Alternatives to It,* New Voices in Biblical Studies (San Francisco: Harper & Row, 1987) 131-53, 187-93.

12. See the outline of the problem by Niels Peter Lemche, "The God of Hosea," in *Priests, Prophets and Scribes: Essays on the Formation and Heritage of Second Temple Judaism in Honor of Joseph Blenkinsopp,* Eugene Ulrich et al., eds., JSOTSup 149 (Sheffield: JSOT, 1992) 241-57. See also Morton Smith, *Palestinian Parties That Shaped the Old Testament,* 2nd ed. (London: SCM, 1987) chap. 2; B. Lang, *Monotheism and the Prophetic Minority* (Sheffield: Almond, 1983) chap. 1; and Smith, *The Early History of God,* chap. 6.

13. See Yee, *Composition and Tradition,* 308-9. Lemche, "The God of Hosea," 255-57, also entertains this possibility.

14. For example, see Ina Willi-Plein, *Vorformen der Schriftexegese innerhalb des Alten Testaments: Üntersuchungen zum literarischen Werden der auf Amos, Hosea und Micha zurückgehenden Bücher im hebräischen Zwölfprophetenbuch,* BZAW 123 (Berlin: DeGruyter, 1971) 244.

The collector of Hosea's oracles played a crucial role in the literary formation of the book. He might have been a disciple of Hosea, or perhaps a scribe to whom the prophet dictated his words. We do not know his identity. Assuming that Hosea uttered more oracles than those actually preserved in the book, the collector's first task was the *selection* of sayings to be recorded for posterity. The book of Hosea is not simply a collection of Hosea's oracles. Rather, the oracles appear in the collector's work as selected traditions, vital enough to be retained. Moreover, the collector was important for the *arrangement* of the various oracles in a particular literary order. Unfortunate for the modern scholar, this order was not chronological. One critical task involves identifying the principles that guided the collector's organization of the material, as well as theorizing dates for it.

The collector thus created the first written tradition regarding Hosea, which later editing expanded, modified, and reinterpreted. Moreover, the collector seems to have been responsible for Hosea 1, the story of Yahweh's command that Hosea marry a promiscuous woman and have children by her. This divine commissioning (whether an actual event or not) marks the beginning of Hosea's prophetic service. Hosea 1 describes Hosea's "call" to be God's spokesperson. The collector had two reasons for prefacing the work with this call narrative. First, he grounded his oracular collection in the life of a particular person: the prophet Hosea. Without this contextualization it would be difficult to attribute the collected oracles to this eighth-century prophet. The collector thus established a stronger connection between the oracles contained in his work and the personality of the prophet.

Second, it was usually thought that a call narrative was written by the prophet to vindicate himself and to legitimate his office before his opponents. According to more recent scholarship, however, call narratives originated with the prophet's tradents, rather than with the prophet himself.[15] By including Hosea 1, the collector authenticated the prophet's ministry and his own work as well. He legitimized Hosea by anchoring his oracles in a selected moment of his ministry: the marriage and parenting the deity commanded. By prefacing his collection with a story of divine commissioning, the collector legitimated himself and the corpus he created. Lacking the call from God that authorizes a prophetic ministry, he carried on the prophet's work (now vindicated by events) by compiling and editing the sayings into a literary tradition for later generations.

The Period of the Josianic Redactor. Commentators often note strong affinities between the prophet Hosea and the tradents responsible for the book of Deuteronomy and the deuteronomistic history (Joshua, Judges, 1 and 2 Samuel, and 1 and 2 Kings). The two share a similar theology. Both insist upon worship of the one God Yahweh (Deut 4:39; 6:4; 1 Kgs 8:60; Hos 2:16-23; 12:9; 13:4). Both describe God's election of Israel (Deut 4:37; 7:6-8; Hos 9:10; 11:1). Both proclaim God's covenantal love of Israel and the people's own loving response (Deut 6:4-5; 7:8; 11:1; Josh 23:11; Hos 2:18-19; 3:1; 10:12; 14:4) and obedience to Yahweh's *torah* (Deut 30:8-10; Josh 1:7-8; 8:30-35; Hos 8:1, 12).

15. B. O. Long, "Prophetic Authority as Social Reality," in *Canon and Authority,* G. W. Coats and B. O. Long, eds. (Philadelphia: Fortress, 1977) 13.

Both vehemently condemn the people's idolatry (Deut 7:2-6; 12:2-4, 29-32; 31:16-22; Josh 24:14-20; Judg 2:11-15; 2 Kgs 17:7-18; Hos 2:8; 4:11-15; 8:5-6, 11; 10:1-2; 11:1-2; 14:8) and summon the people to repentance and return to God (Deut 4:29-31; 30:1-10; Josh 24:23; 1 Kgs 8:22-53; Hos 3:5; 6:1-3; 14:1-2).

Perhaps these similarities can be explained by regarding the prophet Hosea as an innovative theological forerunner of the deuteronomistic groups, an opinion held by those regarding most of the oracles in the book as authentic.[16] Alternatively, one could account for such correspondences by presuming a redaction of the book of Hosea by these circles, who updated and expanded Hosea's oracles for their own generation.[17] In either case, Hosea's oracles bore a fundamental theological relevance for the editors responsible for Deuteronomy and the deuteronomistic history.

The theological relationship between Deuteronomy and the deuteronomistic history was recognized by Martin Noth, who argued that a sixth-century BCE exilic author composed this distinct literary complex.[18] A number of scholars modify Noth's work by positing two major editions of the deuteronomistic history.[19] The first edition (Dtr 1) was produced in the seventh century BCE by a Judean author supportive of the religious reform policies of King Josiah (640–609 BCE). One of the principal themes of Dtr 1 is the crimes of Jeroboam I, the first king of Israel (922–901 BCE), and his northern successors against the cult of Yahweh. Jeroboam I appointed Bethel and Dan as the official sanctuaries of the northern kingdom, rivaling the Temple at Jerusalem. Setting up two golden calves at these holy places, he announced to the people: "You have gone up to Jerusalem long enough. Behold your gods, O Israel, who brought you up out of the land of Egypt" (1 Kgs 12:28). Dtr 1 blames the fall of Israel upon its supposedly "unlawful" cult and climaxes its history in the reforms of Josiah (c. 622 BCE), who tried to rid Judah of its idolatrous cult objects and personnel (2 Kings 22–23; cf. 1 Kgs 13:1-4).

Parts of Hosea can be contextualized in the seventh-century BCE in relation to Dtr 1, particularly in their similar condemnation of Israel's polluted worship. Like Dtr 1, Hosea protests against pilgrimages to northern sanctuaries like Bethel and Gilgal (Hos 4:15; 5:6; 9:15; 10:15), rejecting the calves set up there (Hos 8:5-6; 10:5-6). He denounces idolatrous cult practices, priests who should guarantee liturgical correctness, and the laity (Hos 2:13; 4:17-19; 5:6-7; 6:6; 9:4). He condemns the feasts, new moons, and cultic assemblies that Jeroboam I had established in the north (Hos 2:11; 9:5-6; cf. 1 Kgs 12:32-33). He prophesies

16. M. Weinfeld, "Appendix B: Hosea and Deuteronomy," in *Deuteronomy and the Deuteronomic School* (Oxford: Clarendon, 1972) 366-70.

17. For example, Hans Walter Wolff, *Hosea: Commentary on the Book of the Prophet Hosea*, Hermeneia (Philadelphia: Fortress, 1974) xxxi-xxxii; and Yee, *Composition and Tradition*, 305-13.

18. Martin Noth, *The Deuteronomistic History*, JSOTSup 15 (Sheffield: JSOT, 1981). Originally published in German in 1943.

19. F. M. Cross, "The Themes of the Books of Kings and the Structure of the Deuteronomistic History," in *Canaanite Myth and Hebrew Epic* (Cambridge, Mass.: Harvard University Press, 1973) 274-89; Richard Elliott Friedman, *The Exile and Biblical Narrative: The Formation of the Deuteronomistic and Priestly Works* (Chico, Calif.: Scholars Press, 1981); Richard D. Nelson, *The Double Redaction of the Deuteronomistic History* (Sheffield: JSOT, 1981).

that God will put an end to worship of the baals, with their altars and pillars (Hos 2:11-13, 17; 10:1-2, 8; 13:1-3), a prophecy fulfilled in the later purge under Josiah (2 Kings 23).

The Period of the Exilic Redactor. The second edition of the deuteronomistic history (Dtr 2) was composed during the Babylonian exile (587–539 BCE). This edition brings the nation's history up to date by including the fall of the southern kingdom of Judah. Addressed to the Judeans in exile, it explains the traumatic time of uprooting theologically: The Babylonian exile was the result of a long history of idolatry and faithlessness that began in Israel and continued in Judah.

Sections of the book of Hosea can be situated during this period, either as earlier oracles relevant during the exile or as redactional commentary updating earlier sayings so that they speak to the needs of the exiled people. Hosea 3:4; 9:3, 6-7, 16-17; 11:5-7; and 13:7-16 may refer to the destruction and exile of the north, yet be pertinent for the fall of the south as well.

Noteworthy in Hosea is the theme of repentance/return. On one hand, the nation is called to seek Yahweh and return to God (3:5; 5:15–6:1; 12:6; cf. 2:7; 7:10; 10:12; 14:2). On the other hand, the spiritual repentance of the people and their return to God has its counterpart in the physical return from exile. The spiritual journey back to Yahweh is bound up with the geographical journey back to the land. Hosea 1:11 speaks of a regathering of Israel and Judah under one head. Hosea 3:5 explicitly names this leader as King David, an obviously exilic editorial comment. Hosea 11:11 announces the restoration of the people to their homes. In rich detail, 14:4-7 describes the healing and flourishing of the people back in the land (cf. 6:11b).

The later historical contexts of the collector, the Josianic redactor, and the exilic redactor represent important interpretive stages in the formation of the book of Hosea. The book is the result of an ongoing traditioning process, wherein each stage articulates a voice that recognizes in some way, whether by appropriation or by editing, the value of the Hosean tradition for its own time. Each stage makes its own distinctive imprint on the tradition, transmitting it to a brand-new audience.

ANCIENT ISRAELITE MARRIAGE, METAPHOR, AND THE THEOLOGICAL PROBLEM

In the biblical tradition, different metaphors are used to capture the unique covenantal relationship between God and Israel. Some biblical metaphors draw from the bonds between king and servant, lord and vassal, father and son, and even mother and child, to communicate different facets of the covenantal union. The book of Hosea was the first to employ the metaphor of husband for the deity, casting Israel in negative female imagery as God's adulterous wife.[20] This imaging reflects the historical situation of ancient Israel, where gender relationships were asymmetrical: The man occupied the more privileged

---

20. Parts of this section are similar to my comments in the article, "Hosea," in *The Women's Bible Commentary*, Carol A. Newsom and Sharon H. Ringe, eds. (Louisville: Westminster/John Knox, 1992) 195-202.

position in this society, and the woman was subject to him. Appropriating this socially conditioned relationship as metaphor has deeply affected the theology of the book of Hosea, for this theology interprets the divine as male and the sinful as female. Using this imagery, the prophet describes God's legitimate punishment as physical abuse of the wife by her husband. Interpretive problems arise when the metaphorical character of the biblical image is forgotten.

Theological issues affecting the interpretation of Hosea's marriage metaphors will be highlighted in both the Commentary and the Reflections on the text. As will be seen, the marriage metaphor for the God/Israel covenant becomes problematic for women who continue to be victims of sexual violence. Hosea's marriage metaphor arises from a particular ancient social context. Thus understanding Israel's institution of marriage and its laws regarding adultery is critical to its interpretation.

Two primary features of ancient Israelite society—its patrilineal, patrimonial, patrilocal kinship structure and its honor/shame value system—are especially pertinent to this discussion. Israel practiced a patrilineal kinship ideology, tracing descent through the male line. This ideology was supported by a number of social practices. Power and authority over a particular family household resided with the oldest living male. Ownership of goods and resources lay with this *paterfamilias,* who passed on his assets as patrimony to his eldest son, according to customs of primogeniture.

Marriage arrangements were patrilocal—i.e., the young woman had to leave the household of her birth and enter into the unfamiliar and often hostile abode of her husband's father, adapting herself to it as best she could. Love and romance were not major factors in joining a couple in wedlock. Fathers often used the marriages of daughters to forge or strengthen alliances with other households and larger clan groups.

A new wife occupied an ambiguous position when she entered her husband's household. She retained ties to her own family, who must support her if ever she left her husband's house (cf. Judg 19:2-3). She became a full member of her husband's household only when she bore a son. Furthermore, if the husband was polygamous, his new wife had to contend with other wives, who vied for the husband's attention and the ensuing status it could bring, particularly with the birth of sons. By its patrilineal descent, patrimonial inheritance, and patrilocal residence customs, then, ancient Israel privileged the male and disenfranchised the female in a hierarchy of gender.

In a labor-intensive agricultural society such as Israel's, the birth of children was crucial for survival. Sons were especially valued because they continued the patriline, were beneficiaries of the father, and did not leave the household. In fact, they brought additional human resources into the household in the persons of wives and the potential children they would bear. The wife's primary contribution to the household was to bear legitimate sons to carry on the family name in order to keep limited commodities such as land and other resources within the family.

The sexuality of wives, daughters, and sisters was carefully guarded and controlled, because it comprised the material basis for an ideology of honor and shame that legitimized the androcentric hierarchy of this society. Honor was one's reputation, the value of a person in his or her own eyes *and* in the eyes of his or her social group. Male honor was manifested in wealth, courage, aggression, the ability to provide for one's family and defend its honor, and the frank display of sexual virility. According to the male ideology of honor and shame, women could acquire or be ascribed honor, but their honor differed from that of men. If honor was exemplified through one's personal independence—based on wealth, status, kinship, care of the weak, etc.—then women occupied the lowest rank within this honor system. They were peripheral to the patriline and usually did not inherit any material resources.[21] As a result, they were socially and economically dependent upon men. Their honor was derived from the men with whom they were explicitly connected. Theirs was the honor of the weak, which exhibited itself in deference, modesty, and meekness toward men and in sexual propriety and concern for reputation.[22]

In the Hebrew Bible, shame or disgrace was the very opposite of honor, evoking negative feelings of inadequacy, inferiority, and worthlessness. Like the ideology of honor, notions of shame were divided along gender lines. A man was shamed by his lack of wealth, courage, aggression; by the inability to support his family and protect its honor; and by sexual passivity or impotence. A woman was shamed if she were strong willed, independent, assertive, disrespectful of men, or sexually immodest.

In a patrilineal kinship structure, a large measure of a man's honor depended on a woman's sexual behavior, whether his wife's, daughter's, sister's, or mother's. Men had various strategies for keeping their women (and, by extension, themselves) honorable, such as insisting that women remain veiled in public, segregating them, and restricting their social behavior. A woman's sexual shamelessness constituted a public statement that her husband, father, brother, or son had failed to preserve the family honor by his inability to control her. The male would consequently forfeit his honor in the community.

Adultery was a capital offense in a society that operated under patrilineal and honor/shame-based social systems. In the first place, it violated a man's absolute right to the sexuality of his wife and placed his paternity of her children very much in doubt. In a society governed by a patrilineal kinship structure, a man needed to know for sure that a particular son was his. Second, adultery resulted in a considerable loss of honor for the husband and his household. A "shameless" wife (one who defied his authority) revealed his failure to supervise her sexuality and preserve family honor.

Two types of punishment seem to have been applied to adulterous acts. The first was the stoning to death of both parties (Lev 20:10; Deut 22:22). In practice, however, this punishment was often incurred only by the woman (see Gen 38:24; John 7:53–8:11). According to the law, the couple had to be caught in the act by witnesses in order for

21. An exception would be Num 27:1-11, where the daughters of Zelophehad petition Moses to inherit their father's land.
22. See Lila Abu-Lughod, *Veiled Sentiments: Honor and Poetry in a Bedouin Society* (Berkeley: University of California Press, 1986) chaps. 2–4.

the death penalty to be applied (Deut 19:15). This, of course, was not always feasible. Moreover, the woman was more vulnerable than the man to the accusation, because she could later become pregnant from the union. The second type of punishment is recorded in Hosea, that of publicly stripping the adulteress naked and exposing her shamelessness (Hos 2:2-3; cf. Ezek 16:37-39).

An implicit double standard existed in the biblical evaluation of a man who broke wedlock. Extra-marital activity, which would have been inexcusable for the wife, was tolerated for the husband in many cases. From an honor/shame perspective, a lack of chastity in women placed in jeopardy their own family honor, accumulated in the patriline, whereas a lack of chastity in men threatened the honor of *other* families. A man was not punished for having sex unless an engaged or married woman was involved *and* he was caught in the act (Deut 22:22-29). Engaging the services of prostitutes was acceptable (see Gen 38:12-23; Josh 2:1-7; 1 Kgs 3:16-27). This double standard underscored the issues of honor and legal paternity that so characterized the ideological structure of Israelite society, making the woman the primary offender in adulterous acts.

As we will see, the husband/wife metaphor of the God/Israel covenant in the book of Hosea is embedded with specific, culturally conditioned notions of what it means to be male or female and how each should behave in a particular society. Present-day Euro-American societies are quite different in their understanding of marriage and gender relations. Biblical interpreters and readers must reckon with the adequacy of the husband/wife metaphor in describing the divine/human relationship today.

THE DYNAMICS OF RHETORIC AND METAPHOR

In order to assess the appropriateness of the marriage metaphor (and others) for God's covenant with Israel, one must pay close attention to the rhetoric in which this metaphor is couched. Rhetoric is the art of discourse, either spoken or written, to inform, to persuade, or to move an audience. Prophetic rhetoric is intended to call the nation to judgment, to denounce its social or religious abuses, to criticize its political dealings, to bring the people to repentance and return to God, and to inspire the renewal of their covenantal relationship with the divine. A significant aspect of Hosean rhetoric is his use of metaphor, through which he seizes the imagination of his (male) audience.

A metaphor is a comparison composed of two elements, the lesser known element, the *tenor,* and the better known element, the *vehicle.*[23] In Hosea 1–3, the prophet attempts to convey something profound about the lesser known, God's covenant with Israel, through the vehicle of a better known institution in ancient Israel, the human marriage between husband and wife. (Hosea also uses the metaphor of the parent/child in Hosea 11–13. See the Commentary and Reflections on these chapters.) The elements of the marriage metaphor break down as follows:

23. Cf. "Metaphor," in *A Handbook to Literature,* 5th ed., C. Hugh Holman and William Harmon, eds. (New York: Macmillan, 1986) 298-99.

TENOR: *lesser known*	VEHICLE: *better known*
God's covenantal love	a husband's marital love
Israel's sin of idolatry	a wife's sexual infidelity
God's punishment of Israel	a husband's beating of wife
Israel's repentance/return to God	a wife's repentance/return to her husband
God's renewal of covenantal love	a husband's renewal of marital love

The metaphor of human marriage provides unique access into the depths of God's covenantal relationship with Israel. Understood from a twentieth-century Euro-American perspective (the perspective of many modern biblical scholars), marriage embodies both symbolically and physically the intimacy between two individuals who consciously choose each other out of many possible life partners. It involves a "revelation" on both sides of one's deepest self: one's fears, hopes, desires. This "knowledge," which is often shielded from other people, is bestowed upon the beloved in a daring act of trust. The revelation of this self-knowledge makes one vulnerable to the other. And yet, one will risk this vulnerability and its potential for hurt for the sake of the lover and for the deeper knowledge of self and of the other that love brings. Commitment, intimacy, enduring love, "being there" for the other, physical desire, sexual union—all are bound up in the human institution of marriage. In many ways, this contemporary understanding of marriage is imposed upon the words of Hosea.[24]

However, this modern notion is not what Hosea intends in adopting the marriage metaphor for God's covenant with Israel. Marriage in ancient Israel was certainly not a partnership of equals. Precisely the inequity in such unions determines why Hosea appropriates marriage as a vehicle for the divine/human covenantal relationship. The rhetoric in Hosea is one-sided and directed to a very specific audience: ancient Israelite men. The book of Hosea takes up the marriage analogy to teach these men about the depths of God's covenantal love by appealing to their personal experiences as husbands, as the superior partner in a marriage. In a patriarchal society in which notions of descent, inheritance, marital residence, and honor are intricately bound up with legitimate sons, a faithless wife and her illegitimate children are exceedingly threatening and disruptive. Hosea highlights rhetorically the tremendous effort an ancient Israelite man must make to forgive and take back an unfaithful wife and to accept her children as his own, even if they may have been fathered by another man.[25] To stand by his wife and her children, enduring the social stigma it entails, would be one of the most difficult experiences

---

24. For one example, among many others, of reading the marriage metaphor in Hosea from this twentieth-century perspective, see Karl A. Plank, "The Scarred Countenance: Inconstancy in the Book of Hosea," *Judaism* 32 (1983) 343-54, esp. 345-46.

25. According to Francis I. Andersen and David Noel Freedman, *Hosea,* AB 24 (Garden City, N.Y.: Doubleday, 1980) 187, the text allows for the possibility that Lo-ruhamah might be illegitimate. A faithless wife arouses her husband's suspicions, whether valid or not, about the paternity of his children.

an Israelite man could undergo. And yet, God has precisely this kind of magnanimous love for faithless Israel. God's steadfast love for a people who certainly do not deserve it eventually compels their repentance and return.

The book of Hosea transforms the marriage of a husband to a promiscuous wife into a heuristic vehicle for the covenantal relationship between God and Israel. For modern readers, however, several interpretive problems become evident. In the first place, the metaphor conflates the deity and the human husband. God is cast as an all-forgiving male. The divine becomes a male, and inevitably the male becomes divine. Second, the sinful is embodied in the image of the licentious wife. As is typical in ancient Israelite culture, the female is considered the primary offender in adulterous affairs. In this covenantal metaphor, woman becomes the ultimate transgressor and the epitome of evil as an adulteress and a whore. Third, the metaphor comes perilously close to sanctioning a husband's domestic violence against his wife. The explicit punishment of the wife/Israel by God "for her own good" arises out of God's steadfast love in order "to make her see reason." As scholars point out, Hosea 1 and 3 do not provide any particulars of friction between Hosea and Gomer.[26] Instead, flanking the narrative of God's marriage in Hosea 2, the stories of their marriage are stereoscoped with the stormy relations between God and Israel. Hosea 3 implies what Hosea 2 describes in vivid detail: the physical abuse of Gomer in Hosea's attempts to "love" his adulterous wife into reason. Modeling the behavior of God toward Israel, Hosea isolates Gomer from her lovers (2:8-9; 3:3). He offers Gomer gifts, just as God offers gifts to Israel (2:19; 3:2). He ultimately makes a heroic effort to abstain from sex with Gomer during this period (3:3). What is not explicitly stated is that Hosea, like God, beats his wife into submission. If God's behavior is the model for Hosea, this battering is implied, but not articulated.

ENGLISH AND HEBREW VERSE NUMBERING

At different points in English translations of the book of Hosea, chapter and verse numbering diverges from the original Hebrew text. The Commentary and Reflections will follow the verse numbering found in most English translations. When checking the Hebrew text, however, one should note the following variations:

English trans.	1:10-11	=	Heb.	2:1-2
	2:1-23	=		2:3-25
	11:12	=		12:1
	12:1-14	=		12:2-15
	13:16	=		14:1
	14:1-9	=		14:2-10

26. In particular, see Renita J. Weems, "Gomer: Victim of Violence or Victim of Metaphor?" *Semeia* 47 (1989) 90-91.

BIBLIOGRAPHY

Andersen, Francis I., and David Noel Freedman. *Hosea.* AB 24. Garden City, N.Y.: Doubleday, 1980. A major critical commentary that attempts to resolve textual problems in the book by relating them to Hebrew rhetorical conventions.

Brenner, Athalya, ed. *A Feminist Companion to the Latter Prophets.* Sheffield: Sheffield Academic, 1995. The first half consists of feminist essays on the book of Hosea.

Davies, Graham I. *Hosea.* Old Testament Guides. Sheffield: JSOT, 1993. An introductory volume discussing the religious and historical period of Hosea, his major teachings, the institution of prophecy in Israelite society, Hosea's marriage, and assessment of recent scholarship on Hosea.

———. *Hosea.* NCB. Grand Rapids: Eerdmans, 1992. A commentary based on the RSV, useful in discussing numerous textual problems in the book.

Emmerson, Grace I. *Hosea: An Israelite Prophet in Judean Perspective.* JSOTSup 28. Sheffield: JSOT, 1984. A redaction-critical investigation examining the extent of Judean editing in the book.

King, Philip J. *Amos, Hosea, Micah: An Archaeological Commentary.* Philadelphia: Westminster, 1988. Not a commentary on the texts of these prophets, but a survey of archaeological artifacts and material remains that may help to illuminate selected texts. Helpful in visualizing the cult that Hosea criticizes.

McComiskey, Thomas Edward. "Hosea." In *The Minor Prophets: An Exegetical and Expository Commentary.* Vol. 1. Edited by Thomas Edward McComiskey. Grand Rapids: Baker, 1992. An evangelical commentary presuming Hosean authorship for every oracle in the book. The top half of each page is devoted to an exegetical analysis that governs the author's translation. The bottom half, or exposition, enlarges on the exegetical conclusions reached.

Mays, James L. *Hosea.* OTL. Philadelphia: Westminster, 1969. An excellent commentary, specifically written for "the minister and theological student as they work on the interpretation and understanding of Scripture" (p. vii).

Stuart, Douglas. *Hosea–Jonah.* WBC 31. Waco, Tex.: Word, 1987. This commentary presupposes that the book of Deuteronomy is Mosaic, a product of the second millennium and not of the eighth, seventh, or sixth centuries BCE. Deuteronomy, then, would have directly influenced the prophet Hosea, rather than vice versa.

Ward, James M. *Hosea: A Theological Commentary.* New York: Harper & Row, 1966. Interprets the book primarily as a theological document and "not a personal memoir or chronicle of Israel's history." A very lucid and readable commentary.

Wolff, Hans W. *Hosea.* Hermeneia. Philadelphia: Fortress, 1974. English translation of a 1965 German commentary. A detailed form-critical investigation, valuable in pointing out the problems in the Hebrew text.

Yee, Gale A. *Composition and Tradition in the Book of Hosea: A Redaction Critical Investigation.* SBLDS 102. Atlanta: Scholars Press, 1987. Examines the development of the book through four historical phases, each leaving its own theological imprint on the composition.

OUTLINE OF HOSEA

I. Hosea 1:1–3:5, The Wife/Israel and God

    A. 1:1-10, Hosea, Gomer, and Their Children
    B. 1:11–2:23, The Wife/Israel and Her Husband
    C. 3:1-5, Hosea and Gomer Again

II. Hosea 4:1–11:11, The Son/Israel and God

    A. 4:1–5:7, A Perverse Priesthood, a Wanton Cult, a Licentious People
        4:1-3, A Broken Covenant and a Creation Gone Awry
        4:4-6, A Perverse Priesthood
        4:7-11*a*, Like People, Like Priest
        4:11*b*-14, A Wanton Cult and a Licentious People
        4:15-19, Israel, the Stubborn Heifer
        5:1-7, The Chastising God
    B. 5:8–8:14, A Politics of Self-destruction
        5:8-14, Rending Ephraim and Judah
        5:15–6:3, The Covenantal God Who Heals
        6:4-11, A People Who Transgress the Covenant
        7:1-16, Corruption at Court and Among the Nations
        8:1-14, King, Calf, Cult, and the Covenant
    C. 9:1–11:11, A People's History of Infidelity
        9:1-6, A Festival of Fools
        9:7-9, The Prophet as Fool
        9:10-17, Like Grapes in the Wilderness
        10:1-8, Like a Luxurious Vine
        10:9-15, Like a Trained Heifer
        11:1-7, Like a Rebellious Son
        11:8-11, Journey's End

III. Hosea 11:12–14:9, The Wife and Son/Israel and God

    A. 11:12–13:16, God's Indictment of a Nation
        11:12–12:1, Ephraim Herds the Wind and Pursues the East Wind
        12:2-6, Jacob, the Eponymous Ancestor
        12:7-9, Ephraim's Ill-Gotten Wealth
        12:10-13, Jacob and the Prophet *Par Excellence*
        12:14–13:3, Ephraim's Idolatry
        13:4-11, Yahweh's Feeding and Destroying in the Wilderness
        13:12-14, Ephraim as an Unwise Son

HOSEA 1:1–3:5

THE WIFE/ISRAEL AND GOD

OVERVIEW

Hosea 1–3 are perhaps the most famous chapters in this prophetic book. The intensity of God's covenant with Israel is conveyed dramatically in a metaphor of the marriage between a faithful husband and a faithless wife. The figurative marriage between Yahweh and Israel (Hosea 1–3) provides the interpretive perspective for the rest of the book (chaps. 4–14). As the prism that refracts Hosea 4–14, chaps. 1–3 converge upon the covenantal love of Yahweh for Israel, God's spouse. The unique love of Yahweh forgives the infidelity of the wife when she approaches in repentance.

The narrative of Yahweh and his unfaithful wife (Hosea 2) is situated in a centrally prominent position. Placed before and after the story of God's marriage to Israel are accounts of Hosea's marriage to Gomer (Hosea 1; 3). The tradition of God and the wife Israel becomes a paradigm for the earlier, unresolved story of Hosea's marriage in chap. 1. Highlighted in chap. 2 is the forgiving love of God, who renews covenantal vows with the wayward but repentant wife. Following this characterization of God's marriage with Israel, chap. 3 resolves the conflict entailed in God's command to Hosea to marry a promiscuous woman (chap. 1). Hosea is commanded to *love* his promiscuous wife, just as Yahweh loves Israel. In the context of God's marriage in chap. 2, the human story of Hosea's marriage in chap. 1 is given a "happier ending" in chap. 3.

Hosea 1:2-10 and 3:1-5 provide the only clues to the personal life of the prophet. Nevertheless, it is difficult to separate historical facts about Hosea's marriage from the theological message expressed through it. Much of the literature on Hosea 1–3 is devoted to historical analyses of Hosea's domestic problems, and results have been inconclusive.[27] Do Hosea 1 and 3 form a consecutive narrative of Hosea's marriage? Or is chap. 3 the earlier narrative, since it is voiced in the first person (suggesting autobiography) and since the period of sexual isolation from the wife's lovers and Hosea himself (3:3) precludes the bearing of children described in chap. 1? Are chaps. 1 and 3 simply parallel accounts of the marriage from different sources? Was Gomer really a prostitute? If so, was she a temple prostitute or just an ordinary whore? Was she merely an unfaithful wife? Did Hosea know he was marrying a promiscuous woman, or did Gomer's penchant for illicit affairs emerge only after their marriage?

The different theories advanced to deal with these questions can be summarized briefly.[28] Some scholars interpret the marriage of Hosea and Gomer primarily as an allegory and, therefore, that it should not to be taken literally. Such an interpretation would preserve Gomer's virtue by taking away her existence as an actual woman. In contrast, others think that Hosea literally married an unchaste woman, perhaps even a harlot, and adopted the children conceived through her sexual encounters. Others interpret the command to marry a promiscuous woman proleptically: Gomer was chaste at the time of marriage, but became unfaithful afterward, either as an adulterous wife, an ordinary prostitute, or a cultic prostitute. Some try to vindicate Gomer's reputation by insisting that she should not be equated with the woman in Hosea 3, surmising that Hosea was bidden to take yet another wife who was unfaithful and whose infidelity is unfairly imposed upon Gomer.

27. For a review of the literature, see H. H. Rowley, "The Marriage of Hosea," in *Men of God* (London: Nelson, 1963) 66-67; originally published in *BJRL* 39 (1956–57); and Graham I. Davies, "Hosea's Marriage," in *Hosea,* Old Testament Guides (Sheffield: Sheffield Academic, 1993) 79-92.

28. For a discussion of scholarly debate on these various theories, see Rowley, "The Marriage of Hosea," 66-97; and Davies, "Hosea's Marriage," 78-92.

A variant of this thesis posits that the Gomer in Hosea 1 is of unimpeachable character and claims that she became identified with the prostitute whom Hosea hires (not marries) in chap. 3. Other interpreters argue that Hosea did not actually marry Gomer. The verb "take" (לקח *lāqaḥ*) in 1:2 could mean "marry a wife" or "take a woman (sexually)." Following the latter sense, Hosea merely had sex with two unchaste women: Gomer and the unnamed woman of Hosea 3. These two symbolic actions are not meant to parallel the marriage between God and Israel, described in Hosea 2.

More satisfying than reopening historical questions regarding Hosea's marriage is examining how this marriage functions rhetorically in the text. What prophetic message does Hosea wish to convey rhetorically through his marital woes?

As was mentioned in the Introduction, the story of Hosea's call to ministry and marriage is most likely the work of the collector, who created a structural parallel between the marriages of Hosea/Gomer and Yahweh/Israel. According to the NRSV of 1:2, Hosea is commanded by God to take for himself "a wife of whoredom"[29] and "children of whoredom." In 2:5 the mother is condemned for "playing the whore." These trans-

lations are misleading. The Hebrew noun for "whore," "prostitute," or "harlot" is זנה (*zōnâ*), a cognate of the verb זנה (*zānâ*), whose primary meaning is "to engage in sexual relations outside of marriage." *Zānâ* is a more inclusive term, covering a range of sexual transgressions, including *adultery,* involving a married woman; *fornication,* involving an unmarried daughter, sister, or widow committed under levirate law (see Deut 25:5-6); and *prostitution,* involving women soliciting sex as a means of financial support.

Gomer is a "wife of whoredom" (אשת זנונים *'ēšet zĕnûnîm*) but not because she is a prostitute; she is never labeled a *zōnâ,* the technical term for a prostitute. Rather, she is a "wife of whoredom" because she is habitually promiscuous. Her sexual acts are evaluated pejoratively as being *"like* a whore," although she is not a prostitute by profession. Instead of the NRSV's "wife of whoredom," a more accurate translation would be "wife of promiscuity" (or "promiscuous wife"), or the NIV's rendering, "adulterous wife." Similarly, "to play the whore" (זנה תזנה *zānōh tizneh*) is more correctly rendered "to be promiscuous." When Hosea is commanded to have "children of promiscuity" or "children of unfaithfulness" (NIV), this means that his offspring will inherit the proclivities of their mother as promiscuous or unfaithful children.[30]

---

29. The Hebrew for "wife" (אשה *'iššâ*) can also mean "woman." Thus God could have commanded Hosea to take a promiscuous woman for himself—i.e., to have illicit sex with a woman. However, the literary context seems to draw a structural analogy between Hosea/Gomer and God/Israel. The more appropriate equivalent to God's covenant with Israel is Hosea's marriage to Gomer.

30. For a fuller discussion, see Phyllis Bird, " 'To Play the Harlot': An Inquiry into an Old Testament Metaphor," in *Gender and Difference,* Peggy L. Day, ed. (Minneapolis: Fortress, 1989) 75-94.

HOSEA 1:1-10, HOSEA, GOMER, AND THEIR CHILDREN

NIV	NRSV
1 The word of the LORD that came to Hosea son of Beeri during the reigns of Uzziah, Jotham, Ahaz and Hezekiah, kings of Judah, and during the reign of Jeroboam son of Jehoash[a] king of Israel:	**1** The word of the LORD that came to Hosea son of Beeri, in the days of Kings Uzziah, Jotham, Ahaz, and Hezekiah of Judah, and in the days of King Jeroboam son of Joash of Israel.
²When the LORD began to speak through Hosea, the LORD said to him, "Go, take to yourself an adulterous wife and children of unfaithfulness, because the land is guilty of the vilest adultery in	2When the LORD first spoke through Hosea, the LORD said to Hosea, "Go, take for yourself a wife of whoredom and have children of whoredom, for the land commits great whoredom by forsaking the LORD." ³So he went and took Gomer daughter of Diblaim, and she conceived and bore him a son.

a1 Hebrew Joash, a variant of Jehoash

NIV

departing from the LORD." ³So he married Gomer daughter of Diblaim, and she conceived and bore him a son.

⁴Then the LORD said to Hosea, "Call him Jezreel, because I will soon punish the house of Jehu for the massacre at Jezreel, and I will put an end to the kingdom of Israel. ⁵In that day I will break Israel's bow in the Valley of Jezreel."

⁶Gomer conceived again and gave birth to a daughter. Then the LORD said to Hosea, "Call her Lo-Ruhamah,ᵃ for I will no longer show love to the house of Israel, that I should at all forgive them. ⁷Yet I will show love to the house of Judah; and I will save them—not by bow, sword or battle, or by horses and horsemen, but by the LORD their God."

⁸After she had weaned Lo-Ruhamah, Gomer had another son. ⁹Then the LORD said, "Call him Lo-Ammi,ᵇ for you are not my people, and I am not your God.

¹⁰"Yet the Israelites will be like the sand on the seashore, which cannot be measured or counted. In the place where it was said to them, 'You are not my people,' they will be called 'sons of the living God.'"

ᵃ6 Lo-Ruhamah means not loved.   ᵇ9 Lo-Ammi means not my people.

NRSV

4And the LORD said to him, "Name him Jezreel;ᵃ for in a little while I will punish the house of Jehu for the blood of Jezreel, and I will put an end to the kingdom of the house of Israel. ⁵On that day I will break the bow of Israel in the valley of Jezreel."

6She conceived again and bore a daughter. Then the LORD said to him, "Name her Lo-ruhamah,ᵇ for I will no longer have pity on the house of Israel or forgive them. ⁷But I will have pity on the house of Judah, and I will save them by the LORD their God; I will not save them by bow, or by sword, or by war, or by horses, or by horsemen."

8When she had weaned Lo-ruhamah, she conceived and bore a son. ⁹Then the LORD said, "Name him Lo-ammi,ᶜ for you are not my people and I am not your God."ᵈ

10ᵉYet the number of the people of Israel shall be like the sand of the sea, which can be neither measured nor numbered; and in the place where it was said to them, "You are not my people," it shall be said to them, "Children of the living God."

ᵃ That is God sows   ᵇ That is Not pitied   ᶜ That is Not my people   ᵈ Heb I am not yours   ᵉ Ch 2.1 in Heb

COMMENTARY

The superscription (v. 1) announces the revelation of Yahweh's sacred "word" to Hosea son of Beeri. Although Hosea was ostensibly a northern prophet, v. 1 gives priority to the southern kings of Judah, whose reigns extended far beyond that of the sole Israelite king cited, Jeroboam son of Joash (or Jeroboam II). The Israelite royals contemporary with the Judean kings listed here—Zechariah, Shallum, Menahem, Pekahiah, Pekah, and Hoshea—are omitted. The priority of Judean kings suggests a Judean editing. The phraseology and structure that this verse shares with other prophetic superscriptions indicate that it was part of a joint redaction of the prophetic books. This editing probably occurred during or after the Babylonian exile, when the later prophets can be dated. Moreover, the phraseology is similar to the

editing of 1 and 2 Kings, suggesting a deuteronomistic redaction. The superscription emphasizes that while the revelation was addressed to a particular prophet at a particular historical time, the book in its later, edited state articulates the revealed message of God. As God's word through Hosea spoke to its original audience and to its later Judean audiences, it continues to address us today.

What reason does God give for the shocking injunction for Hosea to marry a wanton woman and have children by her? "The land fornicates by forsaking the Lord" (1:2, author's trans.). The inhabitants of the land have other lovers besides Yahweh. The identity of these lovers is not yet specified.

Responding to God's directive, Hosea takes Gomer, the daughter of Diblaim, for a wife. Although some scholars have regarded Diblaim as Gomer's hometown, or have tried to associate the word with דבלה (dĕbēlâ, "figcakes"), it is most likely the name of Gomer's father. This fact does not reveal anything more about Gomer, however. During the course of their marriage, Gomer bears Hosea three children: a son, Jezreel; a daughter, Lo-ruhamah; and another son, Lo-ammi.

Each child symbolically represents the deteriorating state of the nation. A fruitful plain nestled in the northern hill country, Jezreel was the site of Jehu's brutal massacre of the politically and religiously corrupt house of Omri (1 Kings 21; 2 Kings 9–10). According to the threat implied in the birth of Hosea's son Jezreel, the house of Jehu will be punished for this slaughter (v. 4a).[31] (Indeed, within the time frame of Hosea's historical ministry, the last king of Jehu's dynasty, Zechariah, was assassinated after only six months of rule.) The threat escalates in v. 4b to include the eventual destruction of the entire kingdom of Israel.

The daughter, Lo-ruhamah (lit., "She is not pitied"), symbolically picks up on the latter threat embodied in Jezreel's name—namely, the desolation of the north. Associated with the noun רחם (reḥem, "womb"), "pitied" (רחמה ruḥāmâ) refers to the recipient of God's maternal compassion, which issues forth from the divine womb.[32] However, the daughter's birth signifies that God will no longer have such compassion on the kingdom of Israel.

After weaning Lo-ruhamah, Gomer gives birth to a son, Lo-ammi (lit., "Not my people"). Implied in the son's name is God's declaration to Israel, "You are not my people and I am not your God" (v. 9).[33] The distinctive covenant between God and Israel is articulated by the formula "You are (will be) my people and I am (will be) your God" (Exod 6:7; Lev 26:12-13; Jer 11:4; Ezek 11:20;

14:11; 37:26-27). Lo-ammi symbolizes the nullification of this covenant.

The births of Hosea's three children predict the ruin that will inevitably come upon the north. Nevertheless, in its present redacted state, Hosea 1 exhibits certain interpretive tensions. The threats implied in the birth of each child are mitigated by later editors of the tradition, who reinterpret the story for a new situation. Verse 5 moderates the finality of the nation's fate symbolized in the birth of Jezreel. The eschatological formula "on that day" directs attention to a future event. Instead of terminating the rule of the house of Israel (v. 4), God will "break the bow of Israel." The breaking of the bow signifies not only the destruction of military power but also the end of war and the inauguration of peace (cf. Ps 46:9). The latter interpretation of breaking the bow is certainly the sense of Hos 2:18, which 1:5 anticipates. Moreover, 1:5 reinterprets the symbolic "blood of Jezreel" of 1:4b as a location, the "valley of Jezreel." In this valley, once the site of a bloody massacre, God will abolish all war. The shift from symbol to location foreshadows the wordplay on "Jezreel" (lit., "God sows") in 2:22-23, where God will sow his wife like a seed into the land.

The threat against the house of Israel signified by the birth of Lo-ruhamah ("She is not pitied") is reversed for the house of Judah in v. 7. God will indeed have pity on the southern kingdom. Furthermore, the theme of the "breaking of the bow" is resumed from v. 5 and expanded. No longer will the people depend on military might. God alone will deliver them. Like v. 5, v. 7 anticipates 2:18 where, in the context of a newly ratified covenant, the destruction of weapons of war will begin a new era of peace.

Although the warnings symbolized in Jezreel and Lo-ruhamah are mitigated by vv. 5 and 7, the threat involved with Lo-ammi does not seem to be tempered, if one simply stops at v. 9. The problem of determining the literary conclusion to the birth story of Hosea's children is reflected in the differing chapter divisions of the Hebrew and English texts. The Hebrew text ends chap. 1 at v. 9, corresponding to the switch in tone from doom to hope that begins its next chapter (2:1 Eng. = 1:10). Also, the Hebrew text begins and ends chap. 2 by reinterpreting the names of Hosea's children (MT 2:2-3, 24-25; Eng. 1:11–

31. The negative opinions about Jehu and his dynasty expressed in Hos 1:4 contrast with the more positive assessment by the deuteronomist in 2 Kings 9–10, which credits Jehu with wiping out Baal from Israel by his massacre of Omri's house. Nevertheless, Jehu is censured for not turning away from the sin of Jeroboam in 2 Kgs 10:28-31.

32. Phyllis Trible, *God and the Rhetoric of Sexuality* (Philadelphia: Fortress, 1978) 31-59.

33. The NIV and the NRSV follow an emendation of the MT "Not I AM to you" (לא־אהיה לכם lō '-'ehyeh lā kem) to "not your God" (לא־אלהיכם lō '-'elō hêkem). In the MT the reference to God as I AM echoes Exod 3:14-15, where God reveals the divine name YHWH to Moses through a wordplay on היה (hā yâ, "to be, become"). See Commentary on Hosea 13 regarding the wordplay on 'Ehyeh.

2:1, 22-23). English translations customarily group 1:10–2:1 (MT 2:1-3) as a self-contained unit of hope that contrasts with the negative tone of 1:9 and 2:2 (MT 2:4).

I suggest that the judgment against Israel implied in the name of Hosea's third child, Lo-ammi, finds its mitigation and reversal in v. 10 (MT 2:1). Referring directly to v. 9, "In the place where it was said to them, 'You are not my people [and I am not your God],' " v. 10 proclaims, "it shall be said to them, 'Children of the living God.' " The covenant that was dissolved in v. 9 is renewed in v. 10.[34]

Different interpretive stages then can be detected in Hos 1:2-10. When Israel falls to the Assyrians in 721 BCE, the oracles of Hosea come true. They are preserved by the collector, who joins Hosea 1 (minus vv. 1, 5, 7, and 10) to his prophetic compilation, thus legitimating the ministry of Hosea as well as his own collection of Hosea's sayings. At the stage of the collector, chap. 1 is a story about Hosea's call by God to prophetic ministry. This ministry begins with a series of symbolic actions: marrying a promiscuous woman and siring three children by her. Although the identity of the people's "lovers" is not clear at this point, the marriage represents the land's inhabitants who fornicate by forsaking Yahweh. The three children represent the punishment and destruction that will come upon the northern kingdom because of its promiscuity.

Preserved and circulated in Judah after the fall of Israel, the call story is reinterpreted for a new situation. Verses 5, 7, and 10 presuppose a period in which Judah has experienced the traumas of war and now needs a message of hope. I suggest that these verses coincide with the context of the exilic redactor (587–539 BCE). The punishments embodied in the names of Hosea's children are reversed. God will not completely annihilate the people. Instead, God will eliminate any vestiges of war and bring about a new peace (1:5). God will pour out compassion upon the inhabitants of Judah, stressing again that their salvation does not lie in warfare (1:7). Finally, God will renew the covenant that was annulled by their infidelity. They will become children of the living God (1:10).

34. Hosea 1:10 achieves its reversal of Lo-ammi by means of very clever wordplay in the Hebrew. See Gale A. Yee, *Composition and Tradition in the Book of Hosea: A Redaction Critical Investigation,* SBLDS 102 (Atlanta: Scholars Press, 1987) 68-71.

REFLECTIONS

1. Hosea 1 provides an excellent example of how a prophetic oracle can be appropriated for a new age without negating its original message. We have seen how later redactors contribute to the prophet's words from their distinct experiences of the Word of God. God's Word speaks again to a new place, a new time, and a new audience. The threats symbolized by the children are moderated by expressions of hope, as a new audience that has undergone God's judgment now seeks a message of forgiveness and hope.

Noteworthy is the fact that academic studies usually conclude the call story of Hosea the prophet with the birth of his son Lo-ammi (1:9), ending the unit on a note of foreboding. The Revised Common Lectionary of Christian churches, however, includes v. 10 in its selection from Hosea 1.[35] In the churches' liturgical worship, v. 10 and its reversal of the threat personified in Lo-ammi were recognized implicitly as the end of the story of Hosea's call. Amid feelings of doom and foreboding, God's covenant will be renewed, and the people will again become children of the living God. The prophetic message and its prediction of judgment had to come to pass, however, in order for the people to be moved to action. To realize that God will have compassion upon them, they must recognize that God can also withhold that compassion if they transgress their covenant.

In the lectionary reading, Psalm 85 responds to the theme of hope and forgiveness. The community petitions God to turn away any anger, restoring well-being and the fertility of the

35. Year C, Proper 12; Proper 17 for the Roman Catholic Church and the Anglican Church of Canada.

land. God forgives the iniquity of those who turn to God in their hearts, pardoning all their sins.

2. The usual image of the prophets is that of spokespersons filled with the Spirit to proclaim God's word to the people. Operating under an urgent sense of compulsion, they announce Yahweh's will upon the nation and exhort the people to repent of their sinful ways. They broadcast this message in the Temple, in the marketplaces, in the streets and squares—wherever they can get a hearing. The Hebrew Bible is filled with their eloquent words, denouncing a people, predicting that foreign nations will vanquish them, calling the people to repentance, and describing in vivid detail the Lord's restoration.

Nevertheless, Hosea 1 puts forward another image of the prophet. Notice that Hosea does not speak in chap. 1. Instead of proclaiming God's word to the people through speech, Hosea performs a significant action. His shocking marriage to a promiscuous woman is a sign-act that embodies the iniquity of the people in a way no spoken word can. The Hebrew Bible records other instances where prophets dramatize through bodily actions God's word to Israel. Isaiah, for example, is commanded to walk naked and barefoot in the city of Jerusalem for three years as "a sign and a portent against Egypt and Ethiopia" (Isa 20:3 NRSV; see Isa 20:1-6). Jeremiah is ordered to wear a yoke around his neck to symbolize the Babylonian yoke of slavery that Yahweh will put upon Judah (Jeremiah 27).

Speaking or doing? Words or actions? Which is appropriate in a particular situation? Will God's words be accomplished more by my speaking or by my doing? The prophets offer us two models for action. Some situations require us to speak out—condemning evil deeds and conditions when they occur, exhorting a community to repent and turn to the Lord, or consoling the wounded with gentle words. When words are inappropriate or cannot be found, other occasions demand that we act in ways that will accomplish God's will—feeding the hungry, clothing the naked, or visiting the sick. Our task is to discern which model is the most fitting for the situation.

3. Hosea's profound insight into God's covenant with Israel arises from his own bitter experience of his wife's infidelity. As we will see in the Commentary on Hosea 2, Hosea's gender determines how he envisions the partners of this covenantal relationship. God is perceived metaphorically as the aggrieved husband, and Israel is the selfish, unfaithful wife. Hosea's male experience of female infidelity will affect how he understands the nature of God and the sinful nation.

However, if Hosea had been a woman,[36] commanded to marry a promiscuous man, what form would *her* prophecy have taken? In what would *her* tragedy consist? What kinds of personal grief, disappointments, or sorrows would *she* experience? Would Gomer be a male incapable of making a commitment to a woman, as Israel was in its covenant with God? Would Gomer, like the fornicating Israelites, be unable to sustain a relationship, unfaithful to his wife in his pursuit of other women on the sly? Such are the complaints of many women regarding the men of today. Would Gomer be a "deadbeat dad," siring offspring irresponsibly, neglecting child support payments? Would Hosea have to claim and raise his bastards as her own, as part of her sign-act of God's word? How would Hosea persuade her husband to come back to her? Hosea 2–3 do not provide much help. There, God and Hosea sequester their wives from their lovers. God withdraws the material things needed to sustain the life of his wife and, indeed, chastises her physically in order to get her to "repent." It is very unlikely that these strategies would work for or be desired by a female Hosea.

How would God's message be transformed if the prophet Hosea had been a woman? We

---

36. Female prophets evidently lived and worked in ancient Israel, despite the paucity of biblical references to them. See references to Deborah (Judges 4–5) and Huldah (2 Kgs 22:14-20). Cf. Anna the prophet in Luke 2:36-38.

would visualize the profound relationship between God and Israel from the perspective of a woman, who experiences spousal infidelity in distinctly different ways than does a man.

HOSEA 1:11–2:23, THE WIFE/ISRAEL AND HER HUSBAND

NIV

[11]The people of Judah and the people of Israel will be reunited, and they will appoint one leader and will come up out of the land, for great will be the day of Jezreel.

2 "Say of your brothers, 'My people,' and of your sisters, 'My loved one.'
[2]"Rebuke your mother, rebuke her,
    for she is not my wife,
    and I am not her husband.
Let her remove the adulterous look from her face
    and the unfaithfulness from between her breasts.
[3]Otherwise I will strip her naked
    and make her as bare as on the day she was born;
I will make her like a desert,
    turn her into a parched land,
    and slay her with thirst.
[4]I will not show my love to her children,
    because they are the children of adultery.
[5]Their mother has been unfaithful
    and has conceived them in disgrace.
She said, 'I will go after my lovers,
    who give me my food and my water,
    my wool and my linen, my oil and my drink.'
[6]Therefore I will block her path with thornbushes;
    I will wall her in so that she cannot find her way.
[7]She will chase after her lovers but not catch them;
    she will look for them but not find them.
Then she will say,
    'I will go back to my husband as at first,
    for then I was better off than now.'
[8]She has not acknowledged that I was the one
    who gave her the grain, the new wine and oil,
who lavished on her the silver and gold—

NRSV

[11]The people of Judah and the people of Israel shall be gathered together, and they shall appoint for themselves one head; and they shall take possession of[a] the land, for great shall be the day of Jezreel.

2 [b] Say to your brother,[c] Ammi,[d] and to your sister,[e] Ruhamah.[f]
[2] Plead with your mother, plead—
    for she is not my wife,
    and I am not her husband—
that she put away her whoring from her face,
    and her adultery from between her breasts,
[3] or I will strip her naked
    and expose her as in the day she was born,
and make her like a wilderness,
    and turn her into a parched land,
    and kill her with thirst.
[4] Upon her children also I will have no pity,
    because they are children of whoredom.
[5] For their mother has played the whore;
    she who conceived them has acted shamefully.
For she said, "I will go after my lovers;
    they give me my bread and my water,
    my wool and my flax, my oil and my drink."
[6] Therefore I will hedge up her[g] way with thorns;
    and I will build a wall against her,
    so that she cannot find her paths.
[7] She shall pursue her lovers,
    but not overtake them;
and she shall seek them,
    but shall not find them.
Then she shall say, "I will go
    and return to my first husband,
    for it was better with me then than now."
[8] She did not know

a Heb *rise up from*   b Ch 2.3 in Heb   c Gk: Heb *brothers*
d That is *My people*   e Gk Vg: Heb *sisters*   f That is *Pitied*
g Gk Syr: Heb *your*

NIV

which they used for Baal.

⁹"Therefore I will take away my grain when it
ripens,
and my new wine when it is ready.
I will take back my wool and my linen,
intended to cover her nakedness.
¹⁰So now I will expose her lewdness
before the eyes of her lovers;
no one will take her out of my hands.
¹¹I will stop all her celebrations:
her yearly festivals, her New Moons,
her Sabbath days—all her appointed feasts.
¹²I will ruin her vines and her fig trees,
which she said were her pay from her lovers;
I will make them a thicket,
and wild animals will devour them.
¹³I will punish her for the days
she burned incense to the Baals;
she decked herself with rings and jewelry,
and went after her lovers,
but me she forgot,"

declares the LORD.

¹⁴"Therefore I am now going to allure her;
I will lead her into the desert
and speak tenderly to her.
¹⁵There I will give her back her vineyards,
and will make the Valley of Achor*ᵃ* a door of
hope.
There she will sing*ᵇ* as in the days of her youth,
as in the day she came up out of Egypt.

¹⁶"In that day," declares the LORD,
"you will call me 'my husband';
you will no longer call me 'my master.*ᶜ*'
¹⁷I will remove the names of the Baals from her
lips;
no longer will their names be invoked.
¹⁸In that day I will make a covenant for them
with the beasts of the field and the birds of
the air
and the creatures that move along the ground.
Bow and sword and battle
I will abolish from the land,
so that all may lie down in safety.
¹⁹I will betroth you to me forever;
I will betroth you in*ᵈ* righteousness and justice,

ᵃ15 Achor means *trouble.*   *ᵇ15* Or *respond*   *ᶜ16* Hebrew *baal*
ᵈ19 Or *with*; also in verse 20

NRSV

that it was I who gave her
the grain, the wine, and the oil,
and who lavished upon her silver
and gold that they used for Baal.
⁹ Therefore I will take back
my grain in its time,
and my wine in its season;
and I will take away my wool and my flax,
which were to cover her nakedness.
¹⁰ Now I will uncover her shame
in the sight of her lovers,
and no one shall rescue her out of my hand.
¹¹ I will put an end to all her mirth,
her festivals, her new moons, her sabbaths,
and all her appointed festivals.
¹² I will lay waste her vines and her fig trees,
of which she said,
"These are my pay,
which my lovers have given me."
I will make them a forest,
and the wild animals shall devour them.
¹³ I will punish her for the festival days of the
Baals,
when she offered incense to them
and decked herself with her ring and jewelry,
and went after her lovers,
and forgot me, says the LORD.

¹⁴ Therefore, I will now allure her,
and bring her into the wilderness,
and speak tenderly to her.
¹⁵ From there I will give her her vineyards,
and make the Valley of Achor a door of
hope.
There she shall respond as in the days of her
youth,
as at the time when she came out of the
land of Egypt.

¹⁶On that day, says the LORD, you will call me,
"My husband," and no longer will you call me,
"My Baal."*ᵃ* ¹⁷For I will remove the names of the
Baals from her mouth, and they shall be mentioned by name no more. ¹⁸I will make for you*ᵇ*
a covenant on that day with the wild animals, the
birds of the air, and the creeping things of the
ground; and I will abolish*ᶜ* the bow, the sword,
and war from the land; and I will make you lie

ᵃ That is, *"My master"*   *ᵇ* Heb *them*   *ᶜ* Heb *break*

NIV

in^a love and compassion.
²⁰I will betroth you in faithfulness,
and you will acknowledge the LORD.

²¹"In that day I will respond,"
declares the LORD—
"I will respond to the skies,
and they will respond to the earth;
²²and the earth will respond to the grain,
the new wine and oil,
and they will respond to Jezreel.^b
²³I will plant her for myself in the land;
I will show my love to the one I called 'Not
my loved one.^c'
I will say to those called 'Not my people,^d' 'You
are my people';
and they will say, 'You are my God.'"

^a19 Or with   ^b22 Jezreel means God plants.   ^c23 Hebrew
Lo-Ruhamah   ^d23 Hebrew Lo-Ammi

NRSV

down in safety. ¹⁹And I will take you for my wife
forever; I will take you for my wife in righteousness and in justice, in steadfast love, and in mercy.
²⁰I will take you for my wife in faithfulness; and
you shall know the LORD.

²¹ On that day I will answer, says the LORD,
I will answer the heavens
and they shall answer the earth;
²² and the earth shall answer the grain, the wine,
and the oil,
and they shall answer Jezreel;^a
²³ and I will sow him^b for myself in the land.
And I will have pity on Lo-ruhamah,^c
and I will say to Lo-ammi,^d "You are my
people";
and he shall say, "You are my God."

^aThat is God sows   ^bCn: Heb her   ^cThat is Not pitied
^dThat is Not my people

COMMENTARY

Since Hosea 1:10[2:1] should be regarded as the reversal of the judgment of 1:9, 1:11[2:2] constitutes the proper beginning of the story of God and Israel. The narrative of their "marital" conflicts is placed between the two accounts of Hosea's own marriage. Its central position in the structure of chaps. 1–3 highlights its rhetorical and theological importance for the first division of the book and, indeed, for the remainder as well.

The special story of God's marriage with Israel is framed by a prologue (1:11–2:1) and an epilogue (2:23). These verses form an inclusio of hope around a story of betrayal and violence. They provide a sequence of meditations on the reversed names of Hosea's offspring. Hosea 1:11 predicts the reunification of the separate kingdoms of Judah and Israel under one head. Perhaps this leader is the new Moses, especially since the phrase "come up out of the land" usually refers to the exodus event. A new exodus would envision a return from exile back to the homeland.[37] As will be made explicit in 3:5, the head of the new united kingdom is probably someone of the Davidic dynasty. The reference to the southern monarch points to exilic hopes for the return and restoration of king and kingdom.

"Go up from the land" can also mean "grow up (like plants) out of the land." The prologue (1:11–2:1) leaves indefinite the meaning of the great "day of Jezreel" (יום יזרעאל yôm yizrĕʿeʾl), which qualifies the going up/growing up in the land. Through a wordplay on "Jezreel" in the later epilogue (2:23), however, the great "day of Jezreel" becomes the day when God sows the wife/Israel into the land. Hence, the people will not only go up from the land of exile, but they will also grow up like plants when they are seeded in the land of their homecoming.

2:1. The names of Jezreel's brother and sister, Lo-ammi and Lo-ruhamah, also are reversed. Ammi and Ruhamah in 2:1 form a chiasmus with Ruhamah and Ammi in 2:23, thus delimiting the unit. In 2:23, God announces divine compassion over Lo-ruhamah. Liberated by God as "My people," Ammi can respond in turn by proclaiming, "[You are] my God!" The epilogue thus concludes with the reestablished covenant between Yahweh and the people.

---

37. Cf. the theme of a reunified nation under a king in the exilic text Ezek 37:15-23. Note as well the covenantal formula, "They shall be my people, and I will be their God" (Ezek 37:23 NRSV), which has analogues in Hos 2:1, 23.

2:2-3. The tone of the text changes abruptly from hope in 2:1 to rebuke in 2:2. Hosea 2:2-15[2:4-17] is an indictment (ריב *rîb*) speech by God, set in a legal court and seemingly addressed to Hosea's children. Without the literary context of Hosea 1, added by the collector, the identity of the addressees and their "mother" would be uncertain. Scholars have conjectured that the mother is the goddess Asherah, the city of Samaria, or the matriarch Rachel.[38]

The present context, however, interconnects the prophet's story in Hosea 1 with the metaphorical tale of God and Israel in Hosea 2 so that the two stories essentially become one, creating the powerful marriage metaphor, which articulates the special covenant relationship between God and Israel. In an explicit parallel of 1:9, where the birth of Lo-ammi symbolizes the disintegration of the covenant, God proclaims in 2:2, "She is not my wife,/ and I am not her husband." Playing out the metaphor of marriage, the broken covenant of 1:9 is represented figuratively as a divorce in 2:2. The apparent reason for the divorce? The wife's infidelity.

As stated in the Introduction, the wife was usually regarded as the primary offender in an adulterous affair in ancient Israel, while the "victim" was her dishonored husband. Hence, the religiously pluralistic nation condemned by the prophet metaphorically becomes the faithless wife, Gomer, and Yahweh becomes the disgraced husband, Hosea. On the religious level, the wife's lovers refer to the baals, the once-legitimate Israelite deities thought to bring fertility (2:8, 13, 16-17; see Introduction). On the human level, the "lovers" imply great dishonor for the husband, who apparently could neither provide for the material and sexual needs of his wife nor control her behavior. Both the religious level and the human level converge in Hosea 2. Bracketed by the human story of Hosea's marriage (chaps. 1 and 3), Hosea 2 pushes the marriage metaphor to dangerous limits, wherein Yahweh's legitimate punishment of Israel for breach of covenant is figuratively described as threats of physical violence against the wife.

The first cycle of threats begins in 2:2-3. Yahweh/Hosea enjoins his children to plead with their mother that she "remove the adulterous look from her face/ and the unfaithfulness from between her breasts" (NIV). The NRSV translation, "put away her whoring from her face," is misleading. It suggests that the wife is either an actual harlot, ostensibly wearing some sort of signs on her face to broadcast her profession, or a cultic prostitute, adorned with ritual insignia. Rather, the wife simply puts on cosmetics and jewelry to make herself attractive (cf. v. 13; see also Isa 3:18-23; Jer 4:30; Ezek 23:40). Because her artistic efforts are targeted at her lovers and not at her husband, he berates them as "whorish."

The husband warns his wife that if she refuses to foreswear her adultery, he will (1) strip her naked, (2) make her bare as on the day she was born, (3) make her like a desert, (4) turn her into a parched land, and (5) slay her with thirst (2:3). Although the usual punishment for adultery is death by stoning (Lev 20:10; Deut 22:22; cf. John 7:53–8:11), the parallelism in v. 3, "strip her naked/make her bare," refers to another method of marital chastisement: The husband publicly strips his adulterous wife and shames her (see Ezek 16:37-39). The details, "make her like a desert/turn her into a parched land," underscore the identification made in 1:2 between the unfaithful wife and the land itself. They also emphasize that the provider of life-giving waters for the wife and the land is God the husband. God is able to withhold the rains and ultimately destroy both the wife and the land with thirst.

2:4-5a. The spiraling staircase of threats includes the couple's children, who become deeply infected by their mother's behavior and subsequent condemnation. They are rejected by their father, who, in view of his wife's sexual transgressions, suspects their paternity. Recall from the Introduction that doubts about paternity would terrify a society privileging male descent and inheritance.

2:5b. Although 2:2-23 is essentially the speech of the husband, the wife's words appear at crucial points: 2:5*b*, 7*b*, 12*a*, 16. Nevertheless, one does not really obtain the wife's point of view from this courtroom drama. The words put into her mouth are those that her husband wishes her to say. In this verse, she admits the offense as her

---

38. See William D. Whitt, "The Divorce of Yahweh and Asherah in Hos 2,4-7.12ff," *JSOT* 6 (1992) 31-67; John J. Schmitt, "The Wife of God in Hosea 2," *BR* 34 (1989) 5-18; and Gale A. Yee, *Composition and Tradition in the Book of Hosea: A Redaction Critical Investigation,* SBLDS 102 (Atlanta: Scholars Press, 1987) 124-25.

husband conceives it. Her collapsing marriage results from her pursuit of lovers, whom she thought provided for her welfare. It is all *her* fault. She verbalizes in 2:7*b* her husband's desire that she return to him voluntarily, after recognizing that "it was better with me then than now." To justify the punishment her husband exacts upon her, the wife confesses in 2:12*a* that she has acted just like a low-life whore in her adultery by accepting gifts from her lovers.[39] Finally, after she has been brutally chastised, she spontaneously acknowledges her spouse again as "my husband" and no longer as "my Baal" (2:16). No actual screams of pain or angry protestations against her husband's physical punishment emerge from the wife's lips. Although seemingly given one, the wife has no real voice. In effect, she becomes like a ventriloquist's dummy for her husband, speaking what he wants her to say.

2:6-8. Yahweh/Hosea engages in a three-part strategy to curb his wife's actions. This strategy reflects the social methods used in a patrilineal, honor/shame culture to control women's sexuality (see Introduction). First, the husband segregates his wife from her lovers (vv. 6-7*a*). This enforced seclusion has as its goal the wife's recognition of her absolute dependence on her husband (vv. 7*b*-8).[40] God's isolation of Israel apparently serves as a model for Hosea's sequestering of Gomer in 3:3-4. However, God's actions draw upon the behaviors of Israelite husbands toward their wives, not vice versa.

2:9-13. The second part of the husband's strategy entails a series of physical and psychological punishments for the wife. He will withhold food and clothing from her, reinforcing her vulnerability and reliance upon him (v. 9). He will humiliate her by exposing her genitalia before her lovers, whose sexual and moral impotence is revealed by their inability to rescue her (v. 10).[41] He will put an end to her laughter and festivals (v. 11). He will destroy her vineyards and orchards, making wild animals devour them (v. 12). From his point of view, her public physical degradation and punishment compensate for his own public loss of honor when she "decked herself with her ring and jewelry,/ and went after her lovers,/ and forgot me" (v. 13).

2:14-23. The third part of the husband's strategy to control his wife is the most insidious one, as the reader becomes caught up in the joyous reconciliation of God and Israel. After the wife has been suitably punished, after she has endured various forms of abuse, the husband will seduce her, bring her into the wilderness, speak tenderly to her, and woo her with tokens of love (vv. 14-15). At the theological level, the wife travels on a journey in Hosea 2 that has a twofold destination. On one hand, the wife's physical pursuit of her lovers is thwarted by her husband, in the hope that she will return to him. On the other hand, she embarks on a spiritual journey that moves from alienation from her husband to repentance, and ultimately to a soulful reunion with him. After chastising her, the husband leads her on a trip to the wilderness, where they will be remarried. Finally, she ends her journey back in the land where she will be sown like a seed and take root.

Crucial for the wife's physical and spiritual journey is the stop in the "wilderness," the place where God and Israel first pledged themselves in a covenantal relationship and where, in some traditions (e.g., Jer 2:2; Ezek 16:8-14), they enjoyed their one and only period of marital bliss. The now-repentant wife will reconcile with her spouse in the wilderness, surrendering to him again "as in the days of her youth,/ as at the time when she came out of the land of Egypt" (v. 15). Israel will recognize Yahweh, not as Baal, but as her true husband (v. 16). God, in turn, will forgive Israel's transgressions and betroth her to him again forever (vv. 19-20). The gifts Yahweh gives

---

39. MT = אתנה (*'etnâ*), which is a hapax legomenon. The technical term for a prostitute's wage is אתנן (*'etnan*), which Hosea uses in 9:1 to describe Israel. That Hosea avoids the technical words for "prostitute" and her hire strengthens the argument that Gomer was not an actual prostitute.

40. In an intertextual study of Hosea 2 and the Song of Songs, Fokkelien van Dijk-Hemmes points out that in the Song of Songs, which appears to be focalized in the female, the woman gives food and clothing required for subsistence to the man, while in Hosea 2, which is focalized in the male, the husband provides for the wife, thus reinforcing her dependence on male support. See "Imagination of Power and the Power of Imagination: An Intertextual Analysis of Two Biblical Love Songs: The Song of Songs and Hosea 2," *JSOT* 44 (1989) 81-82.

41. The objectification of female sexuality and descriptions of the wife's insatiability (e.g., 2:5, 7, 13) to make a theological point has been termed prophetic pornography. See T. Drorah Setel, "Prophets and Pornography: Female Sexual Imagery in Hosea," in *Feminist Interpretation of the Bible*, Letty M. Russell, ed. (Philadelphia: Westminster, 1985) 86-95, and "Divine Love and Prophetic Pornography," in Fokkelien van Dijk-Hemmes and Athalya Brenner, *On Gendering Texts: Female and Male Voices in the Hebrew Bible* (Leiden: E. J. Brill, 1993) 167-93.

to her are nothing less than the blessings that will flow from their covenant with each other: righteousness, justice, steadfast love, mercy, faithfulness, and the knowledge of God.

In love again, the couple will renew their covenant/marriage vows, inaugurating a period of cosmic peace, harmony, and bounteous fertility (vv. 18-22; cf. the additions 1:5, 7, 10). The wild animals that threatened to devour the wife's vines and fig trees (v. 14) will become actual partners in this new covenant (v. 18). Moreover, the critical question of paternity is resolved in v. 23. To signify a new covenantal order, Yahweh/Hosea acknowledges the children as his own and renames them. Jezreel now symbolizes the sowing of his mother back into the land. God will have pity on his daughter, She Is Not Pitied, and will declare to Not My People, "You are my people." And he will joyously respond, "My God."

Hosea's nuptial metaphor for the covenant between Yahweh and Israel provides an entrée into the divine/human relationship as no other metaphor can. It engages the reader in a compelling story about a God who is loving, forgiving, and compassionate, in spite of Israel's sinfulness. If Hosea was indeed a religious innovator proclaiming the sole worship of Yahweh against the licit worship of other gods in Israel (see Introduction), then using the metaphor of marriage to convey this monotheistic message was rhetorically daring, revolutionary, and persuasive. Its effectiveness resides in the fact that it profoundly touches upon concerns for fertility, which lie at the heart of the cults of El, Baal, and Asherah. Although accounts of its orgiastic rituals and voracious temple prostitutes are probably fictional, arising more from the libidos of (male) interpreters than from history, the cult's preoccupation with fertility was very real nonetheless. The fruitfulness of the land is critical for an agricultural society in an arid climate. Moreover, human fecundity is essential for the survival of a labor-intensive community with high infant and adult mortality rates.

The marriage metaphor was also serviceable for Hosea's monotheistic teaching because, in addition to fertility, it exploits social concerns for female sexual exclusivity and for paternity. Although men could have more than one wife, women could have only one husband, who was the sole sexual partner. The metaphor grew out of a patrilineal social structure and value system that demanded and enforced the sexual fidelity of a wife to ensure legitimate offspring for her husband.[42]

---

42. One can also argue that monotheism, as a theological construct expressed through the marriage metaphor, contributes to and legitimates an ideology of male superiority. For an anthropological perspective, see Carol Delaney, "Seeds of Honor, Fields of Shame," in *Honor and Shame and the Unity of the Mediterranean,* David D. Gilmore, ed. (Washington, D.C.: American Anthropological Association, 1987) 35-48.

REFLECTIONS

1. Cases like the one described below fill the files of social workers, hospitals, and law enforcement agencies all across the United States:

> Dana used to hide the bruises on her neck with her long red hair. On June 18, her husband made sure she could not afford even that strand of camouflage. Ted ambushed Dana (not their real names) as she walked from her car to a crafts store in Denver. Slashing with a knife, Ted, a pharmaceutical scientist, lopped off Dana's ponytail, then grabbed her throat, adding a fresh layer of bruises to her neck.
>
> Dana got off easy that time. Last year she lost most of her hearing after Ted slammed her against the living-room wall of their home and kicked her repeatedly in the head, then stuffed her unconscious body into the fireplace. Later, he was tearfully despondent, and Dana, a former social worker, believed his apologies, believed he needed her, believed him when he whispered, "I love you more than anything in the world." She kept on believing, even when more assaults followed.[43]

According to a 1992 study by the American Medical Association, as many as one in three

---

43. Jill Smolowe, "When Violence Hits Home," *Time,* July 4, 1994, 19.

women will be assaulted by a domestic partner in her lifetime—four million in any given year. In societies where networks of systemic gender domination exist, wife battering is a frightening expression of a husband's pathological need to maintain power and dominance in the relationship.

Nevertheless, one does not immediately make a connection between marital violence and the story about the God/Israel relationship in Hosea 2. It seems inconceivable to associate the passion that characterizes God's love for Israel with what are euphemistically labeled crimes of passion. The images contained in this story, however, are not gender neutral. If one brackets the fact that Hosea 2 is about the God/Israel relationship, reading it as a story about a male/female relationship, the descriptions of male brutality come suspiciously close to real cases of domestic violence. We cannot simply reverse the images and see God as the faithful wife and Israel as the adulterous husband, since we would have an entirely different scenario. The representation of the battered wife in Hosea was and still is linked to very real situations of women who are continually assaulted by men. Hosea's metaphor makes its monotheistic point at the expense of real women and children who were and still are victims of sexual violence. This abuse of power is not simply a social problem; in Hosea it becomes a theological problem.[44] When the metaphorical character of the biblical image is forgotten, a husband's physical abuse of his wife becomes as justified as is God's retribution against Israel.

Following vivid descriptions of divine punishment (2:9-13), the religious sentiments in 2:14-23 describing God's forgiveness, reconciliation, and covenantal renewal are beautiful and profound. However, the human level on which they are based is very problematic. God's (mis)treatment of Israel eventually ceases when Israel repents; a human husband's abuse of his wife usually does not. Studies have shown that many women remain in abusive relationships because periods of mistreatment are often followed by intervals of kindness and generosity. The husband repents of his battering, begs for his wife's forgiveness, and promises never to lay a hand on her again. This ambivalent strategy intensifies the wife's dependence on the husband. During periods of kindness, her fears are temporarily eased so that she decides to remain in the relationship; then the cycle of abuse begins again. Moreover, the one-sided images of the father's restored relationship with his children in 2:23 belie the trauma real children experience when witnessing their father physically abuse their mother.

Many readers resist making the connection between Hosea 2 and domestic violence, because they find it exceedingly difficult to equate God's just punishment with the violent acts of men. They prefer to restrict themselves to the lofty spiritual themes of God's abiding covenant with Israel, mercy, and forgiveness toward a sinful nation. They forget that these spiritual themes are couched in human terms that describe already dreadful conditions. One could say that these noble theological themes become signified paradoxically by depictions of truly sinful realities. The male violence embedded in the text of Hosea should make readers, both male and female, wary of an uncritical acceptance of its nuptial metaphor.

2. Hosea's marriage metaphor for the God/Israel relationship is often used to prohibit the ordination of women. For example, the 1976 Vatican Declaration on the Question of the Admission of Women to the Ministerial Priesthood points out that God's covenant takes on "the privileged form of a nuptial mystery." Citing the prophets Hosea and Jeremiah (Jeremiah 2) and New Testament texts (Eph 5:22-33; Rev 19:7, 9), this Roman Catholic document states that the nuptial mystery finds its fulfillment in the person of Jesus: "Christ is the Bridegroom; the Church is his Bride, whom he loves because he has gained her by his blood and made her glorious, holy and without blemish, and henceforth he is inseparable from her."[45]

---

44. See James Newton Poling, *The Abuse of Power: A Theological Problem* (Nashville: Abingdon, 1991), who explores different forms of sexual violence as specifically theological problems.

45. *Inter Insigniores* para. 29.

In view of this unfathomable nuptial mystery, the document claims that

> *we can never ignore the fact that Christ is a man.* And therefore, unless one is to disregard the importance of this symbolism for the economy of Revelation, it must be admitted that, in actions which demand the character of ordination and in which Christ himself, the author of the Covenant, the Bridegroom and Head of the Church, is represented, exercising his ministry of salvation—which is in the highest degree the case of the eucharist—*his role* (this is the original sense of the word *persona) must be taken by a man.*[46]

Based on a socially constructed metaphor that conceptualizes God as male and as husband to the wife Israel, the document draws a structural homology with the God/man Jesus, who is bridegroom of the church, his bride. It then asserts the restriction of priestly ordination to men. The argument moves in a "logical" sequence

$$\text{God} \rightarrow \text{God/Man} \rightarrow \text{Man}$$

to exclude women from the ordained priesthood, because they cannot physically represent the person of Jesus as a man in the sacraments. Nevertheless, such arguments reveal how pervasive and tenacious sexism is in our religious institutions. The metaphorical character is forgotten, and the "vehicle" of the metaphor is taken literally. Instead of being the means to convey an understanding of God, the vehicle becomes an end in itself. God is not simply like a male, like a husband, like a father, like a warrior, like a bridegroom. There is literally a male essential in the divine.

3. It may seem that nothing positive can be recouped by allowing the marriage metaphor of the God/Israel relationship to stand. Given the twentieth-century awareness of discrimination and violence against women, one is tempted to reject it completely. Those who take seriously God's revelation in the written Word might prefer to remain on the "spiritual" plane of the text. Others may even deny that violent imagery exists in the text, branding such a reading as "eisegesis." How, then, does one preach on or teach Hosea 2, preserving its integrity as God's Word, yet still reckon seriously with the negative aspects of its nuptial metaphor?

I suggest that a more fruitful approach to Hosea than rejection, blind acceptance, or denial would be to use the text as a "teachable moment."[47] Educators refer to teachable moments as those occasions when instructors respond to a controversy or division that erupts in a classroom of students as opportunities or invitations to learn. The controversy becomes a springboard to explore new issues.

At the most basic level, one can use Hosea 2 as a teachable moment to investigate the institution of marriage in ancient Israel. Not only would such an investigation contextualize the story historically, but also it would lead to a deeper reflection on the nature of marriage in our own time. Students in the classroom or congregations in the synagogue or church would consider the specific ways a contemporary understanding of marriage differs from its ancient Israelite counterpart. Such discussions would inevitably lead to a more profound and honest consideration of present-day gender relationships. Moreover, they would raise consciousness regarding the reality of domestic violence and its various symptoms. Many batterers appear to be functioning normally in the real world. In private, however, it is a different matter. If it is difficult to detect a batterer in real life, it is even more difficult to place God in this position in Hosea 2.

4. One can also use Hosea 2 as a teachable moment to explore the nature of religious language. Such language, even at its most abstract, inevitably expresses its understanding of the deity through models drawn from human experience and relationships. This language is

---

46. Ibid., para. 30; italics added.

47. See also Katheryn Pfisterer Darr, "Ezekiel's Justifications of God: Teaching Troubling Texts," *JSOT* 55 (1992) 110-15, who turns narratives into problems for the student.

highly metaphorical. Students and congregations can learn to distinguish between what is literal and what is figurative and realize that all language about God is the latter. Hosea 2 might be used to illustrate what can happen when religious language is utilized or studied uncritically. Sexism is deeply ingrained in our language. That conceptions of God in our religious language are primarily male, then, is no accident.

5. Simply reversing the gender roles as they are presently depicted in Hosea 2, making God the brutal wife, would be problematic and counterproductive, since the social reality is that most abusers are men. One can reenvision the marriage metaphor of the covenant, however, by creating an entirely new story, casting God as the faithful wife and Israel as the faithless husband. It would be exciting to discover what new shapes this metaphor might take. One fruitful area of reflection would be notions of God's retribution: Does brutal punishment always result in repentance and healing? Does not violence often lead to more violence? Does God send us suffering to chastise us and compel us to repent? What about those who suffer unjustly, those who have not sinned? What other methods might bring about the repentance of a sinful person?

6. Hosea 2 can be used as a springboard to reflect theologically on other metaphors of the divine/human relationship beyond the husband/wife model. In Hosea 11, the prophet will appropriate one drawn from the parent/child relationship. According to the law (Deut 21:18-21), ancient Israelite parents had the right to have their recalcitrant son put to death. Compassion for and bonding with the child, however, prevent Yahweh from doing so (Hos 11:8-9). God transcends human legal institutions that insist on the death penalty for rebellious sons, proclaiming, "for I am God and no mortal,/ the Holy One in your midst,/ and I will not come in wrath" (Hos 11:9*b* NRSV). Moreover, one could also meditate upon the nature of friendship, the betrayal that occurs when that friendship is ruptured, and what needs to be done to mend that rupture. We do not physically punish our friends in order to change their behavior. What can we learn from ordinary friendship that can help us understand the divine/human bond in categories other than punishment and reward?

What are the criteria for determining the appropriateness of a particular metaphor for the God/people relationship? A number of questions can be asked of the metaphor: To whose experience does it speak, and whose experience does it exclude? Whose experiences does the metaphor describe positively, and whose experience does it describe negatively? Is the metaphor fair and just in its representations? How is God represented? Does this portrayal of God resemble any social realities or structures or relations? What is legitimated by this particular portrayal of God?

The challenge in reading Hosea 2 is to open oneself to developing new metaphors of the divine, discovering creative ways to articulate the merciful love of God.

HOSEA 3:1-5, HOSEA AND GOMER AGAIN

NIV

3 The LORD said to me, "Go, show your love to your wife again, though she is loved by another and is an adulteress. Love her as the LORD loves the Israelites, though they turn to other gods and love the sacred raisin cakes."

²So I bought her for fifteen shekels[a] of silver and about a homer and a lethek[b] of barley. ³Then

[a]2 That is, about 6 ounces (about 170 grams) [b]2 That is, probably about 10 bushels (about 330 liters)

NRSV

3 The LORD said to me again, "Go, love a woman who has a lover and is an adulteress, just as the LORD loves the people of Israel, though they turn to other gods and love raisin cakes." ²So I bought her for fifteen shekels of silver and a homer of barley and a measure of wine.[a] ³And I said to her, "You must remain as mine for many days; you shall not play the whore,

[a] Gk: Heb *a homer of barley and a lethech of barley*

NIV

I told her, "You are to live with[a] me many days; you must not be a prostitute or be intimate with any man, and I will live with[a] you."

[4]For the Israelites will live many days without king or prince, without sacrifice or sacred stones, without ephod or idol. [5]Afterward the Israelites will return and seek the LORD their God and David their king. They will come trembling to the LORD and to his blessings in the last days.

a3 Or *wait for*

NRSV

you shall not have intercourse with a man, nor I with you." [4]For the Israelites shall remain many days without king or prince, without sacrifice or pillar, without ephod or teraphim. [5]Afterward the Israelites shall return and seek the LORD their God, and David their king; they shall come in awe to the LORD and to his goodness in the latter days.

COMMENTARY

Hosea 3 is structurally important because it concludes the first section of this prophetic book. Although crucial, it is also the most difficult chapter to interpret. Along with chap. 1, chap. 3 deals with Hosea's marriage. In contrast to the third-person "he" style of chap. 1, chap. 3 employs the first-person "I" style. This change in person has led to opinions that Hosea 3 is autobiographical and, therefore, more authentic and earlier than Hosea 1.[48] These speculations are rather weak, however, since use of the first person does not automatically mean that the chapter was written as an autobiography. Instead, such usage can be the literary device of another author.[49] Moreover, certain phrases and terminology in Hosea suggest that chap. 3 was written later than chap. 1.

Much of the scholarly literature on Hosea 3 deals with historical speculations arising from different opinions about what God commands Hosea to do and what his actions mean (see Commentary on Hosea 1). The strongest arguments understand Hosea 3 as a sequel to Hosea 1 and assume that the adulterous woman in Hosea 3 is Gomer (chap. 1) and not another, anonymous woman.

In its present position, Hosea 3 presupposes the content of Hosea 1–2. The "again" in 3:1 implies the previous narrative of God's directive to Hosea in chap. 1. Verbal and structural similarities exist between God's two commands to Hosea:

1. Yahweh said to Hosea (1:2); Yahweh said to me again (3:1)
2. "Go" (1:2; 3:1)
3. woman/wife (1:2; 3:1)
4. Yahweh in the subordinate clauses (1:2; 3:1)
5. "away from Yahweh" (1:2); "after other gods" (3:1)

Moreover, in both chapters the divine command is followed by an immediate response from Hosea: "he took" (1:3); "I bought" (3:2). The implied return of Hosea's faithless wife (3:3) does not appear in the first account of Hosea's marriage. It is foreshadowed, however, in Israel's return to God (2:9, 15-16). Thus within the context of Hosea 2, the marital narrative of Hosea 3 is more complete.

3:1. The Hebrew text of this verse locates the "again"/ "further"/"once more" between "said" and "go," where it could modify either word or even both. On one hand, v. 1 could mean "The LORD said to me again" (NRSV, following the MT pointing). On the other hand, the verse could be rendered, "Go again and love a woman" (NEB). In the NIV, "again" modifies "love": "Go, show your love to your wife again." Yet, God did not command Hosea to "love" his wife in chap. 1, but to "take" a promiscuous woman as wife.

The most conspicuous difference between the beginnings of chaps. 1 and 3 is the substitution of "love" for "take." The four occurrences of "love" (אהב 'āhab) in 3:1 correspond stylistically to the four occurrences of "promiscuous" (זנה zānâ), used to describe the licentiousness of the

48. Hans Walter Wolff, *Hosea: Commentary on the Book of the Prophet Hosea* (Philadelphia: Fortress, 1974) xxix; Francis I. Andersen and David Noel Freedman, *Hosea,* AB 24 (Garden City, N.Y.: Doubleday, 1980) 292.

49. For example, Daniel 7, as well as the "I AM" sayings in the Gospel of John.

wife and the land in 1:2. Hosea 3:1 plays upon different nuances of the word "love." "Love" characterizes both the profound emotion of Hosea and God *and* the unfaithfulness of Gomer and the children of Israel. The imperative "Love," in God's command to Hosea, is changed to the passive voice to describe the wife ("one loved by a paramour" [NIV, "though she is loved by another"; NRSV, "a woman who has a lover"]). The love that identifies Hosea's devotion to Gomer and God's passion for the Israelites is a covenantal love. In contrast, the love between the wife and her lover and between Israel and its other gods is an adulterous love. With remarkable economy of words, the Hebrew text highlights the magnitude of God's injunction to Hosea. He is bidden to love a wife who makes loves to another, just as Yahweh loves the Israelites who wantonly pursue other gods. One aspect of the play on the word "love" corresponds to the label "promiscuous" in 1:2. The other aspect corresponds to its very opposite: God's covenantal love. The wordplay makes the contrast between marital partners quite striking.

One of the attitudes singled out in 3:1 to illustrate Israel's infatuation with other gods is that they "love raisin cakes" (NRSV; NIV, "sacred raisin cakes"). In 2 Sam 6:19, raisin cakes are distributed to the people as food after the ritual installation of the ark in Jerusalem. Since this allocation of food is not censured in its connection with the cult, it is not clear why for Hosea raisin cakes embody Israel's rejection of Yahweh. One scholar associates the raisin cakes with the cakes of dough made in the image of the Queen of Heaven (Jer 7:18; 44:19).[50] Raisin cakes also may have been an aphrodisiac; the lover in Cant 2:4-5 feeds his beloved raisin cakes as a way to her heart.

3:2. This verse is problematic in that it raises questions about Gomer's present situation. Scholars speculate why Hosea must "buy," "bargain for," or "acquire" her.[51] Is she part of a pimp's stable of prostitutes or a temple prostitute, whom Hosea must purchase in order to secure her release? What is the significance of the "fifteen shekels of silver," the "homer of barley," and the "measure of wine"? (The NRSV adds "measure of wine," reading with the LXX.) And to whom are these paid or given? Do these commodities constitute a bride-price (מהר *mōhar*) paid to Diblaim, Hosea's father-in-law? Why would Hosea have to pay this bride-price if Gomer were already his wife? Has Gomer become someone's personal slave, and are these goods remuneration for buying her back (cf. Exod 21:32)? What is Gomer's status when she returns to Hosea?

The most satisfactory explanation of the money offered is to view Hosea's actions in the light of God's actions in chap. 2. The drama of Hosea's marriage mirrors the story of God and Israel.[52] After repudiating his wife, Hosea strips her of clothes and withholds food from her (cf. 2:2-3, 9-10). According to Exod 21:10, a husband was obligated to furnish food and clothing for his wife. Nevertheless, the question of who provides has become a major bone of contention in Hosea's marriage. Gomer thinks that her lovers supply her food, drink, and clothes (cf. 2:5, 12). Hosea insists that he is the one who has lavished goods upon her for her well-being (cf. 2:8). To drive this point home, Hosea will withdraw support when he rejects her.

When Hosea resolves to forgive Gomer and accept her into his household again, he will give back to her what he has withdrawn: silver to purchase clothes, barley for food, and wine for drink (3:2). Instead of giving a bride-price to Diblaim or payment to a slaveholder, Hosea gives Gomer these gifts directly, just as God imparts covenantal gifts to Israel (2:19). He thus "acquires" her for fifteen shekels of silver, a homer of barley, and a measure of wine.

3:3. This is an exceedingly difficult verse. The NRSV translation is preferable to the NIV, because it is a more accurate rendering of the MT. In order to discipline Gomer, Hosea tells her that she will remain (ישׁב *yāšab*) as his for many days and that she will not have sex with her lovers. Apparently, Hosea will not make love to her either. Hosea's segregation of Gomer from her lovers correlates with God's hedging his wife's way with thorns to frustrate her attempts to contact her paramours (2:6).

50. Jörg Jeremias, *Der Prophet Hosea,* ATD 24 (Göttingen: Vandenhoeck und Ruprecht, 1983) 54.

51. James L. Mays, *Hosea: A Commentary,* OTL (Philadelphia: Westminster, 1969) 57-58; Andersen and Freedman, *Hosea,* 298-300; Wolff, *Hosea,* 61.

52. For what follows, see Walter Vogels, "Hosea's Gift to Gomer," Bib 69 (1988) 412-21.

3:4. The sexual abstinence of Hosea and Gomer is interpreted in in this verse: Israel likewise will live (ישבו *yēšĕbû* [*yāšab*]) many days without its king or prince and without several of its cultic symbols. The pillars, large standing stones set up at shrines since the ancestral period, were part of the licit worship of Israel, although Hosea condemned them (cf. 10:1-2). The ephod was a type of garment worn by priests. The teraphim were probably household gods whose veneration also stretched back to ancestral times. In contrast to his censure of pillars, Hosea's attitude toward the ephod and the teraphim is difficult to determine, since they are not mentioned elsewhere.

3:5. Through a wordplay on *yēšĕbû/yāšab* ("to remain," "to live"), this verse discloses the objective of Israel's political and cultic deprivation: the people's repentance/return (ישבו *yāšubû*). On one hand, the root שוב (*šûb*) may indicate the return from exile. On the other hand, it may signify repentance, returning to God. The physical journey back to the land from exile and the spiritual journey back to God correspond to the wife's own journey, chronicled in Hosea 2. Although the wife seeks lovers, but does not find them along the way (2:7), the children of Israel will seek the Lord their God on their physical and spiritual travels. The references to exile and return, to "David their king"—an expression that is surprising in a northern prophet—and to "the latter days" suggest that this verse originated with exilic redactors.

REFLECTIONS

God's command for Hosea to love an adulterous wife, as God loves Israel, has moved generations of male interpreters to theologize at great length about the pain and suffering Hosea must have experienced in his tumultuous marriage.[53] Countless discussions point out how Hosea would have balked at God's order, yet he overcame his mortification to carry out the divine will. His grief and misery were intended to reflect in a small way the tremendous pathos of God in the face of the people's betrayal. Hosea's anguish has been labeled by Christian interpreters as his "cross," one that finds fulfillment in the cross of Christ. In Hosea's ordeal, we witness the intersection of divine revelation and human experience, gaining a profound insight into God's own wounded heart.[54]

As feminists point out, however, this claim absolutizes and elevates male experience as "human" and overlooks women's distinctive circumstances. Men who have experienced profound love, yet been bitterly hurt by a wife's infidelity, automatically empathize with Hosea's plight. They also have a far easier time translating his experience into divine terms, since the conceptualization of God in the Judeo-Christian tradition has been predominantly male.

Nevertheless, present-day statistics reveal that husbands are twice as likely to be unfaithful to their wives than wives to their husbands. That we have no male counterparts in our vocabulary for "mistress," "concubine," "kept woman," or "the other woman" testifies to the fact that *male* infidelity is the dominant phenomenon. Women whose adulterous husbands lavish gifts on their mistresses and paramours, who are deserted by their spouses for "the other woman," and who must raise children alone in trying economic circumstances because of the flight of the "breadwinner" will have a difficult time sympathizing with Hosea's predicament. Given the sizable occurrence of unfaithful husbands, women face greater challenges in appropriating theological truths when God is depicted as a husband. The gender-specific imagery of Hosea 3 throws up obstacles for women in listening for God's Word.

Women are also in a quandary with expressions of Hosea's "love," intended to persuade Gomer to reconcile with him. One man's love can be a woman's abuse. Hosea imitates Yahweh's methods in trying to convert his wife. Like God, Hosea sequesters Gomer from her

---

53. Cf. F. W. Keene, "Anger and Pain in Hosea," *Continuum* 3 (1994) 207-8; H. Wheeler Robinson, *Two Hebrew Prophets* (London: Lutterworth, 1948); Paul S. Fiddes, "The Cross of Hosea Revisited: The Meaning of Suffering in the Book of Hosea," *RevExp* 90 (1993).
54. Robinson, *Two Hebrew Prophets,* 18-21. More recently, Fiddes, "The Cross of Hosea Revisited," 175-90.

lovers (2:6; 3:3). Like God, Hosea resumes his "provider" role, furnishing her clothing, food, and drink again (2:15-20; 3:2). Moreover, Hosea informs Gomer that he will not have sex with her, just as Israel will exist without its king and cult objects (3:4).

While Hosea 2 clearly describes the physical and emotional violence God inflicts upon his wife to punish her, Hosea 3 is selective in portraying the prophet's chastisement of Gomer: no descriptions of Hosea stripping and humiliating her, no reports of his withholding food and clothing from her, and no accounts of his beating her. If Hosea models God to the fullest extent, these acts of "love" are implied in Hosea 3. The text's silence about these acts coincides with the reality that most cases of wife battering are private, not public, matters.

Through words put into her mouth by her husband, the wife/Israel speaks in chap. 2. Gomer, by contrast, is speechless in chaps. 1 and 3. One wonders about her version of the story. Her muteness only emphasizes the extent to which women have been left out of theological discussions that visualize the deity as male and the sinful as female. As it stands, it is difficult to accept Hosea 3 at face value. What is needed is the creation of new metaphors that express the profound religious truth of God's steadfast love for an undeserving people. As more women become educated in biblical studies, and as more women bring their own experiences into the theological conversation, conceptualizing new metaphors and new stories about God's love becomes a real possibility. Women like Gomer will then be able to find their voice.

HOSEA 4:1–11:11

THE SON/ISRAEL AND GOD

OVERVIEW

The second section, Hosea 4–11, is by far the longest and most difficult section of the book. First, the oracles are not arranged chronologically. One must discern the organizing principle connecting this collection of sayings. Second, the specific historical situations to which these oracles allude are difficult to reconstruct on the basis of the oracles alone. One can only speculate concerning their original contexts. Third, later redactors modified and reinterpreted the oracles for subsequent historical contexts. This later editing must be negotiated in order to find clarity in the material.

In spite of these difficulties, however, major themes emerge from the Hosea 4–11 complex. Like chaps. 1–3, chaps. 4–11 switch from accusation in the form of a legal complaint (2:2; 4:1) to threats of punishment, and then to the proclamation of hope and salvation (3:1-5; 11:8-11). Moreover, a three-part journey motif similar to that found in Hosea 1–3 also appears in Hosea 4–11. Three hope passages in chaps. 4–11 (5:15–6:3; 10:12; 11:10-11) narrate a movement from barrenness to fertility, motivating readers to return to God in repentance. According to the beginning of the complex in 4:3, the symbolic barrenness of the nation is reflected in creation. To prepare for the cosmic covenant that will reverse this sad state of affairs, the three hope passages summon the people to repent and be healed (5:15–6:3) and to till the soil of their hearts to prepare for the abundant fertility that only God can bring (10:12). The spiritual journey in repentance will become the physical journey from exile back to the homeland (11:10-11).

Although parent/child metaphors appear throughout the book, they are concentrated in chaps. 4 and 11, the beginning and end of the second complex. The parent/child metaphor characterizes other aspects of the divine/human covenantal bond, complementing the nuptial metaphor of Hosea 1–3. The most notable of these are God's compassion for and healing of a recalcitrant people.

Hosea 4–11 is rich with other metaphors as well. The prophet describes Israel and Ephraim (the preferred name for the northern kingdom) through various animal and agricultural metaphors, in order to criticize their dealings with other nations.[55] Ephraim, who mixes itself with the peoples, is a half-baked cake (7:8). Ephraim is like a silly, senseless dove, calling to Egypt and going to Assyria (7:11; cf. 9:11). It is a wild ass wandering alone, bargaining for lovers among the nations (8:9). It is a luxurious vine that yields fruit (9:10; 10:1), but then becomes a stricken root that bears nothing (9:16). It is a trained heifer that has plowed wickedness (10:11, 13; cf. 4:16).

In contrast to Hosea 1–3, which condemns the people and the land in general, Hosea 4–11 singles out the nation's leaders for censure: priests (4:4, 9; 5:1; 6:9; 10:5), prophets (4:5; 9:7), king (5:1; 7:3, 5; 8:4, 10), and officials (7:3, 5; 8:4, 10; 9:15; cf. 5:10). Hosea regards as "licentious" the northern kingdom's mercurial political alliances with foreign powers and the intrigue surrounding them (cf. 8:9-10). According to Hosea 6–7, this intrigue centers around a corrupt but influential guild of priests who plot evil in the king's court. The historical context of these sayings seems to be the Syro-Ephraimite war.

Alongside political offenses, chaps. 4–11 denounce the sins that have infected Israel's cult. The licentiousness that describes the wife/Israel and her baal lovers in chaps. 1–3 contaminates worship of the one God, Yahweh, from the reli-

---

55. For a fuller discussion of such metaphors, see Howard Eilberg-Schwartz, "Israel in the Mirror of Nature: Animal Metaphors in the Rituals and Narratives of Israelite Religion," in *The Savage in Judaism: An Anthropology of Israelite Religion and Ancient Judaism* (Bloomington: Indiana University Press, 1990) 115-40.

gious leaders (4:4, 6-8) down to the people themselves (4:9-19; 5:6-7). Just as the wife invests the baals with the silver and gold her husband gives her, so also the people make idolatrous bull calves of silver and gold (8:4-6; 10:5-6; 13:2). Their sacrifices have become occasions for sinning (4:17-19; 8:11-13; 9:4; cf 6:6). Hosea's focus on the cult and the monotheistic worship of Yahweh would be particularly popular during the time of the redactors of the book, when belief in one God and the centralization of worship became normative.

As with chap. 3, Hosea 11 is structurally important because it concludes a major section of the book. It highlights the adventures of the son/Israel. Like the wife/Israel, the son/Israel also experiences a three-part journey. The first is the journey from Egypt (the first exodus), when God first called him from slavery and cared for him in the wilderness (11:1-4). Because of his stubbornness in serving other gods, the son has disowned himself as God's child (11:2). He must make a journey back to Egypt because of his insubordination (11:5-7). God will not leave the son in exile, however. Contingent upon his repentance and return to his parent, the third part of the journey is the son's return from Egypt in a new exodus (11:10-11).

HOSEA 4:1–5:7, A PERVERSE PRIESTHOOD, A WANTON CULT, A LICENTIOUS PEOPLE

OVERVIEW

The oracle contained in 5:1-7 should be included with 4:4-19. Hosea 5:1-7 summarizes the themes of 4:4-19, which focuses on a perverse priesthood, a wanton cult, and a licentious people. Hosea 5:8 begins a new set of oracles, highlighting the political offenses of the land.

Hosea 4:1–5:7 is divided into an introduction (4:1-3) and roughly five oracles (4:4-6; 4:7-10; 4:11-14; 4:15-19; 5:1-7). Although the "I" style appears consistently throughout this unit, abrupt shifts in person, either addressing an audience directly or describing it in the third person (cf. 4:7, 13*b*, 17; 5:1), are probably due to later editorial activity.[56]

56. Gale A. Yee, *Composition and Tradition in the Book of Hosea: A Redaction Critical Investigation,* SBLDS 102 (Atlanta: Scholars Press, 1987) 158-70, 262-72.

Hosea 4:1-3, A Broken Covenant and a Creation Gone Awry

NIV	NRSV
4 Hear the word of the LORD, you Israelites, because the LORD has a charge to bring against you who live in the land: "There is no faithfulness, no love, no acknowledgment of God in the land. [2]There is only cursing,*a* lying and murder, stealing and adultery; they break all bounds, and bloodshed follows bloodshed.	**4** Hear the word of the LORD, O people of Israel; for the LORD has an indictment against the inhabitants of the land. There is no faithfulness or loyalty, and no knowledge of God in the land. [2] Swearing, lying, and murder, and stealing and adultery break out; bloodshed follows bloodshed. [3] Therefore the land mourns, and all who live in it languish; together with the wild animals

a2 That is, to pronounce a curse upon

NIV	NRSV
³Because of this the land mourns,ª and all who live in it waste away; the beasts of the field and the birds of the air and the fish of the sea are dying."	and the birds of the air, even the fish of the sea are perishing.
ª3 Or *dries up*	

COMMENTARY

Hosea 4:1-3 introduces the 4–11 complex, while still preserving obvious links with chaps. 1–3. The "word of the LORD" given to Hosea in 1:1 is now delivered to the people of Israel, who are summoned to hear in 4:1. Like 2:2-15, 4:1-3 constitutes God's legal complaint (ריב *rîb*), this time brought against the inhabitants of Israel. The *rîb* accuses them of lacking three qualities that would manifest their covenantal relationship with God: "faithfulness" (אמת *ʾĕmet*), "steadfast love" (חסד *ḥesed*), and the "knowledge of God" (דעת *daʿat*). These attributes refer to the gifts Yahweh will bestow on his wife when he renews the covenant with all of creation on her behalf (2:18-20). Although the bride is given faithfulness (אמונה *ʾĕmûnâ*, 2:20), the people lack *ʾĕmet*. Steadfast love is missing, and the bride who would come "to know Yahweh" has no such knowledge of God.

The absence of these covenantal qualities gives rise to a number of covenantal violations among the people (4:2). The five crimes singled out (swearing, lying, murder, stealing, and adultery) are prohibited by the Decalogue (Exod 20:1-17;

Deut 5:6-21). Anarchy in the land is epitomized in the vivid image of one bloody deed following another (cf. the bloodshed of Jezreel, 1:4).

The "therefore" (על־כן *ʿal-kēn*) that begins 4:3 highlights the infection of creation itself, resulting from the social iniquity of the land's inhabitants. Human wickedness pollutes nature and all the creatures within it. This cosmic corruption is described as a drought: The land dries up,[57] the inhabitants languish, and creatures perish. The reference to drought sets the tone for Hosea 4–11, accentuating the theme of barrenness that ensues from Israel's covenantal transgressions. The infertility of the land contrasts with previous descriptions of cosmic abundance, flowing from the covenantal reunion of husband and wife (2:18-23). Nevertheless, three hope passages within Hosea 4–11, intermingled with oracles of doom (see Overview to 4:1–11:11), set the stage for the reversal of this barrenness in Hosea 14.

57. אבל (*ʾābal*) can mean "mourn" (NRSV) or "dries up" (cf. note in NIV). Because the subject is the land, the latter interpretation is preferred. See also Joel 1:10-12.

REFLECTIONS

An ecological, "green" consciousness is widespread throughout the world today. In some countries, "green" has even become a party platform. Such a consciousness comes as a positive reaction to troubling times, when biological, chemical, and nuclear weapons capable of wiping out our entire planet are being developed; when we exploit our natural resources without renewing them; when our animals have become or are in danger of becoming extinct because of our carelessness or greed; and when our rivers, our skies, our lakes, and our oceans become polluted with our toxic wastes. Our antiseptic, plastic-wrapped society detaches us from the land. We abandon our farms and concentrate in cities. Our supermarkets distance us not only from the arduous processing of the land's products, but also from the sense of gratitude and respect for what the land has yielded.

In contrast, what is underscored in Hos 4:1-3 is the intimate moral, as well as physical, link between all of creation and a covenanted people. As an agricultural, pre-industrial society, ancient Israel was fully conscious of its interconnection with the land. The way its people lived their lives directly affected the rest of creation. When the people blessed God, the land blossomed forth in lush vegetation. When the people sinned, "the land mourned."

The pollution of our own land provides ample evidence of the brokenness of our society. The destruction of its creatures and its resources indicts us for forgetting "our mother." Hosea 4:1-3 recalls our bonds with the rest of creation and exhorts us to restore the harmony between us by setting our own lives in order.

Hosea 4:4-6, A Perverse Priesthood

NIV

4"But let no man bring a charge,
    let no man accuse another,
for your people are like those
    who bring charges against a priest.
5You stumble day and night,
    and the prophets stumble with you.
So I will destroy your mother—
6   my people are destroyed from lack of
      knowledge.

"Because you have rejected knowledge,
    I also reject you as my priests;
because you have ignored the law of your God,
    I also will ignore your children."

NRSV

4 Yet let no one contend,
    and let none accuse,
for with you is my contention, O priest.[a]
5 You shall stumble by day;
    the prophet also shall stumble with you by
      night,
    and I will destroy your mother.
6 My people are destroyed for lack of
      knowledge;
    because you have rejected knowledge,
    I reject you from being a priest to me.
And since you have forgotten the law of your
      God,
    I also will forget your children.

[a] Cn: Meaning of Heb uncertain

COMMENTARY

Hosea 4:4 begins the first set of oracles in this complex. Crucial for the interpretation of both the first and the second sets (4:4-6, 7-10) is the much disputed 4:4b.[58] Literally, the MT could be read as either "your people are like the contentions of a priest" or "your people are like those who strive with [bring charges against] a priest." The latter sense is followed by the NIV. Nevertheless, it is unclear what these formulations mean precisely when applied to "your people." Also unclear is the identity of the audience addressed in "your people."

Some scholars emend the vowel pointing of the MT to read, "With you is my contention, O priest," an emendation followed by the NRSV.[59] This rendering is preferred, because it fits the context of v. 4 better than the literal translation. Resuming the lawsuit רִיב (rîb) from v. 1, it makes the complaint more precise, directing it against a specific audience: "you, O priest." According to v. 6, this priest, addressed again as "you," will be rejected by God. The identity of this priest is uncertain. Perhaps Hosea is singling out an actual priest during the time of his ministry, or he may be referring to the institution of priesthood. The reference to the office of prophet in v. 5 would strengthen this latter interpretation.

The rîb formulates its indictment against the priest through a contrasting play on five pairs of

58. For a fuller discussion, see Jack R. Lundbom, "Contentious Priests and Contentious People," *VT* 36 (1986) 52-70; and Francis I. Andersen and David Noel Freedman, *Hosea,* AB 24 (Garden City, N.Y.: Doubleday, 1980) 346-50.

59. See Andersen and Freedman, *Hosea,* 346-50.

verbs in vv. 4-6: to contend, to stumble, to destroy, to reject, and to forget.[60] Prohibiting any accusations that others may level, God lays out his own contention against the priest (v. 4). The priest is paired with the prophet, and both will "stumble" and eventually fall (v. 5). These religious leaders share in the current deterioration of Israel's religious life and will be held accountable for it.

The reference to "your mother" in v. 5*b* is often understood to refer to the priest's own mother. However, the parallelism between "your mother" and "my people" in the first colon of v. 6, preserved by the NIV, suggests that "your mother" is Israel. The personification of the nation as the promiscuous wife and mother of Hosea 2 reemerges here. The nation's cultic licentiousness will be a major theme in the following oracular units. Not only does the wife/Israel make an appearance, but the son Ammi ("My people"; cf. 1:9; 2:1, 23) appears as well. In addition to v. 6, Ammi will appear in vv. 8 and 12 (cf. vv. 9, 14).[61]

60. Michael De Roche, "Structure, Rhetoric, and Meaning in Hosea IV 4-10," *VT* 33 (1983) 186-87.

61. If one accepts the MT in 4:4, "my people are like those who contend with a priest," one finds another appearance of Ammi. The only other occurrences of "my people" in Hosea 4–11 are found in 6:11 and 11:7.

The focus on the son (= the people) highlights the parent/child metaphor for the covenant, concentrated here and in Hosea 11, the beginning and end of the second section of the book.[62]

Verse 6 builds to a climax through a series of interlocking parallelisms. Referring to the indictment that there was no knowledge of God in the land (v. 1), God proclaims that Ammi is being destroyed by a "lack of knowledge." This knowledge includes recognition of the one God of Israel, what this God has done for the people, and what this God demands in return. The people's ignorance of all this is due precisely to the priest's rejection of that knowledge. Because he has spurned knowledge, he will be rejected as priest. Like the wife/Israel who forgot Yahweh (2:13), the priest is accused of forgetting God's law (תורה *tôrâ*), the instructions stipulated by the covenant, which he should have transmitted to Ammi. Because the priest has forgotten this *tôrâ*, God will forget his sons, who would inherit his priestly office. (See Reflections at 5:1-7.)

62. On parenthood metaphors for God's covenant, see Gary W. Light, "The New Covenant in the Book of Hosea," *RevExp* 90 (1993) 229-32.

Hosea 4:7-11*a*, Like People, Like Priest

NIV

[7]"The more the priests increased,
　　the more they sinned against me;
　　they exchanged[a] their[b] Glory for something
　　　　disgraceful.
[8]They feed on the sins of my people
　　and relish their wickedness.
[9]And it will be: Like people, like priests.
　　I will punish both of them for their ways
　　and repay them for their deeds.

[10]"They will eat but not have enough;
　　they will engage in prostitution but not increase,
because they have deserted the LORD
　　to give themselves [11]to prostitution,
to old wine and new,
　　which take away the understanding [12]of my
　　　　people."

a7 Syriac and an ancient Hebrew scribal tradition; Masoretic Text *I will exchange*　　*b7* Masoretic Text; an ancient Hebrew scribal tradition *my*

NRSV

[7] The more they increased,
　　the more they sinned against me;
　　they changed[a] their glory into shame.
[8] They feed on the sin of my people;
　　they are greedy for their iniquity.
[9] And it shall be like people, like priest;
　　I will punish them for their ways,
　　and repay them for their deeds.
[10] They shall eat, but not be satisfied;
　　they shall play the whore, but not multiply;
because they have forsaken the LORD
　　to devote themselves to [11]whoredom.

Wine and new wine
　　take away the understanding.

a Ancient Heb tradition: MT *I will change*

COMMENTARY

Hosea 4:7-11a is structured chiastically (ABCB'A'), its center focused on the maxim in v. 9: "And it shall be like people, like priest."

A v. 7 The more they increased . . .

   B v. 8 They feed on the sin of my people . . .

      C v. 9 And it shall be like people, like priest . . .

   B' v. 10 They shall eat, but not be satisfied . . .

A' Because they have forsaken the LORD. . . .

4:7. Building up to the center, the pronoun "they" refers to the priest's sons (v. 6), whom God will forget. (The NIV eliminates the ambiguity of v. 7 by replacing "they" with "the priests.") The more numerous they become, the greater their collective sin. In contrast to the NIV and the NRSV, the MT of v. 7*b* reads "I [Yahweh] will change their glory [כבוד *kābôd*] into shame [קלון *qālôn*]." *Kābôd* and *qālôn* refer to the honor/shame value system held by the ancient Israelites.[63] According to 9:11, Ephraim's honor is identified with its ability to procreate or increase: "Ephraim's glory shall fly away like a bird—/ no birth, no pregnancy, no conception!" Thus in A, the priests' ability to increase or reproduce—in other words, their honor—will be reversed. God will shame them, and they will become a sterile, barren institution.[64]

4:8. The priests "feed on the sin of Ammi [my people]." This feeding could be meant figuratively—i.e., a corrupt parasitical relationship between the priests and the people's sin. The priests, who should lead the people away from sin toward Yahweh, subsist off the people's iniquity instead (cf. v. 6). The verse could also be read literally: The priests gain their livelihood from Ammi's "unorthodox" religious practices (see vv. 11-14).

4:9. The center of the chiasmus functions like a pivot between the two oracular units, vv. 4-6 and vv. 11-14. While vv. 4-6 concentrate on the foundering of the priest and vv. 11-14 highlight the cultic transgressions of the people, v. 9 claims: "It shall be like people, like priest." God will punish both the people and their religious leaders for their evil deeds.

4:10. This verse (B') expands the detail, "feeding upon the people's sin," described in v. 8 (B). Although they eat, they will not be satisfied. The subject apparently is still the priests who either symbolically live off the people's sin or economically profit from their cult practices. The second half of v. 10 (A') resumes the sexual image of v. 7 (A) and anticipates the theme of Ammi's wantonness in the next unit. Like the people, the priests fornicate,[65] but this sinful sexual activity will not lead to procreation. They will be shamed by their inability to multiply. Verse 10 (A') concludes the chiastic unit, detailing the major infraction of the priests: They have forsaken Yahweh to devote themselves to promiscuity.[66]

The literal and symbolic are completely intertwined in this complex of images, making interpretation uncertain. Are the priests literally engaging in illicit sex? If so, some will doubtless procreate children from their unions, making one wonder about the meaning of "they shall fornicate but not multiply." Is the priest's involvement in the cult of Baal, which Hosea condemns as unorthodox, symbolically branded as fornication? If so, the image of sterility refers to the bankruptcy of the priesthood as an institution. The problem of determining what is literal and what is symbolic also affects interpretation of the next oracle, which focuses on the people's wantonness. (See Reflections at 5:1-7.)

---

63. See Introduction. Also, see the use of *kābôd* and *qālôn* in Prov 3:35: "The wise will inherit honor, but stubborn fools, disgrace."

64. See Gen 30:23 and 1 Sam 1:1-11, where barrenness is considered a reproach. Regarding the complex interconnections among priesthood, patrilineal descent, and procreation, see Howard Eilberg-Schwartz, "The Fruitful Cut: Circumcision and Israel's Symbolic Language of Fertility, Descent, and Gender," in *The Savage in Judaism: An Anthropology of Israelite Religion and Ancient Judaism* (Bloomington: Indiana University Press, 1990) 141-76.

65. As was argued in the Commentary on Hos 1:2, זנה *zānâ* covers a range of sexual transgressions, and translations that narrow the meaning to "prostitution" should be avoided. Cf. NIV and NRSV.

66. MT 4:10 has no object for the infinitive "to devote to," "to cherish" (לשמר *lišmōr*). Both the NRSV and the NIV read the first word of 4:11, זנות (*zĕnût*, "promiscuity," "fornication"), as the object of *lišmōr*.

Hosea 4:11b-14, A Wanton Cult and a Licentious People

NIV

11"to prostitution,
to old wine and new,
    which take away the understanding 12of my
        people.
They consult a wooden idol
    and are answered by a stick of wood.
A spirit of prostitution leads them astray;
    they are unfaithful to their God.
13They sacrifice on the mountaintops
    and burn offerings on the hills,
under oak, poplar and terebinth,
    where the shade is pleasant.
Therefore your daughters turn to prostitution
    and your daughters-in-law to adultery.

14"I will not punish your daughters
    when they turn to prostitution,
nor your daughters-in-law
    when they commit adultery,
because the men themselves consort with
        harlots
    and sacrifice with shrine prostitutes—
    a people without understanding will come to
        ruin!"

NRSV

11whoredom.

Wine and new wine
    take away the understanding.
12 My people consult a piece of wood,
    and their divining rod gives them oracles.
For a spirit of whoredom has led them astray,
    and they have played the whore, forsaking
        their God.
13 They sacrifice on the tops of the mountains,
    and make offerings upon the hills,
under oak, poplar, and terebinth,
    because their shade is good.

Therefore your daughters play the whore,
    and your daughters-in-law commit adultery.
14 I will not punish your daughters when they
        play the whore,
    nor your daughters-in-law when they
        commit adultery;
for the men themselves go aside with whores,
    and sacrifice with temple prostitutes;
thus a people without understanding comes to
        ruin.

COMMENTARY

Like the preceding oracle (vv. 7-11a), vv. 11b-14 are arranged chiastically and contain proverbs that deal with the people. While the maxim in v. 9 formed the structural center of vv. 7-10, two "people" proverbs create the outer limits of the chiasmus in vv. 11-14:

A v. 11 Wine and new wine take away the understanding of my people.[67]

A' v. 14 A people without understanding will come to ruin.

The reference to Ammi in v. 11 again recalls Hosea's third child, underscoring the focus on a people who have transgressed God's covenant. According to vv. 12-13 (B), Ammi engages in religious practices that are offensive to Hosea. He consults his עֵץ ('ēṣ, "tree" or "wood") and his מַקֵּל (maqqēl, "branch," "staff," or "rod") to divine God's will. The referents for 'ēṣ and maqqēl are not exactly clear. They may refer to the wooden symbol of the goddess Asherah, who is often associated with trees.[68] They may designate an idol made of wood (Deut 4:28; 28:36; Jer 10:3-5). Given the intertwining of cult and sexuality in this chapter, the staff and the tree could be interpreted as phallic symbols.

Ammi is led astray by "a promiscuous spirit";

---

67. The NRSV follows the MT of 4:12, where "my people" is the subject of the sentence. My reading follows the NIV and the LXX in connecting "my people" with "understanding" in 4:11.

68. For a complete discussion, see Mark S. Smith, *The Early History of God: Yahweh and the Other Deities in Ancient Israel* (San Francisco: Harper & Row, 1990) 80-114.

he fornicates away from Yahweh. We will encounter this spirit again in the next two oracles (4:19; 5:4). The expression conjures up visions of rampant sexuality among the people as they sacrifice on the high places and in the sacred groves. The image of this activity's occurring under shady trees reinforces the licentious aura (v. 13*a*).

At the center of the chiasmus (C) in v. 13*b*, the "cultic fornication" of the son Ammi results in the sexual promiscuity and adultery of the daughters of Israel. In an honor/shame culture, it is the duty of men to supervise the sexuality of their women (see Introduction). If the men are delinquent, their women become lewd. Their sexual abandon profoundly reveals how morally degenerate the male community has become. Therefore, to underscore rhetorically the men's failures, God proclaims in v. 14 that the deity will not punish the sexual offenses of the women of Israel (C'), because the men themselves are guilty of social and cultic sins (B'). On one hand, they frequent prostitutes (social). On the other hand, they sacrifice with hierodules (cultic).

The technical word for "prostitute" (זנה *zōnâ*) is used in v. 14 and is paired in the next colon with קדשה (*qĕdēšâ*; lit., "holy one"). Their pairing leads scholars to assume that *qĕdēšâ* is some sort of cultic prostitute (cf. NRSV and NIV). Until more evidence appears, however, it is premature to assume that *qĕdēšâ* is a woman involved in cultic sexual service. Although *qĕdēšâ* is associated with a cult, her actual function in Israelite sanctuaries is very difficult to reconstruct on the basis of the biblical or extra-biblical texts. Although in

the prophet's mind her rituals involved sexuality, it would be a mistake to accept this at face value. The biblical text is simply too polemical, revealing more about the prophetic mind that leveled the accusation than about actual practices in the cult itself. Until more intelligible and less polemical evidence surfaces, it would be better to translate *qĕdēšâ* as "hierodule," rather than as "cult prostitute." "Hierodule," a word taken from the Greek and meaning "temple servant," preserves the cultic force of the word, but remains neutral regarding sexual aspects, if any, of the woman's ministry.[69]

Many scholars automatically assume that the cultic practices in vv. 11-14 refer to an alien Canaanite fertility cult. As noted in the Introduction, however, many of the religious practices deemed foreign and Canaanite were very much a part of legitimate Israelite cultic activity. If this oracle is original to Hosea, then, the sexual imagery may be part of his overall rhetorical strategy to promote the belief and cultic practice of monotheism. His tactic involves leveling accusations of sexual impropriety against his cultic opponents, in order to define the boundaries of his own monotheistic position.[70] (See Reflections at 5:1-7.)

69. For further study, see Phyllis Bird, " 'To Play the Harlot': An Inquiry into an Old Testament Metaphor," in *Gender and Difference,* Peggy L. Day, ed. (Minneapolis: Fortress, 1989) 84-89, as well as her essay "The Place of Women in the Israelite Cultus," in *Ancient Israelite Religion,* Patrick D. Miller, Jr., Paul D. Hanson, and S. Dean McBride, eds. (Philadelphia: Fortress, 1987) 397-419.

70. For a fuller discussion, see Robert A. Oden, Jr., "Religious Identity and the Sacred Prostitution Accusation," in *The Bible Without Theology: The Theological Tradition and Alternatives to It,* New Voices in Biblical Studies (San Francisco: Harper & Row, 1987) 132-35.

Hosea 4:15-19, Israel, the Stubborn Heifer

NIV	NRSV

15"Though you commit adultery, O Israel,
    let not Judah become guilty.
 	
"Do not go to Gilgal;
    do not go up to Beth Aven.*ᵃ*
And do not swear, 'As surely as the LORD
        lives!'
16The Israelites are stubborn,
    like a stubborn heifer.
	15 Though you play the whore, O Israel,
	    do not let Judah become guilty.
	Do not enter into Gilgal,
	    or go up to Beth-aven,
	    and do not swear, "As the LORD lives."
	16 Like a stubborn heifer,
	    Israel is stubborn;
	can the LORD now feed them
	    like a lamb in a broad pasture?
	
	17 Ephraim is joined to idols—

ᵃ15 Beth Aven means *house of wickedness* (a name for Bethel, which means *house of God*).

NIV	NRSV

How then can the LORD pasture them
   like lambs in a meadow?
¹⁷Ephraim is joined to idols;
   leave him alone!
¹⁸Even when their drinks are gone,
   they continue their prostitution;
   their rulers dearly love shameful ways.
¹⁹A whirlwind will sweep them away,
   and their sacrifices will bring them shame."
	let him alone.
	¹⁸ When their drinking is ended, they indulge in
	   sexual orgies;
	   they love lewdness more than their glory.^a
	¹⁹ A wind has wrapped them^b in its wings,
	   and they shall be ashamed because of their
	   altars.^c

a Cn Compare Gk: Meaning of Heb uncertain   *b* Heb *her*
c Gk Syr: Heb *sacrifices*

COMMENTARY

The fourth oracle, vv. 15-19, is notoriously difficult. Some of the problems can be eased by seeing the unit as an edited composition. The previous oracles, vv. 7-10 and vv. 11-14, focused on the metaphor of the son Ammi/the people. The controlling metaphor for Israel/Ephraim in these verses is that of the promiscuous wife/mother, which first appeared in this section in v. 5. The simile of the heifer in v. 16, the feminine suffixes in v. 18 for "her shields" and "her wings/skirts," and the feminine accusative particle אותה (*'ōtāh*) in v. 19 all reinforce Israel's representation as female.

4:15. Scholars suspect that the reference to Judah in this verse is a secondary expansion of an oracle initially directed to Israel. In its present form, the oracle warns Judah not to emulate its fornicating sister, Israel, by frequenting the northern shrines at Bethel and Gilgal. Bethel ("House of God") is sarcastically called Beth-aven, "House of Evil." Hostility toward these shrines is particularly evident in the commentary of the Josianic redactor, who encouraged worship at the southern sanctuary, Jerusalem. The original oracle did not necessarily condemn the shrines in and of themselves. Rather, it forbade Israel from visiting the shrines hypocritically, while persisting in "fornication."[71]

4:16-17. Verse 16 compares Israel's stubbornness to that of a young female cow. The heifer simile will reappear in 10:11. The NIV and the NRSV translate v. 16*b* as a question, but the interrogative particle is not present in the MT.

The second half of v. 17 is also puzzling. Both the NIV and the NRSV translate הנּח־לו (*hannah-lô*) as "Let him alone." The more usual meaning of נוח (*nûah*) in the hiphil, however, is "to give rest," "to lead," "to make quiet," a rendering confirmed by some of the Greek translations. I suggest that the second halves of both v. 16 and v. 17 be regarded as interpretive commentary by an exilic redactor modifying his received tradition:

> Like a stubborn heifer, Israel is stubborn;
> (But Yahweh will now feed them like a lamb in
>   broad pasture.)
> Ephraim is joined to idols.
> (But he-Yahweh will provide rest for him.)[72]

The image of God shepherding, feeding, and resting the flock is consistent with later exilic thought. For example, Ezek 34:13-15 describes God gathering the Israelites from foreign lands and bringing them back to their own land. God will feed and shepherd them, making them lie down on the mountains of Israel.

4:18-19. These verses are also quite problematic. A minor repointing of the MT in v. 19 renders a more literal translation than either the NIV or the NRSV and preserves the feminine images that they eliminate:[73]

> He [Ephraim of v. 17*a*] falls away with their drinking.
>   They indeed fornicate,
>   They make love continually.
> Shame has wrapped her shields.

---

71. See the discussion in Grace I. Emmerson, *Hosea: An Israelite Prophet in Judean Perspective* (Sheffield: JSOT, 1984) 77-83.

72. Author's trans., repointing the hiphil imperative of *nwh* to the hiphil indicative pf. 3 ms. sg. *hēniah*. For a fuller discussion, see Gale A. Yee, *Composition and Tradition in the Book of Hosea: A Redaction Critical Investigation,* SBLDS 102 (Atlanta: Scholars Press, 1987) 168-69.

73. Ibid., 271-72.

A spirit of lust[74] is in her skirts.
They shall be ashamed because of their altars. (author's trans.)

Israel is accused of being like a stubborn heifer, a metaphor that has connotations of female sexuality.[75] Her dalliance with idols, her inebriation

(cf. v. 11), and her lasciviousness all testify to her stubbornness. In v. 7 God changed the honor of the priests into shame. In v. 12, Ammi was corrupted by a promiscuous spirit. In vv. 18-19, these two themes come together in the striking image of shame wrapping the shields of Israel and a spirit of lust infecting her skirts, employed here as a euphemism for the libidinous organs beneath them. (See Reflections at 5:1-7.)

74. With Francis I. Andersen and David Noel Freedman, *Hosea,* AB 24 (Garden City, N.Y.: Doubleday, 1980) 376, repointing the feminine accusative particle אותה (*'ōtāh*) to *'awwātāh,* "longing," "lust."

75. See עגלה (*'eglâ*) in Judg 14:18 and Jer 50:11. See also the greedy, indolent cows (פרות *pārôt*) in Amos 4:1. The use of פרה (*pārâ*) in Hos 4:16 is dictated by wordplays in 4:16*a*, 17*a*.

Hosea 5:1-7, The Chastising God

<table>
<tr><td>

NIV

5 "Hear this, you priests!
   Pay attention, you Israelites!
Listen, O royal house!
   This judgment is against you:
You have been a snare at Mizpah,
   a net spread out on Tabor.
²The rebels are deep in slaughter.
   I will discipline all of them.
³I know all about Ephraim;
   Israel is not hidden from me.
Ephraim, you have now turned to prostitution;
   Israel is corrupt.

⁴"Their deeds do not permit them
   to return to their God.
A spirit of prostitution is in their heart;
   they do not acknowledge the LORD.
⁵Israel's arrogance testifies against them;
   the Israelites, even Ephraim, stumble in their sin;
   Judah also stumbles with them.
⁶When they go with their flocks and herds
   to seek the LORD,
they will not find him;
   he has withdrawn himself from them.
⁷They are unfaithful to the LORD;
   they give birth to illegitimate children.
Now their New Moon festivals
   will devour them and their fields."

</td><td>

NRSV

5 Hear this, O priests!
   Give heed, O house of Israel!
Listen, O house of the king!
   For the judgment pertains to you;
for you have been a snare at Mizpah,
   and a net spread upon Tabor,
² and a pit dug deep in Shittim;[*a*]
   but I will punish all of them.

³ I know Ephraim,
   and Israel is not hidden from me;
for now, O Ephraim, you have played the whore;
   Israel is defiled.
⁴ Their deeds do not permit them
   to return to their God.
For the spirit of whoredom is within them,
   and they do not know the LORD.

⁵ Israel's pride testifies against him;
   Ephraim[*b*] stumbles in his guilt;
   Judah also stumbles with them.
⁶ With their flocks and herds they shall go
   to seek the LORD,
but they will not find him;
   he has withdrawn from them.
⁷ They have dealt faithlessly with the LORD;
   for they have borne illegitimate children.
Now the new moon shall devour them
   along with their fields.

</td></tr>
</table>

a Cn: Meaning of Heb uncertain   *b* Heb *Israel and Ephraim*

COMMENTARY

The fifth and concluding oracle of this section summarizes many of its ideas: the nation's promiscuity (4:10; 5:3), the promiscuous spirit infecting it (4:12, 19; 5:4), the stumbling of the nation (5:5) vis-à-vis priest and prophet (4:5), the licentious deeds of the people and their leaders (4:9; 5:4), and their lack of knowing Yahweh (4:1, 6; 5:4). Moreover, 5:1-7 reiterates themes found in the Hosea 1–3 complex: illegitimate children (2:5; 5:7), new moons (2:11; 5:7), God's chastisement (2:9-13; 4:9; 5:2), repentance and return (2:7; 3:5; 5:4, 15), and seeking and (not) finding (2:7; 3:5; 5:6, 15). Hosea 5:1-7 anticipates the development of many of these themes in 5:15–6:3, the first hope passage of the three-part journey in chaps. 4–11.

5:1. The opening of chap. 5 recalls 4:1 in exhorting particular audiences to "hear" God's message. The focus of God's judgment is the nation (referred to as the "house of Israel") and its leaders, the priests and the king. Whereas the previous oracles already chided the priests and their cult, the inclusion of the "king" here anticipates the condemnation of political leaders and their intrigue, beginning in v. 8. The three addressees are rebuked by means of three metaphors of ensnarement. Certain geographical locations are singled out, not for their historical or cultic importance, but because they are wordplays on different kinds of traps: "snare" (פח *paḥ*) at Mizpah, "net spread" (רשת פרושה *rešet pĕrûśâ*) upon Tabor, a "pit" (שחטה *šaḥăṭâ*) dug deep at "Shittim" (NRSV). The random location of these places in Israel underscores the fact that the whole nation is becoming corrupt.

5:2-4. The main theme of this final oracle is the chastisement (מוסר *mûsār*) by Yahweh (v. 2). In Hosea 2 God chastises in order to bring about the repentance/return (שוב *šûb*) of the wife. However, Israel and Ephraim have become so promiscuous (v. 3) that their licentious acts do not permit them to return (*šûb*) to God. As described in the two previous oracles, a promiscuous spirit invades them. In contrast to v. 3 where Yahweh knows Ephraim, the people do not know Yahweh (v. 4).

5:5. Recalling the legal imagery that begins this section (4:1), the "pride" that will bear witness against Israel in v. 5a is most likely Israel's own arrogance. Verse 5b continues the legal trope and enlarges the "stumbling" metaphor of 4:5. Not only do priest and prophet stumble (4:5), but also Ephraim and the southern kingdom of Judah founder in their guilt. Consistent with the theme of these oracles, their arrogance and stumbling are linked to a licentious cult (5:6-7).

5:6-7. These verses share a number of commonalities with Hosea 2 and its wife/Israel metaphor. According to Deut 4:28-30, the people are commanded to reject idols. If they "seek" Yahweh with all their heart, they will "find" Yahweh. We were told in Hos 2:7, however, that the wife/Israel sought her baal lovers instead, though God prevented her from finding them in order that she might "return [*šûb*] to her first husband." In v. 6, the people smugly bring their sacrificial animals to "seek Yahweh," but they do not "find" Yahweh; God has already withdrawn from them and their wanton cult. God's withdrawal parallels the husband's withholding of life's necessities from his wife (2:9).

Also particularly apt in this context is the verb בגד (*bāgad*), used to describe Israel's faithless acts in v. 7. In Jer 3:20, *bāgad* characterizes both a wife's infidelity toward her husband and Israel's faithlessness to Yahweh. This nuance of *bāgad* in v. 7 thus recalls the wife/Israel metaphor. Like their mother (2:4-5), the faithless Israelites have borne "illegitimate children" and will be suitably punished. The punishment referred to in the expression "the new moon shall devour them along with their fields," however, is not quite clear. It is possible that the subject of "devour" is Yahweh, resumed from v. 7a, and that Yahweh "will devour the new moon and the fields." In 2:11 Yahweh puts an end to the wife's new moons and festivals and ravages her vines and fig trees. The new moon could refer to a period of time; within a month destruction will come. Or it might be a figurative reversal of 4:8, where the priests "eat"/"devour" the sin of Ammi. In any case, the punishment is correlated with the nation's perverted cult.

REFLECTIONS

1. A consistent topic in this set of oracles is the culpability of Israel's spiritual leaders, the priests, for the corrupt state of the nation. Along with the honor, status, and privileges of priesthood comes enormous responsibility. Instead of instilling the people with the "knowledge of God," however, the priests bear responsibility for their lack of knowledge. It is not merely that the priests are not doing their jobs. Rather, they lead the people further into "promiscuity." They actually live off the people's sin. The priests' hypocrisy and neglect of the people's welfare will result automatically in God's angry judgment.

Hosea 4:4–5:7 describes the priests' transgression through a number of sexual tropes: "fornication," "spirit of promiscuity," "adultery," "frequenting prostitutes," and so forth. The "whoredom" of the priests provokes the "whoredom" of the people. As the Commentary points out, however, it is not clear whether the descriptions of priestly sexual immorality were meant literally or were simply part of Hosea's polemical rhetoric against a cult he condemned.

If the text is interpreted as a literal description of carnal transgressions by priests, one reflecting on the present-day situation might find Hosea's condemnation relevant. A very disturbing form of sexual violence is perpetrated today by persons who are supposedly trusted religious leaders, individuals who should be above reproach. Common in the print and electronic media are scandalous stories of pedophilia among priests and of men who have grown into midlife carrying the guilt of their furtive boyhood encounters with "Father Bill." We hear stories of Sunday school teachers sexually molesting their daughters or sons. We read about ministers and priests who carry on affairs with members of their congregation. Stories of counselors and spiritual directors who sexually exploit their clients are widespread.

The root of these sexual offenses is an abuse of power. Power in and of itself is neutral. It can be used for both very good and very evil purposes. Power is also relational. Some people have more, some less, depending on the social ideologies governing the relationship. In an institutional context such as the church or synagogue, power relationships are determined by the particular roles one has within these structures. In most cases, these roles are hierarchically arranged and specifically defined. Within such an unequal system, the laity entrust power to the clergy to guide their moral and religious lives away from evil and toward the sacred. The present asymmetry of the clergy/lay relation, however, creates occasions for abuse of power. Abuse becomes particularly exacerbated when children are sexually exploited.

Hosea's condemnation of religious leaders is apt for our time. It enjoins us to reflect deeply upon our pastoral ministries and how they help or hinder, assist or obstruct, God's work on this planet. Power accorded to us by virtue of our office brings heavy responsibility. We are called to recognize and confront sexual abuse for those in our care, not contribute to them. We are called to challenge those structures that perpetuate sexual violence, not to collude with them. We are called to reexamine and transform relations of family and gender inequity that can lead to abuse, not to exploit them. Hosea warns us that God will indeed hold us doubly accountable for any failures in our spiritual offices.

2. Hosea pronounces a ringing indictment of those who have wandered away from Yahweh and into other entanglements:

> Israel's pride testifies against him;
>> Ephraim stumbles in his guilt;
>> Judah also stumbles with them.
> With their flocks and herds they shall go
>> to seek the LORD
> but they will not find him;
>> he has withdrawn from them. (5:5-6 NRSV)

Hosea's dramatic depiction in 5:5-6 can be supplemented by an excerpt from Alice Walker's *The Color Purple,* in which the black, sexually abused Celie tells her lover Shug that she no longer writes to God, whom she depicts as a white man who acts "just like all the other mens that I know. Trifling, forgitful and lowdown." Shug tries to correct Celie's misconceptions of the divine:

> She say, Celie, tell the truth, have you ever found God in church? I never did. I just found a bunch of folks hoping for him to show. Any God I ever felt in church I brought in with me. And I think all the other folks did too. They come to church to *share* God, not find God.[76]

Shug's words of wisdom place the notion of "seeking and finding" God into a contemporary perspective. We do not magically find God simply by going to church or synagogue. All religious rituals presuppose a life already charged with the presence of God. We gather in community, as Shug says, to share God, not to find God. We assemble together in order to celebrate God already at work in our lives. We bring God with us into our houses of worship.

In contrast, the Israelites bring their flocks and herds to their liturgies. Evidently that is all they bring. They certainly do not bring God with them. Their lives are empty of God's presence. Hosea's words condemn their hypocrisy and ours when we think that through mere attendance at worship we will automatically find God. Hosea calls us to know God just as God knows us. This knowledge involves a life lived in an intimate covenantal relation with the divine.

76. Alice Walker, *The Color Purple* (New York: Pocket Books, 1982) 199-201.

HOSEA 5:8–8:14, A POLITICS OF SELF-DESTRUCTION

OVERVIEW

Hosea 5:8–8:14 is composed of five oracular units, interlinked through wordplays and resumptions: 5:8-14; 5:15–6:3; 6:4-11; 7:1-16; and 8:1-14. They deal primarily with the internal and external politics of the northern kingdom, although interwoven with theological themes of repentance, return, and restoration (5:15–6:3; 6:11–7:1). A focus on *covenant* (a theme heralded in 4:1-3) particularly distinguishes this political section. The covenantal God rends and strikes down, as well as heals and builds up (5:15–6:3). The covenanted people rebel against their God in their political escapades and continually disobey God's *torah* (6:4-11; 8:1-14).

While the oracles seem to refer to specific historical events, the actual events are very difficult to pinpoint. Many scholars follow Alt's thesis that 5:8–6:6 reflects the time of the Syro-Ephraimite war (c. 735–733 BCE), when the Israelite king Pekah forged an alliance with Syria to repel Assyrian encroachments. Together they attack Judah, which had refused to join their alliance.[77] To explain Hos 5:10, Alt speculated that Judah had invaded Israel at some time during this war. But Alt had to emend the text considerably and conjecture events beyond those recorded in the account of the war in 2 Kings 16, in order to arrive at this interpretation. Moreover, the detail about Ephraim's sending a tribute to Assyria in 5:13 could just as well refer to Menachem's payment to Assyria, prior to the Syro-Ephraimite war (c. 745–736 BCE).

77. Albrecht Alt, "Hosea 5:8–6:6. Ein Krieg und seine Folgen in prophetischer Beleuchtung," *Kleine Schriften zur Geschichte des Volkes Israel II* (München: Beck, 1953) 163-87.

Hosea 5:8-14, Rending Ephraim and Judah

NIV

8"Sound the trumpet in Gibeah,
   the horn in Ramah.
Raise the battle cry in Beth Aven[a];
   lead on, O Benjamin.
9Ephraim will be laid waste
   on the day of reckoning.
Among the tribes of Israel
   I proclaim what is certain.
10Judah's leaders are like those
   who move boundary stones.
I will pour out my wrath on them
   like a flood of water.
11Ephraim is oppressed,
   trampled in judgment,
   intent on pursuing idols.[b]
12I am like a moth to Ephraim,
   like rot to the people of Judah.

13"When Ephraim saw his sickness,
   and Judah his sores,
then Ephraim turned to Assyria,
   and sent to the great king for help.
But he is not able to cure you,
   not able to heal your sores.
14For I will be like a lion to Ephraim,
   like a great lion to Judah.
I will tear them to pieces and go away;
   I will carry them off, with no one to rescue
      them."

[a]8 Beth Aven means house of wickedness (a name for Bethel, which means house of God).   [b]11 The meaning of the Hebrew for this word is uncertain.

NRSV

8 Blow the horn in Gibeah,
   the trumpet in Ramah.
Sound the alarm at Beth-aven;
   look behind you, Benjamin!
9 Ephraim shall become a desolation
   in the day of punishment;
among the tribes of Israel
   I declare what is sure.
10 The princes of Judah have become
   like those who remove the landmark;
on them I will pour out
   my wrath like water.
11 Ephraim is oppressed, crushed in judgment,
   because he was determined to go after
      vanity.[a]
12 Therefore I am like maggots to Ephraim,
   and like rottenness to the house of Judah.
13 When Ephraim saw his sickness,
   and Judah his wound,
then Ephraim went to Assyria,
   and sent to the great king.[b]
But he is not able to cure you
   or heal your wound.
14 For I will be like a lion to Ephraim,
   and like a young lion to the house of Judah.
I myself will tear and go away;
   I will carry off, and no one shall rescue.

[a] Gk: Meaning of Heb uncertain   [b] Cn: Heb to a king who will contend

COMMENTARY

5:8. This verse begins with a command to sound the alarm in Gibeah, Ramah, and Bethel (here derisively called Beth-aven; cf. 4:15), Benjaminite cities in close proximity to each other. The MT literally states, "after you, Benjamin," which the NRSV interprets as "look behind you, Benjamin" and the NIV as "lead on, O Benjamin." The NRSV presumes Alt's conjecture that the enemy was Judah, attacking Benjamin from the south. This assault, however, is not recorded in the 2 Kings 16 account of the Syro-Ephraimite war. The NIV rendition of v. 8 is preferred when read in the light of Judg 5:14, where the phrase "after you, Benjamin" suggests that certain tribes followed Benjamin into battle.

5:9-10. Ephraim and Judah will share parallel fates. Ephraim will become a desolation on the day of God's punishment (v. 9). As a metonymy for the southern kingdom, the princes of Judah are "like those who remove the landmark" (v.

10*a*). Although scholars think this verse refers to Judah's literal annexation of Benjamin,[78] v. 10*a*, like vv. 12 and 14, is formulated as a simile. The princes of Judah are *like* those who remove the boundary marker. According to Deut 27:17, anyone who removes a boundary marker is cursed. Hence, Judah becomes accursed and, like Ephraim, will suffer God's wrath, poured out like water (v. 10*b*).

5:11. Verse 11*b* explains the judgment against Ephraim (v. 11*a*): He was determined to go after צו (*ṣāw*). One wishes that *ṣāw* could clarify the historical background of the oracle, but its meaning is very obscure. *Ṣāw* is interpreted as "idols" by the NIV and emended to שוא (*šāw'*), "vanity," by the NRSV. The NRSV is to be preferred, since the interpretation of *ṣāw* as "idols" is simply too conjectural.

5:12-13. While we may not be able to identify the historical referent of these verses exactly, the rhetoric of the unit clearly places God as the antagonist of Ephraim and Judah. What befalls them will be God's doing. The alarms resounding in v. 8 augur a bleak future for both north and south, as God exacts retribution. Two striking sets of similes cast God in an adversarial role against Ephraim and Judah. They are similar to curses that will afflict the people for their violation of covenant. On one hand, God is "like maggots to Ephraim, and like rottenness to the house of Judah." The NIV rendering of כעש (*kā'āš*) as "like a moth" does not fit the parallelism. The images conveyed in vv. 12-13 are of human disease, death, and decay, especially resulting from a disastrous battle (cf. Jer 30:12-14). This military image is in keeping with the tone set by the call to arms that begins this oracle. The vision of maggots crawling about in festering sores is more apt and frightening in this context than that of a moth. Terrifying lists of diseases and infirmities appear as covenantal curses in Deut 28:21-22, 27-29, 35, 59-61.

When Ephraim and Judah discover their sickness and wounds, they both send tribute to the "great king" of Assyria.[79] With respect to Israelite kings, v. 13 could refer to Menahem's tribute to Tiglath-pileser III, intended to forestall any Assyrian encroachments (c. 738 BCE; see 2 Kgs 15:19-20). It could also allude to the tribute that Hoshea, Israel's last king, paid to Shalmaneser (2 Kgs 17:3). With respect to Judean kings, the reference could point to Ahaz's appeal to Tiglath-pileser III to intervene in the Syro-Ephraimite war (2 Kgs 16:7). Whoever this king is, v. 13 proclaims that "he will not be able to cure you or heal you from your wound." This verse anticipates 6:1, which will assert that it is Yahweh who heals.

5:14. In the second set of similes, God likens the divine self to a lion that violently tears up the two kingdoms (v. 14). The image recalls the covenantal curse of harm inflicted by wild animals (Lev 26:22; Deut 32:24). According to Prov 30:30 the lion is the mightiest and most fearsome of all wild animals. Of the six words for "lion" in Hebrew, Hosea uses four and applies them solely to God: שחל (*šaḥal,* v. 14), כפיר (*kĕpîr,* v. 14), אריה (*'aryēh,* 11:10), and לביא (*lābî',* 13:8). The destruction that the lion wreaks upon the nation will be picked up and mitigated in the next oracle. The bleak words "no one shall rescue" recall the fate of the wife/Israel stripped naked, her private parts visible for all to see: "no one shall rescue her out of my hand" (2:10). (See Reflections at 5:15–6:3.)

---

78. James L. Mays, *Hosea: A Commentary,* OTL (Philadelphia: Westminster, 1969) 89; Douglas Stuart, *Hosea–Jonah,* WBC 31 (Waco, Tex.: Word, 1987) 104.

79. Although the text states that only "Ephraim went to Assyria, and sent to the great king," Ephraim and Judah are very closely paralleled in these verses.

Hosea 5:15–6:3, The Covenantal God Who Heals

NIV	NRSV

[15]"Then I will go back to my place
    until they admit their guilt.
And they will seek my face;
    in their misery they will earnestly seek me."
	[15] I will return again to my place
	    until they acknowledge their guilt and seek my face.
	In their distress they will beg my favor:

NIV

6

"Come, let us return to the LORD.
He has torn us to pieces
but he will heal us;
he has injured us
but he will bind up our wounds.
²After two days he will revive us;
on the third day he will restore us,
that we may live in his presence.
³Let us acknowledge the LORD;
let us press on to acknowledge him.
As surely as the sun rises,
he will appear;
he will come to us like the winter rains,
like the spring rains that water the earth."

NRSV

6

"Come, let us return to the LORD;
for it is he who has torn, and he will heal
us;
he has struck down, and he will bind us up.
² After two days he will revive us;
on the third day he will raise us up,
that we may live before him.
³ Let us know, let us press on to know the LORD;
his appearing is as sure as the dawn;
he will come to us like the showers,
like the spring rains that water the earth."

COMMENTARY

The optimism characterizing 5:15–6:3 seems incongruous with the surrounding negative judgments. Some scholars maintain that 6:1-3 represents a shallow and flawed repentance on the people's part, which God will reject in 6:4-6.[80] However, I suggest reading the Hosean text like a musical score whose notes are read both horizontally in a linear progression and vertically to create chords. Hosea 5:15–6:3 should be regarded with 10:12 and 11:10-11 as the first in a series of contrapuntal voices strategically arranged by a later redactor to prepare for the conclusion of the book. These voices may be original to the prophet Hosea, but their present position is clearly secondary, though consistent with the overall thrust of Hosea 4–11.[81]

The MT of 5:15a reads, "I will go [הלך hālak] and return [שוב šûb] to my place." The verb hālak picks up the hālak in 5:14 of the previous unit. Moreover, šûb will reappear in 6:1, where it will carry the sense of repentance. The intent of God's "going" (departure) is the people's contrition and "seeking" of God's face and favor (5:15b). We have encountered themes of God's withdrawal and the people's seeking before (2:9; 3:3-4; 5:6).

Hosea 6:1 summons the people to "Come

[hālak], let us return [šûb] to Yahweh," resuming and mitigating the threats in 5:13-14. God has torn them to pieces and struck them down (5:14; 6:1). Unlike the "great king," however, the chastising God is the only one who can heal them and bandage their wounds. As with Hosea 2, the period of chastisement when God rends the people is intended to motivate their repentance/return (šûb). This doctrine of correction is particularly characteristic of deuteronomistic and wisdom literature, in which the period of the Babylonian exile was regarded as a traumatic time when the people recognized their guilt and returned to God (cf. Deut 4:29-30; Job 5:17-18).

Scholars have singled out 6:1-3 for special study because of its implications for resurrection theology. Their interpretations can be classified as follows: (1) those who interpret 6:1-3 in the light of the rising from death to life celebrated in Canaanite fertility cults;[82] (2) those who regard the rising in these verses as healing from sickness;[83] (3) those who think that 6:1-3 evinces a doctrine of the resurrection of the body after

80. For example, W. R. Harper, *A Critical and Exegetical Commentary on Amos and Hosea,* ICC (Edinburgh: T. & T. Clark, 1979) 282-83.
81. See Yee, *Composition and Tradition,* 145-58.

82. For a bibliographical survey of the literature, see J. Wijngaards, "Death and Resurrection in Covenantal Context," *VT* 17 (1967) 227-28.
83. Ibid., 228-30; M. Barré, "New Light on the Interpretation of Hos 6,2," *VT* 28 (1978) 129-41, and "Bullutsa-Rabi's Hymn to Gula and Hosea 6:1-2," *Or* 50 (1981) 241-45.

death;[84] and (4) those who construe 6:1-3 as a covenantal resurrection.[85]

Within the context of the whole book, 5:8–8:14 in particular, the notion of covenantal resurrection or renewal is to be preferred. The vocabulary of healing articulates a hope for the renewal of God's covenant, a hope already seen in 2:18, 21-23. The reference to the third day can be understood in the light of Exod 19:11, 15, where it is the pivotal day on which God will establish the covenant with the people on Mt. Sinai. The notion of covenantal renewal is confirmed by 6:3a. The complaints against the people's lack of covenantal knowledge in 2:8; 4:1, 6; and 5:4 are tempered in 6:3a, when the people

are enjoined, "Let us know, let us press on to know the LORD." The opposing theme of covenantal transgression will characterize the next oracular unit, 6:4-11.

Hosea 6:1-3 is the first stage in a three-part movement from barrenness to fertility in chaps. 4–11. Balancing the two similes for God in 5:12, 14 are two similes of the covenantal God drawn from nature. God's appearance is as certain and reliable as the dawn that comes each morning. God comes to the people like the autumn and spring rains, which water the earth. The sun and the rains are necessary ingredients for fruitful agricultural seasons. In contrast to the drought that comes upon the land because of the nation's covenantal infidelity (4:3), the rains will give drink to a thirsty land.

84. Andersen and Freedman, *Hosea,* 420-21.
85. Wijngaards, "Death and Resurrection," 230-39.

REFLECTIONS

All religious language about God involves some sort of comparison with different facets of our limited experiences. In Hosea 1–3, we encountered a husband/wife metaphor expressing the God/Israel covenant. Metaphors like "God is a husband" or "God is a father" are often erroneously taken literally to mean that God is male.

However, with similes such as those in 5:12–6:3, it is easier to remember that religious language consists of tropes drawn from human experience. These tropes, moreover, represent aspects of God's character that are disturbing and strange to modern-day understanding. For example, according to 5:12, God is like maggots, rottenness. Our antiseptic and technological culture preserves us from encountering the horrifying manifestations of death and decay. Yet, maggots and rottenness were very much a part of ancient Israelite experience. Comparing the divine self to such appalling indicators of mortality, Hosea highlights both God's absolute authority over life and death and the scope of Yahweh's terrible judgment: God's very self will bring about Israel's destruction. The image of a rending lion captures the fury and brutality of this destruction (5:14-15a). Today, attacks by wild animals are very much under control. Not so in ancient Israel, which would have completely comprehended the Lord's threat behind the image of a lion, tearing up and carrying off prey to its lair.

Non-human tropes can also convey God's steadfastness, healing, and refreshment. God is as certain as the rising sun, as rejuvenating as the rains (6:3). The ancient Israelites living off the land as farmers, working in an arid, hostile climate, would have appreciated these images of God. Drawn from nature, they are gender-neutral and do not fall into the trap of literalism, as do those dealing with human interpersonal relationships.

Israel's book of Psalms is filled with such non-human tropes. As in Hos 6:3, God is the sun and the life-giving rains (Pss 72:6; 84:11), a shield (Pss 7:10; 18:2; 84:11; 115:9-11; 119:114; 144:2), a chosen portion and cup (Pss 16:5; 119:57), a rock (Pss 18:2, 31; 28:1; 31:2-3; 42:9; 62:2, 6-7; 71:3; 89:26; 144:1), a fortress (Pss 18:2; 31:2-3; 59:9, 16-17; 62:2, 6-7; 71:3; 144:2), and a refuge (Pss 18:2; 28:8; 31:2; 37:39; 46:1; 59:16; 61:3, 62:7-8). God is a light (Ps 27:1), a stronghold (Pss 27:1; 94:22; 144:2), a dwelling place (Ps 91:9), a hiding place

(Ps 119:114), a strong tower (Ps 61:3), a comforting shade (Ps 121:5), and a mother hen protecting its young (Pss 36:7; 57:1; 61:4; 91:4).

We know that God is not actually a rock, a fortress, or a mother hen. These non-human tropes remind us that our language about God is not literal but analogical, not exact or precise but figurative and imaginative. These images reveal the richness and diversity of the Hebrew Bible in describing the deity. They help to depict a God who is beyond words and cannot be exhausted by them. (See also Reflections at 6:4-11.)

Hosea 6:4-11, A People Who Transgress the Covenant

NIV

4 "What can I do with you, Ephraim?
　What can I do with you, Judah?
Your love is like the morning mist,
　like the early dew that disappears.
5 Therefore I cut you in pieces with my prophets,
　I killed you with the words of my mouth;
　my judgments flashed like lightning upon you.
6 For I desire mercy, not sacrifice,
　and acknowledgment of God rather than
　　burnt offerings.
7 Like Adam,[a] they have broken the covenant—
　they were unfaithful to me there.
8 Gilead is a city of wicked men,
　stained with footprints of blood.
9 As marauders lie in ambush for a man,
　so do bands of priests;
they murder on the road to Shechem,
　committing shameful crimes.
10 I have seen a horrible thing
　in the house of Israel.
There Ephraim is given to prostitution
　and Israel is defiled.
11 "Also for you, Judah,
　a harvest is appointed.

"Whenever I would restore the fortunes of my
　people,"

a7 Or As at Adam; or Like men

NRSV

4 What shall I do with you, O Ephraim?
　What shall I do with you, O Judah?
Your love is like a morning cloud,
　like the dew that goes away early.
5 Therefore I have hewn them by the prophets,
　I have killed them by the words of my
　　mouth,
　and my[a] judgment goes forth as the light.
6 For I desire steadfast love and not sacrifice,
　the knowledge of God rather than burnt
　　offerings.

7 But at[b] Adam they transgressed the covenant;
　there they dealt faithlessly with me.
8 Gilead is a city of evildoers,
　tracked with blood.
9 As robbers lie in wait[c] for someone,
　so the priests are banded together;[d]
they murder on the road to Shechem,
　they commit a monstrous crime.
10 In the house of Israel I have seen a horrible
　　thing;
　Ephraim's whoredom is there, Israel is defiled.

11 For you also, O Judah, a harvest is appointed.

When I would restore the fortunes of my
　people,

a Gk Syr: Heb your　b Cn: Heb like　c Cn: Meaning of Heb uncertain　d Syr: Heb are a company

COMMENTARY

6:4. Hosea 6:4-11 interprets the offenses described in 5:8-14 in the light of God's covenant. If 5:15–6:3 is bracketed as the first stage of the journey motif that wends its way through Hosea 4–11, the reference to Ephraim and Judah in this verse links up with the mention of Ephraim and Judah in 5:14. God wonders what to do with these two rebellious nations (cf. 11:8-9). The covenantal love (חסד *ḥesed*) of Ephraim and Judah is as fleeting as the morning fog and the dew, which vanish with sunrise. Utilizing similar imagery from nature, the secondary addition of 6:1-3 will contrast their transitory love with a God whose coming is as dependable as the morning dawn and whose presence is like the invigorating rains.

6:5. Several aspects of Israelite thought surround the striking image of God hewing the people by the prophets and slaying them by the words of God's mouth. The first is the notion of the creative/destructive word. In Gen 1:3, when God says, "Let there be light," light instantly appears. The spoken command and its desired result occur simultaneously. Words of blessing and curse were thought to take effect immediately as they were uttered (cf. Isa 55:11). Moreover, as spokespersons for the deity, the prophets strive to keep the people in a proper covenantal relationship with God. According to 2 Kgs 17:13-14, God warns Israel and Judah through the prophets to repent and keep the law (cf. Jer 35:15). When the people refuse to repent, God cuts them down. Similarly in this verse, the prophetic words to Ephraim and Judah, uttered in God's name, are not idle pronouncements. Just as light simultaneously appeared when God said, "Let there be light," so also God's judgment is like a light that goes forth (cf. v. 3). Hosea 12:10, 13 will return to the theme of the prophets as God's spokespersons and instruments of God's preservation and destruction.

6:6-7. Verse 6 stresses the reason for God's impending judgment. In contrast to the fleeting *ḥesed* of Ephraim and Judah (v. 4), God desires an authentic covenantal love and knowledge of the divine and rejects their meaningless sacrifices (cf. 5:6). It is not the sacrificial system that Hosea condemns, but the dishonesty of its worshipers, whose conduct blatantly contradicts the demands of God's covenant. Verse 7 expands upon the covenant theme, although its meaning is difficult. The NIV follows the MT of v. 7*a* by linking the people's present breach of covenant to the primordial transgression of the first man: "Like Adam, they have broken the covenant." However, because the adverb "there" in v. 7*b* requires a place name and vv. 8-9 focus on crimes committed at other locations, the NRSV emends the text to "at

Adam." According to Josh 3:16, Adam was a city on the Jordan River where the waters were stopped up to allow the Israelites to cross over with the ark on dry ground. Nevertheless, the specific covenantal infraction ostensibly committed at Adam eludes us.

As was pointed out in the discussion of 5:7, the semantic range of the verb בגד (*bāgad,* "to deal faithlessly") includes the wife's marital infidelity toward her husband. *Bāgad* reappears in v. 7*b* in a verbal parallel with the transgression of covenant in v. 7*a*. The sexual/covenantal metaphor alluded to here anticipates the theme of sexual outrages in vv. 9-10.

6:8. The trail of covenantal transgressions, which continues from the city of Adam to the city of Gilead and then on to the Shechem road (vv. 7-9), strikes a dissonant note with the journey back to God in repentance (5:15–6:3). Gilead is the name customarily applied to the Transjordan area. In this verse, however, Gilead is described as "a city of evildoers, tracked with blood." Gilead could be an abbreviation for certain cities in the region of Gilead—e.g., Jabesh-gilead or Ramoth-gilead. In any case, the image of Gilead "tracked with blood" implies a place where murder and anarchy are rampant.

6:9-10. Verse 9 castigates a gang of priests who, like highwaymen concealed in ambush, murder on the Shechem road (see also 4:4-10; 5:1 for accusations against priests). Hosea's precise reference here cannot be reconstructed with certainty.[86] A very ancient sanctuary with a history going back to the period of the ancestors (cf. Gen 12:6-7; 33:18-20), Shechem was the place where Joshua assembled the tribes before his death to renew their covenant with God (Joshua 24). By connecting the offense of murder with a holy place of worship and covenantal renewal, Hosea is perhaps emphasizing with devastating irony how the priesthood, which should guarantee proper worship, sins violently against God's covenant. The complaints against the priests seem to continue in 7:1-7, where the priests evidently encourage the deterioration of the court by debauchery.

86. Cf. Paul A. Kruger, "The Evildoer in Hosea 6:8-9," *JNSL* 17 (1991) 17-22, who argues that instead of reading the text as a historical event, Hos 6:8-9 should be seen as a stylized description of typical evildoers as they are illustrated in the book of Psalms.

Paralleling their crime of murder, the priests commit זמה (*zimmâ*), translated as "monstrous crime" (NRSV) and "shameful crimes" (NIV). When coupled with the verb "to commit," "to do" (עשה *ʿāśâ*), *zimmâ* describes sexual outrages (Judg 20:6; Ezek 16:43; 22:9; 23:48; cf. Lev 18:17; 19:29; 20:14). Just as we are unsure about the precise nature of the murderous crimes the priests commit, so we are also uncertain of their sexual wickedness. Was it rape, incest, adultery, or a combination of these or other sexual sins? The mention of these sexual iniquities leads into God's summary statement in v. 10, which recalls a similar declaration in 5:3: "In the house of Israel I have seen a horrible thing; Ephraim's promiscuity is there; Israel is defiled." The metaphor of the promiscuous wife is again evoked here to reiterate the covenantal infidelity of the nation and its political (5:8-14) and religious (6:9) leadership, a prominent theme of the oracles discussed so far.

6:11. The actual conclusion to Hosea 6 and the beginning of Hosea 7 are disputed. The MT connects the temporal clause "when I would restore the fortunes of my people," with this verse. The NIV and the NRSV, however, connect it with 7:1. With a number of scholars, I suggest that 6:11–7:1a is a later Judean commentary on the prophetic text, which would read: "For you also, O Judah, a harvest is appointed, when I would restore the fortunes of my people, when I would heal Israel."[87]

Harvest is an ambiguous OT image that is used negatively to denote judgment (Amos 8:1; Isa 18:5; Jer 51:33) and positively to embrace a sense of eschatological salvation (Deut 28:4; 30:9). The adverb "also" includes Judah in the destruction of the north and in the hope for a restored and healed nation. Use of the root "to return," "to restore" (שוב *šûb*) and the reference to healing recall similar motifs in 5:15–6:3. The reference to Ammi ("my people"), who is restored and healed, signals the parent/child motif and anticipates the full narrative on this metaphor in Hosea 11, where Ammi turns away from Yahweh and does not know that Yahweh heals them. Moreover, the image of the harvest picks up the agricultural theme and the movement from barrenness to fertility that begin in 6:3, continue in 10:12, and culminate in 14:1-8.

87. Gale A. Yee, *Composition and Tradition in the Book of Hosea: A Redaction Critical Investigation,* SBLDS 102 (Atlanta: Scholars Press, 1987) 178-79, 280-81.

REFLECTIONS

Hosea 5:15–6:6 is the OT lectionary reading for Year A, Proper 5 (Proper 10 for the Roman Catholic Church and the Anglican Church of Canada). This reading is closely connected with the Gospel reading, Matt 9:9-13, 18-26, where the Pharisees complain that Jesus eats with tax collectors and sinners. Jesus compares himself to a physician, who comes to heal the sick, not the healthy. The Gospel story then continues with the healing of the woman suffering from hemorrhages and of the synagogue leader's daughter.

Taken together, the OT and the Gospel readings foreground two necessary aspects in the healing process: repentance and faith. The Hosean reading emphasizes the soul that turns to God in repentance, recognizing its own sinfulness and need for salvation. Nevertheless, this repentance also implies faith, since the soul turns to God (and not to an idol) for its healing and restoration (Hos 6:1-3). The Gospel reading stresses the soul that approaches God in faith. Jesus says to the hemorrhaging woman, "Take heart, daughter; your faith has made you well" (Matt 9:22 NRSV). However, references to tax collectors and sinners and to Jesus as the physician seeking the sick (Matt 9:10-13) underscore the fact that repentance is also at the core of the healing process in the Gospel reading.

Although necessary for healing, true repentance and faith are not exhibited by Ephraim, Judah, and the Pharisees in these OT and NT texts and, therefore, they are condemned. Hosea implies that Ephraim's and Judah's sorrow and piety are insincere and their covenantal love as fleeting as the morning dew (Hos 6:4). God will, therefore, destroy them through the prophetic word. Their hypocrisy infects their sacrificial offerings, which are rejected by God as worthless. God desires steadfast love, not meaningless oblations (6:6). As portrayed by the evangelist, the Pharisees exhibit similar hypocritical attitudes when they deplore Jesus' fellowship with social outcasts (Matt 9:11). Jesus' rebuttal, "Those who are well have no need of a physician, but those who are sick," is very ironic. The Pharisees, ignorant of their own sickness and hypocrisy, are the very ones in need of healing. The tax collectors and sinners whom they censure are, in fact, much better off than the Pharisees are, since these "sinners" have repented of their failings and have acknowledged their need for healing.

Jesus quotes Hos 6:6 to the Pharisees, "Go and learn what this means, 'I desire mercy, not sacrifice.' " According to Matthew, the Pharisees, who are so devoted to the study of the law and the prophets, do not seem to understand them. Hosea's rejection of empty ritual and the divine longing for authentic covenantal devotion are themes that run throughout the prophetic tradition (see Amos 5:21-24; Isa 1:11, 14-15, 43:23-24; Jer 6:19-20; 7:21-23; Mic 6:6-8). This tradition insists that a ritual that does not celebrate a repentant and healed life is meaningless. By citing Hos 6:6, Jesus implies that if the Pharisees truly understood the prophetic tradition, they would not only support his own work among these social pariahs, but minister to them as well.

Hosea 7:1-16, Corruption at Court and Among the Nations

NIV

7 [1]"whenever I would heal Israel,
　the sins of Ephraim are exposed
and the crimes of Samaria revealed.
They practice deceit,
　thieves break into houses,
　bandits rob in the streets;
[2]but they do not realize
　that I remember all their evil deeds.
Their sins engulf them;
　they are always before me.

[3]"They delight the king with their wickedness,
　the princes with their lies.
[4]They are all adulterers,
　burning like an oven
whose fire the baker need not stir
　from the kneading of the dough till it rises.
[5]On the day of the festival of our king
　the princes become inflamed with wine,
　and he joins hands with the mockers.
[6]Their hearts are like an oven;
　they approach him with intrigue.
Their passion smolders all night;
　in the morning it blazes like a flaming fire.
[7]All of them are hot as an oven;
　they devour their rulers.
All their kings fall,
　and none of them calls on me.

[8]"Ephraim mixes with the nations;

NRSV

7 [1]when I would heal Israel,
　the corruption of Ephraim is revealed,
　and the wicked deeds of Samaria;
for they deal falsely,
　the thief breaks in,
　and the bandits raid outside.
[2] But they do not consider
　that I remember all their wickedness.
Now their deeds surround them,
　they are before my face.

[3] By their wickedness they make the king glad,
　and the officials by their treachery.
[4] They are all adulterers;
　they are like a heated oven,
whose baker does not need to stir the fire,
　from the kneading of the dough until it is
　leavened.
[5] On the day of our king the officials
　became sick with the heat of wine;
　he stretched out his hand with mockers.
[6] For they are kindled[a] like an oven, their heart
　burns within them;
　all night their anger smolders;
　in the morning it blazes like a flaming fire.
[7] All of them are hot as an oven,
　and they devour their rulers.
All their kings have fallen;

[a] Gk Syr: Heb brought near

NIV

Ephraim is a flat cake not turned over.
⁹Foreigners sap his strength,
but he does not realize it.
His hair is sprinkled with gray,
but he does not notice.
¹⁰Israel's arrogance testifies against him,
but despite all this
he does not return to the LORD his God
or search for him.

¹¹"Ephraim is like a dove,
easily deceived and senseless—
now calling to Egypt,
now turning to Assyria.
¹²When they go, I will throw my net over them;
I will pull them down like birds of the air.
When I hear them flocking together,
I will catch them.
¹³Woe to them,
because they have strayed from me!
Destruction to them,
because they have rebelled against me!
I long to redeem them
but they speak lies against me.
¹⁴They do not cry out to me from their hearts
but wail upon their beds.
They gather together*a* for grain and new wine
but turn away from me.
¹⁵I trained them and strengthened them,
but they plot evil against me.
¹⁶They do not turn to the Most High;
they are like a faulty bow.
Their leaders will fall by the sword
because of their insolent words.
For this they will be ridiculed
in the land of Egypt."

a14 Most Hebrew manuscripts; some Hebrew manuscripts and Septuagint *They slash themselves*

NRSV

none of them calls upon me.

⁸ Ephraim mixes himself with the peoples;
Ephraim is a cake not turned.
⁹ Foreigners devour his strength,
but he does not know it;
gray hairs are sprinkled upon him,
but he does not know it.
¹⁰ Israel's pride testifies against*a* him;
yet they do not return to the LORD their
God,
or seek him, for all this.

¹¹ Ephraim has become like a dove,
silly and without sense;
they call upon Egypt, they go to Assyria.
¹² As they go, I will cast my net over them;
I will bring them down like birds of the air;
I will discipline them according to the report
made to their assembly.*b*
¹³ Woe to them, for they have strayed from me!
Destruction to them, for they have rebelled
against me!
I would redeem them,
but they speak lies against me.

¹⁴ They do not cry to me from the heart,
but they wail upon their beds;
they gash themselves for grain and wine;
they rebel against me.
¹⁵ It was I who trained and strengthened their
arms,
yet they plot evil against me.
¹⁶ They turn to that which does not profit;*c*
they have become like a defective bow;
their officials shall fall by the sword
because of the rage of their tongue.
So much for their babbling in the land of
Egypt.

a Or *humbles*   *b* Meaning of Heb uncertain   *c* Cn: Meaning of Heb uncertain

COMMENTARY

The fourth oracle of this section is very difficult to interpret on several levels. First, the MT is enigmatic and has been subject to much emenda-tion, as is evidenced by differences in the NIV and the NRSV. I will try to remain exegetically as close to the MT as possible. Second, historical events lying behind the chapter are difficult to reconstruct. The identity of the antagonists in the chapter is not certain. In the present context they seem to be the murderous gang of priests whom Hosea condemns in 6:9. The identities of the king of 7:3, 5 and of the mysterious baker in 7:4, 6 also remain conjectural. Third, sections of the oracle cluster around four metaphors: the hot oven (7:1-7), the cake (7:8-10), the silly dove (7:11-13), and the defective bow (7:14-16). We lack clarity about the rhetorical significance of the metaphors, however, particularly in their historical and cultural referents. For example, why is political scheming compared to a burning oven? Is the baker in 7:4, 6 an actual person involved in court intrigue, the leader of the gang of priests, as has been conjectured,[88] or is he used figuratively in the overall metaphor of the burning oven?

7:1-3. Bracketing 6:11 and the clause "whenever I would heal Israel" from 7:1 as later commentary, the first section begins: "The corruption of Ephraim is revealed,/ and the wicked deeds of Samaria." Several links exist between 7:1 and the previous oracle. Hosea 6:10 states that Yahweh *sees* Ephraim's crimes. According to 7:1, Ephraim's crimes *will be revealed.* Moreover, 7:1 connects with 6:8-9 in the repetition of פעל (*pāʿal,* "do") and גדוד (*gĕdûd,* "bandits"):

6:8	Gilead is a city of evildoers
	(פעלי און *pōʿălê ʾāwen*),
7:1	For they deal falsely
	כי פעלו שקר
	kî pāʿălû šāqer)
6:9	As robbers lie in wait for
	someone
	(וכחכי איש גדודים
	ûkĕḥakkê ʾîš gĕdûdîm),
7:1	And the bandits raid outside
	(פשט גדוד בחוץ
	pāšaṭ gĕdûd baḥûṣ)

These verbal ties suggest that the antagonists described in 7:1-10 are the corrupt group of priests of 6:8-9. Hosea describes their deeds three times as "wickedness"/"evil" (רעה/רע *raʿ*/*rāʿâ*) in 7:2-3, and 15 (cf. 7:1, "wicked deeds of Samaria").

These cult leaders are responsible for the moral deterioration of the royal court. By their instigation the king and his officials become intoxicated with wine, perhaps at a particular festival (7:3, 5). This palacewide state of drunkenness ostensibly prepares for an assassination attempt (7:6-7). The identity of both victims and conspirators is unknown; perhaps Hosea is describing the assassination of King Pekah (2 Kgs 15:30). The statement in 7:7*b*, "all their kings have fallen," may simply be a general summary of the series of *coups d'état* that plagued the north after the death of Jeroboam II (2 Kgs 15:8-31). The text remains obscure.[89]

7:4. The priests are described as adulterers who are like a heated oven. The use of the word "adultery" (root נאף *nʾp*) for the priests, rather than the customary "promiscuity" (זנה/זני *zny/znh*; cf. 4:4-10), creates a wordplay with "baker" (אפה *ʾōpeh*), a figure prominently associated with the oven metaphor. The oven apparently epitomizes the heat resulting from the inebriation (vv. 3, 5), sexual passion, political intrigue (vv. 6-7), or anger caused by the adulterous priests (cf. the emendation of the MT of v. 6 by the NIV and the NRSV). Since the activities of these priests do not appear to be overtly sexual, adultery seems to be a comprehensive trope for indicting and condemning the priests' political machinations.

It is difficult to determine the baker's role at this point, either as part of the oven metaphor or as a historical figure. His role has been glossed over or even eliminated by the NIV and the NRSV. According to both translations of v. 4, the baker does not need to stir (stoke) the fire of the oven. Fire, however, is not even mentioned in the MT of v. 4, which literally reads:

All of them are adulterers;
   like a blazing oven are they.
A baker[90] ceases stirring [or "to be alert"],
   from kneading the dough until it is leavened.

If the baker is not simply part of the metaphor, he could be one of the *dramatis personae* involved in the coup attempts. The stirring (עור *ʿwr*) would be parallel to the task of kneading the dough and would not refer to stoking the oven. More-

---

88. Francis I. Andersen and David Noel Freedman, *Hosea,* AB 24 (Garden City, N.Y.: Doubleday, 1980) 451.

89. See ibid., 447-54, for the different interpretive possibilities for this chapter.

90. Reading בער הם אפה (*bōʿēr hēm ʾōpeh*) for the MT בערה מאפה (*bōʿērâ mēʾōpeh*).

over, the usual meaning of '*wr* in the hiphil is "to rouse," "to wake up," "to be alert." If this is the sense of the reading, then the baker neglected his task of kneading the dough by dozing off.

7:5-6. The scenario is only marginally clarified by these verses. Possibly during a festival,[91] the company of priests somehow causes the royal court to become "sick with the heat of wine," perhaps a euphemism for "very drunk." The crucial detail in v. 5*b*, "He stretched out his hand with mockers," is problematic, because the point of the idiom and its subject are unclear. Perhaps offering more information about the baker, v. 6 literally reads:

When they [the priests] approached in their intrigue,
   like an oven was their heart.
All night their baker slept.
In the morning it [הוא *hû'*] blazed like a flaming fire.

The sleeping baker of v. 6 harmonizes with the description of the drowsy baker in v. 4. Apparently, the crucial role he plays in the conspiracy is sleeping on the job through the night, but how this affects the court or the schemers is uncertain. The NIV and the NRSV emend "their baker" (אפהם *'ōpēhem*) to "their anger/passion" (אפהם *'aphem*). The pronoun *hû'* would then refer to anger that bursts into flame by morning. Besides the problem of departing from the MT, however, the emendation stretches the usual meaning of the verb "to sleep" (ישן *yāšēn*) by reading it as "to smolder." What blazes in the morning is not "their anger," but the oven,[92] which metaphorically symbolizes the priests in their intrigue. This connection is confirmed by the wordplay between "their intrigue" (ארבם *'orbām*) and "blazes" (בער *bō'ēr*) in v. 6.

7:7. In an oblique reference to the assassinations of kings during Hosea's time, this verse describes the rulers as being consumed (אכל *'ākal*) in the conflagration of the plotters' oven. Although the identity of the main characters is difficult to determine and the exact nature of the political treachery perplexing, God clearly voices the ultimate transgression of the people: "None of them calls upon me." This theme of not seeking or calling upon Yahweh amid the disasters that befall the people will recur in vv. 10 and 14.

7:8-9. These verses signal a shift from internal to external politics, from the royal court to the international scene. The tenor of the metaphor switches from priestly conspirators to the politically rash Ephraim; its vehicle, from the oven to what is baked in the oven. Just as cooking ingredients are mixed together, Ephraim is accused of mixing with the nations.[93] Hosea probably refers here to the different political arrangements that the north makes with Syria, Assyria, and Egypt during his ministry. In these alliances, Ephraim is labeled metaphorically as "an unturned cake," one that is baked (or even burnt) on one side, but raw on the other. What Hosea means by this metaphor is not certain. Is Ephraim's foreign policy "half-baked"—i.e., not well thought out? In any case, such a cake is usually not eaten, but tossed out. According to v. 9*a*, however, the foreigners Ephraim mixes with eat away at his strength, as one nibbles a cake. Just as the ruling leaders of the nation are consumed (*'ākal*) by the nefarious schemes of the priests (v. 7), the nation itself is eaten away (*'ākal*) by aliens. The image of gray hairs (שיבה *śêbâ*) sprouting on Ephraim in v. 9*b* seems to depart from the cake metaphor. Usually, a hoary head is valued in the OT (Lev 19:32; Prov 16:31; 20:29). In v. 9*b*, however, gray hair seems to refer to the frailty or loss of strength that comes with age. The cake metaphor can be preserved by understanding *śêbâ* in the light of the Akkadian *šîbu* "mold" (lit., "white hairs," referring to a mold's hairy filaments). Ephraim would thus be like a cake that is not only chomped on by greedy mouths, but also infested with mold.[94] The repetition in v. 9 of the phrase "he does not know it" highlights Ephraim's ignorance of his own deterioration.

7:10. In a summary statement reminiscent of 5:4-6 and its familiar themes, this verse points out that Israel's own pride will testify against him. His arrogance prevents him from repenting and returning to God and seeking God in his foreign affairs.

---

91. Lit., "day of our king" in v. 5*a*. The NIV eliminates the ambiguity by inserting the reference to a "festival."

92. *Bō'ēr*, "to blaze," also describes the oven in 7:4. Moreover, 7:7 describes a "hot" oven.

93. Cf. Num 28:5, 9; Lev 2:4-5 for the culinary use of the verb בלל (*bll*) in the qal.

94. Shalom M. Paul, "The Image of the Oven and the Cake in Hosea VII 4-10," *VT* 18 (1968) 119-20.

7:11-13. The third metaphor in this section compares Ephraim to a silly, senseless dove, fluttering back and forth in its mercurial foreign policy with Egypt and Assyria (v. 11). According to v. 12a, doves are so gullible that they are easily trapped. God appears as a cosmic fowler, throwing a net and pulling Ephraim down, like a bird caught in flight. The NRSV rendering of v. 12b is closer to the MT and is preferred over the NIV, which emends יסר (yāsar, "to chastise," "to discipline") to some form of אסר ('āsar, "to catch," "to imprison," "to fetter"). Although the NIV emendation preserves the entrapped bird metaphor, the literal sense of the NRSV does have meaning in the light of the rest of the book. We have already seen that in Hosea, God's chastisement (מוסר mûsār) has a pedagogical intent to bring about the people's repentance (Hosea 2–3; 5:2; 5:15–6:3). Since the people do not repent and seek God (v. 10), God must now discipline them. Ephraim is compared to a foolish bird that has strayed from its nest and must suffer the consequences (cf. Prov 27:8; Isa 16:2). This image will be reversed by 11:11, which describes people as trembling birds coming from east and west to be returned to their homes by Yahweh.

7:14-16. Verse 14 reiterates the nation's major infraction: They do not cry out to God from their heart (cf. v. 7). Nevertheless, the rest of the verse is difficult. Exegetes often interpret the detail "they wail upon their beds" in the light of their notion of a sexually charged fertility cult. Similarly, they emend the MT's יתגוררו (yitgôrārû, "they become foreigners/sojourners"; cf. NIV) to יתגודדו (yitgôdādû, "they cut themselves"; cf. NRSV). In 1 Kgs 18:28 the same word is used to describe Baal worshipers gashing themselves to compel their god to send fire upon their sacrifice. The misreading could be due to the similarity of the Hebrew letters ר (r) and ד (d). However, this cultic interpretation clashes with the remaining verses, which expand on the final controlling metaphor of this oracle: the defective bow (v. 16). Ephraim's major offenses in this oracle are his political and military involvement with the nations

and neglect of Yahweh. Instead of crying out to God, he turns away (יסורו yāsûrû) from the deity.[95] By flitting from one foreign power to another (v. 11), Ephraim becomes a foreigner or an alien himself in order to procure his grain and wine (v. 14). Reinforcing the military/political imagery in a word-play on יסורו בי (yāsûrû bî, "they turn away from me," v. 14), Yahweh emphatically insists, "But it was *I* who trained [יסרתי yissartî] and strengthened their arms [military might]." *Yissartî*, "I chastised/trained/disciplined," picks up the *mûsār* theology of v. 12b, "I will discipline them according to the report made to their assembly" (NRSV).

Instead of turning to God (שׁוב šûb, v. 10), the people turn (šûb) to לא על (lō ' 'āl), literally, "Not Most High" (v. 16; cf. NIV). The name "Not Most High" parodies the *impotence* of the deity to whom the people turn as they reject Yahweh. Although Yahweh strengthens their might, the people wander after a powerless god. Since this god can do nothing for them, "they have become like a defective bow"—i.e., a bow that has lost it power. Because of their military weaknesses, the leaders will "fall by the sword."

The difficulty of v. 16b, the concluding detail of this oracle and section, is reflected in the translations. The officials fall by the sword because of the "זעם [za'am] of their tongue." *Za'am* usually refers to God's indignation or wrath (Isa 13:5; Jer 10:10; cf. NRSV, "rage of their tongue"). However, the content of these angry words and their target are not clear. The parallelism with "their derision/ridicule" (לעגם la'gām) prompts some to translate za'am as "insolent (tongue)" (cf. NIV). The people's and the leaders' rejection of God will result in their defeat, exile, and ridicule in the land of Egypt, the site of their first enslavement.[96] Verse 16b anticipates later passages that describe God bringing Israel out of Egypt in a new exodus (Hosea 11; 12:9, 13; 13:4-5). (See Reflections at 8:1-14.)

---

95. The NRSV departs from the MT by reading יסרו (yāsōrû, "they rebelled").

96. See Jer 44:12, which has a number of parallels with Hos 7:14-16

Hosea 8:1-14, King, Calf, Cult, and the Covenant

NIV

8 "Put the trumpet to your lips!
An eagle is over the house of the LORD
because the people have broken my covenant
and rebelled against my law.
[2]Israel cries out to me,
'O our God, we acknowledge you!'
[3]But Israel has rejected what is good;
an enemy will pursue him.
[4]They set up kings without my consent;
they choose princes without my approval.
With their silver and gold
they make idols for themselves
to their own destruction.
[5]Throw out your calf-idol, O Samaria!
My anger burns against them.
How long will they be incapable of purity?
[6] They are from Israel!
This calf—a craftsman has made it;
it is not God.
It will be broken in pieces,
that calf of Samaria.

[7]"They sow the wind
and reap the whirlwind.
The stalk has no head;
it will produce no flour.
Were it to yield grain,
foreigners would swallow it up.
[8]Israel is swallowed up;
now she is among the nations
like a worthless thing.
[9]For they have gone up to Assyria
like a wild donkey wandering alone.
Ephraim has sold herself to lovers.
[10]Although they have sold themselves among the
nations,
I will now gather them together.
They will begin to waste away
under the oppression of the mighty king.

[11]"Though Ephraim built many altars for sin
offerings,
these have become altars for sinning.
[12]I wrote for them the many things of my law,
but they regarded them as something alien.
[13]They offer sacrifices given to me
and they eat the meat,

NRSV

8 Set the trumpet to your lips!
One like a vulture[a] is over the house of
the LORD,
because they have broken my covenant,
and transgressed my law.
[2] Israel cries to me,
"My God, we—Israel—know you!"
[3] Israel has spurned the good;
the enemy shall pursue him.

[4] They made kings, but not through me;
they set up princes, but without my
knowledge.
With their silver and gold they made idols
for their own destruction.
[5] Your calf is rejected, O Samaria.
My anger burns against them.
How long will they be incapable of innocence?
[6] For it is from Israel,
an artisan made it;
it is not God.
The calf of Samaria
shall be broken to pieces.[b]

[7] For they sow the wind,
and they shall reap the whirlwind.
The standing grain has no heads,
it shall yield no meal;
if it were to yield,
foreigners would devour it.
[8] Israel is swallowed up;
now they are among the nations
as a useless vessel.
[9] For they have gone up to Assyria,
a wild ass wandering alone;
Ephraim has bargained for lovers.
[10] Though they bargain with the nations,
I will now gather them up.
They shall soon writhe
under the burden of kings and princes.

[11] When Ephraim multiplied altars to expiate sin,
they became to him altars for sinning.
[12] Though I write for him the multitude of my
instructions,

[a] Meaning of Heb uncertain   [b] Or *shall go up in flames*

259

NIV

but the LORD is not pleased with them.
Now he will remember their wickedness
and punish their sins:
They will return to Egypt.
14Israel has forgotten his Maker
and built palaces;
Judah has fortified many towns.
But I will send fire upon their cities
that will consume their fortresses."

NRSV

they are regarded as a strange thing.
13 Though they offer choice sacrifices,[a]
though they eat flesh,
the LORD does not accept them.
Now he will remember their iniquity,
and punish their sins;
they shall return to Egypt.
14 Israel has forgotten his Maker,
and built palaces;
and Judah has multiplied fortified cities;
but I will send a fire upon his cities,
and it shall devour his strongholds.

[a] Cn: Meaning of Heb uncertain

COMMENTARY

8:1-2. Hosea 8:1-14 comprises the fifth and final oracle of the 5:8–8:14 complex. Like 5:8 in the first oracle, 8:1a begins with a command to sound the trumpet at the enemy's approach. The order is accompanied by an ominous description of a great bird over the "house of the LORD," or the sanctuary at Bethel (cf. 4:15; 10:5-6). The NIV's "eagle" and the NRSV's "vulture" connote two separate but not mutually exclusive images. On the one hand, OT references to eagles foreground their strength and speed in swooping down to capture prey (Job 9:26; cf. 2 Sam 1:23). They are often used to describe the enemy that descends upon the people (Jer 48:40; 49:22; Hab 1:8). On the other hand, the hovering vulture conjures up chilling images of scavengers waiting to feast on carrion at battle's end (cf. Prov 30:17).

The people's lack of "knowledge" indicates a broken covenant (2:8; 4:1, 6; 5:4; cf. 6:3). This lack is most evident in their overly confident and insincere declaration: "My God, we—Israel—know you!" (v. 2). Hence, v. 1b summarizes the entire 5:8–8:14 complex by declaring the reason for the enemy's impending approach and Israel's subsequent devastation: They have broken the covenant and transgressed the law (תורה *tôrâ*).

8:3-6. While 6:8–7:16 highlights the conspiracies of cultic priests in the political affairs at court, 8:1-14 underscores the entanglement of kings and princes in the cult. In a nation governed by God's covenant, the domains of religion and politics converge in very real ways. Covenantal infractions in one sphere dramatically affect the other. The illegitimacy of royal leadership is closely linked with its forging from silver and gold the idolatrous "calf of Samaria" (8:4-5). The allusion here is probably to King Jeroboam I's installation of the golden calves at the sanctuaries of Dan and Bethel, which, according to the deuteronomist, was *the sin* leading to Israel's destruction (1 Kgs 12:25–13:34; 2 Kgs 17:14-23).

The MT of v. 5 is difficult. Literally, the verse reads: "He will reject your calf, Samaria." Presumably, the "he" is Yahweh, although God seems to speak in the next sentence: "*My* anger burns against them." The NRSV repoints the MT to read in the passive, "Your calf is rejected," while the NIV repoints to read the imperative, "Throw out your calf-idol." The NRSV is to be preferred, since it balances v. 3. Because Israel has rejected the good, God will reject its cultic symbol, the calf.

A Hebrew wordplay, exploiting the semantic range of the verb "to make" (עשה *ʿāśâ*), underscores the foolishness of Israel, who *makes* useless idols for himself (v. 4) and forgets his own *Maker* (v. 14). Hosea sarcastically points out that a mere artisan *has made* the calf (v. 6). Like all idols, "it is not God," a statement precisely reversing Jeroboam I's declaration to the people when he first erected the calves: "Behold your gods, O Israel, who brought you out of the land of Egypt" (1 Kgs 12:28). Significantly, v. 13 prophesies Israel's return to Egypt because of its unlawful cult. The mocking appellation "Not God" in v. 6

correlates with "Not Most High" in 7:16. While the title "Not Most High" highlights an idol's impotence, "Not God" emphasizes its human manufacture. As a mere object, the calf "shall be broken to pieces."

8:7. To dramatize the hopelessness of the leaders' actions, this verse embarks on a chain of negative logic,[97] punctuated in Hebrew by numerous plays on words. Reading "wind" and "whirlwind" as adverbs instead of as objects, it becomes clear that sowing seeds when it is windy is an exercise in futility. Yet, even if the seeds, which could not be sown in the first place, were to produce grain, this grain could not be reaped because of the whirlwind. Even if the grain that could not be sown were to germinate, it would not put out shoots (NRSV and NIV, "no heads"). And even if this grain put forth shoots against all odds, the shoots would not produce flour. And even if this flour were milled, it would not be baked into cakes. But even if cakes were baked, foreigners would swallow them up (cf. 7:8-9).

The use of "foreigners" (זרים *zārîm*) at the end of v. 7 plays upon "they sow" (יזרעו *yizrā'û*) at the beginning of the verse, thereby tightly connecting the whole. The negative logic of v. 7 anticipates and vividly contrasts the positive declarations in 10:12. The fruit*less*ness of v. 7 opposes the fruit*ful*ness of 10:12, which results from the sowing of righteousness and the reaping of steadfast love.

8:8-10. Verses 8-9 continue the theme of unwise political alliances from the previous oracle by linking the cakes that the foreigners will devour (v. 7) with the devouring of the half-baked cake, Israel/Ephraim, by foreigners (7:8-9). The metaphor shifts from the senseless dove flying to Assyria (7:11) to a wild ass going up to Assyria (v. 9). The Hebrew for "wild ass" (פרא *pere'*) plays upon the consonants in the name "Ephraim" (אפרים *'eprayim*). According to Jer 2:24, the wild ass is characterized by an unbridled sexuality: "In her heat sniffing the wind! Who can restrain her lust?" Verses 9-10 thus depict Ephraim as hiring lovers among the nations. While Hosea 2 epitomizes the wife's lovers as the religious בעלים

(*bĕ'ālîm*), vv. 9-10 enlarge the sexual trope to include foreign nations among Ephraim's lovers. The tribute that his king and princes offer these nations is like the fee a man negotiates with a prostitute (cf. 5:13).[98] Nevertheless, this tribute will become the very weight that oppresses them (v. 10).[99]

8:11-14. In vv. 11-12 the subject shifts from the political treaties and tributes of Israelite royals to concerns about their unlawful cult. But whereas vv. 4-6 focused on the calf of Samaria, vv. 11-13 highlight through clever wordplays in Hebrew the nation's altars and sacrifices. The more Ephraim increased his altars, which were intended for offerings to expiate sin (לחטא *laḥăṭō'*), the more they became the very sites for committing sin (*laḥăṭō'*)! As with vv. 4-5, vv. 11-13 also allude to the iniquitous cult that Jeroboam I established in the north. After installing the calves at Bethel and Dan, he set up worship sites in the various high places and appointed priests to oversee them (1 Kgs 12:31-33).

Continuing the wordplays, God laments that, although Ephraim multiplies (הרבה *hirbâ*) his altars, he ignores the multitudes (רבו *rubbĕw* =*qĕrē'*) of God's תורה (*tôrâ*). The sites for the nation's worship become the places for transgressing God's covenant and law (cf. v. 1). Although Ephraim makes covenants with foreigners (זרים *zārîm*), his own covenant with God is regarded as a foreign or strange thing (זר *zār*, v. 12). Although the theme of God's rejection of Israel's cult has appeared before (4:11-19; 5:6; 6:6), vv. 1-13 articulate the reason for this rejection most explicitly. The sacrificial system does not serve its purpose—i.e., to maintain and preserve the covenant between God and the people. Rather, the system itself becomes the source of their alienation. Moreover, the interweaving of the crimes of priests and kings in Hosea 7–8 reveals that religion and politics are inseparable. Infractions in either domain constitute breaches in covenant and are symbolized by Hosea as sexual promiscuity.

After indicting the nation for its sins, Yahweh announces judgment: "they shall return to Egypt"

---

97. Technically known as "pseudo-sorites." See M. O'Connor, "The Pseudo-Sorites in Hebrew Verse," in *Perspectives on Language and Text: Essays and Poems in Honor of F. I. Andersen's Sixtieth Birthday,* E. W. Conrad and E. W. Newing, eds. (Winona Lake, Ind.: Eisenbrauns, 1987) 244-46.

98. The NRSV is closer to MT in 8:9-10 than is the NIV. The verb יתנו/התנו (*yitnû/hitnû,* "they hire[d])," with the participle "lovers" אהבים *'ăhābîm*) is usually associated with the noun אתנה (*'etnâ*) or אתנן (*'etnān*), "a prostitute's wages" (cf. Hos 2:14; 9:1).

99. The MT of 8:10, followed by the NIV, reads "they will begin." The NRSV repoints the MT to read "they shall writhe" and is to be preferred.

(v. 13). A similar threat appeared in the preceding oracle (7:16). Egypt was the place of the nation's enslavement before Yahweh's liberation of and covenant with Israel. Thus Israel will revert to its former time of misery and affliction before God chose it. Just as the wife/Israel forgot her husband (2:13), so also the nation of Israel forgot its Maker by fashioning idols and making treaties (v. 14). Yahweh will destroy it, in spite of its many fortified cities and strongholds.

REFLECTIONS

1. Hosea uses several terrifying metaphors to describe God's angry retribution against the people. God is like maggots and putrefaction in an open sore (5:12), like a lion that rips and tears at the people (5:14), and like a fowler who traps the birds of the air (7:12). God kills by the very utterance of the divine mouth (6:5). These metaphors present God's punishment as just, because the people have indeed sinned. God would have spared them this chastisement, but "they speak lies against me" (7:13 NRSV). Retribution is inevitable.

Nevertheless, these metaphors make one reflect deeply on God's just retribution and the problem of innocent suffering in our lives. This reflection is as ancient as Job. We often meet people in our ministries and everyday lives who, faced with a terrible tragedy, automatically wonder what wrongs they have committed to prompt God to send them such calamity. A post-Holocaust reading of these texts inquires whether God truly is the source of all suffering. It challenges the prevailing notion that suffering is always God's punishment for sin. Indeed, one response to the Holocaust, during which millions of innocent Jews died in Nazi concentration camps, is to proclaim that there is no God. The frightening alternative is a God who does not care.

A fine line exists between seeing God as one who punishes us for our sins and as one who is the source of all suffering. In popular belief, the latter notion is often conflated with the former. Regarding God as the source of suffering prevents us from grasping an all-important truth that Hosea insists upon: God alone is the source of consolation and healing. Ephraim and Judah sought cures for their illnesses in earthly powers, which proved ineffective (5:13). Only God can heal and bind up wounds. Only God can revive and raise one up (6:1-3). Only God can restore one's prosperity (6:11).

Hosea summons us to a deeper meditation upon the healing and transforming God. He urges us to "press on to know the Lord," not only intellectually with our minds but also existentially in our hearts. Through our day-to-day living, and especially in our moments of suffering, we come to know God as the one who heals and consoles, refreshes and sustains.

2. At different points in this set of oracles, Hosea talks of the nation's sickness and healing (5:12-13; 6:1-3; 6:11–7:1). Although he seems to refer to the bloody wounds resulting from wild animal attacks, sickness can occur at several levels. One can become sick from a virus infecting the body, which succumbs to raging fevers. A person can be mentally ill, with a sickness that is not obvious on one's body, but quite apparent in one's behavior. One can experience a spiritual malaise in which life itself seems meaningless and without hope.

Moreover, sickness is not only an individual, but also a collective affair. For Hosea, sickness affects the whole nation (5:13; 7:1). A nation can be ravaged by war, its women raped, and its people brutalized (cf. 7:16; 8:14). Sickness is apparent in the crime on our streets, where youngsters carry guns for their own protection. Sickness is evinced in the dysfunction and breakup of our families, in domestic and sexual violence, where children are beaten or molested by those who should care for them. Sickness is found in the racism of our society and intolerance and fear of differences. . . . The list goes on.

If sickness occurs at many levels, so too does the healing process. Hosea points out the people's lack of knowledge in several places in this section (7:9; 8:1; cf. 4:1, 6; 5:4). The community neither recognizes its own illness nor remembers the sole source of its cure (7:9-10). The first step in the healing process, then, is recognizing disorder and malady. It is difficult to take this first step. It demands that we become aware of our own sins and accountable for them. So much in our irreligious society prevents us from taking the first step, by deflecting our sinful acts and moral sickness upon something or someone else in a politics of blame—our parents, our home life, our lack of money and resources, etc. There comes a point, however, when we must own up to the sins we have committed and take responsibility for our behavior.

The next level in the healing process is to recognize that only God is the source of all healing. Israel did not know that only God could cure them of their ills. When they discovered their sickness, they "sent to the great king" (5:13 NIV and NRSV) instead, just as we today throw ourselves into material goods, drugs, hedonistic life-styles, and spiritual fads in the hope of becoming well again. Yet, the satisfaction we derive from these various attempts is as fleeting as "the morning dew" (6:4 NIV and NRSV).

Another name for the authentic turning away from sin and turning to God is conversion. At the heart of conversion lies the personal decision to turn to God and reform one's life. It does not reside in external signs of "repentance"—empty sacrifices, burnt offerings, and rituals—which God rejects (6:6; 8:13). These ceremonies are useless unless sin is repudiated and the human heart transformed in the steadfast love and knowledge of God. "Come, let us return to the LORD" (6:1 NRSV).

3. The founders of the United States constitutionally separated the affairs of church from the affairs of state. Nevertheless, Hosea 7–8 provocatively challenge whether this separation is possible in reality. In chap. 7, Hosea lambastes a company of priests who infect the royal court through political intrigue, causing the downfall of kings (7:7, 16) and nation (7:9, 16). In chap. 8, Hosea condemns the idolatrous cult installed by Israel's royal leadership: the molten calf, the numerous altars, and the choice sacrificial offerings. None of these priestly and kingly transgressions, however, is concealed from God: Their wicked deeds "are before my face" (7:2). God will remember their iniquity and punish them for their sins (7:2, 13; 8:13). Hosea vividly depicts the fury of God's punishment. God will pull them down, like a fowler casting a net over a flock of birds (7:12). God will send down fire upon their cities, to devour their fortresses (8:14).

The harshness of Hosea's oracles originates in his profound belief that, along with cultic leadership, political rule falls under God's jurisdiction. Both receive their power and authority from God; both are held accountable to God for the nation's health or deterioration. For Hosea, the people's gravest crime is ignoring the source of their power and rule and seeking their own will. Their own pride convicts them (7:10).

Instead of relegating religion to the individual and otherworldly, these chapters insist that our relationship with God is grounded in the social and the political. God will hold us responsible for living according to the demands of the covenant in these earthly spheres. Through violent images, Hosea reminds us of the consequences of not seeking God. But behind these images is Hosea's alternate vision of a community that actually repents and seeks God—a community that has abolished war and now sleeps secure (2:17; 14:3), has mercy on orphans (14:3), establishes economic fairness and justice (cf. 12:7-8), flourishes as a lush garden and blossoms like the vine (14:7). Hosea insists that our religious beliefs and values can become powerful agents in transforming society for the common good.

HOSEA 9:1–11:11, A PEOPLE'S HISTORY OF INFIDELITY

OVERVIEW

Chapters 9:1–11:11 comprise the third and final complex of oracles contained in Hosea 4–11, concluding the second section of the book with the standard formula for a divine utterance: "a saying of Yahweh." It traces the covenantal transgressions of the Israelite people to their insidious past. If the catchword "Like people, like priest" (4:9) typified the nation in the first complex (4:1–5:7), "Like past, like present" fits this network of sayings.

Hosea 9:1-6 situates these oracles at the autumnal feast of Sukkot (Ingathering or Tabernacles). Although Sukkot celebrates the land's fertility, Hosea prophesies the nation's approaching desolation and barrenness (9:2, 11-12, 14-17; 10:2, 4b, 8, 14; 11:5-6). Sukkot also commemorates the wilderness period after Israel's dramatic flight from Egypt (Lev 23:42-43). It is quite significant, therefore, that Hosea highlights the wilderness period as a positive time of God's care and support of the people (9:10a, 13a; 10:1a; 11:1, 3-4; cf. 2:14-15; 12:9). He radically juxtaposes God's gracious election in the wilderness with the people's iniquity when they settled in Canaan (9:10b, 13b; 10:1b; 11:2). He particularly singles out the "days of Gibeah" (9:9; 10:9), Peor (9:10), Gilgal (9:15), and the settlement period (10:1) as historical markers of the people's sin.

Although most of these sayings focus on judgment and condemnation, themes of exhortation and hope also appear in this complex. Calling the people to "sow for yourselves righteousness" and "seek the Lord," Hos 10:12 becomes the second stage in the journey from barrenness to fertility that began in 6:1-3. The theme of the son Ammi, which begins the Hosea 4–11 section in chap. 4, concludes it in chap. 11. Although God loved the son Ammi, called him out of Egypt, and cared for him in the wilderness, Ammi kept turning to the baals (11:1-2). Nevertheless, God the parent refuses to destroy the rebellious son (11:8-9). In the final stage of their journey (11:10-11), God returns the repentant sons of Israel to their homes. Hosea 11:10-11 parallels 2:23, where God sows the wife/Israel like a seed in the land. Hosea 14:5-7 will later describe Israel's blossoming forth in the land as a luxurious plantation.

Hosea 9:1-6, A Festival of Fools

NIV	NRSV

9 Do not rejoice, O Israel;
    do not be jubilant like the other nations.
For you have been unfaithful to your God;
    you love the wages of a prostitute
    at every threshing floor.
²Threshing floors and winepresses will not feed
      the people;
    the new wine will fail them.
³They will not remain in the Lord's land;
    Ephraim will return to Egypt
    and eat unclean^a food in Assyria.
⁴They will not pour out wine offerings to the Lord,
	9 Do not rejoice, O Israel!
	    Do not exult^a as other nations do;
	for you have played the whore, departing from
	      your God.
	You have loved a prostitute's pay
	    on all threshing floors.
	² Threshing floor and wine vat shall not feed
	      them,
	    and the new wine shall fail them.
	³ They shall not remain in the land of the Lord;
	    but Ephraim shall return to Egypt,
	    and in Assyria they shall eat unclean food.

ª3 That is, ceremonially unclean	ª Gk: Heb *To exultation*

NIV

nor will their sacrifices please him.
Such sacrifices will be to them like the bread of
mourners;
all who eat them will be unclean.
This food will be for themselves;
it will not come into the temple of the LORD.

5What will you do on the day of your appointed
feasts,
on the festival days of the LORD?
6Even if they escape from destruction,
Egypt will gather them,
and Memphis will bury them.
Their treasures of silver will be taken over by
briers,
and thorns will overrun their tents.

NRSV

4 They shall not pour drink offerings of wine to
the LORD,
and their sacrifices shall not please him.
Such sacrifices shall be like mourners' bread;
all who eat of it shall be defiled;
for their bread shall be for their hunger only;
it shall not come to the house of the LORD.

5 What will you do on the day of appointed
festival,
and on the day of the festival of the LORD?
6 For even if they escape destruction,
Egypt shall gather them,
Memphis shall bury them.
Nettles shall possess their precious things of
silver;[a]
thorns shall be in their tents.

[a] Meaning of Heb uncertain

COMMENTARY

We have already seen allusions in Hosea 8 to the calf cult that Jeroboam I established at Bethel. He also instituted a celebration of Sukkot at Bethel to compete with its rival in Jerusalem (1 Kgs 12:32). Scholars commonly agree that the setting of 9:1-6 is the fall festival of Sukkot. Called the "feast of Yahweh" (see Judg 21:19; Lev 23:39; cf. Hos 9:5), Sukkot was an agricultural celebration of the harvesting of grapes and olives that matured in the hot summer sun. It was a joyous occasion during which many imbibed the new wine fermented from recently pressed grapes.[100]

9:1-2. Amid the carousing Hosea proclaims, "Do not rejoice, O Israel!" In its revelry Israel is like the "other nations" (v. 1a), who attribute their harvest of plenty to their fertility gods. In the preceding chapter, Hosea described the foreign nations as Ephraim's lovers (8:9-10). In v. 1b, he returns to the fertility cult that he condemned in chaps. 2 and 4. Participation in this cult causes the nation to become "unfaithful to your God." The "prostitute's pay" for Israel's sexual favors are the products of the threshing floor, which she thinks her "lovers" provide (cf.

2:5, 12). Hosea, however, predicts the barrenness of her threshing floors and emptiness of her wine presses (v. 2; cf. 2:9).

9:3-4. Israel will not be able to call this barren, useless land "home." In a wordplay on ישב/שוב (šûb/yāšab) typical of the book (3:4-5; 11:5-11; 14:2-7), v. 3 declares, "They shall not remain [לא ישבו lō' yēšĕbû] in the land of the LORD;/ but Ephraim shall return [שב šāb] to Egypt." The nation's imminent exile to Assyria is symbolized as a return to Egypt, precisely reversing the exodus event of its salvation history. Israel will regress to the time before its halcyon days with Yahweh in the wilderness, to a time of utter enslavement and misery (cf. 7:16; 8:13).

As strangers exiled to a strange land, the people will eat its unclean food (v. 3b). Hence, their cult must cease, since unclean food is not fit for the worship of Yahweh (9:4; cf. Hos 2:11; Deut 26:14). Hosea compares their sacrifices in exile to "mourners' bread," food associated with a house that death has rendered unclean (cf. Num 19:11-16; Deut 26:14; Hag 2:12-13). Those who consume this bread become defiled. Unacceptable for God's cult, such food is useful only in satisfying one's hunger (v. 4).

100. Roland de Vaux, *Ancient Israel,* vol. 2: *Religious Institutions* (New York: McGraw-Hill, 1965) 495-506.

9:5-6. Thus Hosea's question to the gathered assembly in v. 5 is highly rhetorical: What will you do on God's feast day? Absolutely nothing! The debauched festivals that caused their exile will be ended in that exile. The joy and merriment of their feasts will be turned to sorrow and punishment at their deportation. Even if some from the festival assembly should escape exile by fleeing to Egypt, they will experience another type of gathering. Enlarging upon v. 3 in sinister fashion,

Hosea personifies Egypt as gathering the refugees for burial in Memphis's vast, well-known cemetery. Ironically, on the day when the nation celebrates the wilderness period after its liberation from Egypt, Hosea foretells of the nation's symbolic return to its former site of enslavement and death. The tents of the pilgrims gathered to celebrate will be taken over by prickly weeds. (See Reflections at 9:7-9.)

Hosea 9:7-9, The Prophet as Fool

NIV	NRSV
[7]The days of punishment are coming, / the days of reckoning are at hand. / Let Israel know this. / Because your sins are so many / and your hostility so great, / the prophet is considered a fool, / the inspired man a maniac. / [8]The prophet, along with my God, / is the watchman over Ephraim,[a] / yet snares await him on all his paths, / and hostility in the house of his God. / [9]They have sunk deep into corruption, / as in the days of Gibeah. / God will remember their wickedness / and punish them for their sins.	[7] The days of punishment have come, / the days of recompense have come; / Israel cries,[a] / "The prophet is a fool, / the man of the spirit is mad!" / Because of your great iniquity, / your hostility is great. / [8] The prophet is a sentinel for my God over Ephraim, / yet a fowler's snare is on all his ways, / and hostility in the house of his God. / [9] They have deeply corrupted themselves / as in the days of Gibeah; / he will remember their iniquity, / he will punish their sins.
[a]8 Or *The prophet is the watchman over Ephraim, / the people of my God*	[a] Cn Compare Gk: Heb *shall know*

COMMENTARY

The subject of the oracle changes in vv. 7-9 from God's message to the messenger delivering it. Hosea's threats of the coming days of punishment seem to evoke derisive comments from the festival assembly that interrupts his saying (v. 7). Even though the prophet's threat poetically encloses the mocking words in the text, the prophet himself was probably surrounded by a hostile audience when he actually addressed the revelers. Although v. 8 continues to speak about the prophet, the MT is difficult to decipher, for it begins enigmatically: "Ephraim is a sentinel [or lies in wait] with my God; a prophet is a fowler's

snare." Exactly how does Ephraim function as a sentinel with "my God"? Even more puzzling, in what way does he "lie in wait with my God"? With a minor placement of its accent marker under "prophet," MT would read more sensibly, "A prophet is a sentinel of Ephraim with my God" (cf. NIV and NRSV). Hosea reminds the people that the prophet they call a fool and a madman has a divinely appointed role as a sentinel to warn them about the harsh consequences of their own wickedness (Ezek 3:17-19; 33:7; cf. Hos 8:1).

Verse 8*b* is ambiguous. Does the pronoun "his" refer to the prophet or to Ephraim? Who is the trapper? Who is trapped? How does "his God" relate to "my God" in v. 8a? On one hand, 7:12 describes God as a cosmic fowler who casts a net over birds in flight. By extension, the prophet could be a "fowler's snare" in Ephraim's affairs. According to Jer 6:27, God tells Jeremiah: "I have made you a tester and a refiner among my people so that you may know and test their ways." On the other hand, the text could depict Ephraim as setting a trap for the prophet. Animosity against prophets is quite well documented (Jer 11:18-19; 18:18-23; 20:7-12; Matt 23:37). Supporting the second interpretation, in which Ephraim becomes the ensnarer of the prophet (cf. NIV and NRSV), is the repetition of "hostility" (משטמה *maśṭēmâ*) from the previous verse, where it refers to Ephraim (v. 7). Hosea's first-person use of "my God" could be a rhetorical device to distinguish his own true relationship with God from Ephraim's hypocritical and pernicious connection with the deity and the cult.

According to Hosea, the people's present corruption is rooted in the past (v. 9). This theme will characterize each of the following oracles. Nevertheless, it is difficult to determine the precise meaning of the temporal reference "as in the days of Gibeah." Some scholars connect the expression to Saul's capital at Gibeah and the beginning of the monarchy in Israel (1 Sam 10:26; 14:2; 22:6). Since the context of the expression is the conflict between the people and the prophet as God's messenger, Hosea could be referring to the confrontation between the prophet Samuel and the first king of Israel, Saul.[101]

Hosea will refer to "the days of Gibeah" again in 10:9 in connection with a "war" that will overtake the people in that city. Judges 19–21 describes an inter-tribal war in response to the brutal rape of a Levite's concubine by the inhabitants of Gibeah. The Levite depicts this atrocity as something that "has not happened or been seen since the day that the Israelites came up from the land of Egypt until this day" (Judg 19:30). The internecine war over this crime almost extinguishes one of the tribes. "As in the days of Gibeah," then, may epitomize not only the people's depravity since the establishment of the monarchy, but also the disastrous consequences of not heeding, but persecuting, the prophet sent by God to warn them.

---

101. For a survey of opinions, see Patrick M. Arnold, S.J., "Hosea and the Sin of Gibeah," *CBQ* 51 (1989) 447-78.

REFLECTIONS

1. In chapter 9 Hosea chooses a festival to proclaim his message of doom and condemnation. At a time of much celebration and merrymaking, Hosea proclaims just the opposite: "Do not rejoice, O Israel! Do not exult" (9:1 NRSV). His contemporary Amos, in similar fashion, undermined the revelry of the day of Yahweh (Amos 5:18-20; 8:9-14). Hosea intentionally picks the feast of Sukkot to deliver his prophecy. Usually celebrated for its fruitful production, the threshing floor is condemned as the site of the nation's promiscuity. Because of this licentiousness, the threshing floor and the wine vat will become barren and empty (9:2). The land that provided abundant food and drink will also be emptied of its inhabitants; they will be exiled to Assyria and will consume unclean food (9:3).

By casting such a pall over the festivities, Hosea could be considered a "party pooper," if not for the utter urgency of his message. In order to bring the nation to its senses, he had to subvert an occasion of merrymaking by confronting the people with the harrowing consequences of their collective sins.

2. Hosea offers us impressions about the experiences of a typical prophet. Prophets did not enjoy a life of ease; they did not bask in the people's adoration; their words were not welcomed by their hearers. Instead, prophets were openly disparaged and ridiculed, thrown into prison, run out of town, or even crucified (cf. Matt 23:34-35). Hosea's audience regarded him as an insane fool (9:7). His words fell on deaf ears, and he knew full well the consequences of not being believed. The people will be deprived of religious worship; their festivals will cease (9:4-5). They will be uprooted from their homes to die as strangers in a foreign land (9:3, 6).

It is often said that prophets are well ahead of their time, but it seems more accurate to say that prophets have a special insight into their time. They see the present more clearly and keenly. Consistent with the whole prophetic tradition, Hosea condemns Israel's present social injustice (12:7), religious hypocrisy (5:5-7), moral blindness and licentious behavior (4:10-19), greed (12:8), and the breakdown of basic values in the society (4:1-3).

Like Hosea, Isaiah understood the futility of making political alliances without consulting Yahweh's will (Isaiah 7). In his temple sermon, Jeremiah perceived the intimate connection between justice to Judah's marginalized persons—e.g., alien, orphan, widow, and innocent (Jer 7:5-6)—and proper worship (Jeremiah 7). Amos foresaw the exile of the northern kingdom of Israel because of its present social oppression of the poor (Amos 4). Ezekiel condemned the nation for a history of covenantal transgressions (Ezekiel 16; 23).

The prophets fearlessly called their contemporaries to task to deal with the contemporary situation. They witnessed the deteriorating relations among families, among the races, between the genders, and among the classes. And in the name of God they unmasked these evils before their audiences, warning them of the disastrous results of their present course. They offer us a model to critique the social disorders of our own time.

Hosea 9:10-17, Like Grapes in the Wilderness

NIV

10"When I found Israel,
   it was like finding grapes in the desert;
when I saw your fathers,
   it was like seeing the early fruit on the fig tree.
But when they came to Baal Peor,
   they consecrated themselves to that shameful idol
and became as vile as the thing they loved.
11Ephraim's glory will fly away like a bird—
   no birth, no pregnancy, no conception.
12Even if they rear children,
   I will bereave them of every one.
Woe to them
   when I turn away from them!
13I have seen Ephraim, like Tyre,
   planted in a pleasant place.
But Ephraim will bring out
   their children to the slayer."

14Give them, O LORD—
   what will you give them?
Give them wombs that miscarry
   and breasts that are dry.

15"Because of all their wickedness in Gilgal,
   I hated them there.
Because of their sinful deeds,

NRSV

10 Like grapes in the wilderness,
   I found Israel.
Like the first fruit on the fig tree,
   in its first season,
   I saw your ancestors.
But they came to Baal-peor,
   and consecrated themselves to a thing of shame,
   and became detestable like the thing they loved.
11 Ephraim's glory shall fly away like a bird—
   no birth, no pregnancy, no conception!
12 Even if they bring up children,
   I will bereave them until no one is left.
Woe to them indeed
   when I depart from them!
13 Once I saw Ephraim as a young palm planted in a lovely meadow,[a]
   but now Ephraim must lead out his children for slaughter.
14 Give them, O LORD—
   what will you give?
Give them a miscarrying womb
   and dry breasts.

a Meaning of Heb uncertain

NIV

I will drive them out of my house.
I will no longer love them;
   all their leaders are rebellious.
16Ephraim is blighted,
   their root is withered,
   they yield no fruit.
Even if they bear children,
   I will slay their cherished offspring."

17My God will reject them
   because they have not obeyed him;
   they will be wanderers among the nations.

NRSV

15 Every evil of theirs began at Gilgal;
      there I came to hate them.
   Because of the wickedness of their deeds
      I will drive them out of my house.
   I will love them no more;
      all their officials are rebels.

16 Ephraim is stricken,
      their root is dried up,
      they shall bear no fruit.
   Even though they give birth,
      I will kill the cherished offspring of their
         womb.
17 Because they have not listened to him,
      my God will reject them;
      they shall become wanderers among the
         nations.

COMMENTARY

9:10a. The preceding oracle concludes with the ominous declaration that God will remember Israel's iniquity and punish the people for their sins (v. 9). Verses 10-17 describe God's first act of "remembering," when God revisits Israel's spiritual history and the beginnings of their covenantal relationship. A series of reminiscences will contrast God's election and love for Israel with its continual betrayal. Since the oracle's context remains Sukkot, God's remembering focuses on two themes that the feast commemorates: the wilderness period and fertility. In a simile epitomizing both, God declares, "Like grapes in the wilderness,/ I found Israel" (v. 10a). Since grapes rarely grow in the desert, one would rejoice in and protect this extraordinary example of fecundity. Thus was God's experience when God "found" Israel in the wilderness, made a covenant with them, and protected and sustained them like grapes in a desert land (cf. Deut 32:10; Ezek 16:6-14; Hos 11:1-4).

9:10b. However, this relationship was ruptured at the end of Israel's wilderness journey when Israel "came to Baal-peor," the deity worshiped at Peor, or Beth-Peor, in Moab (see Num 23:28; Deut 3:29; 4:3). According to Num 25:1-5, Israel's first contact with the religion of Canaan began when the Israelites had sexual relations with the women of Moab. These women evidently "seduced" Israel to worship their fertility god Baal as well. Hosea scornfully calls this god בשׁת (*Bōšet*), or "Shame," instead of Baal (cf. NIV and NRSV).[102] In an honor/shame culture such as Israel's, shame was particularly associated with sexual offenses (see Introduction). Guilty of the interchangeable crime of having sex with foreign women and worshiping their gods,[103] the Israelites literally shamed themselves, becoming "detestable like the thing they loved."

9:11-12. What will happen to the honor of Israel/Ephraim? It "shall fly away like a bird" (v. 11). The Hebrew word usually translated as "glory" (כבוד *kābôd*) belongs to the vocabulary of honor and shame (cf. Gen 45:13; Exod 20:12; Prov 3:35; 11:16). In 7:11-12 Ephraim was pictured as a silly, senseless dove flitting off to Egypt and Assyria. In v. 11 Ephraim's glory/honor flutters away, not to political powers, but to the god of fertility. But Ephraim will not be fertile. In another instance of negative logic (cf. 8:7), Hosea

---

102. Later OT copyists substituted the more derogatory term בשׁת *bōšet* ("shame") for the name of the fertility god בעל (*ba'al*). See 2 Sam 2:8; 11:21.
103. Cf. in particular the deuteronomist's judgment over King Solomon's numerous foreign wives in 1 Kings 11.

declares, "No birth, no pregnancy, no conception!" The process of human reproduction is reversed in these words, but the negative logic is clear: Ephraim's women will not conceive, but even if they do, they will not become pregnant; even if they carry a child to term, they will not give birth to it. Should they happen to give birth, they will not rear the child. "Even if they bring up children,/ [God] will bereave them until no one is left" (v. 12). By going off to the god of fertility, Ephraim causes the true God of fertility to "depart from them" and to bring woe upon the nation (v. 12). Prophesied during a celebration of fertility, as was Sukkot, the judgment of infertility would be doubly terrifying to a people whose survival depended on the fruitfulness of their land and women.

9:13. The MT of this verse is very obscure. Closer to the MT is the NIV translation, describing Ephraim "like Tyre" planted in a meadow. The allusion to Tyre may be clarified by Josephus's account of Tyre's revolt against Assyria, resulting in a five-year siege of the city by the Assyrians under Shalmaneser V (725–24 to 721–720 BCE).[104] Similar to the situation at Tyre, Israel's King Hoshea withheld tribute and revolted against Assyria, resulting in the three-year siege of Samaria by the Assyrians (cf. 2 Kgs 17:3-6). Hosea thus prophesies that "Ephraim must lead out his children for slaughter" in order to defend Samaria during this siege.

9:14. Many scholars interpret this verse as Hosea's intercession on Ephraim's behalf, mitigating the threat of v. 13b. Being cursed with barrenness is better than seeing one's children butchered.[105] In view of the infertility theme that characterizes this oracle, uttered at a feast of fertility, however, Hosea's prayer in this verse should be read as a judgment upon the nation, rather than as an intercession.[106] Hosea's curse focuses on the very site of human fecundity: a woman's womb and breasts. Subverting the inter-

cessory form, in which the petitioners beseech God to "give" something for their happiness and welfare (cf. Pss 13:3; 30:9; 29:11; 37:4), Hosea insists that God "give" their women a "miscarrying womb and dry breasts."[107]

9:15. In a second act of remembering, God declares that the people's wickedness "began at Gilgal." In 4:15 and 12:11, God castigates Gilgal for its cultic transgressions. Moreover, Gilgal is the place where Saul was anointed king and where he offered sacrifices, which Samuel the prophet condemned (1 Sam 11:14-15; 13:8-15). God has already censured kings for establishing unlawful worship at Israel's sanctuaries (cf. Hosea 8), and this seems also to be the intent in v. 15a. Reinforcing the criticism of king and cult in 9:15b, God will denounce Israel's leaders as rebels and drive them from the Temple. The "love" that Yahweh used to have for them is now turned to "hate."

9:16. Continuing the agricultural and birth metaphors of vv. 10-12, this verse reiterates God's threat to the nations. The grapevine that once grew miraculously in the desert is now a stricken plant with a shriveled root. A wordplay punctuates God's threat: Ephraim (אפרים *'eprayim*) will no longer bear fruit (פרי *pĕrî*), either on the vine or in the womb. Returning to the negative logic of vv. 11-12, God announces that even if Ephraim, who will no longer bear fruit, should happen to give birth, God "will kill the cherished offspring of their womb."

9:17. As in v. 14, the prophet speaks. Because Ephraim has not listened (שמע *šāma'*) to God, "my God will reject [מאס *mā'as*] them"—i.e., exile Ephraim among the nations. Implied in the clever wordplays of this verse is the covenant between God and the people. According to Deut 4:1, 30, 36; 5:1, the people are called to hear (*šāma'*) and to obey God's commandments. The one who found (מצא *māṣā'*) Israel in the wilderness and ratified a covenant with the people will now reject (*mā'as*) them. (See Reflections at 10:1-8.)

104. Jeffrey K. Kuan, "Hosea 9.13 and Josephus, Antiquities IX, 277-287," *PEQ* 123 (1991) 103-8.

105. James L. Mays, *Hosea*, OTL (Philadelphia: Westminster, 1969) 156; Hans Walter Wolff, *Hosea: Commentary on the Book of the Prophet Hosea* (Philadelphia: Fortress, 1974) 166-67.

106. Deborah Krause, "A Blessing Cursed: The Prophet's Prayer for Barren Womb and Dry Breasts in Hosea 9," in *Reading Between Texts: Intertextuality and the Hebrew Bible*, Danna Nolan Fewell, ed. (Louisville: Westminster/John Knox, 1992) 191-202.

107. Cf. the ancient blessing over Joseph's fertility in Gen 49:25, where God blesses with the "blessings of the breasts and of the womb." Note that Hosea's curse in 9:14 reverses the order: "miscarrying womb and dry breasts."

Hosea 10:1-8, Like a Luxurious Vine

NIV

10 Israel was a spreading vine;
he brought forth fruit for himself.
As his fruit increased,
he built more altars;
as his land prospered,
he adorned his sacred stones.
²Their heart is deceitful,
and now they must bear their guilt.
The LORD will demolish their altars
and destroy their sacred stones.

³Then they will say, "We have no king
because we did not revere the LORD.
But even if we had a king,
what could he do for us?"
⁴They make many promises,
take false oaths
and make agreements;
therefore lawsuits spring up
like poisonous weeds in a plowed field.
⁵The people who live in Samaria fear
for the calf-idol of Beth Aven.ᵃ
Its people will mourn over it,
and so will its idolatrous priests,
those who had rejoiced over its splendor,
because it is taken from them into exile.
⁶It will be carried to Assyria
as tribute for the great king.
Ephraim will be disgraced;
Israel will be ashamed of its wooden idols.ᵇ
⁷Samaria and its king will float away
like a twig on the surface of the waters.
⁸The high places of wickednessᶜ will be
destroyed—
it is the sin of Israel.
Thorns and thistles will grow up
and cover their altars.
Then they will say to the mountains, "Cover
us!"
and to the hills, "Fall on us!"

NRSV

10 Israel is a luxuriant vine
that yields its fruit.
The more his fruit increased
the more altars he built;
as his country improved,
he improved his pillars.
² Their heart is false;
now they must bear their guilt.
The LORDᵃ will break down their altars,
and destroy their pillars.

³ For now they will say:
"We have no king,
for we do not fear the LORD,
and a king—what could he do for us?"
⁴ They utter mere words;
with empty oaths they make covenants;
so litigation springs up like poisonous weeds
in the furrows of the field.
⁵ The inhabitants of Samaria tremble
for the calfᵇ of Beth-aven.
Its people shall mourn for it,
and its idolatrous priests shall wailᶜ over it,
over its glory that has departed from it.
⁶ The thing itself shall be carried to Assyria
as tribute to the great king.ᵈ
Ephraim shall be put to shame,
and Israel shall be ashamed of his idol.ᵉ

⁷ Samaria's king shall perish
like a chip on the face of the waters.
⁸ The high places of Aven, the sin of Israel,
shall be destroyed.
Thorn and thistle shall grow up
on their altars.
They shall say to the mountains, Cover us,
and to the hills, Fall on us.

COMMENTARY

10:1-2. Hosea 10:1-8 enlarges upon themes found in 9:10-17 and 8:1-14: the grape/vine metaphor and the attack against cult, king, and calf. Whereas 9:10 describes Israel as grapes that Yahweh found in the wilderness, 10:1 recalls Israel's settlement in the land, where like a vine it took root and flourished (cf. Ps 80:8-11; Isa 5:1-7; Jer 2:21; Ezek 17:5-6). The more prosperous Israel becomes, however, the more altars and pillars it builds. Although once a legitimate part of Israelite worship (see Introduction),[108] Israel's altars and pillars, along with the high places and the calf of Bethel (vv. 5, 8), are condemned by Hosea as instruments of Israel's deceit and guilt. They will soon be demolished (v. 2).[109] Hosea's cultic castigation will become particularly important about a century later, during Josiah's reform, when, according to the deuteronomist, Josiah

broke the *pillars* in pieces, cut down the Asherim, and covered the sites with human bones. Moreover, *the altar at Bethel, the high place* erected by Jeroboam son of Nebat, who caused Israel to sin—he pulled down that altar along with the high place, crushing it to dust; he also burned the Asherah. (2 Kgs 23:14-15; cf. Deut 7:5; 1 Kgs 13:2-3)

10:3-4. The expression "for now" (כי עתה *kî ʿattâ*) connects v. 3 with the "now" of v. 2. Nevertheless, what is meant in v. 3 when Israel proclaims that now it has no king is difficult to determine. On one hand, the verse could refer proleptically to the time when Israel's monarchy will be abolished because of the nation's guilt. Verse 7 will prophesy the destruction of Samaria's king because of his cultic aberrations. On the other hand, the "king" of v. 3 could refer to Yahweh, whom Israel has rejected as king (cf. 1 Sam 8:7-8). The following clause, "for we do not fear Yahweh," would confirm this interpretation. According to v. 4, those who say "We have no king" are guilty of making covenants of mere words and empty oaths. The background of vv. 3-4 is probably 8:1-4, where Israel's transgression

of the covenant is due to its installation of kings, like Jeroboam I, who do not adhere to God's covenant and flagrantly promote their idolatrous calf cult. Indeed, like the covenantal curse in v. 4*b* and the attack against the calf in vv. 5-6, Deut 29:18 describes idol worshipers as poisonous weeds (ראש *rōʾš*) sprouting among the people.

10:5-6. These verses foretell the fate of the calf set up at the sanctuary at Bethel, which Hosea derisively calls Beth-aven ("House of Evil"; cf. 4:15). The MT literally specifies "calves" of Beth-aven, instead of the singular. Jeroboam I had installed only one calf at Bethel. Hosea employs the plural of "majesty" sarcastically in v. 5, however, to make the point that this "great" calf will soon be taken into exile. When this dreadful event occurs, the inhabitants of Samaria and the idolatrous priests, who have mistakenly placed their hopes in this false object, will be overcome with fear and grief. Hosea intensifies the loss by resuming the vocabulary of honor/shame in an allusion to another past event of Israel's history (cf. 9:10-11). Upon hearing that the ark of the covenant was taken by the Philistines, Phinehas's wife named her newborn infant "Ichabod," symbolizing the fact that "the honor/glory [כבוד *kābôd*] has departed/gone into exile [גלה *gālâ*] from Israel" (1 Sam 4:21). Deliberately contrasting the sacred ark with the profane calf, Hosea contemptuously remarks that the *kābôd* of the calf, its "honor," has gone into exile (*gālâ*), carried off as tribute to fill the coffers of the great king of Assyria (cf. 5:13). The honor or glory of the calf was, in fact, the source of Israel's shame (cf. 9:10, where the Israelites consecrate themselves to "Shame," the Baal of Peor). When its "honor," the calf-idol, is ignominiously taken into exile, Ephraim/Israel will be doubly disgraced (v. 6).

10:7-8. The king, his high places, and his altars will suffer similar fates. The king will be carried away helpless like a chip of wood on turbulent waters (v. 7; cf. Deut 28:36). The high places of Bethel, called the "sin of Israel" by Hosea, will be destroyed.[110] Thorns and thistles

---

108. Cf. Gen 28:18; 31:13; 35:20; Exod 24:4, where the pillars (מצבות *maṣṣēbôt*) are part of the Israelite cult.

109. The NRSV and the NIV add that Yahweh will demolish Israel's altars and pillars, although the MT simply uses "he," leaving open the possibility that Hos 10:2*b* refers to Josiah. See Gale A. Yee, *Composition and Tradition in the Book of Hosea: A Redaction Critical Investigation*, SBLDS 102 (Atlanta: Scholars Press, 1987) 296-98.

110. The deuteronomist continually refers to the calves established by Jeroboam I at Dan and Bethel as the sin that led to Israel's fall (1 Kgs 15:26, 34; 2 Kgs 10:29, 31; 17:21-23).

will overrun its idolatrous altars (cf. 9:6*b*). Those who arrogantly proclaimed that they had no king in Yahweh and did not fear God (v. 3) will cry to the mountains and hills to fall upon them, in order to escape Yahweh's wrath (v. 8).

REFLECTIONS

The context of oracles in Hosea 9–11 is the festival of Sukkot, a celebration of both the fall harvest and the wilderness period of Israel's history. The various metaphors in this section (grapes in the wilderness, the vine, stricken plant, the son nurtured in the desert, etc.) exploit in rhetorically effective ways the significance of the feast for the people. The rebellious people who ignore their roots and the source of their current abundance are contrasted with the God who chose and cared for the son Israel after freeing him from Egypt (see Hosea 11).

Memory plays a crucial role during festal celebrations, since feasts usually commemorate momentous events in the nation's history. In the case of Sukkot, the people remember the time their ancestors spent in the wilderness. Ritual memory provided community with others in the present and continuity with the ancestors. Through ritual acts of remembering, the people "relived" the days when God protected and sustained their forebears in the desert.[111]

Hosea also describes God's acts of remembering during this feast. God remembers finding Israel in the wilderness. The joy of this discovery was like finding grapes in an arid land, and like witnessing the first buds of a fig tree (9:10). Indeed, Israel was like "a young palm planted in a lovely meadow" (9:13 NRSV), a "luxuriant vine" that yields abundant fruit (10:1), and a son who is fed, nurtured, and taught to walk in the wilderness (11:3-4).

God, however, also remembers the people's iniquity and guilt (9:9). Because their evil "began at Gilgal," God will drive them out of the sanctuary (9:15). Because they have sinned "since the days of Gibeah" (10:9 NRSV), God will gather the nations against them (10:10). War will engulf the land, just like the brutal destruction of Beth-arbel, when mothers were dashed to pieces with their children (10:14). The flip side of God's positive memories of finding and nourishing Israel in the wilderness is God's recalling of Israel's insidious periods.

Many lament nowadays how our holidays have become so commercialized and materialistic. We often forget the historical event a festival commemorates, Thanksgiving and Christmas being the most egregious occasions where this forgetfulness occurs. We do have the obligatory ritual of "saying grace" before stuffing ourselves at Thanksgiving. We also have the often lame attempts to put the "Christ" back into Christmas.

However, just as Hosea's God remembers the people's past, a past the revelers apparently have forgotten, so also are we called to remember the past that gives rise to our celebrations in the present. Saying grace is not so important as "doing grace," actually living a grace-filled life and being thankful for it. Putting Christ back into Christmas entails more than displaying a crèche or sending greeting cards illustrating the birth of the Christ child. It means reflecting deeply upon the mysterious source of our salvation and how God became a vulnerable human being in order to achieve that salvation.

Furthermore, just as Hosea's God remembers the people's transgression, so also we are solemnly reminded that we will be accountable when we forget about "doing grace" and "remembering" God, making God, and not our material goods, the central focus of our lives.

---

111. During the Passover celebration before his death, Jesus exhorted his disciples to partake of the bread, his body, "in remembrance of me" (Luke 22:19). When Jesus' words are uttered during eucharistic celebrations, Christians remember/relive the passion, death, and resurrection of Jesus through ritual.

Hosea 10:9-15, Like a Trained Heifer

<table>
<tr><td>

NIV

9"Since the days of Gibeah, you have sinned,
    O Israel,
  and there you have remained.ᵃ
Did not war overtake
  the evildoers in Gibeah?
10When I please, I will punish them;
  nations will be gathered against them
  to put them in bonds for their double sin.
11Ephraim is a trained heifer
  that loves to thresh;
so I will put a yoke
  on her fair neck.
I will drive Ephraim,
  Judah must plow,
  and Jacob must break up the ground.
12Sow for yourselves righteousness,
  reap the fruit of unfailing love,
and break up your unplowed ground;
  for it is time to seek the LORD,
until he comes
  and showers righteousness on you.
13But you have planted wickedness,
  you have reaped evil,
  you have eaten the fruit of deception.
Because you have depended on your own
    strength
  and on your many warriors,
14the roar of battle will rise against your people,
  so that all your fortresses will be devastated—
as Shalman devastated Beth Arbel on the day of
    battle,
  when mothers were dashed to the ground
    with their children.
15Thus will it happen to you, O Bethel,
  because your wickedness is great.
When that day dawns,
  the king of Israel will be completely
    destroyed."

ᵃ9 Or *there a stand was taken*

</td><td>

NRSV

9 Since the days of Gibeah you have sinned,
    O Israel;
  there they have continued.
  Shall not war overtake them in Gibeah?
10 I will comeᵃ against the wayward people to
    punish them;
  and nations shall be gathered against them
  when they are punishedᵇ for their double
    iniquity.

11 Ephraim was a trained heifer
  that loved to thresh,
  and I spared her fair neck;
but I will make Ephraim break the ground;
  Judah must plow;
  Jacob must harrow for himself.
12 Sow for yourselves righteousness;
  reap steadfast love;
  break up your fallow ground;
for it is time to seek the LORD,
  that he may come and rain righteousness
    upon you.

13 You have plowed wickedness,
  you have reaped injustice,
  you have eaten the fruit of lies.
Because you have trusted in your power
  and in the multitude of your warriors,
14 therefore the tumult of war shall rise against
    your people,
  and all your fortresses shall be destroyed,
as Shalman destroyed Beth-arbel on the day of
    battle
  when mothers were dashed in pieces with
    their children.
15 Thus it shall be done to you, O Bethel,
  because of your great wickedness.
At dawn the king of Israel
  shall be utterly cut off.

ᵃ Cn Compare Gk: Heb *In my desire*   ᵇ Gk: Heb *bound*

</td></tr>
</table>

COMMENTARY

Hosea 10:9-15 contains an exhortation entwined within judgments (v. 12). This exhortation represents the second stage in the journey from barrenness to fertility that characterizes Hosea

4–11. The word "Israel" marks the beginning and end of the unit. The beginning, "Since the days of Gibeah you have sinned, O Israel" (v. 9), is connected to the previous oracle by a wordplay on "to the hills" (לגבעות *laggĕbā'ôt*) in v. 8 and by reference to "Gibeah" (הגבעה *haggib'â*) in v. 9. As in 9:9, Hosea regards the "days of Gibeah" as a paradigm of the people's corruption. The expression seemingly alludes to two events: the establishment of the monarchy when Saul set up his capital at Gibeah (1 Sam 10:26; 14:2; 22:6) and the war resulting from the rape of the Levite's concubine (Judges 19–21). According to the start of the oracle, the threat embodied by "the days of Gibeah" will be correlated with these events (v. 9). Israel will again become the site of a horrible war—not a civil war as in Judges 20–21, but a foreign invasion in which nations gather against Israel as instruments of God's punishment (v. 10).[112] According to the end of the oracle, "the king of Israel shall be utterly cut off" (v. 15 NRSV). The monarchy, centered in Gibeah at its inception and responsible for leading Israel into cultic sin, shall be utterly destroyed (v. 15).[113]

10:11. The governing metaphor of vv. 11-14 is that of a trained female calf (עגלה מלמדה *'eglâ mĕlummādâ*), translated by the NRSV and the NIV as "heifer."[114] The word *'eglâ*, designating the condemned calf-idol of Bethel (v. 5), also describes Ephraim in v. 11.[115] The trained heifer contrasts with the depiction of Israel as a stubborn cow (פרה *pārâ*) in 4:16. Yahweh remembers a time when Ephraim was like a docile and obedient heifer, threshing grain without the burden of a yoke over "her fair neck."[116] Ending this freedom, Yahweh will harness Ephraim in order to drive her (NIV). Similarly, Judah must plow, and Jacob must harrow for himself. The

yoking of Ephraim, Judah,[117] and Jacob should be read in the light of 10:5-6 and 8:9-10. Samaria's calf/heifer will be carried away as tribute to the great king of Assyria (10:5-6). The enormous tribute that the people must pay to Assyria will burden the heifer/Ephraim with an oppressive weight (8:9-10). Eventually Ephraim's yoke will become exile itself.

10:13-15. If one brackets v. 12 as a hortatory counterpoint inserted secondarily in to the oracle (see below), then the oracle continues in v. 13, disclosing the reason for the yoking of Ephraim: "you have plowed wickedness, reaped injustice, eaten the fruit of lies." Farming imagery highlights the recurring infertility theme in this set of oracles (8:7; 9:2, 11, 14, 16; cf. 4:3). Yahweh's indictment follows the sequence of land cultivation: plowing, reaping, and eating (cf. 8:7). However, the abstract objects of these actions—wickedness, injustice, deception—are the very opposite of the blessings that should flow from the covenant.

In v. 13, the particle כי (*kî*, "for," "because") reveals the actual covenantal transgression. Instead of trusting in Yahweh, the king representing the nation[118] relies on his own power and warriors (cf. 1:5, 7; 13:10; 14:3). The disastrous consequence of his arrogance is war. Verse 14 repeats the threat of 10:9: like the days of Gibeah, when a civil war almost exterminated a tribe, a terrible war will return against the people. The mighty fortresses upon which they relied will be destroyed (cf. 7:14).

The future destruction of Israel's military strongholds is compared to a past devastation in the people's collective memory: "as Shalman destroyed Beth-arbel on the day of battle." Although the identities of Shalman and Beth-arbel elude us,[119] the battle was evidently an event of unparalleled cruelty and sadism, "when mothers were dashed in pieces with their children." Yahweh warns that the same gruesome atrocities will happen to Bethel, because of its great wickedness (v. 15).

112. Divergences between the NIV and the NRSV in 10:10 are due to difficulties in the MT, but the sense of the verse is clear. God will assemble the nations for a war against Israel to punish them for their "double iniquity." "Double iniquity" could refer to the two events associated with "the days of Gibeah": the war at Gibeah and the establishment of the monarchy. It could also refer to past and present evil for which Israel will be punished. For other meanings, see Yee, *Composition and Tradition*, 210-11.

113. Both 10:7 and 10:15 use the verb דמה (*dmh*, "to be destroyed") in describing the fate of Israel's king.

114. Cf. Jer 31:18, which describes Ephraim as an "untrained calf" (כעגל לא למד *kĕ'ēgel lō' lummād*).

115. עגלה ('*eglâ*) in the *plurale majestatis*. Hosea 8:5-6 and 13:2 use the masculine singular to denote the calf (עגל '*ēgel*).

116. The NRSV is closer to the MT. The NIV unnecessarily emends the MT's על עברתי ('*ā bartî 'al*; lit., "I passed by [or spared] her fair neck") to על על העברתי (*he'ĕbartî 'ōl 'al*, "I will put a yoke upon her fair neck").

117. Against those who remove "Judah" as a gloss, I take the accusation regarding "Judah" as original. Cf. Hos 5:10-14; 12:3.

118. The MT shifts from "you" (pl.) in 10:12-13a to "you" (sing.) in 10:13b-14. "You" (sing.) began the oracle in 10:9a, but was not developed. "You" (pl.) will be resumed in 10:15. It could be that use of the plural indicates an indictment against the whole nation, while use of the singular specifies an indictment primarily against the king, whose downfall is foretold in 10:15.

119. Scholars have suggested the Assyrian kings Shalmaneser I or Shalmaneser V and the Moabite king Salamanu for "Shalman." See James L. Mays, *Hosea*, OTL (Philadelphia: Westminster, 1969) 149.

10:12. As a counterpoint of hope embedded in an oracle of doom, this verse is the second moment in the people's spiritual journey from barrenness to fertility, from exile from the land to being sown back into it (cf. 2:22-23). In the first counterpoint (6:1-3), the people are exhorted to repent and return to Yahweh and are promised thirst-quenching rains for the barren land. Building upon 6:1-3, the agricultural metaphors of v. 12 articulate themes of covenantal preparation: sowing righteousness, reaping steadfast love, and tilling the ground. The sowing motif recalls 2:23, where God will sow the wife/Israel back into the land on the great day of Jezreel. As certain times are proper for tilling and sowing, so it is time to seek the Lord, who will bring life-giving rains. In order to prepare for these coming rains, v. 12 urges the people through triadic imperatives to prepare the soil of their hearts: "Sow for yourselves righteousness, reap steadfast love, break up your fallow ground." Righteousness and steadfast love are precisely the gifts Yahweh will give his wife when their covenant is renewed (2:19). Yahweh and the people must work together in a mutual relationship to bring fertility back to the land, both literally and spiritually. Spring is the proper time for plowing and sowing; it is also "the time to seek the LORD," who will water seeds of righteousness with rains of righteousness. The image of cultivating and seeding for the spiritual preparation of the people anticipates 14:5-7, where the sowing of the people back into the land results in a glorious blossoming.

Hosea 11:1-7, Like a Rebellious Son

NIV

11 "When Israel was a child,
    I loved him,
and out of Egypt I called my son.
[2]But the more I[a] called Israel,
    the further they went from me.[b]
They sacrificed to the Baals
    and they burned incense to images.
[3]It was I who taught Ephraim to walk,
    taking them by the arms;
but they did not realize
    it was I who healed them.
[4]I led them with cords of human kindness,
    with ties of love;
I lifted the yoke from their neck
    and bent down to feed them.

[5]"Will they not return to Egypt
    and will not Assyria rule over them
    because they refuse to repent?
[6]Swords will flash in their cities,
    will destroy the bars of their gates
    and put an end to their plans.
[7]My people are determined to turn from me.
    Even if they call to the Most High,
    he will by no means exalt them."

[a]2 Some Septuagint manuscripts; Hebrew *they*   [b]2 Septuagint; Hebrew *them*

NRSV

11 When Israel was a child,
    I loved him,
and out of Egypt I called my son.
[2] The more I[a] called them,
    the more they went from me;[b]
they kept sacrificing to the Baals,
    and offering incense to idols.

[3] Yet it was I who taught Ephraim to walk,
    I took them up in my[c] arms;
but they did not know that I healed them.
[4] I led them with cords of human kindness,
    with bands of love.
I was to them like those
    who lift infants to their cheeks.[d]
I bent down to them and fed them.

[5] They shall return to the land of Egypt,
    and Assyria shall be their king,
    because they have refused to return to me.
[6] The sword rages in their cities,
    it consumes their oracle-priests,
    and devours because of their schemes.
[7] My people are bent on turning away from me.
    To the Most High they call,
    but he does not raise them up at all.[e]

[a] Gk: Heb *they*   [b] Gk: Heb *them*   [c] Gk Syr Vg: Heb *his*   [d] Or who ease the yoke on their jaws   [e] Meaning of Heb uncertain

COMMENTARY

Just as Hosea 4 begins the Hosea 4–11 section with the image of the son Ammi, chap. 11 will conclude it with Ammi's story in Yahweh's final historical retrospect. Thematic echoes from chap. 2, such as God's love for Israel (2:19-20; cf. 3:1), Israel's exodus from Egypt (2:15), and its worship of the gods of Canaan (2:8, 13), appear in the opening verses of chap. 11. However, the metaphor applied to God is that of the caring parent, rather than the loving husband. The metaphor for Israel is the rebellious son, instead of the adulterous wife.

As in the previous historical retrospects (9:10; 10:11), the wilderness period becomes the idyllic time between God and Israel. The covenant ratified in the wilderness is phrased in the language of kinship. The verb "to call" (קרא *qārā'*) can mean both "to summon" and "to name." Thus when God summons Israel from Egypt, God also names Israel as an adopted son (11:1). In first-person narrative, Yahweh describes a series of nurturing gestures performed on the son's behalf during this time: teaching Ephraim to walk, carrying, healing, leading, lifting, and stooping down to feed the youngster (11:3-4; cf. Deut 32:10-14).[120] In con-

trast to chap. 2, which views God explicitly as husband, the author of chap. 11 does not call Yahweh "mother" or "father." Teaching a son to walk, holding, healing, and feeding him are all activities that *both* parents perform, although one could argue that the primary caregiver during childhood is the mother. Emphasized in the parental metaphor is Yahweh's nurturing, sustaining love.

Just as the wife/Israel "did not know" that her husband, Yahweh, provided for her (2:8), so also the son/Israel "did not know that I [YHWH] healed them" (v. 3; cf. 5:13; 6:1; 14:4). As in the other retrospects, God's election is juxtaposed with Israel's desertion to the gods of Canaan (9:10; 10:1-2). The more God "called" Israel, the more he abandoned God to worship the baals (11:2). The son thus disowns himself from his parent, just as the wife/Israel rejects her husband (2:2a). The son whom God called from Egypt "will return" (שוב *šûb*) to Egypt, because he has refused "to repent" (*šûb*) of his impiety (v. 5). The reality of war, described so unsparingly in 10:9, 14, will come upon him (v. 6). Yahweh laments in the conclusion of this judgment that "My people [Ammi] are determined to turn away [*šûb*] from me." Although they call to the Most High, God will not raise them up (v. 7).[121] (See Reflections at 11:8-11.)

---

120. Although the NIV is closer to the MT, I am following the NRSV reading in the commentary. The MT seems to conflate two images for Israel here: Israel as son and Israel as heifer. The MT description of God lifting the yoke (על *ōl*) from the jaws of Ephraim (11:4) seems to refer to the similar image in 10:11. The reference to the "cords of human kindness" and "bands of love" would then conceivably refer to the reins that control the animal. The NRSV reads עול (*'ûl,* "infant") for *ōl,* which would be more consistent with the metaphor of the son (בן *bēn*) or the youth (נער *na'ar*) of 11:1. The conflation of son/calf motifs is quite possible, however, as is evident in Jer 31:18-20. See the discussion in Yee, *Composition and Tradition,* 216-21.

121. The MT literally reads, "and to על [*'al*] they call him." *'al* could mean "above"; hence the NRSV and the NIV translation, "Most High." Other scholars emend *'al* to *ōl* ("yoke") or to בעל (*ba'al,* "Baal").

Hosea 11:8-11, Journey's End

NIV	NRSV

8"How can I give you up, Ephraim?
   How can I hand you over, Israel?
How can I treat you like Admah?
   How can I make you like Zeboiim?
My heart is changed within me;
   all my compassion is aroused.
9I will not carry out my fierce anger,
   nor will I turn and devastate Ephraim.
For I am God, and not man—
	8 How can I give you up, Ephraim?
	   How can I hand you over, O Israel?
	How can I make you like Admah?
	   How can I treat you like Zeboiim?
	My heart recoils within me;
	   my compassion grows warm and tender.
	9 I will not execute my fierce anger;
	   I will not again destroy Ephraim;
	for I am God and no mortal,

NIV

the Holy One among you.
I will not come in wrath.*
¹⁰They will follow the LORD;
    he will roar like a lion.
When he roars,
    his children will come trembling from the
        west.
¹¹They will come trembling
    like birds from Egypt,
    like doves from Assyria.
I will settle them in their homes,"
    declares the LORD.

*9 Or *come against any city*

NRSV

the Holy One in your midst,
    and I will not come in wrath.*

¹⁰ They shall go after the LORD,
    who roars like a lion;
when he roars,
    his children shall come trembling from the
        west.
¹¹ They shall come trembling like birds from
        Egypt,
    and like doves from the land of Assyria;
    and I will return them to their homes, says
        the LORD.

*Meaning of Heb uncertain

COMMENTARY

11:8-9. The menacing tone of the oracle switches in v. 8, presenting a rare glimpse of God on the verge of destroying the son Ammi, yet balking at the prospect. According to deuteronomic law, both parents could condemn a stubborn, rebellious son before the elders of the city, whereupon he would be stoned to death (Deut 21:18-21). This legal background illuminates the theological intent of v. 8, where God is about to hand over the son to be stoned. God cannot deal with the son in the same way God treated Admah and Zeboiim, two cities destroyed like Sodom and Gomorrah (Deut 29:23). Yahweh's abhorrence of the son's death penalty gives way to a growing compassion. Ultimately, the mother/father God makes a decision: "I will not execute my fierce anger;/ I will not again destroy Ephraim" (11:9*a*). Although the parent has the legal right to have the son killed, compassion for and bonding with the child prevent God from doing so. God transcends human legal institutions, which enforce the death sentence for disobedient sons, proclaiming "for I am God and no mortal,/ the Holy One in your midst,/ and I will not come in wrath" (11:9*b*).[122]

11:10-11. These verses describe the journey's end, when the mother/father God welcomes Ammi back from the lands of his banishment. In 5:14, God is described as a lion (שחל *šaḥal* and כפיר *kĕpîr*), wreaking havoc upon the nations. In v. 10, God appears as a roaring lion (אריה *'aryēh*). God's roaring elicits a corresponding response from Ammi: The sons will come trembling like birds from Egypt and like doves from Assyria (v. 11). God reverses not only the condemnation of v. 5, where Ammi is sentenced to return to Egypt and Assyria (see 7:11; 8:7-13; 9:3), but also the threats embodied in the bird images of 7:11-12 and 9:11-12.

Like the wife/Israel (Hosea 2), the son/Israel embarks on a three-part historical journey in chap. 11. Verse 1 focuses on the past and the journey from Egypt, when God called the son to become Ammi ("My people") in the wilderness. The second stage of the journey, vv. 5-7, centers on the present. Because of his rebelliousness, the son must go into exile to Assyria, symbolized as a return (שוב *šûb*) to Egypt. The third stage of the journey, vv. 10-11, highlights the future. Contingent upon Ammi's repentance (*šûb*), vv. 10-11 describe the "sons" returning (*šûb*) from Egypt and Assyria to their own homes.

122. The MT reads "and I will not come בעיר [*bě 'îr*]." The word *'îr* usually means "city," but can also mean "wrath or rage" (see Jer 15:8). If one interprets *'îr* as "city," then 11:9 could be the reversal of the threat to the cities in 11:6.

REFLECTIONS

1. Hosea continually speaks of the people's "return to Egypt" if they continue in their sinful ways. It is difficult to picture why his hearers would not transform their behavior to avoid such a fate. A return to Egypt means an actual uprooting from the land and captivity in a foreign and hostile country (9:3; 11:5). It means the return to physical slavery, enduring the whips inflicted on one's back by cruel overseers. It means the struggle to exist in squalid living and working conditions (cf. 10:11). It means seeing one's children grow up without a childhood, bent over by toil (cf. 9:12). It means the loss of one's dignity and even one's humanity. Ultimately it means a regressing, a return to a life of hopelessness and despair, a life without freedom and without the ability to make choices.

Throughout chapters 9–11, Hosea summons the people to "remember" their history: how God freed them from slavery in Egypt (11:1); how God chose and protected them in the wilderness (9:10; 11:3-4). Israel, however, refuses to learn from its history and change its course. In very real ways, Hosea's prophecy is fulfilled: Symbolically, Ephraim did "return to Egypt" in its exile by the Assyrians from its beloved land. The Hosean text challenges us to reckon seriously with the religious and political choices before us and to learn the lessons of our own history. One of the most horrifying events of the twentieth century was the holocaust of six million Jews in Nazi concentration camps. Racism, intolerance, and "ethnic cleansing" continue to confront us with the real possibility that the Holocaust can happen again. Hosea warns us that we, too, can "return to Egypt," if we turn a blind eye to racial/ethnic tensions and hostilities in our midst.

2. Several feminists have seized upon Hosea 11 as a rare biblical description of a female God teaching and caring for her son who, filled with maternal compassion, refuses to have her son put to death.[123] Arguing that אִישׁ (*'îš*) in 11:9 literally means "man," and not "humanity," these scholars think that the God of Hosea 11 radically distinguishes herself from men: "For I am God [אֵל *'ēl*] and not man [*'îš*], the Holy One in your midst" (11:9). For them, God rejects male behavior in favor of the female actions and attitudes expressed in Hosea 11.

Their interpretations depend upon some questionable emendations and exegesis of the biblical text.[124] For one thing, *'îš* is not only the Hebrew word for "man," but also serves as a generic term for "humanity," like אָדָם (*'ādām*). The point God makes in 11:9 is that God is not a mortal being who operates under human (Israelite) laws. God transcends these laws in dealing with Israel. The contrast is between creature and Creator and between God and Israel, not between male and female.

Hosea 11 does not call God "mother," but it does not call God "father" either. The chapter highlights a parental love that stresses other dimensions of the God/Israel relationship vis-à-vis the marital love described in Hosea 1–3. Such a love is creative, bringing the child into existence to share in the love between the parents. It is an instructive love that teaches a child to become a better person and to strive for the common good. It is a tolerant and patient love that allows a child to make mistakes and accepts that child back in forgiveness. It is an unconditional love in spite of the child's rebelliousness. It is a corrective love that intervenes when a child strays too far off the path. Finally, it is a healing love that helps bring a wayward child to wholeness.[125]

---

123. Helen Schüngel-Straumann, "God as Mother in Hosea 11," in *A Feminist Companion to the Latter Prophets,* Athalya Brenner, ed. (Sheffield: Sheffield Academic, 1995) 194-218; originally published as "Gott als Mutter in Hosea 11," *TQ* 166 (1986) 119-34; Marie-Theres Wacker, "God as Mother? On the Meaning of a Biblical God-Symbol for Feminist Theology," in *Motherhood: Experience, Institution, Theology,* Anne Carr and Elisabeth Schüssler Fiorenza, eds., *Concilium* 206 (Edinburgh: T. & T. Clark, 1989) 103-11.

124. Siegfried Kreuzer, "Gott als Mutter in Hosea 11?" *TQ* 169 (1989) 123-32.

125. See Kathryn Chapman, "Hosea 11:1-4—Images of a Loving Parent," *RevExp* 90 (1993) 263-68.

3. Hosea 11:1-11 is the final text from the book of Hosea in the Revised Common Lectionary, chosen as the first reading for Proper 13 of Year C (or Proper 18 for Roman Catholics and the Anglican Church of Canada). Thematically, it is more connected to its psalm response (Ps 107:1-9, 43) than to the second reading (Col 3:1-11) or to the Gospel reading (Luke 12:13-21). Hosea 11 concludes with the vivid image of God the roaring lion and God's quaking but repentant children, returning like birds from the faraway lands of their exile. The psalm response picks up the theme of gathering the redeemed from the distant corners of the world. Unlike the recalcitrant son who refused to turn to God (Hos 11:5), the redeemed had "cried out to the LORD in their trouble,/ and he delivered them from their distress" (Ps 107:6 NRSV). The psalm summons the hearer to respond appropriately to God's intervention: with great thanksgiving for God's steadfast love and wonderful works to humankind (Ps 107:8).

HOSEA 11:12–14:9

THE WIFE AND SON/ISRAEL AND GOD

OVERVIEW

Chapters 11:12–14:9[12:1–14:10] make up the third and final section of the book of Hosea. This section takes up and enlarges upon the metaphors that characterize the God/Israel relationship in the two previous sections of the book: the parent/son metaphor of chaps. 4–11 and the husband/wife metaphor of chaps. 1–3. The unwise son brings punishment upon himself for his idolatrous ways, while God the parent equivocates between redeeming and destroying him (Hosea 13; cf. Hosea 11). The repentant wife Israel is rescued from her enslavement by the prophet, brought back to the land (Hosea 12) and planted there, to thrive in blooming splendor under her husband's divine favor (Hosea 14).

As in the preceding two sections, chaps. 12–14 shift from an indictment (ריב *rîb,* 12:2[12:3]) to threats of punishment (chap. 13) to an exhortation to repent and hope for salvation (chap. 14; themes of repentance and hope also appear in 12:6, 9). Hosea's final historical retrospects focus particularly on Jacob, Moses, and the wilderness traditions of the ancestral and exodus stories. He develops these traditions by transforming Jacob the cheat into a paradigm of repentance. Jacob's enforced servitude to marry the woman he loves

parallels Israel's enslavement in Egypt. Nevertheless, through Moses, the prophet *par excellence* and God's deliverer, Jacob's story becomes a bride-rescue story in Hosea 12. Jacob's own conversion beckons readers to "return to your God, hold fast to love and justice, and wait continually for your God" (12:6).

Hosea 12 has undergone a long editorial process of transmission and transformation, which accounts for its differing characterizations of Jacob the patriarch, shifts in tone, and interweaving of various themes. Its separation from Hosea 13 is rather artificial, since the interweaving of themes—e.g., the deliverance of the people from Egypt, their idyllic dwelling in the wilderness, and the parallels between Jacob and Ephraim—continues well into chap. 13 (cf. 12:6, 9 and 13:4-5; 12:2-3 and 13:12-13). Moreover, images of the wind (רוח *rûaḥ*) and the east wind (קדים *qādîm*) beginning in 12:1 connect chiastically with the very end in 13:15 (*qādîm/ rûaḥ-Yahweh*), contributing to the reader's sense of chaps. 12–13 as a unit. Within the Hosea 12–14 complex, chaps. 12–13 constitute God's indictment (and punishment) of a nation, while chap. 14 describes God's blessing of a nation.

HOSEA 11:12–13:16, GOD'S INDICTMENT OF A NATION

OVERVIEW

God's indictment of the nation alternates between historical allusions to Israel's past and correlations with its present state. When discussing the present, Hosea typically refers to the nation

as "Ephraim." The oscillation between past and present can be outlined as follows:[126]

126. Cf. Johan Lust, "Freud, Hosea, and the Murder of Moses (Hosea 12)," *ETL* 65 (1989) 84-85.

Introduction—11:12–12:1:	Ephraim Herds the Wind and Pursues the East Wind
Historical Allusion—12:2-6:	Jacob, the Eponymous Ancestor
Application—12:7-9:	Ephraim's Ill-Gotten Wealth
Historical Allusion—12:10-13:	Jacob and the Prophet *Par Excellence*
Application—12:14–13:3:	Ephraim's Idolatry
Historical Allusion—13:4-11:	Yahweh's Feeding and Destroying in the Wilderness
Application—13:12-14:	Ephraim as an Unwise Son
Conclusion—13:15-16:	The Coming of the East Wind and the Wind of Yahweh from the Wilderness

Hosea 11:12–12:1, Ephraim Herds the Wind and Pursues the East Wind

NIV

¹²Ephraim has surrounded me with lies,
   the house of Israel with deceit.
And Judah is unruly against God,
   even against the faithful Holy One.

12 ¹Ephraim feeds on the wind;
   he pursues the east wind all day
and multiplies lies and violence.
He makes a treaty with Assyria
   and sends olive oil to Egypt.

NRSV

¹²ᵃ Ephraim has surrounded me with lies,
   and the house of Israel with deceit;
but Judah still walksᵇ with God,
   and is faithful to the Holy One.

12 Ephraim herds the wind,
   and pursues the east wind all day long;
they multiply falsehood and violence;
   they make a treaty with Assyria,
   and oil is carried to Egypt.

ᵃ Ch 12.1 in Heb   ᵇ Heb *roams* or *rules*

COMMENTARY

Speaking through the prophet (cf. "me" in 11:12), God begins an indictment of Ephraim/Israel by accusing it of lies and deceit (מרמה *mirmâ*). The reference to Judah in the latter half of 11:12 is difficult, because the meaning of the verb describing Judah's actions with God (רד *rād*), is uncertain. It is usually translated as "walks" or "roams" (so NRSV) and, with the description of Judah as being "faithful to the Holy One," places Judah in a favorable light. The positive reference to Judah is most likely a later addition, foreshadowing other affirmative statements in chaps. 12–13 (12:4*b*-6, 9, 13; 13:4, 14).[127]

The futility of Ephraim's deeds becomes evident in 12:1, where Ephraim attempts to "herd the wind" and "pursue" the east wind. The winds that Ephraim tries to control (12:1) will lash back and ravage him (13:15). The lies and destruction (כזב ושד *kāzāb wāšōd*) that characterize Ephraim's flight to Egypt and Assyria in 7:11-13 also characterize the ill-conceived covenants he makes with them in 12:1.

127. Gale A. Yee, *Composition and Tradition in the Book of Hosea: A Redaction Critical Investigation,* SBLDS 102 (Atlanta: Scholars Press, 1987) 230-31.

Hosea 12:2-6, Jacob, the Eponymous Ancestor

NIV

²The LORD has a charge to bring against Judah;
    he will punish Jacobᵃ according to his ways
    and repay him according to his deeds.
³In the womb he grasped his brother's heel;
    as a man he struggled with God.
⁴He struggled with the angel and overcame him;
    he wept and begged for his favor.
 He found him at Bethel
    and talked with him there—
⁵the LORD God Almighty,
    the LORD is his name of renown!
⁶But you must return to your God;
    maintain love and justice,
    and wait for your God always.

ᵃ2 *Jacob* means *he grasps the heel* (figuratively, *he deceives*).

NRSV

² The LORD has an indictment against Judah,
    and will punish Jacob according to his ways,
    and repay him according to his deeds.
³ In the womb he tried to supplant his brother,
    and in his manhood he strove with God.
⁴ He strove with the angel and prevailed,
    he wept and sought his favor;
 he met him at Bethel,
    and there he spoke with him.ᵃ
⁵ The LORD the God of hosts,
    the LORD is his name!
⁶ But as for you, return to your God,
    hold fast to love and justice,
    and wait continually for your God.

ᵃ Gk Syr: Heb *us*

COMMENTARY

12:2. Yahweh's dispute (ריב *rîb*), which began in 2:2 and continues in 4:4, now concludes in this verse. The main interpretive problem of this indictment is its condemnation of the southern kingdom of Judah, which many scholars regard as a secondary replacement of an original "Israel." Although Hosea includes Judah in his accusation and punishment of Ephraim (5:10-14), the strongest arguments in favor of an original "Israel" would be the parallelism with Jacob here and in 12:12, as well as the wordplay on these proper names (vv. 3-4).

12:3-4b. Selected traditions from the Jacob story become the focus of these verses, although scholars diverge sharply in their interpretations of them.[128] At one level, the text seems to trace the lies and deceit rampant in present-day Ephraim/Israel (11:12) back to the fraud inflicted by its eponymous ancestor, Jacob/Israel. At another level, however, vv. 4-6 seem to present Jacob as a person to be emulated, apparently mitigating the force of Yahweh's *rîb* against Jacob/Israel in v. 3. Rather than opt for either a completely negative

or a positive interpretation, I would argue that both levels are valid in the development of the text.

Verse 3 links the tradition of Jacob's grabbing his brother's heel at birth (cf. NIV) with the pejorative etymology of his name. Responding to Isaac's revelation of Jacob's deceit (מרמה *mirmâ*), a deceit of which his descendants are guilty (11:12), Esau exclaims, "Is he not rightly named Jacob [יעקוב *yaʿăqōb*]? For he has supplanted me [ויעקבני *wayyaʿqĕbēnî*] these two times" (Gen 27:36). Moreover, v. 3 alludes to Jacob's nocturnal struggle with a man at the Jabbok. On that occasion, Jacob received the new name "Israel" because, the man declared, "you have striven with God and with humans and have prevailed" (Gen 32:24-32).

Ambiguity regarding the precise subjects of the verbs in v. 4*bc* creates interpretive problems. If Jacob has just prevailed over the angel, why would he weep and seek his favor? Jacob's weeping at the Jabbok is not recorded in Genesis. If the angel is the subject, then v. 4*b* diverges even more sharply from the Genesis account, which does not relate that the "man" either wept before Jacob or sought his favor. Furthermore, in v. 4*c* the subject

128. See the excellent summary of the problem in Francis I. Andersen and David Noel Freedman, *Hosea,* AB 24 (Garden City, N.Y.: Doubleday, 1980) 594-600.

and object are ambiguous. Did Jacob meet the angel/God at Bethel or vice-versa? The MT states that this person "spoke with us," while the Greek and the Syriac translations (followed by the NRSV and the NIV) have "spoke with him." With whom did this person speak, to "him" or to "us"?

The thematic development of the text becomes apparent when one recognizes the chiastic arrangement of vv. 3-4b:[129]

A In the womb Jacob supplanted his *brother*.
B In his manhood he strove with *God*.
B' He strove with the *angel* and prevailed.
A' He wept and sought (*Esau's*) favor
(cf. Gen 33:4-10)

The subject of each verb is Jacob, whose character is transformed in the progression of the chiasmus. The one who once disinherited his brother (A) now weeps and seeks his favor (A'). This attitudinal change becomes possible only through Jacob's momentous encounter with the divine (B/B').

12:4c-6. The transformation of the patriarch becomes even more obvious in these verses, which presuppose Jacob's dream at Bethel (Gen 28:10-17), where God reveals to him:

"I am the LORD, the God of Abraham your father and the God of Isaac.... Know that I am with you and will keep [*šmr*] you wherever you go, and will bring you back [*šûb*, hiphil] to this land; for I will not leave you until I have done what I have promised [*dbr*] you." (Gen 28:13, 15 NRSV)

129. Following William L. Holladay, "Chiasmus, the Key to Hosea XII 3-6," *VT* 16 (1966) 56-57. For another interpretation that also maintains the tension between a negative and a positive portrayal of Jacob, see Yee, *Composition and Tradition*, 232-37.

These verses are linked to the Genesis tradition not only by subject matter but also through the repetition of significant words: שמר (*šāmar*), שוב (*šûb*), and דבר (*dābar*). Furthermore, these verses exploit various levels of meaning through their ambiguous subjects and suffixes. In v. 4c, the expressions "he found him/us" and "he spoke with him/us" permit a double referent for both subject (God/Jacob) and object (Jacob/the present generation). On one level, God encounters Jacob at Bethel, speaks (*dābar*) with him, reveals the divine name, and enjoins him to repent and return (*šûb*) to God and cherish (*šāmar*) love and justice (v. 6). On another level, God encounters "us" and is revealed to "us," exhorting "us" to repent and adhere to the covenant. On still another level, the repentant Jacob speaks to "us," confesses God's name, and enjoins "us"/"you" to repent, return to God, and keep God's covenant.

Although the prophet indicts Jacob/Israel for his ways (v. 2), he manages through historical references to the Jacob story to communicate hope for the nation and a means by which it can change (vv. 3-6). The eponymous ancestor of Israel, a notorious cheat and liar to whom all of Israel's present sins can be traced, becomes, through his world-changing struggle with God, the nation's paradigm for repentance. He urges his descendants to undergo a similar transformative confrontation with God. The shift from "him" to "us," from the patriarch to the nation, is part of the text's overall design to ground the present sinful generation in its own history and to disclose possibilities for a new future. (See Reflections at 12:10-13.)

Hosea 12:7-9, Ephraim's Ill-Gotten Wealth

NIV	NRSV

7The merchant uses dishonest scales;
    he loves to defraud.
 8Ephraim boasts,
   "I am very rich; I have become wealthy.
 With all my wealth they will not find in me
    any iniquity or sin."
 	
 9"I am the LORD your God,
	7 A trader, in whose hands are false balances,
	    he loves to oppress.
	 8 Ephraim has said, "Ah, I am rich,
	    I have gained wealth for myself;
	 in all of my gain
	     no offense has been found in me
	     that would be sin."*a*
	
	 a Meaning of Heb uncertain

NIV

ₗwho brought youₗ out of[a] Egypt;
I will make you live in tents again,
    as in the days of your appointed feasts."

a9 Or God / ever since you were in

NRSV

9 I am the LORD your God
    from the land of Egypt;
I will make you live in tents again,
    as in the days of the appointed festival.

COMMENTARY

The text moves from the historical Jacob to present-day Ephraim. The metaphor for Ephraim is a merchant who uses dishonest (מרמה *mirmâ*) scales and loves to extort. The use of *mirmâ* here and in 11:12 connects Ephraim with deceptive Jacob, who usurped Esau's rights as oldest son: "Your brother came deceitfully [במרמה *bĕmirmâ*] and he has taken away your blessing" (Gen 27:35). Several wordplays strengthen this connection. In v. 3, Jacob struggled with God in his "manhood" (און *'ôn*). In v. 8, Ephraim boasts of the "riches" ('*ôn*) he has procured through unscrupulous means. He arrogantly believes that nobody will discover his "offense" (עון *'āwōn*).

Challenging Ephraim's cocky egocentrism, "I am rich," Yahweh responds emphatically (note the deliberate use of the pronoun "I" [אנכי *'ānōkî*]) in v. 9 with a revelation of God's name and importance: "I am the LORD your God." While the previous unit began in the past with Jacob and ended with an appeal to the present generation, vv. 7-9 begin in the present and look back to the past. Ephraim is reminded that God has been the nation's deity ("your God") ever since its enslavement in Egypt. The reference to making the people live in tents as in the days of the appointed festival has a double meaning. The festival is most likely Sukkot, as in 9:5-6, where "the day of appointed festival" brings destruction and the pilgrims' tents are overrun by nettles and thorns. On one hand, then, v. 9 is a threat. Boastful Ephraim will be stripped of its wealth and obliterated. On the other hand, v. 9 is also a promise. The wilderness period, which the feast of Sukkot celebrates, was for Hosea an idyllic time when the relationship between God and the nation was in perfect covenantal harmony (cf. 2:14-15; 9:10; 11:1-4). If the people heed the call to repentance by God/Jacob (v. 6), God will restore their covenant. (See Reflections at 12:10-13.)

Hosea 12:10-13, Jacob and the Prophet *Par Excellence*

NIV

10"I spoke to the prophets,
    gave them many visions
    and told parables through them."
11Is Gilead wicked?
    Its people are worthless!
Do they sacrifice bulls in Gilgal?
    Their altars will be like piles of stones
    on a plowed field.
12Jacob fled to the country of Aram[a];
    Israel served to get a wife,
    and to pay for her he tended sheep.

a12 That is, Northwest Mesopotamia

NRSV

10 I spoke to the prophets;
    it was I who multiplied visions,
    and through the prophets I will bring
        destruction.
11 In Gilead[a] there is iniquity,
    they shall surely come to nothing.
In Gilgal they sacrifice bulls,
    so their altars shall be like stone heaps
    on the furrows of the field.
12 Jacob fled to the land of Aram,
    there Israel served for a wife,
    and for a wife he guarded sheep.[b]

a Compare Syr: Heb *Gilead*   b Heb lacks *sheep*

NIV

13The LORD used a prophet to bring Israel up from
Egypt,
by a prophet he cared for him.

NRSV

13 By a prophet the LORD brought Israel up from
Egypt,
and by a prophet he was guarded.

COMMENTARY

The theological focus of this unit is God's creative/destructive word spoken and enacted through prophets in general and through Moses in particular. In Deut 18:15-19, Moses is regarded as the prophet *par excellence.* The shift to the prophets and to Moses is made possible by references to the appointed festival (מועד *môʿēd*) and to dwelling in tents (אהלים *ʾōhālîm*) in the wilderness (v. 9). These allusions evoke images of the tent of meeting (אהל מועד *ʾōhel môʿēd*) in the wilderness, where God spoke to God's servant Moses face to face (Exod 33:9-11). Accordingly, God maintains in v. 10*a* that, since the days of the tent of meeting and of Moses, "I spoke [דבר *dābar*] to the prophets;/ it was I who multiplied visions."

Translations of v. 10*b* diverge regarding what God did or will do through the prophets, because of the different meanings of the Hebrew word אדמה (*ʾădammeh*). On the one hand, God told parables through the prophets (NIV). On the other hand, God will bring destruction through the prophets (NRSV). Given the double entendres that have previously characterized this chapter (cf. vv. 4-6, 8-9), the double meaning of *ʾădammeh* ("to tell parables," "to ruin") is most likely implied here as well. Since the time of Moses, God has sent a succession of prophets to call Israel to conversion. When the nation refuses to repent, God destroys it. A similar thought is expressed in Hos 6:5: "I have hewn them by the prophets,/ I have killed them by the words of my mouth" (NRSV). The agents of God's revelation thus become the agents of God's just punishment.

12:11-12. The appearance of Gilead and Gilgal in v. 11 recalls other references to these sites in Hosea. The qualifier for Gilead (און *ʾāwen,* "iniquity") picks up the wordplay on "manhood/riches" (און *ʾôn*) and "iniquity" (עון *ʾāwôn*) in vv. 3, 8. Hosea 6:8 lambastes Gilead as a "city

of evildoers" (קרית פעלי און *qiryat pōʿălê ʾāwen*). In 4:15, Israel is enjoined not to enter the sanctuaries of Gilgal and Beth-ʾāwen. According to 9:15, Ephraim's evil began at Gilgal.

Moreover, since the Jacob tradition characterizes the next verse, it is not impossible that Gilead and Gilgal are also oblique references to Jacob, who flees to Gilead with his wives to escape his father-in-law, Laban (Gen 31:21-42). He eventually makes a covenant with Laban by setting up a stone heap (גל *gal,* Gen 31:43-53). This covenant centers on Jacob's fair treatment of Laban's daughters and a promise not to marry any other women. In Hos 12:11, the altars of Gilgal will become like stone heaps (גלים *gallîm*) on the furrows of the field (שדי *śāday*). Through a word-play with *śāday,* 12:12 leads into a direct reference to Jacob/Israel and his wife: "Jacob fled to the land of Aram [שדה ארם *śĕdēh ʾărām*], there Israel served [עבד *ʾābad*] for a wife, and for a wife he guarded [שמר *šāmar*]." Hosea identifies Ephraim's harlotous flight and subservience to foreign powers (12:1; cf. 5:13; 8:9) with Jacob's escape to a foreign land to serve for a wife by tending sheep. His labor (עבד *ʾebed*) recalls the time when the nation of Israel was a slave (*ʾebed*) in Egypt (cf. Deut 5:15).

12:13. This negative portrayal of Jacob/Israel is mitigated by this verse, which turns a slave narrative into a bride-rescue story: "By a prophet the LORD brought Israel up from Egypt,/ and by a prophet he was guarded [*šāmar*]." Just as Jacob moved to a foreign country to take a wife and bring her back, so also God travels to a foreign country to take a wife and bring her back.[130] Parallels also are drawn between Jacob and Moses. As with Jacob (vv. 4-5), God reveals the divine name to Moses and speaks with him (v.

130. R. B. Coote, "Hosea XII," *VT* 21 (1971) 401.

9). Moses, the first in a succession of prophets through whom God reveals and executes God's will (v. 10), becomes the chosen agent to lead the wife/Israel up from Egypt and protect (šāmar) her in the wilderness (v. 13).

Through a complex intertwining of wordplays and allusions, then, Hos 12:10-13 combines Jacob/Israel and Moses traditions, as well as ancestral, exodus, and prophetic traditions, in a pointed statement about present-day Ephraim. If the people listen to their patriarchs' injunction to repent (12:6), if they heed the prophets whom God sends (12:10), God will bring them back in a new exodus. As with the wife/Israel in Hosea 2 and the son/Israel in Hosea 11, chapter 12 records a three-stage journey. The first stage is Jacob's journey to a foreign land to find a wife. The second is God's journey to Egypt to rescue the wife/Israel in the first exodus through the prophet Moses. The third is God's journey to the lands of exile to rescue his wife/Israel through the agency of another prophet: Hosea.

REFLECTIONS

Past scholarship on Hosea often flattens Jacob's complex characterization in chapter 12 into either a totally negative or a totally positive portrayal. This binary interpretation of the patriarch blunts the prophet's message. Much more rhetorically effective in presenting a paradigm for a nation's conversion is depicting its ancestor in all of his deceit and betrayal. Jacob sinned despicably against his own family by duping both his brother and his father in order to further his own ambitions. Ephraim was a "chip off the old block" in its offenses.

Through a world-changing encounter with God, however, this epitome of sinfulness and deceit was transformed. His metamorphosis was not easy. The Genesis story relates that Jacob *struggled* with "the man" during the night. The mystics often refer to a "dark night of the soul" as a metaphor for one's struggle with oneself and with the divine. Confronting one's own dark side and heinous actions toward others is frightening in itself. But recognizing that one must be accountable to a higher being for these actions is triply horrendous. Hosea exhorts the nation to undergo its own "dark night of the soul," like its ancestor Jacob. Ephraim is guilty of many transgressions: lying and deceitful activity (11:12–12:1), violence (12:1), unauthorized treaties (12:1), greed (12:7), oppression of the poor (12:7-8), and cultic violations (12:11). As God had spoken through earlier prophets (12:10), God now speaks through Hosea to convict Ephraim of its iniquities and to hold Ephraim responsible for them.

Both the Genesis story and Hos 12:4 relate that Jacob *prevailed.* He not only survived the encounter but also triumphed in it. He was able to seek forgiveness from the brother he had defrauded. God spoke to him again at Bethel, reiterating the promise of land, descendants, and a great name, delivered first to Jacob's ancestor Abraham (Gen 35:9-15; cf. Gen 12:1-3).

Holding up the father of Israel as a model of repentance, God encounters and speaks with us in our own day, as well as during Hosea's time (12:6). Just like Jacob and Ephraim, we, too, are guilty of lies, deceit, violence, greed, and oppression of the poor. We, too, continually mock our religious worship with our hypocrisy. Hosea insists that, if there is hope for sinful Jacob and Ephraim, there is also hope for us. Moreover, at another level of interpretation, the repentant Jacob himself exhorts us to "return to your God, hold fast to love and justice, and wait continually for your God" (12:6). By allowing both positive and negative portrayals of Jacob to cohere side by side, Hosea's teaching of repentance becomes all the more forceful.

Hosea 12:14–13:3, Ephraim's Idolatry

NIV

¹⁴But Ephraim has bitterly provoked him to anger;
  his Lord will leave upon him the guilt of his
    bloodshed
  and will repay him for his contempt.

13 When Ephraim spoke, men trembled;
he was exalted in Israel.
  But he became guilty of Baal worship and
    died.
²Now they sin more and more;
  they make idols for themselves from their
    silver,
  cleverly fashioned images,
  all of them the work of craftsmen.
It is said of these people,
  "They offer human sacrifice
  and kiss*ᵃ* the calf-idols."
³Therefore they will be like the morning mist,
  like the early dew that disappears,
  like chaff swirling from a threshing floor,
  like smoke escaping through a window.

ᵃ2 Or "Men who sacrifice / kiss

NRSV

¹⁴ Ephraim has given bitter offense,
  so his Lord will bring his crimes down on
    him
  and pay him back for his insults.

13 When Ephraim spoke, there was
trembling;
  he was exalted in Israel;
  but he incurred guilt through Baal and died.
² And now they keep on sinning
  and make a cast image for themselves,
  idols of silver made according to their
    understanding,
  all of them the work of artisans.
"Sacrifice to these," they say.*ᵃ*
  People are kissing calves!
³ Therefore they shall be like the morning mist
  or like the dew that goes away early,
  like chaff that swirls from the threshing floor
  or like smoke from a window.

ᵃ Cn Compare Gk: Heb To these they say sacrifices of people

COMMENTARY

12:14–13:1. Hosea moves back to the present in his indictment of Ephraim. In 12:14, he accuses Ephraim of provoking his Lord to anger (הכעיס *hik'îs*; cf. NIV), an expression commonly used to describe God's fury over idol worship (cf. Deut 4:25; 9:18; 31:29; Judg 2:12; 1 Kgs 14:9). The nation's idolatry is the focus of this unit, and God will hold Ephraim accountable for it (12:15). Ephraim had once achieved prominence among the Israelite tribes. When he spoke, people trembled (13:1). However, he incurred guilt בבעל (*babba'al*; lit., "at Baal") and died.[131] The expression "at Baal" most likely refers to a place, Baal-Peor, where at the end of its wilderness journey, the nation was sexually seduced by the women of Moab to worship the fertility god Baal (Num 25:1-18; cf. Hos 9:10).

13:2. The movement from the nation's past to its present idolatry is achieved through the adverb "now" (עתה *'attâ*). The people continue their sinning by casting metal images and silver idols. These idols are condemned as mere works of human manufacture (cf. 8:4-6). The difficulty in v. 2c is reflected in the translations. The NIV's reference to the abomination of human sacrifice is closer to the MT, which can also be rendered: "They who sacrifice people speak to them [the idols]." The calves that are kissed are the cult images installed at Bethel (see 8:5-6; 10:5-6). The kissing of the images seems to be part of the ritual worship of Baal (1 Kgs 19:18).

13:3. God's judgment against the people's idolatry is signaled by "therefore" (לכן *lākēn*). A series of four similes highlights the ephemerality of the nation before the deity. They will be like the morning mist, dew that goes away early, the chaff swirling from the threshing floor, and the smoke that escapes through a window (cf. 6:4) (See Reflections at 13:15-16.).

131. J. Wijngaards, "Death and Resurrection in Covenantal Context (Hos VI 2)," *VT* 17 (1967) 238, suggests that 13:1 may refer to covenantal "death," just as 6:1-3 refers to covenantal resurrection.

Hosea 13:4-11, Yahweh's Feeding and Destroying in the Wilderness

NIV

4"But I am the LORD your God,
⌊who brought you⌋ out of[a] Egypt.
You shall acknowledge no God but me,
    no Savior except me.
5I cared for you in the desert,
    in the land of burning heat.
6When I fed them, they were satisfied;
    when they were satisfied, they became proud;
    then they forgot me.
7So I will come upon them like a lion,
    like a leopard I will lurk by the path.
8Like a bear robbed of her cubs,
    I will attack them and rip them open.
Like a lion I will devour them;
    a wild animal will tear them apart.

9"You are destroyed, O Israel,
    because you are against me, against your
        helper.
10Where is your king, that he may save you?
    Where are your rulers in all your towns,
of whom you said,
    'Give me a king and princes'?
11So in my anger I gave you a king,
    and in my wrath I took him away."

a4 Or *God / ever since you were in*

NRSV

4 Yet I have been the LORD your God
    ever since the land of Egypt;
you know no God but me,
    and besides me there is no savior.
5 It was I who fed[a] you in the wilderness,
    in the land of drought.
6 When I fed[b] them, they were satisfied;
    they were satisfied, and their heart was
        proud;
    therefore they forgot me.
7 So I will become like a lion to them,
    like a leopard I will lurk beside the way.
8 I will fall upon them like a bear robbed of her
        cubs,
    and will tear open the covering
        of their heart;
there I will devour them like a lion,
    as a wild animal would mangle them.

9 I will destroy you, O Israel;
    who can help you?[c]
10 Where now is[d] your king, that he may save
        you?
    Where in all your cities are your rulers,
of whom you said,
    "Give me a king and rulers"?
11 I gave you a king in my anger,
    and I took him away in my wrath.

a Gk Syr: Heb *knew*   b Cn: Heb *according to their pasture*
c Gk Syr: Heb *for in me is your help*   d Gk Syr Vg: Heb *I will be*

COMMENTARY

13:4. Two ambivalent portrayals of God are sketched in this section. The God who fed and nourished the nation in the wilderness is the same God who will destroy it like a savage animal in the wilderness. In deliberate contrast with the people's idolatry, Yahweh reveals the divine name again: "*I* [אנכי *'ānōkî*] am Yahweh your God from the land of Egypt" (author's trans.). Enlarging upon 12:9, Yahweh claims that Israel has known no other god. Besides God there is no other savior, whether an idol

(v. 2) or a king (v. 10), who can deliver them in their time of need.

13:5. Just as Israel knew no other god but Yahweh, so also Yahweh asserts, "*I* [אני *'ănî*] knew you in the wilderness, in the land of drought."[132] On Israel's part, knowledge of God involves a covenantal faith, obedience, and love of the deity. On God's part, it entails the election of Israel and

132. The NRSV reads with the LXX and other versions, "I fed you." The NIV is closer to the MT's "to know," which has the sense of "to care for" in Ps 1:6 and Nah 1:7.

the pledge to love and protect it. God's protection was never so evident as in the wilderness, that arid wasteland where God brought Israel after its enslavement and entered into a covenant with it (cf. 2:14-15). It was the ideal period of the nation's history when it knew no other god but Yahweh and was fed to satisfaction (13:6; cf. 9:10; 11:1-4; 12:9; Deut 8:15-16; 32:10-14).

13:6-9. When the people became sated, however, they forgot God in their arrogance (v. 6; cf. 2:15; Deut 32:18). Hence, the God who preserved Israel in the wilderness will now destroy Israel in the wilderness (vv. 7-8). Because of Israel's hubris, the one whose name was revealed as Yahweh in 12:9 and 13:4 now becomes "I AM" (אהי *'ĕhî*) in 13:7. *'Ehî* is a form of אהיה (*'ehyeh*), which according to Exod 3:14-15 functions as a wordplay on the tetragrammaton, YHWH.[133] In Hos 1:9, God declares, "I am not I AM to you [אנכי לא־אהיה לכם *'ānōkî lō'-'ehyeh lākem*]," a nullification of the covenant symbolized by the birth of Hosea's son "Not My People" (Lo-Ammi). God as *'Ehî* ("I AM") is both being and non-being, simultaneously life-giver and death-dealer. In a series of five similes beginning with *'Ehî*, God compares the divine self to predatory animals that ambush and fall upon their kill in the wilderness (vv. 7-8; cf. 5:14). Although this section does not explicitly mention the covenant, the imagery of devouring animals is characteristic of covenantal curses leveled against the transgressing party.[134] The conflicting picture of God is most evident in v. 9, which can be read: "I will destroy you, O Israel, for in me is your help." The deity becomes both the giver and the taker of life. Verse 9 can also be read, "Your destruction, O Israel, for (you are) against me, against your help," which lays blame for the imminent ruin upon the nation itself (cf. NIV).

13:10-11. Although commentators and translators usually interpret *'ĕhî* in v. 10 as a dialectical variant of איה (*'ayyēh*, "where"), I opt for the multiple reading. On one level, God demands, "Where is your king now, that he may save you?" On another level, v. 10 asserts, "*'Ēhî*/ I AM is/will be your king now, and he will save you." Yahweh already emphasized in v. 4 that the people have no other savior. By means of a wordplay, v. 10 expresses both a sarcastic disillusionment with the human institution of monarchy and an affirmation that *'Ehî* is king precisely because Yahweh, and Yahweh alone, can rescue the people. The giver and taker of life becomes the giver and taker of kings in v. 11. This verse draws upon the anti-monarchic traditions of 1 Sam 8:6-8, where the people are accused of rejecting Yahweh as king, in spite of God's saving activity toward them, "from the day I brought them up out of Egypt to this day." (See Reflections at 13:15-16.)

---

133. For a fuller discussion, see Yee, *Composition and Tradition*, 69-71, 255-58.

134. Cf. 2:18, which describes the renewal of the covenant in terms of the pacification of wild animals, and 4:1-3, where animals are affected cosmically by the nation's transgressions.

Hosea 13:12-14, Ephraim as an Unwise Son

NIV	NRSV
12"The guilt of Ephraim is stored up, his sins are kept on record. 13Pains as of a woman in childbirth come to him, but he is a child without wisdom; when the time arrives, he does not come to the opening of the womb. 14"I will ransom them from the power of the grave[a];	12 Ephraim's iniquity is bound up; his sin is kept in store. 13 The pangs of childbirth come for him, but he is an unwise son; for at the proper time he does not present himself at the mouth of the womb. 14 Shall I ransom them from the power of Sheol? Shall I redeem them from Death?

a14 Hebrew *Sheol*

NIV

> I will redeem them from death.
> Where, O death, are your plagues?
>   Where, O grave,[a] is your destruction?
>
> "I will have no compassion,"

[a]14 Hebrew *Sheol*

NRSV

> O Death, where are[a] your plagues?
> O Sheol, where is[a] your destruction?
> Compassion is hidden from my eyes.

[a] Gk Syr: Heb *I will be*

COMMENTARY

13:12-13. The theme shifts in v. 12 from Yahweh's historical retrospect and future projection on the wilderness period to present-day Ephraim. Just as 12:7-8 connects Ephraim with the Jacob traditions of 12:3-4, so also 13:12-15a joins Ephraim to the Jacob traditions in Hosea 12. Ephraim's iniquity and sin, resulting from his ill-gotten wealth (12:8), are hoarded and stored away (v. 12; cf. Deut 32:34). Hosea 12:12 relates how Jacob fled to Paddam-Aram and served in exchange for a wife. In these verses Ephraim is conceived in their sexual union, linking the present nation to its patriarch Jacob through direct descent. While in his mother's womb, Jacob tries to supplant his brother (12:3). Also portrayed *in utero,* Ephraim is an "unwise son," a witless fetus who hasn't the sense to appear at the cervix at the time of birth (v. 13). The images of Ephraim in the womb recall the paradoxes of Hos 9:10-17, where human (and agricultural) fertility is undermined.

13:14. The equivocation that characterizes chap. 13 culminates in this verse, perhaps one of the most disputed verses in the book. The issue is whether God is life-giver or death-dealer of a nation that refuses to leave the womb. Verse 14a literally reads as a positive assertion of God's intent to ransom and redeem the people from death (NIV), an idea that seemingly conflicts with vv. 12-13. Scholars usually emend the ambiguous אהי (*'ĕhî*) in v. 14b to the interrogative איה (*'ayyēh,* "Where?") and interpret the whole verse as a question insinuating a threat (NRSV; see also v. 10). Read as a question, v. 14a implies that God has the power to ransom and to redeem the people from death, but because of their apostasy, God summons Death and Sheol to wreak their havoc upon them (v. 14b). The ambiguous word נחם (*nōḥam*) would thus signify that "compas-

sion," not "revenge" (cf. TNK), is hidden from God's eyes. Complicating matters in v. 14b, one can read *'ĕhî* as "I am/will be" ("I" speech) or as the name of the deity, *'Ehî*; and one can read דבריך (*dĕbārêkā*) in its usual sense, "your words,"[135] instead of "your plagues." These options render the following possibilities:

> Shall I ransom them from the power of Sheol?
> (I shall ransom them from the power of Sheol.)
> Shall I redeem them from Death?
> (I shall redeem them from Death.)
> Where are your plagues/words, O Death?
> (*'Ehî* is/I am your plagues/words, O Death.)
> Where is your destruction, O Sheol?
> (*'Ehî* is/I am your destruction, O Sheol.)
> Compassion is hidden from my eyes.
> (Revenge is hidden from my eyes.) (author's trans.)

Death and Sheol, the ultimate ends of all human life, are personified here as characters in a drama, in which God appears as the ambiguous *'Ehî.* The dramatic script for these characters is filled with equivocations and questions. Will Ephraim, the unwise son who refuses to be born at the proper time, meet Death and Sheol in an untimely fashion? If so, life and death become interchangeable, and the womb becomes the eternal tomb. Is God the agent of Death, bringing plague and destruction to Ephraim? Verses 7-8 portray God metaphorically like wild animals that stalk, ambush, and fall upon their prey (see also 5:12-14). Does God actually speak the words of Death? According to 6:5, God kills through the words of God's mouth (see also 12:10). Although Yahweh creates all life through the spoken word (Genesis 1), God can end existence by oral command. As in v. 10, *'Ehî,* whose name symbolizes

---

135. On the double meaning of דבריך (*dĕbāreyka,* "plagues/words"), see Francis Landy, "In the Wilderness of Speech: Problems of Metaphor in Hosea," *Biblical Interpretation* 3 (1995) 44.

the essence of life, is both being and non-being, life-giver and death-dealer.

While pondering God's role as the agent of Death, v. 14 also asks whether God is Death's own plague, the one who abolishes Death: "'Ehî is/I am your plague, O Death." Although the sentence is stated indicatively, a question is implied in the slipperiness of דבר (dbr) as either "plague" or "word." God as Death's plague reinforces the divine role as savior, implied in an indicative rendering of v. 14a: "I shall ransom them from the power of Sheol. I shall redeem

them from Death." If God is savior, it is possible to answer the question, "Where are your plagues, O Death?" with a resounding "Nowhere," since "revenge" is hidden from the divine eyes. If God is death-dealer, however, the deity summons Death and Sheol to wreak havoc upon Ephraim, because "compassion is hidden from my eyes." As with the other ambiguities in these chapters, the multivalence of Hosea 13 should be sustained, since all of these possibilities are in some way true and deeply imbedded in the theological drama. (See Reflections at 13:15-16.)

Hosea 13:15-16, The Coming of the East Wind and the Wind of Yahweh from the Wilderness

NIV

15 "even though he thrives among his brothers.
An east wind from the LORD will come,
blowing in from the desert;
his spring will fail
and his well dry up.
His storehouse will be plundered
of all its treasures.
16The people of Samaria must bear their guilt,
because they have rebelled against their God.
They will fall by the sword;
their little ones will be dashed to the ground,
their pregnant women ripped open."

NRSV

15 Although he may flourish among rushes,[a]
the east wind shall come, a blast from the LORD,
rising from the wilderness;
and his fountain shall dry up,
his spring shall be parched.
It shall strip his treasury
of every precious thing.
16b Samaria shall bear her guilt,
because she has rebelled against her God;
they shall fall by the sword,
their little ones shall be dashed in pieces,
and their pregnant women ripped open.

a Or among brothers   b Ch 14.1 in Heb

COMMENTARY

13:15. Hosea's indictment against Ephraim began in 11:12–12:1. Hosea 13:15-16 forms its conclusion. The verb יפריא (yaprî') in v. 15a exploits different possible wordplays on the name "Ephraim" (אפרים 'eprayim). According to Gen 41:52, Joseph names his son Ephraim because "God has made me fruitful [פרה pārâ] in the land of my misfortunes." Verse 15a could thus pick up this tradition and read "He shall flourish [pārâ] among his brothers" (so NIV; the NRSV is based on an emendation of "brothers" to "reeds"). Moreover, 8:9 compares Ephraim, who hires lov-

ers among the nations, to a wild ass (פרא pere') in the wilderness, which cannot contain its lust (cf. Jer 2:24). Yaprî' in v. 15a could then be rendered, "He shall be (sexually) wild among his brothers."[136] The fertility and sexuality embodied by Ephraim's name and by the nation itself will be reversed by counterimages of judgment in the following verses.[137] As the indictment began

136. If פרא (pere') is read as an elative hiphil. See Francis I. Andersen and David Noel Freedman, Hosea, AB 24 (Garden City, N.Y.: Doubleday, 1980) 640-41.

137. The displacement is achieved through the concessive כ (kî) beginning 13:15 (cf. NRSV). The NIV attaches v. 14c to the beginning of v. 15.

with the depiction of Ephraim herding the wind and pursuing the east wind (12:1), it concludes with Yahweh raising up the east wind and a wind from the wilderness.[138] Once a place where the nation was fed and nourished by God (vv. 5-6), the wilderness now produces the sirocco, which will bake the land, drying up every fountain and spring. The windstorms will strip treasuries of the riches that Ephraim had so enthusiastically hoarded (12:8; 13:12).

13:16. In this verse we perhaps discover what happens to Ephraim, who will not leave the womb (v. 13). The sexual promiscuity of Ephraim (v. 15a) becomes incarnate in a feminine personi-

fication of its capital city, Samaria (see Ezekiel 16 for a similar personification of Samaria's southern rival, Jerusalem). Literal and figurative converge in this verse. On the one hand, Samaria will become the site of tremendous destruction and sadistic atrocities, targeting the most vulnerable— children and pregnant women (cf. 10:15). On the other hand, the personification of Samaria as a guilty and rebellious woman is not accidental. Hosea is notorious for his symbolization of the nation's sin as a sexually defiant woman (Hosea 1–3). He represents Samaria as a pregnant woman who will suffer a brutal fate as her punishment. Her swollen belly will be ripped open, and the fruit of her promiscuity, her bastard child Ephraim, torn from her.

---

138. The counterimage is nicely achieved through the distant chiasm between רוח (*rûaḥ*, "wind") and קדים (*qādîm,* "east wind") in 12:1 and *qādîm* and *rûaḥ* in 13:15.

REFLECTIONS

Embedded in the rhetoric of Hosea 13 is a deeply ambivalent and conflicted portrayal of God. Divergences between the NIV and the NRSV translations reveal a Janus-like deity who saves the nation from slavery and feeds them in the wilderness (13:4-6), but at the same time can become like a wild animal in the wilderness that will rip the nation to shreds (13:7-8). God appears as both the giver and the taker of life, the source of being and non-being, the savior and the destroyer (13:9-11, 14). If God is life-giver, God becomes a midwife to Ephraim, who has refused to be born at the proper time (13:12-13). God is like the pious midwives who subvert the pharaoh's evil plans to destroy male Israelite babies (Exod 1:15-22). If God is death-dealer, the divine becomes the pharaoh himself, ordering the slaughter of the infants, ripping open the wombs of women (cf. Hos 13:16).

On the one hand, we can deal with these paradoxes by rationalizing that Ephraim deserved the punishment God meted out. Ephraim forsook God's covenant, cast images for itself and worshiped them (13:1-2), extorted the poor (12:7-8), became allied to foreign nations (12:1), and so forth. God had warned the people through the prophets (12:10), but they persisted in their wickedness. Hence, God's retribution was warranted.

On the other hand, Hosea 13 reminds us of God's impenetrability. We cannot fashion God into our own image and likeness and put God into a box. This was precisely Hosea's accusation against the nation's manufacture of graven idols, gods that were predictable, controllable, and familiar (13:1; see also 10:5-6). For Hosea, God can abolish death and be death's own agent as well. There is a side to God that is altogether strange and "other." Hosea records God's words of destruction not only through past prophets (6:5; 12:10), but also in his own prophetic word. We deny the alien "otherness" of God, depicted by Hosea, at our own peril.

HOSEA 14:1-9, GOD'S BLESSING OF A NATION

OVERVIEW

The metaphor of the son that characterizes chap. 13 gives way to the metaphor of the wife in chap. 14. Perhaps the transition to the wife metaphor is made through the graphic image of a butchered pregnant Samaria, which concludes Hosea's indictment against the nation (13:16). Under the threat of this impending violence, the wife/Israel is exhorted to turn back to her God (v. 1).

In the first section of the book, after the wife's punishment and repentance (2:6-13), 2:23 describes Yahweh's sowing his wife/Israel like a seed into the land. At various points in the second section, Hosea urges the people to repent by utilizing images of the essentials needed to make this seed grow in the land (6:1-3; 10:12). Finally, in this concluding chapter, Hosea depicts the successful results of being sown back into the land. The wife/Israel becomes a lush and luxurious plantation.

Hosea 14:1-9 is divided into three parts. In the first part (vv. 1-3), the prophet calls the nation to repent and return to God. In the second part (vv. 4-8), God speaks, predicting the people's restoration in the land when they repent. The third part (v. 9) summons the wise reader to pay heed to the book as a whole.

Hosea 14:1-3, The Prophet's Call to Repentance and Return

NIV	NRSV
14 Return, O Israel, to the LORD your God. Your sins have been your downfall! ²Take words with you and return to the LORD. Say to him: "Forgive all our sins and receive us graciously, that we may offer the fruit of our lips.ᵃ ³Assyria cannot save us; we will not mount war-horses. We will never again say 'Our gods' to what our own hands have made, for in you the fatherless find compassion."	**14** Return, O Israel, to the LORD your God, for you have stumbled because of your iniquity. ² Take words with you and return to the LORD; say to him, "Take away all guilt; accept that which is good, and we will offer the fruitᵃ of our lips. ³ Assyria shall not save us; we will not ride upon horses; we will say no more, 'Our God,' to the work of our hands. In you the orphan finds mercy."
a2 Or offer our lips as sacrifices of bulls	*ᵃ Gk Syr: Heb bulls*

COMMENTARY

Through characteristic wordplays, Hosea begins this unit with a summons to the nation to repent (שובה *šûbâ*) and return (שובו *šûbû*) to God. The return to the land (ישבו *yēšĕbû,* v. 7) is contingent upon this return to Yahweh. The prophet bids the people to "take words with you and return to the

LORD" (v. 2a), supplying the actual words they should say/take before God (vv. 2b-3). They should ask God to take away the guilt (עון 'āwôn) that made them stumble (vv. 1-2; cf. 12:9; 13:12). In place of this guilt, they will offer penitent words as "the fruit of [their] lips,"[139] renouncing both their political and their religious offenses (v. 3). Their dependence upon other nations is annulled by their declaration: "Assyria shall not save us;/ we will not ride upon horses" (cf. 1:7). Their idolatry is negated by a promise of what they will not say: "We will say no more, 'our God,' to the work of our hands." The orphan who finds mercy (ירחם yĕruḥam) reverses the threat against Israel implied in the name of the daughter, Lo-ruhamah. The redeemed son Ammi will declare to Yahweh alone, "My God" (1:6-9; 2:23). (See Reflections at 14:9.)

139. The first instance of one of the wordplays on the name "Ephraim" appears in this unit: "fruit [v. 2, פרים pĕrîm] of our lips," "blossom" (vv. 6 יפרח yipraḥ and 8 יפרחו yiprĕḥû), "your fruit" (v. 8, פריך peryĕka).

Hosea 14:4-8, God's Rich Plantation

NIV

4"I will heal their waywardness
  and love them freely,
  for my anger has turned away from them.
5I will be like the dew to Israel;
  he will blossom like a lily.
Like a cedar of Lebanon
  he will send down his roots;
6 his young shoots will grow.
His splendor will be like an olive tree,
  his fragrance like a cedar of Lebanon.
7Men will dwell again in his shade.
  He will flourish like the grain.
He will blossom like a vine,
  and his fame will be like the wine from
    Lebanon.
8O Ephraim, what more have I[a] to do with idols?
  I will answer him and care for him.
I am like a green pine tree;
  your fruitfulness comes from me."

a8 Or What more has Ephraim

NRSV

4 I will heal their disloyalty;
  I will love them freely,
  for my anger has turned from them.
5 I will be like the dew to Israel;
  he shall blossom like the lily,
  he shall strike root like the forests of Lebanon.[a]
6 His shoots shall spread out;
  his beauty shall be like the olive tree,
  and his fragrance like that of Lebanon.
7 They shall again live beneath my[b] shadow,
  they shall flourish as a garden;[c]
they shall blossom like the vine,
  their fragrance shall be like the wine of
    Lebanon.

8 O Ephraim, what have I[d] to do with idols?
  It is I who answer and look after you.[e]
I am like an evergreen cypress;
  your faithfulness[f] comes from me.

a Cn: Heb like Lebanon   b Heb his   c Cn: Heb they shall grow grain   d Or What more has Ephraim   e Heb him   f Heb your fruit

COMMENTARY

In this second section, God responds in the first person to a contrite nation. Through other wordplays on šûb, God declares the healing of Israel's disloyalty (משובתם mĕšûbōtōm), because God's anger has turned from them (v. 4). Highlighted between these two assertions is God's announcement, "I will love them freely." Just as the mother/father God healed the son (11:3), so also the hope that God will heal again (6:1-3) finds its fulfillment in v. 4. The theme of God loving this people in spite of their disloyalty reiterates the passionate, tender emotions that Yahweh/husband expressed to his repentant wife (2:19-20; 3:1).

Verses 5-8 describe the results of God's sowing

of Israel back into the land. Just as nourishing rains are crucial for a plantation's growth (cf. 6:3; 10:12), so also Yahweh "will be like the dew to Israel." Perhaps resuming the Jacob tradition of chaps. 12–13, this statement recalls Isaac's blessing over Jacob in Gen 27:28: "May God give you the dew of heaven, and of the fatness of the earth, and plenty of grain and wine." Moreover, the abundance of rain is a manifestation of God's covenant with the people (2:21-23). Only through God's free gift of rain does the plantation of Israel not only survive, but also flourish.

A series of wordplays, particularly on the name "Ephraim," highlight the intimate connection between God and the nation's prospering. Verse 5 uses the divine appellative אהיה (*'ĕhyeh*) in conjunction with Israel's blossoming: "I AM [אהיה *'ĕhyeh*] will be/I will be like the dew to Israel; he shall blossom [יפרח *yiprah*] like the lily." In v. 7, Israel's blossoming (*pārah*) like the vine is prefaced by the return (שוב *šûb*) of Israel, who "will live [ישב *yāšab*] beneath my shadow." The remarkable detail of Israel's residing under God's shade is clarified in v. 8, where Yahweh states:

"O Ephraim [אפרים *'eprayim*], what have I to do with idols? It is I who answer and look after you. I am like an evergreen cypress. Your fruit [*pĕrî*] comes from me" (NRSV; cf. NIV, which is closer to the MT). In an image unique in the whole OT, God is compared to a great tree under whose shade the returning exiles will dwell. This image contrasts with those who play the harlot, making idolatrous sacrifices under trees "because their shade is good" (4:14).

Agricultural and marital metaphors converge in this passage. Compare vv. 5-8 with the erotic love song, the Canticles. In Cant 2:2, the man compares his lover to a lily, just as Yahweh in Hos 14:5 depicts Israel as blossoming like a lily. In Canticles 2–3, the woman compares her lover to an apple tree under which she sits and whose fruit is sweet to her mouth. In vv. 7-8, Ephraim/Israel sits under the shade that God, the evergreen cypress, provides. Rejecting its other deities, Yahweh insists that God answers and looks after Israel. Like a tree that offers protection and nourishment, so God provides fruit (*pĕrî*) and shelter for the people. (See Reflections at 14:9.)

Hosea 14:9, A Summons to the Wise Reader

NIV	NRSV

⁹Who is wise? He will realize these things.
   Who is discerning? He will understand them.
The ways of the LORD are right;
   the righteous walk in them,
   but the rebellious stumble in them.
	⁹ Those who are wise understand these things;
	   those who are discerning know them.
	For the ways of the LORD are right,
	   and the upright walk in them,
	   but transgressors stumble in them.

COMMENTARY

Hosea 14:9, like 1:1, belongs to the latest stages of the book's formation, creating an interpretive frame around the prophetic sayings. Hosea 1:1 situates the book during a particular historical period. Hosea 14:9 exhorts the wise and discerning among present-day readers to study, discern, and appropriate the truths embodied in the work as they "walk in the ways of the Lord," a typically deuteronomic expression referring to obedience to God's commandments (Deut 8:6; 11:22, 28; 19:9).

The "ways of the LORD" are also manifested in the different symbolic and physical journeys recounted throughout the book, teaching the readers narratively about Yahweh's covenant demands. God hedges the wife's "way" with thorns, beginning her journey back to her first husband (2:6-7), which ends in her being sowed and flowering in the land (2:23; 14:5-8). The son who was called from Egypt must journey back to his place of bondage because of his idolatry. Nevertheless, after his chastisement God returns the son to his home in a new Exodus (Hosea 11). Just as Jacob journeyed to a foreign land to rescue a wife, and just as God rescued the wife/Israel through the prophet Moses in the first Exodus, so will God rescue the people again through the prophet Hosea in a new Exodus (Hosea 12).

REFLECTIONS

In Hosea 14 the prophet documents the lush fruitfulness that springs forth in the covenantal rejoining of Yahweh and Israel. He concludes his story of the husband and wife on a very propitious note—or almost a propitious one. What gives pause is the qualifier of God's declaration of love in 14:4 (emphasis added): "I will love them freely, *for my anger has turned from them.*" The reader vividly recalls descriptions of God/husband taking out his wrath on the wife (Hosea 2). Remembering the physical price the wife had to pay to regain her husband's favor, one becomes uncertain about the beautiful metaphors of the wife's abundant fertility. They are built on a series of images that are all too real and painful for many women.

There is perhaps another way of looking at this concluding chapter that is more healing and affirming of gender relations. The well-known female personification of God's own wisdom, woman wisdom herself, is also described as a life-giving tree: "She is a tree of life to those who lay hold of her; those who hold her fast are called happy" (Prov 3:18). Wisdom therefore becomes the tree, under whose shadow Israel will live and flourish (Hos 14:7). Wisdom becomes the tree, whose fruit sustains Ephraim (Hos 14:8). The metaphor of the tree of Wisdom, providing shade and dispensing fruit, gains further support in the next and final verse of the chapter: "Those who are wise understand these things;/ those who are discerning know them./ For the ways of the LORD are right,/ and the upright walk in them,/ but transgressors stumble in them" (14:9 NRSV).

For the wise and discerning, for the abused and the pained, God the husband gives way to the Wisdom of God, woman wisdom as the tree of life. Happy are those who embrace her and receive their fruit from her!

THE BOOK OF JOEL

INTRODUCTION, COMMENTARY, AND REFLECTIONS
BY
ELIZABETH ACHTEMEIER

THE BOOK OF
JOEL

INTRODUCTION

On first reading, the book of Joel may give the impression of being a narrow, nationalistic work that glorifies Israel at the expense of every other nation. Yet, on the basis of Joel 2:28-32, Peter interprets God's action on the day of Pentecost (Acts 2), and Paul makes Joel 2:32 the heart of his gospel (Rom 10:13). Similarly, the church has always turned to Joel 2:12-19 for its lection on Ash Wednesday. Few books are more pertinent to our time; indeed, Joel presents a message that is integral to the Christian gospel at any time, as the Reflections will demonstrate.

We cannot pinpoint the date of the book. A few scholars have termed it as early as the ninth century BCE,[1] and some still argue that it is pre-exilic.[2] Most now are inclined to place it between 500 and 350 BCE. The Babylonian exile and dispersion are in the past, according to 3:1-3. Several passages assume the existence of the Second Temple, the priesthood, and daily sacrifices. There is no mention of a king or royal court, and priests and elders are the community's leaders. The walls of Jerusalem have been restored (2:7, 9) as happened under Nehemiah's direction. Tyre and Sidon have a commercial association with Philistia, known to have been the case before 343 BCE (3:4). The book relies heavily on earlier prophecy, including that of Obadiah, which was not written earlier than the fifth century BCE. No external unrest threatens the community. Thus the evidence seems to point to the conditions of Judah during the Persian period, when it was a tiny subprovince of the Persian Empire.

1. G. Amon, "Die Abfassungszeit des Buches Joel" (Ph.D. diss., Würzburg, 1942); Milos Bic, *Das Buch Joel* (Berlin: Evangelische Verlagsanstalt, 1960).

2. A. S. Kapelrud, *Joel Studies,* UUÅ (Uppsala: Lundequist, 1948); W. Rudolph, "Wann Wirkte Joel?" in *Das Ferne und Nahe Wort: Festschrift Leonhard Rost,* ed. F. Maas, BZAW (Berlin: Töpelmann, 1967) 193-98.

Having said all that, we must acknowledge that establishing a precise date for Joel is not of ultimate importance for its interpretation. The book brings with it a message that was a matter of life or death for Judah, but Joel also deliberately directs that message to every age (cf. 1:3), and thus this prophetic literature is never out of date.

As it now stands in the canon, the book may be regarded as a unity. Earlier scholars[3] divided chapters 1–2:27 from 2:28–3:21, maintaining that the eschatological sections (including all references in chapters 1–2 to the day of the Lord) were later additions to the prophet's work, which originally concerned only a locust plague. However, many interpreters[4] have convincingly shown that the eschatological passages are integral to the book's message and that the book as a whole exhibits a remarkable literary symmetry between its two parts: 2:21-27 promises a reversal of the devastation described in 1:4-20; 3:1-17 describes events of the day of the Lord, foretold in 2:1-11; 2:28-32 portrays the "return" called for in 2:12-17; and 3:17 parallels 2:27. This does not, they believe, preclude later editorial additions (perhaps 3:4-8), and the final shape of the book may be the product of artistic literary arrangement. Nevertheless, the book now presents a unified message for our teaching and preaching.

Joel draws on centuries of Israelite tradition in the framing of his message. Principally, he uses the tradition, familiar from earlier prophecy, of the day of the Lord (Isaiah 13; Ezekiel 30; Obadiah; Zephaniah 1–2; Malachi 4), as well as those of the enemy from the north (Jeremiah 4–6) and of the judgment on foreign nations (Jeremiah and Ezekiel). Sometimes he borrows whole sentences from earlier prophets (e.g., 1:15 from Isa 13:6; 3:16 from Isa 1:2). Sometimes he appropriates smaller word groups (e.g., 3:18 from Amos 9:13; 2:32 from Obadiah 17). But Joel's prophecy is not a stereotyped word from the past. Rather, it is a forceful, sometimes eloquent testimony to the continued working of the prophetic word in history. Not only through immediate revelation to him, but also through the words of earlier prophets, Joel hears God speaking to Judah's present situation. He believes that much foretold in past prophecy has not yet been fulfilled and that the fulfillment is not only being worked out in his time but also stretches on into the future. Indeed, the future that he envisions reaches also into our time and gives to Joel's prophecies their pertinence for our lives.

Joel presents his message in a series of poetic oracles that are sometimes only one strophe or stanza in length (1:2-4; 1:19-20), but that may encompass two strophes (2:18-19, 20; 3:1-3, 4-8; 3:9-10, 11-12; 3:13-14, 15-17), sometimes three (1:5-7, 8-10, 11-12; 1:13, 14, 15-16; 2:12-14, 15-16, 17), or even four (2:1-2, 3-5, 6-9, 10-11). The division of strophes in Hebrew rhetoric can be made on the basis of initial imperative verbs, changes in subject matter, opening exclamations, inclusios, and other such rhetorical devices. Only

---

3. B. Duhm, "Anmerkungen zu den Zwoelf Propheteten," *ZAW* 31 (1911) 1-43, 81-110, 161-204; E. Sellin, *Das Zwölfpropheten Buch,* KAT (Leipzig: Deichertsche, 1922); H. Robinson and F. Horst, *Die Zwölf Kleinen Propheten,* HAT (Tübingen: Mohr, 1938).

4. Principally H. W. Wolff, *Joel and Amos,* Hermeneia (Philadelphia: Fortress, 1977).

---

two passages in the book are in prose (2:30-32; 3:4-8), indicating perhaps Joel's use of traditional prose material.

The prophet couches his message in a number of different forms or genres appropriate to their content. A didactic admonition opens the work (1:2-4), and there are also calls to lamentation (1:5-12; 1:13-16; 2:15-17), a prophetic cry of alarm from the watchmen (2:1-11), a call to repentance (2:12-14), oracles of salvation (2:18-27), oracles against the foreign nations (3:4-8), and apocalyptic fragments presenting signs of the approaching end of history (2:30-31). Such forms are employed with great flexibility, however, often being detached from their original life setting or being combined with other forms.

The Hebrew text of the book is in fairly good shape, so that few emendations are necessary, but anyone who works with the Hebrew text should note that the chapter divisions in the Hebrew differ from those in English versions. Joel 2:28-32 in English versions is 3:1-5 in Hebrew. Similarly, Joel 3:1-21 in English versions is 4:1-21 in Hebrew.

BIBLIOGRAPHY

Allen, Leslie C. *The Books of Joel, Obadiah, Jonah and Micah.* NICOT. Grand Rapids: Eerdmans, 1976. Addresses the full range of history, literary, and theological issues.

Bewer, Julius A. "Commentary on Joel." In *A Critical and Exegetical Commentary on Micah, Zephaniah, Nahum, Habakkuk, Obadiah, and Joel.* ICC. New York: Scribners, 1911. Especially good on philological issues.

Calvin, John. *Commentaries on the Twelve Minor Prophets.* Vol. 2. Edinburgh: Calvin Translation Society, 1896. Theologically astute, pre-critical perspectives.

———. *Joel, Amos, Obadiah.* Edinburgh: Calvin Translation Society, 1896.

Driver, S. R. *The Books of Joel and Amos, with Introduction and Notes.* The Cambridge Bible for Schools and Colleges. Cambridge: Cambridge University Press, 1901. Although dated, this book provides a wealth of historical and linguistic information.

Watts, John D. W. *The Books of Joel, Obadiah, Jonah, Nahum, Habakkuk, and Zephaniah.* The Cambridge Bible Commentary on the New English Bible. Cambridge: Cambridge University Press, 1975. Written for a general audience.

Whedee, J. William. "Joel." In *Harper's Bible Commentary.* San Francisco: Harper & Row, 1988. Brief but insightful, especially on literary issues.

Wolff, Hans Walter. *Joel and Amos.* Hermeneia. Philadelphia: Fortress, 1977. A classic study that gives a comprehensive assessment of the book of Joel.

Outline of Joel

I. Joel 1:1, The Superscription

II. Joel 1:2-12, The Locust Plague

    A. 1:2-4, Tell the Children
    B. 1:5-12, Three Calls to Lamentation

III. Joel 1:13-20, Words to the Priests

    A. 1:13-16, The Approach of God's Day
    B. 1:17-20, The Drought's Effects and a Priestly Prayer

IV. Joel 2:1-11, The Day of God's Army

V. Joel 2:12-17, The Call to Repentance

    A. 2:12-14, The Importance of the Heart
    B. 2:15-17, Instructions to the Priests

VI. Joel 2:18-27, The Restoration of Communion with God

    A. 2:18-20, Covenant Curse Changed to Blessing
    B. 2:21-27, An Oracle of Salvation

VII. Joel 2:28-32, Signs of the Coming Day of the Lord

    A. 2:28-29, The Gift of the Spirit
    B. 2:30-32, Signs in Heaven and on Earth

VIII. Joel 3:1-21, Judgment and Salvation in the Day of the Lord

    A. 3:1-8, The Lord's Case Against the Nations
    B. 3:9-12, The Nations Called to Battle
    C. 3:13-17, The Final Battle and Its Outcome
    D. 3:18-21, The Glorious Future for the Faithful

JOEL 1:1

THE SUPERSCRIPTION

NIV	NRSV
1 The word of the LORD that came to Joel son of Pethuel.	**1** The word of the LORD that came to Joel son of Pethuel:

COMMENTARY

The name "Joel" is found frequently in the post-exilic books of Chronicles, but we know nothing of the prophet Joel other than the name of his father (cf. Jonah 1:1), an unusual fact in the writings of the prophets. Usually there is some indication of the time when the prophet was active (cf. Amos 1:1). The father's name, Pethuel, is found only here, but apparently would have been known to Joel's contemporaries. Some manuscripts have identified Pethuel with Bethuel, the father of Rebekah (Gen 22:22-23), which would give an early date to the book, but there is no good reason for such an identification.

This introductory verse simply states that "the word of the LORD . . . came to Joel," a common statement about God's revelation to prophets (cf. 1 Sam 15:10; 1 Kgs 16:1; Jer 1:2). The word comes from outside of the prophet, not from his own inner musings (cf. Jer 16:15; Ezek 3:1-3).

Joel's name, which means "Yahweh is God," may carry symbolic significance. Although Joel calls Judah to repent of its sins, he never specifies the nature of those sins. But Joel's name, along with 2:27 and 3:17, may indicate that the primary sin that the prophet had in mind was the sin of apostasy, the failure to recognize that Yahweh alone was God.

REFLECTIONS

Joel's prophecy is full of phrases from earlier prophets. It may well be, therefore, that one of the ways God's word came to Joel was through earlier prophets' authoritative words. Through those "lively oracles of God," as the Church of England describes the Bible, God is made known anew, in each new situation.

Certainly, however, fresh words were given by God to Joel, as his book makes clear. And that is significant for our understanding of prophecy. Most commentators have written that the locust plague that ravaged Judah suggested Joel's prophecy to him about the day of the Lord. But that turns the Bible's understanding of prophecy upside down. The prophets did not interpret the Word of God on the basis of the events they witnessed. Rather, they interpreted the events on the basis of the word revealed to them from God. The Word interpreted the events, not vice versa, and it was the function of the prophet to tell, on the basis of the Word of God, just where and when God was at work. For us that means that our times do not interpret the Bible. Rather, the Bible interprets our times.

JOEL 1:2-12

THE LOCUST PLAGUE

OVERVIEW

J oel begins didactically with a three-strophe description of a locust plague that has recently devastated Judah and that has been followed by a drought. Joel commands that the memory of the catastrophes be passed on to future generations, and he calls three groups to mourn, because the catastrophes represent God's covenant curse on the faithless people and their estrangement from God.

JOEL 1:2-4, TELL THE CHILDREN

NIV

²Hear this, you elders;
    listen, all who live in the land.
Has anything like this ever happened in your
        days
    or in the days of your forefathers?
³Tell it to your children,
    and let your children tell it to their children,
    and their children to the next generation.
⁴What the locust swarm has left
    the great locusts have eaten;
what the great locusts have left
    the young locusts have eaten;
what the young locusts have left
    other locusts*a* have eaten.

a4 The precise meaning of the four Hebrew words used here for locusts is uncertain.

NRSV

² Hear this, O elders,
    give ear, all inhabitants of the land!
Has such a thing happened in your days,
    or in the days of your ancestors?
³ Tell your children of it,
    and let your children tell their children,
    and their children another generation.

⁴ What the cutting locust left,
    the swarming locust has eaten.
What the swarming locust left,
    the hopping locust has eaten,
and what the hopping locust left,
    the destroying locust has eaten.

COMMENTARY

1:2-3. Joel questions the inhabitants of Judah and Jerusalem as to whether any of them has ever seen an event comparable to the devastation that a plague of locusts has wreaked in the land of Judah (for the length of time, see 2:25). Both the NRSV and the NIV use the word "elders" (זקנים *zĕqēnîm*) for the people to whom Joel speaks, but the translation probably should be "old men," appealing to their memory of past events. All, including Joel, have been eyewitnesses of the plague, which is almost over. Earlier exegetes sometimes interpreted locust swarms as a symbol of attacking foreign nations, but Joel here refers to real locusts.[5]

5. See H. W. Wolff, *Joel and Amos,* Hermeneia (Philadelphia: Fortress, 1977).

1:4. This verse intimates that the locusts have left the land a barren waste, a phenomenon that travelers to the Near East, who have experienced such plagues, have documented. The locusts have literally threatened Judah's ability to live.

Joel uses four words for locusts: "cutting locust" (גזם *gāzām*), "swarming locust" (ארבה *'arbeh*), "hopping locust" (ילק *yāleq*), and "destroying locust" (חסיל *ḥāsîl*), but despite the NRSV translation of these terms, their meaning is uncertain. *'Arbeh* is the most frequently used term, referring to the fully developed, winged migrating insect of some six centimeters in length. All four terms used together may refer to four stages in the locust life cycle (pupa, adult, wingless larva, winged larva). At a minimum, Joel has piled up terms to emphasize the overwhelming nature of the catastrophe. The three parallel lines, with these four names, reinforce the sense of disaster. Judah has been subject to one swarming, chewing, cutting enemy after another.

The prophet is telling the people nothing that they do not already know, of course. But he bids them pass on accounts of the event to the third and fourth generations and beyond, because the plague is the work of God (cf. Exod 10:4-6, 12-15; Pss 78:46; 105:34-35; Amos 4:9). The word of God has interpreted the event and has revealed it to be a work of judgment (cf. Amos 7:1), calling for repentance (cf. 1 Kgs 8:37). Indeed, the locust plague constitutes God's covenant curse upon the apostate people, as promised in Deut 28:38.

Usually when the OT talks of handing on tradition to the next generations, the good news of God's mighty or saving acts is the subject (cf. Exod 12:26-27; 13:8; Deut 4:9; 6:20-23; 32:7; Pss 22:30; 78:4). Joel also wants the people to pass on the news of God's judgment.

REFLECTIONS

Joel's word from the Lord immediately raises problems for us, because we modern, scientifically minded people do not believe that God effects natural disasters. The prophecies of Joel radically call our customary worldview into question, as does most of the Bible. Throughout the Scriptures God is the Lord of nature, who has created the natural world, who sustains all of its processes, and who uses it for divine purposes (cf. Neh 9:6; Psalm 104; Jer 31:35; Amos 4:7-10). When a natural catastrophe takes place, we therefore need to ask ourselves whether God is trying to call us to repentance, as God was calling Judeans to repentance in the time of Joel.

JOEL 1:5-12, THREE CALLS TO LAMENTATION

NIV

⁵Wake up, you drunkards, and weep!
    Wail, all you drinkers of wine;
wail because of the new wine,
    for it has been snatched from your lips.
⁶A nation has invaded my land,
    powerful and without number;
it has the teeth of a lion,
    the fangs of a lioness.
⁷It has laid waste my vines
    and ruined my fig trees.
It has stripped off their bark
    and thrown it away,

NRSV

⁵ Wake up, you drunkards, and weep;
    and wail, all you wine-drinkers,
over the sweet wine,
    for it is cut off from your mouth.
⁶ For a nation has invaded my land,
    powerful and innumerable;
its teeth are lions' teeth,
    and it has the fangs of a lioness.
⁷ It has laid waste my vines,
    and splintered my fig trees;
it has stripped off their bark and thrown it
        down;

NIV

leaving their branches white.

⁸Mourn like a virgin*ᵃ* in sackcloth
   grieving for the husband*ᵇ* of her youth.
⁹Grain offerings and drink offerings
   are cut off from the house of the LORD.
The priests are in mourning,
   those who minister before the LORD.
¹⁰The fields are ruined,
   the ground is dried up*ᶜ*;
the grain is destroyed,
   the new wine is dried up,
   the oil fails.
¹¹Despair, you farmers,
   wail, you vine growers;
grieve for the wheat and the barley,
   because the harvest of the field is destroyed.
¹²The vine is dried up
   and the fig tree is withered;
the pomegranate, the palm and the apple tree—
   all the trees of the field—are dried up.
Surely the joy of mankind
   is withered away.

ᵃ8 Or young woman   *ᵇ8 Or betrothed*   *ᶜ10 Or ground mourns*

NRSV

their branches have turned white.

⁸ Lament like a virgin dressed in sackcloth
   for the husband of her youth.
⁹ The grain offering and the drink offering are
      cut off
   from the house of the LORD.
The priests mourn,
   the ministers of the LORD.
¹⁰ The fields are devastated,
   the ground mourns;
for the grain is destroyed,
   the wine dries up,
   the oil fails.

¹¹ Be dismayed, you farmers,
   wail, you vinedressers,
over the wheat and the barley;
   for the crops of the field are ruined.
¹² The vine withers,
   the fig tree droops.
Pomegranate, palm, and apple—
   all the trees of the field are dried up;
surely, joy withers away
   among the people.

COMMENTARY

Joel issues a threefold call to weep and wail (v. 5), to mourn or keen (v. 8), to be dismayed and despair (v. 11) over the locusts' ruin of Judah. This is not yet a call to a typical communal fast of lamentation. Instead, the prophet, in this detailed description of the life-threatening situation, attempts to get the populace to understand God's word.

1:5-7. Addressed in the first strophe are intoxicated people, who are least likely to realize that judgment has come upon them. But when the "new wine" or "sweet wine"—that is, the first product of the winepress—is no longer available, surely they too will see the calamity. Joel directs their gaze outward, from their usual preoccupation with their own revelry and satiation to the landscape around them, as if Joel were telling them, "Look! Realize what has happened!"

Verses 6-7 compare the locust plague to an invading army, numberless and overpowering, and to savage beasts with fangs and teeth like saws. Indeed, the image of all vegetation and its produce being cut off predominates in vv. 4-10. The "cutting locust" of v. 4 has "cut off" the sweet wine in v. 5, so that the temple offerings are "cut off" in v. 9, as is the oil in v. 10 ("fails," NIV, NRSV).

According to v. 7, the two sources of fruit—vines and fig trees, which often grew together in the same field—are gone. The locusts have eaten even the bark of the broken trees, leaving them barren and white. But this has been done to God's land and to God's fig trees (cf. "my" in vv. 6-7).

1:8-10. The second strophe's call to lamentation employs a feminine singular imperative ("mourn" or "lament" [אֵלִי *ʾēlî*]) and is probably addressed to Jerusalem, personified as a virgin (cf. 1 Kgs 19:21; Lam 2:13), who is bidden to utter the keening wail used to mourn the dead. The woman has been betrothed, which was the first, binding step in marriage. Thus she had a "husband," as here, but the marriage had not yet been consummated (cf. Gen 29:18-21; Matt 1:18). Jerusalem is to mourn as such a virgin would mourn over the death of her promised husband. As an outward expression of her lamentation, she wears sackcloth, a rough burlap-like material, about her loins.

In this section, the prophet begins to drive home his message by noting that the grain and drink offerings can no longer be furnished for the temple sacrifices (v. 9). The reference is to grain that was moistened with oil and to the libation of wine that normally accompanied the morning and evening burnt sacrifices of lambs (cf. Exod 29:38-40; Num 28:3-8). Since the necessary ingredients are not available, the law of Sinai can no longer be obeyed. In short, Judah can no longer have that communion with God that was prescribed by the Lord. God, the Lord of nature, has cut off the means of fellowship (cf. Amos 8:11-12).

Joel does not criticize Israel's sacrificial worship, as do so many of the earlier prophets (e.g., Isa 1:11, 13; Jer 7:21-22; Hos 6:6; 8:11). For Joel, it is the prescribed and customary means of communion with God, and now it has come to an end. Why would God withdraw this means of fellowship? That is the question Joel wants his compatriots, along with the priests (v. 9), to address.

At the end of v. 10, the prophet drives home the sense of deprivation in a series of three staccato lines: "destroyed the grain,/ dried up the wine,/ cut off the oil"; the sentences become shorter, as if the prophet's words themselves have been cut off, along with everything else.

"Dried up" (אבל 'ābal, v. 10) then anticipates what follows, for in the third stanza, drought replaces the locust plague as another cause of calamity. Certainly the locust plague is in the past, and perhaps Judah has just begun to recover from it. Now the nation faces the additional devastation caused by a lack of rain. But drought too appears to reflect the Lord's will, for rain and the resulting fertility are covenant signs of the favor of God (Deut 28:1-12; Lev 26:3-5, 9-10; 1 Kings 17–18; cf. Jer 14:1-6).

1:11-12. Wheat and barley were the most important cereals in Palestine. Pomegranates from the Jordan Valley were highly prized for their large red juice-yielding fruits. Date palms were abundant, especially around Jericho. We should perhaps read "apricot" instead of "apple" (תפוח tappûah, v. 12), although there were apple trees in Palestine, yielding rather inferior fruit that was nevertheless refreshing and prized for its restorative properties in illness. All of the crops that the farmers had expected have withered, and the farmers despair, for they have nothing to eat or to sell and no seed even for replanting. Harvest, especially the grape harvest, was usually a time for rejoicing (cf. Ps 4:7; Isa 9:3), but like the crops, joy too is dried up (cf. Isa 16:10). The harvest songs are stilled in mouths that are dry as dust and parched with thirst; the very ground itself joins in the mourning (the NRSV has the proper reading of v. 10a).

REFLECTIONS

In the OT's understanding, the natural world is a gift from God, and Israel's land is the primary gift. But the land did not belong to Israel (see Leviticus 25, esp. v. 23; Ps 24:1). Israel was merely the steward of the land, responsible to God for the care and cultivation of its gifts (cf. Gen 2:15); such is the meaning of human "dominion" over the earth in Gen 1:28. Numerous laws in the Torah taught Israel how to treat the land and its gifts (e.g., Exod 20:8-9; Deut 22:6-7; 24:19-22).

Israel was expected to be a faithful steward of the land and its gifts, and if Israel was unfaithful, the land would be taken away from the people. Above all, the people were expected to worship and obey God, the giver of the land.

Certainly Joel's message serves as a warning to us. When we neglect the worship of God or turn away from God, we and all the inhabitants of the earth may suffer under the proximate judgments of the Lord of nature, as Judah suffered—from drought, forest fire, pestilence, devastating storm, and flood. Whence come these ills so out of keeping with a creation that is "very good" (Gen 1:31) unless they are the product of our sins turned back upon our own heads? Further, do not our ecological crises have something to do with our failure to be faithful stewards of God's creation?

The most poignant note in Joel's message, however, is that nature itself is corrupted by human sin. "The ground mourns," reads Joel 1:10*a*. Nature falls with our fall and is done to death with our disobedience (Gen 3:17-18; 9:2; Isa 24:4-6; Jer 12:4). As Paul says, the whole creation groans under the burden of human sin, waiting for its redemption (Rom 8:22). Joel vividly pictures that groaning.

JOEL 1:13-20

WORDS TO THE PRIESTS

OVERVIEW

Because communion with God has become impossible, Joel calls the priests to lamentation and bids them proclaim a public fast of lamentation. The locust plague and drought, which cause even the cattle to mourn, are but the foretaste of the coming day of the Lord. The domestic animals know to cry to the Lord of nature, and Joel furnishes a prayer for the priests to do the same.

JOEL 1:13-16, THE APPROACH OF GOD'S DAY

NIV

13Put on sackcloth, O priests, and mourn;
  wail, you who minister before the altar.
Come, spend the night in sackcloth,
  you who minister before my God;
for the grain offerings and drink offerings
  are withheld from the house of your God.
14Declare a holy fast;
  call a sacred assembly.
Summon the elders
  and all who live in the land
to the house of the LORD your God,
  and cry out to the LORD.

15Alas for that day!
  For the day of the LORD is near;
  it will come like destruction from the
    Almighty.*a*

16Has not the food been cut off
  before our very eyes—
joy and gladness
  from the house of our God?

a15 Hebrew Shaddai

NRSV

13 Put on sackcloth and lament, you priests;
  wail, you ministers of the altar.
Come, pass the night in sackcloth,
  you ministers of my God!
Grain offering and drink offering
  are withheld from the house of your God.

14 Sanctify a fast,
  call a solemn assembly.
Gather the elders
  and all the inhabitants of the land
to the house of the LORD your God,
  and cry out to the LORD.

15 Alas for the day!
  For the day of the LORD is near,
  and as destruction from the Almighty*a* it
    comes.
16 Is not the food cut off
  before our eyes,
joy and gladness
  from the house of our God?

a Traditional rendering of Heb Shaddai

COMMENTARY

Joel now turns to those who are mediators between God and the people—to the priests who serve in the Temple at the altar—and repeats to them what he has previously pointed out to all the inhabitants of the land (v. 7): daily offerings have ceased (v. 13); communion with God has been cut off; the people are suffering under the effects of having lost that bond; God is acting in judgment upon them. Surely, though the people have been blind to the reality of their situation, the "ministers of my God," and "your God," Joel says, will realize what has happened. He calls the priests, therefore, not only to identify with the people in their woes but also beyond that to lead their people in repentance for sin before God.

The wearing of sackcloth was not only a sign of mourning, as in v. 8, but also a sign of penitence (1 Kgs 21:27; Neh 9:1-2; Jonah 3:5-6). Males bared the upper body, so that the chest might be struck in grief (which is the meaning of "lament" [ספד *sāpad*] in v. 13*a*), and sackcloth was girded about the loins. Only in the most extreme circumstance was sackcloth worn at night (v. 13; cf. 2 Sam 12:16, 20).

Joel commands the priests to proclaim, or "sanctify" (קדש *qiddēš*), a fast—that is, they are to make preparations for a public assembly in which the entire population, including old men, women, and children, come together in the Temple to wail, to pray, and to repent of their sins before God (v. 14). Since Joel calls all to gather in the Temple, the community may have been quite small.

Such fasts were called in Israel whenever a national calamity struck—war, famine, pestilence, captivity, here a locust plague and drought (cf. Judg 20:26; 1 Sam 7:6). Usually the fast lasted one day, when the people abstained from food and drink, from sexual relations, and from work and civil affairs, although continuing distress could be commemorated with a fast every year (cf. Zech 7:1-7). The ceremony was characterized by loud wailing and weeping, rending of clothes and striking oneself, falling to the ground, sprinkling oneself with dust and ashes, pouring out water to symbolize tears, and stretching out one's hands to heaven in prayer and supplication to God to forgive and to turn aside the calamity (cf. 1 Sam 7:6; Jer 3:25; 4:8; 6:26; 31:19; Lam 2:10, 19). Always the cry to God accompanied the fast (Ezra 8:21, 23; Neh 9:1-4).

Joel then introduces the most ominous note: The day of the Lord is near (v. 16). The Judeans are suffering not only under the present judgment of locust plague and drought, but they also face a final judgment on the day of the Lord, when God will come to establish divine rule over all the earth.

Israel's belief in the day of the Lord has its roots in the ancient tribal wars against neighboring peoples who attacked Israel during the time of the judges (1220–1020 BCE) and reign of Saul (1020–1000 BCE). Some scholars[6] term such battles "holy wars," because they were conducted according to fixed ritual and cultic rules. But the principal antagonist in such wars was not Israel, but God, who fought with supernatural means at the head of the people (Josh 10:11; 24:7; Judg 5:4-5), inspiring terror and panic among the enemy (Exod 15:14-16; 23:27; Josh 2:9, 24; 5:1; 7:5). Israelites, therefore, believed that God would finally defeat all of their enemies (Deut 20:1-9) and that Israel would enjoy a blessed prosperity in a kingdom of righteousness and peace, ruled by God (cf. Ps 46:4-11; Isa 17:12-14; 31:4-5; 33:17-22). Thus the day of the Lord was thought to be not one specific day, but a time that would include the defeat of all Israel's foes and its everlasting salvation (Isa 32:16-20).

Amos, in the eighth century BCE, was the first to upset this optimistic expectation, for he proclaimed that because of Israel's sins, the day of the Lord would not be a time of salvation for Israel, but of judgment (Amos 5:18-20). Amos was followed in this announcement by Zephaniah (chap. 1), Isaiah (2:6-22), Ezekiel (chap. 7), and Malachi (4:5; 3:1-5; cf. Lam 2:1, 21-22).

Here, Joel joins that prophetic company and proclaims that the day of the Lord has not yet come, but that it is near. Judah has already experienced a "typical" judgment by means of locusts and drought, but it now faces a final

---

6. E.g., Gerhard von Rad, *Holy War in Ancient Israel* (Grand Rapids: Eerdmans, 1991).

reckoning in the day of the Lord. The cessation of daily offerings in the Temple is a sign of the broken relationship. Surely the priests, who lead Judah's worship, can read the meaning of the sign!

REFLECTIONS

When we lose our knowledge of the nature of God, we tend to believe that God never acts in judgment, that there really is no such thing as sin, and that God is a benign and agreeable deity largely committed to helping us out of difficulties and to giving us the best things in life. When true knowledge of God is revealed to us through the Scriptures, however, it becomes clear that God hates sin, will not tolerate it, and will finally do away with it forever in what the Bible calls the Lord's day.

According to the Bible, God has created us for a loving and trusting covenant relationship (Deut 10:12-21; Mark 12:28-34; Rom 12:1-2). Sin constitutes turning away from that relationship and following the devices and desires of our own hearts and minds. And that sin God will not allow, because God is Lord and will be nothing less than Lord over all (cf. Ezek 20:33-38; Phil 2:10-11).

New Testament writers were quite convinced that, on the day of the Lord, to which Jesus and Paul both refer (Mark 13; Matt 25:31-46; Rom 2:5; 1 Cor 1:8; 3:13; 5:5; 2 Cor 1:14; Phil 1:6, 10; 2:16; 1 Thess 5:2), all of us will stand before the judgment seat of God and will be held accountable to God and to Christ for our love and trust and obedience or our lack thereof (Matt 12:36; Rom 14:10-12; 2 Cor 5:10; 1 Pet 4:5).

This passage, which is directed to the priests, shows that the church and its ministers should remember God's judgments and lead in repentance. Far too often the church in our time has acquiesced to the popular culture's belief that God accepts us as we are and never judges us. That is "cheap grace," which preaches "peace, peace, when there is no peace" with God (Jer 6:14; 8:11; cf. 7:4, 8-15).

JOEL 1:17-20, THE DROUGHT'S EFFECTS AND A PRIESTLY PRAYER

NIV

[17]The seeds are shriveled
  beneath the clods.[a]
The storehouses are in ruins,
  the granaries have been broken down,
  for the grain has dried up.
[18]How the cattle moan!
  The herds mill about
because they have no pasture;
  even the flocks of sheep are suffering.

[19]To you, O LORD, I call,
  for fire has devoured the open pastures
  and flames have burned up all the trees of
    the field.

[a]17 The meaning of the Hebrew for this word is uncertain.

NRSV

[17] The seed shrivels under the clods,[a]
  the storehouses are desolate;
the granaries are ruined
  because the grain has failed.
[18] How the animals groan!
  The herds of cattle wander about
because there is no pasture for them;
  even the flocks of sheep are dazed.[b]

[19] To you, O LORD, I cry.
  For fire has devoured
    the pastures of the wilderness,
  and flames have burned

[a] Meaning of Heb uncertain   [b] Compare Gk Syr Vg: Meaning of Heb uncertain

NIV	NRSV.

20Even the wild animals pant for you;
    the streams of water have dried up
    and fire has devoured the open pastures.
	all the trees of the field.
	20 Even the wild animals cry to you
	    because the watercourses are dried up,
	and fire has devoured
	    the pastures of the wilderness.

COMMENTARY

This two-strophe poem (vv. 17-18, 19-20) now further enlarges the picture of the catastrophes to show their effects on the world of nature. Verse 17*ab* is among the few obscure passages in Joel, because it contains words not found anywhere else in the OT. The LXX reads the whole verse as: "The heifers have started at their mangers, the treasures are abolished, the wine-presses are broken down; for the corn is withered." The NIV probably has the best reading, with its reference to drought: Digging shovels find only ungerminated seed. There is no grain, and so the repair of the granary buildings is neglected.

Most pathetic is the plight of the cattle, who wander the barren fields, lowing in their hunger. Even the sheep, who prefer the dry pastures of the steppe and who do not need rich, moist pasture land, stand perplexed (cf. Jer 14:5-6).

Given the desperate situation, Joel composes a prayer for the priests (vv. 19-20). Because it is from God's hand that the judgment has fallen, the cry of lament must be directed to the Lord of nature. The wild beasts know to whom to cry, recognizing their Master (v. 20). Joel wants the priests also to address the Lord and to lead the people in contrition.

Although the reference to "fire" (אֵשׁ *'ēš,* v. 20) might be taken literally in the sense that any vegetation that has recovered from the locust plague has become so dry that it might ignite from the heat of the sun, the image is probably figurative. "Fire" is used throughout the OT to convey an image of God's judgment (Isa 47:14; 66:15-16; Jer 4:4; 5:14), and it is that judgment that has dried up the land.

REFLECTIONS

The innocent animals suffer for our sin. It has always been so (cf. Gen 9:2). For the wickedness of those who inhabit the land, says Jeremiah, "the animals and the birds are swept away" (Jer 12:4 NRSV; cf. Hos 4:1-3; Zeph 1:3). The whole creation groans in travail because humans desert God (Rom 8:22). But the animals know to whom to direct their cry, while we most likely will deny our sinfulness and persist in our evil ways, frantically searching our technology or science, our medical knowledge or political resources for some means of correcting the situation apart from God. Joel reminds us that where God is deserted the forces of death reign.

THE DAY OF GOD'S ARMY

NIV

2 Blow the trumpet in Zion;
    sound the alarm on my holy hill.
Let all who live in the land tremble,
    for the day of the LORD is coming.
It is close at hand—
2   a day of darkness and gloom,
    a day of clouds and blackness.
Like dawn spreading across the mountains
    a large and mighty army comes,
such as never was of old
    nor ever will be in ages to come.

3Before them fire devours,
    behind them a flame blazes.
Before them the land is like the garden of Eden,
    behind them, a desert waste—
    nothing escapes them.
4They have the appearance of horses;
    they gallop along like cavalry.
5With a noise like that of chariots
    they leap over the mountaintops,
like a crackling fire consuming stubble,
    like a mighty army drawn up for battle.

6At the sight of them, nations are in anguish;
    every face turns pale.
7They charge like warriors;
    they scale walls like soldiers.
They all march in line,
    not swerving from their course.
8They do not jostle each other;
    each marches straight ahead.
They plunge through defenses
    without breaking ranks.
9They rush upon the city;
    they run along the wall.
They climb into the houses;
    like thieves they enter through the windows.

10Before them the earth shakes,
    the sky trembles,
the sun and moon are darkened,
    and the stars no longer shine.
11The LORD thunders

NRSV

2 Blow the trumpet in Zion;
    sound the alarm on my holy mountain!
Let all the inhabitants of the land tremble,
    for the day of the LORD is coming, it is
    near—
2 a day of darkness and gloom,
    a day of clouds and thick darkness!
Like blackness spread upon the mountains
    a great and powerful army comes;
their like has never been from of old,
    nor will be again after them
    in ages to come.

3 Fire devours in front of them,
    and behind them a flame burns.
Before them the land is like the garden of
    Eden,
    but after them a desolate wilderness,
    and nothing escapes them.

4 They have the appearance of horses,
    and like war-horses they charge.
5 As with the rumbling of chariots,
    they leap on the tops of the mountains,
like the crackling of a flame of fire
    devouring the stubble,
like a powerful army
    drawn up for battle.

6 Before them peoples are in anguish,
    all faces grow pale.[a]
7 Like warriors they charge,
    like soldiers they scale the wall.
Each keeps to its own course,
    they do not swerve from[b] their paths.
8 They do not jostle one another,
    each keeps to its own track;
they burst through the weapons
    and are not halted.
9 They leap upon the city,
    they run upon the walls;

a Meaning of Heb uncertain   b Gk Syr Vg; Heb *they do not take a pledge along*

NIV

at the head of his army;
his forces are beyond number,
    and mighty are those who obey his command.
The day of the Lord is great;
    it is dreadful.
    Who can endure it?

NRSV

they climb up into the houses,
    they enter through the windows like a thief.

[10] The earth quakes before them,
    the heavens tremble.
The sun and the moon are darkened,
    and the stars withdraw their shining.
[11] The Lord utters his voice
    at the head of his army;
how vast is his host!
    Numberless are those who obey his
        command.
Truly the day of the Lord is great;
    terrible indeed—who can endure it?

COMMENTARY

In 1:15, Joel announced that the day of the Lord was near. He now fills out the picture of that imminent final judgment. Although 2:1-11 may be divided into four stanzas (vv. 1-2, 3-5, 6-9, 10-11), since the poem is bracketed by references to the day of the Lord in vv. 1 and 11, the passage will be treated as a whole.

Four traditions or images predominate in this picture of the day. The first is obviously that of military battle. The Lord speaks through the prophet (v. 1), commanding that the שׁופר (šôpār), "war trumpet," which was made from a curved ram's horn, be sounded to warn the people of the coming enemy (cf. Jer 6:1; Hos 5:8; 8:1). Sentries were stationed on the walls of fortified cities (here Jerusalem), and when the alarm sounded, the news was spread from place to place, and the people gathered within the city walls for protection (cf. Jer 4:5). But the enemy that is approaching, according to Joel, is God's mighty army (vv. 2, 5, 7, 11); and God warns of the attack, even though God is the commander of the host (v. 11).

Some commentators[7] believe that this army refers to the locust horde, but that is doubtful. The locust plague happened in the past, whereas the incomparably greater danger of the day of the Lord still approaches. Certainly, the picture given of the army has been influenced by features of the locust plague, which constitutes the second image Joel uses. The steady and overpowering forward march of the enemy host, their swarming over walls and into houses (v. 9), the desolation left behind them (v. 3), the sound of their eating (v. 5)—all are typical of locust infestations (cf. Rev 9:2-11, which this passage prefigures). But this is no mere locust swarm. This is God's mysterious enemy from the north (see 2:20), also addressed by Jeremiah (1:14; 4:6; 6:1), before whom all the Judeans, all peoples, and the heavens themselves tremble (Joel 2:1, 6, 10). This is God's army, come to destroy God's enemies, before which no one can escape (v. 3, a traditional feature of the day; Amos 5:18-20; 9:1; Zeph 1:18).

The third set of images the prophet employs are traditional features associated with the day of the Lord in other prophetic writings. Verses 1-2 echo Zeph 1:14-15 ("near," "darkness and gloom," "clouds and thick darkness"); v. 6b includes words and phrases from Nah 2:10 ("anguish," "all faces grow pale") and Isa 13:8 ("anguish," "their faces will be aflame"); v. 11 echoes Mal 3:2 ("who can endure") and 4:5 ("great and terrible day"). The description of the day of the Lord was fairly well fixed in earlier

7. See Julius A. Bewer, "Commentary on Joel," in *A Critical and Exegetical Commentary on Micah, Zephaniah, Nahum, Habakkuk, Obadiah, and Joel,* ICC (New York: Scribners, 1911); E. Sellin, *Das Zwölfpropheten Buch,* KAT (Leipzig: Deichertsche, 1922); A. Weiser and Karl Elliger, *Das Buch der zwölf Kleinen Propheten,* ATD (Göttingen: Vandenhoeck und Ruprecht, 1949).

prophetic writings.[8] But Joel was not just copying earlier traditions. Rather, he saw the word of God continuing to work in history, and what he announces is the fulfillment of that earlier word.

The fourth tradition that the prophet uses is that of God's theophany, or appearance (vv. 2, 10). Throughout the OT, God's manifestation always causes cosmic disturbances in heaven and on earth (cf. Exod 19:16-19; Ps 97:1-5; Hab 3:3-11), just as the death and resurrection of Jesus are accompanied by darkness and earthquake, the splitting of rocks, and the opening of tombs (Matt 27:45, 51-52; 28:2). When God leads the army against the foes, the whole cosmos will be affected (cf. Mark 13:24-26), and Joel's final question in v. 11 implies that nothing and no one can remain unscathed by God's final, fearful day.

In v. 2, the NRSV reads that the day will be "like blackness spread upon the mountains"; the NIV says that it will be "like dawn spreading across the mountains." Probably the latter rendering is correct. In that verse, God's army is incomparable, like nothing in the past or in any time in the future (cf. 1:2-3). That day is compared to various military figures and accoutrements in vv. 4-5, but it is only "like" them, as if the prophet were straining at the limits of earthly language (cf. such approximations of the supernatural in Ezek 1:26-28). "Fire" goes before this army and makes a land that was like Eden into a desolate wilderness—a land judged by the burning wrath of the Lord (v. 3), which reverses the thought of Isa 51:3 and Ezek 36:35.

8. For a passage that mentions additional features of the day, read Isa 13:1-13.

REFLECTIONS

We cannot know what God's final judgment of the earth and of its sinful inhabitants on the day of the Lord will be like. The prophets are drawing for us traditional pictures, framed through centuries in Israel's life, and the NT continues to use those pictures. What we do know from both the OT and the NT is that God's final judgment of the world will take place; the NT tells us additionally that on that day the Son of Man will return to set up his kingdom on earth. That judgment is prefigured in the cross of Christ, with its disturbances of the cosmos, and it is promised by our Lord and the apostles. The question of Joel remains apt: "Who can endure it?" (v. 11; cf. Jer 10:10).

THE CALL TO REPENTANCE

OVERVIEW

Although the Judeans are threatened with death by their present catastrophes and by the coming of the day of the Lord, God nevertheless offers them the opportunity to repent and to return to communion with God. As a sign of their sincere willingness to return, Joel instructs the people to hold a fast of lamentation, in which the priests, praying on behalf of the people, plead for God's mercy.

JOEL 2:12-14, THE IMPORTANCE OF THE HEART

COMMENTARY

In the midst of Judah's desperate situation, occasioned by locust plague and drought, and with a final, awful judgment hanging over it, God utters a "but" (a waw adversative in the Hebrew [ן wĕ-]) (v. 12). God speaks in vv. 12 and 13a, as is clear due to the prophetic formula "says the Lord" (found only here in Joel).

God calls the Judeans to return to worship with all their hearts and to rend their hearts and not their garments. The tearing of garments in lamentation was an expression of deep emotion in times of grief, terror, or horror at some misfortune (cf. Gen 37:29, 34; Num 14:6; 2 Sam 3:31; 1 Kgs 21:27; Ezra 9:3), but the expression of repentance in Judah's heart is to be even more emphatic.

The heart in Hebrew idiom symbolizes what the brain symbolizes in language today. The heart was understood as the seat of will and intellect, so that Judah is being asked to turn away from apostasy and return to God in a deliberate act of will. Throughout Israel's history, the deutero-nomic writers and the prophets appealed to their people to love and worship and obey God with all their hearts (cf. Deut 6:6; Jer 4:4; 32:39-40; Ezek 18:31). Here Joel makes the same appeal.

To repent or turn to God has the meaning of "turning around," of going in the opposite direction, so that a person is leading a life different from that before (cf. Isa 9:13; Jer 5:3; Amos 4:6, 8-9; Hag 2:17). But the change Judah is asked to make is based on the nature of God, who will accept the people back into covenant relation, an idea implied by "your God" (v. 13). That latter phrase provides half of the covenant formula, "They shall be my people, and I will be their God" (Jer 32:38 NRSV; cf. Jer 31:33).

The nature of God is set forth in v. 13 in an ancient creedal statement that is found eight other times in the OT (Exod 34:6-7 gives the full form of it; cf. also Num 14:8; Neh 9:17; Pss 86:15; 103:8; 145:8; Jonah 4:2; Nah 1:3). The form here is probably taken from Jonah 4:2, since Joel 4:14 also draws on Jonah 3:9. "Gracious" (חנון *ḥannûn*) is the total goodwill of a superior to an inferior. "Merciful" (רחום *raḥûm*) could be defined as the love of a mother for her child. "Slow to anger" (ארך אפים *'erek 'apayim*) means that God does not immediately punish people for their sins, but waits patiently for repentance and turning. "Steadfast love" (חסד *ḥesed*) is God's faithful, everlasting, loving observance of the covenant bond with the people. On the basis of these qualities in their God, the Judeans will be allowed to return, even though they have earlier deserted their God.

If the people return, God will once again turn to them and *perhaps* restore their grain and wine and oil, for use in their worship (v. 14). But repentance does not coerce God. The Lord is free, and God will be gracious to whomever God chooses to be gracious; God will show mercy to whomever God will show mercy (Exod 33:19; Rom 9:15; cf. 11:33). The decision about renewal is up to God and not human beings. *If* God restores the produce necessary for the resumption of the daily temple offerings, that will be the sign that God has accepted the people into communion once again.

REFLECTIONS

1. Joel 2:12-14 reveals how long-suffering and patient our God is with the covenant people. But even now—in the situation in which you and I stand, in the circumstances in which we find ourselves—the offer of return to fellowship with our God is held out to us.

It is that "but" that makes all the difference—God's refusal to have done with us; God's constant, loving, suffering yearning to give us life instead of death; God's great "nevertheless"; the Lord's refusal to accept the situation as it is, and God's determination to forgive us and to welcome us back, no matter what we have done. There lies all our hope.

2. Joel 2:12-19 is the lection for Ash Wednesday in most churches, and so its call at the beginning of every lenten season is for the rending of our hearts, for that deliberate exercise of will and thought that will turn our lives in opposite directions and point us toward, not away from, our God. Biblical faith involves taking ourselves in hand, making up our minds "even now" to be obedient to God, and then attempting to walk steadfastly, determinedly every day in God's way. None of us can do that apart from the help of God. But the Lord offers us here in Joel and throughout the Scriptures aid in returning to communion. God works in us and with us, but we must also summon our will and thought to repent and change. As Paul would say, we work out our own salvation, but it is God who is at work in us, enabling us to will and to work for God's good pleasure (Phil 2:12-13).

Yet, as Joel and Paul also remind us, we work out our salvation "with fear and trembling" (Phil 2:12 NRSV), for we cannot presume on God or guarantee the Lord's acceptance of us. God is free, and God is Lord, and we are utterly dependent on God's forgiving mercy. When we know that, we approach our God in the humility that is appropriate.

JOEL 2:15-17, INSTRUCTIONS TO THE PRIESTS

NIV

¹⁵Blow the trumpet in Zion,
    declare a holy fast,
    call a sacred assembly.
¹⁶Gather the people,
    consecrate the assembly;
  bring together the elders,
    gather the children,
    those nursing at the breast.
Let the bridegroom leave his room
    and the bride her chamber.
¹⁷Let the priests, who minister before the LORD,
    weep between the temple porch and the altar.
Let them say, "Spare your people, O LORD.
    Do not make your inheritance an object of
        scorn,
    a byword among the nations.
Why should they say among the peoples,
    'Where is their God?'"

NRSV

¹⁵ Blow the trumpet in Zion;
    sanctify a fast;
    call a solemn assembly;
¹⁶   gather the people.
Sanctify the congregation;
    assemble the aged;
gather the children,
    even infants at the breast.
Let the bridegroom leave his room,
    and the bride her canopy.

¹⁷ Between the vestibule and the altar
    let the priests, the ministers of the LORD,
    ·   weep.
Let them say, "Spare your people, O LORD,
    and do not make your heritage a mockery,
    a byword among the nations.
Why should it be said among the peoples,
    'Where is their God?'"

COMMENTARY

As in 1:13-20, Joel turns once again to the priests and orders them to take the leadership in calling the solemn assembly of repentance. The trumpet, or שׁוֹפָר (šôpār, v. 15), does not summon the people to war this time, as in 2:1, but to a religious gathering (cf. Lev 25:9; Ps 81:3). "Sanctify" (קדשׁ qiddēš; cf. 1:14) has the meaning of "set apart for God's purposes," by making complete preparations for worship.

No one is to be exempted, because no one is exempt from the judgment of God on the day of the Lord (v. 16). Newly married men were excused from military service for a year, according to deuteronomic law (Deut 24:5), but the threat here is far greater than that of war. Jeremiah has proclaimed that bride and bridegroom also will be subject to God's eschatological judgment (Jer 7:34; 16:9; 25:10). This is no time for nuptial joy. The bridegroom is to leave that inner room where he was alone with his bride (cf. Judg 15:1; 2 Sam 13:10; 2 Kgs 9:2; Cant 1:4). The bride is to come forth from the cohabitation chamber (Ps 19:5).

Even infants, who have been born into a sinful society (cf. Ps 51:5) are to be carried to the service, and the elderly cannot plead their age as an excuse. (The NRSV is correct in reading זקנים [zĕqēnîm] as "aged" instead of "elders"). All are to be gathered to the Temple as the covenant community.

The priests then are to offer prayers on behalf of the people; apparently it was customary in such circumstances for them to stand in the large space between the porch or vestibule of the inner court (1 Kgs 6:3; 7:21) and the altar of burnt offerings found there (1 Kgs 8:22, 64).

The prayer that Joel furnishes here for the priests is typical of communal laments (cf. Ps 79:4, 8, 10), and the sudden introduction of the concern for the opinion of other nations owes its presence to that tradition (cf. Pss 44:13-14; 115:2; Mic 7:10). Joel's prophecy is firmly embedded in the worship traditions of his people.

The plea has three bases. First, the priests are to appeal to God's pity, which is the import of "spare" (חוס *ḥûs*) in v. 17c. This is the God who "remembers that we are dust," who "does not deal with us according to our sins,/ nor repay us according to our iniquities," who has compassion like a father for his children (Ps 103:10, 13-14 NRSV).

Second, the priests are to appeal to God's covenant relation with the people. The Lord is reminded that the Judeans are "your people" and "your heritage." God has been their God through many centuries, despite their sin. The priests must ask that God's steadfast covenant love continue (cf. Deut 9:26-29; Ps 89:39, 49).

Third, the priests are to remind God that the deity's own honor is at stake. If Judah dies, the foreign peoples will say that God has been unable to save the people (cf. Pss 42:10; 79:10; 89:41, 50; 109:25).

Most commentators[9] assume that the priests and the people respond to Joel's call and repent in an assembly in the Temple. Indeed, some commentators[10] translate vv. 15-17, not as imperatives, but as perfects, indicating that action has already taken place: "They blew the horn in Zion, they sanctified a fast," etc. The NRSV does not adopt this translation, but it does assume, in 2:18-19, that the fast of repentance has taken place and that the Lord then responds in saving action to that repentance. The NIV, on the other hand, implies that everything is still in the future. Joel calls the people to repentance in vv. 15-17, but we are not told the people's response. God's saving answers in vv. 18-19 are promissory: If Judah repents, God will respond in salvation. Certainly what follows in the rest of the book is mostly future tense action. Hence, the NIV's translation is to be preferred. Joel is working out a scenario here of what God will do in order to respond to the people's desperate need. On the basis of that promise of God's future action, the whole book centers on the need for repentance and return to God.

9. So H. W. Wolff, *Joel and Amos,* Hermeneia (Philadelphia: Fortress, 1977).

10. E.g., Julius A. Bewer, "Commentary on Joel," in *A Critical and Exegetical Commentary on Micah, Zephaniah, Nahum, Habakkuk, Obadiah, and Joel,* ICC (New York: Scribners, 1911).

REFLECTIONS

That none of us is exempt from the need for repentance and transformation of our lives before God is perhaps the main thrust of this passage. We have often dropped from our liturgy those preparatory services of self-examination and repentance that used to precede participation in the Lord's supper, just as we have omitted the traditional reading of the Ten Commandments before the supper and the invitation that included the requirement of a desire to walk in newness of life. God loves us and accepts us as we are—we believe—and we come with great confidence to the table.

But our Lord put conditions on our entrance into God's presence, the conditions of reconciliation with our neighbors (Matt 5:23-24), commitment to love God above all else (Mark 10:17-25), and willingness to accept grace when it is offered (Luke 14:15-24). In Joel, Judah has no hope of a future, unless that future be given by God. It is no different for us. Our lives depend on our response to this call for penitence and trust.

Yet, we must not believe that our repentance and turning are automatic guarantees of God's saving favor. Repentance is not a meritorious work that compels God to accept us. When we have done all that is required of us, we are still unworthy servants (see Luke 17:10), and the truly repentant know that they have no goodness of their own to claim, but depend solely on the mercy of God. As the saying goes, the true saint is one who knows that he or she is a sinner.

Finally, we repent and trust God in Christ, not to save our own skins, but because we know that God's work in us will magnify the Lord's glory throughout the earth. Judah's salvation was a glorification of the power and love of the God who continually rescued the people; we know from the Scriptures that God is a great God because of what the Lord did in Israel's life. So, too, will all peoples know how great our Lord is by what God does in our lives. By the Lord's work alone the church becomes the city set on the hill and the light shining in the darkness of this sinful world (see Matt 5:14-16).

JOEL 2:18-27

THE RESTORATION OF COMMUNION WITH GOD

n the following pericopes, God promises to restore to the covenant people the means of communion and to save them on the day of final judgment.

JOEL 2:18-20, COVENANT CURSE CHANGED TO BLESSING

NIV

¹⁸Then the LORD will be jealous for his land
   and take pity on his people.
   ¹⁹The LORD will reply*a* to them:
"I am sending you grain, new wine and oil,
   enough to satisfy you fully;
never again will I make you
   an object of scorn to the nations.

²⁰"I will drive the northern army far from you,
   pushing it into a parched and barren land,
with its front columns going into the eastern sea*b*
   and those in the rear into the western sea.*c*
And its stench will go up;
   its smell will rise."

Surely he has done great things.*d*

*a18,19 Or LORD was jealous . . . / and took pity . . . / ¹⁹The LORD
replied   b20 That is, the Dead Sea   c20 That is, the Mediterranean
d20 Or rise. / Surely it has done great things."*

NRSV

¹⁸ Then the LORD became jealous for his land,
   and had pity on his people.
¹⁹ In response to his people the LORD said:
I am sending you
   grain, wine, and oil,
   and you will be satisfied;
and I will no more make you
   a mockery among the nations.

²⁰ I will remove the northern army far from you,
   and drive it into a parched and desolate
      land,
   its front into the eastern sea,
      and its rear into the western sea;
its stench and foul smell will rise up.
   Surely he has done great things!

COMMENTARY

In Israel's cult, prayers of lament were often followed by expressions of certainty that God would rescue (cf. Pss 6:8-10; 22:21-24; Mic 7:8-10) or by a divine oracle answering the plea (Pss 12:5; 60:6-8; Isa 33:10-12; Hos 14:4-7). Sometimes the plea for rescue could be rejected (cf. Hos 4:4-6) or a condition might be attached (cf. Jer 15:19-21). The prophet presents the response that God will give to the prayer of 2:17 in two strophes, vv. 18-19 and v. 20. Indeed, the Lord's speech in 2:19-22, 24-25, 26d-27 is intended to answer the entire situation pictured in 1:2–2:17. The prophet is foretelling what God will do for those who truly return to God in trust.

That God was "jealous" for the land (v. 18) could be understood to mean that God was "zealous"—the Hebrew word קָנָא (*qānāʾ*) has both

322

meanings. The God of the OT is a zealous God, who is working out a purpose in the world (cf. Exod 20:5; 34:10; Isa 9:7), who has enlisted the covenant people to serve that purpose (cf. Exod 19:3-6; 1 Pet 2:9-10), and who will not be deterred from that purpose by the apostasy of the people or by any foreign threat to their existence. That God spares Israel and does not simply abandon it and enlist some other people is due entirely to the Lord's "pity" for Israel. Nevertheless, God will turn the covenant curse into blessing. The grain, wine, and oil necessary for the daily offerings in the Temple and communion with God will be restored.

Moreover, Judah will experience the day of the Lord, not as a day of judgment, but as one of salvation; the former threat of annihilation has now been reversed. God will remove the "northerner" (הצפוני *haṣṣĕpônî,* v. 20). Some commentators[11] have thought that this word refers only to

11. E.g., Leslie C. Allen, *The Books of Joel, Obadiah, Jonah and Micah,* NICOT (Grand Rapids: Eerdmans, 1976); Wolff, *Joel and Amos;* John D. W. Watts, *The Books of Joel, Obadiah, Jonah, Nahum, Habakkuk, and Zephaniah,* The Cambridge Commentary on the New English Bible (Cambridge: Cambridge University Press, 1975).

the locust hordes, although locusts usually came from the south or southeast. These scholars then picture the locusts being carried into the Dead Sea on the east of Judah and into the Mediterranean on the west by a strong wind, their decaying bodies on the shores causing a stench. But the "northerner" here is much more than the locusts, although the picture may have been influenced by the locust invasion, as it also was in 2:1-10. Rather, the northerner alludes to Jeremiah's mysterious foe from the north (Jer 1:14-15; 4:6; 6:1, 22) and Ezekiel's eschatological Gog (Ezek 38:6, 14-15; 39:1-2), that evil enemy by which God wreaks final judgment on the sinful people. The northerner is not a historical enemy, but God's instrument of wrath. But now God will remove a curse from the people. God's previous judgments on the people have been "great," through historical instruments of locusts and drought, which is the meaning of the last line in v. 20—a still greater act of salvation will come.

JOEL 2:21-27, AN ORACLE OF SALVATION

NIV

21 Be not afraid, O land;
    be glad and rejoice.
Surely the LORD has done great things.
22 Be not afraid, O wild animals,
    for the open pastures are becoming green.
The trees are bearing their fruit;
    the fig tree and the vine yield their riches.
23 Be glad, O people of Zion,
    rejoice in the LORD your God,
for he has given you
    the autumn rains in righteousness.[a]
He sends you abundant showers,
    both autumn and spring rains, as before.
24 The threshing floors will be filled with grain;
    the vats will overflow with new wine and oil.

25 "I will repay you for the years the locusts have
    eaten—
    the great locust and the young locust,

a23 Or / *the teacher for righteousness:*

NRSV

21 Do not fear, O soil;
    be glad and rejoice,
    for the LORD has done great things!
22 Do not fear, you animals of the field,
    for the pastures of the wilderness are green;
the tree bears its fruit,
    the fig tree and vine give their full yield.

23 O children of Zion, be glad
    and rejoice in the LORD your God;
for he has given the early rain[a] for your
    vindication,
    he has poured down for you abundant rain,
    the early and the later rain, as before.
24 The threshing floors shall be full of grain,
    the vats shall overflow with wine and oil.

25 I will repay you for the years
    that the swarming locust has eaten,

a Meaning of Heb uncertain

NIV

the other locusts and the locust swarm[a]—
my great army that I sent among you.
[26]You will have plenty to eat, until you are full,
and you will praise the name of the LORD your
God,
who has worked wonders for you;
never again will my people be shamed.
[27]Then you will know that I am in Israel,
that I am the LORD your God,
and that there is no other;
never again will my people be shamed."

[a]25 The precise meaning of the four Hebrew words used here for locusts is uncertain.

NRSV

the hopper, the destroyer, and the cutter,
my great army, which I sent against you.

[26] You shall eat in plenty and be satisfied,
and praise the name of the LORD your God,
who has dealt wondrously with you. And
my people shall never again be put
to shame.
[27] You shall know that I am in the midst of Israel,
and that I, the LORD, am your God and there
is no other.
And my people shall never again
be put to shame.

COMMENTARY

The oracle is divided into four strophes (vv. 21-22, 23, 24-25, 26-27) in which the speech of God alternates with that of the prophet. One may find the usual form of such an oracle of salvation in Isa 41:8-13, which, unlike the one in Joel, is entirely God's speech. The Isaianic oracle included a statement of God's past dealings with Israel (Isa 41:8-9), an imperative "Fear not!" and a promise of God's intervention (Isa 41:10), a description of the results of God's actions (Isa 41:11-12), and an explanation of God's actions (Isa 41:13). Joel retains part of the form, but uses it with great flexibility.

When God's salvation comes, nature too will be healed. Thus the "soil" (אדמה 'ădāmâ, v. 21; the NIV's "land" is misleading), and the wild animals (v. 22; cf. 1:20) are invited to join in the joy to come. Nature will once again yield its bounty, because God will again give the usual "early" rain of October and November and the "later" rain of March and April, as God had always done before (v. 23).

The NRSV reads לצדקה (liṣdāqâ) as "for your vindication" in v. 23, but the NIV's "the autumn rains in righteousness" is correct. God's gift of rain symbolizes God's righteousness. "Righteousness" (צדקה ṣĕdāqâ) throughout the Bible has to do with the fulfillment of the demands of a relationship, and God promises to fulfill the covenant relation with the people by restoring yearly rains. As a result, the prophet asks the children

of Zion to rejoice, not only over the restoration of the fertility of the ground, but even more so over the restoration of their covenant relation with God as well.

All the hardships that Judah has experienced in the past will be reversed by God's "great" acts (v. 21). The promises of vv. 21-27 exactly match the situation of suffering previously described. The ground will be restored (1:10; 2:21); the wild animals will be fed (1:20; 2:22); joy will return to Judah's worship (1:16; 2:23); drought will be a thing of the past (1:10, 12, 18-20; 2:23); fruit trees will bear (1:12, 19; 2:22); threshing floors and wine vats will be full (1:5, 17; 2:24). All are covenant blessings that God will once more bestow on the repentant and newly faithful people (cf. Deut 11:13-17; 28:3-5, 11-12; Lev 26:3-5). The restoration of crops and rain may have already begun during Joel's time. It is more likely, however, that they are all promises for the future.

In v. 25, the locusts are identified with God's "great army," which is an indication once again that part of the picture drawn in vv. 1-11 was influenced by the locust invasion. Nevertheless, God's final army will be much more than locusts.

The response of Judah to salvation on the day of the Lord will be satisfaction with the goods of life and praise of the name of the Lord its God, who has acted marvelously on Judah's behalf (v. 26). The nations will no longer be able to ask, "Where is their God?" (v. 17; cf. v. 19), for God will be in the midst of it, the covenant God forevermore (v. 19; 3:17), in fulfillment of the ancient promises (cf. Exod 25:8; 29:45; Lev 26:11; 1 Kgs 6:13; Isa 12:6; Ezek 37:27-28; Zeph 3:15, 17; Hos 11:9). Then Israel will know that the Lord is God and that there is no other, for God alone is able to save (v. 27; cf. Isa 45:5-6, 18, 22; 46:9). Israel's apostasy will be finished and forgotten, through a renewed and everlasting covenant (cf. Gen 17:7-8; Hos 2:16-23).

REFLECTIONS

The God who promises in free grace to restore the life of Judah in the time of Joel is the same God who has worked to offer us salvation. Indeed, one could characterize the biblical story as the record of God's actions to restore people to covenant communion. At the beginning of the story, people were created in God's image to have fellowship, as stewards of the "very good" earth, to enjoy the gifts of life and to glorify God (cf. Matt 5:16). God willed for humankind to have abundant life, but that abundant life is possible only in relationship with God. Otherwise we know only chaos, darkness, evil, and finally the void of death.

When people deserted God and tried to make God unnecessary, turning to other sources for life, they brought upon themselves the sterility, hopelessness, lack of joy, and threat of annihilation that Joel so vividly pictures. Worst, they brought the wrath of a God who will be nothing less than Lord over all people and who has the power to judge the entire world.

But running through the Bible's story of God's wrath is the theme of God's constant love and determination to restore people to fellowship and life. But as for Judah, God also has pity for us. And so the glad announcement is that God has come to us and dwelt among us, refusing to desert us (John 1:14). The gospel is that God lives in our midst and walks among us and enters into communion with us (Matt 18:20; 2 Cor 6:16). And the promise is that nothing in all creation will separate those who trust God's work in Jesus Christ from the Lord's loving presence (Rom 8:38-39). In that promise is our assurance of life abundant, both now and hereafter.

Indeed, the promise of faith is that in the final judgment, when God comes to rule over all the earth, we will be accepted as God's people forevermore. God will be with us and will wipe every tear from our eyes; mourning and crying and pain will be done away, and death will be no more (Rev 21:3-4). God gave the first fruits of that promise to Israel through the prophet Joel (2:26-27). God made the promise everlastingly sure through Jesus Christ our Lord.

JOEL 2:28-32

SIGNS OF THE COMING DAY OF THE LORD

OVERVIEW

As precursors of the imminent coming of the day of the Lord, God promises the gift of the Spirit to Judah and signs in heaven and on earth. Those who call on the name of the Lord will be saved on the final day of judgment.

JOEL 2:28-29, THE GIFT OF THE SPIRIT

NIV

28"And afterward,
    I will pour out my Spirit on all people.
Your sons and daughters will prophesy,
    your old men will dream dreams,
    your young men will see visions.
29Even on my servants, both men and women,
    I will pour out my Spirit in those days."

NRSV

28a Then afterward
    I will pour out my spirit on all flesh;
your sons and your daughters shall prophesy,
    your old men shall dream dreams,
    and your young men shall see visions.
29 Even on the male and female slaves,
    in those days, I will pour out my spirit.

a Ch 3.1 in Heb

COMMENTARY

"Afterward" (אחרי־כן *'aḥărê-kēn*) in v. 28 does not indicate that the events of vv. 28-32 will occur after the restorations promised in vv. 18-27. Rather, the word points to that indefinite time of the coming of the day of the Lord, and vv. 28-32 detail events that will precede the day, as signs indicating its nearness.

God promises to pour out the Spirit, on "all flesh," much like one pours out a liquid, although the context indicates that only those in Judah are meant. The Spirit of God throughout the OT was a gift of power, given in order that the recipient might do a particular job for God (see Exod 31:2-5; Judg 6:34; Mic 3:8; Hag 1:14). It is this understanding that Acts 2:4 adopts: The disciples

are given the Holy Spirit in order that they may be witnesses to Christ "to the ends of the earth" (Acts 1:8; 2:4). Prominent as the source of revelation among the early non-writing prophets (e.g., 1 Sam 10:6, 10; 19:20; 2 Sam 23:2; 2 Kgs 2:9), revelation by the Spirit is almost entirely replaced by revelation through the Word in the writing of the classical prophets, until the time of this passage in Joel. In short, the recurrence of prophecy in the Spirit will be a sign that the day of the Lord is near.

Joel emphasizes, however, not the task that will be given to all persons in Judah, but rather the relation of the Judeans to God, as manifested in their ability to prophesy in dreams and visions.

They will have direct communication from God. Once again Joel stresses that the relationship with God will be restored, but here he goes beyond his usual cultic emphases on sacrifices and priests. When such prophecy occurs, the day of the Lord is imminent.

REFLECTIONS

This passage, along with 2:30-32, is quoted in Acts 2:17-21, and it forms part of the lections for the celebration of the day of Pentecost. We should carefully note that the reason for the giving of the Spirit differs in Acts from that found in Joel, as stated in the Commentary. However, the gift of the Spirit as a sign pointing to the imminence of the new age of God's kingdom is pertinent to the interpretation of Acts 2. When the Holy Spirit is poured out on the disciples, gathered in Jerusalem, Acts affirms that the kingdom of God has begun to break into human history. This new reality made its first appearance in the person of Jesus of Nazareth (Luke 11:20). Participation in the life and powers of the new age of the kingdom are now to be offered to all who receive the apostles' testimony to Jesus Christ, both in the first century and in modern times. The day of the Lord, when God will do away with all enemies and usher in the final kingdom of goodness and peace, has not yet come in its fullness, and it will not come until the end of time. We all still face that final judgment. But the day has begun. Christ has ushered it in, and now the answer to Joel's question as to who can endure the coming of the day (Joel 2:12) and who will survive it depends on each individual's stance toward Jesus Christ. "What should we do?" ask those bewildered persons who were present at the day of Pentecost. And the answer from Peter is, "Repent, and be baptized every one of you in the name of Jesus Christ" (Acts 2:38 NRSV). Joel's message of turning and repentance is carried forward in the apostolic tradition of the book of Acts.

The message of Joel is no longer limited to the Judeans, however. Acts 2 breaks the boundaries of Joel 2:28-29, and all persons now are offered the opportunity of turning. The promise is for us and for our children and even for those "who are far away"—Gentiles, from every race and clime (Acts 2:39; see also John 1:12-13; Rom 11:17-24; Gal 4:5-7; Eph 2:11-21).

JOEL 2:30-32, SIGNS IN HEAVEN AND ON EARTH

NIV

30"I will show wonders in the heavens
   and on the earth,
   blood and fire and billows of smoke.
31The sun will be turned to darkness
   and the moon to blood
   before the coming of the great and dreadful
      day of the LORD.
32And everyone who calls
   on the name of the LORD will be saved;
 for on Mount Zion and in Jerusalem
   there will be deliverance,
   as the LORD has said,
 among the survivors
   whom the LORD calls."

NRSV

30I will show portents in the heavens and on the earth, blood and fire and columns of smoke. 31The sun shall be turned to darkness, and the moon to blood, before the great and terrible day of the LORD comes. 32Then everyone who calls on the name of the LORD shall be saved; for in Mount Zion and in Jerusalem there shall be those who escape, as the LORD has said, and among the survivors shall be those whom the LORD calls.

COMMENTARY

True to the apocalyptic tradition, Joel proclaims that the coming of the day of the Lord will be preceded by cosmic and earthly signs (cf. Isa 13:10, 13; Ezek 32:3-8; Mark 13:7-8, 24-25; Luke 21:25). The blood, fire, and smoke of v. 30 probably refer to the burning of cities and the slaughter of their populace. The darkening of the sun and the changing of the moon to blood are to be understood not as natural disasters, such as an eclipse or sandstorm, but as supernatural signs of the approaching day (cf. Amos 8:9). As in Mal 4:5 and Luke 21:25-28, God will give warning of the approaching final judgment.

The only hope of surviving the judgment will be to call on the name of the Lord (v. 32), which means to worship God (Gen 12:8), to acknowledge that one belongs to God (Ps 105:1; Isa 12:4; 44:5; Zech 13:9), and to depend on God for one's life (Prov 18:10; Zeph 2:3). In the light of what has gone before in vv. 12-13, such a calling is not a desperate attempt to save oneself by a last-minute conversion, but the fruit of the dedication of one's whole heart to God.

Obadiah 17 promised earlier that there would be a remnant of the saved left on Mount Zion. Joel here reiterates that promise as part of the tradition handed on to him, which is the meaning of "as the LORD has said" (v. 32). But Joel also adds that persons who call on the name of the Lord are those whom God has called. In short, there is the thought of election here, in which faith is understood, not as a work of human beings, but as a gift from God. The elect have been called by God's free will. The prophet challenges them to respond to their election.

REFLECTIONS

Joel 2:32 promises that all who call upon the name of the Lord will be delivered. Acts 2:21-35 and Rom 10:9-13 interpret the faith that will save in God's final day of judgment as faith in Jesus Christ, who is now "both Lord and Messiah" (Acts 2:36 NRSV). For us, Joel's promise of salvation is to be fulfilled by confessing that "Jesus is Lord" and believing in our hearts that "God raised him from the dead" (Rom 10:9 NRSV). The refuge afforded by Zion in the day of judgment, promised in Joel 2:32, has now given way to the saving effect of Christ's cross and resurrection.

Moreover, Peter promises in Acts 2:38 that faith in Christ will bring the fulfillment of Joel's promise of the gift of the Spirit. In short, the believer will begin now to live in the powers of that new age heralded by the pouring out of God's Spirit (Joel 2:28-29). And the gift of the Spirit, says Paul, is the guarantee of one's salvation in the final judgment (2 Cor 1:22; 5:5; cf. Eph 1:14). So the promise of Joel now is given its final focus and handed on in the faith of the Christian church, which is no longer limited to Israel but spans the world of nations.

That promise, moreover, is to "everyone." No one is excluded—rich or poor, educated or illiterate, old or young, strong or weak, good or bad, you or me. "Everything that the Father gives me will come to you," proclaims Jesus, preserving Joel's thought of election, "and anyone who comes to me I will never drive away" (John 6:37 NRSV). God wills to save the whole world through Jesus Christ (John 3:16).

To "call on the name of the LORD" means, in the scriptures, to tell others what God has done (Ps 105:1; Isa 12:4)—to be witnesses of a worldview that sees everything in the context of God's deeds and character; to be evangels of the glad tidings that God is the ruler yet; to announce to everyone who will listen that he or she too is offered salvation on the day of the Lord. As Paul explains when he uses this verse from Joel, no one can believe unless he or she has heard, and no one will hear unless Christ is proclaimed. And so saving faith in our Lord Jesus Christ will come from what is heard, and what is heard will come from our word about Christ (Rom 10:14-17).

JUDGMENT AND SALVATION IN THE DAY OF THE LORD

OVERVIEW

I n a series of vivid images, Joel now portrays God's final dealings with the nations of the world. First, in a court scene, the nations are declared guilty for their sinful treatment of Israel. Second, though they attempt to war against the verdict, they are then defeated in battle by God's angelic hosts, cut down like grain and trodden upon like grapes in a winepress. Only God can save Judah from a similar fate on the day of the Lord. In God, Judah can find a sure refuge.

JOEL 3:1-8, THE LORD'S CASE AGAINST THE NATIONS

NIV

3 "In those days and at that time,
   when I restore the fortunes of Judah and
      Jerusalem,
²I will gather all nations
   and bring them down to the Valley of
      Jehoshaphat.ᵃ
There I will enter into judgment against them
   concerning my inheritance, my people Israel,
for they scattered my people among the
      nations
   and divided up my land.
³They cast lots for my people
   and traded boys for prostitutes;
they sold girls for wine
   that they might drink.

⁴"Now what have you against me, O Tyre and Sidon and all you regions of Philistia? Are you repaying me for something I have done? If you are paying me back, I will swiftly and speedily return on your own heads what you have done. ⁵For you took my silver and my gold and carried off my finest treasures to your temples. ⁶You sold the people of Judah and Jerusalem to the Greeks,

ᵃ2 *Jehoshaphat* means *the LORD judges;* also in verse 12.

NRSV

3ᵃ For then, in those days and at that time, when I restore the fortunes of Judah and Jerusalem, ²I will gather all the nations and bring them down to the valley of Jehoshaphat, and I will enter into judgment with them there, on account of my people and my heritage Israel, because they have scattered them among the nations. They have divided my land, ³and cast lots for my people, and traded boys for prostitutes, and sold girls for wine, and drunk it down.

4What are you to me, O Tyre and Sidon, and all the regions of Philistia? Are you paying me back for something? If you are paying me back, I will turn your deeds back upon your own heads swiftly and speedily. ⁵For you have taken my silver and my gold, and have carried my rich treasures into your temples.ᵇ ⁶You have sold the people of Judah and Jerusalem to the Greeks, removing them far from their own border. ⁷But now I will rouse them to leave the places to which you have sold them, and I will turn your deeds back upon your own heads. ⁸I will sell your sons and your daughters into the hand of the people of Judah,

ᵃ Ch 4.1 in Heb   ᵇ Or *palaces*

NRSV

that you might send them far from their homeland.

⁷"See, I am going to rouse them out of the places to which you sold them, and I will return on your own heads what you have done. ⁸I will sell your sons and daughters to the people of Judah, and they will sell them to the Sabeans, a nation far away." The LORD has spoken.

NRSV

and they will sell them to the Sabeans, to a nation far away; for the LORD has spoken.

COMMENTARY

The form of this section is best represented in the NIV translation, which sets vv. 1-3 as poetry and vv. 4-8 as prose. God speaks in both parts. The deity engages in a court case against all nations, but once again, this will be a future happening, when God brings final deliverance to the people. The "for" (כִּי *kî*) opening v. 1 closely connects this section with what has gone before. The pouring out of the Spirit and the signs in heaven and on earth have presaged the coming of the day. Now the day's final judgment and salvation are portrayed. The phrase "in those days and at that time" is found elsewhere only in Jer 33:15; 50:4, 20, which also deal with the coming of the kingdom.

3:1-3. These verses set forth the fulfillment of God's promise in Gen 12:3, in which the Lord says to Abram, "I will bless those who bless you, and the one who curses you I will curse" (NRSV). The nations will be judged in terms of their treatment of Israel, who is God's "people" and "heritage" (v. 2).

Three charges are leveled against the nations by God the plaintiff. First, they have scattered God's people among the nations (v. 2), an allusion to the exiles of 722, 597, 587, and 582 BCE (for the latter date, see Jer 52:30). When the northern kingdom of Israel fell to Assyria in 722 BCE, the ten northern tribes were carried into Assyrian exile and disappeared from history, their land then being populated by foreigners. After the Babylonian exiles of 597–582 BCE, many Israelites were dispersed throughout the ancient Near East, although a small number returned to Palestine when released from captivity in 538 BCE at the decree of the Persian ruler Cyrus. Although the

prophets viewed Israel's captivity as the judgment of God on Israel for its sin, according to v. 2, Israel's exile was also the sinful work of the foreign nations.

Second, the foreign nations are to be judged for taking for themselves portions of God's land of Palestine. The land never belonged to Israel, but was loaned to the nation by God, and God is always understood in the OT as the true owner of the land (cf. Lev 25:23; Deut 30:15-20; Ezek 33:23-29). When Assyria and Babylonia claimed the land, therefore, and when aliens from neighboring states took over houses and fields after the fall of Jerusalem (Lam 5:2; Obad 11, 13), they were taking by force what really belonged to God.

Third, the foreign nations are to be judged because they have sold the inhabitants of Judah and Jerusalem as slaves to those merchants and traders who frequently followed conquering armies. Captives, including children, were divided among the soldiers by lot and then were sold for the price of a harlot's hire or for a draft of wine (v. 3). The conquerors have treated the chosen people of God as if they were worth no more than the price of a moment's gratification.

But whoever curses the descendants of Abraham will be cursed by God (cf. Ezekiel 25), and so God declares that God will, in lordly power over them, gather all nations together and bring them down to the valley of Jehoshaphat and go to court with them there (v. 2). The name "Jehoshaphat" means "Jah (a shortened form of Jahweh) judges" and is intended to be symbolic, since there is no valley by that name in Palestine. It cannot be identified with the Valley of Beracah, where King Jehoshaphat won a victory (2 Chr

20:20-28), nor is it the Valley of Gehinnon (Jer 7:31-32). From the fourth century on, it was identified with the Kidron Valley, but that is a narrow wadi and not a plain. Thus the Targum and Theodotian are correct when they read "the plain of judicial decision" and "the country of judgment" respectively, inserting the meaning of the name into the text. In the coming day of the Lord, the Valley of Jehoshaphat is the symbolic name for the place where God will judge all nations.

3:4-8. Some commentators[12] understand these prose verses as a later addition to Joel, and they may well be right. But the verses enlarge on the indictment of 3:1-3 and fit well into their context.

Their theme is the slave trade that Tyre, Sidon, and the five city-states of Philistia carried on with Greece from the fifth century BCE on. We know that Sidon was destroyed by the armies of Artaxerxes III of Persia in 343 BCE and that Tyre fell to Alexander the Great in 332 BCE. The date of 343, therefore, forms the latest date in which the book of Joel could have been compiled. Ap-

12. E.g., H. W. Wolff, *Joel and Amos,* Hermeneia (Philadelphia: Fortress, 1977).

parently some Jews were victims of the slave trade carried on by these coastal cities.

The foreigners are also accused of plundering some of the ornaments and equipment from the Temple and of putting them in their pagan shrines (cf. 1 Sam 5:2; Dan 1:2), although "temples" (היכלות *hêkālôt*) can also have the meaning of "palaces" (v. 5). But the selling of the Jews into slavery is the more serious charge.

The punishment will therefore fit the crime. God will gain the release of Jews enslaved in far-off countries and return them to their homeland, and the Jews will now become the intermediaries, selling the Phoenicians and Philistines to the distant Sabeans (vv. 7-8). Seba is known only as a distant country in the OT, and its location is not specified (cf. Jer 6:20; but archaeological evidence has located it in the southwestern portion of the Arabian peninsula now occupied by Yemen). Joel's point is that Seba is in the opposite direction from Greece and is far away.

Throughout the Bible, God's punishment of sin often takes the form of returning the evil deeds of sinners upon their own heads (cf. 1 Kgs 8:31-32; Jer 50:29; Ezek 35:11; Hab 2:8; Obad 15; Rev 18:4-17; cf. Matt 18:23-35; Rom 1:24-32).

REFLECTIONS

Readers may shrink from the thought in Joel 3:1-8 that God would use evil to punish evil, but the OT is a very realistic book. Evil in our world does beget evil: Hatred breeds hatred; war breeds retaliation; suffering breeds desire for vengeance; oppression breeds lust for power. And as punishment for evil, God sometimes simply lets people suffer sin's consequences or gives them over to it, as much as to say, "All right, if that is what you want, you may have it, full measure and running over."

Joel attests, moreover, that the judgment of God concerns not only individuals, but also the whole world of nations (cf. Amos 1–2). As they have done, so it shall be done to them. International relations are played out in our time and every time against the backdrop of God's sovereignty over the nations, and while some may think that the politicians and economists, the military and multinational corporations are in charge of our world, the prophetic perspective knows better (cf. Matt 25:31-46; 28:18; Rom 13:1-7; Revelation). Joel is prefiguring that final reign of God (Rev 11:15) and the judgment that will precede it.

JOEL 3:9-12, THE NATIONS CALLED TO BATTLE

NIV

⁹Proclaim this among the nations:
Prepare for war!
Rouse the warriors!
Let all the fighting men draw near and attack.
¹⁰Beat your plowshares into swords
and your pruning hooks into spears.
Let the weakling say,
"I am strong!"
¹¹Come quickly, all you nations from every side,
and assemble there.

Bring down your warriors, O LORD!

¹²"Let the nations be roused;
let them advance into the Valley of
Jehoshaphat,
for there I will sit
to judge all the nations on every side."

NRSV

⁹ Proclaim this among the nations:
Prepare war,ᵃ
stir up the warriors.
Let all the soldiers draw near,
let them come up.
¹⁰ Beat your plowshares into swords,
and your pruning hooks into spears;
let the weakling say, "I am a warrior."

¹¹ Come quickly,ᵇ
all you nations all around,
gather yourselves there.
Bring down your warriors, O LORD.
¹² Let the nations rouse themselves,
and come up to the valley of Jehoshaphat;
for there I will sit to judge
all the neighboring nations.

ᵃ Heb *sanctify war*   ᵇ Meaning of Heb uncertain

COMMENTARY

The image of a courtroom case in 3:1-8 is exchanged for a battle scene. Except for the prophet's words in v. 11*d,* God speaks, summoning angelic heralds to carry the message to all nations that they are to prepare for war against the deity. Warriors are to be roused up from their peaceful pursuits and girded for the fray. They should bring all weapons possible, beating their plowshares into swords and their pruning hooks into spears—a deliberate and ironic reversal of the words in Isa 2:4 and Mic 4:3. Even those unfit for battle should consider themselves to be fighting men, for the nations are going to need everyone they can muster to stand against God. Every nation is included (v. 11), and they are to use every possible defense.

But then, God will bring down "warriors," or "mighty men" (גבורים *gibbôrîm*), to the battle scene. The text means that God will bring down angelic hosts to the fight (cf. Ps 103:20; Zech 14:5). The judgment on the nations will be carried out during the ensuing battle in the Valley of Jehoshaphat.

JOEL 3:13-17, THE FINAL BATTLE AND ITS OUTCOME

NIV

13"Swing the sickle,
 for the harvest is ripe.
Come, trample the grapes,
 for the winepress is full
 and the vats overflow—
so great is their wickedness!"

14Multitudes, multitudes
 in the valley of decision!
For the day of the LORD is near
 in the valley of decision.
15The sun and moon will be darkened,
 and the stars no longer shine.
16The LORD will roar from Zion
 and thunder from Jerusalem;
 the earth and the sky will tremble.
But the LORD will be a refuge for his people,
 a stronghold for the people of Israel.
17"Then you will know that I, the LORD your God,
 dwell in Zion, my holy hill.
Jerusalem will be holy;
 never again will foreigners invade her."

NRSV

13 Put in the sickle,
 for the harvest is ripe.
Go in, tread,
 for the wine press is full.
The vats overflow,
 for their wickedness is great.

14 Multitudes, multitudes,
 in the valley of decision!
For the day of the LORD is near
 in the valley of decision.
15 The sun and the moon are darkened,
 and the stars withdraw their shining.

16 The LORD roars from Zion,
 and utters his voice from Jerusalem,
 and the heavens and the earth shake.
But the LORD is a refuge for his people,
 a stronghold for the people of Israel.

17 So you shall know that I, the LORD your God,
 dwell in Zion, my holy mountain.
And Jerusalem shall be holy,
 and strangers shall never again pass through
 it.

COMMENTARY

The section may be divided into two strophes, vv. 13-14 and vv. 15-17, with the particle "for" (כי *kî*) marking the climactic line of the first strophe. Direct speeches of God begin (v. 13) and end (v. 17) the section, with the prophet's comment in between.

3:13. The judgment of the day of the Lord is now loosed in its full fury on those nations that have opposed God's work in Israel. In a series of curt and staccato imperative Hebrew verbs, God commands the angelic warriors to destroy the enemies. The prophet uses two agricultural images: harvesting of grain with a sickle (cf. Isa 17:5; Mark 4:29; Rev 14:15-16, 18-19) and pressing out grapes in a winepress (Isa 63:3; Jer 25:30).

The word for "sickle" (מגל *maggāl*) can also mean "pruning knife," which was used to cut grapes from their vines. With this meaning, the prophet may be alluding entirely to the grape harvest. But both figures—grain and grape harvests—are frequently used of God's judgment (cf. Rev 14:15-20), so the translations in the NIV and the NRSV need not be altered. God's mighty army moves through the enemy forces, cutting them down as a farmer cuts down grain with a scythe. Or God's forces tread down the enemy like a vintner treading out grapes. The picture reminds one most of all of Isa 63:1-6, although in that passage God is the sole warrior crushing the enemy.

So great is the wickedness of the nations that

the juice pressed out from the winepress over-flows the receiving vats. The extent of such evil is emphasized by the final "for" at the end of v. 13.

3:14. The repeated word "multitudes" (המונים *hămônîm*), when read in Hebrew, imitates the confused noise, like a roar or a hum in the distance, rising up from the battlefield.

Significantly, the name of the Valley of Je-hoshaphat is now altered in the prophet's words to "the valley of verdict" or "the valley of deci-sion" (NIV and NRSV). God is now the judge in this court case against the nations, and the verdict on them is ominous. In the last two lines of v. 14, the prophet then steps back from his vision and warns his compatriots once again as he warned them before (1:15; 2:1, 11) that the day of the Lord, with such a judgment for God's enemies, is near. They should heed the call to repentance, therefore (2:12-17).

3:15-16. The picture of the final battle on the day then continues. The darkening of the heav-enly bodies, as in 2:10, will take place on that day. And God, watching the battle scene, will roar from Zion, so that the cosmos will tremble. Verse 16*ab* cites Amos 1:2; all of vv. 13-16*b* are remark-ably similar to Jer 25:30-31. Once again Joel reclaims prophecy from the past and applies it to the present and to the future.

Amid the carnage of God's destruction of the enemies, repentant Judah and Jerusalem can have a refuge (v. 16*d*). And in returning to God, they can find a fortress or stronghold that shields them from all destruction (v. 16*e*; cf. 2 Cor 10:4). Metaphors for such protection are common in the psalms (e.g., Pss 18:2; 46:1; 61:3; 62:7); here they apply to God's protection on the final day.

3:17. The assurance of 2:27 is then repeated in the final line of the second strophe. On that day, Israel will know with absolute certainty that God is its God, that the deity dwells in its midst in the Temple on Zion, and that no alien enemy, whether locusts or human armies, unbelievers or idolaters, will ever enter or defile Jerusalem again (cf. Isa 52:1; Zech 14:20-21; Rev 21:3). Full communion with God will be a reality, and the covenant will be everlasting.

REFLECTIONS

We recoil at the bloody pictures of God's destruction of enemies painted in Joel's book. God is not like that, we say. God is gentle and kind and loving, and would never wipe out opponents as a farmer mows down grain. When we say that, we show no understanding of the scripture, "It is a fearful thing to fall into the hands of the living God" (Heb 10:31 NRSV), because we have little understanding of the nature of God. Thus the scripture's portrayals of the day of the Lord with its final judgment are difficult to comprehend.

But evil and sin are very real, and their forces are very strong, encompassing the ability to torture and degrade, to warp and destroy every form of life. As Ephesians puts it, "our struggle is not against enemies of blood and flesh, but against the rulers, against the authorities, against the cosmic powers of this present darkness" (Eph 6:12 NRSV)—against evil grown so threatening and universal that it is a cosmic shadow darkening the earth. A God who is merely friendly is no match for such evil.

Tertullian knew that. Attacking the heretic Marcion's "good" God, Tertullian wrote, "What a prevaricator of truth is such a god! What a dissembler with his own decisions. Afraid to condemn what he really condemns, afraid to hate what he does not love, permitting that to be done which he does not allow, choosing to indicate what he dislikes rather than deeply examine it! This will turn out an imaginary goodness, for the true God is not otherwise fully good than as an enemy of evil."[13] The God of the Old and New Testaments is an enemy of evil, and while the pictures that Joel and, indeed, all the prophets and the book of Revelation give us of God's destruction of evil may be too bloody for our tastes, they nevertheless encompass the truth that on the day of judgment God will destroy these enemies. We have

13. Tertullian *Against Marcion* I.26-27.

to examine our lives, therefore, as Joel bids us examine them, to ask if we are truly opponents or proponents of God's will. We also should remember that the cross of Christ was no less bloody, when the final victory was won over all the forces of evil, even though in that battle God took on the death due God's enemies.

JOEL 3:18-21, THE GLORIOUS FUTURE FOR THE FAITHFUL

NIV

18"In that day the mountains will drip new wine,
and the hills will flow with milk;
all the ravines of Judah will run with water.
A fountain will flow out of the LORD's house
and will water the valley of acacias.ᵃ
19But Egypt will be desolate,
Edom a desert waste,
because of violence done to the people of Judah,
in whose land they shed innocent blood.
20Judah will be inhabited forever
and Jerusalem through all generations.
21Their bloodguilt, which I have not pardoned,
I will pardon."

The LORD dwells in Zion!

ᵃ18 Or *Valley of Shittim*

NRSV

18 In that day
the mountains shall drip sweet wine,
the hills shall flow with milk,
and all the stream beds of Judah
shall flow with water;
a fountain shall come forth from the house of
the LORD
and water the Wadi Shittim.

19 Egypt shall become a desolation
and Edom a desolate wilderness,
because of the violence done to the people of
Judah,
in whose land they have shed innocent
blood.
20 But Judah shall be inhabited forever,
and Jerusalem to all generations.
21 I will avenge their blood, and I will not clear
the guilty,ᵃ
for the LORD dwells in Zion.

ᵃ Gk Syr: Heb *I will hold innocent their blood that I have not held innocent*

COMMENTARY

3:18. The day of the Lord will bring not only the destruction of God's enemies and the rescue of repentant Jerusalem and Judah, but it will also usher in a paradisiacal existence for the faithful. Borrowing partially on the thought of Amos 9:13, Joel picks up themes from the first chapter of his book and portrays their reversal. Once the sweet wine was cut off (1:5); now the mountains with their vineyards will yield wine in abundance (3:18). Previously there was no milk from the cattle, because they had no pasture (1:18); now the rich grasslands on the hills will furnish an ample supply. During the drought, there was no water anywhere (1:17-20); in God's future, the rivers and wadis of Judah will flow full all year round. Once again, borrowing an earlier prophetic theme, a fountain will flow forth from the Temple and water even the Valley of Shittim (Ezek 47:1-12; cf. Ps 46:4; Zech 14:8; Rev 22:1-2)—a symbol of the life-giving power of God's presence (cf. Ps 36:8; Isa 33:21).

The Valley of Shittim is mentioned nowhere

else in the OT, but the phrase probably refers to that deep and rocky portion of the Kidron Valley or wadi that begins a little northwest of Jerusalem, bends around east of the city, and then continues through a deep gorge southeast toward the Dead Sea. The wadi was usually dry, but acacias grew in abundance in its dry soil; it was sometimes called the Wadi or Valley of the Acacias, as in the NIV.

3:19-20. The portrayal of the reversal of fortunes continues, and the prophet specifies two enemies to be destroyed. Once Judah was a desolation, dry and wasted. Now its enemy Egypt will share that fate (cf. Ezek 29:9, 12; 32:15). Once Edom took advantage of the fall of Judah and Jerusalem to the Babylonians (Obadiah). Now Edom will become nothing but a desolate wilderness devoid of population, while Judah and Jerusalem will be inhabited forever. Both countries are frequently mentioned in prophetic oracles against the foreign nations (cf. Isaiah 34; Jeremiah 46; Ezekiel 30–32). Hence Joel suggests that earlier prophetic words about the destruction of Israel's enemies in the day of the Lord will be fulfilled.

3:21. There is a great deal of uncertainty about the first line of this verse, concerning both the proper translation of the line and its placement. Does it mean that God will avenge the slaying of the people by their enemies, as in the NRSV? Or does it mean that God will forgive any bloodguilt of Judah not already pardoned, as in the NIV? Following the NRSV translation, the line may belong after v. 19, as many scholars have suggested. If the NIV is correct, it must be noted that there has been no previous mention of bloodguilt, and, hence, some scholars would delete the line. Whatever the solution adopted—and neither seems entirely satisfactory—the final promise of the prophet is that God will dwell in Zion.

REFLECTIONS

The promise that Joel finally holds out to those who are faithful to God is the promise of abundant life. The prophet portrays the content of that promise, true to many previous prophetic pictures in the OT, in terms of abundant water and milk and wine (cf. Isa 55:1-3). In line with prophetic and psalmic tradition, he also portrays it in terms of freedom from all enemies and their threats to peace and security (cf. Ps 46:8-11). But above all else, Joel holds out the promise that God will finally defeat all the enemy forces and will dwell in Israel's midst as Lord and source of wondrous life.

In many respects, Joel's message does not sound pleasant to modern ears, for it adamantly reminds us of the fact that we do not control the forces of nature that sustain our lives: God does. And it tells us that we are not autonomous individuals, free to live as we like, but that we are responsible to the God who is sovereign over all nations and persons. It further warns us that we can be done to death by the Lord, who rules nature and history, if we do not confess God's rule and live according to it.

Nevertheless, Joel's message is essentially one of amazing mercy, because it proclaims to us that "even now" (2:12) in our flight from God and our stubborn refusal to obey God's will, God holds the door open to our repentance and return. Judah and Jerusalem in the days of the prophet were no less wandering and sinful than are we, but God's arms were held out to them, inviting them to return.

So God waits for us to respond. As with Judah and Jerusalem in the days of Joel, God waits for us to rend our hearts, to repent, and to receive in faith the salvation that has been offered to us.

The invitation is there. That is what Joel wants us to tell our children (Joel 1:3). The way is open for our return to God. We can stand in the day of the Lord. Abundant and eternal life can be ours in the kingdom.

THE BOOK OF AMOS

INTRODUCTION, COMMENTARY, AND REFLECTIONS
BY
DONALD E. GOWAN

THE BOOK OF
AMOS

INTRODUCTION

THE INFLUENCE OF THE BOOK OF AMOS

here is almost unanimous agreement that the book of Amos is the earliest of the prophetic books. As such, it marks the beginning of a unique tradition in the history of religion: prophecies of the approaching end of the existence of God's people based upon God's judgment of them for failing to live according to the divine standards. The tradition continues from Amos through the books of Hosea, Micah, Isaiah, Zephaniah, and the early parts of Jeremiah and Ezekiel; then it comes to an end. Each of these later works takes up and reasserts the unacceptable message first announced in the book of Amos, but the message of Amos has no predecessors that we can identify. For this reason alone the book has rightly been marked by modern scholarship as one of the most important turning points in the history of the religion of Israel. More obvious to the contemporary reader, however, are two striking characteristics of the book: the power of its language and the passion of its concern for the oppressed. In the nineteenth and twentieth centuries, Amos has been appealed to regularly as the Old Testament's classic statement concerning social justice.

The existence of a prophetic tradition of judgment, from Amos through Ezekiel, shows that in the eighth and seventh centuries BCE Amos's message, with its announcement that God was about to do a new thing in history, had a profound effect on the theology of Israel. In the nineteenth and twentieth centuries CE its social message was taken up with enthusiasm, but during the many intervening centuries, Amos was one of the less influential parts of the canon. It was seldom quoted or even alluded to in Jewish or Christian writings.

The New Testament quotes it twice (5:25-27 in Acts 7:42-43 and 9:11-12 in Acts 15:16-17); it is cited once in the Apocrypha (Tob 2:6 quotes Amos 8:10); and the Mishnah quotes it twice (4:7 in *m. Ta' an.* 3:3 and 9:6 in *m. 'Abot* 3:6).

Once we note the typical ways the Old Testament has been used, prior to the nineteenth century, the reasons for the relative neglect of Amos become clear. Both Jewish and Christian interpreters typically sought messages of comfort and hope in the Old Testament, and there is little of that to be found in Amos. As a source of ethical teaching, the fact that the book contains only one exhortation, with a faint promise (5:14-15; cf. 5:4-6), made it less appealing than other books, which are filled with promises. The central message of the book, "The end has come upon my people Israel" (8:2 NRSV), has not been something many theologians have known how to use. This commentary, however, will attempt to show that Amos is more than a treatise on social ethics and more than an important document for understanding the development of the religion of Israel. It will take Amos's announcement of the impending exile of Israel, interpreted by him as the death of God's people, to be one of history's most profound insights into the true nature of the human dilemma and God's surprising—even shocking—ways of dealing with it. Amos speaks of death; he does not yet know of resurrection, about which the last of the line of judgment prophets spoke (Ezek 37:1-14), but he was the first to announce that Israel must die—the beginning of a new act in the Old Testament's story of redemption.

THE PROPHET AND THE BOOK

We know nothing about some of the prophets except their names (Obadiah, Habakkuk) or their name and place of residence (Nahum). Only the book of Jeremiah contains a lengthy series of stories about the life of a prophet. As for Amos, his book tells us that he came from Tekoa in Judah, that he was somehow associated with shepherds (1:1), and that he had been a herdsman and trimmer of sycamore trees (7:14). We also have the account of a single incident in his life (7:10-17). In spite of such slender evidence, however, other commentaries contain sections in which the life of Amos is reconstructed in various ways. It is clear that we have an almost unavoidable desire to gain access to the personality, experiences, and faith of the individuals responsible for the prophetic books, and that desire is so strong that the most responsible scholars have not hesitated to use their imaginations, along with every clue they can find in the texts of these books, to create biographies they believe to be fair representations of the lives of those prophets.

The "biographical approach" to the prophetic books may affect their interpretation in two different ways, both of them involving circular reasoning. One method attempts to recreate the life of Amos, but depending on the scholar one reads, Amos may have been: (a) a simple Judean shepherd; (b) a well-to-do and prominent citizen, perhaps connected with the Jerusalem Temple; or even (c) a politically important citizen of the northern kingdom. The other method (redaction criticism)[1] decides what the prophet Amos could and could not have said, using criteria derived from the text and presuppositions about the nature of prophecy, and attributes what he could not have said to redactors, after which the remaining passages will represent a consistent message believed to be appropriate for that eighth-century prophet. Some of the redaction critics make no effort to reconstruct a life of Amos (and may deny that this can be done), but I call their work a biographical approach also, for it proceeds on the assumptions that the thought of one individual can be isolated from additions made to it by others, and that it is important to do so.

My work on the prophets has led me to question both of those assumptions and to set aside every effort to recover the "historical Amos," focusing instead on the book of Amos, or what may also be called the Amos tradition. The first assumption fails because of the scarcity of explicit evidence about the life of Amos, which should call for an appropriate scholarly caution. I see no need to be as skeptical of the historicity of stories about the prophets (such as Amos 7:10-17 or Isaiah 7) as some scholars are, but I am skeptical of all efforts to deduce from the words of the prophets either what their personal experiences may have been or clear standards as to what they could or could not have said. The book of Amos may all have come from him, may be mostly his with a few later additions, or may have been heavily redacted. Each of these opinions may be found in the work of very able scholars, but we cannot demonstrate that any one of them is true or false, and since that is the case, some might be driven to the skeptical conclusion that we cannot be sure that any of these words are the very words of Amos.

I prefer to think of this conclusion as cautious rather than truly skeptical, however. It is probably far less important to know exactly what the man Amos said than many have assumed. Certainly, in our time it is hard to avoid that assumption, because we do have a strong biographical interest. The words and stories preserved in the prophetic books lead us to want to know more about these individuals, and seldom has that desire been resisted. But the lives and religious experiences of the prophets seem to have been a subject of little or no interest to the Israelites who collected and produced the final editions of this material. The incidents from the lives of prophets that are contained in these books quite clearly have been preserved because they contain a message from God to Israel, and not because the prophets lived such interesting lives. The great bulk of material concerning Jeremiah's experiences during the last years of Judah might lead us to think otherwise, but there are clues enough in all the books containing stories about the prophets to show us that for Israel it was not the person of the prophet that was important, but the God the prophet represented. The book of Amos is almost anonymous; the pronouns "I" and "me" occur only in 7:1-9, 14-15; 8:1; and 9:1, and that prophetic anonymity ought to be taken seriously.

Thus the question of Amos's occupation (herdsman and trimmer of sycamore trees), which has drawn so much scholarly attention, will be discussed briefly at the appropriate

1. Redaction criticism assumes books such as Amos have come into existence through a gradual process, with the original words of the prophet having been revised by later writers, then supplemented by successive layers of new oracles, in order to make their messages relevant to later times.

place in the commentary (7:14), but will not find a place in this introduction. The words of the book ascribed to him make it clear that Amos did not speak for herdsmen or sycamore trimmers; he spoke for God. We do not know how—or whether—those occupations might have influenced what Amos said, so the efforts to reconstruct that aspect of his life actually contribute nothing certain to our understanding of the words of his book.

Certainly, most of the prophetic books appear to be anthologies, and they may include the words of more than one prophet; but hypothetical reconstructions appear to be so subjective that scholarly caution should lead us to focus on what we have. We have the book of Amos, and we will call that the Amos tradition, rather than trying to identify all or certain parts of it with that person Amos about whom we know so little. Most, if not all, of that tradition makes good sense against a mid–eighth-century BCE background, so the commentary will interpret most of it with reference to the events of that period, without necessarily claiming that the eighth century date proves Amos was its author. The utter newness of the message that God had decreed the end of God's people Israel and the distinctive characteristics of style in the book strongly suggest that one writer was responsible for both its basic message and the ways in which it was expressed, but it should be emphasized again that for ancient Israel authorship seems not to have been a major concern. What was important was the authenticity of the words, which had been confirmed by history. So this commentary will attempt to be guided by Israel's primary interest in preserving the book and accepting it as canonical.

Having found redaction criticism too subjective an approach, this commentary will focus on the more secure results to be obtained from the use of form criticism, elaborated by insights gained from rhetorical analysis, and the study of the history of the traditions that are reused by the prophet.

HISTORY OF THE PERIOD

The superscription of the book (1:1) dates it during the reigns of Uzziah, king of Judah (783–742 BCE), and Jeroboam II, king of Israel (785–745 BCE). The only part of the book that seems to refer to a different period is 9:11-15, although some scholars have dated that section in the eighth-century BCE also, as will be noted in the commentary. The second quarter of the eighth century was a time of relative peace for both nations; both kings are said to have engaged in offensive campaigns to enlarge their territories rather than in defensive action (2 Kgs 14:22, 25-28). A major turn of events came shortly after the death of Jeroboam, with the accession of Tiglath-pileser III to the Assyrian throne in 745. He began to campaign actively in Syria by 740, received tribute from Israel in 738, occupied Galilee and Transjordan in 734 (2 Kgs 15:29), and took Damascus in 732. The government of the northern kingdom had fallen into chaos after Jeroboam's death, with six kings occupying the throne during the 24 years prior to the fall of Samaria. In 722 BCE, Samaria, the capital city of the northern kingdom, fell to the Assyrians under Sargon II.

The book of Amos is thus usually dated between 760 and 750 BCE, after Jeroboam's military successes in Gilead (2 Kgs 14:25; cf. Amos 6:13) and before the rise of Tiglath-pileser III made the Assyrian threat obvious. There is no evidence in Amos of any concern about Assyria; nor is there any reference to the rapid succession of kings in Israel following Jeroboam's death, as there is in Hosea. In Amos 7:11, the prophet is said to have foretold that Jeroboam would die by the sword, which did not happen, so this passage was almost certainly written before Jeroboam's death. Any effort to date the book more exactly than this calls for more explicit evidence than we have. Much has been made of the probability that Amos's ministry took place during a time of prosperity, but the evidence for that comes almost entirely from his own book, so it is inappropriate to describe that as if it were background for the book. What we can deduce concerning the social and economic circumstances to which these words are addressed thus belongs within the commentary. In fact, the most important aspect of the historical setting of Amos is an event that occurred after most (if not all) of the book had been formulated, and that is the end of the northern kingdom in 722 BCE, for the impending death of Israel is the essential message of the book.

THE LITERARY FORM OF THE BOOK OF AMOS

The book of Amos is considered to be one of the masterpieces of Hebrew literature. Only a few major examples of what form criticism and rhetorical analysis have revealed about the style and literary skill of this work can be offered here. The basic unit of speech is usually very short, from one to four sentences, but often these short units are combined into more elaborate structures. Whether the final compiler of the book had a clear plan for the organization of those larger structures is not yet clear, however, so commentaries will present outlines of the book that vary considerably from one another.

Individual Units. The form of speech used most prominently is the announcement of divine judgment combined with a reason, which is usually a description of Israel's sins (e.g., 2:4-5; 3:10-11; 5:11).[2] Either the reason or the announcement may be elaborated, as in 2:6-16. This genre, which occurs frequently throughout the prophetic books, is typically introduced by the messenger formula, "Thus says the LORD." The fact that the prophets use this form of speech more often than any other already tells us something essential about their mission. They seldom rebuke or argue; they seldom entreat or exhort; they have come with an announcement of what God is about to do, claiming that the message has come from God and offering the justification of God's intended act in the reason that goes with the announcement. There are only four exhortations in Amos, and they are severely qualified (4:12; 5:4-6, 14-15; 5:21-24). Other typical prophetic speech forms include the description of a vision (7:1-9; 8:1-3; 9:1-4) and the oracle of promise (9:11-15).

2. Claus Westermann, *Basic Forms of Prophetic Speech* (Philadelphia: Westminster, 1967) 181-88.

Other forms have been borrowed from daily life. Fragments of hymns are cited in 4:13; 5:8-9; and 9:5-6. Amos 4:5; 5:4-6, 14-15 are best understood as parodies of calls to worship. The commentary will show that chapters 1–2 make a new use of the old holy war oracle. A fragment of a funeral song appears in 5:1-2. The most significant feature of these reuses of familiar forms (except perhaps the hymns) is that the prophet has given them a shockingly new meaning, usually reversing what they originally were intended to say.

Larger Structures. The book contains a significant number of carefully organized series of sayings. The longest is the group of eight oracles against the nations in 1:3–2:16. Other series appear in 3:3-8; 4:6-12; 7:1-9. Within a unit, briefer sequences also occur, such as the seven disasters to befall the Israelite army in 2:14-16 and the five efforts to escape from God in 9:2-4. Other patterns of fives and sevens can be found throughout the book.

That the book may be subdivided into major units is suggested by the repetition of key words, such as "Hear!" in 3:1, 13; 4:1; 5:1; 8:4. Rhetorical analysis has found concentric (or chiastic)[3] patterns in 5:1-17 and elsewhere. The discussion offered below does not attempt to decipher the subtle and apparently inconsistent clues to major structures within the book, but will divide it for interpretive purposes according to certain important themes.

TRADITIONS

The prophets were innovators, with a radically new message concerning the approaching end of the way God and Israel had been related, but they made creative use of the traditions by which Israel had lived for a long time. Those of greatest importance for Amos will be noted here.

What has been called "holy war" or "Yahweh war" lies behind the oracles against nations in chapters 1–2 and the "Day of Yahweh" passage in 5:18-20. The battles in Judges and 1 Samuel have been described as following a consistent pattern. They are defensive wars: Israel has been attacked by a superior force, and defeat seems imminent until a charismatic leader announces that God intends to fight for Israel and give the enemy into their hands. Later messages of this type were pronounced under similar circumstances by prophets (1 Kgs 20:28; Isa 7:5-7), and there is additional evidence to show that prophets regularly played a role in assuring the king and his army that God would give them victory (1 Kings 22). The phrase "day of Yahweh" seems originally to have referred to such a day of God's triumph over Israel's enemies. Amos puts such traditions to a new use, announcing that Yahweh is now about to engage in holy war against Israel. Reference to specific aspects of the practice of war appear prominently throughout the book, and since death is a primary result, the practices of mourning for the dead are another tradition upon which Amos draws.

---

3. The simplest chiastic form is the pattern ABB'A'. More elaborate patterns may have a clear midpoint; e.g., ABCDED'C'B'A'.

The hymns that appear in 4:13; 5:8-9; and 9:5-6 introduce elements of the creation tradition to the book. Since they emphasize God's power over nature, they function as part of the book's message that Yahweh is sovereign over all things, and they may be related to Amos's words concerning God's use of nature as a means of judgment (e.g., 4:6-9; 7:1-6).

Although the book does not contain word-for-word citations of any of the laws in the Pentateuch, clear references to specific parts of the legal tradition are recorded there, especially in 5:10-12 and 8:4-6, showing that the prophet was creating no new ethical standards, but that he appealed to what Israel should already have known to be God's will.

THE DISTINCTIVE THEMES OF THE BOOK

Amos represents the earliest collection of the words of a prophet into a book. Discovering what may have led to the creation and preservation of such a collection is thus one way of approaching the question of the distinctive themes of the book. It is logical to begin with the fact that its contents are mostly oracles of judgment. Unlike the earlier prophets, Amos declared that the whole people of Yahweh stood under divine judgment (Amos 3:1-2).

The book of Amos does not speak of reform, but of the end of normal life on the land, not of a better life for the poor but of a time when all will be reduced to despair. Its words of judgment thus should not be carelessly taken up and reapplied to new situations, for seldom is the future as dark for a given people as it was for eighth-century BCE Israel. That does not mean we should not be impressed by Amos's powerful words that claim that oppression of the weak and poor by the rich and powerful stands under the judgment of God. That is part of the message of Scripture for every age, but seldom has it been expressed with the impact of the book of Amos.

There is a great deal of continuity between the emphases of this book and the older traditions of Israel, but all of it has now been skewed by this terrible new message. We may consider what is distinctive in Amos's message concerning God and God's people, the nations, nature, and the future, by observing how what is utterly new ("The end has come upon my people Israel" [8:2 NRSV]) has changed things.

God. The destructive activity of God is emphasized. War dominates the thought of the book, and God is directly involved as the main participant in many passages, with twenty-eight different verbs being used to describe the divine role as warrior and destroyer. Except for 9:11-15, God's positive activity on Israel's behalf is confined to references to the past (2:10-11; 3:1), to temporary reprieves (7:3, 6), and to a highly conditional, partial promise of graciousness (5:15). Elsewhere, God kills (2:3; 4:10; 9:1), destroys (2:9; 9:8), and sends fire (1:4, 7, 10, 12; 2:2, 5), pestilence (4:10), and famine (8:11). This is not a completely new picture of God, for the accounts of the flood in Genesis 6–8, the plagues in Exodus 7–12, and the poems depicting God as a warrior (e.g., Deuteronomy 32; Isaiah 34; Habakkuk 3) also emphasize God's destructive power.

Amos is the only book, however, in which this aspect of God is so dominant, without the emphasis on faithfulness and mercy that almost always accompanies references to judgment elsewhere (e.g., Exod 34:6-7). The book of Amos is thus not to be taken as the last word about the nature of God. It is, rather, an overstatement of the judgmental aspect of God, which can be understood as the natural accompaniment of Amos's discovery that it was all over for Israel. That message was so new, and its implications so terrible, that it had to be stated in the most extreme form possible, and that included extreme statements about God.

God is by no means depicted as an arbitrary or vengeful enemy, however. The divine role as judge is justified again and again by the prophet's use of reason-announcement oracles. God is not described in this book; words like "just," "righteous," and "holy" are not used, in preference for verbs depicting divine destructive activity. That God is the upholder of justice is to be deduced instead from the particular reasons for God's action; for example, "because he [Edom] pursued his brother with the sword" (1:11 NRSV); "because they sell the righteous for silver" (2:6 NRSV); "because you trample on the poor" (5:11 NRSV). God's primary role in this book is to be the judge and the executioner of those persons who have refused to obey divine standards of justice—to which it is assumed God also adheres.

Israel. The wholly new part of Amos's message concerning Israel is the threat of exile (5:5, 27; 6:7; 7:11, 17).[4] Israel had been threatened before with defeat in war as a result of offending God, but there is no clear evidence that anyone prior to Amos spoke explicitly of the possibility that the Israelites might lose the promised land. (It is very doubtful that Leviticus 26 and Deuteronomy 28–29 can be dated earlier than Amos.) The idea is so new that no "theology of exile" appears as yet; deportation is simply announced. Later, Hosea attempted to connect it to Israel's sacred traditions, making exile a temporary return to the wilderness (2:14-15) or a reversal of the exodus, taking Israel back to Egypt (8:13; 9:3; 11:5). The idea created no growing tradition, even in the prophetic books, however, for it was too unthinkable. Once exile had happened, prophets found a way to speak of it as an act of God for the redemption (or re-creation) of God's people, but the materials preserved in Amos are too early to reflect those insights.

The prophet must announce the threat of exile and explain it, even though its ultimate purpose remains hidden. Explaining it does at least mean God continues the effort to remain in conversation with the people: "The Lord GOD has spoken;/ who can but prophesy?" (3:8 NRSV). Regularly the oracles begin with "Hear this word!" but Israel's failure to hear, to understand, and to obey dominates chapters 3–4, and their refusal to behave as the people of Yahweh is documented in chapters 5–6 and 8. Their election had meant Yahweh expected more of them than of the other nations (3:1-2). Yahweh admits

4. Amos's concern is usually for the northern kingdom, but the book occasionally speaks of the traditions of Israel as a whole (2:9-11; 3:1-2; 9:7) or specifically of Judah (2:4-5; 6:1).

it is "my" people upon whom the end will come (8:2), but their failure means something new will have to be done.

The Nations. Amos differs from the other prophetic books in taking up first Yahweh's dealings with all the nations surrounding Israel (except Egypt). The book makes no effort to explain why the nations are responsible to the God of Israel for their actions. Several proposals for the theology underlying Amos 1–2 will be noted in the commentary on those chapters. At this point, let us call these chapters (and 9:7) an expression of the "practical monotheism" of the book. Nothing is said about God's oneness or superiority to other deities, but the book begins with oracles against the nations as a way of asserting that Yahweh has the power to judge all who violate basic principles of justice.

Amos's interest in the relationship of the Gentile nations with Yahweh the God of Israel was taken up by the other prophets (cf. especially Isaiah 14; Ezekiel 28–32), who have left us with the claim that the downfall of nations throughout history must be traced directly to their failure to maintain justice within and among them. We cannot prove those prophets were wrong, for no nation has yet lived up to the standards of the Old Testament God. The litany of disasters in 4:6-12 may be reflected in all of history, which could be understood in the light of Amos's words as God's futile effort to get our attention.

Nature. The meaning of the hymn fragments that appear in 4:13; 5:8-9; and 9:5-6 has been widely discussed,[5] but their relationship to other hymns in the psalter that praise God's creative powers is clear. Elsewhere in the book of Amos, God threatens to turn nature against the people, making it an agent of divine judgment (e.g., 4:7-9; 7:1, 4; 8:8-9; 9:3b), and the hymns may have been included as reminders (since they are traditional language) that nature belongs to God, who thus has the power to use it according to the divine will. That general statement also includes the possibility that God may choose to make nature one of the primary agents of blessing, as in 9:13-14. That blessing cannot be expected until after the judgment has fallen, however.

The Future. The debated aspects of Amos's view of the future are two: Does the book offer any possibility of averting the doom it announces? Is there any way of integrating the promises of 9:11-15 with the negative message that dominates the rest of the book?

Only twice does the book contain an exhortation accompanied by a promise: "Seek the LORD and live" (5:6 NIV) and "Seek good and not evil,/ that you may live," followed by "it may be that the LORD, the God of hosts,/ will be gracious to the remnant of Joseph" (5:14, 15 NRSV). Some scholars have claimed this proves that Amos did not announce irrevocable judgment, but Hunter's thorough exegetical work supports those who say that at best the book does no more than hope that a few who are truly faithful may survive the coming disaster.[6] There is no future for the nation of Israel.

5. J. L. Crenshaw, *Hymnic Affirmations of Divine Justice: The Doxologies of Amos and Related Texts in the Old Testament*, SBLDS 24 (Missoula, Mont.: Scholars Press, 1975); Thomas Edward McComisky, "The Hymnic Elements of the Prophecy of Amos: A Study of Form-Critical Methodology," *JETS* 30 (1987) 139-57; J. D. W. Watts, "An Old Hymn Preserved in the Book of Amos," *JNES* 15 (1956) 33-39.

6. A. Vanlier Hunter, *Seek the Lord! A Study of the Meaning and Function of the Exhortations in Amos, Hosea, Isaiah, Micah, and Zephaniah* (Baltimore: St. Mary's Seminary and University Press, 1982) 56-105.

The second question involves consistency. The biographical approach will ask whether the same person could have announced both 9:8-10 and 9:11-15. Many scholars find that impossible to imagine; others ascribe the different messages to different parts of the prophet's career. Eschewing the biographical approach, we should reformulate the question so as to ask whether the book makes sense with this ending; in fact, these verses do not contradict the message of judgment in the rest of the book. They presuppose the fall of the "booth of David," the ruin of cities, and exile. The reference to David suggests a concern not for Amos's time, but for the end of the Davidic monarchy in the sixth century BCE. Even if these verses were produced in the eighth century, however, the promises they contain were not for the people of that time, for those people were on their way to death.

The new message of the book of Amos is that exile from the promised land is imminent. That means that a radically new stage in God's saving work is about to begin. It looks like the end of it, for Amos's word is "death," but eventually Ezekiel will add "resurrection" (Ezek 37:1-14). There is no hint of that in Amos, but it is important to deal with the Amos tradition as having always been a part of the larger prophetic tradition. These words introduce a new act in the history of salvation, leading us to ask why death must be the route God will take next. But it is not the last act, and Amos must always be read as part of the whole story of exile and restoration.

BIBLIOGRAPHY

Commentaries:

Andersen, Francis I., and David Noel Freedman. *Amos.* AB 24A. Garden City, N.Y.: Doubleday, 1989. A detailed study focusing on the literary characteristics of the book and attempting to reconstruct the career of Amos. Difficult to use because of its length and organization.

Harper, William Rainey. *A Critical and Exegetical Commentary on Amos and Hosea.* ICC. Edinburgh: T. & T. Clark, 1905. The classic statement of the historical-critical approach, which dominated the first half of the twentieth century.

Martin-Achard, Robert. *The End of the People of God: A Commentary on the Book of Amos.* ITC. Grand Rapids: Eerdmans, 1984. A theological commentary by one of the foremost French interpreters of Amos.

Mays, James L. *Amos: A Commentary.* OTL. Philadelphia: Westminster, 1969. Perhaps the most useful brief commentary.

Paul, Shalom. *Amos.* Hermeneia. Philadelphia: Fortress, 1991. The most useful extended commentary. Thorough, based on sound scholarship and demonstrating good judgment.

Wolff, Hans Walter. *Joel and Amos.* Hermeneia. Philadelphia: Fortress, 1977. Contains much valuable material, but is the classic statement of the redaction-critical approach to the book, which now seems superseded by more recent works.

Other Resources:

Auld, A. G. *Amos.* Old Testament Guides. Sheffield: JSOT, 1986. A survey of recent research.

Hasel, Gerhard F. *Understanding the Book of Amos: Basic Issues in Current Interpretations.* Grand Rapids: Baker, 1991. Another survey, reaching more conservative conclusions than those found in Auld.

Van der Wal, A. *Amos: A Classified Bibliography.* 3rd ed. Amsterdam: Free University Press, 1986.

OUTLINE OF AMOS

I. Amos 1:1—2:16, The Divine Warrior

    A. 1:1-2, Superscription and First Epigram
    B. 1:3–2:16, Holy War Again
         1:3–2:5, The Seven Nations
         2:6-16, The Oracle Against Israel

II. Amos 3:1–4:13, Israel's Inability to Hear

    A. 3:1-2, Epigram: Israel Is Different
    B. 3:3-8, Not Without a Witness
    C. 3:9–4:3, Luxury and Injustice
    D. 4:4-13, Religion as Usual, While the World Crumbles

III. Amos 5:1-27, The Death of Israel

    A. 5:1-2, A Funeral Song
    B. 5:3, The Remnant Defined Again
    C. 5:4-6, The Death of the Sanctuaries
    D. 5:7, No Justice . . .
    E. 5:8-9, His Name Is Yahweh
    F. 5:10-13, No Justice in the Gate
    G. 5:14-15, Is There a Chance?
    H. 5:16-17, Mourning in the Streets
    I. 5:18-20, Darkness, Not Light
    J. 5:21-27, What Does God Require?

IV. Amos 6:1-14, Life as Usual—with Disaster Near

    A. 6:1-7, Complacent Extravagance
    B. 6:8-11, Fragments Concerning the Disaster
    C. 6:12-14, Complacency Unfounded

V. Amos 7:1-17, Visions and a Confrontation

    A. 7:1-9, Three Visions
    B. 7:10-17, Priest Confronts Prophet

AMOS 1:1–2:16

THE DIVINE WARRIOR

AMOS 1:1-2, SUPERSCRIPTION AND FIRST EPIGRAM

1 The words of Amos, one of the shepherds of Tekoa—what he saw concerning Israel two years before the earthquake, when Uzziah was king of Judah and Jeroboam son of Jehoash[a] was king of Israel.

²He said:

"The LORD roars from Zion
  and thunders from Jerusalem;
the pastures of the shepherds dry up,[b]
  and the top of Carmel withers."

[a1] Hebrew *Joash*, a variant of *Jehoash*   [b2] Or *shepherds mourn*

1 The words of Amos, who was among the shepherds of Tekoa, which he saw concerning Israel in the days of King Uzziah of Judah and in the days of King Jeroboam son of Joash of Israel, two years[a] before the earthquake.

²And he said:

The LORD roars from Zion,
  and utters his voice from Jerusalem;
the pastures of the shepherds wither,
  and the top of Carmel dries up.

[a] Or *during two years*

COMMENTARY

1:1, The Superscription. The title of the book of Amos is unusual in several respects. Unlike the superscriptions of most of the prophetic books, Amos is said to have "seen" the words. A similar expression also occurs in Isa 2:1; Mic 1:1; and Hab 1:1. The expression may be explained by the fact that visionary experiences are recorded in Isaiah 6; Jeremiah 1; 24; Ezekiel 1–3; 8–11; 37; 40–48; Amos 7; and Zechariah 1–6, and the books of Obadiah and Nahum are entitled "visions." Although there is still some debate about this, the evidence is strong that all the canonical prophets were visionaries, "ecstatic personalities,"[7] so it would have been natural for the editors who provided these titles to have associated the prophets' receipt of words from the Lord with visionary experiences.

7. Johannes Lindblom, *Prophecy in Ancient Israel* (Oxford: Basil Blackwell, 1962) 122-37; R. R. Wilson, "Prophecy and Ecstasy: A Reexamination," *JBL* 98 (1979) 321-37.

The title is also unusual in offering information about Amos's apparent occupation. He was "among the shepherds of Tekoa," evidently meaning that he was one of the them. The word נֹקֵד (*nōqēd*) occurs elsewhere in the OT only in 2 Kgs 3:4, where it is used of King Mesha of Moab. This suggests the word denoted sheep breeders or the owners of substantial flocks, not ordinary shepherds. The word also occurs in cultic contexts in the Ugaritic texts, and this has led to suggestions that Amos raised sheep for the Jerusalem Temple or even that he was a temple official; but these interpretations all try to make too much of a single, rather rare word. Amos's occupation and social status are too uncertain to be used with any confidence as a key to the interpretation of the book (see Introduction).

Tekoa, Amos's home, was about six miles south of Bethlehem and twelve miles south of Jerusalem, with the fertile hills of Judah to the west and the wilderness that slopes down to the Dead Sea immediately to the east. According to 2 Chr 11:5-6, it was one of the cities fortified by Rehoboam in order to guard the eastern border of Judah (cf. Jer 6:1). Efforts to make Amos a citizen of the northern kingdom, from a Tekoa in Galilee, have not been persuasive to many scholars.

The fact that the Judean king Uzziah is mentioned first suggests that the superscription was the work of an editor in Judah. Comparison with the similar references to kings in Isa 1:1; Hos 1:1; and Mic 1:1 also suggests that Amos's ministry did not extend beyond the reigns of Uzziah (773–c. 736 BCE) and Jeroboam (785–745 BCE), since later kings of Judah are included in those lists.

Finally, a more specific reference to the date of Amos's work is provided in the words "two years before the earthquake." The earthquake must have been severe, since Zech 14:5, written several hundred years later, refers to it. Evidence for substantial earthquake damage at Hazor, which excavators have dated to 760 BCE, correlates well with other evidence for the date of Amos.

1:2, The First Epigram. These two powerful lines introduce the God of the book of Amos as the one who has come to judge the earth, waging holy war against the enemies of justice and compassion. Its poetic structure, with two exactly balanced lines, and with a surprise element in the second line, identify it as an epigram. The comparison of God's voice with the roar of a lion might lead one to expect a description of fear and flight or of the taking of prey, but the second line speaks instead of drought.

The first line reappears with the identical words in Joel 3:16 [MT 4:16], and a similar expression also occurs in Jer 25:30, reminding us that this is hymnic language, which each of these prophets has doubtless taken over from the cult. In Pss 18:13[14]; 29:3-9; 46:6[7]; 68:33[34], we find evidence that one of the ways Israel praised Yahweh was to associate God's powerful voice with the destructive forces of nature—ordinarily the thunderstorm, with its wind and lightning. Elsewhere the book of Amos will quote other fragments of nature hymns as reminders of God's awesome power (4:13; 5:8-9; 9:5-6); but the hymns in Amos appear in contexts of judgment, not of praise. With its unexpected second line, the first epigram of the book introduces two of its major themes: the overwhelming power of God and mourning on the earth. Usually mourning would have a human subject, but here it is the result of the wilting of pastures during a time of drought. The mourning of pastures points ahead to the mourning of human beings as a result of God's power exercised in judgment of their sins (Amos 5:16; 8:8, 10; 9:5). Carmel is mentioned in parallel to the pastures, since it was thought of as one of Israel's most fertile places (Cant 7:5; Isa 33:9; Nah 1:4).

Amos seldom refers to Judah (1:2; 2:4-5; 6:1; 9:11), and the use of "Zion" here has led to considerable discussion of the originality of this passage. The first line was clearly borrowed from the Jerusalem cult—not surprising if Amos was a Judean. There is not enough evidence in the book to claim that this verse is part of a program advocating Jerusalem as the only legitimate Yahwistic sanctuary, but neither does it seem necessary to say that a Judean would not have addressed people of the northern kingdom in this way. The epigram was very likely an independent prophetic saying that may or may not have originated with Amos. What is important is not its authorship but its appropriateness as an introduction to the theology of the book.

REFLECTIONS

Amos begins with a concise warning of what is to come. This is to be a book about Yahweh, and about one particular aspect of the character of God. It is an aspect of God that some people, past and present, have made too much of, caricaturing the "Old Testament God" as a wrathful judge in contrast to the merciful God of the New Testament. The book of Amos would seem to justify such a one-sided view; but Amos is only part of the canon, and this book was produced at a time when that side of God's character was about to be manifested. This is a book about the death of Israel and about God's role in that death. That is not an understanding of God that the New Testament "corrected," however, for the New Testament also has a great deal to say about death. Paul, for example, speaks of it thirty-six times in Romans 5–8. Unlike Paul, however, for Amos it may have simply meant the end of God's work with God's people. It is doubtful that Amos knew anything of redemption beyond Israel's death. Only the work of the prophets who followed him shows how the mourning of which he spoke became part of God's redemptive work.

How Amos could have delivered so terrible a message and maintained his faith we do not know, but we do know that Israel found this book, with its words of judgment throughout, to be the word of God to them, and Israel maintained its faith. We are thus challenged to take the terror that rings through these initial words as part of the reality of the way God and God's people are related. There are also times in the experience of contemporary believers when all seems to be coming to an end, and it is not clear what God may intend to do beyond that end.

AMOS 1:3–2:16, HOLY WAR AGAIN

OVERVIEW

Amos is the only prophetic book to begin with oracles against foreign nations, to organize such oracles strictly in a series using the same form for each one (cf., however, Ezekiel 25), and to associate oracles against Judah and Israel with those against the nations by using the identical form. Although the oracles against the nations in other books (Isaiah 13–23; Jeremiah 46–51; Ezekiel 25–32; etc.) have largely been neglected, the distinctive features just noted account for the considerable attention scholars have devoted to those in Amos.[8] Most scholars agree that the oracles were originally produced as a series, although a few have claimed that they were delivered separately, on different occasions. There is little agreement on whether they all were produced in the eighth century BCE. The most doubts are expressed about the Judah oracle, and the oracles against Tyre and Edom are also frequently dated later. Reasons based on content will be discussed in connection with each passage. The structure of these three passages differs from the oracles against Damascus, Gaza, Ammon, and Moab, and this has also been appealed to as evidence for later authorship. The announcement

of punishment is shorter ("I will send fire on . . . and it shall devour the strongholds of . . . ," v. 4), and there is no concluding formula ("says the LORD"). But careful rhetorical analyses of the eight oracles have shown that they are all related to one another in structure and word usage, while each one also differs in various ways from the others.[9] More sophisticated structural considerations tend to support the original unity of the series, but it will be seen that the contents of the Judah oracle raise significant questions about its place with the others.

More significant questions about the oracles against the nations are these: Since they are not addressed to the nations, are they really messages for Israel? They accuse the nations of crimes for which Yahweh will judge them, but on what grounds can the nations be held accountable to Yahweh, the God of Israel? Why should the collection of Amos's words have been introduced with messages concerning foreign nations? Analysis of the form of speech used and the traditions that lie behind the oracles will go a long way toward answering these questions.

Form. Each oracle begins with the messenger formula: "Thus says the LORD." It is so named because it was used to introduce letters and

8. John Barton, *Amos's Oracles Against the Nations: A Study of Amos 1:3–2:5,* SOTSMS 6 (Cambridge: Cambridge University Press, 1980); Paul Noble, "Israel Among the Nations," *HBT* 15 (1993) 56-82; note the special attention given them in Shalom Paul, *Amos,* Hermeneia (Philadelphia: Fortress, 1991) 11-30.

9. John H. Hayes, *Amos: The Eighth-Century Prophet* (Nashville: Abingdon, 1988) 50-55; Paul, *Amos,* 11-27.

proclamations in ancient Near Eastern cultures. The message itself takes the reason-announcement form, which is the most widely used genre in the prophetic literature.[10] Each reason has two parts: first the formula, "For three transgressions of . . . and for four I will not turn it back," and then a citation of a single crime (except for Israel, where a sequence of crimes is listed). The numerical formula appears frequently in the wisdom literature (Job 5:19-26; 33:14-18; Prov 6:16-19; 30:15-31; Sir 23:16-21; 25:7-11; 26:5-6, 28; 50:25-26), and is easily understood as a teaching technique. The numbers probably do not mean, "I have forgiven three of your crimes but cannot forgive the fourth." Nor should three and four be added to get the perfect number seven, as some have suggested. "For three—no, four" is best understood as an effective way of referring to the multiple offenses for which the nations are responsible to God.

The Hebrew of 1:6 does not say, "I will not revoke the punishment" (NRSV) or "I will not turn back my wrath" (NIV), but simply, "I will not turn it back" (לא אשיבנו *lō' 'ăšîbennû*). What "it" refers to is not immediately obvious, unless it is referring ahead to the punishment that will be announced (so NIV, NRSV). This is a carefully formulated, portentous, somewhat mysterious statement that God has passed the sentence and judgment is forthcoming. The word translated "transgressions" or "sins" (פשע *peša'*) is a term often used in political contexts to mean "rebellion," although it is used of other sins as well. It is one of the stronger words for sin and seems fully appropriate when used of Israel's rebellion against the covenant relationship. But here it is used of the nations, and with this word Amos already seems to claim some previous relationship between Yahweh and the nations, which they have violated and to which Yahweh now intends to hold them responsible.

Many efforts have been made to explain the order of the oracles, which follow no neat geographical pattern; neither is it possible to associate the crimes cited with any known pattern of historical events. None of the proposals is obviously correct, and none of them actually adds anything to our understanding of the message of the whole

unit. What is most important is the inclusion of Judah and Israel (2:4-5, 6-16) by the use of the same introductory formulas. This brings the chosen people into the realm of universal judgment announced by the previous series of six oracles against foreigners. But the use of the basic prophetic reason-announcement genre when speaking of the nations also seems to bring them into the realm of people who are accountable to Yahweh, people whose destiny must also be a part of the prophetic message. This leads to consideration of the tradition lying behind the oracles against the nations in the prophetic books.

Tradition. Evidence from the OT (1 Kgs 12:24; 2 Kgs 3:18-19; 6:8-10, 21-22; 7:1; 13:15-19) and from extra-biblical sources[11] shows that prophets were consulted concerning the will of God before battle (1 Kings 22), and sometimes they offered unsolicited oracles (1 Kings 20). In all cultures of the ancient world it was considered essential to know that the god was going with the army before a battle. In that respect, all war was "holy war."[12] In early times, the message of assurance from Yahweh is not said to have come from a prophet (Judg 20:23, 27-28; 1 Sam 14:37; 23:2), but during the monarchy prophets carried out that important role. Of special interest is 1 Kgs 20:28, since it is a reason-announcement oracle, like those in Amos 1–2, and it occurs in a setting reminiscent of Israel's early wars: "Because the Arameans have said, 'The LORD is a god of the hills but he is not a god of the valleys,' therefore I will give all this great multitude into your hand, and you shall know that I am the LORD" (NRSV). That this is an accurate reflection of prophetic activity in the ninth and eighth centuries BCE, and not merely the creation of the deuteronomistic historian, is shown by the appearance of the same genre in a similar setting in Isa 7:5-9. The same form appears again in Isa 37:29, associated with the Assyrian invasion of 701 BCE (cf. also Isa 10:15-16; Jer 49:1-2; Zeph 2:8-11). Later forms of this kind of oracle continued to be produced during the exilic and post-exilic periods, isolated from the setting of war.

10. Claus Westermann, *Basic Forms of Prophetic Speech* (Philadelphia: Westminster, 1967) 142-61, 169-76.

11. J. F. Craghan, "Mari and Its Prophets: The Contributions of Mari to the Understanding of Biblical Prophecy," *BTB* 5 (1975) 32-55.

12. Gerhard von Rad, *Holy War in Ancient Israel* (Grand Rapids: Eerdmans, 1991); Gwilym H. Jones, "The Concept of Holy War," in *The World of Ancient Israel*, ed. R. E. Clements (Cambridge: Cambridge University Press, 1989) 299-322.

There is no evidence that Amos 1–2 was produced during a time when Israel was threatened by all six of the nations named here, and if these chapters are in fact to be dated during the reign of Jeroboam II, there was no military threat at all. Furthermore, Judah and Israel are included in the series, so it is no traditional promise of victory. There is evidence in the contents of the oracles, however, to support the indications from form criticism that Amos was making a revolutionary new use of the prophetic holy war oracle. War dominates the thought of each of the first six oracles. The crimes of Damascus, Edom, Ammon, and Moab are war crimes, and that may also be true of Gaza and Tyre. Whenever the punishment is described at length (1:5, 8, 14-15; 2:2-3, 14-16) it is described as defeat in battle. The vivid description of the flight of soldiers in 2:14-16 reminds us of the panic that accompanied the appearance of the divine warrior on the battlefield in holy war ideology (e.g., Exod 23:27-28; 1 Sam 14:15). The announcements in the first seven oracles begin with the threat that God will send fire that will consume walls and strongholds. That this is expected to be something more than the fires kindled by armies as they laid siege to fortified cities and overran them is shown by the prophets' references to divine fire elsewhere (Isa 10:16-17; Jer 17:27; 21:14; 50:32; Ezek 39:6; Hos 8:14).

Evidence from both form and content thus indicates that Amos is making use of Israel's holy war traditions, but for a new purpose. Although efforts have been made to find parallels to his series of oracles in treaty curses or tribal poems, there is in fact no clear parallel, and it seems most likely that the series itself is a new creation. The other completely new feature, of course, is the inclusion of Judah and Israel as enemies of the divine warrior.

War and its effects were well known to Amos and his audience, for allusions to aspects of war appear not only in chaps. 1–2 but also in 3:11; 4:2-3, 10; 5:3, 18-20; 6:7-8, 13-14; 7:11, 17; and 9:4, 10 as well. Palestine has been a land that has known conflict from as far back in history as we can trace, and the earliest records of the existence of nations show them making war with one another. If Amos is to claim that Yahweh, God of Israel, also holds sovereignty over the surrounding nations, then Yahweh must have something to do with war, because that is what nations do.

Amos may have drawn upon an old tradition for that: The story of the exodus from Egypt claimed that Yahweh had made war against the pharaoh within his own land (in the accounts of the plagues) and had sealed the victory in the wonder at the sea (Exodus 14–15). Yahweh had become a warrior as an *advocate* for the oppressed: the slaves descended from Abraham, to whom Yahweh had promised a homeland. To fulfill that promise it was not enough to punish and defeat the oppressor, Egypt. Israel became a nation, but a nation needs a homeland, and they believed God also fought for them to defeat the Canaanites (Joshua 6; 10:10-13; Judg 4:15). But Amos now extends and transforms those old war traditions. He makes sweeping claims for the sovereignty of Yahweh over both the nations and nature itself, and 1:3–2:3, with its threat of holy war in which Yahweh will be victorious over all of Israel's neighbors, is one way of doing that. Amos represents the beginning of the kind of comprehensive claims for the sovereignty of Yahweh over all nature and history that reached their climax in Second Isaiah, and Amos sums up the key to the intentions of this sovereign God for humanity in the words "justice" and "righteousness" (5:24). Amos could not find these qualities in either the nations or Israel, however.

God was thus no longer about to make war for traditional reasons. The true holy war oracles tended to cite an offense against God or the people as the reason for war (cf. 1 Kgs 20:28; Isa 7:5-7). The offenses cited now are against individuals, and that is true also of the oracle against Israel (but not Judah). The six nations are cited for war crimes, so God already appears as the judge of human warmaking. Israel is accused of crimes against its own citizens, in the immediate context of a reminder of the exodus (2:10), and that seems to be the key to the theology of this section. These two clues lead us to an unusual motive clause in the covenant code of Exodus. Old Testament law is characterized by the frequent appearance of motive clauses, reasons why

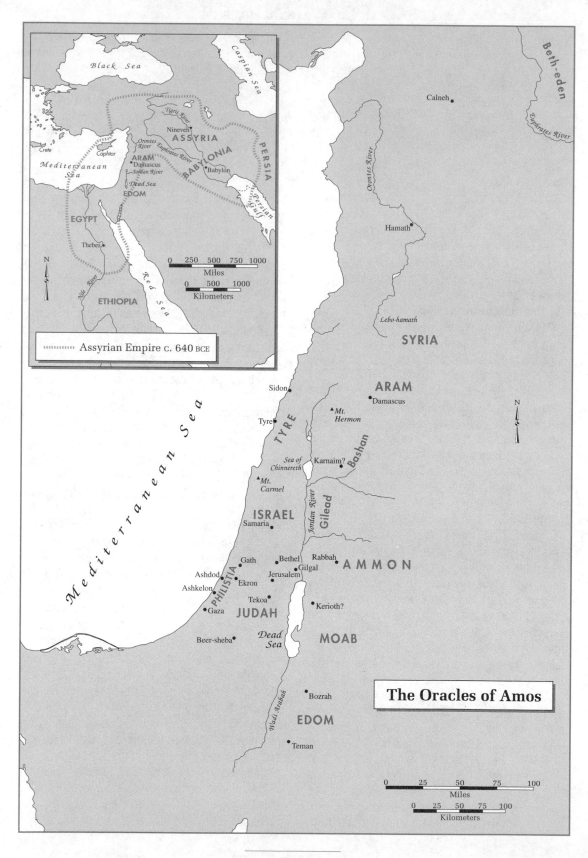

Black Sea

Caspian Sea

Tigris River

Nineveh

ASSYRIA

Orontes River

Euphrates River

BABYLONIA

PERSIA

Crete

Caphtor

Damascus

ARAM

Jordan River

Babylon

Mediterranean Sea

Dead Sea

EDOM

Persian Gulf

EGYPT

Thebes

Nile River

Red Sea

ETHIOPIA

N

0   250   500   750 1000
Miles

0   500   1000
Kilometers

Assyrian Empire c. 640 BCE

Beth-eden

Euphrates River

Calneh

Orontes River

Hamath

Lebo-hamath

SYRIA

Sidon

ARAM

Damascus

Tyre

Mt. Hermon

TYRE

N

Sea of Chinnereth

Karnaim?

Bashan

Mt. Carmel

Jordan River

Gilead

ISRAEL

Samaria

Gath

Bethel

Rabbah

AMMON

Ashdod

Ekron

Gilgal

PHILISTIA

Jerusalem

Ashkelon

Tekoa

Kerioth?

Gaza

JUDAH

Dead Sea

MOAB

Beer-sheba

Bozrah

EDOM

Wadi Arabah

Teman

The Oracles of Amos

Mediterranean Sea

0   25   50   75   100
Miles

0   25   50   75   100
Kilometers

a particular law should be obeyed.[13] They may call upon the Israelites to remember what God has done for them so as to respond in gratitude (Deut 15:12-15). They may appeal to generally accepted truths or common sense (Deut 12:23; 20:19). Or they may offer promises (Deut 12:25). Only once, in the laws of Exodus–Deuteronomy, is a dire threat of direct, divine punishment used as a motive clause:

You shall not wrong or oppress a resident alien, for you were aliens in the land of Egypt. You shall not abuse any widow or orphan. If you do abuse them, when they cry out to me, I will surely heed their cry; my wrath will burn, and I will kill you with the sword, and your wives shall become widows and your children orphans. (Exod 22:21-24 NRSV [MT vv. 20-23])

Amos does not cite any part of this text word for word, but its spirit reappears in his book in a new form. Amos has taken its insistence that God intervenes in human life with fury when the weak are oppressed and has applied it now to the nations as well as to Israel.

This offers another way of explaining why Amos thought the nations were accountable to Yahweh. The most common suggestion is based on Amos's implicit monotheism, saying Amos assumed that all people were subject to Yahweh's judgment, whether or not they knew Yahweh's laws. But that interpretation has always raised questions of fairness. More likely is the claim that there were certain generally acknowledged ideas of unacceptable behavior in warfare that Amos could appropriately have assumed would be known to other nations. A recent theory proposes that all six nations were part of an idealized Davidic empire and that they were being condemned for treaty violations.[14] The motive clause in Exod 22:21-24 offers another option, which is reinforced by the reminder of the exodus in Amos 2:10: Yahweh takes the role of advocate, intervening in human affairs as the enemy of oppressors. This is the role Yahweh plays in the book of Exodus. Pharaoh does not know Yahweh (Exod 5:2) and acknowledges no responsibility to Yahweh, but Yahweh has become the pharaoh's enemy on behalf of those who have cried out for help (Exod 2:23).

Shortly after the time of Amos, Isaiah added another element to the picture. Instead of acting directly, God uses the plans and forces of Assyria in order to accomplish God's purpose, without the Assyrian king's knowledge and, in fact, contrary to that king's intentions, and then (as in Amos 1–2) judges Assyria for the war crimes it commits in the process (Isa 10:5-19; cf. Isa 37:22-29; note the reappearance of the holy war oracle in Isa 37:29). Later, Jeremiah claimed that God was using, and would judge, Nebuchadnezzar in the same way (Jer 25:8-14). The prophetic interpretation of wars of conquest was also used in Deuteronomy to account for Israel's wars against the Canaanites. Then, Israel was the nation used by God to judge Canaan's wickedness (Deut 7:1-5; 9:1-6). But each agent of God's judgment will also be judged!

Some interpreters have read the oracles against the foreign nations (and the one against Judah) as simply a lead-in to the oracle against Israel, imagining Amos stirring up the crowd at Bethel with his declarations that God was about to punish first one, then another of the traditional enemies, then confronting them with the shocker—Israel also! In this reading, the responsibility and fate of the nations is of no great significance; Amos's interest is Israel. The prominence of this passage at the beginning of the book and the care with which it has been formulated suggest, however, that it should be interpreted in the broader context of the OT's interest in the nations.

There is a fascinating tension in what the OT says about the nations.[15] They are usually enemies, but the "nationalistic" outlook, which looks forward to and celebrates the defeat of the nations, is not the only point of view to be found in the OT. The first eleven chapters of Genesis speak of humanity in general, without showing any special interest in Israel. That leads to the promise to Abraham in Gen 12:2-3, which in-

13. B. Gemser, *The Importance of the Motive Clause in Old Testament Law*, VTSup 1 (Leiden: Brill, 1953) 50-66; Donald E. Gowan, "Reflections on the Motive Clauses in Old Testament Law," in *Intergerini Parietas Septum (Eph. 2:14): Essays presented to Markus Barth on His Sixty-fifth Birthday*, ed. D. Y. Hadidian, PTMS 33 (Pittsburgh: Pickwick, 1981) 111-27.

14. For the international ethic theory, see John Barton, *Amos's Oracles Against the Nations: A Study of Amos 1:3–2:5*, SOTSMS 6 (Cambridge: Cambridge University Press, 1980). For the Davidic empire theory, see Max Polley, *Amos and the Davidic Empire: A Socio-Historical Approach* (New York: Oxford University Press, 1989). For a critique of both theories, see Paul Noble, "Israel Among the Nations," *HBT* 15 (1993) 56-82.

15. For the ambiguity concerning the nations, see Donald E. Gowan, *Eschatology in the Old Testament* (Philadelphia: Fortress, 1986) 42-54.

cludes a promise to the nations. Israelite law included special emphases on the importance of ensuring the welfare of sojourners (resident aliens) in their midst (e.g., Exod 22:21[20]; 23:9; Lev 19:33; Deut 24:17). Visions of a better future in the prophetic books often display a remarkable openness to the nations, looking forward to a time when all people will live together in peace (e.g., Isa 2:2-4; Mic 4:1-4). Elsewhere prophets thought other nations would have a future similar to the future Yahweh had decreed for Israel, with exile followed by restoration (Isa 23:15-18; Ezek 29:9b-16; cf. Isa 19:19-22, which is reminiscent of the way Israel's history is described in Judg 2:11-23). The most remarkable outlook of all appears in Isa 19:23-25, which speaks of a time of equality for Israel with its worst enemies, Assyria and Egypt, when God will bless "Egypt my people, and Assyria the work of my hands, and Israel my heritage" (NRSV).

These passages show that for the prophets the nations were more than just foils for their real interest—Israel. The nations also were important to Yahweh (as Amos 9:7 will affirm), so their place at the beginning of the book of Amos must be

taken seriously. For Amos, they stand under judgment, without any mitigation thereof; that is clear. If the reading offered above is correct—that Amos presents Yahweh here primarily in the role of an advocate for the suffering, who intends to intervene wherever on earth cruelty seems to flourish unchecked, then one need not assume that this new use of the holy war oracle means that Amos thought the nations already knew Yahweh's standards. Neither does one need to assume that he has to be saying that Yahweh is simply enforcing standards already devised by humans. An advocate may need to intervene with force on behalf of the oppressed, regardless of the standards (or lack of them) recognized by the oppressor. Amos may have thought the approaching defeat of Damascus and other foreign armies was intended as a divine lesson, aimed at getting the message across for the first time, even as he spoke of disasters that should have had the same effect on Israel (4:6-11). If this was his understanding, he might well have concluded each oracle as the prophet did in 1 Kgs 20:28: "Then you will know that I am Yahweh" (author's trans.). But that is a favorite theme of other prophets, not of Amos.

Amos 1:3–2:5, The Seven Nations

NIV	NRSV

³This is what the LORD says:
"For three sins of Damascus,
    even for four, I will not turn back ˪my wrath˩.
Because she threshed Gilead
    with sledges having iron teeth,
⁴I will send fire upon the house of Hazael
    that will consume the fortresses of
        Ben-Hadad.
⁵I will break down the gate of Damascus;
    I will destroy the king who is in^a the Valley
        of Aven^b
and the one who holds the scepter in Beth Eden.
    The people of Aram will go into exile to Kir,"
                  says the LORD.
⁶This is what the LORD says:
"For three sins of Gaza,
    even for four, I will not turn back ˪my wrath˩.
Because she took captive whole communities
	³ Thus says the LORD:
	For three transgressions of Damascus,
	    and for four, I will not revoke the
	        punishment;^{a}
	because they have threshed Gilead
	    with threshing sledges of iron.
	⁴ So I will send a fire on the house of Hazael,
	    and it shall devour the strongholds of
	        Ben-hadad.
	⁵ I will break the gate bars of Damascus,
	    and cut off the inhabitants from the Valley
	        of Aven,
	    and the one who holds the scepter from
	        Beth-eden;
	    and the people of Aram shall go into exile
	        to Kir, says the LORD.
	
	⁶ Thus says the LORD:

^{a}5 Or the inhabitants of ^{b}5 Aven means wickedness.	^{a} Heb cause it to return

NIV

and sold them to Edom,
[7] I will send fire upon the walls of Gaza
that will consume her fortresses.
[8] I will destroy the king[a] of Ashdod
and the one who holds the scepter in
Ashkelon.
I will turn my hand against Ekron,
till the last of the Philistines is dead,"
says the Sovereign LORD.
[9] This is what the LORD says:

"For three sins of Tyre,
even for four, I will not turn back ⌊my wrath⌋.
Because she sold whole communities of captives
to Edom,
disregarding a treaty of brotherhood,
[10] I will send fire upon the walls of Tyre
that will consume her fortresses."

[11] This is what the LORD says:

"For three sins of Edom,
even for four, I will not turn back ⌊my wrath⌋.
Because he pursued his brother with a sword,
stifling all compassion,[b]
because his anger raged continually
and his fury flamed unchecked,
[12] I will send fire upon Teman
that will consume the fortresses of Bozrah."

[13] This is what the LORD says:

"For three sins of Ammon,
even for four, I will not turn back ⌊my wrath⌋.
Because he ripped open the pregnant women of
Gilead
in order to extend his borders,
[14] I will set fire to the walls of Rabbah
that will consume her fortresses
amid war cries on the day of battle,
amid violent winds on a stormy day.
[15] Her king[c] will go into exile,
he and his officials together,"
says the LORD.

2 This is what the LORD says:

"For three sins of Moab,
even for four, I will not turn back ⌊my wrath⌋.
Because he burned, as if to lime,
the bones of Edom's king,
[2] I will send fire upon Moab
that will consume the fortresses of Kerioth.[d]

NRSV

For three transgressions of Gaza,
and for four, I will not revoke the
punishment;[a]
because they carried into exile entire
communities,
to hand them over to Edom.
[7] So I will send a fire on the wall of Gaza,
fire that shall devour its strongholds.
[8] I will cut off the inhabitants from Ashdod,
and the one who holds the scepter from
Ashkelon;
I will turn my hand against Ekron,
and the remnant of the Philistines shall
perish,   says the Lord GOD.

[9] Thus says the LORD:
For three transgressions of Tyre,
and for four, I will not revoke the
punishment;[a]
because they delivered entire communities
over to Edom,
and did not remember the covenant of
kinship.
[10] So I will send a fire on the wall of Tyre,
fire that shall devour its strongholds.

[11] Thus says the LORD:
For three transgressions of Edom,
and for four, I will not revoke the
punishment;[a]
because he pursued his brother with the sword
and cast off all pity;
he maintained his anger perpetually,[b]
and kept his wrath[c] forever.
[12] So I will send a fire on Teman,
and it shall devour the strongholds of
Bozrah.

[13] Thus says the LORD:
For three transgressions of the Ammonites,
and for four, I will not revoke the
punishment;[a]
because they have ripped open pregnant
women in Gilead
in order to enlarge their territory.
[14] So I will kindle a fire against the wall of
Rabbah,

---

a8 Or inhabitants   b11 Or sword / and destroyed his allies   c15 Or /
Molech; Hebrew malcam   d2 Or of her cities

a Heb cause it to return   b Syr Vg: Heb and his anger tore perpetually   c Gk Syr Vg: Heb and his wrath kept

NIV

Moab will go down in great tumult
    amid war cries and the blast of the trumpet.
³I will destroy her ruler
    and kill all her officials with him,"
                           says the LORD.

⁴This is what the LORD says:
"For three sins of Judah,
    even for four, I will not turn back ⌐my wrath⌐.
Because they have rejected the law of the LORD
    and have not kept his decrees,
because they have been led astray by false gods,ᵃ
    the godsᵇ their ancestors followed,
⁵I will send fire upon Judah
    that will consume the fortresses of
          Jerusalem."

ᵃ4 Or *by lies*   ᵇ4 Or *lies*

NRSV

    fire that shall devour its strongholds,
with shouting on the day of battle,
    with a storm on the day of the whirlwind;
¹⁵ then their king shall go into exile,
    he and his officials together,
                        says the LORD.

2   Thus says the LORD:
    For three transgressions of Moab,
    and for four, I will not revoke the punishment;ᵃ
because he burned to lime
    the bones of the king of Edom.
² So I will send a fire on Moab,
    and it shall devour the strongholds of
          Kerioth,
and Moab shall die amid uproar,
    amid shouting and the sound of the
          trumpet;
³ I will cut off the ruler from its midst,
    and will kill all its officials with him,
                    says the LORD.

⁴ Thus says the LORD:
    For three transgressions of Judah,
    and for four, I will not revoke the
          punishment;ᵃ
because they have rejected the law of the LORD,
    and have not kept his statutes,
but they have been led astray by the same lies
    after which their ancestors walked.
⁵ So I will send a fire on Judah,
    and it shall devour the strongholds of
          Jerusalem.

ᵃ Heb *cause it to return*

COMMENTARY

1:3-5. The series probably begins with Damascus because this Aramean city-state had been the only serious recent enemy of Israel (2 Kgs 13:3). Gilead, a high and wooded area east of the Jordan River, was claimed by the Israelite tribes of Gad and half of Manasseh, but it was subject to attack from Ammon to the south and Damascus to the north. By Jeroboam's time, Gilead had been restored to Israelite control (2 Kgs 14:25). The incident referred to thus probably occurred some years before the time of Amos. "Threshing sledges of iron" (v. 3) were probably sledges made of wood, with teeth of iron or basalt (still called "iron" by the Arabs), which were dragged over the harvested grain on a threshing floor. Many interpreters have taken this to be a literal reference to torture, but Shalom Paul has cited Assyrian texts that use the same expression metaphorically, referring to the thoroughness of their victories over other armies.[16] Since "Gilead," rather than people, is said to have been threshed, Amos probably is referring in general terms to the cruelty of the Arameans' complete suppression of the area. (Compare the simile in 2 Kgs 13:7: "like the dust at threshing" [NRSV].) The subject in Hebrew is "they," not "she" (NIV; see also 1:6, 9). The judgment will fall not only on Damascus, but also on two places that cannot yet be identified. Beth Eden might be the Aramean city-state called Bit-Adini in Assyrian inscriptions, but that is 200 miles northeast of Damascus, and it seems doubtful that Amos would have associated it with a crime against Gilead. Most commentators guess that the Valley of Aven should be associated with the site later known as Baalbeck, a little north of Damascus.

The word "exile" (גלה *gālâ,* v. 5) appears early in the book. Amos threatens a deportation of the Arameans to Kir, another locality whose identification remains uncertain (but see Amos 9:7). It is associated with Elam (part of present-day Iran) in Isa 22:6. According to 2 Kgs 16:9 the people of Damascus were in fact exiled to Kir by Tiglath-pileser III (732 BCE). He was the first king to make wholesale deportations of populations a part of his imperial policy, and that continued to be done by his successors and by the Neo-Babylonian kings who followed the Assyrian period. These deportations were more than the usual taking of captives to be impressed into slavery, but involved the resettlement of entire populations (cf. the description in 2 Kings 17). This had been done a few times by earlier Assyrian kings and by the rulers of Urartu (now Armenia), so Amos may have heard of the practice. Later in the book he will introduce it into Israelite thought for the first time as the most fundamental threat to their existence as the people of Yahweh (5:5, 27; 6:7; 7:11, 17).

1:6-8. Gaza, Ashdod, Ashkelon, and Ekron were four of the five Philistine cities. Gath (the fifth city) may have been omitted because at this time it had been absorbed into the territory of Ashdod. During the period of the judges, the Philistines had been Israel's most dangerous enemy, but their military power was broken by David, and they never recovered it. They main-

tained their independence and commercial importance for centuries, but their sending a whole community into exile would not have been a massive deportation as a result of conquest such as the Assyrians carried out. It may have been a raid that led to the capture of the entire population of a town, who were then sold into slavery. There is no record elsewhere of this event, but it must have been considered enough of an atrocity that Amos knew his audience would remember it. Since Uzziah probably controlled the Negev, separating Philistia from Edom, the incident must have occurred before his time (2 Chronicles 26). Since Judah was the nearest neighbor of the Philistines, the victims may have been Judeans, but Amos does not make that explicit. Edom is said to have been the recipient of captives both here and in the oracle against Tyre (1:9), but the oracle against Edom accuses them of another crime. The slaves may have been forced to work in the copper mines of the Arabah, but Edom was also well located to serve as a provider of slaves for the kingdoms of Arabia; and since the territory was largely desert, trade of that kind could have been important to Edom's economy.

1:9-10. Tyre was the most important of the Phoenician cities in the eighth century BCE. The Phoenicians had few natural resources and turned to sea trade as their source of wealth (cf. Ezekiel 27). They were never a warlike people, and relationships with Israel were generally friendly. The other oracles against the Phoenicians in the prophetic books seem to reflect this, for they show a curious mixture of condemnation for the Phoenicians' wealth and pride with elements of lamentation over their downfall (cf. Isaiah 23; Ezekiel 26–28); Isa 23:15-18 even speaks of a future restoration of Tyre. The Phoenicians' activity in the slave trade is referred to again in the post-exilic period in Joel 3:6 [MT 4:6]. The "covenant of kinship" (NRSV) or "brotherhood" (NIV) may refer to the friendly relationships between Tyre and kings David and Solomon in the tenth century (2 Sam 5:11; 1 Kgs 5:1-12; 9:11-14, 27). A treaty ("covenant" ברית *běrît*]) between Solomon and Hiram of Tyre is mentioned in 1 Kgs 5:12 [MT 5:26]. If Amos is referring to that covenant in v. 9, then it is likely that he is accusing the people of Tyre of dealing in Israelite slaves, although once again it needs to be noted that he does not make

16. Shalom Paul, *Amos,* Hermeneia (Philadelphia: Fortress, 1991) 47.

that explicit. Since the treaty with Solomon would have been in the distant past, it is also possible that Amos is referring to a more recent treaty between Tyre and one of its neighbors, so the slaves may not necessarily have been Israelite. The oracle against Moab (2:1-3) shows clearly that Amos is not concerned only with crimes against his own people. Since Tyre is accused of essentially the same crime as Gaza, and since the conclusion of the oracle is shorter than those against Damascus, Gaza, Ammon, and Moab, many commentators have claimed that it is a later addition to the series. Recent arguments for its originality are very persuasive, however.[17]

1:11-12. The oracle against Edom is also dated in the exilic or post-exilic period by many commentators, because of its shorter conclusion and because the later prophets condemn Edom with great indignation for its mistreatment of Judean refugees at the time of the fall of Jerusalem in 587 BCE, and its subsequent annexation of the southern part of Judean territory (Isaiah 34; Jer 49:7-22; Ezek 25:12-14; 35:1-15; Obadiah).[18] The reference to "his brother" (v. 11) makes it clear that a crime has been committed against the Israelites, since tradition traces the ancestry of Edom back to Esau, twin brother of Jacob (Gen 25:23; 36:1). Verse 11 might then be explained by Obad 10-14 and Ezek 35:5. The Genesis account of the uneasy relationship between Jacob and Esau reflects the historical truth of the lengthy hostile relationship between Israelites and Edomites (cf. Gen 27:39-40). Although Israelites called them brothers (Num 20:14; Deut 2:4; 23:7; Obad 10, 12), the Edomites sometimes suffered under Israelite armies (2 Sam 8:13-14; 2 Kgs 14:7), and control of their region was desired because it would afford safe access to Elath, on the Gulf of Akabah (2 Kgs 14:22; 16:6). Edom had its occasional successes, however (cf. 2 Kgs 8:20-22), and the accusation in v. 11 is general enough that it may well refer to a conflict prior to the time of Amos. Bozrah was one of the principal cities in the northern part of the country, and Teman was a part of Edom, used here to represent the whole.

1:13-15. Ammon had claimed Gilead until Saul's victories over the Ammonites (1 Sam 11:1,

11; 14:47). From Amos's accusation, it would appear that during a more recent time of Israelite weakness, before Jeroboam's successes, the Ammonites had made encroachments again. The crime of which Amos accuses them is the most horrifying of all. To destroy a woman with her unborn child was to attack the enemy's next generation. Unfortunately, however, it appears not to have been an uncommon way for soldiers to vent their hatred of their enemy (the same atrocity is alluded to in 2 Kgs 8:12; 15:16; Hos 10:14; 13:16). The judgment announced by the prophet is correspondingly violent, using imagery drawn from the holy war tradition (cf. Jer 23:19; Ezek 13:13). Rabbah was the capital city of the Ammonites, located at the site of the present capital of Jordan, Amman. Exile is threatened for the two nations that had overrun Gilead, Damascus and Ammon, but for some reason, only the king and his officials are mentioned this time.

2:1-3. Moab had been subdued and cruelly treated by David (2 Sam 8:2). The region had been under the control of the northern kingdom until the death of Ahab, when Mesha, king of Moab, rebelled and succeeded in gaining his independence.[19] The account in 2 Kings 3 shows that Israel, Judah, and Edom were allied against Moab at that time, but we have no information about subsequent relationships between Moab and Edom. There is no other record of the incident Amos alludes to, or of any circumstances that may have led to it, but commentators generally agree that it probably involved the desecration of an Edomite king's tomb. Tomb inscriptions in antiquity regularly called down weighty curses upon anyone who might disturb the bones laid therein. The literal reading, "burned to lime" (NRSV), so that what was left of the bones might actually be used to make plaster, is to be preferred to the NIV's "burned, as if to lime," i.e., to a fine dust. This accusation is of the greatest importance for a proper understanding of the whole series. Gilead was claimed by Israel (1:3), and Edom's crime was certainly against Israelites (1:11), and the crimes of Gaza and Tyre may have been against the Israelites as well. This incident, however, was an affair that concerned only Moab and Edom.

---

17. Ibid., 16-26.
18. For details, see ibid., 16-20, 63.

19. See 2 Kgs 1:1; 3:4-27; and the Moabite Stone, in *Ancient Near Eastern Texts Relating to the Old Testament,* 3rd ed. with supplement, ed. J. B. Pritchard (Princeton: Princeton University Press, 1969) 320-21.

Israel could take no offense at it, but Amos claims that the God of Israel did. Kerioth is also mentioned as one of the cities of Moab in Jer 48:24, 41 and the Moabite Stone.

2:4-5. The Judah oracle, like the oracles against Tyre and Edom, uses the short form, without an expansion of the announcement of judgment. It differs from the six previous oracles in that the reason for judgment does not cite a war crime. Amos could have used traditions that contained memories of Judah's complicity in the extremely cruel treatment of its enemies (2 Sam 8:2; 12:31); so Judah could have been judged on the same basis as the other nations. Both Judah and Israel are judged by different standards from the surrounding nations, however, and the epigrammatic statement that follows this section (3:2) seems to have been placed there in part to explain it. Judah's special relationship with Yahweh gave its people standards to live by, and since they have rejected them, now they must be judged by them. There is debate whether the "lies" after which they have gone astray are false gods (so NIV) or idols (i.e., of Yahweh) or false teachings (perhaps of other prophets). It is probably safest to take the word as referring to false teachings of any kind in contrast to the Lord's instruction (torah).

Until recently, most commentators have concluded that the Judah oracle was added to Amos later by an author influenced by the deuterono-mistic school.[20] Its use of the short form, like that of the Tyre and Edom oracles, has already been shown to be no sound basis for a later date. As to the supposed deuteronomistic influence, the commentaries by Shalom Paul and by Andersen and Freedman show that the relationships with deuteronomistic language are by no means as strong as previously supposed.[21] There remains, however, a question of interpretation raised by the fact that the reason for punishment given in this oracle not only differs from those cited against the neighboring nations, but is also strikingly different from the reason in the Israel oracle, which lists a series of specific examples of social injustice. This is the kind of language prophets used to sum up what God expects of the people of God (e.g., 5:24). Other summary statements of this kind (Isa 1:16-17; Hos 4:6; Mic 6:8) suggest that vv. 4-5 would be easier to understand later in the history of judgment prophecy, after Judah's rejection of the Torah had been spelled out in detail. It may thus have been added to the series for the sake of completeness, after the fall of the northern kingdom. Arguments based on the number of oracles are inconclusive, since either seven (excluding Judah) or seven plus one is a significant pattern. The question of authorship cannot be decided, but this oracle seems more likely than any other to come from a later date.

---

20. Paul, *Amos*, 20-26.

21. See ibid.; Francis I. Andersen and David Noel Freedman, *Amos*, AB 24A (Garden City, N.Y.: Doubleday, 1989).

Amos 2:6-16, The Oracle Against Israel

NIV	NRSV
[6]This is what the LORD says:	[6] Thus says the LORD:
"For three sins of Israel,	For three transgressions of Israel,
even for four, I will not turn back ⌐my wrath⌐.	and for four, I will not revoke the punishment;[a]
They sell the righteous for silver,	because they sell the righteous for silver,
and the needy for a pair of sandals.	and the needy for a pair of sandals—
[7]They trample on the heads of the poor	[7] they who trample the head of the poor into
as upon the dust of the ground	the dust of the earth,
and deny justice to the oppressed.	and push the afflicted out of the way;
Father and son use the same girl	father and son go in to the same girl,
and so profane my holy name.	so that my holy name is profaned;
[8]They lie down beside every altar	[8] they lay themselves down beside every altar
on garments taken in pledge.	
In the house of their god	

a Heb *cause it to return*

NIV

they drink wine taken as fines.

⁹"I destroyed the Amorite before them,
  though he was tall as the cedars
  and strong as the oaks.
 I destroyed his fruit above
  and his roots below.

¹⁰"I brought you up out of Egypt,
  and I led you forty years in the desert
  to give you the land of the Amorites.

¹¹I also raised up prophets from among your sons
  and Nazirites from among your young men.
 Is this not true, people of Israel?"

                              declares the LORD.

¹²"But you made the Nazirites drink wine
  and commanded the prophets not to
     prophesy.

¹³"Now then, I will crush you
  as a cart crushes when loaded with grain.

¹⁴The swift will not escape,
  the strong will not muster their strength,
  and the warrior will not save his life.

¹⁵The archer will not stand his ground,
  the fleet-footed soldier will not get away,
  and the horseman will not save his life.

¹⁶Even the bravest warriors
  will flee naked on that day,"

                              declares the LORD.

NRSV

on garments taken in pledge;
and in the house of their God they drink
  wine bought with fines they imposed.

⁹ Yet I destroyed the Amorite before them,
  whose height was like the height of cedars,
  and who was as strong as oaks;
 I destroyed his fruit above,
  and his roots beneath.

¹⁰ Also I brought you up out of the land of Egypt,
  and led you forty years in the wilderness,
  to possess the land of the Amorite.

¹¹ And I raised up some of your children to be
     prophets
  and some of your youths to be nazirites.ᵃ
 Is it not indeed so, O people of Israel?
                              says the LORD.

¹² But you made the nazaritesᵃ drink wine,
  and commanded the prophets,
  saying, "You shall not prophesy."

¹³ So, I will press you down in your place,
  just as a cart presses down
  when it is full of sheaves.ᵇ

¹⁴ Flight shall perish from the swift,
  and the strong shall not retain their strength,
  nor shall the mighty save their lives;

¹⁵ those who handle the bow shall not stand,
  and those who are swift of foot shall not
     save themselves,
  nor shall those who ride horses save their
     lives;

¹⁶ and those who are stout of heart among the
     mighty
  shall flee away naked in that day,
                              says the LORD.

ᵃ That is, *those separated* or *those consecrated*   ᵇ Meaning of Heb uncertain

COMMENTARY

The oracle against Israel is explicitly connected to the preceding series by the introductory formula "For three transgressions . . . and for four, I will not turn it back" (author's trans.), but thereafter it differs in every respect. The reason is

expanded, and it cites neither war crimes nor the standards revealed by Yahweh. Instead, either four or seven (depending on how one counts) specific examples of injustice and a profligate life-style are cited. The Hebrew is also more difficult, unlike the very clear and straightforward language that precedes this section. The reason for punishment (vv. 6b-8) appears to be interrupted by a historical retrospective in vv. 9-11, but that actually leads to a concluding accusation in v. 12, so vv. 6b-12 should be taken as a whole, leading to the announcement of judgment in vv. 13-16.

2:6-8. Four examples of injustice are cited first. The word translated "righteous" (צדיק *ṣaddîq*) in v. 6b, when used in legal contexts, means the one declared to be "right," so Shalom Paul's translation "innocent" is probably the most accurate way to render it here (cf. Exod 23:6).[22] People apparently were being accused of failing to pay their debts and were being sold into slavery on account of it, even though the accusation was not true. The exact meaning of the parallel line is not clear. The pair of sandals for which the needy are sold does not seem to be a good parallel to the silver for which the righteous are sold, since the former would seem to be something of little value. Are the innocent poor being used as a source of wealth, or are their lives considered to be worthless? "Sandals" may be an obscure reference to a legal process involving property of value (see Ruth 4:7-8; cf. Deut 25:9-10), but we cannot be sure what that process actually is from the available evidence.

The syntax of v. 7a is difficult, for the Hebrew seems to say "those who trample on the dust of the earth, on the head of the poor" (השאפים על־עפר־ארץ בראש דלים *haššō'ăpîm 'al-'ăpar-'ereṣ bĕrō'š dallîm*). The NIV guesses it might be intended as a comparison; the NRSV takes "head" to be the object of the verb, leaving the preposition "on" unaccounted for. The imagery is clear enough, even though the grammar is not. The last part of v. 7 is more difficult, since the Hebrew reads, "a man and his father go to the girl." Most interpreters take this to be a reference to sexual intercourse (what else could it mean?), but the usual verb for intercourse is בוא (*bô'*, "go in") and not הלך (*hālak*, "go"), which is used here. Imagination has turned the girl into a cult prostitute, but a prostitute is never referred to as a "girl" (נערה *na'ărâ*) elsewhere in the OT. She might be a slave girl, sexually involved with son and father, and that seems the

most likely interpretation, in spite of the use of the verb "go."[23]

If that was the case, Amos is condemning the men for something not forbidden elsewhere in the OT. This accusation and the two in v. 8 are examples of the profligate life-style of the wealthy, which Amos condemns elsewhere (e.g., 4:1; 6:1-6). Lying down beside every altar (v. 8) is best connected with the subsequent reference to drinking wine in the house of their God, since reclining at feasts is referred to in 6:4. In the prophet's eyes, the place intended for worship seems to have become a place for partying. Under those circumstances, the garments taken in pledge from the poor, who had as yet failed to repay their debt, garments that were supposed to be returned each evening (Exod 22:26-27[25-26]), were not likely to be treated as the law required.

2:9-12. God interrupts the accusations with an emphatic "But I . . ." (v. 9), reminding the people of the contrast between Israelite and divine behavior. The various elements of the Canaanite population are all subsumed under the term "Amorite" here. The full recital of the mighty, saving acts of God includes the patriarchs, oppression in Egypt, exodus, wandering in the wilderness, and settlement in the land (cf. Deut 26:5-9; Josh 24:2-13). Exodus, wilderness, and settlement are mentioned here, then two unique divine acts are added: the gift of prophets and Nazirites (v. 11). Little is known of what the Nazirite was supposed to contribute to Israelite life. The rules for making a temporary nazirite vow are contained in Num 6:1-21, but Samson and Samuel were said to have been lifelong Nazirites (Judg 13:5; 1 Sam 1:22), and it may be that Amos is referring to deliverers such as these from the period of the judges. This leads Amos to add one more citation to his reasons for judgment (v. 12): Israel has rejected those whom God has set apart for special roles intended to benefit the people. In vv. 6b-8, no explicit citations of OT law as we now have it are given, although most of the behavior described is out of keeping with the law's concern for the poor. Israel's treatment of prophets and Nazirites is thus Amos's most explicit citation of their rejection of Yahweh's way, and that leads to the announcement of judgment, which also differs from the seven oracles preceding this one.

22. Paul, *Amos*.

23. For details, see ibid., 81-82.

2:13. The familiar "I will send fire . . . " does not appear. Instead the prophet uses a formula that often introduces God's intervention in history, the force of which is lost in both the NRSV and the NIV. Literally, the Hebrew text reads, "Behold, I am . . . " with a participle following to indicate the immediacy of God's action. But the idiom that follows is not clear. The verb מֵעִיק (mēʿîq; "press," NRSV; "crush," NIV) occurs only here, and the prepositional phrase that follows it would ordinarily be translated "under you," although "your place" (not "in your place," NRSV) is possible. The verb is repeated in the second line, so it must be something a cart full of sheaves of grain does. So scholars have suggested that the Hebrew be rendered "groan," "shake," "cleave" (furrows), or "hinder." The best interpretation would be a reading that would lead into the following verses, which are filled with images of flight. Since earthquake always produces panic, and since there are allusions to earthquakes else-where in the book, perhaps the verse should be translated: "Behold I am causing a quaking beneath you, as a wagon filled with sheaves quakes."

2:14-16. One of Amos's patterns of seven appears in these verses. The swift, the strong, the mighty, the bowman, the swift of foot, the horsemen, and the stout of heart will all become weak and their efforts futile. This is a vivid way of describing the panic that holy war was believed to strike into the hearts of the enemy army. The enemy is not named, but the context allows it to be none other than Israel. Here Amos introduces the expression "in that day" (v. 16), which is used in various ways in the OT. Here very likely it alludes to the Day of Yahweh, a term Amos will redefine in 5:18-20. The expression "Day of Yahweh" is closely associated with the imagery of holy war, as the commentary on 5:18-20 will show.

REFLECTIONS

1. The depiction of God as a warrior is a disturbing one for people today. For most of history, however, God's direct participation in war seems to have been taken for granted, since the use of war to settle national differences was also generally taken for granted. We cannot simply say, however, that Yahweh was thought of as a God of war in ancient Israel without taking seriously the theological problems that thought raises, not only because there is much less popular acceptance of war today than there seems to have been throughout most of history, but also because Scripture makes another claim: that the will of God for the world is *shalom.* Amos does not provide for us the materials to take up the whole question, but he does suggest an approach that may be partly helpful.

In the Overview of Amos 1:3–2:16 the point was made that Amos depicts Yahweh in the role of an advocate who intervenes in human affairs as the enemy of oppressors. It was suggested that this may not have been a completely new idea for Amos, but that he knew of it already from the exodus tradition. Advocates often must use force and may often be operating on different principles from those whom they oppose in order to aid those who need help. Amos claimed that the suffering of those cited in 1:3–2:3, 6-8 now leads the God whose anger rages against oppressors (according to Exod 22:24; Amos does not speak of God's anger) to wage holy war around the entire horizon, and also against the covenant people. How else could Amos have spoken of divine intervention on behalf of the suffering in his time?

For contemporary believers, intervention on behalf of the suffering is ordinarily thought to take place through the work of the people of God, in their efforts to establish justice. There is ample testimony to the necessity of doing that throughout Scripture (e.g., Deut 10:18-19; Ps 82:3; Prov 31:8-9; Isa 1:17; Jer 22:3). But does human intervention also appropriately involve taking destructive action against oppressors? History contains too many examples of nations who very easily assumed their wars were fought in response to God's will. We ought to be able to see better now. If force is repudiated entirely, however, will there be times when we cannot be an advocate for those who need help?

2. As we look through history at the rise and fall of nations, it is possible for us to give economic and military reasons for their successes and failures, with little or no reference to justice, let alone the direct activity of God. In a way, that thought is comforting, for it frees God from association with the dirtiness of politics and warfare. It also makes God irrelevant to much of human life, however, and challenges the claim of the prophets that God does become involved in international politics, and even uses wars to accomplish the divine purpose. Amos spoke of God as the divine warrior (1:4-5; 5:18-20; 6:8) and referred only vaguely to the armies of unnamed nations (3:11; 4:2; 6:14; 7:17; 9:4, 10). For us it is more likely to be God who is anonymous—or working in hiding—in the United Nations and the United States Congress and the plotting of terrorists.

If the nations ever heard of Amos's message, they probably paid it no attention. Amos has little hope that Israel can or will hear it, either. It is also hard for many people today to believe that there is a God who is really taking an active part in international politics, whose will makes any difference at all in the decisions that parliaments, congresses, and dictators make. It may be harder to believe now than in Amos's time, but careful reading and reflection show it was not easy to believe in his time, either. His words were a challenge to the faith of his age: Can you believe that there really is a God greater than the government? Most of the time the evidence seems to indicate the contrary, but those prophets of Israel claimed they had seen something others cannot see. Our reasoning today, as we consider the apparently unbridled power of the great nations, makes it hard to identify a place for God in world affairs, but we do have something eighth-century BCE Israel did not have. We have historical evidence to prove that when the prophets spoke of destruction and exile for Israel, to be followed by the appearance of a new and transformed people in the restoration, they were right. They also said God would be responsible for that destruction and transformation. We cannot prove they were right about that part, but why should we reject it? If we can believe that, then should we not at least keep open the possibility that there is a God who is now involved in more than the lives of individuals (relatively easy for some to believe), a God who also works—secretly—amid the terrors of war and the efforts of those who strive for peace? We seem to have no authentic prophets now who can discern exactly what God is doing, but the words of the prophets of old call upon us to look for the signs.

AMOS 3:1–4:13

ISRAEL'S INABILITY TO HEAR

OVERVIEW

There are structural relationships between chaps. 3–4 and 5–6, but for several reasons it is useful to deal with chaps. 3–4 as a unit. The primary emphasis in the various sections of these chapters is the effort to communicate the certainty of coming disaster to a people who are unwilling to hear and accept such a terrible message. The epigram in 3:2 agrees that Israel stands in a special relationship with God, but insists that does not make them immune from punishment for the sins already described in 2:6-12. The prophet announces this unacceptable message because he is under the divine compulsion to do so (3:3-8). Even the nations can see why Israel stands under judgment (3:9-11). But Israel thinks religion as usual will solve everything (4:4-5), ignoring the disasters around them, which most people would take to be indications they should turn to God asking what has gone wrong (4:6-11). Even though the elements within the unit are loosely connected with one another, it does have a clear beginning and end. At the beginning, the people are told, "Therefore I will punish you" (3:2 NRSV). At the end, the prophet tells them, "Prepare to meet your God" (4:12 NRSV).

It would be only guesswork to try to determine whether Amos himself was the creator of each of these units, or whether he or someone else did the editorial work that has now associated them in this way. The individual units may very well have originated separately, on different occasions, as other commentaries have treated them, but the approach of this commentary is to resist the temptation to imagine where they might have fit into a hypothetical biography of the prophet Amos. Some hints of redactional activity are evident, as the commentary will show, but in contrast to the approaches taken by Wolff and others, it can be concluded that there is nothing in these chapters that could not have come from the eighth century BCE, except possibly 3:7.

AMOS 3:1-2, EPIGRAM: ISRAEL IS DIFFERENT

NIV

3 Hear this word the LORD has spoken against you, O people of Israel—against the whole family I brought up out of Egypt:
²"You only have I chosen
 of all the families of the earth;
therefore I will punish you
 for all your sins."

NRSV

3 Hear this word that the LORD has spoken against you, O people of Israel, against the whole family that I brought up out of the land of Egypt:
² You only have I known
 of all the families of the earth;
therefore I will punish you
 for all your iniquities.

COMMENTARY

This unit is composed of an epigrammatic sentence with a long introduction. Like 1:2, 3:2 is a two-part sentence, beginning with a well-known thought, in this case a reference to the election of Israel, then adding to it an unexpected twist. Although most of Amos's message concerned the present and near future of the northern kingdom, certain passages speak of the historic Israel, which would include the kingdom of Judah in his time. That is made explicit in v. 1, with the reference to the exodus and the emphatic "whole family that I brought up out of the land of Egypt." One may ask whether it comes from later than the time of Amos and was formulated this way in order to reapply his words to Judah. That remains a possibility, but it seems arbitrary to assert that Amos could never have spoken of Israel as a whole. Scholars who have claimed that the reference to the exodus is a sign of deuteronomistic redaction have been shown to be incorrect by studies of the verb used here. The deuteronomistic vocabulary typically uses הוציא (hôṣî') to mean "bring out" of the exodus, but the verb used here is העלה (haʿăleh), meaning "bringing up."[24] The exodus tradition is introduced here, as in 2:10, in order to remind Israel of the moral basis for what is about to be said: They already owe Yahweh

24. J. Wijngaards, "הוציא and העלה: a Twofold Approach to the Exodus," *VT* 15 (1965) 91-102; T. R. Hobbs, "Amos 3,1b and 2,10," *ZAW* 81 (1969) 384-87.

something, for it is by Yahweh's own free will that they were delivered from slavery.

Another tradition is introduced in the epigram, however, for the first part of the sentence clearly refers to the election of the family of Abraham, as recorded in Genesis (e.g., Gen 12:3; 18:18-19; 28:14). The verb translated "known" in the NRSV is more freely rendered "chosen" by the NIV, but this is appropriate, for the Hebrew word ידע (yādaʿ) is used of knowledge of various kinds, including the most intimate sort (Gen 4:1), as well as the establishment and maintenance of a very close relationship (Gen 18:19; Jer 1:5; Hos 13:4). The more technical term for "election" in the OT is בחר (bāḥar), but yādaʿ, used here, speaks of the same divine activity. Usually a reference to God's choice of Israel to be God's people is combined with some aspect of their favored status (cf. Gen 18:17-19), but the second half of the sentence is one of Amos's creative uses of old traditions. The verb translated "punish" (פקד pāqad) can be used of either favorable or unfavorable activity, depending on the situation. It represents God's appropriate response to human behavior, so it might be translated here "hold you accountable for" (cf. TNK). Only here does Amos use the word "iniquity" (עון ʿāwōn) to denote that for which Israel is responsible. ʿAwōn seems to be the darkest of the "sin" words in Hebrew, including in its meaning the act, the resulting guilt, and the punishment that will follow.

REFLECTIONS

1. Many interpreters of Amos have taken 3:2 to be a theme verse for the entire book. In fact, however, it is not as radical or as thoroughgoing as other texts in the book. It does not yet tell us that the relationship between God and Israel has been broken, for this sentence restates the relationship. Neither does it hint at the extent of the devastation to come (cf. 9:1-4). The first indication of that will appear in the epigram at 3:12. The reference to election speaks of a relationship based on grace, for nothing in Genesis suggests that Abraham and Sarah, or their descendants, were chosen because they were somehow better than others. Both the election tradition, based on the stories of the patriarchs in Genesis, and the exodus tradition agreed that the initiative was God's and that all that was asked of the people was a response to God's gracious choice (e.g., Genesis 17; Exod 19:4-6). But the Sinai tradition made it clear that the response was not an optional matter and that the consequences of rejecting the relationship established by God were a most serious matter. "Therefore I will punish you for all your iniquities" (v. 2) thus would not seem to be a radically new idea. Amos's words show that the popular religion of his day, however, seems to have emphasized the election concept so strongly that the second line of his epigram would have struck his hearers as an unacceptable conclusion.

2. Discussions of election in Christian theology have regularly raised the issue of whether that election is for privilege or for responsibility. The difficulty Amos clearly had in getting a hearing (cf. 2:12; 7:10-13) shows that Israelites of his day were convinced it was for privilege. This text is appropriately understood as the transition between chaps. 1 and 2 and the rest of the book. The first two chapters have done something completely new in claiming that God was about to wage holy war against God's own people. The reasons were not traditional offenses—i.e., war crimes—but the people's violations of covenant law. Amos already has acknowledged that Israel is different (see 2:6-12; see also 2:4-5, if part of the original), but where the future is concerned Amos puts them on the same level with the nations. This epigram explains why.

Israel is different in having been given a special relationship with God, including the revelation of how human beings ought to live together in peace and harmony. But for a people (Israel or the church) to believe themselves to be chosen of God, or for individuals to believe themselves to be "the elect," always carries a danger with it. Its positive side must not be forgotten, for it both assures us of God's concern for us and reminds us that it is God who takes the initiative, but the temptation to take election as a sign of superiority (rather than of God's grace for the undeserving), and as justification for claims of privilege is a strong one. Amos's saying in 3:2 is thus an epigram that ought to remain foremost in the mind of anyone who believes in election. "From everyone to whom much has been given, much will be required; and from the one to whom much has been entrusted, even more will be demanded" (Luke 12:48 NRSV).

AMOS 3:3-8, NOT WITHOUT A WITNESS

NIV

3Do two walk together
 unless they have agreed to do so?
4Does a lion roar in the thicket
 when he has no prey?
Does he growl in his den
 when he has caught nothing?
5Does a bird fall into a trap on the ground
 where no snare has been set?
Does a trap spring up from the earth
 when there is nothing to catch?
6When a trumpet sounds in a city,
 do not the people tremble?
When disaster comes to a city,
 has not the LORD caused it?

7Surely the Sovereign LORD does nothing
 without revealing his plan
 to his servants the prophets.

NRSV

3 Do two walk together
 unless they have made an appointment?
4 Does a lion roar in the forest,
 when it has no prey?
Does a young lion cry out from its den,
 if it has caught nothing?
5 Does a bird fall into a snare on the earth,
 when there is no trap for it?
Does a snare spring up from the ground,
 when it has taken nothing?
6 Is a trumpet blown in a city,
 and the people are not afraid?
Does disaster befall a city,
 unless the LORD has done it?
7 Surely the Lord GOD does nothing,
 without revealing his secret
 to his servants the prophets.

NIV	NRSV
[8]The lion has roared— / who will not fear? / The Sovereign LORD has spoken— / who can but prophesy?	[8] The lion has roared; / who will not fear? / The Lord GOD has spoken; / who can but prophesy?

COMMENTARY

This passage is an apparent defense of Amos's mission as a prophet, a claim that he has no choice but to speak what God tells him. It is completely impersonal, with no reference to a call experience (as in Isaiah 6) or any personal claim to be filled with the Spirit (as in Mic 3:8). Amos speaks in general terms, assuming that those who hear understand the phenomenon of prophecy. The structure is carefully formulated, with its regularity varied enough to avoid monotony. There are seven rhetorical questions in vv. 3-6, with the first standing alone and the other six paired (v. 4, two questions concerning lions; v. 5, two questions concerning birds; v. 6, two questions concerning trouble in a city).

The sequence would seem to move logically toward an eighth question, since the pattern seven plus one is used elsewhere in the book and since v. 8 contains a pair of questions formulated in a new way (a statement followed by "who . . . ?"). The prophet adopts the style of wisdom teaching here. Note that this unit has no introduction or conclusion identifying it as the word of God. It appeals to the human reasoning process, as the wisdom literature typically does. A good parallel to this sequence of rhetorical questions appears in Prov 6:27-29:

Can fire be carried in the bosom
    without burning one's clothes?
Or can one walk on hot coals
    without scorching the feet?
So is he who sleeps with his neighbor's wife;
    no one who touches her will go unpunished. (NRSV)

Sequences of this kind are almost always formulated so as to elicit a negative answer, and thus usually speak of impossibilities (cf. Job 6:5-7; 8:11-13; Isa 66:8-9; Jer 18:14; Amos 6:12). By formulating the questions in vv. 3-8 negatively, the expected answer no refers here to the inevitable.

Efforts have been made to take the questions as allegorical, interpreting the two who walk together as God and Israel, the lion in vv. 4 and 8 as God, and so on, but comparison with the same type of rhetorical questions that appear elsewhere makes it much more probable that these figures should be understood as a series of arbitrarily chosen examples of cause and effect.

3:3-5. The first—two walking together (v. 3)—seems to be a trivial case, and probably we should not try to make anything more of it than what it says on the surface. The verb translated "made an appointment" (יעד yāʿad) means little more than "meet" in its other occurrences. No one could argue that two people could walk together if they had not met. Immediate understanding by the listeners/readers of the behavior of lions and birds was also obviously expected. Observation of the way lions hunt helps us not to misunderstand v. 4. The lions roar after the kill, not while they are hunting or attacking. The reference to the trapping of birds is not so clear, since two words for "trap" (פח paḥ and מוקש môqēš) are used in the first line of v. 5. The following reading makes good sense of it: "Does a bird swoop down upon a ground trap if there is no bait for it?"[25] But there is no strong evidence that môqēš is ever used to mean "bait."

3:6. Having reasoned from effect to cause in the first five questions, the prophet changes the interrogative particle in v. 6 and also changes the order from cause to effect: "Is a trumpet blown in a city,/ and the people are not afraid?" This would obviously be the kind of trumpet blast used by watchmen to warn the residents of a city of an approaching army. As the next sentence is translated, however, the order reverts to effect-cause: "Does disaster befall a city,/ unless the

---

25. Shalom Paul, *Amos,* Hermeneia (Philadelphia: Fortress, 1991) 110.

LORD has done it?" The word translated "disaster" (רעה $rā'â$) in both the NRSV and the NIV is often translated "evil," and this is one of the verses that leads to the discussions of whether the OT authors believed everything, including evil, comes from God.[26] Translating the word as "evil" suggests that the prophet is saying that no disaster (or evil) ever occurs except as an act of God. One interpretation of this passage is that this was the widespread belief in Israel, as a result of the claim that Yahweh was the only God. The OT record shows that most Israelites in the pre-exilic period were not monotheists, however. Some biblical authors may have been so insistent that there is only one source for all that exists that they occasionally spoke of Yahweh as the source of evil as well, as in 2 Sam 24:1 (cf. 1 Chr 21:1); Isa 45:7; or Lam 3:38. That may be what Amos is saying here, and those who claim that v. 8 is a later addition say the point of vv. 3-6 is the effort to persuade Israel that disaster in a city was in fact the result of God's activity. But there is another way of reading the question in v. 6*b*. The author may have intended the cause-effect order, like v. 6*a*, and thus have taken evil in its moral sense: "Does evil happen in a city, and

Yahweh not act?" (author's trans.).[27] This attributes a more regular structure to v. 6, and fits perfectly with the rest of Amos's message, so it seems worth considering as an alternate interpretation.

3:7-8. The first line of v. 8 takes up the roaring lion of v. 4 and of 1:2 as a parallel to the voice of God, but the point of the verse is not to be drawn from the imagery. It is simply the cause-effect relationship again: Just as fear is inevitable, so also is the speech of the prophet. These unacceptable words have not been chosen by Amos; he speaks this way because he has no choice.

The view of prophecy reflected by v. 7 is different, claiming that God always makes the divine will known to the people through the prophets, so that the people never need to doubt their status. The deuteronomistic historian's explanation of the fall of the northern kingdom speaks of the work of the prophets in this way (2 Kgs 17:13). But this is a different subject from that of divine compulsion to speak, which evidently is the point of the whole series of rhetorical questions. Thus v. 7 reads like a marginal note added to the text by an early reader.

---

26. See Fredrik Lindstrom, *God and the Origin of Evil: A Contextual Analysis of Alleged Monistic Evidence of the Old Testament,* CBOTS 21 (Lund: CWK Gleerup, 1983) 199-214.

27. Cf. the NEB marginal note: "If there is evil in a city, will not the LORD act?" See M. J. Mulder, "Ein Vorschlag zur Übersetzung von Amos iii 6b," *VT* 34 (1984) 106-8.

REFLECTIONS

1. A major theological issue lies behind this sequence of questions. The rhetoric of cause and effect suggests inevitability, and the conclusion drawn is that when the Lord speaks, the prophet must speak, whether he wills to do so or not. The broader issue is thus the tension between God's will and the wills of humans. Ordinarily the OT speaks of the free will of humans in making their own decisions, for which they remain responsible. In only a few cases, such as the hardening of Pharaoh's heart (Exod 4:21; 14:4), is God said to have interfered with the human decision-making process. But the prophets claim that God has done that in their lives. The experience of a "call," recorded by others (Isaiah 6; Jer 1:4-10; Ezekiel 1–3), but only alluded to by Amos (7:14-15), made their lives no longer their own. It was no great privilege for them, at least as Jeremiah described it (Jer 20:7-12), but what they say about it indicates they believed that somehow God needed them to carry out God's work at that time. Many others who have not been called to be prophets have felt a similar divine compulsion to do God's work, in spite of what their own desires might have been.

History has validated the claims of the Old Testament prophets, but others have claimed that God has spoken to them, commanding them to teach or to do things no right-minded person would accept as the divine will. The claim to possess direct, divine authority thus raises another issue for the believing community, which long ago came to realize it could not just accept every assertion that a person was speaking or acting under divine compulsion. In Israel the issue took the form of questions about whether a person was a true or a false prophet (9th century: 1 Kings 22; 8th century: Hos 4:5; Mic 3:5-7, 11). The church has recognized that when people claim that they have received a divine call, it must judge as best it can whether that call is a valid one, recognizing that the church may err, but that it is not required to accept every claim without examination.

2. The passage raises another perennial issue, without offering a definitive word about it, as the commentary on v. 6*b* has shown. It touches on the problem of evil. The OT never takes up the issue of the existence of evil in the world as a philosophical question—i.e., discussing its origin or how there could be evil in a world created by a good God. Old Testament authors insist that God is good, that God is sovereign, and that evil is real, without being able to reconcile the paradox; and no theologian has yet been able to do that without modifying or giving up one of those three assertions. The commentary noted that in a few places OT authors seem to have weakened the first assertion by attributing both good and evil to God, and also noted that Amos 3:6*b* may be read that way—but it may also be taken differently. The matter should thus not be pursued further here. Rather, Amos 3:6*b* may be taken as an introduction to a passage that occurs later in this section, 4:6-11, which says quite explicitly that God brought one disaster after another upon Israel. The root for "evil," used in 3:6*b* can denote moral evil, as in Amos 5:14-15, but is also used to designate harm or damage of any kind, as in Amos 5:13; 6:3; 9:4, 10. Amos and other biblical writers will not attribute moral evil to God, but they do not hesitate to say that God, the creator and maintainer of everything good, is also a destroyer. In that respect, Amos 3:6*b* says nothing unusual; 4:6-11, however, will call for additional comment on that aspect of the character of God.

AMOS 3:9–4:3, LUXURY AND INJUSTICE

NIV

⁹Proclaim to the fortresses of Ashdod
  and to the fortresses of Egypt:
"Assemble yourselves on the mountains of
    Samaria;
  see the great unrest within her
  and the oppression among her people."

¹⁰"They do not know how to do right," declares
    the LORD,
  "who hoard plunder and loot in their
    fortresses."

¹¹Therefore this is what the Sovereign LORD says:
"An enemy will overrun the land;
  he will pull down your strongholds
  and plunder your fortresses."

¹²This is what the LORD says:
"As a shepherd saves from the lion's mouth
  only two leg bones or a piece of an ear,
  so will the Israelites be saved,

NRSV

⁹ Proclaim to the strongholds in Ashdod,
  and to the strongholds in the land of Egypt,
and say, "Assemble yourselves on Mount*ᵃ*
    Samaria,
  and see what great tumults are within it,
  and what oppressions are in its midst."
¹⁰ They do not know how to do right, says the
    LORD,
  those who store up violence and robbery in
    their strongholds.
¹¹ Therefore thus says the Lord GOD:
An adversary shall surround the land,
  and strip you of your defense;
  and your strongholds shall be plundered.

¹²Thus says the LORD: As the shepherd rescues
from the mouth of the lion two legs, or a piece
of an ear, so shall the people of Israel who live

ᵃ Gk Syr: Heb *the mountains of*

NIV

those who sit in Samaria
  on the edge of their beds
  and in Damascus on their couches.ᵃ"
¹³"Hear this and testify against the house of Jacob," declares the Lord, the LORD God Almighty.
¹⁴"On the day I punish Israel for her sins,
  I will destroy the altars of Bethel;
the horns of the altar will be cut off
  and fall to the ground.
¹⁵I will tear down the winter house
  along with the summer house;
the houses adorned with ivory will be destroyed
  and the mansions will be demolished,"
                    declares the LORD.

4   Hear this word, you cows of Bashan on
      Mount Samaria,
  you women who oppress the poor and crush
      the needy
  and say to your husbands, "Bring us some
      drinks!"
²The Sovereign LORD has sworn by his holiness:
  "The time will surely come
when you will be taken away with hooks,
  the last of you with fishhooks.
³You will each go straight out
  through breaks in the wall,
  and you will be cast out toward Harmon,ᵇ"
                    declares the LORD.

ᵃ12 The meaning of the Hebrew for this line is uncertain.
ᵇ3 Masoretic Text; with a different word division of the Hebrew (see Septuagint) out, O mountain of oppression

NRSV

in Samaria be rescued, with the corner of a couch
and partᵃ of a bed.

¹³ Hear, and testify against the house of Jacob,
    says the Lord GOD, the God of hosts:
¹⁴ On the day I punish Israel for its transgressions,
    I will punish the altars of Bethel,
  and the horns of the altar shall be cut off
    and fall to the ground.
¹⁵ I will tear down the winter house as well as
      the summer house;
  and the houses of ivory shall perish,
  and the great housesᵇ shall come to an end,
                    says the LORD.

4   Hear this word, you cows of Bashan
      who are on Mount Samaria,
  who oppress the poor, who crush the needy,
    who say to their husbands, "Bring
      something to drink!"
² The Lord GOD has sworn by his holiness:
    The time is surely coming upon you,
  when they shall take you away with hooks,
    even the last of you with fishhooks.
³ Through breaches in the wall you shall leave,
    each one straight ahead;
  and you shall be flung out into Harmon,ᵃ
                    says the LORD.

ᵃ Meaning of Heb uncertain   ᵇ Or many houses

COMMENTARY

Three oracles of similar content appear between the carefully organized sequences of rhetorical questions (3:3-8) and plagues (4:6-12). They are not editorially connected with one another; in fact, the first and second are separated by an epigrammatic sentence (3:12). The addressees of the first and second are never identified (they begin with plural imperatives; 3:9, 13), while the third is addressed to the "cows of Bashan." The subject matter of the three is similar enough, however, that they can be dealt with together.

3:9-11, Even the Nations Can See. This section provides an expanded reason/announcement

oracle (vv. 10-11), introduced by a call to some unnamed heralds, commissioning them to appeal to Ashdod and to Egypt to become witnesses against the sins of Samaria. It is unlikely that Amos had any real heralds, earthly or heavenly, in mind. This appeal to the nations was probably for rhetorical effect. His message is for the people of Samaria, even though he speaks of them in the third person. The LXX reads "Assyria" instead of "Ashdod" in v. 9, and some translators and commentators have preferred the former, since its use would pair Israel's two great enemies to the north and to the south. It is unlikely that a scribe who saw "Assyria" in the original text would have altered it to "Ashdod," however, so the latter translation is probably original. Assyria is not mentioned anywhere else in the book, and there is no evidence to show that Amos knew that it would, indeed, be the adversary responsible for the end of the northern kingdom. Ashdod was probably chosen here because it represented the Philistines, for they and the Egyptians had been the two great enemies of Israel, according to early traditions. Later, Ezekiel took up this idea of the nations as witnesses to the behavior of Yahweh's people, claiming as Amos does that it would be scandalous even in the eyes of these nations (Ezek 5:5-8; cf. Ezek 36:16-36).

Samaria had been the capital of the northern kingdom since the time of Omri (9th century BCE), and Amos's reference to the mountains of Samaria probably pictures the emissaries from Ashdod and Egypt in a sort of theater in the round, observing the tumults and oppressions, the violence and the robbery within it. He sums up the indictment in a sweeping accusation: "They do not know how to do right" (v. 10; cf. Jer 4:22). He speaks in generalities now, rather than citing specific cases as in 2:6-16, probably because his emphasis is on the announcement. The announcement in 2:13-16 had been vigorous and impressive, but not very specific, just speaking of the failure and flight of soldiers. This oracle speaks very directly of an adversary who will surround the land and plunder it. Amos does sometimes refer to a human enemy, although more often he speaks of the judgment being executed directly by God. But the human enemy is never named, which is evidence that the oracles of judgment in this book achieved their final form before the Assyrian threat became obvious.

3:12, Epigram: The Remnant Defined.
The first epigram (1:2) was a play on hymnic language; the second (3:2) was based on the reason/announcement genre. In this verse the prophet uses a wisdom genre—i.e., comparison. What makes it epigrammatic is the bitterly ironic play on the word "rescue" (נצל *nāṣal*). Once again we encounter a self-contained, two-part saying, beginning with an apparently straightforward subject, with which something surprising is done in the second part. Amos here refers to customary practice among shepherds. According to Exod

22:13, if someone entrusted with another person's animal claimed it had been killed by wild beasts, he should produce the remains as evidence that he had not sold it or misappropriated it for himself. The animal had scarcely been "rescued," but Amos chose that verb to make his unexpected comparison. In form the sentence is like many to be found in the wisdom literature, which often teaches by making comparisons, as in Prov 26:18-19: "Like a maniac who shoots deadly firebrands and arrows,/ so is one who deceives a neighbor/ and says, 'I am only joking!' " (NRSV). The same genre is used in Isa 31:4, but as a straightforward comparison of two kinds of fierce activity.

Amos does not use the word "remnant" here, but when he does (5:15), one may well recall v. 12 for his definition. "A remnant shall be saved" is more threat than promise for Amos. This is his first statement of the thoroughness of the destruction that is anticipated, for two legs or a piece of an ear are not much of an animal. This part of the epigram, which is clear enough, shows us what to make of the second part, even though the words are very difficult and any translation is guesswork. The NRSV is to be preferred to the NIV. Two different words for "bed" and "couch" are used, and the parallel with the first part of the verse suggests not that the people are sitting on them, but that fragments of these objects are all that will be saved. The most difficult word is דמשק (*dĕmešeq*) the consonants of which are identical with the name "Damascus"; but the Masoretic Text has pointed the word differently, and no one knows what the author intended. The NIV has emended the text to include "Damascus," but the Masoretes who pointed the text obviously had a strong tradition that the word was not "Damascus." The NRSV has simply substituted the vague word "part." Various proposed emendations may be found in other commentaries, but one must admit that at this time the exact meaning of the final clause remains uncertain.

3:13-15, Religion and Luxury.
This oracle begins with a plural imperative, "Hear," as do 3:1 and 4:1, followed by another imperative, "testify against the house of Israel." It cannot be God addressing Amos, since the imperatives are plural; neither can it be Amos addressing Israel, since those being addressed are to testify against Israel. The addressees may thus be the imagined emis-

saries from Ashdod and Egypt, or the heralds hypothesized as the recipients of the command in 3:9. After the commission another reason/announcement oracle appears, with the reason stated in the briefest possible way this time ("for its transgressions," v. 14), so the emphasis on the coming destruction is even stronger than in 3:9-11. This oracle appropriately follows v. 12. A very full title is given to Yahweh at this point: "the Lord Yahweh, God of Hosts." This is the first occurrence in Amos of the much-discussed word צבאות (ṣĕbāʾôt), translated in the customary way "hosts" in the NRSV and replaced by "Almighty" in the NIV. The word sometimes refers to earthly armies and is associated with the concept of God as the divine warrior; at other times it seems to speak instead of heavenly hosts. Amos uses it as a formal title without any specific reference to either.

Bethel appears here for the first time in the book (cf. 4:4; 5:5-6; 7:10, 13). It had been a sanctuary since early times (Gen 28:19), but with the schism between the northern tribes and Judah, Jeroboam I had made it and Dan royal sanctuaries to compete with Judah's holy place, Jerusalem (1 Kgs 12:26-33). Bethel, the sanctuary, and Samaria, the capital city, are the two places most frequently referred to in Amos. No reason is given here for the destruction of the altars of Bethel, but this passage anticipates later condemnations of Israel's practice of worship (4:4-5; 5:4-5, 21-27). Horned altars have been found in the excavations of various sites in Israel.[28] The blood of atonement was to be placed on the horns of the altar (Lev 4:30; 16:18), and two efforts to gain sanctuary by grasping the horns of the altar are recorded in 1 Kgs 1:50 and 2:28. To cut off these horns was thus to destroy the locus of saving power.

The luxurious life that the wealthy had enjoyed as a result of violence and robbery (v. 10) will also come to an end. Changes in altitude in the land of Israel lead to significant changes in climate within a few miles, so those who could afford it might have had a winter home in the valleys and a summer home in the hills; and these were no mere "cottages," for they were decorated with ivory. Remains of such ivory decorations have been found in excavations at Samaria.

4:1-3, From Luxury to Humiliation. This is a reason/announcement oracle, with the people under judgment being addressed in the second person, unlike 3:9-11, 13-15. The oracle is addressed to the "cows of Bashan, who are on Mount Samaria," an expression without parallel elsewhere, so it has been interpreted variously. It seems most likely to be a reference to the wealthy women of the capital city, but the Targum, Jerome, Calvin, and some modern scholars take it to be a feminine metaphor applied either to the leaders of the kingdom or to the people in general. If read the latter way, then the word usually translated "husband" (אדון ʾādôn), which actually means "lord," is likely to be interpreted as a reference to pagan gods, but that by no means makes the passage read smoothly.

The use of bovine imagery to represent people, usually but not always negatively, is not uncommon in the OT (see Ps 22:12[13]; Jer 31:18; Hos 4:16; Mic 4:13). Bashan was noted for its herds and flocks, and although to call a woman a cow is insulting in our culture, one should not assume that Amos used the expression as an insult. In the Song of Solomon, for example, the poet compares his beloved's hair to a flock of goats, her breasts to fawns, and her nose to a tower of Lebanon (Cant 4:1, 5; 7:3-4). Most interpreters, therefore, understand "cows of Bashan" to be a reference to the elite women of Samaria who lived in opulent splendor. Amos did not see the wealthy women of the northern kingdom as passive beneficiaries of the unjust behavior of the men; rather, he says that they have been actively involved in the oppression of the poor. If ʾādôn here means "husband," instead of "lord," an unusual use of the word (only Gen 18:12; Jud 19:26; Ps 45:12), it has been chosen for ironic reasons. These "lords," are ordered about by their wives, whose promiscuous life-style is possible because the poor are oppressed, the needy are crushed.

The reversal of fortune will be a terrible one, as was the fate of all whose cities were overrun by conquerors. The announcement (vv. 2-3) is introduced with a solemn formula: "The Lord GOD has sworn by his holiness," which in effect means swearing by God's own character. (The same form

28. For pictures of these altars, see J. B. Pritchard, *The Ancient Near East in Pictures Relating to the Old Testament* (Princeton: Princeton University Press, 1954) pl. 575; Gaalyah Cornfeld, *Archaeology of the Bible: Book by Book* (New York: Harper & Row, 1976) 142; Philip J. King, *Amos, Hosea, Micah: An Archaeological Commentary* (Philadelphia: Westminster, 1988) 93, 103.

is found in Ps 89:36. For other divine oaths, see Amos 6:8; 8:7.) This announcement is followed by one of the formulas usually chosen by the prophets to indicate an uncertain time in the future: "Behold, days are coming" (NRSV, "The time is surely coming"; cf. elsewhere in Amos 8:11; 9:13). The designation of God as "Lord Yahweh" (אדני יהוה *ʾădōnāy yhwh*) creates a problem for translators, since "LORD" has traditionally been substituted for "Yahweh." The NRSV makes do with "Lord GOD," while the NIV has adopted "Sovereign LORD" where these two words are used together.

The rest of the oracle is fraught with problems. Either the text has been damaged, or Amos has used terms familiar in his time but unknown to us. The women shall be carried away with hooks or ropes, on shields, or in pots or baskets. All of these terms have been suggested in the effort to translate v. 2b. "Hooks" and "baskets" are the translations that have received the most support. If צנות (*ṣinnôt*) does mean "hooks," then the reference is to leading away prisoners with hooks through their noses, a custom documented in ancient Near Eastern art. If it means "baskets," it presumably refers to the disposal of corpses; but conquerors in antiquity tended to brag about leaving the corpses of their enemies lying about unburied. The destination of these captive (or slain) women is also uncertain, for the final word in the Hebrew of v. 3 is unknown. The best guess, represented by both the NRSV and the NIV, is that it is a place called Harmon, which has not yet been located. If that is correct, then capture and exile would appear to be the fate Amos envisions for the women who now enjoy such an opulent life.

REFLECTIONS

These oracles express in various ways the message repeated again and again in the books of the pre-exilic prophets. Because Israel has failed to maintain its side of the relationship Yahweh had established with it, disaster lies near at hand. The message raises a series of theological questions.

1. Other nations accounted for disasters in a similar way, by saying the people had done something to anger their gods, who punished them by causing their defeat in war or some natural calamity. Was there anything different in what Amos said? There is a twofold answer to that question. New is the thoroughness of the destruction of which Amos speaks. The first hint of that appears in the epigram in 3:12; it will be emphasized all the more in 8:2 and 9:1-4. There is a sense of terror in his saying that the national existence of a people is about to come to an end that sets Amos apart from the common theology of the ancient Near East. In addition, this was not an explanation after the fact, as was customary. If the book is dated correctly, between 760 and 750, and if the few facts we have, suggesting the northern and the southern kingdoms were living in relative security and prosperity, are correct, then there was not even a threat of disaster that needed to be explained. Those who insist on accounting for everything on purely human terms will thus want to date the book later, after the Assyrian conquests under Tiglath-pileser III had begun, but if we are willing to allow that God may indeed speak a new word to the people through an inspired person, there is no need to do that.

2. Would not Assyria have come against Israel anyway, for its own empire-building reasons, even if Israel had always maintained a just and merciful society? The modern historian cannot help asking such a question, but the only truly correct answer we can give to it is that we do not know, for that is not what happened. To imagine a different Israel and then project international history on either the same or a different course is to write historical fiction. All we know is what did happen. Israel did not live by the standards of Yahweh, as the prophets understood them, and Assyria did come. Israel's national existence, and later that of Judah, came to an end, but the individuals who survived interpreted the disaster in the light of the message of Amos and the other prophets, and that led to the appearance of a new and reformed community, during and after the exile. That awful experience led them, at any rate, to believe that the prophets were right, and their acceptance of the prophetic interpretation of exile made more of a difference in the history of the world than anything the Assyrians or Babylonians accomplished.

3. Have we the right (or the wisdom and insight) to make a direct application of Amos's message to any contemporary nation or culture? With injustice still rampant, there is a strong temptation for us to do that, but that should be done with caution. Without direct, divine inspiration we cannot know what God is about to do in our immediate future, as Amos did. Amos's work is not simply a document bound to the eighth century BCE, however. There is ample evidence from history of the truth of the Old Testament's insistence that the health of any society can be measured by looking at how the weak and the poor fared within it. History also verifies the Old Testament's insistence that an unhealthy society will not long endure. We cannot make direct applications of the prophetic message in order to predict our future, but we can and should use it to diagnose the health of our society. Amos has spoken in generalities in this section, but two words stand out as keys to the message he offers elsewhere: *poor* and *needy* (4:1). Those words are specific enough. To know whether a society is healthy, do not look at the wealthy homes or the magnificent sanctuaries, but look at the state of the poor and the needy. If the words that go with them are Amos's words—*tumult, oppression, violence*—then there is no health in that society, and where there is no health, death cannot be far away.

AMOS 4:4-13, RELIGION AS USUAL, WHILE THE WORLD CRUMBLES

NIV	NRSV

⁴"Go to Bethel and sin;
    go to Gilgal and sin yet more.
Bring your sacrifices every morning,
    your tithes every three years.^a
⁵Burn leavened bread as a thank offering
    and brag about your freewill offerings—
boast about them, you Israelites,
    for this is what you love to do,"
            declares the Sovereign LORD.
	⁴ Come to Bethel—and transgress;
	    to Gilgal—and multiply transgression;
	bring your sacrifices every morning,
	    your tithes every three days;
	⁵ bring a thank offering of leavened bread,
	    and proclaim freewill offerings, publish
	      them;
	    for so you love to do, O people of Israel!
	            says the Lord GOD.

⁶"I gave you empty stomachs^b in every city
    and lack of bread in every town,
    yet you have not returned to me,"
            declares the LORD.
	⁶ I gave you cleanness of teeth in all your cities,
	    and lack of bread in all your places,
	yet you did not return to me,
	            says the LORD.

⁷"I also withheld rain from you
    when the harvest was still three months
      away.
I sent rain on one town,
    but withheld it from another.
	⁷ And I also withheld the rain from you
	    when there were still three months to the
	      harvest;
	I would send rain on one city,
	    and send no rain on another city;

a4 Or tithes on the third day   *b6 Hebrew you cleanness of teeth*

NIV

One field had rain;
  another had none and dried up.
[8]People staggered from town to town for water
  but did not get enough to drink,
  yet you have not returned to me,"
                     declares the LORD.

[9]"Many times I struck your gardens and
    vineyards,
  I struck them with blight and mildew.
Locusts devoured your fig and olive trees,
  yet you have not returned to me,"
                     declares the LORD.

[10]"I sent plagues among you
  as I did to Egypt.
I killed your young men with the sword,
  along with your captured horses.
I filled your nostrils with the stench of your
    camps,
  yet you have not returned to me,"
                     declares the LORD.

[11]"I overthrew some of you
  as I[a] overthrew Sodom and Gomorrah.
You were like a burning stick snatched from the
    fire,
  yet you have not returned to me,"
                     declares the LORD.

[12]"Therefore this is what I will do to you, Israel,
  and because I will do this to you,
  prepare to meet your God, O Israel."

[13]He who forms the mountains,
  creates the wind,
  and reveals his thoughts to man,
he who turns dawn to darkness,
  and treads the high places of the earth—
  the LORD God Almighty is his name.

a11 Hebrew God

NRSV

one field would be rained upon,
  and the field on which it did not rain
    withered;
[8] so two or three towns wandered to one town
  to drink water, and were not satisfied;
yet you did not return to me,
                     says the LORD.

[9] I struck you with blight and mildew;
  I laid waste[a] your gardens and your
    vineyards;
  the locust devoured your fig trees and your
    olive trees;
yet you did not return to me,
                     says the LORD.

[10] I sent among you a pestilence after the manner
    of Egypt;
  I killed your young men with the sword;
I carried away your horses;[b]
  and I made the stench of your camp go up
    into your nostrils;
yet you did not return to me,
                     says the LORD.

[11] I overthrew some of you,
  as when God overthrew Sodom and
    Gomorrah,
  and you were like a brand snatched from
    the fire;
yet you did not return to me,
                     says the LORD.

[12] Therefore thus I will do to you, O Israel;
  because I will do this to you,
  prepare to meet your God, O Israel!

[13] For lo, the one who forms the mountains,
    creates the wind,
  reveals his thoughts to mortals,
makes the morning darkness,
  and treads on the heights of the earth—
  the LORD, the God of hosts, is his name!

a Cn: Heb the multitude of   b Heb with the captivity of your
horses

COMMENTARY

There are three distinct genres in this section, but there is evidence that they were intended to be understood together. There is no use guessing about the origins of the individual parts, whether vv. 4-5 were originally a separate oracle or what its occasion might have been (e.g. imagining Amos pronouncing it at a feast in Bethel), or whether v. 13 was taken from an already existing hymn (the rest of which may perhaps be found in 5:8-9; 9:5-6). Such reconstructions differ from scholar to scholar because the evidence for them is so scanty, and the process thus becomes highly subjective. What is clear is that at some time, early or late, as the Amos tradition was taking its present form, connective particles were used to tell the reader that these three parts are to be taken together as a coherent message.

4:4-5, Liturgy Is Not the Answer. This is a bitter parody on the calls to worship that were used in Israel. The same imperative, "Come" (באו *bōʾû*; or "enter"), is used twice in Ps 100:2, 4: "Come into his presence with singing. . . . Enter his gates with thanksgiving" (NRSV; cf. Pss 95:6; 96:8). The same root in the hiphil stem means "bring," and it is used in v. 4*b* as it is used in the regulations for sacrifice in Exod 23:19 and Leviticus 1–7. In the psalms, the call to worship typically leads to a description of the goodness of God, introduced by "for" (כי *kî*; e.g., Pss 95:7; 100:5). Verse 5 uses the same particle to introduce a quite different reason: "For so you love to do." Later, Jeremiah will speak of sacrifice with the same kind of ironic command (Jer 7:21).

The royal sanctuary Bethel appears for the second time in the book, now paired with Gilgal (cf. 3:14). The latter place has not as yet been identified with certainty, for the name seems to have been used of several places marked by stone circles. The best known of such sites is associated with the crossing of the Jordan River in the time of Joshua (Josh 4:19; 5:9). This may be the one mentioned in connection with Samuel and Saul (1 Sam 7:16; 11:14). Hosea condemned the cult at Gilgal as severely as Amos does (Hos 4:15; 9:15; 12:11). The offerings Amos lists may have been perfectly legitimate in his time. Leavened

bread may not be burned as an offering, according to Exod 23:18; 34:25; Lev 2:11, but we do not know whether this regulation was in force in the northern kingdom. (The verb in v. 5 is "burn" [קטר *qāṭar*], not "bring," as in the NRSV). Amos does seem to exaggerate in calling for sacrifices every morning and tithes every three days, if the NRSV is correct (the NIV emends to "three years"). These offerings were never called for so often, and some scholars read the time notices differently as "in the morning" and "on the third day,"[29] but the NRSV translation seems appropriate. This exaggeration is part of the parody, but the truly shocking part is the prophet's claim that all this generosity is "transgression," even "rebellion" (ופשעו *ûpiš'û*; cf. 2:4, 6). Elsewhere Amos will explain why sacrifice is inadequate service to God (5:21-24); here it is left unexplained. That he speaks of those who pay assiduous attention to the details of liturgy without thinking about what God really requires is suggested by the section that follows.

4:6-12, Plagues over Israel. The NRSV and the NIV both omit the connective particles (וגם-אני *wĕgam-ʾānî*) at the beginning of v. 6, best translated "but for my part." Amos has described rather extravagantly what the people love to do; now he lists at some length what God has been doing, while they do not realize God has been at work. The list is composed of seven disasters, all but the sixth of them by forces of nature. God's use of nature for corrective purposes has probably led to the addition of v. 13, which identifies God as creator. The famine, drought, blight, locust swarm, pestilence, sword, and overthrow are called "plagues" because it will be of some help to compare them with the account of the plagues in Egypt, even though the only exact parallels are pestilence and locusts. Other parallels are more often cited by commentators. Some have made a great deal of the sequences of curses found in Lev 26:14-33 and Deut 28:15-68, claiming that Amos is carrying out a covenant-cursing ceremony.[30]

---

29. For discussion of these translations, see Paul, *Amos*, 140.
30. E.g., Henning Graf Reventlow, *Das Amt des Propheten bei Amos*, FRLANT 80 (Göttingen: Vandenhoeck & Ruprecht, 1962) 75-90; Walter Brueggemann, "Amos 4,4-13 and Israel's Covenant Worship," *VT* 15 (1965) 1-15.

There are no word-for-word parallels, however, as if he were quoting covenant curses, and furthermore it is not certain whether those two chapters are even as old as the eighth century BCE. Solomon's prayer in 1 Kgs 8:33-53 is more closely related to this passage, since he speaks of a series of potential calamities that may lead his people to turn to the Lord, and he asks God to be forgiving. But each of the plagues in vv. 6-11 was so common in the ancient Near East that Amos may have simply created his own list, since there is no strong evidence for dependence on earlier material.

Once again a pattern of seven elements plus a conclusion appears. The refrain "yet you did not return to me,/ says the LORD" (v. 6) appears only five times in these verses (vv. 6, 8, 9, 10, 11), but patterns of five elements also are frequently used in this book. Famine (v. 6) is described in a way that the NIV translators decided might not be understood by contemporary readers better acquainted with dental hygiene than with hunger. In Amos's time, if one's teeth were clean it meant one had nothing to eat. "Pestilence after the manner of Egypt" (v. 10) may be a specific reference to the fifth plague in Exod 9:3, since the same word is used there. In Exodus, this pestilence is a disease affecting livestock. The "overthrow" in v. 11 may be another of the references to earthquake in this book. The verb הפך (hāpak) is always used when the destruction of Sodom and Gomorrah is mentioned, as here. According to Genesis, those cities were destroyed by fire from heaven (Gen 19:24-25), but the Dead Sea region is an area of frequent earthquake activity, and the use of the verb may reflect Amos's awareness of that.

Disaster would usually lead people to "turn" to Yahweh for help, or "return" to Yahweh in repentance, assuming that they had done something to deserve it (the verb שוב [šûb] is used both ways). But that has not happened in the recent experience of Israel, Amos claims. There is no need to try to put these plagues in any chronological framework; they happened so often in the ancient Near East that we can assume the people would remember something corresponding to each of them. These disasters have had no effect on the religious life of the people, however, and so Amos declares that God is about to do something different. Verse 12 is a puzzling sentence,

because of repetition and vagueness, but it is impressive, nonetheless. The first part is incomplete: "Therefore thus I will do to you. . . . " That is probably because Amos here deliberately echoes the traditional oath formula. An oath was a conditional act of self-cursing—e.g., "If I do not do A, then may B be done to me." The danger of self-cursing was such that often B was left unsaid, as in 1 Kgs 2:23: "So may God do to me, and more also" (NRSV). The same expression was used when the curse was directed against someone else, as in Jer 5:13, and that is probably the best explanation of the incomplete sentence here.

Having alluded to the unstated consequence, Amos then repeats it, "because I will do this to you," and calls for a response from Israel: "Prepare to meet your God, O Israel!" (v. 12b). The two relatively common verbs "prepare" (כון kûn) and "meet" (קרא qārā') occur in two contexts that may be instructive: the covenant-making ceremony in Exodus 19 and in war settings. So several interpreters believe v. 12 is a call to repent in preparation for covenant renewal, thus finding a positive element in Amos's message that occurs nowhere else except possibly 5:4, 6, 14-15.[31] Others take this to be an ironic reversal of cultic preparations for the appearance of God in theophany, since this time it will be for judgment rather than for covenant making.[32] The fact that God the warrior plays such a prominent role in the book of Amos supports understanding v. 12 to be a call to prepare to meet the God who is about to engage in holy war against the people.

4:13, His Name Is Yahweh. The passage concludes with an outburst of hymn-like language, found elsewhere in Amos only in 5:8-9 and 9:5-6. The refrain "Yahweh is his name" (author's trans.), which appears in each of these texts, has suggested that they somehow belong together, and some scholars have reconstructed them as stanzas of the same hymn.[33] Such efforts have not been widely accepted, but the three passages certainly are based on a common tradition associ-

31. Hans M. Barstad, *The Religious Polemics of Amos,* VTSup 34 (1984) 37 75.

32. A. Vanlier Hunter, *Seek the Lord! A Study of the Meaning and Function of the Exhortations in Amos, Hosea, Isaiah, Micah, and Zephaniah* (Baltimore: St. Mary's Seminary and University Press, 1982) 115-22; Max Polley, *Amos and the Davidic Empire: A Socio-Historical Approach* (New York: Oxford University Press, 1989) 144-47.

33. J. D. W. Watts, "An Old Hymn Preserved in the Book of Amos," *JNES* 15 (1956) 33-39.

ated with theophanies (cf. Psalm 18; Nahum 1; Habakkuk 3).[34] They have been called doxologies, because their form, using a sequence of participles to describe the activity of God, can also be found in the language of praise in the psalter (cf. Ps 103:3-5). Since they lead up to an identification of the name of this creator God, however, they may also be compared to the elaborate titles given to gods and kings in other ancient Near Eastern cultures.[35]

The brief text alludes to at least three traditions. God's creative activity (13*a, c*) is described in similar terms in Ps 95:4-5 and Job 9:5-10. The theophanic tradition, which speaks of God's appearance on earth in terms of the most terrifying of natural phenomena, is alluded to in 13*d* in words identical to those in the more fully developed theophany in Mic 1:2-4. Verse 13*b* speaks of declaring to humanity "his thoughts," without

being specific about whether they are God's or those of humans. Actually, the word שׂח (*śēaḥ*) almost never means "thought," but almost always means "complaint" (e.g., Job 10:1; 21:4; Pss 64:1[2]; 142:2[3]; Prov 23:29). It is part of the complaint tradition in Israel, and if that is its meaning here, "his" may refer to God and the passage may allude back to 3:8*b*: the word of God through the prophet, telling the people what God has against them. The conclusion—"Yahweh the God of hosts, is his name!"—probably echoes an old confession of faith in Israel, since a similar sentence, "Yahweh is his name," appears in Exod 15:3 (cf. Ps 68:4[5]). Both contexts speak of God the warrior, and I have suggested that is the implication of Amos 4:12. The verse now functions to conclude the passage (vv. 4-13) in this way: Yahweh, creator of heaven and earth, has been responsible for the disasters that have befallen Israel in the past. Yahweh now is about to hold Israel responsible for their behavior, which they have not bothered to examine, feeling well satisfied with their self-assurances that abundant offerings are all God wants of them.

---

34. James L. Crenshaw, "Amos and the Theophanic Tradition," *ZAW* 80 (1968) 203-15.

35. Francis I. Andersen and David Noel Freedman, *Amos,* AB 24A (New York: Doubleday, 1989) 453; Jeff Niehaus, "Amos," in *The Minor Prophets: An Exegetical and Expository Commentary,* Vol. 1: *Hosea, Joel, and Amos,* ed. T. E. McComiskey (Grand Rapids: Baker, 1992) 407.

REFLECTIONS

1. There is a continuing tradition in Scripture that speaks of the Creator as being also a destroyer. The God who made and sustains the world sometimes uses the powers of nature in order to carry out judgment against humans, and in the process nature is destroyed as well. This passage is a part of that tradition. The classic statement of it is the flood story (Genesis 6–8), and it next appears in the accounts of the destruction of Sodom and the plagues in Egypt, both of which are alluded to by Amos. Other prophets projected it into their pictures of future judgment (e.g., Isa 2:6-22; 24:1-13; Jer 4:23-28), and it was used in the same way in apocalyptic literature (cf. the plagues in Rev 6:12–7:3; 8:7–9:21; 16:2-21). But the flood story already has God admit that destroying the wicked and starting over does not work: "I will never again curse the ground because of humankind, for the inclination of the human heart is evil from youth; nor will I ever again destroy every living creature as I have done" (Gen 8:21 NRSV). Beginning with Abraham, God will try another way; but that will be a lengthy process, and Amos seems to have concluded that it is not working either. Amos does not speak of what must be done, but later Ezekiel will do so, as God promises through him that the day will come when God will give humans a new heart and a new spirit (Ezek 36:26).

2. In the meantime, Amos seems to accept a popular theology that disturbs many of us when we encounter it in contemporary life. That is, when something goes wrong, people now, as then, will ask, "Why is God doing this to me?" or "What have I done to deserve this?" The popular theology in every age assumes that all tragedies are acts of God inflicted on the guilty for the punishment of their sin. Old Testament authors already began to free themselves from that reasoning process (Job; Habakkuk; Isaiah 53), and Jesus claimed it as bad theology (Luke 13:1-5; John 9:1-3), but it persists, among Christians and non-Christians. Better theology insists that we cannot deduce sin from suffering. Much suffering *is* caused by sin, of course. Our own sins rebound upon us, and other people commit sins that affect us. There is much suffering, however, that is not punishment for anyone's sin and is simply the way the world works. The famine of which Amos spoke must have affected the poor even more severely than the rich whose sins he condemned, and the pestilence caused the animals it affected to suffer, but not for their sins. Yet Amos claims there is something very wrong with Israel because these disasters occurred and they did not turn (or return) to God. Note that if he is saying "turn" he may be accusing them of not even bothering to pray to God for help in time of need. He may be saying that when disaster strikes, people ordinarily ask what they may have done wrong. Whether he agrees with that theology or not, he knows that is what they do. But the people of Israel are so dense that they do not even behave like normal people anymore, and God has found it impossible to get their attention. As Mays puts it, "The strategy of punishment has misfired so often that it will be broken off and replaced by a different kind of history."[36] But Amos knows the next act will be the death of Israel. He gives us no hint that he knows of resurrection to follow (Ezek 37:1-14).

3. Ascribing such destructive activity to the God whose love for people has always been praised is very disturbing, but the world in which we live functions by means of destruction, decay, and death. The New Testament seldom speaks of nature that way (although consider Rom 8:20), but it does continue to say that God's work with human beings on earth requires destruction and death. This time it is the destruction of the Son of God, and that puts things in a new light. It means that the Creator does not stand outside that circle of life, death, and new life, but participates in it personally.[37]

36. James Luther Mays, *Amos: A Commentary,* OTL (Philadelphia: Westminster, 1969) 78.
37. For a fuller discussion of this subject, see Donald E. Gowan, *Theology in Exodus: Biblical Theology in the Form of a Commentary* (Louisville: Westminster/John Knox Press 1994) chap. 6, "The Divine Destroyer," 127-67.

AMOS 5:1-27

THE DEATH OF ISRAEL

OVERVIEW

Like the rest of the book, chapter 5 concludes with three clearly distinguishable units: vv. 16-17, 18-20, 21-27. Verses 1-15, however, seem to contain a series of fragments whose relationship to one another challenges understanding. Verse 7 seems to have no relationship with either vv. 4-6 or vv. 8-9. The refrain "the LORD is his name" seems to come in the middle of a hymnic section (vv. 8-9), raising the question of whether v. 9 is part of the hymn. Verse 10 begins with the indefinite subject "they" (not "you," NIV). There are introductory formulas in vv. 1, 3-4, and 16, leaving vv. 7-15 without the usual marks prophetic books use to distinguish units of speech. It appears that vv. 4-6 and vv. 14-15 belong together, but if they do, why were they separated?

Many scholars now seem satisfied with the discovery of a chiastic structure (including vv. 16-17):

A vv. 1-3 Lament
  B vv. 4-6 Exhortation
    C v. 7 Justice
      D vv. 8-9 "The LORD is his name"
    C′ vv. 10-12 (and 13?) Justice
  B′ vv. 14-15 Exhortation
A′ vv. 16-17 Lament[38]

There is evidence for a pattern here, but the proposed outline scarcely solves all the problems of vv. 1-17. The two lines of v. 7 can hardly be said to balance the twelve lines of vv. 10-12, and if v. 13 is a wisdom saying, the pattern does not

account for it. But there are other matters the proponents of the chiastic explanation do not discuss. What does the pattern mean? What could anyone have been trying to say by organizing material this way? It puts the emphasis on "the LORD is his name," but how is that a comment on vv. 1-3, 7, 10-17, which deal with Israel? If vv. 4-6 and 14-15 were originally a unit, why would someone break it up this way unless he were a scribe more interested in patterns than in meaning? That question could be answered by assuming that these verses were in fact originally separate units, but the present isolation of v. 7 cannot easily be accounted for. Surely the prophet or those close to the prophet would not have broken up meaningful speech units, sacrificing meaning over structure.

Other explanations include supposing a series of scribal errors, but most scholars think this calls for too many errors to account for such disruption of continuity. To think of a gradual accumulation of materials in the redaction process equally leaves unanswered questions.[39] If vv. 14-15 are a later work, patterned after vv. 4-6, why would they have been inserted where they are instead of immediately after v. 6? And why would a redactor choose the present location for vv. 8-9, assuming the same person inserted the hymnic materials of 4:13 and 9:5-6 at climactic points in the book?

In the commentary some tentative suggestions will be made about vv. 7 and 13, which if correct would make the section read more smoothly; but like all other efforts there can be no certainty about them. Careful study does not significantly modify the impression that at this point in the

38. See, e.g., J. de Waard, "The Chiastic Structure of Amos V 1-17," *VT* 27 (1977) 170-77; W. A. Smalley, "Recursion Patterns and the Sectioning of Amos," *BT* 30 (1979) 118-27; N. J. Tromp, "Amos V 1-17. Towards a Stylistic and Rhetorical Analysis," *OTS* 23 (1984) 56-84. Cf. Gary V. Smith, *Amos: A Commentary* (Grand Rapids: Zondervan, 1989) 158-59; Shalom Paul, *Amos,* Hermeneia (Philadelphia: Fortress, 1991) 158-59.

39. H. W. Wolff (*Joel and Amos,* Hermeneia [Philadelphia: Fortress, 1977] 231-35) and R. B. Coote (*Amos Among the Prophets: Composition and Theology* [Philadelphia: Fortress, 1981] 1-10) provide good examples of this approach. But note Claus Westermann, "Amos 5,4-6. 14. 15: Ihr Werdet Leben!" in *Ertrage des Forschung am Alten Testament: Gesammelte Studien III* (Munchen: Kaiser Verlag, 1984) 116.

book several brief prophetic sayings have been gathered, perhaps loosely arranged in chiastic form for want of knowing what else to do with them.

There is a certain thematic unity in the chapter, however, which may account for the decision to gather these brief oracles here, even though they did not originally belong together. The atmosphere of death pervades the chapter, from the funeral song of vv. 1-2 through the description of community-wide mourning in vv. 16-17, to the cry of grief (הוי *hôy*, translated "woe" or "alas," v. 18). The specific form of death Israel will take—exile—is introduced in vv. 5 and 27.

The second prominent theme is justice. It is introduced in v. 7, runs right through vv. 10-15, and forms the great climax to vv. 21-24. Although Amos usually speaks in negative terms of what Israel has done wrong, in this chapter we find positive words about what God requires (vv. 4, 6, 14-15, 24), and this is explicitly defined as justice.

Because of the difficulties of structure and consistency of themes in Amos 5, the ensuing commentary will deal with short units, then the reflections at 5:21-27 will offer a single essay on the theology that is most prominent in this chapter.

AMOS 5:1-2, A FUNERAL SONG

NIV

5 Hear this word, O house of Israel, this lament I take up concerning you:

2 "Fallen is Virgin Israel,
    never to rise again,
deserted in her own land,
    with no one to lift her up."

NRSV

5 Hear this word that I take up over you in lamentation, O house of Israel:

2 Fallen, no more to rise,
    is maiden Israel;
forsaken on her land,
    with no one to raise her up.

COMMENTARY

Since the passage is not introduced as a word of Yahweh, perhaps it should be taken as the prophet's lament over Israel. In many places in the prophetic books, no sharp distinction is made between the word of the prophet and the word of the Lord, so it is not inappropriate to think of this song as being also God's lament (cf. Isa 65:1-2; Ezek 18:31*b*; Hos 11:8). It is one of Amos's creatively disturbing uses of material familiar to his listeners. Now he sings a funeral song before the subject has died, and he mourns not the death of an individual but the death of the nation Israel. This song is introduced by the technical term קינה (*qînâ*), used in Israel to refer to dirges (translated here "lamentation"), so we know that v. 2 is to be read as a funeral song. In the song, Amos has made a new use of two of the aspects of death that produced the most intense grief in Israel.

A failure to take seriously enough Amos's own identification of the genre ("funeral song") has led to some painfully literal efforts to explain why Israel is compared with a virgin. The point of the song has nothing to do with qualities that might be associated with a virgin's life; it speaks of the death of a virgin, and that is why Amos makes the comparison. When Jephthah's daughter accepted her father's foolish vow to sacrifice the first living thing to greet him, she asked only to be given time to "bewail her virginity" (Judg 11:37 NRSV). The problem was that she had no children. In ancient Israel, death was not thought of as any great tragedy if one had lived a long life and would leave children behind, for one truly lived on in them.[40] But to die childless meant one

40. R. Martin-Achard, *From Death to Life: A Study of the Development of the Doctrine of Resurrection in the Old Testament* (Edinburgh: Oliver & Boyd, 1960) 16-47.

was really dead. So the pitiful story was preserved of Absalom's construction of a monument to bear his name after him, since his children had apparently died before him (2 Sam 14:27; 18:18). Amos now says that the impending death of Israel is like the death of a virgin, such as Jephthah's daughter: an occasion for the most intense grief.

"Fallen" (נפלה *nāpělâ*) is a term used of death in other dirges (2 Sam 1:19, 25, 27; Isa 14:12; cf. Ezek 29:5; 39:4-5), and the term translated "forsaken on her land" (נטשה על־אדמתה *niṭṭěšâ 'al-'ādmātāh*) also occurs in Ezekiel's description of a body left unburied (Ezek 29:5; 31:12; 32:4). This is the second aspect of death that would produce great distress in Israel. For a body to be left lying in the field unburied was shocking (Deut 28:26; 2 Kgs 9:10; Ps 79:2-3; Eccl 6:3; Jer 8:1-2; 14:16; 16:4, 6; 25:33), and extreme measures might be called for to ensure that this did not happen to a member of one's community (1 Sam 31:11-13; 2 Sam 21:7-14; Tob 1:16-20; 2:3-10). Here Amos has intensified the shock of mourning the death of the nation before it has happened by laying before them the picture of a childless young woman, dead and lying unburied on her land. This verse, and vv. 18-20, are the clearest reflections in the book of how Amos may have been affected by the message he had to give. He was not one of those who enjoys condemning others. These are his cries of grief. A bit later, Hosea 11 will speak of God's own lament over the rebellions of his adopted son. Perhaps Amos, less explicitly, also reflects God's grief. (See Reflections at 5:21-27.)

AMOS 5:3, THE REMNANT DEFINED AGAIN

NIV	NRSV

[3]This is what the Sovereign LORD says:
"The city that marches out a thousand strong
    for Israel
  will have only a hundred left;
the town that marches out a hundred strong
  will have only ten left."
	[3] For thus says the Lord GOD:
	The city that marched out a thousand
	  shall have a hundred left,
	and that which marched out a hundred
	  shall have ten left.[a]
	
	[a] Heb adds *to the house of Israel*

COMMENTARY

Most commentators take this verse to be the second stanza of the dirge, although it has a new introductory formula, it does not continue the imagery of v. 2, it is not a lament, and the verbs are imperfect rather than perfect. It is not quite epigrammatic in character (like 3:2), but reminds us of other short, potent sayings that probably were preserved because they were memorable in themselves. Then they were included in the collection of Amos's words at what seemed to be appropriate places (cf. 1:2; 3:12; 6:8; perhaps 6:9-10). Like 3:12, it anticipates the notion that even in defeat there will be survivors, but its insistence that no more than 10 percent of any army will be left once again defines "remnant" solely as a threat. The MT adds "for the house of Israel" at the end of the verse. The NRSV has dropped that phrase as a probable repetition from v. 4a; the NIV has moved it to an earlier point in the verse. (See Reflections at 5:21-27.)

AMOS 5:4-6, THE DEATH OF THE SANCTUARIES

[4]This is what the LORD says to the house of Israel:

"Seek me and live;
[5] do not seek Bethel,
do not go to Gilgal,
    do not journey to Beersheba.
For Gilgal will surely go into exile,
    and Bethel will be reduced to nothing.[a]"
[6]Seek the LORD and live,
    or he will sweep through the house of Joseph
        like a fire;
it will devour,
    and Bethel will have no one to quench it.

[a]5 Or grief; or wickedness; Hebrew aven, a reference to Beth Aven (a derogatory name for Bethel)

[4] For thus says the LORD to the house of Israel:
    Seek me and live;
[5]   but do not seek Bethel,
    and do not enter into Gilgal
        or cross over to Beer-sheba;
    for Gilgal shall surely go into exile,
        and Bethel shall come to nothing.

[6] Seek the LORD and live,
        or he will break out against the house of
            Joseph like fire,
        and it will devour Bethel, with no one to
            quench it.

COMMENTARY

The promise that persons who seek Yahweh will live seems to be the first suggestion in Amos that there is a chance to avert the judgment that has been presented as inevitable up until now. Is this a significant qualification of the message of the rest of the book? Those who insist that Amos must have been a preacher of repentance claim to find it here and in vv. 14-15, but there is actually little that is positive in vv. 5-6. The point of this passage is that the great sanctuaries are going to be destroyed. The sentence "Seek me and live" (v. 4) appears to be an ironic use of cultic language (cf. Pss 24:6; 27:8; 34:10[11]), quoting the promise one would expect to hear when coming to the sanctuaries, but denying that God will henceforth be found there. Amos does not deny that the people should seek Yahweh or that truly seeking Yahweh will bring the gift of life, but everything he says about worship denies that they have truly been seeking God.[41] Amos will define what he means by seeking God in vv. 15 and 24. The promise of life was a potent one, for in Hebrew the word "life" (חי ḥay) did not mean

just "existence," but the possession of full vitality, health, and even reputation and prosperity.[42] The quotation of the cultic promise "Seek me and live" is more than ironic in a chapter whose main theme is death. It has an almost wistful tone, for Amos knows he is addressing a dying people who have forgotten how to seek the Lord.

The threat of exile reappears here in a puzzling context for readers of English translations, for how could a place, Gilgal, "go into exile" (גלה gālâ)? The expression is not to be taken literally, for Amos is making a play on words, using both the infinitive absolute (גלה gālōh) and the imperfect (יגלה yigleh) of the root גלה glh to echo the sound of Gilgal (גלגל gilgāl). At this point, "exile" is simply another word for death, the destruction of the great sanctuaries. (For the question of whether this conditional promise of life, in the midst of a chapter that largely deals with death, can be taken as consistent with the message of the rest of the book, see Commentary on 5:14-15. See Reflections at 5:21-27.)

41. "Seeking the Lord" may mean (1) asking for a message from God (Gen 25:22; 1 Sam 9:9; 2 Kgs 3:11); (2) going to a sanctuary to worship (Deut 12:5; Hos 5:6); or (3) following the moral requirements of Yahwism (Pss 14:2; 24:3-6; Hos 10:12).

42. See O. Piper, "Life," in The Interpreter's Dictionary of the Bible (IDB), 4 vols. (Nashville: Abingdon, 1962) 4:124-26; H. Ringgren, "Chayah," TDOT 4:324-44.

AMOS 5:7, NO JUSTICE . . .

NIV	NRSV
7You who turn justice into bitterness and cast righteousness to the ground	7 Ah, you that turn justice to wormwood, and bring righteousness to the ground!

COMMENTARY

This verse is not written in the second person, as the NRSV and the NIV translate it. Nor does it have a word corresponding to the "Ah" of the NRSV. Literally, the Hebrew reads, "Those who turn justice to wormwood and cast down righteousness to earth." It seems to call for a main clause, either preceding or following it. Most commentators connect it with v. 10, which then requires an explanation of how vv. 8-9 have come to be inserted into the middle of a sentence. Some supply the exclamation הוי (hôy), which does occur in 5:18, and this accounts for the "Ah" of NRSV. Others connect v. 7 with v. 6, which in Hebrew ends with "Bethel," thus adding an explicit definition of the people in Bethel who are responsible for its coming destruction. Although not widely accepted, this seems to be the simplest explanation of the location of v. 7.[43]

It introduces two key words for this chapter: "justice" (משפט mišpāṭ) and "righteousness" (צדקה ṣĕdāqâ). They occur together here and in 5:24 and 6:12 (mišpāṭ occurs alone in 5:15). "Righteousness" in this context refers to those standards for what is "right" by which God has instructed Israel how to live. "Justice" is then the realization of those standards of life.[44] One of Amos's special concerns is justice in what we would call the court system, as vv. 10-12 make clear.

Wormwood is a shrub that produces a bitter liquid used as a flavoring in absinthe and vermouth. Its English name comes from its use as a vermifuge and insecticide, but the Old Testament never refers to its useful qualities, using it always as a metaphor for bitterness. (See Reflections at 5:21-27.)

43. Richard S. Cripps, *A Critical and Exegetical Commentary on the Book of Amos,* 2nd ed. (London: SPCK, 1955) 183. Mark Daniel Carroll, *Contexts for Amos: Prophetic Poetics in Latin American Perspective,* JSOTSup 132 (Sheffield: Sheffield Academic, 1992) 228; Klaus Koch, "Die Rolle der hymnischen Abschnitte in der Komposition des Amos-Buches," *ZAW* 86 (1974) 504-37.

44. Pietro Bovati, *Re-Establishing Justice: Legal Terms, Concepts, and Procedures in the Hebrew Bible,* JSOTSup 105 (JSOT, 1994); Hemchand Gossai, *Justice, Righteousness and the Social Critique of the Eighth-Century Prophets* (New York: Peter Lang, 1993); Moshe Weinfeld, *Social Justice in Ancient Israel and in the Ancient Near East* (Minneapolis: Fortress, 1995).

AMOS 5:8-9, HIS NAME IS YAHWEH

NIV	NRSV
8(he who made the Pleiades and Orion, who turns blackness into dawn and darkens day into night, who calls for the waters of the sea and pours them out over the face of the land— the LORD is his name— 9he flashes destruction on the stronghold and brings the fortified city to ruin),	8 The one who made the Pleiades and Orion, and turns deep darkness into the morning, and darkens the day into night, who calls for the waters of the sea, and pours them out on the surface of the earth, the LORD is his name, 9 who makes destruction flash out against the strong, so that destruction comes upon the fortress.

COMMENTARY

This is the second of three passages in Amos that use hymnic language to speak of Yahweh's activity as creator (4:13; 9:5-6). The other two form appropriate conclusions to the sections that precede them, but only a few readers can see any natural continuity between 5:7 and 5:8-9. There is a coincidence of verbs, with הפך (hāpak, "turn") used in the first line of v. 7 and the second line of v. 8, but no meaning can be derived from that usage. The best we can make of the location of this verse is to think that whoever put it in its place in v. 8 saw v. 7 as an identification of those people who stand under judgment. Then they were reminded of the cosmic power of the judge who will pronounce the sentence in vv. 10-12 (13?).

The poem moves from creation to destruction: Yahweh is the maker of the two great constellations and the master of time who makes night and day succeed each other. But calling for the waters of the sea and pouring them out on the surface of the earth hardly sounds like the normal, life-giving gift of rain. It sounds, rather, like the flood of Genesis 6–8, and introduces the transition to v. 9, which speaks of God's ability to lay low the mightiest of human works. (See Reflections at 5:21-27.)

AMOS 5:10-13, NO JUSTICE IN THE GATE

NIV

[10]you hate the one who reproves in court
    and despise him who tells the truth.

[11]You trample on the poor
    and force him to give you grain.
Therefore, though you have built stone
      mansions,
    you will not live in them;
though you have planted lush vineyards,
    you will not drink their wine.
[12]For I know how many are your offenses
    and how great your sins.

You oppress the righteous and take bribes
    and you deprive the poor of justice in the
      courts.
[13]Therefore the prudent man keeps quiet in such
      times,
    for the times are evil.

NRSV

[10] They hate the one who reproves in the gate,
    and they abhor the one who speaks the
      truth.
[11] Therefore because you trample on the poor
    and take from them levies of grain,
you have built houses of hewn stone,
    but you shall not live in them;
you have planted pleasant vineyards,
    but you shall not drink their wine.
[12] For I know how many are your transgressions,
    and how great are your sins—
you who afflict the righteous, who take a bribe,
    and push aside the needy in the gate.
[13] Therefore the prudent will keep silent in such
      a time;
    for it is an evil time.

COMMENTARY

Verse 11 is the only certain example of a reason/announcement oracle in chap. 5. Its strict structure is more accurately represented in the NRSV than in the NIV. There are several possible explanations of vv. 10 and 12. They may both be expansions of the reason in v. 11, for similar elaborations of the simple form are found elsewhere. If v. 7 belongs with vv. 4-6, then v. 10

is best understood as such an expansion. If v. 13 is an isolated wisdom saying, as all translations represent it, then v. 12 should also be taken as an addition to the reason. But there is another possible way of reading v. 13 that resolves the mystery of the supposed wisdom saying and also simplifies the structure. Instead of being translated "prudent," the Hebrew word (משכיל *maśkîl*) may mean "prosperous" or "successful" (as in Deut 29:9[8]; Josh 1:7-8; 1 Sam 18:5, 14; 1 Kgs 2:3; 2 Kgs 18:7; Prov 17:8; Jer 20:11; 23:5). The "silence" referred to may be the silence of death (Jer 6:2; 47:5; 48:2; 49:26; 50:30; Ezek 27:32; Zeph 1:11), so it is possible to read vv. 12-13 as a well-structured reason/announcement oracle, with v. 13 saying, "Therefore, the prosperous will be silent (in death) at that time, for it is a time of disaster."[45] If we must read it as the standard translations have always rendered it, however, then it appears to be an ironic comment on the hopelessness of attempting to do anything about injustice in the courts. Perhaps it is even Amos's bitter comment about himself: If he were wiser, he would not be saying these things!

Justice in the gate is the issue throughout this passage. The city gate was the site of most public activity during the day, and it was there that anyone with a complaint could expect to find the elders of the community, who acted as judges because of their knowledge of customary law.[46] The "reprover" who speaks the truth (v. 10) was probably someone who attempted to uphold the cause of the poor person who had no influence in the community when he tried to bring a case against a rich and prominent citizen. Amos knows that too many of the wealthy possess their houses of hewn stone (instead of uncut field stone, used for most Israelite buildings) and their vineyards (v. 11) because of their deliberate mistreatment of their poorer neighbors, perhaps through unfair taxation ("levies of grain") and even bribery, when the influence of status itself was not sufficient. The law of Yahweh, which emphasizes the fair treatment of everyone in the courts (cf. Exod 23:1-3, 6-8), is no hindrance to those who see a chance to get rich at the expense of their neighbors. (See Reflections at 5:21-27.)

45. See J. J. Jackson, "Amos 5,13 Contextually Understood," *ZAW* 98 (1986) 434-35; G. V. Smith, "Amos 5:13—The Deadly Silence of the Prosperous," *JBL* 107 (1988) 289-91; this interpretation is accepted also by Carroll, *Contexts for Amos,* 228.

46. See R. de Vaux, *Ancient Israel: Its Life and Institutions* (New York: McGraw-Hill, 1961) 143-63; H. J. Boecker, *Law and the Administration of Justice in the Old Testament and Ancient East* (Minneapolis: Augsburg, 1980) 21-52.

AMOS 5:14-15, IS THERE A CHANCE?

NIV	NRSV

[14]Seek good, not evil,
    that you may live.
Then the LORD God Almighty will be with you,
    just as you say he is.
[15]Hate evil, love good;
    maintain justice in the courts.
Perhaps the LORD God Almighty will have mercy
    on the remnant of Joseph.
	[14] Seek good and not evil,
	    that you may live;
	and so the LORD, the God of hosts, will be with
	    you,
	    just as you have said.
	[15] Hate evil and love good,
	    and establish justice in the gate;
	it may be that the LORD, the God of hosts,
	    will be gracious to the remnant of Joseph.

COMMENTARY

These verses seem to be located at the appropriate point in the chapter, no matter what their earlier history (or authorship) may have been, for

they now provide a rather narrow and very explicit definition of what is good—namely, establishing justice in the gate. The verbs "seek" (דרש

dāraš) and "live" (חיה *ḥāyâ*) recall vv. 4-6, but otherwise the subject matter is entirely different—the courts, not the sanctuaries. The imperative to seek good and not evil is paralleled by the imperatives "hate evil and love good." The verbs "love" (אהב *'āhab*) and "hate" (שׂנא *śānē'*) in Hebrew often refer very specifically to decisions and not merely to feelings. To love can mean to choose (Prov 8:36; 12:1; Mic 3:2; 6:8; Zech 8:19), and to hate can mean to reject (Mal 1:2-3), so the imperatives call for action and not merely attitude.

The complacency of the audience is referred to here, a theme that will be elaborated in chap. 6. The people have been comfortable with their self-assurance, "God is with us." This was a potent promise, which typically appears in the OT as God's assurance to leaders in times of danger or uncertainty.[47] God could say, "I will be with you," but only a few times do we find the people confidently saying, "God is with us," as a daily certainty (see Pss 23:4; 46:7, 11[8, 12], speaking of times of danger). This passage makes it a conditional promise, not a matter of certainty at all for the present, and potential only if drastic changes are made.

The potential of God's being with them is not very strong, according to v. 15. The "it may be so" of v. 14 (NIV, "Then"; NRSV, "and so") is paralleled by "perhaps"/"it may be" in v. 15, and no future for the whole people of Israel is envisioned even then. Judgment is still inevitable; there is a faint hope for no more than a remnant, and the pitiful condition of the remnant has

been defined in 3:12 and 5:3. But another of the potent promissory words of the OT does appear here: חנן (*ḥānan*), meaning "to be gracious"/ "compassionate," a word that occurs only here in Amos. Could this conditional promise have come from Amos, whose message elsewhere contains no promises for the immediate future?[48] Many interpreters find it difficult to ascribe it to him, and it certainly is distinct from everything else in the book; but one cannot call its message completely contradictory to the rest. Offering the promise to no more than a remnant fits what is said elsewhere (3:12; 5:3; 9:8). There are no guarantees; the best that can be said is "perhaps." Why would even that be said? Perhaps because it is good Israelite theology, so it cannot be called out of place even in a book with as little hope as this one. God's freedom to be gracious was celebrated, even though it did not logically fit with the equal insistence on God's justice (Exod 33:19; 34:6-7; Joel 2:12-14; Jonah 4:2). Israel stands under judgment, but Yahweh is noted for willingness to avert punishment even when it is thoroughly deserved (Exod 32:7-14; Ps 103:6-14). This passage may show that Amos, like others, realized that God is free to change, for God's own reasons (cf. 2 Sam 12:22; Joel 2:14; Zeph 2:3). (See Reflections at 5:21-27.)

48. Two contrary approaches to interpreting this verse: (1) Assuming that the prophets must have been preachers of repentance, this verse is taken as Amos's real message, and all the unconditional announcements of doom must then in truth be conditional. (2) Assuming that Amos was a judgment prophet, without qualification, then 5:4-6, 14-15 could not be from him. For a full discussion, see A. Vanlier Hunter, *Seek the Lord! A Study of the Meaning and Function of the Exhortations in Amos, Hosea, Isaiah, Micah, and Zephaniah* (Baltimore: St. Mary's Seminary and University Press, 1982) 56-105.

47. Donald E. Gowan, *Theology in Exodus: Biblical Theology in the Form of a Commentary* (Louisville: Westminster/John Knox Press 1994) chap. 3, "I Will Be with You," 54-75.

AMOS 5:16-17, MOURNING IN THE STREETS

NIV

¹⁶Therefore this is what the Lord, the LORD God Almighty, says:

"There will be wailing in all the streets
and cries of anguish in every public square.
The farmers will be summoned to weep
and the mourners to wail.

NRSV

¹⁶ Therefore thus says the LORD, the God of hosts, the Lord:

In all the squares there shall be wailing;
and in all the streets they shall say, "Alas! alas!"
They shall call the farmers to mourning,

NIV

NIV

¹⁷There will be wailing in all the vineyards,
for I will pass through your midst,"
says the LORD.

NRSV

and those skilled in lamentation, to wailing;
¹⁷ in all the vineyards there shall be wailing,
for I will pass through the midst of you,
says the LORD.

COMMENTARY

This section is introduced as a word of the Lord, but its form is unusual, for it describes what the near future will be like. Similar pictures of public lamentation appear in Isa 15:3; 16:10; Jer 48:38; and especially Jer 9:17-22. Amos can see a time when death will have affected every part of the community, so that all that can be heard is wailing and the cry of grief. The lamentation will begin on the day when God passes through their midst, a somewhat puzzling statement, since elsewhere in the book judgment is spoken of as God's not

passing by them (Amos 7:8; 8:2). The later references seem to be related to concepts of God's presence of blessing in the midst of the people, but v. 17 is more like the ominous "meeting" with God in 4:12. This may be a reversal of another originally positive tradition, for in Exod 12:12, 23 God is said to have "passed through" Egypt in order to destroy all the firstborn, except those of Israel (cf. Ezek 9:5). (See Reflections at 5:21-27.)

AMOS 5:18-20, DARKNESS, NOT LIGHT

NIV

¹⁸Woe to you who long
for the day of the LORD!
Why do you long for the day of the LORD?
That day will be darkness, not light.
¹⁹It will be as though a man fled from a lion
only to meet a bear,
as though he entered his house
and rested his hand on the wall
only to have a snake bite him.
²⁰Will not the day of the LORD be darkness, not light—
pitch-dark, without a ray of brightness?

NRSV

¹⁸ Alas for you who desire the day of the LORD!
Why do you want the day of the LORD?
It is darkness, not light;
¹⁹ as if someone fled from a lion,
and was met by a bear;
or went into the house and rested a hand
against the wall,
and was bitten by a snake.
²⁰ Is not the day of the LORD darkness, not light,
and gloom with no brightness in it?

COMMENTARY

The funereal atmosphere continues in this section, for careful studies of the outcry (NIV, "Woe"; NRSV, "Alas" [הוי hôy]) have shown that it is typically an exclamation of a grieving person.[49] The

word hôy is close in sound to the outcry in v. 16, and it seems proper to understand vv. 18-20 as the prophet's lamentation over the complacency of those who assume that only good can

---

49. R. J. Clifford, "The Use of hôy in the Prophets," *CBQ* 28 (1966) 458-64; G. Wanke, "'wy und hwy," *ZAW* 78 (1966) 215-18; W. Janzen, *Mourning Cry and Woe Oracle,* BZAW 125 (Berlin: W. de Gruyter, 1972); H.-J. Kraus, "hoj als prophetische Leichenklage uber das eigene Volk im 8. Jahrhundert," *ZAW* 85 (1973) 15-46; H.-J. Zobel, "hoy," *TDOT* 3 (1978)

359-64. Recent claims that it is merely a cry to get attention scarcely explain the use of this word in mourning the dead and the fact that it is usually followed by a third-person reference. The original sense of grief has been lost, however, in some of its latest uses (Isa 55:1; Zech 2:6-7).

come to them, since they are the people of Yahweh (cf. v. 14*b*). The same word is used of the complacent people in 6:1. The "day of Yahweh," which they desire, has been widely discussed, with little agreement as to the origin of the term or its meaning for Amos's audience. It has been associated with the old concept of holy war, hence as a reference to Yahweh's victories in battle. Some scholars have related it to the epiphany of Yahweh in the autumn New Year's festival. Others have denied that it would have been recognized as a technical term of any sort in Amos's time.[50] But certainly Amos is using a term his audience knows, or he could not call it

something they desired. The imagery of light makes it clear that the "day" was a time when Yahweh appeared to bless the people in some way. Its later uses in the prophets are in highly warlike contexts (e.g., Isa 13:6, 9; Jer 46:10; Ezek 13:5; 30:3), so it seems most likely that the "day" was anticipated as a time when Yahweh would once again defeat Israel's enemies in battle. Amos's reversal of the word's meaning here thus recalls his similar reversal of the sense of the old holy war oracles in chaps. 1–2. The change from light to darkness is then vigorously illustrated by two vignettes on the theme "out of the frying pan, into the fire." (See Reflections at 5:21-27.)

50. For its use as an image of holy war, see: J. M. P. Smith, "The Day of Jahweh," *AJT* 5 (1901) 505-33; Gerhard von Rad, "The Origin of the Concept of the Day of Yahweh," *JSS* 4 (1959) 97-108. For it uses as an image of the New Year's festival, see: S. Mowinckel, *Psalmenstudien: Das*

Thronebesteigungsfest Jahwas und der Ursprung der Eschatologie (Kristiania: Dybwad, 1922) II:248, 272, 318-19. For it use as a non-technical term, see: M. Weiss, "The Origin of the 'Day of the Lord' Reconsidered," *HUCA* 37 (1966) 29-60.

AMOS 5:21-27, WHAT DOES GOD REQUIRE?

NIV

21"I hate, I despise your religious feasts;
    I cannot stand your assemblies.
22Even though you bring me burnt offerings and
        grain offerings,
    I will not accept them.
Though you bring choice fellowship offerings,*a*
    I will have no regard for them.
23Away with the noise of your songs!
    I will not listen to the music of your harps.
24But let justice roll on like a river,
    righteousness like a never-failing stream!

25"Did you bring me sacrifices and offerings
    forty years in the desert, O house of Israel?
26You have lifted up the shrine of your king,
    the pedestal of your idols,
    the star of your god*b*—
    which you made for yourselves.
27Therefore I will send you into exile beyond
        Damascus,"
    says the LORD, whose name is God Almighty.

a22 Traditionally peace offerings   *b26 Or* lifted up Sakkuth your
king / and Kaiwan your idols, / your star-gods; *Septuagint* lifted up
the shrine of Molech / and the star of your god Rephan, / their idols

NRSV

21 I hate, I despise your festivals,
    and I take no delight in your solemn
        assemblies.
22 Even though you offer me your burnt offerings
        and grain offerings,
    I will not accept them;
and the offerings of well-being of your fatted
        animals
    I will not look upon.
23 Take away from me the noise of your songs;
    I will not listen to the melody of your harps.
24 But let justice roll down like waters,
    and righteousness like an ever-flowing
        stream.

25Did you bring to me sacrifices and offerings
the forty years in the wilderness, O house of
Israel? 26You shall take up Sakkuth your king, and
Kaiwan your star-god, your images,*a* which you
made for yourselves; 27therefore I will take you
into exile beyond Damascus, says the LORD, whose
name is the God of hosts.

a Heb your images, your star-god

COMMENTARY

Amos has said that frequenting the sanctuaries is equivalent to rebellion against God and seems to have ridiculed the offering of sacrifice (4:4-5). He has also claimed that God is not to be found at Bethel, Gilgal, or Beersheba (5:4-5). Now comes a fierce divine rejection of the way the Israelites have been worshiping. God wants no part of their holy days, of their offerings, or even of their hymns of praise. God wants justice and righteousness.

Is the subject of the passage what is wrong with worship? It was interpreted that way for many years, along with similar texts in Isa 1:10-17; Jer 7:21-23; Hos 6:6; and Mic 6:6-8. It was said that the prophets condemned ritual in favor of pure, spiritual worship, but that interpretation stumbles over the fact that Isaiah also says that God even refuses to hear the prayers of his contemporaries. There is general agreement now that the point of these passages is not what is wrong with worship, but what is wrong with the worshipers. "Let justice roll down like waters" (v. 24) and the comparable conclusions in the other prophets are statements of the preconditions for acceptable worship. Amos does not intend to replace ritual with social action. Rather, what goes on in society must correspond to what is said and done in worship. Amos tells us that God does not accept the worship of those who show no interest in justice in their daily lives.

Once again his vigorous use of imagery appears. Many of the wadis in Israel are dry most of the year, and when it rains they are subject to flash flooding. The wadis are no metaphor to use for justice in the gate, then. Justice should be like the constant streams whose life-giving water can be depended on every day of the year. The verb in v. 24 is a jussive—i.e., it has the force of an impersonal command. No promise, however conditional, is attached to it. It stands, near the very middle of the book, as God's unconditional requirement, if life is to continue. To extend Amos's metaphor, since Israel has failed to maintain justice, it will be the torrent in which they will drown (cf. 5:8*b*).

The last three verses of the chapter are fraught with problems. Some scholars think v. 26 belongs with v. 25; others read it with v. 27. The tense of the verb in v. 26 has been taken as past, present, or future; and v. 27 has been read as both past and future. If the question in v. 25 calls for a negative answer (and it is hard to read it otherwise), how can that be correlated with the Pentateuch, which speaks of many sacrifices in the wilderness? Harper records eight different explanations of the verse. The translation of v. 26 remains uncertain, especially the translation of סכות (*sikkût*) and כיון (*kiyyûn*). Harper lists six different interpretations of this verse.[51]

Since Jer 7:21-22 also seems to speak of wilderness as a time without sacrifice, there may have been an alternate wilderness tradition in Israel, now preserved in only these two places. Amos and Jeremiah may have been referring to a belief that the sacrificial cult was largely of Canaanite origin, as in fact seems to be true. An alternate reading takes the question to mean, "Was it only sacrifice that you brought me . . . ?"

The ancient versions all translate v. 26 in the past tense (cf. Acts 7:42-43), but there is no other hint in the OT that Israel remembered having practiced this kind of idolatry in the wilderness. It might refer instead to the immediate past, to idolatry in Samaria, and this is probably what the NIV intends. Other interpreters take it as an interrogative past tense, continuing the rhetorical question of v. 25 and expecting a negative answer: "Did you lift up . . . ?" But most translators connect it instead with v. 27, making it a reference to the future, to carrying idols with them into exile. The two most commonly suggested renderings of the words *sikkût* and *kiyyûn* are represented by the NRSV and the NIV translations. The NIV takes the words to be derivatives of common Hebrew nouns, while the NRSV considers them to be distorted forms of the names of Assyrian astral deities. If "Sakkuth" and "Kaiwan" are the correct readings, this raises the question of how early the northern kingdom became acquainted with those cults. Neither approach solves all the problems of this verse, which remains the most difficult one in the book of Amos.

The chapter concludes with the explicit threat

---

51. W. R. Harper, *A Critical and Exegetical Commentary on Amos and Hosea*, ICC (Edinburgh: T. & T. Clark, 1905) 136-37.

of exile. "Beyond Damascus" need not be taken as a specific reference to Assyria as the enemy, since Assyria is never mentioned elsewhere in the book. At that time, "beyond Damascus" was just the most likely direction for a deportation from the northern kingdom to take place.

REFLECTIONS

By this point in the book it has become clear that Amos expects the disaster that God will bring upon Israel in the near future to be so extensive that Amos must speak of the nation's death. It is a terrible thought. Consider any of the small nations of the world today, and imagine being a citizen of a neighboring country and going to that small nation to inform its people that soon they would no longer exist as a nation. Worse yet, imagine trying to convince them that this was the will of their god. How could such destruction and death be the will of any god? That is the theological problem Amos and the other pre-exilic prophets created for their people, and the problem remains for us. Let us try to read Amos this way, and then let the rest of Scripture add something to Amos.

Amos was convinced that Israel soon would fall prey to an invader. Israelite theology had taught him to see the hand of God in every event, but he might have theologized that in two different ways. The invader (and Amos does not seem to know it will be Assyria) might be seen as the enemy of God and God's people, and Amos might have spoken of God's forthcoming judgment of them, as later prophets did in their oracles against the nations (e.g., Isa 37:22-29; Jeremiah 50–51; Ezekiel 25). Instead, Amos was inspired to recognize that the daily life of Israel had completely given up the ethical standards of the Yahwistic religion. Whether he thought in terms of "covenant theology" or not, he clearly saw the treatment of the poor in Israel as a fundamental rejection of the relationship that Yahweh had established with Israel, which required obedience not only in worship but also in the maintenance of a just society. We might describe his evaluation in this way: It was an unhealthy society, so sick it could not survive much longer. But Amos spoke in terms of God's activity in history. The death of Israel would not be from "natural causes"; it would be God's work. We must not then conclude that God prefers to work via killing and burning.[52] God allows human beings to chart their own courses, then finds ways to work through, or in spite of, what they do. The Assyrians would have come against Israel anyway, for their own reasons, and the later prophets will insist that God judges the Assyrians for their cruelty, but God has also found ways to accomplish the divine purpose through even such sinful acts. Amos shows no indication that he knows what that ultimate purpose is (unless 9:15-16 is a hint of it). He speaks of death, but later prophets saw beyond that to new life to be created by God even out of the turmoil and agony of empire building in the ancient Near East.

1. *The Meaning of Exile.* Theological reflection on the place the exiling of God's people plays in the message of the whole Bible leads to conclusions that reach far beyond disasters that occurred in the eighth and sixth centuries BCE. Amos dealt with more than an eighth-century crisis. His message is in continuity with the New Testament's depiction of the predicament of humanity as a whole, at least as Paul described it. At first, Israel's loss of the promised land does not appear to be a subject of any interest to New Testament writers, but there is a trajectory concerning the human dilemma and what God is doing about it that can be traced briefly here, from Amos to Paul.

Israel's earlier traditions may have included threats of insecurity and loss of prosperity in the promised land if the people disobeyed the God who had given it to them.[53] Amos, however,

---

52. For Christian theology's treatment of the difficult subject of God's destructive activity, see Donald E. Gowan, *Theology in Exodus: Biblical Theology in the Form of a Commentary* (Louisville: Westminster/John Knox Press, 1994) 152-67.

53. For a study of these texts, see Donald E. Gowan, "Losing the Promised Land: The Old Testament Considers the Inconceivable," in *From Faith to Faith: Essays in Honor of Donald G. Miller on his Seventieth Birthday,* ed. D. Y. Hadidian, PTMS 31 (Pittsburgh: Pickwick, 1979) 247-68.

---

seems to have been the first to claim that they might lose the land itself. He speaks of exile, the deportation of most of the Israelite population to some other country, in 4:3; 5:5, 27; 6:7; 7:11, 17; 9:4. A promise of restoration from exile appears at the very end of the book (9:15), but that may not be as old as the time of Amos, for a theology of exile and restoration is not developed within the book. When the book was produced the idea was evidently still too new to have produced any theological reflection. A short time later, Hosea found a way to speak of it in terms of Israelite theology: Exile becomes a reversal of the classical history of salvation—back to the wilderness (2:14; 12:9) or back to Egypt (Hos 8:13; 9:3, 6). Even though Hosea knew that the actual physical location of the exile would be Assyria (Hos 9:3; 11:11), theologically it would be the negation of the exodus. That raised the question as to whether there might be a new exodus (Hos 11:10-11), a theme developed later by Judean prophets (e.g., Ezek 20:33-44; Isaiah 43).

Deportations, the scattering of whole populations, have occurred again and again throughout history. The twentieth century produced the term "political refugee" as a new way of speaking of exile. Only one such exile has produced a new people, committed to living in obedience to their God, with a Scripture that was the direct result of that exile experience, and that was the Judean exile in Babylonia during the sixth century. Amos does not foresee that, however. The exile of the northern kingdom populace produced no such results, but the Judean prophets who followed Amos saw exile as death, as he did. That God must work through death—of a nation historically; of the Son of God on the cross; or of the sinful self, as Paul put it (Rom 6:4; 7:4; 8:10; cf. Col 2:11-14)—is one of the great mysteries of our troubled relationship with God, which Amos puts on our theological agenda. The New Testament insists that the question is not, Was Israel so bad they had to die? Neither was it, How could the first-century Jews be so bad that Jesus had to die? The question is, What is so wrong with us that Paul must speak of God's work on our behalf as calling for us to die and rise with Christ? Amos already anticipates that question.

2. *Justice as the Basis for a Healthy Society. Justice* is probably the word most often associated with Amos because of 5:24, but the word itself occurs only in 5:7, 15, 24; 6:12. Without question, it is the perversion of justice that Amos has diagnosed as the major cause of Israel's fatal illness. This has brought the book out of its relative obscurity in Jewish and Christian history, with the rise of the social gospel late in the nineteenth century and of liberation theology late in the twentieth. Amos should not be distorted into a social gospel tract, however, for Amos was not a reformer; neither was he a liberation theologian, for "the end has come upon my people Israel" is a strange kind of liberation.

The intensity of his condemnation of the oppression of the poor and the weak has rightly been taken to heart by reformers, however. Any society that can be diagnosed the way Amos saw the northern kingdom can truthfully be said to be one that will not continue to provide abundance for the few at the expense of the many for very long. We are likely to think first of the deficiencies of economic systems, because of the Marxist critique of capitalism and then the failure of Marxist systems; but it is important to notice the strong emphasis Amos puts on failures of the legal system. We are living in a time when respect for legal systems is breaking down, because those systems obviously are not working as they should. The prophets, beginning with Amos, had in Israelite tradition a legal system based on principles of equality to which they could appeal. They were not creating new ethical standards, but were holding up the failures of the present order against the standards of law, which were being widely ignored. Here is a parallel between us and the prophets. Western civilization also has such a legal tradition, which can in fact be traced back in part to the Old Testament. The prophets challenge us not to proclaim the end is near because of our current failures, but to continue to remind our society of our classical principles of justice and to expose the failures to put them into practice, which still leave the poor and the weak without justice.

Amos has no program for change; it was too late for that. He offers an explanation of what has gone wrong and why it is so wrong that God must intervene in a drastic way. Later generations would see that he was right when he said the end was near, and they would accept his explanation of it as true. For them his words became an imperative to take his advocacy of the law with the utmost seriousness, as they saw what failure to establish justice had done. The exilic and post-exilic Jewish communities set about to make sure their society was such that no prophet like Amos need rise again. As long as we are not convinced it is too late and believe we still have a chance, we also should read the book the way those exiles read Amos—as a challenge not to make the mistake ancient Israel made.

LIFE AS USUAL—
WITH DISASTER NEAR

OVERVIEW

This chapter may be divided into three parts, the first and third of which have clear structures. Between them lie three short sayings (vv. 8-11) that are only loosely related to one another. The first unit (vv. 1-7) has some relationships with 5:18-27 in that it is introduced by "alas" or "woe" (הוי *hôy*) and concludes with the announcement of exile, but the rest of the subject matter is different from anything in chap. 5. The materials in this chapter deal primarily with the attitude of those persons who are comfortable and feel sure nothing can disturb that comfort. It is thus reminiscent of those passages in chaps. 3–4 that deal with Israel's inability to hear the prophet's threatening message. These oracles in chap. 6 say little about judgment for the sins of the wealthy (except v. 12). By means of a lament over people who can see nothing about which to lament (vv. 1-7), the recital of a strange tale concerning death (vv. 9-10), and the use of a riddling saying (v. 12), these texts are new efforts to break through the complacency of the comfortable.

AMOS 6:1-7, COMPLACENT EXTRAVAGANCE

NIV	NRSV
6 Woe to you who are complacent in Zion, and to you who feel secure on Mount Samaria, you notable men of the foremost nation, to whom the people of Israel come! ²Go to Calneh and look at it; go from there to great Hamath, and then go down to Gath in Philistia. Are they better off than your two kingdoms? Is their land larger than yours? ³You put off the evil day and bring near a reign of terror. ⁴You lie on beds inlaid with ivory and lounge on your couches. You dine on choice lambs and fattened calves. ⁵You strum away on your harps like David and improvise on musical instruments.	6 Alas for those who are at ease in Zion, and for those who feel secure on Mount Samaria, the notables of the first of the nations, to whom the house of Israel resorts! ² Cross over to Calneh, and see; from there go to Hamath the great; then go down to Gath of the Philistines. Are you better*ᵃ* than these kingdoms? Or is your*ᵇ* territory greater than their*ᶜ* territory, ³ O you that put far away the evil day, and bring near a reign of violence? ⁴ Alas for those who lie on beds of ivory, and lounge on their couches, and eat lambs from the flock, and calves from the stall;

ᵃ Or *Are they better*   *ᵇ* Heb *their*   *ᶜ* Heb *your*

NIV

⁶You drink wine by the bowlful
    and use the finest lotions,
    but you do not grieve over the ruin of Joseph.
⁷Therefore you will be among the first to go into
        exile;
    your feasting and lounging will end.

NRSV

⁵ who sing idle songs to the sound of the harp,
    and like David improvise on instruments of
        music;
⁶ who drink wine from bowls,
    and anoint themselves with the finest oils,
    but are not grieved over the ruin of Joseph!
⁷ Therefore they shall now be the first to go into
        exile,
    and the revelry of the loungers shall pass
        away.

COMMENTARY

This is the second (and last) of the "woe oracles" in Amos (cf. 5:18-20). It has the typical pattern of הוֹי *hôy* followed by a sequence of participles (vv. 3-6), third-person references to the people being lamented. The NRSV has modified the Hebrew slightly, adding "Alas" in v. 4, and the NIV has done more, introducing "you" in place of the third-person references in vv. 1, 3-7. The announcement of judgment in v. 7, which is nicely tied to the preceding verses by the reuse of the roots ראשׁ (*r'š*, "notable" in v. 1; "first" in v. 7) and סרח (*srḥ*, "lounge" in vv. 4, 7), shows that this is a reason/announcement oracle, with the "woe" forming an extended reason. The pattern is interrupted, however, by v. 2, which takes the form of a disputation saying, challenging the audience's presuppositions of security.

Zion is referred to here in v. 1 and in 1:2, but since the rest of the book is unconcerned with Jerusalem its meaning and originality here have been questioned. It cannot simply be discounted as a later addition, since it stands as a parallel to Mount Samaria, so it may simply be a passing reference to the complacency Amos knew existed in both capitals during these years of relative security. (Note Micah's comparison of Samaria and Jerusalem a few years later, Mic 1:5-9.)

The historical reference and the translation of the question in v. 2 remain difficult problems. Calneh and Hamath were Syrian cities, north of Damascus about 100 and 200 miles respectively. Gath was one of the five Philistine cities, and we do not have enough evidence for the history of these regions in the eighth century BCE to know

why these three cities would have been mentioned together. If this is a reference to their conquest by the Assyrians (Hamath in 720 and Gath in 711 BCE), then there would be no point in the rhetorical question, since Samaria fell in 722 BCE. Calneh was conquered by Tiglath-pileser III in 739 BCE, but he had already imposed tribute on the northern kingdom by 738 BCE, so the complacency that dominates this oracle would scarcely have existed that late. Their presence in chap. 6 probably refers to events for which documentation no longer exists.

The question in v. 2 is difficult because in the Hebrew the subject of the first part is left unstated. It could be "Are you better than these kingdoms?" (NRSV) or "Are they better off than your two kingdoms" (NIV; "kingdoms" refers to Israel and Judah). Andersen and Freedman's translation is probably as close to the Hebrew text as possible, making the questions noncommittal:

Are you better than these kingdoms?
Or is their territory greater than yours?[54]

It makes no difference; all will fall.

The life of this complacent ruling class is illustrated at some length by a description of the banquets they enjoy (vv. 4-6). The occurrence of the word מרזח (*mirzaḥ*) in v. 7 ("revelry," NRSV; "feasting," NIV) has led to comparisons of this scene with texts from other ancient Near Eastern cultures that speak of the *marzeah,* a social and religious institution for the wealthy. The *marzeah* owned buildings and vineyards, and its chief ac-

54. Francis I. Andersen and David Noel Freedman, *Amos,* AB 24A (Garden City, N.Y.: Doubleday, 1989) 558.

tivity seemed to be gatherings for feasts that might last several days, with excessive drinking. The texts date from well before to long after Amos's time, so it seems possible that these verses allude to such an institution in Samaria.[55] Some scholars think it focused on wakes for the dead, but the evidence for that being true is weak. Dining in a reclining position became common later, but it seems to have been an unusual feature of these banquets (v. 4*a*). The daily meal of the average

person did not include meat, but the finest meat was found on these tables (v. 4*b*), and the wine flowed so abundantly that Amos says the people drink not from cups but from bowls that were usually used for cultic purposes (v. 6*a*). All of this luxury made any serious thought impossible. Life was good; why worry? Literally, v. 6*b* says that the diners should be prostrate (the root usually refers to sickness), not from too much drink, but because of the ruin of Joseph. So the foremost people of Samaria will remain foremost in the near future, but in a different way: leading the march into exile (v. 7).

---

55. Hans M. Barstad, *The Religious Polemics of Amos,* VTSup 34 (1984) 127-42; Philip J. King, *Amos, Hosea, Micah: An Archaeological Commentary* (Philadelphia: Westminster, 1988) 137-59; J. L. McLaughlin, "The marzeah at Ugarit: A Textual and Contextual Study," *UF* 23 (1991) 265-81.

REFLECTIONS

What is wrong with luxury? Here Amos describes the "beautiful people" of his time, those who had plenty of money and plenty of leisure time in which to enjoy it. He talks of the way that can lead to excess, but the brunt of his concern is not excess itself, but the way it makes serious thought definitely out of place. No one who wants to talk about the state of the poor or the problems of international relations at a Christmas dinner or during the final stages of a cocktail party or with a group of singers at the end of a fraternity banquet is likely to get much of a welcome. No wonder Amos began with "Alas!"

Neither the book of Amos nor the rest of the OT, however, advocates asceticism, the claim that giving up pleasure will in itself make one better. Israel saw pleasure as one of the good gifts for which God is to be thanked, and that includes plenty to eat and drink and comfort and security (see Lev 26:3-10; Ps 72:3, 16; Eccl 2:24-26; 3:12-13; Jer 31:12-14). The attitudes of some Christians that discomfort is protection from temptation and that wealth in itself is something to feel guilty about do not correspond with the OT outlook.

Luxury is a problem when it is gained at the expense of others' misery (4:1-3; 5:11-12; 8:4-6) and when it deadens the mind and the senses to responsibility. Amos focuses on the latter in this chapter, with the former appearing once, in v. 12. What excesses of eating and drinking can do need not be elaborated on here; North American society provides an abundance of examples of the harm those excesses do to the human body and to human relationships. But for Amos it is the effect of luxury—whether excessive or not—on one's mind, on one's attitude toward life and the world, that is identified as the main problem. As long as I am comfortable, why disturb that comfort by worrying about my behavior or about others who are not doing so well? It is far easier for the preacher to comfort the afflicted than to afflict the comfortable, for the latter can simply choose in one way or another not to hear. After all, does not my comfort prove my behavior is all right—and in fact better than others? The sage's desire for a middle way is relevant here, for he recognized the danger of having too much:

> Give me neither poverty nor riches;
>   feed me with the food that I need,
> or I shall be full, and deny you,
>   and say, "Who is the LORD?"
> or I shall be poor, and steal,
>   and profane the name of my God. (Prov 30:8*b*-9 NRSV)

AMOS 6:8-11, FRAGMENTS CONCERNING THE DISASTER

NIV

⁸The Sovereign LORD has sworn by himself—the LORD God Almighty declares:

"I abhor the pride of Jacob
and detest his fortresses;
I will deliver up the city
and everything in it."

⁹If ten men are left in one house, they too will die. ¹⁰And if a relative who is to burn the bodies comes to carry them out of the house and asks anyone still hiding there, "Is anyone with you?" and he says, "No," then he will say, "Hush! We must not mention the name of the LORD."
¹¹For the LORD has given the command,
and he will smash the great house into pieces
and the small house into bits.

NRSV

⁸ The Lord GOD has sworn by himself
(says the LORD, the God of hosts):
I abhor the pride of Jacob
and hate his strongholds;
and I will deliver up the city and all that is
in it.

⁹If ten people remain in one house, they shall die. ¹⁰And if a relative, one who burns the dead,ᵃ shall take up the body to bring it out of the house, and shall say to someone in the innermost parts of the house, "Is anyone else with you?" the answer will come, "No." Then the relativeᵇ shall say, "Hush! We must not mention the name of the LORD."

¹¹ See, the LORD commands,
and the great house shall be shattered to
bits,
and the little house to pieces.

ᵃ Or who makes a burning for him   ᵇ Heb he

COMMENTARY

6:8, 11. Some efforts have been made to understand vv. 8 and 11 as originally belonging together, but it seems more likely that they were once separate, brief sayings, brought together here with the gruesome vignette in vv. 9-10, because each insists there is no escape. The first saying is somewhat like the epigrams elsewhere in the book (e.g., 3:2, 12) because it gives a negative value to the term "pride of Jacob," but it does not have the typical two-part form of the epigram. Here is the second divine oath in the book (cf. 4:2; 8:7), and the saying may have been introduced here in the hope that the power of this oath might shake the complacency described in vv. 1-7. God swears by God's own life, or self (נפשׁ *nepeš*), because there is nothing greater (Gen 22:16; Jer 51:14). It is a surprise in 8:7 when God swears by the pride of Jacob (גאון *gāʾôn*; usually denoting power, wealth, prestige), the very thing God is said to abhor here.

The phrase is used in a positive sense in Ps 47:4: "He chose our heritage for us,/ the pride of Jacob whom he loves" (NRSV). The heritage seems most likely to be the promised land in that reference, and either land or city will fit in v. 8 as a parallel to "strongholds." This is another of Amos's truly shocking statements, if he says that now the Lord despises the promised land.

6:9-10. The tone of the vignette of death (vv. 9-10) is mysterious, and much of the language is puzzling. The situation is not explained; most scholars think it must be the aftermath of a plague, but others think of widespread starvation in a city under siege.[56] "One who burns the dead" is a translation of מסרפו (*měsārěpô*), a word that may also mean "one who burns him (or it)" but

56. John H. Hayes, *Amos: The Eighth-Century Prophet* (Nashville: Abingdon, 1988) 189.

this is not the right spelling for the Hebrew for "burn" (שׂרף *śārap*). The Syriac and rabbinic interpreters took it to be another word for a relative, perhaps the maternal uncle, but there is no early evidence for such a use of the word. In addition to the spelling problem, it is clear from the OT that cremation was not ordinarily practiced in Israel. Those who claim that is what is referred to here say this must have been a special case, because of plague (cf. 1 Sam 31:8-13). At any rate, it appears that two people have come to remove the bones of someone from a house in which ten people have died. Who is speaking from within the house is uncertain. Some take it to be a lone survivor; others think one of the two searchers has gone in and is asked whether he has found anyone alive there.[57]

57. For details on vv. 9-10, see Shalom Paul, *Amos,* Hermeneia (Philadelphia: Fortress, 1991) 214-16.

The warning to that person to be silent, for in such circumstances the name of the Lord must not be mentioned (v. 10), shows that the aim of the story is to create a sense of dread—to attempt to get the listener to imagine a time when suffering was so intense that one might cry out the name of God in anger or cursing, or when one would be so persuaded of the wrath of God that one would be afraid that the very mention of God's name might bring further destruction.

As the book has emphasized from the beginning, Israel's enemy is now Yahweh. Disaster may come via events in nature (e.g., 4:6-9; 8:7-10) or through war (3:11; 6:14), but it is Yahweh who sends disaster in order to carry out the ultimate beneficent aim. (See Reflections on 5:21-27.)

AMOS 6:12-14, COMPLACENCY UNFOUNDED

NIV

¹²Do horses run on the rocky crags?
    Does one plow there with oxen?
But you have turned justice into poison
    and the fruit of righteousness into bitterness—
¹³you who rejoice in the conquest of Lo Debar[a]
    and say, "Did we not take Karnaim[b] by our
        own strength?"

¹⁴For the LORD God Almighty declares,
    "I will stir up a nation against you, O house
        of Israel,
that will oppress you all the way
    from Lebo[c] Hamath to the valley of the
        Arabah."

a13 Lo Debar means nothing.   *b13 Karnaim means horns; horn here symbolizes strength.*   *c14 Or from the entrance to*

NRSV

¹² Do horses run on rocks?
    Does one plow the sea with oxen?[a]
But you have turned justice into poison
    and the fruit of righteousness into
        wormwood—
¹³ you who rejoice in Lo-debar,[b]
    who say, "Have we not by our own strength
        taken Karnaim[c] for ourselves?"
¹⁴ Indeed, I am raising up against you a nation,
    O house of Israel, says the LORD, the God
        of hosts,
    and they shall oppress you from Lebo-hamath
        to the Wadi Arabah.

a Or Does one plow them with oxen   *b Or in a thing of nothingness*   *c Or horns*

COMMENTARY

These verses can be understood as a loosely structured reason/announcement oracle. They begin with two rhetorical questions leading to a conclusion (v. 12), then identify those whom Amos has ridiculed by one of their self-satisfied quotes (v. 13) and conclude with the announcement of judgment. The questions compare the people's behavior in perverting justice with activities no one would attempt in daily life because these actions are so obviously absurd. So the people's behavior appears to Amos, but they are immune to his accusations, confident in their future because of recent military successes, he says.

The first question is clear, but the MT of the second reads simply, "Does one plow with oxen?" (v. 12*a*). The answer to that question is yes, but the first question leads one to expect a second impossibility. It may be that we are supposed to supply "rock" from the preceding question, and the NIV takes it that way. So it would be folly to try to run horses on a crag, and even more foolish to try to plow it. Another possibility is that the consonants translated "with oxen" (בבקרים *babbĕqārîm*) were originally divided (בבקר ים *babbāqār yām*), which would make the question, "Does one plow the sea with oxen?" (so NRSV and most commentaries). Rather than calling injustice sin, as he did previously, Amos now calls it foolishness, for it is as contrary to good sense as the stupid behavior he has just asked the people to consider. This is the final use of the words "justice" (משפט *mišpāṭ*) and "righteousness" (צדקה

ṣĕdāqâ) in the book (cf. 5:7-15, 21-24), but the subject will reappear in 8:4-6.

The words that appear as place names in modern translations (Lo-debar and Karnaim, vv. 13-14) were taken to be common nouns by earlier interpreters, for they can be translated "that which is not" and "horns." Towns by these names can be located east of the Jordan, however, and Amos is punning with their names, pronouncing the first as Lo-debar to make it sound like "Nothingville," and using the fact that "horn" was a common metaphor for strength to say that the people claim they have taken "strength" by their own strength. The quote in v. 13 is an apparent reference to the successes of Jeroboam II in retaking from the Arameans the region east of the Jordan, as recorded in 2 Kgs 14:25, but Amos also holds that up to ridicule as scarcely significant enough to justify the people's feeling as secure as they do.

The enemy remains unnamed, for nowhere in the book of Amos is there clear evidence that Amos knew it would be the Assyrians. The judgment is described as an explicit reversal of fortune here, not the thoroughgoing destruction spoken of elsewhere, but simply the oppression of those self-confident "victors" throughout the whole region they thought they had just made their own.

REFLECTIONS

At the center of this passage lies the issue of wishful thinking. Amos speaks of people who put their trust in a strong military force, thinking prosperity (for themselves) is assured as long as their borders are secure. As long as the enemy can be located outside their borders, the remedy is simple: Keep the army strong, and enjoy life at home. The sickness within can be ignored as long as the parties can continue. But for Amos the measure of the health, the continuing viability of the nation, is justice, and he has seen it turned to poison. There is no "quick fix" for the internal problems of a society that has turned against itself, but in every generation wishful thinking turns to force as its quick fix. The realism of Amos recognized that force will not solve the problems created by the failure to maintain justice for all, but are there not still more wishful thinkers than realists in the world? In the past, extremely severe penalties for stealing did not stop the hungry from stealing when they saw no other way to stay alive. In the present, more police on the streets and mandatory or longer sentences may seem to be a quick and straightforward way to make communities safer; and, indeed, they may have some useful effect. If people in those communities are hungry and hopeless, however, there will still be no peace in the land.

VISIONS AND A CONFRONTATION
OVERVIEW

In chap. 7 the first three examples of a new genre appear. These visions are the only passages in Amos written in the first person, each telling of something Amos has "seen," followed by a word from God (7:1-3, 4-6, 7-9; also 8:1-3; 9:1-4). Some commentators thus call chaps. 7–9 the "Book of Visions," although these chapters include much more than that.

The visions fall into groups. The first and second are told in exactly the same way, the third and fourth are like each other—slightly different from the earlier pair—and the fifth has an entirely different formulation. The fact that visions three and four are separated by the account of the confrontation between Amaziah and Amos has led to various theories of composition based on the assumption that vv. 10-17 must have been inserted at some later time, breaking up an original unit of visions. We can do no more than speculate on whether the visions were originally an uninterrupted unit, and whether vv. 10-17 might once have been located somewhere else in the book. It is possible to understand their present location, however. Two visions with the same form and the same message appear together (vv. 1-3, 4-6). The third vision is followed by a passage with related content, the encounter with Amaziah (cf. vv. 9, 11). Related materials have also been gathered to follow the fourth vision (cf. 8:3, 10). The fifth passage begins with "I saw," but there is little of visionary character about it, and 9:1-4 is essentially an oracle, reemphasizing the message of 8:1-10.

Many efforts have been made to reconstruct the career of Amos from these materials, but they clearly were not recorded with any biographical interest. There is no hint in the visions and the confrontation account of the time in Amos's life and ministry that they actually occurred or even of their relative chronology. The emphasis throughout is on the word Amos received from God; the prophet himself remains in the background. He alludes to what we would speak of as his "call" in v. 15, but those who try to associate the visions with a call experience fail to take seriously enough the complete absence from them of any commission. We cannot say whether the visions occurred all at one time or at intervals, and there is no good evidence to associate them chronologically with the oracles elsewhere in the book. The relationship with vv. 10-17 is thematic. The variety of results produced by those who have attempted a biography of Amos from these materials should convince us that to do so is to misuse them.

AMOS 7:1-9, THREE VISIONS

NIV

7 This is what the Sovereign LORD showed me: He was preparing swarms of locusts after the king's share had been harvested and just as the second crop was coming up. [2]When they had stripped the land clean, I cried out, "Sovereign

NRSV

7 This is what the Lord GOD showed me: he was forming locusts at the time the latter growth began to sprout (it was the latter growth after the king's mowings). [2]When they had finished eating the grass of the land, I said,

NIV

LORD, forgive! How can Jacob survive? He is so small!"

³So the LORD relented.

"This will not happen," the LORD said.

⁴This is what the Sovereign LORD showed me: The Sovereign LORD was calling for judgment by fire; it dried up the great deep and devoured the land. ⁵Then I cried out, "Sovereign LORD, I beg you, stop! How can Jacob survive? He is so small!"

⁶So the LORD relented.

"This will not happen either," the Sovereign LORD said.

⁷This is what he showed me: The Lord was standing by a wall that had been built true to plumb, with a plumb line in his hand. ⁸And the LORD asked me, "What do you see, Amos?"

"A plumb line," I replied.

Then the Lord said, "Look, I am setting a plumb line among my people Israel; I will spare them no longer.

⁹"The high places of Isaac will be destroyed
    and the sanctuaries of Israel will be ruined;
    with my sword I will rise against the house
        of Jeroboam."

NRSV

"O Lord GOD, forgive, I beg you!
    How can Jacob stand?
    He is so small!"
³ The LORD relented concerning this;
    "It shall not be," said the LORD.

⁴This is what the Lord GOD showed me: the Lord GOD was calling for a shower of fire,ᵃ and it devoured the great deep and was eating up the land. ⁵Then I said,

"O Lord GOD, cease, I beg you!
    How can Jacob stand?
    He is so small!"
⁶ The LORD relented concerning this;
    "This also shall not be," said the Lord GOD.

⁷This is what he showed me: the Lord was standing beside a wall built with a plumb line, with a plumb line in his hand. ⁸And the LORD said to me, "Amos, what do you see?" And I said, "A plumb line." Then the Lord said,

"See, I am setting a plumb line
    in the midst of my people Israel;
    I will never again pass them by;
⁹ the high places of Isaac shall be made desolate,
    and the sanctuaries of Israel shall be laid
        waste,
    and I will rise against the house of Jeroboam
        with the sword."

ᵃ Or for a judgment by fire

COMMENTARY

Prophets were called "seers" (using either חזה [ḥōzeh, v. 12] or ראה [rōʾeh, Isa 30:10]) because they were believed to be able to see things other people could not. What they "see" might simply be the location of the lost asses of Saul's father (1 Sam 9:5-10), or they might see completely supernatural events, as in Isaiah 6 and Ezekiel 1. The visions of Amos fall between these extremes. The introduction, "This is what the Lord GOD showed me" (v. 1), indicates that these were no ordinary experiences (cf. Jer 24:1; 38:21; Ezek 11:25; 40:4; Zech 1:20). But Amos saw earthly things for the most part, and the emphasis in each account is not on sight but on the dialogue between the prophet and God. The first two visions follow an identical pattern. God shows Amos an event, involving thoroughgoing destruction; Amos reacts with an appeal; and the Lord relents, saying it shall not be. The events are visionary, not actual, so we need not wonder how Amos could intercede after the locusts had devoured the vegetation. He understood the vision to be a portent of the future.

7:1-3. God first showed Amos a not-unfamiliar event, a locust plague, coming at the worst possible time of the year. The latter growth (v. 1) would be the crops sown in the spring, such as vegetables. If the plague had come earlier, the locusts would have taken the grain crop, which was planted in the fall, but the vegetables would not yet have sprouted. If it came later, the grain would already have been harvested, but at the time indicated the locusts would have taken everything.[58] For Amos's audience, "after the king's mowings" (v. 1) would have provided more precision, but we have no evidence to explain what time of year that was. It is usually interpreted as the first cutting of hay, but in fact hay crops are not grown and harvested in Palestine as they are in other parts of the world.[59] It probably does not refer to the reaping of grain, since a different word is always used for that. The verb used here usually refers to sheepshearing (except Ps 72:6), but that would not be meaningful in connection with a locust plague. Apparently one form of taxation was taking the first part of some crop, and in the vision what was left for the people was destroyed.

Amos assumes this locust plague is God's judgment for their sins. He takes it upon himself to intercede for them, asking God to forgive them (v. 2). Intercession in the OT is a bold act, for it asks forgiveness based entirely on the character of God, rather than appealing to repentance on the part of the people (cf. Exod 34:9; Num 14:19-20; Dan 9:19).[60] The only quality of Jacob (Israel) Amos can hold up is "He is so small" (v. 2). Amos knows smallness should interest the God who rescued slaves from Egypt (Deut 7:7) and takes personally the fate of widows, orphans, aliens, and the poor (Exod 22:21-27[20-26]). The God of Israel is open to such appeals, as the use of נחם (*nāḥam*) in the niphal stem shows. The word does not mean "repent," as in earlier translations (e.g., RSV), for the way we use that word now implies turning from something sinful. In thirty of its thirty-six uses in the niphal stem, God is the subject, and it always refers to changing the mind, so "regret" and "relent" are appropriate translations.[61] Here God relents, saying that the locust plague will not happen (v. 3), but God does not grant Amos's full request—forgiveness. The de-

struction symbolized by locusts is postponed, or perhaps altered, for some time later Amos had a similar, more terrifying vision.

7:4-6. The second vision speaks of no natural event. The divine fire, of which Amos often speaks (1:4, 7, 10, 12, 14; 2:2; 5:6), devours the cosmic ocean itself (Gen 1:2; 7:11; 8:2; Job 38:16; cf. Deut 32:22). The MT seems to read "judgment by fire" (so NIV), but the Hebrew is unusual, suggesting it is the fire that is judged. Changing the word division (from לרב באש *lārîb bāʾēš* to לרבב אש *lĕrābîb ʾēš*) gives the reading "a shower of fire," now preferred by the NRSV and most commentators.[62] Since God had relented in the first vision, but had not said he had forgiven, Amos this time just cries out, "Please stop!" Once again God relents, "This also shall not be" (v. 3).

7:7-9. The third and fourth visions (7:7-9; 8:1-3) follow a slightly different pattern. God shows Amos an object, which means nothing in itself; so Amos does not react. God then asks Amos what he sees, and he replies with a word that becomes the key to the vision for the divine interpretation of that word becomes the message. Amos does not intercede, probably because the message already precludes that. The same type of vision, with the question, "What do you see?" appears also in Jer 1:11-14, where the key words are "almond" (שקד *šāqēd,* interpreted as שקד *šōqēd,* "watching") and "north." The word אנך (*ʾănāk*), used four times, is the key to vv. 7-8. Unfortunately its meaning in this context remains unclear. It is almost certain that *ʾănāk* does not mean "plumb line," and yet all the modern translations and some commentaries continue to use it. The word occurs only here in the OT and is now known to be the Akkadian word for "tin."[63] But what could be meant by a "wall of tin" (v. 7) or "I am setting tin in the midst of my people Israel" (v. 8)? "Plumb line" first appeared as a guess by the medieval commentators Ibn Ezra, Rashi, and Qimhi; it has become the traditional rendering since then, because it enables one to read the text as a judgment oracle. "A wall of plumb line" (חומת אנך *ḥômat ʾănāk*) and "setting a plumb line in the midst of my people" do

58. For details, see ibid., 227.

59. Harold N. and Alma L. Moldenke, *Plants of the Bible* (Waltham, Mass.: Chronica Botanica, 1952) 28-29.

60. Thomas M. Raitt, "Why Does God Forgive?" *HBT* (1991) 38-58.

61. Terence E. Fretheim, "The Repentance of God: A Key to Evaluating Old Testament God-Talk," *HBT* (1988) 47-70; Francis I. Andersen and David Noel Freedman, *Amos,* AB 24A (Garden City, N.Y.: Doubleday, 1989) 638-79.

62. See, e.g., Delbert R. Hillers, "Amos 7:4 and Ancient Parallels," *CBQ* 26 (1964) 221-25.

63. Benno Landsberger, "Tin and Lead: The Adventures of Two Vocables," *JNES* 24 (1965) 285-96.

not read well, however, and translators have added "built with" in order to make some sense of the former expression.[64] The ancient versions show that they knew the term referred to metal of some kind, but they offer no support for the reading "plumb line."[65] It has become one of the favorite terms borrowed from the book of Amos, but it seems likely that Amos himself would not recognize it, so it should be given up.

The pattern of the vision in vv. 7-9 is identical to 8:1-3, which is based entirely on a wordplay between קיץ (*qāyiṣ*, "summer fruit") and קץ (*qēṣ*, "end"). When God asks the prophet to name the object he sees, as in v. 8 and 8:2, the name rather than the object becomes the point of the vision. So it may be that the wall of tin and the tin in God's hand mean no more than the basket of fruit did, but the sound of the word '*ănāk* was intended to recall two very similar roots, אנח ('*ānaḥ*) and אנק ('*ānaq*), both of which mean "sigh."[66]

The mourning in 5:16-17; 8:3, 10 would thus be alluded to here by wordplay. "See, I am setting '*ănāk* [think '*ănaḥ* or '*ānaq*] in the midst of my people Israel; I will never again pass by them" thus bears an intriguing resemblance to "in all the vineyards there shall be wailing,/ for I will pass through the midst of you" (5:17 NRSV), with the verb עבר ('*ābar,* "pass through," "pass by") used in two different senses. There is probably nothing the translator can do with a wordplay on "tin" in English, but an analogy may be suggested: In a vision a wall of silver is seen, and God is standing with silver in hand. That means nothing until God says, "I am putting shivering in the midst of my people."[67] While the verb '*ābar* was used in a threatening way in 5:17, recalling its use in Exod 12:12, God evidently uses it to represent passing over sin in this case (v. 8*b*), as in Mic 7:18 and Prov 19:11, with the ominous words, "never again." There is nothing more for Amos to say.

The wordplay on sighing is elaborated in v. 9 with two verbs often used by the prophets to speak of desolation, waste, and the human reaction to it. The message concerns a subject introduced earlier (5:4-5). "High places" (במות *bāmôt*) were the open air sanctuaries of Canaanite origin. Only here and in 7:16 does Amos use "Isaac" as a reference to Israel. The new subject, for this book, is the prediction of the end of the dynasty of Jeroboam (v. 9*b*). This led to the inclusion in 7:10-17 of the account of Amaziah's meeting with Amos, which was an outcome of that prophecy.

---

64. For a recent effort to defend "plumb line," see H. G. M. Williamson, "The Prophet and the Plumb-Line: A Redaction-Critical Study of Amos vii," *OTS* 26 (1990) 101-21.

65. The LXX uses the word ἀδάμας (*adamas*), meaning "hardened iron," possibly "steel." Aquila translates it as γάνωσις (*ganōsis*), or "gleam." The Vulgate introduces the translation "trowel," but in his commentary Jerome speaks of *stannatum,* "tin."

66. Emendation of the last occurrence of '*ănāk* to read אנחה '*ănāḥâ,* "sighing," may not be necessary. Andersen and Freedman (*Amos,* 754-59) suggest that there may actually be three different roots here, with the first occurrence meaning "plastered" as in the Vulgate, the second and third meaning "tin," and the fourth meaning "grief," but this seems to be a counsel of despair. The Talmud shows that the rabbis already understood the passage as containing a wordplay, connecting '*ănāk* with אנאה ('*ōnā'āh,* "wrong"/"overreaching"). See *b. B. Mes.* 59a.

67. This reading of the vision as based on word association (as also in Andersen and Freedman, *Amos,* 757) is challenged by Wolff (*Joel and Amos,* Hermeneia [Philadelphia: Fortress, 1977] 300-301) and Susan Niditch (*The Symbolic Vision in Biblical Tradition,* HSM 30 [Chico, Calif.: Scholars Press, 1983] 32), who claim that this is an "idea-association" vision, which means that '*ănāk* must have meaning in itself. But the form points toward word association, and the existence of two similar sounding words with the meaning "sigh" means the passage can be read that way with neither emendation nor guesses as to the original meaning of '*ănāk* being required.

REFLECTIONS

1. Prophets in ancient Israel appear to have been identified as such primarily because they had paranormal experiences, mostly visions and auditory experiences. There are still visionaries in our midst today whose "ecstatic personalities" have been studied by psychologists, and their experiences must be carefully distinguished from the hallucinations experienced by the mentally ill.[68] But to have experienced visions today does not put a person in the same league as Amos or Isaiah. It was not the paranormal experience, but the content of the message they received through those experiences that gave their work lasting importance.

Their descriptions of visions bring us as close as we can get to the "process" of divine

---

68. See Johannes Lindblom, *Prophecy in Ancient Israel* (Oxford: Basil Blackwell, 1962) 122-41.

inspiration, however, and that is not very close. There has been much speculation about the way the authors of Scripture achieved their insights, ranging from assuming it was a purely human process to theories of divine dictation that bypassed the human mind completely. The prophets do tell us that some of their insights came through visions in which they heard God speaking. They never indicate whether all the messages they introduced with "Thus says the LORD" came that way, however. It seems likely that they recounted certain visions in answer to the challenges: How do you know this? Who gives you authority to speak this way? Amos's visions are associated in chap. 7 with a challenge to him from Amaziah. He answered the priest: "The LORD took me from following the flock, and the LORD said to me, 'Go, prophesy to my people Israel' " (7:15 NRSV). He may have answered other challenges with, "The LORD showed me." But note that to recount a vision proves nothing, for how can one know that the teller is not self-deceived or lying (cf. Jer 14:14; 23:16; Ezek 13:7)? The messages of the prophets would be validated by history, and not by any claims concerning their origin. Perhaps that is why the prophetic books do not devote much space to visions. The process of inspiration remains a mystery, and the theories concerning the inspiration of Scripture that have approached it from the point of view of the origin of the words may have been working from the wrong direction. For believers, the effect of the words, not their hypothetical origin, proves whether they have been inspired by God. To this day people claim as justification for their actions, "God spoke to me." Sometimes those claims are clearly condemned by the actions themselves, which are cruel or immoral. It is not always that clear, however, but for Christians there is a standard by which to judge every claim to authority: Is the claim in accordance with the clear teaching of Scripture? Amos's audience did not have such a time-tested standard, but we do, and those who follow leaders whose teachings run counter to Scripture do so at their peril.

2. Why would the first two visions have been recorded, when Amos's intercession came to nothing? They are unlike anything elsewhere in the prophetic canon. Jeremiah was forbidden to pray for his people (Jer 7:16; 11:14), suggesting that other prophets did intercede, like Amos; but that negative case is the closest parallel we have to Amos 7:1-6. Perhaps the two pairs of visions (7:1-6, 7-9 and 8:1-3) represent an early way of saying that God's patience had finally run out. Later prophets would express it more explicitly, especially in Ezek 20:5-31, which retells Israel's history as one of continual rebellion. God's patience, willingness to bear with sinners, waiting for them to change, was an attribute of God that Israel gratefully celebrated. That God is "slow to anger, abounding in love and faithfulness" (Exod 34:6 NIV) had become a kind of credo in Israel, for it is repeated numerous times in the Old Testament: "As a father has compassion for his children,/ so the LORD has compassion for those who fear him./ For he knows how we were made;/ he remembers that we are dust" (Ps 103:13-14 NRSV). But that great truth about a great God had been taken as "cheap grace" in the Israel of Amos's time. The two pairs of visions, in which God at first relents but then says "never again," seem to be one of Amos's ways of saying that God's patience had finally run out; no longer would it be as it had been.

3. Several terms are used for forgiveness, both divine and human, in the Old Testament, but Amos uses in 7:2 one of the "theological verbs": סלח (sālaḥ), a word of which God alone is the subject. The commentary noted that the only basis Amos can adduce for his appeal is "Jacob is small." Here is one of the interesting cases in Scripture where the familiar pattern of repentance followed by forgiveness does not apply. It is not the only case. Moses, in interceding for his people, could appeal to nothing in their behavior or attitude to justify forgiveness; intercession was based solely on the character of God (Exod 32:12-14, 32; 34:6-9; Num 14:17-20). The same point of view appears in Daniel's prayer (Dan 9:18-19). Of course, the familiar pattern of forgiveness for those who repent appears frequently (e.g., 1 Kgs 8:30-50;

Isa 55:7; Jer 36:3), but as the prophets considered the possibility of a future for their sinful people they came to the conclusion that God would have to do something first. So we encounter promises of restoration after the judgment in which forgiveness is what makes it possible for people to change (Isa 44:22; Jer 24:7; 31:34; Ezek 36:22-32). This does correspond to the religious experiences of more than a few people: Repentance is the result of realizing that God is forgiving.

The New Testament makes it abundantly clear that it is God who makes the first move, and not we ourselves. Christ's death was not God's response to any human initiative: "While we still were sinners Christ died for us" (Rom 5:8 NRSV). More than any list of our misdeeds, the knowledge of what God has done for us in Jesus Christ convinces us that we are sinners. What made Amos's intercession possible was the conviction that runs through all of Scripture: If there is any hope for us, it is that God is merciful.

AMOS 7:10-17, PRIEST CONFRONTS PROPHET

NIV

[10]Then Amaziah the priest of Bethel sent a message to Jeroboam king of Israel: "Amos is raising a conspiracy against you in the very heart of Israel. The land cannot bear all his words. [11]For this is what Amos is saying:

"'Jeroboam will die by the sword,
    and Israel will surely go into exile,
    away from their native land.'"

[12]Then Amaziah said to Amos, "Get out, you seer! Go back to the land of Judah. Earn your bread there and do your prophesying there. [13]Don't prophesy anymore at Bethel, because this is the king's sanctuary and the temple of the kingdom."

[14]Amos answered Amaziah, "I was neither a prophet nor a prophet's son, but I was a shepherd, and I also took care of sycamore-fig trees. [15]But the LORD took me from tending the flock and said to me, 'Go, prophesy to my people Israel.' [16]Now then, hear the word of the LORD. You say,

"'Do not prophesy against Israel,
    and stop preaching against the house of Isaac.'

[17]"Therefore this is what the LORD says:

"'Your wife will become a prostitute in the city,
    and your sons and daughters will fall by the
        sword.
Your land will be measured and divided up,
    and you yourself will die in a pagan[a] country.
And Israel will certainly go into exile,
    away from their native land.'"

[a]17 Hebrew *an unclean*

NRSV

10Then Amaziah, the priest of Bethel, sent to King Jeroboam of Israel, saying, "Amos has conspired against you in the very center of the house of Israel; the land is not able to bear all his words. [11]For thus Amos has said,

'Jeroboam shall die by the sword,
    and Israel must go into exile
    away from his land.'"

[12]And Amaziah said to Amos, "O seer, go, flee away to the land of Judah, earn your bread there, and prophesy there; [13]but never again prophesy at Bethel, for it is the king's sanctuary, and it is a temple of the kingdom."

14Then Amos answered Amaziah, "I am[a] no prophet, nor a prophet's son; but I am[a] a herdsman, and a dresser of sycamore trees, [15]and the LORD took me from following the flock, and the LORD said to me, 'Go, prophesy to my people Israel.'

[16] "Now therefore hear the word of the LORD.
    You say, 'Do not prophesy against Israel,
    and do not preach against the house of Isaac.'

[17] Therefore thus says the LORD:
    'Your wife shall become a prostitute in the city,
        and your sons and your daughters shall fall
            by the sword,
    and your land shall be parceled out by line;
you yourself shall die in an unclean land,
    and Israel shall surely go into exile away
        from its land.'"

[a] Or *was*

COMMENTARY

The first-person accounts of Amos's visions are interrupted in vv. 10-17 by a third-person account recording Amaziah's report to Jeroboam and his brief dialogue with Amos. The passage has clearly been placed in this location because the only reference to Jeroboam in an oracle of Amos is in 7:9. It can scarcely be called a narrative, for there is no introduction or conclusion, and no action is recorded. The report to Jeroboam is included in order to explain the encounter with Amos, but we are not told whether Amaziah took both actions at the same time or whether one was the result of the other. Nothing is said of what became of Amos. The location was probably Bethel, but even that is not made explicit. We are given a sequence of quotations that do not intend to provide a bit of Amos's biography, but are needed in order to explain Amos's oracle against Amaziah. In the exchange, Amos more or less incidentally refers to a few details of his personal life, and later interest in the man himself has drawn great attention to those few words.

7:10-13. We are first informed of why Amaziah tried to prohibit Amos from preaching in Bethel. He considered Amos's words to be "conspiracy" (קשר *qāšar,* v. 10), a word used more than once in the accounts of plots to overthrow kings in the northern kingdom (e.g., 1 Kgs 15:27; 16:9; 2 Kgs 10:9; 15:10). His evidence (v. 11) is a two-part summary of what Amos had said, threatening Jeroboam II with death and Israel with exile. The latter part certainly represents a major theme in the book, and it is repeated by Amos himself in v. 17, but the former speaks personally of Jeroboam rather than of his house, as v. 9 does. Whether Amaziah may have misquoted Amos is of less interest than two facts: In his response Amos does not correct or deny it, and Amaziah's version of the prophecy is in fact unfulfilled. According to 2 Kgs 14:29, Jeroboam died a natural death, but the collectors and transmitters of the book of Amos felt no need to expurgate or correct these words.

There is no agreement among commentators as to whether Amaziah was offering friendly advice or whether he was by his own (or by royal) authority ordering Amos out of the country. Some think that his use of the term "seer" (חזה *ḥōzeh*)

is demeaning to Amos, but that is not necessarily so, and there is nothing else in his language to show whether he was actually hostile to the prophet. What is important is clear, however: Amaziah had authority over the sanctuary at Bethel and claimed the right to tell Amos he could not prophesy there. It has been noted that he does not call Amos a false prophet, does not deny the truth of what Amos has said. Amos may say anything he likes, but not in Bethel. The Hebrew expression "eat bread there" (ואכל־שם לחם *weʾĕkol-šām leḥem*) does not occur elsewhere, but has probably been interpreted correctly in the NRSV and the NIV as "earn your bread there," presumably meaning earn a living as a prophet.

7:14-15. Amos's reply begins with three noun clauses. In Hebrew a sentence can be formulated with the verb "to be" understood, so a translator has to supply the verb and also decide what tense was intended. The NRSV follows the majority opinion and translates Amos's response in the present tense: "I am no prophet. . . . " The NIV follows a strong minority who translate the Hebrew as, "I was neither a prophet. . . . " The other debated question in v. 14 is whether "prophet" and "prophet's son" are synonymous or mean something different. The full variety of proposed readings need not be included here.[69] The past tense translation takes Amos's response to focus on how he became a prophet: "At one time I was an agriculturalist, but the Lord took me; so I was not a prophet then, but I am now." Most of those who read the sentence in the present tense think Amos was speaking of how he continues to earn his living: "I am not a professional prophet, but. . . . " The issue at the heart of the confrontation is much the same no matter how vv. 14-15 are read, however. Amaziah has claimed authority over where Amos may speak. Amos refuses to acknowledge any such authority, for he is acting neither as a member of any prophetic group[70] nor on his own. He has been

---

69. For good surveys of the discussion, see Hayes, *Amos,* 235-36; Paul, *Amos,* 244-47.

70. "Prophet's son" does not mean that one's father was a prophet. The term "sons of the prophets" was used in ninth century BCE Israel to refer to prophetic groups (2 Kgs 2:3-15; 4:1, 38; 5:22; 6:1; 9:1).

taken away from his normal occupation and sent to the northern kingdom by God. That means not only that he has had no choice in the matter (cf. Amos 3:8), but also that Amaziah has profoundly offended God by resisting Amos.

The word that the NRSV translates as "herdsman" (בוקר *bôqēr*) has puzzled some scholars—so much so that they have been tempted to emend it to "shepherd" (נוקד *nôqēd*), as does the NIV, because the root is elsewhere used with reference to cattle and because in the next verse Amos speaks of following the flock. If he was not a mere shepherd, but an owner of livestock, there is no reason why Amos could not have owned cattle as well as sheep and goats, however. The phrase "dresser of sycamore trees" (בולס שקמים *bôlēs šiqmîm*) occurs nowhere else in the OT, and it has attracted a great deal of attention. The sycamores referred to are a different tree from the North American sycamore. They bear a kind of fig that grows directly out of the large branches of the tree. In Egypt the fruit is incised to hasten ripening and to inhibit the development of wasps, which infect it. It is not known whether this practice was followed in ancient Israel, but this is the usual explanation of Amos's activity. Others have suggested that he gathered the fruit or the leaves as fodder for his animals.[71] But the sycamore is found in low altitudes, on the Mediterranean coast and in the Jordan valley, not at the altitude of Tekoa. Amos had thus evidently been used to moving about the country in the pursuit of his vocation. He mentions it as a response to Amaziah's challenge, "Flee away to the land of Judah, earn your bread there, and prophesy there" (v. 13 NRSV), to make it clear to Amaziah that prophecy is not his main occupation.

7:16-17. The contrast between vv. 15 and 16 should be noted. On the one hand, Amaziah has assumed the right to restrict Amos's prophetic activity, but Yahweh has said, "Go, prophesy to my people Israel." This leads to a clearly formulated reason/announcement oracle in vv. 16-17. The reason quotes Amaziah's own words against him; the announcement is a terrible curse. It is formulated as a prediction, but it is appropriate to call it a curse, because Amos is not being original here. This is the kind of language used in covenant curses in Lev 26:22 (death of children); Deut 28:30 (wife and property); 28:32, 41 (children-captives); and in a self-cursing formula in Job 31:9-10 (wife). We may be tempted to read it as an ill-tempered outburst, but Amos was using traditional language applied to covenant-breakers. Other prophets spoke in similar ways of people who claimed the prophet was not speaking the truth (Jer 28:15-16; 29:31-32; Mic 2:6; 3:5-7).

It is clear that the people of eighth-century BCE Israel still thought in terms of corporate responsibility: Amaziah's whole family would suffer because of his guilt. Since the northern kingdom was not taken over in entirely until 722 BCE, the family may not have suffered this exact fate, but it is an accurate description of what did happen to families at that time. It has seldom been noticed that "Israel shall surely go into exile away from its land" (v. 17) is quoted by the deuteronomistic historian in two prominent places. The historian never mentions Amos by name, but uses this formulation to sum up the ends of both the northern and the southern kingdoms (2 Kgs 17:23; 25:21), affirming the fulfillment of Amos's words.[72]

---

71. For a survey of the data, see Hayes, *Amos*, 237-38. Cf. T. J. Wright, "Amos and the 'Sycamore Fig,'" *VT* 26 (1976) 362-68.

72. Donald E. Gowan, "The Beginnings of Exile-Theology and the Root *glh*," *ZAW* 87 (1975) 204-7.

REFLECTIONS

This passage insists, with some severity, on God's freedom to choose whom to work with and through. The prophet is not free, but is under divine compulsion to speak (cf. 1 Cor 9:16). But Amaziah assumed, as the priest of a royal sanctuary, one of Israel's major institutions, that he had the power at least to decide what should go on there. A study of the various institutions of Israel—kingship, the sanctuaries, the tribe, the family—shows that ordinarily God worked within human structures, but the Old Testament also insists that God from time to time chooses to work from outside those institutions. So the priesthood of the family of Eli was brought to an end in favor of Samuel, not even a member of a priestly family (1 Samuel 1–4); Jacob, the secondborn twin, was chosen rather than Esau (Gen 25:21-26); prophets dared to stand before the Lord's anointed, the king, and say, "You are the man!" (2 Sam 12:7); and Jesus came from Galilee, from a carpenter's family (Matt 13:55; John 7:41, 52).

When God chooses to bypass our institutions, it is inevitable that those who maintain them and benefit from them will resist, as Amaziah did. So the prophets always faced opposition, some of it severe. There is no conclusion to the "story" in 7:10-17. Many assume it marks the end of Amos's ministry in the northern kingdom and that he returned to Judah. Some even speculate that he may have been killed, but once again we see that for Israel it was not what became of Amos that was important, but what became of his words. We know a bit about other prophets' lives. Isaiah retired from prophecy for a time, apparently finding it to be useless (Isa 8:16-22). Jeremiah fervently wished he could retire (Jer 20:9), and instead found himself under house arrest (Jer 36:5) and then thrown into a dry well (Jer 38:6). Others were killed (Jer 26:20-23). So the tradition equating prophecy with martyrdom grew up in Judaism (Matt 23:37; Acts 7:52). Speaking the truth by no means guarantees acceptance, for the truth will be uncomfortable to someone, and if it disturbs the comfort of those in power it will produce serious opposition. Dostoevsky's "The Grand Inquisitor" is the classic depiction of an institution (the church) that has things so well under control that it does not even need Christ anymore.[73]

But opposition is no proof that one has spoken the truth, and that needs to be reemphasized when one thinks about the prophets. More than a few people have succumbed to the temptation of thinking that they are in trouble because they are being "prophetic," when on occasion it is just because they have been undiplomatic, stupid, or wrong. The image of the noble, suffering prophet can be an enticement at times when one needs to pray for the grace to know whether one is standing for the truth, or just being difficult.

73. Fyodor Dostoevsky, *The Brothers Karamazov*, Book V, chap. 5.

AMOS 8:1-14

THE END HAS COME

OVERVIEW

This chapter continues the sequence of visions begun in chap. 7. The form of the fourth vision (vv. 1-3) is identical with that of the third (7:7-9), and like the third it has been supplemented by the addition of related material. The rest of the chapter may be read as a series of explanations of the "end" that is announced to Amos in the vision. An extended reason/announcement oracle follows the vision (vv. 4-8), and the passage beginning "On that day" (vv. 9-10), which may once have been an independent oracle may now be understood as a continuation of the announcement. The two oracles beginning "The time is surely coming" (vv. 11-12) and "In that day" (vv. 13-14) have also been brought together here because of relationships between them. The atmosphere of death that was so prominent in chap. 5 permeates this chapter also, since "end" leads to descriptions of mourning concluding the first two sections (vv. 3, 9-10) and to "they shall fall, and never rise again" at the end of the third. Although parts of this chapter have been taken by some to be reworkings of Amos's words by disciples, because of the reappearance of themes found elsewhere in the book, each of the individual oracles has its own notes of originality, and there is nothing in the chapter that cannot be understood in terms of an eighth-century BCE setting.

AMOS 8:1-3, THE FOURTH VISION

NIV

8 This is what the Sovereign LORD showed me: a basket of ripe fruit. ²"What do you see, Amos?" he asked.

"A basket of ripe fruit," I answered.

Then the LORD said to me, "The time is ripe for my people Israel; I will spare them no longer.

³"In that day," declares the Sovereign LORD, "the songs in the temple will turn to wailing.ᵃ Many, many bodies—flung everywhere! Silence!"

ᵃ3 Or *"the temple singers will wail*

NRSV

8 This is what the Lord GOD showed me—a basket of summer fruit.ᵃ ²He said, "Amos, what do you see?" And I said, "A basket of summer fruit."ᵃ Then the LORD said to me,
"The endᵇ has come upon my people Israel;
　I will never again pass them by.
³ The songs of the templeᶜ shall become
　　wailings in that day,"
　　　　　　　　　　　says the Lord GOD;
"the dead bodies shall be many,
　cast out in every place. Be silent!"

ᵃ Heb *qayits*　　ᵇ Heb *qets*　　ᶜ Or *palace*

COMMENTARY

The meaning of this vision is based on the similarity of sound of two different words, like the vision in Jer 1:11-12. Wordplays in one language are difficult, if not impossible, to translate into another, but the NIV has made an effort to preserve a word-play with "ripe fruit" (קָיִץ *qayiṣ*) and "the time is ripe" (קֵץ *qēṣ*). The NRSV's translation of *qēṣ* as "end" is more literal, but it loses the sense of word-play. As in the third vision, there is no action and what is seen is just an object that requires an interpretation. Some scholars have tried to provide a setting for this vision, assuming that Amos saw a real basket of fruit (figs or olives) harvested late in the summer, thus associating it with the harvest festival of late summer. Amos says it is something the Lord has showed him, however, so the basket of fruit may have been a completely visionary experience, which could have happened any time during the year. The text provides no background for the vision; everything is focused on one word.

Amos saw a basket of *qayiṣ,* a word that means "summer" and that can also be used of the fruit harvested at summer's end (2 Sam 16:1-2; Jer 40:10, 12; Mic 7:1). God responded with the word *qēṣ,* the root of which (קָצַץ *qṣṣ*) means "to cut off."[74] The noun is used of the end of life in Job 6:11 and Ps 39:4[5]; in Dan 8:17, 19; 9:26; 12:4, 6, 9, 13, it is used as an eschatological term. Only rarely is it used to speak of the end of a people (Gen 6:13; Jer 51:13; Lam 4:18; Ezek 7:2-3, 6). Verse 2*b,* therefore, is the most extreme statement in the book of Amos. God accounts for it here as in the third vision: "I will never again pass them by," evidently meaning there will be no more forgiveness.

Just as 7:9 added some necessary words of interpretation to the third vision, so also 8:3 makes it clear that "end" means death. The singing of funeral songs[75] is reminiscent of 5:16-17, and the word translated here "Be silent" (הַס *has*) is the same as the "Hush" of 6:10. The last line of v. 3 seems to be just a disjointed series of outcries (see NIV). The expression "in that day," which occurs here and in vv. 9, 13; 9:11, was sometimes used to introduce an eschatological oracle in later prophetic books, but in this chapter it simply refers to some indefinite time in the future, as it is often used in the OT.

---

74. There is evidence that in the dialect of Hebrew spoken in the northern kingdom the two words would have been pronounced alike, making the wordplay even more impressive. See Al Wolters, "Wordplay and Dialect in Amos 8:1-2," *JETS* 31 (1988) 407-10.

75. The MT does not read smoothly, as it seems to make "songs" the subject of "wail." Most commentators accept the emendation from שִׁירוֹת (*šîrôt*) to שָׁרוֹת (*šārôt*), thus "singing women will wail" (so TNK). The location may have been Temple or palace (TNK); we do not know enough about the roles of these singers in pre-exilic Israel to know where they would be found.

REFLECTIONS

When we take seriously the terror that lies in the word *end,* we see that it is not surprising that Old Testament authors did not use it very often; neither is it surprising that some modern interpreters have tried to read the vision in a less severe way.[76] The word can be used with ease of the enemy Babylon in Jer 51:13, but when it is used of the flood in Gen 6:13 and when Lam 4:18 and Ezek 7:2-3, 6 use it in describing the death of their own nation, Judah, the context is heavily laden with emotion. The author of Lamentations reminds us of the horrors that go along with the reality of a nation's coming to an end. *End*—nothing more beyond this—is one of those absolutes we resist when it involves us, if we can comprehend it at all. It has often been noted that it seems to be impossible for any of us truly to imagine our own death, even though we know everyone dies. But an end will come, nevertheless. Many organizations (churches included) are kept barely alive, long beyond their natural, useful lifespan, because the remaining members cannot acknowledge that the end does come.

---

76. John H. Hayes, *Amos: The Eighth-Century Prophet* (Nashville: Abingdon, 1988) 207-8; K. Koch, *The Prophets: The Assyrian Period* (Philadelphia: Fortress, 1982) 41-44.

In a way *end* seems to be an inappropriate term to use with reference to the people of God, for would not their end mean not only that they have failed but also that God has failed? This is the most disturbing word Amos could have spoken. He does not tell us whether he ever thought in terms of God's failing, but his continuing emphasis on the sovereignty of Yahweh over nature and the nations, as well as over the chosen people, makes it seem unlikely. All Amos can see, in the immediate future, however, is death. Given the forcefulness of the vision, perhaps we should not rush too quickly to the promises of a new future, beyond judgment, that appear in the other prophetic books (and in a small way in Amos 9:11-15), for we also must face absolutes at times, without any more control over them than Amos had over the fate of Israel. Each of us will die, whether we can comprehend that now or not. Cherished relationships will end before we are ready to give them up, and will not be renewed no matter what we do. Groups to which we have devoted our energies will just wither away. We cannot have any more certain knowledge of what lies beyond those endings than Amos did. Yet Scripture speaks of a God who alone transcends those absolutes. God created something new out of the death of the chosen people (Isa 43:19). God refused to allow the death of Jesus to be the end of the redeeming work, but through resurrection brought new life to those who believe in him. God also promises us another kind of new life, after our deaths, something we cannot "know" but can only believe.

Sometimes the word *new* can be almost as threatening as the word *end*. Only a fully committed faith in a God who is in charge—of our lives, of history, of the world—makes it possible for us to hear those words without shuddering.

AMOS 8:4-10, WHY MUST THE END COME?

NIV

[4]Hear this, you who trample the needy
  and do away with the poor of the land,
[5]saying,
"When will the New Moon be over
  that we may sell grain,
and the Sabbath be ended
  that we may market wheat?"—
skimping the measure,
  boosting the price
  and cheating with dishonest scales,
[6]buying the poor with silver
  and the needy for a pair of sandals,
  selling even the sweepings with the wheat.
[7]The LORD has sworn by the Pride of Jacob: "I will never forget anything they have done.
[8]"Will not the land tremble for this,
  and all who live in it mourn?
The whole land will rise like the Nile;
  it will be stirred up and then sink
  like the river of Egypt.
[9]"In that day," declares the Sovereign LORD,

NRSV

[4] Hear this, you that trample on the needy,
  and bring to ruin the poor of the land,
[5] saying, "When will the new moon be over
  so that we may sell grain;
and the sabbath,
  so that we may offer wheat for sale?
We will make the ephah small and the shekel great,
  and practice deceit with false balances,
[6] buying the poor for silver
  and the needy for a pair of sandals,
  and selling the sweepings of the wheat."

[7] The LORD has sworn by the pride of Jacob:
  Surely I will never forget any of their deeds.
[8] Shall not the land tremble on this account,
  and everyone mourn who lives in it,
and all of it rise like the Nile,
  and be tossed about and sink again, like the Nile of Egypt?

[9] On that day, says the Lord GOD,

NIV	NRSV
"I will make the sun go down at noon and darken the earth in broad daylight. ¹⁰I will turn your religious feasts into mourning and all your singing into weeping. I will make all of you wear sackcloth and shave your heads. I will make that time like mourning for an only son and the end of it like a bitter day."	I will make the sun go down at noon, and darken the earth in broad daylight. ¹⁰ I will turn your feasts into mourning, and all your songs into lamentation; I will bring sackcloth on all loins, and baldness on every head; I will make it like the mourning for an only son, and the end of it like a bitter day.

COMMENTARY

After the dreadful message of the fourth vision, further explanation is called for. It is offered in an extended reason/announcement oracle. The introduction is the herald's cry, "Hear this," recalling 3:1; 4:1; 5:1. The reason uses the very words of those being charged, turning their words into a self-accusation (vv. 5-6; cf. 2:12; 4:1; 6:13; 7:16; 8:14; 9:10). The announcement is introduced in a particularly solemn way, with a divine oath (v. 7; cf. 4:2; 6:8; for similar uses of the oath, Jer 44:26; 49:12-13). The following oracle (vv. 9-10) may once have been a distinct unit, but the prophetic books often use "on that day" to link related oracles, and it seems appropriate here to read these verses as an extension of the announcement, which makes the whole of vv. 4-10 a comment on vv. 1-3.

8:4-6. The central chapters of the book speak for the most part of justice in the gate, abuses taking place within the court system; but this passage returns to the world of commerce, of which Amos also spoke in 2:6-8. He uses the same terms for people who are oppressed, "poor" (ענוים 'ǎnāwîm; דלים dallîm) and "needy" (אביון 'ebyôn), and he begins the accusation with the same verb, "trample" (שאף šā'ap). The focus is very explicit in this passage: on cheating in the sale of grain, by measuring it out in containers smaller than they were supposed to be, using heavier weights to calculate the payment due, tampering with the balances used for weighing, and mixing chaff with the product sold.[77] The theme of holy days, said to be of no use to those who pervert justice in

5:21, is taken up in a new way in the saying Amos attributes to these sellers (v. 5a). They hypocritically observe the rest days, new moon and sabbath, restive all the while because those days put limits on their greed. Little is known about the observance of the new moon day (cf. Num 10:10; 28:11-15; Isa 1:13-14; Ezek 46:3; Hos 2:11[13]). It marked the beginning of the month and evidently was a rest day, but the OT says little about it. This passage is one of the earliest references to the observance of the sabbath as a day of rest.

Amos's emphasis on the grain trade seems to be interrupted by v. 6a, which speaks of buying the poor, in terms comparable to the reference to selling the poor in 2:6b. The passage has frequently been considered a later addition for that reason, but Kessler has suggested that the people being accused here were neither grain merchants as such nor slave traders, but were the wealthy who made loans of grain to the poor, cheating as they did so in order to make it all the more certain that the poor would be unable to repay the loans and would have to become debt-slaves (cf. Exod 21:2; 22:24; Lev 25:39-42). He suggests that their sandals may have been taken as pledges for the debt.[78] It is unclear how the poor could have been expected to repay a loan of grain with silver—ordinarily repayment must have been in kind—but the proposal is worth considering.

8:7. What God means by swearing by the pride of Jacob still remains without a fully adequate explanation. Elsewhere God swears by God's own

---

77. The ephah measured a little more than 39 liters (about 10 gallons); the shekel weighed a little over 11 grams (about 0.4 ounces).

78. Rainer Kessler, "Die Angeblichen Kornhandler von Amos VIII,4-7," *VT* 29 (1989) 13-22.

self (Gen 22:16; Amos 6:8), by God's holiness (Amos 4:2), by God's great name (Jer 44:26), or by God's right hand (Isa 62:8). In the midst of the oath in 6:8 God expresses abhorrence at the pride of Jacob, so is 8:7 bitter irony? Others suggest it is a divine epithet, like "glory of Israel" (1 Sam 15:29), or that it refers to the promised land (cf. Ps 47:4[5]), but certainty is not possible. The content of the oath is unusual. This is the only time "not forgetting" is spoken of as a threat. In laments the sufferer will ask why God has forgotten (Pss 13:1[2]; 42:9[10]; 44:24[25]; Lam 5:20), and ordinarily when it is said that God has not forgotten, it is a reassurance (Deut 4:31; 1 Sam 1:11; Pss 9:12[13]; 10:12; 74:19, 23; Isa 49:15). This is another of Amos's reversals of the normal use of an expression, giving special weight to a brief statement, for instead of God's not forgetting divine promises, God says the people's sins will not be forgotten (cf. Isa 43:25).

8:8. God's use of nature itself as an agent of judgment reappears here, with an unusual comparison of an earthquake to the flooding of the Nile. Obviously Israelites all knew about the Nile's annual floods, but it is very unlikely that Amos had ever seen such a flood, and his comparison is more likely based on the surging flash floods in the wadis of Israel. He may have seen the way an earthquake can virtually liquefy certain kinds of soil, making the comparison all the more appropriate.[79]

8:9-10. Another cosmic feature, the solar eclipse, is introduced in these verses, providing a connection between these verses and v. 8. The extended description of mourning ties vv. 4-10 to vv. 1-3. There was a partial eclipse in Israel on June 15, 763 BCE and a total eclipse on February 9, 784 BCE, so Amos's audience would have known the effects of the darkening of the sun at noon.[80] The trembling of the usually solid earth and the darkening of the sun are then associated with the reversal of festivity into mourning and singing into lamentation. This unit and the next both end the way chap. 5 began, with reference to the most severe kind of grief. Here it is called mourning for an only son (cf. Jer 6:26; Zech 12:10), the one in whom one's own character and vitality might have lived on.

This is the last passage in Amos that provides details of Israel's sins, and it calls for additional reflection on Amos's diagnosis of the nation's fatal illness. Was Israel really that bad? Or is this just a way of rationalizing the fact that a great empire was about to move in, as some have claimed? On what basis did Amos find the behavior of Israelites to be so profoundly offensive to God? There is little support for claiming his message is an interpretation of the Assyrian threat, for he shows no awareness of who the invader will be, and he usually speaks of God as the direct agent of destruction. The terms Amos uses for the oppressed and the oppressor also provide little basis for reading the book as the account of a class struggle between landowners and peasants. He speaks of the oppressed as righteous, needy, poor, afflicted (2:6-7; 8:4-6), but he says virtually nothing to describe them. On the contrary, he describes the activity of oppressors, but has almost no special terms to identify them. This makes a striking contrast between Amos and Hosea, who speaks of kings seventeen times, princes eight times, priests four times, and judges twice. Amos speaks of king and priest only in chap. 7, and instead of naming classes of people he frequently identifies his addressees as Israel, the people of Israel, and the house of Jacob or of Israel. He describes with disdain the way the life-style of the wealthy is supported by their oppression of the poor, but he does not name the wealthy as the group guilty of all that has gone wrong. Obviously corruption in the marketplace and the law court are increasing poverty and making the lives of the poor even more miserable, and that is the essence of Amos's diagnosis; but he indicts anyone who turns justice to wormwood, takes bribes, cheats in buying and selling, etc. All of Israel would have been present in the sanctuaries for the great festivals, and he calls the worship of all of them futile. The judgment will not sort out rich from poor, although one of his ironic twists puts the former leaders at the head of the column of exiles (4:3; 6:7). They all stand under judgment, and even the idea of a remnant is used more as a threat than a promise. This is more realistic than any analysis based on class struggle, for not all suffering is the fault of the rich and those in power. The poor also prey on the poor.

---

79. See, for example, the pictures of the 1964 earthquake in Anchorage, Alaska, in *National Geographic* 126.1 (July 1964) 136-37, 149, 154-55.

80. For details, see Shalom Paul, *Amos,* Hermeneia (Philadelphia: Fortress, 1991) 262-63.

REFLECTIONS

Could Israel have been so bad for God to give up on them and start over? As Amos saw it, religion served only to reassure people that everything was all right, when in fact it was not. Religion said: "Be sure to observe the festival days, keep the sanctuaries in good order, and make the proper sacrifices, and that will provide a divine guarantee." Should we say today, "Get prayer back into the public schools, and that observance will make ours a different nation somehow"? Like contemporary society, the Israel Amos diagnosed had evidently lost the standards of public morality that had once been generally accepted and had provided an ethos that enabled people to live together in general harmony. In mid–eighth-century BCE Israel, as in contemporary society, that loss of standards led people to prey on one another—the true enemy was within. From whence, then, could healing come?

AMOS 8:11-14, WORDS OF LIFE AND OF DEATH

NIV

[11]"The days are coming," declares the Sovereign LORD,
　"when I will send a famine through the land—
not a famine of food or a thirst for water,
　but a famine of hearing the words of the LORD.
[12]Men will stagger from sea to sea
　and wander from north to east,
searching for the word of the LORD,
　but they will not find it.
[13]"In that day
"the lovely young women and strong young men
　will faint because of thirst.
[14]They who swear by the shame[a] of Samaria,
　or say, 'As surely as your god lives, O Dan,'
or, 'As surely as the god[b] of Beersheba lives'—
they will fall,
　never to rise again."

a14 Or *by Ashima*; or *by the idol*   b14 Or *power*

NRSV

[11] The time is surely coming, says the Lord GOD,
　when I will send a famine on the land;
not a famine of bread, or a thirst for water,
　but of hearing the words of the LORD.
[12] They shall wander from sea to sea,
　and from north to east;
they shall run to and fro, seeking the word of the LORD,
　but they shall not find it.

[13] In that day the beautiful young women and the young men
　shall faint for thirst.
[14] Those who swear by Ashimah of Samaria,
　and say, "As your god lives, O Dan,"
and, "As the way of Beer-sheba lives"—
　they shall fall, and never rise again.

COMMENTARY

These verses are usually treated as two units because of the expression "In that day" in v. 13, but the phrase is not always used as an introduction (cf. Isa 10:27; Hos 2:18[20]; Amos 2:16; 8:3; Mic 2:4). The subject matter of each part is unusual, for Amos and for the OT. They appear at first to deal with two different subjects, but they may be related: Those who take the futile

oaths of v. 14 shall no longer be able to gain access to the words of Yahweh. The verses can be read as an announcement of judgment (vv. 11-12, 13, 14b) with a reason incorporated in v. 14a. "Seeking" or "finding" the Lord is a not uncommon idea in the OT, but nowhere else does seeking or finding the word (or words) of Yahweh appear. There are some comparable passages that deal with the dire effects of the silence of Yahweh (such as 1 Sam 14:37; 28:6; Ps 74:9; Prov 1:28; Lam 2:9; Hos 5:6; Mic 3:5-7), but no other author imagines a time when an entire population will frantically search for God's word—a word that they apparently found very easy to ignore in Amos's time. This is probably a comment on Israel's persistent refusal to hear Amos's message, the subject dealt with in other ways in chaps. 3–4. Like Saul when he faced his last battle (1 Samuel 28), the people will know, one day, that they need the word of God. But Amos thinks that part of the judgment will be God's total withdrawal of communication with them.

The reference to "thirst" (צמא *ṣāmāʾ*) in v. 13 provides a connection between the two passages, which may at one time have had separate identities. The thirst in this verse may be literal rather than figurative, since vv. 13-14 seem to speak of the demise of even the strongest in the land, the young people. They are condemned for the oaths they take, reminding us of warnings against swearing by another god in Josh 23:7; Jer 12:16; Zeph 1:5. It still is not clear whether the references to Samaria, Dan, and Beersheba concern pagan deities or forms of the Yahwistic cult. A straightforward reading of the Hebrew text leads to "shame (or guilt) of Samaria" (שמרון באשמת *bĕʾašmat šōmĕrôn*) and "the way of Beersheba" (באר־שבע דרך *derek bĕʾēršābaʿ*). Numerous emendations and interpretations of the two expressions have been suggested.[81] The shame of Samaria might be the calf image spoken of by Hosea (Hos 8:6), and that could have been associated with Yahweh, as the calves at Dan and Bethel had been (1 Kgs 12:28-29). The "way of Beersheba" may refer to the pilgrimages made by people of the northern kingdom to that old sanctuary associated with Abraham and Isaac (cf. Amos 5:5). Other readings of the latter phrase are unconvincing, but with a slight emendation the word translated "shame" in the phrase "shame of Samaria" becomes the name of a goddess, Ashimah (see 2 Kgs 17:30). This translation has been adopted by the NRSV, and a few commentators prefer it. Since Amos elsewhere shows almost no interest in the cults of other gods (cf. 5:26), however, but is intently concerned about the futility of the ways Yahweh is being worshiped in Israel, it seems more likely that he is not making reference to paganism, but is giving instead additional examples of apparent piety that he sees to be no better than hypocrisy.

81. Surveyed by Hans M. Barstad, *The Religious Polemics of Amos*, VTSup 34 (1984) 144-91.

REFLECTIONS

Luther's personal experience had taught him well that preaching and hearing the Word of God make the difference between spiritual life and death.

> This is the last blow. It is the worst, the most wretched of all. All the rest of the blows would be bearable, but this is absolutely horrible. He is threatening to take away the genuine prophets and the true Word of God, so that there is no one to preach even if men were most eager to wish to hear the Word and would run here and there to hear it.[82]

Does the contemporary church see in Amos's words such an awful prospect as Luther did? Does the church recognize that its health and vigor, its very life, depends on one thing only—not on efficiency of organization, not on breadth of programs, not on attractiveness of sanctuaries, services, and clergy—but solely on the clear and faithful preaching of the Word of God as found in Scripture? If it does, there is abundant evidence the church as a whole is not doing enough about it. It is bad enough that some individuals claim they need to rewrite Scripture, finding it to be irrelevant to our time, or even wrongheaded as seen from our "enlightened" point of view. It may be worse that large portions of the church itself give lip service to Scripture while finding other things to do in worship and programming. The dilemma Amos sets before us is this: If we ignore the word God has set before us, what more can God do for us?

82. Martin Luther, *Luther's Works*, vol. 18: *Lectures on the Minor Prophets, I. Hosea, Joel, Amos, Obadiah, Micah, Nahum, Zephaniah, Haggai, Malachi* (St. Louis: Concordia, 1975) 182-83.

NO ESCAPE

NIV

9 I saw the Lord standing by the altar, and he said:

"Strike the tops of the pillars
    so that the thresholds shake.
Bring them down on the heads of all the people;
    those who are left I will kill with the sword.
Not one will get away,
    none will escape.
²Though they dig down to the depths of the grave,ᵃ
    from there my hand will take them.
Though they climb up to the heavens,
    from there I will bring them down.
³Though they hide themselves on the top of Carmel,
    there I will hunt them down and seize them.
Though they hide from me at the bottom of the sea,
    there I will command the serpent to bite them.
⁴Though they are driven into exile by their enemies,
    there I will command the sword to slay them.
I will fix my eyes upon them
    for evil and not for good."

⁵The Lord, the LORD Almighty,
    he who touches the earth and it melts,
    and all who live in it mourn—
the whole land rises like the Nile,
    then sinks like the river of Egypt—
⁶he who builds his lofty palaceᵇ in the heavens
    and sets its foundationᶜ on the earth,
who calls for the waters of the sea
    and pours them out over the face of the land—
    the LORD is his name.

ᵃ2 Hebrew *to Sheol*   ᵇ6 The meaning of the Hebrew for this phrase is uncertain.   ᶜ6 The meaning of the Hebrew for this word is uncertain.

NRSV

9 I saw the LORD standing besideᵃ the altar, and he said:

Strike the capitals until the thresholds shake,
    and shatter them on the heads of all the people;ᵇ
and those who are left I will kill with the sword;
    not one of them shall flee away,
    not one of them shall escape.

2 Though they dig into Sheol,
    from there shall my hand take them;
though they climb up to heaven,
    from there I will bring them down.
3 Though they hide themselves on the top of Carmel,
    from there I will search out and take them;
and though they hide from my sight at the bottom of the sea,
    there I will command the sea-serpent, and it shall bite them.
4 And though they go into captivity in front of their enemies,
    there I will command the sword, and it shall kill them;
and I will fix my eyes on them
    for harm and not for good.

5 The Lord, GOD of hosts,
    he who touches the earth and it melts,
    and all who live in it mourn,
and all of it rises like the Nile,
    and sinks again, like the Nile of Egypt;
6 who builds his upper chambers in the heavens,
    and founds his vault upon the earth;
who calls for the waters of the sea,
    and pours them out upon the surface of the earth—
    the LORD is his name.

ᵃ Or *on*   ᵇ Heb *all of them*

COMMENTARY

The book of Amos ends with four passages that have little relationship with one another: 9:1-6, 7-10, 11-12, 13-15. Although 9:1-6 is typically called Amos's fifth vision, it is mostly unlike the visions in 7:1-9 and 8:1-3. God does not "show" Amos anything, and there is no dialogue. The "I saw" of v. 1 functions merely as an introduction, and the rest is a word from God. It is essentially a judgment oracle, without a reason supplied, and it begins in an unusual way, with an imperative addressed to some unnamed person. Some scholars think the prophet is being commanded to "strike the capitals until the thresholds shake" (v. 1), but that is hard to imagine. More scholars think that God is addressing one of the heavenly host (as in 1 Kgs 22:22), but perhaps it is best to understand the imperative as being used simply for rhetorical effect, with the true agent understood to be God.[83]

Even though nothing is made of Amos's claim that he saw the Lord, here, the words are striking enough that something must be said about them. Israel's usual understanding is expressed in Exod 33:20: "No one shall see me and live" (NRSV); John 1:18 reiterates the same conviction: "No one has ever seen God" (NIV). But on rare occasions, the OT does dare to speak of someone's seeing God: Exod 24:10-11; 1 Kgs 22:19; Isa 6:1. The Exodus passage shows an awareness of the danger involved (esp. Exod 24:11a), but what is important about each of these "sightings" (and also texts such as Ezekiel 1) is that even though the writers felt the need to speak of being uniquely close to God, they knew that God remains indescribable. They dare to say something (in stumbling words) about what surrounds the immediate presence of God, but they will go no further.

Amos offers no description of God at all, except to say that he saw the "LORD standing by [or on] the altar" (v. 1). We do not know where this altar was; it is futile to guess about Bethel or Jerusalem as the location, as some have done. The only help Amos gives in locating it is in the destructive words that follow, which remind us of 3:14-15, suggesting this passage begins with the command to destroy a temple. Sanctuaries are not really the

issue here, however, for the point of the passage is the futility of attempting to escape God's judgment. Even the architectural elements mentioned are probably used for effect: destruction from capitals to thresholds—from top to bottom. The difficult line that follows, with the words translated "heads" (ראש *rō'š*) and "those who are left" (ואחריתם *wĕ'aḥărîtām*), may also have introduced those terms in order to suggest the idea of "first to last," or "beginning to end." The sword appears in vv. 1 and 4 as the instrument of death, so war is anticipated, but as usual there are no details: Death will come by the sword of Yahweh.

9:2-4. Amos uses poetic hyperbole to emphasize the inescapability of judgment. Yahweh is sovereign everywhere, including places no human being can ever go.[84] In Ps 139:7-12, the worshiper expresses intense feelings of security in the same way, insisting that there is no place in the cosmos where the presence of God cannot be known. But Amos has reversed the meaning of omnipresence here. In Israelite thought, Sheol was a kind of universal grave, where everyone went upon death (Gen 37:35; Eccl 9:10; Isa 14:9-15; 38:10; Ezek 32:17-32). A lament might say that the dead have no access to God in Sheol (e.g., Ps 6:5[6]; Isa 38:18), but that was probably an emotional reaction to the prospect of death, since other texts insist Yahweh is sovereign also over the realm of the dead (e.g., 1 Sam 2:6; Prov 15:11). Living people neither dig into Sheol nor climb up to heaven, but even if they could, these are Yahweh's territories. Mount Carmel (v. 3) seems to bring us to real life. It was probably chosen not only because of its height, heavy woodlands, and many caves, but more because it is a ridge projecting into the Mediterranean Sea, forming a good contrast with another impossibility: hiding at the bottom of the sea. Reference to the sea gives Amos an opportunity to allude to the old Israelite uses of creation myths from other cultures, which involved God's destruction of a sea monster (e.g., Ps 74:14; Isa 27:1). But in Israelite theology the sovereignty of Yahweh was extended to make what had been an enemy in the old creation materials

---

83. For a survey of readings, see Shalom Paul, *Amos,* Hermeneia (Philadelphia: Fortress, 1991) 274.

84. The Canaanite king Tagi used the same hyperbole in writing to the king of Egypt, in Amarna letter 264: "If we mount up to heaven, or if we descend into hell, our head is in your hand." See *Les Lettres d'El-Amarna: Correspondance diplomatique du pharaon,* trans. Wm. L. Moran et al. (Paris: Les Editions du Cerf, 1987) 489.

no more than God's "obedient serpent" here (and in Gen 1:21; Ps 104:26).

Elsewhere in the book of Amos, exile is the worst fate imaginable (4:3; 5:27; 6:7; 7:11), but the extravagance of this passage claims that God will not be satisfied even with that, and will pursue the captives (שבי *šĕbî*; the only time Amos uses this word rather than גלה *gālâ*), in order to kill them (cf. Ezek 5:1-4, 12). There follows another of Amos's reversals of the usual use of language. Ordinarily, to "set one's eyes" on someone means to look favorably (Gen 44:21; Jer 24:6), but here God's glance means death.

9:5-6. This final, "hymnic" passage in the book functions much like 4:13: to conclude a section reminding readers of the incomparable power of the God who has spoken. As with 4:13 and 5:8-9, vv. 5-6 may once have had a separate existence, but now they are connected with their context by the reappearance of "all of it rises like the Nile" (cf. 8:8) and the use of the root אבל ('*bl,* "mourn"; cf. 1:2; 5:16; 8:8, 10). These verses are scarcely a doxology or a creation hymn, as they have often been called, for their contents speak of nothing but destruction. The melting of the earth may allude to volcanic activity, and the pouring out of water on the earth almost certainly refers to floods rather than to life-giving rain (cf. 5:8*b*).

REFLECTIONS

The Introduction cautions readers of Amos not to take what this prophet says as the whole story about God, and that warning needs to be repeated at this point. Amos's words are focused on a unique crisis in human history. For him, God had become the enemy of Israel, and only occasionally does Amos remind us that it had not always been so (2:9-11; 3:1-2; 9:7). In 9:1-4, God is depicted as the implacable foe, searching out victims wherever they may try to hide.

1. We cannot say which passage was written earlier, Amos 9:1-6 or Psalm 139, but it is good that the two use the same imagery, for the psalm reassures us that Amos 9:1-4 represents only one special case in God's activity. Having seen Amos's inability to get a hearing for his unacceptable message (cf. 2:12; 4:6-13; 6:1-7; 7:10-17), it is easy for us to understand why he would have resorted to the hyperbolic language in this text. He uses language about God's presence and activity throughout the entire cosmos, which would ordinarily be the language of praise, as one more *ad hominem* effort to break through the resistance of his audience. If one insists, Amos 9:1-6 can be read as a description of a tyrannical God; some interpreters even read Psalm 139 that way. But even here the reference to mourning reappears (v. 5) as a reminder that the whole book can be read as a prophetic lament over the failure of God's people—and the prophet speaks for God.

2. It must be emphasized that this is no picture of the whole character of God, but the need for such a message did not evaporate with the exiling of Israel and Judah. It remains a word addressed to those who complacently do as they please, feeling no responsibility to anyone. Zephaniah described such persons long ago:

> At that time I will search
> Jerusalem with lamps,
> and I will punish the people
> who rest complacently on
> their dregs,
> those who say in their hearts,
> "The LORD will not do good,
> nor will he do harm." (Zeph 1:12 NRSV)

This "practical atheism," the notion that God is indifferent to and uninvolved in human concerns, is a far more popular point of view than any theoretical atheism. Over against it must be set Amos's claim that there is a God who is intensely active, and that the day will come when that God cannot be avoided.

LORD OF ALL

NIV

[7]"Are not you Israelites
the same to me as the Cushites[a]?"
declares the LORD.
"Did I not bring Israel up from Egypt,
the Philistines from Caphtor[b]
and the Arameans from Kir?

[8]"Surely the eyes of the Sovereign LORD
are on the sinful kingdom.
I will destroy it
from the face of the earth—
yet I will not totally destroy
the house of Jacob,"
declares the LORD.

[9]"For I will give the command,
and I will shake the house of Israel
among all the nations
as grain is shaken in a sieve,
and not a pebble will reach the ground.
[10]All the sinners among my people
will die by the sword,
all those who say,
'Disaster will not overtake or meet us.'"

[a]7 That is, people from the upper Nile region   [b]7 That is, Crete

NRSV

[7] Are you not like the Ethiopians[a] to me,
O people of Israel? says the LORD.
Did I not bring Israel up from the land of
Egypt,
and the Philistines from Caphtor and the
Arameans from Kir?
[8] The eyes of the Lord GOD are upon the sinful
kingdom,
and I will destroy it from the face of the
earth
—except that I will not utterly destroy
the house of Jacob,
says the LORD.

[9] For lo, I will command,
and shake the house of Israel among all the
nations
as one shakes with a sieve,
but no pebble shall fall to the ground.
[10] All the sinners of my people shall die by the
sword,
who say, "Evil shall not overtake or meet
us."

[a] Or Nubians; Heb Cushites

COMMENTARY

Each verse in this section could be read as a separate saying. There is enough continuity, however, that the verses can be read as a judgment oracle beginning with a disputation speech that contains two rhetorical questions. The questions are intended to undercut objections to what Amos has been saying, based on appeals to the saving history. Two elements serve to connect the four verses: the references to "sinful kingdom" and "all the sinners" in vv. 8 and 10, and the use of a quotation in v. 10, expressing the complacency Amos is attempting to deal with by his rhetorical question in v. 7 (cf. 5:14).

9:7-8. The most striking of all the "reversals"

in the book appears in v. 7, for it even seems to question the belief in election that was appealed to in 3:2. In two questions unparalleled elsewhere in the OT, Amos puts Israel on the same level, in God's sight, with three other nations. Interpreters have differed over whether Amos intended thereby to demote Israel from its special relationship with God (thus denying election), or whether it is a kind of universalistic claim, saying that each nation has its own relationship with God.[85]

85. The various readings are conveniently summarized by W. Vogels, "Invitation a revenir a l'alliance et universalisme en Amos IX 7," *VT* 22 (1972) 223-39.

Most commentaries until those published very recently have made the unfortunate assumption that the Cushites (Ethiopians, so NRSV) were held in contempt by Israelites. There is no evidence for that in the OT, however, and that assumption can be explained only as the projection of modern biases on the material. In the eighth century BCE, Cush referred to the region south of the second cataract of the Nile—Nubia and the Sudan—and during the latter half of the century Cushite kings gained control of all Egypt. Later, Greek authors used the term to refer to Ethiopia, further south.[86] Old Testament authors refer to the area's wealth (Job 28:19; Ezek 30:4), since Nubia was an important source of gold, but Amos probably chose to compare Israel with the Cushites at this point just because it was the most distant place known in Africa. Other authors speak of it as being at the borders of the known world (Esth 1:1; Isa 18:1; Ezek 29:10; Zeph 3:10). The comparison Amos makes can best be understood in terms of the concept of God that was found to lie behind the oracles against the nations in chaps. 1–2. Amos claims that Yahweh is no national deity. God did choose Israel for a special relationship (3:2), but all the nations belong to Yahweh, to the farthest reaches of the earth.

Even the greatest redemptive event in Israel's history, the exodus from Egypt, has had its parallels in the histories of other nations, Amos asserts. He speaks of two neighbors because it was still remembered that they also had migrated into the region about the same time as the Israelites. The Philistines came from the Aegean region (Capthor is probably Crete), and the Arameans had moved up from the Arabian peninsula to north Mesopotamia, then westward to what we now call Syria and Lebanon.[87] Kir might be the city on the Euphrates, south of Carchemish, also known as Emar, since an inscription from that city calls its ruler "king of the people of the land of Qi-ri";[88] but Amos 1:5 and Isa 22:6 suggest it should be a more distant place.

Verse 7 thus resumes one of Amos's sweeping claims for Yahweh, who is more than the God of Israel. It was not the gods of the Philistines and the Arameans who led the people to a new land, as they had thought. The "sinful kingdom" of v. 8 is thus probably not specifically Israel, but any kingdom whose behavior leads Yahweh to intervene as an advocate of the oppressed. If the passage is read this way, it may be possible to understand the exception (v. 8c) as part of the original message. If the sinful kingdom is Israel, as many read it, then "except that I will not utterly destroy the house of Jacob" appears to be a correction, added by a later reader who knew the destruction had not been complete. But if the verse speaks of God's judgment of every sinful kingdom, then v. 8c may just be a reference to that pitiful remnant of which Amos had spoken elsewhere (3:12; 5:3, 15).

9:9-10. Some readers find a new idea represented by the sieve metaphor of v. 9: a sorting out of the righteous from the wicked. If the text really does speak of a faithful remnant it would thus be contrary to the message of the book as a whole and would probably have to be called a later addition. But the meaning of v. 9 is not as clear as one would like. "Shaking" Israel among the nations has been taken by some as a reference to scattering in exile, but one does not use a sieve for scattering. The nations probably appear as witnesses here (cf. 3:9). Sieves have traditionally been used in Middle Eastern agriculture to separate remains of threshing floor debris from the grain itself. Such sieves have been made of crisscrossed leather strips, allowing the grain to fall through and catching the larger objects (Sir 27:4).[89] The question, then, is what צרור (*sĕrôr*, "pebble") actually means. Elsewhere this word occurs only in 2 Sam 17:13, where it is used to mean "stone." If it means that here, then Amos is saying that not one of the wicked will escape, and that fits very well with v. 10. But some think the word should mean "grain," so that Amos is saying that not one of the righteous will be

86. See R. H. Smith, "Ethiopia," in *The Anchor Bible Dictionary*, 6 vols. (New York: Doubleday, 1992) 2:665-66; T. O. Lambdin, "Ethiopia," in *The Interpreter's Dictionary of the Bible*, 4 vols. (Nashville: Abingdon, 1962) 2:176-77; O. Wintermute, "Cush," in *The Interpreter's Dictionary of the Bible, Supplementary Volume* (Nashville: Abingdon, 1976) 200-201.

87. For a discussion of the Philistines, see Trude Dothan, *ABD* 5:326-33. For more on the Arameans, see R. A. Bowman, *IDB* 1:190-93; A. R. Millard, *ABD* 1:345-50.

88. Ran Zadok, "Elements of Aramean Pre-History," *Scripta Hierosolymitana* 33 (1991) 114.

89. Oded Borowski, *Agriculture in Iron Age Israel* (Winona Lake, Ind.: Eisenbrauns, 1987) 66-67.

overlooked. That reading seems to be motivated by the strong desire to find a more positive message than the book really can support. The former reading seems far more likely; note that even though the metaphor leaves us with a picture of a sorting out of the "righteous," the good grain that has fallen through the sieve, Amos has nothing to say about them; his concern is the pebbles, every one of which will be caught by the sieve. In fact we are not told whether any grain does fall through. The pebbles are then defined explicitly by means of a direct quote, as Amos often does (cf. 4:1; 8:5-6), referring again to their complacent refusal to admit their behavior has put them in mortal danger (cf. 5:14; 6:1-3).

REFLECTIONS

This is one of the most startling of Amos's attacks on the complacency of the northern kingdom, for instead of citing acts of injustice or conspicuous luxury at the expense of the poor, he makes his own original use of Israel's most important religious traditions. The exodus is the classic piece of evidence that Yahweh had the power to defeat other, great nations, and Amos reaffirms that in chaps. 1–2. But it was also thought that Yahweh used that power always on Israel's behalf. It is best not to ask whether in 9:7-10 Yahweh degrades Israel to the level of the other nations or elevates the nations to Israel's level. Yahweh's sovereignty over all nations makes God judge of them all, so this is another way of speaking of the inescapability of judgment, which was described so vividly in 9:1-9. One cannot deduce from the exodus, Amos claims, that Yahweh is thereby obligated to protect Israel from disaster without imposing any conditions on Israel. Other nations have also experienced an exodus, and that was the work of Yahweh. But the power of the Philistines had been broken long ago by David, and the Aramean city-states no longer dominated the region as they had in previous generations. To deduce invulnerability from the exodus is thus faulty reasoning, Amos asserts.

It would be moving far beyond anything this text could support to say that Amos was a "universalist," that he believed each nation had its means of access to the true God. Like other prophets, Amos extends the sovereignty of Yahweh over the whole world without claiming the other nations know the true God (note esp. Isa 45:1-4). Hope would be expressed that one day converts to Yahwism would come to Zion from as far away as Cush (Ps 68:31; Zeph 3:9-10). But by making this claim for the universal sovereignty of Yahweh, Amos marks the beginning of serious consideration, by the prophets, of the nations as something more than enemies. The expanded perspective reaches its culmination in Isa 19:18-24, which concludes with the amazing promise that the day will come when Israel and its two archetypal enemies, Egypt and Assyria, will live together in peace, as equals.[90]

This willingness to believe that foreigners, strangers to oneself, to one's customs, and to one's God are as much a concern to our God as we are has been a hard lesson to learn. In Old Testament passages of this kind lie the roots of the early church's willingness to extend the gospel to everyone, without ethnic or ritual limitations. What was the basis for a message of judgment in Amos eventually became the basis for good news. But the possessors of the good news still find it hard to resist the temptation to think that they also possess God. So Amos's words, reminding us that being God's elect lays upon us special responsibilities, still need to be heard.

90. For the twofold view of the nations in eschatology, see Donald E. Gowan, *Eschatology in the Old Testament* (Philadelphia: Fortress, 1986) 42-54.

AMOS 9:11-15

AFTER THE JUDGMENT

OVERVIEW

The book concludes with two short oracles of promise. They are not thematically related, and neither of them shows any close relationship with the rest of the book. Many commentators consider them to be the work of an exilic or post-exilic author, although there have been numerous efforts to show that they could be the words of Amos. These are the only passages from the book that were given much attention by later Jewish and Christian writers, and that is understandable, since those writers tended to look for good news in the Old Testament. They used these verses without regard for their context, and they had no interest in the question of whether they were likely to have been spoken by an eighth-century BCE prophet.[91] The historical and biographical approaches of the nineteenth and twentieth centuries have raised the issue of consistency: Would a prophet whose message was that of thoroughgoing and inevitable judgment have also uttered two unrelated promises? We shall not take up the unanswerable question of what a person in antiquity may or may not have said, but will ask instead whether these oracles show evidence of continuity with the rest of the book and whether they seem to reflect an eighth-century BCE setting.

Arguments that Amos composed these verses tend to appeal to the conviction that he must have had a positive message to offer.[92] The main problems raised by assigning the oracles to an eighth-century date are then dealt with in one of these ways: David was introduced (v. 11) because Amos was a Judean and looked forward to the reuniting of the monarchy, which had been divided after the death of Solomon. This would not be good news to the northern kingdom, so some suggest a continuing memory of Davidic glories in the north, in spite of Jeroboam's present superiority. Others say that the fallen booth does not refer to the tenth-century BCE schism, but to later distresses that befell the Davidic dynasty, or they make it a reference to the future rather than to the past. The "remnant of Edom" (v. 12) is explained by some scholars as the part of Edom not already controlled by Uzziah, according to 2 Kgs 14:22. Reasons for thinking these verses reflect the time of the exile and do not show any strong indications of continuity with the rest of the book will be offered in the commentary. Both oracles are addressed to a situation of loss, promising that the time will come when God will restore what has been lost and will transform the world to make it better than before.

91. E. g., CD 7:15-16; 4QFlor i.11-13; Acts 15:16-17; Augustine *The City of God* 18.28.

92. For a survey of the discussion, see Gerhard F. Hasel, *Understanding the Book of Amos: Basic Issues in Current Interpretations* (Grand Rapids: Baker, 1991) 116-20.

AMOS 9:11-12, A PROMISE FOR JUDAH

NIV	NRSV
[11]"In that day I will restore David's fallen tent. I will repair its broken places, restore its ruins, and build it as it used to be, [12]so that they may possess the remnant of Edom and all the nations that bear my name,[a]" declares the LORD, who will do these things.	[11] On that day I will raise up the booth of David that is fallen, and repair its[a] breaches, and raise up its[b] ruins, and rebuild it as in the days of old; [12] in order that they may possess the remnant of Edom and all the nations who are called by my name, says the LORD who does this.
a12 Hebrew; Septuagint so that the remnant of men / and all the nations that bear my name may seek the Lord.	*a Gk: Heb their b Gk: Heb his*

COMMENTARY

"On that day" means "then," a reference to an indefinite time in the future. This is the only place where a "booth" (סכה *sukkâ*) of David is mentioned, although Isa 16:5 speaks of the tent of David. A comparison of 2 Sam 6:17; 7:2 with 2 Sam 11:11 suggests that the terms "tent" and "booth" might be interchangeable, and each is used metaphorically in the OT to denote shelters of various kinds (booth: Job 36:29; Ps 31:20[21]; Isa 4:5; tent: Isa 33:20; Jer 30:18; Lam 2:4). The references to rebuilding ruins in v. 11*b* suggests that its use here refers to the city of David, as "tent" does elsewhere. The participle "fallen" (הנפלת *hannōpelet*) is most naturally translated in the past tense here (as in 1 Sam 5:3), but those who argue for a date prior to 587 BCE point out that it could also be rendered "falling," and refer to the declining fortunes of the Davidic dynasty. "Booth" would then have to be the family of David rather than the city. Pre-exilic references to the house of David as "fallen" or even in dire distress are almost nonexistent. The best example of concern over the future of the dynasty is Ps 89:38-51[39-52], but it is probably to be dated later than 587 BCE. God's promise to raise up the booth of David finds its closest parallel in Jer 30:9: "But they shall serve the LORD their God and David their king, whom I will raise up for them" (NRSV; cf. Ezek 34:23-24). Nothing in Amos 9:11 has any evident relationship with the rest of the book. Amos shows no interest in the division of the monarchy after Solomon's death and says nothing of the state of the Davidic dynasty or of the fate of Jerusalem. Even the language referring to the ruin and rebuilding of a city is unusual for this book, but it is common in exilic materials (cf. Jer 31:4, 28). Verse 11 would be a meaningful promise in the middle of the sixth century BCE; it is hard to imagine how it could have seemed other than completely irrelevant to people of the northern kingdom 200 years earlier.

The LXX of v. 12 differs significantly from the MT, reading "so that the remnant of men shall seek, and all the Gentiles upon whom my name is called, says the Lord, who shall do these things." The translator has taken אדום (*'ĕdôm*, "Edom") as אדם (*'ādām*, "humanity") and ירש (*yāraš*, "possess") as דרש (*dāraš*, "seek"). Some scholars think the LXX was using a different Hebrew text, perhaps one to be preferred to the MT, but most believe this is one of the translator's "improvements" on the Hebrew. A positive interpretation is offered by some commentators, claiming that *yāraš* here means the inclusion of Edom and the rest of the nations with Israel as future recipients of the covenant promises.[93] But *yāraš* is always

---

93. O. Palmer Robertson, "Hermeneutics of Continuity," in *Continuity and Discontinuity: Perspectives on the Relationship Between the Old and New Testaments, Essays in Honor of S. Lewis Johnson, Jr.*, ed. J. S. Feinberg (Wheaton, Ill.: Crossway Books, 1988) 91-93; Gary V. Smith, *Amos: A Commentary* (Grand Rapids: Zondervan, 1989) 282.

used in an aggressive sense; references to possessing Edom elsewhere always speak of taking over the territory of an enemy (Num 24:17-18; Ezek 36:5; Obad 19). There were frequent wars between Edom and Israel or Judah, so this promise of victory might be pre-exilic, but the term "remnant of Edom" (and the nations) seems to fit best the time when Judah and all its neighbors had suffered under the Babylonians. A sixth-century BCE date would account for one nation's being mentioned by name, for it was Edom's behavior at the time that the Judeans found most reprehensible (Ezek 25:12-14; 35:1–36:7; Obadiah). The parallels between v. 12 and Ezek 36:4-12 are so close that it seems likely that it is the words of another prophet of Ezekiel's time. There is no point of contact between this promise of a victory for the Davidic dynasty over the nations and the rest of the book of Amos.

These verses introduce two of the frequent themes of OT eschatology: the gift of a righteous king in the line of David and victory over the nations whose enmity had made Israel's life precarious through most of its history. Nothing is said about kingship here except to promise its restoration; v. 11 is similar to texts such as Jer 30:9; Ezek 34:23-24; and Hos 3:5. It remains for other passages to clarify why the restoration of kingship was desirable. It could have been because the king's primary responsibility was the establishment and maintenance of justice (Isa 11:1-5; Jer 23:5).

The reference to the nations is an example of Israel's hopes for peace expressed in a very typically human way. Peace seems to require victory over one's enemies as a prerequisite (cf. Lev 26:6-8; Isa 11:14-16; Zephaniah 2; Zechariah 9). It is all the more surprising, then, when the OT sometimes speaks of peace among the nations that does not involve Israel's victory (Isa 2:2-4; 19:24-25; Mic 4:1-4). It is those passages, rather than texts like Amos 9:12, that stand as the OT's continuing challenge to human tendencies to identify peace with victory over an enemy.

The very different meaning that the LXX gave to this verse represents Jewish thinking along these lines. Edom has become humanity, and humanity has become the subject of the verb, which is now "seek" rather than "possess." These changes leave the verb without an object, but perhaps "the LORD" was intended to be understood. If so, the version may reflect an interest in the eventual conversion of the Gentiles, which appears in some post-exilic Jewish literature.[94] That is what appears, at any rate, in the citation of vv. 11-12 in Acts 15:16-17. The problems raised by this New Testament use of a text that is very different from the MT are too extensive to be discussed here.[95] That Yahweh's name would be "called over" (קרא qārāʾ) the remnant of all the nations (indicating that they belong to Yahweh) is a unique expression for the OT, and it may provide the only point of contact between the Hebrew text and the highly creative use made of it by the writer of Acts.

94. Moshe Greenberg, "Mankind, Israel and the Nations in Hebraic Heritage," in *No Man Is Alien: Essays on the Unity of Mankind in Honour of W. A. Visser 't Hooft*, ed. J. R. Nelson (Leiden: E. J. Brill, 1971) 15-40.

95. Walter Kaiser, Jr., "The Davidic Promise and the Inclusion of the Gentiles (Amos 9:9-15 and Acts 15:13-18): A Test Passage for Theological Systems," *JETS* 20 (1977) 97-111; Earl Richard, "The Creative Use of Amos by the Author of Acts," *NTS* 24 (1982) 44-52; Robertson, "Hermeneutics of Continuity."

REFLECTIONS

The historical figure David became a symbol for Judeans of what we would call good government. The Davidic kingship was believed to be a gift of God. So, for Judah, David was more than a political figure; what was said about him and his line was theologically important. Psalm 72 is a beautiful expression of what the Israelites expected God to give them through the rule of a righteous king. Most of the kings who actually ruled were far from ideal (cf. Jeremiah 22), however, and the hope for good government began to be expressed by the prophets in terms of promises of a righteous king to come in the last days (e.g., Isa 9:2-7; 11:1-5; Jer 23:5-6; Ezek 34:23-24; Mic 5:2-4; Zech 9:9-10). These promises have become famous as "messianic prophecies," and they have been associated with the coming of Jesus by Christians since early times, even though Jesus did not come to be a king (John 6:15) and did not establish justice and peace on earth. Jesus fulfilled other Old Testament promises and for that reason was declared to be the Messiah by his followers (e.g., Acts 2:38-39; 10:34-43; 13:38; Romans 4).

The kingship promises have been dealt with in two ways by Christians, from that day to this. (1) They were spiritualized, so as to make them already fulfilled, in Christ's kingship over the soul or his heavenly kingship. For some, this has been enough, and the hope for better government on earth has seemed unimportant. (2) The futuristic tone of the Old Testament texts was not abandoned in Christianity, however, and these prophecies also became part of Christian hope for a second coming of Christ, when he truly will become king over a world of peace. A cautionary word seems appropriate, both for those who are satisfied with the purely spiritual understanding of Christ's kingship and for those who may be fervently looking for the Second Coming: Either point of view may lead to a neglect of the mess this world is in today. The Old Testament messianic hopes insist that God is intensely interested in good government—justice and peace for God's people—and the New Testament says nothing to change that (e.g., Rom 13:1-7; 1 Pet 2:13-17; 3:13-17; cf. the reference to the nations in Matt 25:31-46; Revelation 21–22). If we believe that, what are we to do in the meantime? Certainly our every concern and all that we do ought to correspond, as much as is humanly possible, to what we believe God is at work to accomplish on earth.[96]

In Jewish apocalyptic literature, beginning with Daniel, the nations came to represent political manifestations of the cosmic forces of evil, which God must overcome in order to rid the world of evil (Dan 2:44-45; 7:26-27; 8:25; 10:13, 20-21; 11:45). Hope for the eventual conversion of the nations did not disappear from Jewish thought, however (Tob 14:6-7; *1 Enoch* 10:21; 50:1-3; *T. Levi* 18:9; *T. Naph* 8:1-4). In the NT the apocalyptic view of the nations as the enemies of God's people still appears in Revelation (Rev 16:12-21; 20:7-10; but cf. Rev 21:24; 22:2). The major NT theme is that the old promise to Abraham, that all the nations of the earth would bless themselves in him (Gen 12:1-3; 22:18), had been fulfilled by the coming of Jesus; and Matthew concludes with the great commission, "Go therefore and make disciples of all nations" (Matt 28:19 NRSV). This is not in continuity with Amos 9:12, but it is in keeping with those other OT hopes for the nations, mentioned above.

---

96. E. Jenni, "Messiah, Jewish," *IDB*, 3:360-65; E. Rivkin, "Messiah, Jewish," *IDBSup,* 588-91; S. E. Johnson, "Christ," *IDB*, 1:563-71; Donald E. Gowan, *Eschatology in the Old Testament* (Philadelphia: Fortress, 1986) 32-42, 121-29.

AMOS 9:13-15, A LAND OF PLENTY

NIV

[13]"The days are coming," declares the LORD,

"when the reaper will be overtaken by the plowman
  and the planter by the one treading grapes.
New wine will drip from the mountains
  and flow from all the hills.
[14]I will bring back my exiled[a] people Israel;
  they will rebuild the ruined cities and live in
    them.

a14 Or will restore the fortunes of my

NRSV

[13] The time is surely coming, says the LORD,
  when the one who plows shall overtake the
    one who reaps,
  and the treader of grapes the one who sows
    the seed;
the mountains shall drip sweet wine,
  and all the hills shall flow with it.
[14] I will restore the fortunes of my people Israel,
  and they shall rebuild the ruined cities and
    inhabit them;

NIV

They will plant vineyards and drink their wine;
  they will make gardens and eat their fruit.
15I will plant Israel in their own land,
  never again to be uprooted
  from the land I have given them,"

                              says the LORD your God.

NRSV

they shall plant vineyards and drink their wine,
  and they shall make gardens and eat their
  fruit.
15 I will plant them upon their land,
  and they shall never again be plucked up
  out of the land that I have given them,
                              says the LORD your God.

COMMENTARY

The second promise speaks of restoration from exile (v. 15) and emphasizes the fertility of the land to which the nation will be restored. These are two more of the frequently recurring themes of OT eschatology. Hunger was a perennial threat in the ancient Near East, and the promise that the day will come when there will be no more hunger is expressed in a delightfully extravagant way in v. 13. Ordinarily barley is harvested in March/April and wheat in May/June, but the prospect for the ideal future is that the crops will be so large the harvesters will still be at work in October/November, when plowing for the next planting would be done. Grapes are harvested in August/September, and in the future they will be so plentiful that wine making will overlap planting time (November/December); poetically, the mountains will flow with wine (cf. Lev 26:5; Joel 3:18; for no more hunger, see Ezek 34:25-29; 36:28-36).

Cities and farmland belonged together in antiquity, unlike today, for the walled town was small and most of its inhabitants made their living working the surrounding land. The rest of Amos does not dwell on the impending ruin of Israel's cities, but that did happen after Amos's time, and v. 14 promises the re-establishment of garden and city. The closest parallels to this passage appear in Jeremiah 30–31.[97]

The rest of Amos typically uses נלה (gālâ) to speak of exile, but this text chooses the vivid "plucked up" (נתשׁ nātaš), a term most often used of exile in Jeremiah (ten times). Verse 15 may be

related to Amos's threats of exile in 7:17 and elsewhere and to his description of the destruction of gardens and vineyards in 4:9, but Amos speaks more of the threat to people than to property. If we ask again what this promise meant to Amos's audience—people whose gardens and vineyards were prospering (6:6; cf. 5:11), who could not imagine being plucked up out of their land (6:1)— we find that the close parallels to this verse in Jer 31:27-28 suggest that vv. 13-15 also come from a prophet contemporary with Jeremiah. At that time, when the people had lost all these good things, such a message was needed, as it was not needed in the days of Amos.

The messages of the pre-exilic prophets focused on what their people needed to hear, and that was God's explanation of the destruction and death that lay just ahead. Thus they focused on the certainty of defeat and exile and on Israel's failures, which led God to decide to start over. Those who survived the falls of Israel in 722 BCE and of Judah in 587 BCE at first thought nothing lay ahead of them (cf. Ezek 37:1-14; Lamentations). They needed promises that God intended a new future for them, and such promises began to appear in the words of Jeremiah and Ezekiel, whose work continued after the destruction of Jerusalem. But the survivors who were given new hope by those promises also finally realized that Amos and his successors had been right after all, and they began to try to live according to the divine standards those prophets held up. As those prophetic materials were gathered and put into the books we now have, it seemed appropriate for them to contain the whole story, not just the

97. Cities: Jer 30:18; vineyards: Jer 31:5; gardens: Jer 31:12; "plucked up": Jer 31:28; restored fortunes: Jer 30:3, 18; 31:23.

first act—the death of Israel—and so Amos and most of the other books now conclude with promises. This is not to be understood as a contradiction of his "No," but as an affirmation that the negative was true for the eighth and the sixth centuries BCE, but was not God's last word.

REFLECTIONS

In the past, little attention was paid to the prophetic promises of the transformation of nature, but in a time when the damage human activity has done to nature is finally beginning to awaken our consciences, these passages deserve careful study.[98] The imagery of the garden is a good one for further reflection, for the garden is the classic example of cooperation between humans and nature. Plants can be made more fertile and more beautiful by human activity, when they are protected from insects, weeds, and disease. The result is a better life for humans, because they have worked with nature rather than exploiting it. Later prophets also spoke of "garden cities" (as we might call them) in the future. Cities of the past were small enough that Micah could picture the new Jerusalem as a place where all would sit under their vines and their fig trees (Mic 4:1-4). Ezekiel looked forward to the rebuilding of cities in the promised land after the exile (Ezek 34:25-29; 36:29-36). They would be places where the will of God would be done at last (36:26-27), and that was directly associated with the transformation of nature itself. If Amos did write vv. 13-15, he certainly would have included the necessity of justice in those rebuilt cities, and so this beautiful picture of an ideal future is not complete without the words of Amos that precede it.

The Old Testament theme of hope for the transformation of nature has been largely ignored in Christian tradition, and it has seldom been seen as having ethical implications for the way we treat the natural world.[99] Technology's ability to increase the effectiveness of the curse humans afflict on nature has finally made us aware that it is to our peril to ignore that part of Israel's concern about the future, for it is a subject about which something must be said and done. If understood properly, the hopes of those prophets of old ought to teach us that the material world is not just the stage on which human life is played out, and not just a source of raw materials. God's redeeming work includes nature as well, the prophets claimed. We may not be able to imagine how that can happen, but if we believe that is God's intention there is something we can do about it now. We can take with the utmost seriousness the ability God has given us to be good gardeners, and that God has put us here, like the first human, "to till it and keep it" (Gen 2:15 NRSV).

98. Antonine DeGuglielmo, O.F.M., "The Fertility of the Land in the Messianic Prophecies," *CBQ* 19 (1957) 306-11; Gowan, *Eschatology in the Old Testament,* 97-120.

99. For a helpful survey, see George Hunston Williams, "Christian Attitudes Toward Nature," *Christian Scholar's Review* 2 (1971/2) 3-35, 112-26.

THE BOOK OF OBADIAH

INTRODUCTION, COMMENTARY, AND REFLECTIONS
BY
SAMUEL PAGÁN

THE BOOK OF
OBADIAH

INTRODUCTION

THE BOOK

The book of the prophet Obadiah—the shortest in the Old Testament—presents a clear message of judgment against the people of Edom. It begins with the word "vision" (v. 1), which reveals the prophetic intent, the tone of the message, and the nature of the literature, and it ends with an affirmation of the kingdom and sovereignty of God, a word of hope (v. 21). The prophet elaborates on earlier traditions—e.g., the day of the Lord—and applies them to his immediate historical situation (the Israelite community of Jerusalem), and then to the exile of the people into Babylonia.

Obadiah is one of the least read prophetic writings in the Bible. It is a short book and does not provide much information about the author and the historical setting in which it was written. Moreover, at the literary level, a section of the message of Obadiah (vv. 1b-6) is similar to Jeremiah 49.

The book of Obadiah belongs to a type of literature that heralds God's judgment to come upon the nations near Israel. These prophecies may have been preserved by the cultic circles in Jerusalem. The oracles of judgment against the nations constitute an important element in the biblical prophetic literature. Prophecies against Edom are also found in Isaiah (21:11-12), Jeremiah (49:7-22), Ezekiel (25:12-14), Amos (1:11-12), and Malachi (1:2-5; see also Isa 11:14; Jer 25:21; Lam 4:21; Joel 4:19).

In the Hebrew canon, the book of Obadiah is fourth in order among the minor prophets, between Amos and Jonah. Perhaps this order stems from the fact that Obadiah and Amos have similar themes: both prophets emphasize the day of the Lord. It is important to point out, moreover, that thematic connections are also found with the book of Joel; the proclamation of the day of the Lord presented in Joel 3:2, 14 is included in Amos 9:11-12 and emerges again in Obadiah 15a-21. Some scholars think that Obadiah 1-14 is a commentary on Joel 3:19, and Obadiah 15-21 on Amos 9:12.

In most Septuagint manuscripts, the longer books (Hosea, Amos, Micah) are followed by shorter ones (Joel, Obadiah, Jonah). Such an ordering may reflect a criterion for order based on a book's length. Nonetheless, the length of Obadiah does not seem to be the main reason for placing it between Joel and Jonah in the Septuagint. Instead, the thematic relationship between Joel 3 and Obadiah and the interest in chronology manifested by the translators of the Septuagint were probably more important factors in establishing that order.[1]

It is difficult to determine precisely the date the book was written, since the historical information it provides is scant. Some scholars have proposed the ninth century BCE, referring to the Edomite rebellion against Joram (2 Kgs 8:20-22). Others, however, have placed the composition of the book at a much later date, at the middle of the fifth century BCE, after the exile of the people of Israel to Babylonia, during the Edomite occupation of the Negev.[2]

Nevertheless, historical, literary, and theological analysis of the book suggests the exilic period, particularly the years immediately following the crisis in Jerusalem (687/686 BCE), as the most probable date of the composition of Obadiah. Edom's attitude to the destruction of Jerusalem and the exile of Judahites helps to illumine Obadiah's historical context. Moreover, during that same period—at the beginning of the sixth century BCE—a literature with similar theological and literary tendencies developed (cf. Ps 137:7; Lam 4:18-22; Ezek 25:12-14; 31:1-15). These writings manifest resentment against the Edomites similar to that presented in the book of Obadiah. That anti-Edomite perspective also occurs in subsequent works. For example in 1 Ezra 4:45, the Edomites are identified as the ones who set fire to the Jerusalem Temple, when the Jews were devastated by the Chaldeans.

THE PROPHET

There is not much information about the prophet Obadiah. A tradition included in the Babylonian Talmud[3] identifies him as the servant of Ahab (1 Kgs 18:3-16), allied with Elijah and the protector of the prophets of the Lord (Jerome knew this tradition). Nevertheless, it is difficult to imagine an official of the king in the ninth century BCE who prophesied exclusively concerning relations between Judah and Edom three centuries later. Furthermore, there is no historical basis for equating the two characters. This tradition probably stemmed from the interest, attested in the Talmud, of identifying the author of

---

1. See Hans Walter Wolff, *Obadiah and Jonah: A Commentary* (Minneapolis: Augsburg, 1986) 17-18.
2. Ibid., 18-19.
3. *Sanhedrin* 39b.

each book of the Bible, along with the fact that very little information on this small prophetic book was available.

The Masoretic Text vocalized the name of the prophet Obadiah as עבדיה (*ʿōbadyâ,* "worshiper of Yahweh"; the Septuagint used Αβδιου (*Abdiou*); and the Vulgate rendered the name as *Abdias,* "servant of Yahweh." These variants in pronunciation produce alternate ways of understanding the same name. Some scholars have thought that the name "Abdias," beyond identifying a person, is symbolic. However, in ancient Israel, the name was fairly common. At least twelve people with that name are mentioned in the Old Testament; moreover, Obed, one of the variants of "Obadiah," is applied to six additional persons, including the grandfather of King David (Ruth 4:21-22; Matt 1:5).

Obadiah was a prophet of Yahweh. The prophet probably lived during the sixth century BCE, delivered his message in Jerusalem, and had at least some religious or cultic training. He was familiar with the prophetic traditions of judgment against the nations and was particularly versed in the anti-Edomite language, as seen in the similarities and parallels with Jeremiah 40; Ezek 25:12-14; Joel 1:15; 2:5, 32; 3:3, 17; and Amos 9:12. The style of Obadiah's oracles demonstrates his great communicative ability and literary skill. Perhaps, like Amos (Amos 7:10-15), he was not a professional prophet, but was called by God for a specific task.

The theme of the lordship of Yahweh (v. 21) perhaps echoes the enthronement psalms (Psalms 47; 93; 96–99), which made a prominent contribution to the worship liturgy in the Temple. The historical focus of the book (vv. 11-16) implies that it reflects the political relationship between Judah and Edom, after the catastrophe of 587/586 BCE and Israel's exile into Babylonia. Obadiah may have witnessed the destruction of Jerusalem and the capture of the people of Judah.

JUDAH AND EDOM

The territory of Edom is located to the south of the Dead Sea and is surrounded by deserts to the east and the south. To the west is a mountainous region that extends south to the Gulf of Aqaba. To the north, the Zered stream separated Edom and Moab. This small territory measured approximately seventy miles north to south and fifteen miles east to west. A characteristic of the region is the reddish color of its rocks and mountains; that geological trait may explain its name: אדום (*ʾĕdôm*) signifies this red region.

The Edomites arrived and settled that region around the year 1300 BCE, sometime before the Israelites arrived in Canaan. The history of the relations between these peoples is characterized by animosity and hostility. Edom is regularly included in the catalogue of judgment oracles against the nations that surround Israel.[4]

Some passages of the OT allude to the fraternal relationship between Israel and Edom; they are identified as "brother" peoples (Genesis 25; 27; 36; Num 20:14-21; Deut 2:4-8;

---

4. See B. C. Cresson, "Israel and Edom: A Study of the Anti-Edom Bias in the Old Testament Religion" (Ph.D. diss., Duke University, 1963).

23:7; Jer 49:7-11; Amos 1:11-12; Mal 1:2-4). Two fundamental conclusions can be drawn from these texts: First, the term "brothers" does not always connote a bond of friendship or camaraderie between peoples. Second, the fraternal relationship between Israel and Edom stems from complex events in the histories of these nations.[5] The struggle between the twins in Rebekah's womb (Genesis 25) symbolizes such enmity and hostility between Israel and Edom.

The people of Israel and Edom have displayed great mutual hostility throughout the ages. According to the narrative in Num 20:14-21, the Israelites, on their journey from Egypt to the promised land, requested permission from the king of Edom to pass through that territory, but he refused them permission. That disdainful attitude marked the beginning of intense enmity between the two nations. The resentment reached its peak when Jerusalem was captured by the Babylonians in 587/586 BCE. The Edomites may have joined in the destruction and helped the plunderers of Jerusalem (Ps 137:7). Moreover, the Edomites helped to capture fugitives who had fled from Judah (Obad 14). Because of the lack of solidarity with the neighboring people of Israel, God is determined to punish Edom.

The difficulties and conflicts between the two peoples were evident from at least the time of King David (2 Sam 8:13-14), and possibly even from the time of King Saul, when Edom was listed among Israel's enemies (1 Sam 14:47). This history of enmity continued throughout the monarchic period to the fall of Judah and the destruction of Jerusalem by the Babylonians (2 Kings 25; Obad 11-14).[6]

During the exile and, subsequently, during the Persian period, neither of these peoples was in a political or military position to manifest resentment or conflict. Judah was a minor district in the Persian provincial system, whereas Edom, distant from the main events of the political powers of that day, experienced pressures from Arab groups that were attempting to take possession of its lands.

After the Babylonian exile, a group of Edomites moved to the south of Palestine to protect itself from the Nabataean Arab groups in the area that was later known as Idumaea, a word that derives from "Edom." Herod the Great was known as an Idumean, a term that reflects the hostility of the Jews toward the Edomites and their resentment toward Herod.

LITERARY STRUCTURE

One theory concerning the structure of the book divides the work into two major sections: (1) vv. 1-4, 15b and (2) vv. 15a, 16-21. This theory reflects the thematic and stylistic differences between these two sections. The first part refers to specific historical problems: the destruction of Jerusalem in the year 587/586 BCE and the attitude of the Edomites concerning that crisis. The rest of the work emphasizes eschatological issues related to God's judgment: the coming of the day of the Lord.

5. See W. Brueggemann, *Genesis,* Interpretation (Atlanta: John Knox, 1982); G. von Rad, *Genesis,* OTL (Philadelphia: Westminster, 1972).

6. See J. R. Barlett, "The Land of Seir and the Brotherhood of Edom," *JTS* 20 (1969) 1-20.

According to the scholars who propose this structure, the book portrays a transition from history to eschatology. Moreover, v. 16 presents an abrupt change in the target audience; the first part of the message is addressed to Edom, the second to Judah. Moreover, the second part of the book has been divided into several sections that reveal stylistic differences: v. 15a, vv. 16-18, and vv. 19-21.

A second theory for explaining the literary and stylistic complexities of the book of Obadiah also divides the work into two sections, but recognizes only vv. 1-18 as original to the prophet. Verses 19-21 were added later to emphasize eschatological hope. Some scholars have identified, in the first section of the book, oracles of the prophet that were subsequently compiled and edited to form the book.

Another theory attempts to explain the book as essentially one literary unit. The author developed his message from ideas and themes of numerous oracles spoken earlier against the nations and preserved in Jerusalem and incorporated into Obadiah's prophecy. Obadiah formulated his message in the light of Jerusalem's destruction, the exile, and the reaction of the Edomites during the 587/586 catastrophe.

This commentary divides the book into three major sections: (1) the proclamation of judgment against Edom (vv. 2-9); (2) the indictment and reasons for judgment (vv. 10-14, 15b); and (3) the announcement of the day of the Lord (vv. 15a, 16-21).

By studying the book of Obadiah as a literary unit, one can discover several important elements that are intimately related. There is a gradual progression in the development of the ideas: from the proclamation of judgment on Edom to the description of its sins during Judah's crisis and finally to the general theme of the day of the Lord with respect to the nations and the survival of a remnant of God's people. Nevertheless, the primary theme is God's judgment against Edom. God, according to the message of the prophet, is the Lord of the earth and will see to it that the territory of Judah is returned to God's people.

From a structural and thematic standpoint, the book may also be studied as a set of six short poems in chiastic form. This analysis underscores the theological importance of the work.[7] The chiastic structure, which presents the themes of the poem in parallel form, takes the shape ABCA′B′C′, with the following themes:

A vv. 1-4 God will humble Edom

  B vv. 5-7 Edom will be attacked and abandoned by its allies

    C vv. 8-11 Edom is judged for remaining passive during the slaughter of its brothers and sisters

    C′ vv. 12-14 Edom should not have rejoiced at the defeat of Judah and should not have plundered and delivered up the survivors of the Jerusalem catastrophe

  B′ vv. 15-18 God's people will return to rule on Mount Zion

A′ vv. 19-21 God will save God's people

7. See L. F. Bliese, "Chiastic and Homogeneous Metrical Structure Enhanced by Word Patterns in Obadiah." Unpublished United Bible Societies paper, 1991.

The main emphasis occurs at the center of the book (sections C and C'): Edom will be judged for its attitude against God's people in their time of crisis and need.

OBADIAH'S RELATIONSHIP TO OTHER PROPHETS

This commentary's analysis of the literary unity of the book does not overlook its diverse components and influences from oral and written sources. Perhaps the material used by Obadiah is of ritual or liturgical origin; however, the range of the prophet's thematic and literary resources is difficult to determine.

The relationship between Obadiah and other prophets, particularly Jeremiah, has been the focus of much study and research.[8] Specifically, we can identify similarities between Obad 1-6 and Jeremiah 49. According to some scholars, Obadiah used the oracles of Jeremiah to formulate his own prophetic proclamation. Others believe that the book of Jeremiah includes the material that had been prepared by Obadiah. Both points of view claim that one of the two authors relied on the material of the other.

A better explanation may be that both works rely on prophetic material that already existed in cultic and prophetic circles in Jerusalem. Stylistic and thematic analysis of both works reveals literary, textual, and thematic continuity, which may be explained on the basis of that hypothesis.[9]

1—Parallels:		2—Similarities:	
Obadiah	Jeremiah	Obadiah	Jeremiah
1*a*	49:7	8	49:7
1*b*-4	49:14-16	9	49:22
5-6	49:9-10*a*	16	49:12

Study of Obadiah, moreover, reveals thematic and literary contact with other prophetic books, particularly with Joel, Amos, and Ezekiel. The parallels and similarities again underscore the importance of prophetic material against other nations, which circulated among the prophetic and cultic groups in Jerusalem. The brief oracle against Edom included in Ezek 25:12-14 and the theme of the day of the Lord of Amos 9:12 are clear examples. Obadiah also bears strong similarities to the book of Joel:

Obadiah	Joel
11	3:3
15	1:15
16	3:17
18	2:5
21	2:32

8. See, e.g., Leslie C. Allen, *The Books of Joel, Obadiah, Jonah, and Micah,* NICOT (Grand Rapids: Eerdmans, 1976) 133-36, 140-43.
9. D. Stuart, *Hosea–Jonah,* WBC (Waco: Word, 1987) 415-16.

Such comparisons between Obadiah and Jeremiah and Joel indicate that these prophets used oral or written sources of prophetic oracles against Edom for developing their own message.

THEOLOGY

The theology of the book of Obadiah is intimately related to the historical reality that characterized the prophet's ministry. After the triumph of the Babylonian armies over Judah and Jerusalem, the citizens were left demoralized and humiliated as they had seen their country devastated, national institutions dismantled, and many of their leaders deported (2 Kgs 2:5). The prophet's theology had to take into consideration the political, social, and spiritual condition of the people, while appropriately responding to the theological expectations of the community. After the exile, the community of Judah and Jerusalem struggled to survive, to reorganize national life, and to comprehend the theological implications of the events that had befallen them.

The message of Obadiah is judgment for Edom and hope for the Yahwistic community. Although the work is not a systematic theological treatise and instead the prophetic word in the face of a national crisis,[10] one may identify four important themes.

Divine Justice. After the devastation of Jerusalem in 587/586 BCE, a divine manifestation of judgment against Edom was needed because of its part in Judah's catastrophe.

To balance the theological crisis created by the destruction of Jerusalem, the religious and political center of the Yahwistic community, Obadiah used and developed a theology of divine justice. God would intervene and punish those who had been involved in the plunder of Jerusalem: Edom. In vv. 2-9, Edom's destruction is announced. In vv. 10-14, the nature of Edom's crimes is developed. Verse 15b emphasizes the punishment warranted by Edom's betrayal of Judah and offense against God.

The Day of the Lord. Tied to the theme of God's justice is the theme of the day of the Lord. But this theme is also linked to the idea of holy war—the belief that God is able and willing to intervene to defeat decisively the enemies of God's people. The day of the Lord also implies the judgment and destruction of those enemies as well as victory and salvation for God's people.

The book of Lamentations identifies two important phases in the manifestation of the day of the Lord (Lam 1:21; 2:21-22) during the crisis of 587/586 BCE. The first phase takes place during the fall of Jerusalem, the destruction of the Temple, and the devastation of the Judahite state. The second phase involves the reaction of Judah's enemies to the slaughter and affliction of the people. Obadiah may have taken that double motif from the book of Lamentations and incorporated it into his message against Edom. The destruction of Edom will result from a new manifestation of the day of the Lord: first, because the Edomites had been accomplices to the Babylonians' intervention against Judah and, second,

10. See R. J. Coggins, *Israel Among the Nations: Nahum, Obadiah, Esther,* ITC (Grand Rapids: Eerdmans, 1985) 74-76.

because they had taken advantage of the crisis to plunder and destroy the city. The destruction of Edom is the logical result of the just actions of a God who responds to the needs of people and does not allow injustice to reign. The people of Judah had received the divine penalty for their sins and actions in violation of the covenant. The book of Obadiah presents the theology of the day of the Lord and the manifestation of divine judgment, now applied to the people of Edom.

The Lord of History. The prophet's theology underscores the ability of the God of Israel to intervene in history and to vent the divine furor against the people of Edom. In ancient days, when nations would go to war, they believed their gods would be present in battle. According to that theology, the people of Judah might have been dismayed and frustrated at a God who was not able to defeat the gods of the Babylonians and the Edomites.

Obadiah's theology affirms that the God of Israel was not defeated and will manifest power in history so as to judge the people who have taken advantage of Judah's defeat in order to plunder it and take over its territory. The affirmation that the Lord is God over history runs counter to the Edomites' view of themselves. The destruction of Edom will not be a chance event but the result of the righteous action of the God of history.

The Kingdom of the Lord. The message of Obadiah ends with a statement concerning the people's future. After the national catastrophe, the future of the Jewish community will be radically transformed. The vindication of the people will be a reality, thanks to divine intervention that will restore the national borders and establish a theocracy in the world (vv. 19-20). Mount Zion will be reestablished as the capital of a renewed and liberated people. The book culminates with an ardent affirmation of faith and hope: "the kingdom shall be the LORD's" (v. 21).

THE TEXT OF THE BOOK

The Hebrew text of the book of Obadiah has been quite well preserved. Scholars frequently use the parallel passage of Jeremiah 49 to revise and amend difficult parts of Obad 1-5. That process of revision and textual amendment, however, must be made without violating the literary integrity of either document (see vv. 19-20). The Septuagint can also be of great assistance in studying the text of Obadiah; nonetheless, the Greek vocalization of poetic portions of the Masoretic Text should be used with careful critical judgment.[11]

Textual corrections that should be made to the book include changing the word נחפשׂו (neḥpeśû; "ransacked," NIV; "pillaged," NRSV) from the plural to the singular (v. 6); revocalizing the Hebrew text, in accordance with the ancient versions, to clarify the sense of the text in vv. 7, 13, 17, 21; and, in v. 20, interpreting a strange expression that has been added to the original text. Some scholars maintain that in several places the text has suffered transpositions during the process of textual transmission (e.g., v. 15). Generally,

---

11. See *Preliminary and Interim Report on the Hebrew Old Testament Text Project,* vol. 5. (New York: UBS, 1980) 297-301.

it is believed that the topographical and geographical references in vv. 19-20 were added at an early stage of the text's history.[12] In this evaluation and analysis of the structure and style of the work, the text's integrity is respected so as to avoid inappropriate amendments and transpositions.

12. Allen, *The Books of Joel, Obadiah, Jonah, and Micah,* 137.

BIBLIOGRAPHY

Allen, Leslie C. *The Books of Joel, Obadiah, Jonah, and Micah.* NICOT. Grand Rapids: Eerdmans, 1976. Excellent overall basic commentary.

Clark, David, and Norm Mundhenk. *A Translator's Handbook on the Books of Obadiah and Micah.* New York: United Bible Societies, 1982. Of special interest to those who know Hebrew.

Coggins, R. J., and S. P. Re'emi. *Israel Among the Nations: Nahum, Obadiah, Esther.* ITC. Grand Rapids: Eerdmans, 1985. Commentary with a theological interest.

Limburg, James. *Hosea–Micah.* Interpretation. Atlanta: John Knox, 1988. A commentary oriented to the task of preaching.

Mason, R. *Micah, Nahum, Obadiah.* Sheffield: JSOT, 1991. Up-to-date, concise assessment of issues raised by Obadiah.

Myers, J. "Edom and Judah in the Sixth-Fifth Centuries B.C." In *Near Eastern Studies in Honor of William Foxwell Albright.* Edited by H. Goedicke. Baltimore: John Hopkins University Press, 1971. Provides important historical information.

Snyman, S. D. "Cohesion in the Book of Obadiah," *ZAW* 101 (1989) 59-71. An article that focuses on the issue of literary unity.

Watts, J. D. W. *Obadiah: A Critical Exegetical Commentary.* Grand Rapids: Eerdmans, 1969. A brief but useful study.

Wolff, Hans Walter. *Obadiah and Jonah: A Commentary.* Minneapolis: Augsburg, 1986. A definitive commentary, with focus on critical issues.

OUTLINE OF OBADIAH

I. Obadiah 1, Heading and Introduction

II. Obadiah 2-9, Judgment Against Edom

III. Obadiah 10-14, 15*b*, Crimes of Edom

IV. Obadiah 15*a*, 16-21, Edom on the Day of the Lord

OBADIAH 1

HEADING AND INTRODUCTION

¹The vision of Obadiah.

This is what the Sovereign LORD says about Edom—
We have heard a message from the LORD:
    An envoy was sent to the nations to say,
"Rise, and let us go against her for battle"—

1The vision of Obadiah.

Thus says the Lord GOD concerning Edom:
We have heard a report from the LORD,
    and a messenger has been sent among the nations:
"Rise up! Let us rise against it for battle!"

COMMENTARY

The introduction of the book of Obadiah is brief. It provides no details concerning the prophet's or his ancestors' home; neither does it indicate the date of his message. The content of the book is presented in the form of prophetic oracles, although the title or heading of the book reads "The Vision of Obadiah." The basic meaning of v. 1 is that God has given to Obadiah a message that must be communicated to the people.

The Hebrew word for "vision" (חזון *ḥăzôn*) suggests that Obadiah may have received his message while in some kind of a trance.[13] The literary unity of vv. 1-14, 15a is evident, since these verses deal solely with Edom's sin, blame, and judgment. This unity is also conveyed through the literary style; in this section, the prophet refers to Edom using the second-person singular "you."

God is the foundation of the message of the prophet Obadiah (v. 1b).[14] The expressions "Lord GOD" and "Sovereign LORD" represent the Hebrew phrase אדני יהוה (*'ădōnāy YHWH*), two words that often appear together in the OT.[15]

The main theme of Obadiah's message is judgment on the nation of Edom. According to the biblical accounts, the Edomites were descendants of Esau, Jacob's twin brother (Gen 25:19-26, 36; see also Introduction, "Judah and Edom").

Verse 1 presents an image of the divine council—i.e., a messenger has been sent from that body. In the OT, God is sometimes depicted as a king. One characteristic of ancient Near Eastern monarchs is that they had courts and councils, groups of people who carried out his orders and advised the king. That image was often used in prophetic circles to describe the setting in which the divine revelations came to the prophet (cf. 1 Kgs 22:19-23). According to Obadiah, the divine council had met and had decided to go to battle against Edom. God, in council, has announced an impending judgment on the people of Edom (see Isa 34:5-15; 63:1-6; Ezek 25:12-14; 35:1-15; Amos 1:11-12; Mal 1:2-4).

The book does not clearly indicate the audience to whom Obadiah addressed his message. Much of the prophecy refers to and describes the judgment of the Edomites; the message, however, is presented to the people of Israel, the community of Judea, and not to Edom.

The translations of v. 1b in the NRSV and the NIV offer some stylistic differences, but both present the same essential information: The messenger of God must be sent before those people can hear the message. The Lord is identified both as the source of Obadiah's message and the one who

---

13. Leslie C. Allen, *The Books of Joel, Obadiah, Jonah, and Micah,* NICOT (Grand Rapids: Eerdmans, 1976) 144; Hans Walter Wolff, *Obadiah and Jonah: A Commentary* (Minneapolis: Augsburg, 1986) 33.
    14. Wolff, *Obadiah and Jonah,* 33.
    15. Regarding the understanding and translation of the name of God see "How to Translate the Name," *TBT* 43 (1992) 403-6; the entire edition of this issue of *TBT* is devoted to the study of the name God.

sends the messenger. The image of the messenger may allude to a representative of Judah who visited the neighboring nations and urged them to form a military alliance against Edom. The meaning of the message is, "Get ready! Let us go to war against Edom." The modern translations express the message as an imperative: "Let us go to war against Edom" (author's trans.).

The prophet apparently realizes that the Lord has commissioned him to proclaim a message of judgment: "We have heard a report." Obadiah speaks to the people of Judah using the plural subject "we" to indicate that both the community and the prophet have received the message and must respond to God's revelation. In so doing, the prophet identifies with the everyday realities of the people.

JUDGMENT AGAINST EDOM

NIV

2"See, I will make you small among the nations;
 you will be utterly despised.
3The pride of your heart has deceived you,
 you who live in the clefts of the rocks*a*
 and make your home on the heights,
you who say to yourself,
 'Who can bring me down to the ground?'
4Though you soar like the eagle
 and make your nest among the stars,
 from there I will bring you down,"
 declares the LORD.

5"If thieves came to you,
 if robbers in the night—
Oh, what a disaster awaits you—
 would they not steal only as much as they
 wanted?
If grape pickers came to you,
 would they not leave a few grapes?
6But how Esau will be ransacked,
 his hidden treasures pillaged!
7All your allies will force you to the border;
 your friends will deceive and overpower you;
those who eat your bread will set a trap for you,*b*
 but you will not detect it.

8"In that day," declares the LORD,
 "will I not destroy the wise men of Edom,
 men of understanding in the mountains of
 Esau?
9Your warriors, O Teman, will be terrified,
 and everyone in Esau's mountains
 will be cut down in the slaughter."

*a3 Or of Sela   b7 The meaning of the Hebrew for this clause is
uncertain.*

NRSV

2 I will surely make you least among the nations;
 you shall be utterly despised.
3 Your proud heart has deceived you,
 you that live in the clefts of the rock,*a*
 whose dwelling is in the heights.
You say in your heart,
 "Who will bring me down to the ground?"
4 Though you soar aloft like the eagle,
 though your nest is set among the stars,
 from there I will bring you down,
 says the LORD.

5 If thieves came to you,
 if plunderers by night
 —how you have been destroyed!—
 would they not steal only what they
 wanted?
If grape-gatherers came to you,
 would they not leave gleanings?
6 How Esau has been pillaged,
 his treasures searched out!
7 All your allies have deceived you,
 they have driven you to the border;
your confederates have prevailed against you;
 those who ate*b* your bread have set a trap
 for you—
 there is no understanding of it.
8 On that day, says the LORD,
 I will destroy the wise out of Edom,
 and understanding out of Mount Esau.
9 Your warriors shall be shattered, O Teman,
 so that everyone from Mount Esau will be
 cut off.

a Or clefts of Sela   b Cn: Heb lacks those who ate

COMMENTARY

T his initial section of Obadiah's utterance may be divided into four basic units or paragraphs. The first paragraph (vv. 2-4) announces the fall of Edom; these verses are similar to Jer 49:14-16. The second paragraph (vv. 5-6) clearly and vividly describes the severity of the punishment; this section is similar to Jer 49:9-10. The third paragraph (v. 7) alludes to the betrayal of allies and friends of Israel; this verse also chides Edom for its lack of intelligence or wisdom. The fourth paragraph (vv. 8-9) points up the absoluteness, decisiveness, and completeness of the punishment proclaimed against the nation of Edom.

Verses 2-4, The Fall of Edom. Verse 2. The prophetic message is structured as if it were being addressed directly to the Edomites. This strategy lets the people of Israel know that God is about to punish their traditional enemies.

The Hebrew phrase translated in this text as "I will surely make you least ["small," NIV] among the nations" (NRSV) generally conveys a completed or past idea, particularly in prose texts. In prophetic poetry, however, this verbal form (sometimes known as prophetic perfect) usually refers to the future; the prophet writes about future events as if they have already happened. (It is not always easy to ascertain whether this verb form refers to the past or actually alludes to future events; hence the ambiguity about the situation in vv. 2-7.) Since v. 1 alluded to the enemies who are about to attack Edom, it is better to present the defeat as an event yet to occur. Moreover, since other verbs of this passage refer clearly to the future, it is best to understand all of these verbs as referring to a future time.

The word קָטֹן (*qāṭōn*; NIV, "small"; NRSV, "least") functions as figurative language. It refers not only to the size of the nation, but also to its might, power, and authority.

At the end of v. 2, the phrase "you shall be . . . despised" conveys the idea that Edom will be greatly humiliated. This notion reveals, moreover, the attitude of Israel toward its enemies.

Verse 3. The statement "Your proud heart has deceived you" (זְדוֹן לִבְּךָ הִשִּׁיאֶךָ *zēdôn libbĕkā hiššî'ekā*) translates literally the Hebrew text. The heart connotes the seat of emotions, as has been maintained in the translations. The Edomites were excessively proud of their military might, thinking they could not be defeated. Ironically, it was this sense of self-sufficiency that defeated them.

The expression "live in the clefts of the rock" may indicate the basis of the Edomites' pride; it may also refer to their capital, Sela. In Hebrew, the word סֶלַע (*sela'*) means "rock."[16] The play on

the meaning of the two words cannot be reproduced in English. The city was situated on a plain among high mountains; it was accessible from only one direction. The town of Sela was like a fortress. This physical, geographical peculiarity caused the Edomites to feel sheltered, safe, and proud.

The expression "you say in your heart," which has been translated also as "you say to yourself," intimates the perception the Edomites had of themselves. Confident because their homes were high on the mountains, the Edomites would rhetorically ask: "Who will bring me down to the ground?" The question attests the Edomites' arrogance. The Edomites thought they were so strong that no one could bring them down, but God, in fact, easily defeated them.

Verse 4. This verse provides the prophet's answer to Edom's pride: "Though you soar . . . I will bring you down." (The issue of pride is often stressed in the prophetic oracles against the nations; see Isa 10:5-15; Jer 50:31-32). Verse 4 offers two images: a high-flying eagle and the eagle's nest. The nest is situated in a hidden and inaccessible place. But it is difficult to determine whether the notions of flying high as eagles and building a nest in an inaccessible place elaborate on the same idea. The second part of the verse, which speaks of making a nest among the stars, constitutes a hyperbole, a figure of speech that makes its point through exaggeration.

The imagery of eagles may connote the ability of these birds to fly very high and build their nests in secluded places. But it may also allude to their legendary size and the fact that they are birds of prey. The disloyal attitude Edom displayed in Israel's hour of crisis can be compared to the behavior of eagles (v. 13 condemns Edom for plundering the people of Israel).

The final phrase of the verse, "says [or declares] the LORD," affirms that the Lord is the one who has spoken. This phrase indicates that the people are not hearing Obadiah's words but the message of the Lord.

Verses 5-6, Total Destruction. Verses 5-9 return to the message proclaimed in vv. 2-4: God is going to punish Edom. Unlike vv. 2-4, where God is the agent, now God's punishment will be meted out by Edom's former allies and friends.

The structure of v. 5 is complex.[17] The text

---

16. Allen, *The Books of Joel, Obadiah, Jonah, and Micah*, 147; Wolff, *Obadiah and Jonah*, 48.

17. Allen, *The Books of Joel, Obadiah, Jonah, and Micah*, 148-49.

presents two images and comparisons: One speaks of two thieves, the other of people who harvest grapes. These ideas are parallel and complement each other. Each conveys the main thrust of the verse: There will be partial rather than absolute destruction.

Two problems complicate an understanding of the verse. First, the subjects of the two images are practically synonymous: "thieves" and "plunderers" or "robbers." Second, the first clause of the text is separated from the second by an exclamation that is thematically related more closely to v. 6 than it is to v. 5: "How you have been destroyed!"

To overcome these difficulties in understanding posed by this text, the Good News Bible (GNB) translation has restructured the passage in three steps. First, it has translated the exclamation "How you have been destroyed!" (NRSV) as "But your enemies have wiped you out completely" (GNB) and has placed it at the end of the verse; in this way, the idea of destruction in vv. 5-6 is more clearly tied in to the unit.[18] Second, in the first part of the verse the two words translated as "thieves" and "plunderers" in the NRSV have been incorporated into a single clause: "When thieves . . . they always . . . " (GNB). Third, the GNB conveys the meaning of this verse through affirmations rather than rhetorical questions.

This kind of restructuring not only simplifies the structure of the verse, but it also makes it easier to follow the progression of the prophet's ideas. The two ideas that are compared follow each other without interruption, and the contrast between them and the situation of Edom is set forth by the phrase "But your enemies. . . . "

When a nation suffers a military defeat, usually the destruction is partial. This will not be the case with Edom, which will experience a much more severe and radical destruction. That idea is communicated by the expression "Oh, what a disaster awaits you." Just as Edom's pride is highlighted in vv. 3 and 4, so also v. 5 depicts its rigorous and far-reaching destruction.

In the first line of v. 5, the word "night" is employed because it is the setting and the time in which the Israelites conceived of thieves' breaking in and stealing. Still, the verse emphasizes not

18. D. Clark and N. Mundhenk, *A Translator's Handbook on the Books of Obadiah and Micah* (New York: UBS, 1982) 12-14.

the time the thieves arrive, but their stealthy, aggressive manner.

The expression "would they not steal only what they want?" implies that thieves leave something behind. And the expression "would they not leave gleanings?" may be based on the fact that the grape harvesters neither see nor are able to reach all the grapes on the vines. For Israel, however, the practice of leaving behind a portion of the produce was deliberate. According to Lev 19:11, anyone reaping a harvest should leave some in the field for the poor.

The Hebrew verb נדמיתה (*nidmêtâ*), which has been translated as "have been destroyed," may be another example of the prophetic perfect (see also the verbs in v. 6 and the first three verbs of v. 7). The change from future to past tense in the verbs in NRSV and NIV (vv. 5-7) may obscure the meaning.

According to Gen 36:1, 8, 19, Esau is the forebear of the nation of Edom. In Hebrew, as in the NRSV and the NIV translations, this verse concerning Edom is presented as an exclamation in the third-person singular. The text addresses Edom in the second person throughout the rest of vv. 2-7. The Hebrew text in Obad 6 employs two clauses to convey the basic idea that Edom will be plundered. In v. 6*b*, the NRSV reads "his treasures searched out," and in v. 6*a*, "How Esau has been pillaged." Many of the people's treasures may have been hidden away in the numerous caves located in the rocky fortress of Edom. This text can also be rendered "your treasures have been looted"; the "treasures" perhaps include items of trade and luxury.

Verse 7, Betrayal of Allies. This verse further develops the theme of Edom's destruction. The prophet describes the divine judgment through three basic ideas: "deceived" by allies, antagonism from "confederates" or "friends," and betrayal by "those who ate your bread." The theme of betrayal by allies and against covenants recurs (see vv. 1, 3-4).

The verb tenses in v. 7 require careful examination. Of the four verbs used in the text, three are in prophetic perfect; the fourth is in the imperfect (see Commentary on v. 2). The verse may be translated in the future tense, as the NIV does, to underscore the future implications of the prophet's message.

Divine judgment focuses on the human element in this unit. The "confederates" must be distinguished from the enemies; the former are nations that had promised to help Edom in times of trouble. The expression שֵׁלְּחוּךָ (*šillĕḥûkā*), translated "they have driven you" or "will force you," derives from the verb whose basic meaning is "send" (שלח *šālaḥ*), although in this text it may mean "escort" or "lead." The idea is that Edom's former allies deceived the Edomites and expelled them from their own lands. The prophet contrasts this idea with the treatment of the people of Judah by the Edomites (v. 14).

In the Hebrew text, the first two lines have the same subject, which occurs in the second clause: "your allies." To facilitate the understanding of the passage, the NRSV and the NIV have restructured the text, identifying the subject of the verse in the first line.

In ancient times, alliances or covenants between individuals or peoples were considered sacred; to break a covenant was abominable; moreover, the covenant breaker was severely penalized (see Ps 55:20; Amos 1:9). In v. 7 the prophet points out the nature of Edom's destruction and judgment. The hope and security implied in international alliances would not suffice to halt the approaching divine judgment, because Edom had been unfaithful to an alliance or covenant with Judah.

The third line of the verse is difficult to understand and to translate. It may allude to the lack of solidarity and the grave offense of withholding hospitality. According to ancient Near Eastern customs, hospitality was a responsibility and obligation that created strong ties of solidarity and loyalty (Ps 41:9).[19] In the Hebrew text, the subject of the third line literally means "your bread" (לחמך *laḥmĕkā*). Since this term is thematically related to the preceding idea, the NRSV has rendered it as "those who ate your bread"—that is, "your close friends." Once again, the nature of Edom's treachery is accentuated.

The final portion of the verse reproaches Edom for its lack of discernment and intelligence. Divine judgment will startle Edom. The nation will fall prey to its own false sense of safety and confidence. Edomites apparently refuse to believe that they could be betrayed.

Verses 8-9, Defeat of the Sages and Warriors. These verses contain the oracle that concludes this section (vv. 5-9). Edom's punishment will be conclusive and absolute. The expression "says the LORD" or "declares the LORD" (v. 8), which marks a prophetic oracle, concludes vv. 1-4 and also begins vv. 5-9. In these latter verses, Edom's wisdom and intelligence (v. 8), as well as its military power (v. 9), are criticized.

Throughout vv. 1*b*-9, divine and human actions are intimately related. In vv. 8-9, "the nations" (cf. v. 1*b*), "thieves" and "plunderers" (v. 5), and "your allies" (v. 7) are instruments of the ire of the Lord. According to the text, Edom's catastrophe is the result of divine intervention through God's agents.

One important element in the holy war theology is that God is the secret ally who brings about confusion among the enemy forces. Such confusion affects the enemy's morale and sense of security (Exod 23:27; Deut 7:23; Josh 10:10). "The wise men" and "men of understanding" in Edom will fearfully tremble when God pours out judgment and wrath. Destruction will be total and absolute.

The fate of Teman as a center of wisdom may stem from its geographical position in the Middle East. This important Edomite town held a privileged position in intermediate trade (v. 9). The caravans and merchants from the East used to bring merchandise and folklore to Teman. In the book of Job, Eliphaz, who represents a type of wisdom severely criticized in the work, is from Teman (Job 2:11; cf. Jer 49:7). According to Obadiah's message, Edom's national wisdom is exemplified in its military capacity. The parallelism between Edom and "Mount Esau" (vv. 9, 19, 21) is found only in the book of Obadiah. Teman poetically refers to Edom.

The NIV's rhetorical questions in v. 8 have been translated as affirmative statements in the NRSV. The theme of the day of the Lord, inferred in the phrases "on that day," usually allude to the day of final judgment. It is used here, however, to refer to Edom's punishment. (See Reflections at vv. 15*a*, 16-21.)

19. Allen, *The Books of Joel, Obadiah, Jonah, and Micah*, 152-53.

CRIMES OF EDOM

NIV

¹⁰"Because of the violence against your brother
    Jacob,
  you will be covered with shame;
  you will be destroyed forever.
¹¹On the day you stood aloof
  while strangers carried off his wealth
  and foreigners entered his gates
    and cast lots for Jerusalem,
  you were like one of them.
¹²You should not look down on your brother
  in the day of his misfortune,
  nor rejoice over the people of Judah
  in the day of their destruction,
  nor boast so much
  in the day of their trouble.
¹³You should not march through the gates of my
    people
  in the day of their disaster,
  nor look down on them in their calamity
  in the day of their disaster,
  nor seize their wealth
  in the day of their disaster.
¹⁴You should not wait at the crossroads
  to cut down their fugitives,
  nor hand over their survivors
  in the day of their trouble.

¹⁵"The day of the LORD is near
  for all nations.
  As you have done, it will be done to you;
  your deeds will return upon your own head."

NRSV

¹⁰ For the slaughter and violence done to your
    brother Jacob,
  shame shall cover you,
  and you shall be cut off forever.
¹¹ On the day that you stood aside,
  on the day that strangers carried off his
    wealth,
  and foreigners entered his gates
  and cast lots for Jerusalem,
  you too were like one of them.
¹² But you should not have gloated*a* over*b* your
    brother
  on the day of his misfortune;
  you should not have rejoiced over the people
    of Judah
  on the day of their ruin;
  you should not have boasted
  on the day of distress.
¹³ You should not have entered the gate of my
    people
  on the day of their calamity;
  you should not have joined in the gloating over
    Judah's*c* disaster
  on the day of his calamity;
  you should not have looted his goods
  on the day of his calamity.
¹⁴ You should not have stood at the crossings
  to cut off his fugitives;
  you should not have handed over his survivors
  on the day of distress.

¹⁵ For the day of the LORD is near against all the
    nations.
  As you have done, it shall be done to you;
  your deeds shall return on your own head.

a Heb *But do not gloat* (and similarly through verse 14)   *b* Heb *on the day of*   *c* Heb *his*

COMMENTARY

Verses 10-14, 15*b* comprise a thematic and literary unit. Obadiah, speaking as the interpreter of the divine will, interrelates two themes of capital importance to his prophecy: violence and fraternity. Divine judgment results from Edom's cruel and inhumane treatment of Judah. The text exposes Edom's unjust, unfriendly attitude and proceeds to justify the divine intervention on the basis of those acts of fratricide.

Verses 10-11, Lack of Solidarity. These verses introduce this unit and also relate vv. 1*b*-9 with this new section. The initial words of v. 10, "Because of the violence," emphasize the judgment announced in the preceding section. Verse 11 describes the context in which Edom acted against Israel. The brotherly relationship mentioned in the text is based on the patriarchal accounts (Genesis 25–29; 32; additionally Deut 23:7 clearly states: "You shall not abhor any of the Edomites, for they are your kin" [NRSV; NIV, "brother"]). Judah is expressly called Jacob (v. 10) to underscore the relationship. Even though the relationship between these peoples involved varying levels of hostility, their fraternity presupposes a moral obligation of solidarity that should not be ignored. The term "brother" is not to be taken literally. The Hebrew word conveys the notion of kinship as well as that of a covenant partner.[20]

Edom's violence—that is, its failure to respect the human rights of the Israelites—will be the reason for the destruction and humiliation that will befall the nation. Edom took advantage of Judah's misfortune to vent its resentment and hostility toward the people and their king (see Introduction, "Judah and Edom"). In the prophet's estimation, that act cannot go unpunished.

In v. 11, The expression "You stood aside"/"you stood aloof" conveys the prophet's harsh criticism of Edom's inhumane behavior. This verse carries the heart of Obadiah's charge. Edom acted as an enemy by allying itself with Judah's invaders: "You too were like one of them." The prophet clearly identifies some of the calamities Judah had experienced: "strangers carried off his wealth" and "foreigners entered his

gates/ and cast lots for Jerusalem." During the great catastrophe, Edomites took part in the plundering and violence against Judah. This description sets the stage for vv. 12-14, which present the day of divine judgment as a response to Edom's behavior.

Verses 12-14, 15b, The Day of the Lord. The main theme of these verses is the day of the Lord.[21] The Hebrew term for "day" (יום *yôm*) appears eleven times in vv. 11-15. The repetition of "on the day" gives the text an extraordinary poetic strength, stressing the importance of this motif and emphasizing the gravity of the accusation. The "day of the Lord" theme is tied to the outpouring of divine judgment, particularly against the enemies of Israel. In vv. 12-14, the prophet plainly describes Edom's behavior during the day of judgment, which is referred to as "the day . . . of his misfortune," "of their ruin," "of distress."

The specific "day" occurred in the year 587/586 BCE, when Nebuchadnezzar's armies entered Jerusalem to conquer the city, destroy the Temple, and take the leaders of Judah into captivity in Babylon. That experience marks the beginning of the period called the exile (see Ps 137:7).

The description of Edom's arrogance and pride in the passage alludes to v. 3. Obadiah's criticism, expressed in specific accusations against Edom, refers to historical events that occurred before the destruction of Jerusalem. This section also includes an extensive list of specific indictments against Edom. The expression "you should not have . . . " marks Edom's specific attitudes and actions against Judah: "gloated over your brother," "rejoiced over the people of Judah," "boasted," "entered the gate of my people," "joined in the gloating of Judah's disaster," "looted his goods," "stood at the crossings," and "handed over his survivors." The repetitions, the parallelism, and the consistency of ideas enhance the literary and thematic unity of these verses.

"The gate" (v. 13) is a symbol of God's presence with the people (Pss 87:2; 9:14; 118:20).

---

20. Hans Walter Wolff, *Obadiah and Jonah: A Commentary* (Minneapolis: Augsburg, 1986) 52-53.

21. Leslie C. Allen, *The Books of Joel, Obadiah, Jonah, and Micah,* NICOT (Grand Rapids: Eerdmans, 1976) 154-56; Wolff, *Obadiah and Jonah,* 52-53.

Since the gates of the city were considered inviolable and secure, the act of entering through them symbolized defeat. The destruction of the gates, likewise, symbolizes God forsaking the people (Lam 4:12-13).

Some poetic features of the text are impossible to reproduce in translations. The English versions of this verse, for instance, do not reflect the Hebrew wordplays on the original message; the English "calamity" translates the Hebrew word אידם ('*êdām*), which is similar to Edom.

The list of injustices enumerated in vv. 12-14 ends with Edom's sentence: "As you have done, it shall be done to you" (v. 15 NRSV). This sentence concludes the indictments against Edom as well as the first part of Obadiah's prophecy. (See Reflections at vv. 15*a*, 16-21.)

EDOM ON THE DAY OF THE LORD

NIV

¹⁵"The day of the LORD is near
for all nations.
As you have done, it will be done to you;
your deeds will return upon your own head.
¹⁶Just as you drank on my holy hill,
so all the nations will drink continually;
they will drink and drink
and be as if they had never been.
¹⁷But on Mount Zion will be deliverance;
it will be holy,
and the house of Jacob
will possess its inheritance.
¹⁸The house of Jacob will be a fire
and the house of Joseph a flame;
the house of Esau will be stubble,
and they will set it on fire and consume it.
There will be no survivors
from the house of Esau."
The LORD has spoken.
¹⁹People from the Negev will occupy
the mountains of Esau,
and people from the foothills will possess
the land of the Philistines.
They will occupy the fields of Ephraim and
Samaria,
and Benjamin will possess Gilead.
²⁰This company of Israelite exiles who are in
Canaan
will possess ⌊the land⌋ as far as Zarephath;
the exiles from Jerusalem who are in Sepharad
will possess the towns of the Negev.
²¹Deliverers will go up on*a* Mount Zion
to govern the mountains of Esau.
And the kingdom will be the LORD's.

a21 Or from

NRSV

¹⁵ For the day of the LORD is near against all the
nations.
As you have done, it shall be done to you;
your deeds shall return on your own head.
¹⁶ For as you have drunk on my holy mountain,
all the nations around you shall drink;
they shall drink and gulp down,*a*
and shall be as though they had never been.
¹⁷ But on Mount Zion there shall be those that
escape,
and it shall be holy;
and the house of Jacob shall take possession of
those who dispossessed them.
¹⁸ The house of Jacob shall be a fire,
the house of Joseph a flame,
and the house of Esau stubble;
they shall burn them and consume them,
and there shall be no survivor of the
house of Esau;
for the LORD has spoken.
¹⁹ Those of the Negeb shall possess Mount Esau,
and those of the Shephelah the land of the
Philistines;
they shall possess the land of Ephraim and the
land of Samaria,
and Benjamin shall possess Gilead.
²⁰ The exiles of the Israelites who are in Halah*b*
shall possess*c* Phoenicia as far as Zarephath;
and the exiles of Jerusalem who are in
Sepharad
shall possess the towns of the Negeb.
²¹ Those who have been saved*d* shall go up to
Mount Zion
to rule Mount Esau;
and the kingdom shall be the LORD's.

a Meaning of Heb uncertain   *b* Cn: Heb *in this army*
c Cn: Meaning of Heb uncertain   *d* Or *Saviors*

COMMENTARY

The translation of v. 15 allows the literary structure of the book to be understood in at least two different ways. Some translations link v. 15 to vv. 10-14. In this way, the imminent judgment of God is presented, and the specific example of Edom's punishment is underscored. Verse 15 is the climax of this unit. Another possibility is to begin the new literary and thematic unit with vv. 16-21. That would emphasize the divine judgment of the nations in a general way, and the case of Edom in particular. The NRSV divides the book into four units: vv. 1-4, vv. 5-9, vv. 10-16, vv. 17-21. The NIV makes only two fundamental divisions: vv. 1-14 and vv. 15-21. In my judgment it is important to take into consideration the continuities between vv. 10-14 and v. 15*b* and between vv. 16-21 and v. 15*a*. Possibly, due to some difficulty in the transmission of manuscripts, the clauses of v. 15 were transposed (see Introduction, "Literary Structure").

The final section of Obadiah's prophecy (vv. 15*a*, 16-21) places the divine judgment of Edom in a broader eschatological perspective. The theme of the day of the Lord is given special attention in the climax of the message: God's final victory will be manifested on behalf of the people of Judah.[22] The conquest and destruction of Edom are presented as a sign of God's judgment against that nation and grace for Israel. The historical events that provide the background for this section are the crimes committed by the Babylonian army during the destruction of Jerusalem.

Verses 15a-16. The prophet begins his message by announcing judgment "against all the nations." The word "day," frequently employed in the previous section of Obadiah's prophecy (vv. 12-14), continues and develops the thought of v. 8. While "the day" of vv. 12-14 refers to the specific historical event of the conquest of Jerusalem, vv. 8, 15 speak of the eschatological day of God's final judgment. In this way, the prophet ties the historical moment of Babylonia's triumph over Israel, with the day of divine judgment at some indeterminate future time.

In contrast to the day of sorrow and defeat referred to in vv. 12-14, the new literary and thematic unit presents the day of victory, of vindication, and of rejoicing for the people of Judah. The final defeat of Edom serves as a preamble to the demise and destruction of the human powers that reject the divine power and sovereignty. The day of eschatological judgment is also the day of final victory for God's people.[23]

In v. 16, the idea of divine judgment is likened to a drunk person. The literary image of "drunk on my holy mountain" alludes to the outpouring of God's wrath (Ps 75:8; Jer 25:15-29; Mark 14:36). The image also describes those who drink the bitter cup of divine judgment and are annihilated: "shall be as though they had never been."

The Hebrew verb שׁתה (*šātâ*, "to drink") is used three times in v. 16 to convey the idea of drunkenness. This text may be related to two literary images. The first alludes to the drunken victory celebrations of the conquerors; ancient armies used to celebrate their victories by getting drunk on the alcoholic beverages they had taken as booty. The second literary image has to do with divine judgment, with the image portraying the Babylonian conquest of Jerusalem.

"My holy mountain" or "holy hill" refers to Mount Zion (v. 17), the section of Jerusalem included in the Temple area. "Zion" and "my holy mountain" often refer to all of Jerusalem, when the writer wishes to emphasize the city's religious importance (2 Sam 5:7; Cant 2:6; Isa 1:8).

Until v. 15*b*, the oracles are directed to the people of Edom; in v. 16, the message is addressed to Israel. The reference "as you drank" (second-person plural) is different from the allusions to Edom (vv. 2-15*b*), which were phrased in the second-person singular. Direct address to the people of Israel continues until v. 21.

Verse 17. This verse offers a divine promise of restoration and deliverance. In contrast to the judgment of the nations, announced in v. 16, the prophet now reveals God's purposes for the people. The future of Jerusalem is closely related to that of the nation of Israel. Worship in the Temple redounds in blessing for the whole land of Judah.

22. G. von Rad, *Old Testament Theology,* 2 vols. (New York: Harper & Row, 1965) 2:119-25.

23. Allen, *The Books of Joel, Obadiah, Jonah, and Micah,* 161-63; Wolff, *Obadiah and Jonah,* 64-65.

Such change in the future status of the city symbolized future prosperity for the country. The city will become a place of refuge, "But on Mount Zion will be deliverance" (NIV). The NRSV expresses that idea of salvation with the phrase "on Mount Zion there shall be those that escape." The theme of salvation for a small group or a remnant is particularly prominent in the book of Isaiah; the name of one of the prophet's children, "Shear-jashub" (Isa 7:3), means "a remnant shall return." The same idea of a remnant is found in Isa 4:2 and 10:20.[24] According to v. 17, the temple mount will again be holy. Holiness in Hebrew thought involves the idea of separation or consecration for the purpose of fulfilling a specific function. Although it has ethical and moral implications, the substantial elements of the concept are (1) the state of separation to fulfill some definite purpose (Lev 2:3; 22:2) and (2) the rejection of anything that may hamper that state of separation (Isa 52:1).

"The house of Jacob/ will possess its inheritance" refers to Israelites who will have an opportunity to claim their ancient territorial possessions. After the destruction of Jerusalem, the neighboring peoples took possession of Judah's lands. The judgment against Edom will result in the restoration of land for the people of Judah.

Verse 18. Some scholars connect vv. 17 and 21 for linguistic, thematic, and formal reasons. But this radical restructuring of the biblical text is unnecessary. Verse 18 continues the idea of salvation that began in the preceding verse; in addition, it uses the same phrases as v. 17, e.g., "house of Jacob."[25]

"House of Joseph" may be a poetic allusion to Israel—that is, to the remnant mentioned in v. 17. It may also imply the salvation of the entire people of Israel (Ps 77:15; Zech 10:6).

The promise of the restoration of Judah continues with the language of fire and destruction in v. 18. While the preceding verses relate salvation to the city of Jerusalem, this verse describes that salvation in terms of the destruction of Edom, calling it the "house of Esau." The prophet clearly and forcefully states that the enemies of Israel will

be utterly destroyed: "There will be no survivors/ from the house of Esau."

The images of "fire" and its rare synonym translated "flame" are common portrayals of God's wrath (Exod 15:7; Isa 10:17; Matt 3:12; Luke 3:17). In this context, however, the prophet stresses that the divine judgment will be inexorably applied to the detriment of Edom. Moreover, not only will the Israelites be allowed to respond to their enemies with the same treatment they had received, but also they will be instruments of God in executing judgment. The holy war against the enemies of God will take place through a coalition of nations (v. 1), including Judah (v. 18). Edom will be destroyed, and Judah will actively participate in the process of destruction. The divine judgment shall be categorically executed.[26]

Verse 18 ends with the traditional formula of the prophetic messenger: "The LORD has spoken." The use of this formula identifies the unit (vv. 15*a*, 16-18) as an oracle; the theme present is that of judgment.

Verses 19-21. Some scholars think the final section of Obadiah's message was originally written in prose.[27] In any event, the passage does not reflect traditional poetic style. The prophet affirms that the restoration of Judah includes the promise of reestablishing the ancient territory of Israel. The prophet incorporates the theme of the land to the list of events that demonstrate the final victory of Judah and the final destruction of Edom.

The nations that took advantage of Judah's devastation to take over unjustly their territories must return that land; the divine intervention and the repeated use of the Hebrew verb ירשׁ (*yāraš*, "to possess") evoke the period of the conquest of Canaan, when Israel took possession of the land. The prophet affirms the importance of the Israelites' reclaiming the land occupied by the Edomites.

Verses 19-20. References to the Negev, the desert south of Judah, begin and end this unit. The Edomites, after the destruction of Jerusalem and the deportation of Israel to Babylonia in 587/586 BCE, infiltrated the region located south of Judah and north of Beersheba. During the times

---

24. H. Wildberger, *Isaiah 1–12* (Minneapolis: Fortress, 1991) 24-26; G. von Rad, *Old Testament Theology*, 2 vols. (New York: Harper & Row, 1965) 1:204.

25. Allen, *The Books of Joel, Obadiah, Jonah, and Micah*, 163-66.

26. R. Smend, *Yahweh War and Tribal Confederation* (Nashville: Abingdon, 1970) 26-42.

27. Allen, *The Books of Joel, Obadiah, Jonah, and Micah*, 168-72; Wolff, *Obadiah and Jonah*, 65-68.

of the Maccabees (1 Macc 5:65), the city of Hebron (north of the Negev) was still possessed by the Edomites; the region was then known as Idumaea. The triumph and conquest of Edom, Mount Esau (v. 19), marked the beginning of an era of national restoration.

The Hebrew text is difficult to translate, but the NRSV and the NIV have contributed to a better understanding of the passage. Yet they do not resolve all the problems. In the first place, although not identified explicitly in the text, the subject of the verse is the Israelites, in particular, the remnant of Israel (v. 19). Second, the NRSV's "Shephelah" should not be interpreted as the proper name of a region; the NIV offers a better understanding of the passage, rendering the expression as "people from the foothills." Some scholars feel that the references to Mount Esau and to Shephelah are subsequent commentaries to Obadiah's message, added to emphasize the anti-Edomite character of the writing.

The restoration of Judah will include the reconquest of the ancient territories of Israel: to the south, the Negev; to the west, "the land of the Philistines"; to the north, "the land of Ephraim and the land of Samaria." This triumph will allow Benjamin (i.e., the youngest tribe of Israel) to "possess Gilead."

The first part of v. 20 is also very difficult to translate. The Hebrew phrase החל־הזה (*haḥēl-hazzeh*; lit., "their hosts") has been understood by the NRSV as a reference to the exiles in Halah, a region near Nineveh, a place to which some Israelites had been deported (2 Kgs 17:6). This rendering of the passage highlights the final victory of Judah: the return of the exiled Israelites, even from the most remote places. In contrast, the NIV has translated literally the Masoretic Text. The Hebrew phrase that literally means "who are the Canaanites" (אשר־כנענים *'ăšer-kĕna'ănîm*) has been understood as a reference to the exiled Israelite groups. According to this translation, the exiles are not in Halah but in Canaan. Zarephath, a city near the Mediterranean Sea and about ten miles south of Sidon (1 Kgs 17:9-24), marks an ideal northern point for the reconquest by the

Israelites. Sepharad may refer to Sardis, capital of Lydia, to the west of Asia Minor (modern-day Turkey), although scholars also place it in Spain, Greece, or Media. The passage assures exiles that, although they have been forced to live in remote places, God will bring them again to the promised land.

According to vv. 19-20, Israelites will move in all directions to recover their historical lands. Judah's victory is also a return to the promised land; their triumph over their enemies is an affirmation of the ancient promise of possession of the lands made to Israel's forebears.

Verse 21. This verse concludes the message of prophet Obadiah's book. It includes a note of hope similar to the one added to the book of Amos, which presents the salvation of Israel in connection with its possession of Edom (Amos 9:12; see also Isa 11:14). The Israelites arrived at Mount Zion to rule over the Edomites, who in this verse are again called Mount Esau (vv. 8, 19). The NIV translation has rendered the Hebrew word מושעים (*môšī'îm*) as "deliverers," although it is not common in the Masoretic Text (cf. Neh 9:27); the NRSV has emended the text and used the passive voice ("those who have been saved").

This text, although it could be thematically and literally related to v. 17, presents the book's major theological statement of victory. The final message of the book of Obadiah is one of victory and salvation: "The kingdom will be the LORD's." This theme is also echoed in the last book of the Bible (Rev 11:15). The international war against Edom (v. 1) will end in the recognition of the kingdom of God once and for all. The victory is not a mere nationalistic reawakening but the symbol of divine sovereignty. This affirmation reveals the theological justification of the message of Obadiah. God's victory includes the restoration of God's chosen people and the judgment of their enemies.

This final verse of the book makes several important theological statements: God will raise up deliverers to fulfill God's purpose in history. That victory will be an ultimate triumph over those who oppose the divine will. And victory exemplifies Yahweh's rule in history.

REFLECTIONS

The study of the book of Obadiah illumines some important issues for today's church and believers. It presents a somber criticism of the lack of solidarity, it offers a word of hope for God's people, and it shows the importance of consciously applying religious traditions to the current scene.

1. *Commitment to Meeting Human Needs.* When they observe the behavior of the Edomites, believers see an example of the way God responds to the lack of solidarity with and commitment to the needy, the excluded, and the persecuted of society. The people of Judah were going through a grave crisis, and the Edomites, rather than sympathizing with and responding to the needs of their neighbors, betrayed them in a disgraceful way. They did not heed the cries for help on the part of the people of Judah, and they participated in the plunder and destruction of their neighbors. The Edomites not only ignored the requests for help from Judah, but they also collaborated with the Babylonians. Divine judgment will be the consequence of that unsympathetic attitude.

That theological perspective of the book of Obadiah holds out a great challenge to modern believers: What theological and political posture are we to assume in the face of the needs of the poor, the excluded, and the destitute of society? The prophetic message of judgment on Edom stems from their attitude, first passive and then aggressive, regarding Judah's misfortune. That theological perspective has repercussions today. The lack of solidarity is concretely manifested in the act of joining groups that despoil and wound the needy and underprivileged of society. Such attitudes invite the judgment of God.

A fundamental value found in Latin American liberation theology is its emphasis on the contextualization of the Christian message.[28] Theology ought not to be an academic exercise divorced from the everyday reality of the people but a critical reflection of the life experiences of God's people. Theology, from that liberation theology perspective, encourages and engages in concrete demonstrations of the principles upon which the kingdom of God is founded. According to those criteria, Obadiah presents a vital theological and pastoral challenge. Seeing the people's needs, God's people must react with a sense of responsibility and solidarity. Intercessory prayer is important and welcome when it is accompanied by tangible acts of love that eliminate the causes that foment, favor, and perpetuate conditions of injustice among the destitute of society. The lack of concrete demonstrations of love constitutes an act of betrayal of both God and the people in need.

Obadiah's prophecy challenges believers to address real problems, such as racism and the oppression of socially excluded groups, such as ethnic minorities and homeless persons. The church and believers, faced with those social realities, can neither remain silent nor identify with the system that excludes or oppresses certain segments of society. In a social crisis that ignores the sorrow and pain of large sectors of the poor, and living in a society unwilling to project itself into the future with pluralism and multiculturalism, believers and the churches must provide sufficient space for the creation of more just and equitable institutions. The church institutions themselves must be transformed by kingdom of God values in the midst of society. To ignore the plight of the indigent is one of the reasons why God judged Edom. True theology responds to the needs of the people. If it cannot speak to the daily reality of the community, it is not good theology.

2. *Theology of Hope.* A monumental contribution of Obadiah to believers is the affirmation

---

28. G. Gutiérrez, *A Theology of Liberation: History, Politics, and Salvation* (Maryknoll, N.Y.: Orbis, 1988); C. Mesters, *Defenseless Flower: A New Readings of the Bible* (Maryknoll, N.Y.: Orbis, 1989); A. R. Ceresko, *Introduction to the Old Testament: A Liberation Perspective* (Maryknoll, N.Y.: Orbis, 1992).

and development of a theology of hope. That theology is grounded in the conviction that God is with the people and has the ability and the will to intervene in the history of Israel. The theology of hope is not based on a utopian expectation but rather on the assurance and the confidence that God accompanies the people. That theology is the inspiration for the work of rebuilding the city. The theology of hope does not encourage believers to accept calamities passively; rather it mobilizes them to build a church and a society that show justice to and are supportive of the needy. Such a theology challenges us to dismantle and transform creatively the existing institutions that undermine the kingdom of God.

The theology of hope is demonstrated in concrete, practical ways. The creation of institutions that do not discriminate on the basis of social background, nationality, or ethnicity is one practical way of demonstrating faith and theological commitment. Hope is not just a topic for speculation, for preaching, or for theological reflection; rather it is the basis for liberating actions. Speculation does not contribute substantially to the affirmation of life and justice; only real demonstrations of love can transform the human being and significantly affect society.

As believers accept the challenge of Obadiah's message of hope and commitment, they develop the ministry of the church. The community of believers is the basic environment for the development of programs of solidarity and hope that modern society needs.

3. *The Kingdom of God.* The book of Obadiah ends with an important theological affirmation: "The kingdom shall be the LORD's." This declaration links the prophet's message to the future. The last word of the prophet is not one of destruction and judgment, but a message of hope. At its end, the book provides a positive announcement of the arrival of the kingdom of God. The judgment of Edom will vindicate and exalt God's people. Mount Zion, the symbol of the presence and the revelation of God, will be the capital of a restored nation.

The theme of God's working in the future and God's role in the implementation of the kingdom must not be confined to sermons that stress the eschatological virtues of biblical theology. The building of the kingdom requires people to translate the theological principles of the kingdom into programs that will benefit believers, churches, and humanity in a tangible way.

The creation of the kingdom requires the transformation of our own life situation. It requires the investment of economic and intellectual resources of the church to produce programs that will benefit God's people in particular and humanity in general. The God of the future demands that believers become involved in the development of initiatives that demonstrate the divine commitment to people with needs.

4. *Contextualization of the Message.* One hallmark of Obadiah's message is the way in which it takes old prophetic themes and adapts them to new exilic realities. The prophet does not woodenly repeat the traditional messages of prophets such as Jeremiah. Obadiah revised the oracles in the light of the new social and political realities of the people, and he transformed those messages so as to guide and to educate the community. The true prophetic word is not a repetition of what other people have said; instead it is the result of a careful analysis of the situation, the serious evaluation of the old prophetic traditions, and the humble acceptance of God's revelation.

The repetition of earlier messages does not guarantee that God's word will be proclaimed. Divine revelation is inseparably linked to real situations. God never addresses humanity as "to whom it may concern"; God calls specific individuals and peoples to respond to historic, concrete, and definite situations. The intimate relationship between human need and divine revelation is a fundamental quality of the prophetic message.

God's revelation to North American society at the end of the twentieth century is different from the one received at the beginning of the century. Hence, leaders and congregations must be willing to allow present needs to determine the congregational programs and homiletic topics. Obadiah's message is a good example of the importance of the intelligent adaptation and contextualization of God's message.

One of the challenges North America faces is the development and creation of a multicultural, multilingual, and pluralistic society and church. That kind of church is distinguished by the participation of all of its sectors, respect for divergent opinions, and the incorporation of minority groups into the decision-making processes.

THE BOOK OF JONAH

INTRODUCTION, COMMENTARY, AND REFLECTIONS
BY
PHYLLIS TRIBLE

THE BOOK OF
JONAH

INTRODUCTION

The book of Jonah bombards the reader with verbal activity from the heavens through the sea and the dry land into the netherworld. This noisy story of just forty-eight verses is nevertheless silent about compelling questions: Who wrote it? Under what circumstances? How? When? Where? Why? The silence has invigorated scholars. Of the many topics they debate, six inform this commentary: composition, date, genre, literary features, theology, and purpose.

COMPOSITION

Heterogeneous Elements. Although Jonah is a coherent narrative, heterogeneous elements compose it. The fictitious character Jonah most likely derives from a reference in 2 Kgs 14:25 to the historical "servant" of Yahweh, "Jonah son of Amittai, the prophet, who was from Gath-hepher" (NRSV). Chapter 1 of the book incorporates a virtually self-contained story of sailors delivered from a storm at sea. Chapter 2, the report of Jonah's being swallowed and vomited by a fish, suggests an independent tradition belonging to the genre of miraculous tales. The psalm Jonah prays while in the fish indicates a poetic provenance distinct from the narrative. Chapter 3 incorporates another virtually self-contained story of the Ninevites' being saved from a threat of destruction. Chapter 4, the extended dialogue between Jonah and Yahweh, with few references to the rest of the narrative, suggests yet another tradition, belonging perhaps to tales of holy men brought to accountability (cf., e.g., Num 22:15-35; 1 Kgs 19:1-18).

Linguistic diversity also contributes to the heterogeneous character of the book. It includes the appearance of different divine appellatives: "Yahweh," "Elohim," "ha-Elohim," and "Yahweh Elohim." Although the differences are in some instances explainable, in others they appear arbitrary. For example, the report about the Ninevites appropriately uses the generic "Elohim" for God rather than the distinctive Israelite name "Yahweh" (3:5-10). By contrast, the ending of the story inexplicably introduces the combination "Yahweh Elohim" (4:6), only to drop it subsequently (4:7-11) for the indiscriminate use of "Elohim" three times and "Yahweh" one time.[1]

The Psalm. The presence of the psalm (Jonah 2:2-9) within the prose narrative poses a major compositional problem. For two centuries it has provoked a storm of controversy. Critics debate whether the author of the narrative or a different author composed it. They wonder whether the narrative originated with the psalm or the psalm was added to the narrative. If it was an addition, they seek to determine who included it: the author of the narrative or an editor. Until the last few decades, the dominant stance challenged the pre-critical assumption of literary unity to build the case that an editor inserted the psalm. That stance has now shifted to argue that the psalm belongs to the original story, whether the author composed it or not.[2] But the matter is far from settled.

Scholars who struggle with the status of the psalm have collected an arsenal of criteria by which to render judgment. It includes linguistics, genre, vocabulary, content, context, theology, structural design, plot development, and character portrayal. In the use of these criteria every point set forth elicits a counterpoint and every counterpoint a point. For instance, Vanoni argues against the original inclusion of the psalm because it speaks of deliverance while Jonah is in the belly of the fish; Limburg argues for the original inclusion of the psalm because it speaks of deliverance while Jonah is in the belly of the fish.[3] Different understandings of deliverance yield different understandings of the same setting. From another perspective, Landes and Trible agree that Jonah exhibits a symmetrical design.[4] Landes then contends that the psalm supports the design and so belongs to the original story. Trible contends that the psalm disturbs the design and does not belong to the original story. In contrast to these scholars, Sasson observes that both authors and editors have stakes in establishing symmetry; therefore, this criterion is itself unreliable for determining

---

1. Efforts to solve the problem have not fully succeeded. For bibliography and critique, see Phyllis Lou Trible, "Studies in the Book of Jonah" (Ph.D. diss., Columbia University, 1963; University Microfilm International, order no. 65-7479) 82-87; Jack M. Sasson, *Jonah,* AB 24B (New York: Doubleday, 1990) 17-18.

2. For a summary of the controversy through the 1950s, see Trible, "Studies in the Book of Jonah," 75-82. For more recent discussions, see, e.g., George M. Landes, "The Kerygma of the Book of Jonah," *Int.* 21 (1967) 3-31; G. H. Cohn, *Das buch Jona im Lichte der biblischen Erzählkunst,* SSN 12 (Assen: Van Gorcum, 1969) 25-26, 92-94; James S. Ackerman, "Satire and Symbolism in the Song of Jonah," in *Traditions in Transformation,* ed. Baruch Halpern and Jon D. Levenson (Winona Lake, Ind.: Eisenbrauns, 1981) 213-46; Jonathan Magonet, *Form and Meaning: Studies in Literary Techniques in the Book of Jonah,* BLS 8 (Sheffield: Almond, 1983) 39-54; Hans Walter Wolff, *Obadiah and Jonah,* trans. Margaret Kohl (Minneapolis: Augsburg, 1986) 128-32, 140-42.

3. Gottfried Vanoni, *Das Buch Jona: Literar-und formkritische Untersuchung* (St. Ottilien: Eos Verlag, 1978) 29-35; James Limburg, *Jonah: A Commentary,* OTL (Louisville: Westminster/John Knox, 1993) 31-33.

4. Landes, "The Kerygma of the Book of Jonah," 16-18, 25-30; Trible, "Studies in the Book of Jonah," 184-92.

the status of the psalm in the book.[5] Critics on all sides of the issue use the same criteria to support opposite conclusions.

The traditional debate about the psalm appears to be at a draw. The sociology of knowledge, constantly overturning itself, makes first one way of perceiving and then another more attractive. Current thinking poses the question differently. It does not ask if the psalm is an insertion; instead, it asks how the psalm functions in the story. Function neither requires nor disavows harmony, though many critics assume the former. They interpret the psalm as the genuine piety of Jonah, and they seek continuity between it and the narrative.[6] This commentary, however, ponders dissonance.

Conclusion. Heterogeneous elements in Jonah attest to a rich heritage of traditions that feed the story. Although their provenance belongs to a lost history, their presence shows that the book did not emerge *de novo*. Some traditions may have circulated originally in oral form, as the abundance of repetition in words, phrases, and larger units indicates. But some may have come from written material that itself employed repetition along with other literary devices. In the end, an unknown author appropriated all these diverse traditions to craft a coherent narrative of superb artistry. A composite history produced a unified story. Apart from the unsettled issue of the psalm, the integrity of the whole garners scholarly respect.

DATE

Introduction. Unlike most prophetic literature, Jonah fails to locate itself in a particular historical setting. It has no superscription that places the book in the reigns of the kings of Israel and Judah (e.g., Hos 1:1; Amos 1:1) or in the exile (e.g., Ezek 1:1-3) or in the post-exilic era (e.g., Hag 1:1; Zech 1:1); nor does the story contain references to known historical events.

Proposals. Various efforts to date the book have not succeeded.[7] (1) An older argument that the text contains "Aramaisms" and thus belongs to the post-exilic era falters in the light of philological studies. They show that most of these words are characteristic of northern Israelite-Phoenician usage and further that Aramaic and Phoenician linguistic phenomena were present in Hebrew before, as well as after, the exile. (2) The view that the Hebrew perfect tense in the translation "Nineveh was" (נינוה היתה *nînĕwēh hāyĕtâ,* 3:3) indicates a time long after the city had fallen in 612 BCE falters on a point of grammar. This tense form occurs elsewhere as a feature of Hebrew narrative style rather than as a device for dating (cf., e.g., Gen 29:17; Exod 9:11). (3) The idea that the alleged nonhistorical phrase "king of Nineveh" (rather than king of Assyria) indicates a time after the demise of the Assyrian Empire falters on an invalid assumption. Similar phrases identifying historical kings with their royal residences occur in the Bible (e.g., 1 Kgs 21:1; 2 Kgs 1:3). (4) The proposal that Jonah is late literature because it "quotes" other biblical

---

5. Sasson, *Jonah,* 203-4.
6. E.g., Landes, "The Kerygma of the Book of Jonah," and Limburg, *Jonah,* 31-33.
7. See George M. Landes, "Jonah, Book of," in *The Interpreter's Dictionary of the Bible, Supplementary Volume* (IDBSup) (Nashville: Abingdon, 1976) 490.

books falters on its own reasoning. Literary affinities do not in themselves establish dependency, and dependency does not in itself establish late dating. (5) Equally unreliable are attempts to date Jonah by its theology, whatever an individual critic declares it to be. Nothing anchors the book theologically to a particular period in Israelite history.

With no secure evidence to date Jonah, scholars have wandered throughout seven centuries to find it a home. Two dates set the boundaries. The reference in 2 Kgs 14:23-25 to Jonah son of Amittai in the reign of Jeroboam II posits the eighth century BCE as the *terminus a quo*. The reference in the Wisdom of ben Sira 49:10 to the "book of the twelve" prophets posits the second century BCE as the *terminus ad quem*. Within these boundaries every century has been proposed.[8] Although a majority of opinions clusters around the sixth, fifth, and fourth centuries, it but shows how indeterminate is the date. The book may belong to the pre-exilic, exilic, or post-exilic period. Dating it becomes even more elusive if a history of composition lies behind the present form.

Conclusion. Some critics still try to date Jonah, but others turn from the quest. Decades ago von Rad cautioned against letting conjectures about the matter cloud interpretation.[9] Citing the caution, Limburg minimizes the importance of the issue for understanding the book.[10] Similarly, Sasson finds inconclusive all the arguments and deems the enterprise itself less useful than often assumed.[11] These views govern this commentary. To have available so many centuries for dating undermines the goal of historical specificity and renders any conclusion suspect. Perhaps the best interpretive efforts allow Jonah to move among centuries.

GENRE

Introduction. The single issue on which scholars agree unanimously is the uniqueness of Jonah among the Book of the Twelve Prophets. Unlike all the others, it tells a story about a presumed prophet (though never so called) rather than relating oracles spoken by a prophet. Yet scholarly unanimity shatters as soon as the question of genre arises. Proposed classifications include allegory, didactic story, fable, fairy tale, folktale, historical account,

---

8. A sampling of proposals covers the gamut. For the eighth century, see G. F. Hasel, *Jonah, Messenger of the Eleventh Hour* (Mountain View, Calif.: Pacific Publishing Assn., 1976) 95-98; Yehezkel Kaufmann, *The Religion of Israel,* trans. Moshe Greenberg (New York: Schocken, 1972) 282-86. For the seventh century, see E. F. C. Rosenmüller, *Prophetae Minores* (1827) 344-47. For the sixth century, see George M. Landes, "Linguistic Criteria and the Date of the Book of Jonah," *Eretz Israel* 16 (1982) 147-70. For the fifth century, see Elias Bickerman, *Four Strange Books of the Bible* (New York: Schocken, 1967) 29; Terence E. Fretheim, *The Message of Jonah* (Minneapolis: Augsburg, 1977) 34-37. For the fifth or fourth century, see Leslie C. Allen, *The Books of Joel, Obadiah, Jonah, and Micah,* NICOT (Grand Rapids: Eerdmans, 1976) 185-88. For the fourth or third century, see Wolff, *Obadiah and Jonah,* 76-78. For the third century, see Frederick Carl Eiselen, *The Prophetic Books of the Old Testament,* vol. 2 (New York: The Methodist Book Concern, 1923) 462-67; Andre Lacocque and Pierre-Emmanuel Lacocque, *Jonah: A Psycho-Religious Approach to the Prophet* (Columbia: University of South Carolina Press, 1990) 26-48.

9. Gerhard von Rad, *Old Testament Theology,* 2 vols., trans. D. M. G. Stalker (New York: Harper & Row, 1962, 1965) 2:291-92.

10. James Limburg, *Jonah: A Commentary,* OTL (Louisville: Westminster/John Knox, 1993) 31.

11. Sasson, *Jonah,* 27-28. George M. Landes now concurs that Jonah cannot be dated with precision; see his review of Sasson's book in *JBL* 111 (1992) 130.

---

legend, *Märchen, māšāl,* midrash, myth, novella, parable, parody, prophetic tale, saga, satire, sermon, short story, and tragedy. This broad spectrum indicates confusion about the meaning of genre, lack of standard nomenclature for genres, and different understandings of the same genre. The spectrum attests also to scholarly extravagances and to the peculiar character of Jonah within the canon.

The genres of folktale, parable, satire, and midrash receive attention here. Each of them illumines dominant literary features of Jonah while showing the inadequacy of any single designation to encompass the story.

Folktale. The genre of folktale designates traditional prose stories, oral or written, in which the realms of fantasy and reality mingle freely.[12] Such stories emerge in cultures all over the world, from ancient times to the present.

Folkloristic Motifs. Jonah abounds in folkloristic motifs.[13] Chapters 1 and 2 report the flight of a disobedient man, the threat of a storm at sea, the casting of lots to determine who is the guilty party, the expulsion of the guilty one, the resulting cessation of the storm, and the opportune presence of an animal to save the one thrown overboard.

Parallels to these motifs appear in folk literature of diverse cultures and times. From Buddhist literature comes the story of one Mittavindaka, who, disobeying his mother, puts out to sea.[14] After six days, the ship ceases to move. The sailors cast lots to determine the one responsible for the trouble, and three times the lots fall on Mittavindaka. As the sailors remove him from the ship onto a raft, they express the wish not to perish because of the misdeed of this young man (cf. Jonah 1:14). Thereafter the ship continues without difficulty. In Western literature the Italian tale *Pinocchio* contains several episodes reminiscent of Jonah, including a storm at sea that endangers the boat on which Gepetto, the father of Pinocchio, travels.[15] When the boat sinks, a shark swallows Gepetto. The same fate befalls Pinocchio as he seeks to rescue his father (cf. Jonah 1:17). Although the shark is not a friendly animal, it does save them from drowning. Later they emerge unharmed from the great fish. Stories with comparable motifs appear in the literature of ancient Egypt, Greece, and New Guinea.[16]

Chapters 3 and 4 of Jonah also contain folkloristic motifs. They include the appearance of royalty and nobility contrasted with common people, a royal proclamation that miraculously effects total repentance, the indiscriminate mingling of people and animals, the fantastic growth and demise of a wonder plant, and the timely appearances of worm, wind, and sun to cause distress.

---

12. See Hermann Gunkel, *The Folktale in the Old Testament,* trans. Michael D. Rutter with intro. by John W. Rogerson (Sheffield: Almond, 1987); Stith Thompson, *The Folktale* (Berkeley: University of California Press, 1977); V. Propp, *Morphology of the Folktale,* trans. Laurence Scott, 2nd rev. ed., ed. Louis A. Wagner with intro. by Alan Dundes (Austin: University of Texas Press, 1973); Patricia G. Kirkpatrick, *The Old Testament and Folklore Study,* JSOTSup 62 (Sheffield: JSOT, 1988).

13. For a fuller exposition, see Trible, "Studies in the Book of Jonah," 144-52.

14. See E. Hardy, "Jona c. 1 und Jit. 439," *ZDMG* 50 (1896) 153.

15. Carlo Collodi, *The Pinocchio of E. Collodi,* trans. and annotated James T. Teahan (New York: Schocken, 1985).

16. See Trible, "Studies in the Book of Jonah," 147-49; for other parallels, cf. Bickerman, *Four Strange Books of the Bible,* 9-49.

Parallels abound.[17] In European tales like "Cinderella" and "Brother Frolick's Adventures," royalty interacts with peasantry, and royal decrees are frequently issued for all peoples in a kingdom (cf. Jonah 3:5-7). In such stories as "The Faithful Beasts" and "The Little Tales About Toads," the worlds of animals and humans freely mingle. Wonder plants are central in "The Royal Turnip," "The Enchanted Trees," and "Jack and the Beanstalk." In this last tale, the beanstalk grows up overnight (cf. Jonah 4:10). Folk stories with comparable motifs appear in Burmese, Hindu, and Japanese literature as well.[18]

Problems. Though Jonah contains innumerable folkloristic motifs, several problems attend its classification under this genre. First, altogether absent in folktales but everywhere present in Jonah is the transcendent and omnipotent deity who directs the action. Although the tales allow for the supernatural in the forms of fairies, witches, gremlins, spells, and enchantments, they have no place for the Creator "God of heaven, who made the sea and the dry land" (Jonah 1:9 NRSV). Second, folktales eschew historical and geographical references to use fictitious times, places, and characters. By contrast, the fictitious Jonah borrows his name from an identifiable eighth-century figure (2 Kgs 14:25), and the fictitious story specifies the historical locales of Joppa, Tarshish, and Nineveh (Jonah 2:2-3). Third, folktales privilege entertainment over instruction, but the book of Jonah reverses the emphasis. To call Jonah a folktale is to classify some, but not all, of its content.

Parable. The Concept of Comparison. The Hebrew term משל (*māšāl*) and its Greek equivalent παραβολή (*parabolē*) cover literature as diverse in length and discourse as the proverb (cf. the book of Proverbs), the taunt song (Isa 14:4*b*-21), the dirge (Mic 2:1-5), the woe pronouncement (Hab 2:6-19), the oracle (Num 23:7-10), and the allegory (Ezek 17:3-10; 20:45-48; 24:3-5).[19] Even where the word *māšāl* does not itself occur, the concept extends to brief narratives like Jotham's fable about trees seeking a king (Judg 9:8-15), Nathan's tale about the ewe lamb (2 Sam 12:1-4), the woman of Tekoa's story about her two sons (2 Sam 14:4-43), and Isaiah's song of the vineyard (Isa 5:1-6). In all these instances the comprehensive genre *māšāl* focuses on the idea of comparison between something said and something intended.

Critics who call Jonah a *māšāl* (or parable) identify different comparisons for it. One view holds that Jonah represents recalcitrant Israel compared to Nineveh, which represents the receptive nations of the world. Another sees Jonah as the model of justice compared to Yahweh as the model of mercy. Still another deems Jonah the negative model of reproachable conduct compared to Nineveh, the positive model of repentance, and to Yahweh, the positive model of compassion.[20] These differences tend to undermine the concept of comparison as a stable criterion for deciding the genre of the book.

17. See esp. *The Complete Fairy Tales of the Brothers Grimm,* trans. with intro. by Jack Zipes (New York: Bantam, 1992).

18. See Trible, "Studies in the Book of Jonah," 150-51; for other parallels, see Bickerman, *Four Strange Books in the Bible,* 9-49.

19. See George M. Landes, "Jonah: A Māšāl?" in *Israelite Wisdom: Theological and Literary Essays in Honor of Samuel Terrien,* ed. John G. Gammie et al., (Missoula, Mont.: Scholars Press, 1978) 137-46.

20. Ibid., 146-49.

In measuring Jonah by known parables within the Hebrew Bible, Sasson finds other problems.[21] He notes as a minor point that Jonah exceeds the usual length of a parable and as a major point that Jonah lacks at its conclusion what a standard parable offers—namely, an explanation of the story told. For instance, Nathan interprets for David the meaning of the parable of the ewe lamb with the punch line, "You are the man!" (2 Sam 12:7 NRSV). The woman of Tekoa instructs David in the meaning of her parable of the two sons with the punch line, "In giving this decision the king convicts himself" (2 Sam 14:13 NRSV). Similarly, the song of the vineyard discloses its meaning in the climactic last stanza, which identifies the vineyard as Israel and Judah (Isa 5:7). The conclusion of Jonah, however, does not move to an explanation. Neither the narrator nor Yahweh nor Jonah shifts to another plane of meaning. The plant remains the plant; the Ninevites remain the Ninevites (4:10-11).

Other Concepts. For some scholars the genre of parable pertains more to the internal literary feature of surprise and hyperbole than to comparison.[22] Surprises in Jonah include a prophet's going to a foreign land to deliver his message rather than speaking on his native soil against another nation, the mass conversion of the Ninevites, the violent storm, the miraculous fish, and the wonder plant. These incidents combine the extraordinary and the improbable to yield hyperbole and thus to mark Jonah as a parable. Yet surprise and hyperbole are surely not unique to parables. Folktales, for example, contain them.

For Christian readers prone to draw their understanding of parable from the Gospels, other obstacles prevail in so classifying Jonah. The stories told by Jesus are more economical in detail and length than is the book of Jonah. They are also embedded texts, narratives within larger narratives, but Jonah is an independent narrative. Although like Jonah they contain extravagances, unlike Jonah they report natural rather than miraculous events.[23] Their main characters are less well developed than is the character Jonah. Most tellingly, the stories of Jesus, unlike the story of Jonah, do not include God as a character. From the perspective of the Gospels, then, Jonah is far too theological to be a parable.[24]

In summary, different understandings of what constitutes a parable and different understandings of Jonah as a parable pose numerous difficulties for this classification. As a compromise term, "parable-like" attests the problem.[25]

Satire. The genre of satire uses irony, derision, wit, invective, and related phenomena to attack a specific target.[26] Though the attack has a serious purpose, humor mediates it.

---

21. Sasson, *Jonah,* 335-37.

22. See Allen, *The Books of Joel, Obadiah, Jonah and Micah,* 175-81, who draws upon the redefinition of parable given by Dan Otto Via, Jr., *The Parables* (Philadelphia: Fortress, 1967) 2-25.

23. On natural extravagances, see Mary Ann Tolbert, *Perspectives on the Parables* (Philadelphia: Fortress, 1979) 89-91.

24. For the older understanding of parable as a simple story with a central point and its inapplicability to Jonah, see Trible, "Studies in the Book of Jonah," 158-61.

25. See Brevard S. Childs, *Introduction to the Old Testament as Scripture* (Philadelphia: Fortress, 1979) 419, 421-22.

26. See Northrop Frye, *Anatomy of Criticism: Four Essays* (Princeton, N.J.: Princeton University Press, 1957, 1971) 223-39; Gilbert Highet, *The Anatomy of Satire* (Princeton, N.J.: Princeton University Press, 1962); Leonard Feinberg, *Introduction to Satire* (Ames: Iowa State University Press, 1967).

In the process the grotesque, the absurd, and the fanciful may come into play. A preponderance of these features within a story confirms it as satire.

Most scholars who call the book of Jonah satire view Jonah himself as the target of attack. Overall, he is self-centered and self-willed, mouthing piety incongruous with his behavior. He is narrow minded and rebellious. Reacting with anger to the total success of his own preaching, he becomes a caricature of a prophet.

Satiric Details. Numerous details support a satiric reading of the story.[27] Though the name "Jonah son of Amittai" means "dove son of faithfulness," Jonah descends (1:3, 5) rather than soars; he disobeys rather than remains faithful. In boarding a ship to Tarshish in the west, he takes the opposite direction from Nineveh in the east. The narrator ridicules him by reporting that he snores in the bottom of the ship while the sailors work mightily to outlast the storm (1:5). The non-Israelite captain of the ship further ridicules him by urging him to pray to his own god and by using the same imperatives with which Yahweh has already addressed him, "Arise, call" (1:6; cf. 1:2). Jonah's subsequent answer to the sailors' questions traps him in a contradiction of his own making. He seeks to flee from the presence of Yahweh, whom he acknowledges to be "God of heaven, who made the sea and the dry land" (1:9 NRSV).

The satire continues when Jonah proposes that the sailors hurl him into the sea (1:12). Death by drowning would be a certain way to achieve flight from Yahweh. But the ploy does not work, because Yahweh appoints a fish to swallow Jonah (1:17). Even the negative connotation (cf., e.g., Exod 15:12; Num 16:28-34) of the verb "swallow" (בלע *bāla*ʾ) ridicules him. He does not die but instead prays an incongruous psalm of thanksgiving while in the belly of the fish (2:2-9). The ridicule of Jonah and by Jonah climaxes with the concluding line of the psalm, "Deliverance belongs to the LORD!" (2:9 NRSV). Thereupon Yahweh orders the fish to "vomit" (קיא *qîʾ*) Jonah out. This infelicitous verb delivers its own satire.

Upon reaching Nineveh, Jonah delivers a five-word pronouncement upon the city. It parodies prophetic discourse (3:4). Making no explicit claim to speak "the word of Yahweh," Jonah uses the ambiguous verb "overturn" (הפך *hāpak*; NRSV, "overthrown"). It belies his intention, for Nineveh overturns through repentance, not destruction (3:5-10). Humor attends the city's earnest repentance. The animals, like the human beings, clothe themselves in sackcloth, mourn, and fast. In saving Nineveh, Yahweh undercuts the messenger and his message. So the outcome humiliates Jonah, and he turns angry.

Irony, humor, parody, fantasy, and the absurd permeate the remainder of the story. Jonah uses a credo about God's mercy (4:2-3) to justify his own unmerciful attitude. His

27. For the sketch provided here, see David Marcus, *From Balaam to Jonah: Anti-prophetic Satire in the Hebrew Bible* (Atlanta: Scholars Press, 1995) 1-27, 93-159; Millar Burrows, "The Literary Category of the Book of Jonah," in *Translating and Understanding the Old Testament,* ed. Harry Thomas Frank and William L. Reed (Nashville: Abingdon, 1970) 80-107; James S. Ackerman, "Satire and Symbolism in the Song of Jonah," in *Traditions in Transformation,* ed. Baruch Halpern and Jon D. Levenson (Winona Lake, Ind.: Eisenbrauns, 1981) 227-29; cf. Andre Lacocque and Pierre-Emmanuel Lacocque, *Jonah: A Psycho-Religious Approach to the Prophet* (Columbia: University of South Carolina Press, 1990) 26-48.

petulant behavior defies his pious words. That behavior extends to his sulking outside the city in a self-made booth and under a God-given plant (4:5). Puns, such as the association of the noun "shade" (צל ṣēl) with the verb "to save" (נצל nāṣal), help to support absurd features in the closing incidents: a plant growing up overnight, a single worm causing the plant's instant demise, and the sun beating upon the head of Jonah, who is sheltered presumably by his own booth (4:5-8). Jonah comes across as a ridiculous character, shifting his mood from delight to defiance. Fittingly, the sun attacking his head mocks his hardheadedness.

According to one interpretation, the question at the end of the book (4:10-11) ironically juxtaposes Jonah's self-pity to Yahweh's gratuitous pity for Nineveh.[28] Another proposal finds the irony in similarity. Jonah's self-pity regarding the plant parallels Yahweh's self-pity regarding Nineveh. The deity spares the city for selfish reasons. In that case, however, a satire attacking Jonah ironically becomes a vindication of him—or ironically becomes an attack on Yahweh.

Problems. Although satiric elements mark Jonah, whether they confirm it as satire opens up unsettled and unsettling problems, first between authorial intention and reader response and then among different readers. What authorial indicators secure satire as the genre of the book? Do generally agreed- upon satiric features become a license for inventing others? To what extent is satire in the eye of the beholder? For example, some readers find Jonah's prayer inside the fish an expression of genuine piety, but others deem it distortion and farce. Some readers chuckle to picture animals clothed in sackcloth and sitting upon ashes, but others see pathos and poignancy. How much satire does the book yield and how much do readers contribute? Jonah may have both less and more levity and gravitas than readers intend.[29]

A related problem concerns the target(s) being attacked. Are the sailors being ridiculed in their seeking to appease a storm god by hurling wares to the sea? Are they being ridiculed for lack of nautical acumen when they try to steer the ship to shore during a storm? Are the Ninevites being ridiculed when they command their animals to repent? Is nature being ridiculed when it is commanded to act unnaturally: A fish to swallow and vomit up a human being? A tree to pop up overnight? A single worm to fell a tree? Is Yahweh being ridiculed as a deity who can be duped by instant and mass conversions? Is Yahweh being ridiculed in arguing with angry Jonah? If a reader decides the book is a satire, then it may present more targets than one would like. At any rate, shifting targets decenter the claim that Jonah is the object of attack.[30]

---

28. See, e.g., Burrows, "The Literary Category of the Book of Jonah," 99; Marcus, *From Balaam to Jonah,* 117-19.

29. For contrasting points of view, cf. Jack M. Sasson, *Jonah,* AB 24B (New York: Doubleday, 1990) 329-40, esp. 331, with R. P. Carroll, "Is Humor Also Among the Prophets?" in *On Humour and the Comic in the Hebrew Bible,* ed. Yehuda T. Radday and Athalya Brenner, JSOTSup 92 (Sheffield: Almond, 1990) 169-89, esp. 171, 180-81, and with Judson Mather, "The Comic Art of the Book of Jonah," *Soundings* 65 (1982) 280-91.

30. Note the tension in the claim by Marcus that the book is "a satire on the prophet himself" and the acknowledgment that "the Ninevites are also ridiculed." Is the target, then, so "clearly defined?" (Marcus, *From Balaam to Jonah,* 95, 121-22, 158, etc.).

Yet another problem centers on the character of Jonah. Does it remain constant throughout the book? Is he consistently disobedient, self-centered, and angry? The psalm (2:2-9) challenges this reading, as does the final question (4:10-11). If Jonah's character is not forever static or negative, then even the pronounced satire upon him does not cover the whole story. (See Commentary on 4:10-11.)

Proposals that the book of Jonah is a satire have their limits. The difficulties extend also to the larger question of whether the Hebrews satirized or whether the genre of satire fits biblical literature.[31]

Midrash. Derived from the Hebrew verb דרש (*dāraš*), meaning "to seek" or "to inquire," the noun *midrash* designates a type of literature, oral or written, that explicates a biblical passage. A midrash is a commentary that endeavors to make a particular text meaningful and relevant. Although midrash flourished in rabbinic literature, its origins are earlier. They include references to the midrash of the prophet Iddo in 2 Chr 13:22 and to the midrash on the book of Kings in 2 Chr 24:27.[32]

Proposals. Taking a cue from the latter reference, Karl Budde proposed long ago that the book of Jonah is a midrash on 2 Kgs 14:25.[33] Just as "Jonah son of Amittai, the prophet," spoke favorably about God's goodness to the sinful kingdom Israel, so the story of Jonah uses him to extend the divine mercy to sinful foreigners. Other scholars have seen the book as a midrash on prophetic literature.[34] For instance, the decree against Nineveh provides commentary on oracles against foreign nations in Jeremiah and Ezekiel. Though these oracles appear as absolute, they remain conditional (e.g., Jer 18:7-8; 25:5; Ezekiel 26–28). Accordingly, Jonah's pronouncement of certain doom results in repentance and deliverance (3:3, 10).

Another view holds that Jonah himself provides the text for the midrash.[35] It is the credo he recites about the character of Yahweh as "gracious . . . and merciful, slow to anger, and abounding in steadfast love, and ready to relent from punishing" (4:2 *b*NRSV). Different versions of the credo appear throughout the Bible in different contexts with different meanings.[36] Choosing one version (cf. Joel 2:13), the author of Jonah built the narrative around it.

31. See Jack M. Sasson, *Jonah*, AB 24B (New York: Doubleday, 1990) 331-34, and George M. Landes, review of Lacocque and Lacocque, *Jonah: A Psycho-Religious Approach to the Prophet*, *JBL* 111 (1992) 131. On the related, yet distinct, genre of parody, see John A. Miles, Jr., "Laughing at the Bible: Jonah as Parody," *JQR* (New Series) 65 (1975) 168-81; cf. Adele Berlin, "A Rejoinder to John A. Miles, Jr., with Some Observations on the Nature of Prophecy," *JQR* (New Series) 66 (1976) 227-35. See also Arnold J. Band, "Swallowing Jonah: The Eclipse of Parody," *Prooftexts* (1990) 177-95.

32. On midrash, see Renée Bloch, "Midrash," *Dictionnaire de la Bible*, Supplement 5 (Paris: Librairie Letouzey et Ane, 1957) cols. 1263-1281; Addison G. Wright, *The Literary Genre Midrash* (Staten Island, N.Y.: Alba House, 1967); H. L. Strack and G. Stemberger, *Introduction to the Talmud and Midrash* (Minneapolis: Fortress, 1992) 254-68.

33. Karl Budde, "Vermutungen zum 'Midrasch des Büches der Könige,' " *ZAW* 12 (1892) 37-51.

34. E.g., A. Feuillet, "Les Sources du Livre de Jonas," *RB* 54 (1947) 161-86; A. Robert and A. Tricot, *Guide to the Bible I*, trans. Edward P. Arbez and Martin R. P. McGuire (New York: Desclee, 1960) 506.

35. See Phyllis Lou Trible, "Studies in the Book of Jonah" (Ph.D. diss., Columbia University, 1963; University Microfilm International, order no. 65-7579) 167-68; 273-79.

36. Exodus 34:6-7 is the earliest formulation. Others include Num 14:18; Deut 7:8-10; 2 Chr 30:9; Neh 9:17, 31; Pss 86:5, 15; 103:8; 111:4; 112:4; 145:8; Joel 2:13; Nah 1:3; Neh 9:17, 31. For comparisons, see Gottfried Vanoni, *Das Buch Jona: Literar-und formkritische Untersuchung* (St. Ottilien: Eos Verlag, 1978) 138-41; Sasson, *Jonah*, 280-83; Michael Fishbane, *Biblical Interpretation in Ancient Israel* (Oxford: Clarendon, 1985) 335-50; Thomas B. Dozeman, "Inner-Biblical Interpretation of Yahweh's Gracious and Compassionate Character," *JBL* 108 (1989) 207-23; James L. Crenshaw, *Joel*, AB 24C (New York: Doubleday, 1995) 135-38.

Two literary devices signal the centrality of the credo. First, its content binds the story together. In 1:3, the narrator reports that "Jonah arose to flee to Tarshish" but gives no reason for his flight. In 4:2, Jonah recites the attributes of Yahweh as the reason "why I hastened to flee to Tarshish." The device of delayed information joins the beginning and ending of the story to produce literary and theological coherence. Second, a conventional clause of disclosure introduces the credo: "for now I know that. . . ." It serves a deictic function, directing attention to a climactic utterance (cf. Gen 22:12*b*; Exod 18:11; 1 Kgs 17:24). By using this device, Jonah points the reader and Yahweh to the heart of his problem: a quarrel with the compassionate nature of God.

The story explicates the credo. Chapters 1 and 2 portray Jonah trying to deny or ignore the gracious and merciful God. He attempts physical flight (1:3), psychological flight (1:5*b*), and existential flight (1:12, 15), but each time Yahweh saves him. Chapter 3 shows Jonah capitulating to the gracious and merciful God, who subsequently spares Nineveh. Chapter 4 depicts angry Jonah berating Yahweh for being merciful. Yahweh then takes over, not to berate Jonah but to extend mercy to him. Plant, worm, sun, and wind play their parts in the divine lesson. Through them the gracious God does not allow Jonah to perish. Divine compassion is itself the last word (4:11). From beginning (cf. 4:2*b*) to end, the book comments in narrative form on the ancient credo. The story is a midrash.

Problems. To classify Jonah as a midrash is not without problems, beginning with the word *midrash* itself. Its meaning can be slippery and imprecise.[37] Further, the appearances of the word *midrash* only in the late book of Chronicles (c. fourth century BCE) may imply that the genre was unavailable for earlier traditions. If Jonah was consciously conceived as a midrash, why does the term itself not appear in the story? How appropriate is the credo for encompassing the narrative? Conversely, how appropriate is the narrative for interpreting the credo?

The affirmation of God as "gracious . . . and merciful" links the opening of chapter 1 (1:1-3) to all that transpires in chapter 3. The ending of chapter 3 further links itself to the credo through identical vocabulary and theology: God "repenting of evil" (3:10; 4:2*b*). The credo then becomes the basis for the events of chapter 4. It supplies the rationale for Jonah's anger and his persistent wish to die. Moreover, it accounts for the continuing deeds and words of Yahweh on behalf of Jonah, and it leads to the question about divine pity at the end.

Omitted from this overview, however, is the sea narrative (1:4–2:11). Yahweh's hurling of a ferocious storm that threatens to destroy innocent lives hardly describes the activity of a merciful God who is slow to anger. The subsequent prayer of the sailors recognizes divine power (1:14), it does not acknowledge divine compassion. Even when the outcome

---

37. See Shaye J. D. Cohen, *From the Maccabees to the Mishnah* (Philadelphia: Westminster, 1987) 204-9.

is salvific, neither the sailors nor the narrator invokes the merciful and gracious God. In several respects, then, the sea narrative undermines the credo as the text for the entire story.

But another way of reading claims the credo. It holds that Jonah's behavior throughout the sea crisis is tacit recognition of the merciful God whom he so resents. In other words, he has knowledge that the sailors lack, and his knowledge shapes the narrative. His instructions to them, for instance, carry the hidden assurance of divine mercy (1:12). And the mercy comes with the cessation of the storm. Moreover, the opportune appearance of the fish signals the mercy that Jonah knows about and rejects. From this perspective the credo undergirds the sea narrative. Yet such a reading minimizes the reality of the storm for the sailors as well as the wrathful portrayal of Yahweh.

Conclusion. In its richness, complexity, and distinctiveness, the book of Jonah resists the categorizing endemic to genres. Although the designations folktale, parable, satire, and midrash illuminate the story to varying degrees, none of them embraces it fully. Perhaps the best interpretive efforts allow Jonah freedom to move among genres.

LITERARY FEATURES

Introduction. Jonah is a literary gem. Even a reading in English can detect exquisite properties in its structure, characters, plot, and style. Jonah 1:1 opens, "Now the word of the LORD came to Jonah son of Amittai, saying" (NRSV). Chapter 3:1 repeats these words, except for the appositive, and adds the telling phrase "a second time." The repetition, plus the addition, signals that the narrative falls into two major scenes.[38] At the beginning of each scene appear the primary characters, Yahweh and Jonah. The other characters, all unnamed, come in groups, each with a leader. They divide between the scenes: the sailors and their captain; the Ninevites and their king. Natural phenomena also play major roles: wind, storm, sea, dry land, and fish in scene one; animals, plant, worm, sun, and wind in scene two. The plot moves by divine activities, with human and natural responses marking the turning points. Throughout the narrative a host of literary features enhances the theology. The present discussion offers but an overview.[39]

External Design. Figure 2 shows the external design of Jonah; the observations that follow highlight certain features.[40]

38. On the phrase "a second time" (שנית *šēnît*) as the introduction to parallel units, cf. Gen 22:11 and 22:15.

39. For a full discussion, see Trible, "Studies in the Book of Jonah," 184-202; Phyllis Trible, *Rhetorical Criticism: Context, Method, and the Book of Jonah* (Minneapolis: Fortress, 1994) 107-22. Cf. Kenneth M. Craig, Jr., *A Poetics of Jonah: Art in the Service of Ideology* (Columbia: University of South Carolina Press, 1993); Herbert Chanan Brichto, " 'And Much Cattle': YHWH's Last Words to a Reluctant Prophet," in *Toward a Grammar of Biblical Poetics* (New York: Oxford University Press, 1992) 67-87.

40. See Trible, *Rhetorical Criticism*, 110-11.

Figure 2: External Design: A Study in Symmetry

Scene One: Chapters 1–2
1. Word of Yhwh to Jonah (1:1)
2. Content of the word (1:2)
3. Response of Jonah (1:3)
4. Report on impending disaster (1:4)
5. Response to impending disaster (1:5)
   —by the sailors
   —by Jonah
6. Unnamed captain of the ship (1:6)
   —efforts to avert diaster by
   * action
   * words to Jonah
   * hope
7. Sailors and Jonah (1:7-15)
   —sailors' proposal (1:8ab)
   —sailors' action and its result (1:7cd)
   —sailors' questions (1:8)
   —Jonah's reply (1:9)
   —sailors' response (1:10)
   —sailors' questions (1:11)
   —Jonah's reply (1:12)
   —sailors' action (1:13)
   —sailors' prayer (1:14)
   —sailors' action (1:15ab)
   —result: disaster averted (1:15c)
8. Response of the sailors (1:16)
9. Yhwh and Jonah (2:1-11)
   —Yhwh's action and its result (1:17)
   —Jonah's prayer (2:1-9)

   —Yhwh's response and its result
   * by word (2:10a)
   * by nature: fish (2:10b)

Scene Two: Chapters 3–4
1. Word of Yhwh to Jonah (3:1)
2. Content of the word (3:2)
3. Response of Jonah (3:3-4a)
4. Prophecy of impending disaster (3:4b)
5. Response to impending disaster (3:4b)
   —by the Ninevites

6. Unnamed king of Nineveh (3:6-9)
   —efforts to avert disaster by
   * action
   * words to the Ninevites
   * hope
7. Ninevites and God (3:10)

   —Ninevites' action (3:10ab)

   —result: disaster averted (3:10cd)
8. Response of Jonah (4:1)
9. Yhwh and Jonah (4:2-11)

   —Jonah's prayer (4:2-3)
   —Yhwh's question (4:4)
   —Jonah's action (4:5)
   —Yhwh's response and its result

   * by nature: a plant (4:6abcd)
     sun and
       wind (4:8abc)
   —Jonah's response (4:8d)
   —Yhwh's question (4:9a)
   —Jonah's response (4:9b)
   —Yhwh's question (4:10-11)

(1) The preponderance of repetitions between the openings of scenes one and two (units 1, 2, and 3 in the chart) secures the division as it stresses the commanding power of Yahweh's word. This constant word compels Jonah to respond. His different responses, first disobedience and then obedience, set in motion the actions of both scenes.

(2) The responses of the sailors and the Ninevites (unit 5) correspond in number, order,

and kind, though not in vocabulary. First come contrasting inward responses: the sailors fear; the Ninevites believe. Second come corresponding articulated responses: the sailors cry; the Ninevites call. Third come contrasting outward responses: the sailors throw away; the Ninevites put on. The narrator draws favorable portraits of both groups as they appeal to the deity אלהים ('ĕlōhîm). These portraits contrast strikingly with that of Jonah.

(3) From each group of foreigners emerges its unnamed leader (unit 6). The captain of the sailors makes a brief appearance; the king of Nineveh takes a major role. Their speeches differ, but the conclusions converge in syntax, vocabulary, and theology. Each opens with a rhetorical expression that anticipates but does not guarantee salvation. "Perhaps," says the captain; "Who knows?" says the king. Each uses the designation "the god" (האלהים hā'ĕlōhîm). Each concludes with the words "and we will not perish." The foreign leaders proclaim a theology of hope that understands the freedom of God. They make clear that whereas prayers and other cultic acts are appropriate—indeed, required—responses to impending disaster, the outcome nonetheless belongs solely to the deity.

(4) The verb "perish" (אבד 'ābad), used by the captain and the king, appears in two other places. The sailors use it in scene one (1:14) and Yahweh in scene two (4:10). These four occurrences provide balance and emphasis.

(5) At the endings (unit 9) the verb "appoint" (מנה mānâ; "provided," NIV), appears once in scene one (1:17) and three times in scene two (4:6, 7, 8). Each time Yahweh is the subject, and nature is the object. Each time Yahweh uses nature to deal with Jonah.

(6) Within the external design, symmetry and asymmetry contend. For example, the reports of impending disaster differ in length, type of discourse, and characters (unit 4). The extended focus on the sailors vies with a short look at the Ninevites (unit 7). The ending of scene two exceeds in length the ending of scene one (unit 9). If the overall symmetry produces rhythm, contrast, emphasis, and continuity, the asymmetry disrupts the rhythm to give contrast and emphasis through discontinuity.

Structural and Stylistic Features. (1) Throughout Jonah, sentences with three main clauses, sometimes doubled, produce a rhythm that facilitates the grasping of content (e.g., 1:3-5, 15-16; 3:5, 7c-8a; 4:7). An alternate structure provides variation through the use of four independent clauses (e.g., 2:1-2a, 11; 3:3-4a; 3:6b; 4:5). Occasionally some clauses depart from conventional Hebrew syntax to place subject before verb, a reversal that effects contrast and emphasis. (See Commentary on 1:4, 5, 9.) In direct discourse, three kinds of sentences prevail: imperative, interrogative, and cohortative or jussive. Yahweh (1:2; 3:2), the captain (1:6), the sailors (1:7-8), and Jonah (4:3) use the imperative. The captain (1:6), the sailors (1:7-8, 10-11), the king (3:9), Jonah (4:2a), and Yahweh (4:4, 9-11) all use the interrogative, sometimes directly and other times rhetorically. The sailors (1:7) and most especially the king (3:7-8) use the cohortative or the jussive.

(2) The phenomenon of repetition permeates the story. It emphasizes themes to build unity and cohesion. A number of verbs occur three or more times each: "arise" (קום qûm), "call" (קרא qārā'), "know" (ידע yāda'), "hurl" (טול ṭûl), "fear" (ירא yārē'), "turn"

(שוב *šûb*), "make" (עשה *'āśâ*), "repent" (נחם *nāḥam*), "appoint" (מנה *mānâ*), "go" (בוא *bô'*), "walk" (הלך *hālak*), and "perish" (אבד *'ābad*). Certain nouns and adjectives appear often: "great" (גדול *gādôl*), fourteen times; "evil" (רעה *rā'â*), nine times; "sea" (ים *yām*), eleven times; and "life" or "self" (נפש *nepeš*), three times. Several phrases and clauses appear two or more times: "to flee to Tarshish," "the presence of Yahweh," "that the sea may be quiet," "call to Yahweh or God," "prayed to Yahweh," "is anger good." Six sets of cognate accusatives increase the use of repetition: "fear a fear," "vow a vow," "sacrifice a sacrifice," "call a call," "evil an evil," "delight a delight."

Unusual Vocabulary. Although the many repetitions suggest that the vocabulary is not large, nonetheless it contains a number of unusual words and words used in unusual ways. Five terms are unique to Jonah: ספינה (*sĕpînâ*; the second occurrence of the two words translated "ship" in 1:5), יתעשת (*yit'aššēt*, "will think," 1:6), קריאה (*qĕrî'â*, "calling," 3:2), קיקיון (*qîqāyôn*, "plant," 4:6, 7, 9, 10), and חרישית (*ḥărîšît*, "strong" or "fierce," 4:8). In addition, four verbs take on unique meanings: חשב (*ḥāšab*, "think"), applied to the inanimate object "ship" (1:4); שתק (*šātaq*, "be quiet"), applied to the sea (1:11-12); חתר (*ḥātar*, "dig" or "hollow out"), applied to the activity of rowing (1:13); and זעף (*zā'ap*, "be enraged"), applied to the sea (1:15). Rare also is the noun מלחים (*mallāḥîm*) for sailors (1:5; cf. only Ezek 27:9, 27, 29). (Elsewhere in Jonah the word translated "sailors" is simply אנשים [*'ănāšîm*], "men.") The phrase רב החבל (*rab haḥōbēl*, 1:6), often translated by the single word "captain," literally means "the chief of the ropes." The noun חבל (*ḥōbēl*) occurs only here and in Ezek 27:8, 27-29.

The clustering of unusual vocabulary within chapter 1 bespeaks the distinctiveness of this seafaring incident within the Hebrew Bible. Some of the words also mark the peculiar style of the narrator in conveying information and ideas. To ascribe thought to the ship (1:4) intensifies its plight. To portray the captain as a handler of ropes (1:6) provides a choice detail about the operation of the ship. To describe rowing as "digging" (1:13) shows the desperation of the sailors (or a lack of nautical knowledge by the author?).

Overall, the vocabulary of Jonah is common and simple, unique and varied. It demonstrates a creative use of words and indicates a cosmopolitan outlook.

Rhetorical Devices. The creative use of words includes rhetorical devices. Some are available in translation, but many only in Hebrew. A sampling indicates their diversity and value.

(1) Alliteration, assonance, and related devices provide aesthetic and thematic emphasis. The alternation of the Hebrew particles מה (*mâ*) and מ (*m*) in the four questions that the sailors ask Jonah produces a staccato effect that achieves force and urgency: "What," "where," "what," and "where" (1:8). Jonah's answer, עברי אנכי (*'ibrî 'ānōkî*), pleases the ear as he articulates his national identity, "A Hebrew am I" (1:9). The internal vowels in the phrase חנון ורחום (*ḥannûn wĕraḥûm*) resound in the description of God as "gracious" and "merciful" (4:2d). Repetition and rhyme enclose the opening line of the psalm (2:2). Its first and last words begin with the consonant "q" (ק *qop*) and end with the vowel "i"

(י î; קראתי qārā᾽tî, "I call"; and קולי qôlî, "my voice"). Several devices interplay in the clause "the ship thought itself to break up" (1:4). The two verb forms חשבה להשבר (ḥiššĕbâ lĕhiššābēr, "thought itself to break up") yield assonance with the vowels i, e, a, and i, a, e. These words also exhibit onomatopoeia; they sound like their meaning—namely, boards cracking from the force of water. The entire clause exemplifies prosopopoeia, the representation of an inanimate object by a human attribute.

(2) Chiasm, a syntactic structure that inverts the order of sentences or words, is a favorite rhetorical device. For instance, the narrated discourse in the fish episode begins and ends with sentences that have Yahweh as subject (2:1, 11). Between them come sentences with Jonah as subject (2:11). Thus the pattern is ABB'A'. The report of Jonah's entering Nineveh (3:3-4a) inverts the order of the nouns: Jonah (A), Nineveh (B), Nineveh (B'), Jonah (A'). Beyond single words, chiasms in Jonah extend to entire verses. (See the Commentary on 1:3.)

(3) Merism, the division of the whole into parts, identifies the description of the cosmos as the heavens, the sea, and the dry land (1:9b). The device also occurs in the references to the total population of Nineveh as "from the greatest to the smallest" (3:5) and "the human and the animal" (3:7b).

(4) Synecdoche, in contrast to merism, substitutes parts for the whole. This device identifies the phrase "the herd and the flock," representing the animal population (3:7b).

(5) Puns enliven Jonah.[41] The opposite verbs עלה (῾ālâ, "go up") and ירד (yārad, "go down") play off each other. The evil of Nineveh goes up (῾lh) to Yahweh (1:2); Jonah goes down (yrd) to Joppa, to the ship, and to the hold of the ship (1:3, 5). Jonah goes down (yrd) to the land, but Yahweh brings up (῾lh) Jonah's life from the pit (2:6). A wordplay between the phrase "from his throne" (מכסאו mikkis᾽ô) and the verb "be covered" (כסה kāsâ) assists in depicting the transformation in the king of Nineveh (3:6b). The word טעם (ṭa῾am), rendered "proclamation" in 3:7, carries the concrete meaning of taste and the figurative meaning of judgment. Its use prepares for a pun on the first instruction, "let them not taste" (אל-יטעמו ᾽al-yiṭ῾āmû). The hope that God may "turn from his fierce anger" literally reads "from the burning of his nostrils" (3:9). After God fulfills the hope, Jonah "becomes angry," a description that literally reads, "it burned to him." What God has turned from inflames Jonah. Wordplay gives the incendiary contrast.

(6) A different kind of rhetorical device is the strategy of delayed information. In 1:1-3, Jonah makes no verbal reply to the command of Yahweh. Only much later (4:2) does the reader learn that Jonah did speak at that time, whether within himself or aloud to Yahweh. When Jonah talks to the sailors (1:9), he does not tell them that he is fleeing from Yahweh. Later the narrator supplies the information (1:10). When the plant withers, the narrator does not report Jonah's reaction (4:7). At the end, Yahweh gives it (4:10). The strategy of delayed information contributes to the surprise and suspense of the story.

---

41. See Baruch Halpern and Richard Elliott Friedman, "Composition and Paronomasia in the Book of Jonah," HAR 4 (1980) 79-92.

Imagery. Overview. The storyteller uses a wide range of imagery. Cosmically it extends from the heavens above (1:9) to the dry land and the sea (1:9) to the depths of the netherworld (2:2). Geographically it extends east to west, from Tarshish (1:3) to Nineveh (3:3), with Joppa (1:3) and possibly Jerusalem (2:4, 7) in between. Vivid language presents the horrors of a storm at sea: the ship tossing to and fro, about to be dashed to pieces, and the frantic efforts of the sailors in hurling wares overboard and in rowing (1:4-5, 11, 13). Equally vivid language reports dangers on dry land: the destructive power of wind and sun beating upon the head of Jonah (4:8). Ritual activities enlarge the imagery: lot casting (1:7), mourning (3:5-8*a*), praying (1:14; 2:2-9), sacrificing (1:15; 2:9), vowing (1:15; 2:9), and worshiping in the Temple (2:4, 7). Varieties of life similarly expand the narrative world: people, animals, and a plant. All these images attest to the cosmopolitan purview of the storyteller.

Gender Imagery. Gender imagery in Jonah clusters around the theme of life and death. This subject requires careful explication, beginning with the distinction between grammar and identity. Comparative studies show that grammatical gender is primarily an issue of syntax rather than of sexual identity.[42] Masculine and feminine nouns, whether animate or inanimate, are not in themselves the equivalent of male and female. These linguistic data constrain the interpretation of certain feminine grammatical nouns and verbs in Jonah 1–2 that metaphorically suggest female activity and anatomy.

(1) The feminine noun אֲנִיָּה (*ŏniyyâ*), one of two words used for the ship, first claims attention because it appears before its verb, thereby reversing the usual order of Hebrew syntax (1:4*a*). As already observed, the verb itself, חִשְּׁבָה לְהִשָּׁבֵר (*ḥiššĕbâ lĕhiššābēr*, "thought to break up"), increases attention because it represents an inanimate object with a human attribute. Figuratively, the total combination yields a female persona for the ship: She thinks that she is cracking up.

(2) In the next verse (1:5) occurs the second word for "ship," סְפִינָה (*sĕpînâ*). It appears in the phrase reporting that Jonah went down to "the innards of the ship" (יַרְכְּתֵי הַסְּפִינָה *yarkĕtê hassĕpînâ*, 1:5*b*). Both of these nouns, "innards" and "ship," are gramatically feminine forms. Building upon the female persona of the thinking ship, the phrase suggests (though it does not specify) a uterine image: the inner recesses where Jonah lies in slumber. But the nautical body cannot shield Jonah. His presence in the "womb" of the ship threatens *her* life as well as his own. Destruction invades the place of conception.

(3) The two phrases about Jonah's being in "the belly of the fish" (1:17; 2:1) pose different images tied to different grammatical genders. The masculine plural noun translated "belly" (מֵעֶה *mē'eh*) signifies internal parts. Three places in the Bible it parallels the grammatical feminine noun בֶּטֶן (*beṭen*) to acquire the meaning "womb" (Gen 25:23; Isa 49:1; Ps 71:6; cf. Ruth 1:11). That meaning is excluded in Jonah 1:17, where the word

---

42. See Bruce K. Waltke and M. O'Connor, *An Introduction to Biblical Hebrew Syntax* (Winona Lake, Ind.: Eisenbrauns, 1990) 96-110.

for "fish" (דג *dāg*) is masculine gender; but it acquires validity in Jonah 2:1, where the word for "fish" (דגה *dāgâ*) is feminine gender.

The switch from the masculine to the feminine gender for "fish" has intrigued readers through the centuries.[43] No one knows why it happened, what it means, or if it is important. Nonetheless, like the imagery of "the innards of the ship" (1:5b), the phrase "from the belly of the fish" in 2:1 evokes the womb. Once again, though this time not by his own choice, Jonah resides in a place of conception that harbors destruction. His presence in the ichthyic "womb" threatens his life.

(4) In the psalm that Jonah prays from within the mother fish, he cries to Yahweh "from the womb of Sheol" (מבטן שאול *mibbeṭen šěʾôl*, 2:3a; neither the NIV nor the NRSV chooses this translation). Here the grammatical feminine noun *beṭen* describes the depths of the underworld. The word climaxes the uterine descent (regression) of Jonah, first into the "innards" of the ship, then into the "belly" of the female fish, and at last beneath earth and sea to the "womb" of Sheol, the most deadly of residences. Tied to the verb *yrd* ("went down") in chapters 1 and 2, this imagery embodies the issue of life and death, of womb and tomb.[44]

Summary. Though the book of Jonah is silent on many critical questions, it speaks eloquently as a literary document. Design, structure, style, vocabulary, imagery, character portrayals, plot development, and rhetorical devices fashion an exquisite narrative abounding in interpretive offerings. Consummate artistry bears theological profundities.

THEOLOGY

Complexities mark the theology of Jonah. This overview begins with themes and moves to a narrative scanning of the book.

Themes. Prophetic Call. Jonah's resistance to the call from Yahweh is not unique. Moses shrank from speaking to Pharaoh (Exod 3:10–4:17); Elijah fled from denouncing the regime of Ahab (1 Kgs 19:1-18); Jeremiah recoiled from prophesying to the nations (Jer 1:4-10). Yet Jonah exceeds them all in his defiance. The phrase "from the presence of Yahweh" (1:3) signals not just resistance but outright disobedience. Contrary to the view that Jonah flees because he believes that Yahweh is confined to the land of Israel, the phrase indicates that Jonah recognizes Yahweh's presence and power in Nineveh. To flee from the divine presence is not to escape God but to reject the divine call.

---

43. For proposals, see Sasson, *Jonah*, 155-57.

44. In a quasi-Jungian reading, Ackerman uses the recesses of the ship, the belly of the fish, and the womb of Sheol, along with Nineveh (3:4-10) and the booth (4:5), to argue that Jonah repeatedly seeks shelters that give him a "womb/death-like security" (James S. Ackerman, "Satire and Symbolism in the Song of Jonah," in *Traditions in Transformation,* ed. Baruch Halpern and Jon D. Levenson [Winona Lake, Ind.: Eisenbrauns, 1981] 239-43). In its concern with archetypal rather than metaphorical concepts, that reading diverges from the one proposed here. Neither Nineveh nor the booth offers a womblike metaphor. Nineveh is not described as an enclosed or walled city. Although the booth ostensibly provides Jonah shade as he sits under it, it need not be an enclosed space. Furthermore, Jonah himself builds the booth, unlike the ship, the fish, and Sheol. Again unlike them, the booth occupies the surface of the land; it does not yield imagery of the depths.

Motives vary for resisting a call. Moses and Jeremiah thought themselves inadequate for the task (Exod 3:11, 4:10; Jer 1:6). Elijah feared for his own life (1 Kgs 19:3, 10). Amos and Isaiah found the message too dreadful to announce (e.g., Amos 7:2, 5; Isa 6:9-13). At first Jonah gives no reason for his resistance. Near the end, he offers an explanation that contrasts with those of his predecessors (4:2-3). He is not concerned about his qualifications; he does not fear for his life; and he does not resist because Yahweh commands him to preach doom. Instead, his objection is the certain knowledge that doom for Nineveh can be averted because God repents of evil. Whereas some prophets shrank from preaching because they saw no hope, Jonah refuses because he knows there is hope. Whereas some prophets complained about the wrath of Yahweh (e.g., Jer 20:7-9), Jonah protests the love of God.

The futility of resisting the call also permeates prophetic literature. Yahweh repeatedly overruled the objections of Moses and sent him to Pharaoh. Yahweh evicted Elijah from Mount Horeb and sent him back to Syria and Israel with a political and prophetic mandate. Yahweh held Isaiah and Amos to their respective assignments, and Yahweh bluntly informed Jeremiah that he had no choice. Similarly, Yahweh pursues Jonah on sea and dry land. By the end of scene one, Jonah has exhausted his efforts to disobey. At the beginning of scene two, without a word he goes to Nineveh as Yahweh commands. But his response is at best "giving in," resignation to the inevitable. At worst it is another way of resisting: to oppose through external obedience; to say yes but mean no.

Jonah's behavior after he fulfills his mission recalls Elijah's after the mighty contest on Mount Carmel (1 Kgs 18:20-46). Elijah leaves first his homeland and then the city of Beersheba, sits under a broomtree, and later makes his way to the cave at Mount Horeb. Jonah leaves Nineveh, builds a booth, and in time finds himself sitting under a miraculous plant. Like Elijah, he pleads that Yahweh take away his life (1 Kgs 19:4; Jonah 4:3). But the circumstances differ. Suffering from exhaustion, Elijah is zealous that Yahweh's will will prevail. Suffering from anger, Jonah is defiant that Yahweh's will has prevailed. Along the way, both narratives involve extensive use of nature. Ravens feed Elijah (1 Kgs 17:4-6); a fish swallows Jonah (Jonah 2:1). Wind, earthquake, and fire signify the absence of God for Elijah (1 Kgs 19:11-12); plant, worm, wind, and sun signify the presence of God for Jonah (Jonah 4:7-8).

Elijah and Jonah are alone among the prophets in being sent to foreign lands. Each addresses God out of a sense of dejection and self-pity, and Yahweh responds with questions that the deity later repeats (1 Kgs 19:9, 13; Jonah 4:4, 9). The questions confront the prophets with the folly of self-concern.

Comparisons of Jonah with other prophets highlight the commonalities and particularities in his call. More than the others, he rails against the inevitability of obedience. In capitulation he continues to resist. He even turns the success of his mission into an accusation that itself tests the character of Yahweh to be merciful to a defiant messenger.[45]

---

45. For Jonah as a reflection on prophets and prophecy, see Amos Funkenstein, *Perceptions of Jewish History* (Berkeley: University of California Press, 1993) 64-70. Cf. Band's view that the book is a parody on a prophet's career that over time got reinterpreted to become the reverse—namely, "a prophetic book with a prophetic message" (Arnold J. Band, "Swallowing Jonah: The Eclipse of Parody," *Prooftexts* [1990] esp. 191-94).

Nineveh. As the object of Jonah's mission, Nineveh poses interpretive challenges. According to the table of nations, Nimrod the mighty hunter founded the city (Gen 10:8-12). Zephaniah condemned it for arrogance and forecast its destruction shortly before that event in 612 BCE (Zeph 2:13-15). Nahum assailed it as the "city of bloodshed" (Nah 3:1), described its evil in great detail, and rejoiced in its destruction. From this prophetic perspective, the historical Nineveh was evil incarnate; it justly deserved its fate.

In decisive ways the book of Jonah counters this portrait. (1) Yahweh, the very God in whose name Zephaniah and Nahum prophesied, repeatedly describes Nineveh as "the great city" (1:2; 3:2; 4:11), and the narrator even declares it a city "great to God" (3:3). Although Yahweh once ascribes "evil" to it (1:2), never is it called "the evil city." Indeed, God recognizes that it turns from evil (3:10). (2) The books of Zephaniah and Nahum denounce Nineveh and see its destruction as the will of Yahweh. But the book of Jonah shows no hatred toward the city. Jonah's own quarrel is not with the city but with God. Unlike those prophetic oracles of judgment, the story shows compassion for Nineveh and sees its salvation as the will of Yahweh. (3) Zephaniah and Nahum concentrate exclusively upon the violence of Nineveh. Although the book of Jonah refers to the evil and the violence of the city (1:2; 3:8, 10), it neither details nor dwells on these horrors. Instead, it emphasizes the religious sensitivities of the city. The people of Nineveh believe in God, engage in acts of penance, and repent (3:5-10). The repenting of God (3:10) then confirms these deeds as genuine. (4) Zephaniah and Nahum describe the historical Nineveh; Jonah depicts the legendary Nineveh. Beyond the identity of name and size, the two cities meet, briefly but profoundly, at the place of evil. Then they depart, radically and profoundly, at the place of repentance. As a result, prophetic imagination does not offer two attitudes toward one Nineveh; rather, it dares to offer two Ninevehs and thus to relativize historical certitude.[46]

Ecology. With a focus on human beings and their environment, ecology constitutes a prominent theological theme throughout Jonah. Yahweh first acts as the subject of a verb whose object is nature. The deity hurls a great wind that produces a great storm upon the sea, which in turn threatens the animated ship and its sailors (1:4). Countering the disobedience of one creature, Yahweh sets nature over against many. A single human response precipitates a hostile environment.

The sailors seek to appease the sea by offering it inanimate wares (1:5). Then they seek to escape the storm by returning to dry land (1:13). At last they succeed in calming the sea by sacrificing the culprit Jonah (1:15). They give to nature one of their own. Concerted human deeds restore harmony to a hostile environment. But the sailors take no credit for restoring the ecological balance. Instead, they worship Yahweh (1:16).

The next episode begins with Yahweh again the subject of a verb whose object is nature. The deity appoints a great fish to swallow Jonah (1:17). This animal of the sea mediates

---

46. Cf. the proposal that Nineveh in the book of Jonah be viewed through the lens of the Hellenistic rather than the ancient Near Eastern world. See Thomas M. Bolin, " 'Should I Not Also Pity Nineveh?' Divine Freedom in the Book of Jonah," *JSOT* 67 (1995) 109-20. This proposal is tied to the unstable assumption of a late date for Jonah.

between the deity and the human being. Whether it performs a benign or malignant function remains a moot question. The verbs used for its actions carry negative meanings: "swallow" (בלע *bāla*ʿ) and "vomit" (קיא *qîʾ*). The former suggests that the fish is a hostile environment for Jonah; the latter suggests that Jonah is a hostile substance for the fish. The natural creature rejects the human creature. But the rejection is not an independent move by the fish. As with the swallowing, it happens because Yahweh decrees it.

A contrasting view observes that the psalm (2:1-9) depicts the fish as a friendly environment. It saves Jonah from the hostile sea; it becomes God's answer to Jonah's cry of distress; it is the place where deliverance happens. Yet the Jonah of the prose narrative does not want to be saved. Having sought flight from Yahweh in several unsuccessful ways, he proposes that the sailors throw him into the sea (1:12). From that perspective, drowning would be his salvation; the raging sea would ironically be his rescuer. But the fish thwarts his wish. The natural creature defies the human creature. Yet again, the defiance is not an independent move. Yahweh controls the fish.

The ecological theme continues in Nineveh, but with marked differences. The animals take their orders from the king rather than from God. Moreover, these natural creatures are not instruments for human or divine purposes; instead, they participate with human beings in acts of repentance. The salutation of the royal decree addresses the population as "the human and the animal" (3:7). Then it emphasizes the latter by the accompanying phrase "the herd and the flock." The instruction that follows commands them not to graze and not to drink water. It requires them to dress in sackcloth, to call to God with strength, and to turn from evil. Throughout, the decree treats animals on a par with human beings. The intent is not ridicule but respect, not parody but pathos. Nineveh cares for its animal population. Positing a link between the social and the animal order, the city symbolizes the cultivated earth.[47] An urban environment seeks the well-being of natural creatures.

At the close of the story, under the aegis of divine appointments, nature benevolent and malevolent instructs Jonah. A miraculous plant shades him; he delights in the plant (4:6). A worm kills the plant (4:7); he pities the plant (4:10). A fierce wind blows upon him, and the sun attacks his head; he faints and asks to die (4:8). Yahweh uses these experiences to argue divine pity for Nineveh. God describes the great city as a socionatural environment with humans by the thousands and animals galore. The deity acknowledges what the king knows: In issues of life and death, the animals of Nineveh matter alongside the people. On this strong ecological note, the book ends.

Justice Versus Mercy. Recent efforts to elucidate the theology of Jonah focus on the theme of justice versus mercy.[48] According to this view, Jonah the creature speaks for

---

47. See Funkenstein, *Perceptions of Jewish History,* 66.

48. See, e.g., James S. Ackerman, "Jonah," in *The Literary Guide to the Bible,* ed. Robert Alter and Frank Kermode (Cambridge: Belknap, 1987) 240-42; Athalya Brenner, "Jonah's Poem Out of and Within Its Context," in *Among the Prophets: Language, Image and Structure in the Prophetic Writings,* ed. Philip R. Davies and David J. A. Clines, JSOTSup 144 (Sheffield: JSOT, 1993) 190-92. A variation of this view contrasts justice and sovereignty; see Terence E. Fretheim, "Jonah and Theodicy," *ZAW* 90 (1978) 227-37; Jonathan Magonet, *Form and Meaning: Studies in Literary Techniques in the Book of Jonah* (Sheffield: Almond, 1983) 107-12.

justice, which he finds violated in Yahweh's sparing of Nineveh (4:2). The city deserves punishment; no sudden repentance can compensate for its violence and evil. Yahweh the Creator speaks for mercy, which the deity freely gives to Nineveh. Despite Jonah's pronouncement (3:4), Yahweh has the sovereign right to do as the deity wills—in this case, to be gracious to whom God will be gracious (4:3; cf. Exod 33:19).

This theological formulation holds problems, beginning with the lack of any vocabulary for divine justice on the lips of Jonah—indeed, with the absence of the word "justice" (משפט *mišpāṭ*) from the entire book. Jonah never frames his quarrel with God that way; he never accuses Yahweh of not being just. That view scholars deduce from his accusation that God is merciful (4:2). But objection to mercy does not necessarily mean approval of justice; it may signify, for instance, a desire for vengeance. Moreover, though the attributes of justice and mercy "are not necessarily synonymous,"[49] neither are they necessarily antonymous (cf. Mic 6:8).

If Jonah had wished to promote justice over against mercy, he might have quoted a different version of the credo. In proclaiming Yahweh "merciful and gracious," Exod 34:6-7 juxtaposes God's "forgiving iniquity . . . " with God who will "by no means [clear] the guilty,/ but [visit] the iniquity of the parents/ upon the children . . . to the third and fourth generation" (NRSV; cf. Num 14:18; Nah 1:2-3). In that version, mercy does not exclude judgment. Jonah might have charged, then, that Yahweh acted unjustly in sparing Nineveh, for the deity cleared the guilty rather than visit iniquity upon them. But Jonah does not quote that version, and he does not argue that way. The credo he recites says nothing about iniquity and punishment. It belongs instead to a countertradition (cf. Joel 2:13) that proclaims God "repenting of evil."[50] (The NIV renders the Hebrew "relents from sending calamity" and the NRSV "ready to relent from punishing.") In Ps 103:8-11, the tradition says outright that the "merciful and gracious" Yahweh "does not deal with us according to our sins nor repay us according to our iniquities." Jonah's appropriation of this tradition does not support the contention that he speaks for justice over against mercy.[51]

Another problem afflicts the juxtaposition of justice and mercy. These categories produce one-dimensional readings of both Jonah and God. Jonah becomes thereby the negative model and God the positive.[52] To be sure, abundant evidence discredits Jonah, but he is not altogether a static character. His behavior shifts from taciturn to loquacious and his mood from thanksgiving to delight to anger. Beyond his self-referential focus, Yahweh's attribution of pity to him (4:10) hints at a different facet of his character. The developing portrait of Jonah is not then totally negative. As for Yahweh, the portrait is not altogether

---

49. See Jack M. Sasson, *Jonah*, AB 24B (New York: Doubleday, 1990) 316.

50. See Thomas B. Dozeman, "Inner-Biblical Interpretation of Yahweh's Gracious and Compassionate Character," *JBL* 108 (1989) 207-23.

51. See David Marcus, *From Balaam to Jonah: Anti-prophetic Satire in the Hebrew Bible* (Atlanta: Scholars Press, 1995) 156; cf. Yehezkel Kaufmann, *The Religion of Israel,* trans. Moshe Greenberg (New York: Schocken, 1972) 282-86, who understands that Jonah's formulation contrasts with that of Exod 34:6-7 but still describes the theological issue of the book as "justice versus mercy."

52. See e.g., Brenner, "Jonah's Poem Out of and Within Its Context," 191-92; cf. George M. Landes, "Jonah: A Māšāl?" in *Israelite Wisdom,* ed. John G. Gammie et al. (Missoula, Mont.: Scholars Press, 1978) 149.

positive. Though God repents of evil toward Nineveh, Yahweh endangers innocent sailors. The deity's hurling the great wind (1:4) displays neither justice nor mercy but menacing power. Like Jonah, Yahweh is not a one-dimensional character. Overall, the contrast between justice and mercy does not do justice to the theologies of the book.

A Narrative Scanning. Theologies at Sea. Yahweh first appears as a commanding presence bent on using Jonah to do the divine bidding. God is power, yet power defied. When Jonah disobeys, the deity replaces imperative speech with violent action. Yahweh summons nature to exact vengeance. The deity hurls a wind; it stirs a storm. So excessive is this fury for retaliation that it lashes out indiscriminately, endangering a thoughtful ship and innocent sailors. Although ignorant of the cause of the storm, the captain seeks a theological solution: "Perhaps" the god of Jonah will show favor "so that we do not perish" (1:6 NRSV). In recognizing the sovereign freedom of God, these words turn on irony. The deity from whom the captain seeks salvation is the very deity who threatens disaster. The irony builds when Jonah describes Yahweh as "God of heaven, who made the sea and the dry land" (1:9 NRSV). The traditional formula proclaims the creative power of God while the narrative itself presents the destructive power.

Jonah's orthodox theology evokes from the sailors great fear. The object of their fear is unspecified (1:10), but their experience is terrifying. The sea rages with increasing ferocity. So the sailors pray to the aggrieved and angry deity of Jonah. Asking that they not perish, they affirm the freedom of Yahweh to do as the deity pleases (1:14). The answer to their prayer follows their expelling Jonah to the sea. It ceases to rage. As the sailors respond with proper cultic acts, their fear transfers from the experience of the storm (1:5, 10) to the worship of Yahweh (1:16). After all, violent actions by this God have compelled them to make a human sacrifice in order to be spared a destruction they do not deserve. Divine wrath has manipulated human characters to achieve its end. Throughout the event Yahweh never even speaks to the sailors.

Appointing a fish to swallow Jonah, Yahweh continues to use nature against Jonah. Though the psalm he recites accents deliverance, a destructive portrait of the deity persists. Yahweh has cast Jonah into the sea, away from the divine presence (2:3-4). This coercive God next returns Jonah to dry land, there to confront him again with the commanding presence.

Chapters 1–2 assault characters and readers with conflicting portrayals of God. The creator vies with the destroyer, the punisher with the rescuer. Divine sovereignty and freedom spell vengeance, vindictiveness, and violence. That Yahweh should take cosmic action, hurling upon the sea a terrible wind all because puny Jonah had disobeyed, bespeaks crushing power. (Among other biblical characters, Job would surely understand what Jonah has stirred up.) The benign outcome for the sailors neither lessens nor justifies the use of nature to inflict indiscriminate suffering upon the innocent. This God is made of stern stuff, and it is not the stuff of justice or of mercy. Issues of theodicy flood these chapters.

Theologies in Nineveh. The second time around Yahweh wins over Jonah. Divine power overwhelms human disobedience. Jonah goes to Nineveh. The deity then withdraws to await the response of the Ninevites to Jonah's ambiguous pronouncement. Like the sailors, the Ninevites are god oriented; unlike the sailors, they are not innocent. The king himself acknowledges their evil and violence (3:8). Nonetheless, like the captain, he sounds a cautious note of hope based on a theological premise. If the captain appeals to the possible favor of God, the king appeals to the possible repentance: "Who knows? God may relent . . . so that we do not perish" (3:9 NRSV).

This premise introduces a theology of repentance, new to the story. It sets up a correlation, neither inevitable nor necessary, but yet possible, between human and divine turning. The repentance of the Ninevites may effect the repentance of God. And so it comes to pass. The Ninevites turn from evil; God turns from evil (3:10). In contrast to the dissonant theologies of chaps. 1–2, chap. 3 yields harmony. It works on a *quid pro quo* basis, an equal exchange between God and the people of Nineveh. Mutuality and reciprocity eliminate evil without resorting to punishment. Repentance substitutes for retribution. But the theology of repentance carries disturbing irony. Whereas the sailors experience the fury of Yahweh, the Ninevites experience the saving power.

Divine repentance angers Jonah. It provides the single verbal link to the credo he recites about God's being "gracious and merciful . . . repenting of evil" (4:2). Jonah does not question the authenticity of Nineveh's action; what bothers him is God's matching response. Yet in reciting the credo, Jonah expands the meaning of repentance beyond reciprocity. Rather than being just a correlary to Nineveh's repentance, God's repentance parallels God's mercy. Though different, the theologies of repentance and mercy work well together, binding parts of chapters 3 and 4. Each of them stands in bold contrast to the theologies of retribution and violence that characterize chapters 1 and 2. Strikingly, Jonah himself never complains about the latter, only about the former.

Theologies Beyond Nineveh. As the story moves to its ending, the theological mix becomes more dissonant. A series of natural appointments—plant, worm, and wind—achieves divine purposes. Once again destructive elements emerge within God. Yahweh does not show regard for the plant in its own right; a worm can destroy it with impunity. Just as Yahweh once hurled a great wind upon the sea because of Jonah's disobedience (1:4), so now the deity appoints a scorching wind to disturb Jonah and allows the sun to beat upon his head (4:8). The power of God to manipulate nature for weal or woe continues.

To each of the natural appointments Jonah responds. The first and third responses show him as self-centered. Shaded by the plant, he delights in it. Buffeted by the wind and beaten by the sun, he asks to die. In between, when the plant dies, his response is not reported. It emerges later to become the basis of yet another theology (cf. 4:7 with 4:10), and that theology upsets Jonah's orthodox understanding of mercy.

New vocabulary signals the new theology. In the last two verses of the book, Yahweh introduces the verb חוס (*ḥûs*) with Jonah and then the deity as subject. Most often translated "pity" or "show compassion" (though both the NIV and the NRSV use the weak word "concern"), the verb supplies Jonah's missing response in 4:7 to the death of the plant. He pitied the plant. Unlike the responses that surround it, this one is not self-centered.[53] The response of *ḥûs* signifies disinterested compassion. It shows that there is more to Jonah than Jonah has shown.

By analogy with Jonah, the verb *ḥûs* reports something new about Yahweh. The deity develops the argument through natural rather than revealed theology. It moves from the human to the divine, from the understandable to the mysterious, from Jonah's pity for the plant to Yahweh's pity for Nineveh. Alongside similarities, the argument through analogy carries dissimilarities. Jonah has no power over the plant. He can neither stop its destruction nor restore it to life. But he does pity the plant after its demise. By contrast, Yahweh's pity for Nineveh prevents the city's demise. The deity has total power over the city and its outcome. In exercising that sovereignty, Yahweh acts in a way new to the story. Yet the deity accounts for *ḥûs* not through divine revelation but through human sensibility for the natural world. Jonah's *ḥûs* argues for Yahweh's *ḥûs*. If the analogy is flawed, nonetheless the argument moves the story to another level of theological insight.

In the movement Yahweh acknowledges for the first time a non-utilitarian view of nature. Jonah pities the plant as a plant. His disinterested compassion forms the premise for Yahweh's disinterested compassion in Nineveh. So Yahweh characterizes the city not according to its evil, to its deeds, and to its repentance (see 3:10), but according to its size, to its ignorance, and to its animals. And Yahweh pities these animals as animals. Unlike the fish and the worm, they are not instruments of divine power. "Pity" (*ḥûs*), then, signals a new theology of ecology. If earlier the Ninevites understood the integrity of the animal creation (3:7-8), now Yahweh embraces that understanding.

The theology of 4:10-11 differs from repentance, mercy, and their interplay (though it is compatible with them).[54] As vocabulary new to the story, *ḥûs* distinguishes this understanding of Yahweh from the attributes cited in the credo. Yahweh shows compassion on the city not because it repents but because Yahweh chooses to show compassion on it. The story yields then two theologies of grace. If the first is understandable, the second is inexplicable; it does not fit the orthodox credo. Indeed, it is even more incredulous (*qal wāḥōmer*)[55] than Jonah's compassion for the plant. In this move from understandable to inexplicable mercy, Yahweh the creator affirms a sovereignty and freedom that borders on caprice. And if on this occasion caprice is compassion, what guarantee does Yahweh

---

53. Contra Herbert Chanan Brichto, " 'And Much Cattle': YHWH's Last Words to a Reluctant Prophet," in *Toward a Grammar of Biblical Poetics* (New York: Oxford University Press, 1992) 78-79.

54. See Hans Walter Wolff, *Obadiah and Jonah,* trans. Margaret Kohl (Minneapolis: Augsburg, 1986) 87; Elias Bickerman, *Four Strange Books of the Bible* (New York: Schocken, 1967) 44; David Noel Freedman, "Did God Play a Dirty Trick on Jonah at the End?" *BR* 6 (1990) 26-31; Kenneth M. Craig, Jr., *A Poetics of Jonah: Art in the Service of Ideology* (Columbia: University of South Carolina Press, 1993) 158-59.

55. The rabbinic phrase *qal wāḥōmer* signifies an argument "all the more" (*a fortiori*) than the one from which it precedes. The argument moves from the small to the great (*ad minori ad maius*). See L. Jacobs, "The *Qal Va-ḥomer* Argument in the Old Testament," *BSO(A)S* 35 (1972) 221-27; cf. the Commentary on Jonah 4:10-11.

give that, on another occasion, it will not be destruction?[56] (Again, Job would understand well Jonah's plight.)[57]

Summary. Despite scholarly propensities to derive one consistent message from Jonah, the book reverberates with a cacophony of theologies.[58] Sovereignty, freedom, creation, retribution, vindictiveness, violence, repentance, mercy, pity, and caprice sound major dissonances. Though at places the harshness fades into harmony (primarily chap. 3), as a whole the disjunctions prevail. Yet they belong to a unified composition exquisitely wrought. Rather than taming the dissonances to produce a single theology, those interpretations that allow them to flourish witness best to the story—and to its God.

PURPOSE

The purpose of the Jonah narrative is not known. Far from deterring speculations, however, that ignorance has encouraged them. Two flaws characterize most efforts: tying the purpose to a presumed date and concentrating on parts of the story as if they equal the whole. A survey of major proposals shows the possibilities and limitations of the subject.

Israel and the Nations. The older view that Jonah espouses universalism to combat the nationalism and exclusionism fostered by the reforms of Ezra and Nehemiah has withered for lack of evidence.[59] The book contains no allusions to the reform measures of the fifth century BCE, nor does it portray Jonah as a nationalist. Its universalism is not an attack on Israel; its tone is not polemical; its contents do not report enmity between Israel and the Gentiles.[60] Correspondingly, the book is not a missionary tract to convert non-Israelites. Jonah does not disparage the gods of the sailors or try to make them Yahweh worshipers. Even when, after the storm, they worship Yahweh, they do not repudiate their own gods. Furthermore, the report on the repentance of the Ninevites says nothing about their conversion to Yahwism. The theological vocabulary of chapter 3 restricts itself to the generic term אלהים (’ĕlōhîm, "god"). Unlike Second Isaiah, for instance, Jonah does not denounce foreign deities or proclaim Yahweh as the only God (cf. Isa 44:9-20; 45:14-25). Neither the theme of polemic against nationalistic Israel nor that of conversion for the nations accounts for the purpose of the book.

Although disavowing these particular formulations, some recent attempts sound related ideas. Ackerman thinks Jonah is designed to help Jews in Jerusalem recover from the

---

56. Cooper moves the argument for divine caprice in 4:10-11 toward God's destructive wrath. See Alan Cooper, "In Praise of Divine Caprice: The Significance of the Book of Jonah," in *Among the Prophets: Language, Image and Structure in the Prophetic Writings,* ed. Philip R. Davies and David J. A. Clines (Sheffield: JSOT, 1993) 144-63. See also Thomas M. Bolin, " 'Should I Not Also Pity Nineveh?' Divine Freedom in the Book of Jonah," *JSOT* 67 (1995) esp. 117-20.

57. The relationship of Jonah to wisdom theologies, especially to Job, remains an undeveloped topic. See Wolff, *Jonah,* 87; Leslie C. Allen, *The Books of Joel, Obadiah, Jonah, and Micah* (Grand Rapids: Eerdmans, 1976) 191.

58. Cf. Wolff, *Jonah*: "The writer is not a systematic theologian" (87-88).

59. See R. E. Clements, "The Purpose of the Book of Jonah," VTSup 28 (Leiden: E. J. Brill, 1975) 16-20; cf. Yehezkel Kaufmann, *The Religion of Israel,* trans. Moshe Greenberg (New York: Schocken, 1972) 282-83.

60. See Bickerman, *Four Strange Books of the Bible,* 14-28.

Babylonian exile, to help them reckon with the apparent injustice of God toward their nation in relation to other nations that have not been punished for even greater sins.[61] Fretheim envisions a despairing and even cynical post-exilic community in Jerusalem, dismayed that the God who has let it down nonetheless requires it to give hope to the enemy.[62] Gitay proposes that the story aims to prepare the way theologically for cooperation with foreign rulers during the Babylonian and Persian periods.[63] Allen writes of a "self-centered" post-exilic community whom the book challenges "to face up to the unwelcome truth of God's sovereign compassion for foreigners and beasts."[64] Wolff thinks that Jonah seeks to overcome through irony the "gloomy concern" with themselves of the Jews in the Hellenistic period and so to effect "the assent of the religious egoist to Yhwh's pity for all human beings."[65] Despite scant evidence for all such dates and statements of purpose, their tenacity perdures.

Unfulfilled Prophecy. Another approach holds that Jonah proposes to address the issue of unfulfilled prophecy. Bickerman contrasts Jeremiah's view that human repentance effects divine repentance with Jonah's view that God's word of doom, once spoken, must not be changed.[66] The book of Jonah then surmounts this antithesis. Although Jeremiah and other prophets predicted that God would destroy Jerusalem, a prediction that came to pass, the author of Jonah teaches "the restored and still sinful city" that if God can spare Nineveh, there is yet hope for the salvation of Jerusalem. Rofé adopts a similar reading.[67] Surveying views about the fulfillment of prophecy found in Deuteronomy, Kings, Jeremiah, and Ezekiel, he concludes that the book of Jonah fits this milieu. Yahweh's salvation of Nineveh confirms Jonah in his previous knowledge that, even though he would like Yahweh to keep the divine word, Yahweh repents of evil. Thus Nineveh has a right to exist, apart from the fulfillment of prophecy.[68]

Repentance. Still another approach subordinates unfulfilled prophecy to the theme of repentance. The possibility of repentance mitigates any absolute declaration of destruction. In developing this idea, Clements finds parallels between Jonah and Jeremiah, Ezekiel, and the deuteronomic history.[69] He argues that, in the aftermath of the exile, many leaders asserted the necessity of repentance as the key to Israel's future. Belonging to the same

---

61. See James S. Ackerman, "Jonah," in *The Literary Guide to the Bible,* ed. Robert Alter and Frank Kermode (Cambridge: Belknap, 1987) 234, 242.

62. See Terence E. Fretheim, *The Message of Jonah* (Minneapolis: Augsburg, 1977) 190-91.

63. See Yehoshua Gitay, "Jonah: The Prophecy of Anti-rhetoric," in *Fortunate the Eyes That See,* ed. Astrid B. Beck et al. (Grand Rapids: Eerdmanns, 1995) 203-6.

64. See Allen, *The Books of Joel, Obadiah, Jonah and Micah,* 190-91.

65. See Wolff, *Obadiah and Jonah,* 86.

66. See Bickerman, *Four Strange Books of the Bible,* 38-45.

67. See Alexander Rofé, "Classes in the Prophetical Stories: Didactic Legend and Parable," VTSup 26 (1974) 155-57.

68. Cf. Childs, who posits two editions for the book. The first ties the purpose of accounting for unfulfilled prophecy to the right of the Creator to let mercy override prophecy for the sake of the entire creation; the second amplifies creation theology in terms of the nations, with Nineveh as the case study. Brevard S. Childs, *Introduction to the Old Testament as Scripture* (Philadelphia: Fortress, 1979) 421-26.

69. See Clements, "The Purpose of the Book of Jonah," 20-21.

---

theological scene, the book of Jonah teaches, through the use of Nineveh, this possibility for Israel. The purpose is to show that human repentance elicits divine repentance.

Efforts to locate purpose in the issues of unfulfilled prophecy and repentance underscore important themes that nevertheless fail to encompass the book. They substitute parts for the whole. From the beginning of the sea story in chapter 1 through the expulsion of Jonah from the fish at the end of chapter 2, neither prophecy nor repentance surfaces as a concern. The vocabulary of repentance appears only in chapter 3 and in 4:2. Chapter 4 does not consider the pronouncement of Jonah (3:4), the repentance of Nineveh, or the issue of unfulfilled prophecy. Indeed, at no place does the book even use the word "prophecy." Parts of Jonah may contribute to these topics, but the topics do not themselves define its purpose.

Rejection of Purpose. Certain literary approaches to Jonah question the value or validity of specifying its purpose. Clines proposes that if readers view the book of Jonah as a story, they can relax about seeking its intent. The book may "have nothing in particular to 'teach' but be an imaginative story . . . in which various serious concerns of the author are lightly and teasingly sketched."[70] (But then to sketch these concerns becomes itself a purpose.) Craig acknowledges that the book is "highly charged ideological literature," but he, too, takes pains to deny it a didactic purpose. Instead, it is polyphonic literature in which "several independent and legitimate points of view . . . work and often struggle together to assert themselves." Craig's rejection of the word "didactic" rests on assigning it the meanings of "militaristic" and "doctrinal." Yet he writes that near the end of the story Yahweh offers Jonah "a practical lesson" (itself a didactic word) whose outcome eschews rational coherence to present "the mystery of divine compassion."[71]

Conclusion. The book of Jonah does not disclose its purpose, and speculation has not secured it. This uncertainty matches the meager knowledge about its origin, date, composition, genre, and setting. Nonetheless, the book offers an abundance of literary treasures, theological complexities, and hermeneutical possibilities. It lends itself to multiple uses and readings in a variety of settings and for a variety of purposes.[72] Interpretations that remain faithful to the diversities and the mysteries best convey the challenges that this cacophonous story provides contemporary communities of faith.

70. See David J. A. Clines, "Story and Poem: The Old Testament as Literature and as Scripture," *Int.* 34 (1980) 119. Cf. Marcus, who says that "no message is advocated; rather Jonah himself is satirized" (*From Balaam to Jonah: Anti-prophetic Satire in the Hebrew Bible* [Atlanta: Scholars Press, 1995] 156-58).
71. See Craig, *A Poetics of Jonah,* 159-65.
72. Cf. Sasson, *Jonah,* 326.

BIBLIOGRAPHY

Commentaries:

Allen, Leslie C. *The Books of Joel, Obadiah, Jonah and Micah.* Grand Rapids: Eerdmans, 1976. A brief exploration especially sensitive to literary and theological matters.

Limburg, James. *Jonah.* OTL. Louisville: Westminster/John Knox, 1993. A standard commentary with special interest in the afterlife of Jonah in Jewish, Christian, and Islamic literature and art.

Sasson, Jack M. *Jonah.* AB 24B. New York: Doubleday, 1990. The most comprehensive commentary available, especially strong in textual and philological analysis and in providing relevant material from the ancient Near East and from Jewish sources.

Wolff, Hans Walter. *Obadiah and Jonah.* Translated by Margaret Kohl. Minneapolis: Augsburg, 1977. A commentary that makes available the best of German scholarship.

Literary and Theological Studies:

Craig, Kenneth M., Jr. *A Poetics of Jonah: Art in the Service of Ideology.* Columbia: University of South Carolina Press, 1993. A conversation with poetic theory that illuminates aesthetic and social features of the text.

Fretheim, Terence E. *The Message of Jonah: A Theological Commentary.* Minneapolis: Augsburg, 1977. A study that explicates the message with attention to its homiletical usefulness.

Magonet, Jonathan. *Form and Meaning: Studies in Literary Techniques in the Book of Jonah.* BLS 8. Sheffield: Almond, 1983. An investigation of the many interlocking literary systems that give the book its complexity.

Trible, Phyllis. *Rhetorical Criticism: Context, Method, and the Book of Jonah.* GBS.OTS. Minneapolis: Fortress, 1994. A line-by-line study of the text to illuminate the artistry of its composition.

OUTLINE OF JONAH

I. Jonah 1:1–2:10, Narrative of Flight, Strife, and Return

    A. 1:1-3, Yahweh's Command and Jonah's Response
    B. 1:4-6, Yahweh's Storm and Human Responses
    C. 1:7-16, Efforts of the Sailors to Avert Disaster and the Result
    D. 1:17–2:10, Yahweh, a Fish, and Jonah

II. Jonah 3:1–4:11, Narrative of Mission, Repentance, and Dissent

    A. 3:1-4, Yahweh's Command and Jonah's Response
    B. 3:5-10, Efforts of the Ninevites to Avert Disaster and the Result
    C. 4:1-5, Jonah's Reaction, Yahweh's Reply, Jonah's Departure
    D. 4:6-11, Continuing Struggle Between Yahweh and Jonah

JONAH 1:1–2:10

NARRATIVE OF FLIGHT, STRIFE, AND RETURN

OVERVIEW

Scene one begins with Yahweh speaking (אמר *'āmar*) to Jonah (1:1-2) and ends with Yahweh speaking to the fish (2:10).[73] Four episodes develop the plot. The first (1:1-3) reports Yahweh's command that Jonah go to Nineveh and Jonah's disobedient flight by ship to Tarshish. The second episode (1:4-6) relates Yahweh's sending

a wind upon the sea and the effect of this act upon the sea, the ship, the captain, the sailors, and Jonah. The third (1:7-16) describes efforts by the sailors to avert disaster and ends with the casting of Jonah to the sea, the cessation of the storm, and cultic acts by the sailors. The fourth episode (1:17–2:10) tells of the fish that Yahweh appoints to swallow Jonah, Jonah's prayer to Yahweh from inside the fish, and the expulsion of Jonah to dry land.

73. Where appropriate, the commentary draws upon Phyllis Trible, *Rhetorical Criticism: Context, Method, and the Book of Jonah* (Minneapolis: Fortress, 1994) 123-73.

JONAH 1:1-3, YAHWEH'S COMMAND AND JONAH'S RESPONSE

COMMENTARY

1:1. The story begins abruptly. No historical superscription or any other introduction precedes episode one. Among the Twelve Prophets, Jonah is the only book to open with the word ויהי (*wayyĕhî,* "and was" or "came to pass"), a term

that often begins narratives (e.g., Judg 1:1; Ruth 1:1; Esth 1:1). Such a beginning suggests continuation. Jonah is but one story in an all-embracing narrative about the divine and the human, a narrative whose own beginning is elusive and whose ending remains unwritten. "And it came to pass" signals a tale told *in medias res.* The NRSV and the NIV translate the verb, however, simply as "came."

Reading the story in canonical sequence relates its opening to the preceding book of Obadiah, a vision that proclaims not only the destruction of the nation of Edom, hated by Israel, but also "the day of the LORD . . . against all the nations" (Obad 15). To move from that diatribe to the words "and it came to pass" (Jonah 1:1) leaves the reader wondering whether the implied narrative pause leads to a resumption of hatred, a change of subject, or a reversal of point of view.[74] The answer comes in the telling of the story.

The next phrase, "the word of the LORD," continues prophetic discourse. It comes to "Jonah son of Amittai." The proper names mean "Dove son of Truth (or Faithfulness)." Some critics find in these names an allegory for Israel and its God.[75] In Hos 7:11, for instance, the faithful Yahweh calls the nation Ephraim a "silly dove." Other critics find irony in the names.[76] The character Jonah is anything but a faithful son of Yahweh's truth. Yet another critic derives the name "Jonah" from the Hebrew root ינה (*ynh,* "oppress," "maltreat") and so suggests the pejorative meaning "Destroyer son of Truth" (cf. Jer 46:16).[77]

The proper names come from 2 Kgs 14:25. During the reign of King Jeroboam II (786–756 BCE), "Jonah son of Amittai, the prophet, who was from Gath-hepher" (NRSV) successfully proclaimed the restoration of the border of Israel "according to the word of the LORD." Unlike that historical figure, the fictitious Jonah does not carry the title "the prophet." Interpretations of the omission vary: (1) The title can be assumed. (2) The omission is inconsequential; others among the

twelve minor prophets also lack the title (e.g., Joel, Obadiah, Micah, and Zephaniah). (3) The omission carries a negative meaning; this Jonah does not merit the designation "prophet." Whatever the explanation, Jonah son of Amittai does receive a private communication from Yahweh, for which the prophetic formula "the word of the LORD" (דבר יהוה *dĕbar Yhwh*) prepares the way.

1:2. The content of the "word" follows. Three divine imperatives address Jonah: "arise" (קום *qûm*), "go" (לך *lēk*), "and call" (וקרא *ûqrā'*). The NIV and the NRSV truncate these commands and so obscure subtleties in Jonah's forthcoming response. The first two imperatives constitute conventional speech; they often appear in prophetic commissioning formulae (e.g., 1 Kgs 17:9; 21:18; 2 Kgs 1:3; Jer 13:4-6; 49:28; Ezek 3:22). Not separated by a conjunction, these verbs produce a hurried rhythm that moves from the general command "arise" to the specification of place: "go to Nineveh, the great city." Having denounced in Obadiah the enemy nation Edom, the canon now turns to another enemy of Israel: the nation of Assyria as represented by its capital city, Nineveh. But the description of the city is positive. Yahweh the god of Israel calls it "great," an adjective that conjures up size, strength, and status.

The third imperative (קרא *qĕrā'*), rendered variously as "call," "cry," "proclaim," or "preach," introduces the ambiguous message. The translation "against [her]" for the preposition על (*'al*), which follows the imperative, is legitimate, but "to" is also valid. Similarly, the next word, כי (*kî*), translated as the causal particle "because," may carry an asseverative meaning, such as "indeed" or "surely." The singular feminine pronoun reference "her," translated "it," changes to the masculine plural possessive in the expression "their evil," a change retained in the NRSV, but not in the NIV. The combination of the singular and the plural, the feminine and the masculine, depicts Nineveh as one and many and as gender inclusive. The noun "evil" (רעה *rā'â*; NIV and NRSV, "wickedness") is a comprehensive term used with different meanings throughout the narrative: e.g., for the destructive storm (1:7-8); for a way of life unacceptable to God (3:10); for the anger of Jonah (4:1). Here the unspecified evil of Nineveh

---

74. Cf. Paul R. House, *The Unity of the Twelve,* JSOTSup 97 (Sheffield: Almond Press, 1990) 82-85.

75. Cf. Peter R. Ackroyd, who revives an older interpretation, in *Exile and Restoration,* OTL (Philadelphia: Westminster, 1968) 244-45. On the designation of the entire book as allegory, a designation rejected now by most scholars, see Phyllis Lou Trible, "Studies in the Book of Jonah" (Ph.D. diss., Columbia University, 1963; University Microfilm International, order no. 65-7479) 153-58.

76. See Hans Walter Wolff, *Obadiah and Jonah,* trans. Margaret Kohl (Minneapolis: Augsburg, 1986) 98-99; cf. James Limburg, *Jonah: A Commentary,* OTL (Louisville: Westminster/John Knox, 1993) 38.

77. See Alexander Rofé, "Classes in the Prophetical Stories: Didactic Legend and Parable," VTSup 26 (1974) 156n. 4.

comes "into the presence" (or "face"; NIV and NRSV, "come up before") of Yahweh.

Whether Jonah is to call "to" or "against" Nineveh; whether he is to call because of evil or with the recognition of evil; whether he is to mediate doom, information, or warning—all of this remains unclear. But two matters are certain: The evil of Nineveh faces Yahweh, and Yahweh commands Jonah to "arise, go . . . and call."

1:3. A third matter is also clear: Jonah does not want to go. But at first the text misleads the reader by suggesting that he does obey. The divine imperative "arise" becomes the human indicative "Jonah arose." Then comes the break. Rather than the indicative "he went" (הלך *hālak*), matching the second imperative "go," the infinitive "to flee" (לברח *librōaḥ*) takes over to redirect the plot (cf. 1 Kgs 17:9-10; Jer 13:4-7). Jonah goes, not to Nineveh, but to Tarshish. Different vocabulary and different grammar signify a different—indeed, an opposite—direction. Whether Tarshish is Sardinia, Carthage, a city in Spain, or a geographical metaphor for where Yahweh is not known (cf. Isa 66:19), Jonah's flight subverts Yahweh's command.

The reason for his flight does not appear here. Given the information of v. 2, the reader may speculate that the greatness and the evil of Nineveh intimidate Jonah. A Hebrew "prophet" in a foreign land might well fear for his life. But such speculation gets undercut later when Jonah gives his reason (4:3). This literary strategy of delayed information marks the story at several places (cf. 1:10; 4:7). It fills gaps, builds suspense, and keeps the reader off guard.

Verse 3 forms a magnificent chiasm that translations obscure:[78]

A Jonah arose to flee to Tarshish from the presence of Yahweh
  B and he went down to Joppa
    C and he found a ship
      D returning to Tarshish
    C′ and he paid her fare
  B′ and he went down in it
A′ to go with them to Tarshish from the presence of Yahweh.

All things appear to work well for Jonah: an accessible seaport, a convenient ship, financial solvency, and available space. The repetition of the phrase "to Tarshish" in the beginning (A), middle (D), and ending (A′) of the chiasm underscores the geographical disobedience of Jonah. He flees west instead of going east. The verb "went down" (וירד *wayyēred*) in B begins a process of descent that deepens in B′: first down to Joppa (a seaport on the Israelite coastline) and then down into the ship. The reference to the ship in C reappears in Jonah's paying of her fare in C′. The verb בוא (*bô*), translated "returning" in D and "go" in A′, is different from the verb (*hālak*), translated "go" in v. 2. The difference underscores disobedience: going or returning (*bô*) to Tarshish versus going (*hālak*) to Nineveh.

Although the NIV has Jonah paying "the fare" and the NRSV has him paying "his fare," the Hebrew text employs the feminine possessive pronoun, "her fare" (שכרה *śĕkārāh*), to match the feminine gender of the noun for "ship" (אניה *'oniyyâ*). Ancient rabbis proposed that Jonah paid for the entire voyage, so eager was he to flee.[79] Yet in the structure of the sentence the irony of enclosure overtakes his flight. Even as he seeks to flee "from the presence of Yahweh," that presence surrounds him. What the structure shows, the story verifies. Jonah's flight is futile. (See Reflections at 1:7-16.)

---

78. See Norbert Lohfink, "Jona ging zur Stadt hina us (Jon 4,5)" *BZ* 5 (1961) 200-201.

79. See Louis Ginzberg, *Legends of the Bible* (Philadelphia: The Jewish Publication Society of America, 1956) 604.

JONAH 1:4-6, YAHWEH'S STORM AND HUMAN RESPONSES

NIV

⁴Then the LORD sent a great wind on the sea, and such a violent storm arose that the ship threatened to break up. ⁵All the sailors were afraid and each cried out to his own god. And they threw the cargo into the sea to lighten the ship.

But Jonah had gone below deck, where he lay down and fell into a deep sleep. ⁶The captain went to him and said, "How can you sleep? Get up and call on your god! Maybe he will take notice of us, and we will not perish."

NRSV

4But the LORD hurled a great wind upon the sea, and such a mighty storm came upon the sea that the ship threatened to break up. ⁵Then the mariners were afraid, and each cried to his god. They threw the cargo that was in the ship into the sea, to lighten it for them. Jonah, meanwhile, had gone down into the hold of the ship and had lain down, and was fast asleep. ⁶The captain came and said to him, "What are you doing sound asleep? Get up, call on your god! Perhaps the god will spare us a thought so that we do not perish."

COMMENTARY

Three incidents compose episode two: Yahweh's hurling a storm upon the sea (v. 4), its effect upon the sailors and Jonah (v. 5), and the efforts of the captain to avert disaster (v. 6).

1:4. After Jonah's flight from the divine imperatives, Yahweh reenters the story through a different mode of expression. The deity counters Jonah not in direct words (cf. v. 2) but in indirect action. Yahweh hurls "a great wind upon the sea." Hebrew syntax emphasizes the divine power by reversing the usual order of words to place the subject, "Yahweh," before the verb, "hurl" (טול *ṭûl*). The verb itself introduces a major motif (cf. vv. 5, 12). A chain of cause and effect ensues as the great wind produces a great tempest that threatens to destroy the ship. The portrayal of the inanimate ship as "thinking to break up" is particularly poignant. The words sound like boards cracking from the force of water: חשבה להשבר (*ḥiššĕbâ lĕhiššābēr*).

Though v. 4 is a modest sentence, in contrast to the preceding chiasm, which contains Jonah's disobedience, its three clauses vibrate with menacing force. Yahweh strikes back. Varying the rhythm of the story, the dissonances in structure and content between vv. 3 and 4 harden the opposition between the characters. Yahweh and Jonah have entered a power struggle.

1:5. In their struggle they make victims of innocent sailors. Three independent clauses continue the chain of cause and effect as they report the consequences of the great wind for the sailors. First comes an inward response: They feared. Next comes an outward response in speech: They cried. Then comes an outward response in deed: They hurled. The verb "fear" (ירא *yārē*ʾ) introduces a motif that will gather meanings as the story progresses (cf. vv. 9-10, 16). The verb "cry" (זעק *zāʿaq*) leads to a religious identity that is not Yahwistic, "each man to his god." But the verb "hurl" (*ṭûl*) shows the sailors emulating Yahweh (cf. v. 4). As this deity hurled a wind "upon the sea," so they hurl their wares "to the sea."

An infinitive without a specified object in the Hebrew indicates the purpose of the sailors' action: "to lighten . . . from upon them." Some commentators illumine this phrase by deeming its unspecified object either the ship or its cargo.[80] In other words, the sailors sought to lighten the ship so that it would ride higher on the tempestuous sea (cf. Acts 27:13-20, 38). If questionable nautical procedure, this explanation also founders on the sea of grammar. The word "sea," not "ship," is the nearest antecedent to the unspeci-

---

80. E.g., Leslie C. Allen, *The Books of Joel, Obadiah, Jonah and Micah*, NICOT (Grand Rapids: Eerdmans, 1976) 206; Wolff, *Obadiah and Jonah*, 105, 112; Jack M. Sasson, *Jonah*, AB 24B (New York: Doubleday, 1990) 89, 99.

fied object of the infinitive. Thus the syntax suggests a different interpretation. The sailors tried to appease the sea (a deity?) by hurling to it their wares as sacrificial offerings.[81] This religious act parallels their cries, each to his own god, to yield a sympathetic picture of these innocent victims caught in the power struggle between Jonah and Yahweh.

To contrast Jonah with the sailors, the usual order of Hebrew syntax reverses (cf. v. 4). The subject, "Jonah," precedes its verb. As three independent clauses describe the responses of the sailors, three more describe Jonah's responses. First comes an outward response of action: Jonah went down. Next comes an outward response of inaction: he lay down. Then comes an inward response of inaction: he slept. The verb "went down" (ירד *yārad*) continues Jonah's direction of disobedient descent, from Joppa (1:3*b*), to the ship (1:3), and now to the innards of the ship. The verb "lay down" (שכב *šākab*) suggests that he intends neither words nor action. The verb in the phrase "fell into a deep sleep" (רדם *rādam*) fulfills the intention.

Occurring infrequently in the Hebrew Bible, the verb *rādam* connotes more than ordinary sleep. Septuagintal translators perhaps found a certain humor in its usage here when they described Jonah as snoring (καὶ ἔρρεγχεν *kai erregchen*). By contrast, they translated the same verb in Gen 2:21, where Yahweh causes a "deep sleep" (*rdm*) to fall upon the first creature, as "being in ecstasy" (ἔκστασις *ekstasis*). But neither snoring nor ecstasy conveys the nuance of this word for the developing portrait of Jonah. Most likely, the verb indicates a deep sleep, even a trance, that precedes death (cf. Judg 4:21).[82] "Going down" (*yārad*) to Joppa, to the ship, and to the innards of the ship, Jonah has increasingly separated himself from life. Soon he will propose his own demise (v. 12), and much later he will demand death (4:3). So he went down, and he fell into a deep sleep—the precursor of death.

The verb *yārad* ("went down") and the verb *rādam* ("deep sleep") share two Hebrew consonants: "r" (ר *resh*) and "d" (ד *dalet*). As the first

and last words to describe the activity of Jonah in v. 5, their proximity encourages a play on their sounds: ירד (*yārad*, "went down") and וירדם (*wayyērādam*, "fell into a deep sleep"). This aural association enhances in turn the verbal and thematic links that move *yārad* from physical flight (v. 3) toward psychological escape (v. 5). *Wayyērādam* then takes over both to secure the latter meaning and to suggest yet another move toward death. Altogether the similarly sounding verbs *yārad* and *wayyērādam* contribute to a theology of human defiance in the presence (not "from the presence"; cf. v. 3) of God's relentless power and pursuit.

The symmetry of all the verbs in v. 5, three describing the sailors and three describing Jonah, belongs to an asymmetrical structure and content. The clauses pertaining to the sailors begin with a minimum of words (verb and subject) and then lengthen twice; the clauses pertaining to Jonah begin with a modest number of words and then shrink twice to the minimum of verb and subject. As the activity of the sailors increases, the activity of Jonah decreases. Lying down to sleep in the innards of the ship, he is close to becoming an inanimate object, a replacement for the wares that the sailors have hurled overboard. Perhaps the narrator hints at things to come.

1:6. The import of the verb *rādam* continues as the captain of the ship intrudes upon Jonah's space and sleep. Using a participial form of the word, this officer is the first human character to speak. A colloquial rendering of his Hebrew might be, "What's with you, so soundly sleeping!" An exclamation of surprise, even of indignation, leads to ironic imperatives. The captain orders Jonah to "arise" and "call" to the god whose own command, "arise . . . call," Jonah has already spurned. The verbal repetition subtly undermines Jonah's efforts to flee from the presence of Yahweh. The imperatives then lead to a tentative declarative introduced by the particle "perhaps" (אולי *'ûlay*), which expresses hope. If the gods of the sailors have not heeded cries for help, perhaps the god of Jonah will so that "we do not perish." Through the captain, the crew's fear of perishing has awakened Jonah from the deathlike sleep he had embraced. Yet he remains silent. (See Reflections at 1:7-16.)

81. Trible, "Studies in the Book of Jonah," 210-11; cf. Terence E. Fretheim, *The Message of Jonah* (Minneapolis: Augsburg, 1977) 82-83.

82. See Jonathan Magonet, *Form and Meaning: Studies in Literary Techniques in the Book of Jonah* (Sheffield: The Almond Press, 1983) 67-69; Sasson, *Jonah*, 101.

JONAH 1:7-16, EFFORTS OF THE SAILORS TO AVERT DISASTER AND THE RESULT

NIV

[7]Then the sailors said to each other, "Come, let us cast lots to find out who is responsible for this calamity." They cast lots and the lot fell on Jonah.

[8]So they asked him, "Tell us, who is responsible for making all this trouble for us? What do you do? Where do you come from? What is your country? From what people are you?"

[9]He answered, "I am a Hebrew and I worship the LORD, the God of heaven, who made the sea and the land."

[10]This terrified them and they asked, "What have you done?" (They knew he was running away from the LORD, because he had already told them so.)

[11]The sea was getting rougher and rougher. So they asked him, "What should we do to you to make the sea calm down for us?"

[12]"Pick me up and throw me into the sea," he replied, "and it will become calm. I know that it is my fault that this great storm has come upon you."

[13]Instead, the men did their best to row back to land. But they could not, for the sea grew even wilder than before. [14]Then they cried to the LORD, "O LORD, please do not let us die for taking this man's life. Do not hold us accountable for killing an innocent man, for you, O LORD, have done as you pleased." [15]Then they took Jonah and threw him overboard, and the raging sea grew calm. [16]At this the men greatly feared the LORD, and they offered a sacrifice to the LORD and made vows to him.

NRSV

7The sailors[a] said to one another, "Come, let us cast lots, so that we may know on whose account this calamity has come upon us." So they cast lots, and the lot fell on Jonah. [8]Then they said to him, "Tell us why this calamity has come upon us. What is your occupation? Where do you come from? What is your country? And of what people are you?" [9]"I am a Hebrew," he replied. "I worship the LORD, the God of heaven, who made the sea and the dry land." [10]Then the men were even more afraid, and said to him, "What is this that you have done!" For the men knew that he was fleeing from the presence of the LORD, because he had told them so.

11Then they said to him, "What shall we do to you, that the sea may quiet down for us?" For the sea was growing more and more tempestuous. [12]He said to them, "Pick me up and throw me into the sea; then the sea will quiet down for you; for I know it is because of me that this great storm has come upon you." [13]Nevertheless the men rowed hard to bring the ship back to land, but they could not, for the sea grew more and more stormy against them. [14]Then they cried out to the LORD, "Please, O LORD, we pray, do not let us perish on account of this man's life. Do not make us guilty of innocent blood; for you, O LORD, have done as it pleased you." [15]So they picked Jonah up and threw him into the sea; and the sea ceased from its raging. [16]Then the men feared the LORD even more, and they offered a sacrifice to the LORD and made vows.

[a] Heb They

COMMENTARY

Continuing where their captain left off, the sailors work to avert disaster. In episode three, four incidents report their efforts and the effects: the casting of lots (v. 7), a conversation with Jonah (vv. 8-9), continuing work to reach shore (vv. 10-13), and the resolution (vv. 14-16).

1:7. Speech brings the sailors into focus as they propose the casting of lots to determine who among them is responsible for "the evil" (רעה $r\bar{a}'\hat{a}$; cf. v. 2). Both the NIV and the NRSV, not inappropriately, render this word "calamity." Although nowhere does the Bible report the exact procedure for casting lots, the technique was familiar in the ancient Near East.[83] Perhaps from among a collection of shards, each inscribed with the name of a member of the ship, the sailors choose one. The narrator then reports the result in a sentence whose climactic phrase lays end stress "on Jonah."

Theologically, the use of lots to disclose the truth elevates chance to the level of divine will. The story does not report that Yahweh (or any other deity) directed the outcome of the exercise but simply that the sailors "cast lots, and the lot fell on Jonah" (v. 7c). In a setting of violence, chance alone provides the way to resolve the conflict.[84] But the chance is caused.

1:8-9. The sailors hurl question after question at Jonah. They ask him first about the culprit of the evil in a third-person reference (1:8a). Then they probe his own identity with second-person pronouns in four questions (1:8b). These questions constitute in Hebrew a litany of alliteration. The particles מה (mâ, "what") and מ (m, "from where" or "from what") alternate in queries about his occupation, origin, land, and people. Brevity, rapidity, and repetition produce a staccato effect that lends force and urgency to the interrogation.

For the third time in the story Jonah has been addressed directly. Yahweh's command led to his flight (v. 3); the captain's command met with his silence (v. 6). But now he is caught, and the interrogative mode accomplishes what the imperative has not. Jonah speaks, answering in reverse order to the two kinds of questions asked him. First he tells his identity (v. 9a), and then he hints at his culpability in evil by declaring his fear of Yahweh (v. 9b). Through this reversal, Jonah shapes a structure that traps his identity within the evil he has wrought and the God he fears.

Two rhyming words declare his national identity: עברי אנכי ('ibrî 'ānōkî, "A Hebrew [am] I"). Septuagintal translators offer a different understanding of the first word, based in part on a confusion between the similarly shaped Hebrew letters ר (resh), transliterated by "r," and ד (dalet), transliterated by "d." Where the Hebrew has resh, the Septuagint reads dalet and so produces the

Hebrew word עבד ('ebed), meaning "servant," instead of the word עברי ('ibrî), meaning "Hebrew." The Septuagint then understands the final letter of the word 'ibrî, the letter י (yodh), rendered as part of the vowel "i," to be an abbreviation of the Tetragrammaton, the sacred name YHWH (יהוה). Accordingly, the Septuagint translates the Hebrew as Δοῦλος κυρίου (Doulos kyriou), meaning "Servant of the LORD." Given the actions of Jonah thus far, the translation produces strong irony. This self-declared "servant of the LORD" is defying the command of the Lord.

As Jonah continues to answer the sailors, his words all but hint at his culpability. Invoking the theological formula "the LORD, the God of heaven, who made the sea and the dry land," he proclaims the all-encompassing power of Yahweh, even though the readers (not the sailors) know that he seeks to flee from the divine presence (v. 3). This information Jonah himself fails to report. Moreover, in the structuring of his sentence, he splits the theological formula to insert himself in the middle: "I am fearing" (אני ירא 'ănî yārē'). Carrying the ambiguous meanings of "fear" and "worship" (cf. 1:5, 10), the verb ירא (yārē') sounds an uncertain note. Once again (see above on vv. 8-9) Jonah shapes a structure that traps him. The cosmic God Yahweh surrounds him: "Yahweh God of the heavens I am fearing who made the sea and the dry land." By reordering the sentence to achieve smooth English, the NIV and the NRSV forfeit its irony and misrepresent Jonah.

1:10-13. The verb yārē' links the preceding section to subsequent efforts by the sailors to avert disaster. Literally, they "fear a great fear" (1:10a). This report prefaces a literary structure built on repetition: They designate major motifs, slow down the story, and build suspense. In the structure three speeches continuing the conversation between the sailors and Jonah alternate with narrated discourse.

The first speech belongs to the sailors. They exclaim, "What [מה mâ] is this that you have done!" (v. 10b). The narrator then interrupts to explain, through the strategy of delayed information (cf. v. 3), why they can accuse Jonah. He has already told them of his flight from Yahweh (v. 10c). But by not having this information come directly from Jonah, the storyteller keeps at bay his claim of culpability.

---

83. Cf. Josh 7:14; 1 Sam 10:20-21; 14:36-46; Acts 1:26. See Joh. Lindblom, "Lot-casting in the Old Testament," *VT* 12 (1962) 164-78; Sasson, *Jonah,* 108-10.
84. See René Girard, *Violence and the Sacred,* trans. Patrick Gregory (Baltimore: Johns Hopkins University Press, 1972) 312-14.

The second speech (v. 11) also belongs to the sailors. Following on their exclamation, "What is this that you have done!" they ask Jonah a question: "What shall we do to you?" One deed deserves another. Yet the sailors are not interested in punishing Jonah, but in quieting the sea, which is getting rougher and rougher. Although the NIV places this latter report about the sea ahead of the sailors' question, the Hebrew text puts it at the close, thereby preparing for its reappearance at the close of the entire unit (v. 13).

The third speech is Jonah's answer to the sailors (v. 12). They have addressed him with the exclamatory and the interrogative; he replies with the imperative: "Pick me up and hurl me into the sea." The verb "hurl" and the noun "sea" evoke past actions. Yahweh "hurled" a wind to the "sea" (v. 4), and the sailors "hurled" wares to the "sea" (v. 5). The translations of the NRSV and the NIV lose this connection.

Once asleep in the innards of the ship, Jonah became in effect a substitute for those discarded wares. Now he insists that this ware, namely himself, be "hurled" to the "sea." Having already confessed that Yahweh made the sea (v. 9), Jonah proposes appeasement through human rather than inanimate sacrifice. As the verb "hurl" and the noun "sea" flow from past actions, they prepare for things to come (cf. v. 15). Jonah promises the sailors the result they desire: "Then the sea will quiet down for you" (v. 12; cf. 1:11).

As Jonah continues, he claims his culpability, a claim built on earlier discourse. In v. 7, the sailors wanted to "know on whose account this evil is to us"; now in v. 12 Jonah confesses, "on account of me the great storm is upon you." In v. 10 the narrator says that the sailors "knew"; now in v. 12 Jonah says, "for I know. . . ." In v. 10 the narrator continues, "that [כִּי *kî*] from the presence of Yahweh he was fleeing" (author's trans.); now in v. 12 Jonah continues, "that [*kî*] on account of me the great storm is upon you" (author's trans.).

Yet Jonah does not offer to jump overboard. He prefers instead that the sailors bring about his death. Unwilling to comply, they "dig" (חתר *ḥātar*) to return the ship to dry land. Hardly good nautical procedure, this action portrays desperation. But even as their earlier efforts had failed (cf. v.

5), so now they are unable to reach dry land. The unit closes (v. 13) with the terrifying refrain that "the sea was getting rougher and rougher upon them" (author's trans.; cf. v. 11).

Of the many literary and theological issues that flood this passage (1:10-13), the words of Jonah require careful exegesis. After all, he is a fugitive with unexplained motives. But his movements are clear, no matter how ironic. He wants to flee from the presence of Yahweh so that he need not go to Nineveh. Already he has tried physical flight by ship to Tarshish. It has not worked. Next he has tried psychological flight by sleeping in the hold of the ship. It has not worked. Now, pressed by the sailors, he tries absolute flight through death: "Pick me up and hurl me into the sea."

These words fit the complexities of Jonah's character. He who has disobeyed the commands of Yahweh and ignored the commands of the captain now issues his own. One interpretation holds that Jonah realizes his sin and his guilt and is willing to pay the price through death.[85] Another sees Jonah as altruistic. To save the lives of the sailors, he will sacrifice his own life.[86] But appearances mask the truth. To acknowledge culpability is to continue defiance. Jonah is not calling upon his God, and he is not going to Nineveh. To save the sailors is to confirm himself. Death by drowning will secure for Jonah what he wants: flight from Yahweh. Thus his seeming concern for the sailors camouflages self-concern. His seeming altruism masks egotism. Deception and irony abound in Jonah. They entrap the sailors, whose emotions (v. 10*a*) and efforts (v. 13*a*) surround him.

1:14-16. The resolution of the crisis comes as the sailors try another way. Having failed in their efforts to reach dry land, they "call" (קרא *qārā'*) to Yahweh. The action recalls their first appearance, when each "cried [זעק *zāʿaq*] to his god" (v. 5). Having learned from Jonah who his God is (v. 9), they now do what he has not (cf. v. 6). They pray (v. 14).

Their prayer belongs to the genre of the communal complaint song. It presumes an occasion

85. See Allen, *The Books of Joel, Obadiah, Jonah, and Micah,* 210-11; cf. Fretheim, *The Message of Jonah,* 88-89.
86. Cf. Sternberg, *The Poetics of Biblical Narrative* (Bloomington: Indiana University Press, 1985) 318-19.

of misfortune for a group.[87] Addressed to God, such songs may come from the innocent or the penitent. In general, they include petition, complaint, confession, reason, motivation, vow, description of distress, expression of confidence in God, reference to sacrifice, and thanksgiving for deliverance. Most of these elements appear in this prayer or in the subsequent actions of the sailors.

Structured on Hebrew particles, the prayer contains three sections: invocation, petition, and motivation. The invocation to Yahweh commences with the strong particle אנה ('ānnâ), translated in the NIV and the NRSV as "please." Each of the two parts of the petition begins with the negative particle אל ('al), translated "not." The motivation opens with the particle kî, translated "for."

The sailors view their plight as double jeopardy. If Jonah stays on board, they perish; if they throw an innocent man overboard, they perish. In beseeching Yahweh not to let them "perish" (אבד 'ābad), they repeat the sentiment of the captain (v. 6). Beyond that, they recognize the sovereignty of Yahweh to "do" (עשה 'āśâ) as the deity wishes. Though they themselves have power to do something to Jonah, they return that power to Yahweh. They put the burden on the deity.

Receiving no direct answer to their prayer, the sailors speak no more. Instead, they follow Jonah's instructions to pick him up and hurl him to the sea (v. 15). True to his assurance, the sea ceases its raging. It returns to its passive state before Yahweh's great wind stirred it up. Theologically, the loss of power to inflict danger signifies that the power was never its own but Yahweh's. Structurally, the reversal to the former state rounds off the sequence of events that began just after Jonah's attempted flight. Narratively, the reversal effects the recognition of Yahweh by the sailors and brings closure to their portrait. In their first appearance, they feared (ירא yārē'), each cried to his god, and they hurled wares overboard (v. 5). Here, in their last appearance, those three actions

find resolution in a threefold response to the cessation of the storm. The sailors worship (yārē'), sacrifice sacrifices to Yahweh, and vow vows.

For the sailors, the story has come full circle. From fear that motivated prayer to unnamed deities, they have become Yahweh worshipers. But the story leaves open the question of conversion. From the perspective of the sailors, the worship of Yahweh may mean but the addition of another god to their pantheon.

Although sympathetic, the closing portrait of the sailors comes with ambiguity. Three times the narrator depicts them undertaking acts that may exacerbate the danger: causing a ship to ride higher, rather than lower, in the tempestuous sea (v. 5); digging oars into the water rather than moving them across the top (v. 13); and steering the ship in a storm toward, rather than away from, the shore (v. 13). These acts lend themselves to different interpretations. They may signify desperation and so arouse pity for the sailors. They may signify a desire to cooperate with Yahweh by returning Jonah to dry land and so arouse commendation for the sailors. They may signify lack of nautical expertise and so arouse disparagement of the sailors. Or they may signify a storyteller unfamiliar with seafaring maneuvers.[88]

Whatever the meaning of the sailors' actions, at the syntactic level the narrator diminishes these innocent and appealing characters. The last three clauses describing them (v. 16) shrink in Hebrew from five words (their fearing a great fear of Yahweh) to three (their sacrificing sacrifices to Yahweh) to two (their vowing vows). So the sailors fade. The assurance of their well-being becomes their dismissal. They form but a subplot. Once important as a foil to Jonah, they disappear from the story as he disappears into the sea. For Jonah that sea means not well-being but troubled waters.

---

87. On the genre, see Erhard Gerstenberger, *Psalms: Part 1, with an Introduction to Cultic Poetry,* FOTL 14 (Grand Rapids: Eerdmans, 1988) 245; on the function, see Moshe Greenberg, *Biblical Prose Prayer as a Window to the Popular Religion of Ancient Israel* (Berkeley: University of California Press, 1983) 15-17.

88. On the Hebrews' lack of maritime knowledge, see Elaine R. Follis, "Sea," in *The Anchor Bible Dictionary* (*ABD*), 6 vols. (New York: Doubleday, 1992) 5:1058. For a contrasting view, see Sasson, *Jonah,* 90-92, 105, 130, 139-42.

REFLECTIONS

1. At the beginning, the divine word makes a sovereign claim upon Jonah. The imperative mode is uncompromising. It constitutes a social and political claim that requires him to meddle in the life of a great city. The authoritarian character of the divine speech stands over against human freedom. It defies the concept of negotiating options. Yahweh commands.

2. In Herman Melville's *Moby Dick,* Father Mapple, the preacher at the Whaleman's Chapel in New Bedford, names "wilful disobedience" as Jonah's sin. He observes that God more often commands than seeks to persuade because what the deity wants of us is too hard for us. "And if we obey God, we must disobey ourselves; and it is in this disobeying ourselves, wherein the hardness of obeying God consists."[89]

3. Jonah's protest against the imperative word comes through his feet, not his tongue. Later we learn that he did have a "word" over against Yahweh's word (4:2), but the narrator here portrays his resistance as taciturn flight. He does not pursue dialogue. This behavior contrasts that of such characters as Moses (Exod 3:1–4:17) and Jeremiah (Jer 1:4-8), both of whom talked back to God, and with Isaiah, who too readily spoke assent (Isa 6:8-13). Nevertheless, Jonah's response begins a struggle of faith not to be trivialized by caricature. In fleeing from the divine presence, Jonah presages the mobile disobedience of countless people. If words could describe his departure, they might well draw from the opening lines of Francis Thompson's terrifying poem "The Hound of Heaven": "I fled Him, down the nights and down the days. . . . "

4. The title of Thompson's poem evokes an apt image for the character Yahweh in this opening encounter. God pursues relentlessly, like a hound after its prey. The deity is even wild and unpredictable, endangering not just the culprit but also the blameless, with neither apology nor explanation. The narrative does not flinch from portraying the violence of the sacred.[90]

This portrayal speaks to all who perceive God as arbitrary, vindictive, wrathful, and unyielding power. Their names, known and unknown, are legion: Jacob wrestling with a divine demon at the Jabbok (Gen 32:22-32); Moses becoming the target of an assassination attempt by Yahweh (Exod 4:24-26); three thousand Israelites exterminated for not measuring up to "the LORD's side" (Exod 32:26-28 NRSV); Miriam, punished with a diseased skin by Yahweh (Num 12:2-16); Naomi receiving calamity from the Almighty (Ruth 1:13, 20-21); Saul, tormented by an evil spirit from Yahweh (1 Sam 16:14); and Jeremiah experiencing divine rape (Jer 20:7). In Jonah innocent sailors suffer the destructive power of Yahweh.

5. The violence of Yahweh in perpetrating the crisis contrasts with the passivity of the deity in resolving it. After hurling the wind upon the sea, Yahweh withdraws. The story does not say that Yahweh directed the falling of the lot upon Jonah; that Yahweh received the hurling of Jonah to the sea as a sacrificial offering; or that Yahweh thereupon calmed the sea (1:15). In all these events the deity stays out of the action. The terrifying God absconds.

6. The sailors are innocent victims of God's terror; Jonah is the guilty victim. His struggles with Yahweh threaten others, and his speeches compound the predicament. He declares Yahweh to be "the god of heaven, who made the sea and the dry land" at the same time that he seeks to flee from this deity (1:9). Jonah's flight betrays his words, and his words mock his flight. Moreover, his belated acceptance of responsibility (1:12) belies his concern for others.

89. See Herman Melville, *Moby Dick or the White Whale* (New York: The New American Library, 1961) 57-58.

90. Cf. René Girard, *Violence and the Sacred,* trans. Patrick Gregory (Baltimore: Johns Hopkins University Press, 1972); James G. Williams, *The Bible, Violence, and the Sacred* (San Francisco: Harper, 1989) esp. 129-62.

Ostensibly he offers himself as the sacrificial victim to save the sailors (1:12), but his ulterior motive is to defy Yahweh by being hurled into the sea. Egotism parades as altruism. Jonah manifests the gap between cognitive speech and existential behavior or the gap between faithfulness and deception. His mode of being endangers others and betrays God.

7. In these episodes, hope, justice, and integrity reside not with Jonah or Yahweh but with the captain and the sailors. The captain understands hope as "perhaps" (1:6). Human beings cannot claim God for their own ends, but they can cry out for salvation. Though blameless victims, the sailors never cry injustice. Finding themselves in a dangerous situation not of their making, they seek to solve it for the good of all. Never do they wallow in self-pity, berate an angry god, raise issues of theodicy, condemn an arbitrary world, target the culprit Jonah for vengeance, or promote violence as an answer. The captain and the sailors appeal to the mercy and justice of God even while they are experiencing divine wrath. The outcome vindicates their stance. Overall, their words and their behavior contrast strikingly with many contemporary responses to undeserved suffering.

8. After the crisis the sailors break the rules that govern orthodox Yahwism. They pray prayers, sacrifice sacrifices, and vow vows without cultic apparati or approval. Neither priest nor Temple nor laws of purity proscribe their activity. Nevertheless, they practice authentic worship. These "others" outside covenant faith show a more excellent way. Their mode of being and their behavior release faith from crippling strictures and structures. Counted among their descendants may be all the "others" of gender, class, and ethnicity who perform genuine acts of piety outside prescribed boundaries; all the "others" who seek both their own salvation and the well-being of culprits; and all the "others" who trust the integrity of the god beyond violence (cf. 1:14).

9. Several stories in the New Testament provide comparison and contrast for this sea scene. Jonah sought to flee from God by going to sea; Jesus sought to escape the crowds by going to sea (Mark 4:1, 35-41; cf. Matt 8:24-27). In both instances a great storm threatens the survival of the ship. To meet the crisis, the captain awakens Jonah, who is asleep in the hold of the ship. To meet the crisis, the disciples awaken Jesus "in the stern, asleep on the cushion" (Mark 4:38 NRSV). Like the captain, the disciples are concerned lest they perish. Like the sailors, the disciples are full of fear. The sacrifice of Jonah to the sea results in "the sea ceasing from its raging." The words of Jesus rebuking the wind and commanding the sea result in "the wind ceased, and there was a dead calm" (Mark 4:39 NRSV).

The extended story in Acts 27 of storm and shipwreck also offers numerous comparisons with the Jonah tale. Both incidents occur in the Mediterranean Sea. In Acts a "violent wind" threatens the ship, its cargo, and the lives of its crew and passengers (cf. Jonah 1:4-5). The latter include soldiers and their prisoners, of whom Paul is one. The crew, the pilot, and the owner struggle with various strategies for survival, including traveling close to shore (cf. Jonah 1:13), turning head-on into the wind, and giving way to it. They throw cargo and tackle, and later even wheat, into the sea to "lighten the ship" (cf. Jonah 1:5).

Paul assumes an active role in saving the ship. More confident than the captain in the Jonah narrative, who expresses only hope (1:6), he assures the men that God "has granted safety" to all who are sailing (Acts 27:21-26). But before the ship finally runs aground, the soldiers seek to kill the prisoners so that they cannot escape. A centurion, wishing to save Paul, orders him and others to jump overboard. Paul swims quickly to land. By contrast, Jonah, hurled to the sea by the sailors, finds his "safety" in the belly of a fish (1:15, 17).

Yet another story in Acts echoes an event in Jonah—namely, the casting of lots. Unlike the sailors, who seek to identify a culprit (1:7), the apostles prepare to choose the successor to the betrayer Judas (Acts 1:15-26). Unlike the sailors, they operate not out of chance but out of prayer that the Lord will reveal the chosen one (Acts 1:24). The description of their act, however, parallels the action of the sailors. The sailors "cast lots and the lot fell on Jonah"; the apostles "cast lots . . . and the lot fell on Matthias" (Acts 1:26 NRSV). They immediately embrace Matthias, but the sailors subsequently banish Jonah (1:15).

JONAH 1:17–2:10, YAHWEH, A FISH, AND JONAH

NIV

¹⁷But the LORD provided a great fish to swallow Jonah, and Jonah was inside the fish three days and three nights.

2 From inside the fish Jonah prayed to the LORD his God. ²He said:
"In my distress I called to the LORD,
  and he answered me.
From the depths of the grave*ᵃ* I called for help,
  and you listened to my cry.
³You hurled me into the deep,
  into the very heart of the seas,
  and the currents swirled about me;
all your waves and breakers
  swept over me.
⁴I said, 'I have been banished
  from your sight;
yet I will look again
  toward your holy temple.'
⁵The engulfing waters threatened me,*ᵇ*
  the deep surrounded me;
  seaweed was wrapped around my head.
⁶To the roots of the mountains I sank down;
  the earth beneath barred me in forever.
But you brought my life up from the pit,
  O LORD my God.

⁷"When my life was ebbing away,
  I remembered you, LORD,
and my prayer rose to you,
  to your holy temple.

⁸"Those who cling to worthless idols
  forfeit the grace that could be theirs.
⁹But I, with a song of thanksgiving,
  will sacrifice to you.
What I have vowed I will make good.
  Salvation comes from the LORD."
¹⁰And the LORD commanded the fish, and it vomited Jonah onto dry land.

ᵃ2 Hebrew Sheol   ᵇ5 Or waters were at my throat

NRSV

¹⁷*ᵃ*But the LORD provided a large fish to swallow up Jonah; and Jonah was in the belly of the fish three days and three nights.

2 Then Jonah prayed to the LORD his God from the belly of the fish, ²saying,
"I called to the LORD out of my distress,
  and he answered me;
out of the belly of Sheol I cried,
  and you heard my voice.
³ You cast me into the deep,
  into the heart of the seas,
  and the flood surrounded me;
all your waves and your billows
  passed over me.
⁴ Then I said, 'I am driven away
  from your sight;
how*ᵇ* shall I look again
  upon your holy temple?'
⁵ The waters closed in over me;
  the deep surrounded me;
weeds were wrapped around my head
⁶   at the roots of the mountains.
I went down to the land
  whose bars closed upon me forever;
yet you brought up my life from the Pit,
  O LORD my God.

⁷ As my life was ebbing away,
  I remembered the LORD;
and my prayer came to you,
  into your holy temple.

⁸ Those who worship vain idols
  forsake their true loyalty.
⁹ But I with the voice of thanksgiving
  will sacrifice to you;
what I have vowed I will pay.
  Deliverance belongs to the LORD!"
¹⁰Then the LORD spoke to the fish, and it spewed Jonah out upon the dry land.

ᵃ Ch 2.1 in Heb   ᵇ Theodotion: Heb surely

COMMENTARY

Episode four of scene one threatens to drown readers in problems, most especially the relationship of the psalm (2:2-9) to the narrated context (1:17; 2:1, 10).

1:17–2:1, 10. By itself the context yields an impressive chiasm:

A And appointed Yahweh a great fish to swallow Jonah,

    B and Jonah was in the belly of the fish three days and three nights.

    B′ And prayed Jonah to Yahweh his God from the belly of the fish.

A′ And spoke Yahweh to the fish and it vomited Jonah to the dry land.

In the extremities (A and A′) Yahweh as subject surrounds the unit to control the action. The deity acts upon a great fish, which in turn acts upon Jonah. As mediator between Yahweh and Jonah, the fish keeps distance between them. Appointed by Yahweh and addressed by Yahweh, it relates to Jonah in countermovements: swallow and vomit.

The verb translated "swallow" (בלע *bāla‘*) bears only a negative meaning (e.g., Exod 15:12; Num 16:30, 32, 34).[91] Here it produces a paradoxical, even ironic, message. Although the fish's swallowing of Jonah saves him from drowning, that salvation opposes the death he seeks. The power struggle between Yahweh and Jonah continues, with the deity again thwarting Jonah's defiance. The verb "vomit" (קיא *qî’*), which returns him to dry land, also evokes negative connotations. Rather than using a delicate word for ejection (e.g., פלט *pālaṭ*), the narrator chooses a distasteful image (cf. the use of *qî’* in Prov 23:8; 25:16). The fish does not stomach Jonah. For certain, the entire alimentary process, from outside to inside to outside, contains polarities without digesting them.

Within the boundaries (A and A′) of the chiasm appear matching sentences (B and B′). Jonah was in the belly of the fish three days and three nights;

Jonah prayed to Yahweh from the belly of the fish (1:17b; 2:1a). Besides repeated words and phrases, counter images join these sentences. The belly of the fish connotes the lower world; Jonah's prayer rises to the heavens (cf. 1:9). Descent and ascent meet; death and life contend. The struggle between Yahweh and Jonah extends to the cosmos.

The meaning of the phrase "three days and three nights" stirs debate. Landes proposes that it designates the time span needed for the fish to return Jonah from the netherworld (2:2, 5-6) to dry land.[92] This proposal draws upon his interpretation of certain ancient Near Eastern texts and on his view that the psalm belongs to the original story. The proposal assumes what the prose narrative does not indicate: Jonah was not swallowed by the fish immediately upon being cast into the sea but instead went into the netherworld, where his life was threatened. Further, the proposal seems to assume that the fish was present in the netherworld—at least, it says nothing about the time the fish would need to arrive there.

Ackerman accepts Landes's mythological interpretation but reverses its direction.[93] The phrase "three days and three nights" signifies the time needed for a descent to the netherworld. In other words, the fish swallows Jonah immediately, not to rescue him, but to take him to death. Yet this proposal says nothing about the time needed to bring Jonah back to dry land. Like Landes's interpretation, it seems to require double the time span given in the text.[94]

In contrast to mythological readings that rely upon the psalm to explicate the prose narrative, Limburg offers the straightforward view that the phrase "three days and three nights" marks the length of time it took for the fish to reach the place where it vomited Jonah.[95] The single parallel usage of this phrase in the Bible (1 Sam 30:11-15) suggests that it may have been a substantial length

---

91. See James S. Ackerman, "Satire and Symbolism in the Song of Jonah," in *Traditions in Transformation,* ed. Baruch Halpern and Jon D. Levenson (Winona Lake, Ind.: Eisenbrauns, 1981) 220-21.

92. See George M. Landes, "The Three Days and Three Nights Motif in Jonah 2:1," *JBL* 86 (1967) 446-50.

93. Ackerman, "Satire and Symbolism in the Song of Jonah," 223n. 11.

94. For a critique, see Jack M. Sasson, *Jonah,* AB 24B (New York: Doubleday, 1990) 151-54.

95. See James Limburg, *Jonah,* OTL (Louisville: Westminster/John Knox, 1993) 62. Tradition locates the place on the Lebanese coastline north of Sidon.

of time. The suggestion finds support in the subsequent reference to Nineveh as a "walk of three days" (3:3). If "three days" conveys a great distance, "three days and three nights" conveys a longer time.

The identity of the fish stirs debate. The ancient tradition that a whale swallowed Jonah probably derives from the Septuagintal translation τό κῆτος (to kētos).[96] The Hebrew, however, does not employ a corresponding word for "whale" (e.g., תנים tannîm). Instead, it speaks four times only of a "fish" (דג dāg), the first time of a "great fish."

As discussed earlier, the grammatical gender used for the fish is unstable. In the first two and the last occurrences (1:17; 2:10) the word "fish" is masculine (dāg), but in the third occurrence (2:1) it is feminine (דגה dāgâ). Explanations for the difference range from fantasy to pedantry.[97] Some medieval exegetes proposed that God moved Jonah for a time to a female fish, with its belly full of babies, because he had become too comfortable in the belly of a male.[98] Other commentators have argued that the feminine grammatical ending is a textual mistake. Still others think that the difference in gender makes no difference in the story. Yet the appearance of the feminine form dāgâ after the term מעה (mē'eh), which designates an internal organ, suggests female imagery: "from the womb of the fish." When Jonah prays to Yahweh from within the "mother" fish, Jonah appropriately moves from death to life.

A chain of cause and effect (cf. 1:4-5) binds this chiasm. Yahweh causes a fish to swallow Jonah. The effect is Jonah in the belly of the fish. Jonah's predicament causes his prayer to Yahweh, thus rendering it the effect. In turn, the prayer causes Yahweh to speak to the fish with the effect that the fish vomits Jonah onto dry land.

2:2-9. Despite the literary and theological eloquence of the chiasm in 1:17–2:1, 10, a sequential reading of the text obscures its presence. The psalm intrudes. Embedded in the belly of the fish, unpredictable Jonah prays.

Several peculiarities mark the prayer. First, Jonah disregards structure. He speaks not in the center of the chiasm (i.e., between 1:17 and 2:1) but after its third line (i.e., after 2:1). Second, he fails to respect a correspondence between genre and setting. In a situation of dire calamity, he prays not a lament or complaint song asking to be delivered from danger (as the sailors did in 1:14); instead he prays a psalm of thanksgiving, asserting that he has already been delivered.

Third, Jonah deviates from the conventional vocabulary of the narrative. He uses new words and phrases. Rather than employing the verb "hurl" (טול tûl), as the narrator did in 1:4-5, 15 and Jonah himself did in 1:12, Jonah introduces two other verbs for the same idea: in 2:3 the verb שלך (šālak; NIV, "hurled"; NRSV, "cast") and in 2:4 גרש (gāraš; NIV, "banished"; NRSV, "driven out"). Further, rather than using the phrase "from the presence of the Lord" (1:3, 10), he says "from your sight" (2:4). And never does he use the adjective "great," the word most often occurring in the narrative. Yet this adjective might well have prefaced nouns in the psalm, like "distress," "deep," "flood," and "mountains."

Fourth, Jonah makes claims that do not fit the narrative. He declares that in his distress he "called" (קרא qārā') to Yahweh (2:2). Echoing the captain's command, "call [qārā'] on your god" (1:6 NRSV), these words remind the reader of the opposite. Jonah did not call to his God. Again, differing from the narrated report, Jonah says that Yahweh cast him into the sea and drove him away from the divine sight. But the reader knows that the sailors did the hurling even as Jonah did the fleeing. After depicting Yahweh as his destroyer, Jonah claims that the deity became his deliverer, bringing up his life from the grave. Mouthing salvation received, Jonah remains in mortal danger. He has been swallowed (a negative word) by a big fish in whose belly he dwells.

The extended debate on whether the psalm belonged to the narrative from the beginning or was added later includes replies to all the above observations.[99] The purpose here is not to rehash the dispute but to consider the literary structure

---

96. See Sasson, *Jonah,* 149-51.

97. See ibid., 154-56.

98. See Louis Ginzberg, *Legends of the Bible* (Philadelphia: The Jewish Publication Society of America, 1956) 606.

99. See esp. the discussions by G. H. Cohn, *Das buch Jona im Lichte der biblischen Erzählkunst,* SSN 12 (Assen: Van Gorcum, 1969) 25-26, 92-94; Landes, "The Kerygma of the Book of Jonah," *Int* 21 (1967) 3-31; Ackerman, "Satire and Symbolism in the Song of Jonah," *Traditions in Transformation,* eds. Baruch Halpern and Jon D. Levenson (Winona Lake, Ind.: Eisenbrauns, 1981), 213-246; Hans Walter Wolff, *Obadiah and Jonah,* trans. Margaret Kohl (Minneapolis: Augsburg, 1968), 128-32, 140-42.

and the function of the psalm in the present story. The perspective adopted explores dissonance between the psalm and the narrative.

The psalm forms a chiasm of four stanzas. Stanza A consists of one strophe (v. 2) with two lines; stanza B of two strophes (vv. 3 and 4), each with two lines; stanza B′ of two strophes (vv. 5-6*b* and 6*c*-7), each with three lines; stanza A′ of one strophe with three lines (vv. 8-9). Though of unequal length, the stanzas balance in vocabulary and subject matter. The words "Yahweh" and "voice" recur inversely in stanzas A (v. 2) and A′ (2:9; the NIV loses this connection, but the NRSV retains it). The psalm begins with an entreaty to Yahweh and the report of an answer; it ends with thanksgiving to Yahweh and the exclamation of deliverance.

Similarly, stanzas B (vv. 3-4) and B′ (vv. 5-7) balance. The first lines of their first strophes close with the corresponding pair "the flood surrounded me" and "the deep surrounded me." The last line of each second strophe closes with the identical phrase "your holy temple." Stanza B describes the psalmist's being cast into the sea (v. 3) and his thoughts about the Temple (v. 4). Stanza B′ describes his life under water (vv. 5-6*b*), his rescue, and his prayer coming to the Temple (vv. 6*c*-7). All of these eloquently structured words the reader hears from Jonah as he prays "to Yahweh his God from the belly of the fish."

2:2, Stanza A. In line one of the Hebrew text (cf. NRSV) Jonah begins and ends with himself: "I called . . . to Yahweh" and "he answered me." In the second line he overcomes the third-person distancing of Yahweh by matching another first-person verb, "I cried," with the direct second-person address of God, "you heard." Long after the captain's imperative (1:6), Jonah calls to his God, and he receives from Yahweh an answer. But in having waited to call, he finds himself in a worse situation than the narrative has reported. His cry goes out not "from the belly [*mē'eh*] of the fish" (1:17) but "from the womb [בטן *beṭen*] of Sheol" (v. 2).

Sheol identifies the abode of the dead (cf. Gen 37:35; Ps 88:3). Located under the earth (Num 16:30-33), it has bars to prevent escape (Job 17:16). In some biblical texts it is the place where God is not (Ps 6:15; 88:5, 10-12; Isa 38:18); in others, God reaches even into Sheol (Amos 9:2;

Job 25:6; Ps 138:8). The NIV does not give a close translation, but it aptly conveys Jonah's residence as "from the depths of the grave."

2:3-4, Stanza B. Jonah recapitulates the gravity of his situation and then turns to contrasting thoughts. Unlike the report in the narrative, he accuses Yahweh of casting him into the deep and of having waves and breakers pass over him. These watery words continue to describe a setting of death (cf. Pss 42:7; 69:2, 15; 68:22; 107:24) for which Jonah blames Yahweh. The accusation allows Jonah to cast himself in a favorable light. Despite his banishment from the eyes of God, he continues to look to the holy Temple. The one who has fled from Yahweh asserts his cultic piety. Such dissonance drives a wedge between the psalm and the narrative—or it renders grotesque the developing portrait of Jonah. He affirms what his actions deny.

2:5-7, Stanza B′. Jonah continues to focus on himself and his predicament. He describes the deadly waters reaching to his "neck" (נפש *nepeš*) or "his throat" (see the note in the NIV). The word *nepeš* holds double meaning. Narrowly it designates that part of the body where breath resides; broadly it encompasses the life of Jonah. His descent deepens to the "bars of the netherworld," another description of the abode of the dead (cf. v. 2). Of particular interest is his use of the verb in "I went down" (see the NRSV). This verb, ירד (*yārad*), completes the journey begun when Jonah went down to Joppa (1:3) and continued when he went down into the ship (1:3) and down into the innards of the ship (1:5). Yet the present setting of waters, the deep, weeds, and mountains is strangely incongruent with the belly of a great fish.

At the nadir of misfortune comes the dramatic reversal. The words "you brought up" counter "I went down." Like its opposite, the verb "bring up" (עלה *ālâ*) connects with the prose narrative. The evil of Nineveh has already "come up" (*ālâ*) before Yahweh (1:2); a plant yet to be appointed will "come up" (*ālâ*) to shade Jonah (4:6). In the psalm, deliverance happens swiftly. Jonah emerges from the pit (שחת *šaḥat*), yet another term for the abode of the dead (Pss 16:10; 30:9; Isa 51:14). Addressing "Yahweh my God," he avers that God the destroyer has become God the deliverer. Then he switches from talking about God's activity to confirming himself as the model of piety. He remembered Yahweh, and his prayer came to the holy Temple. First, Jonah looked toward the Temple; this time his prayer has arrived there. Yet all the while he remains in the belly of the fish. Incongruities persist.

2:8-9, Stanza A'. Asserting his own piety leads Jonah to disparage others. He begins the last stanza by inserting a reference that has nothing to do with himself and Yahweh. Without provocation he takes on "those who cling to worthless idols," convicting them of forsaking the loyalty (חסד *ḥesed*) of Yahweh. The word *ḥesed* will appear in the credo of 4:2, where Yahweh is described as "abounding in steadfast love." As a covenant term, *ḥesed* can have a twofold referent, to both human and divine faithfulness.[100] Jonah affirms the faithfulness of Yahweh and of himself while denigrating the faithlessness of others. Unlike them, he will sacrifice and pay his vows to the God who has delivered him. In Hebrew the weight of this contrast shows in the placing of the first-person independent pronoun at the beginning of the line: "but I" (ואני *wa'ănî*).

Who these others are "who cling to worthless idols" Jonah does not say. The description does not fit the sailors, for they have become Yahweh worshipers, sacrificing sacrifices and vowing vows (1:16). Nor does it fit the Ninevites, who will display true piety (3:5-9). The contrast that Jonah sets up with these unidentified others exacerbates the tension between the psalm and the narrative.

And that tension leads Jonah to another incongruous declaration: He climaxes his psalm with "deliverance to Yahweh" while he remains undelivered in the belly of the fish.

The psalm slows down the movement of the plot, heightens the irony, and complicates the character portrayal of Jonah. It shows how distorted is his perception of reality. Contrary to the narrative, he asserts that Yahweh has sought to destroy him, that he has shown true piety in the midst of calamity, that he projects a voice of thanksgiving, and that he has been delivered from danger. The psalm also evinces Jonah's self-centeredness. The first-person singular as subject, object, and possessive dominates throughout. His arrogance peaks when he contrasts himself favorably with idol worshipers. This reference sends the reader back to the sailors and forward to the Ninevites, the two non-Hebraic groups in the story who are outside the "loyalty" (*ḥesed*) of Yahweh. The depiction of them in the narrative belies Jonah's characterization of them in the psalm. Appearing between the genuine worship of the sailors and of the Ninevites, the psalm offers counterfeit piety from loquacious Jonah.

The closing line, "Deliverance belongs to the LORD!" (2:9) elevates the dissonant tone. If isolated, this sentiment might capture a dominant message of the book, but when spoken by Jonah it has a nauseating effect. So Yahweh spoke to the fish and "it vomited Jonah" (2:10). At the end, the psalm plays a role in delivering the fish from an indigestible burden, a deliverance that allows the narrative to begin a second time.

100. See Katharine Doob Sakenfeld, *Faithfulness in Action* (Philadelphia: Fortress, 1985).

REFLECTIONS

1. At the boundaries of this episode (1:17 and 2:10) the unpalatable verbs "swallow" and "vomit" designate the opposite movements of descent and ascent. Even though in world literature these movements signify the theme of death and life (cf., e.g., Dante's *Divine Comedy*), in Jonah the movements do not so neatly match the theme. Life and death are intertwined and sometimes interchanged. Perspective makes the difference for the meaning.

2. Descent themes are traditionally life denying.[101] They signify death and hell. A natural descent leads to death; a punitive descent leads to death in hell. Jonah in the fish descends from this world to a lower world. He "falls" from what is expected of him and so goes under.

101. See Northrop Frye, *Words with Power* (New York: Harcourt Brace Jovanovich, 1990) 229-71.

In the hymn that Father Mapple of *Moby Dick* reads to the congregation in the Whaleman's Chapel, Jonah describes "the ribs and terrors in the whale" as he goes "deepening down to doom." He sees "the opening maw of hell with endless pains and sorrows there."[102] An exchange between two characters in *Angels in America* also captures well the punitive aspects of the situation.[103] One asks what God does when prophets refuse their vision. The other answers, "He. . . . Well, he feeds them to whales."

3. The descent theme terrifies those who struggle with the divine call. For the Jonah story, however, the ambiguity is that the fish signifies both death and reprieve from death. In swallowing Jonah, it prevents him from drowning. Within its confines of death he is alive. The fish keeps him safe until he is deposited upon dry land.

4. As the fish contains Jonah in both death and life, so the psalm he utters within it contains the ambivalent struggle. Does the belly of the fish save him from the waters of death (cf. Ps 69:1-3, 13-15), or is the belly congruent with the waters (Jonah 2:3)? Is the "womb of Sheol" (Jonah 2:2) equivalent to the belly of the fish, or is the belly the place that saves him from Sheol? In proclaiming thanksgiving and deliverance while he is still in the belly (Jonah 2:9), does Jonah thereby regard the ichthyic abode itself as life-giving? Or is he claiming life proleptically even while residing in death? The psalm deepens his struggle as it complicates distinctions between death and life.

5. The psalm speaks to an indissoluble link between suffering and egotism. Jonah's self-assertive actions and attitude have led to his subterranean predicament. Although his prayer of eight verses is ostensibly thanksgiving to God, in it he uses the first-person singular twenty-six times as subject, object, or possessive. None of these references is self-effacing; they are all boastful. Egotism inflicts suffering; suffering fosters egotism. This episode unflinchingly presents an existential predicament.

6. Comparison with the character Job is instructive. Unlike Jonah, Job refuses to mouth pieties in the experience of suffering (e.g., Job 16–17). Instead, he lashes out at God (e.g., Job 23–24). Though Jonah makes that move later (see Jonah 4), it is not apparent while he resides in the fish.

7. Thanksgiving and triumphalism become confused in the psalm. Jonah is exuberant in thanksgiving, proclaiming life in the midst of death and expressing gratitude for divine deliverance. Yet he is also boastful as he exults in piety over against those whom he condemns. Any descent into death that leads to self-exaltation, the excoriation of others, and the flattery of God produces a triumphalism that falsifies faith.

8. This episode hints at disturbing portraits of God, not unlike those suggested by the sea narrative. Yahweh continues to exercise crushing power without words. This silent divine force bends the creation, natural and human, to its sovereign will (a portrait reminiscent of God in Job). But if an angry deity feeds disobedient prophets to the whales, that same deity preserves them for future assignments. Contradictory images persist. The destroyer and the savior God are one.

9. Matthew 12:40 alludes to this episode in Jonah. Some scribes and Pharisees ask Jesus for an authenticating "sign" of himself as teacher. They seek a demonstration of God's power at work through Jesus. In rejecting their request, Jesus makes one exception: "the sign of the prophet Jonah." He draws an analogy between Jonah "in the belly of the sea monster three days and three nights" and the Son of Man, "three days and three nights . . . in the heart of the earth" (NRSV).

---

102. Herman Melville, *Moby Dick or the White Whale* (New York: The New American Library, 1961) 56-57.
103. Tony Kushner, *Angels in America*, Part Two: *Perestroika* (New York: Theatre Communications Group, Inc., 1994) 104.

The marine habitation of Jonah parallels the subterranean depths for the Son of Man. The analogy belongs to death, not to life; to the underworld, not to the resurrection. So Jesus appropriates the descent theme for himself. Strikingly he omits, both in his reference to Jonah's descent and in its application to himself, any mention of God. The overwhelming power of Yahweh renders Jonah powerless, but Jesus' powerlessness at the heart of earth is devoid of God. Neither the destroyer nor the savior God appoints the earth to swallow him. Instead, Jesus' powerlessness stands over against the putative power of an evil generation seeking a sign.

JONAH 3:1–4:11

NARRATIVE OF MISSION, REPENTANCE, AND DISSENT

OVERVIEW

Scene two begins and ends with Yahweh speaking (אמר *'āmar*) to Jonah.[104] Four episodes develop the plot. The first (3:1-4) reports Yahweh's command that Jonah go to Nineveh and Jonah's obedient response. The second (3:5-10) relates Jonah's words, the efforts of the Ninevites to avert destruction, and God's repentant response. The third episode (4:1-5) tells of Jonah's angry reaction, Yahweh's reply, and Jonah's withdrawal. The fourth (4:6-11) presents Yahweh and Jonah confronting each other in deed and word.

104. Where appropriate, the commentary draws upon Phyllis Trible, *Rhetorical Criticism: Context, Method, and the Book of Jonah* (Minneapolis: Fortress, 1994) 175-225.

JONAH 3:1-4, YAHWEH'S COMMAND AND JONAH'S RESPONSE

NIV	NRSV
3 Then the word of the LORD came to Jonah a second time: ²"Go to the great city of Nineveh and proclaim to it the message I give you." ³Jonah obeyed the word of the LORD and went to Nineveh. Now Nineveh was a very important city—a visit required three days. ⁴On the first day, Jonah started into the city. He proclaimed: "Forty more days and Nineveh will be overturned."	**3** The word of the LORD came to Jonah a second time, saying, ²"Get up, go to Nineveh, that great city, and proclaim to it the message that I tell you." ³So Jonah set out and went to Nineveh, according to the word of the LORD. Now Nineveh was an exceedingly large city, a three days' walk across. ⁴Jonah began to go into the city, going a day's walk. And he cried out, "Forty days more, and Nineveh shall be overthrown!"

COMMENTARY

Episode one is a second beginning. Yahweh again commands (3:1-2), and Jonah again responds (3:3-4).

3:1-2. The divine commission, "the word of Yahweh . . . to Jonah" (author's trans.) initiates the plot. Unlike the translations of both the NIV and the NRSV, the three imperatives that follow in Hebrew are identical to those in 1:2: "arise," "go," and "call." Yet this second beginning does not simply duplicate the first. The third imperative leads, not to a causal or asseverative clause (see 1:2), but to a cognate object and a relative clause. It stresses divine authority over Jonah. A literal translation reads, "call to her the calling that I am wording to you." The Hebrew participle rendered "wording" (דבר *dōbēr*) plays off the formula that introduces the commission, "the word [*děbar*] of Yahweh." But the lack of a specific message in the word leaves Jonah and the reader to ponder whether this commission is like unto or different from the first.

The repetition of the imperatives indicates that despite the descent to Joppa, to the ship, to the innards of the vessel, into the sea, into the belly of the fish, into the land of death and despite the ascent to dry land, the agenda announced in 1:1-2 has developed not at all. Indeed, Jonah has thwarted the divine intention. Subplot subverts plot. The power struggle between Yahweh and Jonah continues.

3:3-4a. As in 1:3, the divine imperative "arise" becomes the human indicative "and Jonah arose." On analogy with the first occasion, obedience is not thereby assured. But the next word is telling. Rather than an infinitive signaling disobedience (so 1:3), it is the human indicative that matches the divine imperative "go": "and he went." Indeed, he "went to Nineveh, according to the word of the LORD." The phrase "word of the LORD" forms an inclusion with the opening of the episode (3:1). Although the inclusion locks in the partial obedience of Jonah, it locks out his response to the third imperative, "call." That exclusion leaves open the question of total obedience and so builds suspense.

The narrator heightens suspense through the delaying tactic of changing the subject. Attention shifts from Jonah to Nineveh (3:3*d*), a city "great to God, a walk of three days." The idiom "great to God" offers rich meanings that the translations of the NIV and the NRSV fail to convey. It suggests divine perspective: The greatness of Nineveh impresses even God (great before God). It suggests divine ownership: God rules over Nineveh (great to God). It suggests divine favor: God has ordained the greatness of Nineveh (great because of God). And it suggests divine abode: The greatness of Nineveh qualifies as a residence for God (great for God). The theological greatness of the city exceeds a mere superlative.[105] Human calculations do not suffice; divine standards take the measure.

Divine greatness relates to size: "a walk of three days." Whatever external information the narrator may be drawing upon for this measure-

ment,[106] within the story the description extends in several directions. The noun "walk" (מהלך *mahǎlak*) derives from the verb הלך (*hālak*), already used in the imperative "go" and in the indicative "he went." Thus Jonah "walked" to Nineveh, itself a walk of three days. Through shared vocabulary the peripatetic man meets the enormous city. Its land size prepares for the population of more than 120,000 citizens "who do not know their right hand from their left" (4:11 NRSV). In the immediate context the phrase "a walk of three days" contrasts with Jonah's "walk of one day." The contrast redounds to the credit of Nineveh. Jonah need not work (walk) too hard before the entire city responds to his message. The repetitions, twice each, of the nouns "city," "walk" and "day" in 3:3*b*-4*a* favorably portray Nineveh.

3:4b. Only after shifting attention to Nineveh does the narrator return to the third imperative of 3:2, "call." The return lifts the suspense of whether Jonah's obedience is complete. "Arise" has become "and Jonah arose" (3:3*a*, author's trans.); "go" has become "went" (3:3*a*); now "call" becomes "and he called . . . " (author's trans.). The NRSV and the NIV offer other translations. Nevertheless, exact correspondences in the Hebrew between the divine imperatives and the human indicatives signal perfect obedience on Jonah's part—or so it appears.

"And he called and said, 'Yet forty days and Nineveh will be overturned [נהפכת *nehpāket*]' " (v. 4*b*, author's trans.). These five words in Hebrew are probably the briefest of all prophetic utterances. Yet they abound in problems. Nowhere in the story has Yahweh given Jonah this particular message to speak. Whereas the narrator has verified Jonah's arrival in Nineveh "according to the word of the LORD," the narrator fails to so verify his speech. No standard prophetic formula such as "the word of the LORD," "thus says LORD," or "oracle of LORD," authenticates the pronouncement. If from the perspective of Nineveh a Yahwistic formula would be incomprehensible, from the perspective of Hebrew prophecy its absence merits attention. After all, other prophecies addressed to foreign nations do contain Yahwistic oracular formulae (e.g., Jer 46–51; Ezek 15:1-3; 27:1-2; 28:1; 31:1-2; 32:1-2). Does the absence

---

105. Cf. D. W. Thomas, "A Consideration of Some Unusual Ways of Expressing the Superlative in Hebrew," *VT* (1953) 209-24; Jack M. Sasson, *Jonah*, AB 24B (New York: Doubleday, 1990) 229-30.

106. See Sasson, *Jonah*, 230-31.

of a formula here indicate anything about the veracity or falsehood of Jonah's proclamation? The story does not answer.

The content of the message poses other problems. Unlike conventional oracles (e.g., Amos 1:3–2:16), it omits any reasons for the announcement. Jonah does not tell the Ninevites why they will be overturned. The particle עוד ('ôd, translated in both the NIV and the NRSV as "more") leaves open the exact timing. It may mean "within" or "at the end of." The idiom "forty days," which most often signifies a long, though unspecified, time of trial and testing (e.g., Exod 24:28; 34:28; Num 13:25; 14:33; 1 Kgs 19:8; 1 Sam 17:16; Ezek 4:6), seems incongruous with the urgency of Jonah's prediction.

The Septuagint offers the alternative reading of "three" rather than "forty days." Coordinated with the description of the city as "a walk of three days," it fits the speed with which the Ninevites respond. A modern proposal holds that "forty days" is a parodic device. Jonah intentionally distorts a traditional formula by turning a long time into a short time.[107] The immediate response

of the Ninevites (3:5) suggests that they understand the parody.

Their response plays on the ambiguities of both the verb הפך (hāpak) and the verbal form nehpāket. In many texts, hāpak signifies destruction (e.g., Gen 19:21, 25, 29; Deut 29:22; Jer 20:16; Lam 4:6). Yet in some texts the verb signifies deliverance (e.g., Deut 23:5; Ps 66:6; Jer 31:13). In other words, hāpak overturns itself; it holds countermeanings. Although the NIV and the NRSV properly translate the verbal form nehpāket as passive, "will be overturned" or "overthrown," they might also have properly translated it as reflective: "overturns itself" or "overthrows itself." Grammatical ambiguity allows Nineveh to be both the recipient and the agent of a word whose meaning is itself ambiguous. Placed on the lips of Jonah, the verb and the verbal form produce exquisite ironies. What Jonah proclaims he undercuts. Not unlike his psalm in the belly of the fish, his prediction mocks him. In acting upon his pronouncement, the Ninevites undermine him too. (See Reflections at 3:5-10.)

---

107. See David Marcus, *From Balaam to Jonah: Anti-prophetic Satire in the Hebrew Bible* (Atlanta: Scholars Press, 1995) 126. But cf. Fretheim, who thinks that forty days is a brief time period, Terence E. Fretheim, *The Message of Jonah* (Minneapolis: Augsburg, 1977) 108-10.

JONAH 3:5-10, EFFORTS OF THE NINEVITES TO AVERT DISASTER AND THE RESULT

NIV

5The Ninevites believed God. They declared a fast, and all of them, from the greatest to the least, put on sackcloth.

6When the news reached the king of Nineveh, he rose from his throne, took off his royal robes, covered himself with sackcloth and sat down in the dust. 7Then he issued a proclamation in Nineveh:

"By the decree of the king and his nobles:

Do not let any man or beast, herd or flock, taste anything; do not let them eat or drink. 8But let man and beast be covered with sackcloth. Let everyone call urgently on God. Let them give up

NRSV

5And the people of Nineveh believed God; they proclaimed a fast, and everyone, great and small, put on sackcloth.

6When the news reached the king of Nineveh, he rose from his throne, removed his robe, covered himself with sackcloth, and sat in ashes. 7Then he had a proclamation made in Nineveh: "By the decree of the king and his nobles: No human being or animal, no herd or flock, shall taste anything. They shall not feed, nor shall they drink water. 8Human beings and animals shall be covered with sackcloth, and they shall cry mightily to God. All shall turn from their evil ways and from the violence that is in their hands. 9Who

NIV

their evil ways and their violence. ⁹Who knows? God may yet relent and with compassion turn from his fierce anger so that we will not perish."

¹⁰When God saw what they did and how they turned from their evil ways, he had compassion and did not bring upon them the destruction he had threatened.

NRSV

knows? God may relent and change his mind; he may turn from his fierce anger, so that we do not perish."

10When God saw what they did, how they turned from their evil ways, God changed his mind about the calamity that he had said he would bring upon them; and he did not do it.

COMMENTARY

Episode two leaves Jonah aside to concentrate upon the city of Nineveh. Three incidents organize the section: the response of the people (v. 5); the response of their king (vv. 6-9); the response of God (v. 10).

3:5. Although Jonah never claimed divine authority for his ambiguous pronouncement, in the first incident the Ninevites make a theological response: "they believed [ויאמינו *wayyaʾămînû*] in God" (author's trans.; cf. Ps 78:22). Coming from the Hebrew root אמן (*ʾmn*), this verb puns on the name of Jonah's father, Amittai ("Belief" or "Truth," 1:1). The "calling" by the son of Belief elicits belief in God. New to the story, the verb "believe" was not even used for the sailors who prayed to Yahweh, vowed vows to Yahweh, and sacrificed sacrifices to Yahweh. If that portrayal failed to secure their conversion to Yahwism (despite the use of the sacred name), the portrayal of the Ninevites follows suit. The object of their belief is not Yahweh but Elohim, a generic term for "god" rather than the particular Israelite name. Using divine vocabulary compatible for the Ninevites along with the verb "believe," the narrator reports the radical theological turning of the city, though not its conversion to Yahwism.

Two verbs, "call" and "put," expand on "believe." The word "call" (קרא *qārāʾ*) resounds throughout the story: in the discourses of Yahweh (1:2; 3:2), the captain (1:6), the narrator describing the sailors (1:14), Jonah (2:3), and the narrator now prefacing Jonah's pronouncement (3:4). The preface presages the response. Just as Jonah "called" to the Ninevites, so they "called a fast" (cf., e.g., Ezra 8:21-23; Esth 4:1-3, 15-17; Jdt 4:8-11). They express their believing through a cultic act of penance. For their succeeding act,

the narrator uses a verb new to the story: they "put" (לבש *lābaš*) on sackcloth. The attire belongs to penitential settings (e.g., Esth 4:1-3, Jdt 4:10).

A threefold verbal description of the Ninevites draws upon vocabulary old ("call") and new ("believe," "put") to report their response to Jonah's ambiguous words. At the conclusion the merism "from the greatest to the least" adds nuance and emphasis to their portrait. This all-inclusive idiom also constitutes pleonasm, a rhetorical device employing more words than necessary. It adds fullness to the phrase "the people of Nineveh."

Verse 5 shows that Nineveh has indeed begun to "overturn." But why the people so readily believe in Elohim, the story never explains.[108] Unlike the sailors in the storm at sea, the Ninevites do not confront immediate and unqualified danger. Unlike the sailors after the calming of the sea, the Ninevites have no evidence of divine mercy. They have heard from Jonah only an ambiguous pronouncement that does not even mention God. Nevertheless, they begin to overturn. Their response prepares for a contrast with Jonah in chap. 4. So easily they believe in God; so fiercely he will argue with Yahweh.

3:6. In the second incident news of the deeds of the Ninevites reaches the king. The people have set the agenda; their ruler now follows their lead. The emergence of this unnamed monarch corresponds to the emergence of the unnamed captain in scene one (1:6). But unlike the captain, the king has an expanded role through actions individual and institutional.

A chiasm of four movements constitutes his individual response. At the beginning the king

---

108. On invented reasons, see Sasson, *Jonah,* 244.

"rose from his throne" (A); at the end he "sat in ashes" (A'). In the middle he "removed his robe" (B), and he "covered himself with sackcloth" (B'). These inverted movements provide a striking picture of a monarch. He has "overturned" in dwelling, dress, and dignity.

3:7-9. Only after humbling himself does the king issue an edict to institutionalize the overturning. It is carefully crafted (the NIV and the NRSV obscure the parts). First comes the *authorization* (v. 7b). It names the place (in Nineveh) and the source of the edict (the decree of the king and his great ones). The *salutation* follows. It is comprehensive, addressing the human being and the animal, the herd and the flock (v. 7c). The *corpus* consists of six instructions. Three are negative (not taste, not graze, not drink), and three are positive (cover, call, and turn from evil). The *conclusion* gives the rationale for the instructions. It offers hope, the possibility that God may repent and thus save the Ninevites from perishing.

Choice vocabulary shapes a proper theology. In the authorization, the Hebrew word translated "decree" (טעם *ṭaʿam*) carries the concrete meaning of taste and the figurative meaning of judgment. It builds a pun with the first negative instruction, "let them not taste anything." The first positive instruction, "let them cover themselves in sackcloth," extends to the animals what the people and the king have already done (vv. 5, 6d). The second positive instruction, "let them call [*qārāʾ*] to God," echoes the captain's imperative to Jonah (1:6) and the narrator's description of the sailors (1:14). But the added condition "with strength" (NIV, "urgently"; NRSV, "mightily") prepares for the radical requirement of the last instruction, "let them turn from evil and violence." The verb "turn" (שוב *šûb*) calls for repentance as it plays on the verb "overturn" (הפך *hāpak*, v. 4).

The verb "turn" (*šûb*) also links the instructions to the conclusion. There *šûb* occurs twice, surrounding the parallel verb נחם (*nāḥam*). The NRSV translates *nāḥam* as "change his mind." The NIV drops it altogether while adding the prepositional phrase "with compassion," a phrase unattested in the Hebrew. The sequence *šûb, nāḥam, šûb* shares the single subject "God" to underscore a theology of divine repentance.

The little clause "who knows" prefaces the theology with possibility and uncertainty. Coming after the ordered "turning" (*šûb*) of the Ninevites (v. 8) and before the hoped-for "turning" (*šûb*) of God (v. 9bd), the clause undercuts any idea of human manipulation effecting divine deliverance. In design and content it parallels the sentiments that the captain expressed with the particle "perhaps" (אולי *ʾûlay*, 1:6).

The juxtaposition of human and divine repentance sets up another comparison. The positive instruction that calls for the human beings and the animals to "turn" specifies a movement away from evil and violence. The hope that God may "turn" specifies a movement away from "his fierce anger." In Hebrew the objects of both movements use body language for destructive action. The first instance becomes apparent through the literal translation of the NRSV: "the violence that is in their hands." The second instance hides in the metaphorical translation "fierce anger." The Hebrew reads literally, "from the burning of his nostrils."

Beginning with possibility and uncertainty, the conclusion ends with hope: "so that we do not perish." Matching exactly the outcome desired by the captain (1:6), these words climax and conclude the well-crafted decree of the king.

3:10. The third incident reports the response of God. In Hebrew three independent clauses organize the structure. Subordinate clauses follow the first and the second but not the third clause. God sees "their deeds" (not "what they did" as in the NIV and the NRSV). The explication of the seeing begins with the particle כי (*kî*), which combines the meanings of "how" and "because." Thus the content of the clause functions as apposition and cause. "How they turned" says that the Ninevites carried out the instructions of the edict. "Because they turned" not only reports their repentance but also supplies the motivation for God's subsequent move. In addition to the verb "turn" (*šûb*), the words "way" (דרך *derek*) and "evil" (רעה *rāʿâ*) draw from the last instruction (v. 8) to relate that the Ninevites have done more than perform deeds of penance. They have changed inwardly; they have overturned (but not as Jonah had intended).

Motivated by their turning (*šûb*), God "repented" (*nāḥam*) about the evil. Like the verb *šûb*, the verb *nāḥam* comes from the conclusion of the edit (v. 9), from the royal expression of hope. (By interpreting the verb *nāḥam* as "had compassion," the NIV once again obscures the Hebrew vocabulary to lose the literary links and the theological emphases.) The verbs "turn" and "repent" depict corresponding movements between the Ninevites and God.

Structure and vocabulary indicate, however, that the correspondence is not inevitable. Placed between the two movements, the "who knows" of the king (v. 9) prevents the tidy operation of cause and effect. Moreover, the use of the verb *nāḥam* in v. 10 for God's repenting, rather than the verb *šûb*, used for the Ninevites' turning (cf. vv. 8-9), undercuts the causal principle. Belonging

in this story exclusively to God (vv. 9-10), *nāḥam* differentiates between divine response and human deeds. Although mutual acts by the Ninevites and God eradicate evil, they turn on separate verbs. In other words, God's response comes on God's terms. The divine unpredictable (who knows?) thus subverts potential disaster into deliverance.

Unlike the Ninevites, God does not do evil. The third clause of this passage reiterates the message in negative form: "and he did not do it." As a two-word statement in Hebrew, this report embodies its meaning by not using the term "evil." God abolishes it from the divine vocabulary.

REFLECTIONS

1. The similarities of 1:1-2 and 3:1-2 show the persistence of the divine call. God perseveres no matter how resistant the respondent. In the Bible the experiences of Moses (Exod 3:1–4:17) and Jeremiah (Jer 20:7-9) illustrate the point. In a contemporary version, the words of the angel to the character Prior in *Perestroika* sound the theme. Infected by the AIDS virus, Prior protests that he is not a prophet but "a sick, lonely man." The angel counters, "You can't Outrun your Occupation, Jonah. Hiding from me one place you will find me in another."[109]

2. The persistence of God wears down resistance. From the beginning, the struggle is unbalanced, and so it is not surprising that at the end the deity prevails. The one whom Yahweh has called must go and must speak as commanded (Jer 1:7). The second time around, then, Jonah capitulates, but inwardly he continues to resist (cf. 4:1-3). Similarly, the character Prior comes to the conditional conclusion, "Maybe I am a prophet," only to hold out, a few lines later, a tentative escape: "And if I hate heaven my only resistance is to run."[110] Although God prevails in such power struggles, human defiance persists. Resistance hides within resignation. Divine calls are not comfortable, not even for those who readily assent (cf. Isa 6:8-13).

3. The short speech that Jonah uttered to Nineveh (3:4) illuminates disjunctions among author, text, and listener (or preacher, text, and congregation). If Jonah intended the destruction of Nineveh, he used ambiguous language (as indeed language often is). The Ninevites then exploited the ambiguity. They chose to hear his destructive intention not as an absolute but as an opportunity for repentance. In effect, the listeners took control of the words away from the author and "overturned" their meaning. The congregation found in the preacher's text the possibility of deliverance.

The philosopher Paul Ricoeur has pointed out that a text is itself mute.[111] It comes alive in the speaking and the hearing. Author and reader share the same text, but they may find (or put) different meanings in it. Illustrated so strikingly in the Jonah narrative, this insight shows

109. Tony Kushner, *Angels in America, Part Two: Perestroika* (New York: Theatre Communications Group, Inc., 1994) 104.

110. Ibid., 53-54.

111. Paul Ricoeur, *Interpretation Theory: Discourse and the Surplus of Meaning* (Fort Worth: Texas Christian University Press, 1976) 75-79.

the potential for blessing and curse in the total act of preaching. To appropriate the theological twist that Joseph offered in Egypt (Gen 50:20), an intended harm may become an intended good.

4. From two directions the narrative disavows cause-and-effect thinking. First, the evil of the Ninevites does not bring punishment (even as, conversely, the innocence of the sailors did not thwart danger). Second, the repentance of the Ninevites does not itself effect the repentance of God. Who knows? Human action does not dictate divine response. This realization is both threatening and assuring. So the story disavows a neatly packaged theology. In the nuances lie the mysteries and the meanings.

5. For many commentators the mass repentance of the Ninevites highlights the "never-neverland" quality of the narrative. Not only are we suspicious about such conversions, but we outright reject them as well. (We do not, however, reject stories of mass violence and destruction; they are only too real.) Yet we need to guard against dismissing this particular narrative. In showing the power of the body politic to turn around, it prevents faith from succumbing to cynicism and despair about the world. It models the corporate and social salvation that faith wills to claim for all the cities of the earth.[112] It addresses systemic concerns.

6. Nineveh contributes to an understanding of *civitas* as a community of memory and expectation, of choices and creativities, of cooperation and potential. The citizens "from the greatest to the least" (3:5 NIV) take the initiative. The merism suggests the riches of inclusivity: male and female, royalty and commoner, nobility and peasant, aged and youth, powerful and powerless—indeed, all sorts and conditions of people. The popular response then reaches the monarch of the city. His behavior emulates the people; his decree institutionalizes what they have already done in spontaneity. The entire passage offers a democratic model for governing in which leader and followers interchange roles. If the model seems distant from the secular city, it is no less compelling for communities of faith.[113]

7. In addition to the comparison that Jesus makes in Matt 12:38-41 between the watery abode of Jonah and his own forthcoming sojourn in the heart of the earth, he relates "the sign of Jonah" to the narrative about Nineveh. Jesus accords the people of Nineveh the right to condemn his generation because Nineveh "repented at the proclamation of Jonah" while his generation cannot see that "something greater than Jonah is here" (NRSV). In the Lukan parallel to this text, Jesus declares Jonah himself to be a sign to the people of Nineveh (Luke 11:30), even as the Son of Man is a sign to his generation. And again he accords the people of Nineveh the role of judge against his own generation, which refuses to see that "something greater than Jonah is here." Although the meaning of the phrase "sign of Jonah" remains obscure (for the book of Jonah never uses the phrase), the words of Jesus declare Nineveh a model to be emulated. Through its repentance, the greatness of the city endures.

112. Cf. James Muilenburg, "Biblical Images of the City," in *The Church and the Exploding Metropolis* (Richmond, Va.: John Knox, 1965) 45-59.

113. The portrayal of Nineveh belongs to a significant bibliography on the concept of the city, beginning with Augustine, *The City of God Against the Pagans,* 7 vols., LCL (Cambridge: Harvard University Press, 1957–1972). In the twentieth century, see Lewis Mumford, *The Culture of Cities* (New York: Harcourt, Brace & World, 1938); Jane Jacobs, *The Death and Life of Great American Cities* (New York: Random House, 1961); Harvey Cox, *The Secular City* (New York: Macmillan, 1965); Jacques Ellul, *The Meaning of the City* (Grand Rapids: Eerdmans, 1970), esp. 66-72. See more recently Marshall Berman, *All That Is Solid Melts into Air: The Experience of Modernity* (New York: Simon and Schuster, 1982); Charles N. Glaab and A. Theodore Brown, *A History of Urban America,* 3rd ed. (New York: Macmillan, 1983). On the city in literature, see, e.g., Charles Baudelaire, *The Flowers of Evil and Paris Spleen,* trans. William H. Crosby with intro. by Anna Balakian (Brockport, N.Y.: BOA Editions, Ltd., 1991); Feodor Dostoevsky, *Notes from the Underground and the Gambler,* trans. Jane Kentish with intro. by Malcolm Jones (Oxford: Oxford University Press, 1991); Andrei Bely, *Petersburg,* trans., annotated, and intro. Robert A. Maguire and John E. Malmstad (Bloomington, Ind.: Indiana University Press, 1978).

JONAH 4:1-5, JONAH'S REACTION, YAHWEH'S REPLY, JONAH'S DEPARTURE

NIV

4 But Jonah was greatly displeased and became angry. ²He prayed to the LORD, "O LORD, is this not what I said when I was still at home? That is why I was so quick to flee to Tarshish. I knew that you are a gracious and compassionate God, slow to anger and abounding in love, a God who relents from sending calamity. ³Now, O LORD, take away my life, for it is better for me to die than to live."

⁴But the LORD replied, "Have you any right to be angry?"

⁵Jonah went out and sat down at a place east of the city. There he made himself a shelter, sat in its shade and waited to see what would happen to the city.

NRSV

4 But this was very displeasing to Jonah, and he became angry. ²He prayed to the LORD and said, "O LORD! Is not this what I said while I was still in my own country? That is why I fled to Tarshish at the beginning; for I knew that you are a gracious God and merciful, slow to anger, and abounding in steadfast love, and ready to relent from punishing. ³And now, O LORD, please take my life from me, for it is better for me to die than to live." ⁴And the LORD said, "Is it right for you to be angry?" ⁵Then Jonah went out of the city and sat down east of the city, and made a booth for himself there. He sat under it in the shade, waiting to see what would become of the city.

COMMENTARY

Episode three reports Jonah's reaction to the events in Nineveh (vv. 1-3), Yahweh's question to him (v. 4), and his withdrawal from the city (v. 5). The verb "burn" (חרה *ḥārâ*) in vv. 1 and 4 delimits that incident from the transitional move in v. 5.

4:1. Episode two ended (3:10) with the Ninevites and God turning away from evil (רעה *rā'â*). By contrast, this episode opens with Jonah surrounded by evil (*rā'â*). The Hebrew reads literally, "and it was evil to Jonah an evil great...." Translations lose the contrast and the emphasis by altering the syntax and softening the vocabulary (see the NIV and the NRSV). For the storyteller, however, something more than "displeasure" is happening to Jonah. Indeed, the second half of the sentence reads literally, "... and it burned to him." The description sets Jonah over against God, who has turned "from the burning of his nostrils" (3:9 author's trans.).

4:2-3. Jonah prays a second time, but now in anger. Unlike its parallel in scene one (2:2-9), this prayer fits the narrative context. In genre and structure it resembles not the psalm but the lament of the sailors (1:14). Invocation, corpus, and conclusion organize its parts.

The invocation begins with the emphatic particle "Ah" (אנה *'ānnâ*; NIV and NRSV, "O") as Jonah calls upon Yahweh. The corpus contains rebuke, justification, and motivation. Jonah rebukes Yahweh by alluding to "this my word" that he spoke while he was still in his homeland (cf. Exod 14:12). He then uses this word to justify his haste to flee to Tarshish. Although he employs the narrated discourse of 1:3, he tellingly omits the phrase "from the presence of the LORD." That charade has ceased. Jonah now confronts Yahweh directly. Rebuke and justification lead to motivation. He explains why he fled.

The deictic phrase "for I knew that..." signals the importance of his disclosure. Elsewhere the phrase precedes climactic utterances (e.g., Gen 22:12*b*; Exod 18:11; 1 Kgs 17:24). Jonah employs it to introduce one version of an ancient confession that permeates Scripture.[114] Four rhythmic phrases focus on divine attributes: (1) Employing

---

114. See Exod 34:6-7; Num 14:18; Deut 7:8-10; 2 Chr 30:9; Neh 9:17, 31; Pss 86:5, 15; 103:8; 111:4; 112:4; 145:8; Joel 2:13; Nah 1:3; Neh 9:17, 31.

assonance and pleonasm, the pair "gracious and merciful" (חנון ורחום *ḥannûn wěraḥûm*) signifies succor and love. The adjective (*raḥûm*), akin to the noun רחם (*reḥem*), meaning "womb," holds the particular image of maternal compassion.[115] (2) The description "slow to anger" (ארך אפים *'erek 'appayim*) literally reads "long of nostrils" (cf. Prov 14:29; 15:18; 16:32), an anthropomorphism connoting friendliness and graciousness. It contrasts with "the burning of his nostrils" in 3:9.[116] (3) The expression "abounding in steadfast love" (ורב-חסד *wěrab-ḥesed*) conveys the fullness of benevolence.[117] (4) The characterization "and repenting about the evil" (ונחם על-הרעה *wěniḥām 'al-hārā'â*) undercuts its own malicious object as it evokes vocabulary, themes, and deeds already attributed to God (cf. 3:10; the translations of the NIV and the NRSV fail to preserve the connections).

An ancient and honorable theology motivated Jonah in his flight to Tarshish (1:3). As the reason for his not wanting to go to Nineveh, it accounts for his lack of surprise at what happened in Nineveh. Yet by reciting the confession in anger, Jonah produces an oxymoron. He subverts divine love into accusation, condemns compassion, and demands vindication from the "merciful" God who coerced obedience from him. The ancient confession that motivated his past behavior becomes thereby the momentum for his present request.

In the conclusion of his prayer, Jonah petitions Yahweh to take away his life. The adverb that opens this section, "and now" (ועתה *wě 'attâ*), suggests immediacy and urgency. Having failed to escape the presence of Yahweh through flight to Tarshish, sleep in the innards of the ship, death at the sea or in the belly of the fish, Jonah is this time direct, not devious, in stating his wish. But the request signals no change in his character. In scene one when he explains to the sailors that on his account the tempest is upon them, he never offers to throw himself into the sea. Instead, he proposes that they do it for him. Similarly now, when he wants to die, he does not initiate suicide.[118] Instead, he proposes that Yahweh do it for him. Reasoning that for himself death is better than life, angry Jonah presses his will and logic upon the merciful God, slow to anger.

Appearing near the end of scene two, this prayer fills a major gap in information that occurred near the beginning of scene one: why Jonah disobeyed the divine command. Without the explanation, the reader might have speculated that Jonah fled because he feared for his life. A messenger of doom might suffer the fate of his message. Or he fled, perhaps, because he wanted doom to come upon Nineveh. If he did nothing, it would happen. Or, conversely, he fled because he did not want doom to come upon Nineveh. If he did not proclaim it, it would not happen. But the delayed information that Jonah supplies undercuts all such reasons and so sends the reader back to scene one.

Rereading scene one in the light of vv. 2-3 offers new perspectives. Jonah's knowledge in flight (1:3) of the merciful God encounters Yahweh's unmerciful action in hurling a destructive wind upon the sea. Does Yahweh thereby challenge Jonah's presumption about Yahweh? Or does Jonah's belief account for his deep sleep during the storm? Does he harbor the assurance that Yahweh will not destroy the ship? If Jonah fled because he knew God to be merciful, why did he not share that understanding with the sailors and thus allay their fears? If Jonah knew God to be merciful, what did he hope to achieve in being thrown overboard? Does his self-claimed knowledge undermine the idea that he sought death by drowning? Does it suggest, instead, that he knew God would rescue him? Does his understanding account for his psalm of thanksgiving in the belly of the fish? Throughout, is Jonah using this knowledge for his own self-confirmatory antics? Is he using theological confession to manipulate God? To put the information that Jonah gives in 4:2 back into the gap after 1:3*a* destabilizes interpretations of the story. But is Jonah's speech reliable?

Another approach to his words holds that in the beginning Jonah did not flee for the reason

---

115. See James Limburg, *Jonah: A Commentary*, OTL (Louisville: Westminster/John Knox, 1993) 90-91; Phyllis Trible, *God and the Rhetoric of Sexuality* (Philadelphia: Fortress, 1978) 1-5, 31-59.

116. See M. I. Gruber, *Aspects of Nonverbal Communication in the Ancient Near East*, Studia Pohl 12 (Rome: Pontifical Biblical Institute, 1980) 485, 503.

117. See Katherine Doob Sakenfeld, *Faithfulness in Action* (Philadelphia: Fortress, 1985) 47-52; Gordon R. Clark, *The Word Ḥesed in the Hebrew Bible*, JSOTSup 157 (Sheffield: JSOT, 1993) 247-55.

118. Cf. A. J. Droge, "Suicide," in *The Anchor Bible Dictionary* (*ABD*), 6 vols. (New York: Doubleday, 1992) 6:227-28.

he now cites. After—and only after—he witnessed the outcome in Nineveh, did he resort to this reason and thereupon put it back into the beginning. The gap in 1:3*a* thus becomes a convenience for him. Borrowing from the narrator the technique of delayed information (e.g., 1:10), Jonah fills the gap to his own advantage while still withholding from God, from the narrator, and from the reader the reason why he fled. In other words, Jonah has a secret life. But in public he justifies himself by belatedly chastising God for being merciful. Ostensibly pulling the story together, his explanation may keep it apart.

The question becomes, Can the reader trust Jonah? In answering, the reader may take a clue from God, who has just heard Jonah's rebuke, justification, motivation, petition, and reason, and now replies.

4:4. The reply is as important for what it does not say as for what it says. First, Yahweh does not take on the content of Jonah's prayer. The deity does not acknowledge Jonah's earlier word, does not refer to his flight, does not comment on his theological motivation, and does not reply to his death wish. Yahweh does not answer on Jonah's terms; the deity does not return to the past. Instead, Yahweh focuses on Jonah's mode of being in the present.

Second, Yahweh does not speak with imperatives, the only discourse that the deity has used thus far in the story (1:2; 3:2). Rather than issuing commands to Jonah, Yahweh now asks him a question. Playing off the narrated description at the beginning of the episode, "it burned to him," Yahweh counters, "Is it good it burns to you?" (author's trans.). Despite Jonah's effort to set the agenda, the narrator and the deity surround his prayer with a different focus. The divine question invites him to consider the meaning of his anger. But this rhetorical maneuver does not work.

4:5. Jonah leaves town without a word. Having already informed Yahweh that death is preferable to life, he spurns the divine question and leaves the narrator to report his exit. Some scholars view this verse as another instance of delayed information.[119] They claim it belatedly reports what Jonah did just after his pronouncement in Nineveh (3:4). Yet the verse itself lacks any verbal indicator of delay (cf. 1:10; 4:2). Read as the immediate sequel to v. 4, it shows Jonah breaking off conversation, setting distance, and shifting attention.

In Hebrew four main clauses ending with a subordinate clause relate his diversionary tactic. Verbs of activity begin the first and third clauses: "Jonah went out" and "he made." A single verb of inactivity, "he sat down" (וישב *wayyēšeb*), opens the second and fourth clauses. Altogether these verbs deliver Jonah to the purposive verb of the ending: "until he should see what would happen in the city" (author's trans.). The prepositional phrase "in the city" parallels similar prepositional phrases about the city at the end of the first two clauses (so translated in the NRSV).

Jonah's diversionary tactics are ironically self-defeating. To go out from the city leaves the place where the divine question was asked; yet previous geographical efforts to escape Yahweh's word have failed. To make a booth secures a shelter; yet in the past neither the innards of the ship nor the waters of the sea nor the belly of the fish has secured Jonah from Yahweh. To sit down twice entrenches Jonah's position; yet past efforts at entrenchment have brought expulsion (e.g., 1:6). To see what would happen in the city resists what has already happened; yet from the beginning resistance has not succeeded. Jonah's narrated response to Yahweh's direct question shows habitual defiance while hinting at inevitable defeat. It moves the last episode away from Nineveh, in both geography and content. (See Reflections at 4:6-11.)

119. Cf. Phyllis Lou Trible, "Studies in the Book of Jonah" (Ph.D. diss., Columbia University, 1963; University Microfilm International, order no. 65-7479) 92-102; Sasson, *Jonah*, 287-90.

JONAH 4:6-11, CONTINUING STRUGGLE BETWEEN YAHWEH AND JONAH

NIV

[6]Then the LORD God provided a vine and made it grow up over Jonah to give shade for his head to ease his discomfort, and Jonah was very happy about the vine. [7]But at dawn the next day God provided a worm, which chewed the vine so that it withered. [8]When the sun rose, God provided a scorching east wind, and the sun blazed on Jonah's head so that he grew faint. He wanted to die, and said, "It would be better for me to die than to live."

[9]But God said to Jonah, "Do you have a right to be angry about the vine?"

"I do," he said. "I am angry enough to die."

[10]But the LORD said, "You have been concerned about this vine, though you did not tend it or make it grow. It sprang up overnight and died overnight. [11]But Nineveh has more than a hundred and twenty thousand people who cannot tell their right hand from their left, and many cattle as well. Should I not be concerned about that great city?"

NRSV

[6]The LORD God appointed a bush,[a] and made it come up over Jonah, to give shade over his head, to save him from his discomfort; so Jonah was very happy about the bush. [7]But when dawn came up the next day, God appointed a worm that attacked the bush, so that it withered. [8]When the sun rose, God prepared a sultry east wind, and the sun beat down on the head of Jonah so that he was faint and asked that he might die. He said, "It is better for me to die than to live."

[9]But God said to Jonah, "Is it right for you to be angry about the bush?" And he said, "Yes, angry enough to die." [10]Then the LORD said, "You are concerned about the bush, for which you did not labor and which you did not grow; it came into being in a night and perished in a night. [11]And should I not be concerned about Nineveh, that great city, in which there are more than a hundred and twenty thousand persons who do not know their right hand from their left, and also many animals?"

[a] Heb *qiqayon*, possibly *the castor bean plant*

COMMENTARY

Five incidents organize episode four. The first three report appointments by Yahweh that eventually lead to speech by Jonah (vv. 6-8); the fourth presents a conversation between Yahweh and Jonah (v. 9); the fifth poses a question by Yahweh to Jonah (vv. 10-11).

4:6-8. Near the close of scene one Yahweh appointed (מנה *mānâ*) a fish to swallow Jonah (1:17). Near the close of scene two Yahweh returns to natural appointments (*mānâ*). This time the divine activity expands, and the divine intent is instruction. Yahweh seeks to persuade Jonah through indirection.

Three tightly woven incidents share structure and vocabulary, with one noteworthy omission. First, each incident begins with a divine appointment. Yahweh appoints (*mānâ*) a plant, a worm,

and a wind. Second, each incident reports the effect of the appointment. The plant grows up around Jonah to shade his head and to deliver him from his evil. The worm attacks (נכה *nākâ*) the plant, and it withers. The sun, aided by a strong wind, then attacks (*nākâ*) Jonah's head. Third, the first and third incidents report Jonah's reaction to what has happened. He delighted in the plant; he fainted and asked to die. But the second incident omits this item. How Jonah reacted to the withering of the plant is not recorded. Within the commonalities unfold this and other individual features of the three verses.

4:6. Botanical identification of the plant (קיקיון *qîqāyôn*) is not possible, because the Hebrew word occurs only here in the Bible. Translations range from "gourd" in the Septuagint and "ivy" in the Vulgate to the indeterminate "bush" of the NRSV and "vine" of the NIV.

But the purposes of the plant are clear. The first purpose, "to be a shade" (צל *ṣēl*) upon Jonah, follows immediately upon the shade (*ṣēl*) of the booth.[120] Built by opposing characters, these shelters give Jonah double protection from opposite perspectives. *Under* the booth that he constructed Jonah sits; *above* Jonah's head Yahweh appoints a plant. Although both constructions provide him shade, only the latter seeks "to deliver him from his evil" (author's trans.). The booth confirms him as he is; the plant seeks to save him from himself. Accordingly, the phenomenon of shade offers different meanings.

The second purpose of the plant, "to deliver Jonah from his evil," plays off the description of "evil to Jonah a great evil" in 4:1. For all the other characters—the sailors (cf. 1:7), the Ninevites (3:10), and God (3:10)—evil has already been dispelled. Now the appointed plant aims to remove it from Jonah as well.

His reaction is delight (שמח *śāmaḥ*), a word that occurs twice here, as verb and as cognate object, but nowhere else in the story. The Hebrew translates literally, "And delighted Jonah upon the plant a great delight." Anger once surrounded Jonah (v. 1); delight now replaces it. (This nuance of structure and meaning is lost in the reductionist translation of the NIV and NRSV, "very happy.") Delight may suggest a change in Jonah's character, but the narrator does not say that the plant achieved its stated purpose to deliver Jonah from evil. Shaded by botanical mercy, the delight of Jonah masks his evil.

4:7. This verse shifts attention from the delight of Jonah to the demise of the plant. A worm (תולעת *tôlaʿat*) attacks it, and it withers. One of three grammatical forms (cf. תולע *tôlāʿ*, masculine, and תולעה *tôlēʿâ*, feminine), the feminine *tôlaʿat* identifies an insect that God appoints to destroy plant life. Deuteronomy 28:39 provides a parallel. At the behest of Yahweh, the worm (*tôlaʿat*) will eat the vineyards of disobedient Israel. By divine arrangement nature assaults nature. The worm is the enemy of the plant. As a symbol of destruc-

tion, the worm (*tôlaʿat*) functions elsewhere as a metaphor for a weak (Isa 41:14) or despised (Ps 22:6) person or for despicable humankind (Job 25:6).

The report about the worm begins expansively, with a temporal reference locating the incident at dawn, but then shrinks to a simple clause of two Hebrew words, translated "attacked the plant," and then again to a single word referring to the plant, translated "it withered." The sound of the verb "withered" (וייבש *wayyîbāš*) echoes in Hebrew the sound of the noun "dry land" (היבשה *hayyabbāšâ*) to evoke verbal association with the fish episode (2:10).

Another connection comes through the two natural creatures, the sea and the earth. Like the fish, the worm is God's instrument. Unlike the fish, it mediates not between Yahweh and Jonah but between God and the plant.[121] So it shields the deity from directly perpetrating death. Unlike the fish, whose role is ambivalent, both devouring and saving, the worm has only a negative function. Yet its destructive act belongs to Yahweh's larger purpose of saving Jonah from himself, of teaching him a new and different way of understanding.

As the last word of the verse, the verb "wither" aptly describes the demise not only of the plant but also of the incident. It stops without a reference to Jonah. Specifically, it fails to report his response to the demise of the plant *qua* plant, apart from the consequences for himself. That he had a response becomes clear only in v. 10.

4:8. In returning to Jonah, this incident relates conversely to the subject matter in v. 6. There Jonah enjoyed shade "upon his head"; here he suffers from the sun "upon his head."

The temporal reference that begins the incident relates chiastically to the temporal reference in v. 7. God's appointment of the worm (A) precedes the coming up of the dawn (B); the rising of the sun (B′) precedes God's appointment of the wind (A′). The sun "attacked" (נכה *nākâ*) Jonah, just as the worm has already "attacked" the plant. So the human creature and the botanical creature experience similar assaults, which lead to parallel con-

---

120. This proximity has encouraged some scholars to transpose 4:5 to follow 3:4; see Phyllis Lou Trible, "Studies in the Book of Jonah," (Ph.D. diss., Columbia University, 1963; University Microfilm International, order no. 65-7479) 92-102.

121. In the incidents of the plant and of Jonah, God is once removed from inflicting death and danger. Though divine activity arranges for these eventualities, the verb "attack" (נכה *nkh*) does not have the deity as subject; instead, nature, the worm, and the sun are the subjects. This distinction perhaps contrasts with the directness of Yahweh in hurling (טול *twl*) the storm upon the sea (1:4) and complements the indirectness of Yahweh in having the fish "swallow" (בלע *blʿ*) and "vomit" (קיא *qîʾ*) Jonah, both negative verbs.

sequences. The plant withered; Jonah fainted and asked to die (v. 8*ef*).

All that has happened in these three intertwined incidents (vv. 6-8) returns Jonah at their end to his own words, "Better my death than my life." His first request for death (v. 3), addressed to Yahweh in a prayer, followed upon the deliverance of Nineveh. This second request, addressed to himself, follows upon the sun's attacking his head. The different occasions evince a common theme. Whatever happens contrary to Jonah's will, be it destructive or salvific, tremendous or trivial, impersonal or personal, he would rather die than live with it.

4:9. Just as the ending of v. 8 repeats with variation the theme and vocabulary of v. 3, so parallelism continues as the first half of this verse repeats with variation the theme and vocabulary of v. 4. Again Yahweh poses the question about anger, "Is it good it burns to you . . . ," but this time adds the specific object, "about the plant?" The question comes after the sun has attacked Jonah. It is not about the plant *qua* plant but about the effect of the withered plant upon Jonah as the sun assaults him.

The impressive repetitions between vv. 3-4 and vv. 8*ef*9*a* mirror in miniature the beginnings of the larger story. Scene one opens (1:1-2) with divine commands, to which Jonah responds in disobedience. All that follows but brings the story back, at the opening of scene two, to the same commands (3:1-2). Repetition with variation (the content of the command) gives Jonah another chance. He then responds in obedience. Similarly, here God asks Jonah a second time about his anger but changes its object from the great city Nineveh to the ephemeral plant. Repetition with variation (the object of the anger) gives Jonah another chance.

On the first occasion Jonah responds to the divine question about anger by walking away. He says nothing, but his narrated actions change the subject and the venue (v. 5). He leaves the city and builds a booth. But on this second occasion Jonah responds differently. He stays put and answers the question. He turns the divine interrogative into his own indicative, "It is good it burns to me . . . " (author's trans.). He also escalates the value of his anger, declaring that it is good "unto death" (4:9*b*). Although he does not specify the

plant, his answer in parallel to the question asked suggests an analogy between it and him. In desiring death, Jonah wishes to be like the withered plant. These are his last words in the story. He ends, as his actions began, opposing Yahweh. But Jonah does not have the last word. As the story continues, it moves beyond the mirroring of its two beginnings.

4:10-11. Even though Yahweh speaks no third command to Jonah, the deity does ask him a third question. Its structure, content, and meaning depend on the declarative sentence that precedes it. A close translation of the Hebrew shows the internal composition of these sentences and their relationship to each other.

And said Yhwh,
A You, you pitied for the plant,
  B which you did not plant and did not cause to be great,
    C which became a child of the night and perished a child of the night.
A′ And I, shall not I pity for Nineveh the great city
  B′ which [has] in it many more than one hundred and twenty thousand humans
    C′ who do not know beween his right hand and his left
      D and animal[s] many?

Both sentences contain independent clauses followed by relative clauses. At the beginnings, independent personal pronouns ("you" and "I") emphasize, respectively, Jonah and Yahweh. Matching forms of the verb "to pity" (חוס *ḥûs*) build an analogy between the characters (A and A′). The objects of their pity contrast in the relative clauses: the great size of the plant and the large population of Nineveh (B and B′); the child-plant and an ignorant population (C and C′). At the end of the second sentence, a coda extends the description of the city to its animals.

Balance and imbalance contend in these sentences. The sixteen words of the declarative (v. 10) give the premise for the twenty-three words of the interrogative (v. 11). The distribution matches the weight of the argument. It moves from the small to the large, an argument known in Latin as *a minori ad maius* and in Hebrew as *qal wāḥōmer*.

Literary and theological insights abound. The root for "great" (גדל *gdl*), which in adjectival form occurs more than any other word throughout the story, appears in both sentences. The verb form "to cause to be great" links the ephemeral plant in stature to the perdurable great city of Nineveh (B and A′). The analogy between the size of the plant and the population of Nineveh (B and B′) joins the greatness of the natural and the urban environment. The city then embraces the natural environment through its animal inhabitants. Extending beyond the structural and substantive parallels of the two sentences, the words "animals many" receive the end stress of the entire story (D).

Another analogy relates the childlike plant to the ignorant population of Nineveh (C and C′). Unique to Jonah, the clause presenting the human (אדם ′ādām) "who do not know between his right hand and his left" has puzzled scholars across the centuries.[122] The generic term ′ādām, which designates the population, can signify frailty and mortality (cf. Gen 2:7); however, those meanings alone hardly explicate the attendant description. Efforts to assign it a moral reading—namely, that the Ninevites do not know right from wrong—falter on the very portrayal of the Ninevites in chap. 3. They are moral creatures who turn from their evil, perform acts of penance, and repent. Suggestions that the phrase refers to the mentally deficient, who lack proper discernment, or to young children, who literally do not know right from left, falter for lack of evidence. Yet the latter suggestion may resonate with the double reference to the plant as a "child of the night."

The appearance of the verb "perish" (אבד ′ābad) completes a symmetry of its usage in the two scenes of the story. The captain expresses the hope that "we will not perish" (1:6). The sailors beseech Yahweh that they not "perish" for the life of Jonah (1:14). The king expresses the hope that "we will not perish" (3:9). Now Yahweh describes the plant that "perished a child of the night." Appearing in corresponding places between the scenes, the four occurrences of this verb belong to direct discourse. All the characters, save Jonah, use it. (By contrast, he uses the verb "die" [מות mût], which the other characters never use.)

The controlling verb for the analogy between Jonah and Yahweh is ḥûs, often translated "pity."

Elsewhere in the Bible, ḥûs functions positively in theological contexts to connote the attitude or emotion of sympathy that expresses itself in gracious action toward another.[123] The verb carries strong meaning. Indeed, negative expressions of ḥûs (not showing pity) can signify violence, disaster, and destruction (e.g., Deut 7:16; 19:21; 25:12; Jer 13:14, 21:7). Sometimes the verb appears with the noun "eye" (עין ′ayin) to convey the concept of overflowing tears for the object of sympathy (e.g., Ezek 20:17; cf. Gen 45:16-20; Ezek 16:5). The range of positive expressions includes compassion, benevolence, and mercy.

Altogether new to the Jonah story, the appearance of ḥûs in the last two verses suggests the introduction of new meaning. The meaning accords well with Yahweh's attitude toward Nineveh. But the verb seems inappropriate for Jonah's stance. Nowhere in the story has he shown pity, for the plant or for anything else. Yet on Yahweh's attribution of this verb to Jonah hinges the validity of Yahweh's argument.

Various translations and explanations attest the problem. The rendering "have concern," used in the NIV and the NRSV, is general enough to cover both Jonah's behavior toward the plant (vv. 8-9) and Yahweh's behavior toward Nineveh,[124] but it produces a weak analogy unworthy of the verb ḥûs. The proposal of two different meanings for ḥûs, such as "fret" for Jonah and "have compassion" for Yahweh, is hardly convincing,[125] because the text does not indicate a switch in meaning. Similarly, a resort to the concept of irony, whereby the ascription of ḥûs to Jonah holds the opposite of its true meaning,[126] finds no basis in the text.

Another approach to the problem evokes the technique of delayed information (cf. 1:10; 4:2-3). This proposal returns to the three well-constructed incidents of vv. 6-8. In the first incident (v. 6), when Jonah delighted about the plant, his response was self-serving. The plant provided him

122. Cf. Jack M. Sasson, *Jonah,* AB 24B (New York: Doubleday, 1990) 314-15.

123. For discussion and biblical references, see S. Wagner, "chus," in *Theological Dictionary of the Old Testament* (*TDOT*), ed. G. Johannes Botterweck and Helmer Ringgren, trans. David E. Green (Grand Rapids: Eerdmans, 1980) 4:271-77.

124. Cf. Leslie C. Allen, *The Books of Joel, Obadiah, Jonah and Micah,* NICOT (Grand Rapids: Eerdmans, 1976) 230-35.

125. Sasson appropriates the translation of Jerome, which uses two Latin verbs: *tu doles* ("you grieve") for Jonah and *ego non oarcan* ("shall I not spare") for Yahweh. See Sasson, *Jonah,* 309-10.

126. See Hans Walter Wolff, *Obadiah and Jonah,* trans. Margaret Kohl (Minneapolis: Augsburg, 1986) 173-74.

shade. In the third incident (v. 8), when he fainted and asked to die, his response was also self-serving. He became angry about the plant after the sun had beat upon his head (v. 9*a*). But between these incidents a worm attacked the plant, and it withered (v. 7). Strikingly, the story does not record how Jonah responded to that event: how he responded to the withering of the plant *qua* plant; how he responded before the withering affected him. A gap emerges in the structure and content of the second incident. Only at the close of the story is the gap filled by that most trustworthy character Yahweh, who speaks to Jonah: "You, you pitied the plant" (author's trans.).

Unlike the responses of delight and faint, pity is not self-serving. It is disinterested compassion. Jonah showed sympathy for the withered plant apart from the effect of that withering upon himself. To that incident Yahweh now returns as the deity shapes the closing argument of the book—an argument that does not close the book.

The filling in 4:10 of the gap in v. 7 expands the character of Jonah beyond a one-dimensional portrayal. There is more to Jonah than a stereotype of disobedience and self-centeredness. There is more to Jonah than a caricature for satire and humor. There is more to Jonah than anger. If that more is but glimpsed in the narrative, it is nonetheless grabbed by Yahweh.

The filling of the gap establishes a premise from which Yahweh can argue for divine pity upon Nineveh. And this argument expands in turn the portrayal of Yahweh. Whereas earlier God repented because Nineveh repented, now Yahweh shifts to a theology of pity independent from deeds of repentance. In the shift, Yahweh's attitude and action toward Nineveh exceed anything that Nineveh itself merits.

With Yahweh's question the story stops, but it does not end. Jonah holds over the question the power of an answer. The last word is not spoken. The new verb *ḥûs*, used of human and divine, moves the story beyond its confines.

REFLECTIONS

1. Jonah 4 provides a sustained focus on the phenomenon of anger. The psychophysical language of the burning of the nostrils holds a deep truth about the human condition. A searing emotion inflames the body; the physical manifests the psychological.

2. The divine questions put to Jonah ask about the value or benefit of anger (4:4, 9). Both the interrogative forms and their content recognize anger, but neither affirm nor condemn it. The text does not engage in "should" talk. Jonah is not told that he should be or should not be angry. Instead, he is invited to reflect on the meaning or value of anger.

3. A reader may hear in the divine questions the implied answer that anger is not good for Jonah, but that answer does not forbid Jonah to be angry. The responsibility for the emotion and its consequences resides with Jonah. When he defiantly holds fast to anger, insisting that it is good for him "unto death," he mouths profound truth. Anger leads to destruction. If it is repressed or suppressed, it "burns" the one who contains it; if it is expressed, it "burns" those to whom it is directed. Although anger is an inevitable part of the human condition, the divine questioning offers the opportunity to work it through and to work through it.

4. Yahweh never argues anger with Jonah. Instead, the deity works circuitously to lead him to a different realization. One approach points up the indiscriminate character of Jonah's anger. It happens whether the issue is weighty or ephemeral: the salvation of Nineveh or the withering of the plant. Promiscuous anger discloses the problem of its possessor rather than the justice of his or her causes. Another approach allows Jonah's defiance to stand while juxtaposing an alternative drawn from Jonah himself. Jonah angry unto death counters Jonah compassionate for the plant. Such juxtaposition allows, but does not compel, movement beyond the impasse of anger.

5. The story shows anger rooted in self-confirmatory thinking. Psychologically, Jonah's anger manifests narcissism; theologically, it bespeaks egotism. This anger is the justification of oneself over against a transcendent mode of being and a transcendent God. In a profound way, then, anger belongs to the journey of faith. It shows the human being, in this case Jonah, wrestling with the demonic and the divine and not always being able to separate the two. It shows the titanic struggle that refuses to submit to coercion. (In this respect, Jonah resembles Jacob, Jeremiah, and Job.) Left unsettled is the outcome: whether blessing or destruction, life or death, will result for Jonah.

6. The theme of anger, though not always the vocabulary, belongs to the developing portrait of Yahweh. Scene one shows an angry deity hurling a storm and controlling Jonah. Scene two shows God turning "from the burning of his nostrils" (cf. 3:9-10). The phrase "Yahweh slow to anger" (lit., "long of nostrils") appears in parallelism to "gracious and merciful" (4:2-3). No longer inflamed, Yahweh seeks to lead Jonah away from anger.

7. The text of 4:2-3 shows well the tension between messenger and message. In anger Jonah proclaims Yahweh "slow to anger." What his words affirm, his existence denies. Such a contradiction is familiar. The novelist Zora Neale Hurston presents it powerfully in the character of Jon Buddy Pearson, inspired and inspiring preacher on Sundays who is a "natchel man" the rest of the week, given to many women and to violence against them.[127] As Hurston plays off the Jonah story, the plant becomes the symbol of an untrustworthy man who needs to be cut down. Messenger and message do not match.

8. Illuminating parallels relate the book of Jonah to the story of the prodigal son and the loving father (Luke 15:11-32).[128] God is like the loving parent, Nineveh is like the prodigal child, and Jonah is like the elder child, who resents the merciful acts of the parent.

9. Like much of Jonah, chapter 4 abounds in ecological sermons. The world of nature belongs to God, who uses it at will. A plant represents flora; a worm, fauna. The natural times of day, symbolized by the dawn and the rising of the sun, cooperate with the divine plan. God then whips up the strong wind (cf. 1:4). At the end, however, the divine use of nature yields to respect for the integrity of creation. Jonah pities the withered plant in and of itself, apart from the effect of its withering upon him. He becomes thereby the model for Yahweh, free of self-interest. An ecology of pity becomes the paradigm for a theology of pity, and that pity embraces not just the human population of Nineveh but also its animals. They constitute Yahweh's last word.

10. In chapter 4, Yahweh is persistent but not coercive. Each of the three divine speeches (4:4, 9a, 10-11) poses questions rather than imposes commands. Yahweh is teacher and guide for Jonah. Corresponding to this change comes the shift from a theology of repentance (3:10) to a theology of pity. If the former makes sense, producing coherence between the turning of the Ninevites and the turning of God, the latter moves beyond sensibility. Nineveh evokes pity, not because it turned from evil, but according to its size, its ignorance, and its animals. As a move of grace, Yahweh's last speech bodes well for Nineveh and for Jonah. But is not this move also an act of caprice? If so, does not the freedom of Yahweh allow the possibility of a caprice of destruction as well as of pity?[129] To those disturbing questions the book gives no answer.

11. Abruptly the story of Jonah stops, but it does not end. The divine question awaits an

---

127. Zora Neale Hurston, *Jonah's Gourd Vine* (New York: J. B. Lippincott, Inc., 1934).
128. See José Alonso Díaz, "Paralelas entre la Narración del Libro de Jonás y la Parabola del Hijo Pródigo," *Biblica* 40 (1959) 632-40.
129. Cf. Alan Cooper, "In Praise of Divine Caprice: The Significance of the Book of Jonah," in *Among the Prophets,* ed. Philip R. Davies and David J. A. Clines, JSOTSup 144 (Sheffield: JSOT, 1993) 144-63; Thomas M. Bolin, " 'Should I Not Also Pity Nineveh?': Divine Freedom in the Book of Jonah," *JSOT* 67 (1995) esp. 117-20.

answer. In pondering the matter, the reader who journeyed with Jonah begins to get the point. The reader is Jonah; Jonah is the reader. So the open-endedness of the last verse invites self-understanding and self-transcendence. The story subverts the reader.

❖   ❖   ❖   ❖

EXCURSUS: THE AFTERLIFE OF JONAH

Innumerable references, allusions, and echoes to the story of Jonah appear in diverse settings. Its afterlife continues to yield abundant reflections through juxtaposition, contradiction, and convergence.

(1) Within the books of the Twelve Prophets the fictitious Nineveh of Jonah meets the historical Nineveh of Nahum and of Zephaniah (2:13-15). The repentant Nineveh meets the evil Nineveh; the Nineveh that God spared meets the Nineveh that Yahweh destroyed. In no necessary way, however, does the second Nineveh negate the first. *Post hoc non est propter hoc.* "After this is not because of this." Whatever destructive end God visited on the historical Nineveh, the fictitious Nineveh endures to show a more excellent way for Nineveh and for God.

(2) Connections between the book of Jonah and the apocryphal book of Tobit are tantalizing. In this romance tale, Tobit is a Jew exiled with his family in Nineveh after the Assyrian destruction of Israel. One night his son Tobias stops to wash his feet in the Tigris River, whereupon a "large fish leaped up from the water and tried to swallow the young man's foot" (Tob 6:3 NRSV; cf. Jonah 1:17). Tobias kills the fish, eating some of it but keeping its gall-bladder, heart, and liver for medicinal purposes (Tob 7:16-18; 8:1-3; 11:7-15).

At the end of the story (Tob 14:4), Tobit predicts the destruction of Nineveh. Manuscript traditions contain two versions.[130] In the more reliable, Tobit refers to "the word of God that Nahum spoke about Nineveh" (NRSV); in the other, Tobit refers to "the word of God that Jonah spoke about Nineveh." This confusion (or interchange) of Nahum and Jonah keeps alive the tension between them.

In Tobit, the story of Jonah lives through the setting in Nineveh, the description of a great fish that is both destructive and salvific, and the prediction of Nineveh's demise. The contrast comes through the reports of Nineveh's being saved in Jonah and destroyed in Tobit (Tob 14:15). If Jonah lends meaning to Tobit, Tobit returns meaning to Jonah.

(3) In citing "the sign of the prophet Jonah," Jesus in the Gospel of Matthew refers to Jonah's journey three days and three nights in the belly of the fish and to the repentance of the people of Nineveh (Matt 12:38-42). The parallel in the Gospel of Luke contains only the second of these references (Luke 11:30-32; for comments, see the Reflections at Jonah 1:17–2:10; 3:5-10).

(4) Allusions and echoes of Jonah abound in the early Christian apocryphal tale called The Acts of Andrew and Matthias.[131] The story opens with the apostles' casting lots to decide where they will preach (cf. Jonah 1:7; Acts 1–2). The lot that falls on Matthias sends him to Myrmidonia, the city of the cannibals. Its citizens seize, torture, and imprison him. Within thirty days they plan to slaughter and eat him.

At this point the story begins to play off the Jonah narrative in the Septuagintal version. Just as Yahweh called Jonah to "arise, go" to Nineveh (1:2), so Jesus commands Andrew (and

---

130. See Irene Nowell, "Tobit," in *The New Jerome Biblical Commentary* (*NJBC*), ed. Raymond E. Brown, Joseph A. Fitzmyer, and Roland E. Murphy (Englewood Cliffs, N.J.: Prentice Hall, 1990) 568-71.

131. For a critical edition that includes references to the book of Jonah, see Dennis Ronald MacDonald, *The Acts of Andrew and The Acts of Andrew and Matthias in the City of the Cannibals* (Atlanta: Scholars Press, 1990) 1-169.

his disciples) to "arise, go" to Myrmidonia. They are to rescue Matthias. Like Jonah (Jonah 1:3), Andrew at first resists the divine call but eventually obeys.

Andrew goes down to the sea and finds a ship going to the city (rather than away from it, as Jonah had sought flight to Tarshish). Unlike Jonah (Jonah 1:3), Andrew cannot pay his own fare, much less the cost of the ship. When Jesus, disguised as the captain (cf. Jonah 1:6), asks him how then he expects to board, Andrew confesses faith in "our Lord Jesus Christ, the good God." His words call to mind Jonah's confession to the sailors about his god Yahweh (Jonah 1:9). Rather than arousing fear on the part of the crew (cf. Jonah 1:10), however, Andrew's answer assures him a welcome that includes provision for food. Captain Jesus sends an angel to "the hold of the boat" to bring it up. The location evokes Jonah's going down to the hold of the ship (Jonah 1:5).

The food provides nourishment for enduring the turbulent sea. Unlike the great wind in the Jonah narrative (Jonah 1:4), this turbulence is not a punitive act of God. As a natural occurrence, it threatens the life of neither the ship nor the crew (cf. Jonah 1:4, 11-13). Nevertheless, the disciples, like the sailors in Jonah, are terrified (cf. Jonah 1:5, 10). To quell their fear, these faithful men fall asleep, a posture that links them to the unfaithful Jonah (Jonah 1:5). Meanwhile, Jesus pilots the ship without difficulty. He attributes the basically benign behavior of the sea to the righteous presence of Andrew on board. The unrighteous presence of Jonah on board his ship caused a life-threatening storm (Jonah 1:7, 10).

When Jonah is hurled into the sea, a great fish appointed by God swallows him awake (Jonah 1:17). When Andrew and his disciples leave their ship, angels commanded by God lift them up asleep. Carried in the fish, Jonah descended to the womb of Sheol (Jonah 2:2) before his expulsion onto dry land (Jonah 2:10). Carried by an eagle, Andrew's disciples ascend to paradise before their arrival at the city gate of Myrmidonia.

After leaving the ship, Andrew, like Jonah (Jonah 3:1-2), receives the divine command a second time: "Stand up, go" to the city. Like Jonah (Jonah 3:3), Andrew "rose up and went." Whereas the story of Jonah reports in brief the evil of Nineveh (Jonah 1:2; 3:8, 10), the story of Andrew details at length the evils of Myrmidonia. Similarly, whereas the presence of Jonah in Nineveh comes with few words by him and the narrator (Jonah 3:4), the presence of Andrew in Myrmidonia involves many deeds and many words by the character and the storyteller.

Upon releasing Matthias from prison, Andrew sends him with the disciples out of the city toward the east. Andrew himself continues to walk in the city and eventually sits behind a pillar to see what will happen. These events offer yet more twists on the Jonah narrative. Jonah also walked in Nineveh (Jonah 3:4). Later he left the city, sat down east of the city, and made a booth for himself until he should see what would happen (Jonah 4:5). In Myrmidonia atrocities multiply. Andrew is attacked and left for dead. Out of his unbearable suffering he asks the Lord to command his spirit to leave him, an echo of the angry Jonah asking Yahweh to take away his life (Jonah 4:3, 8). In neither instance does God grant the request. For Andrew the sign of divine care is the sprouting of large fruit-bearing trees. For Jonah the sign of divine care was the appointing of a plant (Jonah 4:6) to shade him (until a worm destroys it).

If Jonah sought the destruction of Nineveh (Jonah 3:4), Andrew seeks to punish those residents of Myrmidonia who have persecuted him. He commands a statue to spew forth water to drown them. It kills not only the guilty men of the city but also their cattle and their children, two groups evocative of the Jonah story (cf. Jonah 3:5, 7-8; 4:11). At one point the water rises to the necks of the men, an image parallel to Jonah's describing waters that enclose him "up to the neck" (נֶפֶשׁ *nepeš*, 2:5).

Like the Ninevites (Jonah 3:5, 8), those who survive Andrew's flood "believe" in God and cry out to the deity. In time, Andrew raises their dead, including "men, women, children, and beasts." This concern for the greatest to the smallest, most especially for animals, resonates again with the story of Jonah (Jonah 3:5, 7-8; 4:11). When Andrew determines to leave the city, the citizens beg him to stay by performing penitent acts. They put ashes on their heads, as did the Ninevites (Jonah 3:6).

Not persuaded by the pleading, Andrew goes his way. Immediately the Lord Jesus confronts him to ask why he has no compassion for the city. The divine interrogative calls to mind Yahweh's questioning of Jonah about Nineveh (Jonah 4:10-11). Jesus then sends Andrew back to Myrmidonia. In returning, he blesses Jesus for not permitting him to leave the city in his rage. The reference to rage matches Jonah in his anger (Jonah 4:1, 4, 9).

The book of Jonah provides numerous leitmotifs as well as specific vocabulary for the shaping of the Acts of Andrew and Matthias. By turn, major sections of the Acts yield an early Christian midrash on the book of Jonah. In myriad ways, Jonah and Jesus meet.

(5) Jewish legend promotes Jonah as the most prominent disciple of the prophet Elisha.[132] It embellishes the biblical story by filling in many gaps.

Among the numerous variations that legend offers on Jonah 1 and 2 are the following: that Jonah fled from his call because he did not wish to be a false prophet; that he joyously paid for the entire cargo to leave land; that the terrible storm at sea injured only Jonah's ship; that the sailors bargained for his life by immersing him at first only to his knees, then to his navel, then to his neck, but finally had to abandon him totally; that at the creation of the world God made the fish that swallowed him; that the fish was as comfortable as a large synagogue, with its eyes as windows so that Jonah could see out; that only when Jonah was transferred to a less desirable fish did he pray; and that after their deliverance the sailors became proselytes in Jerusalem.

Among the numerous variations that legend offers on Jonah 3 and 4 are the following: that when Jonah saw the mercy of God toward repentant Nineveh he sought divine forgiveness for his own flight; that the heat in the belly of the fish left Jonah without clothes and hair, subject to swarms of insects and so needing the protection of the plant; that the sun (not a worm) smote the plant; that Jonah learned his lesson from the plant and recognized God's goodness; that after forty days Nineveh returned to its sinful ways and so incurred the punishment that Jonah had predicted; that God exempted Jonah from death because of his great suffering in the watery abyss, and thus in the end he entered paradise alive.

Jewish legend also gives Jonah an unnamed wife who was renowned for her piety, especially for a pilgrimage to Jerusalem, which, as a woman, she was not obliged to perform. In these many embellishments on the Jonah narrative, imagination fashions another story.

(6) Jonah plays a major part in the holiest day of the Jewish year, Yom Kippur, the day of atonement, when the whole house of Israel, individually and collectively, seeks to cleanse itself before the Lord (cf. Leviticus 16).[133] Since the period of the Mishnah (c. 200 BCE), the universal Jewish custom has been the reading (or chanting) of this book as a highlight of the afternoon service. That time of day is deemed most appropriate for God's receiving the prayers of the people (cf. 1 Kgs 18:29, 36).

The choice of Jonah for this occasion pertains to many themes, most prominently true repentance and divine forgiveness. On its most sacred day, Israel lifts up as the model of repentance not itself, who is like unto the Hebrew Jonah resisting God, but outsiders: pagan sailors and especially penitent Ninevites. From the transformative deeds of these outsiders Israel learns accountability and responsibility. From the divine compassion that spares them, Israel

---

132. See Louis Ginzberg, *Legends of the Bible* (Philadelphia: The Jewish Publication Society of America, 1956) 604-8.

133. See David P. Wright, "Day of Atonement," *ABD*, 2:72-76; Theodor H. Gaster, *Festivals of the Jewish Year* (New York: William Sloane Associates, 1953) 134-86, esp. 170-77; Nahum Sarna, "Why the Book of Jonah Is Read on Yom Kippur," *BR* 6 (1990) 24.

finds reassurance about itself in relationship to God and learns compassion in relationship to others.

Related themes contributing to the prominence of Jonah in this liturgy include its universalistic perspective; its understanding of evil in moral categories; its references to vows, sacrifices, fasting, and other penitential acts; its stress on genuine transformation over against even fervent recitation of creeds (cf. Jonah 1:9; 4:2-3); and its emphasis on the value of all life, human and animal, in the purview of God (cf. Jonah 4:10-11).

(7) The enormous afterlife of Jonah in Jewish, Christian, Islamic, and secular art, music, and literature defies tracking. The story has inspired people, from childhood to old age, in diverse cultures throughout the world.[134]

---

134. References and other materials are available in the following: Wolf Mankowitz, "It Should Happen to a Dog," A Play in One Act (1956), published in *Religious Drama 3,* Intro. by Marvin Halverson (New York: Meridian, 1959) 121-37; "Jonah," *Encyclopaedia Judaica* (Jerusalem: Macmillan, 1971) 10:173-77; Sol Liptzin, *Biblical Themes in World Literature,* (Hoboken, N.J.: KTAV, 1985) 236-49; Henry Summerfield et al., "Jonah," in *A Dictionary of Biblical Tradition in English Literature,* ed. David Lyle Jeffrey (Grand Rapids: Eerdmans, 1992) 409-11; Robert Atwan and Laurance Wieder, eds., *Chapters into Verse* (Oxford: Oxford University Press, 1993) 445-51; David Curzon, ed., *Modern Poems on the Bible* (Philadelphia: The Jewish Publication Society, 1994) 254-67; James Limburg, *Jonah,* OTL (Louisville: Westminster/John Knox, 1993) 9, 99-123; Limburg, "Jonah and the Whale Through the Eyes of Artists," *BR* 6 (1990) 18-25; Lance Wilcox, "Staging Jonah," *BR* 11 (1995) 20-28.

❖   ❖   ❖   ❖

THE BOOK OF MICAH

INTRODUCTION, COMMENTARY, AND REFLECTIONS
BY
DANIEL J. SIMUNDSON

THE BOOK OF
MICAH

INTRODUCTION

T he book of Micah, attributed to an eighth-century Judean prophet, numbers sixth among the twelve minor prophets. Like some other brief biblical books, it is sometimes overlooked. Many Christians are familiar with certain verses from Micah, yet they may not be aware of their source. The promise of a time of peace when nations will "beat their swords into plowshares" (Mic 4:3), the prophecy about a new ruler to come from the town of Bethlehem (5:2), and the response to the question of what the Lord requires of them, signal Micah's importance. But the book also contains other riches worthy of serious study by those wishing to grow in knowledge of Micah's world and of the God whose words the prophet claims to proclaim.

THE PROPHET AND HIS HISTORICAL SETTING

We know very little about the prophet Micah (whose name means "Who is like [Yahweh]?"). A superscription (1:1) associates him with the reigns of three Judean kings: Jotham (742–735 BCE), Ahaz (735–715), and Hezekiah (715–687). Perhaps he was a younger contemporary of the prophet Isaiah. Unlike Jerusalem Isaiah, however, Micah was from Moresheth, a small village lying southwest of Judah's capital city.

Despite its paucity of explicit biographical information, the collection bearing Micah's name discloses something of the prophet's theology and religious fervor: his identification with the poor and oppressed (e.g., 2:9); the certainty that he had been called to prophesy by Yahweh (3:8); and his anger at the Judean leaders responsible for Jerusalem's impending doom (Micah 3). A century later, when the prophet Jeremiah predicted the destruction of Jerusalem and its temple, certain elders of the land quoted Micah's oracle (Mic 3:12) about Jerusalem's demise (Jer 26:18-19). They reminded their audience that King Hezekiah heeded Micah's prophecy and turned to the Lord, averting the disaster that he had predicted. Perhaps the people should likewise take seriously what Jeremiah was saying.

Scholars have attempted to identify the period of Micah's prophetic ministry more specifically. The consensus is that his earliest prophecies preceded the destruction of the city of Samaria and the fall of the northern kingdom of Israel in 722 (1:6-7)[1]. Some have suggested that he began to prophesy in the 730's, though not earlier.[2] Most scholars have associated his threats to the city of Jerusalem with Sennacherib's invasion in 701 BCE, although a minority would confine his career to a shorter span, ending perhaps within a decade after it had begun.[3]

The latter half of the eighth century BCE was a time of great transition. In the first half of that century, both Judah and Israel prospered because the great powers of the ancient Near East, preoccupied with other matters, did not torment them. That situation changed very rapidly after 746, however, when Tiglath-pileser III came to power in Assyria. A succession of short and unsuccessful kingships, foolhardy efforts at rebellion, and the resurgence of Assyrian power in the region led to the fall of the northern kingdom of Israel and its capital city, Samaria, in 722 BCE. Judah avoided a similar fate but paid a high price for its subservience to Assyria—huge tributes, loss of complete independence, and corruption of its traditions by the incorporation of religious practices of the dominant foreign power. Into this time of great change, when the fortunes of God's people had already declined and promised to get even worse, Micah stepped forward to provide a theological interpretation of crucial events facing the nation and its people.

The situation of ordinary citizens was of great concern to Micah. He felt compassion for the poor and dispossessed, and held the leaders responsible for their suffering. We can learn something about the people's social and economic situation from Micah's condemnation of their rulers, merchants, and prophets. Similar words from Micah's contemporary, Isaiah, add to our picture of a society where the rich and powerful used their influence to exploit the vulnerable and to create even greater inequalities of wealth and influence (e.g., Isa 5:8-10; 10:1-2). The economic situation of the poor was further aggravated by programs of armament and fortification in efforts to hold off the threat from foreign empires (see 2 Chronicles 32). The tribute demanded by Assyria from its vassal states also added to the problem. The wealth needed to buy off Assyria had to come from someone, and the poor surely paid more than their share. Further, Jerusalem grew in population at about this time, probably as a result of a large influx of refugees after the fall of Samaria. Archaeological

---

1. See, e.g., James Limburg, *Hosea–Micah,* Interpretation (Atlanta: John Knox, 1988) 3.
2. Hans W. Wolff, *Micah: A Commentary* (Minneapolis: Augsburg, 1990) 2-3.
3. Mays dates Micah's activity to a short time in 701 BCE before Sennacherib's invasion. See James L. Mays, *Micah,* OTL (Philadelphia: Westminster, 1976) 16. Wolff dates Micah's public activity to a short time between 733–722 BCE. See Wolff, *Micah,* 8.

evidence provides limited verification of this picture, which is drawn mostly from biblical material.[4] Chapters 16–19 of 2 Kings provide further details about this time of historical upheaval from the perspective of the deuteronomic historian.

LITERARY CONCERNS

Like other OT books, Micah has been carefully examined by biblical scholars using the methods of analysis common to the trade. Specialists have been, and many still are, preoccupied with matters of authorship and history of composition (redaction).[5] Conservative scholars have tended to attribute to Micah as much of the book as is rationally possible. A majority of scholars, however, have ascribed most of chaps. 1–3, but very little of chaps. 4–7, to Micah (perhaps some verses in chap. 6, and 7:1-7, but virtually nothing in 4–5). The challenge, as they see it, is to locate post-Micah materials in specific times and places and to trace the gradual growth of the book. More recently certain literary approaches, including rhetorical criticism, have encouraged scholars to bracket questions of original authorship and redaction history and to concentrate on interpreting the book as a whole in its final, canonical form.

With the exception of its superscription (1:1), the book of Micah consists of poetry, not prose. Characteristic features of Hebrew poetry—e.g., synonymous parallelism (the repetition of a thought, albeit with important variations in vocabulary, grammatical forms, and syntax; see, for example 3:6), traditional word pairs, metaphors, and similes—appear throughout the book.

Scholars interested in form criticism find examples of many literary genres in the book of Micah: judgment and salvation oracles, lament, lawsuit, disputation speech, prayer, and hymn. The prophet used these various forms drawn from different aspects of life to shape, enliven, and intensify the important messages that he felt called to speak. Many scholars question whether Micah ever spoke the promises of salvation contained in the collection. If his primary calling was to warn of impending doom (as suggested by Jer 26:18), would he have diluted the urgency of that message by concomitantly proclaiming words of hope? Would doing so soften his message, allowing listeners who should repent to fall back on a false security that God would never abandon them after all? We will ponder these questions as we move through the book of Micah.

Efforts to find some unifying principle for the present organization of the book of Micah have led to a number of suggestions. Although shorter units are generally isolated without much difficulty, the task of identifying major structural divisions has proven elusive. The book seems more a collection of materials than a carefully planned, coherent work. Abrupt transitions, sudden shifts between condemnation and promise, and alternations in personal pronouns and gender abound. Yet even scholars who do not discern much overall coherence

---

4. Delbert R. Hillers, *Micah: A Commentary on the Book of the Prophet Micah,* Hermeneia (Philadelphia: Fortress, 1984) 5.

5 See especially Mays and Wolff; Hillers, by contrast, expresses little confidence in the results of redaction criticism.

in Micah must decide how to divide the book into major parts for their analysis of its content. In general, four basic ways to divide the book have emerged.

(1) At first glance, Micah seems to divide into three parts: Chapters 1–3 consist of brief words of judgment against Samaria and oracles against Jerusalem (except for words of promise in 2:12-13); chaps. 4–5 contain words of salvation (except for more hard words of judgment in 4:9-10; 5:10-15); and chaps. 6–7 are a mixture of judgment oracles, leading finally to hope. For this commentary, we will divide Micah into these three major units, although this division leaves some problems with the intrusion of salvation promises in the first section and more judgment oracles in the second section. Many scholars who have divided Micah in this way have assumed that the prophet spoke only judgment oracles and that, therefore, most of what is authentic to Micah appears in the first three chapters.

(2) Several scholars argue in favor of dividing Micah into the following three major units: chaps. 1–2; 3–5; and 6–7. Each section begins with the imperative "hear," indicating the beginning of a major structural unit. Further, each of these three units moves from judgment to hope, a rather common flow seen often in biblical materials. The imperative "hear" also appears in 3:9 and 6:9, but these occurrences are considered by proponents of this view to be of secondary structural importance, echoing 3:1 and 6:1.[6] This way of making sense out of the overall structure of Micah has a certain appeal, though it seems not to deal adequately with the apparent major break between chapters 3 and 4.

(3) Another alternative is to divide the book into two major parts: chaps. 1–5 and 6–7. Again, both of these sections begin with "hear." Further, both begin with a lawsuit in which the prosecutor makes a case against the accused. Mays suggests that the first section is addressed to all nations, offering them a choice between submission and punishment. The second section is addressed to Israel.[7]

(4) A further way to divide Micah entails separating 7:8-20 as a closing liturgy spoken by the people. The other divisions remain the same as in the first hypothesis: Chapters 1–3 expose guilt and pronounce judgment with a brief interpolation in 2:12-13; chaps. 4–5 promise future salvation for Jerusalem and Israel; 6:1–7:7 is the work of a post-exilic social critic making a contemporary application of Micah's message; and 7:8-20 is a liturgical passage.[8]

THE TEXT

Although some scholars complain about the poor state of preservation of the Hebrew text of Micah the overall meaning is usually apparent. There are, however, some passages that are very difficult to translate (such as 1:10-16; 2:7-10; 6:9-12; and 7:11-12), as will become obvious when one compares the differing solutions proposed by the NIV and the

6. Leslie C. Allen, *The Books of Joel, Obadiah, Jonah, and Micah*, NICOT (Grand Rapids: Eerdmans, 1976) 258. Limburg supports this three-part division, *Hosea–Micah*, 159.

7. Mays, *Micah*, 3.

8. Wolff, *Micah*, 17-18.

NRSV translators. Occasionally, translators must acknowledge in a footnote that the Hebrew text is uncertain.

THEOLOGICAL ISSUES

Micah is a rich resource for the theological tasks of the preacher, the teacher, and the pastoral caregiver. Sometimes troubling and sometimes comforting, Micah provides insights into the nature of God and to the way humans relate to God and to each other. Some passages from Micah may strike us as "answers" to our deepest questions of meaning. Other texts disturb us and raise hard questions about what we are doing with our lives. In some cases, Micah may drive us to other biblical texts for words of assurance and a renewed sense of acceptance by God. Theological issues that the reader will encounter in the book of Micah include the following:

1. Despite its brevity, the book of Micah presents a complex variety of ways in which Yahweh relates to humanity. God seemingly acts differently in some situations than in others. God is angry and destructive, but the same God overflows with compassion and pity and comforting promises that abandonment will never be permanent. God is judge and savior, acts in the world and remains hidden, has a special covenant with the people of Israel and cares for the whole world. How can God be all of this and more? What is the true nature of God, the God who remains when all the present terrible events are history?

2. The anger of God is an issue too often avoided. Prophetic books like Micah do not permit us to sidestep it. Many people believe they have experienced God's anger, especially if they have suffered great trials in their own lives. Too often the church has not provided an opportunity for them to think about this issue. The book of Micah gives one an occasion to reflect upon God's wrath.

3. What does God expect from us? Micah answers that question in 6:6-8. Are we saved by our piety, our sacrifices, the way we perform and participate in liturgy? Are we saved by our ethical practices? Can we ever be good enough? What about God's grace and forgiveness? Can we save ourselves through proper understanding, the correct theological formulation, a right reading of the Holy Scriptures? Micah helps us think about these questions, even as we continue to struggle with how to be right before God.

4. The interpretation of disaster and suffering as judgment for sin needs constantly to be examined. Micah clearly states that the calamities the people will endure are the consequence of human behavior. All will suffer, though their leaders are most culpable. When bad things happen, is there always some sin lurking in the background that explains human suffering and sustains our belief in a just God? The doctrine of retribution retains its hold in the lives of many faithful people. The book of Micah gives an occasion to think about it, to see what is valid and what needs critique, what should be applied personally and communally, and what should be rejected as not fitting one's own circumstances.

5. From whom do the prophets (or other proclaimers of a word from God) receive their authority? What makes a prophet true or false? Often, prophets are judged to be true or false on the basis of the accuracy of their predictions (Deut 18:22; Jer 28:9). Why does the message of Micah end up in a canonical book, whereas many of ancient Israel's prophets were either forgotten or remembered only as those with whom true prophets had to contend?

6. The task of the prophet can be very painful. Often the prophets tried to say no when God placed a heavy task upon them. Their message often includes a painful criticism, and the listeners' first impulse is to reject the message and condemn and isolate the messenger. Unless the prophet actually hates those addressed, the message of doom will bring personal pain. Although we know very little about Micah, we can detect in his laments the inner pain that all proclaimers of God's Word must sometimes feel.

7. How does one articulate a message of hope that is honest, realistic, and able to revive the spirit of one who has been crushed? There are wonderful words of hope in Micah. Promises contained there continue to sustain and comfort troubled persons in our own day. The promises of hope in Micah remain a rich pastoral resource.

8. For Christians, the passage about a new ruler to come from Bethlehem (5:2-5) bears special significance. We are uplifted by it every Advent and Christmas season. What does Micah really say about the coming Messiah and the new age? Did Jesus fulfill these prophecies? In what way? Is there still more to come, if Micah's hopes for the future are to be fully realized?

9. When is the appropriate time to speak of hope? This is a very important question for scholars of the book of Micah. Many debates about the authenticity of certain oracles in the book are based on the assumption that Micah would not have issued a word of hope when his main motive was to announce judgment. Could Micah utter doom and hope at the same time? Does hope come only after disaster, when it is no longer appropriate to speak of destruction? When people have lost everything they become desperate to hear words of encouragement. In public preaching and private counseling, when is it time to proclaim the law, the consequences of continuing misdeeds, the need for repentance? Should we wait until someone has finally "hit the bottom" before we begin to speak of hope? The struggle to discern the right word for the right time remains very much with us.

BIBLIOGRAPHY

Allen, Leslie C. *The Books of Joel, Obadiah, Jonah, and Micah.* NICOT. Grand Rapids: Eerdmans, 1976. Writing from a more conservative perspective, Allen opts for unity and authenticity unless doing so proves absolutely untenable. More concerned for theological matters than many commentaries.

Hillers, Delbert R. *Micah: A Commentary on the Book of the Prophet Micah.* Hermeneia. Philadelphia: Fortress, 1984. Hillers brings sociological concerns, data from archaeology, and detailed textual analysis to the discussion of Micah. He proposes that Micah consists of materials connected with a movement of protest and revitalization.

Kaiser, Walter C., Jr. *Micah–Malachi.* Communicator's Bible. Dallas: Word, 1992. Intended for a more conservative audience, this commentary uses the New King James Version as its basic text. It intends to bridge the gap between good scholarship and serious study of the Bible in local religious communities.

Limburg, James. *Hosea–Micah.* Interpretation. Atlanta: John Knox, 1988. Limburg attends especially to those sections of Micah that seem most promising for preaching and teaching. Good theological and pastoral insights for the preacher and teacher.

Mays, James L. *Micah: A Commentary.* OTL. Philadelphia: Westminster, 1976. Very interested in the redaction history of Micah, how it grew from the prophet's own words in order to speak to various situations in the subsequent history of Israel. Considerable scholarly detail, along with helpful theological perspectives.

Wolff, Hans W. *Micah: A Commentary.* Minneapolis: Augsburg, 1990. Similar to Mays in approach and method, but not in conclusions. The methods of form criticism and redaction history are used extensively. Develops the theory that Micah held the office of elder in and for the town of Moresheth.

Outline of Micah

I. Micah 1:1–3:12, Terrible Days Are Coming—for Good Reason

  A. 1:1, Historical Setting
  B. 1:2-7, God's Case Against Israel
  C. 1:8-16, A Call to Lament
  D. 2:1-5, Loss of Inheritance Is God's Response to Injustice
  E. 2:6-11, False Prophets Preach False Assurance
  F. 2:12-13, A Word of Hope Breaks In
  G. 3:1-12, Against Rulers, Priests, and Prophets
    3:1-4, Condemnation of Rulers
    3:5-8, Judgment Against Prophets
    3:9-12, Rulers, Priests, and Prophets Caused This Mess

II. Micah 4:1–5:15, Hope Will Finally Prevail

  A. 4:1-5, Peace, Prosperity, and Security in the Days to Come
  B. 4:6–5:1, Tough Times Ahead, but God's People Will Prevail
  C. 5:2-5*a*, The Promised Ruler from Bethlehem
  D. 5:5*b*-15, God Will Judge and Rescue
    5:5*b*-6, Seven Shepherds and Eight Rulers
    5:7-9, Your Remnant Shall Defeat Your Enemies
    5:10-15, God's Judgment on Israel and Its Enemies

MICAH 1:1–3:12

TERRIBLE DAYS ARE COMING—FOR GOOD REASON

OVERVIEW

The first three chapters of Micah present God's case against the very people whom God had chosen for a special covenantal relationship. Disaster is on the way. Although prophets, priests, and rulers fed the people a false optimism, reality would soon befall them. Micah's task is to alert the people to the danger and to challenge their reliance on the hope that God will always protect them, no matter how flagrant their disobedience. God is well aware of their sin and will soon respond with appropriate anger. God does not act unfairly, without good reason. The people, particularly the leaders, and not God, must be held accountable for terrible, impending events. God has not broken promises, but God's people have not kept their part of the agreement.

After the editorial superscription (1:1), God begins to make the case against Samaria, and then Judah (1:2-7). Samaria's imminent destruction should function as a warning of what will follow for Judah and Jerusalem. Since Micah sees clearly what is coming, he is moved to lament for his own people in the kingdom of Judah (1:8-9). In a very interesting but difficult passage, Micah uses wordplays on the names of several Judean towns in order to articulate the approaching disasters (1:10-15). Chapter 1 ends with a call for Jerusalem (and the people she embodies) to join Micah in the lament.

In chap. 2, the sins that were mentioned in general terms in chap. 1 are described in further detail. Particularly offensive is the greed of the wealthy and the powerful who seize the property and other possessions of those who have no protection against such avarice. In a nice irony, in which the punishment fits the crime, the Lord will now remove the inheritance (the land promised by God to the covenant people) from those who have stolen from persons weaker than they (2:1-5).

With the exception of 2:12-13, most of the rest of this section concentrates on the failures of the rulers, the prophets, and the priests. They are largely responsible for the coming disasters. They have not warned the people about what was coming so that repentance might be possible and calamities averted. They have spoken words that people wish to hear, rather than God's truth (2:6, 11; 3:5-7, 9-12). The rulers have been especially vicious in their treatment of people (3:1-3). Rulers and prophets are singled out for special words of judgment (3:4, 6-7), but the terrible truth is that all will suffer because of what they have done or failed to do. This section, dominated by the theme of appropriate judgment, closes with the prediction that Jerusalem will become a heap of ruins (3:12, the passage remembered by the elders in Jeremiah's day; cf. Jer 26:18).

Micah 2:12-13 disrupts the logic of these first three chapters. Why should words of hope be inserted in the flow of texts about impending destruction? Do we explain it as a liturgical break from the relentless heaviness of doom, as a reminder that punishment is never the final word because God is good or as a reminder that hope is possible even in the face of terrible situations that cannot be changed? Were these words placed by Micah at this point in his book, or were they added by a later redactor?

MICAH 1:1, HISTORICAL SETTING

NIV

1 The word of the LORD that came to Micah of Moresheth during the reigns of Jotham, Ahaz and Hezekiah, kings of Judah—the vision he saw concerning Samaria and Jerusalem.

NRSV

1 The word of the LORD that came to Micah of Moresheth in the days of Kings Jotham, Ahaz, and Hezekiah of Judah, which he saw concerning Samaria and Jerusalem.

COMMENTARY

Since the book of Micah provides virtually no information about the prophet, we are grateful for the few facts added by a later editor in its superscription (1:1). The best guess for placing Micah historically is that his first oracle dates to just before the fall of Samaria (722 BCE) and most of his warnings about Jerusalem belong to the time of the invasion of Assyria's king Sennacherib (701 BCE; see Introduction).

Although both the NIV and the NRSV use the translation "The word of the LORD *came* to Micah," the verb in Hebrew is simply "to be" (היה *hāyâ*). The word of the Lord "was" to Micah. Here is the pointed claim that he spoke not his own word, but God's word, and that fact makes his prophecies worthy of attention and careful reflection.

The Hebrew word "saw" (חזה *hāzâ*) at the end of v. 1 is not the usual word for "see" (ראה *rāʾâ*), but it most often describes instances of prophetic revelation in which the prophet sees more than other people do. The NIV tries to capture this specialized meaning of "see" by adding the word "vision," which is not present in the Hebrew text.

Does Micah see (as the text says) the word of the Lord? Does he hear the word? Or does he see a vision? No matter how it comes to him, the opening verse of Micah assures us that Micah knows God's word and that God speaks through the prophet's mouth.

The name "Micah" is a shorter version of "Micaiah," which means "who is like Yahweh?" This is a very fitting name for this prophet. The promises at the end of the book (7:18-20) ask the question, "Who is a God like you?" Micah is not to be confused with the prophet Micaiah ben Imlah of 1 Kings 22, but he is certainly the prophet mentioned in Jer 26:18. The town of Moresheth is probably the same one mentioned in 1:14 and is located in the Shephalah, between the coastal plain and the hill country, about 25 miles southwest of Jerusalem. We have no further information about Micah beyond what we can deduce from this opening verse, from the prophetic oracles themselves, and from the brief mention in Jeremiah. (See Reflections at 1:2-7.)

MICAH 1:2-7, GOD'S CASE AGAINST ISRAEL

NIV

²Hear, O peoples, all of you,
 listen, O earth and all who are in it,
that the Sovereign LORD may witness against
  you,
 the Lord from his holy temple.

NRSV

² Hear, you peoples, all of you;
 listen, O earth, and all that is in it;
and let the Lord GOD be a witness against you,
 the Lord from his holy temple.
³ For lo, the LORD is coming out of his place,

NIV

³Look! The LORD is coming from his dwelling place;
    he comes down and treads the high places of the earth.
⁴The mountains melt beneath him
    and the valleys split apart,
like wax before the fire,
    like water rushing down a slope.
⁵All this is because of Jacob's transgression,
    because of the sins of the house of Israel.
What is Jacob's transgression?
    Is it not Samaria?
What is Judah's high place?
    Is it not Jerusalem?

⁶"Therefore I will make Samaria a heap of rubble,
    a place for planting vineyards.
I will pour her stones into the valley
    and lay bare her foundations.
⁷All her idols will be broken to pieces;
    all her temple gifts will be burned with fire;
    I will destroy all her images.
Since she gathered her gifts from the wages of prostitutes,
    as the wages of prostitutes they will again be used."

NRSV

and will come down and tread upon the high places of the earth.
⁴ Then the mountains will melt under him
    and the valleys will burst open,
like wax near the fire,
    like waters poured down a steep place.
⁵ All this is for the transgression of Jacob
    and for the sins of the house of Israel.
What is the transgression of Jacob?
    Is it not Samaria?
And what is the high place[a] of Judah?
    Is it not Jerusalem?
⁶ Therefore I will make Samaria a heap in the open country,
    a place for planting vineyards.
I will pour down her stones into the valley,
    and uncover her foundations.
⁷ All her images shall be beaten to pieces,
    all her wages shall be burned with fire,
    and all her idols I will lay waste;
for as the wages of a prostitute she gathered them,
    and as the wages of a prostitute they shall again be used.

a Heb *what are the high places*

COMMENTARY

Micah's first oracle begins with a summons to the peoples of the earth to pay attention, for Yahweh has convened a judicial proceeding and is testifying against them. In fact, following verses set out God's case against Samaria, capital of Israel's northern kingdom, with reference also to Judah and Jerusalem, who are guilty of similar offenses (1:5b). Why are other nations included in Yahweh's summons? God is God of the whole earth, not just these two small countries at the eastern end of the Mediterranean Sea. All the nations of the world are to heed how Yahweh punishes even those who would claim special favors from God. Surely, Yahweh will do no less to those who have been Israel's enemies. As Delbert Hillers observes, God's testimony against the nations ". . . . sets Yahweh's judgment on an individual nation in the context of his universal zeal to establish justice. The fate of God's own people is not the result of caprice, but the carrying out of a broader order."[9]

Verses 3-4 describe Yahweh's appearance (theophany) on earth and its awesome, frightening effects. One does not stand in God's presence without fear of annihilation. Even mountains melt and valleys burst open (1:4) when God comes down to tread upon the high places of the earth (1:3). There is a possible double-meaning to "high places," which could refer either to the mountains that are often associated with theophanies, or more specifically to the pagan shrines to fertility deities set up on high hills throughout the land.

All of this upheaval is a consequence of Israel's sins, manifested in its capital city (v. 5). The reference

9. Delbert R. Hillers, *Micah,* Hermeneia (Philadelphia: Fortress, 1984) 19.

to Jerusalem in v. 5*b* may have been added to the oracle subsequent to its composition. If so, it is an apt addition. Implicit in the text as it stands is the idea that Jerusalem should take particular warning from what happens to Samaria. Most of the rest of the book will address Judah/Jerusalem, because the southern kingdom has chosen to follow in the footsteps of its northern cousin.

In 1:6-7, God shifts roles from prosecuting attorney to judge and pronounces punishment on the guilty party. Samaria shall become ruins, its site reduced to farmland, its foundations exposed.

The destruction of idols and the reference to the wages of a prostitute (1:7) place special emphasis on Samaria's sin of idolatry in pursuing pagan religious practices condemned by the prophet Hosea and others. Jeremiah (3:6-10) and Ezekiel (chaps. 16 and 23) also will apply prostitution imagery to Samaria and Jerusalem, who sell themselves to gain favors from other nations. Though we cannot be absolutely certain what is meant by 1:7*b*, Micah appears to use this same metaphor for Samaria's sins and draws the conclusion that the impending destruction is fitting punishment for her offense.

REFLECTIONS

Already in the first seven verses of Micah, a number of theological issues demand our attention.

1. Who is a true prophet and who is not? Why is Micah remembered as one who received a special revelation so that the editor can say with confidence that these are the words of the Lord? Is it because what was predicted actually happened? The destruction of Samaria certainly occurred as Micah had said. The prophecies about the fate of Judah, however, did not happen until more than a century later.

There is ambiguity in the description of how the word comes to the prophet. The prophet sees, as do others, but somehow perceives deeper meaning in what is seen. The prophet hears, but may not know whether the message comes from outside, audible voices or from words that silently take form within the prophet's mind. Some prophets see visions, but the prophet's gift may be to see a word from God in the ordinary, not only in supernatural experiences of the deity. Neither the method of communication between God and the prophet nor the type or quality of his religious experience separates the true prophet from others who claim to speak for God. Perhaps Micah was remembered as a speaker of God's Word and not a false prophet because God's people remembered his message, and it has continued to speak to them in succeeding generations.

2. Although God is always present in the world, there are momentous times when God's presence is revealed in powerful and unforgettable ways. The faithful often long for some direct encounter with God to settle their uncertainties and give them some specific assistance, but the truth is that God's appearances are often more frightening than comforting. A typical reaction to a theophany in the Bible is to throw oneself on the ground in sudden and acute awareness of both one's sinfulness and one's weakness (e.g., Isa 6:1-5). God's presence among us will not necessarily make things better for us. People who do evil deeds to others and think they are getting away with it do not expect or want God to appear and interfere with their business. When God comes to execute justice, some people will be delivered and vindicated. Others will be punished or, at the least, prevented from further wrongdoing.

3. God is the God of the whole world. And yet God comes to us in the particular, through the history, writings, and promises of an ancient people who felt themselves to be in a special relationship with the one true God. How does God relate to those covenant people and to all other human beings who are part of God's creation? Should the people of the covenant get special favors? Or should they be punished even more severely than the others? Does God use some nations to bring judgment on other nations? Micah struggles with the question of how Israel relates to the other nations and how they all relate to God.

4. God is active in the world. God knows what is happening and will respond with action. Events are not simply a matter of chance or the working out of scientific laws of cause and effect or merely the result of human activity. God is involved in all that happens. No matter how sophisticated we become at explaining all phenomena in terms of the natural world, Micah (and the Bible in general) reminds us that God is a participant and not merely an observer who set up the system but no longer gets in the way. This principle can bring comfort and hope to those who wait for God to bring relief from their distress. It can also bring considerable difficulty when we are confronted with terrible events and wonder whether God has caused them or, at the least, is doing nothing to prevent or remove them.

5. Micah tells us that God punishes people for their sins. That is one way to explain the terrible prospects facing Israel while maintaining the belief that God is just and is active in the world. Many people have been hurt from assuming that senseless tragedy in their lives has been sent to them by a God who is punishing them for known or unknown sins. Others have so rejected this view that they act as if God is indifferent to their behavior and that they will never be accountable for their treatment of other people. It may be wrong to believe that one's personal suffering is necessarily a case of God's punishment. It may be equally wrong to assume that a God of justice, who identifies with the pain and suffering of the world, will never bring punishment on those who have profoundly hurt those whom God loves.

MICAH 1:8-16, A CALL TO LAMENT

NIV

[8] Because of this I will weep and wail;
    I will go about barefoot and naked.
I will howl like a jackal
    and moan like an owl.
[9] For her wound is incurable;
    it has come to Judah.
It[a] has reached the very gate of my people,
    even to Jerusalem itself.
[10] Tell it not in Gath[b];
    weep not at all.[c]
In Beth Ophrah[d]
    roll in the dust.
[11] Pass on in nakedness and shame,
    you who live in Shaphir.[e]
Those who live in Zaanan[f]
    will not come out.
Beth Ezel is in mourning;
    its protection is taken from you.

a9 Or *He*   b10 *Gath* sounds like the Hebrew for *tell.*   c10 Hebrew; Septuagint may suggest *not in Acco.* The Hebrew for *in Acco* sounds like the Hebrew for *weep.*   d10 *Beth Ophrah* means *house of dust.* e11 *Shaphir* means *pleasant.*   f11 *Zaanan* sounds like the Hebrew for *come out.*

NRSV

[8] For this I will lament and wail;
    I will go barefoot and naked;
I will make lamentation like the jackals,
    and mourning like the ostriches.
[9] For her wound[a] is incurable.
    It has come to Judah;
it has reached to the gate of my people,
    to Jerusalem.

[10] Tell it not in Gath,
    weep not at all;
in Beth-leaphrah
    roll yourselves in the dust.
[11] Pass on your way,
    inhabitants of Shaphir,
    in nakedness and shame;
the inhabitants of Zaanan
    do not come forth;
Beth-ezel is wailing
    and shall remove its support from you.
[12] For the inhabitants of Maroth

a Gk Syr Vg: Heb *wounds*

NIV

¹²Those who live in Maroth^a writhe in pain,
        waiting for relief,
    because disaster has come from the LORD,
        even to the gate of Jerusalem.
¹³You who live in Lachish,^b
        harness the team to the chariot.
    You were the beginning of sin
        to the Daughter of Zion,
    for the transgressions of Israel
        were found in you.
¹⁴Therefore you will give parting gifts
        to Moresheth Gath.
    The town of Aczib^c will prove deceptive
        to the kings of Israel.
¹⁵I will bring a conqueror against you
        who live in Mareshah.^d
    He who is the glory of Israel
        will come to Adullam.
¹⁶Shave your heads in mourning
        for the children in whom you delight;
    make yourselves as bald as the vulture,
        for they will go from you into exile.

^a12 *Maroth* sounds like the Hebrew for *bitter.*   ^b13 *Lachish* sounds like the Hebrew for *team.*   ^c14 *Aczib* means *deception.*   ^d15 *Mareshah* sounds like the Hebrew for *conqueror.*

NRSV

        wait anxiously for good,
    yet disaster has come down from the LORD
        to the gate of Jerusalem.
¹³ Harness the steeds to the chariots,
        inhabitants of Lachish;
    it was the beginning of sin
        to daughter Zion,
    for in you were found
        the transgressions of Israel.
¹⁴ Therefore you shall give parting gifts
        to Moresheth-gath;
    the houses of Achzib shall be a deception
        to the kings of Israel.
¹⁵ I will again bring a conqueror upon you,
        inhabitants of Mareshah;
    the glory of Israel
        shall come to Adullam.
¹⁶ Make yourselves bald and cut off your hair
        for your pampered children;
    make yourselves as bald as the eagle,
        for they have gone from you into exile.

COMMENTARY

1:8-9. Biblical prophets are very much involved in the messages they proclaim. They do not enjoy speaking about terrible things that will happen to God's people. Perhaps it is a little easier for Micah (who is from the southern kingdom of Judah) to pronounce doom on the northern kingdom of Israel. But it soon becomes clear to him that what has happened to Samaria will also befall his own people. Judah and Jerusalem are hopelessly sick with an incurable wound (v. 9). It has reached the very gates of Jerusalem (v. 9). The disaster is both imminent and inevitable. Because Micah sees this so clearly, he is moved to lament, howling and wailing like the mournful sounds of the jackal or the ostrich (the NIV understands this to be an owl, v. 8).

Prophets often used the lament form to express their prophecies about coming disaster. They lamented as if something horrible had already happened. For their listeners, the message was contained both in the words and in the acting out of the lament. Certainly, the prophet would attract attention by acting as if everything had gone wrong when most people still thought that things were going along quite nicely. Although the prophets, like Micah, often used the lament form in a formal way to announce their doom oracles, their expressions of pain and mourning were not simply a superficial act. Their pain was real. Micah's statement that he would go barefoot and naked (v. 8) reminds one of Isaiah 20, in which Isaiah walks naked and barefoot for three years as a visible sign of the shame and exile that would come to Egypt and Ethiopia.

1:10-15. Micah announces his lament in 1:8. At the end of this section, he will invite Jerusalem to join in his lament over her children, the Judean towns whose destruction he has proclaimed or predicted in intervening verses (1:16). This is probably the most difficult Hebrew text in the book of Micah, and its many corruptions and obscurities have confounded the best efforts of textual critics. Though certainties elude us, we can offer some observations about its meaning and function.

Most commentators agree that Micah's lament bewails the plight of certain fortified towns and villages lying in the path of an actual or imagined invading army. Several of these towns are mentioned nowhere else in the Bible and are unknown to us (e.g., Shaphir, Maroth, Beth-ezel, and probably Zaanan). Of the towns we can identify, all are located in the Shephalah, southwest of Jerusalem. Second Kings 18:13 (= Isa 36:1) recounts that in the fourteenth year of King Hezekiah, Sennacherib, King of Assyria, captured a number of Judean cities (forty-six according to Sennacherib's Annals) before besieging Jerusalem. In the view of many scholars, Micah's lament fits the historical setting of Sennacherib's campaign against Judah in 701 BCE.[10] Others contend that Micah has simply chosen towns in no particular order whose names can, through puns, be made to bear threatening meanings.[11] Perhaps one need not choose one of these options to the exclusion of the other. I am inclined toward the former, without dismissing the latter.

One is puzzled by the beginning of v. 11, which directs the listeners not to tell of the coming judgment in Gath or to weep. This seems a contradiction if the point is to call people to lamentation (v. 16). Some scholars have tried to solve this difficulty by assuming a faulty text and suggesting some emendations.[12] Others have read the text as is, but have suggested other explanations. The lament over the deaths of Saul and Jonathan in 2 Sam 1:20 has the same imperative: "Tell it not in Gath." The point there is to deprive the Philistines of the occasion to exult (2 Sam 1:20*b*), though Israel is clearly instructed to lament this tragedy. Perhaps this connection to David's lament over Saul and Jonathan has influ-

enced the present form of this difficult text in Micah 1:10.

In some cases, the significance of Micah's word-plays is rather obvious, if one looks at the Hebrew word behind the English translation. In other cases, we can only guess what the prophet had in mind. In the most clearly identifiable puns, the sound of the name of the city sounds like a Hebrew word that helps to describe the approaching calamity. Some of the best examples of this are Beth-leaphrah (בית לעפרה *bêt lě'aprâ*; Beth Ophrah in the NIV), which in Hebrew sounds like "dust" (עפר *'āpār*); Zaanan (צאנן *ṣa'ănān*), whose Hebrew sounds like "to go out" (יצא *yāṣā'*); Maroth (מרות *mārôt*), which sounds like "bitter" (מרה *mōrâ*); Lachish (לכיש *lākîš*), which sounds like "to a team of horses" (לרכש *lārekeš*); and Achzib (אכזיב *'akzîb*), which sounds like "a deceiving brook" (אכזב *'akzāb*). Although we have difficulty detecting the precise meaning of each of these words, the overall message of destruction to the cities of Judah is clear. Further, even though the text seems to have been damaged to some extent in transmission, we still are impressed by the literary skill of the prophet who put together this masterful description of the bleak future awaiting the people of Judah.

1:16. This section closes with an invitation to Jerusalem (and hence to the people she represents) to join Micah in his lament. The severity of the situation calls for extreme ritual acts of lamentation: cutting the hair, and then cutting it again until one is bald as an eagle (or "vulture," NIV). It is uncertain who are the "children of your delight [בני תענוגיך *běnê ta'ănûgāyik*; or "pleasure"]." The NRSV makes a negative judgment about the children by using the translation "pampered children," an interpretation that goes beyond what the text actually says. The NIV's "children in whom you delight" is better. Some have said that these "children" may represent the towns and cities marked for destruction in the preceding succession of word-plays. Others have suggested that this may be an application of this passage to a later time, when Jerusalem had fallen to Babylon and many were sent into exile.

10. See James L. Mays, *Micah,* OTL (Philadelphia: Westminster, 1976) 52-54.

11. Leslie C. Allen, *The Books of Joel, Obadiah, Jonah, and Micah,* NICOT (Grand Rapids: Eerdmans, 1976) 278.

12. Mays, *Micah,* 51.

REFLECTIONS

1. Are there times when repentance is no longer possible, when so much has already happened and so many processes have been put in motion that no matter how people respond to the prophet, nothing can change the outcome? Micah says that Jerusalem's wound is incurable (1:8). If the prophet has already reached that conclusion, then what is the point of preaching doom to the people? What motivates the prophet to continue to warn about what is to come when it is assumed that no one will hear and, even if someone does, it is too late to stop the inevitable? Micah is not the only prophet who had to deal with this question. Jeremiah tries to intercede for the people until God finally tells him that it is too late. God will punish no matter what anyone does (Jer 11:14; 15:1). God tells Ezekiel that the people will not listen to him. Nevertheless, he must speak the word that God has put in his mouth. Whether they hear it or not, they will know that there has been a prophet among them (Ezek 2:5). The message may be of more value to future generations, who seek to understand what God is doing in their time, than it was to those to whom it was first addressed.

When we speak to individuals, congregations, politicians, or environmental polluters about dangers that lie ahead, what is our motivation? Is it to teach them so that changes can be made in time to avert the disasters we foresee? What do we do if they do not respond but go ahead with their destructive behavior? Do we persist in our message, against all odds, simply because it is the truth and needs to be spoken by someone? Maybe there is a time, later on, "after the exile," when people's eyes will be opened. Although it is too late to prevent some suffering, previously neglected words of warning may yet provide insight about how to avoid future pain. Any of us who are concerned to make a better world and avoid suffering can identify with the prophet's task.

2. To be a prophet is a very painful calling. The words that are spoken may be so horrible that the speaker is moved to tears by them. The prophet's pain is even worse than that of others because he sees with such clarity what lies ahead. Others bury their heads in the sand and rely on false assurances that are always available from imitation prophets who are eager to please. Further, the bad news uttered by the prophet will soon arouse the hostility of those who do not like the message and, therefore, hate the messenger.

Biblical prophets felt great compassion for their people. If they hated those whose behavior they condemned, their task would have been easier. In our day, we should beware of prophets of doom who dislike the people they criticize, who predict destruction and almost enjoy the thought of what they describe. Sometimes the biblical prophets, like Jeremiah, were pushed beyond their capacity to remain compassionate to those who responded to their message with ridicule and hatred. But Jeremiah did not begin his ministry with such bitterness, and neither did Micah or other speakers of God's truth who were compelled to speak what was true even when it hurt.

3. Names are very important in the Hebrew Bible. Sometimes names are given to persons or to places as a way to sum up an event that has occurred or a promise that is given (see, e.g., the naming of Jacob's children in Genesis 30; Hosea's children in Hosea 1; Isa 7:14).

In the list of cities in 1:10-15, the prophet reinforces his calamitous message with a clever use of words. Even though there are translation difficulties in this passage, we can see considerable care in the writing of this oracle. The words have been chosen carefully so that the names of the cities reveal something about their own disastrous future. Merely to speak the name of the city is to prophesy what will happen to it. Micah 1:10-15 is a creative literary piece, regardless of the actual historical circumstance of these cities and their ultimate fate.

MICAH 2:1-5, LOSS OF INHERITANCE IS GOD'S RESPONSE TO INJUSTICE

NIV

2 Woe to those who plan iniquity,
to those who plot evil on their beds!
At morning's light they carry it out
because it is in their power to do it.
[2]They covet fields and seize them,
and houses, and take them.
They defraud a man of his home,
a fellowman of his inheritance.

[3]Therefore, the LORD says:

"I am planning disaster against this people,
from which you cannot save yourselves.
You will no longer walk proudly,
for it will be a time of calamity.
[4]In that day men will ridicule you;
they will taunt you with this mournful song:
'We are utterly ruined;
my people's possession is divided up.
He takes it from me!
He assigns our fields to traitors.'"

[5]Therefore you will have no one in the assembly
of the LORD
to divide the land by lot.

NRSV

2 Alas for those who devise
wickedness
and evil deeds[a] on their beds!
When the morning dawns, they perform it,
because it is in their power.
[2] They covet fields, and seize them;
houses, and take them away;
they oppress householder and house,
people and their inheritance.
[3] Therefore thus says the LORD:
Now, I am devising against this family an evil
from which you cannot remove your necks;
and you shall not walk haughtily,
for it will be an evil time.
[4] On that day they shall take up a taunt song
against you,
and wail with bitter lamentation,
and say, "We are utterly ruined;
the LORD[b] alters the inheritance of my
people;
how he removes it from me!
Among our captors[c] he parcels out our fields."
[5] Therefore you will have no one to cast the line
by lot
in the assembly of the LORD.

[a] Cn: Heb *work evil*   [b] Heb *he*   [c] Cn: Heb *the rebellious*

COMMENTARY

2:1-2. The judgment oracle in Mic 2:1-5 exhibits the prophet's predilection for matching divine punishment to human crime: the plight inflicted by wrongdoers will redound upon themselves. It begins with an "alas" saying, a form common to laments over the deceased (and to Israel's prophetic literature; see, e.g., Amos 6:1, 4; Isa 5:8-24; 10:1-4). In this context, the cry introduces an indictment of those who lie awake at night devising new and creative ways to steal the land and homes of others, and then arise in the morning and carry out

their covetous plans without restraint or moral compunction. (Isaiah 5:8 likewise indicts those who "join house to house, who add field to field. . . .") The word "covet" (חמד *ḥāmad*) in v. 2 is the same word that appears in the Decalogue (Exod 20:17 and Deut 5:21). Hence, their land-grabbing strategies violate the very heart of the covenant between God and Israel. What begins as an inner attitude leads to terrible acts. Such oppressors, Micah charges, think themselves free to take what they want. But they shall soon discover that Yahweh has plans for them, even as they have plans for satisfying their greed. The same Hebrew root (חמד *ḥmd*) is used for the plans of the wicked and God's plans for them (vv. 1 and 3).

Land and land ownership held a special place in Israel's traditions. According to Joshua 14–21, the land was divided among Israel's tribes and families, but God remained its true owner. It was handed down from generation to generation as a sacred trust; and laws were established to prohibit seizure of another's property. Hence, as Delbert Hillers observes, the actions of those whom Micah indicts were "an assault on the basic structure of the people of God":

The economic and social ideal of ancient Israel was of a nation of free landholders—not debt-slaves, share-croppers, or hired workers—secure in possession, as a grant from Yahweh, of enough land to keep their families. "Each under his own vine and his own fig tree" summarizes the ideal. Other ideals, such as jus-tice, mutual love and fidelity, a close-knit family, and so on, depended on achievement of this sort of eco-nomic security. If the family land was lost, little other economic opportunity remained.[13]

2:3-5. The prophetic indictment of vv. 1-2 is followed in vv. 3-5 by the announcement of a three-fold punishment (introduced by "there-fore"). Those who have abused their power will no longer walk with pride. Rather, Yahweh in-tends to bend them beneath the yoke of captivity. They will suffer humiliation as the victors mock

them with taunt songs and parodies of their own laments (v. 4). The people's inheritance, once divided among the tribes of Israel, will be par-celled out to others (v. 4). Who are these "cap-tors" (NRSV) or "traitors" (NIV) who will receive portions of Israel's inheritance. Some scholars have thought that Micah had Assyria in mind, expecting that the nation would fall to Sen-nacherib. Others have concluded that whenever the text speaks of loss of land and exile, the reference must be to the later Babylonian conquest in 586 BCE and, therefore, a subsequent addition to Micah's oracle from more than a century later.[14] While a few texts in Micah surely reflect a time after the fall of Jerusalem, we cannot assert with absolute certainty that such is the case here.

Once the land has been lost and given to others, there will be no one in the assembly of the Lord to divide the land by lot. These words may have reminded Micah's listeners of the story of the conquest of Canaan under Joshua. Accord-ing to Joshua 18, after the land lay subdued before them, Joshua sent out men to explore, to divide the land into seven parts, and to bring back descriptions of each division. When they returned, "Joshua cast lots for them in Shiloh before the LORD; and there Joshua apportioned the land to the Israelites, to each a portion" (Josh 18:10 NRSV). What was done by Joshua at the birth of the nation will now be undone. The land will go to someone else.

13. Hillers, *Micah*, 33.

14. E.g., Mays, *Micah*, 65.

REFLECTIONS

1. Does the punishment always fit the crime? Prophets like Micah make a forceful case for a just God who is active in the world. Those assertions about God are often challenged when terrible things happen in a world that is supposedly governed by a good God. Micah's answer to that challenge is to hold firm his belief in God's justice and power, but to give a rationale for the punitive action that God will take. God is moved to punish the people because of great provocation from them. God is in control even when events take a nasty turn. If God is not working for justice, then we are all at risk in a world where nothing makes sense except the whims (and covetousness) of those with the power and determination to turn their desires into reality.

We sometimes categorize the prophets of the Bible as purveyors of a very dismal message of punishment sent by a harsh and unyielding God. Oracles of doom dominate the message of the pre-exilic prophets. It was their unwanted and unhappy task to interpret terrible events and see the hand of God even in what is unpleasant. If we follow their pattern and understand all disasters (for individuals, for groups, and for whole nations) to be the result of God's action against human sin, we run the risk of oversimplification. Micah knew that many people suffer not because of God's doing but because of the evil done by other human beings. Those singled out in 2:1-5 (and again in chap. 3) are particularly guilty and will pay for their sin in ways that are exactly right for their crimes. But Micah has a realistic view of the corporate inter-relationships of society. He knows that many innocent people will also suffer along with the guilty when the inevitable punishment comes.

The punishment does fit the crime. God is just, and God is at work. In this world, however, sometimes the innocent suffer and the evil prosper. A universal application of a cause-and-effect theory of retribution will not explain all the suffering of the world. Nevertheless, the prophet's message of a just God who will not tolerate abuse of others remains as a hope for the future, if not yet a present reality.

2. Although Christians do not identify fully with the OT promises about land and the tragedy of losing one's inheritance, this area is worth exploring more fully. One needs only to open the newspaper to see continuing battles between various ethnic groups over their attachment to the land (e.g, Northern Ireland, the former Yugoslavia, indigenous peoples in the Americas or Australia, and the ancient land of Israel itself). Palestinians and Jews exchange assertions that God gave them the land thousands of years ago. For many in our day, a close connection exists between identity and ownership of the land. In the late twentieth century, in the North American Midwest, many farms that had been owned by the same family for over a century were lost to bankers and large corporations. Lives were shattered and consumed by guilt and shame because those who had been entrusted with the legacy of past generations lost it. In some cases, that guilt was justified, but not always, and not to the extent that it afflicted these farmers.

These examples point to the continuing, powerful symbolism of land and property in an increasingly urban world. When those ancient land grabbers, whom Micah condemns, seized the property of the weak and the vulnerable, they were robbing people of their life, their soul, their identity.

MICAH 2:6-11, FALSE PROPHETS PREACH FALSE ASSURANCE

NIV

[6]"Do not prophesy," their prophets say.
  "Do not prophesy about these things;
  disgrace will not overtake us."
[7]Should it be said, O house of Jacob:
  "Is the Spirit of the LORD angry?
  Does he do such things?"

  "Do not my words do good
  to him whose ways are upright?
[8]Lately my people have risen up
  like an enemy.
You strip off the rich robe
  from those who pass by without a care,
  like men returning from battle.

NRSV

[6] "Do not preach"—thus they preach—
  "one should not preach of such things;
  disgrace will not overtake us."
[7] Should this be said, O house of Jacob?
  Is the LORD's patience exhausted?
  Are these his doings?
  Do not my words do good
  to one who walks uprightly?
[8] But you rise up against my people[a] as an
      enemy;
  you strip the robe from the peaceful,[b]
  from those who pass by trustingly

[a] Cn: Heb *But yesterday my people rose*   [b] Cn: Heb *from before a garment*

NIV

⁹You drive the women of my people
  from their pleasant homes.
You take away my blessing
  from their children forever.
¹⁰Get up, go away!
  For this is not your resting place,
because it is defiled,
  it is ruined, beyond all remedy.
¹¹If a liar and deceiver comes and says,
  'I will prophesy for you plenty of wine and
    beer,'
  he would be just the prophet for this people!"

NRSV

  with no thought of war.
⁹ The women of my people you drive out
  from their pleasant houses;
from their young children you take away
  my glory forever.
¹⁰ Arise and go;
  for this is no place to rest,
because of uncleanness that destroys
  with a grievous destruction.ᵃ
¹¹ If someone were to go about uttering empty
    falsehoods,
  saying, "I will preach to you of wine and
    strong drink,"
  such a one would be the preacher for this
    people!

ᵃ Meaning of Heb uncertain

COMMENTARY

This interesting passage gives us a glimpse of the opposition that faced Micah and his message. The text is very difficult to translate, particularly vv. 8 and 10, as is apparent when one compares translations. Micah begins by quoting his opponents' command not to preach negative and despairing words (v. 6) and their argument that a patient and just God would not do the terrible things the prophet proclaims (v. 7). Micah responds that they have violated God's justice and can no longer count on divine patience and their special relationship with God to insulate them from the punishment that is coming (v. 8). Though the text is not entirely clear in vv. 8-10, Micah describes in greater detail the offenses they have committed. The list sounds similar to what Micah said in vv. 1-5, condemning their theft of property and possessions. They have acted as enemies to their own people, and the consequences fall most heavily upon the innocent, the women, and the children. Micah concludes this section with a sarcastic comment about what kind of preachers would be welcomed by these people (v. 11). They want someone who will speak falsehood, who will promise what they want to hear, who will dull their sensitivities with false

optimism just as one escapes reality under the influence of wine and beer.

The prophets dared to criticize those in authority, whether economic, political, or religious leaders. And so it is not surprising that the Bible contains many references to opponents of prophets. The command not to preach reminds us of Amaziah's warning to Amos (Amos 7:10-13) not to prophesy in Bethel because it was the "king's sanctuary." The word translated as "preach" or "prophesy" (נטף *nāṭap*) in vv. 6 and 11 is not the most common Hebrew word for "prophesy" (נבא *nābāʾ*) but is sometimes used in parallel with that word and can be considered a synonym (e.g., Ezek 21:2; Amos 7:16).

We cannot be sure exactly who are Micah's opponents in this debate. Perhaps they are the prophets who have sold their integrity for the rewards of pleasing their audience. They will hear more from Micah in the next chapter. More likely, the opponents are those persons whom Micah condemns as robbers in vv. 1-5 and again in vv. 8-10. They have relied on God's promise of security as interpreted by the prophets and preachers of the time. They are convinced that Micah must be wrong. God made a covenant with them, promising to protect them from their enemies. Do not the ancient traditions teach about a forgiving and merciful God, slow to anger and willing to forgive (see, e.g., Exod 34:6-7, which Micah's opponents may have known well)? Micah seems to preach against God's promises, destroying the people's morale, distorting the message of hope. And so Micah's challengers see themselves as God's defenders over against this negative upstart, this prophet who speaks only of doom.

When catastrophe strikes, even when it is understood as God's punishment, innocent people suffer along with the guilty. Verse 9 speaks specifically about women and children who will bear the suffering that results from the sins of others. Women will be driven from their homes. Young children will lose their inheritance, their future. Micah is filled with righteous anger not only because the perpetrators of evil bring punishment on themselves (which is just, after all), but also because they have brought extreme pain, hardship, and suffering to the innocent.

Verse 10 contains another reference to the upcoming punishment as removal from the land,

Israel's inheritance from God. The word for "rest" (מנוחה *měnûḥâ*) in v. 10 has a specialized use in conjunction with the promised land (see Deut 12:9; Ps 95:11) and is virtually a synonym for the word "inheritance" (נחלה *naḥălâ*) in v. 2.[15] For Hillers,[16] the oppressors' exploitation of the poor itself defiles the land (Num 35:34; Deut 21:23). Mays claims that v. 10 has been reinterpreted by redactors in light of the Babylonian exile; hence, "uncleanness" refers to idolatry, a major cause of the expulsion of Judah's population from its inheritance (Jer 19:13; Ezek 22:5, 15; 24:13; 36:25, 29; 39:24).[17] The condemnation of uncleanness and defilement (v. 10) is language usually used to describe idolatry. So the sins of Judah include social injustices against other people as well as the practice of false religion. The two usually go together.

15. James L. Mays, *Micah*, OTL (Philadelphia: Westminster, 1976) 71-72.
16. Delbert R. Hillers, *Micah*, Hermeneia (Philadelphia: Fortress, 1984) 36-37.
17. Mays, *Micah*, 71-72.

REFLECTIONS

God's people long for assurance that God will not abandon them when they do evil things. But if they become too complacent in that assurance, God will remind them that disobedience has negative consequences. On the one hand, God is gracious, accepting, forgiving. God does not ask us to meet any impossible standard in order to be included and loved. Overly scrupulous persons need not drive themselves to despair trying to be good enough to persuade God to love them. On the other hand, God cares deeply about how we live in relationship with God, with other human beings, and with the whole creation. When we engage in destructive behavior, God is hurt and (dare we say?) angry. A God who is never angry in response to human sin would be a God who does not care, who lacks compassion, who is willing to turn away from the creation and ignore its pain.

Both parts of this picture of God are true. In some ways, Micah's opponents are right when they emphasize the long-suffering, patient God. And surely Micah is also right. But who is right at a particular time and place? What is the right message for Micah's time or for our own time? Too often people fix their attention on the wrong message for them. The perpetrators of injustice in Micah's day do not need more words of assurance about a God who accepts them without any qualifications, as if it follows from that assertion that God will ignore their evil deeds. Likewise, the person who is tormented by guilt and shame does not need to hear more about how worthless and inadequate he or she is. Rather, that person needs the strong message of acceptance by a gracious God. These images of God may seem to be conflicting, and it is hard to hold them together without over- or underemphasizing one or the other. People are conditioned to hear only part of the message. The truth that is the right word for me at one time in my life may not be the right word at another time. How does one sort all this out? It is not easy. It is particularly difficult for preachers who are called to speak an appropriate word of God to a variety of human situations.

Micah's opponents were not entirely wrong. They understood part of the message. But for that time and place, Micah was the true prophet. Those who spoke only of peace and security in the face of human evil and impending doom were not true messengers of God's word. The question remains for students of the book of Micah as to whether it was ever the right time for Micah himself to speak of promise and hope instead of doom and destruction. Or are the words of hope, placed here and there in the book, the work of others who express a new word for a later time?

MICAH 2:12-13, A WORD OF HOPE BREAKS IN

NIV	NRSV
12"I will surely gather all of you, O Jacob; I will surely bring together the remnant of Israel. I will bring them together like sheep in a pen, like a flock in its pasture; the place will throng with people. 13One who breaks open the way will go up before them; they will break through the gate and go out. Their king will pass through before them, the LORD at their head."	12 I will surely gather all of you, O Jacob, I will gather the survivors of Israel; I will set them together like sheep in a fold, like a flock in its pasture; it will resound with people. 13 The one who breaks out will go up before them; they will break through and pass the gate, going out by it. Their king will pass on before them, the LORD at their head.

COMMENTARY

For a majority of commentators, Mic 2:12-13 constitutes an oracle of salvation in the midst of pronouncements of gloom. Similar to Mic 4:6-8 and consistent with other, exilic expressions of hope (e.g., Jer 23:3; 31:8-10; Ezekiel 34; Isa 40:11), it depicts Yahweh as a shepherd who gathers the flock (Israel) from the fold of captivity and leads it to freedom. The following commentary adopts this line of interpretation. We note, however, that Mays understands the text differently, arguing that "YHWH is not 'the breaker' who breaks walls of captivity to rescue his flock, but the one who breaks down the fortified gate of Jerusalem and leads them out through it . . . The siege and fall of the city is the work of YHWH as King of Israel. The exile is a manifestation of his sovereignty and not his defeat."[18]

18. Ibid., 75-76.

If, as most commentators aver, 2:12-13 is an expression of hope, why is it located at this point in the book, surrounded by doom oracles?

The first three chapters of Micah are primarily messages of impending destruction. So why this interruption in the flow at the end of chapter 2? Did Micah ever speak these words? If he did, were they placed here by him or by someone who put the book together in its present form? Are they the product of a later redactor, inserted because in a time of great suffering readers of the book needed to be reminded that God's last word is one of hope, not complete abandonment and perpetual punishment?

There are at least three possibilities concerning the authorship of this passage: (1) It was written by Micah, who perhaps had in mind Judah's deliverance from complete destruction at the hands of Sennacherib, the invading Assyrian king, in 701 BCE. (2) Micah wrote it, but at a time later than the other oracles in chaps. 1–3. According to this view, it represents a different period in the prophet's thinking, most likely related to the fact that Jerusalem did not fall to Sennacherib after all. Its present placement is the work of later editors during the book's final stage of literary composition.[19] (3) The material dates from a time much later than Micah, most likely from the exilic period. It fits that historical situation and has many parallels to other prophetic expressions of hope from that time.[20]

Whether one identifies Micah as the speaker of these words or not, the question remains as to why they should be placed here. Some scholars (including Allen and Limburg) view these verses as an important clue to the structure of the book.[21] They divide the book into three parts: chaps. 1–2; 3–5; and 6–7. Each section begins with the Hebrew imperative "Hear" (שמעו šim'û; or "Listen"). And each moves from doom to salvation, from punishment to hope. This movement is very common in biblical prophetic collections and in lament psalms (e.g., Psalms 3; 13; 28; 55). The book progresses from doom to hope three times. Others divide the book between chaps. 3 and 4 for similar reasons. Most of the bad news appears in the first three chapters, and most of the hope is in the rest of the book, again flowing from punishment to salvation.

There is no clear explanation for the presence of this word of hope in the midst of doom oracles. One may suspect that it was not placed there by Micah but is the work of some later editors of the book. Although they accepted Micah's interpretation of their history, the unrelenting condemnations of the book almost cried out for a word of hope in the midst of the tragedy. Is God going to get us out of this dreadful situation? Is this the end of our story? Why wait until the end of chapter 3 or the end of the book for a word of hope? Tell us now that God remains on our side and will deliver us from pain and suffering, whether we deserve it or not. The book of Lamentations proclaims a word of hope in the midst of terrible circumstances (see Lam 3:19-33). For readers of Lamentations, and possibly also for exilic readers of Micah, the occasion for lament had not yet ended. They did not know how the story would turn out. A reminder that God would not leave them forever in their present state could give them hope.

19. Leslie C. Allen, *The Books of Joel, Obadiah, Jonah, and Micah*, NICOT (Grand Rapids: Eerdmans, 1976) 301.
20. Mays, *Micah*, 76.
21. Allen, *The Books of Joel, Obadiah, Jonah, and Micah*, 257-58; James Limburg, *Hosea–Micah*, Interpretation (Atlanta: John Knox, 1988) 159.

REFLECTIONS

How does one speak of hope to people who see no future, no way out, nothing but more of the same or worse? Like Micah, we may try to analyze the situation. How did we get into this mess? Whose fault is it? Can we learn something so that it will not happen again? Or we can enter into the lament with those who suffer, empathizing with them, helping them to find both words and permission to articulate their devastation. All this—our rationalizing about the cause and our willingness to hear the complaint—may in some subtle ways help to rebuild hope.

But can we be more direct, more specific? What can we promise? Perhaps our listeners are in such despair that they discount our cheerful words of hope as trivial, false optimism, or unrealistic. Can we confidently assert that the war will finally end, that age-old hostilities will cease, that an individual can change lifelong patterns of behavior, that the rains will come (or stop) or the cancer will disappear or God will act in response to our prayers? Some days our efforts to speak a word of hope will be met with some success. We will see signs of new courage and confidence as we go forward into the unknown. At other times our best efforts may be met with indifference, even hostility, as if we have not realized just how bad things really are. Whether Micah ever spoke direct words of hope, his book raises for us the very important question of how and when to speak of a future that, in its immediate prospects, seems only gloomy.

MICAH 3:1-12, AGAINST RULERS, PRIESTS, AND PROPHETS

OVERVIEW

Chapter 3 contains a ringing indictment of the leaders of society, the establishment, the "pillars" of the community. They have the responsibility for leading the people in a way that would ensure their safety and well-being. Instead, they made life miserable for the people and brought the whole nation to the brink of a terrible catastrophe. The chapter divides itself neatly into three parts: vv.

1-4, words against the political and judicial leaders; vv. 5-8, words against the prophets and other recipients of special revelation; and vv. 9-12, a summary condemnation of all leaders who have failed, closing with Micah's astounding prediction that the sacred city of Jerusalem will become a pile of ruins.

Micah 3:1-4, Condemnation of Rulers

NIV	NRSV
3 Then I said, "Listen, you leaders of Jacob, 　you rulers of the house of Israel. Should you not know justice, ² you who hate good and love evil; who tear the skin from my people 　and the flesh from their bones; ³who eat my people's flesh, 　strip off their skin 　and break their bones in pieces; who chop them up like meat for the pan, 　like flesh for the pot?" ⁴Then they will cry out to the LORD, 　but he will not answer them. At that time he will hide his face from them 　because of the evil they have done.	**3** And I said: 　Listen, you heads of Jacob 　and rulers of the house of Israel! Should you not know justice?— ² you who hate the good and love the evil, who tear the skin off my people,ᵃ 　and the flesh off their bones; ³ who eat the flesh of my people, 　flay their skin off them, break their bones in pieces, 　and chop them up like meatᵇ in a kettle, 　like flesh in a caldron. ⁴ Then they will cry to the LORD, 　but he will not answer them; he will hide his face from them at that time, 　because they have acted wickedly. *a* Heb *from them*　*b* Gk: Heb *as*

COMMENTARY

The chapter begins "And I said," as if Micah were reporting at a later time about some earlier event in his ministry. The phrase seems out of place at the beginning of this chapter. Some interpreters dismiss it as a later addition for which we have no explanation. Others regard it as a relic of an autobiographical section (such as Hos 3:1-5 or Isaiah 6) that has now been lost. If one accepts that Mic 2:12-13 was inserted into the book at a later time, then it is possible that this opening phrase links Micah's confrontation with evildoers in 2:6-11 with the series of condemning oracles in chap. 3. Micah rejects their command that he cease preaching such a message uttering even more detailed words of accusation and fitting punishment.[22]

3:1-3. The people being addressed in vv. 1-4 are the rulers, the heads, the political and judicial leaders of the people. They were appointed to uphold the law, to see that all citizens were treated equally and fairly, regardless of their wealth or status within society. Micah asks the biting question, "Should you not know justice?" (v. 1*b*). No wonder that the covetous land grabbers of 2:1-5 have been so successful in their devious schemes. They have had the government authorities, particularly those who oversee the judicial system, on their side. Micah uses particularly offensive language to describe the viciousness of their action and its effect on the people (vv. 2*b*-3). They have acted like cannibals preparing other humans for a meal as a butcher tears, flays, breaks, and chops up animals. The language is probably not to be taken as a literal description, but as a dramatic way of describing the horrible

abuse committed by those who should have defended the rights of those less powerful than they. Micah's outrage is magnified by his identification with the people in their suffering, as seen again in his reference to them as "my people" in v. 3.

3:4. In each of the three sections of chap. 3, a description of the offense is followed by a pronouncement of the appropriate punishment. As already noted, Micah has a great sense of "poetic justice" such that the offenders' deeds turn back on them in ways that are just, even ironic. The rulers who failed to hear the cry of persons who came to them pleading for justice will soon experience God's refusal to answer their cry for help. Micah does not specify the nature of the calamity in v. 4; instead he emphasizes the turning of the tables on those who now need help. They will receive a response from God that is as indifferent as was their own. The Hebrew word for "cry out" (זעק *zā'aq*) is often used as a technical word for an appeal to a judge. It also expresses special pleas to God (as in Pss 22:5; 107:13, 19; 142:6). When anyone in dire straits cries for help, the absence or silence of God can be terrifying, leaving little reason to hope. Biblical laments express in many ways the fear that God will hide God's face and withdraw God's presence (see Pss 13:1; 27:7-10). Often, Yahweh's presence seems most elusive when it is most desired. According to Micah, this will surely be the fate of the unjust rulers. (See Reflections at 3:9-12.)

22. Mays, *Micah,* 77-78.

Micah 3:5-8, Judgment Against Prophets

NIV	NRSV

[5]This is what the LORD says:
"As for the prophets
  who lead my people astray,
if one feeds them,
  they proclaim 'peace';
if he does not,
  they prepare to wage war against him.
[6]Therefore night will come over you, without
      visions,
  and darkness, without divination.
The sun will set for the prophets,
  and the day will go dark for them.
	[5] Thus says the LORD concerning the prophets
	  who lead my people astray,
	who cry "Peace"
	  when they have something to eat,
	but declare war against those
	  who put nothing into their mouths.
	[6] Therefore it shall be night to you, without
	     vision,
	  and darkness to you, without revelation.
	The sun shall go down upon the prophets,
	  and the day shall be black over them;
	[7] the seers shall be disgraced,

NIV

⁷The seers will be ashamed
and the diviners disgraced.
They will all cover their faces
because there is no answer from God."

⁸But as for me, I am filled with power,
with the Spirit of the LORD,
and with justice and might,
to declare to Jacob his transgression,
to Israel his sin.

NRSV

and the diviners put to shame;
they shall all cover their lips,
for there is no answer from God.
⁸ But as for me, I am filled with power,
with the spirit of the LORD,
and with justice and might,
to declare to Jacob his transgression
and to Israel his sin.

COMMENTARY

3:5. In this section, Micah attacks people who claim to have a special revelation from God. They have misused their gifts, he says, selling them to the highest bidder. Those who can pay always receive a good word. Those who cannot put food in the mouths of the prophets become their enemies (v. 5). There are inferences to holy war in the Hebrew word that is translated as "to declare" (or "to prepare for" [קדש‎ *qādaš*]) war in v. 5. The prophets are more receptive to what people want to hear than they are to God's actual message. After all, there are no material rewards for harsh words like those spoken by Micah. The victims of an unjust system of government and religion cannot pay the prophets to speak up on their behalf. The wealthy and powerful people, by contrast, are able to reward those who perform their dirty work. Further, they can make it very unpleasant for anyone who challenges them.

3:6-7. In his recital of punishment, Micah uses several different words for these supposed bearers of a revealed word from God. The technical word for "prophet" (נביא‎ *nābî'*) appears in vv. 5, 6, and 11. (It was not used in 2:6-11.) This word likely originated with the emergence of kingship in Israel to describe persons who advised the king about God's will (e.g., stories of Samuel and Saul in 1 Sam 9-15, Nathan and David in 2 Samuel 12, Micaiah ben Imlah and Ahab in 1 Kings 22). The word "seer" (חזה‎ *hōzeh*, v. 7) probably had a distinct meaning in earlier times, but in many biblical texts it functions as virtually a synonym for "prophet" and is often used in parallel with that word (*nābî'*). The "diviner" (קסם‎ *qōsēm*, v. 7) is usually condemned because of the methods

that he used to receive a divine word. These methods (which included the reading of various omens—sticks, arrows, livers of animals, astrology, etc.) were generally considered by Israel (or at least by the biblical authors) to be foreign practices that were unacceptable ways to receive a revelation from God. The prophets usually received their messages in more subjective ways (dreams, voices, visions, etc.) rather than by manipulating exterior devices. In this passage, Micah seems not to make these distinctions. He lumps together all intermediaries in the same condemnation. Whether their gifts of perception, clairvoyance, and predicting the future are legitimate is beside the point. Micah is less concerned with their method than with their willingness to sell themselves, their skills, and their influence for a price.

Again, the punishment will fit the crime. They will remain in darkness with no light, no vision, no revelation. Since they have ignored God's authentic word in their efforts to please those who reward them, they will no longer receive a word from God. Prophets with no vision, no revelation, no divine words to convey to the people have lost their reason for being. Nothing is left for them but to be publicly disgraced and to live out their lives in shame. The meaning of "cover their lips" (v. 7 NRSV), which is a literal translation, is uncertain. The NIV translates the Hebrew as "cover their faces" to continue the theme of shame and disgrace, even though that is not precisely what the text says. The phrase may assert that they have no word to speak. Some scholars have pointed to a few passages that indicate that covering the lips is a ritual of mourning (see Lev 13:45; Ezek 24:17, 22).[23]

3:8. Micah now steps forward to distinguish himself from these other intermediaries whom he has just condemned. Biblical prophets were not embarrassed to speak forthrightly about their calling. They were often challenged to defend themselves against those who questioned their status as authentic prophets of the Lord. They *knew* that God had called them for a special task. They did not claim any special gifts for themselves apart from the certainty that God had called them. Often, in accounts of their call, the prophets protested their inadequacy (see, e.g., Isa 6:5; Jer 1:6; also Moses in Exod 3:13–4:17). Micah was different from false purveyors of a divine message because (he asserted) he was filled with power, the Spirit of the Lord, justice, and might. None of his opponents could honestly claim all that. Further, his specific assignment was to declare to Israel its sin. Micah was not doing this for personal gain. God's word had found him, and he could not back away from the task God had given him. We have no account of Micah's call (compare Isa 6:1-8; Jer 1:4-10; Ezekiel 1–3; Hosea 1–3; possibly Amos 7:1-9). Verse 8, however, describes how the prophet understood his calling and his mission. (See Reflections at 3:9-12.)

23. E.g., Allen, *The Books of Joel, Obadiah, Jonah, and Micah*, 313.

Micah 3:9-12, Rulers, Priests, and Prophets Caused This Mess

NIV	NRSV

[9]Hear this, you leaders of the house of Jacob,
    you rulers of the house of Israel,
who despise justice
    and distort all that is right;
[10]who build Zion with bloodshed,
    and Jerusalem with wickedness.
[11]Her leaders judge for a bribe,
    her priests teach for a price,
    and her prophets tell fortunes for money.
Yet they lean upon the LORD and say,
    "Is not the LORD among us?
    No disaster will come upon us."
[12]Therefore because of you,
    Zion will be plowed like a field,
Jerusalem will become a heap of rubble,
    the temple hill a mound overgrown with
        thickets.
	[9] Hear this, you rulers of the house of Jacob
	    and chiefs of the house of Israel,
	who abhor justice
	    and pervert all equity,
	[10] who build Zion with blood
	    and Jerusalem with wrong!
	[11] Its rulers give judgment for a bribe,
	    its priests teach for a price,
	    its prophets give oracles for money;
	yet they lean upon the LORD and say,
	    "Surely the LORD is with us!
	    No harm shall come upon us."
	[12] Therefore because of you
	    Zion shall be plowed as a field;
	Jerusalem shall become a heap of ruins,
	    and the mountain of the house a wooded
	        height.

COMMENTARY

3:9. Micah brings this section to a startling climax. He has more words for the rulers and the prophets. This time he also includes the priests in his criticism. Every area of society—business, government, and religion—is corrupt. Those who should act on behalf of the people have instead brought them much misery and they are responsible for the punishment that God will soon send on the city and the nation.

3:10-12. Since Jerusalem was built with bloodshed and wrongdoing, it is only fitting that the city should be reduced to a pile of rubble and a wooded hill (v. 12; recall 1:6). What was built out of violence will be destroyed by violence.

Again, the punishment is a fitting consequence of the crime. We cannot be sure exactly what Micah means in v. 10 when he says that the city was built with bloodshed. He may have in mind the aggressive seizing of property (2:1-5) or the forced labor and heavy taxes needed to carry out programs of fortification and other building projects (see the Introduction).

Micah has now added priests to the list of those who are willing to sell their integrity and their God-given responsibilities for a price (v. 11). The priest was a teacher of the law, responsible for seeing that the sacred traditions were passed on faithfully from one generation to the next. If the priest will not teach what is right and true, the judges and other government officials will not execute the law fairly, and if God's messengers are more concerned with pleasing people than with listening to God, then society is in grave danger. It is only a matter of time until destruction comes.

Micah knows that his word of impending doom will be met with pious statements about God's faithfulness: "Surely the Lord is with us." God will not let anything bad happen to the chosen people, they think. They see themselves as the ones who trust, rely, "lean" on God. Are they not God's special people? It is blasphemy, heresy, the fearful fantasy of one with little faith to suggest that God would let the holy city, the place of God's dwelling among the people, be destroyed (v. 12). And so Micah's opponents cry "peace" when it is not a time for peace (as did Jeremiah's opponents in Jer 6:14; 8:11; 28). They quote ancient words of assurance in order to excuse their violation of the covenant. They use part of their religious heritage in a perverse way to avoid accountability and to reject the words of one of God's true prophets.

Micah's listeners were truly shocked by his pronouncement concerning Jerusalem. It was still remembered a century later when some of the elders cautioned that Jeremiah should be heeded just as King Hezekiah had heeded Micah's word and repented. The Lord then turned aside the disaster that Micah had promised (Jer 26:18-19). Was Micah's prediction actually fulfilled? The Jeremiah text interprets the survival of Jerusalem as a result of repentance that was prompted by Micah's prophecy. So one could say that Micah's prediction was effective, even though the disaster did not occur when he expected it. Jerusalem was destroyed by the Babylonians in the time of Jeremiah, so one might say that Micah's prophecy was correct, though delayed for awhile. Yet, Jerusalem, in spite of a history of conflicts that continue to our day, has never been reduced to a plowed field or a hill "overgrown with thickets" (v. 12 NIV). Since biblical times, there has always been a city there.

REFLECTIONS

1. Micah understands the corporate nature of retribution, even as he also expects individuals to be punished appropriately for their sins. The leaders of society are particularly guilty, and Micah clearly articulates a punishment that is commensurate with their wrongdoing. But when evil is at work in a society, everyone suffers, not merely those singled out for special retribution. The sin of others brings pain to the innocent. Micah's people have already suffered because of their leader's deeds (described in 2:1-5; 3:1-4). If Jerusalem is totally destroyed, many good and faithful people will suffer along with the perpetrators of injustice. We are all interconnected. Wrong that is done against one will have, eventually, a negative effect on all. If we stand idly by while some are treated unfairly, in the belief that it has nothing to do with us, we may be in for an unpleasant surprise.

When we generalize from the Bible to interpret the suffering of the world, we do well to remember what Micah tells us. People will pay for the wrong they have done to others. But not all suffering can be explained as punishment for sin. Some may be the consequence of victimization and abuse by the wicked and the powerful. Other suffering may be the result of living in communities, where the misdeeds of one person or of corrupt institutions and systems will have a ripple effect, bringing undeserved suffering to many.

2. The first three chapters of Micah are very critical and condemning of leaders who abuse their power and authority. These texts do not make us comfortable, and we often avoid them. The church has often decided that the condemning side of the prophet's message is intended for someone else, either ancient or modern. When the prophet begins to speak about hope for the future, then we are ready to listen. We are much more congenial to Micah 4–5 than we are to Micah 1–3.

We ought to listen to the whole book of Micah. Even harsh words that we intuitively reject may be helpful to us. Sometimes it is kinder to warn people that their behavior is destructive, that they are hurting themselves and others, than to remain silent because we do not wish to offend. There may be more love in a well-placed warning than in passive permissiveness that sees the danger ahead and says nothing. This was the challenge facing the prophets, who, once they knew what was coming, were accountable to share that message with others.

3. Micah raises difficult questions about how the leaders in society can be fair and just to all and not only to those who pay their salaries. The problem is more subtle than taking a bribe or selling your ideas to the highest bidder. The politician receives money from special interests, who then expect favors, however quiet the pressure. The lawyer may be more concerned for his or her clients' self-interests than for a larger sense of truth and justice. The preacher is hired (we may think of it as a "call") by a congregation who, since they pay the pastor's salary, expect to be comforted and uplifted, and probably do not enjoy being scolded from the pulpit. Anyone can rationalize what he or she does and says (and does not say). Old Testament prophets have a single-mindedness that may seem excessive. Their lack of compromise and extreme sensitivity to injustice in all forms is "unrealistic." The effect of their preaching was usually to offend people rather than to change them. It would not work if we tried that, we think. That may well be true, but, at the least, the prophet raises for us the question, For whom do we actually work? To whom are we finally accountable? The prophet knew the answer: God.

4. Can any group, society, or nation claim a special relationship with God that makes it immune from the consequences of its members' actions? Micah's listeners took great offense at his prediction that Jerusalem would be destroyed. When the Babylonians did destroy the Temple, the palace, the monarchy, and the nation, the religious people had to go back to the drawing board and try to figure out what this calamitous event meant. The writings of Micah and other pre-exilic prophets were of great help in that task. If even God's special people and holy place can be destroyed, can anything be immune? Will there always be a United States of America, Western culture, even Christianity? Will God intervene to stop us from self-destructive behavior? Will there be a time when it is too late to avert the disaster? Surely, many in our day would react to Micah's audacious prophecy about Jerusalem with outrage, cries of heresy, and hostility if their own particular "Jerusalem" were under attack.

5. Words of faith can be perverted to bring a false message. In Mic 2:7, God's attribute of patience is used as a disclaimer against Micah's pronouncement of impending punishment. Again, in 3:11*b*, God's promise to be with the people is used as an argument against Micah's dire predictions. The promise of God's constant presence is, in itself, somewhat ambiguous. It can be heard as either good news or bad news. Many people have found comfort from sensing the presence of God when they have gone through difficult or dangerous times (see Psalms 23; 139). Others will hear warning or threat in the idea of God's presence. No matter where we go or what we do we cannot escape God's scrutiny (see Amos 9:2-4; cf. Isa 7:14; 8:5-10). Evildoers may think they are getting away with their crimes, that God has not noticed, that there will be no accountability. God's presence is something they do not want, because it threatens their freedom to do whatever they desire without fear of retribution. (Cf. Reflections on 1:2-7).

Micah's opponents have heard only the positive side of the affirmation of God's presence. Micah warns them not to take false assurance from this because there is a negative side to what they perceive as a word of protection. God has seen what they have done. God does not like it, and dire consequences are on the way. Micah's opponents self-righteously claim that he has not relied on the Lord as they have done. When used in the wrong context, even words of comfort and hope can become self-serving and a rationalization for excusing oneself from proper accountability. (See the Reflections on 2:6-11.)

The problem remains for preachers and teachers and prophets and other interpreters of the Word of God: Is this the right word for this person (or these people) at this time and in this situation? In a sense, Micah's opponents are quoting the Scripture against him and his message (just as the devil quotes the Bible to Jesus to tempt him to try another way to carry out his mission in Matt 4:1-11). Not every passage in the Bible is immediately valid for every person at all times. The wise spokesperson for God, like Micah, is the one who can determine the right word for the right time.

MICAH 4:1–5:15

HOPE WILL FINALLY PREVAIL

OVERVIEW

In chapters 4–5 of Micah, hopeful words dominate, in contrast to the prevalence of the judgment oracles in the first three chapters. The distinctions are not absolutely clear, however. In 2:12-13 we see the intrusion of a word of hope in the prophecies of doom, and chaps. 4–5 contain both announcements of impending suffering and assurances of Israel's eventual deliverance from all its enemies. Although better times are promised, there is also a clear recognition that much trouble must be endured before hopes will be realized. These and other indications suggest an audience that is facing imminent exile or perhaps already has been dispersed and scattered among the nations. The mention of Babylon in 4:10 has led many scholars to conclude that most of the words in these chapters come from just before or during the Babylonian exile, with some passages (such as 4:1-4) as late as post-exilic times.[24] Others who claim Mican authorship for the entire book date this material to the threatened invasion by the Assyrians under Sennacherib in 701 BCE. The

Assyrians are specifically mentioned in 5:5b.[25] Although they date Micah to this time in history, some of these scholars believe it was possible for Micah to speak about specific names and events lying far in the future, such as the Babylonian exile in 586 BCE.[26] (See the discussion about predictions in biblical prophecy in Reflections on 4:6–5:1.)

Throughout chaps. 4–5 we see a strong desire for relief from oppression, a return of what was lost (and maybe something even better), a world in which God reigns supreme, God's sovereignty is recognized by all and justice is finally a reality. The desire for justice is sometimes very closely related to a human desire for vengeance on enemies who have caused (and will, for a time, continue to bring) great hurt to God's people. In these chapters, God's relationship with the nations of the world ranges from their peaceful inclusion in God's plan to harsh punishment.

24. James L. Mays, *Micah,* OTL (Philadelphia: Westminster, 1976) 95-104.

25. Leslie C. Allen, *The Books of Joel, Obadiah, Jonah, and Micah,* NICOT (Grand Rapids: Eerdmans, 1976) 341.

26. Walter C. Kaiser, Jr., *Micah–Malachi,* Communicator's Bible (Dallas: Word, 1992) 61-63.

MICAH 4:1-5, PEACE, PROSPERITY, AND SECURITY IN THE DAYS TO COME

4 In the last days

the mountain of the LORD's temple will be established
as chief among the mountains;
it will be raised above the hills,
and peoples will stream to it.

4 In days to come
the mountain of the LORD's house
shall be established as the highest of the mountains,
and shall be raised up above the hills.
Peoples shall stream to it,
2   and many nations shall come and say:

NIV

[2]Many nations will come and say,
"Come, let us go up to the mountain of the
    Lord,
  to the house of the God of Jacob.
He will teach us his ways,
  so that we may walk in his paths."
The law will go out from Zion,
  the word of the Lord from Jerusalem.
[3]He will judge between many peoples
  and will settle disputes for strong nations far
    and wide.
They will beat their swords into plowshares
  and their spears into pruning hooks.
Nation will not take up sword against nation,
  nor will they train for war anymore.
[4]Every man will sit under his own vine
  and under his own fig tree,
and no one will make them afraid,
  for the Lord Almighty has spoken.
[5]All the nations may walk
  in the name of their gods;
we will walk in the name of the Lord
  our God for ever and ever.

NRSV

"Come, let us go up to the mountain of the
    Lord,
  to the house of the God of Jacob;
that he may teach us his ways
  and that we may walk in his paths."
For out of Zion shall go forth instruction,
  and the word of the Lord from Jerusalem.
[3] He shall judge between many peoples,
  and shall arbitrate between strong nations
    far away;
they shall beat their swords into plowshares,
  and their spears into pruning hooks;
nation shall not lift up sword against nation,
  neither shall they learn war any more;
[4] but they shall all sit under their own vines and
    under their own fig trees,
  and no one shall make them afraid;
for the mouth of the Lord of hosts has
    spoken.

[5] For all the peoples walk,
  each in the name of its god,
but we will walk in the name of the Lord our
    God
  forever and ever.

COMMENTARY

This beautiful oracle speaks of a time when all the people of the world live in peace and harmony. They will recognize the one true God, seek to learn what God expects from them, and no longer pursue war as a means of settling disputes (God will now arbitrate all conflicts between nations). Individuals will be left alone to live in prosperity on their own land.

Since this passage occurs in a very similar form in Isa 2:2-4, scholars have long debated the connection between the two texts. Did Micah quote Isaiah or vice versa? Or is the saying originally independent of both prophets, inserted in each book either by the prophet or by later editors? There are differences of opinion on this issue, but the theory of an independent saying incorporated into both collections seems most likely. Because of the nature of the promise and its placement in direct contrast to the terrible judgment on Jerusa-

lem in 3:12, it seems most reasonable that 4:1-5 is an exilic or post-exilic expression of hope. The destruction of Jerusalem and oppression by foreign tyrants is not the end of the story.

4:1-2. Micah 4:1-5 is a direct answer to the oracles of punishment in previous chapters, especially the climax in 3:12. The shame of Jerusalem will be replaced by the glorification of the city and the Temple (v. 1). The temple mount in Jerusalem will now become the highest of the mountains, a dramatic description of the new status of the once humiliated Jerusalem. Anyone who has actually been to Jerusalem knows that there are higher hills close to the site of the Temple. What does this mean? Do mountains grow bigger? Hyperbolic language like this gives a kind of eschatological, "end of the world" feel to this passage, especially if one is prone to think of it literally and not as a metaphor for the renewed and increased authority of the city and its Temple.

Those who had mocked Israel and its people's claims to be the special people of the one true God (who had ostensibly been unable or unwilling to save them from disaster) now will recognize that Israel's God is indeed the God of the universe. Just as Israelites had long made their pilgrimages to the holy city, so also now streams of people from all nations will join them (vv. 1-2). The nations of the world will come willingly to learn about this God so that they, too, may "walk in his paths" (v. 2). No coercion here will be necessary. It will be their own decision to come to Zion because they know it is the right and only place to go. (We are reminded of Jeremiah's vision of the new covenant that will be written on individuals' hearts so that everyone will know what to do and will do it [Jer 31:33-34].)

4:3. In the wake of the nations' decision to follow Yahweh, there will be peace. Wars will end once and for all. God will judge directly without the intrusion of sinful human institutions. Since preparation for war will no longer be necessary, instruments of violence can be converted into useful implements of agriculture.

4:4. This verse does not appear in the Isaiah version of this saying. The Micah text adds this appealing move from the big picture of world peace and justice to its effects on individuals, now free to enjoy life in peace and security. No more war, no enemies to fear, no injustice to threaten family and property—what a wonderful world that would be!

4:5. This verse has the feel of a liturgical ending attached to the saying. It is an admission that this vision of hope has not yet appeared on earth. Other nations continue to follow their own gods. The time for universal allegiance to the God of Israel lies still in a distant and uncertain future. But the worshiping congregation that lives in this hope commits itself to continue walking in the way of the Lord until the promise is fully realized.

REFLECTIONS

What is the relationship between realistic, earthly, achievable hopes and those that stretch our imagination beyond what humans have ever been able to accomplish? Is world peace possible? The dust hardly settled on the end of the cold war before the United States and other nations were off fighting in some remote corner of the world that we hardly knew existed. Hostility and greed seem to exist as long as human beings live on the planet. Those who work to bring peace and security into this world, whether at the level of families, neighborhoods, or nations, have good reason to be discouraged and even to abandon their efforts. Are we to continue to work for goals that we know are not possible through purely human effort? Is Mic 4:1-5 a call to action, a reminder of our task and responsibility? Or is it something for which we can only wait patiently until God takes steps that are possible only for God? Or is it in some way a combination of both doing and waiting?

These questions are not easily resolved. Throughout the history of the church, faithful people have come to different conclusions about the extent of their involvement in efforts to improve a world that is very resistant to change. Some have given up on this world altogether and have read texts like this one purely as the hope for the end of the world and the new age, when all that is wrong will finally be made right.

MICAH 4:6–5:1, TOUGH TIMES AHEAD, BUT GOD'S PEOPLE WILL PREVAIL

NIV

⁶"In that day," declares the LORD,
"I will gather the lame;
   I will assemble the exiles
   and those I have brought to grief.
⁷I will make the lame a remnant,
   those driven away a strong nation.
The LORD will rule over them in Mount Zion
   from that day and forever.
⁸As for you, O watchtower of the flock,
   O stronghold^a of the Daughter of Zion,
the former dominion will be restored to you;
   kingship will come to the Daughter of
      Jerusalem."

⁹Why do you now cry aloud—
   have you no king?
Has your counselor perished,
   that pain seizes you like that of a woman in
      labor?
¹⁰Writhe in agony, O Daughter of Zion,
   like a woman in labor,
for now you must leave the city
   to camp in the open field.
You will go to Babylon;
   there you will be rescued.
There the LORD will redeem you
   out of the hand of your enemies.

¹¹But now many nations
   are gathered against you.
They say, "Let her be defiled,
   let our eyes gloat over Zion!"
¹²But they do not know
   the thoughts of the LORD;
they do not understand his plan,
   he who gathers them like sheaves to the
      threshing floor.
¹³"Rise and thresh, O Daughter of Zion,
   for I will give you horns of iron;
I will give you hoofs of bronze
   and you will break to pieces many nations."
You will devote their ill-gotten gains to the LORD,
   their wealth to the Lord of all the earth.

^a8 Or hill

NRSV

⁶ In that day, says the LORD,
   I will assemble the lame
and gather those who have been driven away,
   and those whom I have afflicted.
⁷ The lame I will make the remnant,
   and those who were cast off, a strong
      nation;
and the LORD will reign over them in Mount
      Zion
   now and forevermore.

⁸ And you, O tower of the flock,
   hill of daughter Zion,
to you it shall come,
   the former dominion shall come,
   the sovereignty of daughter Jerusalem.

⁹ Now why do you cry aloud?
   Is there no king in you?
Has your counselor perished,
   that pangs have seized you like a woman in
      labor?
¹⁰ Writhe and groan,^a O daughter Zion,
   like a woman in labor;
for now you shall go forth from the city
   and camp in the open country;
   you shall go to Babylon.
There you shall be rescued,
   there the LORD will redeem you
   from the hands of your enemies.

¹¹ Now many nations
   are assembled against you,
saying, "Let her be profaned,
   and let our eyes gaze upon Zion."
¹² But they do not know
   the thoughts of the LORD;
they do not understand his plan,
   that he has gathered them as sheaves to the
      threshing floor.
¹³ Arise and thresh,
   O daughter Zion,
for I will make your horn iron

^a Meaning of Heb uncertain

NIV

5 Marshal your troops, O city of troops,[a]
   for a siege is laid against us.
They will strike Israel's ruler
   on the cheek with a rod.

NRSV

and your hoofs bronze;
you shall beat in pieces many peoples,
   and shall[a] devote their gain to the LORD,
   their wealth to the Lord of the whole earth.

5[b] Now you are walled around with
         a wall;[c]
   siege is laid against us;
with a rod they strike the ruler of Israel
   upon the cheek.

[a]Gk Syr Tg: Heb *and I will*   [b]Ch 4.14 in Heb   [d]Cn Compare
Gk: Meaning of Heb uncertain

COMMENTARY

4:6-8. Words of promise continue in v. 8. Jerusalem is addressed first as *Migdal-'eder* (NRSV "tower of the flock"; NIV "watchtower of the flock"). This place name, which elsewhere appears only after the conclusion of the story of the death and burial of Rachel at Bethlehem (Gen 35:21), evokes the image of Israel as Yahweh's flock (Isa 40:11; Jer 13:17, 20; Zech 10:3). *'ōpel* appears originally to have designated the old city of David. "In Isa 32:14," Mays notes, " *'ōpel* is associated with watch-tower and it may be used here as a kind of synonym to 'citadel of the flock,' as well as one of the old names associated with the city."[27] Hence, this verse employs traditional epithets to remind the city of its past and to assure its inhabitants that they shall again have a future. Its dominion, its kingship, and its status as the capital city will all be restored.

Some commentators have, on the basis of Gen 35:21, connected the phrase "tower of the flock" with Bethlehem. Following this line of reasoning, v. 8 could be addressed to both Bethlehem and Jerusalem. The promise of the restoration of dominion would then involve both the reconstruction of Jerusalem and a new king from Bethlehem, the hometown of David (see Mic 5:2). This may be reading too much into "the tower of the flock," but it is possible.[28]

4:9-10. Several scholars, including Allen and Mays,[29] have noted a series of sayings in 4:9-13

(and possibly into chap. 5) that contrast the movement from "now" to "then," from present distress to coming deliverance. Now you cry aloud and writhe like a woman in the pains of childbirth, but your exile in Babylon will turn out to be the means and the place of your redemption. The reference to the king (who is also called the counselor) in v. 9 implies that the king has not yet been removed, but there is little hope that he can do anything to avert the terrible events that are coming. The word "redeem" (גאל *gāʾal*) in v. 10 has an ancient usage in which the next of kin was responsible for seeking vengeance and restoration for one who could no longer do it for himself (sometimes because of death). Later, the word was used extensively to speak about God's activity to "redeem" those who had gone into exile (particularly in texts from Isaiah 40–55).

4:11-13. Now many nations are gathered against Jerusalem, gloating over its defilement (v. 11). But they do not know God's plans (v. 12). Like the schemers in 2:1-3, they will find that while they were making their own plans, God had something else in mind. God gathers them together, not to gawk at the humiliation of Israel, but to be crushed by Israel (v. 12). Jerusalem, like a threshing ox, will pulverize them with iron horns and hooves of bronze (v. 13). The image is violent. The Israelites' switch from victim to conqueror is extreme. Holy war language is used to describe how the spoils of war will be "devoted" (חרם *ḥāram*) to the Lord, rather than kept

---

27. Mays, *Micah,* 103.
28. Kaiser, *Micah–Malachi,* 57-58.
29. Allen, *The Books of Joel, Obadiah, Jonah, and Micah,* 335; Mays, *Micah,* 104.

for personal gain (see Joshua 7 and 1 Samuel 15 as examples of this practice).

5:1. This verse (4:14 in the Hebrew text) causes some difficulty in translation (cf. NRSV with NIV). Further, it is uncertain whether to connect it with what precedes or what follows. It is possible that it presents a third in the series of sayings from "now" to "then," which move from present distress (the ruler of Israel is struck on the cheek) to the coming of a new king from the line of David (v. 2). In order to emphasize the importance of the messianic prophecy of 5:2-5*a* by treating it as a separate section, the discussion here ends this section with 5:1.

Throughout chaps. 4–5, then, one finds a mix of judgment and hope, with the emphasis on hope that comes after the judgment has run its course. The prophet does not promise that all suffering and pain, surely some of it deserved, can be avoided. But the message moves beyond immediate misfortunes to a glorious future that God has in mind for the people. Whether Micah himself ever made that move is debatable. But if he did not, it is clear that those who read his words in a later time found it necessary to articulate God's promises for the future in order to complete the prophetic ministry that Micah had begun. It is no less the Word of God if it is spoken by a follower of Micah and not by the great prophet himself.

REFLECTIONS

1. How far into the future does a biblical prophet see? The beautiful picture of a world free from war and all that can harm us is certainly a long look into a future that reaches even beyond history. But it is poetic, visionary, lacking in precise details that can be located in a particular time and place. When the prophet gets specific, mentioning Babylon or Assyria, or talks of returning from exile, the logical assumption is that he is speaking about the immediate future, to people in his own time. For reasons such as this, the majority of scholars believe that most (if not all) of Micah 4–5 comes from a time later than Micah, when a new situation called for a different message.

There is a huge difference of opinion among Christians on this matter, however. If one begins with the assumption that God can and does give specific information about the distant future, then it is not inconceivable that Micah could make predictions about the exile in Babylon, the return from that exile, the birth of Jesus, and even details about the end time. The mention of Babylon in 4:10 would not be evidence for a later dating but proof that God gives prophets precise information about events that will occur decades or even centuries in the future. It follows, then, that there may be predictions about our own day hidden in the ancient biblical texts if we have the wisdom and the spiritual guidance to find them.[30]

Proponents of these two approaches to the reading of biblical prophecy are so different in their starting assumptions that it is very difficult for them to understand one another and to be sympathetic to the other's position on the predictive capabilities of biblical prophets.

2. We have some excellent texts in 4:6–5:1 for speaking hope to people who are in the midst of great distress. The repetitive movement from suffering to hope reminds us that God is at work to see that our individual life pilgrimage will move in the same direction. Although hope seems beyond present thought or feeling, the prophet's words repeat again and again the liberating intention of God not to let people remain trapped in their experience of exile. It is important to note that these hopeful words from Micah do not belittle the reality of suffering. Nor do they promise a quick fix, a way to bypass the pain yet to be endured before the dawn of better days. Sufferers appreciate a word that takes their pain seriously. They will give credibility to the speaker of words of hope who has not attempted to sell an easy solution without being honest about the pain.

---

30. See Kaiser, *Micah–Malachi*, 61-63, for an example of how a scholar from this perspective looks at these texts.

3. God can use human intentions, whether for good or for evil, to accomplish what God wills. There is a complicated relationship between human freedom and the working out of God's will. Human beings may think they are doing exactly what they want, but they will be surprised when they see that God has used their actions to bring about an altogether different result. In Mic 4:11-13, the nations gather to watch the desecration of Jerusalem, only to find that God has brought them together so that Israel can take vengeance against them. What a surprise! God takes our human decisions, out of good motives or bad, and works toward goals of justice, peace, and mercy. Human sin makes God's task more difficult, but God's intention is always toward the good. This point is made with great artistry at the end of the Joseph story when Joseph tells his brothers, "Even though you intended to do harm to me, God intended it for good" (Gen 50:20 NRSV). Similarly, the terrible deed of the crucifixion of Jesus, intended by government and religious officials and ordinary citizens to remove Jesus forever from the scene, becomes for a Christian the means by which God saves the human race.

4. How should we treat our enemies? Should we seek vengeance on them? Does justice not demand that those who have committed terrible atrocities pay for what they have done? The violence that is suddenly turned against the nations in 4:13 is troublesome to many of us who are uncomfortable with God as judge, punisher, avenger. How can a God of mercy and forgiveness also endorse such acts of violent retaliation? The same God who receives the nations of the world, who teaches them, and who settles their disputes in 4:1-4 now lures nations into a place where they will be slaughtered by Israel. One wonders whether excessive calls for vindication against enemies reveals more about the interpreters of God than what God actually thinks or feels. How much of God's anger and execution of punishment is actually projection onto God by a battered and humiliated people? This possibility may divert some of the violence that the Bible ascribes to God. But we must be careful not to explain away and deny altogether the possibility of God's anger. To do so would be to fall into the trap with Micah's audience, who believed that their special status with God made them immune from God's negative judgment (Mic 2:6-7; 3:11). A God who is never angry would be a God who has no compassion and empathy for those who suffer at the hands of others. God's anger is the other side of God's love and concern. To be in relationship with a God who truly cares about people and what they do means running the risk that God may sometimes be angry. The good news is that anger is never the last word. The movement in Micah and throughout Scripture is always from judgment to forgiveness, from punishment to mercy, from suffering to hope.

MICAH 5:2-5a, THE PROMISED RULER FROM BETHLEHEM

<table>
<tr><td>

NIV

2"But you, Bethlehem Ephrathah,
    though you are small among the clans[a] of Judah,
out of you will come for me
    one who will be ruler over Israel,
whose origins[b] are from of old,
    from ancient times.[c]"

</td><td>

NRSV

2a But you, O Bethlehem of Ephrathah,
    who are one of the little clans of Judah,
from you shall come forth for me
    one who is to rule in Israel,
whose origin is from of old,
    from ancient days.

</td></tr>
<tr><td>

a2 Or *rulers*   b2 Hebrew *goings out*   c2 Or *from days of eternity*

</td><td>

a Ch 5.1 in Heb

</td></tr>
</table>

NIV

[3]Therefore Israel will be abandoned
    until the time when she who is in labor gives
        birth
and the rest of his brothers return
    to join the Israelites.
[4]He will stand and shepherd his flock
    in the strength of the LORD,
    in the majesty of the name of the LORD his
        God.
And they will live securely, for then his
        greatness
    will reach to the ends of the earth.
[5] And he will be their peace.

NRSV

[3] Therefore he shall give them up until the time
    when she who is in labor has brought forth;
then the rest of his kindred shall return
    to the people of Israel.
[4] And he shall stand and feed his flock in the
    strength of the LORD,
    in the majesty of the name of the LORD his
        God.
And they shall live secure, for now he shall be
        great
    to the ends of the earth;
[5] and he shall be the one of peace.

COMMENTARY

The promise of a new ruler to come from the town of Bethlehem is very familiar to all Christians and is often cited during the Advent and Christmas seasons. The wise men quote Mic 5:2 in response to Herod's question about where the Messiah will be born (Matt 2:6). Bethlehem is the hometown of David. To locate the birthplace of the new king in David's town is to see in him the continuation of the ancient promises that God had given to David (see, e.g., 2 Sam 7:16-17). Although Israel endured the reigns of some terrible kings and, in fact, would see the loss of the monarchy entirely at the hands of the Babylonians in 586 BCE, hope remained that God had not withdrawn the promise that a son of David would always sit on the throne. At the time of Jesus, many Jews still looked for such a Messiah, and texts like Mic 5:2 encouraged this expectation among the people.

The promise of 5:2-5a comes at the end of a series of sharp contrasts between present defeat and a glorious future (see the same movement from "now" to "then" in 4:9-13). The meaning of the first half of 5:1 is uncertain, but the ending of the verse is clear: The king of Israel will be struck on the cheek and disgraced by some enemy. Verses 2-5a, then, respond to this degradation with a strong statement that a new ruler will come to turn the situation around completely. The present remains a time of suffering, and it may get worse before relief comes, but the people

should not lose heart. Again, the movement is from suffering to salvation, from defeat to victory.

The mention of both Bethlehem and Ehpratha (see Ruth 1:2; 1 Sam 17:12; Ps 132:6) makes a double connection with David, including both geographic location and family identification. The small size of Bethlehem reminds one of a common biblical theme: When God is about to do something great, human estimates of status, size, power, and influence are completely irrelevant. In fact, God often deliberately chooses someone whom we would probably dismiss as the most unlikely candidate for carrying out God's mission (see Gideon's protests in Judg 6:15; Saul in 1 Sam 9:21; and the selection of David in 1 Sam 16:1-3). This theme continues in the New Testament stories of the humble origins and the humiliating crucifixion of the one whom Christians claim as Messiah.

In v. 2, the specific Hebrew word for "king" (מלך *melek*) is not used; rather the writer uses a more general word for "ruler" (מושל *môšēl*). This may be due to an ongoing discomfort in Israel with the institution of kingship, which many considered to be a foreign import with overtones of idolatry and disrespect for God as the true king of Israel (see 1 Samuel 8). God says that this new ruler will be "for me" (v. 2), finding strength and authority in the Lord (v. 4) and not in his own power. This new king will subordinate himself to the true ruler of Israel. By depending utterly on

God, he will ensure that the people dwell securely. No other power (even to "the ends of the earth") will be able to contend against a nation led by such a king (v. 4).

The new ruler "shall stand and feed his flock in the strength of the LORD" (v. 4a). Shepherd was a common metaphor in the ancient Near East. Israel borrowed this language to describe its own rulers and particularly to speak about David and his descendants. David was, in fact, a shepherd, both literally as one who tended his father's sheep and figuratively as the model king of Israel. Sometimes God, as the true king, was also identified as a shepherd in Micah (2:12; 4:6-8) and elsewhere in the OT (e.g., Psalm 23; Ezekiel 34). Jesus' followers drew on this same tradition when they identified him as the good shepherd (see John 10:1-18).

The word "messiah" (משיח *māšîaḥ*) is not used in Mic 5:2-5a, yet it is often called a messianic text. The Messiah would be someone anointed for a special office. Most often this word refers to kings, and it occurs most frequently in the stories of David. The word "messianic" has come to be used to describe hope for a new leader who will come from the family of David to guide the people from present oppression and suffering to a glorious victory.

The last part of v. 2 indicates that the origin of this promised ruler stretches back nearly three centuries to the covenant God made with David. The promise is old. Now it appears to be in jeopardy as foreign powers (Assyria or Babylon, depending on when one dates this oracle) threaten to remove the king and wipe out the nation. But God does not break promises. They may be put in abeyance for a time, largely because of the sin of the leaders of the people, but God will fulfill them in ways even more wondrous than first imagined. Some Christians interpret the ancient origin of the new ruler as a statement about the pre-existence of Jesus, who was with God from the beginning. For such persons this passage is much more significant for its anticipation of the distant future, the birth of Jesus and his second coming, than it is as a word to the immediate

historical situation facing Micah or for redactors who updated his book to speak to changing times.

Verse 3 perhaps gives a clue to the dating of this prophetic word. Like other promises in chaps. 4–5, it states that there must be a waiting period before Israel's fortunes are reversed. Two things will happen before the bad ceases and the good begins. When the one who is in labor gives birth and when the rest of his kindred return, then the new ruler will appear and the great new reign will start. Who is in labor? Is it the mother of the new king? Many scholars have thought so and have read this verse in connection with Isa 7:14 and 9:6. If this interpretation is correct, does that mean that the wait will be over when that baby has grown to majority and is able to take office? Or is this a far distant glimpse of the virgin Mary, a prediction of the birth of Jesus? It is easy to see why this text is popular for Christians who have applied Micah's words to the story of Jesus.

Should one instead read this text in connection with Mic 4:9-10? The present is painful, like the terrible ordeal of a woman in labor. But the pain of childbirth ends, and there is joy when a child is born into the world. This is the theme running through much of Micah 4–5: the present pain is real, but deliverance will come and it will be wonderful. This seems to be the most logical reading of 5:2-5a, and it leads to the conclusion that it is probably addressed to people either about to enter into exile or already in exile. Some have suggested that the return of all the kinsmen could be understood as hope for the reunification of the tribes of the northern kingdom of Israel with the southern kingdom of Judah. If so, it could be dated to the Assyrian threat in the time of Micah and not to the later Babylonian conquest.[31] More likely, these verses are an admonition to exiles in Babylon to wait, like a woman in labor who knows there will be a happy ending to her pain, until they are able to return home. Then a new king will be enthroned and they will live securely, for "he shall be the one of peace" (v. 5a NRSV; NIV, "And he will be their peace").

31. E.g., Leslie C. Allen, *The Books of Joel, Obadiah, Jonah, and Micah*, NICOT (Grand Rapids: Eerdmans, 1976) 345.

REFLECTIONS

1. Who is the new king from Bethlehem who will come to rule as God's representative on earth? There are at least two obvious answers to this question, depending on one's basic assumptions. It is either Jesus or the one to be crowned king after the exiles have returned and the Davidic monarchy is restored. On the one hand, Christians have so long associated this text with the birth of Jesus that it is hard to read it without making that connection. Lectionaries of Advent readings have reinforced that understanding of Mic 5:2. Many Christians read Old Testament prophecies without worrying too much about their meaning in the original setting. They are more interested in them as predictions, pointers, foreshadows of what was to come in the person of Jesus and the future of the church. They see Jesus in many passages throughout the Old Testament, but most notably in texts like this one.

On the other hand, it is equally obvious to many readers of Micah that this prophecy was a word of hope intended to address the distress of people who lived in a particular time and place. God will finally send some decent rulers to relieve their terrible situation, defeat their enemies, provide security for the future, and rule with some integrity. Whether the context is the time of Micah or the later Babylonian oppression, the hopes are earthly, concerned for the here and now, relating ancient promises to contemporary experiences.

So some would say that the coming king is obviously Jesus. The prophecy looks forward to his birth or, perhaps, to his second coming, when the time of waiting will be over and the reign of God will finally be achieved in all its glory. Others say that the text is obviously talking about an earthly king. After they return from exile, God will reestablish the monarchy in a restored capital of Jerusalem. Up to the present time, this has not happened. Although the city and the Temple were rebuilt, never again has a son of David ruled as king in Jerusalem.

2. Can a biblical text that seems obviously to be addressed to specific people in ancient times somehow be freed from its earliest historical context so that it can continue to speak a word from God to a world that constantly faces new challenges? The book of Micah may contain words that are pertinent not only to hearers in Micah's day, but also to those facing exile in Babylon and, still later, to the followers of Jesus who search the Scriptures to find passages that help them interpret who Jesus is. Micah also speaks to us who live in a time and place far distant from the great eighth-century BCE prophet. Of course, Micah was not talking to us. We are not his first audience, but our questions are not unlike those raised by his listeners. Our sins are similar. Our need for a word of warning and a glimmer of hope beyond the present ordeal is great. And so we stretch the meaning of the ancient text so that it speaks directly to us. At times we may see more than is actually there, no doubt, more than Micah meant to say. We need to be attentive to our tendency to read what we want the text to mean and not what the text actually says. But the text is not limited to the vision of Micah or his editors. The Spirit continues to work in the reading of the Scripture within communities of faithful people. New understandings of God's will for us in our time and place are possible. Although we see things that the original speaker never imagined, we may, in fact, be in touch with a word from God.

MICAH 5:5b-15, GOD WILL JUDGE AND RESCUE

Micah 5:5b-6, Seven Shepherds and Eight Rulers

NIV

When the Assyrian invades our land
    and marches through our fortresses,
we will raise against him seven shepherds,
    even eight leaders of men.
[6]They will rule[a] the land of Assyria with the
    sword,
    the land of Nimrod with drawn sword.[b]
He will deliver us from the Assyrian
    when he invades our land
    and marches into our borders.

[a]6 Or *crush*   [b]6 Or *Nimrod in its gates*

NRSV

If the Assyrians come into our land
    and tread upon our soil,[a]
we will raise against them seven shepherds
    and eight installed as rulers.
[6] They shall rule the land of Assyria with the
    sword,
    and the land of Nimrod with the drawn
    sword;[b]
they[c] shall rescue us from the Assyrians
    if they come into our land
    or tread within our border.

[a] Gk: Heb *in our palaces*   [b] Cn: Heb *in its entrances*   [c] Heb *he*

COMMENTARY

This short section causes some confusion in the continuity of chapter 5. The best guess is that it was an independent war song expressing confidence that leaders (seven or eight or however many we may need) will emerge to ensure victory over any invading power. We may wonder how this passage fits with the preceding announcement of the new ruler from Bethlehem. The sense of boastfulness in the old war song seems to be at some variance with what has just been said about the new king. The ruler from Bethlehem will save the people because he has been chosen by God and will receive power and authority directly from God. The emphasis is on God's power to save, not on humans' boasting about their ability to resist any enemy attack. Will these seven or eight shepherds, whoever they are, be subservient to the new ruler who in turn is completely subordinate to God?

The mention of Assyria might seem to support

scholars who think that this oracle comes from the time of Micah, perhaps at the occasion of the invasion by Sennacherib. Oracles from Micah 1–3 probably date from that time. But it is very unlikely that Micah would introduce a war song boasting of Israel's ability to fend off an invasion. Micah's main point in those chapters is the destruction of Jerusalem (3:12). Some interpreters argue that the placement of 5:5b-6 immediately following 5:2-5a suggests a much later date. "Assyria" may be understood as a code name for any great power that might threaten Israel after the new king has begun his reign.[32] In that case, the promised security from all enemies is similar to the assurance of 4:1-4. Genesis 10:8-11 mentions Nimrod as the son of Cush and connects him with Babylon, Assyria, and other locations in Mesopotamia. (See Reflections at 5:10-15.)

32. James L. Mays, *Micah,* OTL (Philadelphia: Westminster, 1976) 119.

Micah 5:7-9, Your Remnant Shall Defeat Your Enemies

NIV

[7] The remnant of Jacob will be
    in the midst of many peoples
like dew from the LORD,
    like showers on the grass,
which do not wait for man
    or linger for mankind.
[8] The remnant of Jacob will be among the nations,
    in the midst of many peoples,
like a lion among the beasts of the forest,
    like a young lion among flocks of sheep,
which mauls and mangles as it goes,
    and no one can rescue.
[9] Your hand will be lifted up in triumph over your
        enemies,
    and all your foes will be destroyed.

NRSV

[7] Then the remnant of Jacob,
    surrounded by many peoples,
shall be like dew from the LORD,
    like showers on the grass,
which do not depend upon people
    or wait for any mortal.
[8] And among the nations the remnant of Jacob,
    surrounded by many peoples,
shall be like a lion among the animals of the
        forest,
    like a young lion among the flocks of sheep,
which, when it goes through, treads down
    and tears in pieces, with no one to deliver.
[9] Your hand shall be lifted up over your
        adversaries,
    and all your enemies shall be cut off.

COMMENTARY

These verses seem to assume that Israel has been scattered among the nations, but it is possible that "surrounded by many peoples" (vv. 7-8) merely refers to the geographical location of Israel. Most scholars believe this is an exilic saying that addresses questions about the future of the remnant of God's chosen people and how they are to relate to the other nations of the world. Certain Old Testament prophets (especially Isaiah and Jeremiah) refer to the "remnant" that will be left when God's punishment has run its course. This might have been heard as a threat that many people would be destroyed and *only* a remnant would survive. But, more often, it is perceived as a word of hope. God will not destroy the people completely. God will not give up on the covenant but will begin a new phase in Israel's history after the cleansing and refining of the people have taken place (see Jer 31:7-9). The story of God and Israel goes on. Israel has a future.

What is to be Israel's role in the future? In this short passage, we see a sharp contrast between a positive and a negative effect of Israel on its neighbors. According to v. 7, the remnant will be like dew or rain, considered life-giving gifts from God in that semi-arid part of the world. But in v. 8, the image changes to that of a lion let loose to slaughter animals of the forest or, even worse, to tear into a flock of sheep with no one to inhibit the devastation. Some commentators have associated this saying with Gen 12:3, the promise that Abraham's descendants will be a blessing to some and a curse to others. The emphasis falls on God as the initiator of both positive and negative aspects of Israel's role. Dew and rain come without any human effort or control (v. 7*b*). Similarly, it is by God's action that all enemies will be removed in that great time in the future (v. 9) when swords are reworked into plowshares, all nations will turn to the one true God (to whom the remnant of Israel bears witness), and the new king reigns in peace as God's appointed ruler. All of these themes from chaps. 4–5 come together as we approach the end of this section of Micah. (See Reflections at 5:10-15.)

Micah 5:10-15, God's Judgment on Israel and Its Enemies

NIV

¹⁰"In that day," declares the LORD,
"I will destroy your horses from among you
and demolish your chariots.
¹¹I will destroy the cities of your land
and tear down all your strongholds.
¹²I will destroy your witchcraft
and you will no longer cast spells.
¹³I will destroy your carved images
and your sacred stones from among you;
you will no longer bow down
to the work of your hands.
¹⁴I will uproot from among you your Asherah poles*a*
and demolish your cities.
¹⁵I will take vengeance in anger and wrath
upon the nations that have not obeyed me."

a14 That is, symbols of the goddess Asherah

NRSV

¹⁰ In that day, says the LORD,
I will cut off your horses from among you
and will destroy your chariots;
¹¹ and I will cut off the cities of your land
and throw down all your strongholds;
¹² and I will cut off sorceries from your hand,
and you shall have no more soothsayers;
¹³ and I will cut off your images
and your pillars from among you,
and you shall bow down no more
to the work of your hands;
¹⁴ and I will uproot your sacred poles*a* from
among you
and destroy your towns.
¹⁵ And in anger and wrath I will execute vengeance
on the nations that did not obey.

a Heb Asherim

COMMENTARY

The movement back and forth between promise and judgment takes another turn in these verses. Most often, we have observed a flow from bad news to good news, but this passage breaks that pattern. Verses 10-14 speak about what must be done to remedy the faithlessness of Israel. The last verse is a harsh word about the fate of all nations who remain disobedient to God.

5:10-14. These verses list a number of things that God will do to remove false securities, idolatries, objects of misdirected trust to which Israel has often turned instead of relying on the one true God. There is a repetition of the Hebrew word "cut off" (כרת *kārat*; NIV, "destroy"). First, all dependence on military armaments will be removed (vv. 10-11). If God is on their side, they need not concern themselves with arming and fortifying for war. If God is not on their side, no amount of preparation will prevent their defeat. Second, God will destroy all false religious practices, including sorcery, soothsaying, and other foreign means of manipulating a word from God (v. 12; see Exod 22:18; Lev 19:26; Deut 18:9-14; 1 Sam 28:3-10), as well as pillars and poles that are symbols of pagan fertility rites (v. 13). In short, God will remove all of those distractions, false

hopes, and securities that divert the people from trusting and obeying the only power that can provide true and lasting security. Verses 10-14 make clear the need for the people to change, to be purified. If Israel is to live in safety and as a model to other nations, these radical surgeries, performed directly by God, will be necessary. Although surgery is never a pleasant experience, one could read vv. 10-14 as good news, not as a threat of punishment. If Israel (or any nation) cannot prosper while captivated by the false gods of military armaments or useless religious practices, then God is doing the people a favor by "cutting" them off.

5:15. With regard to the rest of the world, God also will take action. The mood seems to change in this verse as God vows to act in anger and wrath bringing vengeance on nations that do not obey. If this oracle originated in exilic times, as many think, it may reveal a strong desire for vindication on the part of exiles. God may have punished Israel and Judah for good reason, as Micah and other prophets have made clear, but justice will not be fully served until Babylon is held accountable for its cruelty and oppression of God's people.

REFLECTIONS

1. Micah 4–5 is much concerned with how Israel is to relate to other nations and how the God of Israel will deal with the whole world (see Reflections on Mic 1:2-7). The Babylonian exiles, suffering under foreign rule, struggled with what it meant to be God's chosen people when God was using evil nations to punish them. One might conclude that the Israelites would have been better off to be one of the nations that God used to exact retribution than to be the special people who were the recipients of that punishment. What will God do next? Will Assyria or Babylon ever have to answer to God for their atrocities? Is not the God of Israel the Lord of all the nations? Will there be vindication, a chance for renewal, a return home with some guarantee of security and stability so that the Babylonians and the Assyrians of the future will not be able to continue their cruel deeds?

In their better moments, the people of Israel could begin to see that perhaps they had a mission to the nations, to be a blessing to them, like dew or gentle rain on the grass. Isaiah 40–55 clearly moves in this direction, as does Mic 4:1-4 and 5:7. God does intend good things for other nations and not only for Israel. But there will also be a negative judgment on those nations who refuse to obey once they have heard the truth about the holy God of Israel. Israel carried the message, both in words from God and in its own history, that God is steadfast in love and quick to forgive but will not compromise with evil. So Israel could be a blessing or a curse, depending on the response of the nations to what God's people both speak and do.

2. The list of false securities that God will purge (5:10-14) has a familiar, contemporary ring to it. Idolatry is not simply a matter of setting up statues or using symbols borrowed from very different and incompatible religious traditions. To place one's hope and ultimate security in any thing or person or idea that is less than God is to be guilty of idolatry. Even rigid adherence to a set of theological principles or blind faith in a certain denomination or a saintly church leader can become idolatry if it substitutes partial knowledge about God for trust in that one who, unlike all human imitations, will never let us down.

God intends to remove military armaments because of our tendency to be lured into a false sense of security by them. We can say much about how this has been evidenced in the last several decades. And God's condemnation of human ways of conjuring a word from God through sorcery and soothsaying is of special interest in a time of intense, but often misguided, searches for spirituality. Much that is called "new" spirituality in our day has incorporated ancient practices that were condemned by our spiritual ancestors at least as far back as the time of Samuel and Saul (see 1 Sam 28:3-10). In these days, as in Micah's time, we need to watch for subtle idolatries and religious practices that divert our attention away from God and onto human inventions that may make us feel good for a time but will ultimately fail us.

3. God's anger is a frightful prospect (see Reflections number 4 on 4:6–5:1). When God speaks of executing vengeance, we shudder as we relate that possibility to our experience with human emotions of hatred and the desire for revenge. It is better to use words like *vindication* and *justice* rather than *vengeance* as we try to express the conviction that God will not tolerate disobedience and will, in the end, make all things right. When God comes to bring justice, vindication, or vengeance, some will be happy and some will be terrified. God's justice is a two-edged sword. Those who have been oppressed, enslaved, or hurt in some way will be joyful because their torment has ended. They will be free at last. The perpetrators of evil will be justly punished or, at least, not allowed to continue their terrible deeds. When God comes, the former will see justice as vindication. The latter will perceive it as vengeance.

MICAH 6:1–7:20

FROM JUDGMENT TO HOPE

OVERVIEW

Chapters 1–3 consist primarily of prophetic proclamations that terrible disasters are coming as fitting punishment for the disgraceful behavior of Israel's leaders, with a little interlude of hope at the end of chapter 2. Chapters 4–5 are mostly promises that things will get better, but not until difficult times, already set in motion, have run their course. Now, in this closing section of the book, we again see a mixture of judgment and hope, but hope as the last word. Many of the themes raised in earlier chapters are recapitulated here. One of the three most famous passages from Micah is the response to the question, "What does the Lord require of you?" (6:8; the other most quoted passages from Micah are 4:1-4 and 5:2-5a).

Chapter 6 begins with a covenant lawsuit, in which mountains and hills will serve as the jury that decides either for the Lord or for God's people in the controversy between them (6:1-2). God begins by reciting a short summary of the great acts that God performed on behalf of the people (6:3-5). In a style resembling the question-and-answer formula of an entrance liturgy, the people ask what Yahweh requires of them, and they are given an answer (6:6-8). God speaks again and recites once more a list of Israel's offenses (6:9-12) that cannot be tolerated. God has no choice but to bring on the punishment that the people so clearly deserve (6:13-16). Yahweh's case is clear. What God has done, and will do, to the people is appropriate and just under the circumstances.

Chapter 7 begins with a lament over the decadence of society (7:1-7). One is reminded of the prophet's lament in 1:8-9. The book ends with what is often identified as a closing liturgy, making the final transition from suffering to hope, from punishment to forgiveness. This theme recurs throughout the book; thus it is not surprising that the book should end on a positive note. The fortunes of Israel and its enemies will be reversed (7:8-17). The final passage is a wonderful expression of belief in a forgiving, caring, compassionate, and faithful God (7:18-20). With that conviction about God as a foundation, hope is possible even in the most miserable life situations.

MICAH 6:1-16, GOD'S CASE AGAINST ISRAEL (AGAIN)

Micah 6:1-2, Introduction

NIV	NRSV

6 Listen to what the Lord says:
 	
"Stand up, plead your case before the
  mountains;
  let the hills hear what you have to say.
²Hear, O mountains, the Lord's accusation;
	6 Hear what the Lord says:
	Rise, plead your case before
	  the mountains,
	  and let the hills hear your voice.
	² Hear, you mountains, the controversy of the
	  Lord,

NIV

listen, you everlasting foundations of the
earth.
For the LORD has a case against his people;
he is lodging a charge against Israel."

NRSV

and you enduring foundations of the earth;
for the LORD has a controversy with his people,
and he will contend with Israel.

COMMENTARY

The Lord invites Israel to plead its case before the jury of mountains and hills. Yahweh's people wonder whether God is just when they are punished while other, more wicked nations continue to prosper. Maybe God (or the prophet or others) has heard such complaints about injustice (see Hab 1:12-17) and it is time, in response, again to make the case for why God is bringing punishment. This is a lawsuit against those who have broken the covenant. The form is borrowed from ancient Near Eastern treaties in which the dominant king recites the benefits he has bestowed on his vassals, and then proclaims blessings for obedience and penalties that will follow disobedience. The subject states pledge their allegiance, know-ing full well the consequences of rebelling against their master. Israel has broken the covenant; God has not. If disasters are now the result of that disobedience, God cannot be declared unjust. The mountains and the hills will be the jury. Let them decide. They have been around a long time. They have seen all the evils that humans have done from the beginning of time. They were present when the covenant was made, and they witnessed the pledges that have now been broken (see Deut 4:26; 30:19; 31:28; 32:1; Ps 50:4; Isa 1:2 for instances of heaven and earth being called as witnesses to covenant making). (See Reflections at 6:13-16.)

Micah 6:3-5, What God Has Done for the People

NIV

3"My people, what have I done to you?
How have I burdened you? Answer me.
4I brought you up out of Egypt
and redeemed you from the land of slavery.
I sent Moses to lead you,
also Aaron and Miriam.
5My people, remember
what Balak king of Moab counseled
and what Balaam son of Beor answered.
Remember ⌊your journey⌋ from Shittim to Gilgal,
that you may know the righteous acts of the
LORD."

NRSV

3 "O my people, what have I done to you?
In what have I wearied you? Answer me!
4 For I brought you up from the land of Egypt,
and redeemed you from the house of
slavery;
and I sent before you Moses,
Aaron, and Miriam.
5 O my people, remember now what King Balak
of Moab devised,
what Balaam son of Beor answered him,
and what happened from Shittim to Gilgal,
that you may know the saving acts of the
LORD."

COMMENTARY

God now speaks directly to make a case. One can almost hear a note of hurt, wonderment, and pleading in God's opening question (v. 3). There is a wonderful play on words in Hebrew in the juxtaposition of the very similar words "to weary" (לאה *lāʾâ*) and "to bring up" (עלה *ʿālâ,* vv. 3-4).[33] The great God who delivered the people from Egypt has somehow become burdensome to them. God recites a short version of a salvation history, a kind of creed that recalls key periods in Israel's history when God's activity was seen most clearly (Josh 24:5; 1 Sam 12:8; Ps 105:26). It is very unusual for Miriam to be listed along with Moses and Aaron in such a list of God's mighty acts.

King Balak had hired Balaam to speak a curse against Israel, but it turned into a blessing (Numbers 22–24). "From Shittim to Gilgal" (v. 5) must refer to the crossing of the Jordan into the promised land. Shittim is east of the Jordan, and Gilgal is on the west. If the people will only remember these and other saving acts of God, they will never waver from following God's way, and, consequently, life will continue to go well for them. "To remember" (זכר *zākar*) in texts like this means to identify fully with the ancient stories, to know that they are not remote tales from long ago but are living examples of the ongoing presence and power of God in every age. (See Reflections at 6:13-16.)

33. In their hiphil forms in vv. 3-4, these two words sound very similar.

Micah 6:6-8, What God Expects in Return

[6]With what shall I come before the LORD
  and bow down before the exalted God?
Shall I come before him with burnt offerings,
  with calves a year old?
[7]Will the LORD be pleased with thousands of rams,
  with ten thousand rivers of oil?
Shall I offer my firstborn for my transgression,
  the fruit of my body for the sin of my soul?
[8]He has showed you, O man, what is good.
  And what does the LORD require of you?
To act justly and to love mercy
  and to walk humbly with your God.

[6] "With what shall I come before the LORD,
  and bow myself before God on high?
Shall I come before him with burnt offerings,
  with calves a year old?
[7] Will the LORD be pleased with thousands of
  rams,
  with ten thousands of rivers of oil?
Shall I give my firstborn for my transgression,
  the fruit of my body for the sin of my soul?"
[8] He has told you, O mortal, what is good;
  and what does the LORD require of you
but to do justice, and to love kindness,
  and to walk humbly with your God?

COMMENTARY

6:6-7. God has done all these things for the people. Now the people ask what God expects in return. In vv. 6-7, an individual raises the question for the whole community. What can we do to please God, especially at those times when we have gone astray and need to make things right with God again? Many commentators have noted that the dialogue in these verses is like an en-

trance liturgy, such as in Psalms 15 and 24. A religious official, probably a priest, responds to questions about who may approach the holy space, what one must do to please God and to be acceptable to the Most High. In vv. 6-7, the questions are all related to participation in Israel's sacrificial cult. What constitutes an acceptable offering: year-old calves, rams, "rivers of oil," even the worshiper's firstborn? The questions about quantity gradually rise to ridiculous levels ("thousands of rams" or "ten thousand rivers of oil" in v. 7a). Then, at the end, there is a qualitative jump with the suggestion that God may even require the giving of a human life (v. 7b). God had once asked that of Abraham, but then prevented Abraham from completing that terrible sacrifice (Genesis 22). Israel had looked in horror at the practice of human sacrifice (see Deut 12:31; 18:10; Jer 19:5; Ezek 16:20). The questions push the point to the extreme: Does anything suffice to move God to accept me, particularly when I have defied God, repented, and wish to return to a closer relationship?

6:8. The answer changes the question. This often happens in the biblical story (God's "answer" to Job in Job 38–41 is a classic example). The people's questions were preoccupied with what they could do to please God through religious ritual and ceremony. Micah is in good company with other prophets when he clearly states that God is more interested in the way people live their everyday lives than in their religious practices. Amos even says that God "hates" such superficial efforts of piety if they are not accompanied by lives dedicated to justice and righteousness (Amos 5:21-24).

The threefold summary of what God expects (v. 8) is a general summary, leaving the details to further explication. Several very important biblical words appear here. "Justice" (משפט *mišpāṭ*) is something that people do. It is not enough to wish for justice or to complain because it is lacking. This is a dynamic concept that calls on God's

people to work for fairness and equality for all, particularly the weak and the powerless who are exploited by others. "Kindness" translates a Hebrew word (חסד *ḥesed*) that is very common in the Bible, but its meaning can hardly be conveyed by any single English word. It has to do with love, loyalty, and faithfulness. It can be used to describe the key element in relationships, whether in marriage or between human friends or between God and humanity. It is not enough to maintain covenant faithfulness (whether on the human level or between humans and God) out of duty or fear of punishment. Israel is to "love" (אהב *'āhab*) God— to be faithful to its covenant partner—as God loves Israel. There is no resentment, as if manipulated or coerced by another (whether God or human). Israel's relationship of faithfulness to God is motivated by love. Some scholars have pointed out that the word "humbly" (from צנע *ṣn'*) might better be understood as "carefully" or "circumspectly."[34] The key word in this verse is "walk" (הלך *hālak*). We are to walk with God, careful to put God first and to live in conformity with God's will. Our life pilgrimage is likened to a walk with God as our constant companion.

These key verses from Micah are about lifestyle, one's total outlook on life, and one's ethical values. They reject the simplistic notion that there is one thing Israel can do (ritually or otherwise) to make things right between God and the people. (See Reflections at 6:13-16.)

---

34. James Limburg, *Hosea–Micah,* Interpretation (Atlanta: John Knox, 1988) 192.

Micah 6:9-12, What God Cannot Tolerate

NIV

[9] Listen! The LORD is calling to the city—
    and to fear your name is wisdom—
    "Heed the rod and the One who appointed
        it.[a]
[10] Am I still to forget, O wicked house,
    your ill-gotten treasures
    and the short ephah,[b] which is accursed?

a9 The meaning of the Hebrew for this line is uncertain. b10 An ephah was a dry measure.

NRSV

[9] The voice of the LORD cries to the city
    (it is sound wisdom to fear your name):
    Hear, O tribe and assembly of the city![a]
[10] Can I forget[b] the treasures of wickedness in
        the house of the wicked,
    and the scant measure that is accursed?
[11] Can I tolerate wicked scales

a Cn Compare Gk: Heb *tribe, and who has appointed it yet?*
b Cn: Meaning of Heb uncertain

NIV

¹¹Shall I acquit a man with dishonest scales,
    with a bag of false weights?
¹²Her rich men are violent;
    her people are liars
    and their tongues speak deceitfully."

NRSV

    and a bag of dishonest weights?
¹² Your*ᵃ* wealthy are full of violence;
    your*ᵃ* inhabitants speak lies,
    with tongues of deceit in their mouths.

ᵃ Heb *Whose*

COMMENTARY

God speaks again. The people have been told that Yahweh requires justice, loving-kindness, and a humble walk with God. If that is true, then the behavior of the people demonstrates that they have not lived up to that standard. God has no choice but to move against them. God cannot forget or tolerate the wickedness that is so prevalent, particularly in the cheating, stealing and lying that goes on in the name of commerce (vv. 10-12). God would be untrue to God's own self if such evil were allowed to continue with no response. If the jury is still listening, the evidence is clear. God is acting justly. The people are in the wrong and deserve punishment. If they cry out in their suffering that God is unjust, then they need to take another look at the total picture as presented in chapter 6. The contrast between what God has done for the people and what they have done in response should remove any doubt about God's justice. (See Reflections at 6:13-16.)

Micah 6:13-16, What God Is Moved to Do

NIV

¹³"Therefore, I have begun to destroy you,
    to ruin you because of your sins.
¹⁴You will eat but not be satisfied;
    your stomach will still be empty.*ᵃ*
You will store up but save nothing,
    because what you save I will give to the
        sword.
¹⁵You will plant but not harvest;
    you will press olives but not use the oil on
        yourselves,
    you will crush grapes but not drink the wine.
¹⁶You have observed the statutes of Omri
    and all the practices of Ahab's house,
    and you have followed their traditions.
Therefore I will give you over to ruin
    and your people to derision;
    you will bear the scorn of the nations.*ᵇ*"

ᵃ14 The meaning of the Hebrew for this word is uncertain.
ᵇ16 Septuagint; Hebrew *scorn due my people*

NRSV

¹³ Therefore I have begun*ᵃ* to strike you down,
    making you desolate because of your sins.
¹⁴ You shall eat, but not be satisfied,
    and there shall be a gnawing hunger within
        you;
you shall put away, but not save,
    and what you save, I will hand over to the
        sword.
¹⁵ You shall sow, but not reap;
    you shall tread olives, but not anoint
        yourselves with oil;
    you shall tread grapes, but not drink wine.
¹⁶ For you have kept the statutes of Omri*ᵇ*
    and all the works of the house of Ahab,
    and you have followed their counsels.
Therefore I will make you a desolation, and
        your *ᶜ* inhabitants an object of hissing;
    so you shall bear the scorn of my people.

ᵃ Gk Syr Vg: Heb *have made sick*   *ᵇ* Gk Syr Vg Tg: Heb *the statutes of Omri are kept*   *ᶜ* Heb *its*

COMMENTARY

God will now act out of justice and righteousness. In fact, the process has already begun (v. 13). What follows is a series of what are sometimes called futility curses, in which one's best efforts and hard work lead only to frustration and the loss of what one had hoped to achieve or acquire. They appear in the OT as sanctions (curses) that will befall those who break the covenant (see Deut 28:30-31, 38-40; Lev 26:26). The text in v. 14*b* is very difficult. Both the NIV and the NRSV connect it with the insatiable hunger mentioned in v. 14*a* and interpret it as an extension of that idea. Others have thought that it speaks about childbirth. It will be difficult to conceive children, and those few who are born will perish by the sword.[35] In ancient Israel, one achieved a kind of immortality in leaving children behind. It was a great calamity to be left without offspring.

Other oracles of punishment in Micah provide clues about historical context. If Assyria or Babylon is mentioned by name, or if the message seems addressed to people already scattered in exile, then we can draw some conclusions about when these words were spoken. In vv. 13-16, the context is less certain. Famine and crop failure could result from natural causes, such as drought or pestilence. Or crops could be lost to a rampaging army. The mention of the sword in v. 14 may refer to an invasion by Assyria or Babylon, but we cannot be sure which one, if either. In v. 16, Omri and his son Ahab (notorious for his conflicts with Elijah in 1 Kings 18; 21:17-29) are named as both a condemnation ("you have followed their ways," NIV and NRSV) and as a prophecy that Judah's fate will be like that of Samaria. The word "followed" is the same word as "walk" (הלך *hālak*) in v. 8. The people have chosen to walk with Omri and Ahab rather than with the Lord. No wonder disasters are imminent. With regard to dating, v. 16 belongs sometime between the fall of Samaria (722 BCE) and the fall of Jerusalem (586 BCE). The closer it is to the former date, the more likely that it is a word from Micah rather than a later editor.

The NIV reads the end of v. 16 as "the scorn of the nations," choosing an alternate text. The NRSV translates the Hebrew text literally: "the scorn of my people." The NIV, however, seems to make better sense. Its reading is synonymous with the preceding line and similar to many biblical expressions of the humiliation and ridicule heaped on the nation that is defeated and sent into exile.

35. James L. Mays, *Micah,* OTL (Philadelphia: Westminster, 1976) 143; and Leslie C. Allen, *The Books of Joel, Obadiah, Jonah, and Micah,* NICOT (Grand Rapids: Eerdmans, 1976) 380.

REFLECTIONS

1. How can persons know that they are right with God? (See the section "Theological Issues" in the Introduction.) The familiar text from Mic 6:6-8 gives us some ways to think about this perennial faith question. Clearly, God makes demands on those whom God calls into community. But which comes first: God's actions to form the community or meritorious behavior that earns acceptance from God? Many biblical texts, including this one, place the initiative with God. It was God who brought the slaves out of Egypt, led them safely through the wilderness into the promised land, and made them a people. God called, loved, and made a commitment to them without requiring them to attain some preliminary standard of ethics, piety, or knowledge. But now they are God's people and are expected to live accordingly, particularly with regard to justice, love, and faithfulness to God and to each other. If they are unable or unwilling to do so, there will be unpleasant consequences. That does not mean that God has stopped loving them, but negative results are inevitable when people live out of conformity with the way God has constituted the world.

What God requires is both easier and harder than the questions of vv. 6-7 imply. It is easier because there is nothing that we need to do (or are able to do) to make ourselves sufficiently worthy to approach God. It is harder, because what God expects of us is a dedication of our whole lives, not just outward and occasional acts of piety. There is really nothing new here. God has already told the people what is good (v. 8a). They have the teachings of Moses and the great stories of deliverance through God's graceful action. Their fascination with ceremony and sacrifice may actually hide a reluctance to come to terms with what they already know, with what is truly important.

If one is in right relationship with God (walking humbly with God), one need not worry overmuch about what to do to win approval or forgiveness for sinful indiscretions. If one is not right with God, no liturgical ceremony, sacrifice, act of generosity, or rigid adherence to theological absolutes will be sufficient.

2. Is God just? When terrible things happen to people, even to those who seem least deserving, how do we reconcile attributes of God (e.g., power and justice) that appear to be in contradiction? If God is powerful and at work to influence earthly events (such as the exodus, the blessing by Balaam, the safe crossing of the Jordan), then why does God cause (or allow?) disasters that crush God's own people? Does God actually interfere in the life of the planet, or is God merely a frustrated bystander like the rest of us? Is there a middle position that affirms God's influence but admits that it is modified by human freedom?

Throughout the years, faithful people have struggled with the question of theodicy, the effort to find a rational defense of God's justice within the reality of horrible circumstances. In a sense, God has been on trial many times throughout the centuries, as in the dispute between God and the people in Micah 6. Any jury (mountains or hills or the people of Israel or the Christian church) should look carefully at the evidence. In doing so, they may come to the same conclusion as the book of Micah: God is, indeed, just. The people sinned to the point where God had no choice but to punish the offenders. If God did not act to punish the guilty and vindicate the oppressed, it would have been a denial of justice.

In pastoral work and in our preaching, we are wise to treat theories of theodicy with some caution. Enthusiastic efforts to clear God of charges of injustice and to argue against denials of God's power may lead to untrue accusations against human beings. In times of suffering, when all are looking for someone to blame, we may save God's reputation only by increasing the guilt of humanity, both individually and collectively. (See Reflections number 5 on 1:2-7; Reflections number 1 on 2:1-5; Reflections number 1 on 3:9-12; and Job 13:1-12.)

3. Is God hurt by the rejection of those whom God has called and loved? In 6:3-5, God's defense reminds us of the lament of parents who have done everything possible to prepare their children for happy and successful lives, only to be puzzled, offended, and grieved by their rebelliousness. What to do? Is punishment the proper course? Will it help? A parent who continues to love a misbehaving child does not want to hurt the child, but cannot let matters go on without intervention. Parents think that required discipline is more painful to them than to their child, but very few recipients of punishment ever believed that.

Just as the prophet does not like to be the messenger of menacing news to the people he loves, so also God does not enjoy inflicting punishment, even if the people deserve it. So God has a problem, too, when people are disobedient. God also feels pain. We can see examples of God's grief and sorrow in the Pentateuch (e.g., Gen 6:5-6), in other prophetic writings (e.g., Jer 3:19-20; 4:19-22; 5:7-9; Hosea 11), and certainly in the suffering God of the New Testament.

MICAH 7:1-7, THE PROPHET'S LAMENT OVER THE DECADENCE OF SOCIETY

NIV

7 What misery is mine!
I am like one who gathers summer fruit
at the gleaning of the vineyard;
there is no cluster of grapes to eat,
none of the early figs that I crave.
[2]The godly have been swept from the land;
not one upright man remains.
All men lie in wait to shed blood;
each hunts his brother with a net.
[3]Both hands are skilled in doing evil;
the ruler demands gifts,
the judge accepts bribes,
the powerful dictate what they desire—
they all conspire together.
[4]The best of them is like a brier,
the most upright worse than a thorn hedge.
The day of your watchmen has come,
the day God visits you.
Now is the time of their confusion.
[5]Do not trust a neighbor;
put no confidence in a friend.
Even with her who lies in your embrace
be careful of your words.
[6]For a son dishonors his father,
a daughter rises up against her mother,
a daughter-in-law against her mother-in-law—
a man's enemies are the members of his own
household.
[7]But as for me, I watch in hope for the LORD,
I wait for God my Savior;
my God will hear me.

NRSV

7 Woe is me! For I have become like one
who,
after the summer fruit has been gathered,
after the vintage has been gleaned,
finds no cluster to eat;
there is no first-ripe fig for which I hunger.
[2] The faithful have disappeared from the land,
and there is no one left who is upright;
they all lie in wait for blood,
and they hunt each other with nets.
[3] Their hands are skilled to do evil;
the official and the judge ask for a bribe,
and the powerful dictate what they desire;
thus they pervert justice.[a]
[4] The best of them is like a brier,
the most upright of them a thorn hedge.
The day of their[b] sentinels, of their[b]
punishment, has come;
now their confusion is at hand.
[5] Put no trust in a friend,
have no confidence in a loved one;
guard the doors of your mouth
from her who lies in your embrace;
[6] for the son treats the father with contempt,
the daughter rises up against her mother,
the daughter-in-law against her mother-in-law;
your enemies are members of your own
household.
[7] But as for me, I will look to the LORD,
I will wait for the God of my salvation;
my God will hear me.

[a] Cn: Heb *they weave it*   [b] Heb *your*

COMMENTARY

The oracle of punishment in 6:13-16 is followed by a poignant lament. We are reminded of the lament over the fate of Samaria and the spread of disaster to Jerusalem in 1:8-9. Some scholars have supposed that the speaker of this lament is Jerusalem in response to the warning it has just received.[36] It

seems more likely, however, that the prophet is lamenting, not only for himself but as the spokesperson for God. If Micah is, indeed, speaking (and there is no compelling reason to doubt that), we have here another rare look inside the prophet's mind and heart. In this passage, the prophet's agony is less related to the terrible events soon to

36. Mays, *Micah,* 151.

come than to the deplorable state of society, which has precipitated the disaster.

7:1-4. Society has deteriorated both in its public (7:1-4) and its private (7:5-6) spheres. Anyone who searches for an honest and faithful person will be as disappointed as one who is hungry and comes to the vineyard or orchard after all the fruit has been picked (v. 1). The best of the citizens are like briars and thorns (v. 4). We can only imagine what the worst are like. The list of their sins—preying on one another, doing evil, taking bribes, misusing power, and perverting justice (vv. 2-3)—is similar to what we have seen elsewhere in Micah's prophecies (e.g., Mic 2:2, 8-9; 3:9-11). Other biblical characters also searched vainly for a few—or even one—honest and upright persons in desperate attempts to show that a condemned people are not completely decadent and, perhaps, to avert God's punishment (see Gen 18:23-33; Jer 5:1). But it is to no avail, and it is too late. The day of punishment, seen already by their watchmen (prophets like Micah?), is at hand (v. 4).

7:5-6. Not only public life has dissolved into greed and abuse of power, but even private arenas of friendship and family have been infected by the general dissolution of the society as well. No one can be trusted. Even a husband and wife, locked in the intimate embrace of their own bed, dare not share their deepest thoughts and feelings with each other (v. 5). The solidarity and security of the nurturing family is gone as intergenerational hostilities flare up (v. 6; see Jesus' predictions of the family strife that will precede the end time in Matt 10:21, 35-36; Luke 12:51-3; Mark 13:12). No wonder the prophet is moved to lament.

7:7. As bad as things are, the lament ends with a word of hope. As with other laments throughout the psalter, the flow is from complaint to acceptance to praise. God has heard, God will do something, and, therefore, one can still hope. Hebrew has a number of words that can be translated as "hope." The word "wait" (יחל *yāḥal*) can just as well be rendered "hope" (v. 7*b*). "To wait" is "to hope," if one knows for what or for whom one is waiting. Hope is not always expressed in terms of specific content. Rather, the basis of hope is a relationship of trust, confidence that the God to whom Israel has turned in the past will not forever abandon the people to their present distress. How the deliverance will come and when remain beyond human vision. But Israel lives in hope because it knows who God is (see Commentary on 7:18-20).

REFLECTIONS

1. Once more we are reminded of the burden that the prophet must carry (see Reflections number 2 on 1:8-16). The prophet sometimes uses the lament form as a way to pronounce a disaster that has not yet occurred. But this is more than a clever use of a literary form. The true prophet loves his people and is pained by the message he must bear and is sometimes driven to a genuine lament that expresses his suffering. Jeremiah is best known for this, but we also see it here, yet briefly, in Micah.

2. The prophet is alienated from his own society. His critical analysis of all that is wrong puts him in a position against the people with whom he lives. When he begins to speak, that alienation grows as his listeners resist the message and the messenger. The gap between prophet and people is particularly obvious in this passage. There is not one decent person among them. If even the best of them is awful, how bad are the worst of them?

If we put ourselves in the place of Micah's audience, we can imagine our response to his critique of society. Who does he think he is, anyway? Why is he so alienated? Perhaps he had an unhappy childhood and is projecting his hostility on all of us. How do we understand prophets of doom in our own day? They often look like people who are already at odds with society. Do we take seriously their message or dismiss them as self-righteous, angry, perhaps paranoid cranks? Is their message true, a sharp picture of reality, or merely symptomatic of their own failure to be fully socialized? In our day, there is no shortage of prophets of doom.

How do we respond? Are we any better at distinguishing between true and false prophets than were Micah's hearers?

MICAH 7:8-20, THE CLOSING LITURGY

OVERVIEW

The book of Micah ends with what scholars agree is a closing liturgy. It concludes the book on a hopeful note and makes Micah's prophecies usable in public worship. It assumes a time when the nation has already fallen and is sitting in darkness (v. 8), enemies are gloating (vv. 8, 10), and the wall of the city has been destroyed (v. 11). This points to a time after 586 BCE. Most scholars date it late in the exilic period or the early post-exilic times because of the people's willingness to accept the prophet's assignment of blame (v. 9) and because the text expresses a more confident mood about the future than would have been possible early in the exile.[37] Now the people begin to believe that the message of judgment so prominent in Micah is not the end of the story. They look ahead to a time when God will bring about a new deliverance that will rival the great saving event of the exodus.

This passage is identified as a liturgy, in part, because more than one voice is heard. Personified Jerusalem speaks in vv. 8-10. In vv. 11-13 a priest, or some other religious functionary, responds. Verses 14-17 express the people's appeal to Yahweh; and verses 18-20 express their praise of God, who forgives their sins.

37. James Limburg, *Hosea–Micah,* Interpretation (Atlanta: John Knox, 1988) 193.

Micah 7:8-17, The Fortunes of Israel and Its Enemies Reversed

NIV	NRSV

⁸Do not gloat over me, my enemy!
    Though I have fallen, I will rise.
Though I sit in darkness,
    the LORD will be my light.
⁹Because I have sinned against him,
    I will bear the LORD's wrath,
until he pleads my case
    and establishes my right.
He will bring me out into the light;
    I will see his righteousness.
¹⁰Then my enemy will see it
    and will be covered with shame,
she who said to me,
    "Where is the LORD your God?"
My eyes will see her downfall;
    even now she will be trampled underfoot
    like mire in the streets.
 	
¹¹The day for building your walls will come,
    the day for extending your boundaries.
¹²In that day people will come to you
	⁸ Do not rejoice over me, O my enemy;
	    when I fall, I shall rise;
	when I sit in darkness,
	    the LORD will be a light to me.
	⁹ I must bear the indignation of the LORD,
	    because I have sinned against him,
	until he takes my side
	    and executes judgment for me.
	He will bring me out to the light;
	    I shall see his vindication.
	¹⁰ Then my enemy will see,
	    and shame will cover her who said to
	        me,
	    "Where is the LORD your God?"
	My eyes will see her downfall;ᵃ
	    now she will be trodden down
	    like the mire of the streets.
	
	¹¹ A day for the building of your walls!
	
	ᵃ Heb lacks *downfall*

NIV

from Assyria and the cities of Egypt,
even from Egypt to the Euphrates
    and from sea to sea
    and from mountain to mountain.
¹³The earth will become desolate because of its
        inhabitants,
    as the result of their deeds.

¹⁴Shepherd your people with your staff,
    the flock of your inheritance,
which lives by itself in a forest,
    in fertile pasturelands.ᵃ
Let them feed in Bashan and Gilead
    as in days long ago.

¹⁵"As in the days when you came out of Egypt,
    I will show them my wonders."

¹⁶Nations will see and be ashamed,
    deprived of all their power.
They will lay their hands on their mouths
    and their ears will become deaf.
¹⁷They will lick dust like a snake,
    like creatures that crawl on the ground.
They will come trembling out of their dens;
    they will turn in fear to the LORD our God
    and will be afraid of you.

ᵃ14 Or *in the middle of Carmel*

NRSV

In that day the boundary shall be far
        extended.
¹² In that day they will come to you
    from Assyria toᵃ Egypt,
and from Egypt to the River,
    from sea to sea and from mountain to
        mountain.

¹³ But the earth will be desolate
    because of its inhabitants,
    for the fruit of their doings.

¹⁴ Shepherd your people with your staff,
    the flock that belongs to you,
which lives alone in a forest
    in the midst of a garden land;
let them feed in Bashan and Gilead
    as in the days of old.

¹⁵ As in the days when you came out of the land
        of Egypt,
    show usᵇ marvelous things.

¹⁶ The nations shall see and be ashamed
    of all their might;
they shall lay their hands on their mouths;
    their ears shall be deaf;
¹⁷ they shall lick dust like a snake,
    like the crawling things of the earth;
they shall come trembling out of their
        fortresses;
they shall turn in dread to the LORD our
        God,
    and they shall stand in fear of you.

ᵃOne Ms: MT *Assyria and cities of*   ᵇCn: Heb *I will show him*

COMMENTARY

7:8-10. God's people have been disgraced and humiliated by what has happened to them. Their honor has been defiled. Further, God has been mocked by the enemy's sarcastic question, "Where is the LORD your God?" (v. 10), implying either weakness or indifference on God's part. Some have associated the taunting enemy with Babylon, but most have seen this as a reference to Edom, which caused Judah great anguish by its reaction to Jerusalem's downfall.[38] (See Ps

137:7; Isa 34:8-10; Lam 3:14; 4:21; Obad 12.) Israel's desire for vindication (vv. 8-10, 16-17) may be tarnished by more than a little of its own anger, but it also reflects concern for God's honor if perpetrators of evil against God's people were not held accountable. They had come to accept the truth of Micah's indictment. They have indeed deserved God's judgment (v. 9*a*). But now they expect God, if justice is to be fully executed, to become their advocate and to judge other nations by the same standards used to measure the conduct of Israel (v. 9*b*).

38. Ibid., 193; Allen, *The Books of Joel, Obadiah, Jonah, and Micah*, 394; Mays, *Micah*, 158.

7:11-13. In vv. 11-12, a priest or other religious spokesperson seems to step forward and pronounce specific words of good news. The wall will be rebuilt. The boundary will be extended, perhaps to the ideal borders of David's and Solomon's reigns (or further), from Egypt on one side, to the great empires of Mesopotamia on the other (see Ps 72:8; Zech 9:10). And people will be on the move from everywhere back to Jerusalem (v. 12). Most likely this is a reference to the return of the Babylonian exiles, but it could also be a reference to the time when all pagan nations will come to Jerusalem to learn about the one true God (as Mic 4:1-4). If so, the passage begins to take on eschatological overtones, looking into the far distant future when God will act to correct all that is wrong with the world.

7:14-15. These verses address God as the shepherd (see Mic 2:12; 5:4), urging God to let the people again feed in Bashan and Gilead. These areas were noted for their excellent pasture land (Num 32:1; Jer 50:19). They had been lost to Israel since the eighth century BCE. This is another expression of the people's hope for return to the land that had been promised to them from ancient times but had fallen under foreign domination.

Verse 15 contains a direct reference to the exodus from Egypt, that great act of deliverance which had achieved creedal significance as the premier act of God on behalf of the people. Now they ask God again to do marvelous things to accomplish their salvation from exile in foreign lands and to bring all the world into proper subjection to the one true God (vv. 16-17). Besides this explicit mention of the exodus in v. 15, there are other appeals to the exodus tradition in vv. 18-20.

7:16-17. When the nations realize who God is, they will be ashamed, completely humiliated, filled with fear. They will turn to God in fear and dread, not in hope and trust, as in 4:1-2. It is as if Micah 4 gives a longer view of the future, a willingness to look beyond the more immediate pains of exile and subjugation and desire for revenge to a time when all nations will be reconciled under the rule of the one true God.

Micah 7:18-20, Hope in God Remains

NIV	NRSV

[18]Who is a God like you,
  who pardons sin and forgives the
    transgression
  of the remnant of his inheritance?
You do not stay angry forever
  but delight to show mercy.
[19]You will again have compassion on us;
  you will tread our sins underfoot
  and hurl all our iniquities into the depths of
    the sea.
[20]You will be true to Jacob,
  and show mercy to Abraham,
as you pledged on oath to our fathers
  in days long ago.
	[18] Who is a God like you, pardoning iniquity
	  and passing over the transgression
	    of the remnant of your[a] possession?
	He does not retain his anger forever,
	  because he delights in showing clemency.
	[19] He will again have compassion upon us;
	  he will tread our iniquities under foot.
	You will cast all our[b] sins
	  into the depths of the sea.
	[20] You will show faithfulness to Jacob
	  and unswerving loyalty to Abraham,
	as you have sworn to our ancestors
	  from the days of old.
	
	a Heb *his* *b* Gk Syr Vg Tg: Heb *their*

COMMENTARY

The liturgy ends with a glorious hymn that brings everything in the book of Micah to a proper focus. The opening question of v. 18 reminds us of the meaning of Micah's name: "Who is like

Yahweh?" (author's trans.). Such rhetorical questions about God are not uncommon in the OT (e.g., Exod 15:11; Pss 77:13; 71:18-19). The exodus reference from the "Song of the Sea" again links the expectations of the people singing this hymn with the wondrous acts of God in the escape from Egypt. There is hope for the future in remembering what God has done in the past.

Many key words and ideas about God are crowded into the final three verses of Micah. There are words about God's character—forgiving, not holding on to anger, delighting in mercy, compassionate, faithful, and loyal. Many scholars have seen a connection between vv. 18-20 and Exod 34:6-7.[39] These two passages share several words for human rebellion and disobedience: sin, iniquity, transgression. And each has several ways to describe what God will do about sin: pardon, pass over, tread underfoot, throw into the depths of the sea—another possible allusion to the exodus and the crossing of the sea (Exod 15:1-5). The bottom line is that God is merciful and forgiving. The bad times are over. God's anger had been stirred by the people's faithlessness and the wrong done to the weak and powerless. But God's true nature again comes to the fore. The ancient promises will never be broken (v. 20). If one faces the future with faith in a God like this, hope is possible no matter what experiences the world might bring.

39. Limburg, *Hosea–Micah*, 196; Allen, *The Books of Joel, Obadiah, Jonah, and Micah*, 403; Mays, *Micah*, 167.

REFLECTIONS

1. Throughout Micah, there is a constant tension between justice and mercy. God is a righteous God and will not tolerate evil. Punishment is inevitable if sinful behavior persists. The world makes moral sense. God cannot abandon God's own standards of justice. And yet, God is constantly pulled in the direction of forgiveness and mercy. God is also in pain when people disobey, and God can see the terrible consequences awaiting them. God wants to forgive and move on to better things if people will give at least some hint of repentance, some opening into which God can move to relax the rigid standards of absolute justice.

This tension between justice and mercy shows up even in the structure of the book. Mercy and forgiveness break through in the midst of the horrible proclamations of doom in chapters 1–3. Although chapters 4–5 primarily stress the positive word about a forgiving God, judgment is still present. Evil consequences are already at work and will need to run their course. And in chapters 6–7, again we see a mix of judgment and hope, but, in the end, hope has the last word.

Since the received word from God is a mix of good news and bad news, those of us who are called to be contemporary bearers of God's Word need constantly to be alert to the times and situations of our audience so that we speak the truth and do not try to resolve the tension by proclaiming only one side of the message. We need to be mindful of Micah's critique of the religious leaders of his day who had part of the message right but who failed to warn their people of the dangers ahead (see Reflections on 2:6-11).

2. Having said all this, we are grateful that the conclusion of the book of Micah maintains (as do innumerable passages throughout the Bible) that the best description of God uses words like *mercy, forgiveness, faithfulness, compassion, loyalty,* and *love.* The world is full of people who do not know that about this God, but who may have heard about the punishing, avenging God. The end of Micah needs to be proclaimed loudly and clearly to put in proper perspective the hard words found earlier in the book.

THE BOOK OF NAHUM

INTRODUCTION, COMMENTARY, AND REFLECTIONS
BY
FRANCISCO O. GARCÍA-TRETO

THE BOOK OF
NAHUM

INTRODUCTION

NINEVEH AND ASSYRIA

The book of Nahum presents a difficult question to readers of the Bible. Why does Nahum, a Judean prophet, focus his attention on the fortunes of Nineveh, a distant Mesopotamian city? Simply to say that Nineveh was one of the major cities of Assyria and the main residence of the last Assyrian kings does not explain its importance for the author of this Hebrew poem. The fall of Nineveh in 612 BCE must have been one of the most momentous events during the time when the book of Nahum was written. Still, it is a challenge to understand the strong antipathy the poet manifests against the city and his joy at its doom.

Situated on the banks of the Tigris River, in today's northern Iraq, ancient Nineveh's remains lie beneath two mounds, Kuyunjik and Nebi Yunus, in what is now the city of Mosul. The Nineveh of Nahum's time was the premier city of the Late Assyrian Empire, from which Ashurbanipal (668–627), the last powerful king of Assyria, reigned. The Late Assyrian Empire comprised the reigns of six major kings and lasted from the second half of the eighth century BCE to the fall of Nineveh in 612 BCE.[1] It was precisely these six kings who cast the strongest shadows upon the political and cultural existence of Israel

---

1. The fifteen years or so between the death of Ashurbanipal and the fall of Nineveh remain obscure to historians. Two kings seem to have ruled the rapidly collapsing empire, Ashur-etel-ilani and Sinsharrishkun, but little is known of their reigns. For three years after the fall of Nineveh, another, Ashur-uballit II, was nominally the last king of Assyria, until the last elements of the Assyrian army were defeated and dispersed in 609 BCE.

and Judah. Relatively unimportant in themselves, these two kingdoms found themselves, along with a number of their Syro-palestinian neighbors, caught up in an expansionist Assyrian policy, which aimed at Assyrian control of Egyptian trade.

Figure 3: The Late Assyrian Kings

Tiglath-pileser III ("Pul")	744–727 BCE
Shalmaneser V	726–722
Sargon II	721–705
Sennacherib	704–681
Esarhaddon	680–669
Ashurbanipal	668–627 (631?)
The Collapse	626–609
Ashur-etil-ilani	630?–627?
Sinsharrishkun	626–612
Ashur-uballit II	611–609

The first of the six kings was Tiglath-pileser III, who invaded Palestine and captured Gaza in 734. As 2 Kings 15–16, for example, shows "Pul" (a diminutive of the name "Tiglath-pileser") exacted tribute from both Israel and Judah. From then on, Assyria remained a major and generally unwelcome player in the politics of the Palestinian states. His successor, Shalmaneser V, reigned for only four years, but was the one who conquered the Northern Kingdom in 722. In the same year, Sargon II put an end to Shalmaneser's life and reign.

Sargon II was the founder of Assyria's last dynasty. His son Sennacherib was the Assyrian king who devastated Judah in 701, sacked Lachish and other cities, and exacted heavy tribute from Hezekiah after besieging him in Jerusalem "like a bird in a cage," as Sennacherib's annals boast. He also chose to make Nineveh his capital, where he erected a magnificent royal palace as his residence and seat of government. The darkest years of Assyrian vassalage for Judah were those of the long reign of Hezekiah's son Manasseh (687–642), who ruled in Jerusalem under three Assyrian overlords: Sennacherib, Esarhaddon, and Ashurbanipal. While the deuteronomistic history's judgment on Manasseh as the worst of the kings of Judah (2 Kings 21) does not mention Assyria, it stands to reason that Judean nationalists, as well as Yahwistic monotheists, would have considered Assyria to be the wellspring of Manesseh's treason and apostasy. Sennacherib successfully crushed a long-standing Babylonian rebellion, and his forces destroyed the city of Babylon in 689. Esarhaddon, coming to the throne in 680, misguidedly turned his attention to the conquest of Egypt, which the Assyrian army invaded in 671. Assyria's armed might was fearsome, and Assyrian propaganda sought to inspire fear as a means of augmenting that might. Esarhaddon's westward move nevertheless constituted a serious mistake that led to irreducible Egyptian resistance and, more dangerously, pulled forces away from the eastern frontiers where the real threat to Assyria's survival lay.

Ashurbanipal managed temporarily to undo some of the worst results of his predecessor's policies, successfully quelling Babylonian rebellion and waging war against Elam, but with the mixed result of freeing the hand of the Medes to become a greater threat to Assyria. Ashurbanipal also inherited Esarhaddon's Egyptian entanglement, as a result of which the sack of No-Amon (the Egyptian capital city of Thebes) by the Assyrians, referred to in Nah 3:8-10, took place in 663.

Babylonia was to be Assyria's nemesis, destined to bring about the destruction of Nineveh. The Babylonians had long harbored rebellion against domination by their northern neighbors. Nabopolassar, who became king in Babylon in 626, formed an alliance with the Medes and brought the rule of Assyria to an end in a war highlighted by the fall of the cities of Asshur in 614 and of Nineveh in 612.

It is easy to see how a Judean consciousness, formed by well over one hundred years of Assyrian hegemony and buttressed by brutal militarism and propaganda, could react with elation at the news of Assyria's collapse. The Judahites perceived that Yahweh had accomplished Nineveh's downfall. What could be more natural than to cast the defeat of a long-hated oppressor as the long-sought after deliverance finally granted by "a jealous and avenging God"?

THE STRUCTURE OF THE BOOK

Sketching an outline of Nahum's forty-seven verses has not been a simple task, as a comparison of three of the standard English commentaries makes clear. Perhaps the least helpful attempt is that of Charles L. Taylor, who simply distinguished "the Acrostic Poem (1:1-9)" from "the Long Poem (1:11–3:19)" and bridged the gap between these two parts with "a Series of Marginal Notes (1:10, 12, 13, 15, 2:2)."[2] More detailed, and certainly more helpful, are the more recent proposals of Elizabeth Achtemeier and J. J. M. Roberts, both of whom apply form-critical categories in their analyses of the composition.[3] On the one hand, Achtemeier recognizes 1:1 as a title, and then distinguishes six sections: (1) an opening hymn (1:2-11); (2) an oracle against Balial/Nineveh (1:12-15); (3) a judgment oracle in the form of a prophetic vision (2:1-13); (4) a woe oracle (3:1-7); (5) a taunt song (3:8-13); and (6) a final oracle (3:14-19) in two parts: a taunt song (3:14-17) and a funeral dirge (3:18-19). On the other hand, after the superscription (1:1), Roberts identifies four related oracles: (1) one "of reassurance to Judah (1:2–2:1)"; followed by (2) an "oracle threatening the Assyrian king (2:2-14)"; then (3) "a hoy-[woe] oracle against Nineveh (3:1-17)"; and, finally, (4) another "against the king of Assyria (3:18-19)."

2. Charles L. Taylor, Jr., "Nahum," in *The Interpreter's Bible* (Nashville: Abingdon, 1956) 6:957-969.
3. Elizabeth Achtemeier, *Nahum–Malachi* (Atlanta: John Knox, 1986); and J. J. M. Roberts, *Nahum, Habakkuk, and Zephaniah,* OTL (Louisville: Westminster/John Knox, 1991).

Nonetheless, a powerful poetic composition such as Nahum, with its strong thematic integrity, demands a sustained reading from beginning to end. The theme is the fall of Assyria, which Nahum interprets as Yahweh's act of deliverance for his people Judah and defeat of his/their enemy Assyria. One's reading of Nahum must be informed, to be sure, by the perspectives and conclusions of critical analysis, but it must also allow literary sensibility full play. The poetic power of Nahum depends in great part on the cumulative impact of image upon image, metaphor upon metaphor. This accumulation of images rises to a pitch close to incoherence as the poet describes the destruction of the Assyrian capital and the fate of its inhabitants. Although analysis of the individual elements in the composition helps the reader to understand the poet's craft, only a sustained reading of the book as a whole will let the interpreter feel its literary power.

In agreement with Roberts, I recognize a main break at the end of 1:15 (2:1 in the Masoretic Text), which divides the poem into two major sections. The theme of the first part (1:2-15) is the appearance of Yahweh as the divine avenger, a warrior who defends the people and destroys their assailants, challenges the Assyrian enemy, who has dared to oppress Judah, and proclaims victory and salvation to Judah. The second section of Nahum (2:1–3:19) envisions the downfall of Nineveh, portraying it so vividly that the poetry takes on an almost incantatory character, as if it were an attempt to bring the events to pass magically by visualizing them. Certain formal elements used by the poet characterize parts of both sections—the incomplete alphabetic acrostic (1:2-8) in the first or the woe-oracle (3:1-17) in the second—but the presence of these elements is not to be taken as grounds for marking major discontinuities within the sections. Nahum in this sense works as a collage, assembling literary material in the service of a larger poem.

THEME

The theme that Nahum's poetry so powerfully expresses—the avenging wrath of Yahweh redressing Assyrian oppression and abuse of power by Nineveh—will raise serious questions for theologically and ethically sensitive readers, particularly in the light of the horrors of war motivated by nationalism and tribalism. It is clear that the church has not been able easily to integrate Nahum's message into its liturgical usage; Nahum shares with Obadiah the dubious distinction of being the only prophetic books that do not appear in the Revised Common Lectionary, and probably for similar reasons. Elizabeth Achtemeier makes a strong attempt to face the problem in the introduction to her commentary by insisting that we let Nahum "be a book about God," and that Nahum's message then must be that God, the sole arbiter of human history, will not let the wicked go unpunished. In her analysis, the use of "evil" (רעה *rāʾâ*) in 1:11 and 3:19 forms an inclusio that not only frames but also provides the theological key to the book: "evil introduced and evil done away form the inclusio of the thought of the book."[4]

---

4. Achtemeier, *Nahum–Malachi*, 5-7.

Such a reading raises questions and leaves unanswered issues about the theology of Nahum. Can God's punishment of violence and oppression partake of that same violence and oppression? What difference is there between the Assyrians and their foes the Medes and Babylonians? Or, as Isaiah 10 recognizes, if Assyria's depredations have been committed as "the rod of [God's] anger," no matter how guilty Assyria is, is not its crime at least in part an initiative of divine justice? Such a notion implicates God in human acts of violence and death-dealing destruction, which are always impossible to qualify as absolutely good.

Another aspect of the ethical problem that Nahum poses is the lack of distinction the book makes between the guilty and the innocent, even (especially) among the Ninevites. There is no lack of examples of a much more precise sense of justice in the Hebrew Bible. Where, for example, is the overriding concern for the life of guiltless human beings (even in Sodom!) that Abraham expresses and that God agrees to in Genesis 18? Or the intellectual struggle to devise a scheme of personal condemnation or vindication according to personal guilt or innocence (even among the exiles) of Ezekiel 18? Finally, where is the lesson of God's love for all life (even in Nineveh), which the hapless prophet is taught in the last verse of the book of Jonah: "And should I not be concerned about Nineveh, that great city, in which there are more than a hundred and twenty thousand persons who do not know their right hand from their left, and also many animals?" (Jonah 4:11 NRSV)? Perhaps the book of Nahum might serve to spur the church toward ethical and theological discussion of these issues, on which no one can claim that this book speaks the last, or the most unexceptionable, word.

DATE AND PROVENANCE

The book cannot have been written before the fall of Thebes in 663 BCE, to which it alludes in 3:8. Moreover, the book seems to anticipate the fall of Nineveh, rather than report it, so that it must have been written before 612. Most scholars narrow this fifty-year window by assuming that the expectation of the fall of Nineveh probably developed after Nabopolassar and the Medes had actually begun to demolish Assyrian military power, so that shortly before 612 is the most likely judgment. A Judean provenance is likely, and given the genre of the work, we may assume that it was produced by a prophet-poet. But as the section on the superscription will suggest, nothing can be said for certain about the author.

BIBLIOGRAPHY

Achtemeier, Elizabeth. *Nahum–Malachi*. Interpretation. Atlanta: John Knox, 1986. Especially concerned with theological and hermeneutical issues.

Cathcart, Kevin J. "Nahum, Book of." In David Noel Freedman, ed., *The Anchor Bible Dictionary*. New York: Doubleday, 1992. 4:998-1000. A recent and authoritative introduction to the book of Nahum.

Roberts, J. J. M. *Nahum, Habakkuk, and Zephaniah: A Commentary.* OTL. Louisville: Westminster/John Knox, 1991. Focuses on exegetical and critical matters.

OUTLINE OF NAHUM

I. Nahum 1:1, The Superscription

II. Nahum 1:2-15, The Divine Warrior

    A. 1:2-8, The Acrostic Theophany
    B. 1:9-15, Salvation and Doom Announced

III. Nahum 2:1–3:19, The Fate of Nineveh

    A. 2:1-10, The Scatterer
    B. 2:11-13, The Lion Hunt
    C. 3:1-3, Woe to the City of Bloodshed!
    D. 3:4-7, The Humiliated Prostitute
    E. 3:8-11, Are You Better Than Thebes?
    F. 3:12-19, Final Diatribe

THE SUPERSCRIPTION

NIV	NRSV
1 An oracle concerning Nineveh. The book of the vision of Nahum the Elkoshite.	**1** An oracle concerning Nineveh. The book of the vision of Nahum of Elkosh.

COMMENTARY

The first verse, often called the "title" of the book, identifies its contents and genre as well as its author as either the prophet-poet stated them or, more likely, a later editor assessed them. The word משא (*māśśā'*), translated "oracle," identifies eighteen passages in the prophetic books (see, e.g., Isa 13:1; 15:1; 19:1) whose contents appear to constitute instances of a specific genre of prophetic speech.[5] That genre has been characterized as a form that responds to a feeling of doubt, within the Israelite community, about what God intends in a particular historical situation. The *māśśā'*, then, clarifies those intentions, as the prophet addressed the community. The topic of the *māśśā'* is the specific nation, city, people, or historical circumstance that precipitates the question.

In the case of Nahum, the topic is the (perhaps imminent or impending) fall of Nineveh. The basis for the answer is the specific revelation that the prophet seeks and receives about the topic, perhaps what, in the case of Nahum, is referred to by the words "the book of the vision." The vision provided the basis for the prophetic answer to the request for clarification about the deity's intention. That answer typically addresses both the community and the object of divine action, a circumstance that in Nahum at times produces ambiguity about who is being addressed. The NIV translators have sought to resolve that ambiguity, for example, by interpolating "O Nineveh" (1:11) or "Nineveh" (1:14; 2:1; see also 1:8) at certain junctures in the text, a procedure that yields a translation more specific than the original text and that thereby diminishes its allusive power.

Nothing is known about the prophet Nahum as an individual. His name means "comfort" or "consolation" and may be an abbreviated form of "Nehemiah," which means "Yahweh is my consolation." Nahum's hometown, Elkosh—whose exact location is unknown—appears to have been located in southwest Judah. (See Introduction on the approximate dates of his activity.)

5. Richard D. Weis, "Oracle," in *The Anchor Bible Dictionary* (New York: Doubleday, 1992) 5:28-29. See also R. Weis, "A Definition of the Genre Maśśa' in the Hebrew Bible" (Ph.D. diss., Claremont, 1986).

THE DIVINE WARRIOR

OVERVIEW

The first section of the poem focuses on the awesome figure of Yahweh the warrior, making an appearance to deliver Judah by smashing Judah's oppressors. An acrostic poem hymns the theophany, followed by a proclamation of doom and of salvation to the respective parties.

NAHUM 1:2-8, THE ACROSTIC THEOPHANY

NIV

²The LORD is a jealous and avenging God;
the LORD takes vengeance and is filled with
wrath.
The LORD takes vengeance on his foes
and maintains his wrath against his enemies.
³The LORD is slow to anger and great in power;
the LORD will not leave the guilty unpunished.
His way is in the whirlwind and the storm,
and clouds are the dust of his feet.
⁴He rebukes the sea and dries it up;
he makes all the rivers run dry.
Bashan and Carmel wither
and the blossoms of Lebanon fade.
⁵The mountains quake before him
and the hills melt away.
The earth trembles at his presence,
the world and all who live in it.
⁶Who can withstand his indignation?
Who can endure his fierce anger?
His wrath is poured out like fire;
the rocks are shattered before him.
⁷The LORD is good,
a refuge in times of trouble.
He cares for those who trust in him,
⁸ but with an overwhelming flood
he will make an end of ₍Nineveh₎;
he will pursue his foes into darkness.

NRSV

² A jealous and avenging God is the LORD,
the LORD is avenging and wrathful;
the LORD takes vengeance on his adversaries
and rages against his enemies.
³ The LORD is slow to anger but great in power,
and the LORD will by no means clear the
guilty.

His way is in whirlwind and storm,
and the clouds are the dust of his feet.
⁴ He rebukes the sea and makes it dry,
and he dries up all the rivers;
Bashan and Carmel wither,
and the bloom of Lebanon fades.
⁵ The mountains quake before him,
and the hills melt;
the earth heaves before him,
the world and all who live in it.

⁶ Who can stand before his indignation?
Who can endure the heat of his anger?
His wrath is poured out like fire,
and by him the rocks are broken in pieces.
⁷ The LORD is good,
a stronghold in a day of trouble;
he protects those who take refuge in him,
⁸ even in a rushing flood.
He will make a full end of his adversaries,ᵃ
and will pursue his enemies into darkness.

ᵃ Gk: Heb *of her place*

COMMENTARY

Both in form and in content, the first verses of Nahum evoke ancient liturgical traditions. Alphabetic acrostics—i.e., compositions in which the first word of each line or stanza begins with a successive letter of the alphabet—are relatively frequent in biblical psalmody and wisdom literature.[6] While most of the examples of the form now found in the Bible are of exilic and post-exilic origin—and post-biblical usage is attested from the writings of the Qumran sectarians as well—Psalms 9–10 (a single composition) and Nahum 1:2-8 attest to the use of the form in pre-exilic Judah. Nahum appears, therefore, to begin by either quoting or parodying a form that does not belong to the standard repertory of prophecy, but to the realm of liturgy. This in itself is not unusual, given the well-known prophetic device of poetic imitation of funeral dirges, lawsuits, love songs, and the like. Nahum's acrostic, like a number of others in the Bible, does not reach across the complete alphabet, but only halfway, to כ (*kaph*) or the English letter "k," with certain irregularities

6. See Wilfred G. E. Watson, *Classical Hebrew Poetry: A Guide to its Techniques*, JSOTSup (Sheffield: JSOT, 1984) 190-200. Watson identifies Nah 1:2-8; Psalms 9; 10; 25; 34; 37; 111; 112; 119; 145; Prov 31:10-31; Lamentations 1–4; and Sir 51:13-20 as the alphabetic acrostic compositions in the Bible.

(the ד [*dālet*], "d," is missing in v. 4, and the order of the first two words in v. 6 has to be switched in order to have the line begin with ז [*zayin*], "z").

Robert Alter has said that poetic language in prophetic literature aligns "statements that are addressed to a concrete historical situation with an archetypal horizon,"[7] a horizon whose outer limit is myth. The theophany of vv. 2-8 is a case in point: The events relating to the impending fall of the Assyrian Empire are aligned against the "archetypal horizon" of the basic ancient Near Eastern myth of the divine warrior, emerging to do battle against his enemies. These enemies are identified, at times, with the forces of chaos that threaten the order of creation, with death-dealing drought, or with the human adversaries who threaten the nation. As in Canaan, Babylonia, and Assyria, variations of this basic myth were easily incorporated into the royal ideology of Judah (e.g., Psalms 2; 68; 110).

1:2-3. Verse 2 is dominated by the triple utterance of the words נקם יהוה (*nōqēm YHWH*), literally "revengeful [is] Yahweh," which produces an incantatory effect; it is as if the prophet were

7. Robert Alter, *The Art of Biblical Poetry* (New York: Basic Books, 1985) 146.

Figure 4: The Hebrew Alphabet

א	ʾāleph	ט	ṭêt	פ	pē ʾ
ב	bêt	י	yôd	צ	ṣādê
ג	gîmel	כ	kaph	ק	qôph
ד	dālet	ל	lāmed	ר	rêš
ה	hē ʾ	מ	mēm	שׂ	śîn
ו	wāw	נ	nûn	שׁ	šîn
ז	zayin	ס	sāmek	ת	tāw
ח	ḥêt	ע	ʿayin		

(In alphabetic acrostics, the letters *śîn* and *šîn* are treated as a single letter.)

evoking, by naming it, this particular epiphany of a retributive god. The first line of the verse, moreover, brackets two of these statements between two expressions (אל קנוא 'ēl qannô' and בעל חמה ba'al ḥēmâ) that, while usually translated "a jealous God" and "wrathful," recall at the same time the names of El and Baal[8] and the ancient Canaanite mythology, which appears clearly in v. 4. In the second half of v. 2, the third nōqēm YHWH introduces the objects of Yahweh's vengeful wrath as the adversaries, who in the first half of v. 3 are identified as "the guilty." The NRSV brings out the proper nuance by translating "the LORD is slow to anger but great in power," a better rendition of the Hebrew than the NIV's "and great in power."

The second element of the acrostic, beginning with the letter ב (bêt), is the second half of this verse, which begins with בסופה (bĕsûpâ), "in the whirlwind." It is perhaps better to recognize a hendiadis[9] here and translate the verse as: "his path is in the stormy whirlwind, and the clouds are the dust he treads." The image evoked is that of an aroused and angry Yahweh, striding forward in the upper regions of the atmosphere to confront the enemies. This image makes a smooth transition to the cosmic and nature images that fill the rest of the acrostic theophany.

1:4. References to "the sea" (ים yām) and "the rivers" (נהר nāhār) in the first line of this verse draw on the background of ancient Canaanite myth, which underlies many passages of the Hebrew Bible. Psalm 29 provides a telling example. There the enemies vanquished by God are identified as "the waters" (v. 3) and as "the flood" (v. 10). The Ugaritic texts, in particular, use the same terminology of "sea" and "river" to name the enemies vanquished by Baal the warrior. Nahum's use of this terminology is allusive; the sea and the rivers simply dry up before Yahweh's rebuke, and they do not appear as actual foes doing battle.

The second line of v. 4, as it now appears in the MT, breaks the acrostic, since its first word does not begin with ד (dālet, "d"), leading to the critical suggestion that אמלל ('umlal), the verbal form that both begins and ends the line, should be replaced in the first instance by the roughly synonymous דללו (dālĕlû). Both the NRSV and the NIV seem to follow this suggestion, rendering the two verbs as "wither" and "fade." The image of the withering of the highlands of Bashan, Carmel, and Lebanon provides an appropriate transition between the theme of the drying of the waters that precedes it and that of the shaking of the mountains, which follows.

1:5-8. Verse 5 comprises the ה (hē', "h") and ו (wāw, "w") lines of the acrostic, ushering in a complex of themes (shaking mountains, melting hills, trembling of the earth and its inhabitants) that recalls the language of theophanies such as Ps 18:7-15 (see also 2 Sam 22:8-16). Verse 6, with a simple emendation to restore זעמו (za'mô, "his indignation") to the first place in the clause, becomes the ז (zayin, "z") line, followed in the second half of the verse by the ח (ḥêt "ḥ") line, which begins with חמתו (ḥămātô), "his wrath." After the allusions to earthquake and volcanic eruption (vv. 5-6), v. 7 introduces a serene image of Yahweh as a stronghold, a high place where people find refuge from the waters of the flood. The NRSV's translation is preferable here, reading 8a as the concluding line of v. 7, rather than attempting to relate it to the rest of 8, as the NIV has it. Verse 7 presents the ט (ṭêt, "ṭ") and the י (yôd, "y") elements of the acrostic, with the minor emendation of dropping the initial ו (wāw, "and") from the second line. The verb ידע (yāda') has the primary meaning "to know," but the sense "to be concerned about," "to care about" is well attested, and it is probably what should be read here: "he cares about those who take refuge in him." Verse 8b begins with כ (kaph, "k"), the last letter of the acrostic: "he will make an end" (כלה יעשה kālâ ya'ăśeh). The MT presents a problem with the reading "her place" (מקומה mĕqômāh), which does not permit a straightfoward interpretation, given the absence of a referent for the pronoun. The NIV's reading, "Nineveh," has no apparent textual support. Emendations have been suggested, for example to "his foes" (קמיו qāmāy; see the NRSV), but it

---

8. The word אל ('ēl) is ambiguous, since it can be either a general term for "god" or the name of the high god, El, of the Canaanite pantheon. In similar manner, the word בעל (ba'al), literally "lord" or "owner" (here used in the expression "owner of wrath," i.e., "wrathful") could also refer to Baal, the Canaanite god.

9. A hendiadis is a literary device in which two terms are conjoined in order to express a single idea. It is from the Greek for "one by means of two."

seems best to follow Roberts's suggestion[10] and read, without having to make any changes to the consonantal text, "opposition" (*mĕqûmāh*), an abstract noun that does not otherwise appear in the Hebrew Bible but would be a perfect regular derivation from the verbal root in question: "he will put an end to opposition, and pursue his enemies into darkness."

10. J. J. M. Roberts, *Nahum, Habakkuk, and Zephaniah*, OTL (Louisville: Westminster/John Knox, 1991) 43.

REFLECTIONS

As with a number of psalms (e.g., Ps 19:7-15) the theophany in Nahum presents us with a vision of God that is both sublime and problematic. The power of the ancient, awe-inspiring images is still there, even when we experience them at a significant historical and cultural distance. There is something deeply appealing about a vision of a retributive God who finally comes to set things right, to defend the people against their enemies, to subdue the unruly powers, and to establish sovereign rule over the nations. There is great comfort in the conviction that evil will be brought to a final reckoning.

A problem remains, however, with the image of a "jealous" and "avenging" God; if left as the only divine representation on which to build a theology, such an image would result in a figure more demonic than godlike. Nahum's divine warrior is so deeply rooted in Judean nationalism, so intently focused on the utter destruction of the people's enemy, that it is hard to imagine that, even for Nahum's time, this was all that could be said about God. A merciless God, more precisely, an image of God that does not take into account God's love for all humankind, becomes a demonic God.

Along with this problem, there remains the ever-present danger that persons who read these words will take it into their heads to decide who is God's enemy, thereby demonizing their fellow human beings. It is very tempting to turn real grievances harbored against others into occasions for thinking that God is on our side alone, thereby forgetting that God cares for all people. As general jubilation over the Persian Gulf War demonstrated, our society is more than ready to celebrate a victory and not count the cost in "enemy" lives, in this case tens of thousands of Iraqis, certainly many more than those who perished in the fall of Nineveh.

NAHUM 1:9-15, SALVATION AND DOOM ANNOUNCED

NIV	NRSV

[9]Whatever they plot against the LORD
    he[a] will bring to an end;
    trouble will not come a second time.
[10]They will be entangled among thorns
    and drunk from their wine;
    they will be consumed like dry stubble.[b]
[11]From you, ⌞O Nineveh,⌟ has one come forth
    who plots evil against the LORD
    and counsels wickedness.
	9 Why do you plot against the LORD?
	    He will make an end;
	    no adversary will rise up twice.
	10 Like thorns they are entangled,
	    like drunkards they are drunk;
	    they are consumed like dry straw.
	11 From you one has gone out
	    who plots evil against the LORD,
	    one who counsels wickedness.
	
	12 Thus says the LORD,

a9 Or What do you foes plot against the LORD? / He *b10 The* meaning of the Hebrew for this verse is uncertain.

NIV

¹²This is what the LORD says:

"Although they have allies and are numerous,
  they will be cut off and pass away.
Although I have afflicted you, ₍O Judah,₎
  I will afflict you no more.
¹³Now I will break their yoke from your neck
  and tear your shackles away."

¹⁴The LORD has given a command concerning you,
    ₍Nineveh₎:
  "You will have no descendants to bear your
    name.
I will destroy the carved images and cast idols
  that are in the temple of your gods.
I will prepare your grave,
  for you are vile."

¹⁵Look, there on the mountains,
  the feet of one who brings good news,
  who proclaims peace!
Celebrate your festivals, O Judah,
  and fulfill your vows.
No more will the wicked invade you;
  they will be completely destroyed.

NRSV

"Though they are at full strength and many,ᵃ
  they will be cut off and pass away.
Though I have afflicted you,
  I will afflict you no more.
¹³ And now I will break off his yoke from you
  and snap the bonds that bind you."

¹⁴ The LORD has commanded concerning you:
  "Your name shall be perpetuated no longer;
from the house of your gods I will cut off
  the carved image and the cast image.
I will make your grave, for you are worthless."

¹⁵ᵇ Look! On the mountains the feet of one
  who brings good tidings,
  who proclaims peace!
Celebrate your festivals, O Judah,
  fulfill your vows,
for never again shall the wicked invade you;
  they are utterly cut off.

ᵃ Meaning of Heb uncertain   ᵇ Ch 2.1 in Heb

COMMENTARY

The utter futility of opposing God, of trying to frustrate God's designs in history, is the theme of this subsection. To plot against God is dangerous as well, and the description in v. 10 may well apply to the results of one's attempting to do so: self-ruin and destruction.

It is very difficult to determine with certainty whether Judah or Nineveh is being addressed in this section. A common way to deal with the ambiguity of these verses has been to suppose that they are a miscellaneous collection, produced when some redactor inserted verses (e.g., 1:10, 12-13, 15; 2:2)[11] into a text that is otherwise addressed to Assyria. A better choice, however, is to read the text as it stands, hearing in it the dual message of salvation and doom as a sort of musical chord in which both notes sound together in dissonance. The NRSV and the NIV differ in their reading strategies for this passage; the latter tries

to specify the addressees by inserting "Nineveh" in vv. 11 and 14, as it also inserts "Judah" in vv. 12 and 15. The NRSV prefers, correctly in my judgment, to preserve the ambiguity of the text and does not attempt to identify those who are addressed.

The verb in the first line of v. 9 must be read as a second-person plural "you" (NRSV) and not emended to a third-person "they" (NIV). The sense of the poem does not require such an emendation. The poetic voice addresses all comers: "Why do you [anybody] plot against the LORD?" as it boasts of God's prowess as a warrior: "He will make an end; no adversary [lit., no hostility][12] will rise up twice." The boast continues in v. 10, which in three striking images suggests the result of the thrashing Yahweh gives the enemies—from entanglement to unconsciousness to complete destruction. All of this is conveyed with wonderful

---

11. So Charles L. Taylor, Jr., "Nahum," *The Interpreter's Bible*, 12 vols., ed. George Buttrick, (Nashville: Abingdon, 1956) 6:960-62.

12. Reading with modern interpreters צרה (*sārāh*) as an abstract noun derived from the same root as צר (*sār*), "adversary."

Hebrew alliterations of ס (*sāmek*), "s," in the first two cases and in שׁ (*šîn*), "*š*," in the third, reinforcing the portrayal of the slumping losers, suggesting perhaps the hissing of the implied fire that "consumes" them like stubble. We may in fact detect here an instance of the striking stylistic device that Nahum displays elsewhere, e.g., in 3:2-3, where separate images are piled one on top of another to form a total impression without much regard for a formal syntactical connection, but with powerful artistic effect.

Verse 11 addresses the antagonist directly, though not with the specificity that the NIV's insertion of "O Nineveh" effects. While the feminine singular form of address ("from you") certainly fits an allusion to a city (feminine in Hebrew), that city is not necessarily Nineveh.[13] It seems better to preserve as deliberate the ambiguity of the referent that the text offers at this place. The ominous figure who emerges (or "goes out") in v. 11 is characterized, in two participial clauses, as one "who plots evil against the LORD" and "who counsels wickedness." The first expression in v. 11 is a fairly common combination of verb and object (e.g., Gen 50:20; Esth 9:25; Jer 26:3; 36:3; Mic 2:3). The second one is unique as a combination, even though בליעל (*bĕliyyā'al*), the word translated "wickedness" in v. 11 by both the NIV and the NRSV, occurs a total of twenty-seven times in the Hebrew Bible, and once again in Nahum (2:1).[14] In either case, whether wicked or deadly, the counsel forms a fitting parallel to the evil plot against the Lord, mentioned in the first half of the verse.

Rather abruptly, the next two verses (12-13) introduce an oracle of salvation, the only oracle introduced by the otherwise frequent (225 other instances in the prophetic book) formula "thus says the LORD" (כה אמר יהוה *kōh 'āmar YHWH*). The NRSV's rendering of שלמים (*šĕlēmîm*) as "at full strength" (lit., "complete") seems better than the NIV's "they have allies," for which the verb must be assumed. Both translations choose to ignore the repeated וכן (*wĕkēn,* "and thus, and

so"), but it would be better to translate "Though they are at full strength and *thus* many, *even so* they will be cut off and pass away" in the first part of v. 12. The Lord, ultimate source of the people's affliction, promises that it is now over (12*b*), because "now" (ועתה *wĕ'attâ,* v. 13) God will break the yoke and snap the bonds that bind them. Both the NRSV and the NIV prefer to follow the vocalization of the MT (in spite of the defective spelling מטה [*mōṭē(h)*] for מוטה [*mōṭē(h)*]) and read *mōṭē(h)* as "yoke" rather than "staff," which would have been the expected translation of the consonantal text. The *mōṭe(h)*) is not the common "yoke" used for binding two animals to the plow or cart (usually על *'ōl*). The uses of the word in Isa 58:6, 9 and Jer 28:10, 12, suggest a sort of slave collar, which, along with the "bonds" (NRSV) or "shackles" (NIV), constitutes a powerful metonymy for oppression. The Lord continues to speak directly in the second person. The one addressed is, according to the pronominal suffix ("from you" מעליך *mē'ālāyik*]), a feminine singular subject, once again befitting either a city (Jerusalem) or Judah, to whom the word of liberation is addressed.

Verse 14 begins with a change in voice. Once again, as in the "thus says the LORD" of v. 12, we hear momentarily about the prophet: "the LORD has commanded concerning you," with a change in addressee, signaled by the use of a second-person masculine singular pronominal suffix for the "you" in the MT. It is not likely, then, that "Nineveh" is the one addressed, as the NIV intercalation of the name suggests, but rather an individual who represents the oppression that the Lord has just promised to break, most probably the king of Assyria. The gist of the divine decree occurs in three clauses, all of them assailing in some way the king's dynastic power, which of course the fall of Nineveh will epitomize. Both the NRSV and the NIV prefer to spell out the meaning of the first clause. Hence their translations ignore the vivid idiom, which can be read more literally as Roberts does, "Seed will not be sown from your name again."[15] The destruction of the images "from the house of your gods" fits well in this context, once we remember the very close association that ancient Near Eastern mon-

---

13. Roberts, *Nahum, Habakkuk, and Zephaniah,* 52-54, e.g., argues for a Judean audience.

14. Scholars disagree on the etymology of בליעל (*bĕliyya'al*). Some relate the word either to the idea of "worthlessness" (בלי יעל *bĕli ya'al* can be read as "without worth," and hence "wickedness") or derive it from the verbal root בלע (*bl'*), "swallow," linking the term to the idea of Sheol, the abode of the dead, as "the Swallower." See Theodore J. Lewis, "Belial," in *The Anchor Bible Dictionary* (New York: Doubleday, 1992) 1:654-56.

15. Roberts, *Nahum, Habakkuk, and Zephaniah,* 43.

archies (Judean as well as Assyrian) claimed between the king and the deity or deities who legitimated their rule. In the case of Assyria, the usual list of legitimating deities included Ashur, Sin, Shamash, Bel, Nebo, Nergal, and Ishtar, which Nahum, using the typical polemic strategy of Yahwistic prophecy, reduces to "carved images" and "molten images." The third clause, which the NRSV and the NIV render "I will make/prepare your grave, for you are worthless/vile," is certainly better rendered "I will make your grave a refuse heap," as newly discovered linguistic evidence suggests.[16]

Verse 15 (2:1 MT), which explicitly addresses Judah, returns to the theme of the announcement of good news, personified in the figure of the messenger, or more precisely, in a form of synecdoche (a literary device in which the part stands for the whole), as the *feet* of the messenger standing on the mountains to make his proclamation. This striking figure probably influenced the author of Isa 52:7. If we ask further about the identity of the מבשׂר (*mĕbaśśēr,* or "messenger"),

Yahweh may be a possibility. The figure appears "on the mountains" to broadcast his victory, in a fitting conclusion to the first section of Nahum's poem, which began with a theophany. The *mĕbaśśēr* may, in theory, be an announcer of either good or bad news, but the context and the parallel expression "who proclaims peace" (משמיע שלום *maśmîaʿ šālôm*) make clear that the former is meant. Still, it is clear that the *šālôm* announced will result from the imminent military destruction of Assyria's power and the ruination of its capital, Nineveh. Hence the proclamation of Yahweh's victory is good news for Judah alone. A more immediate result of the promulgation of *šālôm* will be ritual observance: Judah is called to celebrate festivals (חגים *ḥaggîm*) and to fulfill vows (נדרים *nĕdārîm*), both technical terms pertaining to the cult. The "wicked"—or "wicked one"—who will no longer invade Judah is, once again, בליעל (*bĕliyyāʿal*; see Commentary on v. 13), probably the king of Assyria, who will be utterly destroyed ("cutting off," a frequent idiom in this sense; see also Commentary on v. 12).

---

16. See Kevin J. Cathcart, "Nahum, Book of," in David Noel Freedman, ed., *The Anchor Bible Dictionary* (New York: Doubleday, 1992) 4:998.

REFLECTIONS

There are more words of comfort in this section than anywhere else in the book of Nahum. Perhaps here we come closest to hearing the best that Nahum has to offer: words from a God who comforts the afflicted, who promises freedom from the bonds of slavery, who brings good tidings and proclaims peace, a God who calls liberated people to celebration and festivity. There are also strong words of condemnation: God stands against the afflicters, the enslavers, the wicked violators of the rights of others. God has taken sides. The question is, Which side is which? We have seen too much, in the past and in our own time, of the ugly and the twisted results of mixing nationalism or tribalism into our determination of who are God's people and who are God's enemies. No single people or nation or race or civilization can claim an exclusive right to God's favor and protection. None of us has the right to gloat and rejoice over the destruction of human life, particularly the lives of those who by accident of birth or history come to be defined for us as enemies.

To say this is to understand that we can no longer read Nahum as the nationalistic poem that it clearly was for its author. We should, perhaps, take a clue from Augustine, who envisioned the two cities, that of God and that of human sin, intertwined to the point of not being easily separable along the lines of national states or specific peoples. It is at the level of beliefs, commitments, attitudes, and inclinations that the "cities" distinguish themselves, particularly as these shape our behavior toward our neighbor.

Nahum's words cry out not so much against Assyria as against oppression, not so much against Nineveh as against wickedness. He favors not just the poor of ancient Judah, not just the enslaved of ancient Israel. He is concerned for all poor, all homeless, all exiled, all oppressed people in every time and place. "Look! On the mountains the feet of one who brings good tidings, who proclaims *šālôm!*" To some, it is a message of hope; to others, it is a summons to judgment. Perhaps the best commentary on Nahum's meaning here is Matt 25:31-46, in which acts of justice and compassion to "one of the least of these" determine who shall inherit the kingdom of God.

THE FATE OF NINEVEH

NAHUM 2:1-10, THE SCATTERER

NIV

2 An attacker advances against you,
 ˻Nineveh˼.
Guard the fortress,
watch the road,
brace yourselves,
marshal all your strength!

²The Lord will restore the splendor of Jacob
 like the splendor of Israel,
though destroyers have laid them waste
 and have ruined their vines.

³The shields of his soldiers are red;
 the warriors are clad in scarlet.
The metal on the chariots flashes
 on the day they are made ready;
 the spears of pine are brandished.ᵃ

⁴The chariots storm through the streets,
 rushing back and forth through the squares.
They look like flaming torches;
 they dart about like lightning.

⁵He summons his picked troops,
 yet they stumble on their way.
They dash to the city wall;
 the protective shield is put in place.

⁶The river gates are thrown open
 and the palace collapses.

⁷It is decreedᵇ that ˻the city˼
 be exiled and carried away.
Its slave girls moan like doves
 and beat upon their breasts.

⁸Nineveh is like a pool,
 and its water is draining away.
"Stop! Stop!" they cry,
 but no one turns back.

⁹Plunder the silver!

NRSV

2 A shattererᵃ has come up against you.
 Guard the ramparts;
watch the road;
gird your loins;
 collect all your strength.

² (For the Lord is restoring the majesty of Jacob,
 as well as the majesty of Israel,
though ravagers have ravaged them
 and ruined their branches.)

³ The shields of his warriors are red;
 his soldiers are clothed in crimson.
The metal on the chariots flashes
 on the day when he musters them;
 the chargersᵇ prance.

⁴ The chariots race madly through the streets,
 they rush to and fro through the squares;
their appearance is like torches,
 they dart like lightning.

⁵ He calls his officers;
 they stumble as they come forward;
they hasten to the wall,
 and the manteletᶜ is set up.

⁶ The river gates are opened,
 the palace trembles.

⁷ It is decreedᶜ that the cityᵈ be exiled,
 its slave women led away,
moaning like doves
 and beating their breasts.

⁸ Nineveh is like a pool
 whose watersᵉ run away.
"Halt! Halt!"—
 but no one turns back.

⁹ "Plunder the silver,

ᵃ3 Hebrew; Septuagint and Syriac / the horsemen rush to and fro
ᵇ7 The meaning of the Hebrew for this word is uncertain.

ᵃ Cn: Heb scatterer   ᵇ Cn Compare Gk Syr: Heb cypresses
ᶜ Meaning of Heb uncertain   ᵈ Heb it   ᵉ Cn Compare Gk: Heb
a pool, from the days that she has become, and they

NIV

Plunder the gold!
The supply is endless,
    the wealth from all its treasures!
[10]She is pillaged, plundered, stripped!
    Hearts melt, knees give way,
    bodies tremble, every face grows pale.

NRSV

plunder the gold!
There is no end of treasure!
    An abundance of every precious thing!"

[10] Devastation, desolation, and destruction!
    Hearts faint and knees tremble,
all loins quake,
    all faces grow pale!

COMMENTARY

Yahweh will carry out the design on Nineveh by means of a human adversary. The second section begins with a descriptive introduction of this enemy, who is presented at the moment of the successful conclusion of a siege. It is, of course, almost certain that the poet has the Babylonians and their Median allies in mind as the historical enemies who will actually carry out the attack. In describing the attackers, the poet uses vivid and pictorial language, instead of a more neutral description of the onslaught, which had yet to take place.

2:1. The foe is first characterized as the מֵפִיץ (*mēpîṣ*). The enemy is thus called "a scatterer"; the NIV's interpretation based on this ("an attacker"), even though it unnecessarily weakens the image by generalizing it, is to be preferred to the NRSV's "a shatterer."[17] The city[18] under siege hopes to prevent the scattering of its people, which v. 8 (MT 9) nonetheless vividly portrays. The rest of v. 1 is taken up with a series of imperatives in which the poet mimics the ineffectual orders with which the doomed Ninevite garrison attempts to ready itself for the onslaught. Such language emphasizes the futility of resistance: This is Nineveh's last hour.

2:2. Prosaic and clearly intrusive in its context, this verse is probably not part of the original poem, but a comment or gloss from a later redactor; the NRSV sets it off in parentheses. Reference to "the majesty of Jacob as well as the majesty of Israel" (NRSV; NIV, "splendor") is puzzling, given

the identity of Jacob and Israel, on the one hand, and, on the other hand, the usually negative connotation of the expression גְאוֹן יַעֲקֹב (*gěʾôn yaʿăqōb*; or גְאוֹן יִשְׂרָאֵל *gěʾôn yiśrāʾēl*), normally translated "the pride of Jacob" or "the pride of Israel."[19]

2:3. This verse turns from the shouted commands in v. 1 to a graphic description of the enemy army's awesome approach. The first half of the verse is clear; it refers to the red shields and scarlet dress of the advancing army. This is no ragtag rabble, but a well-equipped army, uniformed in expensively dyed cloth. The second half of the verse presents some difficulties, which stem from our relative ignorance of terminology apparently having to do with military equipment. The first of these terms is פְּלָדוֹת (*pělādôt*), a rare word that both the NRSV and the NIV translate as "metal," which may be a Persian loan word for "steel."[20] It might refer to the shiny steel fittings of the chariots and their harnesses, flashing in the sun. The second problem word is בְּרֹשִׁים (*běrōšîm*), usually identified as the wood of a cypress tree; the word's primary meaning is clear, but the author is apparently using it in a special sense here.[21] The NRSV follows the Septuagint's reading (οἱ ἱππεῖς *hoi hippeis* [Hebrew פָּרָשִׁים *pārāšîm*]) and translates "the chargers," but the emendation does not seem necessary. Either the NIV's reading ("the spears of pine") or Seow's suggestion that it refers to the juniper frames of

17. Based on an emendation to a form derived from נפַץ (*nāpaṣ*), "to shatter."

18. The singular feminine pronominal suffix to the word translated "against you" points to the city being addressed.

19. Roberts, *Nahum, Habakkuk, and Zephaniah*, 64. See, e.g., Amos 6:8 or Hosea 5:5.

20. Ibid., 57.

21. The cypress tree is the *Cupressus sempervirens*. Some have suggested that *beros* is the Aleppo pine (*Pinus halepensis*, so the NIV) or the juniper (*Juniperus phoenicea*).

the chariots[22] seems a better choice. Either case presents an example of synecdoche, in which a part is used to represent the whole.

2:4. The chariots are most likely the same ones the author of the poem has so far described—that is, those of the invaders. Nahum now imagines their rushing through the streets and squares outside the main wall, apparently describing an early stage of a progressive disintegration of Nineveh's defenses from the outside inward. The attack will culminate in v. 6 with the fall of the palace in the center of the city. Suddenly seen up close, the chariots that glinted and flashed in the sun from a distance now look like fiery torches or lightning, unleashed on the first houses of the city. The poet does not envision a long siege, but a catastrophic sudden attack that penetrates the city's defenses as if they did not exist.

2:5-6. The description of the attack continues, shifting from the chariots to the powerful image of the invading commandos in a stumbling, headlong rush for the wall under the defenders' attack. Simultaneously, the besieging archers set up their movable defensive shield (NRSV, "mantelet"), from which they give the shock troops protective fire for their attempt to scale the wall. The attack's success is cryptically portrayed in the two images of v. 6: the "river gates" (whether these are to be understood as gates in the defensive wall or as flood gates is not clear) are thrown open, and the palace (or "the temple," a reading that the Hebrew word ההיכל [*hahêkāl*] allows) "melts," the literal meaning of the verb מוג (*mûg*), which the NRSV renders as "trembles" and the NIV as "collapses." The juxtaposition of these images alludes to the language of 1:4-5, where "the rivers" are among the defeated enemies of Yahweh, who also "melts" the hills; thus these verses relate the downfall of Nineveh to the theophany of the victorious Yahweh in the first chapter.

2:7-10. The next four verses paint a word picture of the immediate aftermath of the city's downfall. Their theme is simply put: Nineveh's people will be enslaved and exiled, and its riches will be plundered by the invaders. The first part of v. 7 is difficult to the point of being unintelligible, so some degree of emendation seems nec-

essary for translation.[23] The RSV, for example, reads, "its mistress is stripped, she is carried off," a reading that the NRSV and the NIV abandon, the former to read "It is decreed that *the city* be exiled,/ *its slave women* led away," and the latter, "It is decreed that *the city*/ be exiled and carried away." I have italicized the elements that these translations must supply, either from the general context (the city) or from the next clause (its slave women).

It is precisely the reference to "her serving women" (אמהתיה *'amhōtêhā*) that persuades me to prefer a reading like the RSV's and to see in v. 7 a reference to a regal "mistress," whether human or divine, now about to go into exile along with her retinue of maidservants.[24] If, as suggested above, the היכל (*hêkāl*) of v. 6 is to be read "temple," the image of its mistress being led into captivity may envisage the goddess Ishtar, patron deity of Nineveh, being carried away by the enemy amid the cries and breast-beating of her priestesses. The capture and removal of the images from a defeated enemy's temple is a practice well attested in Assyrian and Babylonian warfare. In either case, the motif constitutes a powerful figuration of the exile of the inhabitants of Nineveh.

The powerful simile of this verse provides a variation on the same theme: Nineveh, its walls breached and its gates open, is like a ruptured reservoir whose waters stream out unchecked. In the second part of the verse, the poem shifts from visual to auditory means of expression as we hear the futile commands to halt. The defeated army and the people of Nineveh are likened to "her waters," as they stream in panic to avoid capture. The verbal form נסים (*nāsîm*, "they flee"), applied to the waters' action in the first half of the verse, really fits humans better than waters.

In verse 9 the poet continues to make use of sound images, as we hear the victors shouting orders (the repeated imperative "Plunder . . . plunder" [בזו . . . בזו *bōzzû . . . bōzzû*]), to loot and plunder in the streets of the defeated city. The quick but vivid sketch of the fall of Nineveh that

---

22. See Roberts, *Nahum, Habakkuk, and Zephaniah,* 58.

23. The option of reading the text without emendation is adopted by the translators of the TNK. That translation is: "And Huzzab is exiled and carried away. For a variety of readings that have been suggested for הצב (*huṣṣab*), see ibid., 60. Roberts's own translation is "the princess is made to stand among the captives" (55).

24. See the RSV's textual note appended to v. 7: "*Its mistress* is either Nineveh's queen or its patron goddess Ishtar."

began in v. 1 concludes in v. 10 with a rush of words, which, far from attempting the ordered sense of a statement, seem instead to carry the emotional power of a curse or an incantation. One must hear the first phrase בוקה ומבוקה ומבלקה (*bûqâ ûmĕbûqâ ûmĕbullāqâ*) in order to appreciate the malevolent effect of the repeated alternation of *b* and *q* in Hebrew, reminiscent of full-throated spitting as the poet execrates the fallen city. Both the NRSV ("Devastation, desolation, and destruction!") and the NIV ("She is pillaged, plundered, stripped!") attempt, to their credit, to represent this powerful effect in their translations. The rest of v. 10 constitutes a list of physical manifestations of emotional distress, which sums up the wretchedness of the defeated Ninevites.

REFLECTIONS

Something about the combination of sight and sound in this masterpiece of imaginative description reminds us, uncannily, of the way in which television has so often brought us images of warfare, of ruin and devastation of cities, and of the desperate plight of human beings caught up in these events. Far from resembling the carefully sanitized and orchestrated portrayals of violence in some World War II–era movies, which glorified warfare in the long tradition of Western literature and art, Nahum brings to mind the gory incoherence of the chaotic images that began to reach us from Vietnam and from Bosnia. War, indeed, is hell.

After the first, inevitable moment of distancing, of feeling thankful that such violence is not happening where you live or to you, but over there and to them, come the empathy and the pity and the inevitable recognition that we are all the same and that it is, indeed, happening to us. We can begin to understand the pain and distress that many military veterans, who have seen too much violence, must try to deal with for the rest of their lives. All forms of violence against human beings, no matter the scale or the circumstances, are ultimately assaults on all humans and on the image of God in all of us. Nahum in all probability did not intend to arouse in his readers empathy and pity for the people of Nineveh, but he comes close, with his skill in description, to making it inevitable and to strengthening the case against violence.

NAHUM 2:11-13, THE LION HUNT

NIV

[11]Where now is the lions' den,
    the place where they fed their young,
where the lion and lioness went,
    and the cubs, with nothing to fear?
[12]The lion killed enough for his cubs
    and strangled the prey for his mate,
filling his lairs with the kill
    and his dens with the prey.

[13]"I am against you,"
    declares the LORD Almighty.
"I will burn up your chariots in smoke,
    and the sword will devour your young lions.
    I will leave you no prey on the earth.
The voices of your messengers
    will no longer be heard."

NRSV

[11] What became of the lions' den,
    the cave[a] of the young lions,
where the lion goes,
    and the lion's cubs, with no one to disturb
        them?
[12] The lion has torn enough for his whelps
    and strangled prey for his lionesses;
he has filled his caves with prey
    and his dens with torn flesh.

[13]See, I am against you, says the LORD of hosts, and I will burn your[b] chariots in smoke, and the sword shall devour your young lions; I will cut off your prey from the earth, and the voice of your messengers shall be heard no more.

[a] Cn: Heb *pasture*   [b] Heb *her*

COMMENTARY

After the graphic description of the city's downfall in 2:1-10, the reader comes to the central portion of the second section, where two forceful, sustained images liken Assyria's defeat to Yahweh's hunting down of a pride of lions (2:11-13) and to the public degradation of a prostitute (3:4-7), both actions marked by the explicit threat, "I am against you" (2:13; 3:5). These images effectively bracket the central woe oracle in 3:1-3, with its echo of the description of 2:1-10. Lions appeared frequently in Assyrian official art, notably in the lion hunt scenes in wall reliefs, many of them from Ashurbanipal's palace at Nineveh, in which the king is depicted ritually hunting lions. King Ashurbanipal, in particular, was proud of his accomplishments as a lion hunter, and he even had a royal preserve established in which he kept lions imported from Syria for his hunts. The lion also appears frequently in association with Ishtar, a deity associated with war as well as with human sexuality. Ishtar was one of several such goddesses in the ancient Near East who were spoken of in terms of prostitution by the Israelite prophets. Nahum seems to draw from these Near Eastern sources for his devastating images.

Nahum takes on a sardonic tone in vv. 11-12,

as the poet asks, "Where now is the lions' den?" referring to the Assyrian king and his court. Nahum continues with an extended metaphor in which Nineveh, formerly the safe haven of the Assyrian lion, where it and its mate and cubs found refuge and where they stored their plunder, provides the obvious answer to the rhetorical question. The NRSV's references to "prey" and "torn flesh" ("kill" and "prey," NIV) probably allude to the enormous amount of wealth that the Assyrians exacted from their vassals or plundered from their conquests, much of which had gone into the building of Nineveh's palaces and temples. Verse 13 introduces the challenge, "See, I am against you" (הנני אליך hinĕnî 'ēlayik), of the divine warrior, the "LORD of hosts" (יהוה צבאות YHWH ṣĕbā'ôt), speaking to Assyria's military power. The challenge mixes martial and leonine images together ("chariots" and "messengers" with "young lions" and "prey"), thus clearly referring to the images of the preceding verse as well as stating the plain historical meaning of the challenge: Yahweh will destroy the military and hegemonic power of Assyria. The hunter has become the prey—or better, the former lion hunter is now the dying lion.

REFLECTIONS

There is, of course, wisdom in the saying that "those who live by the sword shall die by the sword," and that is one way of looking at the meaning of the lion oracle. Human history is littered with the ruins of empires that, like Assyria, tested that truism. To think of that impersonal principle as the controlling force in human affairs, however, does nothing more than envisage an endless succession of swordbearers, forever overthrowing and being overthrown.

Nahum's faith, on the other hand, insists that it is God, not some impersonal principle, that brings about retribution: "I am against you, says the LORD of hosts." This reading of history through the eyes of faith puts an end to the fatalism, or even the cynicism, that the "endless cycle" view can produce. God is active in human history. God has a plan and a purpose for human history. God's people can look forward to a time when swords will be beaten into plowshares, spears into pruning hooks, when that plan and that purpose are fulfilled in true and lasting peace. It is a hope, and as such it is not yet realized; but people of faith find in that hope the encouragement they need to work for the establishment of peace and justice in the world.

NAHUM 3:1-3, WOE TO THE CITY OF BLOODSHED!

NIV

3 Woe to the city of blood,
full of lies,
full of plunder,
never without victims!
²The crack of whips,
the clatter of wheels,
galloping horses
and jolting chariots!
³Charging cavalry,
flashing swords
and glittering spears!
Many casualties,
piles of dead,
bodies without number,
people stumbling over the corpses—

NRSV

3 Ah! City of bloodshed,
utterly deceitful, full of booty—
no end to the plunder!
² The crack of whip and rumble of wheel,
galloping horse and bounding chariot!
³ Horsemen charging,
flashing sword and glittering spear,
piles of dead,
heaps of corpses,
dead bodies without end—
they stumble over the bodies!

COMMENTARY

3:1. The poet's voice is again heard in this verse, responding to the divine utterance of the preceding verse with a section that begins with a compact woe oracle. The woe oracle is a form of Hebrew prophetic utterance that typically begins, as in v. 1, with the interjection הוֹי (*hôy*; NRSV, "Ah!"; NIV, "Woe"). Such language probably had its origins in a form of ritualized curse, in which the opening exclamation is followed by a statement of the nature of the behavior that prompted the execration.[25] The verse is thus not to be read as an expression of grief over the demise of Nineveh, but rather as performative speech that vents anger. In the case of the prophetic woe oracle, it is, of course, God's anger that brings calamity. Nineveh is bluntly addressed as a "city of bloodshed" (the NRSV is to be preferred here to the NIV's "city of blood" as a translation of עִיר דָּמִים [*'îr dāmîm*])—that is to say, execrable

as responsible for unlawful deaths. To that charge are also added deceit and plunder. The last term in the verse, טֶרֶף (*ṭārep*; NRSV, "plunder"; NIV, "victims") alludes to the lion imagery of the preceding section (2:13), where it occurs following the use of the related verb in the first clause of 2:12. Ordinarily the verb means "to tear" and refers to the action of wild animals in killing their victims, hence the usual meaning of the noun *ṭerep* is "prey."

3:2-3. These verses interject very effectively a return to the scene of the devastation of Nineveh, from which the poem looked away at the end of 2:9. Using the same frenzied audiovisual descriptive style as in 2:1-9, the poet gives the reader a last view of the dying city, where the invading army has turned from looting and plunder to massacring the population. We hear in v. 2— before we see them—the terrifying noise of the chariots charging through the streets: cracking whips, rumbling wheels, clattering hooves, crashing frames. Then we see in v. 3 the cavalry charging the crowd (flashing swords, glittering spears) and the gruesome result of their work: "piles of dead,/ heaps of corpses,/ dead bodies without end—/ they stumble over the bodies!"

25. Claus Westermann already suggests this in *Basic Forms of Prophetic Speech* (Philadelphia: Westminster, 1967) 190-98. See also Waldemar Janzen, *Mourning Cry and Woe Oracle*, BZAW (Berlin: Walter de Gruyter, 1972). Janzen seeks the origin of the "woe" in a "lamentation-vengeance pattern" arising from funeral laments for people killed by violence, where "the woe-cry can undergo a metamorphosis from grief and mourning to accusation, threat, and even curse" directed at the slayer (27-39).

NAHUM 3:4-7, THE HUMILIATED PROSTITUTE

NIV

⁴all because of the wanton lust of a harlot,
    alluring, the mistress of sorceries,
who enslaved nations by her prostitution
    and peoples by her witchcraft.

⁵"I am against you," declares the LORD Almighty.
    "I will lift your skirts over your face.
I will show the nations your nakedness
    and the kingdoms your shame.
⁶I will pelt you with filth,
    I will treat you with contempt
    and make you a spectacle.
⁷All who see you will flee from you and say,
    'Nineveh is in ruins—who will mourn for
        her?'
    Where can I find anyone to comfort you?"

NRSV

⁴ Because of the countless debaucheries of
        the prostitute,
    gracefully alluring, mistress of sorcery,
who enslaves^a nations through her
        debaucheries,
    and peoples through her sorcery,
⁵ I am against you,
    says the LORD of hosts,
    and will lift up your skirts over your face;
and I will let nations look on your nakedness
    and kingdoms on your shame.
⁶ I will throw filth at you
    and treat you with contempt,
    and make you a spectacle.
⁷ Then all who see you will shrink from you and
        say,
    "Nineveh is devastated; who will bemoan her?"
    Where shall I seek comforters for you?

^a Heb *sells*

COMMENTARY

The amplified woe of vv. 1-3 is followed by a section (vv. 4-7) in which, as in 2:11-13, an embodiment of Nineveh/Assyria is directly castigated by Yahweh: "I am against you!" (הנני אליך *hinĕnî ʾēlayik,* v. 5; cf 2:13). A striking change of imagery marks this section, however. Earlier, Nineveh was the den of the Assyrian lion, whose military power Yahweh defeated; in the present case, Nineveh is a prostitute whom Yahweh will publicly humiliate and shame. As a counterpart to the former case, where the lion symbolized Nineveh's armed might, the present figure condemns the entrapping seductiveness (the "sorcery" [כשף *kesep*] of v. 4) of Nineveh's diplomatic and commercial alliances (cf. v. 16). Also, consistent with the standard prophetic cliché of calling the worship of "other gods" prostitution, the figure may offer a sardonic portrayal of the goddess Ishtar, representing her city, as the whore in disgrace. Once again, in v. 5, Yahweh appears to speak directly the words of condemnation: "I am against you." Then, in graphic detail, Yahweh

describes the humiliation to which Nineveh will be subjected.

The first image of such humiliation (v. 5) uses formal parallelism to convey a solemn tone, making the content somehow even more appalling. The description leaves little to the imagination: Yahweh lifts Nineveh's skirts over her face, to expose her private parts ("your nakedness"//"your shame") to the entire world's ("nations"//"kingdoms") contemptuous gaze. Adding insult to injury in the three following parallel clauses, Yahweh will "defame" Nineveh (שקצים [*šiqquṣîm*], rendered as "filth" by both the NRSV and the NIV, can also mean "abominations," and the idiom used here, "I will throw *šiqquṣîm* upon you" can mean "I will defame you"). Yahweh will treat Nineveh with contempt and make her a spectacle. The desired result of all this vilification is predicted in v. 7: Nineveh is told that the sight of the city will be enough to make onlookers flee, voicing the belief that no one will mourn its fate. Yahweh's voice ends the section with the rhetorical question, "Where shall I seek comforters for you?" There is, of course, no possible answer; not even Yahweh can find mourners for Nineveh's destruction.

REFLECTIONS

In response to this portrayal of the humiliation of what was once the mightiest power in the ancient world, conventional wisdom would respond: "The bigger they are, the harder they fall." The equivalent Spanish proverb adds: "Everyone makes firewood of the fallen tree." Nahum insists, once again, that just as the downfall of Assyria's power was God's doing, so also would the loss of its reputation and its fall into universal contempt be God's doing: "I am against you!"

Precisely at this point, however, today's reader must question Nahum's choice of poetic expression for God's activity. Disturbing as the images of God the warrior are in their appeal to warlike violence, the image of God's humiliation of the prostitute is particularly abhorrent to modern readers. Nahum clearly speaks as a male representative of a patriarchal culture in which women's sexuality was to be controlled totally by fathers or husbands. Hence the prostitute, who was not so controlled, became a quasi-demonic figure, a dangerous temptress, the very antithesis of the "good" (i.e., controlled) woman. Many women and men in the church today have come to recognize that patriarchal views about such control and resulting demonization have caused enormous harm to women. Add to this the harm that an image of God abusing and humiliating a woman can do, and it is clear that these verses in the book of Nahum must be treated as dangerous territory. The God of human history is as much obscured here as revealed, in images that cannot rise far enough above the limitations of their originating culture.

NAHUM 3:8-11, ARE YOU BETTER THAN THEBES?

NIV

8Are you better than Thebes,[a]
   situated on the Nile,
   with water around her?
The river was her defense,
   the waters her wall.
9Cush[b] and Egypt were her boundless strength;
   Put and Libya were among her allies.
10Yet she was taken captive
   and went into exile.
Her infants were dashed to pieces
   at the head of every street.
Lots were cast for her nobles,
   and all her great men were put in chains.
11You too will become drunk;
   you will go into hiding
   and seek refuge from the enemy.

[a]8 Hebrew *No Amon*   [b]9 That is, the upper Nile region

NRSV

8 Are you better than Thebes[a]
   that sat by the Nile,
with water around her,
   her rampart a sea,
   water her wall?
9 Ethiopia[b] was her strength,
   Egypt too, and that without limit;
   Put and the Libyans were her[c] helpers.

10 Yet she became an exile,
   she went into captivity;
even her infants were dashed in pieces
   at the head of every street;
lots were cast for her nobles,
   all her dignitaries were bound in fetters.
11 You also will be drunken,
   you will go into hiding;[d]
you will seek
   a refuge from the enemy.

[a] Heb *No-amon*   [b] Or *Nubia*; Heb *Cush*   [c] Gk: Heb *your*
[d] Meaning of Heb uncertain

COMMENTARY

From the powerful symbolic attack on the emblems of Assyrian power that 2:11–3:7 represent, the poem turns to historical allusion in v. 8 to convict Nineveh of the hopelessness of her situation as well as to argue by implication for the justice of her downfall. In 633 BCE, more or less half a century before the fall of Nineveh, the Assyrian army had ravaged and plundered נא אמון (*Nō ʾAmôn*) in Egypt, known in English by its Greek name, Thebes. Nahum takes some license in v. 8 with the actual location of the city, which had grown up on both banks of the Nile and can hardly be said to have had waters around it as a defensive wall. The NIV handles the references in v. 9 to Thebes' connection to כוש (*kûš*; NIV, "Cush"; NRSV, "Ethiopia"; another possible translation is "Sudan") and to Egypt, on the one hand, and to Put and the Libyans on the other, better than does the NRSV. The pairing of these terms corresponds to Egypt's political situation in the seventh century: It counted on powerful allies, which, when all was said and done, could give no aid. Put—even though the exact meaning of the term is not clear—is frequently paired with, and may be identical to, Libya. More important, during the reign of the Sudanese (or 25th) Dynasty, Egypt and Cush were united. During the reign of the pharaohs of this dynasty, Thebes had gained new prosperity and had become immensely wealthy as the site of the great temple of the god Amon, whom the citizens of that city especially revered. In the process of this development, of course, Thebes had also become a prime target for Assyrian looting. In a few, but chillingly effective, images, v. 10 depicts the brutal Assyrian enslavement and exile of Thebes' people: babies, who would be an impediment on the march, are brutally killed as their families are herded to the top of each street (see Ps 137:9 for another instance). Neither the nobles nor the officials escape enslavement and exile in fetters. It is now Nineveh's turn to suffer what it had once inflicted. Verse 11 returns to the unusual image of a drunken stupor, which was used in 1:10 to characterize the state of Yahweh's enemies and is used here to describe the suffering of Nineveh's people in a cringing, demoralized rout.

REFLECTIONS

"Are you better than Thebes?" These must be terrible words to face. Nation or individual, are you better than those whom you oppressed and brutalized? It is clear that Nahum intends to mark the similarity of Thebes with Nineveh in the parallels he implies between their defenses, situation by a river, and allies. Besides, who would know better than Assyria how a mighty city like Thebes could be conquered? In a context where all, whether nations or individuals, are reduced to being mutual predators, all in turn must become prey. This is just as true in the world of international affairs as it is in personal interactions that take place in the microcosm of a workplace.

Nahum seems to be appealing to the conscience of Assyria, not to convince it to change its behavior, but to convict it of its crimes, and to confront it with the inevitability of retribution. The better alternative, no less valid because it remains implicit, would be to work for a context of cooperation and mutual support, where indeed the question "Are you better than Thebes?" would be irrelevant.

NAHUM 3:12-19, FINAL DIATRIBE

NIV

¹²All your fortresses are like fig trees
    with their first ripe fruit;
when they are shaken,
    the figs fall into the mouth of the eater.
¹³Look at your troops—
    they are all women!
The gates of your land
    are wide open to your enemies;
    fire has consumed their bars.

¹⁴Draw water for the siege,
    strengthen your defenses!
Work the clay,
    tread the mortar,
    repair the brickwork!
¹⁵There the fire will devour you;
    the sword will cut you down
    and, like grasshoppers, consume you.
Multiply like grasshoppers,
    multiply like locusts!
¹⁶You have increased the number of your
        merchants
    till they are more than the stars of the sky,
but like locusts they strip the land
    and then fly away.
¹⁷Your guards are like locusts,
    your officials like swarms of locusts
    that settle in the walls on a cold day—
but when the sun appears they fly away,
    and no one knows where.

¹⁸O king of Assyria, your shepherds^a slumber;
    your nobles lie down to rest.
Your people are scattered on the mountains
    with no one to gather them.
¹⁹Nothing can heal your wound;
    your injury is fatal.
Everyone who hears the news about you
    claps his hands at your fall,
for who has not felt
    your endless cruelty?

^a18 Or *rulers*

NRSV

¹² All your fortresses are like fig trees
    with first-ripe figs—
if shaken they fall
    into the mouth of the eater.
¹³ Look at your troops:
    they are women in your midst.
The gates of your land
    are wide open to your foes;
    fire has devoured the bars of your gates.

¹⁴ Draw water for the siege,
    strengthen your forts;
trample the clay,
    tread the mortar,
    take hold of the brick mold!
¹⁵ There the fire will devour you,
    the sword will cut you off.
    It will devour you like the locust.
Multiply yourselves like the locust,
    multiply like the grasshopper!
¹⁶ You increased your merchants
    more than the stars of the heavens.
    The locust sheds its skin and flies away.
¹⁷ Your guards are like grasshoppers,
    your scribes like swarms^a of locusts
settling on the fences
    on a cold day—
when the sun rises, they fly away;
    no one knows where they have gone.

¹⁸ Your shepherds are asleep,
    O king of Assyria;
    your nobles slumber.
Your people are scattered on the mountains
    with no one to gather them.
¹⁹ There is no assuaging your hurt,
    your wound is mortal.
All who hear the news about you
    clap their hands over you.
For who has ever escaped
    your endless cruelty?

^a Meaning of Heb uncertain

COMMENTARY

The last eight verses of Nahum are an address of Yahweh, directed first to Nineveh (vv. 12-17) and then to the king of Assyria (vv. 18-19). After the impassioned pitch of the preceding sections, the tone now seems somewhat calmer, the images less harrowing and more commonplace. The theme is the inevitability of Assyria's defeat, taken for granted almost as if it has already happened.

3:12-13. These verses begin by pointing out the hopelessness of Assyria's military predicament before the advancing enemy. The fortresses of Assyria are ripe for the plucking, says the simile of v. 12, like fig trees full of ripe fruit that will not require much effort on the eater's part. Verse 13 elaborates on the same theme by pejoratively comparing the soldiers (עם 'am; lit., "people," which both the NRSV and the NIV render as "troops") of Assyria to women, and immediately following the comparison with the image of the "gates of your land" being "wide open" to the enemy. Even though the prophet refers primarily to the burned wooden beams that would have been used to bar the gates, perhaps there are also overtones of rape. Nineveh is quite literally defenseless, its fall inevitable.

3:14-15a. After the images of vv. 12-13, v. 14 is clearly ironic. The series of commands (feminine imperative forms are used, so we must assume that the city is being addressed) usually pertains to early preparations for withstanding a siege. Here they come only after it is clear that they are too late to be of any use. What good is it now to think of adequate stores of water or of hurriedly making bricks to strengthen the fortress walls? The first part of v. 15 answers the implied question: In the strongholds, the Assyrians will try desperately but pointlessly to defend themselves. But "fire will devour you,/ the sword will cut you off./ It will devour you like the locust." That is to say, the destruction of the city will be carried out with the devastating thoroughness of a swarm of locusts destroying a field.

3:15b-17. A series of variations on the locust theme follows, beginning with the end of v. 15, where, ironically and even more impossibly, the city is commanded to multiply its people like locusts, in order to face the threat. Here the emphasis is on the capacity for rapid numerical increase, rather than destructiveness, of locusts.

Verse 16, though enigmatic, continues the use of the locust imagery. The "merchants" or "traders" of the city (the Hebrew word רכלים [rōkĕlîm] is clear, but its exact referent is less so), numerous as the stars of heaven, are now going to fly away, as molting locusts having shed their skin. (The NRSV correctly translates פשט [pāšat] as "sheds its skin," a reading that is preferable to the NIV's "strip the land.") Since merchants were usually among the best-informed classes of ancient societies, and since they would tend to try to escape being captured and losing their wealth, perhaps the poet refers to the sudden flight of the Assyrian and foreign traders from the doomed city, leaving behind the empty shells of their abandoned shops. Numerous as they were in Nineveh, their multitude will have been more like transient locusts than fixed stars.

The final variation occurs in v. 17, this time referring to the sudden flight of court officials. The prophet uses the striking metaphor of the dispersal of a swarm of locusts, sluggishly settled on a fence because of the night's cold, but then warming up and disappearing as the sun rises. The precise sort of officials meant by the words מנזריך (minnĕzārayik) and טפסריך (tapsĕrayik), rendered "your guards" and "your scribes" by the NRSV and "your guards" and "your officials" by the NIV, is somewhat unclear. The terms are apparently based on Assyrian words. Cathcart supports the suggestion that Assyrian manzazē and tupšarru, the words in question, may mean "augurs and astrologers," court officials expert in interpreting omens of all sorts in order to offer the king guidance for his actions.[26] The idea that they, too, have suddenly disappeared and that "no one knows where they have gone" takes on a truly ominous timbre; these are the people whose business it is to know what the future is about to bring.

3:18-19 Yahweh addresses the king directly and charges him with failure in the most fundamental duty of kingship: protecting his people.

26. Kevin J. Cathcart, "Nahum, Book of," in David Noel Freedman, ed., *The Anchor Bible Dictionary* (New York: Doubleday, 1992) 998.

The metaphor of the king as the shepherd of the people and of the people as the flock of the king is one of the basic concepts of the ancient Near East. Verse 18, therefore, is a serious indictment of the king of Assyria, whose government has collapsed in a stupor, leaving the people defenseless, like a scattered flock wandering in the mountains. Not only is the king a failure at his task, but also he is condemned to death (v. 19). The monarch is mortally wounded and hears, as it were from his death bed, the claps of joy at his demise from all those who have been touched by his endless cruelty. A failure to his people, for whose annihilation he is held responsible, he dies detested by his former victims. As is his fate, so also is Nineveh's. Yahweh has exacted vengeance on the city as well.

REFLECTIONS

A strong poetic work such as the book of Nahum has undeniable power and beauty, and it has much to tell us about the attitudes and understandings of its time. If it were simply a seventh-century BCE Hebrew poem that was recovered by archaeologists after being unknown for centuries, scholars would certainly study it; we would recognize its artistic merit. We could then regard it as a museum artifact, safely ensconced in a glass case. The problem, of course, is that this ancient poem has been handed down as part of the Jewish and Christian canons; in both synagogue and church, Nahum has the status of a work that believers must take into account as being in some way revelatory.

The absence of Nahum from the lectionary presents an implicit confession that Nahum is a book that makes the church uncomfortable, one that it seldom, if ever, opens. The attitudes toward violence that the prophet betrays in his theology of a jealous and avenging God raise serious questions for believers. Nahum's vision of the divine warrior coming to destroy Nineveh in retribution for Assyrian oppression fails ultimately to rise above justifying yet another instance of brutal human warfare, with its vividly portrayed consequence of human misery. How can we identify such violence and such misery as God's doing? How can we celebrate, as Nahum seems to suggest, the wholesale destruction of human life as an act of God?

In like manner, Nahum's reflection of patriarchal attitudes toward women, current in his society, particularly in the abhorrent picture of God's humiliating and abusing Nineveh as a prostitute, present serious problems to our religious sensitivity. How could we possibly go on, even by implication, teaching those attitudes? We are very much aware of the harm that such images have caused to women, and of the distortions these images have introduced into our social relations and into a theological understanding of our sexuality.

In his 1991 Gifford Lectures James Barr, speaking about the similarly problematic biblical concept of the "ban" (חרם, ḥērem), offers words that apply to Nahum as well. We must not read the Bible in ways that condone ideas that identify wickedness with a particular people or race or nation. We cannot accept the concept that wickedness justifies mass destruction. Above all, says Barr, we must reject "the belief that religious commands override morality and that it is good for us that this should be so."[27] To read the book of Nahum, then, we must prepare to listen to, but at the same time to argue with, this ancient poet. Such argument, in fact, is present in biblical books like Jonah or Ruth, which convey very different attitudes toward foreigners and toward women. Let our reading of Nahum stimulate us to take up the ethical and theological tasks the prophet poses. Let us not forget that there is much more to be said in our continuing conversation with the word of God as it struggles to express itself through the words of human beings.

27. James Barr, *Biblical Faith and Natural Theology* (Oxford: Clarendon, 1993).

THE BOOK OF HABAKKUK

INTRODUCTION, COMMENTARY, AND REFLECTIONS
BY
THEODORE HIEBERT

THE BOOK OF
HABAKKUK

INTRODUCTION

he message of Habakkuk has become known to the church primarily through a single phrase, "the just shall live by faith" (2:4), the phrase quoted by the apostle Paul in his letter to the Romans (1:17 KJV). In fact, the brief section of Habakkuk in which this phrase occurs, Hab 2:1-4, along with Hab 1:1-4, are the only texts from Habakkuk selected for public reading in Christian worship in the Revised Common Lectionary. This key phrase, though brief and quoted by Paul without reference to the larger context of which it is a part, lies at the heart of the prophet's message and provides a useful starting point for interpreting the book of Habakkuk. This phrase can only be understood fully, however, through an examination of its place in the book of Habakkuk as a whole and of its relationship to the concrete experiences of the prophet.

THEOLOGICAL ISSUES

Habakkuk's central concern for justice places him solidly in the tradition of Israel's prophets. Like his predecessor Isaiah and his contemporary Jeremiah, Habakkuk calls attention to and criticizes the miscarriage of justice in the political, judicial, and economic institutions of Judah and of its capital, Jerusalem. Also in the tradition of Israel's prophets, he predicts the demise of this unjust society as the result of coming events in which God will punish its unjust leaders and reestablish equity and proper order.

Unlike other prophets in the biblical canon, however, Habakkuk gives prominent attention to a persistent and troubling problem that challenges this prophetic confidence in God's justice: the perseverance of injustice in the world. Even in the very events and agents understood by Habakkuk as instruments by which divine justice will be done, injustice seems to be present. Real-world politics appear to be continually at odds with the prophetic passion for justice and faith in God's just rule. This problem, maintaining a belief in God's just rule in spite of an unjust world, is the central issue around which the book of Habakkuk as a whole has taken shape.

The challenge of believing in the ultimate power of justice in a world that appears to be overwhelmingly unjust is one of the most difficult existential struggles the religious person must face. Among biblical writers, Habakkuk was not alone in wrestling with it. Job, to whom Habakkuk is often compared, faces this issue more directly perhaps than does any other biblical figure, though within the context of his own family rather than in the wide realm of international politics, with which Habakkuk is concerned. The book of Job explores the religious crisis of a good and honest man who experiences a series of unprovoked catastrophes that force him to challenge the views in Israel's wisdom traditions of God's just rule. Such challenges are also raised in the context of Israelite worship. In the psalms of lament, the most common psalm type in the psalter, psalmists cry to God based on experiences of suffering and misfortune and plead for God to rectify wrongs and restore order. On occasion, a prophetic figure, such as Habakkuk's contemporary, Jeremiah, will question God's reliability and administration of justice in the world. But these occasions are rare in prophetic literature. No prophet confronts the issue of a just God and an unjust world in the direct and forceful way that Habakkuk does.

LITERARY STRUCTURE

The literary structure within which this topic is explored in the book of Habakkuk is built on a debate between the prophet and God, composed of two arguments. In the first argument, the prophet opens the debate with a complaint deploring the lack of justice in Judean society and God's failure to act against it (1:2-4). God responds by describing an astonishing, imminent event: a Chaldean invasion, designed to bring down Judah's corrupt government and put an end to its unjust policies and practices (1:5-11). In the second argument, the debate moves to a new level. The prophet again initiates the exchange with a complaint, this time questioning the justice of the divine plan itself: the Chaldean invasion. In his second complaint, Habakkuk describes the corruption of the Chaldeans, the very instrument by which God planned to render judgment and restore justice (1:12–2:1). Again, God responds, thereby completing the second exchange of speeches.

But just here, in the second divine response, the high point toward which the debate between the prophet and God has been building—the point at which the final resolution of Habakkuk's problem is expected—we encounter the book's key literary and exegetical challenges. The first of these challenges is the deciphering and translation of the difficult Hebrew in God's brief response to Habakkuk (2:2-4). Does it contain a new divine argument or merely promise a response in the future, one that is to be found perhaps in the subsequent sections of the book? The second major challenge is the relationship to the preceding debate of the literary units that follow this response. The first of these units is neither a prophetic complaint nor a divine response, but a collection of sayings spoken by conquered nations and peoples to ridicule the Chaldean oppressor (2:5-20). The second of these units, introduced by a superscription, often a sign of later editorial activity (3:1) and accompanied by musical notations characteristic of the book of Psalms (3:1, 3, 9, 13, 19), is an elaborate victory hymn describing God's appearance as a conquering warrior (3:2-19). The way in which one understands the relationship of these concluding literary sections to one another and to the previous dialogue determines to a great extent the way in which one interprets the ultimate message of the book.

The basic picture of the shape of the book of Habakkuk and its message that emerges from this exegesis discloses three stages of literary and theological development in the book's compilation. The first is represented by the judgment speech delivered to Judah (Hab 1:5-11), expressing the traditional prophetic theology of divine justice according to which Judah's sins will be justifiably punished by a foreign invader. The second stage is the incorporation of this oracle into the elaborate debate (Hab 1:12–2:4), in which this traditional theology of divine justice is questioned and then reconstructed in the second divine response (2:1-4) and in the wisdom of conquered peoples (2:5-20). The third stage involves the addition by later disciples of Habakkuk of an archaic victory hymn interpreted as the future intervention of God to restore absolute justice on earth (3:1-19). Within the framework of such a literary and theological development lie the most reliable clues for understanding the full sense of Habakkuk's claim: "The just shall live by his faith" (2:4 KJV).

HISTORICAL SETTING

Habakkuk has provided little concrete data to identify the historical events and political situation that led to his religious crisis and ensuing debate with God. The superscription of the book (1:1) contains no information, as do many superscriptions of prophetic books (Isa 1:1; Jer 1:1-3), about the particular kings within whose reigns the prophet spoke. Further, the language in which Habakkuk conducts the debate at the heart of the book is general and archetypal in nature. The key players in the political drama that raised such serious questions for Habakkuk—unrestrained oppressors and helpless victims—are regularly designated by the nonspecific terms "the wicked" and "the righteous" (1:4, 13; 2:4; cf. 3:13).

The starting point for understanding the book within a particular historical period is its one concrete political reference: the mention of the Chaldeans in 1:6. "Chaldean" is the name used by biblical historians (2 Kgs 25:1-13; 2 Chr 36:17) and prophets (Jer 21:4; Ezek 23:23) for the Neo-Babylonians under the rule of the powerful king Nebuchadnezzar II (605–562 BCE), who sacked Jerusalem in 597 and destroyed it completely in 586 BCE. These Neo-Babylonians first became a major force in the ancient Near East under the rule of Nebuchadnezzar's father, Nabopolassar, who declared himself king of Babylon in 626 BCE.

Habakkuk's prediction of an invasion of Babylonian armies (1:5-11) certainly predated their first siege of Jerusalem in 597 and probably also their first appearance in the coastal plain adjacent to Judah in 604 BCE. Otherwise, the prediction would hardly have been astonishing or unbelievable (1:5). On the other hand, a Neo-Babylonian invasion of Judah would not have been even conceivable until 605 BCE, when the Babylonians defeated the Assyrians and the Egyptians at Carchemish, four hundred miles north of Jerusalem, to establish their supremacy in the west. It is likely, therefore, that Habakkuk's announcement of the Chaldean invasion was delivered between these events, in 605–604 BCE, the fifth year of the reign of Jehoiakim, king of Judah, whose corrupt regime is described in 1:2-4.[1]

The central question that drives the book of Habakkuk—the persistence of injustice, even in the divine judgment on Judah at the hands of the Chaldeans—logically arises, however, from Habakkuk's firsthand experience of the Chaldeans themselves. Thus the description of abuses by the Neo-Babylonian invader in Habakkuk's second complaint (1:12–2:1) and the composition and compilation of the debate with God over divine rule in chaps. 1 and 2 derive from the period between Nebuchadnezzar's first invasion in 597 and his destruction of Jerusalem in 586 BCE, the era of the reign of Zedekiah, a Judean placed in power by the Neo-Babylonian regime. Habakkuk's career and his fervent struggle with divine justice are to be viewed, therefore, against the backdrop of the final, turbulent days of Jerusalem and its great Davidic dynasty.

The historical period within which the victory hymn in chap. 3 was composed and became part of the book of Habakkuk has been the subject of much discussion and debate. An earlier generation of scholars, represented in the bibliography by G. A. Smith, believed the poem to have been composed and added to Habakkuk in the post-exilic period, long after Habakkuk's career, the fall of Jerusalem, the Babylonian exile, and the initial efforts by the returned exiles to rebuild Jerusalem and Judah. Most contemporary scholars, including Achtemeier, Gowen, Haak, and Roberts as cited in the bibliography, have by contrast come to regard this hymn as an authentic work of Habakkuk himself, composed during the final, troubled days of Jerusalem, which gave rise to his debate with God in chaps. 1–2. A sizable body of evidence suggests, however, that the hymn in Habakkuk 3 is an archaic composition, added to the corpus of Habakkuk in the post-exilic period in order to emphasize God's final victory over evil. This evidence will be described in the commentary.

1. J. J. M. Roberts, *Nahum, Habakkuk, and Zephaniah,* OTL (Louisville: Westminster/John Knox, 1991) 82-84, 95.

SOCIAL LOCATION

No direct information is provided in the book's superscription, or in Habakkuk's speeches themselves, that allows us to determine the social location of this prophet or his family within Judean society. Because his speeches share certain features of the psalms, and because chap. 3 contains musical annotations characteristic of the psalter, some have suggested that Habakkuk was a cult prophet—that is, a prophet employed by the Temple to deliver divine oracles within the liturgies and rituals of this institution.[2] The evidence is not decisive, with scholars differing on Habakkuk's relationship to the Temple and its priestly officials. Habakkuk's own struggle with the question certainly arose out of his prophetic office (1:1), as it did for Jeremiah; but the influence of the Temple upon his thought is more difficult to assess. As the biblical evidence from the psalter, from Job, and from Jeremiah, mentioned above, indicates, the question of God's justice and reliable rule in the world was raised in a variety of social contexts in ancient Israel. In the end, the problem of believing in the ultimate power of justice in an unjust world is such a basic one that it transcends particular social locations and political crises.

2. Sigmund Mowinckel, *The Psalms in Israel's Worship,* trans. D. R. Ap-Thomas (New York: Abingdon, 1967) 2:93, 147, 150; J. H. Eaton, "The Origin and Meaning of Habakkuk 3," *ZAW* 76 (1964) 144-71.

BIBLIOGRAPHY

Achtemeier, Elizabeth. *Nahum–Malachi.* Interpretation. Atlanta: John Knox, 1986. A brief commentary focusing on the theology and biblical context of the book.

Gowen, Donald E. *The Triumph of Faith in Habakkuk.* Atlanta: John Knox, 1976. A theological study addressed to laypeople.

Haak, Robert D. *Habakkuk.* VTSup 44. Leiden: Brill, 1991. A detailed analysis of the text and of the political background of Habakkuk.

Hiebert, Theodore. *God of My Victory: The Ancient Hymn in Habakkuk 3.* HSM 38. Atlanta: Scholars Press, 1986. The more technical argument for the interpretation of Habakkuk 3, presented here.

Roberts, J. J. M. *Nahum, Habakkuk, and Zephaniah.* OTL. Louisville: Westminster/John Knox, 1991. A thorough, historical commentary focusing on the textual issues, historical background, and key themes of the book in its original setting.

Smith, George Adam. *The Book of the Twelve Prophets.* Volume 2 of *The Expositor's Bible.* London: Hodder and Stoughton, 1898. A still useful commentary reflecting an earlier generation of Habakkuk scholarship.

OUTLINE OF HABAKKUK

I. Habakkuk 1:1, Superscription

II. Habakkuk 1:2–2:4, The Debate Between Habakkuk and God

    A. 1:2-11, The First Argument
        1:2-4, Habakkuk's First Complaint: The Miscarriage of Justice in Judah
        1:5-11, God's First Response: The Chaldeans, God's Instrument of Judgment

    B. 1:12–2:4, The Second Argument
        1:12–2:1, Habakkuk's Second Complaint: The Chaldeans' Corrupt Regime
        2:2-4, God's Second Response: The Reliability of God's Rule

III. Habakkuk 2:5-20, The Fall of Tyranny

IV. Habakkuk 3:1, Superscription

V. Habakkuk 3:2-19, God's Cosmic Reign

HABAKKUK 1:1

SUPERSCRIPTION

NIV	NRSV
1 The oracle that Habakkuk the prophet received.	**1** The oracle that the prophet Habakkuk saw.

COMMENTARY

Prophetic books customarily begin, as do modern books, with the facts of publication: title, author (occasionally including family, hometown, and occupation), and date (identified by the name of the king during whose reign the prophecy was delivered). About the author, we are provided a name (Habakkuk) and an occupation (prophet), but no date, a fact that has led to some disagreement about the historical circumstances that gave rise to this literature. The title of Habakkuk's work, "oracle" (משׂא *maśśā'*), derives from the common verb "lift up" or "raise" (נשׂא *nāśā'*) and may well have as its basic sense a communication brought to public attention—that is, a message lifted up, a voice raised.[3] The custom of referring to such a message as having been "seen" (cf. Isa 1:1; Nah 1:1) may derive ultimately from the visionary experiences traditionally associated with the prophets.

3. Roberts, *Nahum, Habakkuk, and Zephaniah*, 86.

HABAKKUK 1:2–2:4

THE DEBATE BETWEEN HABAKKUK AND GOD

HABAKKUK 1:2-11, THE FIRST ARGUMENT

Habakkuk 1:2-4, Habakkuk's First Complaint: The Miscarriage of Justice in Judah

NIV

²How long, O LORD, must I call for help,
    but you do not listen?
Or cry out to you, "Violence!"
    but you do not save?
³Why do you make me look at injustice?
    Why do you tolerate wrong?
Destruction and violence are before me;
    there is strife, and conflict abounds.
⁴Therefore the law is paralyzed,
    and justice never prevails.
The wicked hem in the righteous,
    so that justice is perverted.

NRSV

² O LORD, how long shall I cry for help,
    and you will not listen?
Or cry to you "Violence!"
    and you will not save?
³ Why do you make me see wrongdoing
    and look at trouble?
Destruction and violence are before me;
    strife and contention arise.
⁴ So the law becomes slack
    and justice never prevails.
The wicked surround the righteous—
    therefore judgment comes forth perverted.

COMMENTARY

The speech that opens the book of Habakkuk resembles the beginning of a psalm of lament, in which a worshiper in distress appeals for divine aid (e.g., Psalms 3; 12; 22). Habakkuk's speech begins with an address to God (1:2), the traditional opening of a lament, and employs a phrase commonly used in laments: "How long?" (עד־אנה ʿad-ʾānâ; see, e.g., Ps 13:1-2; cf. Ps 74:10). Habakkuk's speech continues, as does a typical lament, with the complaint proper, a statement of the problem experienced by the speaker (1:3-4). Here, however, the resemblance of Habakkuk's speech to the lament ends. While a psalm of lament proceeds with some combination of additional elements—a confession of trust in God, a petition to God to intervene (expressed with imperative verb

forms), and a concluding vow of praise anticipating God's intervention—Habakkuk's speech incorporates only the lament's two opening sections.[4] In this truncated lament, however, we can see the basic shape of the prophet's major concern.

From the final summary statement in Habakkuk's complaint, it is clear that he is concerned about the perversion (lit., "twisting," "bending" [עקל ʿāqal]) of justice in Judean society (1:4). But the language in which this injustice is described and in which its perpetrators ("the wicked" [רשע rāšāʿ]) and its victims ("the righteous" [צדיק ṣaddîq]) are identified is so general that it has been

4. For an introduction to the psalms of lament, see Bernhard W. Anderson, *Out of the Depths: The Psalms Speak for Us Today,* rev. ed. (Philadelphia: Westminster, 1983) 63-105.

impossible for scholars to reach a consensus about the precise kind of corruption lamented in this speech. A popular position among a past generation of scholars was to see here the oppression of Judah by a foreign power, such as the Assyrian Empire.[5]

More often, the disorder described in Habakkuk's complaint has been interpreted against the backdrop of internal Judean politics. This disorder has been viewed as the suppression of a pro-Jehoahaz, pro-Babylonian party by the pro-Jehoiakim, pro-Egyptian party in power,[6] or as the restriction of prophetic activity and speech.[7] In Habakkuk's repeated references to violence and lawlessness, the modern reader might be predisposed to see indications of the rise of crime and the loss of law and order.[8] For a variety of reasons, however—and these would not exclude some of the options just mentioned—the injustice Habakkuk deplores in this speech is best understood as the abuse of power in the administration of King Jehoiakim, whose reign in Judah from 609–597 BCE is chronicled by the deuteronomistic historian in 2 Kgs 23:34–24:7 and referred to repeatedly, with prophetic scorn, by Habakkuk's contemporary, Jeremiah.

In the first place, the exploitation of the poor and the less privileged by the rich and powerful is a fundamental concern among Israel's prophets, and the language Habakkuk uses here is appropriate for documenting such a situation. The terms "violence" (חמס *ḥāmās*) and "destruction" (שׁוד *šōd*; better "plunder" in 1:2-3) are used as a pair by other prophets to describe the ruthless accumulation of wealth by political officials (Ezek 45:9; Amos 3:10; cf. Mic 2:4). Even the verb "cry" (זעק *zāʿaq*; "[I] cry to you, 'Violence!' " [v. 2]) is customarily used in the Bible as an appeal for help by the oppressed (e.g., Exod 2:23; Ps 22:5; cf. Isa 5:7, where another form of the same word occurs). The words "strife" (ריב *rîb*) and "contention" (מדון *mādôn*) derive from the legal sphere of Judean society. They appear to describe

stresses in Judah's judicial system brought on by irresponsible litigation or the failure to administer justice properly.

Even Habakkuk's use of the term "righteous" (צדיק *ṣaddîq*) for the victims of such abusive policies may identify them as society's poor and marginalized. Although a general, nonspecific term in itself, "righteous" occasionally refers to the poor in prophetic discourse (e.g., Isa 29:20-21; Amos 2:6-7; 5:1). Habakkuk's mention of the righteous being surrounded reflects the severe restrictions and limitations on the freedom of the corrupt regime's victims, perhaps including restrictions on prophetic activity and speech itself. Such abuses of power are ultimately to blame, according to Habakkuk, for a society in which justice is absent and the law ineffectual (1:4).

Further support for such an interpretation can be found among Judah's historians and prophets, who attribute to Jehoiakim a regime in which such oppressive policies are pursued. Jehoiakim is accused of dishonest gain (Jer 22:17). He is charged with using forced, unpaid labor for building his own lavish residence, and with demanding heavy payments from Judah's citizenry to support his Egyptian alliance (2 Kgs 23:35; Jer 22:13). Furthermore, the king is implicated in the obstruction of justice (Jer 22:13), in the shedding of innocent blood (2 Kgs 24:4; Jer 22:17), and in the murder of prophets (Jer 26:20-23). A written record of the prophecy of Jeremiah, Habakkuk's contemporary, was destroyed by Jehoiakim piece by piece in his own fireplace (Jeremiah 36). Jehoiakim's regime was, in fact, deposed as a result of the Babylonian invasion Habakkuk predicts in the oracle of 1:5-10.

The critique of social injustice present in Habakkuk's complaint is typical of prophetic speech, but the literary form in which that critique is expressed here is somewhat unusual. The most common form within which such a prophetic critique is delivered is the judgment speech, a two-part address drawn from the judicial sphere, in which an indictment, outlining the people's sins, is followed by a sentence, prescribing punishment for them (e.g., Isa 5:8-10; Amos 1:3-5; 2:6-16).[9] In a judgment speech, the prophet as-

5. See the summary of this view by George Adam Smith, *The Book of the Twelve Prophets*, vol. 2 of *The Expositor's Bible* (London: Hodder and Stoughton, 1898) 115-124.

6. Defended recently by Robert D. Haak, *Habakkuk*, VTSup 44 (Leiden: Brill, 1991) esp. 107-49.

7. J. Gerald Janzen, "Eschatological Symbol and Prophetic Existence in Habakkuk," *CBQ* 44 (1982) 394-414.

8. Noted in the recent commentary by Ralph L. Smith, *Micah–Malachi* (Waco, Tex.: Word, 1984).

9. On the prophetic judgment speech, see Claus Westermann, *Basic Forms of Prophetic Speech* (Louisville: Westminister/John Knox, 1991) 129-94.

sumes the role of the court messenger or herald, delivering to the public the verdict of the presiding judge: a list of sins for which the defendant has been found guilty, followed by the sentence imposed by the judge on their account. In such a literary form, the prophet adopts God's perspective on the world, indicting injustice, proclaiming its punishment, and affirming divine rule with all of the authority, power, and certainty of the heavenly court.

Habakkuk, however, has selected the opening stanzas of a lament with which to describe the injustices of Judean society. It is a fateful choice. In doing so, Habakkuk has abandoned the divine perspective common in prophetic discourse and has assumed instead the role of the victim whose case has not been redressed by divine intervention and who can only appeal to God for aid in a prayer of lamentation. In such a literary context, the abuses in Judean society are viewed not as crimes already judged but as injustices that have gone unseen and unpunished. God's administration of justice in the world is immediately posed as a problem rather than assumed as a certainty. Habakkuk's first sentence, his address to God, which begins his lament, drives the point home. With his opening words, Habakkuk accuses God directly of being inattentive and inactive.

Habakkuk's selection of a lament rather than a judgment speech with which to begin his work sets the tone for the entire book. Such a response to the experience of injustice is not unique among Israel's prophets. It is probably better known from the so-called confessions (better, "laments") of Jeremiah, in which Jeremiah complains bitterly to God for not acting to judge the wicked and for allowing Jeremiah to suffer their torments (e.g., Jer 15:10-21; 20:7-18). But in no prophetic corpus does the *problem* of divine justice set the terms for the book as a whole, as they are set for this book by the opening lines of Habakkuk's lament.

REFLECTIONS

Two key traits of biblical religion are embedded in Habakkuk's opening lament: the concern for social justice and the willingness to argue with God.

1. One of the great legacies of the prophetic movement, reflected clearly in Habakkuk's opening critique of Judean society, is its absolute commitment to social justice. Authentic religion, according to the prophets, was not merely a matter of personal spirituality or of the ritual activity of worship. It required a public dedication to principles of fairness and equity in political, judicial, and economic life. Habakkuk's central theological concerns involve public affairs often relegated today to the secular world: the inequities in the judicial system, the economic exploitation of the poor by the wealthy, the breakdown of social order. Habakkuk considered these "secular," social affairs to be those in which God held Judah primarily responsible for its ethical behavior.

Moreover, the prophets demanded such standards of fairness and equity especially of those who wielded political and economic power: Israel's kings, priests, judges, and its wealthiest citizens. When social unrest increases, it is easy for a society to blame its poor, who are often disproportionately involved in crime and in prison populations. It requires much more courage to hold accountable, as did Habakkuk, society's elite and powerful figures and organizations, who customarily protect the privileged and institutionalize the disparity between rich and poor. In the eyes of Israel's prophets, the real cause of social conflict was to be placed, not at the feet of the poor, but in the corridors of power, where the policies that structure a society, in just or unjust ways, are formulated and executed.

Prophets such as Habakkuk provided one of the strongest and most persuasive critiques of the abuse of power and one of the clearest defenses of the underprivileged and the marginalized that is to be found in Western literature. On the contemporary scene, this prophetic concern is represented powerfully by liberation theologians. Living in countries whose populations have been exploited by oppressive regimes, such theologians have recognized clearly the real political implications of the prophetic concern for social justice. "The God of the Bible," asserts the Peruvian theologian Gustavo Gutiérrez, "is a God who takes sides with the poor and liberates them from slavery and oppression."[10] James Cone, an African American theologian, makes a similar claim: "The doing of theology, on the basis of the revelation of Yahweh, must involve the politics which takes its stand with the poor and against the rich."[11]

2. The other trait of biblical religion prominent in Habakkuk's opening speech is his argument with God. Having taken his stand with the victims of injustice, Habakkuk is prepared to defend their cause, even to the point of questioning God's handling of their case. Such a direct challenge to God arises out of a tradition of arguing with God, much more prominent in the OT than in the NT. Biblical figures like Moses (Exodus 3–4), Jeremiah (1:4-10), Job, and the psalmists argue with God. These arguments are ways of dealing openly and honestly with the discrepancy all persons face at one time or another between the facts of human experience and the ideals and visions of religious faith. They arise not out of hostility or indifference to religious faith, but out of a passionate search for the ways of God in the world. There are times when patience, an honorable and enduring virtue, is abandoned by biblical authors in order to pursue this search properly.

The reason for Habakkuk's argument is the discrepancy he faces—spelled out clearly already in his opening lament—between belief in a just God and the experience of an unjust world. In Habakkuk's eyes, the divine judge appears either uninterested or unable to do justice in the world. This problem, the problem of theodicy, has been put in no simpler and starker terms than it was put by Nickles in Archibald MacLeish's adaptation of Job, *J.B.*:

> If God is God He is not good,
> If God is good He is not God.[12]

If God is really God—in control of the world—God cannot be good or just and also allow injustice and suffering to exist and to endure. If God is really good and just, God cannot be in control of such a corrupt world.

The religious person may confront such a crisis as urgently in private and personal tragedies as in massive social catastrophes. It is the problem Habakkuk faced by the miscarriage of justice under Jehoiakim's administration in the final days of the Davidic dynasty. It is the basis of his argument with God, an argument taken up in one form or another, privately or publicly, by every believer who experiences firsthand the pain of oppression or the suffering of the innocent.

10. Gustavo Gutiérrez, "Biblical Overview of the Sources of Liberation Theology," in *The Power of the Poor in History* (Maryknoll, N.Y.: Orbis, 1983) 7.

11. James H. Cone, "Biblical Revelation and Social Existence," in *God of the Oppressed* (San Francisco: Harper & Row, 1975) 65.

12. Archibald MacLeish, *J.B.* (Boston: Houghton Mifflin, 1956) 11.

Habakkuk 1:5-11, God's First Response: The Chaldeans, God's Instrument of Judgment

NIV

5"Look at the nations and watch—
    and be utterly amazed.
For I am going to do something in your days
    that you would not believe,
    even if you were told.
6I am raising up the Babylonians,*a*
    that ruthless and impetuous people,
who sweep across the whole earth
    to seize dwelling places not their own.
7They are a feared and dreaded people;
    they are a law to themselves
    and promote their own honor.
8Their horses are swifter than leopards,
    fiercer than wolves at dusk.
Their cavalry gallops headlong;
    their horsemen come from afar.
They fly like a vulture swooping to devour;
9   they all come bent on violence.
Their hordes*b* advance like a desert wind
    and gather prisoners like sand.
10They deride kings
    and scoff at rulers.
They laugh at all fortified cities;
    they build earthen ramps and capture them.
11Then they sweep past like the wind and go on—
    guilty men, whose own strength is their god."

a6 Or *Chaldeans*   *b9* The meaning of the Hebrew for this word is uncertain.

NRSV

5 Look at the nations, and see!
    Be astonished! Be astounded!
For a work is being done in your days
    that you would not believe if you were told.
6 For I am rousing the Chaldeans,
    that fierce and impetuous nation,
who march through the breadth of the earth
    to seize dwellings not their own.
7 Dread and fearsome are they;
    their justice and dignity proceed from
        themselves.
8 Their horses are swifter than leopards,
    more menacing than wolves at dusk;
    their horses charge.
Their horsemen come from far away;
    they fly like an eagle swift to devour.
9 They all come for violence,
    with faces pressing*a* forward;
    they gather captives like sand.
10 At kings they scoff,
    and of rulers they make sport.
They laugh at every fortress,
    and heap up earth to take it.
11 Then they sweep by like the wind;
    they transgress and become guilty;
    their own might is their god!

a Meaning of Heb uncertain

COMMENTARY

The speech that follows Habakkuk's opening lament represents a widely used, conventional genre of prophetic discourse: the announcement of judgment. The announcement of judgment, often but not always following an indictment in a judgment speech, describes God's sentence on the guilty. The sentence announced in this speech is the invasion of the Chaldeans. While the Chaldean invasion predicted here is not explicitly identified as God's judgment on Judah, the standard form and content by which this event is described indicate that it does, indeed, represent such a prophetic announcement. The speech is addressed to the entire Judean populace, as the plural imperatives ("look," "see," etc.) in its opening lines indicate (v. 5).[13] As is customary in this genre, the announcement of judgment is presented as a speech by God in the first person (1:6; cf. e.g., Jer 4:6 and Amos 6:14, where the same grammatical construction—first-person pronoun plus participle—is employed). After this divine declaration to act, the nature of the intervention is described in third-person narrative verse (vv.

13. English, unlike Hebrew, does not distinguish between singular and plural second-person forms, such as the imperative verbs here.

6-11). As is the case in many prophetic judgment speeches, God punishes a corrupt Judean government by allowing it to fall at the hands of a foreign army (cf. Isa 10:28-32; Jer 4:5-31).[14]

Habakkuk's description of the Chaldean army's approach reflects the familiar realities of ancient Near Eastern warfare and the behavior of imperial governments. The special attention to horses, horsemen, and their speed in the vivid imagery of vv. 8-9 accurately reflects the fact that the great armies of Near Eastern antiquity were built around horse-drawn chariots and cavalry, upon which armies relied for mobility in battle. The mention of fortresses and earthworks in v. 10 depicts the common practice of laying siege to walled cities and the construction of massive earthen ramps used to assault the walls.[15]

The imperialist goals for which such an army was built are emphasized in this speech. The Babylonians defer to no one. They have earned their own honor, and they make their own laws (v. 7). Their power, in their eyes, rivals God's (v. 11). They seize and annex neighboring territories (v. 6), and they capture and deport their citizenry (v. 9). They scoff at rulers and their fortresses (v. 10). Before such expansionist policies, the small, peripheral kingdom of Judah is defenseless, and its demise is inevitable. These images of the invincibility of God's instrument of punishment underline for Habakkuk's listeners the certainty of God's judgment.

In its identification of a foreign nation as God's instrument for the punishment of injustice and the restoration of justice in Judah, this speech positions Habakkuk directly in the mainstream of prophetic thought. From the first of the writing prophets, Amos (c. 760 BCE), prophets had regarded the invasion of enemy armies as just punishment for the unjust practices within the societies of the kingdoms of Israel and Judah. According to such thought, the God of the prophets was in control of the world, directing international and domestic politics so that justice would be done. In the concrete details of history, in the rise and fall of nations and regimes, one could see the hand of God, ensuring that the wicked were punished and the righteous rewarded. In just such terms does Habakkuk view the Chaldean offensive in this speech.

Several features of this speech suggest that Habakkuk's announcement of judgment was originally composed independently of the literary context in which it is now found. First, it is not addressed to the prophet, whose complaint precedes it, but to Judean society as a whole, as the plural imperatives ("look [ראו *rĕ'û*] . . . watch [הביטו *habbîṭû*] . . . be utterly amazed [התמהו תמהו *hittammĕhû tĕmāhû*]" [NIV]) and the pronouns ("your" [כם- *-kem*]) that introduce the speech make plain (v. 5). Second, an announcement of judgment, as noted above, is a conventional form of prophetic discourse, occurring commonly by itself or as the second part of a judgment speech following an accusation or indictment. It does not usually function as a response to a lament, the role it plays in its current literary setting in Habakkuk. Third, the speech lacks a transition linking it to the preceding lament, like the transition used later to link God's second response to Habakkuk's second lament (2:2).

If indeed this announcement of judgment was once delivered independently, outside of the context of the argument with God as a part of which it is now included, it represents a simple affirmation of the traditional prophetic confidence in God's just rule. On its own terms—or perhaps once following a prophetic indictment—the speech asserts unequivocally God's just administration of the world's affairs. Such an unwavering belief in divine justice in human society is characteristic of prophetic thought. Its presence within the bounds of this speech suggests that Habakkuk began his career with this same unwavering belief. This announcement of judgment was likely first delivered in 605–604 BCE, a few years before the invasion of the Chaldean armies in 597 BCE, an invasion that would challenge Habakkuk's faith in God's just rule.

Positioned now as part of the prophet's argument with God, this announcement of judgment takes on a new role. Following Habakkuk's lament, it is now a response to a problem, not an unquestioned principle of faith; it is an argument in a debate, not a proclamation of assumed truth. As such, this speech still defends mainline prophetic theology. It asserts that the injustice of

---

14. On the announcement of judgment, see Westermann, *Basic Forms of Prophetic Speech,* 149-61, 169-86.

15. The conduct of war in the ancient Near East, especially in Israel's history, is described with analysis and photographs of ancient warfare imagery by Yigael Yadin, *The Art of Warfare in Biblical Lands,* 2 vols. (New York: McGraw-Hill, 1963).

Judean society detailed in Habakkuk's lament will be fairly punished by God through the agency of Nebuchadnezzar's armies. But this theology has now been repositioned as one argument, though a traditional and honorable one, within a larger debate—a debate, as it turns out, that is not to be settled with this response.

If this speech was indeed composed by Habakkuk as a traditional announcement of judgment, and secondarily used as part of Habakkuk's argument with God, it reveals a development in Habakkuk's thought about divine justice in the world.

Originally secure in traditional prophetic theology, which interpreted such foreign invasions as God's just punishment of a sinful Judah, Habakkuk's firsthand experience of this event led him to question its justice. Between the composition of the speech, as an announcement of judgment, and its present literary context, as a response to Habakkuk's complaint, we see the first development in the prophet's thought, a move from the certainty of prophetic theology to a struggle with the facts of human existence.

REFLECTIONS

By identifying the Chaldeans as the instrument of God's justice, Habakkuk expands the social context of his theological reflection from Judah's domestic situation to the international scene. This broad international setting and the military conflicts within it provide the concrete context within which Habakkuk's exploration of the problem of justice will be pursued in the remainder of the book. Habakkuk's statement of the problem and the resolution of it are worked out, not in the context of a private and personal religious experience, but in terms of the wide public world of international politics. This context cannot be dismissed or spiritualized without altering the message of the book. At the same time, the problem of justice is such a fundamental one that insights gained in the public arena may cast light upon the most private and individual of struggles.

In its current position, as a response to his complaint about the miscarriage of justice in Judean society, Habakkuk's announcement of judgment defends, if temporarily, the traditional biblical position on the issue of theodicy. According to this position, God rules the world justly. Moreover, this just rule can be discovered in the concrete events of world history. The wicked are punished and the righteous protected by a deity who directs events in the world toward these ends. This is the basic orientation of the prophets, as it was of other biblical authors. Biblical historians interpreted the fortunes of the kingdoms of Israel and Judah in these terms (e.g., 2 Kings 17). Israel's wisdom circles counseled that

> The wicked are overthrown and are no more,
>   but the house of the righteous will stand. (Prov 12:7 NRSV)

The psalmists appealed for divine aid on this basis:

> O let the evil of the wicked come to an end,
>   but establish the righteous,
> you who test the minds and hearts,
>   O righteous God. (Ps 7:9[10] NRSV)

This doctrine—that God directs affairs toward just ends—pervades biblical literature and is fundamental to biblical thought. Applied to the scene of world politics, as Habakkuk does, it is at once a reassuring and troublesome doctrine. On the one hand, belief in God's just rule challenges the view that history is driven by blind chance or, worse yet, by the powers of evil. It asserts that behind the rise and fall of nations is a power ensuring justice and directing national affairs to a proper end. On the other hand, such a belief is almost impossible to work out within the vagaries of real politics, in which the conflict of national self-interests determines international events. Where is the hand of God to be found in such affairs?

One thing that can be said for the prophets, as for Habakkuk here, is that they refused the easy and almost universal practice of identifying God's rule exclusively with the policies of their own country. They often dared to identify God's justice with the enemy, a claim that would be regarded as seditious and unpatriotic today as it was in Habakkuk's day, when his contemporary Jeremiah was imprisoned for espousing it (Jeremiah 37–38). Wherever located, religious people have always wished to affirm God's just rule, in spite of the ambiguities of real international politics. This tension, however, became too great for Habakkuk, whose next argument takes up this crisis of faith.

HABAKKUK 1:12–2:4, THE SECOND ARGUMENT

Habakkuk 1:12–2:1, Habakkuk's Second Complaint: The Chaldeans' Corrupt Regime

NIV

¹²O Lord, are you not from everlasting?
  My God, my Holy One, we will not die.
O Lord, you have appointed them to execute judgment;
  O Rock, you have ordained them to punish.
¹³Your eyes are too pure to look on evil;
  you cannot tolerate wrong.
Why then do you tolerate the treacherous?
  Why are you silent while the wicked
  swallow up those more righteous than themselves?
¹⁴You have made men like fish in the sea,
  like sea creatures that have no ruler.
¹⁵The wicked foe pulls all of them up with hooks,
  he catches them in his net,
he gathers them up in his dragnet;
  and so he rejoices and is glad.
¹⁶Therefore he sacrifices to his net
  and burns incense to his dragnet,
for by his net he lives in luxury
  and enjoys the choicest food.
¹⁷Is he to keep on emptying his net,
  destroying nations without mercy?

2 I will stand at my watch
  and station myself on the ramparts;
I will look to see what he will say to me,
  and what answer I am to give to this complaint.ᵃ

ᵃ1 Or and what to answer when I am rebuked

NRSV

¹² Are you not from of old,
  O Lord my God, my Holy One?
Youᵃ shall not die.
O Lord, you have marked them for judgment;
  and you, O Rock, have established them for punishment.
¹³ Your eyes are too pure to behold evil,
  and you cannot look on wrongdoing;
why do you look on the treacherous,
  and are silent when the wicked swallow
  those more righteous than they?
¹⁴ You have made people like the fish of the sea,
  like crawling things that have no ruler.

¹⁵ The enemyᵇ brings all of them up with a hook;
  he drags them out with his net,
he gathers them in his seine;
  so he rejoices and exults.
¹⁶ Therefore he sacrifices to his net
  and makes offerings to his seine;
for by them his portion is lavish,
  and his food is rich.
¹⁷ Is he then to keep on emptying his net,
  and destroying nations without mercy?

2 I will stand at my watchpost,
  and station myself on the rampart;
I will keep watch to see what he will say to me,
  and what heᶜ will answer concerning my complaint.

ᵃ Ancient Heb tradition: MT We   ᵇ Heb He   ᶜ Syr: Heb I

COMMENTARY

With this speech, Habakkuk begins the second argument in his dialogue with God. Habakkuk complains to God for the second time, employing again elements of the psalm of lament. This lament begins, as did his first (1:2-4), with a direct address to God (1:12-13a), and it continues with the complaint proper, the statement of the problem Habakkuk faces (1:13b-17). In the address, Habakkuk affirms God's immortal nature and holy character, contrasting it in the complaint that follows with the unjust realities of Habakkuk's own circumstances. Once again, then, Habakkuk employs the first two elements of the conventional lament for his complaint. In this case, however, he concludes his appeal with the expectation of a response (2:1). The book of Habakkuk thus begins to take the shape of a dialogue or a debate, in which a new complaint demands a new response.

As in his first lament, Habakkuk uses the non-specific terms "righteous" (צדיק *ṣaddîq*) and "wicked" (רשע *rāšāʿ*) for the just and the unjust individuals or parties of whom he speaks (1:13). In this second lament, however, the identity of the wicked who harass the righteous is the Chaldean Empire, described in 1:5-11, rather than Jehoiakim's government, criticized in 1:2-4. Several pieces of evidence support this interpretation. In the first place, the third-person singular masculine pronouns ("he," "his") and verb forms ("he gathers," "he rejoices," 1:15), by which the wicked person is identified in this speech, continue the third-person singular masculine forms of 1:6-11. They refer to the term "nation" (NRSV)/"people" (NIV), used of the Chaldeans in 1:6. These pronouns and verb forms in 1:6-11 have all been translated in the plural ("they"/"their") in both the NRSV and the NIV. Second, the imperialistic character of the wicked in 1:12-17 reflects the description of Chaldean policies and practices in the prediction of their invasion in 1:5-11. The same sort of ruthlessness, military power, and expansionist greed are emphasized in both speeches. Thus the wicked in this lament are not the wicked of the first lament, the corrupt government of Jehoiakim in Judah. They are, rather, the Chaldeans, the very instrument designated by

God to render judgment upon Judah's oppressive government (1:12b).

Whereas Habakkuk's opening lament (1:2-4) addressed issues of justice in the political, judicial, and economic structures of his own society, his second lament addresses issues of justice on the international scene. These issues are addressed from the perspective of a citizen of a small, poor country whose destiny is determined and whose people are exploited by the imperialistic goals of one of the ancient Near East's superpowers. Habakkuk condemns such typical characteristics of imperialism as massive military machines (1:15-16a; cf. 1:11), the concentration of wealth derived from conquest and control of weaker nations (1:16b), and the disregard for the welfare of native populations that are brought into the sphere of imperial domination (1:14-15, 17). Above all, he laments the unimportance of human life under such a government, comparing conquered people to the fish of the sea—hooked, snared in nets, gathered up, and dragged to their death (1:14-15).

This vivid description of the oppression experienced by people under imperial rule suggests that Habakkuk himself may have known of it firsthand. If so, Habakkuk's second lament, and the crisis that motivated his debate with God, comes from a new period in Habakkuk's career, the period after the Babylonian invasion he predicted (1:5-11) had actually occurred (597 BCE). Jehoiakim died on the eve of this assault, and the new king, his son Jehoiachin, was deported by the Babylonians. Zedekiah was installed in his stead, and Judah was brought into the sphere of Babylonian influence and control. This new set of circumstances presented a new challenge to Habakkuk's conception of divine justice.

This new challenge arises from Habakkuk's recognition that the instrument of judgment by which God intended to restore justice to Judean society was itself corrupt and oppressive. Although Jehoiakim's regime had fallen on the eve of the Babylonian attack, the Neo-Babylonian Empire, that brought it down, was even more corrupt and godless than the government it had replaced. God's intervention had not created its intended effect. The cause of justice had not been advanced. One unjust government had been replaced by another, more unjust than the first. Thus Habakkuk challenges traditional prophetic theology, which interpreted the incursion of the enemy as God's legitimate punishment for sin and as an instrument of God's just rule. This challenge led to Habakkuk's debate with God, a debate that has given shape to the book as a whole.

The tension Habakkuk saw between traditional prophetic theology and his actual experience is heightened by his contrast between the character of God and the nature of the world in this lament. On the one hand, Habakkuk emphasizes God's absolute righteousness. God is eternal,[16] and God is holy—so holy that evil of any kind is intolerable to God (1:12-13a). On the other hand, Habakkuk documents the reign of evil in the world (1:13b-17), an evil that appears to go unchallenged by the deity (1:13b). Habakkuk even appears to blame God for creating humanity as an ungoverned mass, ripe for exploitation by those in power (1:14). The discrepancy between God's absolute holiness and the complete absence of God's holiness in the world appears irreconcilable.

In the final word of his second lament, Habakkuk describes the challenge he has posed to God and to traditional theology as a "complaint" (2:1). Such a translation subdues a stronger and sharper Hebrew term (תוכחת *tôkaḥat*), which means "argument," "reproof," "rebuke." The same term is used earlier in this lament to describe God's "punishment" or judgment of Judah at the hands of the Babylonians (1:12b). Habakkuk is thus more than a complainer or malcontent. He is a debater in an argument, one who stands in judgment of traditional views about God's ways with the world.[17]

---

16. Read with the NRSV's "You shall not die" (לא תמות *lōʾ tāmût*) in the second line of 1:12. It provides a proper poetic parallel to the declaration of God's eternal character in the first line of 1:12. The actual Hebrew text, "We shall not die" (לא נמות *lōʾ nāmût*), reflected in the NIV, represents one of eighteen instances in which the early scribes who preserved the text believed it had been altered to avoid disrespect to the deity. In this case, even the implication that God might die in this assertion to the contrary was considered irreverent.

17. Read "and what he will answer" (ישיב *yāšîb*; NRSV) in the final line of 2:1, an alternative textual tradition reflected in the Syriac translation. This reading suitably parallels the preceding line in this poetic unit and reflects the basic concern of the entire verse. The actual Hebrew text, "and what I will answer" (אשיב *ʾāšîb*), reflected in the NIV, appears to represent a corruption arising out of a concern to soften the prophet's bold challenge to God.

REFLECTIONS

Habakkuk's second lament presents two critiques: one of colonial rule and the other of a basic dogma in biblical faith—God's administration of justice in the world.

1. In describing the Babylonians, Habakkuk attacks the kinds of imperialistic policies that have been a part of international politics throughout history and that, in the modern era, have been practiced in one form or another by rich and powerful industrialized nations. These policies include the building of massive military machines; the expansion of political influence and control over smaller, neighboring countries; and the exploitation of the resources and the populace of these countries for political security and economic gain. Resistance to the injustices of such colonial policies, the modern equivalents of those Habakkuk criticized, can be found in twentieth-century independence and liberation movements in Africa, Asia, Latin America, and the former Soviet Union.

As the citizen of a small, colonialized country, Habakkuk forces the contemporary American reader to look at international politics from the other side—from the side of the poorer nations whose governments and economies have come under the control of the world's larger, richer nations. In this way, Habakkuk challenges the modern reader to reconsider the standards of justice inherent in these colonial relationships, especially as those standards affect the well-being of the citizens of poor nations. Habakkuk's second lament becomes thereby a call to reconsider, on the basis of biblical standards of equity and justice, the relationship between wealthy, industrialized nations and the Third World nations.

2. For Habakkuk, the unrestrained expansion of imperial power undermined confidence in

God's just rule of the world. It signified to Habakkuk a failure of the biblical theology of justice, that God punishes the wicked and protects the righteous. It is the same sense of the failure of traditional doctrine expressed by Job, on the basis of the personal misfortunes he experienced. The central biblical doctrine of God's fair treatment of the wicked and the righteous, defended with understandable conviction by Job's three friends, is rendered invalid by Job's experience.

The insight toward which Habakkuk and Job are both driven, in the one case by international events and in the other by the tragedy of a single life, is the recognition that the problem of evil in the world cannot be explained entirely by the biblical theology of reward and punishment, espoused by prophets, sages, historians, and psalmists alike. For Habakkuk, the awful abuses of colonial governments proved that the traditional theology of reward and punishment did not work itself out in people's lives. In the real world of Chaldean occupation, the wicked went unpunished and the righteous went unrewarded. The righteous are, in fact, surrounded and swallowed up (1:4, 13). In such an ambiguous and disordered world, is it possible to maintain confidence in divine justice? If it is possible, what would such a concept of divine justice look like? Habakkuk and Job ask such questions. Such are the questions asked by any religious person who is brought face to face with real injustice, with debilitating oppression, or with unprovoked personal tragedy that robs life of its sense and purpose.

Habakkuk 2:2-4, God's Second Response: The Reliability of God's Rule

NIV

[2]Then the LORD replied:
"Write down the revelation
and make it plain on tablets
so that a herald[a] may run with it.
[3]For the revelation awaits an appointed time;
it speaks of the end
and will not prove false.
Though it linger, wait for it;
it[b] will certainly come and will not delay.

[4]"See, he is puffed up;
his desires are not upright—
but the righteous will live by his faith[c]—

a2 Or *so that whoever reads it*   b3 Or *Though he linger, wait for him; / he*   c4 Or *faithfulness*

NRSV

[2] Then the LORD answered me and said:
Write the vision;
make it plain on tablets,
so that a runner may read it.
[3] For there is still a vision for the appointed time;
it speaks of the end, and does not lie.
If it seems to tarry, wait for it;
it will surely come, it will not delay.
[4] Look at the proud!
Their spirit is not right in them,
but the righteous live by their faith.[a]

a Or *faithfulness*

COMMENTARY

This brief text is particularly crucial for the book as a whole. As God's second response to the prophet, it promises to provide the resolution of Habakkuk's criticism of traditional prophetic theology (1:12–2:1)—that is, his questioning of God's just rule. Furthermore, in this divine speech we encounter the well-known phrase "the just shall live by . . . faith" (v. 4 KJV), by which the message of Habakkuk has been largely mediated to the church, since Paul first quoted it in his letter to the Romans (1:17). Due primarily to this phrase, vv. 1-4 (paired with 1:1-4) are the only texts from Habakkuk selected for the Revised Common Lectionary.

Unfortunately, this text is the shortest speech in the book of Habakkuk and in many respects the most difficult to translate. This difficulty arises from a Hebrew text that is at times apparently damaged or disturbed (e.g., v. 4a) and at other times sound but hard to understand (e.g., v. 2b).[18] Given the brevity of the response and the difficulties in translation, scholars have differed on whether these verses actually contain a divine message or merely advise the prophet to wait for it.[19] However one decides this issue, God does make certain demands of the prophet that have a direct bearing on the larger issue with which the book is dealing. And these demands, it is generally agreed, are primarily concerned with the matter of faithfulness, trustworthiness, or reliability (NRSV, NIV, "faith") with which the speech concludes (v. 4b).

2:2. Before we take up this important concept, and with it the significance of the phrase "the just shall live by . . . faith," we must examine the instructions that lead up to it. The first thing Habakkuk is told to do is to write down the vision, or revelation, so that it is clearly visible on tablets. The reason for this order is ostensibly given in the following line: "So that one reading it may run." The NIV translation ("so that a herald may run with it") is better than the NRSV's ("so that a runner may read it"). But what sort of running is this? It has been suggested that, the message being written so plainly, even someone running by could read it, or that "running" be understood metaphorically as reading quickly. This running has also been understood as running in terror from the oncoming judgment predicted in the vision, or conversely as running, or living, in the light of the divine promises contained in the vision.[20]

But I believe we should understand this image instead within the self-understanding of the prophets as messengers, heralds who "ran" to deliver the messages entrusted to them by their sovereign (the interpretation adopted in the NIV). Such an understanding of "run" is present in Jeremiah's description of prophetic behavior: "I did not send the prophets,/ yet they ran;/ I did not speak to them,/ yet they prophesied" (Jer 23:21 NRSV; cf. 2 Sam 18:19-27; 2 Chr 30:6, 10; Esth 3:13, 15; Jer 51:31; Zech 2:3 for the use of "run" in this sense). Taken in this way, v. 2 means that Habakkuk is commissioned to record the vision in order to carry it and announce it to the people.

2:3. Another reason for recording Habakkuk's vision, a reason that appears to be taken up directly in the next verse, is the common concern among the prophets about the reliability of the visions they received. At several times in his career, for example, the prophet Isaiah's visions are put in writing before the divine acts announced in them have actually occurred—before, in fact, it appears at all likely that such events could actually take place (see Isa 8:1-4, 16-17; 30:8-11). In these cases, the written record of the vision serves as an official affidavit or guarantee to verify the trustworthiness of the vision's content. Later, when the events have come to pass, the document provides indisputable confirmation of the truthfulness of prophetic revelation.

Habakkuk's vision seems to be characterized as such a guarantee or affidavit in v. 3. This is particularly obvious if one translates, as many prefer now to do, the Hebrew term עוד (ʿôd; rendered "still" by the NRSV and "awaits" by the NIV) as "witness" in v. 3a and the term יפח (yāpēaḥ; rendered "speaks" by the NRSV and the NIV) in v. 3b as "testifier," so that this poetic couplet would read: "For the vision is a witness for the appointed time, and a testifier of the end—it does not lie."[21] The vision is thus described as a reliable pledge that God will act in the future. Although its fulfillment may appear to be delayed, the vision will not prove false; it will inevitably come to pass.

2:4. The concern for reliability and trustworthiness continues into this verse, which brings this brief divine speech to an end and represents the core of its message. Contained within the two lines of this verse is a contrast between two

18. J. A. Emerton discusses some of the key problems in "The Textual and Linguistic Problems of Habakkuk II.4-5," *JTS* 18 (1977) 1-18.

19. Contrast Elizabeth Achtemeier, *Nahum–Malachi,* Interpretation (Atlanta: John Knox, 1986) 41-48, with J. J. M. Roberts, *Nahum, Habakkuk, and Zephaniah,* OTL (Louisville: Westminster/John Knox, 1991) 107-12.

20. Ralph L. Smith, *Micah–Malachi* (Waco, Tex.: Word, 1984) 105; Roberts, *Nahum, Habakkuk, and Zephaniah,* 109; Robert D. Haak, *Habakkuk,* VTSup 44 (Leiden: Brill, 1991) 56; J. Gerald Janzen, "Eschatological Symbol and Prophetic Existence in Habakkuk," *CBQ* 44 (1982) 405.

21. Reading עד (ʿēd, "witness") for עוד (ʿôd, "yet," "still") and taking יפח (yāpēaḥ) as the noun "testifier." See Roberts, *Nahum, Habakkuk, and Zephaniah,* 105-6; Haak, *Habakkuk,* 55-56; and J. Gerald Janzen, "Habakkuk 2:2-4 in the Light of Recent Philological Advances," *HTR* 73 (1980) 53-78.

individuals, the second of whom, described in v. 4b, is the righteous person. But the first line (v. 4a) is difficult and obscure in Hebrew. Many proposals have been suggested for the meaning of the phrase and the identity of the individual here contrasted with the righteous.[22] The Hebrew as it stands reads, "Look, his life [NRSV, "spirit"; NIV, "desires"] is swollen [and] is not upright in him" (or "does not go straight in it"). The NRSV and the NIV take the verb "swollen" (עפל 'āpal), which occurs only here in the OT, metaphorically, to mean "puffed up" or "proud," thus suggesting that the proud individual is to be contrasted with the righteous person in v. 4b. But this is a speculative interpretation of 'āpal. Of the alternate readings that have been suggested, I particularly like J. J. M. Roberts's proposal, based on his understanding of the consonants, customarily read as the single word "swollen," instead as two different terms. He reads: "Now the fainthearted, his soul will not walk in it" (that is, in the vision's message).[23] This reading explains the extant Hebrew text and provides a fitting contrast to the endurance of the righteous, of which the following line speaks.

In this last line of God's response, we meet the principal theme of the speech in the well-known phrase "the just shall live by . . . faith" (both the NRSV and the NIV translate צדיק [ṣaddîq] as "righteous" instead of as "just"). A proper understanding of this phrase rests upon the interpretation of its final term, the Hebrew word אמונה ('ĕmûnâ) and the pronominal suffix attached to it, customarily translated "his faith" (the NRSV avoids the masculine pronoun by rendering the term as "their faith"). The translation "faith," used by both the NIV and the NRSV, although traditional, is a potentially misleading rendering of

the Hebrew because of its connotations as belief in a doctrine or as an inner posture toward God to be contrasted with an outer observance of the law. The term 'ĕmûnâ actually refers to the quality of firmness, steadiness, steadfastness, or fidelity, a meaning that has been relegated to the footnotes in both the NRSV and the NIV.[24] It is the kind of loyal commitment admired in people (e.g., Prov 12:17) and believed, moreover, to be a primary aspect of God's own character (e.g., Ps 89:1-2). If the antecedent of the third-person singular masculine pronominal suffix attached to this term is the righteous person mentioned in this line, v. 4b would mean that the righteous live or survive in the world through their faithfulness, through their fidelity to God, and through their steadfast endurance. On the other hand, if the antecedent of this pronominal suffix is the vision that has been the subject of the speech up to this point, then v. 4b would read, "the righteous shall live by its faithfulness," that is, by the reliability or trustworthiness of the vision itself.

Whether one takes this phrase to describe the faithfulness of the righteous or the trustworthiness of God's vision, the concern for fidelity is paramount here. At a time when the wicked are in control, when the vision describing God's intention to reestablish justice has not yet become a reality, Habakkuk is called in the interim to trust God's assurances and to remain faithful. This divine command to Habakkuk may be taken as the actual content of Habakkuk's vision, or one might read it as God's requirement of the prophet as he awaits the vision. In either case, Habakkuk is directed to maintain a faithful commitment to God's justice and to persist in its principles, even when such justice appears to be absent in the world around him. Such is the message of God's second response.

---

22. The major proposals are summarized by Emerton, "The Textual and Linguistic Problems of Habakkuk II.4-5," 1-18.

23. Roberts, *Nahum, Habakkuk, and Zephaniah,* 105-7. Roberts reads עפלה ('uppĕlâ, "swollen") as עף לה (' aplōh), "the one who faints before it." I would not employ, however, as does Roberts, the term "soul," a Greek conception not characteristic of OT thought.

24. The choice of "faith" over "faithfulness" may have been made by the translators to preserve the traditional (KJV) and familiar use of "faith," or to be consistent with the translation "faith" where Hab 2:4 is quoted in the NT (Rom 1:17; Gal 3:11; Heb 10:38).

REFLECTIONS

1. In his poem "Manifesto: The Mad Farmer Liberation Front," Wendell Berry expresses an insight nearly the same as that in Hab 2:4: "Be joyful though you have considered all the facts."[25] Like Habakkuk, Berry proposes neither a simple solution nor a complete resolution of the problem of injustice. But there is here a hardheaded, thoughtful, and profound response to it. The righteous, the sincerely religious, those who long and work for justice and righteousness receive the strength to go on, not because the world itself is just or because it rewards those who work for justice, but because these persons possess a larger vision of the way things should be. They possess the vision, as did Habakkuk, of God's just reign. There will always be a discrepancy between such a vision and the real world. But the truly righteous place greater trust in the truth and in the reliability of that vision than in the brute facts of existence.

When Hab 2:4 is quoted in the NT, this sense of faithful endurance extends in new directions. Habakkuk's challenge of living faithfully between the promise of justice and its fulfillment in sixth-century BCE Judah is appropriated and applied to Christian experience, the experience of living between the announcement of the kingdom of God in the life and preaching of Jesus and its actual establishment on earth. For the early Christians, who were regularly persecuted, this was a period of suffering that demanded great trust in the reliability of God's promises in Jesus' message, the sort of trust that inspired one to endure in spite of the circumstances. This is the kind of situation the Letter to the Hebrews describes, counseling Christians to endure in the face of persecution and suffering, quoting in support of this advice the divine admonition to Habakkuk in 2:3-4 (Heb 10:32-39, esp. vv. 37-38).[26]

Paul also regards Christian existence as a life lived between the inauguration of salvation in Jesus, the first fruits of new life, and the ultimate salvation of the world to come (e.g., 1 Cor 15:20-28). His understanding of faith includes the notion of confidence in God's promises. Yet when he enlists Hab 2:4 ("the righteous will live by . . . faith" [KJV]) for his theology, he does so to argue that salvation is a gift of God, gained not by faithfulness to the law, but by faith in Christ—that is, belief in God's saving deed in Jesus. Such is the sense in which Paul uses Hab 2:4 when he employs it as his theme text for the Letter to the Romans (Rom 1:16-17), and when he argues to the Galatians that no one is justified by obedience to the law but by faith in Christ (Gal 3:10-11). Thus Paul has taken a term, originally signifying patient trust and endurance, to mean belief, a posture of assent, to be sharply contrasted with deeds of righteousness. Such a dichotomy was not present in Habakkuk's thought. Paul has reused a phrase urging trust and endurance to advance his new understanding of salvation and of the place of Jews and Gentiles within it.[27]

2. The text in which this phrase occurs, along with Hab 1:1-4, is the only text from Habakkuk selected for the Revised Common Lectionary, a selection that likely reflects both the use of this phrase in the NT and the judgment that within it lies the heart of the prophet's message. Paired with Hab 1:1-4, Hab 2:1-4 is used twice, as the OT reading for Proper 22 and for Proper 26 of Year C. For Proper 26, the OT reading from Habakkuk is part of a semicontinuous sequence of OT readings from the prophets and, therefore, has no intended or actual relationship to the Gospel story of Zacchaeus, with which it is linked. It does have a clear resonance in the selection from Ps 119:137-144, in which God's righteousness is

25. Wendell Berry, "Manifesto: The Mad Farmer Liberation Front," in *Collected Poems* (San Francisco: North Point, 1984) 151-52.

26. Harold W. Attridge, *The Epistle to the Hebrews,* Hermeneia (Philadelphia: Fortress, 1989) 297-304.

27. Joseph A. Fitzmyer, *Romans,* AB 33 (Garden City, N.Y.: Doubleday, 1993) 137-38, 253-68; Krister Stendahl, *Paul Among Jews and Gentiles* (Philadelphia: Fortress, 1976) 23-40.

contrasted with the psalmist's mistreatment and suffering at the hands of his or her enemies and in which the psalmist affirms commitment to God's precepts in spite of his or her anguish.

For Proper 22, Hab 1:1-4 and 2:1-4 are intentionally paired with Luke 17:5-10, which contains two relatively independent elements, one of which is a saying on the power of Christian faith (Luke 17:5-6). After the disciples ask to have their faith increased, Jesus responds by describing the power of genuine faith: It is powerful enough to uproot the giant sycamore tree. This kind of faith is not so much the endurance in troubled times of Habakkuk but belief in Jesus, or even in the charismatic power to perform miracles.[28] Yet there is in this exchange between the disciples and Jesus something of the ethos present in Habakkuk's dialogue with God. The disciples appeal for more faith, struggling, as did Habakkuk (1:1-4), for a greater understanding and a deeper trust in the ways of God. And Jesus responds to the disciples, as did God to Habakkuk (2:1-4), that the power of God is absolutely reliable, so that what seems completely impossible will come to pass. It is both appropriate and ironic that the Psalm alternative to the Habakkuk text for Proper 22, Year C, is Ps 37:1-9, a wisdom psalm contrasting the wicked and the righteous in support of the traditional theology with which Habakkuk is wrestling so rigorously:

> For the wicked shall be cut off,
> but those who wait for the
>   LORD shall inherit the land.
> (Ps 37:9 NRSV)

Thus the legacy of Habakkuk's struggle, "the just shall live by . . . faith[fulness]," challenges the truly religious person to remain committed to the larger vision of God's justice and purpose in the face of circumstances that appear to contradict its truth. The tension between this vision and the real world was stretched nearly to the breaking point by Habakkuk's experiences in sixth-century BCE Judah, as it was for many persecuted Christians in the Roman Empire. Each tragedy, whether individual or communal, revives this tension and directs us to reconsider the power of Habakkuk's vision of faithful and steadfast endurance.

---

28. Joseph A. Fitzmyer, *The Gospel According to Luke*, AB 28 and 28A (Garden City, N.Y.: Doubleday, 1981, 1985) 1136-43.

THE FALL OF TYRANNY

NIV

⁵indeed, wine betrays him;
  he is arrogant and never at rest.
Because he is as greedy as the grave[a]
  and like death is never satisfied,
he gathers to himself all the nations
  and takes captive all the peoples.
⁶"Will not all of them taunt him with ridicule
and scorn, saying,
  "'Woe to him who piles up stolen goods
  and makes himself wealthy by extortion!
  How long must this go on?'
⁷Will not your debtors[b] suddenly arise?
  Will they not wake up and make you
    tremble?
  Then you will become their victim.
⁸Because you have plundered many nations,
  the peoples who are left will plunder you.
For you have shed man's blood;
  you have destroyed lands and cities and
    everyone in them.

⁹"Woe to him who builds his realm by unjust gain
  to set his nest on high,
  to escape the clutches of ruin!
¹⁰You have plotted the ruin of many peoples,
  shaming your own house and forfeiting your
    life.
¹¹The stones of the wall will cry out,
  and the beams of the woodwork will echo it.

¹²"Woe to him who builds a city with bloodshed
  and establishes a town by crime!
¹³Has not the LORD Almighty determined
  that the people's labor is only fuel for the fire,
  that the nations exhaust themselves for
    nothing?
¹⁴For the earth will be filled with the knowledge
  of the glory of the LORD,
  as the waters cover the sea.

¹⁵"Woe to him who gives drink to his neighbors,
  pouring it from the wineskin till they are
    drunk,

a5 Hebrew *Sheol*   b7 Or *creditors*

NRSV

⁵ Moreover, wealth[a] is treacherous;
  the arrogant do not endure.
They open their throats wide as Sheol;
  like Death they never have enough.
They gather all nations for themselves,
  and collect all peoples as their own.

⁶Shall not everyone taunt such people and,
with mocking riddles, say about them,
  "Alas for you who heap up what is not your
    own!"
  How long will you load yourselves with
    goods taken in pledge?
⁷ Will not your own creditors suddenly rise,
  and those who make you tremble wake up?
  Then you will be booty for them.
⁸ Because you have plundered many nations,
  all that survive of the peoples shall plunder
    you—
because of human bloodshed, and violence to
    the earth,
  to cities and all who live in them.

⁹ "Alas for you who get evil gain for your
    houses,
  setting your nest on high
  to be safe from the reach of harm!"
¹⁰ You have devised shame for your house
  by cutting off many peoples;
  you have forfeited your life.
¹¹ The very stones will cry out from the wall,
  and the plaster[b] will respond from the
    woodwork.

¹² "Alas for you who build a town by bloodshed,
  and found a city on iniquity!"
¹³ Is it not from the LORD of hosts
  that peoples labor only to feed the flames,
  and nations weary themselves for nothing?
¹⁴ But the earth will be filled
  with the knowledge of the glory of the LORD,

a Other Heb Mss read *wine*   b Or *beam*

NIV

so that he can gaze on their naked bodies.

¹⁶You will be filled with shame instead of glory.
  Now it is your turn! Drink and be exposed*a*!
The cup from the LORD's right hand is coming
    around to you,
  and disgrace will cover your glory.

¹⁷The violence you have done to Lebanon will
    overwhelm you,
  and your destruction of animals will terrify
    you.

For you have shed man's blood;
  you have destroyed lands and cities and
    everyone in them.

¹⁸"Of what value is an idol, since a man has
    carved it?
  Or an image that teaches lies?
For he who makes it trusts in his own creation;
  he makes idols that cannot speak.

¹⁹Woe to him who says to wood, 'Come to life!'
  Or to lifeless stone, 'Wake up!'
Can it give guidance?
  It is covered with gold and silver;
  there is no breath in it.

²⁰But the LORD is in his holy temple;
  let all the earth be silent before him."

a16 Masoretic Text; Dead Sea Scrolls, Aquila, Vulgate and Syriac (see also Septuagint) and stagger

NRSV

as the waters cover the sea.

¹⁵ "Alas for you who make your neighbors drink,
  pouring out your wrath*a* until they are
    drunk,
  in order to gaze on their nakedness!"

¹⁶ You will be sated with contempt instead of
    glory.
  Drink, you yourself, and stagger!*b*
The cup in the LORD's right hand
  will come around to you,
  and shame will come upon your glory!

¹⁷ For the violence done to Lebanon will
    overwhelm you;
  the destruction of the animals will terrify
    you—*c*
because of human bloodshed and violence to
    the earth,
  to cities and all who live in them.

¹⁸ What use is an idol
  once its maker has shaped it—
  a cast image, a teacher of lies?
For its maker trusts in what has been made,
  though the product is only an idol that
    cannot speak!

¹⁹ Alas for you who say to the wood, "Wake up!"
  to silent stone, "Rouse yourself!"
Can it teach?
See, it is gold and silver plated,
  and there is no breath in it at all.

²⁰ But the LORD is in his holy temple;
  let all the earth keep silence before him!

a Or poison   b QMs Gk: MT be uncircumcised   c Gk Syr: Meaning of Heb uncertain

COMMENTARY

In 2:5-20 we encounter a new form of literature and a new section of the book as a whole. The viewpoint reflected here is neither the first-person perspective of the prophet in the complaints nor the first-person perspective of God in the responses that make up the preceding debate. In these verses we hear a new speaker: the nations who have been overrun and who now break their silence to address their oppressor (vv. 5-6*a*). The tyrant who is addressed, though not named explicitly, must be the same Babylonian Empire that overwhelmed Judah, since the behavior attributed to it by the nations—e.g., the plunder and bloodshed of many peoples (v. 8)—reflects the characterization of Babylon by Habakkuk earlier in the book (1:5-17).

These verses actually contain a collection of five speeches or sayings, each focusing on a trait of Babylonian imperialism: (1) the accumulation of wealth, vv. 6*b*-8; (2) the search for security, vv. 9-11; (3) the use of violence, vv. 12-14; (4) the pursuit of fame and honor, vv. 15-17; and (5) the confidence in idols, vv. 18-20. Each saying begins with the Hebrew term הוי (*hôy*; NIV, "Woe"; NRSV, "Alas"), followed by a participial verb form ("the one who . . . "), which begins the description of a typical practice of the Babylonian tyrant. Speeches 1, 2, and 4 follow a uniform scheme in which the nations address Babylon directly in the second person ("you") and describe a reversal of fortune for the Babylonian Empire. The third and fifth speeches lack these elements and are anomalous in other ways; speech 5, for example, employs the introductory expression *hôy* in the body of the speech (v. 19) rather than at the beginning. It is thus difficult to be sure we possess these two sayings in their original form. The collection of speeches in its entirety is preceded by an introduction, which identifies the addressee, the speaker, and the literary genre of the speeches themselves (vv. 5 6*a*).

Three terms in v. 6*a* identify the genre of the speeches found in the collection that follows. The first of these terms (משל *māšāl*), rendered in both the NRSV and the NIV with the verb "taunt," is the title used to designate the short wisdom sayings collected in the book of Proverbs (e.g., Prov 1:1; 10:1). Because this term can be used to identify someone as a negative example or lesson (e.g., Jer 24:9), as is the case with the Babylonian oppressor here, translators have often given the term a negative twist, "taunt," in their rendering of this verse. In its simplest sense, however, it designates an astute observation, a terse statement of popular wisdom, like those gathered in the book of Proverbs. The designation of these wisdom sayings also as "words of reproach" (NRSV, "mocking"; NIV, "ridicule") refers to their ridicule of the tyrant's pretensions. Their further designation as "riddles" may refer to the paradoxical character of the theme of reversal in them, a theme that is at once based on ordinary experience and at the same time almost inconceivable in the face of absolute, imperial power. The word *hôy*, with which each speech begins, originates in funeral lamentations

and is employed widely by the prophets to introduce statements on the demise of the guilty.[29]

In each of the five proverbial sayings in this short collection, a paradoxical reversal of fortune is described with the aim of ridiculing the pretensions of imperial power. In the first (vv. 6*b*-8), the tyrant's acquisition of wealth through the exploitation of the economies of conquered peoples is lampooned. A day is described in which this unjustified wealth will be reclaimed by those from whom it was taken, thereby reducing the oppressor to the poverty of the oppressed. This reversal of fortune is cleverly embedded in the Hebrew term for the economically exploited in v. 7*a*. This term, נשכיך (*nōšěkêkā*), may be translated either "debtors" (lit., "those who pay interest"), as the NIV has done, or "creditors" (lit., "those who charge interest"), as the NRSV has done. In fact, both meanings may be intended here, since v. 7 describes debtor nations rising up to become creditor nations, thus subjecting the oppressor's economy to exploitation by others.

In the four sayings that follow, other trappings of imperial power are ridiculed as illusory or transitory. One of these is the search for security (vv. 9-11). The tyrant, guilty of widespread violence ("cutting off many peoples," v. 10*b*), tries to protect himself from recriminations by building an impenetrable residence. In this case, the very materials acquired unjustly to build the residence (v. 9*a*) take up the cry of the oppressed (the same verb for "cry" [זעק *zāʿaq*] Habakkuk himself uses in 1:2) to haunt the oppressor in the "safety" of his fortress.

Another pretension of power ridiculed in these sayings is the pursuit of glory and honor (vv. 15-17). The imperial drive for honor, according to this saying, leads inevitably to shame. The description of the reversal in this case is achieved through the use of two conventional images of shame: drunkenness and nakedness (cf., e.g., Lam 4:21), used first for the tyrant's vanquished populations (v. 15), but then unexpectedly of the tyrant himself (v. 16). Whereas the active parties in the preceding reversals were the impoverished peoples (vv. 7-8) and ill-gotten gain (vv. 9, 11), here it is the world of nature. The tyrant's quest for fame is described in v. 17 as "violence done to

---

29. Richard J. Clifford, "The Use of *Hôy* in the Prophets," *CBQ* 28 (1966) 458-64.

Lebanon," a reference to the harvesting of Lebanon's great mountain forests, revered in antiquity and considered symbolic of greatness and glory (Isa 2:12-13; 35:2; such a crime is attributed to the Babylonian Empire in Isa 14:8). With an observation frighteningly modern in an age of environmental crisis, a ruined nature is pictured as turning around to bring down the empire that destroyed it (v. 17).

REFLECTIONS

The controlling theme of these speeches as a whole is the fall of tyranny. In them, imperial power is described as a system that has within it the seeds of its own destruction. The fall of tyranny results from forces set in motion by the ruthlessness of tyranny itself. No one has put this theme more succinctly than has George Adam Smith in his commentary on these sayings: "Tyranny is intolerable. In the nature of things it cannot endure, but works out its own penalties. By oppressing so many nations, the tyrant is preparing the instruments of his own destruction. As he treats them, so in time shall they treat him. . . . Tyranny is suicide."[30]

Placed in the book of Habakkuk after the dialogue between God and the prophet and, in particular, immediately following God's final response to the prophet's questions, this collection of sayings about the suicidal nature of tyranny adds another dimension to the resolution of Habakkuk's distress over injustice in the world. By designating these speeches as proverbs of universal wisdom, by placing them in the mouths of the nations of the world, and by describing in them the forces that inevitably undermine imperial power, Habakkuk claims that there exists, in the common fund of human experience and wisdom, evidence for a principle of justice operative in the world that in the end destroys all tyrannical power and pretension.

The book of Habakkuk thus sets forward two resources for coping with the problem of injustice in the world and for maintaining confidence in God's just rule. One is the personal, prophetic vision of the reliability of God's rule and the ultimate power of justice (2:2-4). The other is the record of history itself, which shows that the most blatant kinds of injustice, described here in terms of imperial power, do not endure (2:5-20). The juxtaposition of these two sections of the book allows Habakkuk to contrast the trustworthiness of the vision of God's just rule with the transitoriness of the reign of the unjust tyrant.

The enduring wisdom of these sayings ridiculing the pretensions of imperial power is perhaps most clearly to be observed in the modern era in those forces that have undermined colonialism during the latter half of the twentieth century: the independence movements of Africa and Asia, the liberation movements in the Americas, and the demise of totalitarianism in the Soviet Union and Eastern Europe. In these modern political movements can be seen the disintegration of imperialism of one kind or another, an imperialism whose policies so impoverished its subjects—taking their wealth, their dignity, their security—that it could not endure. For citizens of debtor nations or peoples, as was Habakkuk, such wisdom is a source of hope and empowerment. But for citizens of wealthy creditor nations, such wisdom is a sober reminder of the serious consequences of national and international policies or practices that enrich through exploitation.

Such are the lessons of these sayings on the national and international scene today. But one might also consider the wisdom of these sayings at a personal, individual level as well. The main pursuits of the tyrant ridiculed in these sayings—wealth, security, fame—are by no means unique to the dictator. They might be described as the elemental drives of much human endeavor. Thus the tyrant cannot be viewed as a strange and distant character but as an image of ordinary humanity and the desires that consume its energy and dictate its actions. For all obsessed with these values, these sayings have two cautionary points. In the first place, wealth,

---

30. G. A. Smith, *The Book of the Twelve Prophets,* vol. 2 of *The Expositor's Bible* (London: Hodder and Stoughton, 1898) 144.

security, and fame are, in the end, transitory phenomena, conditions that cannot be ensured. In the second place, when gained at the expense of others, they carry with them the seeds of their ruin. Within the sayings, therefore, are expressed serious reservations about those common human goals—ever greater wealth, security, fame—in pursuit of which humanity invests much of its time and energy.

HABAKKUK 3:1

SUPERSCRIPTION

COMMENTARY

The superscription attributing chapter 3 to Habakkuk appears to certify this chapter as an authentic composition of the prophet to whom chapters 1–2 are attributed (1:1). But for many scholars, this second superscription has had just the opposite effect, raising questions about the authorship of the text it introduces and about the relationship of this text to Habakkuk 1–2. Headings such as this are not always reliable. In prophetic collections, such superscriptions occasionally attribute later compositions to earlier prophets who could not have composed them (e.g., Isa 13:1; Jer 46:1). In the psalms, superscriptions attributing authorship are commonly later additions, based on subsequent exegesis interested in locating the text in a precise historical setting.[31]

The comparison of this superscription to psalm titles is not coincidental, since Hab 3:1 also contains a musical notation, "on/according to Shigionoth," found elsewhere only in the superscription of Psalm 7. In fact, other notations in Habakkuk 3, the reference to the musical director and to stringed instruments (v. 19*b*) and the repeated use of "Selah" (vv. 3, 9, 13), are common in psalms but unknown in prophetic literature. This evidence raises the possibility that Habakkuk contains a psalm later attributed to Habakkuk and then added to his corpus. Such secondary attribution of psalms to prophetic figures is not unknown, since four psalms in the Septuagint (Psalms 145–148) were ascribed to Haggai and Zechariah.

31. See Brevard S. Childs, "Psalm Titles and Midrashic Exegesis," *JSS* 16 (1971) 137-50.

God's Cosmic Reign

NIV

²Lord, I have heard of your fame;
    I stand in awe of your deeds, O Lord.
Renew them in our day,
    in our time make them known;
    in wrath remember mercy.

³God came from Teman,
    the Holy One from Mount Paran.   *Selah* ª
His glory covered the heavens
    and his praise filled the earth.
⁴His splendor was like the sunrise;
    rays flashed from his hand,
    where his power was hidden.
⁵Plague went before him;
    pestilence followed his steps.
⁶He stood, and shook the earth;
    he looked, and made the nations tremble.
The ancient mountains crumbled
    and the age-old hills collapsed.
    His ways are eternal.
⁷I saw the tents of Cushan in distress,
    the dwellings of Midian in anguish.

⁸Were you angry with the rivers, O Lord?
    Was your wrath against the streams?
Did you rage against the sea
    when you rode with your horses
    and your victorious chariots?
⁹You uncovered your bow,
    you called for many arrows.   *Selah*
You split the earth with rivers;
¹⁰   the mountains saw you and writhed.
Torrents of water swept by;
    the deep roared
    and lifted its waves on high.

¹¹Sun and moon stood still in the heavens
    at the glint of your flying arrows,
    at the lightning of your flashing spear.
¹²In wrath you strode through the earth
    and in anger you threshed the nations.
¹³You came out to deliver your people,

NRSV

² O Lord, I have heard of your renown,
    and I stand in awe, O Lord, of your work.
In our own time revive it;
    in our own time make it known;
    in wrath may you remember mercy.
³ God came from Teman,
    the Holy One from Mount Paran.   *Selah*
His glory covered the heavens,
    and the earth was full of his praise.
⁴ The brightness was like the sun;
    rays came forth from his hand,
    where his power lay hidden.
⁵ Before him went pestilence,
    and plague followed close behind.
⁶ He stopped and shook the earth;
    he looked and made the nations tremble.
The eternal mountains were shattered;
    along his ancient pathways
    the everlasting hills sank low.
⁷ I saw the tents of Cushan under affliction;
    the tent-curtains of the land of Midian
        trembled.
⁸ Was your wrath against the rivers,ª O Lord?
    Or your anger against the rivers,ª
    or your rage against the sea,ᵇ
when you drove your horses,
    your chariots to victory?
⁹ You brandished your naked bow,
    satedᶜ were the arrows at your
        command.ᵈ   *Selah*
You split the earth with rivers.
¹⁰ The mountains saw you, and writhed;
    a torrent of water swept by;
    the deep gave forth its voice.
    The sunᵉ raised high its hands;
¹¹ the moonᶠ stood still in its exalted place,
    at the light of your arrows speeding by,
    at the gleam of your flashing spear.
¹² In fury you trod the earth,
    in anger you trampled nations.

ª3 A word of uncertain meaning; possibly a musical term; also in verses 9 and 13

ª Or *against River*   ᵇ Or *against Sea*   ᶜ Cn: Heb *oaths*
ᵈ Meaning of Heb uncertain   ᵉ Heb *It*   ᶠ Heb *sun, moon*

NIV

to save your anointed one.
You crushed the leader of the land of
wickedness,
you stripped him from head to foot.   *Selah*
¹⁴With his own spear you pierced his head
when his warriors stormed out to scatter us,
gloating as though about to devour
the wretched who were in hiding.
¹⁵You trampled the sea with your horses,
churning the great waters.

¹⁶I heard and my heart pounded,
my lips quivered at the sound;
decay crept into my bones,
and my legs trembled.
Yet I will wait patiently for the day of calamity
to come on the nation invading us.

¹⁷Though the fig tree does not bud
and there are no grapes on the vines,
though the olive crop fails
and the fields produce no food,
though there are no sheep in the pen
and no cattle in the stalls,
¹⁸yet I will rejoice in the LORD,
I will be joyful in God my Savior.

¹⁹The Sovereign LORD is my strength;
he makes my feet like the feet of a deer,
he enables me to go on the heights.

For the director of music. On my stringed
instruments.

NRSV

¹³ You came forth to save your people,
to save your anointed.
You crushed the head of the wicked house,
laying it bare from foundation to roof.ᵃ
Selah
¹⁴ You pierced with theirᵇ own arrows the headᶜ
of his warriors,ᵈ
who came like a whirlwind to scatter us,ᵉ
gloating as if ready to devour the poor who
were in hiding.
¹⁵ You trampled the sea with your horses,
churning the mighty waters.

¹⁶ I hear, and I tremble within;
my lips quiver at the sound.
Rottenness enters into my bones,
and my steps trembleᶠ beneath me.
I wait quietly for the day of calamity
to come upon the people who attack us.

¹⁷ Though the fig tree does not blossom,
and no fruit is on the vines;
though the produce of the olive fails,
and the fields yield no food;
though the flock is cut off from the fold,
and there is no herd in the stalls,
¹⁸ yet I will rejoice in the LORD;
I will exult in the God of my salvation.
¹⁹ GOD, the Lord, is my strength;
he makes my feet like the feet of a deer,
and makes me tread upon the heights.ᵍ

To the leader: with stringedʰ instruments.

ᵃ Meaning of Heb uncertain   ᵇ Heb his   ᶜ Or *leader*
ᵈ Vg Compare Gk Syr: Meaning of Heb uncertain   ᵉ Heb *me*
ᶠ Cn Compare Gk: Meaning of Heb uncertain   ᵍ Heb *my heights*
ʰ Heb *my stringed*

COMMENTARY

Because of these unusual characteristics of Habakkuk, interpreters have focused on the overriding issue of this chapter's authorship and its relationship to the Habakkuk of chapters 1–2. An earlier generation of scholars, represented in the bibliography by George Adam Smith, considered these characteristics of Habakkuk 3 as indicators of separate authorship. These scholars typically regarded this chapter as a late liturgical composition, added to the corpus of Habakkuk in the post-exilic era, at least a century after chapters 1–2 were composed.[32]

Today, by contrast, most scholars regard Habakkuk 3 as a composition of the seventh-century BCE

32. G. A. Smith, *The Book of the Twelve Prophets*, vol. 2 of *The Expositor's Bible* (London: Hodder and Stoughton, 1898) 126-28.

prophet Habakkuk and as an original part of the dialogue between the prophet and God around which the book is organized. The dialogical structure of the chapter—the prophet's prayer (v. 2), followed by a description of God's appearance (vv. 3-15), followed by the prophet's response (vv. 16-19)—is considered similar to the complaint-response pattern in chapters 1–2. And some scholars think the divine appearance itself (vv. 3-15) is the actual content of the vision Habakkuk had been commanded to record in 2:2. The chapter's unique psalm-like notations are then explained as Habakkuk's appropriation of psalm forms, or regarded as psalm directions later added to a prophetic composition.

In spite of the popularity of such recent views, the unique features of Habakkuk 3 still argue strongly for its separate authorship. Even more persuasive than the peculiar psalmic notations is the archaic quality of the style and content of the poem, a quality that suggests this poem is a composition much older than the rest of the book of Habakkuk. The style of the poem, in particular its pattern of verb tenses for past narrative and its verse structures, resembles most nearly the oldest poetic compositions in the OT. The same is true of its content. Its depiction of God's theophany at, and march from, a southern mountain (vv. 3-7) and its explicit imagery of God's battle as a conflict between storm and sea (vv. 8-15) find their closest parallels in the corpus of Israel's earliest poetry (e.g., Exodus 15; Deuteronomy 33; Judges 5). Such evidence suggests that the poem in Habakkuk 3 is an ancient composition, originating perhaps as early as Israel's premonarchic era. In form and content, it appears to be a hymn of victory, celebrating God's intervention as the reason for the success of Israel's armies.[33]

3:2, 16-19. This hymn is encompassed by a literary framework, which encloses the recitation of God's deeds and is composed from the first-person perspective of the poet. The Masoretes, who supplied vowels for the consonantal Hebrew text, understood v. 2, the hymn's introduction, as a prayer. They interpreted the last three lines of the verse as a request made by the prophet to God, reading an imperative verb (NRSV, "revive";

NIV, "renew") followed by two jussive forms imploring God to act. The NRSV and the NIV have emphasized this interpretation by rendering the verbs in all three lines as imperatives. But the early Greek and Aramaic versions do not read imperative or jussive forms here, raising the question as to whether these lines are actually to be understood as an appeal to God. According to the pattern of verb tenses in the remainder of the poem, the verbs in v. 2 may be read simply as past narrative ("you made yourself known . . . you remembered mercy"), representing the poet's introductory description of the acts of God in the recitation that follows.

The conclusion of the poem (vv. 16-19) represents a return to the first-person perspective of the poet, reflected in the introduction (v. 2). It begins with the same verb that opens the introduction: "I heard . . . " (שמע šāma‘). While in the introduction the poet anticipates the recitation of the theophany that follows, in the conclusion the poet responds to it. This response includes a mixture of fear at the awesome spectacle and power of God's appearance (v. 16) and joy at the victory that God has accomplished (vv. 18-19).

3:3-15. These verses narrate a theophany, a direct appearance of God. This theophany represents, in fact, the most detailed and elaborate one in the OT (cf. Exodus 15; 19; Judges 5; Psalms 18; 29; Isaiah 6). To describe God and God's activity, the poet interweaves imagery from two spheres of life, the spheres we have now come to distinguish rather neatly as history and nature. God is described in terms of a pre-eminent image of power in human society, the soldier or man of war. God marches into battle with military escort in front and behind (v. 5). God rides a chariot, driving its horses into the conflict (vv. 8, 15). God uncovers the bow, lets the arrows fly, and brandishes a sword (vv. 9, 11). This vivid presentation of God as a warrior attributes the victory of Israel's own armies (vv. 12-13, 18-19) to God's presence among them, fighting on their side to ensure their success.

Woven into this image of God as a warrior are images drawn from the world of nature. God appears in the form of the thunderstorm. God's chariot is identified with the rolling storm cloud, drenching the earth with torrents of water (v. 10). God's weaponry—arrows and spear—is identified

---

33. A more detailed explanation of this viewpoint can be found in chap. 3 of T. Hiebert, *God of My Victory: The Ancient Hymn in Habakkuk 3,* HSM 38 (Atlanta: Scholars Press, 1986) 81-128.

as lightning bolts striking the land (vv. 11-12). God's adversary, furthermore, is identified as the sea and the rivers (vv. 8-15). This imagery of the conflict between storm and sea is drawn from a conventional ancient Near Eastern motif in which the supreme deity, in the form of a thunderstorm, subdues Sea, an adversarial deity representing chaos, and thereby establishes order in the cosmos and guarantees life to its people.[34] By employing the imagery of this traditional motif and interweaving it with the political imagery of the warrior, the poet has founded God's control of historical affairs within God's control of cosmic orders.

This presentation of God as a warrior, subduing the forces of chaos in the cosmos and bringing victory and security to God's people, is particularly characteristic of two kinds of literature in the OT: Israel's old victory hymns, which make liberal use of the ancient Near Eastern conflict motif, and late apocalyptic compositions, which reappropriate this motif to describe God's future intervention in the world to destroy the powers of wickedness once and for all and to establish the uncontested reign of God on earth. Such an apocalyptic divine warrior can be found, for example, in the postexilic portions of Isaiah (e.g., Isa 59:15b-20; 63:1-6) and in the additions to Zechariah (e.g., Zech 9:1-17; 14:1-21). By the addition of such hymns to older prophetic material, the editors aimed to extend and enrich these older visions with the affirmation that God was planning to enter the realm of history in a decisive event that would destroy evil completely and establish the just rule of God forever.[35]

It is within the context of such apocalyptic thought and its fervent expectation of God's decisive intervention in human affairs that the addition of the poem in Habakkuk 3 to the rest of the corpus can be best understood. The editors of Habakkuk's prophecy, rather than composing a new hymn to anticipate God's absolute victory, took an old hymn celebrating God's reign over the cosmos and history and reinterpreted it as testimony to the future. The pattern of verb forms, used in archaic poetry for past narrative, may in fact be read with such a future orientation, according to the conventions of later Hebrew grammar.[36]

By adding such a poem to the text and by reading it as a description of the coming apocalypse, the editors of Habakkuk raised the prophet's hope for justice to another dimension, a new dimension of reality that entered biblical thought with the dawn of the apocalyptic consciousness in the post-exilic era. Habakkuk's confidence in the trustworthiness of God's promises (2:2-4) and the nation's wisdom about the suicidal forces within tyranny (2:5-20) were linked to the ordinary world of human politics and affirmed the reality of God's rule in this realm. The poem in Habakkuk 3, however, takes this affirmation one step further. Read as an apocalyptic hymn, it asserts that the future will bring the end of historical evil and the inauguration of God's cosmic reign.

Understood in this light, Habakkuk 3 adds an apocalyptic resolution to the problem of injustice, raised by the prophet. This chapter states that not only does the vision of God's justice sustain the righteous (2:2-4), not only does the self-destructive character of injustice give the righteous hope (2:5-20), but also the hope of the righteous is strengthened by the confidence that God is bringing the world's affairs to a decisive conclusion, a conclusion in which God's just rule—for which Habakkuk longed and struggled—will be unconditionally established.

34. The best examples are the Babylonian creation epic, Enuma Elish, and the Baal cycle from the Canaanite city of Ugarit, both found in *Ancient Near Eastern Texts Relating to the Old Testament,* ed. James B. Pritchard, 3rd ed. (Princeton: Princeton University Press, 1969) 60-72, 129-42.

35. Paul D. Hanson, *The Dawn of Apocalyptic* (Philadelphia: Fortress, 1975) esp. 123-34, 203-28, 292-324.

36. See Hiebert, *God of My Victory,* 129-49.

REFLECTIONS

1. If, indeed, the ancient hymn of victory in Habakkuk 3 has taken on the apocalyptic overtones suggested in the commentary, then it provides an early example of the resolution to the problem of justice taken in apocalyptic thought, which emerged at the end of the OT period and became an important strain in Judaism and an essential component of the Christian vision. According to the apocalyptic point of view, the injustices of history, such as those about which Habakkuk so eloquently complained, could be rectified only through a decisive intervention of God that would end history and inaugurate an age in which God's reign would be absolute. This new age was often associated with life after death, with another sphere of existence in which the righteous would be finally rewarded and the wicked punished. In the Christian apocalyptic vision, the new age, inaugurated and confirmed by the resurrection of Jesus, will be ushered in by the second coming and the final judgment.

In such a theology, the problem of injustice in a world ruled by a just God is dealt with in a more radical and absolute way than in the counsel of faithfulness (2:2-4) or of the suicidal nature of injustice (2:5-20), found earlier in the book of Habakkuk. In apocalyptic thought, the righteous are promised complete vindication. But this vindication must await another world. It will not be part of this one. The perspective from which the problem of injustice is viewed has been significantly broadened to include a new sphere of existence beyond this earthly life. In this context, the affirmation that "the just shall live by . . . faith" takes on a new sense. It becomes an admonition not only to remain faithful within the injustices of this world but also to await the vindication God has promised the righteous in the next world. This is exactly the new point that the apocalyptic editors wished to make with their inclusion of this hymn in the Habakkuk corpus. And it is the hope with which many Christians have invested the phrase "the just shall live by . . . faith."

2. Since Habakkuk 3 contains one of the most detailed and vivid descriptions in the Bible of an appearance of God, its images of God deserve attention. Perhaps the most prominent is the image of God as a warrior. The conception of the warrior God that dominates Habakkuk 3 presents a difficult theological issue. On the one hand, it is a powerful way of affirming God's power and control over earthly affairs. It also reflects the truth that in the world in which we live, justice does not come about by inaction and passive accommodation to things as they are. It must be won through conflict and struggle and by the single-minded purpose of the dedicated soldier. On the other hand, however, this image identifies God with warfare, the most destructive and deadly of human institutions, an institution that has been defended as just and necessary through the ages but that is susceptible to great abuses and has inflicted untold suffering upon the innocent. The prophet Habakkuk, as did other prophets, guarded against the selfish, chauvinistic use of the image of the divine warrior—"God is on our side"—by affirming the possibility that God fought with the enemy (1:5-11). But he saw quite clearly that this did nothing to mitigate the horrors of war (1:12-17). However they are resolved, the powerful ambiguities in the image of God as warrior must be squarely faced by religious people today.

The other dominant divine image in Habakkuk 3 is that of the thunderstorm. This is not an uncommon image for the divine in ancient Near Eastern thought, and it undoubtedly derives from the sense of God's presence and power in the rain, upon which the dry-land agricultures in the Mediterranean world depended. Such must have been the case for Israel as well. This is worth special attention in an era of environmental crisis in which we are being forced to reexamine our own attitudes toward nature and the valuation of nature within our religious traditions. Biblical faith has customarily been described as a historical faith, centered on a deity active in history and in the historical pilgrimage of God's people, for which nature provides a mere backdrop or stage. But the emphasis in Habakkuk 3 that God is present in the phenomena of nature should cause us to rethink such traditional views and to reexamine the place of the natural world in biblical faith.

THE BOOK OF ZEPHANIAH

INTRODUCTION, COMMENTARY, AND REFLECTIONS
BY
ROBERT A. BENNETT

THE BOOK OF
ZEPHANIAH

INTRODUCTION

THE PROPHET AND THE SETTING OF HIS MINISTRY

The book of Zephaniah stands in the ninth position of the collection of Hebrew prophetic literature called the Book of the Twelve. Zephaniah's three chapters represent the collected oracles or divinely inspired sermons of the late seventh century BCE prophet Zephaniah ben Cushi. All that we know about Zephaniah ben Cushi comes from the title or introduction to this work and from inferences drawn from the oracles.

In the style typical of such collections, the title or opening verse identifies the author by name and background, the date and location of his activity, plus a basis for speaking in God's name. Zephaniah 1:1 tersely gives the call or right to speak simply as "The word of the LORD that came to Zephaniah," followed by a genealogical lineage going back some four generations to an ancestor named Hezekiah, and then concludes by locating this ministry during the reign of King Josiah (640–609 BCE).

The unusually long genealogy—the norm is one or two generations—suggests that the last name is of special significance. It may point to King Hezekiah (715–687 BCE) himself, the last reforming king before Josiah. Moreover, the prophet's full name, Zephaniah ben Cushi, is noteworthy because in usual Hebrew parlance "Cushi" means "African" and prefixed with the word בן (ben, "son"/"child of") suggests an African heritage. The name "Zephaniah" represents a combination of the divine name prefaced with a form of the Hebrew word whose meaning is "hide" or "protect" (צפניה ṣĕpan-yāh), thus "Yahweh protects."[1]

---

1. On the name "Zephaniah," see Adele Berlin, *Zephaniah*, AB 25A (New York: Doubleday, 1994) 64-65, and J. J. M. Roberts, *Nahum, Habakkuk, and Zephaniah*, OTL (Louisville: Westminster/John Knox, 1991) 165-66.

The rest of what we know about Zephaniah ben Cushi must be gleaned from the content of his preaching. Given his knowledge of the city (1:10-13), its temple rites (1:7-8), and it hierarchy (1:8-6; 3:3-4), plus his concern (1:12-13) and compassion (3:7, 14, 17) for its citizenry, Zephaniah must have been a Jerusalemite with connections to its Temple and the royal family. The dominant motif and single-minded message of his preaching, the coming day of the Lord, both as judgment (1:7–2:4) and as salvation (3:9-20), derives from cultic rites of the Jerusalem Temple. The sins of the community singled out for attack in his oracles as the root causes of the impending destruction—idolatry, syncretism, and the adoption of foreign dress and customs—are among those prohibited during the reforms of Josiah (2 Kgs 23:4-14). These in turn correspond to sins attacked in the deuteronomic law code (Deuteronomy 12–26), which was rediscovered and then promulgated under Josiah.

The content as well as the imagery found in Zephaniah's oracles reflects the union of ancient northern, pre-monarchic Yahwistic traditions of holy war and the divine warrior, plus equally ancient southern Jerusalem/Zion traditions of Yahweh as creator and as king. This merger was fostered after the fall of the northern kingdom (722 BCE) under the reform movements of Hezekiah and, subsequently, Josiah. The literary history of Deuteronomy reflects this joining together of traditions. The prophetic voices of Isaiah and Micah, followed some seventy years later by Zephaniah ben Cushi and then Jeremiah, each in his own way preached a message marked by wrathful vindication wrought by a divine warrior and divine promise associated with Jerusalem/Zion. More specifically, Zephaniah's oracles on the coming day of the Lord exhort one to do what is right and to reject what is wrong or face dire consequences (cf. the ancient Sinai covenant tradition in Deut 30:19), while also concluding with confident assurances for the faithful and with hymns celebrating God as king (3:12-18).

The historical and political setting of Zephaniah's ministry can be reconstructed from evidence present in the central unit of the book, the oracles against the (foreign) nations (2:5-15; 3:8). These accounts of God's dealings with Judah's near and distant neighbors not only give some inkling of the geopolitics of the ancient Near East during the seventh century BCE, but also mark the transition within the book of Zephaniah between the message of doom and the message of hope. Indeed, this unit itself opens on the note of judgment and ends just prior to Zephaniah's promises to Judah and Jerusalem, which are prefaced with a word of hope for the nations (3:9).

The oracle against the nations is a standard part of the prophetic repertoire, occurring in Amos 1–2, Isaiah 13–23, Jeremiah 46–51, and Ezekiel 25–32. The earliest example of an oracle used against a foreign nation is found in the story of the Moabite seer Balaam, who, though called upon to curse the invading Israelites, instead blesses them on their way into the promised land (Numbers 22–24). This account from the pre-monarchic period is set within the context of holy war, where it is God who fights on behalf of the Israelites.

This same setting continues in the monarchic period when Isaiah opens his oracles against the nations by calling for holy war against Babylon (Isa 13:1-16).

Zephaniah ben Cushi's oracles against Judah's near neighbors (2:5-11), inhabitants of the Palestinian land bridge linking Asia in the north with Africa to the south, reflect the changed political situation within the region when young Josiah was placed on the throne of Judah in 640 BCE (2 Kgs 21:19-26; 22:1-2). Assyria, which had destroyed the northern kingdom of Israel and forced surviving Judah in the south to pay tribute, to cede territory, and to adopt Assyrian cult figures and other practices, was now in decline and no longer the dominant power within Syria-Palestine. This opening segment of the oracles against the nations assumes that Judah's servile status has passed and can now be interpreted as an opening salvo in the nation's efforts to regain territory lost to its neighbors during the Assyrian hegemony (2:7-9).[2]

The oracles against Judah's more distant neighbors, Cush/Nubia—rulers of Egypt during Hezekiah's reign who had helped to thwart Assyria's capture of Jerusalem (2:12) and hated Assyria to the north (2:13-15)—likewise give hints of their geopolitical setting. Assyria had captured Thebes in 633 BCE, spelling the end of the Cushite 25th Dynasty of Egypt. Still, Assyria's own capital, Nineveh, would fall not many years later in 612 BCE. Oracles linking these events occur in Zephaniah's later contemporary, Nahum (Nah 3:8-13). Likewise, the setting of Zephaniah's oracles is clearly one in which the prowess of Cushite Egypt has passed, though still remembered, and the fate of Assyria has already been sealed. However, Zephaniah does not consider the next major international power, even though his later contemporaries within the prophetic movement, Habakkuk and then Jeremiah, will point to the rise of the Neo-Babylonians.

Zephaniah's was the first prophetic voice to be raised in Judah against its people's disobedience to God since the time of Isaiah, some seventy years earlier during Hezekiah's reign. Isaiah's oracles against the nations (Isaiah 13–23) included a warning to Hezekiah against an alliance with the Cushite rulers of Egypt (Isaiah 18), since elsewhere Isaiah proclaimed Assyria as God's chastening rod, later itself to be judged (Isa 10:5). Zephaniah 2:12-15 shows that both powers were in decline toward the end of the seventh century BCE, thereby giving Josiah and the deuteronomic reformers the hope of bringing Judah back to religious and political independence and renewed obedience to God.

Zephaniah's ministry, therefore, is best located in the city of Jerusalem at the very beginning of Josiah's deuteronomic reform movement, approximately between 630 and 620 BCE, close in time to the prophet Nahum's oracles celebrating the fall of Nineveh in 612 BCE (Zeph 2:13-15). Given the vivid descriptions of the sins being condemned and the single-minded earnestness of Zephaniah's proclamation of the devastating day of the Lord, it appeared likely that this preaching preceded the full implementation of the reforms and, indeed, may have helped to inspire and guide the direction of the sought-for changes

---

2. See Duane L. Christensen, "Zephaniah 2:4-15: A Theological Basis for Josiah's Program of Political Expansion," *CBQ* 46 (1984) 669-82; cf. the critique by Berlin, *Zephaniah*, 119-20.

in Jerusalem and Judah. Josiah's father, Amon (642–640) was killed in a palace coup. Josiah himself was placed on the throne by the "people of the land" (2 Kgs 21:24 NRSV) when he was only eight years old (2 Kgs 22:1). With the discovery of the "book of the law" in the eighteenth year of his reign (2 Kgs 22:3-20), its authentication, and its promulgation (2 Kings 23), the reform began in 621 BCE. The core of the book of Deuteronomy (Deuteronomy 12–26) became the basis of purifying Judah of the idolatry, paganism, and loss of faith in God's will to act (2 Kings 22–23) resulting from Assyrian hegemony, which had been aided by Manasseh's and Amon's ready compliance. The reform effort was dealt a serious setback, however, with the untimely death of Josiah (609 BCE), who was killed in battle when attempting to stop Egyptian forces from aiding Assyria.

THE BOOK OF ZEPHANIAH: ITS COMPOSITION, FORM, AND STYLE

The book of Zephaniah is composed of the collected oracles of the prophet arranged according to subject matter, thereby yielding three major literary units: (a) oracles of divine judgment against Judah and Jerusalem (1:2–2:4); (b) oracles of divine judgment against the nations (2:5–3:8); and (c) oracles of divine promise to the nations and to Judah and Jerusalem (3:9-20). The literary form called "oracle" is the biblical prophets' stock-in-trade. It is the vehicle through which the prophet proclaims the divinely inspired Word of God to God's covenanted people.

Zephaniah's later contemporary, Jeremiah, sets the oracle within its proper context as one of several means of inspired leadership through which God directs the covenant community:

Instruction [תורה *tôrâ*] shall not perish from the priest, nor counsel [עצה *'ēṣâ*] from the wise, nor the word [דבר *dābār*] from the prophet. (Jer 18:18 NRSV)

Priestly *torah*, or law, is like catechism or instruction in God's commandments. Its equivalent in Greek would be διδαχή (*didachē*, "teaching"). Wisdom teachers provide counsel, advice, or guidance in human affairs based upon their vast store of empirically gained knowledge. The prophet is given a word or profound insight into the contemporary state of the divine-human relationship, which he or she feels compelled to express in as effective a way as possible. Again, it is Jeremiah who summarizes both the prophetic compulsion to speak and the dire consequences for the speaker and the audience as expressed in the imagery of the divine word as a consuming fire (Jer 5:14; 20:8-9).

The oracles of judgment and of promise presuppose the covenant relationship between God and the Hebrew people that was established under the leadership of Moses at Mount Sinai. God and people are yoked together as long as the people obey the commandments or covenant stipulations, which demand exclusive loyalty to Yahweh alone and just dealings with one's neighbor. Whereas obedience leads to life in the land of promise, disobedience leads to expulsion from the land, bondage, and death. The sanctions for maintaining covenantal loyalty are understood by all to be blessings of life or curses of death (e.g., Deuteronomy 28). Therefore, when Zephaniah ben Cushi preached a stern message of doom and disaster to a disobedient society, his audience knew the covenantal context out of which he spoke. Likewise, the faithful, humble remnant whom he singled out within that decadent society also knew that he spoke not only of judgment, but also of the promise that lay beyond the chastening and purifying destruction about to befall Judah and Jerusalem.

The oracles against the nations, though addressed to those outside the Sinai covenant bond, are also to be understood within a wider covenant context acknowledged by the Israelite community. The Israelites realized that their God was indeed Lord of the nations and that the divine word applied to all peoples, as in the Noah covenant (Genesis 9) and again as in the table of nations (Genesis 10), which shows how all nations are related. On the one hand, while it is the case that judgment against the nations is due them for attacking God's people and taking the promised land God had given them as part of their covenant bond (i.e., Zeph 2:8-9 against Moab and Ammon), it is also true that these oracles are motivated out of the belief that a universal or natural law of justice is at work, which no nation can violate without punishment. The oracles against the nations with which Amos opens his attack on the injustices of Judah and Israel (Amos 1–2) are replete with examples of threats against the nations for what we would call crimes against humanity and common human decency.[3]

This fundamental belief in God's lordship in the life of the covenant community, extending even to the nations of the earth, means that for prophet and for people the power of the divine word enunciated through the oracle was such that it not only foretold what was to be, but also helped to initiate the process of the oracle's fulfillment. The oracle was in essence a sentence of judgment handed down in the heavenly court, where God was judge and the prophet an officer of the court, announcing its decrees of guilt or innocence, of sentencing to death or imprisonment or release. Each prophet gave his or her statement about the particular crimes or covenant infractions of which the community was guilty, which was then followed by the judgment or punishment. Although the idiom of the law court was the chief social setting or institutional context of the prophetic oracle of judgment or that of promise, language of priestly ritual and of wisdom advice was also borrowed to drive home the statement of charges and impending punishment.

The form of Zephaniah ben Cushi's oracles follows the pattern that reflects the court of law, with terms and images also taken from temple ritual and school. His sermons are set in Jerusalem on the occasion of a major pilgrimage festival, most likely Ingathering (Tabernacles/Booths). With the dramatic image of God sweeping the earth clean, Zephaniah opens his diatribe about Judah's and Jerusalem's idolatry and religious syncretism. After getting the people's attention, the prophet introduces his central message about the coming day of the Lord by using an even more startling image, which has been borrowed

3. Amos 1:3, 6, 9, 11, 13 list the crimes against humanity of Israel's neighbors.

from the temple ritual: sinners are the sacrifice and the fierce executors of God's will are invited guests (1:7-9). Zephaniah ben Cushi's close association with the ruling elite of Jerusalem enabled him to describe in vivid detail their sins against God as well as to capture the repetitive cadence of priestly ritual in his portrayal of the day of judgment as one full of terror and dread (1:14-16). The temple ritual celebrating God's advent as the divine warrior who destroys the enemies of the covenant community had been a festive occasion of great joy. However, Amos, preaching before the fall of the northern kingdom, had already warned that the sins of the people made them God's enemies and thus the objects of God's wrath (5:18-24).

Punishment for people who break the covenant with God takes many forms, usually occuring as military defeat. However, the prophet reaches back into ancient covenantal tradition to extend the repertoire of sentences for the many crimes of which his people are found guilty. These are expressed in various ways using the imagery of the reversal of creation (1:2-3; 2:4), denial of the fruits of one's labor (1:13), and barrenness of the land (2:8-11, against Moab; 2:13-15, against Assyria).

For all the stern single-mindedness of the prophet, he apparently pleads with those whom he addresses within this courtroom-like setting. Twice at the conclusion of the oracles against the nations when Jerusalem is addressed, Zephaniah laments that the city has not learned from experience—that is, has not accepted "correction"/"instruction" (מוסר *mûsār*), an expression borrowed from the didactic rhetoric of the wisdom teachers (3:2, 7).[4] Among the resources such wisdom counsel provides is the ability to learn from life's experiences, here, perhaps, the fate of the northern kingdom and of other cities destroyed by God.

The central motif of the book of Zephaniah is the coming of the day of the Lord as a time of terrifying judgment against Judah and all the earth (1:14-18). The day of the Lord (יום־יהוה *yôm-Yahweh*) is the central referent around which the final canonical shape of the collected oracles is formed. In the oracles of judgment (1:2–2:4) the warnings of impending doom (1:7-13) repeatedly include the phrase "on that day" (1:7*a*, 8*a*, 9*a*, 10*a*; "at that time," 1:12*a*), and then in the description of that terrible moment itself (1:14-18), "day of the Lord" or simply "day" recurs cascade-like or as a thundering avalanche in practically every verse. The exhortatory pleading that follows (2:1-4), almost like a brief respite from the terrifying preceding scene, concludes this first unit of the book with a grace note, "perhaps you may be hidden/ on the day of the LORD's wrath" (2:3*b* NRSV).

The oracles against the nations (2:5–3:8), threatening universal destruction, similarly refer to "the day when I arise as a witness" (3:8 NRSV), but lead immediately into the oracles of promise with which the book ends (3:9-20). They open with the expressions "at that time" (3:9*a*) and "on that day" (3:11*a*). The tone changes dramatically in the promises, since now it is an occasion for rejoicing over God's just vindication that converts the nations (3:9) and allows the humble remnant to live in peace (3:11-13).

4. Examples of wisdom tradition's use of "correction"/"instruction" (*mûsār*): Prov 1:2, 3, 7-8; 10:17; 15:32-33; 23:12, 23.

This central and unifying motif—the day of the Lord—is clearly expressed within the milieu of the Jerusalem Temple with which Zephaniah ben Cushi is closely related. The prophet has chosen a festival occasion such as Ingathering, when many pilgrims come to Jerusalem and the temple complex, at which to make his proclamation that the time of God's judgment against the sinful community was drawing near. The punning language in the Hebrew text—i.e., the opening image of God sweeping the earth of its inhabitants, essentially reversing the process of creation (1:2-3)—is closely related to the terminology for the festival of Tabernacles or Ingathering. The sins outlined and condemned (1:4-5) are closely related to the temple personnel and the observance of religious practices that profane the proper worship of God.

Another bold and imaginative device is the announcement of a special sacrifice in the Temple, where sinful Judah is the sacrificial offering and the invited guests are the appointed forces of its destruction (1:7-9). Zephaniah ben Cushi even adopts the priestly call to worship, "Be silent [הס *has*] before the Lord GOD!" (1:7*a*, as in the well-known invocation of Hab 2:20). Similar features occur in the festive calls to choral song (3:14) and in the priestly oracles that report God has heard the penitent's call for divine succor, "Do not fear . . . " (3:16*b*; cf. the salvation oracles in Isa 40:9; 41:10, 13; 43:1, 5). Furthermore, the language of the psalms, the hymnody of the Temple, seems to be reflected in oracles against the nations' judgment of foreign gods (2:11; cf. Ps 82:6-7) and in the affirmation that God is king in the oracles of promise (3:15*b*; cf. the enthronement psalms' proclamation of God as universal king, Psalms 93; 96–99).

Understanding this cultic setting helps one to understand the essential unity in these collected oracles, even as they move from announcement of doom to promise of peace, from a message for Judah/Jerusalem to words addressed to all nations. Within the general announcement of doom, the reader may also find authentic, though muted, signs of hope. These are the words to the humble remnant (2:3, 7, 9) and the reassurance of God's continued stabilizing influence within a corrupt society (3:5*a*), as well as the potential that the people may learn from the disasters, that they can take "correction"/"instruction" (*mûsār*, 3:7). Even the reversal of the Noah covenant (Gen 9:11) in Zeph 3:8*b* prepares the audience for the possibility of something good in the future: the lifting of the curse of many languages (Gen 11:9) in the promise of changed speech among the nations (Zeph 3:9). This motif marks the sudden and dramatic transition from words of judgment to words of promise, using an image of God reversing creation. Since the collected oracles began using this device (Zeph 1:2-3), one may understand it as a rhetorical tool with which the prophet's audience was familiar and thus could easily grasp.

Moving from the universal to the particular, as in the opening oracles, the prophet then announces that "on that day" (3:11) the sentence of judgment against Jerusalem will be reversed for the humble remnant (3:11-13). The concluding victory song of joy (3:14-20) echoes these notes of changed circumstances. A temple choir is invoked to sing that Yahweh is king (3:14), as in the enthronement psalm (see Psalms 96; 98–99). Moreover, one hears a priestly oracle of blessing, "Do not fear" (3:16*a* NRSV), doubtless reminiscent of the solemn assembly that Amos condemned as premature (Amos 5:18-24). However, on the other side of judgment, this ceremony was appropriate, since it conformed to God's agenda of release. Zephaniah ben Cushi, who plumbed the depths of terror awaiting the wicked, could also envision another future for the humble remnant that survived.

The book of Zephaniah is marked by a distinctive literary style and poetic technique. Except for the superscription (1:1), the entire collection of oracles is written in poetic form. Assonance and repetition are key poetic devices in this work. The introductory oracle on universal destruction (1:2-6), for example, repeats the word "sweep" (Hebrew root אסף 'sp) four times, twice in the opening verse for added emphasis (אסף אסף 'āsōp 'āsēp), "I will utterly sweep away." The use of "from the face of the earth" and "humans"/"humanity" (1:3) is an example of paronomasia, or repetition of similar sounding words, since the Hebrew for "earth" and "human" (אדמה 'ădāmâ and אדם 'ādām) sound very much alike. Similarly, the repetition of the expression "day of the LORD" (yôm-Yahweh) in the following oracle (1:7–2:4) is used for poetic effect. Assonance and a punning wordplay stand at the end of this oracle as a conclusion and as a transition to the oracles against the nations (2:5-15) that follow. Thus "Gaza shall be deserted [עזה עזובה 'azzâ 'ăzzûbâ] . . . and Ekron shall be uprooted [ועקרון תעקר we'eqrôn tē'āqēr]" (2:4 NRSV), using similar sounds respectively for the place name and its attending verb.

Powerful metaphors, dramatic imagery, and clever turns of phrase occur throughout the book of Zephaniah. The literary devices that attend the prophet's great sermon on the day of the Lord (1:7–2:4) have had a lasting affect upon subsequent understanding of the universal day of judgment. Among the images used are the call to the sacrifice, where sinners are the offering and the invaders are invited guests (1:7), and the portrayal of God searching Jerusalem with lanterns to expose those who drink their lives away in the belief that God does not care and will not intervene (1:12). The depiction of God's appearance as warrior in that central oracle on the great day of judgment is one of the great poems to be found in the Bible. Indeed, it has influenced liturgies for the burial of the dead in Western Christianity through the medieval Latin hymn "Dies Irae" ("Day of Wrath"). Zephaniah ben Cushi's proclamation of the divine intervention as a day of great distress emerges out of a veritable cascade of nouns modifying the bass note-like repetition of the word "day" (יום yôm):

That day will be a day of wrath,
a day of distress and anguish,
a day of ruin and devastation,
a day of darkness and gloom,
a day of clouds and thick darkness,
a day of trumpet blast and battle cry. (1:15-16a NRSV)

The prophet also has a penchant for drawing striking examples from the natural order to illustrate realities within the social order. Thus, for example, corrupt officials and judges are called "roaring lions" and "evening wolves" (3:3), while God's sure and righteous presence is likened to the dependability of the sunrise.

"Every morning he renders his judgment,/ each dawn without fail" (3:5*b* NRSV). For all of his single-minded, dispassionate announcement of doom that would befall the wicked community, the prophet also envisions the righteous who pursue life under God's reign in pastoral serenity (3:13). Likewise, in the concluding victory song of release, there is a depiction of God as king and victorious warrior who rejoices and exults in the midst of the redeemed (3:17). Perhaps Zephaniah ben Cushi's audience was thus reminded of the account of King David dancing before the ark as it was brought to Jerusalem (2 Sam 6:12-15) or, perhaps, of the enthronement psalm in which nature rejoices over God's reign as righteous judge (Ps 98:7-9).

TEXT

The Hebrew manuscript tradition, called the Masoretic Text, upon which our English translations of the book of Zephaniah are based, is in very good condition. This is doubtlessly the result of the early collection and transmission into written form of Zephaniah's oracles by those who were drawn to the prophet's message and were intent upon seeing that it was preserved, especially until the time of its fulfillment. Such a motivation for preserving the words of a prophet is clearly noted in Zephaniah ben Cushi's later contemporary Habakkuk (Hab 2:2-3), and also in Jeremiah (Jer 36:27-32).

The earliest translation of the Hebrew manuscript, the Greek translation known as the Septuagint, which emerged from the Alexandrian diaspora community in third-century BCE Egypt, generally reflects and, therefore, supports the authenticity of the Masoretic Text. The Dea Sea Scrolls or Qumran Palestinian Hebrew MSS from the last two centuries BCE also reflect the consonantal text of the MT.

The few difficulties that do occur for the translator and interpreter of the Hebrew text are, for the most part, due to a lost or obscure meaning of a Hebrew word or a corruption of the text because of scribal or transmission errors. A literal translation of the MT behind Zeph 3:18, for example, does not make much sense. The NIV attempts to stay close to the MT in its translation of 3:18, with an alternative reading placed in its note on this verse. The NRSV follows the LXX and the Syriac Version of the Old Testament (Syr), opening this verse with the final line of 3:17*c*, as indicated in its notes. Other examples of these two approaches in the NIV and the NRSV to obscure texts in Zephaniah are to be found in the treatment of Zeph 1:4*b* and 3:17*b*. The latter involves the much-debated question of what to do with the MT's "he will be silent in his love," when the context—the lines immediately before and after—suggests, as in the LXX and the Syr, that it be read as "he will renew you in his love" (3:17*b* NRSV). The NIV, however, translates "he will quiet you with his love."

BIBLIOGRAPHY

Achtemeier, Elizabeth. *Nahum–Malachi*. Interpretation. Atlanta: John Knox, 1986. Commentary on Zephaniah with focus on contemporary issues.

Africa in Antiquity: The Arts of Ancient Nubia and the Sudan. 2 vols. New York: Brooklyn Museum, 1978. Comprehensive study of Nubian artifacts from all periods, with definitive essays.

Ancient Civilizations of Africa. Edited by G. Mokhtar. Berkeley: University of California Press, 1990.

Ball, Ivan J. *Zephaniah: A Rhetorical Study.* Berkeley, Calif.: Bibal, 1988. The content of Zephaniah is examined through the approach of rhetorical criticism.

Bennett, Robert. "Africa." In *Oxford Companion to the Bible.* Edited by Bruce Metzger and Michael Coogan. New York: Oxford, 1993.

———. "Africa and the Biblical Period," *HTR* 64 (1971) 483-500. Surveys of African presence and impact during major biblical periods.

Ben Zvi, Ehud. *A Historical-Critical Study of the Book of Zephaniah.* BZAW 198. Berlin: DeGruyter, 1991. Detailed study of the text of Zephaniah, using the historical-critical method.

Berlin, Adele. *Zephaniah.* AB 25A. New York: Doubleday, 1994. A new translation with references from rabbinic and other sources.

House, Paul. *Zephaniah: A Prophetic Drama.* JSOTSup 69. Sheffield: Almond Press, 1988. Unique study of Zephaniah as a dramatic presentation.

Kapelrud, Arvid. *The Message of the Prophet Zephaniah: Morphology and Ideas.* Oslo: Universitetsforlaget, 1975. Study of the linguistic and conceptual elements within Zephaniah.

Kitchen, Kenneth. *The Third Intermediate Period in Egypt.* Warminster: Aris & Phillips, 1973. Extensive survey of Egyptian sources on the Nubian, 25th Dynasty of Egyptian pharaohs.

Rice, Gene. "The African Roots of the Prophet Zephaniah." *JRT* 36 (1979). Survey of the historical-critical approach to the topic.

Roberts, J. J. M. *Nahum, Habakkuk, and Zephaniah.* OTL. Louisville: Westminster/John Knox, 1991. Philological form-critical and historical-critical analysis of Zephaniah.

Taylor, Charles, "Zephaniah." In *The Interpreter's Bible.* Vol. 6. Nashville: Abingdon, 1956. Representative of earlier approaches to the text, with Howard Thurman as homilist.

Thurman, Howard. *Deep River and The Negro Spiritual Speaks of Life and Death.* Richmond, Ind.: Friends United Press, 1975. Seminal interpretation of the inner meaning of the Spirituals.

———. *A Track to the Water's Edge: The Olive Schreiner Reader.* New York: Harper & Row, 1973. Thurman introduces American readers to writings of the white South African feminist.

Tutu, Desmond. *The Words of Desmond Tutu: Selected by Naomi Tutu.* New York: Newmarket, 1989. Tutu's daughter selects key thoughts of her Nobel laureate and archbishop father.

Washington, James M., ed. *Conversations with God: Two Centuries of Prayers by African Americans.* New York: HarperCollins, 1994. Extensive selection of prayers from all periods and diverse voices.

OUTLINE OF ZEPHANIAH

I. Zephaniah 1:1, The Word of the Lord to Zephaniah ben Cushi

II. Zephaniah 1:2–2:4, Oracles Against Judah and Jerusalem

    A. 1:2-6, Announcement of God's Judgment of Judah
    B. 1:7-13, Warnings of the Coming Day of the Lord
    C. 1:14-18, The Great Day of the Lord
    D. 2:1-4, Pleas to Judah

III. Zephaniah 2:5–3:8, Oracles Against the Nations

    A. 2:5-15, Announcement of Judgment on the Nations
    B. 3:1-5, The Wickedness of Jerusalem
    C. 3:6-8, Concern for Jerusalem and Announcement of Universal
        Judgment

IV. Zephaniah 3:9-20, Oracles of Promise of Universal Conversion and of Salvation for Jerusalem

    A. 3:9-13, Promises of Universal Conversion and of Salvation for
        the Remnant of Judah
    B. 3:14-20, Victory Song of Joy for Jerusalem

THE WORD OF THE LORD TO ZEPHANIAH BEN CUSHI

NIV

1 The word of the LORD that came to Zephaniah son of Cushi, the son of Gedaliah, the son of Amariah, the son of Hezekiah, during the reign of Josiah son of Amon king of Judah:

NRSV

1 The word of the LORD that came to Zephaniah son of Cushi son of Gedaliah son of Amariah son of Hezekiah, in the days of King Josiah son of Amon of Judah.

COMMENTARY

The very first line of the book of Zephaniah, by an editor of the collected sayings of the prophet, serves both as the title and as the introduction to the words of Zephaniah ben Cushi. It locates the prophet in time and place and authenticates his right to speak in God's name. Within this single verse, Zephaniah ben Cushi is identified as being called by God to speak to the people of Judah during the reign of King Josiah (640–609 BCE). His lineage stretches back four generations to an ancestor named Hezekiah, who may have been the king of Judah (715–687 BCE) bearing the same name. Given the content and context of Zephaniah's words, he appears to have been influenced by the political and religious message associated with King Hezekiah and the prophets Isaiah and Micah of that former generation. Zephaniah ben Cushi was closely aligned with the reform policies of King Josiah of his own era and with the activities of his contemporaries, the prophets Nahum and Jeremiah.

The genealogy of Zephaniah ben Cushi is unique in that it spans four generations. The norm is typically two generations. This atypical genealogy, therefore, highlights the name "Hezekiah" all the more.[5] This possibility of a royal ancestry illumines the other noteworthy aspect of the prophet's lineage: his African ancestry. In Hebrew, the word "Cushi" (כושי *kûšî*), in antiquity and today, means "African." This form of the word, whether taken as a proper name or as an ethnic designation, regularly points in biblical usage to Israel's darker hued neighbors to the south, peoples from Egypt and the extended regions of the Nile valley. Egyptian texts use the name "Kush" for the cataract region of the Upper Nile.[6] This usage is attested in the account of the dispute between Miriam and Moses over Moses' Cushite (NRSV, "Ethiopian") wife (Numbers 12). The term "Cushite" also designates the soldier in King David's service who brought word of Absalom's death (2 Samuel 18). Indeed, Zephaniah's later contemporary, Jeremiah, attests to royal court officials of African ancestry in the service of Josiah's successor, King Jehoiakim (609–597 BCE)—i.e., "Jehudi son of Nathaniah son of Shelemiah son of Cushi [בן־כושי *ben-kûšî*]" (Jer 36:14 NRSV), and the well known "Ebed-melech" (NRSV, "the Ethiopian" [*kûšî*]), who rescued Jeremiah from the dungeon (Jer 38:7).

During Hezekiah's reign, there were strong diplomatic and military ties between Judah and the

---

5. Robert R. Wilson, *Prophecy and Society in Ancient Israel* (Philadelphia: Fortress, 1980) 279-80; see also Adele Berlin, *Zephaniah,* AB 25A (New York: Doubleday, 1994) 65-67; and J. J. M. Roberts, *Nahum, Habakkuk, and Zephaniah,* OTL (Louisville: Westminster/John Knox, 1991) 165-66.

6. *Africa in Antiquity: The Arts of Ancient Nubia and the Sudan,* 2 vols. (New York: Brooklyn Museum, 1978) 1:75-78; 2:43-63; see also *Ancient Civilizations of Africa,* ed. G. Mokhtar (Berkeley: University of California Press, 1990) 141-84. The region of southern Africa called Kush by the Egyptians subsequently becomes the kingdom of Kush.

Cushite 25th Dynasty rulers of Egypt, when Judahite kings attempted to ward off an Assyrian invasion. The one pharaoh clearly named in the Bible, "King Tirhakah of Ethiopia" (2 Kgs 19:9 NRSV; מֶלֶךְ־כּוּשׁ melek-kûš, "King of Nubia/Cush"), is the ally against whom the Isaiah 18 oracle is directed.[7] Indeed, Zephaniah ben Cushi uses the same phrase, "beyond the rivers of Ethiopia [Cush/Nubia]" to describe the ancestral home of the 25th Dynasty Egyptian rulers (Zeph 3:10a NRSV; cf. Isa 18:1, 7). Further, the prophet's vanguard role in rousing support for Josiah's reforms may have been influenced by an ancestor identified with Hezekiah and his reforms (2 Kgs 18:1-8) almost a century earlier.

The meaning of the name "Zephaniah" is also significant, since it encapsulates a major theme found in the prophet's oracles, "Yahweh protects [the righteous]" (Zeph 2:3; 3:12). The prophet's name consists of two elements: an abbreviated form of the divine name Yah(weh), prefaced with a verbal form of the Hebrew root צפן (ṣpn), meaning "hidden"/"protected" and by extension also "treasured."[8] This is the same Hebrew root used when the psalmist affirms, "In the shelter of your presence you hide them/ from human plots" (Ps 31:20 NRSV).

Three other figures in the Hebrew Bible bear the name "Zephaniah," all of whom hold priestly positions. They are (a) a Kohathite ancestor of Heman, a singer in the levitical choir of the Temple (1 Chr 6:36); (b) a priest who was involved in the interactions between King Zedekiah (597–587 BCE) and Jeremiah prior to the fall of Jerusalem (Jer 21:1; 29:25, 29; 37:3) and executed by the Babylonian captors of Jerusalem in 587 BCE (Jer 52:24-27//2 Kings 25:18-21); and (c) the father of Josiah, a high priest who returned from the Babylonian exile during the rebuilding of the Temple, perhaps to be identified with the slain priest of the same name (Zech 6:10-14).

From all of this we discover the strong associations that this name bears among those who hold a priestly office and have close ties with the royal household. The call to announce the word of the Lord, the special ancestry and lineage of the prophet, and even the theophoric construction of the name, "Yahweh protects," all reinforce the particular message of this late seventh-century BCE prophet.

---

7. Kenneth A. Kitchen, *The Third Intermediate Period in Egypt* (Warminster: Aris & Phillips, 1973) 383-93. On the Empire of Kush, see *Ancient Civilizations of Africa,* 161-84.

8. Adele Berlin, *Zephaniah,* AB 25A (New York: Doubleday, 1994) 64, see also n. 4 of the present commentary.

REFLECTIONS

A later collector and editor of the words of the prophet Zephaniah ben Cushi, as was the custom, added a superscription indicating the time, the place, the lineage, and the nature of the prophet's call to preach. The who, what, where, when, and why questions are still being put to this prophet as his words confront us today. However, as is often the case with the Scriptures, we latter-day questioners discover that certain questions are turned upon us as well. Our own identities get caught up in the search for the person who is presuming to confront us with God's word for humankind.

The very name "Zephaniah," whose Hebrew original means something like "God protects" or even "treasures," speaks volumes in itself. This name touches the much-discussed issues of self-esteem and respect for the dignity of fellow human beings. If we believe that God protects and treasures those who hear the divine word and trust in it, then it follows that we will hear the prophet's message of coming destruction in a certain way. The impending doom, as will become clear in our study of the prophet's oracles, is universal. No one will escape, but there will be survivors. Thus we are all held responsible before the divine judge for our actions and our attitudes toward others. For all of its sternness—when mercy seems to be silenced—the oracle of doom can point to the other side of punishment. Correction and a changed heart become a pronouncement of release and a call to rejoice.

The other part of the prophet's name, indicating his African ancestry—son of Cushi—can also challenge our identity, our self-esteem, and our view of other human beings. The conventional meaning of the phrase "son of Cushi" points to one's having African ancestry, as do the geopolitics of that era, when Egypt was ruled by its Cushite/Nubian neighbors from the Upper Nile region, modern-day southern Egypt and Sudan. This situation is attested in 2 Kings 19, Isaiah 18, Nahum 3, and in a proverb indicating long and widespread familiarity with Africans: "can Ethiopians [Cushites] change their skin . . .?" (Jer 13:23a NRSV). Some commentators on the "ben Cushi" of Zephaniah's ancestry challenge the conventional meaning by positing an ancient mythic source or simply by ignoring it and thereby not raising the issue of foreign background.[9] That God uses a foreigner, an African, someone of mixed ancestry to proclaim the divine word to late seventh-century BCE Judah raises many questions about our own identity in our relationship with God and with our neighbors. Given the movements of nations and peoples over this land corridor between Africa, Europe, and Asia in antiquity as well as today, it seems highly unlikely that we can transport back in time our visions of a homogeneous society, or at least one in which certain players are locked out or locked in to subservient roles.

As we attempt to determine what this superscription means to us today, we must begin by asking ourselves about our reaction to this name. What forces within us are at work to shape a particular attitude or predisposition to resist or to reject the interpretation suggested above? Denial, rejection, surprise, consternation, or simply a pause to consider one's feelings—all are possible reactions as we are confronted with the possibility, even probability, of Zephaniah's African or mixed-race heritage.

9. Berlin, *Zephaniah,* 66, 111-13; Gene Rice, "The African Roots of the Prophet Zephaniah," *JRT* 36 (1979) 21-31.

ORACLES AGAINST JUDAH AND JERUSALEM

ZEPHANIAH 1:2-6, ANNOUNCEMENT OF GOD'S JUDGMENT OF JUDAH

NIV

2"I will sweep away everything
from the face of the earth,"
declares the LORD.
3"I will sweep away both men and animals;
I will sweep away the birds of the air
and the fish of the sea.
The wicked will have only heaps of rubble[a]
when I cut off man from the face of the
earth,"
declares the LORD.

4"I will stretch out my hand against Judah
and against all who live in Jerusalem.
I will cut off from this place every remnant of
Baal,
the names of the pagan and the idolatrous
priests—
5those who bow down on the roofs
to worship the starry host,
those who bow down and swear by the LORD
and who also swear by Molech,[b]
6those who turn back from following the LORD
and neither seek the LORD nor inquire of him.

a3 The meaning of the Hebrew for this line is uncertain.   b5 Hebrew
Malcam, that is, Milcom

NRSV

2 I will utterly sweep away everything
from the face of the earth, says the LORD.
3 I will sweep away humans and animals;
I will sweep away the birds of the air
and the fish of the sea.
I will make the wicked stumble.[a]
I will cut off humanity
from the face of the earth, says the LORD.
4 I will stretch out my hand against Judah,
and against all the inhabitants of Jerusalem;
and I will cut off from this place every remnant
of Baal
and the name of the idolatrous priests;[b]
5 those who bow down on the roofs
to the host of the heavens;
those who bow down and swear to the LORD,
but also swear by Milcom;[c]
6 those who have turned back from following
the LORD,
who have not sought the LORD or inquired
of him.

a Cn: Heb sea, and those who cause the wicked to stumble
b Compare Gk: Heb the idolatrous priests with the priests
c Gk Mss Syr Vg: Heb Malcam (or, their king)

COMMENTARY

The first words of the oracle concerning God's coming judgment occur in the form of God's own first-person announcement of universal destruction that will befall the entire earth. This divine self-disclosure sets forth the theme of Zephaniah ben Cushi's message of God's intention to break in upon human history to mete out justice to the nations, especially to wayward Judah. The dual focus of this opening oracle is reflected in God's role as creator, returning the world to its original state (1:2-3) and as divine warrior-judge, reaching forth to destroy disobedient, idolatrous Judah (1:4-6).

The oracle opens abruptly with imagery of God sweeping the creation clean. In a reversal of the order of creation in Genesis (Gen 1:20-26), all humans, animals, birds, and fish are threatened with destruction. All of this will come to pass because of the "wicked" (1:3c), particularly Judah's breaking of the Sinai covenant commandments to worship God alone and not to serve other gods (1:4-6). The latter is implied in the enumeration of the sins of idolatry (1:4); of syncretism, or mixing other religious observances with the worship of Yahweh (1:5); and the sin, especially of the elite classes, of no longer caring for divine instruction and of thinking that God does not care (1:6; specified in 1:12). The oracle addresses these errant persons, but because they are the leaders, the priests, and the teachers of the community, the whole society is doomed.

The theological framework upon which this opening oracle is based is none other than the covenant relationship established between God and the Israelites at Mount Sinai under the leadership of Moses. The ritual of a sacrificial meal ratified this bond between God and the people (Exodus 6 and 24), but stipulations of total obedience to God were attached in the form of commandments (Exod 20:1-17//Deut 5:6-21) and law codes (Exod 20:22–23:33, Covenant Code; Deuteronomy 12–26, Deuteronomic Code). The prophet is thus using the language of indictment against Judah for breaking the commandments to worship God alone in order to awaken his audience to the awful fate that awaits them. This oracle represents the opening salvo in Zephaniah ben Cushi's war against the paganism that had taken hold of Judah during the subservience of Manasseh (687–642 BCE) and Amon (642–640 BCE) to their Assyrian overlords. Indeed, Zephaniah's first words may have ignited the spark behind Josiah's movement to reform his nation, as described in 2 Kings 22–23. The Deuteronomic Code upon which the reform movement was based actually opens with a call for the destruction of pagan shrines and practices (Deut 12:1-12). Such idolatry is cited in Zeph 1:4 as a cause for the nation's impending destruction.

1:2. The first words that the prophet's audi-

ence heard in Hebrew: "I will utterly sweep away . . ." (אָסֹף אָסֵף 'āsōp 'āsēp, 1:2a), based on two Hebrew roots (אסף 'sp and סוף swp, respectively), provide a fine example of assonance. The prophet is clearly alluding to the great deluge of the Noah story, in which the flood waters swept away all the inhabitants of the earth. This verse sounds an ominous warning that universal destruction will return as the fate of wayward humankind. Although the two Hebrew roots in combination connote destruction (swp means "come to an end" or "cease"; 'sp means "gather and take away" or "remove"), however, alone the root 'sp has another connotation of being collected and gathered together not only for removal, but also for assembly, for being brought into the company of others, (cf. Mic 2:12: "I will surely gather . . . " [NRSV]).

Zephaniah ben Cushi's audience may not have remembered Micah's oracle, but it is likely that they would have heard in Zephaniah's opening oracle an allusion to the great festival of Ingathering (Booths/Tabernacles; אסיף 'āsîp), which shares the same Hebrew root, 'sp. Of the ancient pilgrimage festivals in the cultic calendar originating at Sinai (Exod 23:16; 43:22), Unleavened Bread (Passover), Weeks (First Fruits/Pentecost), and Ingathering, the latter was the most important and best attended. It was popularly called the "feast of Yahweh" (Lev 23:39) or simply "the feast" (Ezek 45:25; 1 Kgs 8:2, 65). This festival commemorates God's protection of Israel during the wilderness wanderings (Lev 23:39-43) and was the occasion on which Solomon dedicated the Temple in Jerusalem (1 Kings 8). It may well have been the occasion on which Zephaniah ben Cushi chose to utter his oracle, since crowds gather for the event and since purification of Solomon's Temple and the concentration of all worship therein were two of the major goals of the deuteronomic reforms (2 Kings 23). Furthermore, this festival under its other name, Booths/Tabernacles, was the occasion for the future ingathering of all nations to Jerusalem to worship God (Zech 14:16), a vision that Zephaniah also held for the future (3:9-10).

1:3. The prophet's audience could not have missed the ominous consequences of God's decision to sweep away all creation, with the possible allusion to ending God's protective care associated with the festival of Ingathering. Zephaniah was part of a prophetic tradition that, before him (Hos 4:1-3) and just after him (Jer 4:23-26), could announce that the God of the Sinai covenant with Israel could bring life to an end for those who broke the commandments laid down by Moses. The concluding phrase of this opening oracle, "I will cut off humanity/ from the face of the earth" (v. 3), reminds the people of the curses upon all who break faith with God (Deut 28:15-68), especially that found in Deut 6:15, which reflects the language of the Josiah reform movement that Zephaniah ben Cushi supported and very likely helped to initiate.

1:4-6. The oracle continues by making specific charges against Judah and Jerusalem. As if in a court of law, the indictment lists three specific charges for which God will punish this community: (1) idolatry, transferring their trust to Canaanite fertility gods (בעלים *bĕ ʿālîm,* 1:4*b*); (2) syncretism, mixing worship of other gods with worship of Yahweh—namely, "the host of the heavens" and Milcom (1:5); and (3) indifference to God, not calling on God or—as becomes clearer later (1:12)—thinking that God does not care (v. 6). Zephaniah understands such cynicism as a malady of the upper classes, the leaders, that had infected all elements within the society.

The conditions that the prophet was attacking in this and his subsequent speeches resulted from nearly seventy years of political and religious subservience that Manasseh and Amon had given their Assyrian overlords. The voice of prophecy had ceased with the close of the ministries of Isaiah and Micah at the beginning of the seventh century BCE. Hezekiah (715–687 BCE) had worked to build the defenses of the city. He used his alliance with the Cushite 25th Dynasty pharaohs to ward off Assyrian capture of Jerusalem. In addition, he instituted religious reform by purifying the Temple of foreign elements (2 Kings 18–20). Jerusalem was indeed spared then, but Hezekiah's successors, Manasseh and Amon, gave in to Assyrian pressure, permitting many foreign religious and social customs to permeate the land (2 Kings 21). The collapse of Assyria and the palace coup that brought Josiah (640–609 BCE) to the throne set the stage for the reform movement, based on the rediscovered Deuteronomic Code (Deuteronomy 12–26), to be introduced in 621 BCE (2 Kings 22–23). This moment was the window of opportunity during which Zephaniah proclaimed the coming day of the Lord in order to purge the community of the results of years of social and religious neglect.

REFLECTIONS

The opening oracle in the book of Zephaniah juxtaposes the two ways God communicates with humankind: (1) as creator to creatures, addressing us in terms of our common or shared humanity as members of the family of nations; and (2) as clan or tribal deity, calling out to us as an individual group marked by a shared historical, political, geographic, and religious—or here, covenantal—identity. Zephaniah ben Cushi demonstrates that God does indeed care, contradicting the cynics and the skeptics of every age, by having God speak out directly: "I care enough to intervene in nature and in your history" (see Zeph 1:2-6).

1. The prophet presupposes among his hearers an awareness both of the Noah covenant, linking humanity as a family of nations with God (Genesis 9–10), and the Sinai covenant mediated by Moses, yoking freed Hebrew slaves and their companions with God as a new people and a religious congregation (Exodus 19–24). We latter-day hearers of the Word are put on notice about and are challenged to come to terms with the complexity of how God communicates with us. God transcends our sectarian, denominational, ethnic, or national perceptions of the deity. Our accountability to the divine will extends beyond our separate identities as Christian, Jew, Muslim, Catholic, Protestant, Orthodox, Reformed, Conservative, Shiite, Sunni, Hindu, Buddhist, and beyond, whatever our Eastern or Western recognition of God. Although it was not of the same order as suggested here, an example of the complexity of dual religious claims upon us is found in Paul's agonizing over the pull of his Jewish and

Christian covenantal ties and his conclusion that the one has not abrogated the other (Romans 11).

Zephaniah 1:2-6 forces us to view our responsibilities as citizens of planet earth in terms of the global village imagery. We are linked to one another beyond the historical boundaries of religion, race, class, and nation. The popular slogan "Think globally, act locally" moves us beyond merely local or more narrowly defined parochial concerns. Zephaniah ben Cushi has discerned that the sinfulness of the one community has consequences for all creation.

2. The threat of reversing the process of creation, thus linking Judah's sins with universal destruction, should also remind us of our culpability in a whole set of environmental crises confronting the world. Zephaniah ben Cushi was indeed prescient in linking universal destruction with rampant idolatry and cynicism among the populace and its leaders (1:2-6), and thereby exposing our hand in the destruction of nature. Pollution and the depletion of natural resources may not be the same as God's sweeping life off the earth, but from Zephaniah's perspective, we are held accountable.

The root causes of extinction of life forms today may be laid at the feet of human, nationalistic pride. Instead of tending the earth, we have arrogated to ourselves the right to exploit its resources. Idolatry has become ideologically based domination—such as racism, sexism, classism, and the like—which denies the supremacy of God along with any sense of equality with one's neighbor. Syncretism exists as ritualistic expressions of such ideologies, going beyond explicit attacks, such as burning crosses, swastika graffiti, and racial slurs, into more subtle but equally lethal assumptions about a person or group simply on the basis of color, sex, or language. Such lack of respect for God and for other human beings is translated into an even deeper antipathy toward the earth. The cycle spirals on: as we treat creation, so we treat its creatures. Cynicism and skepticism about the existence of any greater force or power in control of life lead to stultifying indifference. Scottish exegete George Adam Smith in the late nineteenth century captured the awful consequences of social and religious indifference: "Here is evidently the same public temper, which at all periods provokes alike the despair of the reformer and the indignation of the prophet: the criminal apathy of the well-to-do classes sunk in ease and religious indifference. . . . The great causes of God and Humanity are not defeated by the hot assaults of the Devil, but by the slow, crushing, glacier-like mass of thousands and thousands of indifferent nobodies. God's causes are never destroyed by being blown up, but by being sat upon."[10]

10. George Adam Smith, *The Book of the Twelve Prophets,* vol. 2 (New York: Doubleday, 1929) 52-54.

ZEPHANIAH 1:7-13, WARNINGS OF THE COMING DAY OF THE LORD

NIV	NRSV
7Be silent before the Sovereign LORD, for the day of the LORD is near. The LORD has prepared a sacrifice; he has consecrated those he has invited. 8On the day of the LORD's sacrifice I will punish the princes and the king's sons	7 Be silent before the Lord GOD! For the day of the LORD is at hand; the LORD has prepared a sacrifice, he has consecrated his guests. 8 And on the day of the LORD's sacrifice I will punish the officials and the king's sons and all who dress themselves in foreign attire.

NIV

and all those clad
in foreign clothes.
⁹On that day I will punish
all who avoid stepping on the threshold,ᵃ
who fill the temple of their gods
with violence and deceit.

¹⁰"On that day," declares the LORD,
"a cry will go up from the Fish Gate,
wailing from the New Quarter,
and a loud crash from the hills.
¹¹Wail, you who live in the market districtᵇ;
all your merchants will be wiped out,
all who trade withᶜ silver will be ruined.
¹²At that time I will search Jerusalem with lamps
and punish those who are complacent,
who are like wine left on its dregs,
who think, 'The LORD will do nothing,
either good or bad.'
¹³Their wealth will be plundered,
their houses demolished.
They will build houses
but not live in them;
they will plant vineyards
but not drink the wine."

ᵃ9 See 1 Samuel 5:5.   ᵇ11 Or the Mortar   ᶜ11 Or in

NRSV

⁹ On that day I will punish
all who leap over the threshold,
who fill their master's house
with violence and fraud.

¹⁰ On that day, says the LORD,
a cry will be heard from the Fish Gate,
a wail from the Second Quarter,
a loud crash from the hills.
¹¹ The inhabitants of the Mortar wail,
for all the traders have perished;
all who weigh out silver are cut off.
¹² At that time I will search Jerusalem with lamps,
and I will punish the people
who rest complacentlyᵃ on their dregs,
those who say in their hearts,
"The LORD will not do good,
nor will he do harm."
¹³ Their wealth shall be plundered,
and their houses laid waste.
Though they build houses,
they shall not inhabit them;
though they plant vineyards,
they shall not drink wine from them.

ᵃ Heb who thicken

COMMENTARY

This second of the nine oracles in the book of Zephaniah introduces the concept of the day of the Lord in its ritual manifestation as a day of divine sacrifice (1:7-8), defines it further as a time of punishment for those who have introduced foreign customs into the land (1:8-9), draws a picture of the anguished reaction of the Jerusalem populace (1:10-11), and concludes with a special warning of coming disaster for the faithless, indolent rich (1:12-13). There is an ominous repetition of the words "day of the LORD" (יום־יהוה *yôm-Yahweh*), or its surrogate "that day/time" (1:7, 8, 9, 10, 12), as the prophet enunciates the crimes and the punishment of the leaders (1:8-9) and the rich (1:12-13), separated only by an interval on the anguish of the city (1:10-11).

Although the theme of crime and punishment predominates in this warning on the coming day of the Lord, suggesting a life setting or societal context of the law court, the oracle's opening designation that this is the day of the Lord's sacrifice (1:7-8) may point also to the Temple as a proper setting for this oracle. Generally, biblical scholars have defined the prophetic role as the messenger of God's decisions, based on the covenant in the divine court of law. In prophetic oracles, the charges are set forth as the reasons for the punishments that are being announced. Moses, the prototype of the prophet in the covenant breaking and covenant renewal incidents at Mount Sinai (Exodus 32–34) and the later prophet Micaiah, who informs King Ahab of his fate (1 Kgs 22:13-14), are classic examples of what the prophet does, whom he serves, and the social/religious context in which the prophet's ministry is performed. Accounts of the call to prophecy in Isaiah 6 and Jeremiah 1 emphasize this same theme of the prophet as a messenger or officer of the divine court. The vision of the Ancient One sitting in judgment (Dan 7:9-14) graphically portrays the divine court in action. From such a perspective, this oracle of Zephaniah can thus be understood as a bill of indictment with sentences of judgment attached (Zeph 1:8-9, 12-13).[11]

This second oracle yields a few glimmers of insight into the background and social standing of Zephaniah ben Cushi. The oracle's first words, "Be silent |הם *has,* similar in sound and meaning to the English "hush"] before the Lord GOD!" (1:7), are a typical priestly call to worship, invoking silence in the presence of God. Zephaniah's later contemporary, Habakkuk, used the same expression as an introduction to the appearance of God, which has become a standard invocation to worship:

The LORD is in his holy temple;
 let all the earth keep silence [*has*] before him!
(Hab 2:20 NRSV)

This text from Habakkuk and the references to sacrifice (זבח *zābaḥ*) in vv. 7*b*-8*a,* together with references to consecration or purification of the guests in v. 7*b,* all suggest that the prophet is conversant with temple rites and priestly terminology. He uses it to good effect as a very successful means of getting his audience's attention, while putting them on notice that God is about to appear. Furthermore, he employs a striking image of an active deity to introduce the oracle; here, God is preparing to offer sacrifices (vv. 7-8), whereas before (vv. 2-3) God was sweeping the earth of all life. And here, too, the ominous image of creation's being reversed is replicated and intensified by the implied meaning that the audience being addressed was to be the sacrificial offering and that—just as awful—the invited guests were the enemy invaders sent by God as instruments of the imminent destruction.

The rest of this oracle reveals Zephaniah ben Cushi's keen firsthand knowledge of the deadly weaknesses of the officials and the princes, exemplified in their importation of foreign dress styles (v. 8) and adoption of pagan practices in the temple rituals (v. 9; cf. vv. 4-5). We discover both

Zephaniah's knowledge of the city neighborhoods and their inhabitants in his account of the anguish of the populace (vv. 10-11) and his familiarity with the indolent life-style of the wealthy, even down to his ability to verbalize their cynical thoughts (vv. 12-13). The prophet was obviously a Jerusalemite who moved among the elite class within the society, but he was conversant as well with the merchants and ordinary folk. Given his own pedigree, perhaps pointing back to the household of Hezekiah (v. 1), the reference to "the king's sons" (v. 8*a*) may imply his continued access to the royal household. This reference might also place the time of Zephaniah's ministry as early in the reign of Josiah (640–609 BCE), soon after a palace coup brought the young Josiah to the throne (2 Kgs 21:23–22:20). The princes referred to may thus have been relatives of the deposed Amon.[12]

1:7-9. The oracle commences with the riveting portrayal of God as a high priest about to offer sacrifice, with the implication that Judah is the sacrifice and the invited guests are the designated armies of destruction (v. 7). Whereas the first oracle opened with God directly addressing the people (1:2-4), in this second sermon the prophet speaks as priest calling the community to worship with a ritual invocation to silence in the presence of God (v. 7*a*). The prophet has very effectively equated the newly introduced phrase "day of the LORD" with the actual appearance of God to perform the act of sacrifice, the slaughter of sinful Judah. Lest that point be missed by the audience, God finally speaks in first-person address to stipulate the offenses, to identify who is to be punished and why (vv. 8-9). Zephaniah ben Cushi, in the tradition of the prophet as messenger of decrees from God the divine judge, places the charges of covenantal infractions and the sentences of punishment clearly and very effectively before the people. Moreover, he intensifies the moment by putting it in the context of the real presence of God during sacrifice and names that occasion, the day of the Lord (vv. 7-9; see also vv. 10-12).

The charges spelled out are not as frivolous as they may sound to modern ears: lavish, "trendy,"

11. Claus Westermann, *Basic Forms of Prophetic Speech* (Philadelphia: Westminster, 1967) 169-200.

12. Berlin, *Zephaniah,* 79; J. J. M. Roberts, *Nahum, Habakkuk, and Zephaniah,* OTL (Louisville: Westminster/John Knox, 1991) 178.

imported attire (v. 8b) and an old superstitious practice of the Philistines cited in 1 Sam 5:5 (Zeph 1:9a). They represent rejection of tradition and the influx of foreign, specifically syncretistic, practices among the leaders—within the royal household and the priesthood who shape the community's identity. These offenses represent practices from Manasseh's time (2 Kings 21) that Josiah sought to remove (2 Kings 23). These forms of syncretism and idolatry exposed Judah to the curses of doom for the disobedient (Deut 28:15-68).

1:10-11. The prophet's attention shifts from the sins of the leaders to a look at the effect of divine wrath upon the city and its inhabitants, concluding with the reappearance of God, searching Jerusalem with lamps in order to expose the complacent skeptics (1:12-13).

The prophet goes into some detail as he traverses the city, recording how it is taking in the announcement of impending disaster. Our best knowledge about Jerusalem's structure at the time of Zephaniah comes from the post-exilic accounts of the repair and rededication of the city walls (Nehemiah 3; 12). Zephaniah ben Cushi's sympathy is with the populace. From among them will come a cry from the Fish Gate, a wail from the Second Quarter, a loud crash from the hills, and a wail from the inhabitants of the Mortar (v. 10). Huldah, the prophetess who authenticated the law book that became the foundation for the deuteronomic reforms, lived in the Second Quarter (2 Kgs 22:14). These neighborhoods mentioned in v. 10 were more or less on the northerly side of Jerusalem, which would have been especially vulnerable to enemy attack. This part of the oracle portrays the disruption of city life and its commerce resulting from a military attack. The vignette concludes with a description of the expected commercial chaos: "all the traders have perished;/ all who weigh out silver are cut off" (v. 11).

1:12-13. In order to dramatize the fate of those skeptics who say that God does not care enough to mete out justice, the prophet introduces the ominous image of God carefully searching the darkened city with lamps to ferret out the indolent rich people. Zephaniah ben Cushi has skillfully crafted the conclusion of his second oracle on the coming day of the Lord so that the deity, here portrayed as a warrior searching for his prey—a military search and destroy mission—speaks in the first person:

> I will search Jerusalem with lamps,
> and I will punish the people. v. 12a)

High drama continues with a statement of the cynics' true thoughts (v. 12b). Their complacent life-style condemns them to the awful futility curse (v. 13), set forth in Deut 28:30, 38-40.

Three key elements in this concluding segment merit further explanation: (1) the image of the lamp, (2) the idiom "rest complacently on their dregs" (v. 12), and (3) the curse against the wealthy (v. 13). In addition to its more mundane functional use as a source of light, the lamp (נר *nēr*) is used in a positive metaphorical way, signifying God's Word, as in the familiar verse from the book of Psalms: "Your word is a lamp to my feet/ and a light to my path" (Ps 119:105 NRSV). In the wisdom tradition, lamps are equated with parental guidance: "For the [parent's] commandment is a lamp and the teaching a light" (Prov 6:23 NRSV). In these verses from Zephaniah, however, the plural is used, "lamps," connoting that God and the invading troops on the search-and-destroy mission are one. No one can hide from God, because "Darkness is as light to [God]" (Ps 139:12b NRSV). God has no need of torches to search someone out. This verse from the psalter further supports the view that the prophet and the audience alike understood the image of God's searching the darkened city with "lamps" as really referring to an invading army that functioned as an instrument of God's wrath.

The expression "who rest complacently on their dregs" (v. 12b) portrays the decadent and indolent life-style of skeptics who blaspheme God by saying that God does not care enough to render justice in life. The Hebrew word הקפאים (*haqqōpĕ'îm,* lit., "thicken," "congeal") originated from the wine-making process, in which new wine was left to stand with the dregs or sediment or lees of the grapes long enough to enhance the wine's color and body, but then is drawn off before the wine becomes too thick and syrupy. Zephaniah uses this terminology to compare these people with wine that has become spoiled because it has sat too long with the dregs.[13]

---

13. Berlin, *Zephaniah,* 87-88; Roberts, *Nahum, Habakkuk, and Zephaniah,* 176.

The curse pronounced over the rich is taken from the ancient curses in Deuteronomy 28. It is called a futility curse, because in it an individual is denied the benefits of his or her labor. As in Amos 5:11, this reversal of fortune constitutes poetic justice for those who have oppressed the poor through heartless exploitation. Although less explicit than his predecessor Amos, Zephaniah condemns those whose wealth comes through the unjust treatment of others.

The announcement of the advent of the day of the Lord was initially introduced in the first oracle with God's threat to sweep all life from the earth (vv. 2-3), but was then reinforced by God's announcing a sacrifice at which Judah was to be the sacrificial offering and an invading enemy God's guests (v. 7). The progression from the creator's threatening to reverse creation to the high priest's sacrificing his people has now advanced to the portrayal of God as a military invader searching Jerusalem with lamps to find and destroy prey (v. 12).

Zephaniah ben Cushi has reversed the positive roles of God as the creator and sponsor of the system of ritual sacrifice. Such a reversal conforms to covenant rhetoric: "I call heaven and earth to witness against you today that I have set before you life and death, blessings and curses. Choose life" (Deut 30:19 NRSV). These words, used as part of a covenant renewal ritual, were known throughout the community, as were the blessings for obedience and curses for disobedience (v. 13; cf. Deuteronomy 28). The prophetic focus on the negative images of God was a clever reminder to Zephaniah's audience that their rejection of God's commandments was the reason why God was about to appear, not as savior, but as destroyer of the community. This second oracle's bold use of divine images, no less than its repetition of the key words "day" and "time" (vv. 7-10, 12), serves as prelude to what follows.

REFLECTIONS

This second oracle in the book of Zephaniah works to change Judah's perception of reality: from death-dealing complacency that blinds one to the truth to a courageous look at what lies ahead. The prophet, as always, tries to help his audience see and begin to confront what really is going on within their community. What often comes across as an abrasive, shrill voice is really a wake-up call into reality. And that reality within is one that is about to self-destruct or to be destroyed by forces over which the community no longer has any control. Consequently, in order even to begin to deal with the coming reversal of fortunes, the prophet works to change attitudes and perceptions about what actually is happening or soon will happen to the community.

1. Zephaniah ben Cushi is quite clever in initiating this process of change through what today might be called role reversal. The sacrificial system that was used to ensure the ongoing presence of God within the community is taken over by God's acting as high priest in order to offer up the sinful community as a sacrifice. The manipulators of the presence of the divinity become manipulated and punished instead by the very God whom the sacrificial system purported to hold close. Furthermore, the invited "consecrated guests," whose identity is left ambiguous, may have been Judah, invited to witness its own sacrifice, or, equally disheartening, its enemies, appointed as the instruments of God's punishment. However this element may be interpreted, the whole scene is presented in the service of an ultimate wake-up call to what is about to happen on the fast-approaching day of the Lord.

In its contemporary manifestation, such a bold statement in the name of confronting society or any individual community with the real truth about itself would more often than not be rejected and labeled obscene or ungodly. The bearer of the message would be judged deranged and would be dismissed with pejoratives like "whistle blower" and "loose cannon." This is the fate of the prophet today. Nevertheless, the message of this oracle is clear and still potent:

Reality, things as they truly are, must be faced if there is to be any hope of survival from the social, economic, or moral disasters about to come.

2. Howard Thurman, an African American preacher, mystic, and theologian wrote the reflections on Zephaniah for *The Interpreter's Bible.*[14] But he addressed elsewhere the issue of righting wrongs within his society, particularly in the light of role reversal or changing the way one can move from a relationship of inequality to one of equality. Thurman argued that changing a stereotypical role of being oppressed is the only way the underclass can end the dominance of the overclass and move into a relationship of equality. Although speaking then of racism, his universal approach to equality in life makes his insight applicable to other "isms," such as sexism and classism.

Using Jesus' admonition to "let your 'Yes' be 'Yes,' and your 'No,' 'No'" (Matt 5:37 NIV), Thurman counsels the disinherited always to speak the truth and stop using deceit as a means of survival in a master-servant relationship—that is, saying what is perceived to be inoffensive as a means of survival or to curry favor with a boss or persons claiming authority. By breaking this cycle of deceit, one has the opportunity to tip the scales of imbalance in one's favor, since one has abandoned the role of underdog based upon one's own acquiescence and has taken a stance of everyone's being on a level field, looking one another in the eye.

In a prose poem on the conflicting values of deception and honesty, Thurman captures Zephaniah ben Cushi's call for us to take the risk of confronting reality with changed perceptions of self, of God, and of God's will for us:

> The word—Be genuine!
> Let your words be yea, yea; nay, nay!
> All else, obscures truth,
> Tempting one to betray the Eternal.
> What a hard word for the weak!
> It brings down around their heads
> The great fortress of defense
> Against embattled power
> . . . .
>
> There is a point beyond which one cannot go,
> Without yielding his right to try again.
> To play God false to save one's skin,
> May jeopardize all there is that makes one whole,
> "What would a man give in exchange for his soul?"[15]

14. Howard Thurman, "Zephaniah," in *The Interpreter's Bible,* ed. George Buttrick, 12 vols. (Nashville: Abingdon, 1956) 6:1013-1034.
15. Howard Thurman, "The Greatest of These," in *Deep River and The Negro Spiritual Speaks of Life and Death* (Richmond, Ind.: Friends United, 1975) 50-52. Copyright © 1975 by Howard Thurman. Reprinted by permission of The Thurman Trust.

ZEPHANIAH 1:14-18, THE GREAT DAY OF THE LORD

NIV	NRSV

[14]"The great day of the LORD is near—
    near and coming quickly.
Listen! The cry on the day of the LORD will be bitter,
    the shouting of the warrior there.
[15]That day will be a day of wrath,
	[14] The great day of the LORD is near,
	    near and hastening fast;
	    the sound of the day of the LORD is bitter,
	    the warrior cries aloud there.
	[15] That day will be a day of wrath,
	    a day of distress and anguish,

NIV

a day of distress and anguish,
a day of trouble and ruin,
a day of darkness and gloom,
a day of clouds and blackness,
[16] a day of trumpet and battle cry
against the fortified cities
and against the corner towers.
[17] I will bring distress on the people
and they will walk like blind men,
because they have sinned against the LORD.
Their blood will be poured out like dust
and their entrails like filth.
[18] Neither their silver nor their gold
will be able to save them
on the day of the LORD's wrath.
In the fire of his jealousy
the whole world will be consumed,
for he will make a sudden end
of all who live in the earth."

NRSV

a day of ruin and devastation,
a day of darkness and gloom,
a day of clouds and thick darkness,
[16] a day of trumpet blast and battle cry
against the fortified cities
and against the lofty battlements.

[17] I will bring such distress upon people
that they shall walk like the blind;
because they have sinned against the LORD,
their blood shall be poured out like dust,
and their flesh like dung.
[18] Neither their silver nor their gold
will be able to save them
on the day of the LORD's wrath;
in the fire of his passion
the whole earth shall be consumed;
for a full, a terrible end
he will make of all the inhabitants of the
earth.

COMMENTARY

Zephaniah ben Cushi provides one of the great biblical portrayals of a judgment day in this poem. It opens abruptly with the simple statement that the great day is fast approaching, and then it clearly identifies the terrible presence of God as the destroying warrior (v. 14). The ensuing two verses supply graphic details about the frightening aspects of combat: darkness and gloom, trumpet and battle cry as the cities' defenses are being stormed (vv. 15-16). The focus in the concluding lines shifts from the elements of warfare to that of the devastation wrought upon the populace (vv. 17-18). This third oracle describes for sinful Judah and Jerusalem the frightful consequences of God's appearance.

Several different poetic devices contribute to the power of this statement. In the opening verse, God is identified with the avenging warrior, specifically causing thunderous noise and blood-curdling shrieks of warfare (v. 14b). The Hebrew word translated "sound" or "Listen! The cry" (קול qôl) is the same word that in hymnic texts signifies the very "sound"/"noise"/"voice" of God:

The voice of the LORD [קול יהוה qôl Yahweh] is over
the waters;
. . . .
The voice of the LORD is powerful;
the voice of the LORD is full of majesty.
(Ps 29:3-4 NRSV)

Zephaniah uses this Hebrew term with ritual connotations to describe the "day of the LORD."

Immediately following this riveting introduction to the book's third oracle, the prophet underscores the power of God's intervention by using ritual-like extended repetition of the word "day" (יום yôm):

That day will be a day of wrath,
a day of distress and anguish,
a day of ruin and devastation,
a day of darkness and gloom,
a day of clouds and thick darkness,
a day of trumpet blast and battle cry.
(1:15-16a NRSV)

Indeed, it may well have been this solemn repetition that led to the adaptation of these verses, through the Latin of the Vulgate translation, into the great medieval hymn *Dies irae* ("Day of Wrath"), composed by Thomas of Celano. The impact of this technique, along with the poem's emphasis on the event as a day of final judgment, ensured its use in Western liturgical tradition for the burial of the dead.

A third poetic technique employed in this oracle is the juxtaposition or intermingling of images—terrestrial and celestial, historical and cosmic, particular and universal—throughout, but particularly in the concluding section (vv. 17-18). God as divine warrior, for example, is described not only in the language of military activity—e.g., "trumpet blast" and "battle cry" as siege tactics (v. 16)— but also in the first-person speech: "I will bring such distress upon people/ . . . because they have sinned against the LORD" (v. 17). Just as in the ancient hymns of the exodus liberation (Exod 15:1-18, 21) and of holy wars to conquer the promised land (Judges 5), so also here the divine warrior controls the natural elements and uses "darkness and gloom . . . clouds and thick darkness" (v. 15*b*) from God's cosmic arsenal to do battle. One may discern the consequences of such an array of military and cosmic weaponry in distress-related blindness from the unnatural darkness and in the depiction of total carnage, scattered blood and flesh (v. 17). Further, no one can use a bribe as a means of escaping "the day of the LORD's wrath" (v. 18*a*). Finally, the "fire" of divine passion at this moment of vindication can neither be quenched nor contained, and hence it consumes the whole earth and all humankind (v. 18*b*). What begins as judgment against the covenant people Judah engulfs "all the inhabitants of the earth," thereby signifying that this particular occasion has devastating universal consequences.

The first biblical reference to the day of the Lord occurs in the book of Amos. That prophet impugned the northern kingdom's celebration of the day of the Lord as a cultic ceremony in which the people expected God to do battle with God's enemies (Amos 5:18-24). The second and third oracles of Zephaniah (Zeph 1:7-13, 14-18) along with other sections, such as the oracles against the nations (Zeph 2:5–3:8), expand Amos's critique of the misplaced confidence and joyful anticipation of God's appearance as divine warrior. In both situations, Amos and Zephaniah understood the people as enemies of God because of their disobedience to the commandments demanding loyalty to God and proper treatment of their kinsfolk.

The origins of the day of the Lord concept and related rituals are wrapped in obscurity. Some scholars think there was a ritual theophany symbolizing God's presence to vindicate the claims of the Sinai covenant. Such a ritual may have originated in ancient tribal rites of holy war (Judges 5) or equally ancient ceremonies for the new year ensuring God's rule for the good of the nation. This new year festival may be reflected in certain so-called enthronement hymns (Psalms 93; 96–99). In any event, the day of the Lord concept and ritual encompass God's rule over the nations as well as over Judah/Israel, thus providing a backdrop both for oracles against Judah and the nations and for oracles of salvation, each of which is present in the book of Zephaniah.

REFLECTIONS

The book of Zephaniah is best known for its portrayal of the day of the Lord, a final judgment day for those who have broken covenant with God. The brief, though graphic, depiction of doomsday for Judah drives home the fact that it is the moment of divine vindication, silencing once and for all those who have thought that God does not care for creation and community enough to intervene to mete out justice. Cosmic destruction is the focal point of the day of the Lord. This day is circumscribed, however, as a moment in time with a beginning and an end. Moreover, its placement in the collection of oracles indicates that there is a future.

Zephaniah's indictments of the people charge that the opposite of love is not hate, but indifference and apathy. God's judgment as divine justice shows just how much God does care and actively works to ensure that there will be a future, or more explicitly a future relationship, between creator and creature, deity and people. For those to whom justice has been denied, there is now the possibility—the "perhaps" of the ensuing oracle—of a future and a hope. The day of the Lord does not represent the end of the world or the suspension of natural laws. Zephaniah and the prophets who came after him link survival after this momentous event with a future establishment of divine rule.

When speaking of prophets like Zephaniah, Klaus Koch notes: "By criticizing social, political and cultic conditions as intolerable, they relativized the ultimate importance of the divinely given past. . . . The prophets certainly do not reject the view of a salvation history as such, but they do establish that Yahweh's work has still to be perfected. . . . In order really to know God as he is . . . one must experience the future revolution."[16] Out of the ashes arises, not nothingness, but the possibility of a new future.

16. Klaus Koch, *The Prophets,* vol. 1: *The Assyrian Period* (Philadelphia: Fortress, 1982) 163.

ZEPHANIAH 2:1-4, PLEAS TO JUDAH

NIV

2 Gather together, gather together,
O shameful nation,
2before the appointed time arrives
and that day sweeps on like chaff,
before the fierce anger of the LORD comes upon
you,
before the day of the LORD's wrath comes
upon you.
3Seek the LORD, all you humble of the land,
you who do what he commands.
Seek righteousness, seek humility;
perhaps you will be sheltered
on the day of the LORD's anger.

4Gaza will be abandoned
and Ashkelon left in ruins.
At midday Ashdod will be emptied
and Ekron uprooted.

NRSV

2 Gather together, gather,
O shameless nation,
2 before you are driven away
like the drifting chaff,[a]
before there comes upon you
the fierce anger of the LORD,
before there comes upon you
the day of the LORD's wrath.
3 Seek the LORD, all you humble of the land,
who do his commands;
seek righteousness, seek humility;
perhaps you may be hidden
on the day of the LORD's wrath.
4 For Gaza shall be deserted,
and Ashkelon shall become a desolation;
Ashdod's people shall be driven out at noon,
and Ekron shall be uprooted.

a Cn Compare Gk Syr: Heb *before a decree is born; like chaff a day has passed away*

COMMENTARY

The fourth oracle is addressed to sinful Judah in what appears to be a last prophetic effort to bring the community to its senses before the day of the Lord catastrophe actually occurs. This oracle concludes with a graphic portrayal (2:4) of the fate of Judah's Philistine neighbors as further inducement for the humble within the community to pray to God for their deliverance. It is as if the

divine pathos through its empathy with the covenant people were recoiling at the horror that was about to befall them. Through the prophet, God pleads with at least a faithful remnant that they turn and be saved from the dreadful destruction that is coming (2:3).

The prophetic oracle not only details the sins of the community that subject it to the sentence of death and destruction, which Zephaniah in his role as messenger of the divine judgment is duty-bound to deliver, but it also includes an exhortation for the people to turn from their sinful ways. It is not always clear whether the pleas originate from the personal empathy of the prophet for his neighbors or whether the divine empathy is being expressed, as, for example, Hosea 11 speaks of God's continued compassion for God's own rebellious people. Sometimes the community remains ungrateful despite all that God has done for it (cf. Mic 6:1-5) as a prelude to what is required of the community (Mic 6:6-8). Zephaniah ben Cushi appears to express concern for the citizens of Jerusalem, whose lives are about to be turned upside down (Zeph 1:10-11; 2:1-3).

2:1-2. This fourth oracle opens with an exhortation for the sinful nation to gather itself together, not for an assembly—but given the meaning of the first two words, based upon the Hebrew noun for "straw" (קַשׁ *qaš*), hence "gather"/"collect [straw]"—for burning. A threat is implied here, a threat that the gathering will enable a fire to blaze up (2:1). The nation finds itself in a flammable situation. The reality of just how close is that moment is driven home with the threefold repetition of the word "before,"[17] leading up in crescendo sequence to the words "the day of the LORD's wrath" (יום אַף־יהוה *yôm 'ap-Yahweh,* v. 2).

2:3. The focus of the oracle narrows down to the "humble of the land," who might survive the coming conflagration. The humble (ענו *'ānāw*) are those people who have remained faithful to God, those led and taught by God (cf. Ps 25:9). They are urged to prepare themselves for the advancing onslaught by fulfilling three moral demands: to seek God, righteousness, and humility (ענוה *'ānāwâ*). Prophetic oracles often contain admonitions to change and to take up positive behavior—in other words, to turn and repent. One of the most famous threefold admonitions is found in Mic 6:8:

He has told you, O Mortal, what is good;
  and what does the LORD require of you
but to do justice, and to love kindness,
  and to walk humbly with your God? (NRSV)

Amos concludes his declaration that the day of the Lord would be a disaster for Israel with the equally well-known admonition: "But let justice roll down like waters,/ and righteousness like an ever-flowing stream" (Amos 5:24 NRSV). Zephaniah also provides constructive advice for times such as these (vv. 1-3).

The possibility of survival for the humble faithful is held out in the word "perhaps" (אוּלי *'ûlay,* v. 3c). The same word in this usage appears in Jeremiah in anticipation of coming disaster (Jer 20:10; 26:3). Also in Jeremiah, the possibility of being "hidden" on that day is expressed in Jeremiah's oracles of promise to his rescuer, Ebed-melech the Ethiopian: "But I will save you on that day, says the LORD . . . you shall have your life as a prize of war, because you have trusted in me, says the LORD" (Jer 39:17a, 18b NRSV). The promise here is that Ebed-melech may survive the coming disaster. His life, seen through the perspective of a combatant, is his booty or prize of war. In the face of impending doom, there is hope for the future from the merciful God.

2:4. The first word of this verse is the conjunctive particle "for" (כי *kî*), which grammatically links this verse with what precedes it, thereby making it serve as an illustration of the fate awaiting wayward Judah.[18] Zephaniah ben Cushi's last cry to Judah concludes with a poignant personification of the neighboring Philistine cities as an abandoned, defenseless woman. This metaphor provides further motivation for Zephaniah's hearers to join the humble in obedience to God as a possible means of survival. The extended imagery is intended to match deuteronomic exhortative speech (cf. Jeremiah 39 on Ebed-melech's fate). The emphasis on eliciting a response from the hearer helps to explain the characteristic piling up of words and expressions, as opposed to the terse style of the prophetic oracle. Here the poetic artistry is not so much a message of impending doom as it is part of deuteronomic reform preaching, attempting to elicit a change within the recalcitrant community.

The prophet pulls out all the stops in his sermonic repertoire to catch and hold the attention of his audience. Five different elements or techniques help Zephaniah achieve this goal: (1) The

---

17. The Hebrew of the first of these three phrases reads "[before] a decree is born" (לדת חק *ledet ḥōq*). The NRSV's "[before] you are driven away" is based on an emendation of the Hebrew text.

18. See James Muilenberg, "The Linguistic and Rhetorical Usages of the Particle כי in the Old Testament," *HUCA* 32 (1961) 135-60.

introductory "for" alerts the audience what follows addresses them, even though foreign neighbors are mentioned. "Ah" (הוי hôy), with which v. 5 begins, introduces a whole new oracle form: oracles against the nations. (2) Each of the four fates is introduced in a staccato manner, with the name of each of the cities, not unlike the impact achieved by the fourfold repetition of "day" in the oracle on the day of the Lord (1:15-16a). (3) Chiastic (crisscross) symmetry also binds the verse together, since in Hebrew the first and last cities, Gaza and Ekron, begin with the same letter of the Hebrew alphabet, ע ('ayin), and the two middle cities, Ashkelon and Ashdod, each begin with the Hebrew letter א ('āleph). (4) Alliteration (repetition of similar sounds) and punning between the first and last cities provide a sonic framework in Hebrew: "Gaza shall be deserted [עזה עזובה 'azzâ 'ăzzûbâ] . . . and Ekron shall be uprooted (ועקרון תעקר wĕ 'eqrôn tē 'āqēr). (5) Perhaps most striking of all is the extended use of the metaphor of the wife in various stages of distress or bereavement for each of the four cities: jilted before marriage; abandoned after marriage; divorced; and made barren.

The marriage metaphor applied to Judah/Israel is found elsewhere in prophetic literature (Isa 54:4-8; Jeremiah 3; Hosea 1–3), but it had not been used of other nations. Perhaps in doing so here Zephaniah is not only emphasizing the broken covenantal relationship between God and the people, as in the reversal of relationships in the call to ritual sacrifice (1:7) and in the day of the Lord itself (1:12a, 14-16), but also envisioning a new historical role for the nations.

REFLECTIONS

1. This fourth oracle unit from Zephaniah ben Cushi has a significantly changed tone; it is more an impassioned plea than were the earlier stern warnings. Does this changed attitude reflect the prophet's feelings toward his own people, or can one speak of a divine empathy or pathos here? The Jewish exegete and theologian Abraham Heschel wrote of the divine pathos in contradistinction to the Greek philosophical view of a distantly removed and passionless God:

> The preoccupation with justice, the passion with which the prophets condemn injustice is rooted in their sympathy with divine pathos. The chief characteristic of prophetic thought is the primacy of God's involvement in history. History is the domain with which the prophets' minds are occupied. They are moved by a responsibility for society, by a sensitivity to what the moment demands. . . . To the biblical mind the implication of goodness is mercy. Pathos, concern for the world, is the very ethos of God. This ethical sensitivity of God—not the ethical in and for itself—is reflected in the prophets' declarations. Prophetic morality rests upon both a divine command and a divine concern. Its ultimate appeal is not the reasonableness of the moral law, but to the fact that God has demanded it and its fulfillment is a realization of God's concern.[19]

2. Scripture witnesses to God's initiating and reaching out to establish a relationship with nature and with humankind. Throughout Zephaniah there is some ambiguity, as in this opening call, for example, where it is unclear whether the prophet intends to call the people to "gather together" for safety, to better hear his message, or to be better kindling for the coming conflagration. But this ambiguity adds to the passion of the response to the call—a good homiletical device—and passion rather than apathy is at the heart of what the prophet is addressing. Behind the prophet stands God! Positive advice is given ("seek"), and a promise is proffered ("perhaps"), along with further motivation via the example of the fate of the Philistine cities. In other words, the prophet works to achieve the ultimate goal of making a way for the people's survival. What stands out is the empathy, or shared pain, behind the exhortatory pleas of the prophet and of the one in whose name he speaks.

19. Abraham J. Heschel, *The Prophets,* vol. 1 (New York: Harper & Row, 1962) 218-19.

Howard Thurman expresses a similar thought, but from the human side of the results of pain shared with God set forth in the Spiritual "Were You There When They Crucified My Lord?":

At last there is worked out the kind of identification in suffering that makes the cross universal in its deepest meaning. It cuts across differences of religion, race, class, and language, and dares to affirm that the key to the mystery of the cross is found deep within the heart of the experience itself. "Were you there when they crucified my Lord?/ Were you there when they crucified my Lord?/ Oh! sometimes it causes me to tremble, tremble, tremble;/ Were you there when they crucified my Lord?" The inference is that the singer was *there:* "I know what he went through because I have met him in the high places of pain, and I claim him as my brother." Here again the approach is not a conceptual one, but rather an experimental grasping of the quality of Jesus' experience, by virtue of the racial frustration of the singers.[20]

20. Thurman, *Deep River and The Negro Spiritual Speaks of Life and Death,* 27.

ORACLES AGAINST THE NATIONS

OVERVIEW

The second section of Zephaniah is a special form of prophetic speech called "oracle against the (foreign) nations." It is a pronouncement of doom against Israel and Judah's neighbors because of their sins against God and God's elect. This particular form of prophetic speech is found in Isaiah 13–23, Jeremiah 46–51, and Amos 1–2. These oracles can be recognized easily, because they are addressed to the nations and often open with the exclamatory cry הוי (*hôy,* "Ah"/"Alas"/"Woe!"). This type of oracle is closely related to the ideology of holy war and the day of the Lord tradition because they, too, proclaim that God strides forth as the divine warrior to punish those who violate God's covenant. The curse uttered against a foreign nation appeared to be a sign of blessing for either Israel or Judah.

In the eighth century BCE, however, the prophet Amos began to change this perception when he listed Israel as one of the enemies of God. The oracles against the nations in Amos 1–2 served as an introduction to an enumeration of the northern kingdom's sins against God and as an announcement of its destruction. Amos reiterated this idea that the sinful elect were also subject to God's wrath and that ritual celebrations of God's appearance in the midst of the community, such as on the day of the Lord, would no longer be festivals of joyful blessing, but of defeat and gloom (Amos 5:18-24).

Zephaniah ben Cushi understood the day of the Lord tradition as a fast-approaching disaster for Judah and used it as a preaching tool on behalf of the late–seventh-century BCE deuteronomic reform movement (Zeph 1:7–2:4). Zephaniah also placed the tradition within a universal context (Zeph 1:2-6). His oracles against the nations provide still another extension of the consequences of the day of the Lord for all peoples. The divine wrath spills over onto the nations (Zeph 2:5-15), but this universal extension of doom also becomes the occasion and the opportunity for universal salvation (Zeph 3:6-13).

ZEPHANIAH 2:5-15, ANNOUNCEMENT OF JUDGMENT ON THE NATIONS

NIV	NRSV

[5]Woe to you who live by the sea,
    O Kerethite people;
the word of the LORD is against you,
    O Canaan, land of the Philistines.
 	
"I will destroy you,
    and none will be left."
[6]The land by the sea, where the Kerethites[a] dwell,
 	
a6 The meaning of the Hebrew for this word is uncertain.
	[5] Ah, inhabitants of the seacoast,
	    you nation of the Cherethites!
	The word of the LORD is against you,
	    O Canaan, land of the Philistines;
	    and I will destroy you until no inhabitant is
	        left.
	[6] And you, O seacoast, shall be pastures,
	    meadows for shepherds
	    and folds for flocks.

NIV

will be a place for shepherds and sheep pens.
[7]It will belong to the remnant of the house of
Judah;
there they will find pasture.
In the evening they will lie down
in the houses of Ashkelon.
The LORD their God will care for them;
he will restore their fortunes.[a]

[8]"I have heard the insults of Moab
and the taunts of the Ammonites,
who insulted my people
and made threats against their land.
[9]Therefore, as surely as I live,"
declares the LORD Almighty, the God of Israel,
"surely Moab will become like Sodom,
the Ammonites like Gomorrah—
a place of weeds and salt pits,
a wasteland forever.
The remnant of my people will plunder them;
the survivors of my nation will inherit their
land."

[10]This is what they will get in return for their
pride,
for insulting and mocking the people of the
LORD Almighty.
[11]The LORD will be awesome to them
when he destroys all the gods of the land.
The nations on every shore will worship him,
every one in its own land.

[12]"You too, O Cushites,[b]
will be slain by my sword."

[13]He will stretch out his hand against the north
and destroy Assyria,
leaving Nineveh utterly desolate
and dry as the desert.
[14]Flocks and herds will lie down there,
creatures of every kind.
The desert owl and the screech owl
will roost on her columns.
Their calls will echo through the windows,
rubble will be in the doorways,
the beams of cedar will be exposed.
[15]This is the carefree city
that lived in safety.
She said to herself,

a7 Or *will bring back their captives*   b12 That is, people from the
upper Nile region

NRSV

[7] The seacoast shall become the possession
of the remnant of the house of Judah,
on which they shall pasture,
and in the houses of Ashkelon
they shall lie down at evening.
For the LORD their God will be mindful of them
and restore their fortunes.

[8] I have heard the taunts of Moab
and the revilings of the Ammonites,
how they have taunted my people
and made boasts against their territory.
[9] Therefore, as I live, says the LORD of hosts,
the God of Israel,
Moab shall become like Sodom
and the Ammonites like Gomorrah,
a land possessed by nettles and salt pits,
and a waste forever.
The remnant of my people shall plunder them,
and the survivors of my nation shall possess
them.
[10] This shall be their lot in return for their pride,
because they scoffed and boasted
against the people of the LORD of hosts.
[11] The LORD will be terrible against them;
he will shrivel all the gods of the earth,
and to him shall bow down,
each in its place,
all the coasts and islands of the nations.

[12] You also, O Ethiopians,[a]
shall be killed by my sword.

[13] And he will stretch out his hand against the
north,
and destroy Assyria;
and he will make Nineveh a desolation,
a dry waste like the desert.
[14] Herds shall lie down in it,
every wild animal;[b]
the desert owl[c] and the screech owl[c]
shall lodge on its capitals;
the owl[d] shall hoot at the window,
the raven[e] croak on the threshold;
for its cedar work will be laid bare.
[15] Is this the exultant city

a Or *Nubians*; Heb *Cushites*   b Tg Compare Gk: Heb *nation*
c Meaning of Heb uncertain   d Cn: Heb *a voice*   e Gk Vg: Heb
desolation

NIV	NRSV

"I am, and there is none besides me."
 What a ruin she has become,
     a lair for wild beasts!
 All who pass by her scoff
     and shake their fists.
	that lived secure,
	 that said to itself,
	     "I am, and there is no one else"?
	 What a desolation it has become,
	     a lair for wild animals!
	 Everyone who passes by it
	     hisses and shakes the fist.

COMMENTARY

The fifth oracle opens with the distinctive wail or cry of curse/lament, "Ah!" or "Woe" (הוי *hôy*, v. 5*a*). The nations over whom this cry is uttered are listed according to their geographical proximity to Judah, moving outward according to the points of the compass: the Philistine cities along the seacoast to the west (vv. 5-7); Moab and Ammon beyond the Jordan Valley and the Dead Sea to the east (vv. 8-11); the distant nation of Cush/Ethiopia to the south (v. 12); and Assyria to the north (vv. 13-15). The near neighbors sharing the relatively narrow Palestinian land bridge are named first, followed by the great powers in Africa to the south and then Asia to the north. The cry uttered by the prophet against the nations expresses a range of human emotions—from anger for what they have done against Judah to lament over the destruction that awaits them for their deeds. One may compare it to the priestly ritual curse (ארור *ʾārûr*) leveled against covenant law breakers (Deut 17:13-26; 28:15-20). Isaiah effectively used this cry to attack the moral depravity among his own people: "Woe [*hôy*] to those who call evil good and good evil" (Isa 5:21-22 NRSV; cf. Isa 5:8, 11, 18, 20). Whether used as the ultimate human invective or a profound funerary lament (cf. 1 Kgs 13:30; Jer 34:5), this cry constitutes an effective verbal warning of tragedy that awaits.

2:5-7. The Philistine cities and inhabitants of the region (originally from Crete ["Cherethites," v. 5*a*]) are threatened with extinction and their land left only as pasturage (vv. 5-6). The concluding line of this segment of the oracle, however, speaks of a restored or surviving remnant of Judah who will possess this abandoned region (v. 7). This expectation may reflect another aspect of the Josianic reform movement, which included not only a return to pre-Assyrian observance of the Yahwistic religion, but also reclamation of lands lost during the Assyrian occupation (2 Kings 23). In the preceding oracle (vv. 1-4), the Philistine cities were cited as motivation to the remnant of Judah to reform itself as a means of survival (v. 4). In the present oracle, the cry against this territory has a positive message: The area will become a refuge for the remnant of Judah.

2:8-11. As for the neighbors to the east, Moab and Ammon, the fifth oracle charges them with taunts and threats against God's elect and expansions within the land of promise (v. 8), for which God will send destruction upon them (vv. 9-11). The Septuagint translates the MT's "their [my people's] territory" as "my territory" (v. 8*b*), making clear that expansion at Judah's expense violates the Sinai covenant's protection of that territory and thus constitutes an offense against God. This claim may reflect that Josiah's political as well as religious changes had been put into place ("survivors of my nation shall possess them" [v. 9]) with iconoclastic reforms (v. 11).[21] The idea of Yahweh's sovereignty over the nations works itself out in the destruction of the nations' gods (Ps 82:6-7).

2:12. The Nile Valley kingdoms to the south, Egypt and Cush/Ethiopia, are only briefly noted and remembered as the Cushite (or Nubian, as they called themselves) 25th Dynasty of Egypt (751–656 BCE). Egypt loomed large in the Hebrew imagination, not only as the ancestors' place of bondage, but also as the traditional place of sanctuary during political distress (1 Kgs 11:26-40) and of sustenance in the time of famine (Genesis

---

21. Duane L. Christensen, "Zephaniah 2:4-15: A Theological Basis for Josiah's Program of Political Expansion," *CBQ* 46 (1984) 669-82; Adele Berlin, *Zephaniah*, AB 25A (New York: Doubleday, 1994) 119.

37–50). In addition, Egypt was Judah's military ally (see Hezekiah's alliance with "Tirhakah, king of Cush," 2 Kgs 19:9). Isaiah describes in graphic detail the Nubian emissaries' return home "beyond the rivers of Nubia" (Isa 18:1, author's trans.; cf. NRSV, "Ethiopia"; NIV, "Cush" [כוש *kûš*]) after their meeting with Hezekiah.

The brevity of the oracle in v. 12 may reflect proximity to the events surrounding Hezekiah, Isaiah, the Cushite pharaoh, and the Assyrian Sennacherib's lifting of the siege of Jerusalem (2 Kings 19), as well as the capture of the Egyptian/Cushite religious capital of Thebes by the Assyrian Ashurbanipal (633 BCE). The fall of Thebes was well noted in prophetic literature, especially by Zephaniah's contemporary Nahum, who, while singing the defeat of the Assyrian capital, Nineveh (621 BCE), could lament: "Are you better than Thebes [נא אמון *Nō'-'āmôn*]/ that sat by the Nile,/ with water around her,/ her rampart a sea,/ water her wall?/ Ethiopia [*kûš*] was her strength,/ Egypt too . . ." (Nah 3:8-9*a* NRSV). The interchangeability of Nubia/Cush with Egypt is also part of Israelite hymnic tradition as it recounts the mighty acts of God on Israel's behalf: "He struck all the first born in Egypt,/ the first issue of their strength in the tents of Ham" (Ps 78:51 NRSV). Therefore, Zeph 2:12 is not, as some have suggested, merely an editorial gloss to fill up the points of the compass in this set of oracles against the nations. Rather, it evoked strong recollections of the Cushite rulers of Egypt.[22]

2:13-15. The oracle against Assyria turns to the north, the traditional route of invading armies. One of Jeremiah's visions included a symbolic cauldron spilling over from the north (Jer 1:13), followed by the divine threat, "Out of the north disaster shall break out on all the inhabitants of the land" (Jer 1:14 NRSV). Similarly, Zephaniah uses this final oracle against the nations for his longest and most heated word against an old and feared aggressor: "And he will stretch out his hand against the north,/ and destroy Assyria;/ and he will make Nineveh a desolation,/ a dry waste like the desert" (v. 13). Assyria was the destroyer of Israel, the northern kingdom, and the oppressor of surviving Judah in the south. Zephaniah was in the forefront of this effort, and his oracles on the day of the Lord sought to revive among Judah the covenant loyalty that might save it and provide hope for the future.

The oracle against Assyria fits into this same program by designating Assyria's sin as arrogance against God (v. 15*a*). It provides a theological and political basis for removing all aspects of the Assyrian period of rule in the land. This unit, therefore, concludes with an extended statement about Assyria's pride in placing itself above God: "Is this the exultant city/ that lived secure,/ that said to itself,/ 'I am, and there is no one else'?" (v. 15*a*). On the international (universal) scene, this insolent thought may be compared to the Jerusalemite who thought God did not care (1:12). Zephaniah joins his contemporary Nahum in exulting over the fall and destruction of Assyria's capital, Nineveh. Nahum's "All who hear the news about you/ clap their hands over you" (Nah 3:19*b* NRSV), parallels Zephaniah's, "Everyone who passes by it/ hisses and shakes the fist" (v. 15*c*). At this point, the oracle against the nations is both a curse against those defeated by God and a blessing for God's people in their time of distress.

---

22. Contra J. J. M. Roberts, *Nahum, Habakkuk, and Zephaniah,* OTL (Louisville: Westminster/John Knox, 1991) 202. For other interpretations, see Adele Berlin, *Zephaniah,* AB 25A (New York: Doubleday, 1994) 111-14, 120-24. The graphic depiction of Nubian emissaries returning to their homeland in Isa 18:1-2, 7 suggests a familiarity with the Cushites. It correctly locates them in the upper reaches of the Nile, where the Blue and the White Niles converge, soon joined by the Atbara near the fifth cataract (Isa 18:1). It goes on to note their reputation as conquering warriors, their distinctive height, and their "smooth" (NRSV), "smooth-skinned" (NIV) appearance (Isa 18:2). The Hebrew word behind this last characteristic feature is מורט (*môrāṭ*), used also of the "burnished bronze" (NRSV and NIV) or glistening vessels of Solomon's Temple (1 Kgs 7:45). The prophet means to indicate that the darkly bronzed skin of the Nubians also glistens in the sun. African American writer James Baldwin, in recounting his growing up in Harlem, attests to this racial characteristic. Of boys playing stick ball in the street, he notes, "The cold sun made their faces like copper and brass" (*Go Tell It on the Mountain* [New York: Dial Press, 1963] 32).

For ancient Near Eastern references to the Cushites throughout the biblical period, see Robert Bennett, "Africa and the Biblical Period," *HTR* 64 (1971) 483-500. See also *Ancient Civilizations of Africa,* ed. G. Mokhtar (Berkeley: University of California Press, 1990) 33-61, on the "Africanness" of the ancient Egyptians.

REFLECTIONS

1. The oracles against the nations affirm God's rule over the nations. They include two often divergent perspectives. The one that predominates in the prophetic oracles sees the nations as enemies encroaching upon the political and territorial integrity of the people of God. There is, however, another perspective on the nations, which views them as a family of nations of which the people of God are also members. Hints of this ecumenical aspect are found in the ancient Genesis accounts of Noah's sons repopulating the earth and in the accompanying chart or table of nations (Genesis 9–10). Some of the temple hymnody reflects this latter point of view, such as Psalm 47, of a more nationalistic bent, and Psalm 82, a prophetic call for universal justice. This range of biblical testimony attests to both the human lens through which the divine word is refracted and at times a vision that seems to be less self-conscious of its identity as the people of God.

As lord of the nations, God holds all peoples responsible for what is right and wrong. Thus Amos 1–2 condemns Israel's neighbors for their excesses in warfare. Also, the prophet Nahum can exult over the fall of the hated Assyrian capital, Nineveh, while at the same time uttering words of regret at the fall of Cushite Thebes (Nah 3:8-9). It appears that the endemic concern for self is held in check so that concern for other human beings can be expressed, especially in the oracles against the nations. In these oracles, the cry, "Ah!" is truly a funereal lament of loss or at least sympathy for the agony of another people. Such is the perspective implied in Zephaniah ben Cushi's lament over Cush (2:12) and even in Isaiah's grudging admiration, more lament than curse, of Hezekiah's ally, Cush (Isa 18:1).

2. But what of the real anger that spills over when nation goes to war with nation or two people are in conflict with each other? The oracles against the nations raise this issue for us today, especially where nationalism and issues of cultural or racial domination are involved. Anger at and resistance to oppression of any kind cause people to lash out at their offending neighbor and lead that neighbor to strike back at the threat. The prophetic oracles of doom against the nations include a rich store of invectives, curses, and punishments to draw from as the prophet seeks ways to express the divine anger as well as the human hurt. This storehouse is the repertoire of ritual curses leveled against covenant law breakers, as found, for example in Deuteronomy 28, but also in the curse or imprecatory psalms (Pss 58:6-9; 109:6-20; 137:9; 139:19-22).

C. S. Lewis's comments on the curse psalms may help us to deal with the matter of expressing anger in the face of oppression and, still worse, the suppression of anger. Lewis wrote during the World War II air raids on London and had to engage his nation's anger at its attackers. The language of the first half of the twentieth century may seem dated today, but the truth of his comments on this issue is still vital. He makes two salient points about the biblical cursing of one's enemy: First, while the offender may be guilty of provoking one's anger, it is a worse crime to forbid the offended one to protest his or her situation with an expression of anger. Second, it is equally appalling—Lewis calls it "a most alarming symptom"—when there is an absence of anger as indignation in the face of inhumanity against other human beings:

> For we can still see, in the worst of their maledictions, how these old poets were, in a sense, near to God. Though hideously distorted by the human instrument, something of the Divine voice can be heard in these passages . . . doubtless [God] has for the sin of those enemies just the implacable hostility which the poets express. . . . In that way the relentlessness of the Psalmists is far nearer to one side of the truth than many modern attitudes which can be mistaken, by those who hold them, for Christian charity.[23]

23. C. S. Lewis, *Reflections on the Psalms* (New York: Harcourt Brace, 1986) 32.

ZEPHANIAH 3:1-5, THE WICKEDNESS OF JERUSALEM

NIV

3 Woe to the city of oppressors,
rebellious and defiled!
[2] She obeys no one,
she accepts no correction.
She does not trust in the LORD,
she does not draw near to her God.
[3] Her officials are roaring lions,
her rulers are evening wolves,
who leave nothing for the morning.
[4] Her prophets are arrogant;
they are treacherous men.
Her priests profane the sanctuary
and do violence to the law.
[5] The LORD within her is righteous;
he does no wrong.
Morning by morning he dispenses his justice,
and every new day he does not fail,
yet the unrighteous know no shame.

NRSV

3 Ah, soiled, defiled,
oppressing city!
[2] It has listened to no voice;
it has accepted no correction.
It has not trusted in the LORD;
it has not drawn near to its God.

[3] The officials within it
are roaring lions;
its judges are evening wolves
that leave nothing until the morning.
[4] Its prophets are reckless,
faithless persons;
its priests have profaned what is sacred,
they have done violence to the law.
[5] The LORD within it is righteous;
he does no wrong.
Every morning he renders his judgment,
each dawn without fail;
but the unjust knows no shame.

COMMENTARY

The oracles against the nations near their conclusion with an oracle against Jerusalem, specifying the sins that make it an enemy of God and subject it to divine judgment. This sixth oracle quite pointedly opens with the traditional lament/curse cry against the nations: "Ah [הוי *hôy*], soiled, defiled,/ oppressing city!" (v. 1). What follows is an extended bill of indictment, first summarized in general terms, that Jerusalem has rebuked the messenger-prophet and rejected God (v. 2). Then the specific community leaders who have broken God's law are named (vv. 2-4). This unit ends with a statement affirming God's continuing presence for good, but acknowledges the persistence of the unjust (v. 5).

This oracle highlights Zephaniah ben Cushi's particular interest in Jerusalem and the failure of its leaders to guide the city on the path of obedience to God. The verses pinpoint the corrupting influences of Jerusalem's designated leaders:

judges, prophets, and priests. Following in the tradition of Isaiah (Isa 1:21-26) and Micah (Mic 3:1-11), Zephaniah exposes the corruption in high places, causing the populace to ignore the prophetic "voice" (קול *qôl*) or word of God, to reject the wisdom counselor's advice or "correction" (מוסר *mûsār*), and to disobey the priestly torah or instruction (תורה *tôrâ*) to trust in and draw near to (i.e., worship) God (v. 2). The corruption of the city results directly from its leaders' failure to live up to their designated roles and responsibilities (cf. Jer 18:18; Zephaniah's special concern for Jerusalem may be reflected in a kindred oracle from Ezekiel [Ezek 22:23-30]).

The prophet reiterates the failure of the leaders (vv. 3-4) by exposing their dereliction of duty in contrast to God's faithfulness and righteousness (v. 5). The contrast is between the failed, now illegitimate rule of the debased rulers and the life-giving presence of the God of justice. The justice system receives special attention, the corrupt courts run by officials likened to "roaring lions" and judges characterized as "evening wolves" (v. 3). The temple is no better, since prophets cannot be relied upon to speak the truth or priests to know and teach the law (v. 4). By contrast, "The LORD within it [the city] is righteous;/ he does no wrong" (v. 5a) and is as dependable as the rising sun—or better, is the one responsible for the order of nature and of society: "Every morning he renders his judg-ment,/ each dawn without fail" (v. 5b). Morning was the time when justice was dispensed at the city gates or the open space within the walled city. The rulers held court, but even if corruption prevailed in that designated space—so the prophet affirms—the one who rules the heavens and is responsible for sustaining the natural order will see that justice ultimately prevails. This affirmation concludes the oracle on the wicked city and sets the stage for the last oracle of judgment in these collected words of Zephaniah ben Cushi.

REFLECTIONS

1. Charles DeGaulle, leader of the Free French government in exile during the Second World War, contrasted his status as the legitimate voice of France against what he called the legal, but illegitimate, voice of the Vichy government, which the Nazi invaders had set up during their occupation of France. The image of sinful Jerusalem calls to mind a similar contrast between the failed and hence illegitimate rulers who were the legal guardians of the society and the as yet unacknowledged legitimate rule of the city, which the prophet affirmed was being exercised by God (2:5).

In this sixth oracle, Zephaniah ben Cushi challenges us to recognize the difference between established guardians and leaders of society and the fulfillment of the duties they have been called to exercise within society. There is often a gap between the legitimate expectations of persons, for example, seeking justice in the courts, and the reality or their perception of being denied a fair hearing or the rudiments of due process. Prophet, priest, and wisdom counselor in ancient Jerusalem translate today into government, which includes the justice system, religious institutions, and the humanistic sciences, including medical, psychological, and social services. Earlier on, the prophet (1:10-13) let us know that this infrastructure also included business, finance, and industry.

In his comparing leaders to "roaring lions" and "evening wolves" who leave nothing until the morning (3:3), the prophet underscores the problem of greed. The soul of a community and the fabric of a society cannot continue intact if justice, right dealings, respect, and honesty are lacking among its leaders.

2. During the civil rights movement of the 1950s and 1960s, Dr. Martin Luther King, Jr., spoke out for the legitimate claims of African Americans and others against the illegitimacy of legally established discriminatory laws and practices. The condemnation of what is wrong is not the only word of the prophetic voice, for that voice also addresses the reality of God's continuing presence in life. It is just as important to point to and witness on behalf of the divine hand still at work so as to keep hope alive and to energize the reformers.

James A. Forbes, Jr., pastor of the Riverside Church, New York City, captured the essence of this affirming faith in his 1990 prayer commemorating Martin Luther King, Jr., Day: "Because our needs are so great today, and your care so constant, we know that you are rebuilding the network of compassion around new visionaries who you have assembled for this hour. Surprise us with the discovery of how much power we have to make a difference in our day:—a difference in the way citizens meet, greet, respect, and protect the rights of each other.—a difference in the breadth of our vision of what is possible in humanization, reconciliation, and equalization of results in our great city.—a difference in the way government, business, and labor can work together, for justice and social enrichment.—a difference in our response to the needy, and a difference in our appreciation for those who give of themselves for the surviving and thriving of our beautiful people . . . This is our fervent and sincere prayer. Amen."[24]

24. James M. Washington, ed., *Conversations with God: Two Centuries of Prayer by African Americans* (New York: HarperCollins, 1994) 260-61.

ZEPHANIAH 3:6-8, CONCERN FOR JERUSALEM AND ANNOUNCEMENT OF UNIVERSAL JUDGMENT

NIV

[6]"I have cut off nations;
 their strongholds are demolished.
I have left their streets deserted,
 with no one passing through.
Their cities are destroyed;
 no one will be left—no one at all.
[7]I said to the city,
 'Surely you will fear me
 and accept correction!'
Then her dwelling would not be cut off,
 nor all my punishments come upon her.
But they were still eager
 to act corruptly in all they did.
[8]Therefore wait for me," declares the LORD,
 "for the day I will stand up to testify.[a]
I have decided to assemble the nations,
 to gather the kingdoms
and to pour out my wrath on them—
 all my fierce anger.
The whole world will be consumed
 by the fire of my jealous anger.

[a]8 Septuagint and Syriac; Hebrew *will rise up to plunder*

NRSV

[6] I have cut off nations;
 their battlements are in ruins;
I have laid waste their streets
 so that no one walks in them;
their cities have been made desolate,
 without people, without inhabitants.
[7] I said, "Surely the city[a] will fear me,
 it will accept correction;
it will not lose sight[b]
 of all that I have brought upon it."
But they were the more eager
 to make all their deeds corrupt.

[8] Therefore wait for me, says the LORD,
 for the day when I arise as a witness.
For my decision is to gather nations,
 to assemble kingdoms,
to pour out upon them my indignation,
 all the heat of my anger;
for in the fire of my passion
 all the earth shall be consumed.

[a] Heb *it* [b] Gk Syr: Heb *its dwelling will not be cut off*

COMMENTARY

The seventh poetic unit continues the theme of the preceding segment, the wickedness of Jerusalem, but with a significant difference. Here, God addresses the city directly in first-person speech, and—instead of listing the awful things it has done to precipitate the divine wrath—God recounts the divine acts of destruction upon other cities in the expressed hope that Jerusalem would learn therefrom and change its ways (vv. 6-7a). However, instead of accepting correction, the city continues along its path to oblivion (v. 7b), so that God announces a final sentence of universal destruction by fire (v. 8). This final oracle is similar in tone and in intent—up to a point—to the divine pleas to Judah (2:1-4) that followed the announcement of the cataclysmic day of the Lord (1:14-18) and that also concluded the book of Zephaniah's first major unit: oracles against Judah and Jerusalem (1:2–2:4). In both places, a final word to turn and perhaps be saved is uttered to the city: "Seek the LORD . . . " (2:3 NRSV); and "fear me . . . accept correction" (3:7). The motivation to change in 2:4 was the metaphor of the woman in distress (the Philistine cities) and in 3:6 the divine warrior's ravishing of the cities (unnamed). A final and more ominous parallel occurs in the call to assemble as the occasion for the final, universal conflagration (2:1 and 3:8*b*).

3:6-7. This seventh oracle opens with God's speaking directly to Jerusalem, recounting the way God has destroyed the enemy cities in order that Jerusalem might learn that God does indeed care and will act to vindicate the divine will against scoffers in Judah who set themselves above God (1:12-13) and against blasphemers among the nations (2:10-11, Moab and Ammon; 2:15, Assyria). The language used in v. 6 returns to the traditional terminology used in judgment curses against Judah (1:3*b*, 4*b*) and against the nations (2:4*a*, 9*a*, 13*a*, 15*b*). Although the Hebrew behind the English of v. 7 is obscure, the sense is clearly that all of the foregoing evidence of God's active presence should awaken the city to a sense of the error of its way and its thoughts about God. From this, the people of Jerusalem will understand why destruction is about to befall them as well. A key

word (v. 7) borrowed from the wisdom tradition is "correction" (מוסר *mûsār*), an openness to learning from experience and from observation, an ability the people sorely lack.

3:8. The final word on the judgment about to befall Jerusalem and the nations is introduced by "therefore" (לכן *lākēn*), a word closely associated with the announcement of the sentence handed down to those judged guilty of sins against God or God's anointed ones.[25] This judgment reintroduces the eschatological language of the day of the Lord (יום־יהוה *yôm-Yahweh)* as the oracle ends on the note of the coming universal judgment: "the day when I arise as a witness."

The call to assembly at the conclusion of the oracles against the nations parallels the earlier call for Judah to assemble for judgment (2:1). This is the moment when Judah and Jerusalem share the fate of the nations, since they are now counted among the enemies of God. Yet, from another perspective on the unity of the family of nations (Genesis 9–10), the specific punishment of this people can have only negative consequences for the rest of the nations. The divine judgment from the Lord of the earth can only be universal in scope. Recalling the Noah covenant (Gen 9:1-11), promising that a deluge shall never again destroy the earth, the prophet sees "the fire" next time(3:8*b*; see also 1:18*b*)!

---

25. As in Isa 8:7; Jer 5:14; 7:20; Mic 3:4. See Claus Westermann, *Basic Forms of Prophetic Speech* (Philadelphia: Westminster, 1967) 149.

REFLECTIONS

1. God's final plea to Jerusalem is a call for the city to learn from the many events going on around it. The prophet in particular is trying to interpret to the city and the nation that destruction is about to befall them not because God has abandoned them, but rather that God is confronting the people with opportunities to correct their self-destructive course and craft a new beginning for the future. Confronting Jerusalem is not unlike the intervention process in confronting an alcoholic or a substance abuser in today's society. Intervention involves bringing to consciousness all of the worst and all of the best in order to save the abusers and those who are bound in one way or another to the substance abuser. In the case of the city, as with the modern tragedy, many others are deeply affected, so the attempted correction and change in behavior involves an extended family of participants.

God, therefore, is addressing a total community, its central core and its many appendages and dependencies. We, too, should pause, take caution, and not rush to individualize a contemporary application of this biblical word, but acknowledge the extensive network surrounding the power abusers. Whole institutions and systems can reflect the alcoholism of their leaders, so that a vast network of co-dependency can attend and serve the needs and wishes of the one addicted to alcohol, drugs, power, and the like. The "tough love" that counsels apparent abandonment and isolation of abusers by those closest to them is a key element in the correction process. The pain of tough love is borne by the victims as well as by the victimizer, by the extended family members as well by the individual.

God's pleas to power abusers, as found in Zeph 2:1-4 and 3:6-7, confront the harsh reality—despite their many *mea culpas* and denials of wrong intent—that their sin is idolatry of self or self-centered arrogance. They are like Nineveh, who could say, "I am, and there is no one else" (Zeph 2:15*a* NRSV), or like the indolent scoffer who thinks, "The LORD will not do good,/ nor will he do harm" (Zeph 1:12*b* NRSV). One remedy for this form of life-threatening cancer is, of course, its total annihilation, as revolutionaries like to say, by any means necessary. The biblical witness, despite our modern sensibilities—doubtlessly stemming from our own vested interests—is not averse to this form of remedy. The oracles of doom are genuine and have been verified by history. Yet even in the midst of the harsh reality of divine wrath, there is prophetic witness to divine mercy as a part of divine justice.

2. The grace note struck even in the midst of doom is the possibility of survival proffered for some, even as they, too, affirm that justice must and will be done. This is the statement of faith uttered by Zephaniah ben Cushi: "Every morning [God] renders [God's] judgment,/ each dawn without fail" (3:5*b* NRSV). That pebble drop of affirmation sends out ever widening ripples of faith, so that, faced with the destruction of Jerusalem, the book of Lamentations can sing:

> The steadfast love of the LORD never ceases,
>   his mercies never come to an end;
> they are new every morning;
>   great is your faithfulness. (Lam 3:22-23 NRSV)

The great hymn of Thomas O. Chisholm, "Great Is Thy Faithfulness," based on Lamentations, evokes in all who sing it the reaffirmation of faith in God's power to save in the face of destructive forces, such as the injustices of oppressive social institutions. The hymn's chorus takes up anew Zephaniah ben Cushi's affirmation of God's eternal justice:

> Morning by morning new mercies I see;
> All I have needed thy hand hath provided;
> Great is thy faithfulness, Lord unto me!

Oracles of Promise of Universal Conversion and of Salvation for Jerusalem

ZEPHANIAH 3:9-13, PROMISES OF UNIVERSAL CONVERSION AND OF SALVATION FOR THE REMNANT OF JUDAH

NIV

9"Then will I purify the lips of the peoples,
  that all of them may call on the name of the
    LORD
  and serve him shoulder to shoulder.
10From beyond the rivers of Cush[a]
  my worshipers, my scattered people,
  will bring me offerings.
11On that day you will not be put to shame
  for all the wrongs you have done to me,
  because I will remove from this city
    those who rejoice in their pride.
  Never again will you be haughty
    on my holy hill.
12But I will leave within you
  the meek and humble,
  who trust in the name of the LORD.
13The remnant of Israel will do no wrong;
  they will speak no lies,
    nor will deceit be found in their mouths.
  They will eat and lie down
    and no one will make them afraid."

a10 That is, the upper Nile region

NRSV

9 At that time I will change the speech of the
    peoples
  to a pure speech,
  that all of them may call on the name of the
    LORD
  and serve him with one accord.
10 From beyond the rivers of Ethiopia[a]
  my suppliants, my scattered ones,
  shall bring my offering.

11 On that day you shall not be put to shame
  because of all the deeds by which you have
    rebelled against me;
  for then I will remove from your midst
    your proudly exultant ones,
  and you shall no longer be haughty
    in my holy mountain.
12 For I will leave in the midst of you
  a people humble and lowly.
  They shall seek refuge in the name of the
    LORD—
13   the remnant of Israel;
  they shall do no wrong
    and utter no lies,
  nor shall a deceitful tongue
    be found in their mouths.
  Then they will pasture and lie down,
    and no one shall make them afraid.

a Or Nubia; Heb Cush

COMMENTARY

This eighth oracle introduces the third and final segment of the book of Zephaniah. It marks a significant change in tone and content: from words of imminent doom to promises of hope. Also, as in the first oracle, the prophet addresses both Judah and humankind, with a universal statement preceding a word to the covenant community. The central focus of the universal message is that "at that time" God will give a new, common speech to the nations so that they can praise God with "pure speech" and in "one accord" (שכם אחד *šěkem 'eḥād*; lit., "one shoulder"; v. 9). This promise reverses the confusion of tongues among the nations as spoken of in the story of the Tower of Babel (Gen 11:1-9). At the heart of the promise to Judah is another reversal of fortune, in which the faithful remnant will replace the haughty blasphemers (vv. 11*b*-12).

3:9. The new word of promise is clearly located in time, for in prophetic eschatology God's activity always happens within the arena of history. The divine will is fulfilled within recognizable time and space, hence the significance of the opening words: "At that time . . ." (כי־אז *kî-'āz*; lit., "for then"). Indeed, one could say this word of blessing fulfills the promise made in the oracle against Moab and Ammon: "and to him shall bow down,/ each in its place,/ all the coasts and islands of the nations" (2:11*b* NRSV). The threat of universal destruction, which overflowed from the fire of God's wrath against Jerusalem, is reversed so prayer can be lifted to God. The lifting up of prayer may even be suggested by the key phrase "call on the name of the LORD" (בשם יהוה קרא *qěrā' běšēm Yahweh*), a stock deuteronomic phrase used in Solomon's dedication of the Temple as "the house for the name of the LORD" (1 Kgs 8:20 NRSV).

3:10. This universal promise is made more specific by locating its origin in the upper reaches of the Nile Valley, near Cush, still remembered as the superpower ally who helped thwart the Assyrian destruction of Jerusalem (2 Kgs 19:1-13). The phraseology and promise of this verse recall the oracle of Isaiah 18 and the temple hymn: "Let Ethiopia [כוש *kûš*] hasten to stretch out its hands to God" (Ps 68:31 NRSV). The promise here is

one of conversion rather than nationalistic exploitation, as might be implied in Isa 45:14, which speaks of the wealth of the nations being given to Jerusalem.

Is this call to Cush truly a conversion or a summons to Hebrew exiles of the diaspora to return home? Clearly this passage signifies the bringing of new people into the service and worship of Yahweh. Such a missionary or proselytizing thrust existed from time to time in Israel. The conversion of non-Israelite peoples in their midst is attested from the exodus and wilderness wanderings (Exod 12:38) up to the conquest of the promised land via the trickery of the Gibeonites (Joshua 9). Ruth signifies David's Moabite ancestry (Ruth 1:16-18), Isa 2:2-4 predicts a universal conversion, and Isa 49:6 signals Israel's mission as "a light to the nations" (לאור גוים *lě'ôr gôyim*).

Amos hints at other non-Israelite covenant and exodus experiences, "Are you not like the Ethiopians to me,/ O people of Israel? says the LORD./ Did I not bring Israel up from the land of Egypt,/ and the Philistines from Caphtor and the Arameans from Kir?" (Amos 9:7 NRSV). Of the Zion songs, the enigmatic Psalm 87 has the nations register on the holy mount as if it were the navel of the earth: "Among those who know me I mention Rahab and Babylon;/ Philistia too, and Tyre, with Ethiopia— 'This one was born there,' they say" (Ps 87:4 NRSV). Perhaps most important, Zephaniah ben Cushi may be reflecting on his own African heritage as a witness to this call to conversion.

3:11-13. The next section heralds the promise of a new age for Judah (v. 11's "on that day" is parallel to "at that time," v. 9) and for the faithful remnant. This part of the eighth oracle makes clear that the idolatry and skepticism that were attacked as the root causes of Judah's approaching demise have now been removed (v. 11). It is as though the fire of the divine wrath had been a purifying flame, like the coals used in Isaiah's purification ritual (Isa 6:6-7), leaving only the humble and those who call upon "the name of the LORD" (v. 12). The faithful who have survived the devastating onslaught of the day of the Lord (2:14-18) now move forward to take the places of those who have been consumed in the sacrificial flames (1:7). Their constancy and truthfulness have seen them through to their present state of blessing and joy reserved for those who keep covenant with God. Indeed, their present situation is close to the promise held forth in the oracle against the Cherethites (Cretans; 2:7).

The faithful remnant to whom the prophet also preached (2:3, 7) were not spared the sacrificial holocaust of the day of the Lord, but had the resources to come through it alive, finding it not their end, but rather a threshold to the new age. The promise in this oracle exceeds the reversal of fortune for the faithful remnant as it is the vindication of those who, like Zephaniah ben Cushi, attempted to bring about fundamental change within the religious and political life of late seventh-century BCE Judah.

REFLECTIONS

1. The universal thrust in this oracle of Zephaniah ben Cushi is amazing. God invites all peoples of the earth, from farthest Cush to God's own covenanted people, here called "remnant of Israel" (שארית ישראל *šĕ'ērît yiśrā'ēl*), a phrase referring to the religious community that survived the catastrophe that befell Jerusalem. This envisioned future is not a remake of the old order of enmity between peoples and nations, but is a new beginning, based on a new ethic and means of dealing with one another. The changed or pure speech that unifies peoples is defined more fully, for here relationships are not based on wrong dealings, lies, and deceitful speech (vv. 9a, 13a). Rather, this new society is based on trust of neighbor and the institutions of government, which would include commerce, health care, insurance, banking, and labor practices. The unifying factor behind this reformation is the promise or expressed hope that—like God, so people—the nations will worship the one true God (v. 9b).

2. The conversion of the nations begins with the conversion of Cush "beyond the rivers of Ethiopia" (v. 10a; cf. Isa 18:1, 7). This ancient African superpower exercised a profound influence on the Israelite imagination through the eighth- and seventh-century BCE prophets, who reflected upon its role during the declining years of the Davidic monarchy. The experience of exile and growing diaspora communities, such as at Alexandria in the Nile Delta, also contributed to sustained interest in Egypt and Cush of the Nile. The nascent Christian movement saw its pentecost experience as the occasion for expansion, and it, too, looked south into Cush for early conversions. Early church historian Eusebius of Caesarea, for example, saw the conversion of the Cushite official in Acts 8:26-39, which preceded the conversion of the Roman soldier Cornelius (Acts 10), as symbolizing the beginning of the spread of Christianity.[26]

This interpretation of Zephaniah ben Cushi's identity and the subsequent impact of 3:10 on the conversion account in Acts 8:26-39 help to correct Eurocentric readings of history that exclude Africa's formative role in the development and spread of Jewish and Christian religious traditions. The acknowledgment and acceptance of Nubia/Cush (the NRSV uses the Greek equivalent, Ethiopia), along with its near neighbor and racial relative, Egypt, as being in and of Africa correct misinformed and often politically motivated views of African inferiority. The biblical witness holds an entirely different view of Egypt and Cush—namely, that they were important African players in the then international political and cultural scene. Ancient hymnic tradition equated Egypt with Ham: "He struck all the firstborn in Egypt,/ the first issue of

---

26. See *The Ecclesiastical History of Eusebius Pamphilus, Bishop of Caesarea,* trans. Christian F. Cruse (Grand Rapids: Baker Book House, 1955) 50: "For as the annunciation of the Saviour's gospel was daily advancing, by a certain divine providence, a prince of the queen of the Ethiopians, as it is a custom that still prevails there to be governed by a female, was brought thither and was the first of the Gentiles that received of the mysteries of the divine word from Philip. The apostle, led by a vision, thus instructed him and he, becoming the first fruits of believers throughout the world, and is said to have been the first, on returning to his country, that proclaimed the knowledge of God and the salutary abode of our Saviour among men. So that, in fact, the prophecy obtained its fulfillment through him: 'Ethiopia stretched forth her hands unto God.'" This history dates from about 350 CE. More popular depictions are found in Timothy Kendall, "Kingdom of Kush," *National Geographic* (November 1990) 96-124, and David Roberts, "Out of Africa: Artwork of Ancient Nubia," *Smithsonian* (June 1993) 90-100. See also nn. 6 and 7 of the present commentary. For the worldwide renown of the late Kushite or Meroitic empire, see *Ancient Civilizations of Africa,* 167-82.

their strength in the tents of Ham" (Ps 78:51 NRSV). Cush within the prophetic literature was neither distant nor exotic, neither outlandish nor odd, but accessible and familiar (so Isaiah 18 and 20; Jer 13:23; Amos 9:7; Nah 3:8-9; and Zeph 1:1; 2:12; 3:10).

Unfortunately, the effects of pseudo-scientific racial theories from the nineteenth century CE, supposedly proving the inherent inferiority of blacks, are still among us. These racial theories are comparable to the lies and deceit that marked the enmity Zephaniah ben Cushi predicted would cease in the coming reign of God. The oracle in Zeph 3:9-13 should give heart to reformers today who work for local and international peace, because it is a clarion call for removing racist, sexist, and nationalistic ideologies based on lies and deceit and the fear they engender.

3. When fear is swept away, all things become possible, through the efforts of many people performing many brave acts against their oppressors and making conscious efforts to rid themselves of an externally imposed self-hatred. African American theologian Howard Thurman, who unlocked the faith and wisdom of the slave sorrow songs or Spirituals, was also a prophetic visionary when he introduced American readers to the writings of Olive Schreiner, a white South African feminist and opponent of racism in the nineteenth century. In *A Track to the Water's Edge: The Olive Schreiner Reader,* Schreiner tells the tale of a woman in the desert trying to make it to the distant land of freedom, but who is blocked by a deep-flowing river. An elder counsels her:

> "Have you seen the locusts how they cross a stream? First one comes down to the water-edge, and is swept away, and then another comes and then another, and then another, and at last with their bodies piled up a bridge is built and the rest pass over." She said, "And, of those who come first, some are swept away, and are heard of no more; their bodies do not even build the bridge. And are swept away, and heard of no more—and what of that? he said. "And what of that—" she said. "They make a track to the water's edge." "They make a track to the water's edge ." And she said, "Over that bridge which shall be built with our bodies, who will pass?" He said, "The entire human race."[27]

27. Howard Thurman, ed., *A Track to the Water's Edge: The Olive Schreiner Reader* (New York: Harper & Row, 1973) 56.

ZEPHANIAH 3:14-20, VICTORY SONG OF JOY FOR JERUSALEM

NIV

[14]Sing, O Daughter of Zion;
    shout aloud, O Israel!
Be glad and rejoice with all your heart,
    O Daughter of Jerusalem!
[15]The LORD has taken away your punishment,
    he has turned back your enemy.
The LORD, the King of Israel, is with you;
    never again will you fear any harm.
[16]On that day they will say to Jerusalem,
    "Do not fear, O Zion;
    do not let your hands hang limp.
[17]The LORD your God is with you,

NRSV

[14] Sing aloud, O daughter Zion;
    shout, O Israel!
Rejoice and exult with all your heart,
    O daughter Jerusalem!
[15] The LORD has taken away the judgments
        against you,
    he has turned away your enemies.
The king of Israel, the LORD, is in your midst;
    you shall fear disaster no more.
[16] On that day it shall be said to Jerusalem:
    Do not fear, O Zion;
    do not let your hands grow weak.

NIV

he is mighty to save.
He will take great delight in you,
  he will quiet you with his love,
  he will rejoice over you with singing."

18"The sorrows for the appointed feasts
  I will remove from you;
  they are a burden and a reproach to you.*a*
19At that time I will deal
  with all who oppressed you;
I will rescue the lame
  and gather those who have been scattered.
I will give them praise and honor
  in every land where they were put to shame.
20At that time I will gather you;
  at that time I will bring you home.
I will give you honor and praise
  among all the peoples of the earth
when I restore your fortunes*b*
before your very eyes,"

                    says the LORD.

*a18 Or "I will gather you who mourn for the appointed feasts; / your
reproach is a burden to you   b20 Or I bring back your captives*

NRSV

17 The LORD, your God, is in your midst,
  a warrior who gives victory;
he will rejoice over you with gladness,
  he will renew you*a* in his love;
he will exult over you with loud singing
18 as on a day of festival.*b*
I will remove disaster from you,*c*
  so that you will not bear reproach for it.
19 I will deal with all your oppressors
  at that time.
And I will save the lame
  and gather the outcast,
and I will change their shame into praise
  and renown in all the earth.
20 At that time I will bring you home,
  at the time when I gather you;
for I will make you renowned and praised
  among all the peoples of the earth,
when I restore your fortunes
before your eyes, says the LORD.

a Gk Syr: Heb *he will be silent*   *b* Gk Syr: Meaning of Heb uncertain   *c* Cn: Heb *I will remove from you; they were*

COMMENTARY

The ninth and concluding oracle in the book of Zephaniah consists of a call to Jerusalem. The city is to rejoice that its sentence of destruction has been lifted and that God, proclaimed as "The king of Israel, the LORD" (מלך ישראל יהוה *melek yiśrā'ēl Yahweh,* v. 15*b* NRSV), is in its midst. Then, God directly addresses the joyous assembly, making similar statements of reassurance (vv. 18-20).

3:14-18. Verses 14-17 commence with a call by an unidentified voice for Jerusalem to rejoice, not unlike a priestly word of assurance to suppliants that their plea to God has been heard. Such a priestly oracle of blessing is assumed in the dramatic shift from lament to joyous confidence (e.g., Ps 22:22-26). Moreover, oracles of blessing are actually cited in Isa 43:1, 5; 44:2, 8. The city is addressed, using ritual terms of endearment: "Sing aloud, O daughter Zion" (v. 14). Such parallel usage is also found in the poignant ritual laments for fallen Jerusalem in the book of Lam-

entations (Lam 2:13, 15, 18). The prophet offers proclamation of release in clear, measured speech befitting a courtroom scene: Your judgment is removed; your enemies, the vehicles of the wrath of God, are turned away. The king (warrior) is in your midst; but now you need not fear disaster, as in the day of the Lord (v. 15).

The message of these verses reminds one of the great announcement of release from the Babylonian captivity: "Speak tenderly to Jerusalem,/ and cry to her/ that she has served her term,/ that her penalty is paid" (Isa 40:2 NRSV). In the language of Isaiah ben Amoz (Isa 6:5), barely seventy years before Zephaniah's time, God is called the king (מלך *melek*; see Psalms 47; 95). God's presence in the midst of the community spells peace rather than disaster. The poet offers a priestly word of blessing and release: "Do not fear, O Zion" (v. 16; cf. Isa 41:10; 43:1, 5). Not only does the redeemed community rejoice over its God and king (v. 15), but also God rejoices over the redeemed (v. 17*b*), as in the book of Isaiah (Isa 62:5*b*; 65:19*a*). Zephaniah's language of the people's joy over God as king and ruler of the nations reflects the words of the psalms proclaiming God as king (Psalms 47; 95) as well.

Such similarities between Zephaniah and the language and thought of the temple cultic tradition unite these oracles of promise with the earlier words of judgment, which are also located in the temple ritual (Zeph 1:7-8, 14-16; 2:3, 11; 3:5). The same is also true of the use of language from the courtroom, where God's decision to destroy (3:8) has now been dropped and the sentence commuted (3:15*a*). The oracles of Zephaniah ben Cushi, whether foretelling doom or hope, are couched in images and terms borrowed from the Temple and the law court, where God is respectively high priest and supreme judge. The deity authorizes curses for those who disobey the covenant and blessings for those faithful to the commandments. This reflects the language and thought of covenant, which was important in Josiah's reform movement.

The closing words of v. 17*b* are difficult to interpret, since the Hebrew behind "he will renew you in his love" (NRSV)/"he will quiet you with his love" (NIV) literally reads: "he will be silent in his love" (באהבתו יחריש *yaḥărîš bĕʾahăbātô*). The English is based on the reading from the Septuagint, which gives a sense closer to the thought expressed in the lines immediately preceding and following the verse. The reference to

the "warrior who gives victory" directs our thoughts to the divine warrior figure present in chaps. 1–2. However, in the circumstances reflected in this call to rejoice (see v. 15), the holy war against the covenant breakers is past and the faithful are now victorious. If one follows the Septuagint Hebrew (as in NRSV), which links the opening phrase of v. 18*a* with the close of v. 17*b*, one discovers the contexts for the call to rejoice and the ritual foretaste of the future release—namely, the festival uniting the closing of this collection of oracles with its beginning (1:2-3, 7) and the allusions there to the feast of Ingathering (Booths/Tabernacles).[28]

3:19-20. The last words in the book of Zephaniah center around the themes of restoration and return for the oppressed, the lame, and the outcast (v. 19), with the promise of return, restoration, and praise "among all the peoples of the earth . . . says the LORD" (v. 20). These promises may reflect the sentiments of a post-exilic editor; they have not occurred elsewhere in Zephaniah but are found in Isaianic passages from after the return from captivity (Isa 56:8; 62:7). Such additions usually account for the final editorial working of a collection, which often provides the title at the beginning of a book and an appended comment at its conclusion.

28. A parallel construction and setting may be found in ritual reenactments, so Hos 12:9, "I am the LORD your God/ from the land of Egypt;/ I will make you live in tents again,/ as in the days of the appointed festival" (NRSV).

REFLECTIONS

All of the main characters in the oracles of Zephaniah ben Cushi are present in the closing segments of his collected words: God, Judah/Jerusalem, the nations—but with a dramatic difference. Here, joy is the key to unlocking the message of God to Israel, to the nations, and to all of us today. The promise expressed here is that all nations, along with God's elect, will with one voice call on the divine name. The real reversal of fortune is not located solely in getting back what was lost in the meting out of divine justice, but in changed relationships between the main protagonists. The heavy sentence of judgment has been commuted, thereby making way for a future that is different from the past. For some of the privileged few today, this is shocking and not the way the justice system is supposed to work. Nevertheless, the word that ultimately came to this prophet of doom was more about the future than about the past, and more about those who will inherit the future than about those who will be punished. It is the faithful who rejoice and—perhaps most shocking—it is the God who commutes judgment sentences who also rejoices among those who have been released to live another day and in another way.

The interlinking of God, Israel, and the nations under which Zephaniah ben Cushi presents his vision of the future is a challenge to groups and races and religions and ideologies that continue to preach all kinds of separation today. Two sayings of South African Archbishop Desmond Tutu capture what truly causes God to rejoice as peoples and nations learn to live together in unity:

> Africans believe in something that is difficult to render in English. We call it *ubutu, botho*. It means the essence of being human. You know when it is there and when it is absent. It speaks about humaneness, gentleness, hospitality, putting yourself out on behalf of others, being vulnerable. It embraces compassion and toughness. It recognizes that my humanity is bound up in yours, for we can only be human together. . . .
>
> . . . In our African language we say "a person is a person through other persons." I would not know how to be a human being at all except I learn this from other human beings. We are made for a delicate network of relationships, of interdependence. We are meant to complement each other. All kinds of things go horribly wrong when we break that fundamental law of our being. Not even the most powerful nation can be completely self-sufficient.[29]

29. Desmond Tutu, *The Words of Demond Tutu: Selected by Naomi Tutu* (New York: Newmarket, 1989) 71, 73. Cf. Psalm 133 on the blessedness of unity.

THE BOOK OF HAGGAI

INTRODUCTION, COMMENTARY, AND REFLECTIONS
BY
W. EUGENE MARCH

THE BOOK OF
HAGGAI

INTRODUCTION

ittle is known about the man for whom the book of Haggai is named. No family name or other information is provided here or in the only other place where Haggai is mentioned, Ezra 5:1; 6:14. His name seems etymologically related to the Hebrew stem חגג (*ḥgg*), which means "make a pilgrimage" or "observe a pilgrimage feast." H. W. Wolff suggests that the name, found often in extra-biblical, post-exilic sources, was popular because it was "an allusion to the birth on a feast day of the person so named."[1] Three other persons with names related to this stem are mentioned in the Bible: Haggith, 2 Sam 3:4; 1 Kgs 1:6, 11; 2:13; 1 Chr 3:2; Haggiah, 1 Chr 6:30; and Haggi, Gen 46:16; Num 26:15.

The absence of a family name suggested to Carol Meyers and Eric Meyers that Haggai had family connections that would have been problematic for the prophet if they were publicly announced.[2] David Petersen, on the other hand, considered the absence of genealogical detail concerning Haggai a deliberate means of focusing attention on the divine authority by which the prophet spoke.[3] Nonetheless, for whatever reason, Haggai, like Amos, Habakkuk, and Obadiah before him, is not provided with a lineage.

Efforts have been made to develop some kind of biographical profile for Haggai based on other details in the book. Early Jewish and Christian sources assumed that Haggai was

---

1. Hans Walter Wolff, *Haggai*, trans. Margaret Kohl (Minneapolis: Augsburg, 1988; German edition in *BK* series 1986) 37.
2. Carol L. Meyers and Eric M. Meyers, *Haggai and Zechariah 1–8*, AB 25B (Garden City, NY: Doubleday, 1987) 8.
3. David L. Petersen, *Haggai and Zechariah 1–8*, OTL (Philadelphia: Westminster, 1984) 18-19.

a man at least seventy years old on the basis of Hag 2:3, but, according to Janet Tollington, this verse actually makes no claim concerning the prophet's age.[4] On the one hand, on the basis of his use of agricultural images, Haggai has been identified as a Judahite farmer who never left Palestine. On the other hand, he has been portrayed as one of those persons who returned from the exile determined to lead restoration efforts and overcome the lethargy of those who had escaped exile and remained in Judah. In truth, however, all such efforts to identify Haggai remain speculative. There is just not sufficient evidence within the book to draw a biographical sketch.

Probably the only thing that can be said for certain of Haggai is that he was remembered as a prophet with authority. Five times Haggai is called "the prophet" (Hag 1:1, 3, 12; 2:1, 10). The messenger formula, "thus says the LORD," employed so often in the prophetic literature, is prominent in Haggai as well (fully in Hag 1:2, 5, 7; 2:6, 11; abbreviated in Hag 1:8; 2:7, 9). The divine oracle formula, "says the LORD" or "saying of the LORD," is likewise frequent in this book (Hag 1:9, 13; 2:4, 9, 14, 17, 23). Haggai addressed both the governor and the high priest as one with authority (Hag 1:1, 12, 14; 2:2, 4). He dealt with matters of priestly teaching as one who stood outside the priestly circle but who, nonetheless, deserved a hearing (Hag 2:10-14). Unlike the professional cultic prophets prevalent before the Babylonian exile, whose false optimism had been so harmful to the nation, Haggai presented a message of hope grounded in the hard reality of a destroyed land. Although some have tried to associate Haggai with the prophets (sometimes called cultic prophets) who lived at or near Israel's shrines and who participated regularly in the worship there, it seems best to understand him as being outside of those circles. Rather, Haggai is best associated with the long tradition of classical prophets raised up by God to proclaim the Lord's word to Israel.[5]

One further aspect of Haggai's role as prophet should be noted. As already mentioned, he was closely linked to Zechariah in Ezra 5–6. The two prophets were pictured working in Jerusalem at the same time and toward the same goal. Yet there is no reference to the other prophet in either Haggai or Zechariah. This enigmatic silence only underscores the vagueness of detail concerning Haggai the prophet. Petersen is indeed correct that, with so little biographical data, attention must be centered upon the message rather than the messenger.[6]

HISTORICAL CONTEXT

The work of Haggai, according to the book itself, was concentrated between August 29, 520 BCE, and December 18 of the same year, the second year of the reign of Persian King Darius (Hag 1:1, 15; 2:1, 10). Scholars basically accept these dates as authentic and

4. Janet E. Tollington, *Tradition and Innovation in Haggai and Zechariah 1–8,* JSOTSup 150 (Sheffield: JSOT, 1993) 52-53.

5. See ibid., 61, 76; Wolff, *Haggai,* 16-17.

6. Petersen, *Haggai and Zechariah 1–8,* 18-19.

believe the book was compiled in its present form only a short time after the prophet spoke, certainly before 515 BCE, when the work on the Temple initiated at Haggai's urging was completed.

That the Temple could be rebuilt and that life in Jerusalem could resume with a degree of safety and modest prosperity was the result of Persia's defeat of the Babylonians. When his army conquered the city of Babylon in 538 BCE, Cyrus the Persian ended the harsh Babylonian rule that had prevailed in most of Mesopotamia and Syria-Palestine for over seventy years (612–538 BCE). Very quickly Cyrus set about reorganizing the administration of not only Babylon but also the vast empire Babylon had established. Further, early in his reign, Cyrus issued a decree, now preserved in what is known as the Cyrus Cylinder. The decree ordered the return of sacred images and temple furniture taken by the Babylonians as spoils from the numerous cities they had conquered. This decree effected the return of some Judahite exiles with a mandate and financial support to reconstruct the Temple (Ezra 1:2-4; 6:2-5). This decree may also explain why the writer of Second Isaiah, rejoicing at the prospect of the return from exile, conferred upon Cyrus the title of "Messiah," the Lord's "anointed" (Isa 45:1).

Cyrus was succeeded by Cambyses, his son, who ruled eight years (530–522 BCE). Cambyses extended Persian control into Egypt. While on his way home from his western military campaign, he received word of a revolt and suddenly died. The circumstances of Cambyses' death are unclear, but one of his officers, Darius, a blood relative although not a son, took over.[7] Darius returned home and put down the revolt. For the next two years, Darius dealt with rebellion in a number of cities. Then, with his rule finally established, Darius I the Great guided the Persian Empire until his death in 486 BCE.

Under Cyrus's administrative plan, Judah was governed as a large satrapy (province) called "Babylon and Beyond the River." "Beyond the River" had Samaria as its administrative center. Due to Cambyses' ambitions in Egypt, Syria-Palestine began to evolve into a separate district. By the time Darius I took over, a "governor" (פחה *peḥâ*) named Ushtani was in charge of the whole satrapy of "Babylon and Beyond the River," while a subordinate named Tattenai (also called *peḥâ* in Ezra 6:6, 13) administered that part of the satrapy called "Beyond the River." It is likely that the pressure to remove Judah from Samaria's direct administrative control began when Zerubbabel was appointed and dispatched to Judah around 523–522 BCE, though full regional autonomy was not to be realized until later in the fifth century.[8]

The socioeconomic situation of Judah at the time of Haggai can only be described broadly. Recent studies, well summarized by Petersen, highlight three aspects of the situation.[9] First, the economy was not particularly productive. Jerusalem, the major market and trading center of the region, was still recovering from the devastation of 587 BCE. Limited labor resources and relatively poor land combined to produce minimal economic

---

7. Ibid., 22.
8. Ibid., 24-27.
9. Ibid., 28-31.

return. Agricultural specialization in wine and olives became necessary in order to survive, but the end result of the specialization was the entrenchment of the more wealthy over against the poor.

A second phenomenon that dominated Judah's society was the concentration of community life around the Temple. As primarily the royal chapel of the monarchy before the exile, the Temple had played an important, though much more limited, role. The people as a whole did not go to the Temple. It was the sanctuary of the king and his household. After the people's return from the exile, however, the Temple became the center of social and economic activity in a way never seen during the days of the kings. Such temple-centered civil societies became typical all across Syria-Palestine during the Persian period. Judah's relatively sparse population and small territory (smaller than the state of Rhode Island), centered economically, socially, politically, and religiously around Jerusalem, made the Temple the religious and civic symbol it had never been before.

Finally, land distribution and administration took on a new look in the post-exilic community. When families had been exiled in 587 BCE, their land had been taken by people who had remained. When the deportees began to return under the auspices of the Persian authorities, conflicts inevitably arose. Elsewhere in the Persian Empire a new institution was developing that was adapted to the circumstances of Judah. Known as the בית אבות (*bêt 'ābôt*), the "fathers' house," it functioned as a collective, holding and administering land. In theory, members of a particular "house" were related genealogically from tribal times, but this was more myth than reality. Membership lists for some of these "houses" (e.g., Neh 7:61-62) indicate that people who had been in exile were integrated with those who had stayed behind. Thus land, taken possession of by those to whom it had not originally belonged, was shared with the returnees whose families had once been landowners. These collectives became the institution by which land was redistributed, and some measure of stability and productivity was brought back into the land.

During Haggai's time there was no longer a society defined by national borders with its own king and national religion. Rather, a community organized in landholding collectives with the Temple of the Lord as its administrative, economic, and religious center began to emerge. The shape of the society was not nearly as clear in Haggai's era as it would become one hundred years later. The prophet's task was to assist in these early stages of the process by pressing the need for rebuilding the Temple, and this he did vigorously.

THE BOOK OF HAGGAI

The most immediate impression that the book of Haggai makes on the reader is its chronologically ordered set of five units, presenting speeches made by the prophet and the circumstances of those speeches. Unlike most of the other prophetic books, which appear primarily as collections of unconnected, undated oracles, Haggai exists more in the form of a narrative or a drama. The narrative has five episodes: Hag 1:1-11; 1:12-15*a*; 1:15*b*–2:9; 2:10-19; 2:20-23, with a date assigned to each unit. In the two brief chapters that comprise this book, a narrative spanning approximately three and one-half months is presented and arranged according to the appropriate dates:

Hag 1:1	first day, sixth month, second year of King Darius	August 29, 520 BCE
Hag 1:15*a*	twenty-fourth day, sixth month, second year of King Darius	September 21, 520 BCE
Hag 1:15*b*–2:1	twenty-first day, seventh month, second year of King Darius	October 17, 520 BCE
Hag 2:10	twenty-fourth day, ninth month, second year of King Darius	December 18, 520 BCE
Hag 2:20	twenty-fourth day, ninth month, second year of King Darius	December 18, 520 BCE

It seems clear that the book is intended to preserve and interpret words spoken by a prophet at critical points in the history of the community.

The type of narrative found here may be characterized as "brief apologetic historical narrative."[10] During the sixth century BCE, the distinctive style of prose represented here developed and may also be seen in other historical works influenced by the deuteronomists. Other examples of such a genre are found in 2 Kings 22–23; and Jeremiah 26; 36; 37–41. The book of Haggai aims to remember the positive community achievement represented by the rebuilding of the Temple and to emphasize Haggai's role in that event. Thus it might well be entitled, according to Petersen, "The story of Haggai's involvement in the restoration of Judah."[11]

There is wide agreement that the composition of the book had at least two phases: the preservation of the words of the prophet, probably by a disciple, and then the development of the narrative structure in which the present material is presented. The completion of the narrative was accomplished not long after the events remembered, and certainly before the temple project was completed (515 BCE). The narrative was fashioned by supplying a connective framework that provided context and, to a degree, interpretation (cf. Hag 1:1,

10. Ibid., 35, citing W. Rudolph, *Haggai–Sacharja 1–8/9–14—Maleachi,* KAT (1976).
11. Ibid., 34.

3, 12-13*a*, 14-15; 2:1-2, 10, 20-21*a*).[12] R. Mason has rightly demonstrated the many connections of the Haggai narrative with the deuteronomists (as opposed to relationships with the chronicler, which has been suggested by others).[13] Apart from debate concerning the original placement of Hag 2:15-19 and its possible connection to Hag 1:15*a*, there is general agreement on the date of the basic composition of Haggai.[14]

The message of Haggai is straightforward: Rebuild the Temple and therein witness and give testimony to the reign of God, both in the present and in the future. This twofold character of the message needs to be remembered. If only the present context is emphasized, the book might be read as too mundane, too concerned with the obvious need to rebuild the community. With the future (some would say eschatological) dimensions in mind, however, Haggai's words remind his hearers that the work of God's people always points beyond the present moment to the continuation of God's work and fulfillment of all the divine purpose.

12. Janet E. Tollington, *Tradition and Innovation in Haggai and Zechariah 1–8,* JSOTSup 150 (Sheffield: JSOT, 1993) 23; but for different suggestions, see Carroll Stuhlmueller, *Rebuilding with Hope: A Commentary on the Books of Haggai and Zechariah,* ITC (Grand Rapids: Eerdmans, 1988) 14; and Hans Walter Wolff, *Haggai,* trans. Margaret Kohl (Minneapolis: Augsburg, 1988; German edition in *BK* series 1986) 18.

13. R. Mason, "The Purpose of the 'Editorial Framework' of the Book of Haggai," *VT* 27 (1977) 415-18.

14. Wolff, *Haggai,* 59-62.

BIBLIOGRAPHY

Commentaries:

Meyers, Carol L., and Eric M. Meyers. *Haggai and Zechariah 1–8: A New Translation, Introduction, and Commentary.* AB 25B. Garden City, N.Y.: Doubleday, 1987. A careful treatment of historical, linguistic, and stylistic matters important for understanding both prophetic books here considered.

Petersen, David L. *Haggai and Zechariah 1–8.* OTL. Philadelphia: Westminster, 1984. A comprehensive commentary that combines a review of significant scholarship with excellent historical and literary insight.

Stuhlmueller, Carroll. *Rebuilding with Hope: A Commentary on the Books of Haggai and Zechariah.* ITC. Grand Rapids: Eerdmans, 1988. A helpful examination of the content and theological significance of Haggai and Zechariah for the church.

Wolff, Hans Walter. *Haggai.* Translated by Margaret Kohl. Minneapolis: Augsburg, 1988; German edition in *BK* series 1986. A careful analysis of the text, language, setting, and intention of Haggai with excellent bibliography up to 1984.

Other Suggested Studies:

Mason, R. "The Purpose of the 'Editorial Framework' of the Book of Haggai," *VT* 27 (1977) 413-21. A very useful summary of previous work and a thoughtful suggestion for understanding the composition and structure of the book of Haggai.

Tollington, Janet E. *Tradition and Innovation in Haggai and Zechariah 1–8.* JSOTSup 150. Sheffield: JSOT, 1993. A provocative, fresh appraisal of the composition, authority, and theological implications of Haggai and Zechariah 1–8.

OUTLINE OF HAGGAI

I. Haggai 1:1-11, Build for God's Glory

II. Haggai 1:12-15*a*, They Obeyed the Lord

III. Haggai 1:15*b*–2:9, Take Courage and Work

IV. Haggai 2:10-19, From This Day On

V. Haggai 2:20-23, Like a Signet Ring

BUILD FOR GOD'S GLORY

NIV

1 In the second year of King Darius, on the first day of the sixth month, the word of the LORD came through the prophet Haggai to Zerubbabel son of Shealtiel, governor of Judah, and to Joshua[a] son of Jehozadak, the high priest:

²This is what the LORD Almighty says: "These people say, 'The time has not yet come for the LORD's house to be built.'"

³Then the word of the LORD came through the prophet Haggai: ⁴"Is it a time for you yourselves to be living in your paneled houses, while this house remains a ruin?"

⁵Now this is what the LORD Almighty says: "Give careful thought to your ways. ⁶You have planted much, but have harvested little. You eat, but never have enough. You drink, but never have your fill. You put on clothes, but are not warm. You earn wages, only to put them in a purse with holes in it."

⁷This is what the LORD Almighty says: "Give careful thought to your ways. ⁸Go up into the mountains and bring down timber and build the house, so that I may take pleasure in it and be honored," says the LORD. ⁹"You expected much, but see, it turned out to be little. What you brought home, I blew away. Why?" declares the LORD Almighty. "Because of my house, which remains a ruin, while each of you is busy with his own house. ¹⁰Therefore, because of you the heavens have withheld their dew and the earth its crops. ¹¹I called for a drought on the fields and the mountains, on the grain, the new wine, the oil and whatever the ground produces, on men and cattle, and on the labor of your hands."

a1 A variant of *Jeshua*; here and elsewhere in Haggai

NRSV

1 In the second year of King Darius, in the sixth month, on the first day of the month, the word of the LORD came by the prophet Haggai to Zerubbabel son of Shealtiel, governor of Judah, and to Joshua son of Jehozadak, the high priest: ²Thus says the LORD of hosts: These people say the time has not yet come to rebuild the LORD's house. ³Then the word of the LORD came by the prophet Haggai, saying: ⁴Is it a time for you yourselves to live in your paneled houses, while this house lies in ruins? ⁵Now therefore thus says the LORD of hosts: Consider how you have fared. ⁶You have sown much, and harvested little; you eat, but you never have enough; you drink, but you never have your fill; you clothe yourselves, but no one is warm; and you that earn wages earn wages to put them into a bag with holes.

7Thus says the LORD of hosts: Consider how you have fared. ⁸Go up to the hills and bring wood and build the house, so that I may take pleasure in it and be honored, says the LORD. ⁹You have looked for much, and, lo, it came to little; and when you brought it home, I blew it away. Why? says the LORD of hosts. Because my house lies in ruins, while all of you hurry off to your own houses. ¹⁰Therefore the heavens above you have withheld the dew, and the earth has withheld its produce. ¹¹And I have called for a drought on the land and the hills, on the grain, the new wine, the oil, on what the soil produces, on human beings and animals, and on all their labors.

COMMENTARY

1:1. This opening scene of Haggai, as are those that follow, is very precisely dated, this one to the first day of the sixth month in the second year of Darius I (522–486 BCE), or August 29, 520

BCE.[15] This dating is interesting because it is so specific. For the most part, prophetic materials elsewhere in the Bible set events and oracles only in general time periods (cf. Isa 1:1; Hos 1:1). More precise datings occur (Isa 6:1; Amos 1:1), but nothing like those found in Haggai and Zechariah. On this date in summer, Haggai's work began, and it came to an end three and one-half months later in December.

The date cited here is significant for two reasons. First, it is well into the second year of Darius's reign, after he had been able to quell a series of revolts that had followed the death of Cambyses and Darius's accession to the throne in 522 BCE. By 520 BCE, the tumult had passed and stability had been restored. Second, the first day of the month was traditionally set aside for special sacrifices (Num 28:11-15), but in the absence of an altar or temple, such special feast days were impossible to observe in a ritually appropriate manner.

Besides Darius, three other people are identified by name in this first episode: Haggai, the prophet; Zerubbabel, the governor; and Joshua, the high priest. As noted in the Introduction, little is known about Haggai other than that he was recognized as a prophet with authority. Five times Haggai is explicitly identified as "prophet" (1:1, 3, 12; 2:1, 10; see also Ezra 5:1; 6:4). The biblical account does not disclose whether Haggai was among the deportees who returned from Babylon after the exile or whether he was from among those who had remained behind in Palestine. That he was a prophet is clear. His was a divinely appointed task.

Zerubbabel was a returnee. According to Ezra 2:2, he, along with Jeshua (probably an Aramaic variant spelling of "Joshua") and others, led a sizable group (Ezra 2:64-65) back to Judah from Babylon in 538 BCE, after King Cyrus of Persia had granted permission and encouragement (Ezra 1:2-4). Apparently Zerubbabel was born in Babylon and given an Akkadian name ("Zerbabilu"). His lineage is not completely clear. In this passage and in Ezra 3:2, his father is Shealtiel, the eldest son of Jehoiachin (also known as Jeconiah), the Davidic king taken into captivity by the Babylonians in 597 BCE (2 Chr 36:9-10). In 1 Chr 3:19, however, Zerubbabel's father is known as Pediah, the third son of Jehoiachin. Petersen, following Rudolph's suggestion of a levirate marriage, understands Zerubbabel to be a nephew of Jehoiachin.[16] At some point, Zerubbabel was given the title "Governor of Judah," a title used of him only here and in Hag 1:14; 2:2, 21. The duties of "governor" (פחה *pehâ*) were probably not as fully developed in Judah in 520 BCE as they became a century later.[17] Despite the several uncertainties here noted, Zerubbabel was a very important person, a man of Davidic lineage and authorized by the Persian authorities to lead the Judahite community in a reorganization and restoration of its institutions.

The third person named in this passage is Joshua (the name means "the Lord is salvation"), son of Jehozadak (in Ezra 3:2, the Aramaic form of this name is "Jeshua son of Jozadak"). He was the grandson of Seraiah, the "chief priest" who was killed at the time of Jerusalem's destruction in 587 BCE (2 Kgs 25:18; 1 Chr 6:14-15). Joshua is listed, as already noted, among the returnees in 538 BCE (Ezra 3:2). The title he carries in Haggai, "high priest" or "great priest" (הכהן הגדול *hakkōhēn haggādôl*), clearly attests to his authority. Joshua appears to be the first to serve as high priest, a position that became of utmost importance in the centuries that followed.[18]

In Hag 1:1, 3, the author uses a distinctive phrase to describe the prophet's relation to the word of the Lord. Usually in the prophetic literature, the "word of the LORD" (דבר יהוה *dĕbar YHWH*) happens or comes "to" (אל *'el*) a prophet (e.g., Jer 1:4; Hos 1:1; Mic 1:1). Haggai 2:10, 20 uses this phrase as well (the NIV more correctly

---

15. After the Babylonian Exile, the calendar of the Assyrians and the Babylonians was adopted by the Judahites, although the pre-exilic Israelite calendar was still employed for religious purposes. Whereas the Israelite New Year's Day and the Day of Atonement, for instance, were celebrated in the fall, in the Babylonian calendar, New Year's was celebrated in the spring. Consequently, late August occurs in the sixth month of the Babylonian calendar instead of the twelfth month, as it would have in the pre-exilic Israelite calendar. And the Judahite New Year's Day was located in the seventh month of the Babylonian calendar, whereas it was obviously in the first month of the pre-exilic calendar. Further, the calendar no longer is related whatsoever to the Judahite kings, since there are none. Rather, reference is made simply to the only king who mattered—namely, Darius, ruler of the Persian Empire.

16. David L. Petersen, *Haggai and Zechariah 1–8*, OTL (Philadelphia: Westminster, 1984) 45; cf. Hans Walter Wolff, *Haggai*, trans. Margaret Kohl (Minneapolis: Augsburg, 1988; German edition in *BK* series 1986) 38.

17. Petersen, *Haggai and Zechariah 1–8*, 45-46; but see Wolff, *Haggai*, 39, for a different opinion.

18. Petersen, *Haggai and Zechariah 1–8*, 46.

renders the Hebrew than does the NRSV). In Hag 1:1, 3; 2:1, however, the "word of the Lord" is transmitted "by" or "through" (בְּיַד *bĕyad*) the prophet (lit., "by the hand of the prophet"). Such an instrumental use of the preposition became more common after the exile in the deuteronomistic sections of Kings and in the chronicler's history.[19] This phrase emphasizes the mediatorial function of the prophet and places attention on the prophetic message.

1:2-11. These verses contain two messages from the prophet, even though these messages now function as one. The longer, and probably earlier, message is a word to the people, preserved in Hag 1:7-11. The shorter message, Hag 1:4-6, is part of a disputation. They have been combined and presented by the final editor as a word given directly to the leaders of the people: Zerubbabel the governor and Joshua the high priest. Haggai's basic appeal was straightforward: Since the leaders and the people had built houses for themselves, they should honor God by rebuilding the Temple.

Haggai speaks to the leaders because "these people" deny that the time has come to rebuild the Temple (Hag 1:2). The identity of "these people" (lit., "this people" [הָעָם הַזֶּה *hāʿām hazzeh*]) is not clear. The term "remnant of the people" (Hag 1:12, 14), employed in the following scene, might imply some distinction between those persons who had returned from exile and those who had remained in Judah. Since Zerubbabel and Joshua are responsible for the whole Judahite population, however, "these people" probably are best understood here as referring to the whole community. All stand under the indictment of the Lord for their failure to rebuild the Temple, a project begun eighteen years earlier and still uncompleted (Ezra 1:2-11; 3:1-7; 5:16).

The prophet then moves to the heart of the issue. In disputational style, v. 4 poses an ironic question in which Haggai contrasts the houses the people live in with the ruined Temple of the Lord. The term translated "paneled" (סְפוּנִים *sĕpûnîm*) in the NRSV and the NIV does not necessarily connote high quality furnishings. Rather, the emphasis is on the state of completion.[20] The people have

"finished" dwellings while the Lord's house is very much "unfinished." Indeed, the temple is "desolate," in "ruins" (חרב *ḥārēb*).

In v. 6, the prophet poses a series of contrasts (cf. v. 9). In each instance the emphasis is on the unsuccessful character of the action attempted. The plural indicates that the people are addressed: "You have sown much, and harvested little." This type of language is related to what are termed "futility curses" in international treaties of the era.[21] On the basis of such futility curses, if the treaty or covenant is violated, then the guilty party will experience the type of frustration represented in v. 6. No matter what is attempted, it will come to nothing.

Located twice within this narrative is the command that the people reflect upon their situation: "Consider how you have fared" (vv. 5, 7 NRSV); "Give careful thought to your ways" (vv. 5, 7 NIV; שִׂימוּ לְבַבְכֶם [*śîmû lĕbabĕkem*]). What is at stake is the need to focus, literally to "set the heart." The "heart" is the organ of thinking and will in Hebrew psychology. The people are enjoined, on the one hand, to reflect, to decide, and then to act in the light of what has and has not been happening to them (vv. 4-6). Their own current experiences of frustration should prompt them to listen to the word of the Lord. On the other hand, they are to contemplate a different mode of operation, to consider doing something that they have not done before. They are to go to the mountains, where they are to gather wood in order to begin rebuilding the temple (vv. 7-8). The result of this action will be fulfilling rather than frustrating to them.

Still, what Haggai's people face at the present is a devastating drought (vv. 9-10). Since it would not be unusual to find Palestine dry at the end of August, when this narrative is dated, the drought must have been going on for an extended period. Because the Lord's Temple lies devastated (v. 9; cf. v. 4 [*ḥārēb*]), the land, the people, and indeed all living things now suffer the killing weight of drought (v. 11; חרב *ḥōreb*]). This play on words is hardly accidental. Because the people hurry to their own houses and ignore the ruined

---

19. Wolff, *Haggai*, 37.
20. Carol L. Meyers and Eric M. Meyers, *Haggai and Zechariah 1–8*, AB 25B (Garden City, NY: Doubleday, 1987) 23-24.

21. See Petersen, *Haggai and Zechariah 1–8*, 50, citing D. Hillers, *Treaty Curses and the Old Testament Prophets*, BibOr 16 (Rome: Pontifical Biblical Institute, 1964) 28.

Temple, disaster has come upon them in the form of a drought (vv. 9b-11).

The implication from the very beginning is that the present circumstances could be different if the people would only heed the word brought by the prophet. In v. 8 this is made explicit. If they will rebuild the Lord's house, God promises to "take pleasure in"—that is, to accept—the people's effort (v. 8 [ארצה] 'erṣeh from the root רצה rṣh]). The term is often used in connection with the acceptance or rejection of sacrifice (Amos 5:22; Mic 6:7). Before the Temple rebuilding is even begun, it is declared acceptable to God. No matter what the outcome of the people's efforts, the prophet declares that the Lord will take pleasure in it.

Further, the Lord will "be honored" (v. 8, אכבד 'ekkābĕdā, a niphal form of the root כבד kbd, meaning "to honor," "to glorify") by their work. The idea that deities needed temples/houses in which to dwell was very important in antiquity. The Baal cult, which existed for many centuries, saw the building of Baal's temple as a major concern. Thus to provide God a temple was imperative. But Haggai's reason is somewhat different from simply to secure a place for the Lord to live. The aim is to bring honor to God. Rather than continue in a hostile, drought-provoking relationship, the people can honor their God if they will but rebuild the Temple. All the world will learn of the Lord when the Lord's house is restored.

A very distinctive term for God, יהוה צבאות (YHWH ṣĕbā'ôt), rendered as "LORD of hosts" (NRSV) or "LORD Almighty" (NIV), is used repeatedly (vv. 2, 5, 7, 9; 2:4, 6-9, 11, 23). This language derives originally from the theology and cult of the early monarchy and the Jerusalem Temple.[22] In the post-exilic restoration period, Judah had neither king nor Temple. Hence, Haggai used the term to emphasize the power and sovereignty of the Lord over the whole world, including even the Persian king.[23] The Lord of hosts is no longer bound only to Judah and the Jerusalem Temple, since the deity has people in Babylon and in Egypt as well as in Palestine. The Lord of hosts will be honored by the rebuilding of the Jerusalem Temple, but will never again be limited to that structure.

22. See Janet E. Tollington, *Tradition and Innovation in Haggai and Zechariah 1–8*, JSOTSup 150 (Sheffield: JSOT, 1993) 65-70.
23. See Meyers and Meyers, *Haggai and Zechariah 1–8*, 18-19.

REFLECTIONS

1. The attention to historical detail and to historical context is neither accidental nor incidental. By remembering the declaration of a divine word in this way, a claim is made about the arena of God's action. God was concerned about the very real world of politics and religion, of self-serving and self-giving human beings. Human beings were challenged to act responsibly, the leaders receiving the first words of the prophet. God acted through a human named Haggai, whom some no doubt knew in all his humanity. The message delivered was quite mundane, directing that a building project be begun or completed. This event was important as a step along the way of faithfulness, but it was not climactic in itself.

Most of God's challenges to human allegiance, to us, come in quite historically specific moments, this-worldly events through people and for people. The Protestant Reformation began when one particular man, Martin Luther, in one historical situation decided to respond to what he understood God to be saying through Scripture. The civil rights movement in the 1950s and 1960s in the United States began when one particular woman, Rosa Parks, in a very specific context, knowing herself to be God's, refused to participate any longer in the degrading practice of consigning black people to the back of the bus. Such human deeds continue to be the measure of our faithfulness to God and the means by which the divine will is made manifest in the world.

2. Behind the straightforward appeal of Haggai for the leaders and people to rebuild God's Temple was the prophet's desire to honor the Lord. Circumstances had demonstrated that God did not need a temple as a dwelling. The reality of God's presence with and purpose for the people had become clear despite the destruction of the Temple. Thus Haggai presents the idea of rebuilding the Temple, not as a magical means of gaining divine approval, but as a way of honoring God.

Haggai identifies an important issue: human devotion and willingness to work on behalf of God. Haggai challenges his people to give God more, not less, than they were giving themselves. Fund raising is often disclaimed as untimely or inappropriate, but Haggai's logic is simple and difficult to dispute: What is good enough for us is certainly the minimum we should present to God in our thankfulness and praise.

3. The Lord of hosts was God of all gods and ruler of all kingdoms. A temple was an appropriate testimony to the wonder of God's continuing relationship to God's people and the people of all the world. It was a visible reminder to all the world that the Lord of hosts was God of heaven and earth. The Temple was a place chosen by God where human beings could expect to encounter God, to be challenged and renewed by the divine presence. Thus Haggai's call to rebuild the Lord's Temple was a declaration of God's presence and authority.

This claim is reinforced with yet another. Although the new calendar, with its reference to Darius, acknowledged human historical reality, the assertion that the Lord of hosts had delivered a divine word by a prophet Haggai set all reality under the domain of the Lord. God, as understood here, is no tribal deity hopelessly limited to the stony hills of Judah. God is the Lord of hosts, God of all gods, and ruler of all kingdoms.

4. Does God really cause drought? Does God intervene in human history by directly punishing a people in the manner here suggested? Certainly the writers of the Bible thought God to be this way. To get caught up in an argument about whether such a view is good or bad, true or false, however, is to miss the point. Haggai was not trying to expound or defend a doctrine or philosophy of divine causality. A prophetic speech was not the place for such an effort, and neither, probably, is a sermon.

Haggai's assertion about God's judgment was aimed at getting the people to recognize that their behavior mattered to God. Their failure to honor God displeased God. Haggai's word was heard because the people had a guilty conscience. This particular drought became a symbol of punishment because the people recognized their own disobedience. It is important not to generalize, however, and suggest that every drought is divine punishment for specific sins. Indeed, it is problematic to claim that any drought or other form of hardship is the result of divine displeasure. Nonetheless, drought as a symbol of the brokenness of creation and the need for divine healing and restoration remains a powerful image.

HAGGAI 1:12-15a

THEY OBEYED THE LORD

NIV

¹²Then Zerubbabel son of Shealtiel, Joshua son of Jehozadak, the high priest, and the whole remnant of the people obeyed the voice of the LORD their God and the message of the prophet Haggai, because the LORD their God had sent him. And the people feared the LORD.

¹³Then Haggai, the LORD's messenger, gave this message of the LORD to the people: "I am with you," declares the LORD. ¹⁴So the LORD stirred up the spirit of Zerubbabel son of Shealtiel, governor of Judah, and the spirit of Joshua son of Jehozadak, the high priest, and the spirit of the whole remnant of the people. They came and began to work on the house of the LORD Almighty, their God, ¹⁵on the twenty-fourth day of the sixth month

NRSV

12Then Zerubbabel son of Shealtiel, and Joshua son of Jehozadak, the high priest, with all the remnant of the people, obeyed the voice of the LORD their God, and the words of the prophet Haggai, as the LORD their God had sent him; and the people feared the LORD. ¹³Then Haggai, the messenger of the LORD, spoke to the people with the LORD's message, saying, I am with you, says the LORD. ¹⁴And the LORD stirred up the spirit of Zerubbabel son of Shealtiel, governor of Judah, and the spirit of Joshua son of Jehozadak, the high priest, and the spirit of all the remnant of the people; and they came and worked on the house of the LORD of hosts, their God, ¹⁵on the twenty-fourth day of the month, in the sixth month.

COMMENTARY

1:12-14. The scene shifts with these verses. The time is three and one-half weeks later than the previous unit, September 21, 520 BCE (v. 15a). Those involved include Zerubbabel, Joshua, and Haggai the prophet, as earlier (v. 1), but now the author explicitly mentions also the "remnant of the people" (vv. 12, 14). This short unit is designed to demonstrate that the prophetic word, the divine message, was received and acted upon with the aid of God's Spirit.

Haggai's initial word had been directed to Zerubbabel, the Persian-appointed official ("governor"; cf. Commentary on 1:1), and Joshua, the high priest. Zerubbabel's title is not used in v. 12 (cf. 1:1, 14; 2:2, 21), but there is no question that the same two officials identified previously are the subjects here. "The remnant of the people," however, designates an additional recipient of Haggai's words. The term "remnant" (שארית *šĕʾērît*) typically refers specifically to those who returned from exile (Jer 43:5). In this passage, the term probably refers to those people who had

returned from Babylon and among whom Zerubbabel and Joshua, as returnees themselves, had the most influence.[24]

The initial response of Zerubbabel, Joshua, and the "remnant of the people" was twofold: They "obeyed," and they "feared" (v. 12). The Hebrew term וישמע (*wayyišmaʿ*) literally means "and he heard," but hearing the word or voice of God meant in Hebrew "to obey." If one did in fact "hear," one would then "obey." There can be no true "hearing" without "heeding." Thus the people being addressed "heard," and they "obeyed." They also "feared" the Lord. The Hebrew term וייראו (*wayyîrĕʾû*) connotes that they were properly "awed" before the Lord, who had sent Haggai (cf. Ps 34:11; Prov 3:7). They recognized God's awesome power and amazing constancy. The Lord had maintained a relationship with them, even though their ancestors had not acted as they had been so clearly commanded (Deut 4:25-31). They

24. Wolff, *Haggai*, 52.

obeyed, and they feared before God (v. 12). But there was a need for assurance from and empowerment by God. Otherwise their awe was in danger of becoming a numbing, paralyzing dread.

In response to the people's fear, the prophet delivers an often repeated message, God's assuring declaration: "I am with you" (v. 13). As in the first scene, Haggai the prophet conveys the divine message of assurance to Zerubbabel, to Joshua, and to the "remnant of the people." This form of assurance echoes the traditional oracle of salvation (see Isa 41:10, 13; 43:1, 5; 44:2, 8). Such a promise of divine protection and support was intended to bolster and encourage the recipient. To obey the Lord was costly, but the divine presence was graciously offered as encouragement.

An additional title, "messenger," is given to Haggai in this passage (v. 13). The Hebrew term מלאך (mal'ak) is rarely used to describe a prophet, although the name "Malachi" (מלאכי mal'ākî) means "my messenger" (Mal 1:1; 3:1; cf. 2 Chr 36:15-16). The "messenger" spoke "by" or "with" the Lord's "message" (במלאכות bĕmal'ăkût). To hear the messenger was tantamount to hearing the "voice of the LORD their God," for so were the prophets perceived (Deut 18:18-19; Jer 42:4-6; 43:1-7). The idea was either that Haggai's message was God's message or that Haggai spoke as one commissioned by the Lord.

The Lord "their God" (three times in Hag 1:12, 14) not only sent the messenger, but also "stirred up" the hearers. By repeating the names of those already mentioned (v. 12), the prophet underscores the significance of this divine act. The "spirit" of each is awakened, aroused, spurred to action (cf. Isa 41:2, 25; 45:13; 50:4). Because of this divine stirring, they came and worked (lit., "they did a work"). The Hebrew term for "work" (מלאכה mĕlā'kâ) recalls the term mal'ak. With the messenger's assurance ("message" [mal'ăkût]), they turned to the task of rebuilding (mĕlā'kâ) the Temple, the house of the Lord of hosts (v. 14).

1:15a. This verse presents a problem. It seems appended awkwardly to the preceding verses. Usually the date formula is situated at the beginning of a unit (so 1:1; 2:1, 10, 20). The unusual position of the date in v. 15a has prompted some to argue that it originally was linked as the introduction to Hag 2:15-19.[25] While the suggestion to link these passages is interesting, no ancient manuscripts support such a radical rearrangement of the text. Clearly the second half of the verse (v. 15b) belongs with Hag 2:1. Rather than dislocating v. 15a by moving it to the next chapter, it seems best to understand it as concluding the unit that began at v. 12.

25. Ibid., 59-60.

REFLECTIONS

1. God's prophet is God's messenger. The messenger is the medium of God's voice, but not in any spiritualistic sense of the term *medium*. Haggai was a human being to whom a message was entrusted. God, through Haggai, called the leaders and the people to the task of rebuilding the Temple. As in most other places in the Bible, there is no information, and apparently no interest, in how the message was given to Haggai. There is nothing to support or deny the various doctrines concerning the inspiration of Scripture; such doctrines have too often served to distract and divide so many who love God and seek to serve the Lord. How the prophet received the word is simply not an issue in this text. What is important is the message itself. That is the point of concentration. Anything that diverts interest away from the message is to be ignored.

God continues to charge individuals and communities with speaking and living the divine message. Their task is faithfully to proclaim by word and by deed God's will and purpose. The messengers will always prove imperfect, but without claiming to be more or less than they are, their task (our task?) is to deliver God's message within all the ambiguities that mark the contemporary situation.

2. In response to the prophetic word, the leaders and the people "obeyed" and "feared" the Lord. Obedience and fear are strongly emphasized in this passage. For Israel, to hear God's commandments was to live by that instruction. For Israel, hearing was not a neutral act, not just the physical act of receiving and interpreting sound patterns. Hearing, rather, required response—namely, to do God's will, to obey. In the call "Hear, O Israel," repeated through the centuries in Jewish liturgy, Israel is commanded to heed the instruction of the Lord God, thereby loving God alone and living in God's way (Deut 6:4-9). In a much different context, the letter of James reflects a similar understanding in its admonition to "be doers of the word, and not merely hearers" (Jas 1:22 NRSV).

Additionally, however, there is the need for fear, a profound sense of awe that acknowledges human creaturehood, with all its limitations, in the presence of the Lord of hosts. The idea is not that of crawling before God or claiming absolute worthlessness. Rather, the point is to acknowledge God as God, as inherently other than humankind and all else that God has created. Isaiah 55:6-9 lyrically expresses the basis for the proper fear or awe of God. But if this awe-filled sense of God's grandeur is too much for someone and leads to a sense of helplessness or worthlessness, ironically the only remedy is the mysterious, sometimes frightening presence of God that brings assurance and empowerment. It is this fear and this obedience that Haggai's message evoked.

In a time and context in which both obedience and fear (awe) are considered marks of weakness, it is difficult to envision a response pleasing to God. The Bible does not suggest that God desires a mindless, cringing allegiance. Rather, the aim is people who in respect and gratitude intentionally accept and are guided by God's ways.

3. The response to Haggai's message was neither immediate nor only a matter of human willpower. The dating of this passage suggests that more than three weeks passed before work actually got underway. Those involved apparently were moved by the prophet's call to rebuild the Temple (1:8, 12), but they didn't begin work immediately. What took place between Haggai's first confrontation with the people and the actual beginning of the restoration of the Temple is not clear. Probably planning and preparation were necessary; the work had to be organized.

But the text is quite clear that something else was necessary as well. The work got underway when the Lord "stirred up the spirit" of the leaders and the people. For the task to be accomplished, God's inspiration was needed, and it was given. Human will was crucial, but human intention was not then and is not now sufficient apart from divine assistance.

How God "stirred up the spirit" of the people is not made clear. Perhaps Haggai's prophetic challenge played a role; perhaps individual hearts were touched by the divine. But by whatever means, divine inspiration, then as now, was a critical factor in the community's response.

TAKE COURAGE AND WORK

NIV

²15in the second year of King Darius. On the twenty-first day of the seventh month, the word of the LORD came through the prophet Haggai: ²"Speak to Zerubbabel son of Shealtiel, governor of Judah, to Joshua son of Jehozadak, the high priest, and to the remnant of the people. Ask them, ³'Who of you is left who saw this house in its former glory? How does it look to you now? Does it not seem to you like nothing? ⁴But now be strong, O Zerubbabel,' declares the LORD. 'Be strong, O Joshua son of Jehozadak, the high priest. Be strong, all you people of the land,' declares the LORD, 'and work. For I am with you,' declares the LORD Almighty. ⁵'This is what I covenanted with you when you came out of Egypt. And my Spirit remains among you. Do not fear.'

⁶"This is what the LORD Almighty says: 'In a little while I will once more shake the heavens and the earth, the sea and the dry land. ⁷I will shake all nations, and the desired of all nations will come, and I will fill this house with glory,' says the LORD Almighty. ⁸'The silver is mine and the gold is mine,' declares the LORD Almighty. ⁹'The glory of this present house will be greater than the glory of the former house,' says the LORD Almighty. 'And in this place I will grant peace,' declares the LORD Almighty."

NRSV

2 In the second year of King Darius, ¹in the seventh month, on the twenty-first day of the month, the word of the LORD came by the prophet Haggai, saying: ²Speak now to Zerubbabel son of Shealtiel, governor of Judah, and to Joshua son of Jehozadak, the high priest, and to the remnant of the people, and say, ³Who is left among you that saw this house in its former glory? How does it look to you now? Is it not in your sight as nothing? ⁴Yet now take courage, O Zerubbabel, says the LORD; take courage, O Joshua, son of Jehozadak, the high priest; take courage, all you people of the land, says the LORD; work, for I am with you, says the LORD of hosts, ⁵according to the promise that I made you when you came out of Egypt. My spirit abides among you; do not fear. ⁶For thus says the LORD of hosts: Once again, in a little while, I will shake the heavens and the earth and the sea and the dry land; ⁷and I will shake all the nations, so that the treasure of all nations shall come, and I will fill this house with splendor, says the LORD of hosts. ⁸The silver is mine, and the gold is mine, says the LORD of hosts. ⁹The latter splendor of this house shall be greater than the former, says the LORD of hosts; and in this place I will give prosperity, says the LORD of hosts.

COMMENTARY

This third episode is dated to October 17, 520 BCE, one month later than the preceding one. This day, the twenty-first of the seventh month, happens to be the seventh day of the great eight-day autumn festival, the Feast of Booths, which begins on the fifteenth day of the seventh month (Lev 23:33-36, 39-43; Num 29:12-38). This very significant feast day celebrates the harvest and God's sustaining care.

During the Feast of Booths, or the Feast of Sukkot, Israelites celebrated Solomon's bringing the ark of the covenant into the Temple and the Temple's dedication (1 Kgs 8:1-13, 62-66). But as the name implies, the Feast of Booths also commemorates Israel's release from bondage in Egypt and the people's dwelling in booths as they traveled to Sinai (Lev 23:42-43). The reference in 2:5*a* to the exodus thus seems consistent in this passage and provides grounds for retaining these words, even though the Septuagint does not include them.[26]

The word of the Lord again comes "through" or "by" the prophet Haggai (cf. 1:1). Haggai speaks again to the same audience as in the previous scene: Zerubbabel, Joshua, and the "remnant of the people" (Hag 2:2). In 2:4, however, a different term for the people is introduced: "people of the land" (עם הארץ *'am hā'āreṣ*). The precise meaning of the Hebrew term is disputed. It seems to have first referred to the wealthy landed class of pre-exilic days (2 Kgs 21:14; 23:30). By the time of Ezra, however, some years after Haggai, it was used to refer to those people who were actively hostile to the rebuilding of the Temple, and not to those who had been in exile (Ezra 4:1-5). Probably Haggai used the term to refer to people who had stayed behind and had taken over the land vacated by people taken into exile.[27] In this passage, Haggai addresses "all" of "the people of the land," which may imply that the audience was composed of both persons who had never left Palestine and those who had returned from exile (2:4).

Although work had begun on the rebuilding project, some of the people were critical and dissatisfied. Reflected in the prophet's questions in v. 3 are the people's complaints. Apparently some of the older members of the community did not have much good to say about the new structure they saw emerging (2:3). Although sixty years had passed, they could still remember what the Temple looked like before it was destroyed in 587 BCE. Haggai addressed their cynicism and disappointment directly: "Is it not in your sight as nothing?" (v. 3). He admitted that the Temple did not look like much yet. By so doing he silenced the complainers and challenged them, along with all the others, to have confidence in what God was about to do.

The prophet next turns to positive exhortation (v. 4). The "now" (עתה *'attâ*) of v. 3, used in connection with the disappointment of perceived reality (namely, the unimpressive nature of the new temple) is put aside with the second "now" that begins v. 4. "Now" a new resolve is to be made. Three times Haggai enjoins the leaders and the people to "take courage" or to "be strong" (חזק *ḥăzaq*). The leaders and the people, all the people of the land, needed to disregard the negative comments and continue with the task. "Take courage, and work!" (see v. 4) Why? Because "I am with you, says the LORD of hosts" (v. 4). As in the preceding passage (1:13), the prophet's primary response to uncertainty or withdrawal of commitment on the part of his audience was the affirmation of God's presence. Indeed, God's "Spirit," the very presence of God, already "abides" or "remains" among the community. Just as they were assured that God would take pleasure in their work no matter what they did (1:8), so also now they are assured that God's Spirit is already among them. God was in their midst, and thus they had nothing to fear (v. 5*b*; cf. 1:13).

Verses 6-9 constitute a second reason for the people to take courage and work. Not only is God's Spirit in their midst, but also the Lord of hosts is about to act once again. The language of v. 6*a* connotes that the anticipated event is imminent. This is not the eschatological "day of the LORD," even though it has sometimes been so interpreted. Rather, this is an imminent intervention by God for a very specific purpose: that the treasure of the nations will come, providing splendor to the restored Temple (v. 7).

The imagery used to describe God's action is reminiscent of the theophanic tradition, the tradition of God's appearing accompanied by the cataclysmic shaking of the heavens and the earth (Exod 19:18; Judg 5:4-5; Ps 18:7-15). But in this passage nature and nations do not just react by trembling at God's approach, as in the theophanic tradition. Rather, the Lord of hosts is pictured as shaking the heavens and the earth, the sea and the dry land, all creation, and the nations as well (vv. 6-7). The term "shake" (רעש *rā'aš*) is used at times to refer to an earthquake (Amos 1:1). But the root *r'š*, when used in the more specialized verb form Hiphil as in v. 7, may refer to the shaking of historical institutions (cf. Isa 14:16; Ezek 31:16). There is no reason why the participle מרעיש (*mar'îš*) need be translated in the future tense. God "shakes" the nations in order that the Temple may once again become splendid (v. 7).

Verse 7 presents interesting terminology. The

26. See David L. Petersen, *Haggai and Zechariah 1–8,* OTL (Philadelphia: Westminster, 1984) 66.

27. See Hans Walter Wolff, *Haggai,* trans. Margaret Kohl (Minneapolis: Augsburg, 1988; German edition in *BK* series 1986) 78-79.

word translated as "splendor" (NRSV) or "glory" (NIV) is כבוד (*kābôd*). While *kābôd* sometimes refers to God's presence (Exod 40:34; Ezek 10:18-19), in this passage it means "honor" or "wealth." God is going to fill the Temple with wealth or with the splendor that comes from beautiful and expensive appointments. Indeed, the "splendor" and "glory" of the new Temple will exceed that of the first one (v. 9). People who remember the former glory will be amazed (v. 3).

The "glory" or "splendor" will be achieved because God's shaking of the nations will bring the "treasure of all nations" or "the desired of all nations" to fill the Temple. The difference between the NRSV and the NIV translations reflects various understandings of חמדת (*hemdat*). If the term is translated as it stands in the MT text, then it is a singular feminine construct form of "desire" (cf. 2 Sam 9:20). The Vulgate translation understands the term as a reference to the Messiah, who, as "the desire of all the nations," would one day return to the Temple. Christians have incorporated this understanding in the hymn "Come, Thou Long-Expected Jesus."

There is a major problem with this interpretation, however, since the singular noun is the subject of a plural verb, "they will come" (ובאו *ûbā'û*). With a slight change in the way the Hebrew is pronounced, this problem can be elimi-

nated. Instead of *hemdat*, the editors of *BHS* suggest *hămudōt*, a reading supported by the Septuagint. Such a plural form is found in Gen 27:15 and Ezra 8:27, where it refers to precious, desirable things. Hence, the term can be translated as "treasure of all nations" (NRSV) and understood, in part, as a reference to the treasures that once were taken away from the Temple (2 Kgs 25:13-17). These would now be returned with even more than what had originally been taken (Ezra 1:5-11; cf. Isa 60:8-18). As a result, the glory and splendor of the Temple are assured.

Two comments remain concerning this unit. First, Hag 2:8 boldly affirms that the treasure, the "silver and the gold," belong to God. Lest there be any misunderstanding or misappropriation of the wealth that would bring splendor to the Temple, the text affirms God's ownership of the Temple and its glory. God alone was the provider of the Temple's splendor. Second, Hag 2:9 affirms that God's intention is to establish "peace" or "prosperity." The point is that when God gives this שלום (*šālôm*), the hard times described in the opening scene (1:6, 9-11) will be brought to an end. Hostilities will cease. The community will be restored. Wholeness will return. Shalom, which includes both peace and prosperity, will result.

REFLECTIONS

1. It was no accident that the prophet addressed the people on this day. Tradition and expectation are brought together at such commemorative moments. Old symbols can be reframed for new messages. The very occasion of the festival was a message of continuity beyond destruction, hope, and thanksgiving, even in the midst of despair. Haggai's word on this occasion was a challenge to the present for the sake of the future in the midst of a celebration of the constancy and generosity of the Lord.

For Jews today, the celebration of Sukkot testifies to the ongoing care of God for the world and all its peoples in an age of great skepticism and disbelief. For contemporary Christians, Easter functions in somewhat the same way by enabling us to face the destructive reality of death with a word of promise and renewal that points beyond the grave. In our hearing such a declaration of God's constancy and generosity, once again can hope, thanksgiving, and renewal be manifested among God's people for the sake of all God's creatures.

2. Language about God's shaking of creation, including the nations, is obvious in this passage. There are two ways that such imagery can be appropriated. The negative way is to consider this language as strictly end-of-time, as impressive but not relevant in the present, scientifically oriented world. Some people take such language as proof of an underdeveloped or misconceived understanding of God. Such an approach underscores the difference between ancient and modern worldviews.

A more positive reading, however, draws upon the fact that in ancient Israel the same language could be used to describe the activities of a terrible king, utterly human, the king of Babylon, who at the height of his powers had made nations shake and the earth tremble (Isa 14:16-17). This understanding of the language suggests that God's activity does not have to be read literally or eschatologically.

The hyperbole can be heard for what it is. God's intervention may be understood as being brought about by human beings. The text emphasizes that God will bring about the return of the previous liturgical and ornamental items that were stripped from the earlier Temple, and these will then be used to create an even more splendid Temple. Metaphor it clearly is, but hardly nonsense. Human hands are still most frequently the means of divine agency.

3. God cared about Judah and the people Haggai addressed. Therefore, restoration was assured—about this, the people could be certain. But God's intention went beyond the repair of a destroyed temple. God desired to bestow blessings and would not settle for less. The early post-exilic community was poor and struggling. They had worked hard during the nearly twenty years since the exiles had been allowed to return to rebuild Jerusalem. While many had at least adequate housing, the drought of 520 BCE had made life all the more difficult. Haggai's principal foes were older folk, perhaps well-meaning at one level, who kept comparing the memory of a glorious past with their experience of a mediocre to poor present. The "good old days" seemed so much better (and perhaps actually were), but that was now immaterial.

The task of each generation is to take courage in God's goodness and to work on behalf of God's purposes. Loyalty and dedication are measured by the degree of willingness to stick to the task. Discouragement and depression are contagious and need to be resisted. Haggai was certain that whatever the restored Temple was to be, it would be better than the heap of stones then standing in Jerusalem's center. God wanted dedication to the task, not nostalgia for the past.

Thus God's gracious word to Haggai not only assured the people that the Temple would be made splendid, but also that the ill health of the community, its economic weakness, its vulnerability, would be replaced by God's "peace." *Shalom,* peace, is a rich term that includes restoration of health, cessation of hostilities, and enrichment of individual and community life, prosperity in the richest sense of the term. God's ongoing commitment is to establish shalom in this world—God's richest blessing.

God's peace, however, is never disembodied. It always occurs in real space among real people. There is not only a spiritual side but also, of equal importance, a material side. To suggest that only the soul is important to God is to ignore prophetic texts (e.g., Isa 25:6-8; 61:1-4; 65:17-25) and Gospel accounts (e.g., Matt 25:31-46) alike. The announcement of God's shalom always carries this twofold (spiritual and material) meaning.

FROM THIS DAY ON

¹⁰On the twenty-fourth day of the ninth month, in the second year of Darius, the word of the LORD came to the prophet Haggai: ¹¹"This is what the LORD Almighty says: 'Ask the priests what the law says: ¹²If a person carries consecrated meat in the fold of his garment, and that fold touches some bread or stew, some wine, oil or other food, does it become consecrated?'"

The priests answered, "No."

¹³Then Haggai said, "If a person defiled by contact with a dead body touches one of these things, does it become defiled?"

"Yes," the priests replied, "it becomes defiled."

¹⁴Then Haggai said, "'So it is with this people and this nation in my sight,' declares the LORD. 'Whatever they do and whatever they offer there is defiled.

¹⁵"'Now give careful thought to this from this day on[a]—consider how things were before one stone was laid on another in the LORD's temple. ¹⁶When anyone came to a heap of twenty measures, there were only ten. When anyone went to a wine vat to draw fifty measures, there were only twenty. ¹⁷I struck all the work of your hands with blight, mildew and hail, yet you did not turn to me,' declares the LORD. ¹⁸'From this day on, from this twenty-fourth day of the ninth month, give careful thought to the day when the foundation of the LORD's temple was laid. Give careful thought: ¹⁹Is there yet any seed left in the barn? Until now, the vine and the fig tree, the pomegranate and the olive tree have not borne fruit.

"'From this day on I will bless you.'"

[a]15 Or to the days past

¹⁰On the twenty-fourth day of the ninth month, in the second year of Darius, the word of the LORD came by the prophet Haggai, saying: ¹¹Thus says the LORD of hosts: Ask the priests for a ruling: ¹²If one carries consecrated meat in the fold of one's garment, and with the fold touches bread, or stew, or wine, or oil, or any kind of food, does it become holy? The priests answered, "No." ¹³Then Haggai said, "If one who is unclean by contact with a dead body touches any of these, does it become unclean?" The priests answered, "Yes, it becomes unclean." ¹⁴Haggai then said, So is it with this people, and with this nation before me, says the LORD; and so with every work of their hands; and what they offer there is unclean. ¹⁵But now, consider what will come to pass from this day on. Before a stone was placed upon a stone in the LORD's temple, ¹⁶how did you fare?[a] When one came to a heap of twenty measures, there were but ten; when one came to the wine vat to draw fifty measures, there were but twenty. ¹⁷I struck you and all the products of your toil with blight and mildew and hail; yet you did not return to me, says the LORD. ¹⁸Consider from this day on, from the twenty-fourth day of the ninth month. Since the day that the foundation of the LORD's temple was laid, consider: ¹⁹Is there any seed left in the barn? Do the vine, the fig tree, the pomegranate, and the olive tree still yield nothing? From this day on I will bless you.

[a] Gk: Heb since they were

COMMENTARY

This fourth episode is dated to December 18, 520 BCE, two months later than the prophet's previous word. There was nothing special about the date—no appointed festival, no special moment in Israel's history to remember. The significance of the day is found in the events of the day itself. On this day the Lord's word came "to" (אֶל *'el*) and not "through" Haggai (v. 10; cf. 1:1, 3; 2:1). On this day something very special happened (v. 15). On this day a new period of divine blessing began, according to the prophet, a renewal of the relationship between God and Haggai's community.

2:10-14. The opening section of this unit presents two questions that Haggai is told to place before the priests for a "ruling" (NRSV), or "what the law says" (NIV). Haggai is following time-established custom when he asks for a "decision" or "instruction" (תורה *tôrâ*). But Haggai's request is designed, in turn, to instruct the community (v. 11). The form of the questions posed, by the custom he follows, requires a "yes" or "no" response on the part of the priests. The setting seems to be described in Leviticus with respect to the duties assigned the Aaronites (Lev 10:10-11).

The first question centers on the extent to which "holiness" (קדש *qōdeš*) is transferable (v. 12). Clearly anything that came into direct contact with consecrated meat within a holy place was made "holy" (Lev 6:26-29). But, Haggai asks, "Does it go any further?" If meat that had been made holy by an act of consecration was taken away from the altar to be eaten at home (cf. Lev 7:16-17) and then inadvertently came in contact with other food in the house, did these things become holy? The priests' answer is clear: "No" (v. 12).

The second question probes the issue of uncleanness. The Hebrew is cryptic. The subject of the verb טמא־נפש (*těmē'-nepeš*), usually translated "defiled" or "unclean by contact with a dead body," apparently is a shorter form of a priestly term designating someone who is unclean because he or she has come in contact with a corpse (see Num 5:2; 6:6; 9:10; 19:11, 13). Such ritual uncleanness was one of the three most dangerous types of uncleanness with which the community had to contend (Num 5:2-4). The answer to Haggai's query as to whether someone in such a state of uncleanness could contaminate others was quite clear, according to the priests: "Yes" (v. 13).

The conclusion Haggai announces to the people on the basis of the teaching received from the priests is that "every work of their hands" is thus unclean (v. 14). The offerings presented "before" or "in the sight of" the Lord were tainted and

unacceptable. Although the offerings might have been conducted by "holy" priests, their holiness was not sufficient to overcome the ritual uncleanness of the setting. Thus the offerings were rendered unclean, and they, in turn, made every work of the people's hands unclean.

Two major interpretations have been advanced to explain the situation behind these verses. Wolff, following Rothstein, has argued that the expressions "this people" and "this nation" referred to the Samaritans. According to Ezra 4:1-5, the Samaritans had sought to participate in the rebuilding of the Temple but were prohibited by Zerubbabel, Joshua, and other leaders in the community. By this reading, Haggai's words may be understood possibly as part of the reason why the Samaritans were rejected. As people of mixed lineage, the Samaritans were considered unclean by those who had gone into exile and had returned. Thus, if the Samaritans participated in the rebuilding project, their uncleanness would have contaminated the whole project, making it unacceptable to God.[28]

Petersen, on the other hand, who stands with the majority of interpreters, puts forward another and more convincing interpretation. The real problem was not with the Samaritans (whose conflict with the Judahites likely did not become severe until much later) but with the altar upon which the Judahites were making their sacrifices. The central altar in the temple complex had at least been desecrated, if not utterly destroyed, by the Babylonians when they captured Jerusalem (2 Kgs 25:8-10; Lam 4:14-15). Indeed, according to the prophet Ezekiel, the Temple had become defiled even before the Babylonians had entered it to such a degree that the presence of God was withdrawn (Ezek 8:5-18). Haggai's concern, according to Petersen, was that the altar was being used even before the Temple was rebuilt, but without the proper ritual purification (cf. Ezra 3:1-7). Thus the offerings presented on it were made unclean.

The references, then, to "this people" and to "this nation" in v. 14 are to the same audience mentioned previously (1:2, 12; 2:2, 4), and the problem was that they had brought offerings, "the work of their hands," that had become unclean

28. Wolff, *Haggai,* 92-94.

because the great altar had not yet properly been cleansed of its defilement.[29]

2:15-19. A dramatic shift occurs in v. 15, marked by ועתה (*wĕ ʿattâ*; NRSV, "but now"; NIV, "and now"). As in Hag 1:5, this term connects what follows with what has preceded, but with a decided change of focus. "From this day on" things will be different (vv. 15, 18). The people are to "consider," to take to heart what is about to happen (cf. Hag 1:5, 7). No longer will provisions placed in storage be diminished by unexplained causes (v. 16), nor would crops be destroyed by God-sent plagues (v. 17). Rather, "from this day on," from December 18, 520 BCE, a new era of prosperity is on the horizon (vv. 18-19).

29. Petersen, *Haggai and Zechariah 1–8,* 79-85.

What is so important about this day? In the language of v. 15, on this day "a stone was placed upon a stone" or "a stone was laid on another." On this day, "the "foundation of the LORD's temple was laid" (v. 18). Work had already begun earlier (Hag 1:12-15), but the actual setting of the foundation stone and rededication of the Temple, including its cleansing from defilement, took place on December 18 (cf. Ezra 3:10-13; Zech 4:9). According to custom, a stone from the previous Temple was put in place as part of the foundation of the new structure, thereby assuring continuity with the past as the community moves toward the future. Prayers and sacrifices are offered. Thereby the necessary ritual purification of the Temple and its altar is accomplished. A new order, from Haggai's perspective, has begun.

REFLECTIONS

1. The issue of cultic holiness or contamination may not seem especially relevant to people today. The contagious and dangerous character of some diseases, such as the Ebola virus, is an appropriate matter of concern, but worry over whether something is cultically (religiously) clean or unclean will not stir many today. Nonetheless, the apprehension in Haggai's time over cultic contagion was as real as that experienced by many persons now (usually out of ignorance) over the virus that produces AIDS. That something could become holy merely by contact with the holy or unclean by contact with something defiled was a matter of significance for Haggai's people. Thus the way one dealt with things clean and unclean mattered.

What is at stake is attitude. If one believes something is unclean or off limits, then it is unclean for that person and should not be handled, and certainly not presented to God (cf. Rom 14:14). To disregard God's way and still come before God as if nothing is wrong is offensive to God (cf. Jer 7:8-15). Where an obvious duty (like repairing and rededicating the Temple) is ignored or refused, or where people willingly accept contamination by contact with the unclean, God's people are not presenting themselves as a "living sacrifice, holy and acceptable to God" (Rom 12:1 NRSV). Knowing what is acceptable to God and then choosing to ignore or violate that knowledge renders one "unclean." Those who come before God with an uncaring or scornful attitude concerning such "uncleanness" risk God's holy displeasure.

Although definitions and modes of what is holy/profane and clean/unclean may change, allegiance to God and the commitment to live life before God are still of utmost importance. The manner in which people choose to serve or not to serve God is the issue.

2. The work of the people's hands was unclean and unacceptable because of the context in which they worked. Because the altar and the Temple were unclean, all that the people did was unclean. They may not have been aware of their uncleanness. They may not even have been able to avoid becoming unclean. Nonetheless, by their participation, willing or unwilling, in worship at an unclean altar and temple, their offerings became tainted and unacceptable.

Ignorance of the law is no excuse, as the saying goes. When a person today fails to report income properly, before the law he or she is guilty. If someone supports a government that is unjust or exploitative, that person shares in the guilt. The wrongdoing may go unrecognized or unacknowledged, as was the case among all too many Christians in Europe and the United States during the Nazi persecution of the Jews between 1933 and 1945, but the wrongdoing is nonetheless real and destructive.

Sometimes systems become so bad, so corrupt, that they must be rejected outright. Sometimes there is no way to cooperate or to compromise with corruption. Sometimes fundamental, context-altering changes have to be made before anything clean or good can be brought forth. Corporate wickedness/uncleanness is much more difficult to recognize (after all, everyone is doing it) and to change (after all, it's a way of life) than is individual behavior. Sexism, racism, ageism—such social wrongdoings all too often go unchallenged among God's people, thereby tainting all the good they try to do.

3. "But now"—circumstances can always change. What had appeared as an unchangeable situation was altered by an act of fidelity. History is replete with examples of sudden, unexpected changes. One of the most dramatic was the collapse of the Soviet Union in the early 1990s and the dissolution of what appeared a mighty and almost invincible superpower. Suddenly, almost overnight, the whole balance of world politics, economy, and military alliance was undone. The consequences, good and bad, continue to unfold, but whatever the outcome, it is clear that there has been a dramatic and unanticipated change in circumstances.

Insofar as a choice can be made, to follow God's way is more likely than not to lead to good things. Still, the faithful in times of trouble will look ahead and hope for the "but now." Likewise, in good times the faithful will watch lest complacency and self-satisfaction lead to disaster. God's "but now" is a reminder that circumstances can change dramatically and that evil will not prevail forever.

4. Setting the cornerstone or foundation of a building is perhaps the most significant moment in the creation of a new structure. Certainly this was the case when the destroyed and defiled Temple of the Lord in Jerusalem was rededicated. Christians often have taken this ceremony as a metaphor for the establishing of the church as a new Temple founded on Jesus Christ, the cornerstone (Eph 2:20; 1 Pet 2:4-6). Further, seeing Ps 118:22 as a reference to Jesus, Christians have claimed that though some have rejected the precious stone and have stumbled on it, such is not the case with those who have followed Jesus (Acts 4:11; Rom 9:33; cf. Mark 21:42; Luke 20:17). Obviously Haggai did not have such things in mind when he pronounced his word, for it was intended for his own day. But religious tradition reshapes and reinterprets the words of one generation for another. Thus, while not Haggai's original intent, it is understandable how the Christian tradition would use his language and imagery in proclaiming the wonder of the establishment of the church founded upon Jesus Christ, God's cornerstone.

LIKE A SIGNET RING

NIV

²⁰The word of the LORD came to Haggai a second time on the twenty-fourth day of the month: ²¹"Tell Zerubbabel governor of Judah that I will shake the heavens and the earth. ²²I will overturn royal thrones and shatter the power of the foreign kingdoms. I will overthrow chariots and their drivers; horses and their riders will fall, each by the sword of his brother.

²³"'On that day,' declares the LORD Almighty, 'I will take you, my servant Zerubbabel son of Shealtiel,' declares the LORD, 'and I will make you like my signet ring, for I have chosen you,' declares the LORD Almighty."

NRSV

20The word of the LORD came a second time to Haggai on the twenty-fourth day of the month: ²¹Speak to Zerubbabel, governor of Judah, saying, I am about to shake the heavens and the earth, ²²and to overthrow the throne of kingdoms; I am about to destroy the strength of the kingdoms of the nations, and overthrow the chariots and their riders; and the horses and their riders shall fall, every one by the sword of a comrade. ²³On that day, says the LORD of hosts, I will take you, O Zerubbabel my servant, son of Shealtiel, says the LORD, and make you like a signet ring; for I have chosen you, says the LORD of hosts.

COMMENTARY

A second episode is dated to December 18, 520 BCE. As before, the word came "to Haggai," though the term "the prophet" is not repeated (v. 20; cf. 1:1, 3, 12; 2:1, 10). The word was to be announced only to Zerubbabel, the governor of Judah. The previous word was presumably spoken to the people (v. 14), but this book's concluding word to Zerubbabel in his capacity as political leader is spoken privately.

2:21-22. The unit actually preserves two oracles, the first more general (vv. 21-22), and the second quite specific (v. 23). The first begins with words that echo Haggai's October oracle: The Lord is "about to shake the heavens and the earth" (v. 21; cf. v. 6). The NRSV translates מרעיש (*mar'îš*) "about to shake," while NIV renders it as "will shake." The term in question is a Hiphil participle and does not require a future translation. Thus translating it in the present tense better conveys the meaning here and in the following verse. "I shake," "I overthrow," and "I destroy," all refer to God's past activity, which may also occur again. God "overthrew" Sodom and Gomorrah (Gen 19:25, 29; Isa 13:19; Amos 4:11). God

had the power to overthrow enemy chariots, sending them to destruction as the deity had delivered Israel from Egypt (v. 22; cf. Exod 14:28; 15:4-5, 19, 21). In the language of holy war, God sets enemy against enemy in order to triumph (v. 22; cf. Judg 7:22; Ezek 38:21). Petersen, noting a number of other points of parallel as well, rightly concludes that Haggai's rhetoric "places him squarely within the standard discourse of Israel's classical prophets."[30]

2:23. The first oracle primarily affirms that the Lord who addressed Zerubbabel through Haggai, the Lord of heaven and earth, exercises dominion over the kingdoms of the nations as well (vv. 21-22). The second oracle is much more specific and concerns Zerubbabel alone (v. 23). The connection between the two is made with the phrase "on that day" (ביום ההוא *bayyôm hahû'*). Together these two oracles link God's rule of the world with the specific intent to assign Zerubbabel a very special role in that rule. "On that day" should not be construed as some indefinite or eschatological day. Rather, it is a particular day on which

30. Ibid., 99.

God chooses Zerubbabel, governor of Judah, as God's agent.

The language used about Zerubbabel is subtle but clear to those who know the tradition. Haggai never called Zerubbabel a king or a prince, titles that would have raised profoundly troubling political questions. Haggai 1:1 had already referred to the one king that mattered in Judah's history at that time—namely, Darius. But the special relationship between God and Zerubbabel, the grandson of Jehoiachin, the last Davidic king to sit on the throne in Jerusalem, is nonetheless explicit and powerful. God "takes" Zerubbabel, "chooses" him (v. 23). The Lord calls Zerubbabel "my servant" (עבדי 'abdî), a term especially used as a Davidic title (2 Sam 7:5; 1 Kgs 11:32, 36; Ezek 34:23; 37:24-25), but a term Jeremiah had also used of Nebuchadnezzar (Jer 25:9; 27:6) and that Isaiah had bestowed upon Cyrus (Isa 45:1). Further, the Lord makes Zerubbabel "a signet ring" (v. 23; the NIV's "like my signet ring" is certainly a reasonable translation, but the pronoun "my" does not occur in the Hebrew text).

The term "signet ring" (חותם hôtām) bears special importance. The signet ring was actually a seal in the form of either a cylinder or a scarab. It could be worn on the finger or on a chain around the neck or arm. It was used to validate important documents and procedures. To set one's seal in witness to a proceeding was legally binding. For the Lord to make Zerubbabel like a signet ring, therefore, was a powerful image.

One other biblical text provides important background for understanding this verse. In Jer 22:24-26, Jeremiah reports that Jehoiachin, the king of Judah, will be taken into exile. The image Jeremiah uses is striking. Even if the king were "the signet ring on my [God's] right hand," he would

be torn off and given into the hands of the Babylonians (Jer 22:24 NRSV). In contrast, Haggai may now be suggesting that God is supporting the Davidic heir. The signet ring (symbolizing King Jehoiachin) that was torn from the Lord's hand would now be replaced by Jehoiachin's grandson Zerubbabel, a new signet ring, to exercise authority on behalf of God.

The claim here is subtle but strong. Haggai does not challenge Persian authority, but he does put it into perspective. Darius was the king, but it was God who shook the nations and ruled over them. In the world's eyes, Zerubbabel was governor of Judah, but to God he was the divine signet ring authorized to act on behalf of God in rebuilding the Temple and, perhaps, in accomplishing even greater things in the days ahead.

In the Old Testament, Zerubbabel is mentioned only in a limited number of texts outside of Haggai and always in relation to the reconstruction of Jerusalem and the Temple (see, e.g., 1 Chr 3:19; Ezra 2:2; 3:2, 8; 4:2, 3; 5:2; Neh 7:7; 12:1, 47; Zech 4:6, 7, 9-10). It remains one of the great puzzles that, after reaching the zenith ascribed to him here by Haggai, nothing more is known about the activities of Zerubbabel. To Haggai he appeared as a very special man chosen and designated by God, but apart from a story found in the apocryphal book of 1 Esdras (3:1-5:3), which probably is not historical, and a reference in Sirach (49:11-12), the only other references to this man occur in the genealogies of Jesus (Matt 1:12-13; Luke 3:27). For his own day, Zerubbabel was surely a symbol of hope and the ongoing care of God. For later generations, he was a reminder that God always works through specific human beings toward the accomplishment of the divine purpose.

REFLECTIONS

1. Although the main concern of Haggai the prophet was the rebuilding and rededication of a relatively insignificant temple in a small district in the backwaters of the Persian Empire (at least as far as world opinion would have judged it), the real issue is the worldwide dominion of the Lord of hosts. Israel was always tempted to believe that the Lord was concerned only with Israel. Moreover, the countries surrounding and often dominating Israel believed that the Lord of hosts, if a god at all, was certainly only a local and lesser deity.

But, according to Haggai, this God is able to shake the foundations of the universe, to overthrow kingdoms, and to rearrange the power structures of the world. Obviously such an affirmation can be made only through faith. Jews and Christians have made such a claim across the centuries, celebrating in anticipation the fullness of God's reign and the inevitable elimination of evil. Many people may now question the very reality of God, but people of faith continue to share Haggai's conviction of God's worldwide dominion.

2. God ensures a continuity from past to future. Haggai remembers and alludes to God's dramatic interventions in the past, the overthrow of mighty nations and cities, and the delivery of Israel from bondage. Haggai is confident that God will lead the people into the future. This passage is neither a call to revolution nor an appeal to an eschatological end. These words encouraged people in the present. Haggai aimed to enable the people to learn from their past what to expect in the future. God is the basis of both past and future and the guide and strength for the present.

3. Once again, Haggai makes an obvious point: God works through people. Zerubbabel is acknowledged as God's very special agent. Zerubbabel as servant carries foward God's promise to David. Zerubbabel as signet ring is granted authority as God's proxy, the right to sign in God's place. From a human point of view, this amazing display of divine engagement has at least two effects. On the one hand, it demonstrates the high regard God has for humankind. As the culmination of creation, in the very image of God, humans are God's special love (Gen 1:26-30; Ps 8:3-8). With all human beings God stands in everlasting covenant (Gen 9:8-17). It is with and for humans that God's presence is made manifest in this world (Exod 24:9-18; John 1:14). On the other hand, it means that divine action is always troublesomely ambiguous, veiled as it is in human flesh. The Davidic heir, Zerubbabel, no doubt recognized this. Certainly another in David's lineage lived with this reality five centuries later as he grew up in Nazareth of Galilee.

THE BOOK OF ZECHARIAH

INTRODUCTION, COMMENTARY, AND REFLECTIONS
BY
BEN C. OLLENBURGER

THE BOOK OF
ZECHARIAH

INTRODUCTION

The book of Zechariah comes next to last in the "Book of the Twelve," or what are sometimes called the minor prophets. The literature now gathered under the name of Zechariah exists in at least two quite distinct parts. Since the seventeenth century, scholars have argued that some or all of chaps. 9–14 was written by someone other than the author of chaps. 1–8 and that the two sections were written at different times. Joseph Mede noted that Matt 27:9 attributes the statement about the thirty shekels of silver in Zech 11:13 to Jeremiah. In defense of the New Testament's accuracy, Mede argued that Zechariah 9–11 was indeed written by Jeremiah, a century earlier than Zechariah.[1] Since Medes' time, the substantial differences between chaps. 1–8 and all of 9–14 have led all but the most conservative scholars to see these two parts of the book as coming from different hands. That view is followed in this commentary. Thus the major structural division in the book occurs between chaps. 1–8 and 9–14, which reflect sections now known as First and Second Zechariah.

FIRST ZECHARIAH

Structure, Form, and Composition. Within chaps. 1–8 a series of eight visions (1:7–6:15) is framed by a pair of sermons. The first of these sermons (1:1-6) is brief and retrospective. It reports a call to repentance, modeled on the preaching of the "former prophets" to the forebears, and the community's positive response. In style and vocabulary,

1. See J. Baldwin, *Haggai, Zechariah, Malachi* (Atlanta: John Knox, 1986) 63.

vv. 1-6 strongly resemble the second, much longer sermon that comprises chaps. 7–8. There, too, the preaching of the former prophets is of key importance, as is the refusal of the forebears to respond to their words. This lack of a response led to Yahweh's judgment, devastation, and the difficult circumstances from which Yahweh now promises to deliver the community (7:8-14; 8:1-8). However, nowhere in the longer sermon, or in the visions, is there a call to repentance like that of 1:3: "Return to me, says the LORD of hosts, and I will return to you" (NRSV). On the contrary, in both the sermons and the visions the reversal of communal fortunes is Yahweh's own initiative (8:11). The precise language of 1:3 occurs elsewhere only in Mal 3:7, although it shares the perspective of the prophetic speeches in Chronicles (e.g., 2 Chr 30:6; cf. Joel 2:12-14). It seems that Zechariah's editors have composed a brief sermon on the basis of chaps. 7–8, but from a different theological perspective, which now serves as a preface to the visions: Yahweh's gracious announcements in the remainder of First Zechariah—especially Yahweh's promises to "return" (1:16; 8:3)—are now prefaced by, and predicated on, the community's repentance or return to Yahweh. In this way, Zechariah's editors have interpreted Zechariah in the direction of Haggai.

These editors have done so as well by providing a chronological framework for both the sermons and the visions in the superscriptions to each part (1:1, 7; 7:1), which link Zechariah's activity with Haggai's. The first chapter of the book of Haggai attributes the community's ills to its ignoring the Temple, which "lies in ruins" (Hag 1:9 NRSV), and exhorts them to rebuild it (1:8). Conversely, Haggai's second chapter attributes the community's dramatically improved fortunes to the people's beginning to work on temple reconstruction (Hag 2:15-19). Haggai's exhortation in chap. 1 is dated in the sixth month, and his reflections in chap. 2 are dated in the ninth month (2:10, 18). The redactors of Zechariah placed Zech 1:2-6 squarely between these two dates, sometime in the eighth month (1:1). In this way, they urge us to interpret the community's "return" in Zech 1:6 along lines provided by Haggai 1, as the theological premise of what Zechariah sees in his visions.

At the heart of First Zechariah are the visions, dated late in the eleventh month (1:7). They are arranged in chiastic fashion, with the first and the last visions framing the others. As explained in the commentary to chap. 1, the arrangement of the visions corresponds to their varying foci; in the first (1:8-17) and last (6:1-8) visions, the focus extends to the whole world. The focus first narrows to Judah and then to Jerusalem and finally to the lampstand—symbol of Yahweh's presence—in chap. 4; it then expands outward again to encompass the whole world. At one stage in the book's composition, this arrangement probably included seven visions, with chap. 4 as their center and pivot.[2] These visions, excluding chap. 3, are variations on a common pattern, in which Zechariah converses with an interpreting angel:

1. Zechariah reports a vision: "I saw. . . . "
2. He describes a sign: "and there before me was/were. . . ."

2. Carol L. Meyers and Eric M. Meyers, *Haggai and Zechariah 1–8,* AB 25B (New York: Doubleday, 1987) liv-lvii.

3. He asks: "What is this/are these?"
4. The angel identifies the sign: "This is/these are. . . . "
5. The angel interprets the sign.[3]

Chapter 3 departs significantly from this pattern to focus on Joshua the high priest. This chapter was probably added secondarily, increasing the number of visions to eight and giving them this arrangement:

(1) 1:8-17 Horses and riders patrolling the earth
    (2) 1:18-21 Four horns and four smiths
    (3) 2:1-5 Jerusalem without limits
        (4) 3:1-10 Joshua the high priest
        (5) 4:1-6a, 10b-14 The lampstand
    (6) 5:1-4 A flying scroll
    (7) 5:5-11 A flying ephah
(8) 6:1-8 Horses and chariots patrolling the earth

The addition of chap. 3 is not the only way in which editorial activity has affected the character of the visions. Intruding into what is now the fifth vision is an oracle addressed to Zerubbabel (4:6b 10a), described in Haggai as the "governor of Judah" (Hag 1:1). The oracle in Zechariah 4 identifies Zerubbabel as the temple builder, a role assigned in Zech 6:9-15 to an anonymous but expected "branch"—a royal figure from David's line, also expected in 3:8. Editorial activity here reflects uncertainty and perhaps disagreement about the role of Zerubbabel, to whom Haggai attaches extraordinary expectations (Hag 2:20-23). Further, there is some evidence that the first three visions, in chaps. 1 and 2, were once an independent collection. With their accompanying oracles (1:14-17; 2:6-13[10-17]), these visions respond to the distress expressed in 1:12, envisioning Yahweh's return to Jerusalem, the elimination of oppression by the nations, Yahweh's action against Babylon and the nations, and the gathering of Jerusalem's people—and people from the nations—as God's people, culminating with Yahweh's dwelling in Zion. As a response to these things, all flesh is to be silent (2:13). With what was, at one stage in the formation of the book, the next vision (chap. 4), Zechariah has to be roused as if from sleep, suggesting that the visions in chaps. 4–6 were added to form a collection of seven, with chap. 3 added subsequently as a supplement to chap. 4.

The visionary material in First Zechariah includes oracles as well. These are identified by formulae introducing them or within them, including "thus says Yahweh" (messenger formula, 1:14), "says Yahweh" (oracle formula, 2:5), and "the word of Yahweh came to . . . " (revelation formula, 4:8). The oracles in chaps. 1–2 are integrally related to the content of the visions they follow, by interpreting or expanding on them. The oracular

---

3. Michael Fishbane, *Biblical Interpretation in Ancient Israel* (Oxford: Clarendon, 1985) 448.

conclusion to chap. 3, in vv. 6-10, issues in an address to Joshua, as is also the case with Zerubbabel in 4:6-10 a. In contrast, the oracular conclusion (6:9-15) to the vision sequence bears a less evident relation to the vision preceding it.

The oracles that follow Zechariah's visions constitute an extended sermon. How they function structurally or rhetorically is explained in the Commentary on chap. 7. In chaps. 7–8, Zechariah is not a seer of visions but a prophet and an interpreter of the tradition. The superscription in 7:1 dates the sermon approximately two years after the visions. In its content, and especially in what it promises for the future, the sermon is closely related to the material in chaps. 1–2.

The Date and Setting of First Zechariah. Each of the superscriptions in First Zechariah, like those in Haggai, dates the material in the reign of Darius, king of Persia, either to his second year (1:1, 7) or to his fourth (7:1). These correspond to 520 and early 519, and to 518 BCE. Darius was third in the succession of Persian emperors, the first of whom, Cyrus, led Persia in displacing Babylon as the imperial power controlling the Mediterranean region. Cyrus made it Persian policy, after 539 BCE, to repatriate populations that had been exiled to Babylon, a policy celebrated in Ezra 1:1-4. The policy continued under Cambyses and then Darius, who assumed the throne in 522 BCE. He secured his reign against militant opposition in 520, the year assigned to Zechariah's first sermon and his visions. The Persian policy toward exiles, especially under Darius, was motivated by more than benevolence. It was designed to foster loyalty in the provinces and to provide efficient means of imperial control, including the collection of revenues. To this end, Darius supported or mandated the reconstruction of provincial institutions—religious, social, and economic—under authorized local leadership. Central among these institutions, in Judah's case as elsewhere, was the Temple; by Persian design, it was the administrative, cultic, and financial center of an essentially agrarian economy.

Under Persian organization, Judah (or in its Aramaic form, "Yehud") was part of the satrapy "Beyond the River," administered from Babylon. Whether it had provincial status, with its own governor, is a matter of dispute, but it does seem probable. According to Ezra, Zerubbabel and Joshua led a group of the *golah*—Jewish exiles—from Babylon to Judah and two years later initiated the rebuilding of the Temple (Ezra 2:1-2; 3:8-9). Haggai assumes that Zerubbabel and Joshua were Judah's leaders, as governor and high priest (Hag 1:1). In that case, and also by Persian design, it was members of the *golah,* repatriated from Babylon, who assumed civic and cultic authority in Judah, most of whose population had not been exiled. But in the Persian period, following the Babylonian conquest earlier in the sixth century BCE, Judah was only a fraction of its former self. In area, it comprised approximately 900 square miles, about the size of the greater Chicago metropolitan area, with a population only a third as large as it was earlier. Jerusalem's population, perhaps six or seven thousand before its destruction in 586 BCE, numbered only a few hundred in 520.[4] Zechariah's expectation that Judah's towns would overflow with goods (1:17), and that Jerusalem's population would exceed the capacity

4. Meyers and Meyers, *Haggai and Zechariah 1–8,* 24-25; and the same authors, "Demography and Diatribes: Yehud's Population and the Prophecy of Second Zechariah," in *Scripture and Other Artifacts,* ed. M. Coogan, J. Exum, L. Stager (Louisville: Westminister/John Knox, 1994) 268-85.

of any walls (2:4[8]; cf. 8:5), takes on new light in view of these data; he expects that Yahweh will reverse present conditions and past ones.

Basic Themes in First Zechariah. (1) Reversal is itself a persistent theme of chaps. 1–8. It is expressed within the visions, where Yahweh will reverse the relative situations of Judah/Jerusalem and the nations (1:14-17), and in the long sermon, where the reversal of Judah's fortunes is joined with a reversal of Yahweh's stance toward the community (8:10-13).

(2) But reversal, whether in the abstract or in relation to specific circumstances, is subordinate to Zechariah's implicit and explicit claim that Yahweh is "lord of the whole earth" (4:14). This claim does not easily comport with that of an empire like that of the Persians. Zechariah affirms the sovereignty of Israel's God.

(3) In the logic of the Zion tradition, in which Zechariah stands, Yahweh's lordship— Yahweh's dominion—is exercised from the divine dwelling place, Zion. In this regard, everything, and every kind of reversal, depends on God's return to Zion, which Zechariah's visions and sermons announce. God is specially related to a certain place.

(4) Within the community, leadership will be shared between the high priest and a royal figure (3:8-10; 4:10b-14; 6:9-15). However, one does not have the sense that this is a real-life political program. Rather, the "civic" authority is the subject of future expectation, of a messianic sort associated with David. In both 3:8-10 and 6:9-15, the priests are principally to bear witness to the promise of this coming "branch" of David.

(5) The Temple will be the locus of Yahweh's presence and dominion, symbolized by the lampstand in chap. 4. However, unlike Haggai, Zechariah nowhere urges the community to initiate or to continue building the Temple. Its reconstruction, under charge of the royal "branch," will correspond to the newly ordered world that Zechariah envisions and announces.

(6) This newly ordered world has a social and moral character that contrasts with the past and the present. The land will be purged of its guilt (3:9) and of its wickedness (5:1-11). In the future, truthfulness, justice, and peace will characterize the people of Judah (8:10-19). Moral transformation is not the condition of God's return, but results from it.

(7) Throughout, First Zechariah expects that other nations will be included in the glorious future promised to Judah and Jerusalem. Robbed of their destructive powers (1:18-21[2:1-4]) and witnessing to God's presence, they will be included among Yahweh's people (2:15[11]; 8:20-23). As with several other themes, this one deserves to be called eschatological.

Zechariah the Prophet. The literature associated with him provides few details about Zechariah. The superscriptions (1:1, 7) identify Zechariah as the son of Berechiah and the grandson of Iddo. The book of Ezra describes Zechariah as the close colleague of Haggai (Ezra 5:1-2; 6:14). Indeed, Ezra never mentions one without the other. This view is reflected in the editing of Zechariah 1–7, which coordinates, through the chronological references, Zechariah's activity with Haggai's. In one detail, Ezra disagrees with the superscriptions in Zech 1:1, 7. While these name Berechiah as Zechariah's father and Iddo as his grandfather, Ezra 5:1 and 6:14 say that Zechariah was the "son of Iddo." They make no mention of Berechiah. Perhaps Iddo was a family name. The names "Iddo" and "Berechiah" are used frequently in the OT, and there is no way to determine from which family Zechariah the prophet descended.

SECOND ZECHARIAH

Second Zechariah (chaps. 9–14) presents a complex and often discordant vision of the future, and in a literary style vastly different from those of First Zechariah. Apart from chap. 11, the prophetic persona so prominent in First Zechariah is completely absent from these chapters, as are any concrete references to their occasion. They refer to no identifiable person, no Zerubbabel or Joshua, and no Zechariah; they provide sparse and uncertain clues to their date; and the religious, social, and political concerns they address can be inferred only with great difficulty, and only tentatively. If our Bibles did not bind these latter chapters together with the first eight, we may find few reasons to connect them with Zechariah.[5] Indeed, some have suggested that Zechariah 9–11; 12–14; and Malachi are a three-part prophetic collection, two parts of which are now joined artificially to Zechariah 1–8.[6] Among the reasons for this suggestion is the presence in Zech 9:1; 12:1; Mal 1:1 of a phrase that occurs in each of these verses and nowhere else; it can be translated: "oracle of the word of Yahweh,"[7] though neither the NIV nor the NRSV translates it this way.

Structure, Form, and Composition. The material in these chapters is visionary, in the broadest sense of the term—it envisions the future. Of course, this is true of much prophetic literature and particularly of First Zechariah. However, two interrelated features of Second Zechariah mark its unusual visionary character. First, to articulate the vision, it refers extensively to other OT texts. Envisioning the future is here a literary and even an exegetical activity.[8] To some extent, this is true of First Zechariah as well; its visions and oracles draw especially on Isaiah and Jeremiah (see Commentary on chaps. 1 and 2). But in contrast to the symmetrical arrangement of visions and oracles of Zechariah 1–6, Second Zechariah exhibits a profusion of genres: "invectives, threats, heraldic odes, promises, extended metaphors, symbolic actions," and others, in a form more "anthology-like" than symmetrical.[9]

Second, as a way of envisioning the future, Zechariah 9–14 *re*-envisions the past. For example, the poems in chaps. 9 and 10 not only draw from earlier texts, but also portray the future as a recapitulation and thus as a restoration, without a single specific reference to present circumstances. The description of Yahweh's march in 9:1-8 could be set in

5. But see Rex A. Mason, "The Relation of Zech. 9–14 to Proto-Zechariah," *ZAW* 88 (1976) 227-39.
6. D. Peterson, *Zechariah 9–14 and Malachi,* OTL (Louisville: Westminster/John Knox, 1995) 2-3.
7. Eugene H. Merrill, *Haggai, Zechariah, Malachi: An Exegetical Commentary* (Chicago: Moody, 1994) 240.
8. Katrina J. A. Larkin, *The Eschatology of Second Zechariah* (Kampen: Pharos, 1994) 27-39.
9. Meyers and Meyers, *Haggai and Zechariah 1–8,* 46-47.

almost any period of Judah's history,[10] and 10:11 speaks as if Assyria and Egypt were still the world's great imperial powers. The past, and precisely God's action on behalf of Israel, is paradigmatic, and these poems draw from earlier texts to construct the paradigm. The narrative in 11:4-14 complicates this paradigm, suggesting conflict and disintegration rather than restoration. Although it is an autobiographical narrative, this text can be read as a symbol of Israel's history—and its future. Even the ominous announcements in 12:2-3 and 14:1-2 that the world will gather for war against Jerusalem recapitulate the past. Once before, "all the kingdoms of the earth" fought against Jerusalem (Jer 34:1; Zech 12:3), with exile the result (Zech 14:2). On the other hand, the future envisioned in Zechariah 12, and much more so in chap. 14, is not simply a restoration; it is utopia.[11] While restoration leaves intact conditions that can lead again to disintegration and exile, the utopian future of chaps. 12 and 14 eliminates those conditions. Here the future becomes radically discontinuous with the past, and such radical discontinuity involves violent conflict. These chapters depict a world at war, with its focus on Jerusalem. In Second Zechariah, the ordered world of First Zechariah is fractured, awaiting a new ordering.[12]

These observations make plausible the suggestion that Second Zechariah comprises two collections, chaps. 9–11 and 12–14, each designated as "an oracle" (משא *maśśā'*). The differences between them involve style and rhetoric, as well as content. For example, the first collection makes extensive use of subordinate causal or explanatory clauses introduced by כי (*kî*, "because" or "for"), characteristic of prophetic speech. This conjunction occurs twenty times in chaps. 9–11, but only four times in 12–14, three of them in 13:3-5. By contrast, the phrase "on that day" punctuates chaps. 12–14, where it occurs seventeen times (in reference to the future, it occurs only at 9:16 within chaps. 9–11).

Still, the material within each of these collections (9–11; 12–14) is not all of a piece. The narrative of 11:4-14 departs abruptly from the eschatological visions in chaps. 9–10, and the continuity between and within those two chapters is editorial. Forming a part of this continuity is the motif of sheep (or the flock) and shepherds, which first appears in 9:16. It is picked up again in 10:2 and then in 11:1-3, and is explored at length in 11:4-14. Finally, in 11:15-17, the shepherd suffers a violent punishment. Similarly, chaps. 12 and 14 present different scenarios of the future, and they are separated by 13:2-6, which predicts the elimination of prophets. But chap. 13 has links to both chap. 12 and chap. 14. The elimination of prophets is joined to the cleansing offered the house of David (12:10; 13:1-2), and the stabbing of prophets (13:3) echoes the stabbing or piercing of an anonymous victim in 12:10. The conclusion of chap. 13, in vv. 7-9, envisions another kind of cleansing, by fire, which will kill one-third of the population. This motif introduces the war and exile of 14:1-2. For these reasons Zechariah 13 is pivotal within the second collection (chaps. 12–14), which is distinct from 9–11.

---

10. P. Hanson, *The Dawn of Apocalyptic* (Philadelphia: Fortress, 1975) 316.

11. Shemaryahu Talmon, "The Concept of Masiah and Messianism in Early Judaism," in *The Messiah: Developments in Earlier Judaism and Christianity,* ed. James H. Charlesworth (Minneapolis: Fortress, 1992) 79-115.

12. Brevard Childs, *Introduction to the Old Testament as Scripture* (Philadelphia: Fortress, 1979) 483.

While it is evident that chaps. 9–11 and 12–14 are two collections, their independence is only relative. In its concluding verses, chap. 13 returns to the sheep/shepherd motif of chaps. 9–11. In 13:7 the shepherd is struck with a sword and the sheep scattered. This is the only occurrence of the motif in chaps. 12–14, and it echoes 11:17; there, too, the shepherd encounters a sword. The act of violence against the shepherd has a different meaning in the two passages, but it does forge a connection between the two larger collections, or "oracles." Just as chap. 13 is pivotal within chaps. 12–14, so also chap. 11 is pivotal between chaps. 9–10 and 12–14.

Date and Setting. It is clear in Zech 11:17 and 13:7 that the shepherd is a figure of leadership of or within the community. This is not obvious in 10:2, and it is not the case in 11:1-3. Neither is it made explicit in either 11:4-17 or 13:7-9 exactly what leader(s) or what form of leadership—civil, cultic, prophetic—is in view. However, Zechariah 11 and the larger context of chap. 13 strongly suggest conflict within the community—i.e., within the community that can be described as Yahweh's sheep (9:16). Since the work of Otto Plöger,[13] and more recently of Paul Hanson, it has become common to interpret Second Zechariah against the background of intra-communal conflict. Such interpretation is rendered problematic by the very obscurity of the texts, by the absence of concrete references to people or events, and thus by permanent uncertainty about the times and circumstances in which these texts were written, collected, edited, and published. However, it seems clear enough that there is a conflict between the future as restoration, envisioned in chaps. 9–10, and the utopia envisioned in chaps. 12 and 14. And it may be that the nature of that conflict is reflected in chaps. 11 and 13.

Second Zechariah cannot be dated with any certainty; in addition, its several chapters, or parts of them, may come from different times. Proposals range from the seventh to the second century BCE. The commentary on chaps. 12–14 assumes that these materials are related to changes in Persian policy toward Judah and Jerusalem at the time of Nehemiah, just after the middle of the fifth century BCE. At this time, Persia sought to strengthen its control over, and military defenses within, the eastern Mediterranean area and to more effectively centralize the administration of Judah in Jerusalem.[14] Such social changes as these efforts brought about do not explain Second Zechariah, but they provide a plausible occasion for the violence and salvation that Jerusalem is expected to suffer, according to chaps. 12 and 14.

Theological Issues. Second Zechariah attests quite diverse expectations of the future. But in all cases the future depends on the action of God. Second Zechariah is a radically theocentric text; the only action it expressly enjoins on the community is to rejoice, and this injunction is addressed to Zion/Jerusalem at the entrance of its king (9:9). As in First Zechariah, the Zion tradition is prominent here, especially in chaps. 9 and 14. As do Zechariah's visions, Second Zechariah expects a future royal figure in the line of David.

---

13. Otto Plöger, *Theocracy and Eschatology* (Oxford: Blackwell, 1968) 78-96.
14. Carol Meyers and Eric Meyers, *Zechariah 9–14*, AB 25C (New York: Doubleday, 1993) 20-23.

But this expectation, clearly expressed in 9:9-10 and implicit in 10:4-5, becomes complicated in chaps. 11–13 and is entirely absent from chap. 14. And again, like First Zechariah, the second part of the book envisions a world newly ordered, re-created, by God's initiative. But it comes to see the way to the future as fraught with conflict, suffering, and death. Perhaps for that reason Second Zechariah figures prominently in the NT's passion narratives.

BIBLIOGRAPHY

Achtemeier, Elizabeth. *Nahum–Malachi.* Interpretation. Atlanta: John Knox, 1986. Includes a brief commentary on Zechariah oriented to preaching.

Baldwin, Joyce. *Haggai, Zechariah, Malachi.* Tyndale Old Testament Commentaries. Downers Grove, Ill.: Inter-Varsity, 1972. Thoroughly informed, insightful, and compact.

Calvin, John. *Commentaries on the Twelve Minor Prophets,* vol. 5. Grand Rapids: Eerdmans, 1950. Remarkably sober and scholarly for its time, it remains a valuable resource for Christian interpreters.

Hanson, Paul D. *The Dawn of Apocalyptic.* Philadelphia: Fortress, 1975. An influential and technical study that interprets Second Zechariah's community as dissenting from the priestly leadership in Judah, as represented by First Zechariah. Relates Second Zechariah to the beginnings of apocalyptic literature.

Larkin, Katrina J. A. *The Eschatology of Second Zechariah.* Kampen: Pharos, 1994. Disagrees with Hanson and relates Second Zechariah to the interpretive activity of wisdom circles.

Luther, Martin. *Lectures on the Minor Prophets.* Vol. 3: *Zechariah; Luther's Works,* vol. 20. St. Louis: Concordia, 1973. Contains two full commentaries, Luther's lectures of 1526 and 1527. Displays Luther's Law-Gospel hermeneutic.

Mason, Rex. *The Books of Haggai, Zechariah, and Malachi.* CBC. Cambridge: Cambridge University Press, 1977. The commentary on Zechariah is very brief, but especially valuable for showing Zechariah's use of earlier biblical tradition.

————. *Preaching the Tradition: Homily and Hermeneutics After the Exile.* Cambridge: Cambridge University Press, 1991. Contains a thorough literary examination of Zechariah in relation to similar material in Chronicles and Ezra–Nehemiah.

Merrill, Eugene H. *Haggai, Zechariah, Malachi: An Exegetical Commentary.* Chicago: Moody, 1994. A conservative evangelical commentary, critically informed and thorough, with an eye to the NT.

Meyers, Carol L., and Eric M. Meyers. *Haggai and Zechariah 1–8,* and *Zechariah 9–14* AB 25B, 25C. New York: Doubleday, 1987, 1993. With Petersen's, the definitive commentary on Zechariah in English. Nothing is omitted.

Mitchell, Hinckley G. *A Critical and Exegetical Commentary on Haggai and Zechariah.* ICC. Edinburgh: T. & T. Clark, 1912. An old standard.

Petersen, David L. *Haggai and Zechariah 1–8.* OTL. Philadelphia: Westminster, 1984; *Zechariah 9–14 and Malachi.* OTL. Louisville: Westminster John Knox, 1995. With the Meyers's, the definitive commentary in English. (The commentary on Zechariah 9–14 was published too late to be used here.)

Redditt, Paul L. *Haggai, Zechariah, Malachi.* NCB. Grand Rapids: Eerdmans, 1995. (Published too late to be used here.)

Smith, Ralph L. *Micah–Malachi.* WBC. Waco: Word, 1984. Especially useful for its brief, but thorough, references to past scholarship.

OUTLINE OF ZECHARIAH

I. Zechariah 1:1–8:23, First Zechariah

    A. 1:1-6, Return to Me, and I Will Return to You

    B. 1:7–6:15, Zechariah's Visions

        1:7–2:17, Visions of Global Transformation

            1:7-17, The First Vision: Yahweh Is Returning to Jerusalem

            1:18-21, The Second Vision: Four Horns and Four Smiths

            2:1-5, The Third Vision: An Expansive Jerusalem

            2:6-13, Babylon and Zion

        3:1–4:14, Visions of Restoration and Divine Presence

            3:1-10, The Fourth Vision: Joshua the High Priest, the Satan, and the Branch

            4:1-14, The Fifth Vision: A Golden Lampstand and Zerubbabel

        5:1-11, A Flying Scroll and an Ephah Flown Away

            5:1-4, The Sixth Vision: A Flying Scroll

            5:5-11, The Seventh Vision: This Is the Ephah

        6:1-8, The Eighth Vision: The Four Winds of Heaven

        6:9-15, The Priest and the Branch

    C. 7:1–8:23, A Long Sermon on Fasting and Celebration

        7:1-6, Shall I Go On Mourning?

        7:7-14, This Is the Message of the Prophets

        8:1-8, It May Well Seem Impossible

        8:9-13, Let Your Hands Be Strong

        8:14-15, I Have Purposed to Do Good

        8:16-17, These Are the Things to Do

        8:18-19, Fasting Will Be Celebration

        8:20-23, We Have Heard That God Is with You

II. Zechariah 9:1–14:21, Second Zechariah

    A. 9:1–11:17, Promises of Restoration and a Narrative of Disintegration

        9:1-17, The Restoration of Zion

            9:1-8, An Itinerary of Disempowerment

            9:9-10, The Entry of Zion's King

            9:11-17, War Resumes

        10:1-12, The Restoration of Judah and Israel

        11:1-3, Trees and Shepherds Wail

        11:4-17, The Shepherd's Story

    B. 12:1–14:21, War, Purification, and Re-creation

        12:1–13:1, War and Purification

        12:1-8, War Against Jerusalem

FIRST ZECHARIAH

ZECHARIAH 1:1-6, RETURN TO ME, AND I WILL RETURN TO YOU

NIV

1 In the eighth month of the second year of Darius, the word of the LORD came to the prophet Zechariah son of Berekiah, the son of Iddo:

[2]"The LORD was very angry with your forefathers. [3]Therefore tell the people: This is what the LORD Almighty says: 'Return to me,' declares the LORD Almighty, 'and I will return to you,' says the LORD Almighty. [4]Do not be like your forefathers, to whom the earlier prophets proclaimed: This is what the LORD Almighty says: 'Turn from your evil ways and your evil practices.' But they would not listen or pay attention to me, declares the LORD. [5]Where are your forefathers now? And the prophets, do they live forever? [6]But did not my words and my decrees, which I commanded my servants the prophets, overtake your forefathers?

"Then they repented and said, 'The LORD Almighty has done to us what our ways and practices deserve, just as he determined to do.'"

NRSV

1 In the eighth month, in the second year of Darius, the word of the LORD came to the prophet Zechariah son of Berechiah son of Iddo, saying: [2]The LORD was very angry with your ancestors. [3]Therefore say to them, Thus says the LORD of hosts: Return to me, says the LORD of hosts, and I will return to you, says the LORD of hosts. [4]Do not be like your ancestors, to whom the former prophets proclaimed, "Thus says the LORD of hosts, Return from your evil ways and from your evil deeds." But they did not hear or heed me, says the LORD. [5]Your ancestors, where are they? And the prophets, do they live forever? [6]But my words and my statutes, which I commanded my servants the prophets, did they not overtake your ancestors? So they repented and said, "The LORD of hosts has dealt with us according to our ways and deeds, just as he planned to do."

COMMENTARY

This opening section of Zechariah comprises a brief sermon that serves as a preface to the visions that extend from 1:7 through chap. 6. Moreover, it exhibits striking similarities of language and style to the much longer sermon on fasting and celebration in chaps. 7–8. These two sermons, of vastly different length, encompass Zechariah's visions.

Framing the sermon itself are two editorial components, the superscription (v. 1) and a report (v. 6) that the people repented or "(re)turned" (שׁוב *šûb*).

This is exactly what Zechariah, speaking in Yahweh's name, urged them to do, so that Yahweh would return to them (v. 3). In heeding God's Word, the people acknowledge their identity with the ancestors—the ancestors' ways and deeds (v. 4) they acknowledge as their own (v. 6*b*). But in repenting they distinguished themselves from their ancestors, to whom the former prophets had delivered the same message but without success (v. 4). This provoked Yahweh's anger (v. 2), which is the occasion of the plural "you" in v. 2.

In the course of the sermon, the words that had overtaken the ancestors also overtake their descendants (v. 6a). Zechariah's preaching joins the people with their ancestors, and it also links Zechariah with the former prophets. This latter connection is evident in the way Zechariah makes earlier prophets' words his own. The citation in v. 4 of the former prophets is not only a synopsis of earlier prophetic preaching, but also a direct allusion to Jer 25:5: "Turn . . . from your wicked ways and from your wicked deeds" (cf. Ezek 24:14). Moreover, these words of Jeremiah are themselves a quotation of even earlier prophets, of Yahweh's "servants the prophets" (Jer 25:4; Zech 1:6a). And the observation in v. 4 that the ancestors disregarded the prophets mirrors the similar complaint in Jer 25:3-4, 7 ("but you would not listen"). The sermon thus locates Zechariah within a prophetic tradition. However, the sermon incorporates other biblical texts as well. For example, the language of Zechariah's rhetorical question in v. 6a echoes that of the curses in Deuteronomy 28. Moses, in Deut 28:45, warns that curses will come upon Israel, *overtaking* them if they do not observe the commandments and *statutes* Yahweh *commanded* (cf. Deut 28:2, 15). Each of the terms in italic type appears in v. 6a. Even the people's response—as God has *purposed*

to do with us, so God has done (v. 6b)—mirrors another text; in lamenting the destruction of Jerusalem, Lam 2:17 affirms that "Yahweh has *done* what he *purposed*" (Jer 24:8; 51:12).

The sermon is a tissue of quotations and allusions.[15] It derives its content and its authority from earlier words of Yahweh. But it derives its force from the rhetorical questions Zechariah poses in vv. 5-6a. These elicit assent: Yes, the ancestors are gone, and so even are the prophets; but Yahweh's words and statutes do not suffer the same mortality. They endure, even after overtaking our ancestors.

The people's repentance, their (re)turning, which opens them to God's own return, is a fitting preface to the visions that follow. They consistently announce and depict Yahweh's return to Zion. According to the superscription (v. 1), Zechariah's sermon came in the autumn of Darius's second year (520 BCE), shortly after Haggai and Zechariah, along with many others, came from Babylon to Judah. It was a new community in a new place, uncertain of its future and its past. Zechariah's sermon offers them both.

---

15. Rex Mason, *Preaching the Tradition: Homily and Hermeneutics After the Exile* (Cambridge: Cambridge University Press, 1991) 199-205.

REFLECTIONS

The opening verses of Zechariah present the reader with a crystallization of the entire prophetic drama: God's anger at God's people (1:2), the call to repentance and return to Yahweh (1:3-5), and the people's repentance (1:6). This brief sermon should not be read simply as a harsh indictment or severe warning and hence as inappropriate words for a group of people in need, not of judgment, but of hope. Rather, hope is precisely what Zechariah offers here. It is not a glib hope, grounded in simple optimism, but a hope grounded in the community's identity as God's people and their share in the history of that people.

This history is formed not only by God's words and statutes, but also by the people's continuing refusal to heed those words. In 1:1-6, Zechariah accuses the people of nothing and makes no threats. Instead, he confronts the people with the same words constantly proclaimed by the former prophets and invites the people to return to God (1:4). When the people do repent and return to Yahweh (1:6), their words make no reference to the ancestors. Instead of locating the cause of their present situation in their ancestors' failures (cf. Lam 5:7, "Our ancestors sinned; they are no more, and *we* bear *their* iniquities"), they refer directly to *our* ways and *our* deeds, and to what Yahweh has done with *us*.

The community's repentance in 1:6, then, is not simply a question of corporate guilt. Rather, their repentance acknowledges that God's enduring Word from the past is addressed to them in the present moment, that they belong to the ongoing story of God's judgment and promise.

The words "return to me and I will return to you" provide more than a call to repentance; they are an invitation to reunion. The book of Zechariah thus opens with an invitation to its first readers and to contemporary readers to claim their identity as God's people and to return to the God who defines their lives and is the source of hope for their present and their future.

ZECHARIAH 1:7–6:15, ZECHARIAH'S VISIONS

OVERVIEW

To move from Zechariah's sermon (1:1-6) to the visions that follow is to enter a different and unfamiliar world. Here horses range the earth, and women with wings fly. It is a visionary world alive with motion and urgency, and with deep purpose. Zechariah envisions a restoration of Judah and Jerusalem, the civic and cultic life of the community and its institutions, its leadership, and its spirit. But he envisions all of this as the restoration of sacred space and thus as the restoration, or re-creation, of that space where heaven and earth converge. Jon D. Levenson refers in this regard to the "homology of temple and created world," reflected in biblical accounts of creation and of the construction of the sanctuary. The Old Testament depicts "the sanctuary as a world, that is, an ordered, supportive, and obedient environment," and "the world as a sanctuary, that is, a place in which the reign of God is visible and unchallenged, and his holiness is palpable, unthreatened, and pervasive."[16] It is this homology that lies behind Zechariah's visions, or rather before them. What he envisions is its restoration—not only, and not in the first place, of the Temple but also of the world. This conception is reflected in the arrangement and scope of the visions themselves.[17]

At the outer limits of the vision sequence (chaps. 1 and 6), the whole world is in view, while at the heart (chap. 4) is a single lampstand and the Temple. The focus of the visions moves inward from the periphery to the center, and then back to the periphery. At both extremes of this movement, at the beginning and at the end, things are at rest and quiet. But in between, the world has changed. This is what Zechariah envisions and struggles to discern. The form of the visions reflects not only the obscurity that Zechariah confronts, but also the power somehow at work behind it. He is protected from both by the intermediary, an angel, who interprets what Zechariah glimpses and stands between him and the Lord. Typically, Zechariah sees a sign: something that he can describe, but not identify. The interpreting angel speaks with Zechariah, identifies the sign, and interprets it.[18] It is a process of revelation through conversation, often issuing in oracles. Following angelic conversations, Zechariah regains his prophetic voice.

16. Jon D. Levenson, *Creation and the Persistence of Evil: The Jewish Drama of Divine Omnipotence* (San Francisco: Harper & Row, 1988) 82, 86.

17. Carol Meyers and Eric Meyers, *Haggai and Zechariah 1–8,* AB 25B (New York: Doubleday, 1987) liv-lvii.
18. Michael Fishbane, *Biblical Interpretation in Ancient Israel* (Oxford: Clarendon, 1985) 447-50.

Zechariah 1:7–2:17, Visions of Global Transformation

OVERVIEW

This section of First Zechariah is composed of three visions and a series of oracles. They form a coherent unit within the larger vision cycle. The announcement in 2:13[17], with its injunction to silence, is a coda to this unit, oriented around a common theme: God's action against the nations and for Jerusalem/Zion and Judah. The first vision (1:8-13) portrays the scene from which the promise of this action emerges, and the coda in 2:17[13] announces its inauguration: Yahweh has stirred or "roused himself from his holy dwelling." Yahweh's movement is from dwelling to dwelling. In 1:14 Yahweh announces that "I am returning" to Jerusalem, and in 2:14[10] promises to dwell there.

Zechariah 1:7-17, The First Vision: Yahweh Is Returning to Jerusalem

NIV

[7]On the twenty-fourth day of the eleventh month, the month of Shebat, in the second year of Darius, the word of the LORD came to the prophet Zechariah son of Berekiah, the son of Iddo.

[8]During the night I had a vision—and there before me was a man riding a red horse! He was standing among the myrtle trees in a ravine. Behind him were red, brown and white horses.

[9]I asked, "What are these, my lord?"

The angel who was talking with me answered, "I will show you what they are."

[10]Then the man standing among the myrtle trees explained, "They are the ones the LORD has sent to go throughout the earth."

[11]And they reported to the angel of the LORD, who was standing among the myrtle trees, "We have gone throughout the earth and found the whole world at rest and in peace."

[12]Then the angel of the LORD said, "LORD Almighty, how long will you withhold mercy from Jerusalem and from the towns of Judah, which you have been angry with these seventy years?" [13]So the LORD spoke kind and comforting words to the angel who talked with me.

[14]Then the angel who was speaking to me said, "Proclaim this word: This is what the LORD Almighty says: 'I am very jealous for Jerusalem and Zion, [15]but I am very angry with the nations that feel secure. I was only a little angry, but they added to the calamity.'

[16]"Therefore, this is what the LORD says: 'I will return to Jerusalem with mercy, and there my house will be rebuilt. And the measuring line will be stretched out over Jerusalem,' declares the LORD Almighty.

[17]"Proclaim further: This is what the LORD Almighty says: 'My towns will again overflow with prosperity, and the LORD will again comfort Zion and choose Jerusalem.'"

NRSV

[7]On the twenty-fourth day of the eleventh month, the month of Shebat, in the second year of Darius, the word of the LORD came to the prophet Zechariah son of Berechiah son of Iddo; and Zechariah[a] said, [8]In the night I saw a man riding on a red horse! He was standing among the myrtle trees in the glen; and behind him were red, sorrel, and white horses. [9]Then I said, "What are these, my lord?" The angel who talked with me said to me, "I will show you what they are." [10]So the man who was standing among the myrtle trees answered, "They are those whom the LORD has sent to patrol the earth." [11]Then they spoke to the angel of the LORD who was standing among the myrtle trees, "We have patrolled the earth, and lo, the whole earth remains at peace." [12]Then the angel of the LORD said, "O LORD of hosts, how long will you withhold mercy from Jerusalem and the cities of Judah, with which you have been angry these seventy years?" [13]Then the LORD replied with gracious and comforting words to the angel who talked with me. [14]So the angel who talked with me said to me, Proclaim this message: Thus says the LORD of hosts; I am very jealous for Jerusalem and for Zion. [15]And I am extremely angry with the nations that are at ease; for while I was only a little angry, they made the disaster worse. [16]Therefore, thus says the LORD, I have returned to Jerusalem with compassion; my house shall be built in it, says the LORD of hosts, and the measuring line shall be stretched out over Jerusalem. [17]Proclaim further: Thus says the LORD of hosts: My cities shall again overflow with prosperity; the LORD will again comfort Zion and again choose Jerusalem.

[a] Heb and he

COMMENTARY

1:7. The superscription repeats the information about Zechariah provided in 1:1. It also assigns a precise date to the visions, some three months after the sermon that precedes them. This would be in the winter of 519 BCE, five months after construction work on the Second Temple had begun (Hag 1:15). This superscription, like all of those in Haggai and Zechariah, is the work of editors. They understood the visions to be God's word at a critical moment in history. In one respect, the moment is one embedded in Persian history: the second year of the Persian king Darius. But that history is transcended and subverted in the visions. The present may bear the name Darius, but it is Yahweh who stamps the future.

1:8-13, Vision One. Zechariah's first vision moves in dramatic fashion to its climax in v. 13, where Yahweh is overheard speaking gracious and comforting words to the interpreting angel. This angel is Zechariah's intermediary in the visions, but in this first vision the process of mediation is especially complex.[19] Indeed, the words Yahweh speaks in v. 13 follow a series of dialogues that constitute the vision's drama. Zechariah is one participant in these dialogues; farthest removed from him is Yahweh, who only speaks to, and is only addressed by, angels. Zechariah has no direct access to Yahweh, but depends on intermediaries. These include the interpreting angel, of course, but also one identified as the angel of Yahweh (v. 11). While Zechariah overhears what is said to and by this Yahweh-angel (vv. 11-12), his own dialogue is only with the interpreting angel—and with a man "standing among the myrtle trees" (v. 10). This man, first introduced as being on horseback (v. 8), seems to command the horses, whom he identifies and who themselves speak in v. 11. They report to the Yahweh-angel, who then speaks plaintively to Yahweh (v. 12). It is this speech, this complaint, that provokes God's gracious and comforting words to the interpreting angel. Everything else in First Zechariah depends on these words and on the one who speaks them.

In this first vision, Zechariah's eyes open, at night, on a scene whose figures are already in place: the man on horseback and the horses behind him. It is important to note first that they are among the myrtles in what NRSV translates as "the glen" and the NIV as "a ravine." The precise meaning of the Hebrew word מצלה (*mĕṣulâ*) is in doubt, however. It derives from a word meaning "the deep," as in the depths of the sea—a place, indeed a power, at the extremity of the world and at the extreme limits of life (see Exod 15:15; Pss 69:2[3], 15[16]; 107:24; Jonah 2:3[4]). Reference to the deep in v. 8 reinforces the darkness implied by the myrtles, which Zechariah sees at night, and contributes to the numinous quality of the scene.[20] The myrtles in the deep here seem to shroud the presence of Yahweh, which is sometimes associated with darkness (1 Kgs 8:10-13; cf. Exod 20:21; 2 Sam 22:10 [= Ps 18:9(10)]; Ps 97:2). The luxuriant growth of myrtles is also suggestive of Eden, the garden of God (Isa 51:3; Ezek 27:23; 28:13). Finally, the angelic activity in this vision reminds one of Jacob's dream in Genesis 28. Jacob exclaimed that the site of his dream was the "gate of heaven" (Gen 28:17). Zechariah is situated in such a liminal space, a fluid boundary between heaven and earth.

The imagery Zechariah employs here is not merely ornamental to the content of the vision. He pictures a quiet and peaceful scene, even edenic, corresponding exactly to the report in v. 11 that the whole world remains quiet. But the scene is also fraught with the mystery and power of the deep. The quietness among the myrtles is not languid, but tense and highly charged. Horses arrayed behind a mounted rider—as if in military formation—bring the report. The horses are now at rest, after patrolling the earth, but the rider remains mounted; heaven remains mobilized.

This mounted rider and the horses behind him are the figures composing the vision's sign. They are what Zechariah asks the interpreting angel to identify. In fact, however, it is the rider, the man on horseback, who provides the identification; and it is the series of dialogues beginning in v. 11 that

---

19. Carol Meyers and Eric Meyers, *Haggai and Zechariah 1–8*, AB 25B (New York: Doubleday, 1987) 118.

20. Cf. David L. Petersen, *Haggai and Zechariah 1–8*, OTL (Philadelphia: Westminster, 1984) 139. It is interesting that in an Aramaic inscription, "Abyss" (מצלה *mĕsulâ*) is a deity paired with "Springs." See *TSSI* 2.7iA.11-12.

interpret the sign. This leaves the man on horseback without explicit identification.

Several features of the vision report allow the reader to identify the mounted rider with the Yahweh-angel. First, within the visions, only angels address human beings (e.g., 1:14; 2:8[4]; 3:6); such communication is appropriate to the function of angels as intermediaries and messengers. But in v. 10 the mounted rider seems to address Zechariah. Second, both the mounted rider and the Yahweh-angel are identified as "standing among the myrtle trees" (vv. 8, 10-11). Third, the position of the other horses behind the mounted rider, who speaks for them, suggests that he commands them. But, at the same time, the horses report directly to the Yahweh-angel, which suggests that he is their commander. And, fourth, it is this angel who communicates their report directly and immediately to Yahweh (v. 12). Thus the identity of the mounted rider—the man on a red horse—merges with that of the Yahweh-angel.

It is not entirely strange that a human figure should turn out to be an angel. Of the three men who visit Abraham and Sarah (Genesis 18), two of them turn out to be angels (Gen 19:1) when they come to Sodom. The New Testament also warns of this possibility (Heb 13:2). But it is strange that horses should speak, as they seem to do in v. 11. Perhaps this implies that these horses, too, have riders (the horses in the final vision [chap. 6] are hitched to chariots, but no riders [or drivers] are mentioned). What matters is what Zechariah's vision report tells us about these horses. First, it gives four colors for the horses, even if two of them turn out to be red (v. 8)! If these colors, or those in 6:2-3, had some significance, it has been lost. What remains significant is the number 4; it symbolizes totality, as do heaven's four winds in 2:6[10] and 6:5, and the four horns and smiths in 1:18-21[2:1-4]. Second, the text tells us that these horses had patrolled the whole earth; and that, third, Yahweh had commissioned them to do so (vv. 10-11). The horses are Yahweh's agents, and they have unlimited, universal range. Clearly, these are no ordinary horses.

Here it pays once more to compare this first vision to the last one in chap. 6. In both the first and the last visions, horses are described as patrolling the earth and as expressly commissioned

to do so (1:10-11; 6:7). In chap. 6, the horses appear after presenting themselves "before the LORD of all the earth" (6:5 NRSV). This same language occurs in Job 1:6-7; 2:1-2, where the "divine beings" (lit., "the sons of God") present themselves to Yahweh after patrolling the earth. That is to say, the horses in Zechariah's first and last visions act just as do the divine beings of Job 1–2. The Old Testament often portrays God as being accompanied by a retinue, which goes under a variety of names, including "sons of God" (see, e.g., Job 1–2; Ps 29:1). Sometimes this retinue appears as a deliberative body, or council, as in 1 Kgs 22:20-22 and Isa 6:8. Significantly, both of these texts envision God enthroned among a host (1 Kgs 22:19; Isa 6:1-3). In 1 Kgs 22:19, Micaiah sees "the host of heaven" standing or "stationed" before Yahweh, prepared to offer counsel and to do Yahweh's bidding. I suggest that Zechariah's first vision (not to mention his last one) portrays the four-colored horses, including the mounted rider-angel, as Yahweh's "host."

There is no precedent in the Old Testament for associating horses with the heavenly host. However, archaeologists have uncovered in the vicinity of Jerusalem a substantial number of horse figurines, most of them with riders.[21] These figurines are not part of any official cult, from which they would have been proscribed, but probably functioned in family worship and present popular piety. Othmar Keel and Christopher Uehlinger interpret these figures as personifications of the "host of heaven."[22] They also suggest that this "host" can be personified as the "angel of Yahweh" (so 2 Kgs 19:35). This is precisely what happens in Zechariah's first vision. In v. 12, after receiving the horses' report, the Yahweh-angel addresses God with the epithet "O LORD of hosts." While the epithet is pervasive in Zechariah's oracles, it occurs only here within the visions

21. John S. Holladay, Jr., "Religion in Israel and Judah Under the Monarchy: An Explicitly Archaeological Approach," in *Ancient Israelite Religion: Essays in Honor of Frank Moore Cross,* ed. Patrick D. Miller, Jr., Paul D. Hanson, S. Dean McBride (Philadelphia: Fortress, 1987) 249-99. Ephraim Stern provides pictures of representative figurines in *Material Culture of the Land of the Bible in the Persian Period, 538–332* B.C. (Warminster: Aris & Phillips/Jerusalem: Israel Exploration Society, 1982) 167.

22. Othmar Keel and Christopher Uehlinger, *Göttinnen, Götter und Gottessymbole: Neue Erkenntnisse zur Religionsgeschichte Kanaans und Israels aufgrund bislang unerschlossener ikonographischer Quellen,* QD 134 (Frieburg: Herder, 1993) 396-98. On p. 398 they make explicit reference to Zech 1:7-11.

proper. The Yahweh-angel addresses Yahweh as the Lord of that host whom the angel personifies, who have done Yahweh's bidding, and who now report to Yahweh. It seems, then, that Zechariah draws on both Old Testament tradition and popular religious customs in envisioning God's global reconnaissance as Lord of the earth and of heaven's host.[23]

This metaphor of heaven's host, with Yahweh as its Lord, is military in character. In Josh 5:13-15, Joshua is confronted by the commander of Yahweh's host, whose sword is drawn. Horses and riders themselves symbolize war (e.g., Pss 33:17; 76:6[7]; Hag 2:22 promises that "the horses and their riders shall fall, every one by the sword of a comrade" [NRSV]). In Zechariah's first vision the horses and the rider(s) do not wage war; they only report, after global reconnaissance, that the whole world remains quiet, peaceful, at rest.

We might expect such a report to be greeted with great joy, as it is in Isa 14:5-7: "The LORD has broken the staff of the wicked,/ the scepter of rulers . . . that ruled the nations in anger/ with unrelenting persecution./ The whole earth is at rest and quiet;/ they break forth into singing" (NRSV). But in Zechariah's first vision, no such act of deliverance has produced the world's quietness. That the whole earth remains at rest provokes not joy, but complaint. The Yahweh-angel's complaint in v. 12 makes clear that the world at rest may be attributed to Yahweh, and that it reflects the continuing absence of Yahweh's compassion.

The angel opens his protest with a question, "How long?" (v. 12). The question does not necessarily indicate a lament, at least not in a formal sense. It occurs frequently in expressions of wearied frustration or exasperation, as in Exodus 10, which expresses God's frustration with Pharaoh (Exod 10:3) and the frustration of Pharaoh's viziers (Exod 10:7). Similarly, in Num 14:27 and Hos 8:5, Israel has driven Yahweh to exasperation (cf. Jer 23:26). Proverbs 1:22 and 6:9 express exasperation with fools and "lazybones" (NRSV). Naturally, such wearied frustration can issue in

lamentation, so that "How long?" is both an expression of distress and an appeal to Yahweh for help (Pss 6:4[3]; 74:10). However, especially in contexts similar to that of Zech 1:12, the question, "How long?" has a surprisingly literal character. Isaiah's question in his vision is met with an exact answer: "Until cities lie waste" (Isa 6:11 NRSV). In Daniel, angels pose the same question and receive a mathematically precise answer (Dan 8:13-14; 12:6-7). In these visionary scenes, both the prophet's question (Isa 6:11) or that of an intermediary—an interpreting angel (v. 12; cf. Dan 8:13; 12:6; 4 Ezra 4:35, 39)—and the answer to it are part of the text's message. The whole visionary scene frames the future disclosed within it, and thus both past and present are subject to Yahweh's determination. This is already presupposed in the question, "How long?" which expects a precise answer. It is not the expression of a merely formal lament; the question is by no means rhetorical. To the contrary, the purpose of posing the question is precisely to reveal its answer. In the case of both Zechariah and Daniel, the answer is drawn from Jeremiah (Dan 8:13; 12:7).

In asking, "How long?" the angel adds a reminder that Yahweh has been angry with, or has cursed, Jerusalem and Judah's towns "for seventy years now" (v. 12; see also 7:5). This is a clear allusion to Jer 25:11-12 and 29:10, where Jeremiah announces a seventy-year period of Babylonian hegemony, followed by a return from exile. It may be that the Jeremiah texts intend this seventy years to be read in a general way, perhaps as extending through three generations (Jer 27:6-7). Isaiah announces a seventy-year punishment of Tyre (Isa 23:15-17), suggesting that the seventy-year period is a kind of formula. But Zechariah gives Jeremiah's seventy years a literal interpretation.[24] For these seventy years, God has withheld mercy, and the whole earth still remains at rest.

The language of v. 12 leaves it uncertain whether Yahweh remains angry with Jerusalem and Judah's towns, or whether they remain under Yahweh's curse. The word used here (זעם *za'am*) can have either sense. In other OT texts (Num 22:11-12; 23:7-8; Prov 24:24) this word occurs

23. For the association of heaven's host with "Yahweh of hosts," see E. Theodore Muller, Jr., "Host, Host of Heaven," in *The Anchor Bible Dictionary,* 6 vols. (New Doubleday, 1992) 3:301-4. Muller notes that, in Ps 103:20-21, Yahweh's host includes Yahweh's messengers (or angels) and "mighty warriors" (302).

24. See Michael Fishbane, *Biblical Interpretation in Ancient Israel* (Oxford: Clarendon, 1985) 481.

in conjunction with others that plainly mean "curse." In Ps 7:12[11] and Dan 11:30, anger seems to be in view. Perhaps Zechariah means to trade on the ambiguity. In any event, Yahweh is responsible for the misery of Jerusalem and Judah's towns, or more properly, for alleviating it—now.

The vision then reaches its climax in v. 13; Yahweh speaks "gracious words." In so doing, Yahweh uses language attested in Jer 29:10, in which Yahweh says, "I will fulfill to you my promise" (NRSV) after the seventy years have been completed. "Gracious words" and "my promise" are both translations of the Hebrew expression "[my] good words" (cf. Jer 29:10; 33:14). Thus Yahweh implicitly acknowledges the divine promise. In adding that these words were comforting, Zechariah alludes to Second Isaiah (e.g., Isa 40:1). He does so repeatedly in the oracles that follow.

1:14-17. The oracles that follow the first vision are integral to it. They provide the content of God's speech to the interpreting angel (v. 13). Moreover, they take up every element of the Yahweh-angel's concern: the absence of divine compassion (v. 16); the situation of Jerusalem and of Judah's towns (vv. 16-17); and Yahweh's anger/curse (vv. 15, 17). The first oracle (vv. 14-16) is fully developed, consisting of a commission (v. 14a), an announcement (v. 16), and the basis for the announcement (vv. 14b-15). The second oracle (v. 17) is abbreviated.[25] It includes Judah's towns, now called Yahweh's, among the beneficiaries of Yahweh's return, and it forms a summary conclusion; v. 14 speaks of Jerusalem and Zion, while v. 17 speaks of Zion and Jerusalem.

For the first and only time in the sequence of visions, Zechariah is expressly commissioned to speak. The interpreting-angel acts as the mediator of God's word; he acts on Yahweh's behalf, instructing Zechariah to proclaim in Yahweh's name—in the name of the Lord of hosts. The angel does not say to whom Zechariah is to proclaim the message. These oracles seem to remain wholly within the visionary context. Zechariah is to proclaim, first, that Yahweh is both very zealous, or jealous, for Jerusalem and for Zion and very angry with the nations.

The meanings "zealous" and "jealous" are both implied in the word קָנָא (qānā'). Zeal/jealousy combines singular devotion with single-minded determination. This combination leads to action on behalf of its object and against whatever would compromise its integrity or threaten it.[26] Exemplars are Phineas (Num 25:11, 13) and Elijah (1 Kgs 19:10-16). Phineas's singular devotion to Yahweh led to "impassioned action" (TNK) against an Israelite and a Midianite woman (Num 25:10-13). Elijah's zeal for God led him to oppose the royal court of Samaria. Yahweh's zeal for the divine name leads to action for Israel and against the nations (Ezek 39:25). In Isa 37:32, the zeal of Yahweh of hosts accomplishes what is promised regarding Jerusalem and Zion, despite the contrary plans of a more powerful nation. So here in vv. 14-15, Yahweh's zeal, or jealousy, for Jerusalem/Zion has its counterpart in Yahweh's anger at the nations, and it will issue in the actions promised in these oracles.

The nations with whom God is angry are at ease. This is an unmistakable reference to the world at rest in v. 11. In v. 15, however, this rest, this peace, is exposed as reflecting complacency, even contempt (cf. Job 12:5; Ps 123:4; Isa 32:9; Amos 6:1). Yahweh shifts the blame from the divine to the earthly, the international realm. In acknowledging God's own, temporally limited anger, Zechariah draws on the Isaiah tradition. In Isa 10:25, Yahweh promises that the divine anger, expressed in Assyria's aggression, will soon come to an end. The term "anger" in this verse (and in Isa 10:5) is the nominal form of same word the Yahweh-angel uses in v. 12 (za'am). In Isa 57:17-18, God acknowledges having been angry, but promises to repay with comfort (cf. Zech 1:17). And Isa 54:7-8 contrasts the brevity of God's abandonment and anger with God's promised compassion, all of it addressed to Zion (see also Isa 60:10; cf. Zech 1:16). Similarly, v. 15b proclaims that, while Yahweh was angry at Jerusalem/Zion, the now contemptuously complacent nations have allied themselves with the disaster.[27] It serves their purposes.

---

25. David L. Petersen, *Haggai and Zechariah 1–8,* OTL (Philadelphia: Westminster, 1984) 152.

26. M. Luther, *Lectures on the Minor Prophets,* vol. 3, *Zechariah,* in *Luther's Works,* vol. 20 (St. Louis: Concordia, 1973) 175.

27. In every instance, the construction עזר + ל (*zr + l*), which NRSV translates "made . . . worse," means "come to the aid of" someone; in martial contexts, it means to act as an ally. On the syntax of Zech 1:15b, see GKC #158b.

God's purpose, which Zechariah is commissioned to proclaim, is to return to Jerusalem with compassion. Yahweh's compassion and comfort (vv. 13, 16-17) are not merely consoling. They are, rather, indicative of Yahweh's determination to change—to rearrange—things; they have political—indeed, geopolitical—overtones (note the occurrences of "comfort" in Isa 51:3, 12, 19; 52:9, in the context of Isa 51:1–52:12). The Persian officials, under whose governance Zechariah envisions the future, would take no offense at what he announces: that God is returning to Jerusalem and that God's house will be rebuilt.[28] Both are in strict accord with the Persian policy of restoring local, provincial cults. It is only that Zechariah and the Persian rulers understand the name "Yahweh" in different and incompatible ways. For the Persians, Yahweh is a local deity; for Zechariah, Yahweh is the Lord of hosts and Lord of the whole earth. Persia is, by implication, merely one of the complacent nations.[29] These oracles do not elaborate on their geopolitical overtones. Global rearrangements are an important but derivative concern, because—in the logic upon which Zechariah draws—they depend on Yahweh's return to Jerusalem.

The adverb "again" occurs four times in v. 17, repetition that emphasizes that Zechariah is announcing a restoration—the restoration of order. This is an act of creation. It is in this sense that we should understand the announcement that Yahweh will comfort Zion. As noted earlier, the language of comfort (and compassion) is at home in the latter part of Isaiah, in which it is part of the larger semantic domain of suffering. But the semantics of suffering assume a different character when it is Zion that suffers and Yahweh who comforts. Yahweh acts, not as therapist or counselor, but as king; and Zion is not a client, but the

city and the people (Isa 51:16) with whom Yahweh is identified. So Isaiah's announcement that "the LORD has comforted his people" (Isa 52:9 NRSV) follows as a consequence of the announcement that "your God reigns" (Isa 52:7 NRSV), an announcement addressed explicitly to Zion. And when Isaiah exhorts heaven and earth to celebrate, because God has extended comfort and compassion to the suffering people, Zion's exaltation and the correlative submission of kings and queens follow as a result (Isa 49:13, 22-23). And when Isaiah announces that Yahweh will comfort the people in Jerusalem, as a mother comforts her children, it follows that Yahweh's anger (as in Zech 1:12) will be directed to Yahweh's enemies (Isa 66:13-14). In Zechariah 1, the Lord comforts Zion by returning to Jerusalem and restoring it—not just as a viable city, but as the dwelling place of Yahweh of hosts, Lord of the whole earth.

The concluding promise in v. 17—that Yahweh will again choose Jerusalem (see 2:16[12]; 3:2)—complements the promises of Yahweh's return, the rebuilding of the Temple and Jerusalem, and Yahweh's comfort of Zion. It draws language from traditional sources (e.g., Pss 78:68; 132:13; cf. 2 Chr 6:6). These texts stress the permanence of God's choice, and thus of Jerusalem/Zion. Psalm 78:69 says that Yahweh "built his sanctuary like the heights, like the earth he has founded it forever." In Ps 132:14, the Lord says of Zion, "This is my resting place [or throne] forever." Babylon's destruction of Jerusalem and of the Temple cast doubt on this permanence and on Yahweh's choice. This doubt is given definitive expression in the theological judgment of 2 Kgs 23:27b: "I will reject this city that I have chosen, Jerusalem, and the house of which I said, My name shall be there" (NRSV). Zechariah 1 announces that this rejection, the expression of Yahweh's anger and curse, was temporary and is ended, and that Yahweh's house will be rebuilt. Yahweh will again choose Jerusalem and comfort Zion.

28. The verb שבתי (šabtî), "I am returning," is a performative perfect, which both announces and initiates an action. Paul Joüon and T. Muraoka, *A Grammar of Biblical Hebrew*, Subsidia Biblica 14, 2 vols. (Rome: Pontifical Biblical Institute, 1991) #112f, g.
29. Petersen, *Haggai and Zechariah 1–8*, 112.

REFLECTIONS

1. Zechariah's visions confront the contemporary reader with a world of obscure and fantastic images—of figures moving and speaking urgently at the intersection of heaven and earth. These images may entertain or perplex us, but it is important not to lose sight of what

Zechariah was doing. What he portrays in his visions is the restoration of the world to its proper order. But more than that, in the midst of a world that seems to reflect only disorder and confusion, Zechariah envisions, imagines, and constructs an alternative. He is engaged not only in constructive theology, but also in preaching.[30] He invites those hearing him to imagine, to envision, and to inhabit the world according to what it will become on God's initiative.

In consequence, Zechariah's rhetoric is daring. It exploits notions and imagery—the host of heaven, for example—that other prophets found reason to condemn (cf. Jer 8:2). But any language we use to speak of God, and especially to speak of God's relation to our world, to us, and to our deepest uncertainties, is fraught with danger and risks violating its own limits. That is, the need to speak about God in ever-changing circumstances can bring the speaker to the limits of what conventional speech can communicate about God, so that the speaker must risk using daring language to speak of God.

2. Zechariah takes that risk, confronting a situation unprecedented in the tradition on which he draws. He stands in the tradition of the prophets, but no prophet before him had to address a community that felt the full weight of the prophetic tradition and its judgments, and who now had to forge a common life in circumstances different from those any earlier prophet had addressed (see Introduction for a review of the historical and social context of Zechariah). This community needed no warning of God's punishment; they labored under its effects. They were not merely threatened with God's abandonment; they lived with its reality. And they stood to suffer no rebuke for undue confidence in the Temple, which lay in ruins. In these circumstances, Zechariah did not simply repeat prophetic tradition or follow past conventions. Rather, he reread the prophetic traditions in the light of his present crisis and used the images of those traditions to envision a new reality for the present day. His visions and daring rhetoric are thoroughly grounded in "biblical tradition." Indeed, the tradition everywhere provides the material of Zechariah's imagination. He is no less an exegete than a visionary. The visions and oracles of the first two chapters are an exposition of Second Isaiah, especially of Isaiah 54, and of Jeremiah. Out of this treasure, Zechariah brings what is old and what is new (cf. Matt 13:52).

Zechariah's prophetic vision thus arises from the conversation between past tradition and present crisis. It is this conversation that shapes both his constructive theological work and his preaching, as it can for the theological and pastoral life of the contemporary church.

30. Petersen, *Haggai and Zechariah 1–8,* 115.

Zechariah 1:18-21, The Second Vision: Four Horns and Four Smiths

NIV

[18]Then I looked up—and there before me were four horns! [19]I asked the angel who was speaking to me, "What are these?"

He answered me, "These are the horns that scattered Judah, Israel and Jerusalem."

[20]Then the LORD showed me four craftsmen. [21]I asked, "What are these coming to do?"

He answered, "These are the horns that scattered Judah so that no one could raise his head,

NRSV

18[a]And I looked up and saw four horns. [19]I asked the angel who talked with me, "What are these?" And he answered me, "These are the horns that have scattered Judah, Israel, and Jerusalem." [20]Then the LORD showed me four blacksmiths. [21]And I asked, "What are they coming to do?" He answered, "These are the horns that scattered Judah, so that no head could be raised;

a Ch 2.1 in Heb

NIV	NRSV
but the craftsmen have come to terrify them and throw down these horns of the nations who lifted up their horns against the land of Judah to scatter its people."	but these have come to terrify them, to strike down the horns of the nations that lifted up their horns against the land of Judah to scatter its people."[a] [a] Heb *it*

COMMENTARY

The scope of the second vision remains international. Using the image of four horns, it refers to the nations (Deut 33:17; Ps 132:17; Lam 2:3, 17; Ezek 29:21). Yet the focus moves from the whole earth (1:11) to Judah, Israel, and Jerusalem (1:19), and finally to Judah itself (1:21). In this way the second vision returns to the theme of Yahweh's anger at the nations (1:15). More broadly, this second vision continues the theme of reversal, introduced in 1:14-15: The powerful nations will be disempowered.

1:18-19[2:1-2]. In these verses (as in the following vision, and in 5:1 [cf. 5:5]; 5:9; and 6:1), Zechariah "lifts his eyes" and sees something. This does not imply that what he sees is overhead, but only that he lifts his gaze to see what is before him. What he sees are four horns, seemingly just as mundane as horses standing in a myrtle grove. And consistent with these visionary conventions, Zechariah asks his interpreting angel to identify these four horns.

The angel describes what the horns have done (cf. 1:10). The verb of which the horns are the subject is זרה (*zārâ*), which can mean either "to scatter" or "to winnow" (see Ruth 3:2). If it means "to scatter," then the national powers in question are those that have sent Judah, Israel, and Jerusalem into exile. But such punishment is Yahweh's prerogative, and it is odd to hold the nations culpable for what Yahweh promises to do (Lev 26:33) and claims to have done (Ezek 36:19).[31] The angel does not clarify the matter. Instead, and quite remarkably, Yahweh intervenes.

1:20-21[2:3-4]. The Lord intrudes in the vision

to show Zechariah a second and correlative sign: four smiths, one for each of the horns. It is not unprecedented that Yahweh shows a prophet the sign that Yahweh then interprets (Jer 24:1; Amos 7:1, 4, 7; 8:1). Verse 19 includes all the "horns" that have scattered/winnowed Yahweh's people. Just as Daniel will do later on, compressing four successive empires into the spatial form of one great statue (Daniel 2), so also Zechariah brings together Israel's historical oppressors in the image of four horns. But in v. 21 Yahweh provides a second, narrower definition of the horns, as those who had acted specifically against the land of Judah. Here it seems clear that not exile, but oppression is the key problem. The "horns" have made it impossible for the people *in* Judah to raise their heads. They have winnowed Judah (Jer 15:7).

Whenever the horns are the subject of זרה (*zārâ*; NRSV, "scattered"), the TNK translates this verb as "tossed." This seems entirely appropriate to the action of horns, and appropriate as well to the sense of this second vision; these horns have tossed Judah. It is also appropriate that the smiths will terrify the horns. They will throw down the horns of the nations that have raised a horn against the land of Judah. There is symmetry in this action; when the nations raised their horns, no one in Judah could raise a head. The smiths will throw down the raised horns. Smiths are usually artisans (2 Sam 5:11), but Ezekiel speaks of artisans—smiths—of destruction (Ezek 21:36[31]), just as Isaiah speaks of Yahweh's smith, who forges destructive weapons (Isa 54:16). Such are the smiths of Zechariah's second vision. Notably, these smiths will not destroy the nations; they will cut off their horns. The nations themselves have an important place in the oracles that conclude Zechariah 2, a place among the people of God. The nations, even those that have

---

31. Christian Jeremias, *Die Nachtgesichte des Sacharia*, FRLANT 117 (Göttingen: Vandenhoeck & Ruprecht, 1977) 22-23. The verb occurs twelve times in Ezekiel with reference to exile; in each case Yahweh is the one who "scatters" (in Ezek 5:2, Ezekiel scatters hair to symbolize exile).

oppressed Judah, are not destroyed; they are pacified. Their capacity for violent oppression is cut off.

Zechariah does not specify which nations are in view. By implication (there are four horns), he includes all nations, insofar as they have oppressed Judah. Does this vision, along with the oracles following the first one (vv. 14-17), imply an expectation that Judah would be free of Persian domination? Almost certainly, yes. But it presents no call to arms. The smiths who terrify and throw down the horns are not identified with any earthly power; they are Yahweh's agents, as are the horses in chaps. 1 and

6. Neither do Zechariah's visions offer an explicit critique of Persian rule. Rather, they argue for the restoration of the world to its proper order: the order of creation. Pacifying the nations is part of that restoration, and for Zechariah, Persia is the regnant international power. Eshmunazar, fifth-century BCE king of Sidon, refers to the Persian emperor as "lord of kings."[32] For Zechariah, Yahweh is Lord of the whole earth (Zech 4:14; 6:5). The theology expressed in the visions has no room for an empire other than Yahweh's. (See Reflections at 2:6-13.)

32. *TSSI* 3.28.18, 108, 113.

Zechariah 2:1-5, The Third Vision: An Expansive Jerusalem

2 Then I looked up—and there before me was a man with a measuring line in his hand! ²I asked, "Where are you going?"

He answered me, "To measure Jerusalem, to find out how wide and how long it is."

³Then the angel who was speaking to me left, and another angel came to meet him ⁴and said to him: "Run, tell that young man, 'Jerusalem will be a city without walls because of the great number of men and livestock in it. ⁵And I myself will be a wall of fire around it,' declares the LORD, 'and I will be its glory within.' "

2[a] I looked up and saw a man with a measuring line in his hand. ²Then I asked, "Where are you going?" He answered me, "To measure Jerusalem, to see what is its width and what is its length." ³Then the angel who talked with me came forward, and another angel came forward to meet him, ⁴and said to him, "Run, say to that young man: Jerusalem shall be inhabited like villages without walls, because of the multitude of people and animals in it. ⁵For I will be a wall of fire all around it, says the LORD, and I will be the glory within it."

a Ch 2.5 in Heb

COMMENTARY

The third vision returns to the theme of 1:16, though formally this vision differs from all the others. It shows Zechariah taking extraordinary initiative. Rather than asking an angelic intermediary to identify the sign, Zechariah *asks the sign itself*; he asks the "man with a measuring line in his hand" (NRSV). The scene lacks all the numinous qualities of the first vision and even the mystery of the second. What Zechariah sees is entirely mundane: He sees a surveyor and asks him where he is going. Even the language is unusually straightforward. The verb "to go" (הלך

hālak) is used only here to describe the movement of a figure in the visions. Typically, these figures "come forward," or appear, and in each case it is a heavenly being or a non-human figure within the vision. In 2:3 (twice) and 5:5 it is an angel; in 5:3, the "curse"; in 5:5-6, the "ephah"; in 5:9, two winged women; in 6:1, 6 (three times), heavenly chariots; in 6:5, the four winds of heaven; in 6:7-8, horses. Here the figure is an ordinary surveyor whom Zechariah asks an everyday question: Where are you going?

The surveyor's answer—to determine the

length and breadth of Jerusalem—would seem to be the sign's interpretation (provided by the sign itself!). That is, it would seem to signify that Jerusalem will be rebuilt, as promised in 1:16. But it is the surveyor's answer that brings his conversation with Zechariah into the visionary context; it attracts the interpreting angel to the scene (2:3). This angel and another one "come forward" with some urgency. The message that the interpreting angel gives the other angel, to be conveyed to the surveyor, interprets the sign. First, the interpreting angel identifies the man as a נער (na'ar), not necessarily a "young man" but probably an official.[33] Second, the angel distinguishes the surveyor's "measuring line" from the "line stretched out over Jerusalem" (1:16). The surveyor's measurements are intended for the construction of a wall to enclose Jerusalem and defend it. The first is impossible and the second unnecessary.

The impossibility is due to Jerusalem's future vast population. Like ancient Nineveh, Jerusalem will have myriad people and cattle (2:4[8]; Jonah 4:11). Second Isaiah also promises a vast population for Jerusalem (Isa 49:18-20; 54:1-3), whose

citizens will complain: "The place is too crowded for me; make room for me to settle" (Isa 49:20). Yet although the extraordinary increase in Jerusalem's population will make walls impossible, at the same time the city will be left defenseless. Indeed, the angel chooses his terms carefully in saying that Jerusalem will live like "unwalled villages." In Ezek 38:11, villages are unwalled because the people live in safety, having no need of walls, "and without bars and gates." In Zechariah's third vision walls are unnecessary, because Yahweh will be a wall of fire around Jerusalem.

The picture of Yahweh as a wall of fire recalls Isa 4:5, where Yahweh creates a canopy of cloud and fire to protect Zion. The Isaianic text is the more evocative, since it mentions "all the glory there" in Zion. However, in Zechariah's third vision it is God who will be glory in Jerusalem. Consistently in this first cycle of visions (chaps. 1–2), the Lord promises to be present in Jerusalem—not only to rebuild and to protect Jerusalem, not only to be present in the Temple, but to be fully, gloriously, and powerfully present in the city.[34] Under these conditions, as Zechariah envisions them, a surveyor in the employ of a wall-contractor faces certain unemployment. (See Reflections at 2:6-13.)

33. In some biblical texts and seal inscriptions a נער (na'ar) is a functionary. N. Avigad points, for example, to 2 Sam 9:9-10; 19:9, and to seals and bullae from Palestine. See Avigad, "The Contribution of Hebrew Seals to an Understanding of Israelite Religion and Society," in *Ancient Israelite Religion: Essays in Honor of Frank Moore Cross*, ed. Patrick D. Miller, Jr., Paul D. Hanson, S. Dean McBride (Philadelphia: Fortress, 1987) 195-208.

34. Petersen, *Haggai and Zechariah 1–8*, 171-72.

Zechariah 2:6-13, Babylon and Zion

NIV	NRSV
[6]"Come! Come! Flee from the land of the north," declares the LORD, "for I have scattered you to the four winds of heaven," declares the LORD. [7]"Come, O Zion! Escape, you who live in the Daughter of Babylon!" [8]For this is what the LORD Almighty says: "After he has honored me and has sent me against the nations that have plundered you—for whoever touches you touches the apple of his eye— [9]I will surely raise my hand against them so that their slaves will plunder them.[a] Then you will know that the LORD Almighty has sent me.	6Up, up! Flee from the land of the north, says the LORD; for I have spread you abroad like the four winds of heaven, says the LORD. [7]Up! Escape to Zion, you that live with daughter Babylon. [8]For thus said the LORD of hosts (after his glory[a] sent me) regarding the nations that plundered you: Truly, one who touches you touches the apple of my eye.[b] [9]See now, I am going to raise[c] my hand against them, and they shall become plunder for their own slaves. Then you will know that the LORD of hosts has sent me. [10]Sing and rejoice, O daughter Zion! For lo, I will come and dwell in your midst, says the LORD. [11]Many nations shall
[a]8,9 Or *says after . . . eye:* 9 "*I . . . plunder them.*"	[a] Cn: Heb *after glory he* [b] Heb *his eye* [c] Or *wave*

NIV

10"Shout and be glad, O Daughter of Zion. For I am coming, and I will live among you," declares the LORD. 11"Many nations will be joined with the LORD in that day and will become my people. I will live among you and you will know that the LORD Almighty has sent me to you. 12The LORD will inherit Judah as his portion in the holy land and will again choose Jerusalem. 13Be still before the LORD, all mankind, because he has roused himself from his holy dwelling."

NRSV

join themselves to the LORD on that day, and shall be my people; and I will dwell in your midst. And you shall know that the LORD of hosts has sent me to you. 12The LORD will inherit Judah as his portion in the holy land, and will again choose Jerusalem.

13Be silent, all people, before the LORD; for he has roused himself from his holy dwelling.

COMMENTARY

Just as Zechariah took the initiative in the third vision, so also he seems to do in the oracles that follow it. They are not commissioned, and there is no explicit indication of who is speaking. The two oracles in 2:6-7[10-11], each beginning with הוֹי (*hôy,* "Hey!"), follow naturally the two preceding visions. Zechariah 2:8-9[12-13] interprets these *hôy* oracles in terms of the reversal first adumbrated in 1:14-15 and continued in the second vision (1:18-21[2:1-4]). The instruction to Zion to rejoice (2:10[14]) forms a provisional conclusion to the first visionary cycle, grounded in the announcement of Yahweh's coming (cf. 1:16) and the divine promise to dwell in Jerusalem's midst (2:9[5]). However, the remaining oracular material, through the end of chap. 2, interprets the preceding visions and oracles in a particular way. It returns to the theme of the nations, specifically in order to include "many" of them among Yahweh's people and to define Yahweh's special relationship with Judah; and it reaffirms Yahweh's decision "again" to choose Jerusalem (2:16[12]; cf. 1:17).

Hôy oracles like those in vv. 6-9[10-13] occur frequently in the prophetic literature. The word *hôy* is an interjection, a call to attention. Only in v. 6[10] is it repeated; and only in 2:6 and in Isa 55:1 is it followed immediately by an imperative, in this case, "Flee!" Clearly, these oracles convey a sense of urgency, and the repeated *hôy* ("Hey! Hey!") echoes the repeated imperatives in Isaiah 51–52: "Awake, awake!" (Isa 51:9); "Rouse, rouse yourself!" (51:17); "Awake, awake!" (52:1); "Depart, depart!" (52:11). The last text listed

commands people to leave Babylon, as does Zech 2:7[11]. The urgency behind this instruction lies in Zechariah's second and third visions, to which the *hôy* oracles stand in a complementary relation. The instructions in these oracles follow from what Zechariah has just envisioned.

If that much is clear, much else remains ambiguous. For example, these oracles do not make explicit to whom they are addressed. The "you" to whom Zechariah speaks is plural and (apart from 6:15) is the only such direct address in all of 1:7–6:15. Although v. 6[10] implicitly identifies the audience as those whom Yahweh has "spread like the four winds of heaven," it is not obvious what "spread" (פרשׂ (*pārēś*) means in this case. Also, it is difficult to know whether v. 7[11] addresses Zion who is living in Babylon or whether it instructs Babylon's citizenry to escape *to* Zion.

2:6[10]. On the first matter, interpreters tend to agree that "I spread you out" refers to Yahweh's dispersion of the people in exile.[35] But there are two difficulties with this view. First, the word *pāraś* nowhere else refers to exile. Typically, and frequently, the Bible uses the word "scatter" (סער *sāʿar*) in referring to exile and dispersion, as does Zechariah (7:14). "Spread" is a neutral term, almost always used of spreading hands in prayer or petition. Second, "I spread you out" is here given as the reason why "you" should flee the north country. That Yahweh sent people into exile and dispersion hardly serves as a reason why they should now flee the north country. Besides,

---

35. Ps 68:14[15] is the only instance in which פרשׂ (*pārēś*) is used to mean "disperse": God dispersed enemy kings in Jerusalem.

that Israel—the descendants of Jacob—should themselves "spread out" to the north, indeed, to all four directions, is God's explicit promise to Jacob in Gen 28:14 (using a different verb).

We should note that two of the expressions used in v. 6b [10b]—the "four winds of heaven" and "the north country"—occur again in the final vision (6:5, 8). There the horses and chariots are identified as the four winds of heaven, and one of them puts Yahweh's Spirit at rest in the north country. If Yahweh's agents are the four winds of heaven, which Yahweh sends out to patrol the earth (6:7), what does it mean that Yahweh has spread the people out *like* the four winds of heaven? The ambiguity is both ineradicable and intentional. Hints of exile and dispersion are clear, but both logic and syntax suggest that, not exile, but return is at stake. Even the means of returning to Jerusalem is provided; to be spread out like the winds of heaven is the ability to fly, to flee *from* the north country. After all, the four winds of heaven are horses and chariots, which can and do roam the earth.

2:7[11]. The second matter (Whom does this verse address?) is just as ambiguous. There are (in Hebrew) no prepositions in this verse: no *to* and no *from*. "Zion" may be vocative: "Hey, Zion!" In that case, Zion is urged to escape Babylon. But the other nouns in the verse could also be vocatives: "Hey . . . residents of daughter Babylon!" In that case, the people of Babylon are urged to flee to Zion. The first alternative has the advantage of consistency, since the verses that precede and follow (vv. 6, 8-9[10, 12-13) address Yahweh's people. It seems, then, that Zion here personifies God's people, as it does in Isa 51:16.[36] Some part of that people, of Zion, is apparently resident in Babylon, whence they should escape (Jer 51:6). Since Babylon is surely one of the horns to be thrown down by the smiths (1:21), there is every good reason to escape it—that is, to escape the administrative center of the Persian Empire, of which Judah is a province.

2:8-9[12-13]. The reversal announced in the second vision is explicit in the oracle's elaboration, which provides further reason for escaping Baby-

lon and other nations as well. This elaboration concerns the nations that have plundered "you," on the principle that "whoever touches you touches the apple of my own eye." The same sentiment is expressed in Jer 30:16; Ezek 39:10; Deut 32:9-10 employs similar imagery in putting Israel at the center of God's attention. But here the imagery is uniquely physical; the exploitation of Judah or Zion, of God's people, is a poke in the pupil of God's eye. In response, Yahweh's hand is waving over the nations; those who had plundered will themselves be plunder, the spoils of war, to the very people they had enslaved (2:13[19]). In this act of reversal, Yahweh alone will embody the action of the four smiths, fulfilling the anger at the nations that was first announced in 1:15.

The oracle concludes with Zechariah referring to himself: "you will know that Yahweh of hosts has sent me." The same kind of statement occurs in 2:11[15]; 4:9; and 6:15, so it appears to be a formula—a vindication formula, attesting Zechariah's status as a genuine prophet of God.[37] In all cases but 4:9, the formula occurs with reference to the nations, or to those who come from the nations. In 2:11[15], it is addressed to Zion, but it is uncertain whom Zechariah addresses in 2:9[13]. However, the "you" is plural, as is the case in all of 2:6-9[10]13]. This suggests that Zechariah is speaking to those whom Yahweh has urged to flee the north country and to escape Babylon, those whom the nations have taken as spoil, or plundered. This may help to explain the enigmatic and hardly translatable phrase in 2:8[12], which the NRSV renders as "after his glory sent me." I suggest the translation: "after glory Yahweh sent me to the nations who plundered you." In that case, Zechariah is borrowing the language of Jer 25:15, 17, where Jeremiah speaks of having been sent by Yahweh to the nations. In Haggai, "glory" (כבוד *kābôd*) means wealth, specifically the wealth of nations, which will come to Jerusalem (Hag 2:7, 9). It has the same meaning in post-exilic Isaiah texts (Isa 60:13; 61:6; 66:12). In that case, the glory of which Zechariah speaks in 2:12[18] is just the

36. Petersen, *Haggai and Zechariah 1–8*, 176-77; cf. Carol Meyers and Eric Meyers, *Haggai and Zechariah 1–8*, AB 25B (New York: Doubleday, 1987) 164.

37. Except in Zech 2:13[9], the formula concludes with "to you." Comparable statements occur in Jeremiah and Ezekiel, and all of them may depend on Deut 18:21-22. See Janet E. Tollington, *Tradition and Innovation in Haggai and Zechariah 1–8*, JSOTSup 150 (Sheffield: JSOT) 70-75.

plunder that the nations will become. This enigmatic phrase then participates in the great reversal—the transformation—to which Zechariah links his vindication as a prophet.

2:10-12[14-16]. Corresponding to the transformation of international arrangements that the visions and oracles of chap. 2 announce is a contrast between two daughters: "daughter Babylon" in v. 7[11], and "daughter Zion" in v. 10. While the first of these personified cities stands under the threat of God's hand, the second has cause to rejoice. In three other Old Testament texts, Zion is instructed to sing or shout for joy. Twice, Yahweh's presence in Zion's midst is the reason for rejoicing (Isa 12:6; Zeph 3:14-15); in Isa 54:1-3 it is the promise of a vast increase in Zion's population. Both reasons are cited in vv. 10-11[14-15]. The announcement of God's coming returns to the theme of 1:16. But in v. 10[14] this announcement accompanies the promise that Yahweh will dwell in Zion's midst. Indeed, the promise is repeated in the very next verse, where it follows a second announcement: Many nations will join themselves to Yahweh (v. 11[15]).

The repetition of "I will dwell in your midst" is striking, and so is the notice that the inclusion of the nations will happen "on that day." This adverbial phrase occurs elsewhere in First Zechariah only at 3:10. Together, these features suggest that vv. 11-12[15-16] expands an oracle that had concluded in v. 10[14]. The suggestion gains support from the repetition, v. 11[15], of the vindication formula that appear first in v. 9[13]. The purpose of this expansion is to include within the promise of Yahweh's dwelling in Jerusalem those "many nations" that will join themselves to Yahweh. In other words, the work of the smiths in the second vision and the reduction of the nations to plunder in 2:7-9[11-13] is not the end of the matter; many of them will join themselves to Yahweh on that day. This expectation about the nations is in fundamental agreement with later parts of the Isaiah tradition (Isa 14:1-3; 56:1-8; cf. 66:19b-21), and with the conclusion of Zechariah's sermon (8:20-23). Accordingly, the prophet's vindication is tied not only to the Lord's action *against* the nations—the reversal of plunderer and plundered that v. 9[13] announces—but also to the *inclusion* of those many nations who join themselves to Yahweh (2:11[15]).

The full inclusion of these nations is explicit in the promise that "they will be my people." This is the first half of a statement of fundamental importance in Israelite traditions: "They will be my people, and I will be their God" (e.g., Deut 7:6; 14:2; 2 Sam 7:23; Jer 24:7; 32:38; Ezek 11:20; 37:23; cf. Zech 8:8; 13:9, and the commentary on those texts). This expression is commonly called the covenant formula. However, nowhere else does it refer to some group other than Israel (or Judah), and nowhere else does only the first part of the formula occur. Here in Zechariah, the second part of the formula ("I will be their God") is replaced with "and I will dwell in your [Zion's] midst."[38] In other words, the God who will dwell in Zion is the God whose people includes many nations. This represents a rereading of the oracle in v. 7[11], now understood as urging Babylon's citizenry to escape. Where could they go but to the Lord, and hence to Zion? The syntax of that oracle permits such a reading, as suggested above. But this rereading leaves uncertain the special status of Judah, the apple of God's eye.

To resolve this uncertainty, this verse promises that Yahweh will inherit Judah as the divine portion in the holy land. In this case, Judah refers to the people, not to the territory. Regularly in Old Testament tradition, the people are Yahweh's heritage or inheritance (Deut 32:9; Ps 106:40; Isa 47:6). While Yahweh's land is Israel's heritage (1 Kgs 8:36), the people are Yahweh's heritage (1 Kgs 8:51). Among all the nations who will be God's people, God's special possession and heritage and inheritance is Judah. Elsewhere this special relation among the nations is expressed in terms of priesthood. Among all the nations who are God's, Israel enjoys the status of priests (Exod 19:6; Isa 61:5-6). That the land (lit., the ground) is holy derives solely from God's presence there (cf. Exod 3:5). This claim, too, is a reversal, and it represents a transformation. What was desecrated (cf. Ps 74:7) is now called holy. But the transformation corresponds exactly to what Zechariah first announced (1:17). Yahweh will again choose Jerusalem.

2:13[17]. The first cycle of visions and oracles concludes with the solemn notice that God is roused from the holy dwelling. Everything that is

---

38. Meyers and Meyers, *Haggai and Zechariah 1–8*, 169.

announced and promised in the visions and oracles of Zechariah's first two chapters depends on this arousal and on this movement. Yahweh's "holy dwelling" may refer to the Temple (as in Ps 26:8) or to heaven (Deut 26:15). In Ps 68:4-5[5-6] God, riding on the clouds, is "in his holy dwelling." None of these descriptions is conceptually at odds with the notion that Yahweh dwells in Zion's midst. Clearly, Zech 2:13[17] and its context see no tension between Yahweh's holy dwelling in heaven, on the one hand, and, on the other, Yahweh's dwelling in Zion—precisely what 2:10-11[14-15] promises. It is Yahweh's stirring from heaven, stirring into action, that initiates the fulfillment of what the whole of the first vision cycle announces and promises and expects, including the promise that Yahweh will dwell in Zion's midst. In prospect of this stirring, this rousing of Yahweh—and of the transformations and reversals it will effect—all flesh is enjoined to silence (Hab 2:20; Zeph 1:7).

REFLECTIONS

1. The reality envisioned and proclaimed in Zech 1:18–2:13 discloses some forms of peace as counterfeit. A world stable and at rest need not be a world genuinely at peace. Zechariah's concerns remain within the orbit of Judah and its future, but from this particular perspective he envisions the disarmament of powers that exploit and oppress. Even then, however, he does not escape the logic of reciprocal violence, of the plundered becoming the plunderers. Neither does the book of Revelation, which quotes Zechariah in asking vengeance for martyrs (Rev 6:10).

It is all the more remarkable, therefore, that Zechariah envisions, and God promises, not the destruction of the nations or the establishment of an imperial Jerusalem, but the *inclusion* of the nations among God's covenant people. In his commentary on Zechariah, Martin Luther called this a miracle second to none.[39] The inclusion of the nations is one of the hallmarks of Zechariah's eschatological vision. All notions of power and dominance will be redefined in the future envisioned here, as the nations are transformed from agents of destruction (1:18-21) to witnesses to God's presence in the world (2:11). It is the power of Yahweh alone that gives shape to the future, and it is to the recognition of this theological reality that Zechariah calls the people.

This "miracle" of the inclusion of the nations, of one's enemies, in the fullness of God's promises suggests an alternative vision for living in the world. Is there in what Zechariah here announces the basis for transcending the tit-for-tat logic of reciprocal violence that we see daily around the globe? If one can live out of and into this eschatological vision of a world in which many nations are united as one people, the answer to that question may be yes.

2. The image that closes the first cycle of visions and oracles, God stirring in God's holy dwelling (2:13), provides a visual illustration of the theological reality that undergirds all of Zechariah's words: The promised future derives from the initiative of God. These visions are single-mindedly theological. That is, the depth and breadth of Zechariah's imagery are all in the service of his revelation of God and his evocation of the presence of God for God's people. For all the intensity, dynamism, and imaginative scope of Zechariah's rhetoric, the first cycle concludes with the summons to a hushed silence in response to Yahweh's presence. This summons is no less urgent and demanding in the contemporary moment than it was in Zechariah's day.

---

39. M. Luther, *Lectures on the Minor Prophets*, vol. 3, *Zechariah*, in *Luther's Works*, vol. 20 (St. Louis: Concordia, 1973) 210.

Zechariah 3:1–4:14, Visions of Restoration and Divine Presence

OVERVIEW

The first two chapters of Zechariah envisioned a transformation of the international order, which will benefit Zion/Jerusalem, where God promises to be present. Now, chaps. 3–4 (which are paired at the center of the vision sequence) address the mode and the symbols of God's presence. Their focus is restricted to Jerusalem, especially on the leadership of the restoration community. That leadership is both priestly and royal. These chapters go so far as to identify the leaders in question: Joshua the high priest (chap. 3) and Zerubbabel the temple builder (chap. 4). Both are rooted firmly in history; they figure prominently in Haggai's prophecies and in Ezra's account of the Temple's reconstruction (Ezra 3:2-9; 5:2). At the very center of the vision sequence, the fourth and fifth visions gain an unusual degree of specificity. They treat issues and people central to the project of Judah's restoration in the Persian period. Not only was it a matter of restoring a ruined city or of rebuilding Judah's towns, but it also involved the restoration of Judah's central institutions, including priesthood and Temple as symbols and media of divine presence.

In Israel as well as throughout the ancient Near East, temple building was a task for kings. Zechariah is not shy about this, and he makes unmistakable allusions to kingship—perhaps to a restored Davidic monarchy—in both chap. 3 and 6:9-15. Temple and kingship are intertwined with creation in the theology on which Zechariah draws. Thus Ps 78:69 can speak of Yahweh building "his sanctuary like the heavens, like the earth that he founded forever."[40] In Psalm 89 the Davidic king is God's agent in maintaining the cosmic order that God brought about in creation (Ps 89:10-13, 20-26[9-12, 19-25]).

When the central section of the fifth vision (4:6*b*-10*a*) names Zerubbabel as *the* temple builder, it joins Haggai in attaching royal, even messianic, expectations to this scion of the Davidic house (Hag 2:6-9, 20-23). But in chap. 3, which stands now as a fourth vision, the royal figure called "Branch" is unnamed (3:8); and chap. 6, which also refers to this unnamed "Branch" and temple builder, expects him in the future (6:12-13). There is, then, some tension among the visions on this point. The structure of chap. 4 clearly reflects that tension, as we shall see.

40. Jon D. Levenson, *Creation and the Persistence of Evil: The Jewish Drama of Divine Omnipotence* (San Francisco: Harper & Row, 1988) 87. The verb "founded" (יסד *yāsad*) in this verse is from the same root as that attested in Zech 4:9.

Zechariah 3:1-10, The Fourth Vision: Joshua the High Priest, the Satan, and the Branch

<table>
<tr><td>

NIV

3 Then he showed me Joshua[a] the high priest standing before the angel of the LORD, and Satan[b] standing at his right side to accuse him. [2]The LORD said to Satan, "The LORD rebuke you, Satan! The LORD, who has chosen Jerusalem, rebuke you! Is not this man a burning stick snatched from the fire?"

[3]Now Joshua was dressed in filthy clothes as he stood before the angel. [4]The angel said to those

a1 A variant of Jeshua; here and elsewhere in Zechariah means accuser. *b1 Satan*

</td><td>

NRSV

3 Then he showed me the high priest Joshua standing before the angel of the LORD, and Satan[a] standing at his right hand to accuse him. [2]And the LORD said to Satan,[a] "The LORD rebuke you, O Satan![a] The LORD who has chosen Jerusalem rebuke you! Is not this man a brand plucked from the fire?" [3]Now Joshua was dressed with filthy clothes as he stood before the angel. [4]The angel said to those who were standing before him,

a Or the Accuser; Heb the Adversary

</td></tr>
</table>

NIV

who were standing before him, "Take off his filthy clothes."

Then he said to Joshua, "See, I have taken away your sin, and I will put rich garments on you."

[5]Then I said, "Put a clean turban on his head." So they put a clean turban on his head and clothed him, while the angel of the LORD stood by.

[6]The angel of the LORD gave this charge to Joshua: [7]"This is what the LORD Almighty says: 'If you will walk in my ways and keep my requirements, then you will govern my house and have charge of my courts, and I will give you a place among these standing here.

[8]"'Listen, O high priest Joshua and your associates seated before you, who are men symbolic of things to come: I am going to bring my servant, the Branch. [9]See, the stone I have set in front of Joshua! There are seven eyes[a] on that one stone, and I will engrave an inscription on it,' says the LORD Almighty, 'and I will remove the sin of this land in a single day.

[10]"'In that day each of you will invite his neighbor to sit under his vine and fig tree,' declares the LORD Almighty."

[a]9 Or *facets*

NRSV

"Take off his filthy clothes." And to him he said, "See, I have taken your guilt away from you, and I will clothe you with festal apparel." [5]And I said, "Let them put a clean turban on his head." So they put a clean turban on his head and clothed him with the apparel; and the angel of the LORD was standing by.

[6]Then the angel of the LORD assured Joshua, saying [7]"Thus says the LORD of hosts: If you will walk in my ways and keep my requirements, then you shall rule my house and have charge of my courts, and I will give you the right of access among those who are standing here. [8]Now listen, Joshua, high priest, you and your colleagues who sit before you! For they are an omen of things to come: I am going to bring my servant the Branch. [9]For on the stone that I have set before Joshua, on a single stone with seven facets, I will engrave its inscription, says the LORD of hosts, and I will remove the guilt of this land in a single day. [10]On that day, says the LORD of hosts, you shall invite each other to come under your vine and fig tree."

COMMENTARY

This fourth vision, concerned with Joshua the high priest, is an addition to the sequence of seven night visions. While it is most closely related to the fifth vision (chap. 4), the fourth vision is also linked grammatically and thematically to the visions and oracles in chaps. 1–2. First, the subject of the initial verb ("*he* showed me" [יַרְאֵנִי *yarʾēnî*]) is not identified. It could be either Yahweh or the interpreting angel. This oblique introduction serves primarily to include chap. 3 within the sequence of visions. Second, v. 2 identifies Yahweh as the one who "chooses Jerusalem," a reference to the promises in 1:17 and 2:12[16]. Third, the "holy land" (or "ground") of 2:12[16] is of concern in 3:9 as well. This last verse is part of the complex oracular conclusion to chap. 3.

The same Yahweh-angel who speaks to Joshua in the body of the vision (3:4) also speaks to him in oracles (3:6-10). The entire fourth vision (with its oracles) is related to chap. 4 by dint of the sign in 4:1-5, and especially with the figures mentioned in the interpretation of that sign: the two "sons of oil" or "anointed ones" (4:14). One of them is Joshua.

3:1-2. Verse 1 introduces Joshua as the high priest. This title appears rarely outside of Haggai and Zechariah. However, the deuteronomistic history refers to a high priest in two places. Jehoiada is referred to as high priest (2 Kgs 12:7) during the reign of Jehoash (9th cent. BCE), and Hilkiah has that title (2 Kgs 22:4, 8; 23:4) in the reign of Josiah (7th cent. BCE). Both were associated with temple repair and reform, which makes them appropriate models for Joshua. Jehoiada serves as a model in another respect.

The visionary scene opens in the heavenly court; Joshua stands before the Yahweh-angel, and the satan (שָׂטָן *śāṭān*) stands at Joshua's right hand to accuse (שָׂטָן *śāṭān*) him. (The Hebrew actually reads הַשָּׂטָן [*haśśāṭan*], a word that includes the definite article; hence, I refer to "the" satan, unlike NRSV and the NIV.) In Ps 109:6, too, the accuser stands at the right hand of the defendant. Typically, in scenes of the heavenly court, God sits enthroned while heavenly beings stand in attendance (2 Kgs 22:19 [= 2 Chr 18:18]; Isa 6:1; Ezek 1:26–2:1; Dan 7:8-10; cf. Jer 23:18). In the book of Zechariah, the satan is one of the attendants in the heavenly court (3:1, 4). The imagery here is consistent with that of the first and last visions, where Yahweh's agents patrol the earth. They do so as well in Job 1:6-7; 2:1-2, where one of these agents is the satan. He is not yet an independent figure who acts against God, as in the New Testament (and cf. 1 Chr 21:1), but perhaps a kind of policeman and prosecuting attorney for the heavenly court. The satan's charge against Joshua is not made explicit, but he evidently challenges Joshua's fitness as high priest. Remarkably, it is Yahweh who speaks in Joshua's defense. In chap. 3, the distinction between Yahweh and the Yahweh-angel is so blurred that, in v. 2, Yahweh speaks as if the angel were addressing, even invoking, Yahweh!

Twice, God is invoked to rebuke the satan. The invocation is repeated in order to identify God as "Yahweh who chooses Jerusalem." This identification is crucial, both in reiterating the promises of chaps. 1–2 and in reference to Yahweh's rebuke of the satan. Yahweh describes Joshua as a "brand rescued from the fire." This phrase clearly alludes explicitly to Amos 4:11, which describes the survivors of a conflagration as a brand—a smoldering stump—rescued from the burning (cf. Isa 7:4). Joshua the high priest has been rescued from Jerusalem's destruction, but barely; his grandfather Seraiah was executed by Nebuchadnezzar (2 Kgs 25:18-21), and his father, Jehozadak, was exiled in Babylon. Prophetic indictments of the priesthood were withering, and the priests were held significantly to blame for Jerusalem's destruction. Indeed, Lamentations reports the complaint of those left to suffer in a ruined Jerusalem—namely, that the "iniquities" (עָוֹן *ʿāwôn*) of the priests and the sins of the prophets had provoked God to consume Zion's foundations with fire (Lam 4:11-13). The sentiment doubtless remained alive in Jerusalem; the satan articulates it. But just as Yahweh again chooses Jerusalem, so also Joshua's iniquity or guilt (*ʿāwôn*) will be removed (3:4).

3:3-5. The removal of Joshua's guilt is the fourth vision's sign. It is a symbolic action that follows the satan's rebuke. Joshua's filthy clothes are removed, and he is given a clean "turban" and "festal apparel." These are apparently symbols of office, though not specifically of priestly office.[41] Although Joshua's cleansing recalls the rites of purification for priestly investiture (Lev 8:6-10), Joshua is already the high priest. His cleansing resembles that of Isaiah (Isa 6:1-7). Notably, the removal of Isaiah's guilt (*ʿāwôn*) permits him access to the heavenly court, where he receives a divine commission (Isa 6:8-9). This is also the case in this chapter, in which the interpretation of the sign consists of a new commission for Joshua: He is given certain administrative responsibilities, as symbolized by his apparel and access to the heavenly court—on condition.

3:6-10. The Yahweh-angel interprets the sign, addressing Joshua in an oracle that begins with a pair of conditions (v. 7). The first seems general enough—to walk in God's ways—and the second refers to routine priestly responsibility for guarding the sanctuary. However, both conditions were earlier addressed to Solomon as part of his royal assignment (1 Kgs 2:3; 3:14). Further, Joshua's assignment in v. 7*b* seems to extend to what were formerly royal prerogatives. Judah's kings exercised considerable control over God's house and its courts, including its iconography (2 Kgs 16:10-16; 21:5; 23:11-12). The angel's oracle to Joshua, then, assigns an expanded sphere of responsibility to the high priest. It says nothing, however, about Judah's governor (Zerubbabel, according to Haggai) or about the civic administration of Judah as a Persian province; there is no place here for a mere governor.

Instead, the angel addresses Joshua again (vv. 8-10) and includes Joshua's priestly colleagues in this address, giving them an entirely new role. The angel calls these priests omens, portents (Isa

---

41. Elizabeth E. Platt, "Jewelry, Ancient Israelite," *ABD* 3 (1992) 823-34.

8:18; Ezek 12:6) of what Yahweh is doing—namely, "bringing my servant, Branch" (v. 8). This announcement, to which the priests are testimony, relates to something Yahweh has already done: placed a seven-eyed stone before Joshua (v. 9a). Further, it includes what Yahweh will do—remove the land's "guilt" (NRSV) or "sin" (NIV), or its punishment (ʿāwôn, v. 9b)—and what will follow as a consequence of all this (v. 10). This expansion on the angel's oracle comprises another series of signs, which the angel and Zechariah leave the reader to interpret. Implicitly, they refer the reader to other biblical texts. Jeremiah uses the arboreal image of a branch to refer to the future king, who will be of legitimate, i.e., Davidic, lineage (Jer 23:5; 33:15; cf. Isa 11:1). In this context Jeremiah refers explicitly to David as Yahweh's servant. Joshua and his colleagues are signs or omens that God is bringing an unnamed scion of David's house: a king.

These other texts help to explain the stone already placed before Joshua. It is part of the royal insignia, which has two parts (Ezek 31:21, though the terms vary). One part is a crown or diadem, and the other part is precious stones. Thus stones (jewels) adorn the diadem in 9:16. In 2 Sam 12:30, David finds Milcom's crown with a precious stone in it. In 2 Kgs 11:12, Jehoiada the high priest crowns Jehoash with royal insignia: diadem and jewels.[42] Zechariah 6:9-15 says that both Joshua the priest and the coming royal branch will have crowns and thrones, but in chap. 3 Joshua is already given insignia of high priestly office (vv. 4-5). Although Exod 28:36 includes in these insignia a rosette of gold, inscribed "Holy to Yahweh," Zech 3:9 reserves the stone to the unnamed royal branch. Yahweh, who is bringing this branch, is also engraving the stone, which does not necessarily imply a written inscription. The seven eyes on the stone may be what Yahweh is engraving. Seven eyes are also significant in the fifth vision (see Commentary on 4:10b), but here they are part of the branch's insignia. In Zechariah's numerology, "seven" symbolizes totality or completeness (cf. Gen 2:1-4). That the stone has been put in front of Joshua is explained by

the example of Jehoiada. Surreptitiously, and in defiance of illegitimate but regnant authority, this earlier high priest crowned the legitimate scion of David's house, Jehoash, giving him the royal insignia (diadem and jewels; 2 Kgs 11:4-12). When the branch comes, the high priest will present to him the royal insignia: the stone. For now, Joshua and the priests are omens, signs, pointing to a future symbolized by the stone.

That the branch's coming will coincide with the removal of Judah's guilt and punishment is to be expected. Jeremiah promised such (Jer 33:8) on the way to promising both a Davidic "branch" and an enduring priesthood (Jer 33:15-18). This forgiveness will happen in one day, just as there is one stone before Joshua. This consistency emphasizes the relation between the appearance of the branch and the future of the land. But "in one day" could also be translated "on the first day" (ביום אחד bĕyôm ʾeḥad). The allusion to creation may be intended, and reflected as well in the seven eyes of the branch's stone, in the sevenfold structure of Zechariah's visions, in the seven-branched lampstand of the central vision (chap. 4), and in Yahweh's Spirit being set at rest in the seventh vision. The re-establishment of legitimate, Davidic rule in Judah signifies the dawn of a new creation. Such an event will result ("on that day") in the kind of peace and prosperity promised in v. 10. This is expressly part of Jeremiah's promise (Jer 33:6-7), and it naturally follows on just and legitimate rule (1 Kgs 4:24[5:5]; Hos 2:12[14]; Mic 4:4).

The oracles in chap. 3 anticipate a future in which the high priest and a royal branch exercise a form of joint rule. The chronicler gives historical precedent for this in the reign of Jehoshaphat. He created a judicial institution in Jerusalem, administered jointly by priestly and royal representatives, though with different spheres of responsibility (2 Chr 19:1-11).[43] Zechariah 3 says nothing about the responsibilities of the coming branch, but 6:9-15 assigns him the role of temple builder. A shared administration is envisioned in chap. 4 as well, which also addresses temple building.

---

42. For the proper translation of this verse, see Mordechai Cogan and Hayim Tadmor, *II Kings*, AB 11 (Garden City, N.Y.: Doubleday, 1988) 128.

43. Joseph Blenkinsopp, *Ezra–Nehemiah*, OTL (Philadelphia: Westminster, 1988) 151, with reference to Ezra 7:25-26.

REFLECTIONS

Zechariah has announced that God will again dwell in Zion's midst. The OT knows that God's presence is not limited to one place, nor is it in the control of officials or institutions. The writer of a familiar psalm confesses that even "in the darkest valley" God is present (Ps 23:4). Yet against this backdrop of God's omnipresence, the OT also knows that God chooses to act and to be known in concrete moments and to employ particular earthen vessels in the service of that choice. God thus chooses Joshua the high priest. This third chapter of Zechariah invites three reflections.

1. God chooses, not a pure vessel, but a solid one. Joshua has his accuser, and the satan is right: Joshua's clothes are filthy. He is unfit for office. And just as prosecutors represent the people, doubtless the satan did as well. But God's decision respecting Joshua issues in neither a sentence nor a program of rehabilitation. Rather, God changes Joshua's clothes. Joshua could never make himself fit for the divine office he holds or the tasks to which God calls him. Could anyone? Even so, the God who is transforming the world can transform Joshua and remove his guilt. Nothing suggests that this will make Joshua faultless; indeed, he is charged with responsibilities he may neglect or flout. Earthen vessel he will remain, and it is as earthen vessel that Joshua is fit in God's eyes and in God's court for the task he is assigned and permitted to carry out.

This story of Joshua gives a personal face to Zechariah's vision of God's transformative power. The cosmic meets the individual in this narrative, as the God whom the world is to greet with hushed silence is shown to be the same God who dresses the high priest in clean garments and commissions him for work among the people. Joshua does not warrant his election; indeed, the narrative goes to great lengths to underscore his complete unworthiness. As in the first cycle of visions, Joshua's election once again highlights God's initiative in the unfolding of God's promises. This vision thus invites the reader to entertain the complex interrelationship of grace, election, and call in the lives of God's people.

2. The vision of Zech 3:1-10 adds a new dimension to the first cycle of visions by adding historical specificity to their cosmic scope. As noted in the commentary, the restoration envisioned in chap. 3 is quite concrete: the restoration of the monarchy. The symbols of branch and stone suggest even more concretely the restoration of the Davidic monarchy. The eschatological future for which Zechariah yearns and to which he summons his people is not some vague, general promise of the future, but is grounded in the concreteness of the people's own experience. God's eschatological promises do not render the people's history and the hopes to which that specific history gives rise irrelevant or obsolete. Rather, Zechariah challenges the people to view their history and their hopes through the lens of God's promises, so that the concreteness of the community's experience becomes the vessel for the fulfillment of God's promises. The eschatological promise of a restored creation will occur, not apart from, but through the concreteness that has always marked God's dealings with God's people.

3. Given its predominant concern with the priesthood, Zechariah 3 ends on a strikingly material note. Vines and fig trees symbolize prosperity and peace. Micah says that in the future, people will sit under their *own* fig trees with no one to make them afraid (Mic 4:4). Zechariah says something slightly different. Despite the NIV and the NRSV translations, he does not tell who owns the vines and trees. Rather than everyone's sitting under his or her own vines and trees, according to Zechariah, neighbors will invite each other, in Calvin's words, "to have their repast" under vines and fig trees.[44] Zechariah thus envisions a communal repast, without expressed concern for whose vineyard is whose.

---

44. John Calvin, *Commentaries on the Twelve Minor Prophets,* vol. 5 (Grand Rapids: Eerdmans, 1950) 104.

That such social well-being and fellowship attend the coming of the Branch, the Messiah, seems altogether natural to Zechariah. Yet Calvin and Luther, who identify the Branch with Jesus Christ, seem to fall short of Zechariah's vision in calling this well-being and fellowship only spiritual.[45] The gap between Zechariah and these Christian interpreters raises important and sometimes difficult questions for Christian readers. Does one lose anything of the concreteness and scope of Zechariah's eschatological vision if one insists on an exclusively christocentric reading of his symbolism? Does a christocentric reading of the messianic symbols here require a spiritualizing of the vision of social well-being? To put it another way, can Christian readers affirm the radical vision of social and communal fellowship that characterizes Zechariah's vision of eschatological fulfillment of the messianic age? In order to understand what it means to claim Jesus as Messiah, as the Branch, it seems incumbent upon Christian readers to explore and inhabit the richness of messianic hopes within Judaism.

45. Luther, *Lectures,* 221.

Zechariah 4:1-14, The Fifth Vision: A Golden Lampstand and Zerubbabel

NIV

4 Then the angel who talked with me returned and wakened me, as a man is wakened from his sleep. [2]He asked me, "What do you see?"

I answered, "I see a solid gold lampstand with a bowl at the top and seven lights on it, with seven channels to the lights. [3]Also there are two olive trees by it, one on the right of the bowl and the other on its left."

[4]I asked the angel who talked with me, "What are these, my lord?"

[5]He answered, "Do you not know what these are?"

"No, my lord," I replied.

[6]So he said to me, "This is the word of the LORD to Zerubbabel: 'Not by might nor by power, but by my Spirit,' says the LORD Almighty.

[7]"What[a] are you, O mighty mountain? Before Zerubbabel you will become level ground. Then he will bring out the capstone to shouts of 'God bless it! God bless it!'"

[8]Then the word of the LORD came to me: [9]"The hands of Zerubbabel have laid the foundation of this temple; his hands will also complete it. Then you will know that the LORD Almighty has sent me to you.

[10]"Who despises the day of small things? Men will rejoice when they see the plumb line in the hand of Zerubbabel.

a7 Or Who

NRSV

4 The angel who talked with me came again, and wakened me, as one is wakened from sleep. [2]He said to me, "What do you see?" And I said, "I see a lampstand all of gold, with a bowl on the top of it; there are seven lamps on it, with seven lips on each of the lamps that are on the top of it. [3]And by it there are two olive trees, one on the right of the bowl and the other on its left." [4]I said to the angel who talked with me, "What are these, my lord?" [5]Then the angel who talked with me answered me, "Do you not know what these are?" I said, "No, my lord." [6]He said to me, "This is the word of the LORD to Zerubbabel: Not by might, nor by power, but by my spirit, says the LORD of hosts. [7]What are you, O great mountain? Before Zerubbabel you shall become a plain; and he shall bring out the top stone amid shouts of 'Grace, grace to it!'"

[8]Moreover the word of the LORD came to me, saying, [9]"The hands of Zerubbabel have laid the foundation of this house; his hands shall also complete it. Then you will know that the LORD of hosts has sent me to you. [10]For whoever has despised the day of small things shall rejoice, and shall see the plummet in the hand of Zerubbabel.

"These seven are the eyes of the LORD, which range through the whole earth." [11]Then I said to him, "What are these two olive trees on the right and the left of the lampstand?" [12]And a second

NIV

"(These seven are the eyes of the LORD, which range throughout the earth.)"

¹¹Then I asked the angel, "What are these two olive trees on the right and the left of the lampstand?"

¹²Again I asked him, "What are these two olive branches beside the two gold pipes that pour out golden oil?"

¹³He replied, "Do you not know what these are?"

"No, my lord," I said.

¹⁴So he said, "These are the two who are anointed to*ᵃ* serve the Lord of all the earth."

ᵃ14 Or two who bring oil and

NRSV

time I said to him, "What are these two branches of the olive trees, which pour out the oil*ᵃ* through the two golden pipes?" ¹³He said to me, "Do you not know what these are?" I said, "No, my lord." ¹⁴Then he said, "These are the two anointed ones who stand by the Lord of the whole earth."

ᵃ Cn: Heb gold

COMMENTARY

With his fifth vision, Zechariah returns to a pattern more typical of the visions outside chap. 3. He describes a scene—a lampstand, lamps, and olive trees—and asks the interpreting angel to identify it. That the interpreting angel has to rouse Zechariah as if from sleep (v. 1) distinguishes this vision from the rest. In an earlier arrangement of the book, it probably formed the keystone of the seven-vision sequence. That arrangement is now disturbed by chap. 3, with which it now forms a pair. Moreover, the arrangement of chap. 4 seems itself to have been altered. As the angel begins to identify what Zechariah has seen, he turns abruptly to address Zerubbabel (v. 6). Then Zechariah himself delivers an oracle concerning Zerubbabel (v. 8), which concludes with the vindication formula (as at 2:9, 11[13, 15]). Finally, in the last part of v. 10, the angel identifies "these seven" as the eyes of Yahweh, referring to the seven lamps of the lampstand (v. 2). The Zerubbabel material in vv. 6b-10a thus intrudes in the middle of the lampstand vision.[46]

4:2-5. What Zechariah sees is not easy to describe.[47] He calls it a golden lampstand, or menorah, but it is not the familiar menorah. It has a bowl at its top and seven lamps, which are also at its top. Perhaps they are arranged around the top, at the edge of the bowl. Each of the seven lamps has seven spouts or lips, each of which would hold a wick. Zechariah's lampstand is clearly related to the one Moses built for the tabernacle (Exod 25:31-37). But the tabernacle lampstand, the model for the later menorah of Judaism, had six branches. It is like a tree; its imagery is arboreal and floral. Zechariah's lampstand has no such imagery, but it shares with the tabernacle menorah the function of a lamp: illumination. In both cases, the illuminating and life-giving presence of God is at the heart of the symbol.

Although Zechariah's lampstand lacks the arboreal imagery of the tabernacle menorah, two olive trees flank it (v. 3). More precisely, they flank the "bowl" atop the lampstand. This term, "bowl" (גלה *gullâ*), describes another ritual object. At the front of the Temple, to guard its entrance, Solomon built two massive pillars, which he named Jachin and Boaz (1 Kgs 7:21). Atop the pillars were capitals, each with a "bowl" surrounded by representations of lotus flowers and pomegranates

46. Van der Woude defends the current order of 4:1-14, as does Merrill. See A. S. van der Woude, "Zion as Primeval Stone in Zechariah 3 and 4," in *Text and Context: Old Testament and Semitic Studies for F. C. Fensham*, ed. W. Claassen, JSOTSup 48 (Sheffield: JSOT, 1988) 237-48; Eugene H. Merrill, *Haggai, Zechariah, Malachi: An Exegetical Commentary* (Chicago: Moody, 1994) 157-59. However, I do not find their arguments from syntax persuasive.

47. Carol Meyers and Eric Meyers, *Haggai and Zechariah 1–8,* AB 25B (New York: Doubleday, 1987).

(1 Kgs 7:19-22, 41-42). These, too, are like trees. In placing a bowl atop the lampstand, Zechariah alludes to the Temple, the site of God's presence. But he does so in the Temple's *absence.* Instead of blossoming pillars with bowls at the right (south) and left (north) of the temple entrance (1 Kgs 7:21), Zechariah sees two olive trees at the right and the left of the lampstand's bowl. These olive trees do not provide the fuel—olive oil—for the lamps. Instead, together with the lamps and their divine, celestial light, they symbolize divine presence and sacred space, illumination, fertility, and creation. And like the pillars at the Temple's entrance, they flank "the gate of heaven."[48]

4:6-10a. Before the angel can interpret this imagery for Zechariah, he delivers an oracle to Zerubbabel, governor of Judah (Hag 1:1). The terms with which the angel initially addresses Zerubbabel (v. 6) suggest battle. Zerubbabel has a battle to wage, but not by might—or with an army (Exod 14:4)—and not by (military) power. These same terms occur in Ps 33:16: "A king is not saved by his great army [or might], a warrior is not delivered by his great power." Instead, Yahweh's Spirit, by which God created the world (Ps 33:6), will assist Zerubbabel. These notions are thoroughly at home in Jerusalem and its Zion theology.

Zechariah's foe is the "great mountain," which will be leveled by Zerubbabel (v. 7). Given the explicit statement that Zerubbabel's hands have laid the foundation of this (Yahweh's) house and will carry it to completion (v. 9), it seems plausible that the great mountain is simply the rubble of the destroyed Temple. He achieves victory by bringing out a stone, which is greeted with unanimous acclamation (v. 7). Similar rejoicing (not unlike that of 2:10[14]) greets another stone (NRSV, "plummet") in Zerubbabel's hands (v. 10a). The angel's oracle and Zechariah's give obscure names to these stones, which English translations typically render as adjectives. It is a near consensus among contemporary interpreters that these names, and the whole of this Zerubbabel "intrusion," reflect Mesopotamian ceremonies accompanying temple (re)construction.[49]

This text in Zechariah's fifth vision makes two clear claims. The first is that Zerubbabel acts as the temple builder. The second and correlative claim is that Zerubbabel will complete the Temple. In other words, he is (like Solomon) David's heir to the throne of Judah; he represents the dawn of the messianic age. These claims help to explain the presence of this material in the fifth vision. Very simply, Zerubbabel, and no one else, is constructing the place—the house—for God's presence as symbolized by the lampstand and the olive trees. Haggai, for one, had messianic expectations for Zerubbabel (Hag 2:20-23). Others were less sanguine. Haggai addresses those to whom the Temple in construction seems as nothing (2:3), while Zechariah adverts to people who despise "the day of small things" (v. 10). So far as it concerned Zerubbabel, their modesty or skepticism was justified. Ezra reports that "the elders of the Jews," not Zerubbabel, completed the Temple (Ezra 6:14). The governor who apparently succeeded him, Elnathan, was not of David's line. An inscription from the vicinity of Jerusalem suggests that a woman named Shelomith was Elnathan's administrative associate. Shelomith was Zerubbabel's daughter (1 Chr 3:19).[50] Zerubbabel's fate is unknown.

4:10b-14. As was noted earlier, Zechariah dissociates the expected Davidic ruler from Zerubbabel (chap. 3). The same is true of these verses, the interpretation of Zechariah's fifth vision, and 6:9-15. The angel first identifies "these seven" as the eyes of Yahweh ranging over the whole earth (v. 10b). This "seven" refers to the seven-lipped lamps of v. 2. Their association with eyes is appropriate, since they illuminate. Like the sun, Yahweh's eyes see everything, bring it to light, and examine (Ps 19:4-6[5-7]). Like the horses of chaps. 1 and 6, and the satan in Job 1:7; 2:2, they encompass the whole earth. The precise expression is repeated in 2 Chr 16:9, where "Yahweh's eyes range the whole earth to strengthen those completely true to him" (author's trans.). In that context, God's eyes discovered that King Asa of Judah had not been completely true. Thus these eyes play both a

48. Tryggve N. D. Mettinger, *The Dethronement of Sabaoth,* ConBOT 18 (Lund: Gleerup, 1982) 111.

49. See David L. Petersen, *Haggai and Zechariah 1–8,* OTL (Philadelphia: Westminster, 1984) 240-44. Antti Laato matches every detail of the text with such ceremonies, in "Zechariah 4, 6b-10a and the Akkadian Royal Building Inscriptions," *ZAW* 106 (1994) 53-69.

50. Nahman Avigad, *Bullae and Seals from a Post-Exilic Judean Archive, Oedem* 4 (1976) 11-13; Shemaryahu Talmon, "Ezra and Nehemiah," in *The Interpreter's Dictionary of the Bible,* 327.

supportive and an investigatory role in God's administration of the whole earth.[51]

Satisfied, Zechariah asks about the olive trees (vv. 3, 11) and then asks another question in v. 12. This second question introduces new terms and confusing imagery.[52] Zechariah did not report seeing any branches (or channels) or golden pipes. Regardless, the angel answers that "these"—the two olive trees—are (literally) "the two sons of oil" and that they attend the Lord of the whole earth (v. 14). Zechariah's (or the angel's) terms are carefully chosen. Those who attend or stand by the Lord are members of the heavenly court (3:8), just as the mounted rider/Yahweh-angel is stationed, or stands, among the myrtles (1:8, 11). Moreover, in 3:8 Joshua is promised conditional access to the members of this court. Here in 4:14, two people—symbolized as olive trees—are included among the Lord's attendants. Neither of them is named. It is unlikely that they are called "anointed." The term for "oil" here (יצהר *yiṣhār*) is used neither for anointing oil nor for lamp oil. It typically occurs together with "grain" and "new

wine" as symbols of fertility and prosperity (e.g., Num 18:12; Deut 7:13; Jer 31:12; Joel 2:19). At the same time, the expression "sons of" (בני *běnê*) sometimes designates an affiliation or membership in a guild. In pre-exilic Judah there was an office, or function, "son of the king."[53] We could understand these "two sons of oil" as ministers of prosperity, because they attend the Lord.

This judgment is not entirely at odds with the difficult question of v. 12, which pictures golden pipes draining "gold" (MT) from the olive trees. Neither is it at odds with the splendid depiction of the future in 3:10. The light that dawns with the lampstand in chap. 4, and thus with the presence of God, signals the revival of worship in a sacred space. But it also—and just because of that—signals the renewal of the world. This fifth vision depends on and reflects the transformations and reversals that Zechariah's first two chapters envision. Like the supplementary fourth vision, it envisions a joint administration—a diarchy—within a world whose only Lord is God. Zerubbabel's role in achieving this vision is undeniable, and his disappearance is not the end of the vision.

51. The seven eyes may reflect what, according to Xenophon and Herodotus, is a Persian institution: the eyes and ears of the king, a system of informants useful for policing a vast empire. See A. L. Oppenheim, " 'The Eyes of the Lord,' " *JAOS* 88 (1968) 173-79; Michael Fishbane, *Biblical Interpretation in Ancient Israel* (Oxford: Clarendon, 1985) 450.

52. Petersen, *Haggai and Zechariah 1–8*, 234-37.

53. Gabriel Barkay, "A Bulla of Ishmael, the King's Son," *BASOR* 290-91 (1993) 109-14.

REFLECTIONS

1. In this problematic chapter, Zechariah once again treads a dangerous path. Paul Hanson has called it "ignominious." Hanson judges that Zechariah put prophecy "in the uncritical service of a specific, political system" and wedded his own fate in part to the fate of Zerubbabel.[54] This is a harsh judgment. Is Hanson right?

Zechariah's prophecy concerning Zerubbabel is certainly reason for pause—and a warning. But did Zechariah's vision of a priestly-royal administration put prophecy in greater danger, or was it any less critical than, for example, Jeremiah's prophecy of a restored and everlasting Davidic monarchy and levitical priesthood? For that matter, did not the apostles and do not Christians wed their fate to the fate of Jesus Christ? And was it not the fate of Zechariah and Zerubbabel to be drawn into the service of Christian scripture and witness to Jesus Christ? Zerubbabel, who disappeared from history, reappears in the genealogy of Jesus (Matt 1:12; Luke 3:27). In order to envision the present and future when both were obscure, Zechariah risked particularity—perhaps excessive particularity. But the Jewish community he helped to create (Sir 49:11) endured, and it endures still.

An issue that this fifth vision puts before the church is that of the concrete particularity of Scripture's witness. The texts of the Old and New Testaments did not emerge in a historical vacuum. Each of them participates fully in the historical circumstances in which it was produced

54. P. Hanson, *The Dawn of Apocalyptic* (Philadelphia: Fortress, 1975) 247.

and, in most instances, to which it was articulated. With the prophetic literature, in which one of the prophet's goals was to redescribe the events of history so that political realities would be understood also as theological realities, the conjunction of historical contingency and theological claim is particularly acute. How does one hear the Word of God when the claims of the prophets are read centuries later, when the events of which they spoke—whether of the Babylonian exile, the Persian restoration, or Zerubbabel's completion of the Temple—are but a distinct memory?

This Zerubbabel vision stands as a reminder to those who are tempted to interpret Scripture as a disembodied word, and as witness to that Word, which exists apart from the real people who produced it, who transmitted it as a part of Scripture, and who read and hear it today. The challenge for the theological interpreter is to read this visionary text as the concrete and particular claim of Zechariah, whose voice joins the chorus of scriptural witnesses to the enduring Word.

2. The themes that Zechariah strikes and the imagery he uses throughout the first four chapters are redolent of creation. We moderns are prone to limit creation to a distinct "natural" realm or order. Throughout the OT and Zechariah, the order of creation extends to political arrangements, worship, the Temple—even to the future—because God is the author of it all. And all of it is in the service of life, which God the creator sustains. The arboreal and celestial imagery associated with the lampstand and the Temple, symbols of divine presence, reflects a wholesome union of nature and grace. Zechariah places before the reader a powerful creation theology. This theology should not seem strange to those for whom the divine presence is associated with eating bread and drinking wine, yet another wholesome union of nature and grace.

3. In addressing Zerubbabel, Zechariah (or the angel) uses martial terms and imagery, as if Zerubbabel were going to war. Building the Temple, just initiating its construction, is pictured as an immense and even dangerous task. Zerubbabel will not accomplish this task with the might and power that a royal figure usually commands, however. Rather, he is to put himself in the service of God's Spirit. It is difficult to understand, and even harder to believe, that the Spirit of God can and does prevail in place of power and might. Contemporary instincts often run in the opposite direction. Even if we confess that by the Spirit of God the world was created, it is easier to think of this Spirit as a subtle influence than as the world-creating and transforming power of the Lord of hosts. It can hardly be accidental that Zechariah, who did think of God's Spirit in this way, could also envision a reality seriously at odds with, but also truer than, that of his dispirited compatriots and the empire that ruled them. In this faith, confidence, and vision, Zechariah was indeed a prophet.

Zechariah 5:1-11, A Flying Scroll and an Ephah Flown Away

OVERVIEW

Zechariah's fifth vision (chap. 4) marked a shift in the pace of the vision sequence. All of the other visions display movement, which is sometimes urgent. But the lampstand is stationary. As the symbol of divine presence, it represents a provisional goal of the movement displayed in the preceding visions and announced in the oracles that accompany them.

Beginning with the sixth vision (5:1-4), things are once more on the move. Objects, signs, appear on the visionary scene and move away from it. The term "to go out" or "to appear" (יצא *yāṣāʾ*) occurs thirteen times in the last three visions, but elsewhere only in the third vision (2:7[3]). The urgent movement of that vision resumes in chap. 5. Zechariah again lifts his eyes (5:1), as he had done in the second and third visions (1:18[2:1]; 2:1[5]), and sees something in motion: a flying scroll. The sixth vision thus resumes the pace of earlier ones, but it reverses the direction of their focus. The visions in chaps. 1–4 move from the periphery, "the whole earth," to the center. With chap. 5, the scope of the visions begins to expand until, in the final vision (6:1-8), it again embraces the whole earth.

This shift in pace and scope is directly related to the provisional goal that the visions achieved in chap. 4. First, the fifth vision concludes with a reference to Yahweh as "Lord of the whole earth" (4:14). Precisely where the scope of the visions is most tightly focused, their universal scope is adumbrated. Second, God's presence, as symbolized by the lampstand, requires the absence—the removal or elimination—of certain other things; in chap. 5, Zechariah envisions this process of elimination. Thus these two visions participate in the creation of sacred space.

Zechariah 5:1-4, The Sixth Vision: A Flying Scroll

NIV

5 I looked again—and there before me was a flying scroll!

[2]He asked me, "What do you see?"

I answered, "I see a flying scroll, thirty feet long and fifteen feet wide.[a]"

[3]And he said to me, "This is the curse that is going out over the whole land; for according to what it says on one side, every thief will be banished, and according to what it says on the other, everyone who swears falsely will be banished. [4]The LORD Almighty declares, 'I will send it out, and it will enter the house of the thief and the house of him who swears falsely by my name. It will remain in his house and destroy it, both its timbers and its stones.'"

[a]2 Hebrew *twenty cubits long and ten cubits wide* (about 9 meters long and 4.5 meters wide)

NRSV

5 Again I looked up and saw a flying scroll. [2]And he said to me, "What do you see?" I answered, "I see a flying scroll; its length is twenty cubits, and its width ten cubits." [3]Then he said to me, "This is the curse that goes out over the face of the whole land; for everyone who steals shall be cut off according to the writing on one side, and everyone who swears falsely[a] shall be cut off according to the writing on the other side. [4]I have sent it out, says the LORD of hosts, and it shall enter the house of the thief, and the house of anyone who swears falsely by my name; and it shall abide in that house and consume it, both timber and stones."

[a] The word *falsely* added from verse 4

COMMENTARY

The close connection between the fifth vision (chap. 4) and the sixth is indicated by a stylistic awkwardness. Twice, Zechariah refers to what "he said," but this *he* is never identified (cf. 3:1). Obviously, it is the interpreting angel who addresses Zechariah, but the angel has not been mentioned since early in chap. 4 (4:5). It is as if the sixth vision simply continues the fifth. But the content of these two visions is radically different, and within the chiastic arrangement of the visions, Zech 5:1-4 (vision 6) balances 2:1-5[5-9] (vision 3). A part of this balance is achieved poetically.

In 2:1[5], Zechariah sees a surveyor with a measuring line, while in 5:1 he sees a flying scroll. In Hebrew, there is assonance between these terms: חבל מדה (*ḥebel middâ*, "measuring line"), and מגלה עפה (*měgillâ 'apâ*, "flying scroll"). Although the surveyor in the third vision intends to determine the *width and length* of Jerusalem, in the sixth vision Zechariah records the *length and width* of the scroll. This inversion of terms corresponds to an inversion of another kind. In the third vision, the surveyor's intentions are thwarted: The restored Jerusalem's dimensions will be unlimited, and Yahweh will be a protective wall of fire in place of walls. In the sixth vision, the scroll has precise dimensions, and its range extends beyond Jerusalem (5:2); however, the sixth vision is not concerned with any external threat, but with the threat of internal corruption. The flying scroll symbolizes that threat and, at the same time—rather, in the course of the vision—its elimination.

5:1-2. Like its counterpart in chap. 2, Zechariah's sixth vision introduces an apparently mundane sign: a scroll. But while the surveyor (chap. 2) is just an everyday surveyor, the scroll *flies.* And it is immense: twenty cubits by ten, or roughly thirty feet by fifteen feet. Clearly, this is no ordinary scroll. Do its dimensions have any significance?[55] The vestibule at the front of Solomon's Temple was twenty cubits by ten cubits (1 Kgs 6:3), and for centuries interpreters have sought to connect this feature with Zechariah's scroll.[56] Also, the monumental cherubim over the ark, deep within the Temple, were ten cubits high, and their combined wingspan was twenty cubits (1 Kgs 6:24-27). The winged cherubim suggest flight, and the ark contained the tablets of the law (1 Kgs 8:6-9), which included prohibitions against theft and the false use of God's name—both implicitly condemned in v. 4. But Zechariah gives the dimensions of a flying scroll, not of winged creatures flying it. And nothing in vv. 1-3 suggests that the scroll is (a copy of) God's law, or even that it appears at Yahweh's initiative. Both signs, the scroll and the ephah (NRSV, "basket"), have an initially neutral value. A scroll is just a document, and an ephah just a unit of measure, like a book and a bushel. The ephah that appears in v. 6 clearly does *not* come from Yahweh. Neither does the scroll in vv. 1-2, which appears as an oath or a curse in v. 3. Its immense size is connected with the notice in v. 3 that it "goes out over the face of the whole world [ארץ *'ereṣ,* "earth" or "land"]." In other words, it is ubiquitous.

5:3. In this respect, the scroll is like the sun. Indeed, its "going out over the whole earth/land" is like the description of morning in Gen 19:23: "The sun had gone out over the whole earth when Lot came to Zoar" (cf. Judg 5:31). Comparison with the sun is apt in this context. Among Israel's neighbors, the sun was a deity particularly concerned with law and justice. The Old Babylonian king Hammurabi refers to the sun god Shamash ("Sun") as "the mighty judge of heaven and earth" in his famous law code. Indeed, Hammurabi refers to himself as "the king of justice, to whom Shamash committed law."[57] The sun is associated with justice, in part because it brings everything to light. This notion is reflected in Psalm 19, which describes the sun's circuit as extending from one end of heaven to the other, so that "nothing escapes its heat" (Ps 19:7[6]). In its very next verse, the psalm turns to praise of Yahweh's law, which is perfect and "illumines the eyes" (Ps 19:9[8]).

The legal character of the scroll is explicit in the angel's identification of it as an oath or a curse, or perhaps an imprecation (אלה *'ālâ*). The term is at home in legal proceedings, where the plaintiff's claim is published as an imprecation (Lev 5:1; cf. Judg 17:2). The guilty party, or the one accused, is obligated to respond (1 Kgs 8:31), as are any material witnesses. Testimony of any kind is to be sworn, and false testimony is condemned (Lev 5:20-24; Prov 29:24). This is to assure that guilt or innocence can be fairly determined (1 Kgs 8:32). According to the covenant code (Exod 20:22–23:33), in the absence of witnesses an oath determines innocence concerning the loss of another's property (Exod 22:9-11[8-10]). In these events, an oath is a serious matter. Like the sun, it should bring everything to light on behalf of justice. That this is not the case in vv. 1-3 is obscured by the translations, according to which the thief and swearer will be "banished" or "cut off" (v. 3). The term so translated (נקה *niqqâ*) refers, not to the future, but to the past or to what has been and is the case. It does not mean "banished" or "cut off," but "held innocent" or "acquitted." In other words, the oath exculpates both every thief and anyone giving sworn testimony.

55. Carol Meyers and Eric Meyers, *Haggai and Zechariah 1–8,* AB 25B (New York: Doubleday, 1987) 280-83.

56. Martin Luther, *Lectures on the Minor Prophets,* vol. 3, *Zechariah,* in *Luther's Works,* vol. 20 (St. Louis: Concordia, 1973); 233-35; cf. John Calvin, *Commentaries on the Twelve Minor Prophets,* vol. 5 (Grand Rapids: Eerdmans, 1950) 128; Hinckley G. Mitchell, *A Critical and Exegetical Commentary on Haggai and Zechariah,* ICC (Edinburgh: T. & T. Clark, 1912) 168-69.

57. *ANET,* 178, 179.

The grammar in v. 3 is unusual, but the translations may be correct in suggesting a scroll with writing on both sides; in other cases, the combination מזה ... מזה (*mizzeh . . . mizzeh*) means "this side and the other" (e.g., Exod 37:8; Josh 8:33). In Exod 32:15, this expression refers to the two tablets of the law, "written on the front and on the back." The scroll handed to Ezekiel is likewise written on both sides (Ezek 2:9-10, using different terms). If this verse does describe a scroll written on both sides, then the two sides provide the text of an oath: One side absolves thieves, and the other absolves those who give sworn testimony, thieves included. However, the point seems to be, not that the scroll is written on both sides—if it is flying, the back side would remain illegible—but that the acquittal of thieves, on one hand, has its correlate in the acquittal of anyone who gives sworn testimony or who swears ignorance, on the other hand. In either case, the judicial/legal system has become a machine for issuing verdicts of innocence. Testimony is worthless, so justice is corrupted; it is not administered (cf. 3:7).

Notably, "swearing" occurs neither in the name of Yahweh nor of any other deity. Neither is it said to be false swearing. The categories "true" and "false" are irrelevant, because every oath guarantees an innocent verdict. Under these conditions, the vast oath-bearing scroll going out over the land is not the judicial sun, which brings everything to light. Instead, it casts a shadow over the land, letting justice fall into that vast gray area where distinctions are impossible. Under these circumstances, the scroll is not a light, but a foil—a cover-up.

5:4. Circumstances and the character of the scroll change in this verse, in which the sixth vision abruptly changes voice. This is the only place within the visions at which God is quoted in oracular fashion. This oracular speech constitutes the vision's interpretation. In a sense, Yahweh commandeers the vision and its interpretation. This formal intrusion corresponds to the content: Yahweh commandeers the scroll/oath. Now, in the oracular interpretation, it is Yahweh who brings it out for a particular purpose. Now the oath will return as a curse. Now, just as the sun brings everything to light so that "nothing escapes its heat," so also the scroll/oath/curse will enter, lodge in, and consume the house of the thief and the house of the one who swears falsely and in God's name.

Zechariah does not here envision structural changes in the administration of justice; instead, he envisions the elimination of its perversion. Henceforth, thieves will be strictly accountable, as will those who give testimony. The vision provides scant clues about specific social conditions it may be addressing. It may well be that this early period of Judah's restoration, when new institutions were being created or old ones restored, offered opportunities for fraud. It may also be that, when families coming from Babylon claimed property occupied and claimed by Judean families, charges and countercharges of theft were common, all of them backed by sworn testimony. Yet, fraud and false testimony are matters of concern in every period of Israel's history, to judge from the Old Testament.

In v. 4, the "curse" does not devolve on the entire community, even though it may harbor thieves and liars.[58] Zechariah here severs the connection, explicit in Deuteronomic parlance, between the curse and the covenant—Yahweh's contracted relation with Israel (Deut 29:11-14[12-15]). In Zechariah, it is the thief and the liar who will suffer; the curse lodges in their houses and consumes them. It does not threaten the "house" of Judah. Thus the curse is here entirely positive; it works for the community's benefit. Nowhere in Zechariah's visions, or anywhere in First Zechariah, is there a word of judgment or threat directed against the community. The scroll, in the form of a devouring curse, eliminates one internal threat to the community's well-being—just as Yahweh's wall of fire (2:9[5]) eliminates external ones.

---

58. Mitchell, *Haggai and Zechariah,* 170.

REFLECTIONS

1. A community or a nation safe from external threat is not automatically secure. Historical and contemporary evidence abounds that the threat of aggression and even the reality of oppression by an external power can conceal the seeds of internal ruin. When that threat and that reality vanish, these seeds gain opportunity to grow into a corrupting and destructive force. Internal corruption is as great a threat as an external enemy, and is even more insidious to the well-being of a community. Zechariah is acutely aware of this. What would it matter, finally, that Judah was free from international aggressors and oppressors, if the seeds of its destruction lay within? A corrupt judicial system, the routine perversion of justice, and the absence of justice are no less a threat, and no less oppressive, than is occupation. As a result, in this vision Zechariah envisions the elimination of this corrupt system by the action of God alone.

It is instructive that Zechariah relies on God to commandeer the scroll, transforming it from an instrument of injustice to the opposite. He does not rely on or defer to the emperor in this internal matter; he does not treat it as a matter of imperial state. Zechariah's sixth vision thus provides an interesting lens through which to reflect on the history of the church and its often compromised relationship with imperial states. Freed from the threat of persecution, and declared first legitimate and then official, the church relied on the emperor (and then the prince) to eliminate not enemies without, but dissenters within. This, too, was a form of corruption. The contemporary church may be flirting with a similar form of corruption when it allies itself with the state and asks the power of the state to promulgate and enforce its laws.

2. It would be a mistake to interpret Zechariah's sixth vision only in negative terms. This vision builds on what was already well known in Israelite law: that theft and false testimony were prohibited, that acts of injustice against one's neighbor were prohibited. The specific prohibitions against fraud are contained in the holiness code at Lev 19:11-15, which culminate in the summary injunction, "You shall love your neighbor as yourself" (Lev 19:18 NRSV). The same prohibitions and the same summary injunction appear in Rom 13:9, "Love your neighbor as yourself" (cf. Eph 4:22-29).

Zechariah's sixth vision thus symbolically depicts the elimination of fraud from the community's life, and as the texts cited above show, this opens the way to a community built on love of neighbor. There is no tension, in any of these texts, between love and justice. In all of them, justice is the form love takes.

3. The whole biblical tradition condemns false swearing, of course, but strands of the NT prohibit swearing altogether (Matt 5:33-37; James 5:12). Swearing is prohibited, because what we affirm or testify is either true or false, and nothing we could swear by can either change the fact or confirm it. The truth of one's spoken word should be enough ("Let your 'Yes' be yes and your 'No' be no"). Given the presence of traditions in the Bible against swearing oaths to back up one's word, it is curious that when we officially and solemnly swear, it is with our hands on the Bible. By the default of public practice, the Bible has come to function more or less as the scroll does in Zech 5:1-4. It is placed in the position to exonerate those who testify falsely.

Zechariah 5:5-11, The Seventh Vision: This Is the Ephah

NIV	NRSV
⁵Then the angel who was speaking to me came forward and said to me, "Look up and see what this is that is appearing."	5Then the angel who talked with me came forward and said to me, "Look up and see what this is that is coming out." ⁶I said, "What is it?" He said, "This is a basket[a] coming out." And he said, "This is their iniquity[b] in all the land." ⁷Then a leaden cover was lifted, and there was a woman
⁶I asked, "What is it?"	
He replied, "It is a measuring basket.[a]" And he	

a6 Hebrew *an ephah*; also in verses 7-11

a Heb *ephah*   b Gk Compare Syr: Heb *their eye*

NIV

added, "This is the iniquity[a] of the people through-out the land."

[7]Then the cover of lead was raised, and there in the basket sat a woman! [8]He said, "This is wickedness," and he pushed her back into the basket and pushed the lead cover down over its mouth.

[9]Then I looked up—and there before me were two women, with the wind in their wings! They had wings like those of a stork, and they lifted up the basket between heaven and earth.

[10]"Where are they taking the basket?" I asked the angel who was speaking to me.

[11]He replied, "To the country of Babylonia[b] to build a house for it. When it is ready, the basket will be set there in its place."

[a]6 Or appearance   [b]11 Hebrew Shinar

NRSV

sitting in the basket![a] [8]And he said, "This is Wickedness." So he thrust her back into the basket,[a] and pressed the leaden weight down on its mouth. [9]Then I looked up and saw two women coming forward. The wind was in their wings; they had wings like the wings of a stork, and they lifted up the basket[a] between earth and sky. [10]Then I said to the angel who talked with me, "Where are they taking the basket?"[a] [11]He said to me, "To the land of Shinar, to build a house for it; and when this is prepared, they will set the basket[a] down there on its base."

[a] Heb ephah

COMMENTARY

The theme of elimination continues in the seventh vision, as another internal threat is removed. The angel expressly identifies this threat as "wickedness" (v. 8), which is removed through the agency of two winged women (vv. 9-11). It is not obvious, however, what "wickedness" means in this vision, whose imagery is both fantastic and difficult to decode. The complexity of this vision's imagery is reflected in its form. Four times in this vision the interpreting angel identifies or interprets something for Zechariah (the seventh vision includes nearly one-third of all the angel's speeches). There is no complex process of mediation, as in the first vision with its multiple speakers; here the complexity involves the imagery itself. As in the fifth vision (chap. 4), the angel takes the initiative, asking Zechariah what he sees. In chap. 4, Zechariah responded with an elaborate and detailed description of the sign, but now he can describe nothing. He can only ask, "What is that?" (v. 6). Zechariah's question echoes among his readers.

To Zechariah's question the angel responds by identifying the sign. "This," he says, "is the ephah that is going out" (v. 6). Structurally, the remainder of the vision divides into two parts. In vv. 6-8 the angel identifies the complex sign. In vv. 9-11

the vision then expands (Zechariah sees something else) to include two women who bear the ephah away. This expansion further interprets the sign. The first part of the vision (vv. 6-8) has its own elaborate structure. After identifying what Zechariah cannot describe—the ephah—the angel seems to interpret it: "This," he says, "is their eye in all the earth/land [ארץ *'eres*, v. 6*b*]." Next, Zechariah himself sees the sign and describes two additional features: a lead disk that is lifted and a woman sitting in the ephah. This the angel identifies as "wickedness" (v. 7). The first part of the vision concludes with the interpreting angel, not speaking, but taking action—the only time in the book. He thrusts the woman into the ephah and thrusts the lead disk, now called a lead stone, onto the ephah's mouth (v. 8). After this the winged women carry the ephah to Shinar.

An ephah is a unit of dry measure, perhaps about a bushel. It is also a container of equivalent size for measuring grain or flour. What Zechariah sees is, obviously, a container, for a "woman" is sitting inside it (v. 7). What kind of container is uncertain, perhaps a basket or a jar. Neither is it certain that the ephah is of standard size; after all, it contains a woman—or perhaps a figurine or image of a woman. The angel's preliminary interpretation of the ephah ("this is their eye") only provokes more questions. Most translations and commentaries follow the LXX and the Syriac in reading "their iniquity" (עונם *ʿăwōnām*) instead of "their eye" (עינם *ʿēnām*).[59] In that case, the ephah would represent "their iniquity in all the land" of Judah. However, First Zechariah contains no such general indictments. In the entire book, the term *ʿāwōn* occurs only in chap. 3, where it refers to Joshua (3:4) and to the guilt or punishment of "that land," which Yahweh will remove in one day (3:9). Achieving greater clarity about what Zechariah sees here, and what the angel identifies and interprets, requires attention to the vision's expansion and interpretation in vv. 9-11 and to its place in the visionary sequence.

In v. 9, Zechariah describes something new: two winged women carrying the ephah away. The angel explains that they are going to build a house—a shrine or sanctuary—for it in Shinar, where it will sit on a base constructed for it (vv. 9-11; cf. Isa 40:18-20; Jer 10:2-4). The ephah, including its component parts, will apparently be venerated in the land of Shinar. "In the land of Shinar" evokes Gen 11:2, where the people build a city and a tower "in the land of Shinar," which turns out to be Babel (=Babylon; Gen 11:9). The ephah, then, is an object of veneration, at home among the nations whose origin and symbol is Babylon. That the ephah is here a religious object bears on the interpretation of the vision's beginning (vv. 5-8).

Zechariah's seventh vision has a dual context. This vision follows immediately the sixth one (vv. 1-4), but the second vision (1:18-21[2:1-4]) functions as its structural counterpart in the chiastic arrangement of the visions. As noted above, the sixth vision is remarkable for lacking an explicit mention of the interpreting angel. Just as remarkable is the angel's inclusion, in the seventh vision, among the things "appearing" or "going out" (יצא *yāṣaʾ*, v. 5). Elsewhere, he "appears" ("comes forward") only in the middle of a vision (2:3[7]). His appearance here to initiate the seventh vision links it closely with the preceding vision of the scroll/curse. That sixth vision ended with the curse devouring the house of the thief and false swearer. Now the angel instructs Zechariah (the

only time in the visions) to see what else is appearing on the scene: the ephah. Evidently, we are to see some connection between the concerns of these two visions.

Perhaps something of that connection is provided by the second vision (1:18-21[2:1-4]), to which the seventh corresponds structurally. There the issue was the nations who had raised their horns against Judah so that the people of Judah could not raise their heads—i.e., the vision concerned Judah's oppression by the nations. And the corresponding seventh vision, according to vv. 9-11, concerns a religious object—the ephah—belonging to the nations. If the second vision helps us to understand the connection between the sixth vision and the seventh, we should be able to see some association among oppression, unaccountable theft, and the ephah.

As Petersen has noted, "ephah" is often qualified by a term like "just" or "honest."[60] Israel is to have but one honest ephah—a common standard for measuring grain and determining payment (Lev 19:36; Deut 25:14; Ezek 45:10-13; Amos 8:5; Mic 6:10). A false ephah, or more than one measure, would constitute theft. An ephah has to do with money. This helps to explain the term "disk" (ככר *kikkār*, translated "cover") in v. 7. The same term can mean "talent," a weight of around 65 pounds for measuring precious metals in scales. In v. 8, this lead disk or talent becomes a lead *stone*, a disk weighing one talent. The passages that mandate an honest ephah also mandate honest scales and "stones" (Lev 19:35-36; Deut 25:13-15; Ezek 45:10; Mic 6:10-11). Like the ephah, the lead disk/talent/stone connotes money. Nothing within the seventh vision suggests that its ephah and its talent are false or non-standard. However, the imagery does suggest that money is at issue, as is the illicit veneration of a "foreign" deity. Moreover, the literary placement of this vision suggests as well that issues of oppression and theft are in view.

We should notice, first, that the ephah and its disk/stone are borne off to Shinar, where the nations and their rebellion against God have their origin. Second, the association between oppressive injustice—including both theft and false swearing—and worship of alien gods is a commonplace

---

59. But cf. Meyers and Meyers, *Haggai and Zechariah 1–8*, 297-98.

60. David L. Petersen, *Haggai and Zechariah 1–8*, OTL (Philadelphia: Westminster, 1984) 255-56.

in the prophets. Hosea (Hos 4:2-14) and Jeremiah (Jer 7:4-10) expound on it. Jeremiah makes explicit that exploitation and offerings to Baal and other gods go hand in hand. Hosea expressly links false or "empty" oaths (cf. Zech 5:3-4) with veneration of an image: "the calf of Beth-aven." Moreover, Hosea promises that this "thing" will be carried to Assyria as tribute (Hos 10:3-6; Ezek 7:20-21), much as the ephah, including its "stone," will be carried to Shinar (Zech 5:9-11).

As a province, Judah had to pay heavy taxes to the Persian Empire (Neh 9:36-37). Meeting that burden proved onerous, especially when it was combined with support of rapacious provincial officials (Neh 5:7) and chronically poor agricultural yields (Neh 5:3; Hag 1:6). Significantly, it was the Persian king Darius who imposed standard weights throughout the empire, for the purpose of paying taxes in silver; taxes were to be assessed "according to the Babylonian talent."[61]

The ephah and its talent/stone symbolize the corrosive internal effects of domination by the complacent nations who allied themselves with the disaster (1:15) and have exploited Judah (1:21[2:4]). These internal effects, eliminated in the sixth and seventh visions, have an economic dimension, as we have seen. They also have a religious or cultic dimension, as is clear from vv. 9-11. At the heart of the seventh vision (vv. 6-8), the ephah and its lid acquired yet another level of meaning.

Zechariah sees a woman sitting "in the midst of" the ephah (vv. 7-8). Zechariah sees only "this certain woman," but the angel does identify her: "This is Wickedness," he says. "Wickedness" (הרשעה *hāriš'â*) means wrongdoing in general, but in Deuteronomy and Ezekiel it is especially associated with the nations (Deut 9:4-5; Ezek 5:6). In Ezekiel it is also associated with Jerusalem's "abominations" (Ezek 5:11), the veneration of alien gods (cf. Deut 7:25-26). Jeremiah also speaks of abominations in Judah and Jerusalem, twice in contexts that describe worship of the "Queen of Heaven" (7:10-18; 44:1-27). According to Jeremiah, this worship involved making incense offerings, pouring libations, and baking cakes "marked with her image" (Jer 44:19 NRSV). It is not obvious which female deity is here nominated

"Queen of Heaven," but the Phoenician Astarte is a good candidate. She was officially introduced into Israel by Solomon (1 Kgs 11:5-7), and her worship included the baking of cakes.[62] She was also referred to as "queen," and specifically as "holy."[63] However, it is unlikely that, in Judah, the identity of Astarte was kept distinct from that of Asherah, a deity frequently mentioned in the OT. One of Asherah's epithets was apparently קדש (*quds̆û*), or "holiness."[64]

These details bear on the interpretation of vv. 7-8. The ephah houses a woman identified as "wickedness"—a direct contrast with, and denial of, the epithet "holy" or "holiness." If the ephah signals devotion to the deity, then we might expect it to contain flour for baking something in her honor. In that case, the lid—the disk—might serve as a baking platter. The term ככר (*kikkār*), translated "disk" or "talent" or "covering" literally means "loaf" of bread (e.g., 1 Sam 2:36), including bread for offerings.[65] Zechariah's vision does not clarify these matters; rather, its imagery is sufficiently rich and ambiguous to evoke a variety of associations. The angel does not pause over them, but packs the woman into the ephah and puts the lead stone on its mouth. With wickedness thus safely housed, two winged women appear to bear it away (v. 9).

Why two *women?* This is also unclear, but Jeremiah's description of the worship of the "Queen of Heaven" may provide a clue. It involved whole families (Jer 7:10-18), but women seem to have taken particular initiative in it (Jer 44:15, 19). Second Kings 23 may provide another clue. In its catalog of illicit objects that Josiah removed from the Temple, it refers also to women—apparently part of the temple personnel—who were "weaving houses there for Asherah" (v. 7 MT). Perhaps the ephah is, in this instance, a plaited or woven basket, a house (cella) for the deity, for use in household shrines.

61. Steven Shawn Tuell, *The Law of the Temple in Ezekiel 40–48,* HSM 49 (Atlanta: Scholars Press, 1992) 114. Tuell is citing Herodotus.

62. Susan Ackerman, *Under Every Green Tree: Popular Religion in Sixth-Century Judah,* HSM 46 (Atlanta: Scholars Press, 1992) 26; Brian Peckham, "Phoenicia and the Religion of Israel: The Epigraphic Evidence," in *Ancient Israelite Religion: Essays in Honor of Frank Moore Cross,* ed. Patrick D. Miller, Jr., Paul D. Hanson, S. Dean McBride (Philadelphia: Fortress, 1987) 84.

63. *TSSI* 3.33A.6, 9.

64. John Day, "Asherah," *ABD* 1 (1992) 484; Frank M. Cross, *Canaanite Myth and Hebrew Epic* (Cambridge, Mass.: Harvard University Press, 1973) 34; Johannes C. de Moore, "אשרה *'ǎšērāh*," *TDOT* 1 (1974) 438-44.

65. *CAD* 8 (1971) 49-50. See *ANEP* #150.

The two winged women carry it to Shinar, there to provide it a shrine, a permanent house on a secure foundation.

All of this helps in interpreting "their eye" (v. 6b). In its immediate context, "their" has as its antecedent the thief and false swearer of v. 4. In the structural arrangement of the visions, "they" can also be the nations. Syntactically, "their eye" refers to the ephah and everything associated with it. Once more, Ezekiel is instructive. In 20:8, Ezekiel refers to "the detestable things of their eyes," which he identifies with "their ancestors' idols" on which "their eyes were set" (Ezek 20:24). Contrasted with these eyes is Yahweh's eye, "which spared them" (Ezek 20:17; cf. Ezek 18:6-27). God's eyes have been mentioned already in Zechariah (2:12[8]; 4:10b; the former text refers to Yahweh's special concern for Judah, while the latter refers to God's administration of the whole earth). Here there is a contrast between "their eye" and Yahweh's eyes "in the whole earth."[66] Thieves and false swearers, like the nations—and like those who venerate the nations'

gods—have their eye on—that is, they rely for their security on—what is being eliminated.

Zechariah's most complex and difficult vision marks, at its end, a shift in the movement of the visions. The second and third visions move from the periphery, the whole earth, to the center. At this center, the fourth and fifth visions focus on Jerusalem and the Temple. The focus expands again in the sixth and seventh visions, which have apparently to do with Judah. With the flight of the women bearing the ephah to Shinar, however, the visionary movement pushes suddenly toward the extreme periphery. This prepares for the eighth and final vision, whose scope is once more the whole earth. We may wonder, then, about the references in vv. 3, 6 to "the whole land," and "the entire land" (NRSV). Both of these could be rendered "the whole earth," as elsewhere in the visions (1:11; 4:10, 14; 6:5). Certainly, chap. 5 is concerned with the situation in Judah and Jerusalem, but we may see in its ambiguous references to the whole land/earth the adumbration of a broader concern—a much wider sacred space.

---

66. Eugene H. Merrill, *Haggai, Zechariah, Malachi: An Exegetical Commentary* (Chicago: Moody, 1994) 172-73.

REFLECTIONS

1. According to the interpretation offered above, Zechariah regards the ephah, along with all it contains and variously represents, as the debris resulting from domination. For Zechariah, the ephah is what unfortunately remains from a long history of oppression and occupation, as symbolized by the four horns/nations of 1:18-21[2:1-4]. In envisioning the removal of the ephah from Judah, Zechariah is reclaiming and reenvisioning the identity of Judah. He is engaged in defining the people of Judah as Yahweh's people "on the holy land" (2:12[16]).

Definition includes boundaries; identity involves boundary formation. The ephah lies outside the boundaries of the holy land. These boundaries are not spatial, but religious. They are determined by Yahweh's presence to a community defined as Yahweh's "portion" (2:16[12]). To a people defined as belonging to God, and on this ground defined as holy, some things are incompatible and alien. Indeed, they are foreign. The ephah thus symbolizes for Zechariah what was alien, what led to defeat and bondage in the first place. To reestablish the community's identity, whatever is alien must be removed.

All communities of faith mark boundaries as a way of establishing their identity, although those conversations often take place in language more prosaic than Zechariah's vision of the ephah. Social, moral, and theological boundaries are always under discussion, not only about what should be excluded, but also about what is and must be included. Conclusions reached in these discussions change with time and circumstance. For example, the bronze serpent fashioned by Moses at the command of God (Num 21:16-29) was later destroyed by Hezekiah in faithfulness to the same God. It had become something alien, associated with idolatry (2 Kgs 18:4). Judgments about what is alien and to be excluded, and what is faithful and to be included, are always subject to charges of idolatry. Martin Luther judged certain longstanding, entirely indigenous practices of the church to be idolatrous, representing its Babylonian captivity. Some of Luther's contemporaries judged him to have made Scripture an idol.

In these respects, Zechariah is part example, part instructor. His words provide an example as they present one way to approach questions of boundary definition, of claiming what is faithful and of removing what contains within it the residues of corruption, oppression, and injustice. His words are instructive in that the ephah presents not just pristinely religious connotations, but also economic ones. In a similar vein, the NT defines greed as idolatry (Eph 5:5; Col 3:5). The vision of the ephah can instruct the church to envision its own boundary markers with respect to greed.

2. By far the most troubling element of Zechariah's seventh vision is the role women play in it. The woman inside the ephah is identified as wickedness, and two other women bear it away. The text nourishes a larger biblical and otherwise traditional tendency to view "the feminine as evil,"[67] or as temptation to evil, beginning with interpretations of Eve. This tendency is alive in Proverbs, which warns against the temptations of a woman (the opposite of Wisdom) who is "strange" and "foreign," as in Prov 6:24 (cf. NRSV).[68] Zechariah's vision shares in this characterization of female wickedness as foreign, apparently identifying the principal woman as a foreign deity. Even with this qualification, however, there is no avoiding what is plain in this text: Women especially are associated with this particular wickedness.

The outright misogyny in this text cannot be ignored. To do so is to collude with Zechariah and the traditions on which he draws in their depiction of women. One approach to this text is to say along with a character in Flannery O'Connor's story "The Violent Bear It Away,"[69] "That's all a prophet is good for—to admit somebody else is an ass or a whore." Or one may attempt to find a meaning that works around the depiction of women as evil. Calvin, for example, admits not knowing why women carry the ephah away, "except it was that Jews might know that there was no need of any warlike preparations, but that their strongest enemies could be laid prostrate by weak and feeble instruments; and thus under the form of weakness [God's] own power would be made evident."[70] Yet note that in this "positive" reading of the role of the women in this text, Calvin's own prejudices and presuppositions about women seep through, so that women's "weakness" is substituted for their "wickedness."

There is no simple solution to the disturbing attitude toward women proclaimed in this text. At the very least, the contemporary interpreter must name the problem for what it is and struggle with the question of how to hear the Word of God in a text that identifies a woman as wickedness.

---

67. David L. Petersen, *Haggai and Zechariah 1–8,* OTL (Philadelphia: Westminster, 1984) 257.

68. Harold C. Washington, "The Strange Woman of Proverbs 1–8 and Post-Exilic Judean Society," in *Second Temple Studies 2: Temple Community in the Persian Period,* ed. Tamara C. Eskenazi and Kent H. Richards, JSOTSup 175 (Sheffield: JSOT, 1994) 217-42.

69. Flannery O'Connor, *The Collected Works* (New York: The Library of America, 1988) 355. The title is from Matt 11:12 (KJV).

70. John Calvin, *Commentaries on the Twelve Minor Prophets,* vol. 5 (Grand Rapids: Eerdmans, 1950) 138.

Zechariah 6:1-8, The Eighth Vision: The Four Winds of Heaven

NIV	NRSV
6 I looked up again—and there before me were four chariots coming out from between two mountains—mountains of bronze! [2]The first chariot had red horses, the second black, [3]the third white, and the fourth dappled—all of	6 And again I looked up and saw four chariots coming out from between two mountains—mountains of bronze. [2]The first chariot had red horses, the second chariot black horses, [3]the third chariot white horses, and the fourth chariot

NIV

them powerful. [4]I asked the angel who was speaking to me, "What are these, my lord?"

[5]The angel answered me, "These are the four spirits[a] of heaven, going out from standing in the presence of the Lord of the whole world. [6]The one with the black horses is going toward the north country, the one with the white horses toward the west,[b] and the one with the dappled horses toward the south."

[7]When the powerful horses went out, they were straining to go throughout the earth. And he said, "Go throughout the earth!" So they went throughout the earth.

[8]Then he called to me, "Look, those going toward the north country have given my Spirit[c] rest in the land of the north."

[a]5 Or winds   [b]6 Or horses after them   [c]8 Or spirit

NRSV

dappled gray[a] horses. [4]Then I said to the angel who talked with me, "What are these, my lord?"

[5]The angel answered me, "These are the four winds[b] of heaven going out, after presenting themselves before the Lord of all the earth. [6]The chariot with the black horses goes toward the north country, the white ones go toward the west country,[c] and the dappled ones go toward the south country." [7]When the steeds came out, they were impatient to get off and patrol the earth. And he said, "Go, patrol the earth." So they patrolled the earth. [8]Then he cried out to me, "Lo, those who go toward the north country have set my spirit at rest in the north country."

[a] Compare Gk: Meaning of Heb uncertain   [b] Or spirits   [c] Cn: Heb go after them

COMMENTARY

The eighth and last vision has a structural counterpart in the first vision (1:8-13). Horses figure prominently in the imagery of both visions, and both have the whole earth in view. Also similar is the setting of the first and last visions, in proximity to the presence of God; both visions depict a scene at the gate of heaven. In both, Zechariah is situated in a liminal space, where the boundary between heaven and earth is fluid. If there were originally only seven visions (excluding chap. 3), they had the lampstand vision (chap. 4) as their pivotal focus. There God's presence is concretely symbolized and concentrated, even localized, at the sacred center—in a temple furnishing. The Temple, too, is a gate of heaven. At both ends of the vision sequence, Yahweh's presence extends to the extreme periphery, to the whole earth. In this way the structure of the visions corresponds to the "homology of temple and created world" that they envision.[71] What they envision is, more properly, the restoration and re-creation of this homology (see the Commentary on 1:8-13).

6:1-4. The first vision depicts an edenic scene,

71. Jon D. Levenson, *Creation and the Persistence of Evil* (San Francisco: Harper & Row, 1988) 82.

shrouded in a mysterious darkness that fits both a world at rest and the difficulty of "seeing" what this scene might mean. In the first vision, the horses and riders are stationary; they have returned from a reconnaissance mission and stand among the myrtles. In the last vision, this tense quietness is shattered; the horses burst like the sun from between two mountains—bronze mountains (6:1)—and they are drawing chariots. They are not returning from reconnaissance, but going out on a mission that they complete. They finish a work of creation that Zechariah has envisioned along the way and that ends with Yahweh's Spirit appropriately at rest (6:8).

In marked contrast to the seventh vision, where Zechariah can neither name nor describe what he sees, here he is in full possession of his visionary and descriptive powers. He sees four chariots, horses of four colors, and two mountains of bronze. When Zechariah asks his interpreting angel to identify this sign ("What are these?" [v. 5]), the angel identifies the horse-chariot combinations, but not the bronze mountains.

Interpreters have associated these mountains with those from between which the Mesopotamian sun god Shamash comes forth every morning.[72] These mountains can also be represented as doors,[73] appropriate to the gate of heaven.[74] This solar connotation of the two bronze mountains, and chariots proceeding from between them, gains strength from comparison with 2 Kgs 23:11, which refers to "horses that the kings of Judah had dedicated to the sun"; to these were joined "chariots of the sun." Solar imagery is applied to Yahweh in many places throughout the OT.[75] Isaiah 60, for example, describes Yahweh's presence in Zion as the dawn or sunrise (Isa 60:1-3). In this connection, when commenting on the sixth vision (5:1-4), I pointed to Psalm 19, where the sun "goes out" (יצא *yāṣā'*), as do the horses and chariots in the eighth vision (6:1). It seems that they go out in every direction but east. If the east is their point of origin, they would have no reason to go there; in 8:7, "east" is זרח השמש (*zĕrah haššemeš*), or "sunrise." Given the biblical and other evidence, it makes sense to think of the two mountains in 6:1 as being ablaze with the rising sun.[76] This imagery is appropriate to the last vision, since the first one—if not all of them— came at night (1:8). Zechariah's visions conclude with the dawn.

The chariots in the final vision offer a further contrast to the first one. Horses and chariots typically represent military armament (e.g., Isa 31:1), and it is likely that the chariots have a martial character in vv. 1-8. That Yahweh is in command of chariots is attested in other texts, including Ps 68:17[18]. In Patrick Miller's translation, the verse reads, "The chariots of 'Yahweh' were two myriad, a thousand the warriors/archers of the Lord, when he came from Sinai with the holy ones." As Miller comments, "it is obviously the divine army here which marches forth to fight for Israel."[77] This divine army is elsewhere referred to as Yahweh's "host(s)." In this respect, the last vision returns to the imagery of the first.

In both visions, God's agents have patrolled the earth (1:11-12; 6:7).

The horses and riders—and the Yahweh-angel—in Zech 1:8-12, as well as the horse-drawn chariots in 6:1-8, portray Yahweh's host. In these instances, the imagery is both royal and martial. Its martial character is heightened in the last vision by the presence of chariots. Rather than returning, they are going out. They do so, in the last vision, *after* presenting themselves to "the Lord of the whole earth" (v. 5; cf. Job 1:6-7; 2:1-2). In contrast to the first vision, the mission of God's agents in chap. 6 begins—it does not end—in consultation with Yahweh. The solar imagery, with which Yahweh's "host" is here connected, reinforces the point and defines the mission.

6:5. The mission is adumbrated in the interpreting angel's identification of the sign: "these are the four winds of heaven." This need not indicate a departure from the solar imagery that seems otherwise present in this vision. In two texts, God's chariots are associated with wind (Isa 66:15-16; Jer 4:11-13).[78] But in these texts, chariots and wind (using different terms) are instruments of judgment and destruction; neither of these elements is in view in Zechariah's final vision. On the other hand, the "four winds" have already been mentioned in 2:6[10], as has "the north country" (6:8). The former text contains hints of both exile and dispersion, on one hand, and of return and the means of return, on the other hand—return precisely from "the north country." What was in chap. 2 "like" the four winds of heaven "are" those winds in chap. 6. In the last vision, these winds—Yahweh's hosts— have the character of dawn. We may compare Psalm 80, where Yahweh of hosts is associated with the sun (Ps 80:7[8] implores the "God of hosts" to "restore us; let your face *shine,* that we may be saved").

6:6-7. Zechariah's description of the sign (vv. 2-3) and the angel's identification of it in these verses are fraught with difficulties. Zechariah seems to describe horses of four colors, while the angel identifies only three; the angel says nothing about the "red" horses. The term the NRSV translates as "gray" (אמצים *'ămuṣṣîm,* v. 3) it renders "steeds" in v. 7. In both cases the NIV

72. *ANEP* #685. A. L. Oppenheim, "The Eyes of the Lord," *JAOS* 88 (1968) 176.

73. *ANEP* #683.

74. Petersen, *Haggai and Zechariah 1–8,* 268.

75. J. Glen Taylor, *Yahweh and the Sun: Biblical and Archaeological Evidence for Sun Worship in Ancient Israel,* JSOTSup 111 (Sheffield: JSOT, 1993) 111; Mark S. Smith, *The Early History of God: Yahweh and the Other Deities in Ancient Israel* (San Francisco: Harper & Row, 1990) 115-24.

76. Carol Meyers and Eric Meyers, *Haggai and Zechariah 1–8,* AB 25B (New York: Doubleday, 1987) 319-20.

77. Patrick D. Miller, Jr., *The Divine Warrior in Early Israel,* HSM 5 (Cambridge: Harvard University Press, 1975) 108, 109.

78. Petersen, *Haggai and Zechariah 1–8,* 156-66.

uses the translation "powerful." Moreover, the syntax in vv. 6-7 is very obscure.[79] In my judgment, the red horses are not identified for the same reason that the direction "east" is not named: The red horses have nowhere to go. The NIV's translation seems best: All the horses are powerful, and they all "went out" (v. 7a). There is one more problem that the translations ignore: According to the angel, the black horses *are going* to the north, while the white and dappled horses *have gone* to the west and south. The black and northbound horses (with their chariots) put Yahweh's Spirit at rest in the north country, from which it is necessary and now possible to flee (2:6[10]).

6:8. In spite of the decidedly martial character of this vision's imagery, there is no war to be fought. Indeed, the term "set . . . at rest" (הניחו *hēnîḥû*) is commonly used in texts that describe Israel's freedom from war as rest from all enemies (e.g., 2 Sam 7:1). By the same token, Jeremiah describes national enemies as coming from "the north," whether it is Babylon, the enemy of Judah (Jer 6:22), or the enemies of Babylon itself (Jer 50:9). From Judah's perspective and Jeremiah's, war always comes from the north, historically and naturally, given the regional topography. But Zechariah, based on the angel's interpretation, describes the black horses as going *to* the north country, where they set God's Spirit at rest— where they establish peace and from whence exiles

will return. Just so, according to Jeremiah, Israel and Judah will return from "the land of the north" (Jer 3:18).

With Yahweh's Spirit at rest, the movement of and within the visions comes to an end. All of the going out and coming forward, the appearing and coming out, all of the motion that dominates the last three visions culminates and concludes with the movement of the horses and chariots. They are the four winds of heaven. Since the movement ends with God's wind/Spirit at rest, the vision returns to the world at rest of 1:11. The words for "rest" are different in 1:11 and 6:8, but their meaning overlaps; they appear together in 2 Chr 14:5-7[4-6], which describes Judah's freedom from war as "peace" and "rest" (NRSV). The world is at peace when Zechariah first sees in the night, and it as at peace when the visions conclude. But the world has changed. International, internal, and cosmic order have been re-created. Sacred space has been restored.

In the last verse of the last vision (v. 8), the interpreting angel summons Zechariah. Typically, such language conveys a military summons (Judg 4:10). Here it seems to express the angel's astonishment, which he urges Zechariah to share, and thus also the astonishment of Zechariah's readers—who are elsewhere urged to believe the impossible (8:6). The angel's, and Zechariah's, final instruction is to "See!" Everything has now become transparent. And the angel's voice here merges completely with Yahweh's, just as the angel vanishes.

79. Eugene H. Merrill, *Haggai, Zechariah, Malachi: An Exegetical Commentary* (Chicago: Moody, 1994) 188-89.

REFLECTIONS

1. As he did in chap. 1, Zechariah once more exhibits an impressive boldness in his use of imagery. In reflection on the theological significance of this imagery, it is important to bear in mind the difference between a literary image and an icon, not to mention the equally important difference between an icon and an idol. Zechariah does not suggest that some material representation should count as an image of God or be understood as embodying the physical presence of God. But neither does he limit his vision of God by restricting his imagination to conventional images and language about God. What Zechariah here envisions exceeds every expectation. The vitality of his imagery throughout the visions provides the reader with a glimpse of the vitality of his understanding of God and God's relationship to the created order. Zechariah treads boldly and imagines even what could otherwise be forbidden.

Zechariah is a provocative model for the preacher. He put all of his imaginative and imagistic gifts and resources into the service of his prophetic announcement of God's word for his day. The almost complete absence of didactic address and explicit exhortation in these visions stands in marked contrast to the rationalist, empiricist, and frequently coercive proclamation often heard in the contemporary church. Zechariah did not talk and teach about God; rather, in his often fantastical images, Zechariah painted a picture of a world thoroughly shaped by the sovereignty of God. Zechariah trusted in the power of the vivid and imaginative language of his visions to evoke the presence of God for his listeners and, indeed, to bring them into God's presence.

2. What Zechariah imagines is a created world—cosmos—ordered to God's rule and purpose. This order extends even and especially to the north country, the seat and font of disorder. Is such a vision at all realistic? Did the sociopolitical relations of the late sixth-century BCE world correspond in any discernible respect to the order of God's creation as perceived by Zechariah? There is no contesting that Zechariah was a visionary, but did his visions—did this last one—bear any relation to the "real" world? Are these texts only a vision?

We can only suppose how Zechariah might have responded to such a question. We may gain a fresh vantage point on this question if we address it to visionary language with which, at least nominally, the contemporary Christian is more familiar and comfortable— e.g., Paul's language of cross and resurrection. While on the surface this language may seem light-years removed from Zechariah's visions, a closer examination of how Paul envisions the world through the use of this language suggests some crucial overlaps. Paul declares that God was in Christ reconciling the world to himself (2 Cor 5:19). Does this vision of God's reconciling action in the world bear any closer correspondence to the "real" events of the first century CE than does Zechariah's vision of God's sovereign, reconciling acts? Would an objective reading of the first-century CE world produce the same conclusions as those envisioned by Paul in 2 Corinthians? In Paul's view, the cross, in combination with the resurrection, provides the governing image of a created world ordered to God's rule and purposes. Anyone at home with the interpretive logic of cross and resurrection can be patient with Zechariah's imagination.

3. Now the world, the cosmos is ordered. What then? What follows from this? Now God's Spirit is at rest. What do *we* do in consequence? If, as has been suggested, there were originally seven visions, with the last completing the world's recreation, then what should follow is rest. If God's Spirit rested, then so should God's people. What follows from restored creation, then, not simply temporally but as a consequence, is sabbath. Sacred rest. Nothing is quite so hard to believe as this: Everything that truly matters, and on which the world and its future utterly depends, is accomplished without our effort. Indeed, it is even accomplished in spite of us. We, therefore, can only rest and bear witness to what is nowhere and in no respect obvious, yet is in every respect true.

Zechariah 6:9-15, The Priest and the Branch

NIV

9The word of the LORD came to me: 10"Take ⌊silver and gold⌋ from the exiles Heldai, Tobijah and Jedaiah, who have arrived from Babylon. Go the same day to the house of Josiah son of Zephaniah. 11Take the silver and gold and make a crown, and set it on the head of the high priest, Joshua son of Jehozadak. 12Tell him this is what the LORD Almighty says: 'Here is the man whose

NRSV

9The word of the LORD came to me: 10Collect silver and gold[a] from the exiles—from Heldai, Tobijah, and Jedaiah—who have arrived from Babylon; and go the same day to the house of Josiah son of Zephaniah. 11Take the silver and gold and make a crown,[b] and set it on the head of the high priest Joshua son of Jehozadak; 12say to him: Thus says

[a] Cn Compare verse 11: Heb lacks *silver and gold*   [b] Gk Mss Syr Tg: Heb *crowns*

NIV

name is the Branch, and he will branch out from his place and build the temple of the LORD. [13]It is he who will build the temple of the LORD, and he will be clothed with majesty and will sit and rule on his throne. And he will be a priest on his throne. And there will be harmony between the two.' [14]The crown will be given to Heldai,[a] Tobijah, Jedaiah and Hen[b] son of Zephaniah as a memorial in the temple of the LORD. [15]Those who are far away will come and help to build the temple of the LORD, and you will know that the LORD Almighty has sent me to you. This will happen if you diligently obey the LORD your God."

[a]14 Syriac; Hebrew *Helem*   [b]14 Or *and the gracious one, the*

NRSV

the LORD of hosts: Here is a man whose name is Branch: for he shall branch out in his place, and he shall build the temple of the LORD. [13]It is he that shall build the temple of the LORD; he shall bear royal honor, and shall sit upon his throne and rule. There shall be a priest by his throne, with peaceful understanding between the two of them. [14]And the crown[a] shall be in the care of Heldai,[b] Tobijah, Jedaiah, and Josiah[c] son of Zephaniah, as a memorial in the temple of the LORD.

15Those who are far off shall come and help to build the temple of the LORD; and you shall know that the LORD of hosts has sent me to you. This will happen if you diligently obey the voice of the LORD your God.

[a] Gk Syr: Heb *crowns*   [b] Syr Compare verse 10: Heb *Helem*
[c] Syr Compare verse 10: Heb *Hen*

COMMENTARY

With this section, one leaves the world of the visions and returns to one that Zechariah inhabits with everyone else, including Joshua the high priest. Here Zechariah receives, not a vision, but an oracle with instructions. These instructions concern matters already addressed in chaps. 3–4: temple construction and the community's dual leadership.

The structure of the oracle proper (vv. 10-15) consists of two units. The first and much larger unit gives instruction regarding a crown or crowns (vv. 10-14). This unit itself divides into instruction to make crowns and to crown Joshua (vv. 10-11); an oracle to Joshua regarding the "Branch" (vv. 12-13); and instruction regarding the other crown (v. 14). The second unit consists of only v. 15, which promises help from "far off" in building the Temple. It also contains Zechariah's signature "self-vindication" formula (see Commentary on chap. 2).

In formal terms, vv. 9-15 are an oracle, but unlike the oracles in chaps. 1–3, this one does not interpret or extend the imagery in the vision preceding it. Indeed, this oracle has only an artificial literary connection with the last vision. The introductory revelation formula ("the word of Yahweh came to . . . ") occurs within the visions only

at 4:8, within an oracular interruption of the fifth vision. However, this formula occurs in each of First Zechariah's superscriptions (1:1, 7; 7:1) and in the fasting and celebration sermon that concludes First Zechariah (e.g., 7:4, 8). This suggests that the placement of vv. 9-15 after the last of Zechariah's visions is editorial. However, it is not accidental. The oracle depends on the whole visionary sequence. Its content depends on what has been accomplished in the visions, particularly in the concluding eighth vision. With its references to the four winds of heaven and the north country, the last vision echoes Zech 2:6[10], which urges flight from the land of the north. On one reading of 2:7[11], that flight is to Zion. It is significant, therefore, that Zechariah is instructed to go to the גולה (*gôlâ*), exiles who have come from Babylon (v. 10).

6:10-11. "The exiles" here designate a distinct group, just having arrived from Babylon. The term occurs only here in First Zechariah, which elsewhere makes no explicit distinctions among groups in the population. By the time of Nehemiah and Ezra, some seventy years later, the *gôlâ* referred to a genealogically defined group who (or whose families) had come from Babylon. This group controlled Judah's internal affairs, including land tenure and administration of the Temple (see Ezra 10:8). It also guarded its membership by excluding, in principle, families who had not been in Babylon—in other words, all Judeans whose families had remained in the land—and those without the proper genealogy (Ezra 2:61-63). Exactly when this social structure began to take the shape it assumed under Nehemiah and Ezra remains unclear. However, it is nonetheless striking that Zechariah here refers to a group as the *gôlâ*. In its general meaning, "the exile(s)," it applies to Zechariah himself and to both Joshua and Zerubbabel among those Zechariah has been addressing in his visions and oracles. According to the dates in Ezra 3:8 and Zech 1:7, Joshua and Zerubbabel would have come to Judah two years earlier.

Zechariah is instructed to "take [לקח *lāqaḥ*; NRSV, "collect"] silver and gold from the *gôlâ* (v. 10). Contrary to the translations, v. 10 does not specify what he is to take from them. In priestly legislation the term *lāqaḥ* refers to taking an offering; in Exod 25:23-28 Moses is to collect commodities, including precious metals, from the people to build the sanctuary. The term has a similar sense here. The offering is to be received from three people, Heldai, Tobijah, and Jedaiah, who are not further identified. Zechariah is then told to go alone to the house of Josiah son of Zephaniah. It is at Josiah's house that Zechariah is to make crowns of silver and gold, placing one of them on the head of Joshua (v. 11). This coronation seems to replicate the scene in 3:4-5, where Joshua receives the insignia of high priestly office; but there he receives a turban. In chap. 3 he is merely Joshua, here he is identified as the son of Jehozadak.

It is significant that Josiah is associated with Zephaniah, the name of the deputy priest to Seraiah (2 Kgs 25:18), and that Joshua is associated with Jehozadak, who was Seraiah's son (1 Chr 5:39-40[6:13-14]). Both Zephaniah and Seraiah were executed by Nebuchadnezzar (2 Kgs 25:18-21). Here their descendants collaborate with Zechariah in Joshua's coronation. Following it, Zechariah delivers an oracle to Joshua (v. 12).

6:12-14. This oracle seems also to replicate chap. 3. Both 3:8 and 6:12 address Joshua about the "Branch." In 3:8 the Branch's coming is promised, and Joshua and his priestly colleagues are signs of that promise. The grammar of v. 12 implies that the Branch is present: "Here is a man, 'Branch' is his name." While 3:8-10 mentions nothing about the Temple, 6:13-14 stresses that it is precisely the branch, and no one else, who will build the Temple. This focus recalls 4:6b-10a, which stresses that Zerubbabel, who had begun the reconstruction of God's house, will complete it; but in neither 3:8-10 nor 6:12-14 is Zerubbabel mentioned. If the temple builder is the branch, and if Zerubbabel will complete construction of God's house, then surely Zerubbabel would be the branch. His omission here is striking. It has led to suggestions that his name has been eliminated from vv. 12-14, which originally included him, and even that the branch is actually Joshua himself—improbably, since the oracle is addressed to Joshua. Zerubbabel's disappearance remains a mystery. It leaves the branch unidentified, while promising that he will "branch out from his place" (cf. Jer 33:15). And it promises that, as the branch grows, so will the Temple: He will build the "Temple" (היכל *hêykāl*), but more precisely the central and largest room in the house of Yahweh, located between the vestibule and the most holy place.

Consistent with both 3:6-10 and 4:1-6a, 10b-14, the oracle in chap. 6 leaves the two-person leadership model intact. But, as in chap. 3, the priest is given administrative authority in anticipation of a royal branch who is not yet—or is no longer—on the scene. Still, this arrangement is to be temporary. In the future, the branch—the royal figure—will rule with royal authority (cf. Num 27:20), and both he and the priest will have thrones, to which crowns seem appropriate. Moreover, there will be an accord—a "counsel of peace"—between them (v. 13). The term occurs nowhere else in the OT, but it recalls another term, "covenant of peace" (Isa 54:10; Ezek 34:25; 37:26), which signifies the cessation of hostility, threat, or danger.[80]

On my reading, v. 14 has one crown, which is not on Joshua's head.[81] It is to be placed in the Temple, the very thing the Branch will build, as a reminder. The translations indicate that the

---

80. Bernard F. Batto, *Slaying the Dragon: Mythmaking in the Biblical Tradition* (Louisville: Westminster/John Knox, 1992) 157-59.

81. Meyers and Meyers, *Haggai and Zechariah 1–8*, 362-63; cf. Petersen, *Haggai and Zechariah 1–8*, 273.

crown(s) will be given (to the care of) the same people named in v. 10, as a memorial to them (although two of their names are mysteriously changed in 6:14 MT). The syntax, however, suggests that this is not a memorial, but a reminder to Heldai, Tobijah, and Jedaiah (Exod 13:9; 17:4; Num 10:10; Josh 4:7).[82] And this reminder will be in the Temple. Only priests could enter the "temple," as Uzziah learned painfully (2 Chr 26:16-21). If Heldai, Tobijah, and Jedaiah can be reminded by something in the Temple, then they are priests. From them—from these members of the *gôlâ*—were taken offerings that included silver and gold for the making of crowns, one of which went to Joshua; the other would remain in the Temple.

According to 3:1-5, Joshua's status as high priest was contested. It was reaffirmed there and is again in 6:10-14. Perhaps the *gôlâ* priests had their own views about who was qualified to be high priest. Perhaps they viewed dual leadership as inimical to Persian interests, especially if one partner bore such royal, messianic expectations as Haggai attached to Zerubbabel (Hag 2:21-23). These *gôlâ* priests would have returned to Judah after Darius had secured his throne and with his sponsorship. Zechariah addresses them with pro-

phetic authority: Joshua is the crowned and authorized priest. The priest will share a throne with the promised branch—if not Zerubbabel, then someone else—whose crown will remain in the Temple as a reminder.

Zechariah's hopes seem not to have materialized as he expected. In Ezra's report of the Temple's completion (Ezra dates it in March 515 BCE), neither Joshua nor Zerubbabel is mentioned, but only the "elders of the Jews" (Ezra 6:14-15). Both Joshua and Zerubbabel have vanished, but still Haggai and Zechariah are credited with inspiring the entire effort, from beginning to end (Ezra 5:1; 6:14).

6:15. The concluding verse of the oracle promises that many "far off" will come to assist in the Temple's construction. Zechariah does not identify these who are far off, but the term seldom refers to Jews (Isa 46:12; cf. Isa 33:13; 66:19). The promise in this concluding verse of the vision sequence anticipates the conclusion of Zechariah's sermon in 8:20-23. It also echoes Zechariah's oracle in 2:11[15]. As in the latter case, the promise is joined with the self-vindication formula: "then you [plural] will know." Here Zechariah departs from the form of the oracle and addresses a broader audience, even as he includes those far off.

82. Rodney R. Hutton, "Jedaiah," *ABD* 3 (1992) 654.

REFLECTIONS

In this passage, the reader again is brought into the sphere of Jewish messianic hopes and expectations (see Reflections on 3:1-10). As noted in the commentary above, these messianic hopes are expressed in complex ways within the oracle of Zech 6:9-15—in particular, the coronation of the Branch-messiah and the construction of the Temple. For the Christian reader, who identifies messianic hopes solely with the person of Jesus, the richness and complexity of the messianic expectations expressed in this oracle may seem at best baffling, at worst obsolete and irrelevant. Yet these messianic expectations were part of a vital conversation within Second Temple Judaism that shaped the theological perspectives of those first-century CE Jewish Christians who understood Jesus as the fulfillment of their messianic hopes. This Zechariah oracle, then, affords contemporary Christians the opportunity to experience the intensity, desire, and yearning of Jewish messianic theologies despite the difference in perspective concerning the fulfillment of those expectations. Zechariah's sure hope in the accomplishment of God's messianic age testifies powerfully to his faith in God.

ZECHARIAH 7:1–8:23, A LONG SERMON ON FASTING AND CELEBRATION

OVERVIEW

Nearly two years after the word of Yahweh had come to Zechariah and inspired visions, it came again, to inspire a sermon—this according to the superscriptions in Zech 1:7 and 7:1. The sermon, comprising all of chaps. 7–8, forms the third and final section of First Zechariah. The first section comprised a brief sermon based on this longer one. The date assigned to it, the fourth day of the ninth month in Darius's fourth year (7:1), corresponds to December 7, 518 BCE. This is the latest of the dates given in Haggai and Zechariah. Recent commentaries tend to interpret Hag 2:10, 18 as pointing to a temple dedication or refoundation ceremony on December 18, 520 BCE.[83] Ezra 6:15 says that the Temple was completed in March of 515 BCE. If these dates are correct, Zechariah's sermon comes midway between the beginning and the completion of work on the Temple.

Zechariah, in his sermon, refers to the day when the Temple's foundation was laid; moreover, he attaches signal importance to it (8:9; cf. Hag 2:18). It seems natural that, at this midway point, the people of Judah would need encouragement to complete what must have seemed an onerous and ill-timed project (Hag 1:2-6). Zechariah does offer encouragement, associated with the laying of the Temple's foundations (8:9-13). He nowhere expressly encourages the people to work on the Temple, however, or mentions the Temple-construction project apart from the retrospective reference in 8:9. The Temple was clearly important to Zechariah; the visions and their oracles indicate so. But it is not the point of his sermon to urge the community to persevere in its construction. The rhetorical goal of Zechariah's sermon is not to urge the Judeans to do something extraordinary, but to convince them of what Yahweh has done, is doing, and will do.

In achieving this rhetorical goal, Zechariah adverts to none of the preceding visions, but the language of the sermon reflects, at key points, the oracular material in chaps. 1–2. The announcement of Yahweh's return to Jerusalem (1:16) is echoed in 8:3, 15. The promise that Yahweh will dwell in Jerusalem (2:10, 11[14-15]), is echoed in 8:3, 8. The inclusion of "many nations," promised in 2:11[15] (cf. 6:15) resonates with and is dramatically expanded in 8:20-23. Thus the sermon incorporates and reiterates the promises associated with the first cycle of visions. Earlier, the promises are part of the theme of reversal, first introduced in 1:14-15, where Yahweh's anger turns to zeal for Jerusalem/Zion. Precisely that reversal is the sermon's point and provides its structure: a reversal from past to future, from God's great anger at the ancestors (7:12) to Yahweh's great zeal for Zion and return to Jerusalem (8:2-3, 14-15).

Like the visions, the sermon moves in chiastic fashion from the periphery (A), to the center, and back to the periphery (A'). At its inception in 7:4-6, the sermon (B) addresses the matter of fasting, to which it finally returns (B') in 8:18-19. From fasting, the sermon turns (C) to the ancestors' *mis*conduct in 7:7-12*a,* and then returns (C') to the community's conduct in 8:16-17. From the issue of misconduct—of the ancestors' disobedience—the sermon turns (D) to judgment against the ancestors, in 7:12*b*-14, with which it contrasts (D') salvation in the present and future in 8:1-8, 14-15. These latter verses enclose the sermon's hortatory center (E) in 8:9-13. The exhortation itself refers both to the past (8:10//7:12*b*-14) and to the future (8:11-13*a*), with the present being pivotal (8:9). With its framework in 8:1-8, 14-15, this hortatory section (8:9-13) emphasizes the reversal to which the larger sermon points. Finally, at the extreme periphery, in 7:2-3 (A) and 8:20-23 (A'), people come *from* the periphery—as an embassy—to "entreat Yahweh's favor." The first embassy (A) raises the question of fasting, which occasions the sermon, while the latter

83. E.g., Petersen, *Haggai and Zechariah 1–8,* 88-90.

embassy (A′) follows the answer to that question. In between, everything has changed.

A Embassy with question about fasting (7:1-3)
  B God's answer concerning fasting (7:4-6)
    C Ancestors' misconduct (7:7-12*a*)
      D Judgment against the ancestors (7:12*b*-14)
        E Exhortation (8:9-13)
      D′ Salvation in the present and future (8:1-8, 14-15)
    C′ The community's conduct (8:16-17)
  B′ God's edict concerning fasting (8:18-19)
A′ Embassy to seek the Lord (8:20-23)

The sermon's structure reflects its theme of reversal: the qualitative difference between past and future. Both structure and theme disclose an important part of the sermon's logic. Fasts may remain (one in 7:3, two in 7:5, and four in 8:19), but their character will be wholly different: no longer fasts of mourning, but fasts of celebration. Social-moral norms that summarize prophetic preaching were important in the past, and they will continue to be so in the future; but whereas ignoring them in the past produced judgment (7:9-10), salvation inaugurated in the present will enable adherence to them (8:16-17). The moral integrity of the community is not a condition of Yahweh's beneficent action on its behalf, but one of its fruits. Between the miserable conditions described in 7:14; 8:10 and their reversal in 8:4-5, 12-13 comes Yahweh's promise (8:2-3) and decision to initiate a reversal (8:14-15). The sermon lacks the brilliant imagination of the visions, but its conjunction of theology and rhetoric is profound.

At the same time, its style is forbidding. The formulae that signal oracular speech ("thus says Yahweh of hosts" [messenger formula]; "the word of Yahweh came to . . . " [revelation formula]; "says Yahweh" [oracle formula]) occur with unprecedented frequency in the sermon, nineteen times all together, and sometimes in rapid succession (8:2, 3, 4, 6, 7, 9).[84] This is stylistically heavy handed, but it serves a rhetorical purpose. The *revelation formula* is a structuring device; it occurs at major stages in the sermon. First, it intro-

duces the sermon, locating it (at least) two years after the visions (7:1). The details that follow in 7:2-3 report questions that help to define the basic issue. Second, it introduces Zechariah's own address to the community (7:4), in which he persuasively redefines the issue through rhetorical questions that expose the questions of 7:2-3 as concealing a misunderstanding of the past, present, and future. Third, it introduces a recapitulation of prophetic preaching, the negative response to it, and the consequences of that response (7:8). Fourth, it introduces Zechariah's own proclamation (8:1), which reverses the consequences of the preceding unit. Fifth, it introduces Zechariah's definitive answer to (or redefinition of) the questions reported in 7:2-3 (8:18).

The revelation formula not only authorizes directly Zechariah's responses to a question about ritual (7:4; 8:18), but also (and at the same time) authorizes his interpretation and continuation of the prophetic tradition (7:8; 8:1)—to interpret the past, but also to interpret the present and the future. Zechariah's rhetoric thus makes explicit and implicit claims about his prophetic authority: He is authorized by receiving Yahweh's word, and his own words are those of the prophets before him.

The *messenger formula* is also a significant feature in the structure of the two chapters, frequently (in chap. 8) distinguishing smaller units. It also serves the rhetorical function of claiming divine authority for extraordinary claims. The messenger formula occurs but once in chap. 7 (7:9) in conjunction with the revelation formula. This is the case also at 8:1, 18. These are the decisive stages within the sermon: Zechariah's recapitulation of the former prophets (7:9); his claims about what Yahweh is now doing, the results of Yahweh's action (8:1); and his definitive response to the questions that are the occasion of, and are included within, the sermon (8:18).

In Zech 8:2-8, the messenger formula sets apart each of a series of claims. This series includes another rhetorical question (v. 6) that acknowledges the extraordinary nature of the surrounding claims and, at the same time, elicits the community's acknowledgment that this is no reason to disbelieve them. This implied acknowledgment involves one further claim, introduced by the messenger formula in 8:7, which summarizes

---

84. David J. Clark, "Discourse Structure in Zechariah 7:1–8:23," *BT* 36 (1985) 328-35.

Zechariah's proclamation to this point. Then in 8:9, the messenger formula authorizes Zechariah's exhortation, which includes both instruction and further claims about the future. In 8:14, the messenger formula authorizes Zechariah's proclamation, recapitulating the past, announcing the future, and making his own a summary of prophetic preaching that corresponds to one he quoted in 7:9-10. Finally, in 8:20, the messenger formula authorizes extraordinary claims about the international response to what Zechariah has claimed, on divine authority, about Yahweh's impending actions regarding Jerusalem.

The use of quotative, oracular formulae, then, secures the point that his extraordinary claims are not Zechariah's own. Each of them, and especially every individual claim about Jerusalem's future (in chap. 8), is divinely authorized. By means of the repeated messenger formula, the claims in 8:2-8 are set apart from each other, each duly authorized in an ascending order that reaches its crescendo in 8:8*b*: "They shall be my people and I will be their God, in faithfulness and in righteousness." This remarkable use of the formula "thus says . . . " is characteristic of Persian royal procla-

mations beginning with Darius, in which it has a similar function.[85] Instead of "thus says Darius," however, Zechariah says, "Thus says the LORD."

There is no genre in OT literature that can be clearly defined as "sermon."[86] Nevertheless, First Zechariah presents this section as an extended public oral performance aimed at persuading a particular audience to adopt a new understanding of itself concerning the actions and intentions of God, which it announces, and to believe and act accordingly. Moreover, this announcement, and the suasive rhetoric accompanying it, includes and depends on exposition of and continuity with an authoritative tradition: the prophets. Such a speech can be viewed as a sermon, even if it lacks an explicitly liturgical context. This sermon is, at least in part, a literary creation. Some of its components (esp. 8:9-13) may be of independent origin. Still, the whole of 7:1–8:23 works as a sermon.

85. Samuel A. Meier, *Speaking of Speaking: Marking Direct Discourse in the Hebrew Bible*, VTSup 46 (Leiden: Brill, 1992) 291-93.
86. Rex Mason, *Preaching the Tradition: Homily and Hermeneutics After the Exile* (Cambridge: Cambridge University Press, 1991) 141-43.

Zechariah 7:1-6, Shall I Go On Mourning?

NIV

7 In the fourth year of King Darius, the word of the LORD came to Zechariah on the fourth day of the ninth month, the month of Kislev. ²The people of Bethel had sent Sharezer and Regem-Melech, together with their men, to entreat the LORD ³by asking the priests of the house of the LORD Almighty and the prophets, "Should I mourn and fast in the fifth month, as I have done for so many years?"

⁴Then the word of the LORD Almighty came to me: ⁵"Ask all the people of the land and the priests, 'When you fasted and mourned in the fifth and seventh months for the past seventy years, was it really for me that you fasted? ⁶And when you were eating and drinking, were you not just feasting for yourselves?' "

NRSV

7 In the fourth year of King Darius, the word of the LORD came to Zechariah on the fourth day of the ninth month, which is Chislev. ²Now the people of Bethel had sent Sharezer and Regem-melech and their men, to entreat the favor of the LORD, ³and to ask the priests of the house of the LORD of hosts and the prophets, "Should I mourn and practice abstinence in the fifth month, as I have done for so many years?" ⁴Then the word of the LORD of hosts came to me: ⁵Say to all the people of the land and the priests: When you fasted and lamented in the fifth month and in the seventh, for these seventy years, was it for me that you fasted? ⁶And when you eat and when you drink, do you not eat and drink only for yourselves?

COMMENTARY

An embassy comes to "entreat Yahweh's favor"—typically, to plea for mercy (2 Chr 33:12; Jer 26:19). It is not clear who commissioned this embassy or exactly whom it included, however; the MT has only "Bethel," which the English translations interpret as "the people of Bethel." On the other hand, "Bethel" may be part of a larger name: "Bethel-sharezer." "Bethel" is the name of a deity in Jer 48:13, as in Phoenician texts. It also occurs in the names of Jews at Elephantine in Egypt, and in Babylonian inscriptions. Jeremiah attests a Nergal-sharezer, whose name includes the name of the god Nergal (Jer 39:3, 13). This Nergal-sharezer is called "Rab-mag," a title denoting a royal official, and some scholars have suggested that Zechariah's "Regem-melech" is a corruption of "Rab-mag."[87] In that case, Bethel-sharezer the Rab-mag would have sent emissaries to Jerusalem.[88] Bethel was remembered as a place of mixed worship. The Assyrians repatriated an Israelite priest to Bethel, where he taught exiles from various countries to worship Yahweh—which they did, still venerating their native deities (2 Kgs 17:26-34). It may be that Bethel, in v. 2, has this significance and that Sharezer and Regem-melech are significant because their names are not Jewish. In the structure of the sermon, this embassy from Bethel foreshadows a more global one from the multitude of nations (8:20-23); both embassies come "to entreat Yahweh's favor." This one from Bethel, where Yahweh is known, asks about ritual practice.

The practice in question is "mourning" and "devotion" (not "abstinence," NRSV or "fasting," NIV) in the fifth month. The term used by the embassy from Bethel, הנזר (*hinnāzēr*), nowhere in the OT designates a public or private rite and nowhere else means "fasting" (Lev 22:2; Ezek 14:7; Hos 9:10). The rites occurred in the fifth month, most likely commemorating the Temple's destruction (2 Kgs 25:8)—an event they had mourned for "all these years." They ask, "Shall we continue?" To this question, and to the Bethel embassy, Zechariah offers no answer. Their inquiry provides Zechariah the occasion for a public sermon, which he addresses to the entire population, including the priests. He takes up the issue of fasting (v. 5)—not only such rites as the Bethel embassy may have practiced, but fasting and lamentation in both the fifth and the seventh months. The latter fast evidently commemorated the murder of Gedaliah (2 Kgs 25:25; Jer 41:1-3). Pointedly, Zechariah notes that both fasts have been going on, not just for many years, but "for these *seventy* years" (v. 5, italics added).

The reference to seventy years (v. 5) occurs earlier (1:12). There the angel reminded God that Jerusalem and Judah's cities have suffered under Yahweh's anger or curse without mercy "for seventy years now." As an interpretation of Jer 25:11-12; 29:10, the completion of seventy years augurs a reversal, which Zechariah announces in 1:14-17. His comments on fasting (vv. 5-6) are governed by this reversal, which will redefine the character of fasting. At the sermon's beginning, his remarks on fasting are enigmatic. They consist of two rhetorical questions. The first elicits acknowledgment that "No, it was not for Yahweh that we fasted," and the second that "Yes, it is we who eat and who drink." Despite Isa 58:3-6 and its criticism of fasts, Zechariah criticizes neither the fasts nor the people.[89] As Isaiah 58 illustrates, fasting was a response to adversity and constitutes a plea for God's intervention (Isa 58:3, 9; Joel 2:12-15). Zechariah alludes to such adversity in 7:8, 14; 8:4-5. In this light, fasting seems appropriate. Since the seventy years are over, Yahweh is announcing a reversal (8:1-8). Now celebratory eating and drinking seem appropriate. (See Reflections at 8:20-23.)

---

87. Peter R. Ackroyd, *Exile and Restoration,* OTL (Westminster: John Knox, 1968) 206-7.

88. 2 Kgs 19:37 (= Isa 37:38) claims that Sennacherib had two sons, Adram-melech and Shenazar, whose names are similar to those in Zech 7:2.

89. Richard Elliott Friedman, "The Prophet and the Historian: The Acquisition of Historical Information from Literary Sources," in *The Poet and the Historian,* ed. R. E. Friedman, HSS 26 (Chico, Calif.: Scholars Press, 1983) 1-12.

Zechariah 7:7-14, This Is the Message of the Prophets

NIV

7" 'Are these not the words the LORD proclaimed through the earlier prophets when Jerusalem and its surrounding towns were at rest and prosperous, and the Negev and the western foothills were settled?' "

8And the word of the LORD came again to Zechariah: 9"This is what the LORD Almighty says: 'Administer true justice; show mercy and compassion to one another. 10Do not oppress the widow or the fatherless, the alien or the poor. In your hearts do not think evil of each other.'

11"But they refused to pay attention; stubbornly they turned their backs and stopped up their ears. 12They made their hearts as hard as flint and would not listen to the law or to the words that the LORD Almighty had sent by his Spirit through the earlier prophets. So the LORD Almighty was very angry.

13" 'When I called, they did not listen; so when they called, I would not listen,' says the LORD Almighty. 14'I scattered them with a whirlwind among all the nations, where they were strangers. The land was left so desolate behind them that no one could come or go. This is how they made the pleasant land desolate.' "

NRSV

7Were not these the words that the LORD proclaimed by the former prophets, when Jerusalem was inhabited and in prosperity, along with the towns around it, and when the Negeb and the Shephelah were inhabited?

8The word of the LORD came to Zechariah, saying: 9Thus says the LORD of hosts: Render true judgments, show kindness and mercy to one another; 10do not oppress the widow, the orphan, the alien, or the poor; and do not devise evil in your hearts against one another. 11But they refused to listen, and turned a stubborn shoulder, and stopped their ears in order not to hear. 12They made their hearts adamant in order not to hear the law and the words that the LORD of hosts had sent by his spirit through the former prophets. Therefore great wrath came from the LORD of hosts. 13Just as, when I[a] called, they would not hear, so, when they called, I would not hear, says the LORD of hosts, 14and I scattered them with a whirlwind among all the nations that they had not known. Thus the land they left was desolate, so that no one went to and fro, and a pleasant land was made desolate.

a Heb *he*

COMMENTARY

The structure of this unit comprises an introduction (v. 7), in which Zechariah adverts to the "words of the former prophets" (cf. 1:4); a summary of those words (vv. 9-10); a report of the people's response to the prophets (vv. 11-12a); and the consequences of that response (vv. 12b-14). All of this unit refers to the past, and it describes adversity (v. 14) as the reversal of an earlier prosperity (v. 7). Behind this reversal is the people's rejection of the former prophets' words. In his recital of the past, Zechariah speaks prophetically; he speaks *as* a prophet by quoting the prophets.[90] His quotation of the former prophets

90. Carol Meyers and Eric Meyers, *Haggai and Zechariah 1–8,* AB 25B (New York: Doubleday, 1987) 396.

is preceded by the *revelation formula* (v. 8), and it includes the *messenger formula* (v. 9a). This combination does not occur again until 8:18-19, when Zechariah returns to the matter of fasting.

The words of the prophets (vv. 9-10) are an epitome of standard, even commonsense, social norms drawn from a variety of OT texts. They move from obligations (v. 9) to prohibitions (v. 10), in each case stressing mutuality. One finds primary concern for the socially marginalized, the widow, the orphan, the alien, and the poor, who are to be included in the definition of mutuality ("each other"), and hence of the community. These norms were known everywhere—outside Israel as well as within—which makes it all the more reprehensible that the ancestors rejected them. Only extraordinary stubbornness could account for this, as Zechariah points out (vv. 11-12*a*) in language found frequently in Chronicles (2 Chr 15:1-7; 20:15; 33:10).[91]

The consequences of this rejection—i.e., the routine practice of injustice, oppression, and evil—seem so natural as to be inevitable: desolation, with everyday traffic, people going "to and fro" (v. 14; cf. 2 Chr 15:5), rendered impossible. This Zechariah understands, not as divine ratification of natural consequences, but as God's action. The streets of the city are abandoned, not just

91. See Rex Mason, *The Books of Haggai, Zechariah, and Malachi,* CBC (Cambridge: Cambridge University Press, 1977) 49-51.

because they are dangerous, but because there are so few people to walk them. God's judgment has included dispersion, precisely the reversal of earlier conditions, when Jerusalem and Judah were full of people (v. 7). This dispersion and all these judgments are the consequence of rejecting the former prophets' words (v. 13). Those words Zechariah is divinely authorized to appropriate as his own (v. 8). If he can authoritatively recite the past as the cause of present adversity, then he can authoritatively announce the future. If the past involved a reversal from prosperity to adversity, then the future involves a reversal of the opposite kind. (See Reflections at 8:20-23.)

Zechariah 8:1-8, It May Well Seem Impossible

NIV

8 Again the word of the LORD Almighty came to me. [2]This is what the LORD Almighty says: "I am very jealous for Zion; I am burning with jealousy for her."

[3]This is what the LORD says: "I will return to Zion and dwell in Jerusalem. Then Jerusalem will be called the City of Truth, and the mountain of the LORD Almighty will be called the Holy Mountain."

[4]This is what the LORD Almighty says: "Once again men and women of ripe old age will sit in the streets of Jerusalem, each with cane in hand because of his age. [5]The city streets will be filled with boys and girls playing there."

[6]This is what the LORD Almighty says: "It may seem marvelous to the remnant of this people at that time, but will it seem marvelous to me?" declares the LORD Almighty.

[7]This is what the LORD Almighty says: "I will save my people from the countries of the east and the west. [8]I will bring them back to live in Jerusalem; they will be my people, and I will be faithful and righteous to them as their God."

NRSV

8 The word of the LORD of hosts came to me, saying: [2]Thus says the LORD of hosts: I am jealous for Zion with great jealousy, and I am jealous for her with great wrath. [3]Thus says the LORD: I will return to Zion, and will dwell in the midst of Jerusalem; Jerusalem shall be called the faithful city, and the mountain of the LORD of hosts shall be called the holy mountain. [4]Thus says the LORD of hosts: Old men and old women shall again sit in the streets of Jerusalem, each with staff in hand because of their great age. [5]And the streets of the city shall be full of boys and girls playing in its streets. [6]Thus says the LORD of hosts: Even though it seems impossible to the remnant of this people in these days, should it also seem impossible to me, says the LORD of hosts? [7]Thus says the LORD of hosts: I will save my people from the east country and from the west country; [8]and I will bring them to live in Jerusalem. They shall be my people and I will be their God, in faithfulness and in righteousness.

COMMENTARY

Consequently, following Zechariah's recital of the past in 7:7-14, the future will bring Jerusalem's repopulation. Not only will Jerusalem again

be full of people, but conditions will be peaceful as well. People will grow old there, and children will play in the squares (vv. 4-5). These conditions will follow from Yahweh's return to Zion to dwell in Jerusalem (vv. 2-3). What Zechariah here announces echoes the oracles in 1:14-17; 2:10-12[14-16] and expands on them. Jerusalem will be called "faithful city" (עיר־האמת '*ir-hā'ĕmet*), and Yahweh's mountain, Zion, will be called "holy mountain" (הר־הקדש *har haqqodeš*). The first designation is unique, though it resembles Isa 1:21: "faithful city" (קריה נאמנה *qiryâ ne'ĕmānâ*). Zion is often called the Lord's holy mountain, where Yahweh dwells (e.g., Joel 4:17). Some late prophetic texts expect Zion/Jerusalem to be given a new name. In each case, the new name expresses the restoration of God's relationship to the city and, consequently, of the city's restoration as well: "I delight in her" (Isa 62:2, 4); "Yahweh is our righteousness" (Jer 33:16); "Yahweh is there" (Ezek 48:35). Zechariah does not give Zion/Jerusalem a new name, but his designations signal the same kinds of restoration. Just as the Lord is returning to dwell in Jerusalem, so also Yahweh will bring "my people" back to dwell there (vv. 3, 8). Just as the restored city will be "faithful" and the mountain "holy," so also God's relationship with them will be restored, in faithfulness and righteousness (vv. 3, 8; cf. Isa 48:1). The full covenant formula appears here (see Commentary on 2:11[15]): "they will be my people, and I will be their God." This pronouncement, too, is a reversal, from the mutually severed relationship (7:13) to its restoration in mutuality and integrity (8:8).

In the course of describing this very different future, Zechariah counters a possible reservation: What Yahweh announces through Zechariah will seem too hard—so hard as to be impossible (v. 6). This reservation is attributed to "the remnant of this people," a term that appears again in vv. 11-12, but nowhere else in Zechariah (cf. Hag 1:12, 14; 2:2). In each case it appears in a reference to the future, contrasted with the past. Zechariah makes clear his reference to the future by adding "in those days" (cf. NRSV), as in v. 23. According to v. 11, the future is beginning "now." By referring to the people as a remnant, Zechariah again signals a change from the adversity produced by the past and still affecting the present. That change will include God's saving "my people" from countries east and west (v. 7). Those who witness this and see Jerusalem restored (vv. 4-5) may consider it too hard—impossible. How much more impossible would it seem in prospect? Zechariah counters the reservation theologsically, or God does, by posing a rhetorical question: "Shall it also seem impossible to me?" A similar question occurs twice in the OT. In Gen 18:14, announcing that Sarah will bear a son, Yahweh asks, "Is anything impossible for God?" In Jer 32:27, after promising that the land will again flourish (Jer 32:15), Yahweh asks, "Is anything impossible for me?" In that same chapter, Jeremiah confesses that the Lord "made the heavens and the earth"; clearly, "Nothing is impossible for you" (Jer 32:17). (See Reflections at 8:20-23.)

Zechariah 8:9-13, Let Your Hands Be Strong

NIV

9This is what the LORD Almighty says: "You who now hear these words spoken by the prophets who were there when the foundation was laid for the house of the LORD Almighty, let your hands be strong so that the temple may be built. 10Before that time there were no wages for man or beast. No one could go about his business safely because of his enemy, for I had turned every man against his neighbor. 11But now I will not deal with the remnant of this people as I did in the past," declares the LORD Almighty.

12"The seed will grow well, the vine will yield its fruit, the ground will produce its crops, and

NRSV

9Thus says the LORD of hosts: Let your hands be strong—you that have recently been hearing these words from the mouths of the prophets who were present when the foundation was laid for the rebuilding of the temple, the house of the LORD of hosts. 10For before those days there were no wages for people or for animals, nor was there any safety from the foe for those who went out or came in, and I set them all against one other. 11But now I will not deal with the remnant of this people as in the former days, says the LORD of hosts. 12For there shall be a sowing of peace; the vine shall yield its fruit, the ground shall give its

NIV	NRSV
the heavens will drop their dew. I will give all these things as an inheritance to the remnant of this people. [13]As you have been an object of cursing among the nations, O Judah and Israel, so will I save you, and you will be a blessing. Do not be afraid, but let your hands be strong."	produce, and the skies shall give their dew; and I will cause the remnant of this people to possess all these things. [13]Just as you have been a cursing among the nations, O house of Judah and house of Israel, so I will save you and you shall be a blessing. Do not be afraid, but let your hands be strong.

COMMENTARY

Some form of this unit was probably an independent piece before being included in the sermon.[92] It is self-contained, beginning and ending with the exhortation, "Let your hands be strong" (vv. 9, 13). It reprises the theme of reversal that characterizes the whole sermon (vv. 10-11, 13). Further, it has verbal links with Haggai—e.g., "the foundation of Yahweh's house was laid" (v. 9; Hag 2:18); "people and animals" (v. 10; Hag 1:11); "the heavens . . . their dew" (v. 12; Hag 1:10). These, along with the content of the passage, have led some scholars to conclude that the prophets to whom Zechariah refers in v. 9 are Haggai and himself[93] or Haggai alone or even that it is a quotation of Haggai.[94] The similarities with Haggai are undeniable, but the text is Zechariah's own. Haggai's purpose is to persuade the people and their leaders to build God's house (Hag 1:7). Zechariah's purpose is entirely compatible, but different.

8:9a. The introduction to the passage is redactional, composed to join it with the larger sermon. Zechariah addresses "those hearing these words from the mouths of the prophets." "Hearing" presents a *double-entendre.* First, when Zechariah quoted the former prophets in chap. 7, his quotation included the observation that Yahweh called through the prophets, but the ancestors "did not hear" (7:7, 13). Those whom Zechariah now addresses *are* "hearing." In each case, the word means "to listen" and "to heed." Second, Meyers and Meyers have pointed out that hearing "from the mouth of" a prophet can mean hear-

ing the written (dictated) words of a prophet.[95] It has this meaning in Jer 36:24, which is a verbal parallel to v. 9a: *"those hearing* [in these days] (all) *these words* [of the prophets]."[96] Moreover, the Jeremiah text refers to the preceding words, which Baruch had read "from the mouth of" (as dictated by) Jeremiah (Jer 36:4-6). Verse 9a refers to the words of the prophets that Zechariah has been proclaiming (quoting), not just in chap. 7, but in 8:1-8 as well. These latter words expand on the visions and oracles in chaps. 1–2, which draw heavily on prophetic tradition, a tradition still being formed in Zechariah's day.

8:9b. It is in this light that we should understand the reference to the Temple's (re)foundation. The conjunction of v. 9a with v. 9b has produced some difficult syntax, perhaps best rendered as "when the foundation of Yahweh's house was laid, for the building of the temple." In other words, these prophetic words have been heard consistently from Zechariah since the laying of the foundations. Now there is every reason to "let your hands be strong." This exhortation need not indicate a specific, material task. It is roughly equivalent to "take courage" (so TNK) or "have faith" (Isa 35:3; cf. 2 Chr 15:1-7; Zeph 3:16). Zechariah urges the people to continue heeding, trusting the prophetic word, whose instrument he is. Zechariah does not exhort the people to work on the Temple or on anything else; rather, he urges them to take the Temple's founding as a sign of the reversal to which he has been pointing since the beginning of chap. 8, and implicitly since

92. David L. Petersen, *Haggai and Zechariah 1–8*, OTL (Philadelphia: Westminster, 1984) 305.
93. J. Baldwin, *Haggai, Zechariah, Malachi* (Atlanta: John Knox, 1986) 151.
94. Meyers and Meyers, *Haggai and Zechariah 1–8*, 420.

95. Ibid., 419-20.
96. Bracketed words are Zechariah's, the one in parentheses is Jeremiah's, and those in common are italicized.

his enigmatic remarks on fasting in 7:5-6. Zechariah did not regard temple construction as unimportant. Rather than regarding it as an obligation to be urged on his audience, he considered it the sign of a new day and a reason to believe the promises he makes, in continuity with earlier prophetic words.

8:10-12. This relationship to earlier prophets seems to be confirmed by v. 10, which points once more to conditions in the past, "before those days," and by v. 11, which contrasts "now" with "former times," as in "former prophets" (7:7, 12). The former times were characterized by the social chaos that the prophetic summary in 7:9-10 should prevent; it was not safe to go about, because of enemies, and—as God's judgment—people were set against each other. There was no *shalom* (v. 10). By contrast, *shalom* will charac-

terize the future, extending even to the agricultural realm (v. 12).

8:13. This unit ends by promising a different kind of reversal, extending to both houses, Israel and Judah. This is not a political reference, but a theological one. Technically, there was no house of Israel; it vanished under Assyrian conquest. One could now allude to Israel in a curse: "May you be like the house of Israel"—i.e., suffer its fate. Given its adversity, Judah could function similarly. The reunion of the house of Israel with the house of Judah, both returned from dispersion, remained an object of prophetic hope (e.g., Jer 3:18). In that case, these houses will function in a blessing: "May you be like the houses of Israel and Judah." Having drawn once more on the prophets, Zechariah concludes: "Do not be afraid, but let your hands be strong."

Zechariah 8:14-15, I Have Purposed to Do Good

COMMENTARY

These verses, together with vv. 1-8, provide a framework, joining vv. 9-13 to the larger sermon. They resume the promises of vv. 1-8. At the same time, they repeat the concluding encouragement of v. 13: "Do not be afraid." As the basis for this encouragement, they return to the matter of ancestral disobedience and consequent judgment (7:7-14; cf. 1:2-6), but only in order to contrast it with "these days," in which Yahweh purposes to do good to Jerusalem and the house of Judah. The contrast is emphasized by the twofold use of the verb "purpose" (זמם *zāmam*). Everywhere else in the OT this word refers to God's determination

to punish.[97] It is used that way in v. 14, but in v. 15 the divine purpose is reversed. That reversal is also explicit in the "Just as" of v. 14 contrasted with the "so now" of v. 15. This construction also occurs in v. 13, and, with exactly the opposite connotations, in 7:13. There, just as God called and the people refused to hear, here they would call and Yahweh would not hear. This is not an eschatological hope, but the reiteration of what has been announced. There is no reason for fear. (See Reflections at 8:20-23.)

97. Petersen, *Haggai and Zechariah 1–8,* 309.

Zechariah 8:16-17, These Are the Things to Do

[16]"These are the things you are to do: Speak the truth to each other, and render true and sound judgment in your courts; [17]do not plot evil against your neighbor, and do not love to swear falsely. I hate all this," declares the LORD.

[16]These are the things that you shall do: Speak the truth to one another, render in your gates judgments that are true and make for peace, [17]do not devise evil in your hearts against one another, and love no false oath; for all these are things that I hate, says the LORD.

COMMENTARY

Zechariah offers another summary, parallel to his previous summary of prophetic social norms (7:9-10), whose rejection brought calamity and adversity. This one differs in details, but has the same structure, moving from obligations to prohibitions. This movement also has a pivot. Speaking truth to each other is obligatory (v. 16), while each plotting the misfortune of the other is prohibited. Again, mutuality is stressed, but in this instance, Zechariah speaks on his own prophetic authority. His opening words, "These are the things that you shall do," are virtually identical to those of Moses: "These are the things Yahweh has commanded you to do" (Exod 35:1), and "these things" are equivalent to "these words" that stand at the head of Moses' legal instruction

(Exod 24:3; 34:27). Zechariah's language stands in continuity with a tradition of prophetic instruction to which he has already made reference (7:9-10). That his instruction to the community in vv. 16-17 is so markedly similar to his citation of prophetic tradition in chap. 7 shows that Zechariah envisions no new law or new covenant, but faithfulness to what Yahweh's prophets proclaimed in the past (7:7). While the former prophets admonished a prosperous community that was ruined by its unfaithfulness and Yahweh's ensuing wrath, Zechariah here defines the social/moral rudiments of a community whose current adversity provides the occasion of Yahweh's promises. (See Reflections at 8:20-23.)

Zechariah 8:18-19, Fasting Will Be Celebration

[18]Again the word of the LORD Almighty came to me. [19]This is what the LORD Almighty says: "The fasts of the fourth, fifth, seventh and tenth months will become joyful and glad occasions and happy festivals for Judah. Therefore love truth and peace."

18The word of the LORD of hosts came to me, saying: [19]Thus says the LORD of hosts: The fast of the fourth month, and the fast of the fifth, and the fast of the seventh, and the fast of the tenth, shall be seasons of joy and gladness, and cheerful festivals for the house of Judah: therefore love truth and peace.

COMMENTARY

Zechariah returns to the putative topic of his sermon: fasting (cf. 7:4-6). Far from criticizing the practice of fasting, he adds two more fasts to the

number he gave in 7:5, which was already double the number about which the Bethel embassy inquired. These additional fasts in the fourth and tenth months may be Zechariah's invention for rhetorical purposes, though Jewish tradition assigned them to different episodes in Jerusalem's destruction.[98] Zechariah's point is that in the future fasting will be oriented, not to sin, divine wrath, tragedy, and devastation, but to celebration of what Yahweh has done for the house of Judah. This is a reversal of the very definition of fasting: not abstinence and mortification, but joy. It does not answer the Bethel embassy's inquiry; instead, it redefines the present. It does not alter the reality that, whether fasting or eating and drinking, it is people doing it, and not for Yahweh. It merely

places both fasting and eating/drinking in the light of a future that Zechariah's sermon announces and defines as Yahweh's.

It follows, therefore, that this community should love truth, or faithfulness, and peace (v. 19). These terms occur repeatedly in the sermon (7:9; 8:3, 8, 10, 12, 16, 19). They describe the character and consequence of Yahweh's action (vv. 3, 12) and the character of the community itself (v. 16). It is singularly appropriate that these are qualities to be cherished. This brief exhortation at the conclusion of the unit does not qualify the celebratory nature of future fasting. Truth and peace are themselves to be celebrated. (See Reflections at 8:20-23.)

98. Richard Elliott Friedman, "The Prophet and the Historian: The Acquisition of Historical Information from Literary Sources," in *The Poet and the Historian,* ed. R. E. Friedman, HSS 26 (Chico, Calif.: Scholars Press, 1983).

Zechariah 8:20-23, We Have Heard That God Is with You

NIV

20This is what the LORD Almighty says: "Many peoples and the inhabitants of many cities will yet come, 21and the inhabitants of one city will go to another and say, 'Let us go at once to entreat the LORD and seek the LORD Almighty. I myself am going.' 22And many peoples and powerful nations will come to Jerusalem to seek the LORD Almighty and to entreat him."

23This is what the LORD Almighty says: "In those days ten men from all languages and nations will take firm hold of one Jew by the hem of his robe and say, 'Let us go with you, because we have heard that God is with you.'"

NRSV

20Thus says the LORD of hosts: Peoples shall yet come, the inhabitants of many cities; 21the inhabitants of one city shall go to another, saying, "Come, let us go to entreat the favor of the LORD, and to seek the LORD of hosts; I myself am going." 22Many peoples and strong nations shall come to seek the LORD of hosts in Jerusalem, and to entreat the favor of the LORD. 23Thus says the LORD of hosts: In those days ten men from nations of every language shall take hold of a Jew, grasping his garment and saying, "Let us go with you, for we have heard that God is with you."

COMMENTARY

In the oracles that follow the third vision, Zechariah conveyed Yahweh's promise that "many nations will devote themselves to Yahweh, and become his people" (2:11[15]; cf. 6:15). The sermon omits any such reference to the nations until its end. Here peoples and the inhabitants of many cities will consult one another, exactly in the manner of Isa 2:3 (cf. Mic 4:2): "Come, let us go" to entreat Yahweh, exactly as the Bethel embassy had done (v. 21; cf. 7:2). That former

small embassy foreshadows this latter, universal one. Whereas the tiny Bethel embassy came to inquire specifically of the priest and prophets, "in those days"—in the future—ten people of every nation will grasp the edges of each Jew's garment. They will not consult with each other but with the Jews: "Let us go with you, because we have heard that God is with you" (v. 23).

Those to whom Yahweh called through the prophets did not hear (7:13); those to whom Zechariah speaks are hearing (8:9); and, thanks to what God is doing, even people who do not speak Hebrew will have heard: God is with you. What the nations here attest is what Zechariah's sermon claims.

REFLECTIONS

1. Zechariah's long sermon exhibits sound homiletical and pastoral practice. It treats seriously a question of current, pressing concern. It is not a question that Zechariah has invented, but one put to him by the people to whom it matters (7:2-4). In treating the question seriously, Zechariah does not offer a simple official ruling: "Yes, you should continue to mourn"; or "No, your ritual mourning is no longer appropriate." Neither does he treat the question as of only incidental concern, peculiar to the people or person who posed it. Rather, he sees in the question something important for all the people, priests included. Moreover, Zechariah sees what is at stake in the question—not some concealed motives lying behind it, but what is actually at stake in the question itself.

Zechariah recognizes that the question, "Shall we mourn?" is about the present life of the community of faith. The question asks whether the present is determined by the past. It is Zechariah's homiletical and pastoral genius here to take the community's concern about their *past* and *present* and open it up to a message of hope about their *present* and *future*. By situating the community's whole present—its adversity and its concerns—in relation to the past and to the future, Zechariah redefines the present. Zechariah's language about past and future is grounded in the concreteness of God's story with God's people. Zechariah redefines the community's present by proclaiming what God has done, is doing, and will do.

2. The sermon also exhibits good theology. Consistent with the rest of the OT, Zechariah proclaims that salvation (8:7, 13) is at God's initiative, by God's own action (8:3), the result of God's own decision (8:15), consistent with God's faithfulness (8:8). Indeed, God's decision to save—to give "the house of Judah" a life and a future it could not create on its own—derives solely and absolutely from the character of God. No reason for God's decision is offered, no basis proffered, no grounds whatever that might lie outside God's own self: "I *have purposed* in these days to do good to Jerusalem and to the house of Judah" (8:15). God's graciousness toward Jerusalem and Judah is rooted in God's identity and not in any action that Judah has taken. In the NT, this gracious freedom of God acquires the name "gospel," and in Zech 8:14-15 one sees the enactment of "the gospel beforehand" (cf. Gal 3:8).

3. Yet this sermon contains more than the proclamation of God's grace. As noted in the commentary, on the authority of the prophets and of his experience of the divine word, Zechariah carefully delineates the grounds of God's judgment, whose effects the community still suffers. Those grounds are summarized as disobedience and as an incredibly adamant rejection of God's instruction made known to the people through the prophets (7:7-12). This instruction was neither unusual nor onerous. It was beneficent and charted the way to a healthy and whole community: Practice authentic justice; exhibit mutuality and compassion; do not defraud the socially vulnerable; do not plot each other's harm (7:9-10). Why the ancestors, living in prosperity, would reject such minimal and even obvious conditions of a community's well-being was as incredible in Zechariah's day (cf. Isa 5:8-9; 10:1-4) as it remains in ours.

Unlike the exercise of God's grace, then, the exercise of God's judgment can be traced to the community's rejection of these fundamentals of community life. This balance between God's grace and God's judgment can be illustrated by reference to the parable found in Matt 18:23-35. The parable recounts how a king forgives the debts of one of his slaves "out of pity for him" (Matt 18:23-27). Yet this very same slave, when he encounters one of his debtors, will not forgive the man's debts but instead has him cast into prison (18:28-30). When the king learns of the slave's actions, he rescinds his former agreement and hands the man over to be tortured until he pays off his debt. The man had received grace in the king's act of social and economic justice toward him, yet he would not enact the same basic tenets of social justice toward his debtor. The social practices outlined in Zech 7:9-10 give the community the opportunity to respond in kind to the grace God extends to them. When they reject those practices, they reject the grace that lies at the heart of God and in so doing become a people of desolation (7:14).

4. We should not be surprised that Zechariah offers his own prophetic, divinely authorized, Moses-like instruction (8:16-17). As with Moses, this instruction—the law—follows God's gracious (re)turn. Moses did not offer the law as God's condition for the Hebrews' liberation from Egyptian bondage. What need does a slave have of a law? Rather, law is concomitant with freedom, which it enshrines and protects. It is not imposed as the *condition* of freedom, at least not in the Bible. In Zechariah's sermon, law follows the announcement of God's free determination to benefit Jerusalem and Judah (8:15-16). It comes, properly, as a gift, not at all as a burden. How could the injunction to "render in your gates judgments that are true and make for peace"—i.e., judgments that make for communal well-being—count as a burden? Zechariah's proclamation of the law belongs to his proclamation of the gospel. It is his joyous announcement of the possibility for just and faithful living that has been given to the community by its God.

5. At the heart of Zechariah's sermon is the suspicion that this is all too wonderful and simply unbelievable. It is impossible. The NT, too, knows of this suspicion. It is not possible for a camel to pass through the eye of a needle or for anyone to be saved (Matt 19:24-26; Mark 10:25-27). In responding to this suspicion and despair, Jesus alludes to Zech 8:6. He does not at all deny, but rather affirms that, indeed, this is impossible. But like Zechariah, Jesus reminds his listeners that "possibility" is a concept properly applied to human capacities. It has no application to God. For Zechariah, this theological perspective erodes the limits of what we are able to imagine and believe. He does not commend some kind of positive or possibility thinking; he commends attention to God and to what God has promised. God's promises redefine what it is possible to imagine and believe.

SECOND ZECHARIAH

ZECHARIAH 9:1–11:17, PROMISES OF RESTORATION AND A NARRATIVE OF DISINTEGRATION

OVERVIEW

Chapter 9 opens the second part of Zechariah with a vision of Yahweh's triumphal march, the restoration of Zion and its king, and a battle for Zion's dispersed people. This promising vision of restoration continues in chap. 10, with a hint of trouble in 10:2. In 11:4-17, trouble is the focus, and the genre changes to prophetic autobiography. By the end of chap. 11, the community finds itself in the kind of desperate situation to which First Zechariah envisioned and proclaimed the solution.

Zechariah 9:1-17, The Restoration of Zion

OVERVIEW

Zechariah 9 comprises three units, with vv. 9-10 pivotal among them. The first unit (vv. 1-8) describes Yahweh's north-to-south march from Syria, along the Mediterranean coast through Phoenicia and Philistia, concluding at the Temple ("my house," v. 8). Following the entrance of Zion's king and the pacification of Ephraim, Jerusalem, and the nations (vv. 9-10), the third unit announces war (vv. 11-17). Given the peace achieved in vv. 1-10, the martial character of this third unit is striking. It may have been composed later and added to the chapter. However, it does not overturn the two units that precede it; in fact, it depends on them, as the commentary will explain.

Zechariah 9:1-8, An Itinerary of Disempowerment

NIV	NRSV
An Oracle	An Oracle.
9 The word of the LORD is against the land of Hadrach and will rest upon Damascus— for the eyes of men and all the tribes of Israel are on the LORD—[a]	**9** The word of the LORD is against the land of Hadrach and will rest upon Damascus. For to the LORD belongs the capital[a] of Aram,[b] as do all the tribes of Israel; 2 Hamath also, which borders on it,
[a]1 Or *Damascus. / For the eye of the LORD is on all mankind, / as well as on the tribes of Israel,*	[a] Heb *eye* [b] Cn: Heb *of Adam* (or *of humankind*)

NIV

[2]and upon Hamath too, which borders on it,
and upon Tyre and Sidon, though they are
very skillful.
[3]Tyre has built herself a stronghold;
she has heaped up silver like dust,
and gold like the dirt of the streets.
[4]But the Lord will take away her possessions
and destroy her power on the sea,
and she will be consumed by fire.
[5]Ashkelon will see it and fear;
Gaza will writhe in agony,
and Ekron too, for her hope will wither.
Gaza will lose her king
and Ashkelon will be deserted.
[6]Foreigners will occupy Ashdod,
and I will cut off the pride of the Philistines.
[7]I will take the blood from their mouths,
the forbidden food from between their teeth.
Those who are left will belong to our God
and become leaders in Judah,
and Ekron will be like the Jebusites.
[8]But I will defend my house
against marauding forces.
Never again will an oppressor overrun my people,
for now I am keeping watch.

NRSV

Tyre and Sidon, though they are very wise.
[3] Tyre has built itself a rampart,
and heaped up silver like dust,
and gold like the dirt of the streets.
[4] But now, the Lord will strip it of its possessions
and hurl its wealth into the sea,
and it shall be devoured by fire.

[5] Ashkelon shall see it and be afraid;
Gaza too, and shall writhe in anguish;
Ekron also, because its hopes are withered.
The king shall perish from Gaza;
Ashkelon shall be uninhabited;
[6] a mongrel people shall settle in Ashdod,
and I will make an end of the pride of
Philistia.
[7] I will take away its blood from its mouth,
and its abominations from between its teeth;
it too shall be a remnant for our God;
it shall be like a clan in Judah,
and Ekron shall be like the Jebusites.
[8] Then I will encamp at my house as a guard,
so that no one shall march to and fro;
no oppressor shall again overrun them,
for now I have seen with my own eyes.

COMMENTARY

This first unit of chap. 9 has four constituent parts: (1) vv. 1-2, an introduction that places God (or God's word) in Syria; (2) vv. 3-4, concerning Tyre; (3) vv. 5-7, concerning the Philistines; and (4) v. 8, Yahweh's encampment at the Temple. Each marks a point along Yahweh's itinerary.

9:1-2. The term "oracle" (משא *maśśā'*), followed by "the word of Yahweh," appears in v. 1 and in 12:2 and Mal 1:1, a combination unique to these three texts. It seems to combine two ways of introducing prophetic oracles. The revelation formula ("the word of Yahweh came to . . . ") is characteristic of Haggai and First Zechariah, while the term *maśśā'* occurs twelve times as the heading of Isaiah's prophecies against the nations (Isaiah 13–23).[99] The use of this combination differs among the two Zechariah texts and

that of Malachi, however. In Mal 1:1 it is clearly a superscription, identifying the subject of the oracle, Israel, and its recipient, Malachi. Zechariah 12:1 also names the subject, again Israel, but no recipient. Instead, this superscription concludes with an oracle formula, "says Yahweh," in which "Yahweh" forms the subject of participles describing the Lord as creator. Thus the superscription of 12:1 issues directly in a brief hymn of praise.

In v. 1, the terms "oracle" and "word of Yahweh" are also joined syntactically with what follows. Together, they form the subject of "is against the land of Hadrach," and they are the antecedent of "*his* [or its] resting place" (cf. NRSV, "will rest"). Here Zechariah is alluding to several earlier texts. First, the eighth vision of First Zechariah concludes with God's Spirit *at rest* in the north country (6:8). The words "resting place" and "at rest" derive from the same root. In v. 1,

99. Beth Glazier-McDonald, *Malachi: The Divine Messenger,* SBLDS 98 (Atlanta: Scholars Press, 1987) 24-27.

the direction of God's movement is reversed, and Yahweh's presence is represented by word rather than by spirit. This function of Yahweh's word can be compared with Isa 9:7[8]: "the Lord sent a word to/against Jacob, and it fell upon Israel." Second, Zechariah is here playing on the word "oracle" (*maśśā'*), which can also mean "burden." It derives from the verb "to lift" (נשא *nāśā'*) Indeed, the first occurrence of this term involves just such a play on words. In 2 Kgs 9:25, Jehu instructs his aide to "lift" the body of Joram, because Yahweh had "lifted" (uttered) a "burden" (oracle) against him. Ezekiel also plays on the same words. In Ezek 12:1-16, "oracle" alludes to picking up baggage for exile.[100] This background helps to explain the term "resting place" (מנוחה *měnûḥâ*) in v. 1. In Jer 51:59, "resting place" means billet or quarters, and Seariah is called the quartermaster, or chief of the resting place, in charge of securing overnight quarters on Zedekiah's journey to Babylon. In this verse, Yahweh is on a journey, with Damascus the first stop.

In no way are vv. 1-8 or the rest of chaps. 9–11 concerned specifically about Hadrach, Damascus, or all of Syria. Hadrach, Damascus, and Hamath (v. 2) are the first and northernmost points on an itinerary of national disempowerments, which Yahweh works in order to secure the people against threat of invasion or oppression (v. 8). In its use of the term "oracle" with reference to Damascus, v. 1 makes a third textual allusion, to Isa 17:1-7. Isaiah's oracle concerns the destruction of Damascus and Israel, but concludes with this announcement: "On that day, humankind will look to their maker, and their eyes will be to(ward) the holy one of Israel." This expectation helps to explain the claim of v. 1, that "the eye of humankind is on [or it belongs to] Yahweh" (cf. NRSV, which emends the text). The eye of humankind is, by itself, a metaphor of human greed and arrogance, of claims to self-determination opposed to God's own prerogative, as is clear from Isa 2:11-12 (cf. Prov 27:20). This reference to all humans also helps to account for the inclusion in v. 2 of Tyre (Tyre and Sidon considered as one, as in Jer 47:4), which was famous for its wealth, its pride, and its wisdom (Ezek 27:12, 33;

28:1-17). In spite of that, God lays claim to the eye of all humankind (cf. Zech 5:6).

Included in this category of all humankind are "all the tribes of Israel" (v. 1). The syntax here is very difficult, and the reference to all of Israel's tribes is enigmatic; apart from Ezek 48:19, it is unique among the prophets. Naturally, Israel would be included among those whose eyes are on, and whose attention belongs to, Yahweh. Also (according to v. 10), the territory of the former northern kingdom, Israel, would be included in the extent of the king's dominion. By tradition, this domain included everything west of the Euphrates (1 Kgs 5:4[4:24]). But more than a territorial point is being made here. "All the tribes of Israel" occurs just twenty-three times in the Bible, eight times in Kings and Chronicles; in each of these latter cases it refers to God's choice of Jerusalem, and at least implicitly to the Temple (e.g., "the city that Yahweh had chosen out of all the tribes of Israel, to put his name there" [1 Kgs 14:21]). Given the reference to Yahweh's house in v. 8 and the focus on Zion/Jerusalem in vv. 9-10, which expressly includes Ephraim, "all the tribes of Israel" in v. 1*b* anticipates the festal procession of Zion's king. It is this procession for which Yahweh's procession southward prepares.

Verses 1-2 stand as a theological claim or confession at the head of what follows. In Hebrew, "Yahweh" does not serve as the subject of a verb in these verses; Yahweh's action begins in v. 4. It is action against Tyre, which vv. 1-2 introduce.

Just prior to the mention of Tyre, and just after reference to all the tribes of Israel, v. 2 speaks of Hamath, which "borders on" (the only verb in vv. 1-2) Damascus and the land of Hadrach. Indeed, Hamath lay between Damascus and, to its north, Hadrach. The name "Hadrach" occurs only here in the Bible; it is known only from Aramaic and Assyrian inscriptions, none of which mention the place after 698 BCE.[101] Zechariah begins Yahweh's procession at a northern point that probably no longer existed under that name at the time of its writing. Indeed, Yahweh's procession southward in vv. 1-8 seems to reflect that of an Assyrian king of the eighth century BCE,

100. Walther Zimmerli, *Ezekiel I*, Hermeneia (Philadelphia: Fortress, 1979) 273.

101. Benedikt Otzen, *Studien über Deuterosacharja*, ATDan 6 (Copenhagen: Munksgaard, 1964) 99. See *ANET* 282-83, 655-56.

Tiglath-pileser III.[102] In scripting the future, Zechariah reconstructs a paradigmatic past—and assigns both to God.

9:3-7. These verses describe the rearrangement of political realities along the Mediterranean coast, moving from Tyre in the north and concluding with Ekron, the city nearest Judah. As do vv. 1-2, vv. 3-7 draw on a store of prophetic oracles against the nations, including oracles against Tyre and the Philistine cities (e.g., Isaiah 23; Ezekiel 26–28; Amos 1:1-10). In Zechariah, all of these cities lose their sovereignty, and Tyre is burned.

9:3-4. While v. 2 mentions Tyre's wisdom, v. 3 refers to its wealth, silver and gold amassed as a measure for defending against Yahweh's march. These defensive measures include the construction of a rampart, but no such measures will avail. While older prophetic texts lie behind these verses, they have been composed with poetic skill, which makes precise translation difficult. In Hebrew, the term "rampart" (מצור *māṣôr*) is a play on the name "Tyre."[103] "Mire of the streets," which here describes the amount of Tyre's silver and gold (v. 3), is everywhere else a metaphor of defeat in battle (cf. 10:5). The language of v. 4 is ambiguous; it may refer to either economic loss or military defeat (e.g., the NRSV's "cast her wealth into the sea" could also be translated "defeat her army at sea"). Only at the beginning of v. 3 and at the end of v. 4 is the language unambiguously military.[104] In between, framed by defensive measures and their futility, Tyre loses its vaunted wealth.

9:5-7. Tyre's demise produces terror in the Philistine cities (v. 5), who had close ties with Tyre (cf. Jer 47:3-5). With each city named in v. 5, the terror is compounded, from Asheklon to Gaza to Ekron, until the reason is made explicit: Ekron's hope, and that of the other cities, has withered (v. 5*a*). Their "hope" (מבט *mabbāṭ*) was Tyre, just as in an earlier time Egypt had been Ashdod's hope (see Isa 20:5, the only other place where the word occurs). The remainder of v. 5 moves in reverse order, from Ekron to Gaza to

Asheklon; Gaza's king will vanish, and Asheklon will be uninhabited, or without a ruler.[105] Either the whole population or their rulers will flee these cities (there is precedent for both; see Amos 1:8; Zeph 2:4-7).

Ashdod is the next city mentioned (v. 6), and with the same ambiguity. The first words of the verse are difficult, since the meaning of the subject ("mongrel people"/"foreigners") is uncertain, and the verb could be translated "will settle" or "will rule." In the latter case, the subject is singular. It may refer to an illegitimate or an unwanted ruler. This seems likely, since the latter part of the verse means, "I will cut off the sovereignty [pride] of the Philistines" (cf. 10:11*b*; Isa 13:19). The eighth-century BCE Assyrian king Sargon II recorded that Ashdod's king fled at his advance, leaving wife and children behind.[106] Abdication was a typical response of Philistine rulers under threat. In any event, the goal of Yahweh's action against Philistia is not depopulation, but cleansing and incorporation.

Yahweh acts toward Philistia only by removing its sovereignty (v. 6) and removing blood and detestable things from its mouth (v. 7). "Detestable things" can include idolatry and other illicit cultic practices, but blood in the mouth refers more specifically to eating meat from which the blood has not been drained (see Gen 9:4; Deut 12:16). Since the detestable things are said to be between the teeth, the text most likely refers to eating proscribed meat. The goal of this cleansing is the incorporation of a Philistine remnant: "They will remain—yes, even they!—for our God." Although Amos had promised that every last Philistine would perish (Amos 1:8), and Zephaniah had promised that the Judeans would expropriate abandoned Philistine property (Zeph 2:6-7), Zechariah departs from these sources. The fate of the Philistines is to be a clan—perhaps a regiment—in Judah and Ekron, like a Jebusite. No other prophet mentions the Jebusites (cf. 2 Sam 6:5-8). Perhaps Zechariah has in mind Josh 15:63, which reports that the Jebusites, original inhabitants of Jerusalem, "live in Jerusalem with the people of Judah to this day." Just so, Ekron will live with and be part of the people of Judah.

9:8. Nothing is said in vv. 1-7 about precisely

---

102. J. J. M. Roberts, "The Old Testament's Contributions to Messianic Expectations," in *The Messiah: Developments in Earlier Judaism and Christianity,* ed. James H. Charlesworth (Minneapolis: Fortress, 1992) 44-45.

103. Ralph L. Smith, *Micah–Malachi,* WBC (Waco, Tex.: Word, 1984) 253.

104. Carol Meyers and Eric Meyers, *Haggai and Zechariah 9–14,* AB 25C (New York: Doubleday, 1993) 99.

105. Ibid., 109-10.
106. See *ANET,* 285.

how any of this will come about—how Tyre will be defeated or who will burn it; how the Philistine cities will come to have different and non-royal leadership; how the people will be persuaded to abandon cultic practices; or how they will be incorporated into Judah. No armies accompany Yahweh on the march, but that march reaches its goal and achieves its provisional aim in this verse. Here God speaks (as in vv. 6-7) promising to encamp "at my house." This encampment, too, has a martial character and purpose. God will act as a guard or sentry (1 Sam 14:12), to ensure that what Yahweh has already achieved in disempowering (demilitarizing) the nations will not be undone. No one will march back and forth (cf. 7:14), and no oppressor again will overrun God's people.

Yahweh's encampment stands in contrast to the temporary billet, or resting place, of v. 1 (the terms חֲנִיתִי [wĕḥānîtî, v. 8] and מְנֻחָתוֹ [mĕnuḥātô, v. 1] have a certain assonance). Verse 8 returns to v. 1 in a second way. Although the first verse speaks of the eye of humankind, in v. 8 Yahweh concludes with "now I have seen with *my* eyes." In 4:10*b*, God's seven eyes roam the earth, whereas in 9:8 God has completed an itinerary. Whatever prospects Syria, Phoenicia, the Philistines, and even all the tribes of Israel might have envisioned for themselves or for each other, Yahweh's eyes now have brought a new order and will govern it. (See Reflections at 9:9-10.)

Zechariah 9:9-10, The Entry of Zion's King

COMMENTARY

Paul Hanson has suggested that 9:1-8 corresponds to elements of a ritual pattern in which God engages in battle, is victorious, and comes to the sanctuary or Temple. In some texts, this pattern includes a victory shout, a procession, and "the manifestation of Yahweh's universal reign."[107] These elements are present in these verses. Whether these verses form part of a ritual pattern, they clearly presuppose vv. 1-8. Yahweh's march has made possible what vv. 9-10 announce, drawing again on earlier texts.

The announcement begins with instruction to Zion/Jerusalem. Zion had been instructed to rejoice already in 2:10[14], because God was coming to dwell in Zion. This same instruction, with the same reason, also occurred in an earlier text that identifies Yahweh as "the king of Israel"

107. P. Hanson, *The Dawn of Apocalyptic* (Philadelphia: Fortress, 1975) 299-315.

(Zeph 3:14-15). Indeed, rejoicing and shouting for joy are especially associated with the celebration of God as king (see Psalms 47; 96; 98).[108] Zechariah draws on this tradition, but v. 9*a* instructs Zion/Jerusalem to rejoice and shout at the entrance of a human king, not of Yahweh as king.

In this expectation of a human king, unprecedented in biblical texts of the later Persian period, Zechariah does draw on precedent. Ezekiel promised a future Davidic king who would rule a united Israel and Judah (Ezek 37:22, 24). Jeremiah issued a similar promise, using the name "Branch" to refer to a future Davidic king (Jer 23:5; 33:14-22). First Zechariah appropriated that name (3:8) and applied it to the temple builder (6:12), with royal associations in both cases. In Zech 4:9, these are attached expressly to the Davidic Zerubbabel, who was the focus of Haggai's royal-messianic promises (Hag 2:20-23). Verses 9-10 give Zion's future king no name, but the language makes evident that he will be a scion of David's house.

These verses allude to a number of earlier biblical texts.[109] First, v. 9*b* says that the king will be "righteous" (NRSV, "triumphant"). A more adequate translation may be "legitimate." The term צדיק (*ṣādîq*) is used in Jer 23:5 to describe the "Branch," specifically to say that he will be a legitimate heir of David. Second, the king will be riding "a colt, the foal of an ass." This refers to Gen 49:10-11, Jacob's blessing of Judah, which Zech 9:9 interprets as a dynastic promise: The king who comes from the tribe of Judah will have "a colt . . . the foal of a donkey." Third, vv. 9-10 use the language of Psalm 72 to expand on Gen 49:10: "the obedience of the peoples will be his." As does Ps 72:11, Zech 9:10 expects that the Davidic king will exercise universal dominion: "from sea to sea, and from the river [Euphrates] to the ends of the earth." Fourth, the extent of the future king's dominion and the peace that characterizes it (Zech 9:10) reflect Solomon's kingdom. Solomon, David's immediate heir, ruled from the Euphrates to the Mediterranean and enjoyed "peace on all sides" (1 Kgs 5:4[4:24]; see Commentary on Zech 9:1). In drawing on earlier texts, Zech 9:9-10 evokes the memory of a former time and envisions its restoration.

The king whom Zion is to greet will not be just another monarch like Solomon, however. While Ps 72:12 expresses hope that the king will save the needy, or the "humble," in Zech 9:9 it is the king who is "saved" (NRSV, "victorious") and who is "humble," riding on a donkey. Riding a donkey is not necessarily a sign of humility, but a donkey is quite different from a war horse (v. 10). Here, v. 9 seems to have in mind Ps 33:16-17: "a king is not *saved* by his military strength," and "the horse is useless for salvation." This king, whom Zion will greet, comes in peace; more precisely, he comes in the light of the salvation and peace that Yahweh has already achieved (vv. 1-8) and in the light of Yahweh's action in v. 10. Here God speaks once more, promising to "cut off" armaments from Jerusalem and Ephraim.

Again in v. 10, Zechariah draws on tradition, as represented in Pss 46:9[10]; 76:3[4], where Yahweh makes a universal end of war and destroys the instruments of war in defense of Zion.[110] Once before (v. 7) God promised to "cut off" something, the detestable practices of the Philistines, which will permit their inclusion as a clan and a remnant for God in Judah. Now Yahweh promises to cut off, to eradicate, the instruments of war, not universally, but from Jerusalem and Ephraim. They have no need of weapons, nor does Zion's king, because God has already pacified the entire region from the Euphrates to the Mediterranean and has secured the Temple (vv. 1-8). On this basis, Zion's legitimate king can declare international peace.

---

108. Ben C. Ollenburger, *Zion: The City of the Great King,* JSOTSup 41 (Sheffield: JSOT, 1987) 34-35.

109. See Michael Fishbane, *Biblical Interpretation in Ancient Israel* (Oxford: Clarendon, 1985) 501-2; Meyers and Meyers, *Zechariah 9–14,* 125-26, 129.

110. Ollenburger, *Zion,* 141-42.

REFLECTIONS

1. Zechariah 9:1-10 presents an eschatological vision of restoration. It imagines what does not yet exist as the restoration of a remembered past. This text thus invites the reader to think about the interrelationship of memory and hope, of past and future. Memory here is not only the source of imagination but its product as well, and both are fueled by tradition. The author of these verses uses earlier texts (see Commentary) to construct a paradigm that covers both past and future: both Solomon of the past and Zion's future king. Yet the future is not simply a re-creation of the past. Rather, the envisioned and desired future constitutes restoration of what *cannot* now exist; only Yahweh can bring it and will bring it, acting alone. And it is because of Yahweh's initiative that the future differs from the past and Solomon from the future king. The future envisioned in 9:1-10 is *eschatological.* It belongs to God.

2. The imagery with which this eschatological future is envisioned may surprise and even discomfit the contemporary reader. Yahweh's march to the Temple (9:1-8) is described in militaristic language, so that Yahweh appears as the ultimate conqueror. Yahweh's march to the Temple involves both war and peace, but they occur in a relationship determined by God's purpose and goal: peace. In 9:1-7, only the proud and wealthy Tyre stands in opposition to this goal, amassing its defenses against Yahweh. Because of this opposition, Tyre alone is the object of Yahweh's war. As in Isa 2:12, God is "against all that is proud and arrogant," which Tyre symbolizes. So also it is only pride, the sovereignty of the Philistines, that Yahweh cuts off. War is not the necessary means to peace; rather, these verses suggest that it is a consequence of opposing peace, of opposing Yahweh's ultimate purpose for Israel and for the world.

3. Zechariah 9:9 is the first of several passages in Second Zechariah quoted or alluded to in the NT. All four Gospels use this verse in portraying Jesus' "triumphal entry" into Jerusalem, and precisely his entry as king (Matt 21:9; Mark 11:9-10; Luke 19:38; John 12:13). But this text serves the Gospels in another way, by describing the king as riding a colt (according to the LXX). The kind of animal Jesus rides (in Matt 21:5, a donkey *and* a colt!) signals for the evangelists the character of his kingship. John makes this clear, making his quotation of Zech 9:9 read, "Do not fear, daughter of Zion. See your king is coming, sitting on a donkey's colt!" (John 12:15). While the crowd in Matthew hails Jesus as the Son of David (Matt 21:9), Matthew cites Zech 9:9 to stress that the king is humble. In this respect, the Gospels do not misinterpret their text. Zion's king is, like Solomon, a royal son of David, but without military power.

Zechariah 9:11-17, War Resumes

NIV	NRSV

[11]As for you, because of the blood of my covenant with you,
    I will free your prisoners from the waterless pit.
	[11] As for you also, because of the blood of my covenant with you,
	    I will set your prisoners free from the waterless pit.

[12]Return to your fortress, O prisoners of hope;
    even now I announce that I will restore twice as much to you.
	[12] Return to your stronghold, O prisoners of hope;
	    today I declare that I will restore to you double.

[13]I will bend Judah as I bend my bow
    and fill it with Ephraim.
  I will rouse your sons, O Zion,
    against your sons, O Greece,
    and make you like a warrior's sword.
	[13] For I have bent Judah as my bow;
	    I have made Ephraim its arrow.
	  I will arouse your sons, O Zion,
	    against your sons, O Greece,
	    and wield you like a warrior's sword.

[14]Then the LORD will appear over them; his arrow will flash like lightning.	[14] Then the LORD will appear over them,

NIV

The Sovereign LORD will sound the trumpet;
   he will march in the storms of the south,
¹⁵ and the LORD Almighty will shield them.
They will destroy
   and overcome with slingstones.
They will drink and roar as with wine;
   they will be full like a bowl
   used for sprinkling^a the corners of the altar.
¹⁶The LORD their God will save them on that day
   as the flock of his people.
They will sparkle in his land
   like jewels in a crown.
¹⁷How attractive and beautiful they will be!
   Grain will make the young men thrive,
   and new wine the young women.

^a15 Or *bowl,* / *like*

NRSV

   and his arrow go forth like lightning;
the Lord GOD will sound the trumpet
   and march forth in the whirlwinds of the
      south.
¹⁵ The LORD of hosts will protect them,
   and they shall devour and tread down the
      slingers;^a
they shall drink their blood^b like wine,
   and be full like a bowl,
   drenched like the corners of the altar.

¹⁶ On that day the LORD their God will save them
   for they are the flock of his people;
for like the jewels of a crown
   they shall shine on his land.
¹⁷ For what goodness and beauty are his!
   Grain shall make the young men flourish,
   and new wine the young women.

^a Cn: Heb *the slingstones*   ^b Gk: Heb *shall drink*

COMMENTARY

This third unit of chap. 9 has a loose connection with the preceding verses. It begins abruptly with Yahweh's address to Zion, "As for you also" (v. 11). Thus it resumes the address to Zion, begun in v. 9. It also introduces something entirely new. Yahweh addresses Zion again in v. 12, "I will restore to you double," and for a third time in v. 13, "I will make you like a warrior's sword." Contrary to the announcement of peace in v. 10, vv. 11-13 promise war. The reason for this war is given in v. 12: to restore double to Zion. Verses 11-12 indicate the nature of the restoration: Zion's prisoners, "prisoners of hope," are being freed by Yahweh and are urged to return to the stronghold or fortress. To accomplish this hoped-for return of Zion's prisoners, God will use Judah and Ephraim as a bow, the very instrument eradicated in v. 10, and will rouse, or wield, their sons against those of Greece (v. 13). The battle itself, preceded by Yahweh's theophany (v. 14), is envisioned in v. 15*a* and followed by celebration and prosperity (vv. 15*b*-17).

9:11-13. All of this will happen because of the blood of Zion's covenant (v. 11*a*). "Blood of [the] covenant" occurs in only one other place,

Exod 24:8, where it describes Moses dashing the blood of sacrificed bulls on the people who have promised to obey the covenant he has just read to them (Exod 24:7). In consequence, Moses calls this blood "the *blood of the covenant* that Yahweh makes with you on the basis of all these words." The blood of the covenant symbolizes the people's acceptance of it, their agreement to be bound by it. The logic of v. 11 is quite different. Here Zion's blood is in view, and it is on the basis of Zion's "covenant blood" (REB) that Yahweh promises to act, releasing its prisoners.

The conjunction of covenant and freedom for prisoners recalls promises made in connection with the servant in Isa 42:6-7; 49:8-9. The latter text also envisions a return to Jerusalem (Isa 49:9-23), as does Isaiah 54, which speaks of God's covenant of peace with Zion in promises that its population will be vastly increased (Isa 54:1-10), a concern latent in Zech 9:11-17. Similarly, Isaiah 61 announces release to prisoners (Isa 61:1), an everlasting covenant (Isa 61:8), and a *"double portion"* in the land" (Isa 61:7; cf. Zech 9:12). None of these texts, however, speaks of Zion's covenant as does Ezek 16:61, from which the expression in Zech 9:11 may derive. But in expanding that expression to include blood, Zech 9:11 seems to interpret Jer 51:34-36. There Zion/Jerusalem, complaining that it has been devoured and emptied by Nebuchadnezzar, utters an oath: "May my blood be upon the inhabitants of Chaldea." In response, Yahweh promises Zion, "I will take up your cause and exact vengeance for you." In Zechariah's interpretation, Zion's oath of blood and Yahweh's promised vengeance form a covenant, which is the basis of the announcements in 9:11-13.

The first of these announcements concerns the release of prisoners "from the waterless pit." The same phrase occurs in Jer 34:8, referring to Jeremiah's imprisonment. But also and more suggestively Joseph's brothers put him in "a waterless pit" before selling him to merchants bound for Egypt (Gen 37:24), where he became a slave and a prisoner (Gen 39:1, 20-22).[111] Allusion to Joseph makes sense in this context, not only because the release of prisoners is at stake, but also because Joseph was the father of Ephraim. Ephraim, the former northern kingdom, is included in the dominion of Zion's king (vv. 9-10) and among those who count as Zion's prisoners, the return of whom will count as double restoration for Zion/Jerusalem. In chaps. 9–10, a reunited Israel (Joseph/Ephraim) and Judah is the object of hope (as it is in Jeremiah 31; Ezekiel 34; 37; Zech 8:13). Moreover, chap. 9 envisions a populous Jerusalem (as does, e.g., Isaiah 54; Zech 8:7-8). In fact, the population of early Persian-period Jerusalem probably numbered less than five hundred.[112] Nehemiah, in the fifth century BCE, had to institute a lottery to populate the city (Neh 7:4-5; 11:1-2). Zechariah stakes Jerusalem's *double* restoration, not on a lottery, but on a battle that will free prisoners.

Ephraim is also included, with Judah, among Zion's sons whom Yahweh wields in war against the sons of Greece (v. 13). The mention of Greece here has led some scholars to date this text and even all of chap. 9 in the time of (or after) Alexander the Great, who conquered the region in 332 BCE. However, Joel 3:6, from the Persian period, charges that Tyre, Sidon, and the Philistines "sold the sons of Judah and the sons of Jerusalem to the sons of the Greeks."[113] The language is strikingly similar to that of v. 13. Further, Yahweh promises to "rouse" the Judeans and return them from the far-off place where they have been sold (Joel 3:7), i.e., from Greece or Ionia. The biblical name "Javan," which appears in both v. 13 and Joel 3:6 ("Javanites"), refers literally to Ionia, a Greek area of southwest Asia Minor, but also more generally to all Greece. It is from here, according to Joel, that Yahweh will "rouse" (עור *'ûr*) the Judeans; 9:13 uses a different stem of the same verb: "I will arouse your sons." Neither Joel nor Zechariah envisions a war of liberation against an occupying Greek army. Rather, Zech 9:11-15 envisions a war to bring prisoners from Javan/Greece home to Zion, which has been secured already (9:1-10). Javan is known for its trade in human beings, but it also connotes a place that is far off. In Isa 66:19-20, Javan is the most distant place from which the nations will bring diaspora Jews to Jerusalem. Joel, too, emphasizes Javan's remoteness from Judah and Jerusalem, a sense we should probably also perceive in Zech 9:13. Yahweh has already marched from the east and north to Jerusalem; now Yahweh will bring back prisoners from the western reaches.

9:14-15. God will wield Judah and Ephraim as an archer wields a bow (v. 13); they are the bow, but it is Yahweh's arrow that guarantees victory (v. 14). Here military terms are absorbed into the language of theophany (cf. Hab 3:11; Pss 18:5[4]; 144:5-8), but the battle is real. Yahweh will protect Zion's warriors, and "they will destroy; they will suppress the sling-stones" (v. 15*a*; cf. NIV, NRSV). Sling stones were launched from catapults mounted on city walls (2 Chr 26:15). Assyrian reliefs depicting the assault against Lachish show archers mounting ladders and protected by siege machines against a hail of stones, many of which have been removed from excavations at Lachish.[114] Yahweh's archers or Yahweh the archer prevails against the sling stones.

---

111. Michael Fishbane, *Biblical Interpretation in Ancient Israel* (Oxford: Clarendon, 1985) 502.

112. Meyers and Meyers, *Haggai and Zechariah 9–14*, 353.

113. Hans Walter Wolff, *Joel and Amos*, Hermeneia (Philadelphia: Fortress, 1977) 77-78.

114. *Oxford Bible Atlas*, ed. Herbert G. May, John Day (New York: Oxford University Press, 1989) 104-5.

Celebration follows. The picture here is of drunken revelry (NIV), not drinking blood (NRSV). Although blood is suggested by reference to the horns of an altar, the word "blood" does not occur in the text, and consuming blood was strictly forbidden (Lev 17:10-12).

9:16-17. The conclusion returns only implicitly to Zion's prisoners. That Yahweh will "save them" may refer either to the warriors (vv. 13-15) or to the prisoners (vv. 11-12). In 8:7, 13; 10:6, to save means to rescue from captivity and diaspora, and that is its likely meaning here. Yahweh will save them "as the flock of his people," which suggests the action of a shepherd gathering lost sheep. This will happen "on that day," a phrase that occurs only here in chaps. 9–11. I suggest that a specific day is in view, especially since v. 16b is a causal clause: "because the stones of a crown are glittering on [Yahweh's] land." The word "glittering" is a verbal form of the word "signal" (נס nûs) in Isa 11:10-12, where the "root of Jesse"—like the Branch, a king in the line of David—will signal return from diaspora. Similarly, in Zech 9:16 the crown jewels, glittering on Yahweh's land, will signal the release of prisoners from the farthest reaches. In this way, all of vv. 11-15 depend on the appearance of Zion's king in vv. 9-10 and thus ultimately on Yahweh's itinerary in vv. 1-8.

Peace and prosperity will result (v. 17). Grain and new wine are traditional symbols of plenty—indeed, of life—and of peace. In Gen 27:28, Isaac blesses Jacob with the prospect of grain and new wine, and Moses' blessing in Deut 33:28 associates a land of grain and new wine with safety and peace. Where these symbols and these commodities nourish young men and young women, there is a future.

REFLECTIONS

1. For the author of 9:11-17, the peace achieved in the earlier parts of the chapter is by itself complete. The situation is analogous to that of chap. 1, where the whole world is at rest, but inappropriately so. In 9:1-10, Judah and Israel are freed from the threat of oppression, and Jerusalem has its king; but Zion's people remain prisoners far away from the land. Restoration remains unfinished if it does not include the release of prisoners and their return. Zion's peace is provisional until the prisoners are free. The sign of peace and restoration is evident in the goodness and abundance of grain and wine (9:17). These verses underscore the communal dimensions of eschatological restoration (see also Reflections at 3:1-10). The fullness of God's peace and presence is known only when all, not just some, parts of community life are restored to wholeness. It is not possible, Zechariah suggests, to speak about the coming of God's restoration in individualistic terms. God works for and desires the restoration of community.

2. This passage has its echo in the NT, which refers to the blood of the covenant (9:11). In Luke's account of the last supper, Jesus says of the wine, "This . . . is the new covenant in my blood" (Luke 22:20; cf. 1 Cor 11:25). To be sure, echoes of the covenant language of Exod 24:8 and Jer 31:31 sound here, but given the prominence of Zechariah 9–14 in the Gospel passion narratives, it is also important to read these words in the light of the blood of Zechariah's covenant. Hebrews says that it was "by the blood of the eternal covenant" that "the God of peace" raised Jesus from the dead (Heb 13:20). In a further echo of the language of Zechariah, Hebrews also comments, speaking to Christians, that "you have come to Mount Zion" and "to Jesus" (Heb 12:22, 24). The connections with Zech 9:11-17 suggest a new way for Christians to think of their identity in Christ. Perhaps we should think of ourselves not as Zion's warriors sent to liberate prisoners, but the other way—as those far off, graciously included in the number of Zion's children because of the blood of the covenant (Zech 9:11).

Zechariah 10:1-12, The Restoration of Judah and Israel

NIV

10 Ask the LORD for rain in the springtime;
it is the LORD who makes the storm clouds.
He gives showers of rain to men,
and plants of the field to everyone.
²The idols speak deceit,
diviners see visions that lie;
they tell dreams that are false,
they give comfort in vain.
Therefore the people wander like sheep
oppressed for lack of a shepherd.

³"My anger burns against the shepherds,
and I will punish the leaders;
for the LORD Almighty will care
for his flock, the house of Judah,
and make them like a proud horse in battle.
⁴From Judah will come the cornerstone,
from him the tent peg,
from him the battle bow,
from him every ruler.
⁵Together they*a* will be like mighty men
trampling the muddy streets in battle.
Because the LORD is with them,
they will fight and overthrow the horsemen.

⁶"I will strengthen the house of Judah
and save the house of Joseph.
I will restore them
because I have compassion on them.
They will be as though
I had not rejected them,
for I am the LORD their God
and I will answer them.
⁷The Ephraimites will become like mighty men,
and their hearts will be glad as with wine.
Their children will see it and be joyful;
their hearts will rejoice in the LORD.
⁸I will signal for them
and gather them in.
Surely I will redeem them;
they will be as numerous as before.
⁹Though I scatter them among the peoples,
yet in distant lands they will remember me.
They and their children will survive,
and they will return.

a4,5 Or ruler, all of them together. / 5They

NRSV

10 Ask rain from the LORD
in the season of the spring rain,
from the LORD who makes the storm clouds,
who gives showers of rain to you,*a*
the vegetation in the field to everyone.
² For the teraphim*b* utter nonsense,
and the diviners see lies;
the dreamers tell false dreams,
and give empty consolation.
Therefore the people wander like sheep;
they suffer for lack of a shepherd.

³ My anger is hot against the shepherds,
and I will punish the leaders;*c*
for the LORD of hosts cares for his flock, the
house of Judah,
and will make them like his proud
war-horse.
⁴ Out of them shall come the cornerstone,
out of them the tent peg,
out of them the battle bow,
out of them every commander.
⁵ Together they shall be like warriors in battle,
trampling the foe in the mud of the streets;
they shall fight, for the LORD is with them,
and they shall put to shame the riders on
horses.

⁶ I will strengthen the house of Judah,
and I will save the house of Joseph.
I will bring them back because I have
compassion on them,
and they shall be as though I had not
rejected them;
for I am the LORD their God and I will
answer them.
⁷ Then the people of Ephraim shall become like
warriors,
and their hearts shall be glad as with
wine.
Their children shall see it and rejoice,
their hearts shall exult in the LORD.

⁸ I will signal for them and gather them in,
for I have redeemed them,

a Heb them   b Or household gods   c Or male goats

NIV

¹⁰I will bring them back from Egypt
and gather them from Assyria.
I will bring them to Gilead and Lebanon,
and there will not be room enough for them.
¹¹They will pass through the sea of trouble;
the surging sea will be subdued
and all the depths of the Nile will dry up.
Assyria's pride will be brought down
and Egypt's scepter will pass away.
¹²I will strengthen them in the LORD
and in his name they will walk,"
declares the LORD.

NRSV

and they shall be as numerous as they were
before.
⁹ Though I scattered them among the nations,
yet in far countries they shall remember me,
and they shall rear their children and return.
¹⁰ I will bring them home from the land of Egypt,
and gather them from Assyria;
I will bring them to the land of Gilead and to
Lebanon,
until there is no room for them.
¹¹ They^a shall pass through the sea of distress,
and the waves of the sea shall be struck
down,
and all the depths of the Nile dried up.
The pride of Assyria shall be laid low,
and the scepter of Egypt shall depart.
¹² I will make them strong in the LORD,
and they shall walk in his name,
says the LORD.

^a Gk: Heb *He*

COMMENTARY

The material in this section was originally independent of chap. 9, to which it has been linked by the reference to God's people as a flock (9:16; 10:2-3). Chapters 9 and 10 share common themes, including both legitimate royal leadership in Judah and the restoration of Israel; but they develop them differently. They constitute parallel rather than successive visions. It seems that 11:1-3 was composed as a poetic appendix to chap. 10. As does 10:10, 11:1-3 refers to Lebanon and concludes with the shepherd motif of 10:3. Apart from these verbal associations, 11:1-3 celebrates what 10:3-12 envisions. Of course, 11:1-3 now introduces the shepherd narrative of 11:4-14(17), and 10:2 appears to have that narrative, and perhaps even chap. 13, in view.

Zechariah 10:1-2, Ask the Lord, Not Diviners. The first two verses of chap. 10 are not so obviously related as translations may suggest. At the same time, v. 3 introduces something, different from v. 2, that continues through the remainder of the chapter.

10:1. Chapter 10 opens with poetic praise of Yahweh as creator. Yahweh is the one who gives

rain in the spring (or late) season, who makes thunderbolts and rain showers, and thus vegetation. That Yahweh is depicted as producing thunderbolts, rain, and vegetation is unique to 10:1 and Job 38:25-27. The latter text declaims God's singular capacity to give the world its mysterious order. Such is certainly, if obliquely, a major issue in 10:3-12. One may contrast the rain that Yahweh gives to the drying-up of the Nile (v. 11). Egypt's agriculture, and hence its life, did not depend on seasonal rains but on the Nile's annual flood. But v. 1 does not discriminate; the rains that Yahweh gives are "for them," and the vegetation "for everyone."

10:2. This verse appears to proceed from the initial words of v. 1, "Ask from Yahweh . . . ," to which it contrasts the consulting of teraphim and diviners (cf. Jer 14:14). These have proffered only lies, vain dreams, and empty consolation. For that reason, the people wandered like sheep, and they suffer now because there is no shepherd. Since wandering is what a shepherd usually does with a flock (see Jer 31:24), the verse apparently anticipates v. 3b, which speaks of Judah as Yahweh's flock. They wandered, and suffer, without a shepherd (v. 2*b*). "Without a shepherd" elsewhere refers to the absence of leadership and (except for Num 27:17, regarding Joshua) to the absence of royal leadership (1 Kgs 22:17 = 2 Chr 8:16; Ezek 34:8, 23). Verse 4 addresses this problem, as did Zech 9:9-10 in quite different terms. The author of v. 2 blames this condition on the consultation of fraudulent diviners rather than of Yahweh. As a consequence, there is no shepherd such as David, whom Yahweh chose from among the sheepfolds to shepherd Judah and Israel (Ps 78:52, 70-72; cf. Jer 23:1-6).

Zechariah 10:3-12, Judah's Victory and Israel's Return. Verse 3*a,* which declares Yahweh's anger at the shepherds and the rams (rendered "leaders"), does not follow easily from v. 2. The problem is that there is no shepherd, yet in v. 3*a,* shepherds are the objects of Yahweh's anger. Evidently, these are not the same shepherds. Although "shepherds" almost always refers to Judah's own leaders, Jer 12:10-11 speaks of the "many shepherds" who have devastated Judah, referring to invading nations (similarly, Jer 49:19; 50:44).[115] In Isa 14:9 and Ezek 39:18, "rams"/"leaders" are international rulers and kings. Hence 10:3*a* refers to the nations and their leaders who rule Judah and keep Israel in dispersion. Verses 10-11 correlate the end of Assyrian and Egyptian sovereignty with Israel's return to the land. By contrast, v. 4 expresses Yahweh's attention to the shepherds and leaders, with the promise of legitimate royalty from Judah's house.[116] Thus vv. 4-12 follow and expand on both parts of v. 3, including the final clause: Judah's character as Yahweh's proud war horse.

The remainder of the chapter exists in two parts: Verses 4-6*a* concern the house of Judah, whereas vv. 6*b*-11 concern the house of Joseph (Ephraim, v. 7), or Israel. Verse 12 stands as a coda, referring to both houses. The transition in v. 6 is marked by Yahweh's first-person speech and even more by the different actions of Yahweh regarding the two houses: "I will strengthen the house of Judah, while the house of Joseph I will save; I will return them" to the land. God will strengthen Judah, or make it superior, in a battle that v. 5 describes. In turn, Judah's success in battle depends on the promise of a cornerstone and a tent peg from Judah (v. 4).

10:4-6a. "Cornerstone" (פִּנָּה *pinnâ*) is elsewhere a metaphor for a ruler (Judg 20:2), including royalty (Ps 118:22; Isa 19:13). "Tent peg" (יָתֵד *yātēd*) is more obscure, but Isa 20:20-25 uses the term to describe Eliakim, who bears the keys to David's house and is Yahweh's servant. Eliakim is a tent peg bearing, temporarily, the weight of royal responsibility. The cornerstone/tent peg comes from Judah's house, indicating that royalty from David's line is at issue in v. 4 (cf. the use of "Branch" in 3:8; 6:12). Finally, restoration of royal leadership is indicated by the term "commander" (נֹגֵשׂ *nôgēś*; NIV, "ruler"), which Isa 9:3[4]; 14:4 uses in reference to kings who have conquered Judah. This is the same word translated "oppressor" in 9:10. Zechariah 10:4 is the only place in the Bible where the term has a positive connotation and refers to a native ruler. Its decidedly martial character is appropriate to the context, in which Judah's Davidic line will also be a "battle bow."[117] In the future, Judah will no longer be governed by the shepherds and leaders with whom Yahweh is angry. Instead, Judah will have its own legitimate ruler and army.

This Judahite army will fight successfully, thanks to Yahweh's presence (vv. 5-6*a*). They will throw horse riders, or cavalry, into confusion ("shame"), as Yahweh does to Israel's foes (Ps 44:8[7]). Riders on horses symbolize Judah's presumably superior military foes (cf. Ezek 38:15; Hag 2:22). The latter text joins the promise that these will be overthrown with a messianic announcement to the Davidic Zerubbabel. A similar conjunction is apparent in vv. 4-5, but with a reverse logic. Here, the confounding of a cavalry follows, rather than precedes, the presence of a cornerstone and a tent peg.

Curiously, the enemy with a confounded cavalry is not identified (the battle seems otherwise to lack an enemy). According to v. 5, Judah will be like warriors; they will trample and fight, for Yahweh will be with them. But they neither trample nor fight anyone.[118] With alien shepherds and leaders under Yahweh's care (v. 3*a*) and its

115. William McKane, *A Critical and Exegetical Commentary on Jeremiah,* vol. 1, ICC (Edinburgh: T. & T. Clark, 1986) 274-78.

116. Carol Meyers and Eric Meyers, *Haggai and Zechariah 9–14,* AB 25C (New York: Doubleday, 1993) 198-202.

117. Eugene H. Merrill, *Haggai, Zechariah, Malachi: An Exegetical Commentary* (Chicago: Moody, 1994) 272-74; cf. Zech 9:10, 13.

118. Meyers and Meyers, *Zechariah 9–14,* 234-35.

own royal and military leadership restored, Judah's enemies are confounded and ephemeral.

10:6b-11. Attention shifts to Israel, to the house of Joseph/Ephraim, in these verses. There are two subunits here, vv. 6b-8 and vv. 9-11. In each one, Yahweh promises to bring Israel back to the land (vv. 6, 10) and to gather them from their places of exile (vv. 8, 10). Both of these actions are subsumed under the term "to save"(ישׁע *yāša‘*) in v. 6, which governs all that follows. God's promises to save Israel are based in divine compassion. Such sentiment is expressed in Yahweh's declaration, "I am their God and I will answer them" (v. 6).

The first element in this declaration resembles part of the covenant formula, which is encountered partially in 2:15[11] and fully in 8:8: "They will be my people, and I will be their God." The full formula occurs again in chap. 13, together with an expansion of the second element of Yahweh's declaration in 10:6: "They will call on my name, and I will answer them" (13:9). The declaration in v. 6 differs from these others in one crucial respect. In chaps. 2, 8, and 13, Yahweh promises to be "their God" after the nations or the exiles come to Jerusalem, or after a calamitous purging in Judah. Here, Yahweh says, "I am their God," speaking of a group—Israel—that is in exile and has been in exile since 721 BCE. That Yahweh is their God provides the basis for the promised return and gathering.

Although v. 6 introduces and governs both units, through v. 11, it also provides a transition to the martial imagery in vv. 7-8. With Yahweh as subject, the verb "rejected" (זנח *zānaḥ*) occurs most frequently in the psalms in the context of defeat (e.g., Pss 44:10-12[9-11]; 74:1-10; cf. Lam 2:7). In this context, rejection consists of abandonment to national, military foes. Israel will be as if Yahweh had not done this; consequently, and by contrast, Israel/Ephraim will be like a warrior reveling in victory (v. 7; cf. 9:15). As in the case of Judah, this is a victory without a palpable victim. The poet emphasizes Yahweh's intention to gather Israel, having redeemed them from the powers that hold them captive (v. 8a; cf. Jer 31:11).

The last sentence in v. 8 should be translated, "They [Israel] will multiply as before."[119] This un-

derstanding sets the context for the promise in v. 10 that Israel's population will overflow even the agriculturally inhospitable lands of Lebanon and Gilead. However, this promise depends on v. 9, which opens the second unit of vv. 6-11. Most interpreters emend the beginning of the verse to read, "Though I scattered [or sowed] them among the peoples," referring to the scattering of Israel after 721 BCE. But in the MT (and LXX and Vg) the verb has a future tense, and Yahweh's "sowing" of Israel or Judah always has the positive sense that the people or their prosperity will increase (Jer 31:27; Ezek 36:9; Hos 2:25[23]). It is interesting to observe that Nahum tells the Assyrian king that seed will not again be sown from his name—i.e., his name will not be perpetuated (Nah 1:14). Exactly the opposite is promised Israel in 10:9; Yahweh will sow them, even among the peoples. Even in the most remote places they will remember Yahweh and sustain their children and will return (v. 9).[120]

The final verse in this unit (v. 11) recalls the exodus—here a second exodus from Assyria and Egypt. It abruptly ends Yahweh's first-person speech (vv. 6-10) to describe Yahweh's way through the sea (in MT and Vg, the verbs are third-person singular, with Yahweh as subject). Psalm 77 uses this imagery to refer to the first exodus, in which Yahweh led Israel "like a flock" through the mighty waters (Ps 77:17-21[16-20]). In v. 11, the Lord strikes the waves and dries up the Nile's waters (cf. Isa 37:25). As a result, Assyria loses its sovereignty ("pride") and Egypt its scepter. Elsewhere in the OT, nations are characterized as mighty, roaring waters (Isa 17:12-14). Against such, God acts as creator, imposing order on chaos, subduing enemies, and establishing Israel and its king (Pss 33:6-14; 89:9-27[8-26]). In these texts, as in v. 11, cosmic and political order are joined. This allusion to creation resonates with claims about Yahweh as creator, as articulated in v. 1.

10:12. The coda returns to v. 6, both of which promise that Yahweh will strengthen the people, now including both Judah and Israel. Thus united and strengthened, they will move in Yahweh's name. This statement resembles that of Mic 4:5,

---

119. Meyers and Meyers, *Zechariah 9–14,* 215.

120. On the verb translated "sustain," see Norbert Lohfink, "Deuteronomy 6:24; לחיתנו [*lĕḥayyōtēnû*] 'To Maintain' Us," ed. M. Fishbane, E. Tov (Winona Lake, Ind.: Eisenbrauns, 1992) 111-19.

"We will walk in the name of our God forever." Here the verb is reflexive, however, as it is in 2 Sam 7:7, where God says, "I have moved about among all the tribes of Israel" without being located in one sanctuary. The statement in this verse evinces not only continued devotion to Yahweh, but also the expansive freedom that Yahweh promises to grant Judah and Israel.

REFLECTIONS

1. That Yahweh is the creator (10:1) may seem like an abstraction when compared with the details and problems of history. Indeed, in some ways language about creation is an abstraction, a diversion from political and military matters depicted in Zech 10:3-12. Zechariah begins by diverting our attention to Yahweh as the creator and sustainer of life. Everything depends on the creator. As in Psalm 136, there is no discontinuity between Yahweh the creator "who gives food to all flesh" (Ps 136:25) and Yahweh who delivers Israel from their enemies (Ps 136:10-24). In Zech 10:1, Yahweh brings the spring rain, a timely rain at the end of the growing season. Since Yahweh is sowing a late crop (10:9), spring rains will be essential.

The presence of creation theology in a text that also articulates the vision of restoration in the concrete language of nations and armies points to the theological complexity and density of Israel's language and experience of God in its life. While many in the contemporary church feel that choices must be made in order to identify *the* appropriate language about God, the faithful of Israel suffered under no such illusion. God was glimpsed in the spring rain as well as in the political struggles of one people and one nation. Zechariah's eschatological vision encompassed both; the restoration of God's peace and reign exceeded any one set of images and theological yearnings.

2. Zechariah 10 fully endorses the restoration envisioned in chap. 9. The program of restoration in chap. 10 gives full attention to Ephraim (Joseph/Israel), fleshing out references that were enigmatic in chap. 9 (e.g., 9:10, 13). Yahweh will save and restore the people of Ephraim to their land. This restoration attests to the remarkably durable memory of Israel's exile and dispersion and to the equally durable hope for its restoration. To be sure, this memory and hope cohere with the expectations that a son of David—another Solomon—will administer a united kingdom (9:9-10). But this hope is given a theological basis in Yahweh's mercy and thus in Yahweh's changed disposition.

The description of God's behavior in these verses is remarkable. In intense anger, Yahweh banished Israel "from his presence" (2 Kgs 17:18; cf. Zech 10:3). But now, in compassion, God will regard them as not rejected (Zech 10:6). Ultimately this hope *and* God's compassion and capacity for change are grounded in the divine self: "Because I am Yahweh." The text adds "their God," not as a qualification or extension, but because Yahweh is never other than Israel's God. Theologies that adhere to a strict notion of the immutability of God miss the power of the witness of this text. The intimacy of Yahweh's connections with the chosen people is evident in God's willingness to change for them, to have compassion where God had once willed judgment.

Zechariah 11:1-3, Trees and Shepherds Wail

NIV	NRSV
11 Open your doors, O Lebanon, so that fire may devour your cedars! ²Wail, O pine tree, for the cedar has fallen; the stately trees are ruined! Wail, oaks of Bashan; the dense forest has been cut down! ³Listen to the wail of the shepherds; their rich pastures are destroyed! Listen to the roar of the lions; the lush thicket of the Jordan is ruined!	**11** Open your doors, O Lebanon, so that fire may devour your cedars! ² Wail, O cypress, for the cedar has fallen, for the glorious trees are ruined! Wail, oaks of Bashan, for the thick forest has been felled! ³ Listen, the wail of the shepherds, for their glory is despoiled! Listen, the roar of the lions, for the thickets of the Jordan are destroyed!

COMMENTARY

Should we read this text in the context of chap. 10 or in the context of 11:4-17? Contemporary scholarship is divided on the answer, and each side can mount good arguments.[121] The larger literary context determines how we regard the shepherds of v. 3 and, indeed, the entire poem. Does it celebrate what 10:3-12 promises, or does it foreshadow the conflicts of vv. 4-14 and the shepherd's fate in v. 17? As a transitional piece in the larger collection of 9:1–11:17, it does both. This is not just an ambivalent literary judgment; it recognizes the ambiguity of the shepherd motif in Second Zechariah.

This short poem combines two kinds of imagery. In vv. 1-2, the imagery is arboreal: Lebanon's cedars, the cypress, the oaks of Bashan, the thick forest. Such imagery is also present in v. 3, which refers to the dense foliage (the "pride" or "thicket") of the Jordan. Here we find pastoral language. It is the shepherds who will wail, as Bashan's oaks do in v. 2, and it is lions that will roar, because they will lose their cover when Jordan's thickets are destroyed.

This pastoral imagery works at more than one level. First, the geographical references to Lebanon and Bashan recall 10:10, which promises that Israel will expand into and beyond Lebanon and Gilead, to the south of Bashan. To make Lebanon and Bashan hospitable to agriculture and grazing would require their deforestation, which vv. 1-2

envision (cf. Mic 7:14).[122] But the imagery of vv. 1-3 works at a second, symbolic level. In Isa 2:13 the cedars of Lebanon and oaks of Bashan are among the proud and lofty things that will be brought low when Yahweh is exalted (cf. Ps 29:9-5). As symbols of pride and strength, the cedars of Lebanon and other trees represent nations (so Amos 1:8). In Ezek 17:3, the cedar of Lebanon is Judah's king. Ezekiel 31 describes Assyria as a cedar of Lebanon, which Yahweh cut down and sent to Sheol to join the other trees (the nations) that were Assyria's allies and victims (Ezek 31:3, 16-17). Isaiah depicts God's defense of Jerusalem against an invading army, probably Assyrian, using similar imagery: Yahweh will cut down the tallest trees and the thickets of the forest, "and Lebanon with its majestic trees will fall" (Isa 10:33-34). Zechariah, too, speaks of Lebanon's majestic trees (v. 2). Against the background of Isaiah and Ezekiel, Zechariah's imagery possesses a political quality.

This seems especially clear in v. 3, which refers again to the shepherds. They will wail, because their "glory" is ruined. The Hebrew words translated "majestic" (אדרים 'addirîm) in v. 2 and "glory" (אדרתם 'addartām) in v. 3 are cognate. In the OT, neither verse explicitly mentions trees, but the context of v. 2 strongly suggests that "majestic [ones]" refers to Lebanon's majestic cedars. However, in v. 3, the term used for "glory" (אדרת

---

121. Katrina J. A. Larkin, *The Eschatology of Second Zechariah* (Kampen: Pharos, 1994) 293-95.

122. Meyers and Meyers, *Haggai and Zechariah 9–14,* 240.

'adderet) means in other places "robe" or "mantle" (see 13:4; in Jonah 3:6, it refers to the Assyrian king's royal robe). The same veiled allusion to sovereignty occurs in the last part of v. 3, where the young lions roar because the thickets of the Jordan are ruined. What is here translated "thickets" (גאון *gā'ôn*) is in 10:11 the pride or sovereignty of Assyria. Zechariah borrows the term "thickets"/"pride of the Jordan" from Jeremiah, to whom it is otherwise unique. The borrowing is deft. In Jer 49:19; 50:44, Yahweh promises to come like a lion from the thickets of the Jordan against a safe pasture (Edom and Babylon) and asks, "Who is the shepherd who can stand before me?" By taking over the phrase "thickets of the Jordan," Zech v. 3 alludes both to pride/sovereignty and to the shepherds whom Yahweh opposes. To make the political reference evident, Zechariah changes Jeremiah's "lion" to "young lions," a metaphor for kings.

Yahweh, too, can act the part of a young lion. In Jer 25:34-38, Yahweh will strike out like a young lion against the ruler of all nations, the shepherds and "majestic ones of the flock" (cf. v.

2). Just as in Jer 25:34, 36, the shepherds will wail (v. 3). But in Zechariah the young lions are rulers, who wail along with the shepherds. Both are deprived of their majesty, as are Lebanon's cedars.

Structurally, v. 1 governs the poem: Fire will consume Lebanon's cedars, and the wailing of v. 2 is in response to that event. It is a response analogous to that of the Philistines upon the destruction of Tyre (9:3-7). The imagery shifts in v. 3. It is impossible to correlate either the trees of vv. 1-2 or the shepherds and lions of v. 3 with specific nations and rulers. The whole of 11:1-3 celebrates what is envisioned and announced in 10:3-11 (esp. 10:11). Still one cannot detect precise allusions to nations like Assyria and Egypt. The cedar(s) of Lebanon (v. 1) are the prime example: What ruler or what nation in Second Zechariah's era could count as a cedar of Lebanon? Rather, and especially in view of its dependence on earlier prophetic texts, Zech 11:1-3 constructs a paradigm of Yahweh's action against what is proud and lofty, especially in a political sense.

REFLECTIONS

The first two verses of Zechariah 11 depict an ecological disaster. Trees function here as figures of power and pride. In another biblical text, the cedars of Lebanon rejoice at the death of a tyrant, because he will no longer come to cut them (Isa 14:8). Here, too, cedars are a figure, but kings did cut them: Solomon built the Temple with them (1 Kgs 5:13). Within the figurative language of Zech 11:1-2, we glimpse a recognition that political and demographic rearrangements, including those sponsored by Yahweh, have natural consequences. Some of these consequences we would recognize as disastrous. This text thus reminds us that human activity does not exist in a vacuum. On the contrary, human activity, and particularly human deployment of power and might, is inextricably bound to the life of the natural world. What was true in Zechariah's time is even more true today. Human decisions and actions concerning war, international alliances, consumerism, and the way nations allocate their economic resources impinge upon more than other human beings. The consequences are felt throughout the created order. All creation groans for its redemption (Rom 8:22).

Zechariah 11:4-17, The Shepherd's Story

NIV

4This is what the LORD my God says: "Pasture the flock marked for slaughter. 5Their buyers slaughter them and go unpunished. Those who sell them say, 'Praise the LORD, I am rich!' Their own shepherds do not spare them. 6For I will no longer have pity on the people of the land," declares the LORD. "I will hand everyone over to his neighbor and his king. They will oppress the land, and I will not rescue them from their hands."

7So I pastured the flock marked for slaughter, particularly the oppressed of the flock. Then I took two staffs and called one Favor and the other Union, and I pastured the flock. 8In one month I got rid of the three shepherds.

The flock detested me, and I grew weary of them 9and said, "I will not be your shepherd. Let the dying die, and the perishing perish. Let those who are left eat one another's flesh."

10Then I took my staff called Favor and broke it, revoking the covenant I had made with all the nations. 11It was revoked on that day, and so the afflicted of the flock who were watching me knew it was the word of the LORD.

12I told them, "If you think it best, give me my pay; but if not, keep it." So they paid me thirty pieces of silver.

13And the LORD said to me, "Throw it to the potter"—the handsome price at which they priced me! So I took the thirty pieces of silver and threw them into the house of the LORD to the potter.

14Then I broke my second staff called Union, breaking the brotherhood between Judah and Israel.

15Then the LORD said to me, "Take again the equipment of a foolish shepherd. 16For I am going to raise up a shepherd over the land who will not care for the lost, or seek the young, or heal the injured, or feed the healthy, but will eat the meat of the choice sheep, tearing off their hoofs.
17"Woe to the worthless shepherd,
　who deserts the flock!
May the sword strike his arm and his right eye!
　May his arm be completely withered,
　his right eye totally blinded!"

NRSV

4Thus said the LORD my God: Be a shepherd of the flock doomed to slaughter. 5Those who buy them kill them and go unpunished; and those who sell them say, "Blessed be the LORD, for I have become rich"; and their own shepherds have no pity on them. 6For I will no longer have pity on the inhabitants of the earth, says the LORD. I will cause them, every one, to fall each into the hand of a neighbor, and each into the hand of the king; and they shall devastate the earth, and I will deliver no one from their hand.

7So, on behalf of the sheep merchants, I became the shepherd of the flock doomed to slaughter. I took two staffs; one I named Favor, the other I named Unity, and I tended the sheep. 8In one month I disposed of the three shepherds, for I had become impatient with them, and they also detested me. 9So I said, "I will not be your shepherd. What is to die, let it die; what is to be destroyed, let it be destroyed; and let those that are left devour the flesh of one another!" 10I took my staff Favor and broke it, annulling the covenant that I had made with all the peoples. 11So it was annulled on that day, and the sheep merchants, who were watching me, knew that it was the word of the LORD. 12I then said to them, "If it seems right to you, give me my wages; but if not, keep them." So they weighed out as my wages thirty shekels of silver. 13Then the LORD said to me, "Throw it into the treasury"a—this lordly price at which I was valued by them. So I took the thirty shekels of silver and threw them into the treasurya in the house of the LORD. 14Then I broke my second staff Unity, annulling the family ties between Judah and Israel.

15Then the LORD said to me: Take once more the implements of a worthless shepherd. 16For I am now raising up in the land a shepherd who does not care for the perishing, or seek the wandering,b or heal the maimed, or nourish the healthy,c but devours the flesh of the fat ones, tearing off even their hoofs.
17 Oh, my worthless shepherd,
　who deserts the flock!

aSyr: Heb it to the potter　bSyr Compare Gk Vg: Heb the youth
cMeaning of Heb uncertain

NRSV

May the sword strike his arm
and his right eye!
Let his arm be completely withered,
his right eye utterly blinded!

COMMENTARY

The poem in vv. 1-3 celebrates the loss of sovereignty and power that nations and their rulers (shepherds) have suffered, as those were depicted in 10:3-12. At the same time, vv. 1-3 provides a transition into the narrative of vv. 4-14 and its conclusion in vv. 15-17. Here the focus of Second Zechariah shifts from international affairs and the restoration of Judah and Israel to matters internal to the community. The shepherds are not kings of other nations, but leaders within Judah. Read as an introduction to vv. 4-17, the poem in vv. 1-3 acquires quite a different sense. It portends the internal dissolution that vv. 4-17 narrate and that chaps. 12–14 extend and variously resolve.[123] Already, 10:2 prepared for this reading and for the description of Judah as a shepherdless flock. Verses 4-17 pursue that description in narrative fashion.[124]

Only here within chaps. 9–14 (perhaps excepting 14:5) does the author assume a prophetic persona. The messenger formula, so common to First Zechariah, occurs only in 11:4, where Yahweh instructs Zechariah to tend the sheep. Yahweh issues further instructions in vv. 13 and 15. Moreover, the entire text is a first-person report; it is an autobiographical narrative. In constructing it, Zechariah draws heavily on Jeremiah and Ezekiel. These earlier prophets made extensive use of the shepherd metaphor (esp. Jer 23:1-8; Ezekiel 34). Both of these texts criticize Judah's shepherds for their neglect of the flock, and both envision a restored Davidic house as the solution (Jer 23:5-6; Ezek 34:23-30). Zechariah 11 seems to endorse the criticism, if not the solution, but its use of the shepherd/flock metaphor is rather free. Further, the two staffs that Zechariah takes

as his insignia (11:7) recall the two sticks that Ezekiel took to symbolize the enduring union of Judah and Israel (Ezek 37:15-28). In chap. 11, that union is fractured (v. 14). However, it is unlikely that Zechariah is engaged in a "polemical dialogue with the Ezekielian vision of the future."[125] If a polemic is involved, it is more directly with the vision of the future expressed in chaps. 9–10, which expect a restored Judah and Israel under traditional, Davidic leadership.

Zechariah 11:4-17 is made up of three sections: (1) vv. 4-6, Zechariah's commission and the rationale for it; (2) vv. 7-14, the execution of that commission; and (3) vv. 15-17, a second commission, of which Zechariah's actions in vv. 7-14 are exemplary or paradigmatic. These three parts of the narrative are integrally related, with vv. 15-17 serving as an interpretation of the whole. Notably, in v. 15 Yahweh instructs Zechariah to "take up again the tools of a foolish shepherd." In other words, in vv. 4-14 Zechariah has acted the role of a foolish shepherd, a role assigned him in vv. 4-6. In vv. 16-17, Yahweh tells Zechariah that his actions have been not just paradigmatic, but portentous: They portend those of a worthless shepherd, who—just as Zechariah did (v. 9)—will abandon the flock. This is a shepherd whom Yahweh alone will raise up, but will nevertheless punish (v. 17), a sequence that corresponds to Yahweh's enigmatic purposes as announced in vv. 4-6.

11:4-6. In the report of his commission, Zechariah refers to "Yahweh, my God" (v. 4). This peculiar expression anticipates 13:9, when the survivors of an extreme judgment will themselves affirm, in response to Yahweh's own affirmation of them, that "Yahweh is my God." But in chap. 11, Zechariah stands alone in this relation, which issues in a commission to "shepherd the sheep

---

123. P. Hanson, *The Dawn of Apocalyptic* (Philadelphia: Fortress, 1975) 335-37.

124. Paul L. Redditt, "The Two Shepherds in Zechariah 11:4-17," *CBQ* 55 (1993) 676-86.

125. Hanson, *The Dawn of Apocalyptic*, 345.

destined for slaughter." This term for "slaughter" (הרגה *hărēgâ*) occurs only in 11:4, 7 and in Jeremiah, who asks God to treat the wicked as "sheep for slaughter . . . on the day of slaughter" (Jer 12:3; cf. Jer 7:32; 19:6). In Zechariah's case, it is those buying the sheep who slaughter them with impunity, while those selling the sheep get rich and bless Yahweh for it (v. 5*a*). Tending the sheep are shepherds who have no pity on them (v. 5*b*). The pronouns in the MT suggest that "their" (masc.) refers to those who sell and buy the sheep, while "them" (fem.) refers to the sheep. In other words, the shepherds are in the employ of the sheep traders and have no pity on the sheep they tend—sheep destined for slaughter (cf. Ezek 34:3). All of this Yahweh tells Zechariah in assigning him to shepherd the sheep.

Yahweh gives the reason for this assignment in v. 6, which briefly abandons the shepherd/sheep metaphor: "Because *I* will no longer have pity on the land's inhabitants" (reading "land" with the NIV, rather than "earth"). Strangely, the pitiless and presumably contemptible shepherds of v. 5 represent the stance Yahweh is now taking, leaving people at the mercy of one another and captive to the will of their king. "Into the hand of a king" means defeat and captivity (Judg 3:8), of which Nebuchadnezzar is the best example. In Jer 21:7, Yahweh promises to give Jerusalem's survivors into the hands of King Nebuchadnezzar, and "he shall strike them down with the edge of the sword; he shall not pity them, or spare them, or have compassion" (NRSV). In this respect, Nebuchadnezzar was the exact instrument of God's own pitiless judgment: "I will not pity or spare or have compassion" on the people of Jerusalem (Jer 13:4; cf. Ezek 5:11). Yahweh's stance in 11:6 recalls an earlier time and past judgments. The result will be similar to the situation described in 7:14 and 8:10: anarchy, oppression, and devastation. Here God offers no grounds for this stance. Yahweh seems to contribute to the deplorable state of affairs described metaphorically in v. 5, promising that "I will deliver no one" (v. 6).

11:7-14. Based on his commission, along with its distressing rationale, Zechariah enacts his role. He shepherds the sheep destined for slaughter, and he does so "on behalf of the sheep merchants" (v. 7).[126] The buyers and sellers of v. 5 are here sheep merchants (v. 11), and Zechariah would presumably serve their interests, as did the shepherds in v. 5. But the first part of the narrative (vv. 7-9) tells a more complicated story. After becoming the shepherd, Zechariah performs three actions: (1) He takes two shepherd's staffs and names them Favor (or Pleasantness) and Unity, (2) he eliminates "the three shepherds," and (3) he abandons the sheep.

11:7-9. The names Zechariah gives his two staffs gain added significance in vv. 10-14, but here they indicate the positive and beneficial character of Zechariah's shepherding—beneficial for the sheep, which the staffs protect and guide, keeping the flock together. Zechariah eliminates (with the suggestion of violence) the three shepherds, presumably those in the employ of the merchants.

It has proven futile to try to identify these three shepherds, or to determine why there are three.[127] Certainly, they represent leaders in the community, and perhaps all of them, but the text leaves matters open. However, it is in the interest of the sheep that Zechariah eliminates these shepherds. So it is surprising that Zechariah next reports (v. 8*b*): "I could no longer bear them, and they were fed up with me." He refers not to the three shepherds, but to the sheep, and their mutual disgust prompts his resignation (v. 9): "So I said, 'I will not shepherd you.' " He abandons the sheep to death, to loss, and to self-destruction. In doing so, Zechariah opens the way for the disastrous situation Yahweh announces in v. 6.

11:10-14. The remainder of the narrative describes Zechariah's subsequent actions, framed by breaking his staffs, Favor (v. 10) and Unity (v. 14). Between these actions, Zechariah discusses his wages with the sheep merchants (vv. 12-13). To all of this, Zechariah's action in v. 9 (abandoning the flock) is the backdrop.

In explaining his breaking the two staffs, Zechariah again departs from, or modifies, the sheep/shepherd metaphor. Breaking the first, Favor, he explains as annulling "the covenant I made with all the peoples." This recalls the covenant of peace God promises in Ezek 34:23-25; 37:24-26, a covenant that will leave Israel and Judah secure in the land, safe from predators. In

---

126. Carol Meyers and Eric Meyers, *Haggai and Zechariah 9–14*, AB 25C (New York: Doubleday, 1993) 261-62.

127. Hinckley G. Mitchell, *A Critical and Exegetical Commentary on Haggai and Zechariah*, ICC (Edinburgh: T. & T. Clark, 1912) 306-7.

Ezekiel, this promise reverses current circumstances, in which the shepherds "do not shepherd the sheep" (Ezek 34:3), just as Zechariah now does not do. But Ezekiel also promises that Israel and Judah will be gathered from all over into a single, united nation under one Davidic shepherd (Ezek 37:21-24). This fraternal relation, too, Zechariah annuls, as he explains in breaking the second staff, Unity (v. 14). What Ezekiel promises for the future, seconded in Zechariah 9–10, Zechariah here treats as a reality that is to be annulled.[128]

A "covenant with all the peoples" (v. 10) is attested nowhere else. On the basis of vv. 7-8, one would expect this covenant to have been for the benefit of the sheep, for their protection, on analogy with Ezekiel's covenant of peace (cf. Hos 2:18[20]).[129] Its annulment again exposes the sheep to the dire consequences now adumbrated in vv. 9 and 16. This act is intended for the benefit of the sheep merchants, freed to prey on the sheep. The merchants recognize it as Yahweh's word (v. 11), just as, in v. 5, the sheep sellers blessed Yahweh for their gain. Consequently, these merchants are prepared to pay Zechariah a lordly sum, thirty shekels of silver, after he invites them to judge whether he merits any wage at all (vv. 12-13). Obviously, both they and Zechariah regard his resignation to have benefited them.

For the first time since v. 4, Yahweh speaks to Zechariah and tells him what to do with his wages: cast them to the potter, or to the treasury. The textual witnesses are confusing; the MT reads "potter," the Syriac "treasury," the LXX "furnace" or "foundry" (Matt 27:5-8 preserves both "potter" and "treasury"). In all events, Zechariah's wages were deposited in the Temple, which suggests that "treasury" is the better reading. Priests are in charge of this treasury (2 Chr 29:6-9; Neh 7:69-70 = Ezra 2:68-69; Mal 3:8). It may also be significant that Zechariah describes the thirty shekels to be his value in their eyes. Leviticus 27 specifies the number of shekels equivalent to the "life-worth" of various individuals, who could donate that amount to the sanctuary/Temple as

a way of redeeming their "life" from obligatory devotion to temple service.[130] According to one interpretation, "the valuation of persons" was a kind of maintenance tax for the Temple (2 Kgs 12:4[5]).[131] Zechariah's value was estimated at thirty shekels, which he paid to the temple priests and which freed him from further obligation. (In Nehemiah 5, debt slavery exacerbated by heavy taxation and rapacious "governors" prompted reform measures, over which the priests had charge [Neh 5:12].)

In this narrative, the larger concerns and hopes regarding Judah's autonomy and security, along with the restoration of a united kingdom of Judah and Israel, stand alongside oblique references to internal conflicts. Still the sheep merchants have no fixed identity. They could be "all the peoples" with whom the shepherd has contracted to preserve the sheep. They could be the priestly administrators of the Temple-centered economy. And they could be the civil, even Persian, administrators of the Judean province. All of these may be seen as preying on the sheep, who detest the shepherd's leadership (v. 8*b*). In the end, hope for a united Judah and Israel is broken, as is the covenant with all the peoples. In chap. 12, "all the peoples" come in siege against Jerusalem (12:2). Zechariah's last reported act in chap. 11 is to break the staff Unity; after 12:1, Second Zechariah does not again mention Israel.

11:15-17. Zechariah's abdication is to be temporary, since God commissions him to take up again the instruments of a foolish shepherd (v. 15). The entire narrative in vv. 4-14 is exemplary. It resembles judgments pronounced in Ezekiel, in Jeremiah, and, before that, in Isaiah (Isa 9:13-20[19-21]). Yahweh is "raising up" another shepherd. In Jeremiah and Ezekiel, this raising up provides reason for hope, but not here. Yahweh is now raising up a shepherd in the manner that Zechariah has demonstrated: one who abandons the flock to the depredations (vv. 9, 16) that characterized Israel's shepherds of the past (cf. Ezek 34:1-10). This shepherd is not just foolish; he is worthless and is to be struck with a sword and rendered powerless (v. 17).

In this second commission, Yahweh calls Zechariah

128. P. Hanson, *The Dawn of Apocalyptic* (Philadelphia: Fortress, 1975) 343-45.

129. André Caquot, "Breve remarques sur l'allegorie des Pasteurs en Zacaharie 11," *Melanges bibliques et orientaux en l'honneur de M. Delcor*, ed. A. Caquot et al. (Neukirchen-Vluyn: Neukirchener Verlag, 1985) 45-55.

130. Baruch A. Levine, "Leviticus," *ABD* 4 (1992) 318.

131. Mordechai Cogan and Hayim Tadmor, *II Kings,* AB 11 (New York: Doubleday, 1988) 135-37.

to take up again "the equipment of a . . . shepherd." The term occurs elsewhere only in 1 Sam 17:40, where it refers to David's equipment. Likewise, only David has shepherd's staffs (v. 7; cf. 1 Sam 17:40-43). If chap. 11 is implicitly critical of the priestly establishment, it is also suspicious of hopes lodged in a shepherd like David. These criticisms do not spare prophets, for it is expressly as a prophet that Zechariah enacts his role. He abandons the sheep (the community) to predation and destruction (v. 16) of the sort that Ezekiel describes (Ezek 34:1-10) and that characterized Judah's last kings (Jer 22:6-30). In chap. 11, there is no redeeming office—not even a faithful population—in which hope may be lodged. Hence, these verses set the stage for the violent expectations of chaps. 12–14.

REFLECTIONS

Its interpreters have been inclined to regard Zech 11:4-17 as among the most complex texts in the OT. Its difficulties run very deep, indeed—presenting the reader with disturbing images of prophecy and of the role of political and religious leaders in the safekeeping of a people.

1. Interpreters have seen in this text the reflection of events from virtually every century of Israel's history, from the exodus to the Roman conquest. They have identified the three shepherds of 11:8 with everyone from Moses and his siblings to Judas Maccabeus and his.[132] Thus Zechariah's words are both a reflection on the past and a projection of the future. Chapters 9–10 have also regarded Yahweh's past action, and Israel's own past, as paradigmatic, envisioning a future restoration. Zechariah 11 complicates that vision. The past remains paradigmatic, but as a paradigm of dissolutions and Yahweh's judgment, not of restoration.

In one respect, Zechariah follows his primary exemplar, Ezekiel's oracle against the shepherds (Ezekiel 34). "Here too," Walter Zimmerli says of Ezekiel 34, "in marked distance from what is merely contemporary, the oracle is directed to the history of Israel as a whole."[133] Of course, Zechariah means also to say something contemporary, something about the present and the future. But what Yahweh says about the future in 11:15-17 reflects "the history of Israel as a whole." The future will continue the past that has been enacted in Zechariah's own narrative (11:4-14).

Does this oracle simply underscore the familiar adage "Those who forget their history are doomed to repeat it"? Perhaps. But the theological dynamics of this text seem richer and more complex than that. In the details of this narrative and its symbolism, Zechariah holds a mirror up to the faith community in which it can see not only its past, but also its present. As in the poem of Zech 11:1-3, this narrative presents a dense portrait of actions and their consequences, of brokenness with God and brokenness in human community. Israel is allowed to read its history through God's eyes and to see how far it has fallen from God's hopes for God's shepherds. It is a sobering picture. The contemporary reader is left to wonder who in its context has the strength and honesty to summon the church to its future by telling it the sobering story of its history.

2. To read the first-person singular voice of this oracle as "Zechariah" is a construction of the narrative and of its location in the book. More than that, the autobiographical narrative (11:4-17) constructs a prophet as a character in the text, one who hears and acts with authority in accord with the words "thus says the LORD." In their symbolic actions and proclamations, prophets before Zechariah have represented Yahweh's judgment and the people who suffer it. But in astonishing fashion, Zechariah here represents those shepherds who tire of their flock

---

132. Mitchell, *Haggai and Zechariah*, 306-7.
133. Walter Zimmerli, *Ezekiel 2*, Hermeneia (Philadelphia: Fortress, 1983) 214.

and abandon it (11:9) and of the shepherd who will behave so and suffer the sword as a result (11:15-17). The word of the Lord thus calls Zechariah to enact and to embody the lamentable history (and future?) of Israel's shepherds as a whole. The writer has created a bleak picture of the life of God's people. Such a perverse prophetic commission seems to undercut the very authority of the prophet on which it depends. What, then, is the future of prophecy and the prophet? Zechariah 11 places this question before the faith community, but does not supply an answer. The answer seems to come in chap. 13, in which the shepherd is killed for the future of the flock (13:7-9).

3. Zechariah 11:12-13 plays a small, but nonetheless pivotal role in the Gospel passion narratives. In Matthew's account of Judas's betrayal of Jesus, the monetary sum for which Judas betrays Jesus, thirty pieces of silver, is drawn from Zechariah 11 (cf. Matt 26:16). Matthew is alone among the evangelists in including this detail (Matt 27:7-10). What is the significance of linking Judas's wages for betraying Jesus with the wages of the foolish shepherd? Perhaps Matthew attests that Judas, like the foolish shepherd of Zechariah 11, is determined to destroy the flock, in this case by destroying Jesus the shepherd. (The description of Judas as a thief in John 12:6 also identifies Judas as one whose actions threaten the safety of the flock; see John 10:1, 8, 10.)

ZECHARIAH 12:1–14:21, WAR, PURIFICATION, AND RE-CREATION

OVERVIEW

The superscription at the head of chap. 12 introduces a second collection comprising the remainder of Second Zechariah. The superscription itself issues first in an oracular formula ("says Yahweh"), which in turn introduces a hymn in praise of God the creator (see Commentary on 9:1). The language of this brief hymn is traditional, with its closest parallels in Second Isaiah. There, too, God is described as stretching out the heavens, founding the earth (Isa 51:13) and giving breath to people (Isa 42:5; cf. Ps 104:2, 5, 29). The specific language at the end of 12:1 ("who forms the spirit of humankind within") is appropriate to 12:10, where Yahweh promises to pour out a spirit of favor and supplication. However, in this first verse the human "spirit" is equivalent to breath and thus to life: Yahweh creates the heavens and the earth and gives life to people. This is not something that God has done only in the past; the participles in this verse describe Yahweh's character and Yahweh's capacity to do something new. The language is redolent of a new

creation and in this respect anticipates chap. 14 as much as it introduces chap. 12.

While the material in chaps. 12–14 is disparate, it features the repeated use of "on that day." This phrase fits the increasingly utopian character of this material with its eschatological scenarios of what will transpire "on that day." In addition, the phrase plays a significant role in structuring the material.[134] In the MT it has two different forms: "on that day" and "it will be on that day." The longer form, with the verb (typically not represented in translations), frequently introduces larger structural or logical units. For example, following the announcement in 12:1-2, "it will be on that day" (12:3) introduces a unit that extends through 12:8, which is itself divided into smaller units that describe what will happen "on that day" (12:4, 6, 8). Similarly, 12:9 introduces a unit that extends through 13:1.

134. David J. Clark, "Discourse Structure in Zechariah 9–14: Skeleton or Phantom?" in *Issues in Bible Translation,* ed. Philip C. Steine, UBS Monograph Series 3 (London: United Bible Societies, 1988) 64-80.

Zechariah 12:1–13:1, War and Purification

Zechariah 12:1-8, War Against Jerusalem

NIV

An Oracle

12 This is the word of the LORD concerning Israel. The LORD, who stretches out the heavens, who lays the foundation of the earth, and who forms the spirit of man within him, declares: ²"I am going to make Jerusalem a cup that sends all the surrounding peoples reeling. Judah will be besieged as well as Jerusalem. ³On that day, when all the nations of the earth are gathered against her, I will make Jerusalem an immovable rock for all the nations. All who try to move it will injure themselves. ⁴On that day I will strike every horse with panic and its rider with madness," declares the LORD. "I will keep a watchful eye over the house of Judah, but I will blind all the horses of the nations. ⁵Then the leaders of Judah will say in their hearts, 'The people of Jerusalem are strong, because the LORD Almighty is their God.'

⁶"On that day I will make the leaders of Judah like a firepot in a woodpile, like a flaming torch among sheaves. They will consume right and left all the surrounding peoples, but Jerusalem will remain intact in her place.

⁷"The LORD will save the dwellings of Judah first, so that the honor of the house of David and of Jerusalem's inhabitants may not be greater than that of Judah. ⁸On that day the LORD will shield those who live in Jerusalem, so that the feeblest among them will be like David, and the house of David will be like God, like the Angel of the LORD going before them."

NRSV

An Oracle.

12 The word of the LORD concerning Israel: Thus says the LORD, who stretched out the heavens and founded the earth and formed the human spirit within: ²See, I am about to make Jerusalem a cup of reeling for all the surrounding peoples; it will be against Judah also in the siege against Jerusalem. ³On that day I will make Jerusalem a heavy stone for all the peoples; all who lift it shall grievously hurt themselves. And all the nations of the earth shall come together against it. ⁴On that day, says the LORD, I will strike every horse with panic, and its rider with madness. But on the house of Judah I will keep a watchful eye, when I strike every horse of the peoples with blindness. ⁵Then the clans of Judah shall say to themselves, "The inhabitants of Jerusalem have strength through the LORD of hosts, their God."

⁶On that day I will make the clans of Judah like a blazing pot on a pile of wood, like a flaming torch among sheaves; and they shall devour to the right and to the left all the surrounding peoples, while Jerusalem shall again be inhabited in its place, in Jerusalem.

⁷And the LORD will give victory to the tents of Judah first, that the glory of the house of David and the glory of the inhabitants of Jerusalem may not be exalted over that of Judah. ⁸On that day the LORD will shield the inhabitants of Jerusalem so that the feeblest among them on that day shall be like David, and the house of David shall be like God, like the angel of the LORD, at their head.

COMMENTARY

The first part of chap. 12 describes a future battle involving the nations of the earth against Jerusalem, while in vv. 9-12 Yahweh promises to open a new initiative with the house of David and Jerusalem's inhabitants. The announcement of this initiative concludes in 13:1, which provides a transition to the discussion of the elimination of prophets (13:2-6).

Yahweh intends to make Jerusalem a "cup of reeling." The image of nations, or of Jerusalem, drinking from the cup of Yahweh's wrath is familiar (Isa 51:17-22; Jer 25:15-28). But none of the other texts uses the word סַף (*sap*), which occurs here. It can mean a "cup" for cultic use, but more commonly it means "threshold" (e.g., Isa 6:4; Jer 35:4). The image of all the peoples stumbling or reeling over Jerusalem's threshold is congruent with the same people injuring themselves trying to lift the "stone" Jerusalem (v. 3). The picture is of peoples and nations invading Jerusalem to plunder it.[135] Yahweh designs such reeling to benefit Jerusalem. It is at their own initiative that all of the world's nations come against Jerusalem (cf. 14:2), but Yahweh's intentions override theirs.

The second verse includes Judah in the siege against Jerusalem, but in a syntactically difficult, secondary way. It is hard to imagine siegeworks laid against a province or a population. This part of the verse anticipates the role of Judah in vv. 4-7.

Judah is especially prominent in vv. 1-7 and is referred to in four ways: as Judah (vv. 2, 7), as the "house of Judah" (v. 4), as the "clans of Judah" (vv. 5-6), and as the "tents of Judah" (v. 7). The latter two terms occur nowhere else in the OT (see below). "House of Judah" is common in the OT and occurs in both First and Second Zechariah, typically paired with the "house of Israel" (8:13; 10:6). In vv. 5, 7, however, Judah is clearly distinguished from the house of David and the "inhabitants of Jerusalem." Indeed, v. 7 acknowledges the potential for rivalry between these bodies. That there were religious and social conflicts between different groups in Persian-period Judah is evident from texts like Isaiah 56–66 as well as First and Second Zechariah (see Commentary on Zechariah 3; 6; 11). While conflicts over membership in the community, participation in the cult, land tenure, leadership, and power may lie behind chap. 12, they are not explicit. More directly relevant may be the efforts of Nehemiah, appointed by the Persians, to refortify Jerusalem and to give it "a new status . . . as an urban center within the imperial system."[136] In the mid-fifth century BCE, local power was vested in the heads of landed, paternal estates ("houses of the fathers"), whereas Jerusalem and the Temple served as a cultic and administrative center.[137] Since Jerusalem was also the seat of the Persian provincial administration and taxation, the possibility of tension existed. It would be exacerbated by new tax burdens due to refortification and the garrisoning of Persian troops. Chapter 12 does not exploit that tension, or potential rivalry, but ameliorates it: Judah will not suffer from the greater glory of David's house and the inhabitants of Jerusalem (v. 7).

Meyers and Meyers prefer to render the latter as "leaders of Jerusalem," rather than "inhabitants," to designate the entire royal bureaucracy under the patronage of the house of David.[138] The issue turns, in part, on the translation of יֹשְׁבֵי (*yōšĕbê*), which can bear either meaning (see Commentary on 9:5-6). The Meyerses argue that these verses reflect pre-exilic political organization projected onto the future; in the fifth century BCE, there was no Davidic house bestowing patronage on a royal bureaucracy in Jerusalem. The question of translation aside (I will use "inhabitants"), Zechariah envisions a restored, if chastened, Davidic house and a Jerusalem freed, with Judah's help, from any external oppression.

The creation of such a community is described in vv. 3-6. Following Yahweh's announcement in v. 3, "on that day" Yahweh promises to render armaments (horses and riders) harmless (v. 4), striking them with panic, madness, and blindness. The terms "panic" and "blindness" occur only here and in Deut 28:28 in a catalog of curses, where Yahweh threatens to strike Israel with these afflictions and let their enemies defeat them if they are faithless. Here that curse is reversed and applied to Israel's enemies. By contrast, Yahweh's eyes will open on the house of Judah, thereby extending the metaphor of 9:8.

The "clans of Judah" respond to this promise, affirming (the text is difficult) that the inhabitants of Jerusalem have strength "in Yahweh of hosts, their God" (v. 5). The affirmation is appropriate, given the association of Yahweh of hosts with Jerusalem/Zion and its defense, but the phrase

---

135. Meyers and Meyers, *Haggai and Zechariah 9–14*, 313.
136. Kenneth G. Hoglund, *Acahaemenid Imperial Administration in Syria-Palestine and the Missions of Ezra and Nehemiah*, SBLDS 125 (Atlanta: Scholars Press, 1992) 224.

137. Harold C. Washington, *Wealth and Poverty in the Instruction of Amenemope and the Hebrew Proverbs*, SBLDS 142 (Atlanta: Scholars Press, 1994) 156-65.
138. Meyers and Meyers, *Zechariah 9–14*, 324-25.

"their God" is striking. It does not suggest that Judah worshiped another God. Instead, the clans of Judah recognize Yahweh's intention to preserve Jerusalem (vv. 2-3), and they respond. More properly, Yahweh responds (v. 6), in the same terms as in vv. 2-3. There, Yahweh says twice, "I will make Jerusalem . . . " while here it is "I will make the clans of Judah. . . . " Yahweh's actions are, in this respect, the same toward Judah as toward Jerusalem. Everything depends on those actions. Yahweh will make Judah's clans like fire; a "flaming torch among the sheaves" recalls Samson's strategy against the Philistines (Judges 15).

Two consequences follow in v. 6b. First, Judah will conquer ("consume") "all of the surrounding peoples." This forms an inclusio with v. 2, where "all of the surrounding peoples" establish a siege against Jerusalem. Second, "Jerusalem will again dwell in its place, Jerusalem." In this apparent redundancy, the first "Jerusalem" likely refers to the population and the second to the city. Concerns for the repopulation of Jerusalem, using similar terms, are expressed elsewhere (Isa 44:26; Jer 17:25) as well as in Zech 2:4[8].

To guard against any aggrandizement by the Davidic house and the people of Jerusalem, Yahweh will "save the tents of Judah first" (v. 7). "Tents" occurs here in marked contrast to "clans" in vv. 5-6. Tents are not inferior dwellings, but homes, to which soldiers return after battle (e.g., 2 Sam 20:22) or to which people return after a national assembly (1 Kgs 8:66). Judah's clans are more like regiments involved in battle, while tents are appropriate to permanent dwellings on the land. With the qualification expressed in v. 7, David's house and Jerusalem are described in the grandest possible terms. "On that day," with Yahweh as a protecting shield (cf. 9:15), even Jerusalem's most bumbling citizen will be like David, who will be "like God" (v. 8). Such a claim (eerily reminiscent of the serpent's in Gen 3:5) was not unknown in the ancient world. A Babylonian prophecy from the sixth century BCE foresees that, after a succession of kings fail to do so, a new king will "provide justice in the land." His dynasty will endure forever, and "the kings of Uruk will exercise rulership like the gods."[139] However, this claim for David is immediately modified: "like an *angel* of Yahweh," a description applied to David in 2 Sam 19:27[28]. In that text, Mephiboseth, grandson of Saul, acknowledges David's power to do as he pleases and David's compassion in giving him a place of honor. The comparison forms a fitting transition to Zech 12:9–13:1.

139. Hermann Hunger and Stephen A. Kauffman, "A New Akkadian Prophecy Text," *JAOS* 95 (1975) 372-73.

Zechariah 12:9–13:1, Victory and Mourning

NIV

9"On that day I will set out to destroy all the nations that attack Jerusalem.

10"And I will pour out on the house of David and the inhabitants of Jerusalem a spirit[a] of grace and supplication. They will look on[b] me, the one they have pierced, and they will mourn for him as one mourns for an only child, and grieve bitterly for him as one grieves for a firstborn son. 11On that day the weeping in Jerusalem will be great, like the weeping of Hadad Rimmon in the plain of Megiddo. 12The land will mourn, each clan by itself, with their wives by themselves: the clan of the house of David and their wives, the clan of the house of Nathan and their wives, 13the

a10 Or *the Spirit*   b10 Or *to*

NRSV

9And on that day I will seek to destroy all the nations that come against Jerusalem.

10And I will pour out a spirit of compassion and supplication on the house of David and the inhabitants of Jerusalem, so that, when they look on the one[a] whom they have pierced, they shall mourn for him, as one mourns for an only child, and weep bitterly over him, as one weeps over a firstborn. 11On that day the mourning in Jerusalem will be as great as the mourning for Hadad-rimmon in the plain of Megiddo. 12The land shall mourn, each family by itself; the family of the house of David by itself, and their wives by themselves; the family of the house of Nathan by

a Heb *on me*

NIV

clan of the house of Levi and their wives, the clan of Shimei and their wives, 14and all the rest of the clans and their wives.

13 "On that day a fountain will be opened to the house of David and the inhabitants of Jerusalem, to cleanse them from sin and impurity."

NRSV

itself, and their wives by themselves; 13the family of the house of Levi by itself, and their wives by themselves; the family of the Shimeites by itself, and their wives by themselves; 14and all the families that are left, each by itself, and their wives by themselves.

13 On that day a fountain shall be opened for the house of David and the inhabitants of Jerusalem, to cleanse them from sin and impurity.

COMMENTARY

12:9-10a. This verse begins a new unit, closing off the international conflict of vv. 2-6 with Yahweh's summary statement: "On that day, I will all but destroy the nations coming against Jerusalem." Yahweh's posture toward the nations may be contrasted with Yahweh's new initiative toward the house of David and the inhabitants of Jerusalem: "I will pour out a spirit of favor and supplication" (v. 10a; similar references to pouring out the spirit occur in Ezek 39:29; Joel 2:28-29; in each case it is God's Spirit). Here it is a decidedly human spirit that is poured out (cf. Ezek 36:26). "Spirit" is often a metaphor for enabling power, and so here the spirit enables favor and supplication.

12:10b-11. Both translation and interpretation of these verses are difficult. It is possible to read, "they will look to me whom they have pierced," meaning that David's house and Jerusalem had pierced Yahweh.[140] But piercing (דקר *dāqar*) elsewhere in the OT always means physical violence and usually death (e.g., Num 25:8; 1 Sam 31:4); it does so expressly in 13:3. The mourning described in vv. 10b-12 is mourning "for him," the one pierced or stabbed. It seems preferable to take the MT's object marker before the relative pronoun as indicating an accusative of respect, allowing one to translate "concerning the one whom they pierced" (cf. LXX.)[141] But who was the victim?

He is not identified, and no precise identifica-

tion is possible. Instead of identifying the victim, the text describes the character and the extent of mourning over his death. It characterizes the mourning by comparing it first with that for an only and firstborn son. Only two individuals are described as only children: Isaac (Genesis 22) and Jepthah's unnamed daughter (Judges 11; cf. Jer 6:26; Amos 8:10). Abraham had every intention of sacrificing Isaac, and Jephthah needlessly sacrificed his daughter to fulfill a vow that he hoped would bring him victory in war. For the same purpose, Mesha, king of Moab, sacrificed his firstborn son, the crown prince, and won a reprieve from Israel's army (2 Kgs 3:27). Verse 10 draws David's house and Jerusalem's citizens into this circle of sacrifice.

Second, the text compares the mourning in Jerusalem to that of Hadad-Rimmon in Megiddo's plain. Hadad was the Syrian storm god, elsewhere known as Baal, and Rimmon was apparently a deity as well (2 Kgs 5:18). The reference here is geographical, however, and Hadad-Rimmon is likely an unknown place in the plain of Megiddo. That is where Josiah was killed by Pharaoh Necho in an ill-advised and tragic battle. The chronicler reports that Josiah was mourned by all Judah and Jerusalem and that Jeremiah composed laments for him that were being sung in the chronicler's day (fifth century BCE; see 2 Chr 36:20-25).[142] The mourning for this unknown victim will be like that for King Josiah. Closer to hand may be the memory of Gedaliah's assassination, which was still commemorated (7:5). Gedaliah, whom Neb-

---

140. Eugene H. Merrill, *Haggai, Zechariah, Malachi: An Exegetical Commentary* (Chicago: Moody, 1994) 320.
141. Paul Joüon and T. Muraoka, *A Grammar of Biblical Hebrew* (Rome: Pontifical Biblical Institute, 1991) #125 ("accusative of limitation or of specification").

142. Merrill, *Haggai, Zechariah, Malachi*, 323.

uchadnezzar left in charge of Judah, was stabbed to death by Ishmael, a member of the royal (Davidic) house (Jer 41:1-3).[143] These comparisons suggest that the unidentified victim in v. 10 had, or is given, royal status.

12:12-14. The extent of mourning, as described in these verses, seems to support suggestions about the victim's royal status. For purposes of mourning, the land is divided into families or clans, four of which are named. The families of David and Levi (or the Levites) represent royal and priestly leadership. Those of Nathan and Shimei are more obscure, since the Bible records several people of each name. One Nathan is a son of David (2 Sam 5:14), and a Shimei is the descendant through Gershom of Levi (Exod 6:17; Num 3:21). Why Zechariah chooses these rather obscure names is uncertain, but David/Nathan, Levi/Shimei seem to form pairs of royal and priestly families, representing the leadership of what can be called the house of David and the inhabitants of Jerusalem—a category that includes the remaining, unnamed families (v. 14). Their mourning, led by the official classes, is like that for an only son and crown prince, and for a king of Judah, whom they have stabbed.

143. Meyers and Meyers, *Haggai and Zechariah 9–14,* 341.

Yet this is not official public mourning; each family mourns alone, men and women by themselves. This picture stands in marked contrast to the public lamentation for Josiah, which expressly included both male and female singers (2 Chr 35:25). Indeed, the victim is not just anonymous, but entirely absent after v. 10. The text focuses entirely on the community's (on Jerusalem's) leadership and the qualities of favor and supplication that the spirit poured out by Yahweh will enable.

13:1. The promise of this verse is, like the mourning in 12:11-14, concomitant with the announcement in 12:9-10. On that day there will be a fountain for cleansing. Here, too, there are strong parallels with Ezek 36:25-29, a text that informs the continuation of the chapter in vv. 2-6. But this verse also looks back to 12:10, to the stabbing. Its terms are familiar from priestly legislation; Num 19:11-20 describes water provided for cleansing, specifically from impurity and uncleanness incurred by touching a dead body. David's house and Jerusalem's inhabitants will be cleansed of this defilement, which Hag 2:13-14 describes as contagious. Notably included among the defiling corpses in Numbers 19 is one "pierced with a sword" (Num 19:16), a piercing חלל (*ḥll*) suffered by the servant in Isaiah 53:5, 10).

REFLECTIONS

1. Zechariah 12 offers an alternative vision of the future, and the difficult narrative in chap. 11 has prepared for this. There Zechariah, enacting the role of shepherd, broke the covenant with all the peoples and the fraternity between Judah and Israel. In chap. 12 all the peoples come to prey on Jerusalem, and Judah alone is left to act in its defense.

This is an odd and unsettling vision of the future, as God is depicted as initiating both the attack on Judah and Judah's victory over its enemies. As in chap. 11, the picture of God and of the relationship between God and God's people is complex. Zechariah's vision knows almost no restraints; that is, the consequences of the breach in the covenant are painted on a large canvas with bold and sweeping strokes. In interpreting this vision in the contemporary setting, it is of the utmost importance to remember that this text is an expression of Zechariah's prophetic *vision* and not an objective reading of international history. The interpreter needs to struggle with this vision to discover what Zechariah is saying about God and God's people and not read it as a flat prophecy about international conflagration and the ultimate salvation of a chosen people. The broad strokes with which Zechariah paints this picture show that, for him, one could never domesticate questions about relationship with and fidelity to God. According to Zechariah, nothing about God and Judah's relationship with God is "done in a corner" (cf. Acts 26:16). Everything is at stake in the faith community's relationship with its God.

2. It is tempting to see in the anonymous victim of 12:10 a scapegoat, along the lines of René Girard's theory of mimetic desire, rivalry, and sacred violence.[144] It is simpler, though, to see in this victim someone who stood in the way—perhaps the way of the exaltation of the house of David. It is important to remember that, in the reality of fifth-century BCE politics, exaltation was itself only a matter of hope, but such hope is no small matter. To challenge powerfully held convictions about the future also challenges convictions about the present. Such challenges are dangerous. Prophets in Israel's history could so attest, and that line of challengers does not end with the biblical record. Centuries of martyrs and millions of victims, most as anonymous as the victim of Zech 12:10, attest to the dangers inherent in challenging long-held political and religious convictions.

3. It is no surprise that Zech 12:10 has left its imprint on the NT. Indeed, it is surprising that only John 19:37 adverts directly to the piercing, when referring to the actions of the Roman soldiers that "fulfilled" Zech 12:10 (cf. Rev 1:7). The terms "only" and "firstborn" in v. 10 are given christological significance in the NT and lie in the background of the use of this text in the Gospel of John (cf. John 1:18). The LXX renders the term "only" as "beloved" or "favored," as the TNK translates this verse.[145] In the designations of Jesus as the beloved Son (Matt 3:17; Luke 9:35) and as the firstborn—of Mary (Luke 2:7) or of a large family (Rom 8:29), or of all creation (Col 1:15)—one hears echoes of Zech 12:10.

144. See René Girard, *Things Hidden Since the Foundation of the World* (Stanford, Calif.: Stanford University Press, 1987).
145. Jon D. Levenson, *The Death and Resurrection of the Beloved Son* (New Haven: Yale University Press, 1993) 25-31.

Zechariah 13:2-9, Prophet and Shepherd Removed

OVERVIEW

Zechariah 13:2-9 exists in two parts. The first (vv. 2-6) describes the elimination of prophets and prophecy. The second part of the chapter (vv. 7-9) is an oracle addressed to a sword that will strike Yahweh's shepherd. These verses thus return to the shepherd metaphor of chap. 11 (particularly to 11:17). At the same time, they provide a transition to chap. 14, in which an eschatological scenario begins with the kind of event announced in 13:8-9*a*.

Zechariah 13:2-6, If Anyone Prophesies

NIV	NRSV
[2]"On that day, I will banish the names of the idols from the land, and they will be remembered no more," declares the LORD Almighty. "I will remove both the prophets and the spirit of impurity from the land. [3]And if anyone still prophesies, his father and mother, to whom he was born, will say to him, 'You must die, because you have told lies in the LORD's name.' When he prophesies, his own parents will stab him.	[2]On that day, says the LORD of hosts, I will cut off the names of the idols from the land, so that they shall be remembered no more; and also I will remove from the land the prophets and the unclean spirit. [3]And if any prophets appear again, their fathers and mothers who bore them will say to them, "You shall not live, for you speak lies in the name of the LORD"; and their fathers and their mothers who bore them shall pierce them through

NIV

4"On that day every prophet will be ashamed of his prophetic vision. He will not put on a prophet's garment of hair in order to deceive. 5He will say, 'I am not a prophet. I am a farmer; the land has been my livelihood since my youth.*' 6If someone asks him, 'What are these wounds on your body*?' he will answer, 'The wounds I was given at the house of my friends.' "

*5 Or *farmer; a man sold me in my youth*   *6 Or *wounds between your hands*

NRSV

when they prophesy. 4On that day the prophets will be ashamed, every one, of their visions when they prophesy; they will not put on a hairy mantle in order to deceive, 5but each of them will say, "I am no prophet, I am a tiller of the soil; for the land has been my possession* since my youth." 6And if anyone asks them, "What are these wounds on your chest?"* the answer will be "The wounds I received in the house of my friends."

a Cn: Heb *for humankind has caused me to possess*   *b* Heb *wounds between your hands*

COMMENTARY

13:2. The first verse of chap. 13 had announced the opportunity of cleansing for the House of David and Jerusalem's inhabitants. Verse 2 then opens a new unit by interpreting v. 1 from the perspective of Ezek 36:25-26. In Ezekiel, Yahweh promises a new spirit, as in Zech 12:10, but the deity also will sprinkle Israel with water to cleanse them from their "uncleanness" and from their idols (Ezek 36:25). The term "uncleanness" (נדה *niddâ*) appears 13:1. Verse 2 then associates it with idols, as does Ezekiel (using a different term for "idols"). Yahweh promises to cut off the names of the idols from the land so that they will not be remembered (v. 2a). It then repeats the term in association with the prophets: "also the prophets and the spirit of uncleanness I will expel from the land." The land will be purified when it is free of idols, prophets, and the "spirit of uncleanness." By implication, it is this spirit to which the prophets respond, instead of to Yahweh's Spirit, as in 7:5.

13:3-6. Prophets and prophesying constitute the theme of these verses. Verse 3 follows as a consequence of v. 2; its grammatical subjects are the father and mother of anyone who prophesies. Verse 4 introduces a new unit within vv. 2-6, whose subject is prophets. Verses 4-6 report the response of prophets to the situation described in vv. 2-3, with prophets under threat of expulsion or death.

13:3. The action of parents in this verse is directed against "anyone who again prophesies."

Parents will assign the death penalty (based on a charge of speaking lies in Yahweh's name) and will execute it themselves. The prophets Jeremiah and Ezekiel excoriate other prophets for speaking lies in Yahweh's name and prophesying without being sent by Yahweh to do so (Jer 14:14; 23:16; 27:15; Ezek 13:6-8). Verse 3 suggests that anyone who prophesies now falls into that category and is thus subject to death. Deuteronomy 18:15-22 stipulates death for a prophet who speaks in God's name what God did not instruct him to speak. The test of such speaking is whether what the prophet announces in Yahweh's name in fact occurs (cf. Deut 13:1-5[2-6]). The parents apply no such test; they will stab their offspring "when he prophesies." Prophesying is now defined as lying.

The irony here goes beyond the condemnation of prophecy within a prophetic text. Ready as they were to condemn false prophets, earlier prophets also vigorously condemned those who would prevent prophets from prophesying (see Jer 11:19-22; Amos 2:12; Mic 2:6-7). In v. 3, the threat is reversed, and parents treat an offspring who prophesies as the House of David and as Jerusalem's inhabitants treated the unnamed victim of 12:10. In chap. 12, this act was followed by mourning, men and women separately. Here there is no mourning, but fathers and mothers act in concert, privately, immediately, and on their own initiative.

13:4-6. This second unit of 13:2-6 reports in carefully chosen words the response of prophets "on that day." The text of these verses is cryptic and full of allusions. The governing statement occurs in v. 4a: "The prophets will be ashamed, each one of his vision when he prophesies." "When he prophesies" (v. 4) repeats the last word (in the MT) of v. 3. There is good reason, then, for shame—and for fear. Accordingly, a prophet will take actions to avoid being identified as a prophet: First, in order to deny that he is a prophet, he will not wear a hairy mantle (v. 4b); second, he will say that he is not a prophet but a tiller of the soil who has owned his ground from youth (v. 5); third, he will say that he received the wounds on his back in the house of his friends (v. 6).

The first action (v. 4b), not wearing a hairy mantle, is expressly "in order to deny." The verb כחש (kāḥaš) has no object (cf. Gen 18:15, where "Sarah denied"). The mantle itself evokes the prophet Elijah, famous for his mantle (1 Kgs 19:13). The prophet could also be identified by his hairy garment. The term "hairy mantle" is used elsewhere only of Esau (Gen 27:25). Thus there is in v. 4b an apparent reference to the prophet Elijah, with an allusion to Esau and a secondary allusion to his brother, Jacob, who feigned Esau's hairy mantle in order to deceive Isaac (Gen 27:5-23, 35). Likewise, in the second action there is an evident reference to the prophet Amos, whose words are quoted: "I am not a prophet" (v. 5; Amos 7:14). The prophet in v. 5 also adds that he is a "tiller of the soil." This is said of no individual in the OT except Cain

(Gen 4:2).[146] To reinforce the allusion to Cain, the prophet says, "I have owned the land from my youth," or, according to the MT, "a man acquired me from my youth," as a servant to till the soil.[147] The verb in the MT is קנה (qānâ). In Gen 4:1, Eve uses the term to explain the name "Cain." Cain's occupation as "tiller of the soil" (Gen 4:2) is expressly contrasted with that of his brother, Abel, who was a "shepherd of sheep" and history's first murder victim. Thus Zech 14:5 refers to the prophet Amos and also to Cain, with a secondary allusion to his brother, Abel, whose occupation coincides exactly with that assigned to Zechariah in 11:4. The text of 13:4-5 uncovers the very deceptions it describes, and it exposes a prophet who, in shame and with reasonable fear, denies what he is.

The denial continues with the third action (v. 6), when the prophet is asked about the wounds on his back. He answers, enigmatically, that he was "struck" (cognate in the OT with "wounds") in the house of his friends—those who love him. The answer may allude to v. 3, and thus to the stabbing inflicted by parents.[148] It also points forward to v. 7, where a sword is ordered to "strike" Yahweh's shepherd. (See Reflections at 13:7-9.)

146. K. Larkin, *The Eschatology of Second Zechariah* (Kamper: Pharos, 1994) 172.
147. Eugene M. Merrill, *Haggai, Zechariah, and Malachi: An Exegetical Commentary* (Chicago: Moody, 1994) 333.
148. Hinckley G. Mitchell, *A Critical and Exegetical Commentary on Haggai and Zechariah,* ICC (Edinburgh: T. & T. Clark, 1912) 339.

Zechariah 13:7-9, The Sheep Will Scatter

NIV	NRSV
7"Awake, O sword, against my shepherd, against the man who is close to me!" declares the LORD Almighty. "Strike the shepherd, and the sheep will be scattered, and I will turn my hand against the little ones. 8In the whole land," declares the LORD, "two-thirds will be struck down and perish; yet one-third will be left in it. 9This third I will bring into the fire; I will refine them like silver and test them like gold.	7 "Awake, O sword, against my shepherd, against the man who is my associate," says the LORD of hosts. Strike the shepherd, that the sheep may be scattered; I will turn my hand against the little ones. 8 In the whole land, says the LORD, two-thirds shall be cut off and perish, and one-third shall be left alive. 9 And I will put this third into the fire, refine them as one refines silver, and test them as gold is tested.

NIV	NRSV

They will call on my name
    and I will answer them;
I will say, 'They are my people,'
    and they will say, 'The LORD is our God.'"
	They will call on my name,
	    and I will answer them.
	I will say, "They are my people";
	    and they will say, "The LORD is our God."

COMMENTARY

This semi-poetic unit returns to the shepherd metaphor in v. 7, which it then interprets and expands in vv. 8-9. It is cast as an oracle, with the oracle formula in vv. 7-8. Verse 7 includes Yahweh's epithet: "says the LORD of hosts." In Second Zechariah this full form otherwise occurs only in v. 2, which suggests that vv. 7-9 are an interpretive complement to vv. 3-6. Indeed, the relation between these two parts of chap. 13 is analogous to that between 11:4-14 and 11:15-17.

13:7. The oracle opens by addressing a sword, "Awake!" In some contexts, this signals a call to battle (Judg 5:12), but here the sword is called to perform an execution. Yahweh first identifies the victim as "my shepherd" and as one who is "my associate" (NRSV). The latter term (עמית 'āmît) is somewhat obscure. It occurs elsewhere in the OT only in Leviticus (11 times), where it designates a fellow community member with whom one stands in a relation of mutuality and reciprocity (e.g., Lev 19:11; 25:17). Yahweh commands the sword to attack the shepherd, "my associate" (v. 7). Naturally, the shepherd does not open his mouth. Yahweh next states the purpose of this execution: so that the sheep will be scattered. A good shepherd would prevent this. Yahweh's hand will be against not only the shepherd and not only the mature, perhaps culpable sheep, but also the little ones of the flock, an image Zechariah draws from Jer 49:20; 50:45.

13:8-9. In the two concluding verses of chap. 13, Zechariah abandons the shepherd/sheep metaphor to describe the fate of the people, divided into thirds. The image derives from Ezek 5:1-12, where Ezekiel performs a symbolic act to depict the fate of Jerusalem at the hands of the Babylonians: A third will die from pestilence and famine, a third will fall to the sword, and a third will be scattered at the point of a sword (Ezek 5:12). Zechariah takes Ezekiel's prophetic depic-

tion of what did happen, in 587 BCE, as paradigmatic of what will happen in the future. However, he modifies the image to focus on the one-third who will be left in the land. These face a refining fire (v. 8), which will produce precious metals (cf. Num 31:23; Mal 3:2-3); more, it will result in an intimate relationship with Yahweh. Many biblical texts describe this relationship in terms of Israel's call and Yahweh's ready answer (e.g., Ps 81:7[8]; Isa 65:24; Jer 33:3) and its fracture as calling that receives no reply (7:13). Here the relationship is sealed in reciprocal covenant terms: the covenant formulae, which recall 2:11[15]; 8:7-8; 10:6 (see Commentary on 10:6).

Only here in Second Zechariah does Yahweh refer to the community as "my people." Following the calamity and the purging described in vv. 8-9a, the surviving remnant ("my people") will stand in relation to Yahweh as did the shepherd (*"my* shepherd, *my* close associate," v. 7) whose death permits their scattering and leads to their redemption. The verbs and pronouns in v. 9b are all singular, as if the community will embody the shepherd, who even in 11:4 would call Yahweh "my God." Zechariah 13 reaches back beyond chap. 11 to 10:2, which associates divination and false prophecy with the absence of a shepherd and a wandering flock. In Jeremiah, Yahweh charges that Judah's swords have devoured its prophets (Jer 2:30), and Zech 13:2-3 expects prophets will be expelled and that their parents will stab anyone who prophesies, while in 13:4-6 a prophet practices deception to conceal his identity and the source of his wounds. In this light, the sword against Yahweh's own shepherd gains new significance (v. 7). His death accomplishes not just the cleansing of David's house and Jerusalem's citizens, but a final scattering, death, and refining (vv. 7-9). It also invites fresh consideration of the one stabbed in 12:10, mourned like an only (or favored) child. Such mourning is predicted in threats of judgment in Jer 6:26 and Amos 8:10. Amos follows this immediately with the threat of famine: "not of bread. . . , but of hearing Yahweh's words," which will be everywhere sought

but nowhere found (8:11-12). He says this in the context of a conflict with the royal house of Jeroboam, whose priest Amaziah forbade Amos from prophesying at the sanctuary and palace (7:12-13).

REFLECTIONS

1. The picture of prophecy in Zechariah 13 is bleak. Zechariah is not the only, or the first, biblical text to attest contempt for the prophets, but in other texts the contempt is usually specific (see Jer 23:25-40; Ezek 13:1-12) and frequently focuses on the distinction between true and false prophecy (Jer 20:6; 28:15; 40:16; 43:2). It is too easy to identify the prophet in Zech 13:4-6 as false. With such an identification, one then could label the prophet's denial of the prophetic vocation (vv. 4-5) as the result of a flaw in the prophet's character. But the oracle in Zechariah 13 does not allow for such an easy solution. This oracle depicts a situation in which prophecy disappears, in which a prophet will be stabbed by his parents, in which the death of a prophet yields benefits to the community only through its own consequent dissolution, division, and reduction. By simple virtue of being a prophet, the prophet is placed in a murderous context. Why would or should anyone seek a prophetic ministry?

This bleak view of the prophet's fate has important echoes in the NT. In Luke 13:34, for example, Jesus laments over Jerusalem's reputation for killing prophets, "Jerusalem, Jerusalem, the city that kills the prophets and stones those who are sent to it" (see also Matt 23:31-37; Luke 11:46-52). The parable of the vineyard (Matt 21:33-46; Mark 12:1-12; Luke 20:9-19), in which the servants and the son of the landowner are killed, shares the same view of the fate that awaits prophets.

2. In Zech 13:7-9, the shepherd, God's compatriot, is to be struck down in order that the flock will be scattered (cf. Zech 11:15-17). A third will remain to be God's own, purified people. It is hardly surprising that the NT draws on this text. We may see the verse reflected in John 10:11, where Jesus says, "I am the good shepherd. The good shepherd lays down his life for his sheep." The shepherd in Zechariah 13 did not lay down his life, however; it was taken from him (cf. John 10:18). Matthew and Mark take note of this element, but in their Gospels the personified sword of Zech 13:7 gives way to the one who wields it (Matt 26:31; Mark 14:27). Unlike in Zechariah, the scattering is not the purpose of the striking, but its result. The Zechariah text is used to portend Peter's denial and Jesus' abandonment by his followers at his death.

Zechariah 14:1-21, The Exaltation of the King

OVERVIEW

Chapter 14 presents the final and climactic vision of Second Zechariah. In its depiction of a war against Jerusalem involving all the nations, it resembles chap. 12. The relation between these two chapters is similar to that between chaps. 9 and 10, but the differences between chaps. 12 and 14 are noteworthy. In chap. 14 there is no

mention of David's house or of any future royal figure; no allusion to a shepherd or to prophets or to priests or to any human leader. To a degree unlike any other text in Zechariah, this chapter celebrates Yahweh as king; in fact, *only* here in Zechariah is Yahweh referred to as king, and that three times (14:9, 16, 17). Accordingly, Zechariah

14 has a universal perspective. Whereas 12:11-14 refers to the leading families (or clans) who mourn a victim, 14:17 refers to the families of the entire earth, who will come to Jerusalem. Corresponding to its universal perspective is the chapter's focus on Jerusalem, the geographic source of dominion over the world.

This chapter may be divided into two sections: vv. 1-11 and 12-21. In place of the formulaic "on that day," which occurs frequently within chap.

14, the first verse announces that Yahweh's day is coming. This moment introduces the convergence of all nations at Jerusalem, where Yahweh brings them for war, and issues in a transformation of cosmic proportions. A major break occurs at v. 12, as indicated by syntax. Here attention turns to the fate not just of those nations that warred against Jerusalem, but of all the nations. They will come again to Jerusalem, but now to prostrate themselves before the king.

Zechariah 14:1-11, War and Transformation

NIV

14 A day of the LORD is coming when your plunder will be divided among you.

²I will gather all the nations to Jerusalem to fight against it; the city will be captured, the houses ransacked, and the women raped. Half of the city will go into exile, but the rest of the people will not be taken from the city.

³Then the LORD will go out and fight against those nations, as he fights in the day of battle. ⁴On that day his feet will stand on the Mount of Olives, east of Jerusalem, and the Mount of Olives will be split in two from east to west, forming a great valley, with half of the mountain moving north and half moving south. ⁵You will flee by my mountain valley, for it will extend to Azel. You will flee as you fled from the earthquake[a] in the days of Uzziah king of Judah. Then the LORD my God will come, and all the holy ones with him.

⁶On that day there will be no light, no cold or frost. ⁷It will be a unique day, without daytime or nighttime—a day known to the LORD. When evening comes, there will be light.

⁸On that day living water will flow out from Jerusalem, half to the eastern sea[b] and half to the western sea,[c] in summer and in winter.

⁹The LORD will be king over the whole earth. On that day there will be one LORD, and his name the only name.

¹⁰The whole land, from Geba to Rimmon, south of Jerusalem, will become like the Arabah. But Jerusalem will be raised up and remain in its

NRSV

14 See, a day is coming for the LORD, when the plunder taken from you will be divided in your midst. ²For I will gather all the nations against Jerusalem to battle, and the city shall be taken and the houses looted and the women raped; half the city shall go into exile, but the rest of the people shall not be cut off from the city. ³Then the LORD will go forth and fight against those nations as when he fights on a day of battle. ⁴On that day his feet shall stand on the Mount of Olives, which lies before Jerusalem on the east; and the Mount of Olives shall be split in two from east to west by a very wide valley; so that one half of the Mount shall withdraw northward, and the other half southward. ⁵And you shall flee by the valley of the LORD's mountain,[a] for the valley between the mountains shall reach to Azal;[b] and you shall flee as you fled from the earthquake in the days of King Uzziah of Judah. Then the LORD my God will come, and all the holy ones with him.

6On that day there shall not be[c] either cold or frost.[d] ⁷And there shall be continuous day (it is known to the LORD), not day and not night, for at evening time there shall be light.

8On that day living waters shall flow out from Jerusalem, half of them to the eastern sea and half of them to the western sea; it shall continue in summer as in winter.

9And the LORD will become king over all the earth; on that day the LORD will be one and his name one.

---

[a]5 Or ⁵My mountain valley will be blocked and will extend to Azel. It will be blocked as it was blocked because of the earthquake ᵇ8 That is, the Dead Sea ᶜ8 That is, the Mediterranean

[a] Heb my mountains ᵇMeaning of Heb uncertain ᶜ Cn: Heb there shall not be light ᵈ Compare Gk Syr Vg Tg: Meaning of Heb uncertain

NIV

place, from the Benjamin Gate to the site of the First Gate, to the Corner Gate, and from the Tower of Hananel to the royal winepresses. [11]It will be inhabited; never again will it be destroyed. Jerusalem will be secure.

NRSV

10The whole land shall be turned into a plain from Geba to Rimmon south of Jerusalem. But Jerusalem shall remain aloft on its site from the Gate of Benjamin to the place of the former gate, to the Corner Gate, and from the Tower of Hananel to the king's wine presses. [11]And it shall be inhabited, for never again shall it be doomed to destruction; Jerusalem shall abide in security.

COMMENTARY

As in 12:1-6, in chap. 14 all the nations come to Jerusalem for war. However, this time they come because God gathers them (v. 2). It is a day for Yahweh (v. 1), as the chapter makes clear. Why, then, does it spell disaster for Jerusalem? The disaster is first adumbrated in terms of war spoils taken from Jerusalem and divided, the prerogative of a victorious army (Ps 68:12[13]; Isa 33:23), and then described in more specific terms. The city will be captured, the houses plundered, and the women raped (v. 2). These, too, are the common and deplorable accompaniments of war and, in Israel's experience and Judah's, so was exile. Here, half of the city will go into exile, while the rest remain. The text offers no reason why some people will be exiled and others not; it does not characterize either group, and neither does it suggest that Jerusalem is being judged for an offense against God. However, chap. 14 does describe the reordering, the re-creation of social, political, ecological, and cosmic structures on Yahweh's day. As part of that reordering, certain polarities are eliminated;[149] e.g., night and day will become one continuous light (v. 7); Yahweh will be one with one name universally revered (v. 9); and the polarities of holy and profane will no longer apply in Jerusalem and Judah (v. 21). In contrast, new divisions are introduced: like the population of Jerusalem, the Mount of Olives will be divided in half (v. 4); a freshwater stream from Jerusalem will divide in half (v. 8); the nations united in v. 1 are reduced to chaos (v. 13) and divided into families (v. 17). The division in Jerusalem's population occurs as part of this re-

ordering. It prepares for the holiness that will ultimately characterize Jerusalem and Judah (cf. Zeph 3:8-12).

14:1-5. The taking of spoils from Jerusalem is reversed in v. 14, but this hardly mitigates the disaster of vv. 1-2. Neither does the announcement that God will march forth and fight against those nations that Yahweh has brought against Jerusalem (v. 3). The fighting, "as Yahweh fights on the day of battle," is not described here, although the theme is picked up retrospectively in v. 12. Yahweh's march ends on the Mount of Olives (v. 4), which "stands opposite the temple area and is about 100 feet higher than Jerusalem itself."[150] In a remarkably anthropomorphic image, Yahweh's feet will be on the mountain. The mountain takes the place of the ark, or of Jerusalem itself, as God's footstool (Pss 99:5; 132:7; cf. Exod 24:8). The scene culminates in v. 9 with Yahweh as king over all the earth. But before and after v. 9 come topographical and cosmic changes that begin with the mountain dividing across its east-west axis, its now twin peaks moving north and south respectively (v. 5). The apparent purpose of this geological innovation is to open a gorge to the east of Jerusalem through which the people can escape the devastation,[151] as they did from the earthquake that Amos mentions (Amos 1:1). Here the prophet's voice intrudes, referring to Yahweh as "my God" (cf. 11:4; 13:9) in a promise that Yahweh will come and that all the "holy ones" will be with the people in their escape. This is apparently a reference to the holy

---

149. P. Hanson, *The Dawn of Apocalyptic* (Philadelphia: Fortress, 1975) 377.

150. Warren J. Heard, Jr., "Olives, Mount of," *ABD* 5 (1992) 13.
151. See Carol Meyers and Eric Meyers, *Haggai and Zechariah 9–14*, AB 25C (New York: Doubleday, 1993) 424-27.

ones in Yahweh's martial retinue,[152] who accompany Yahweh's march from Sinai. In that march, too, Yahweh became king (Deut 33:2-5).

14:6-9. Concomitant with this event come two other changes, one in the cosmos, the other in Jerusalem's ecology (vv. 6-8). The first alters creation itself, ending its ordered pattern of cold and heat, day and night, "as long as the earth endures" (Gen 8:22). The second produces a stream of fresh, living, water, with its source in Jerusalem, half of which flows to the Dead Sea and half to the Mediterranean. These two changes create ideal agricultural conditions, especially as the fresh water flows into the Dead Sea. That theme continues in v. 10, but the reference to water flowing from Jerusalem is juxtaposed with the theme of Yahweh's kingship (v. 9). Traditions rooted in Jerusalem depict Yahweh as king over all the earth (Ps 47:3-8[2-7]), enthroned over the subterranean seas (Ps 29:10), and Zion, God's dwelling, as nurtured by a river and streams (Ps 46:3[2]).[153] Verse 9a draws on that tradition,

while v. 9b alludes to the Shema (Deut 6:4-5). When Yahweh exercises dominion ("becomes king") over all the earth on Yahweh's day, that dominion will be both universal and exclusive; God will not be invoked by another name.

14:10-11. Returning to the theme of vv. 6-8, and particularly the fresh or living waters of v. 8, v. 10a announces the transformation of Judah; it will be like the Arabah or plain. In the background is Ezekiel's vision of a river flowing eastward from below the Temple's threshold into the Dead Sea and spilling over into the Arabah, the arid region to the south. The river will bring life everywhere it flows; its banks will be lined with fruit trees, and the stagnant waters of the Dead Sea will be filled with various fish. The trees will bear fruit monthly, since they are irrigated by water that flows from the Temple (Ezek 42:1-12). Judah can expect such an existence when the land becomes a plain, all the way from the north (Geba) to the south (Rimmon). Jerusalem, by contrast, will be lifted up in its place. (See Reflections at 14:12-21.)

---

152. Hanson, *The Dawn of Apocalyptic*, 375.
153. Ben C. Ollenburger, *Zion: The City of the Great King*, JSOTSup 41 (Sheffield: JSOT, 1987) 50-52.

Zechariah 14:12-21, The Nations Come to Jerusalem

NIV

[12]This is the plague with which the LORD will strike all the nations that fought against Jerusalem: Their flesh will rot while they are still standing on their feet, their eyes will rot in their sockets, and their tongues will rot in their mouths. [13]On that day men will be stricken by the LORD with great panic. Each man will seize the hand of another, and they will attack each other. [14]Judah too will fight at Jerusalem. The wealth of all the surrounding nations will be collected—great quantities of gold and silver and clothing. [15]A similar plague will strike the horses and mules, the camels and donkeys, and all the animals in those camps.

[16]Then the survivors from all the nations that have attacked Jerusalem will go up year after year to worship the King, the LORD Almighty, and to celebrate the Feast of Tabernacles. [17]If any of the peoples of the earth do not go up to Jerusalem to

NRSV

[12]This shall be the plague with which the LORD will strike all the peoples that wage war against Jerusalem: their flesh shall rot while they are still on their feet; their eyes shall rot in their sockets, and their tongues shall rot in their mouths. [13]On that day a great panic from the LORD shall fall on them, so that each will seize the hand of a neighbor, and the hand of the one will be raised against the hand of the other; [14]even Judah will fight at Jerusalem. And the wealth of all the surrounding nations shall be collected—gold, silver, and garments in great abundance. [15]And a plague like this plague shall fall on the horses, the mules, the camels, the donkeys, and whatever animals may be in those camps.

[16]Then all who survive of the nations that have come against Jerusalem shall go up year after year to worship the King, the LORD of hosts, and to

NIV

worship the King, the LORD Almighty, they will have no rain. ¹⁸If the Egyptian people do not go up and take part, they will have no rain. The LORDᵃ will bring on them the plague he inflicts on the nations that do not go up to celebrate the Feast of Tabernacles. ¹⁹This will be the punishment of Egypt and the punishment of all the nations that do not go up to celebrate the Feast of Tabernacles.

²⁰On that day HOLY TO THE LORD will be inscribed on the bells of the horses, and the cooking pots in the LORD's house will be like the sacred bowls in front of the altar. ²¹Every pot in Jerusalem and Judah will be holy to the LORD Almighty, and all who come to sacrifice will take some of the pots and cook in them. And on that day there will no longer be a Canaaniteᵇ in the house of the LORD Almighty.

ᵃ18 Or part, then the LORD   ᵇ21 Or merchant

NRSV

keep the festival of booths.ᵃ ¹⁷If any of the families of the earth do not go up to Jerusalem to worship the King, the LORD of hosts, there will be no rain upon them. ¹⁸And if the family of Egypt do not go up and present themselves, then on them shallᵇ come the plague that the LORD inflicts on the nations that do not go up to keep the festival of booths.ᵃ ¹⁹Such shall be the punishment of Egypt and the punishment of all the nations that do not go up to keep the festival of booths.ᵃ

20On that day there shall be inscribed on the bells of the horses, "Holy to the LORD." And the cooking pots in the house of the LORD shall be as holy asᶜ the bowls in front of the altar; ²¹and every cooking pot in Jerusalem and Judah shall be sacred to the LORD of hosts, so that all who sacrifice may come and use them to boil the flesh of the sacrifice. And there shall no longer be tradersᵈ in the house of the LORD of hosts on that day.

ᵃ Or tabernacles; Heb succoth   ᵇ Gk Syr: Heb shall not   ᶜ Heb shall be like   ᵈ Or Canaanites

COMMENTARY

14:12-15. The first section of chap. 14 ends with the promise that Jerusalem will be inhabited and that, without any threat of future destruction, it will remain secure (v. 11). With that, the chapter returns to the matter of "all the peoples that have fought against Jerusalem." Verse 12 introduces the matter by promising a plague on these peoples, and v. 15 extends this plague to the animals in (presumably, military) camps. Separating these verses is a brief description of the battle "on that day" (vv. 13-14), referring to vv. 1-2. Here the plundering is reversed, and the wealth of all the surrounding nations will be gathered up in Jerusalem (v. 14; cf. Hag 2:6-9). "Yahweh's great panic," will fall on the battle participants (v. 13; cf. Deut 7:23; 2 Chr 20:22-25). Each enemy will clutch at the hand of the other, but in the confusion each will end up raising a hand against the other. It is from this perspective that one should understand the statement in v. 14a that "even Judah will fight against Jerusalem." The clause נלחם ב (*nilḥam bĕ*), followed by a noun, elsewhere

(including v. 3) always means "to fight against." The translation is hardly in doubt, and the distinction between Judah and Jerusalem was encountered in 12:1-8. We do not have here an indication of warring factions within the post-exilic community.[154] Rather, the confusion brought about by Yahweh's great panic is so great that neighbor is fighting neighbor, and even Judah is fighting Jerusalem.

14:16-17. Verse 16 resumes the motif present in v. 12: the nations that came up *against* Jerusalem. They will now make annual pilgrimages *to* Jerusalem to bow down to King Yahweh of hosts.[155] The expectation that the leaders of subject nations would make a pilgrimage to honor a new king is known in the ancient world and in the OT (Ps 72:8-11 attests to such an expectation). In Isaiah 40–66, this motif is transferred to Zion, which replaces the king as the reason for a pilgrimage (Isa 45:14; 49:22-23; 60:4-14). In all of these texts (apart from Isaiah 49), the nations

154. Hanson, *The Dawn of Apocalyptic*, 392.
155. Meyers and Meyers, *Haggai and Zechariah 9–14*, 466.

bring with them gifts, or their wealth, to the king's or to Zion's benefit. In Zechariah 14 the nations' wealth has already been gathered (v. 14). The international pilgrimage is to keep the festival of booths. This autumnal festival was a likely setting for the enthronement psalms (e.g., Pss 93 and 97), which celebrate Yahweh's kingship.[156] If so, Zechariah associates the autumnal festival of booths with an international pilgrimage to honor King Yahweh of hosts, a title or name that occurs only in vv. 16-17 (cf. Isa 6:5).

14:18-19. In v. 18, Zechariah once more mentions a plague (cf. vv. 13, 15), perhaps identifying the withholding of rain as a plague to punish any of the earth's families (or clans) that do not make the pilgrimage required in v. 16. The text of v. 18 is difficult. Part of the difficulty is that withholding rain from Egypt, watered by the Nile, would hardly be a punishment, much less a plague. Regardless, Egypt is here singled out, perhaps because it was the origin of the exodus, of which the festival of booths was to be a reminder (Lev 23:43). That all the nations are required to come to Jerusalem for a festival represents a significant transformation, since Lev 23:42 restricts it to citizens of Israel and Neh 8:17 limits it to those who were members of the *golah*.

14:20-21. Corresponding to this extension of the autumnal festival to all the nations is the extension of holiness to everything in Jerusalem and Judah. The inscription "Holy to Yahweh," reserved in priestly literature for the diadem on the high priest's turban (Exod 39:28-30), will in the future adorn even horses' bells. Any cooking pot will do for boiling sacrificial meat, even though Lev 6:24-30 carefully regulates the treatment of such pots used in the sin offering and Ezek 46:20-24 assigns priests to guard the sanctity of boiling meat for sacrifice. Verses 20-21 eliminate such concerns, along with the "graded holiness" that informed priestly understanding.[157] The defining function of the priests was to distinguish between the holy and the profane (Lev 10:10), a distinction no longer important. Hence, there is no mention of priests; v. 21 speaks only, and in the most general terms, of "all those who sacrifice." The transformations in Jerusalem's cult (vv. 16-21), are no less profound than the topographical and cosmological transformations depicted in vv. 5-10.

The last sentence in chap. 14, and in Zechariah, says that there will be no more traders or merchants in Yahweh's house. As in chap. 11, "merchants" is here an entirely appropriate translation of the MT's "Canaanite" (cf. Isa 23:8). The Temple had been a site of commercial activity in the past, and the priest received payments of silver from sin and guilt offerings (2 Kgs 12:4-16). But in the Persian period, and by Persian design, the Temple was the very center of the Judean economy and functioned as a kind of central bank. Zechariah envisions the end of all such commerce "on that day."

---

156. Ollenburger, *Zion,* 24-52.

157. The phrase is Jacob Milgrom's ("Sacrifices and Offerings, OT," IDBSup [1976] 763-71).

REFLECTIONS

1. Zechariah 12–14 began with praise of Yahweh as creator (12:1). This last chapter gives some indication of what such praise may entail. At the least, it points to a potential difference between a theology of creation and a theology of God the creator. Jeremiah, no wooden traditionalist himself, secured his vision of the future by appealing to the very permanence of a fixed order of creation (Jer 31:35-36; 33:20-21, 25-26), while Zechariah regards the created order as malleable in a future that is only now disclosed. Creation, in its dependable orderliness, is no longer the symbol and touchstone of reliability (cf. the whirlwind speeches of Job 38–41). Its place is taken by God's promises, to be realized in a future that depends utterly on God, as creator and re-creator of heaven and earth.

2. That this re-creation involves, even if only in its initial moments, such recognizable but still monstrous depredations as pillage, rape, and exile gives reason for pause and grounds for objection. But the objection needs to be raised at the proper point—at the one and only point in this entire chapter where Yahweh speaks in the first person, "I will gather all the nations for war" (14:2). Here Zechariah writes out of national memory and experience, and might agree with the judgment of David R. Blumenthal that "one cannot reject God," a judgment that Blumenthal roots in "the doctrine of creation and covenant: God is creator, and God is in a covenant with us that cannot be nullified. . . . For this reason we do not reject God; we learn to cope with God and God's actions."[158] As noted many times in the commentary, Zechariah's visions are not merely an attempt to cope with Persian domination; they represent his coping with God. Even in his most utopian, most freely imaginative moment, Zechariah still does not imagine a way to a future without war, and he cannot imagine war as anything but what it has always been even in God's hands. Contemporary readers may want to shy away from such a vision of God's future, but we do much better to use Zechariah's vision as a lens through which to reflect honestly on how the contemporary faith community, too, employs images of violence and warfare in its visions of the future.

3. In its vision of the future, Zechariah 14 is thoroughly inclusive: All the nations are included in the celebration of Yahweh's kingship, and everything in Jerusalem and Judah is included in the sphere of holiness. Second Zechariah thus ends on the same inclusive note as does First Zechariah (8:20-23). In Zechariah 8, people from everywhere—the multitude of nations—seek the way to Jerusalem on their own initiative, simply because they have heard that God is with the Jews. But in Zechariah 14, the nations—the families of the earth—come, and are compelled to come, as survivors. In the course of chapter 14 they are transformed from aggressors to survivors, and then to God's devotees. It is a powerful vision of God's sovereignty.

4. Interpreters have long recognized the role of Zechariah 14 in Mark's account of Jesus' entry into Jerusalem (Mark 11). Jesus begins on the Mount of Olives (Mark 11:1), which is where God stands in Zech 14:4. Entering Jerusalem, in a way that reflects Zech 9:9, Jesus is hailed as king (Mark 11:9-10), echoing Zech 14:9. Jesus comes finally to the Temple (Mark 11:15), as all people do in Zech 14:20-21. In the Temple, Jesus drives out those engaged in trade (Mark 11:15-16), interpreting Zech 14:2 as does the Targum to Zechariah. It may be true, as Paul Brooks Duff says, that in its difference from Zechariah 14—in the contrast of Jesus' entry with that of the divine warrior in Zechariah—Mark 11 redefines the nature of messiahship and messianic expectation.[159] But Zechariah 14 has already redefined messianic expectation by eliminating it: Kingship is exclusively and exhaustively Yahweh's prerogative, and it is not delegated, even in modified or redefined form, to any anointed human representative. And in Mark, two chapters later, when Jesus is on the Mount of Olives (Mark 13:3; again echoing Zech 14:4), he tells his disciples that the way to the future will involve war and suffering no less awful than that envisioned by Zechariah, before the "Son of man comes with great power and glory" (Mark 13:26). The NT provides no handy escape from what may offend us in Zechariah 14. There, too, we have to cope with God, our only hope.

---

158. David R. Blumenthal, *Facing the Abusing God: A Theology of Protest* (Louisville: Westminster/John Knox, 1993).
159. Paul Brooks Duff, "The March of the Divine Warrior and the Advent of the Greco-Roman King: Mark's Account of Jesus' Entry into Jerusalem," *JBL* 111 (1992) 55-71.

THE BOOK OF MALACHI

INTRODUCTION, COMMENTARY, AND REFLECTIONS
BY
EILEEN M. SCHULLER, O.S.U.

THE BOOK OF

MALACHI

INTRODUCTION

Malachi is the final book in the collection of the Twelve Prophets. Although the order of these books may have varied when the Bible was copied in manuscript form, in present-day Christian Bibles, Malachi concludes the entire prophetic section and is the final book of the whole of the Old Testament. As such, many readers have seen it as a transition to the New Testament, as "the skirt and boundary of Christianity" to use Tertullian's phrase. In most Hebrew manuscripts and in modern Jewish Bibles, Malachi functions differently: It is "the seal of the Prophets." It concludes both the Book of the Twelve (Hosea–Malachi) and the larger unit of Prophets (Joshua–Malachi), and it is followed by the section called Writings.

The book of Malachi is a relatively short collection of fifty-five verses. As expected in a book that belongs to the corpus of Prophets, in it we find words from God delivered through a human agent, words of both judgment and salvation, directed to "Israel" (1:1), either to the people as a whole or to the priests specifically (1:6; 2:1). But we also hear the voices of the people and the priests in response. Indeed, one of the distinctive features of the book is the way that priests and people articulate their questions and state their complaints in a way that sets up the dynamic of an ongoing dialogue. Finally, in addition to the words of God and the words of the people, the book also includes a brief editorial introduction (1:1), one verse of narration (3:16), and an epilogue (4:4-6).

Many readers have the sense that with the book of Malachi the prophetic corpus per se and the OT as a whole end not with a bang, but with a whimper. The book does not belong to the time when Israel and Judah were political powers on the stage of the world

Figure 5: Historical Setting of the Prophetic Books

Date*	Events	Prophet	Kings of Israel	Kings of Judah	Kings of Assyria/Babylon/Persia	References
					Kings of Assyria	
			Jehoahaz (816–800)		Adad-nirari III (810–783)	
805	Assyria defeats Damascus, opening the way for sixty years of Israelite and Judean expansion, a growing luxury class, and economic and religious excesses		Joash (800–785)	Amaziah (?)		*ANET* 282
		Jonah**	Jeroboam II (785–745)	Uzziah (?)	Shalmaneser IV (782–773)	
					Ashur Dan (772–755)	
		Amos (760)			Ashur-nirari IV (754–745)	
		Hosea (750–724)		Jotham (?–742)		
745	Renewed Assyrian campaigns against Aram and Palestine		Zechariah, Shallum (745)		Tiglath-pileser III (744–727)	2 Kgs 15:10
745–724	Political unrest in Israel: assassinations of Zechariah, Shallum, Menahem, Pekahiah, and Pekah		Menahem (745–736)			2 Kgs 15; ANET 282
		Isaiah of Jerusalem (738–701)	Pekahiah (736–735)	Jehoahaz I (742–727)		
735–733	Syro-Ephraimite War; Ahaz pays tribute to Assyria		Pekah (735–732)			2 Kgs 16:5-8; Isa 7:1–8:15; 2 Chr 28:5-21
732	Damascus destroyed by Assyria, Aram becomes an Assyrian province; Israel made a vassal state	Micah (730–700)	Hoshea (732–723)	Hezekiah (727–698)	Shalmaneser V (726–722)	2 Kgs 16:2; *ANET* 282
722	Israel defeated by Assyria; Hoshea imprisoned				Sargon II (721–705)	2 Kgs 17:3-4
721	Samaria destroyed by Assyria, population deported					2 Kgs 17:5-6; 18:9-12; *ANET* 284-86
713–711	Assyria defeats coalition led by Ashdod					Isa 20:1-6; *ANET* 286-87
705	Hezekiah joins coalition against Assyria				Sennacherib (704–681)	*ANET* 287-88
701	Coalition defeated by Assyria; Jerusalem spared					2 Kgs 18:13–19:37; 2 Chr 32:1-22; *ANET* 287
				Manasseh (697–642)		
689	Babylon destroyed by Assyria					
679–671	Assyrian campaigns against Egypt and Phoenicia Manasseh remains loyal to Assyria				Esarhaddon (680–669)	*ANET* 290-93
					Ashurbanipal (668–627)	
663	Thebes destroyed by Assyria					Nah 3:8-10; *ANET* 295
				Amon (642–640) Josiah (639–609)		
		Zephaniah (630–620)				

*All dates are approximate.

**Based on 2 Kgs 14:25; the book of Jonah and the events that it reports are difficult, if not impossible, to date.

Date*	Events	Prophet	Kings of Israel	Kings of Judah	Kings of Assyria/Babylon/Persia	References
					Kings of Babylon	
626	Babylon gains freedom from Assyria; Josiah's "deuteronomic reform"	Jeremiah (627–583)			Nabopolassar (626–605)	*ANET* 304 2 Kgs 23:1-25; 2 Chr 34:1-33
614	City of Asshur destroyed by Medes					*ANET* 305
612	Nineveh destroyed by Medes and Babylonians	Nahum (612)				
609	Josiah killed; Judah under Egyptian control	Habakkuk (609–597)		Jehoahaz II (609)		2 Kgs 23:29-30, 33-35;
	Defeat of Assyrian and Egyptian forces at Haran			Jehoiakim (608–598)		2 Chr 35:20-24
605	Defeat of Egyptian forces at Carchemish and Hamath				Nebuchadnezzar (605–562)	Jer 46:1-12; *ANET* 307
604	Babylon gains control of Syria, Palestine, and Phonecia					
601/600	Egypt defeats Babylonian army; Jehoiakim withholds tribute					2 Kgs 24:1 *ANET* 564
598/597	Babylonians besiege Jerusalem; first deportation			Jehoiachin (598–597)		2 Kgs 24:8-17; 2 Chr 36:10; *ANET* 564
590/589	Zedekiah withholds tribute	Ezekiel (593–573)		Zedekiah (597–586)		2 Kgs 24:20 *b*; 2 Chr 36:13
587	Jerusalem falls; Gedaliah appointed governor; second deportation	Obadiah (?)		Gedeliah (586–581?)		2 Kgs 25:1-24; 2 Chr 36:17-21 Jer 52:1-30; *ANET* 564
582/581	Gedaliah assasinated; third deportation					2 Kgs 25:25-26; Jer 40:7–42:18; 52:30
561	Jehoiachin released from prison; remains in Babylon				Evil-merodach (562–560)	2 Kgs 25:27-30; Jer 52:31-34
					Kings of Persia	
550	Cyrus the Persian begins campaigns against Lydia and Media	Second Isaiah (550–538)			Cyrus (559–530)	*ANET* 305-6
538	The city of Babylon surrenders to Persia					*ANET* 315-16 2 Chr 36:22-23; Ezra 1:1–2:70
	Edict of Cyrus; first return of exiles led by Sheshbazzar; Rebuilding of Temple begun, but soon halted					Ezra 3:8–4:5
526/525	Persia defeats Egypt					
522	Accession of Darius; Temple rebuilding resumed	Haggai (520); Zechariah (520–518)			Darius (522–486)	Ezra 5:1–6:12
516/515	Temple completed and rededicated					Ezra 6:13-18
		Malachi (?) Second Zechariah (c. 450)				
458	Ezra travels to Jerusalem (?)					Ezra 7:1–8:36
445	Nehemiah travels to Jerusalem	Joel (?)				Neh 2:1-11

*All dates are approximate.

empires, but comes from the post-exilic period, when Judah (or Yehud, as it was sometimes called) had been reduced to a minor administrative unit in the vast Persian Empire.[1] The book is written in what is, at best, elevated and crafted prose, though not devoid of imagery and structure. This is not the rich lyrical poetry of a prophet like Isaiah. Throughout much of the book the prophet is concerned with details of animal sacrifice, the payment of tithes, bored priests, unfaithful husbands, and complaining laity. What deliverance is promised will come in the distant future when the Lord "will come to his temple" (3:1 NIV), but the description of that final eschatological scenario is frustratingly brief and sparse in imaginative detail. Some sections (esp. 2:10-16) are very difficult to interpret, and individual verses (e.g., 2:15) are hopelessly corrupt in the Hebrew so that only a combination of emendation and guesswork yields any intelligible meaning. The prophet is quoted directly only twice in the NT (Mal 1:2-3 in Rom 9:13 and Mal 3:1 in Mark 1:2/Matt 11:10/Luke 7:27), and only small selections from Malachi are included in most Christian lectionaries (usually Mal 3:1-4; 4:1-2).

And yet the book is not without strength or appeal. Many years ago G. von Rad warned about the modern tendency to judge the later prophets against some artificial norm of a "great age of prophecy" and find them wanting, precisely because they are not Isaiah, Jeremiah, or Ezekiel. Von Rad concluded that "the only proper question is whether these prophets, in giving the message they did, were true ministers to their day."[2] Some years before Malachi, the prophet Zechariah had aptly described this period after the exile, when Israel had lost its king and political independence and was struggling to learn new ways to survive, as "the day of small things" (Zech 4:10 NRSV). It was in "this day of small things" that Malachi continued the established prophetic tradition and introduced new perspectives for his time and for the generations to come.

Within these four short chapters, for example, we find a particularly rich and creative reworking and integration of the major covenant themes that inspired the earlier prophets.[3] The passion for justice, the concern for the widow and orphan and laborer of the eighth-century prophets is combined with a focus on Temple, cult, and priesthood that both reflects and addresses the centrality of these institutions for the post-exilic community. In line with similar developments in Joel, Zechariah 9–14, and Isaiah 56–66, Malachi 3–4 attests to a lively eschatological expectation and introduces certain new concepts (such as the "book of remembrance" [3:16]) connected with the firm hope that "the day is coming" (4:1 NRSV). Throughout subsequent centuries in Second Temple Judaism, Malachi's description of the "covenant with Levi" (2:4 NRSV) played a formative role in the development of a rich body of literature around the figure of Levi (e.g., *Jubilees* 30–32, the *Testament of Levi,* and the Aramaic Levi Document). Similarly, the promise that Elijah

---

1. The precise status of the territory of the former kingdom of Judah and the city of Jerusalem within the Persian Empire remains a matter of scholarly debate. For a good summary of the issues and alternatives, see D. Petersen, *Zechariah 9–14 and Malachi,* OTL (Louisville: Westminster John Knox, 1995).

2. G. von Rad, *Old Testament Theology,* vol. 2 (London: SCM, 1975) 278-79.

3. See S. L. McKenzie and H. N. Wallace, "Covenant Themes in Malachi," *CBQ* 45 (1983) 549-63.

will come "before the great and terrible day of the LORD" (4:5 NRSV) generated a wealth of legends and traditions in Judaism and was of crucial importance for the early Christian community as it sought to understand both John the Baptist and Jesus and the relationship between them (see Matt 11:10-14; Mark 9:13; Luke 7:24).

AUTHOR, DATE, AND HISTORICAL CONTEXT

Scholars have long debated whether "Malachi" is to be taken as the personal name of a specific prophet or as a title, "my messenger" (מלאכי *mal'ākî*), derived from the expression in 3:1: "See, I am sending my messenger" (NRSV). I will follow established convention and use Malachi as a name, but as the commentary at 1:1 discusses in greater detail, this does not imply that we can know anything about the specific individual who was the intermediary in the transmission of these words from God. These oracles are basically anonymous and function independently of the person of the prophet.

Similarly, the book of Malachi is curiously ahistorical. There are no references to specific persons or events that would enable us to situate these words on the larger stage of world history, and many of the abuses the prophet condemns are generic to almost any period of biblical—or human—history. There is general consensus that the book comes from the time after the Babylonian exile; the references to a governor (not a king) in 1:8 and to the destruction of the kingdom of Edom (1:2-5) as well as certain linguistic features all point to the period of the Persian Empire (539–332 BCE). The date is certainly somewhat later than the prophets Haggai and Zechariah—that is, after the reestablishment of the Temple in 515 BCE.

Often these oracles are fixed more precisely in the decades immediately before Ezra and Nehemiah, c. 480–450 BCE. It is certainly true that many of the abuses condemned in Malachi are related to major concerns of the books of Ezra and Nehemiah: provision for sacrifices(Neh 10:32-39; 13:31; Mal 1:6-14); payment of tithe (Neh 10:37-39; 13:10-14; Mal 3:8-12); definition of community boundaries through regulation of acceptable marriage partners (Ezra 9–10; Neh 11:23-27; Mal 2:10-12); exploitation of the disadvantaged (Neh 5:1-13; Mal 3:5). Moreover, it is generally assumed that Malachi came first and was relatively ineffectual with his prophetic message, so that real reform was effected only with the concrete measures enacted by Ezra and Nehemiah. Although such a scenario is not impossible, it is much more speculative than often admitted and depends on a multitude of assumptions.[4] Many of the issues in Malachi are not as similar in detail to conditions at the time of Ezra–Nehemiah as appears on first glance, and such generic abuses could have been found at almost any time during the Persian period.

In addition to reading Malachi through the lens of Ezra–Nehemiah, scholars have looked for other clues that might establish a more precise date for the prophet: linguistic analysis of the

---

4. For an attempt to relate Malachi very specifically to Ezra and Nehemiah, see W. J. Dumbrell, "Malachi and the Ezra-Nehemiah Reforms," *Reformed Theological Review* 35 (1976) 42-52. Another proposed dating for Malachi is to place him precisely in the years between the first and second visits of Nehemiah to Jerusalem—that is, immediately after 433 BCE (as argued most recently by P. A. Verhoef, *The Books of Haggai and Malachi,* NICOT [Grand Rapids: Eerdmans, 1987] 156-60).

Hebrew language in the book; the relative placement of Malachi 3–4 on an evolutionary line of development of eschatological scenarios; comparison of the language with the technical terminology of the Deuteronomic and Priestly codes. But attempts to use such criteria for dating Malachi have proved problematic and fundamentally inconclusive. Recently some commentators have turned to the work of archaeologists, historians, and social scientists for help in understanding Jewish life under Persian domination.[5] Studies of settlement patterns and the size and material culture of sites in the early part of Persian rule do support the sense gleaned from the book of Malachi of a small and relatively poor community, without solid economic resources or great hopes, a community that could well ask, "Where is the God of justice?" (2:17 NRSV) and expect vindication only in a future day of direct divine intervention. Yet a certain caution must be exercised when attempting to draw precise sociological and historical conclusions from these oracles. Malachi is a prophet and, as such, condemns specific abuses in society from the perspective of God's law and the fundamental covenant reality of Israel's existence. It is simplistic, however, to conclude that his depiction of laxity, corruption, unfaithfulness, and indifference reflects the total reality of life under the rule of the Persian Empire.

Furthermore, it is surely significant that these oracles were not handed down with reference to specific historical events. In pointed contrast to the editorial process that produced the books of Haggai and Zechariah—one that judged the oracles of Haggai and Zechariah could be understood only by knowing the exact year, month, and day of their deliverance (Hag 1:1; 2:1, 10, 20; Zech 1:1, 7; 7:1)—the process of collecting and editing that led to the book of Malachi never considered such knowledge essential to reading these words of the Lord. If we take that editorial process seriously, we are in fact discouraged from seeking such historical precision, or at least assuming that such knowledge would somehow be the key to understanding this material.

TEXT, FORM, AND STRUCTURE

The Hebrew text of Malachi presents few major problems that seriously affect the meaning. Fragments from Mal 2:10–4:6 have been preserved as part of one of the Minor Prophets scrolls found at Qumran from about 150–125 BCE.[6] Perhaps a few words in another manuscript are from Mal 3:6-7.[7] These are our earliest Hebrew copies of the book, and they preserve some interesting divergent readings and perhaps a different order for the whole collection,[8] but they will not dramatically change our understanding of the book.

5. For an exploratory effort to raise many of these questions, see the two volumes of collected essays edited by P. Davies, *Second Temple Studies 1: Persian Period,* JSOTSup 117 (Sheffield: Sheffield Academic, 1991), and T. C. Eskenazi and K. H. Richards, *Second Temple Studies 2: Temple Community in the Persian Period,* JSOTSup 175 (Sheffield: Sheffield Academic, 1994). For a recent survey of the literature, see T. C. Eskenazi, "Current Perspectives on Ezra-Nehemiah and the Persian Period," *Currents in Research 1* (1993) 59-86.

6. 4QXII[a]. For a preliminary discussion of the most significant fragments, see R. E. Fuller, "Text-Critical Problems in Malachi 2:10-16," *JBL* 110 (1991) 47-57.

7. 4QXII[c]. The Qumran manuscripts of the Twelve Prophets will be published by R. E. Fuller in *Discoveries in the Judaean Desert* (Oxford: Clarendon, forthcoming).

8. In 4QXII[a], the last verses of Malachi are followed by another column of text that seems to come from Jonah. This order is not attested in any other manuscripts.

In this commentary, the focus is on the final form in which the book now exists. Scholars have sometimes tried to separate the original core of prophetic material from the secondary additions by a redactor.[9] Yet apart from the superscription in 1:1 and the final verses in 4:4-6, there is little consensus on what might be secondary additions (1:12-14; 2:11-12; 3:1 b-4; 3:13–4:3 are most frequently proposed as secondary). In any case, this short book gives little evidence of having undergone as lengthy and complex a process of development as is often postulated for other prophetic books.

The formation of the book cannot be separated from the question of how the Book of the Twelve (the "Minor Prophets") was put together. Indeed, some scholars suggest that the very existence of Malachi as a separate book (rather than as an anonymous collection of oracles or as a continuation of the material in Zech 9:1 and 12:1) came about precisely at the stage when the prophetic material was organized so that there would be exactly twelve books.[10] However, so little is known about the whole process of the formation of the Book of the Twelve that elaborate reconstructions about how this larger context shaped the book of Malachi are highly speculative and abstract.

Certain features of the book's structure are puzzling in the light of how the rest of the prophetic corpus is arranged. For instance, the traditional prophetic formula "thus says the LORD of hosts" occurs some twenty-two times, but it does not delineate short individual oracular units in the same way as in an earlier book like Amos. Although at times the phrase seems to be scattered at random, the repetition of this classic formula makes the book sound "prophetic," even though the individual units are quite different in form and structure from anything found in other prophetic literature.

The book falls clearly into six distinctive units of varying length: 1:2-5; 1:6–2:9; 2:10-16; 2:17–3:5; 3:6-12; 3:13–4:3. There is a basic common structure to each unit: an opening affirmation, whether in the form of a statement or a question; a response that calls into question in some way what was said; and an explication and amplification that reaffirms the initial word. But within this general pattern, there is considerable diversity and fluidity in the way each unit is developed.

Perhaps the most distinctive feature of the book is the repeated use of questions— twenty-two in only fifty-five verses. The questions are not all of one type. Some are rhetorical with a self-evident reply: "Is not Esau Jacob's brother?" (1:3 NRSV); "Did not one God create us?" (2:10 NIV); "Will anyone rob God?" (3:8 NRSV). Others are accusatory: "If then I am a father, where is the honor due me?" (1:6 NRSV); "When you offer blind animals in sacrifice, is that not wrong?" (1:8 NRSV). The most profound question, "Where is the God of justice?" (2:17 NIV), is not put to God directly, but quoted indirectly: "Yet you say . . . 'Where is the God of justice?' " (2:17 NRSV). The questions put directly to

9. For example, see P. L. Redditt, "The Book of Malachi in Its Social Setting," *CBQ* 56 (1994) 240-55. Redditt delineates core oracles and secondary additions and draws conclusions about the sociological setting of both.

10. J. Nogalski, *Redaction Processes in the Book of the Twelve*, BZAW 218 (New York: Walter de Gruyter, 1993) 182-212. Nogalski sees a very close link between the material in Malachi and Zechariah 1–8 and seeks to explain how it became separated in the formation of the Book of the Twelve.

God are most often "how" questions: "How have you loved us?" (1:2 NRSV); "How have we despised your name?" (1:6 NRSV); "How have we polluted it [you]?" (1:7 NRSV); "How have we wearied him?" (2:17 NIV); "How shall we return?" (3:7 NRSV); "How do we rob you?" (3:8 NIV); "How have we spoken against you?" (3:13 NRSV).

Although the genre has been described variously as "prophetic disputation," "discussion," "catechetical," or "lawsuit," none of these terms really fits the book as a whole. Other prophets certainly made use of questions (e.g., Isa 40:27-28; Jer 2:14, 23, 29, 32; Amos 5:20; Mic 2:7; Hag 1:4; 2:3; some twenty-five questions in Zechariah 1–8), but in these prophets the questions are not as central to the entire book as they are in Malachi. It is difficult to decide precisely how much this format reflects the prophet's actual style of speaking and how much it is a literary and rhetorical device, perhaps stemming from the stage when the material was put into written form. What is certain is that a new style of prophetic discourse is in the process of development, a style both more dialogical and more argumentative than in the earlier prophets.

BIBLIOGRAPHY

Recent Commentaries:

Achtemeier, Elizabeth. *Nahum–Malachi.* Interpretation. Atlanta: John Knox, 1986. A commentary for teaching and preaching. Presents an unusual view of the form of the book as a court case tried before the priest in the Temple.

Glazier-McDonald, Beth. *Malachi: The Divine Messenger.* SBLDS 98. Atlanta: Scholars Press, 1987. A close study of the Hebrew text from a literary-historical perspective.

Kaiser, Walter C., Jr. *Malachi: God's Unchanging Love.* Grand Rapids: Baker Book House, 1984. A teaching commentary written from the evangelical perspective that uses the book of Malachi as a model for how to do exegesis.

Petersen, David L. *Zechariah 9–14 and Malachi.* OTL. Louisville: Westminster/John Knox, 1995. A major scholarly commentary. Offers a distinctive perspective by treating the ten chapters of Zechariah 9–14 and Malachi 1–4 as a single body of material.

Redditt, Paul L. *Haggai, Zechariah, Malachi.* NCB. Grand Rapids: Eerdmans, 1995. A short scholarly commentary that places particular emphasis on the editorial composition of the book of Malachi.

Smith, Ralph L. *Micah–Malachi.* WBC 32. Waco, Tex.: Word, 1984. A basic scholarly commentary that summarizes the work of many earlier scholars, with excellent bibliographies on each section of the book.

Verhoef, Pieter A. *The Books of Haggai and Malachi.* NICOT. Grand Rapids: Eerdmans, 1987. Written from the perspective of evangelical scholarship; distinctive in its use of structural analysis.

Specialized Studies:

Hugenberger, Gordon Paul. *Marriage as Covenant: A Study of Biblical Law and Ethics Governing Marriage, Developed from the Perspective of Malachi.* VTSup 52. Leiden: E. J. Brill, 1994. A very detailed study of Mal 2:10-16 that makes a sustained argument for the view that Malachi understands marriage as a covenant.

Mason, Rex. *Preaching the Tradition: Homily and Hermeneutics After the Exile.* Cambridge: Cambridge University Press, 1990. Examines the similarities between the style of Malachi and the preaching of the Levites in the books of Chronicles, the speeches in Ezra–Nehemiah, and other post-exilic prophets.

O'Brien, Julia M. *Priest and Levite in Malachi.* SBLDS 121. Atlanta: Scholars Press, 1990. Focus on the understanding of priesthood in the book of Malachi and the post-exilic period.

OUTLINE OF MALACHI

I. Malachi 1:1, Superscription

II. Malachi 1:2–4:3, Six Units

    A. 1:2-5, The God of Love

    B. 1:6–2:9, Accusation Against the Priests

    C. 2:10-16, Accusation of Unfaithfulness

    D. 2:17–3:5, The God of Justice

    E. 3:6-12, Accusation Concerning Tithes

    F. 3:13–4:3, The Righteous and the Wicked

III. Malachi 4:4-6, Epilogue

MALACHI 1:1

SUPERSCRIPTION

NIV

1 An oracle: The word of the LORD to Israel through Malachi.[a]

[a]1 Malachi means *my messenger*.

NRSV

1 An oracle. The word of the LORD to Israel by Malachi.[a]

[a] Or *by my messenger*

COMMENTARY

This short verse stands outside the regular structure of the discourse, which begins in 1:2. It is similar to other superscriptions in the Book of the Twelve, and is probably the work of the redactor of the entire collection.

We read a superscription expecting certain basic information to aid us in contextualizing the oracles that follow. Above all, we expect to find the name of the prophet who acted as the intermediary in the divine-human communication. The superscription in Malachi both defeats and fulfills that expectation. There is a fundamental ambiguity about whether "Malachi" is a personal name or a title, "my messenger." The Septuagint, for instance, has translated ביד מלאכי (*běyad malʾākî*) as ἐν χειρὶ ἀγγέλου αὐτοῦ (*en cheiri angelou autou*), "at the hand of his messenger." Targum Jonathan adds: "whose name is called Ezra the scribe." The early Christian work 5 Esdras, when listing the Twelve Prophets, concludes with "Haggai, Zechariah and Malachi who is also called the messenger of the Lord" (1:40). Although linguistically the form *malʾākî* is not impossible for a personal name, no such name is attested elsewhere in the Hebrew Bible or in ancient Semitic sources. It is unlikely that the superscription is preserving simply a historical fact about an individual who was serendipitously called at birth by a name so appropriate to his designed role in life. Yet the fact remains that the redactor chose an expression that readily lent itself to being treated as a proper name. Thus this collection of oracles was no longer perceived as being anonymous, even though the superscription provides no access to the historical prophet.

The language of "messenger" as a designation for the prophet is significant. Just as in the early days of prophecy there was a change in terminology so that "the one who is now called prophet [נביא *nābîʾ*] was formerly called a seer [ראה *rōʾeh*]" (1 Sam 9:9), so also in the Persian period, those formerly called "prophet" increasingly became known by the designation "messenger." Haggai, for instance, is designated as both "prophet" (1:1, 3, 12; 2:1, 10) and "messenger" (1:13); the chronicler uses both terms for the long series of figures sent by God in the past (2 Chr 36:15-16); in Second Isaiah, "servant" and "messenger" become synonymous (Isa 42:19; 52:7). Yet even as the messenger language situates the book firmly in prophetic tradition, it also recalls the heavenly "angelic" (מלאך *malʾāk*) through whom God communicates (Gen 16:7; 22:11; Exod 3:2; Zech 1:9) and acts (Exod 23:20-23; 33:6; Isa 63:6). Furthermore, the priest, precisely in his role as teacher, is also understood as "the messenger of the LORD of hosts" (Mal 2:7 NRSV). And distinctive to Malachi is the promise of an unidentified messenger still to appear before the Day of the Lord: "See, I am sending my messenger to prepare the way" (3:1 NRSV). It is unlikely that the redactor meant to identify these oracles simplistically with the words of this eschatological messenger. But by using the designation "my messenger," the redactor has drawn the anonymous prophet into a whole network of figures past, present and future—prophetic, priestly, and divine.

The collection is called in Hebrew an "oracle" (משא *maśśāʾ*). Whatever the original sense of the term ("lifting up of the voice" or "burden"), this word became a technical term in the circles that edited the prophets (cf. the superscriptions in Isa 13:1; 17:1; 19:1; Nah 1:1; Hab 1:1). The specific combination of "oracle" with "the word of the LORD" is found only here and in Zech 9:1 and 12:1, and it points to some common editorial history for these particular collections.

In designating the audience as "Israel," the redactor sets Malachi in the same framework as Deuteronomy, the only biblical book addressed to "all Israel" (Deut 1:1). In the epilogue (Mal 4:4; see Commentary there), the entire prophetic collection is brought into relationship with the statutes and ordinances given "at Horeb for all Israel" (NRSV). Thus already in the superscription we are alerted to the influence of Deuteronomy and deuteronomistic thought in almost every segment of the book. One may discern such influence in specific vocabulary (the terminology for the priests), distinctive themes (love, fear), and the overarching framework of covenant, blessing, and curse.

REFLECTIONS

1. Why are we given so little information about the prophet? Indeed, when we turn to the prophetic books, it is often with the expectation that in this part of the Bible we can come to know a specific individual who has had immediate and direct communication with the divine. It is not by chance that for many people the favorite prophetic books are Jeremiah or Amos or Hosea, books in which the "person" of the prophet and at least some events of his life stand out more clearly (though even in these books modern critical scholarship tends to be very skeptical about our ability to recover the "real life" of the prophet).

But for many of the prophets, including Malachi, virtually nothing is known about their life or their call to prophecy or their personality. Already in the Second Temple period, this was perceived as a lacuna. A rich tradition of legendary material developed and eventually found written expression in works like "The Lives of the Prophets,"[11] a work that fills some of the gaps about "the names of the prophets and where they are from, and where they died and how, and where they lie."

2. In framing the book between the poles of Israel/all Israel (1:1; 4:4), the editors help us to make one of the basic interpretive moves required of any modern reader. The prophet addressed concrete individuals ("priests who despise my name" [1:6 NRSV]; "those who feared the LORD" [3:16 NIV]) in a specific situation eat a specific time. The editor already understands these words as being addressed far more broadly, not just to the small community in the province of Yehud, but to Israel, the whole of the twelve tribes. When we attempt to hear these words as speaking in some way to us today, in circumstances so radically different in time and place from Malachi's original context, we are only continuing a process already begun in the book itself.

In only a superficially more sophisticated way today, we often attempt to read "behind the text" to recover details of the social status and life story of the prophet—though Malachi has proved singularly resistant to all but the most speculative and general reconstructions (e.g., since Malachi speaks so highly of the Levites, he must have been a Levite). Such an approach reads against what the Bible itself considers important. The absence of personal and biographical information can focus our attention on what we do have and know: the words that came through the prophet. Precisely because we know so little about the human agency through which this word came to us, the word can stand, above all else, as a word of God.

---

11. This Jewish work, preserved in Christian sources, can be found in the *Old Testament Pseudepigrapha*, ed. J. Charlesworth, 2 vols. (New York: Doubleday, 1985) 2:379-99, esp. 394-95. The account about Malachi is brief, telling of his birth in Sopha and his early death. According to this source, his name "means 'angel'; for he was indeed beautiful to behold" (16:2).

MALACHI 1:2–4:3

SIX UNITS

MALACHI 1:2-5, THE GOD OF LOVE

NIV

2"I have loved you," says the LORD.
"But you ask, 'How have you loved us?'
"Was not Esau Jacob's brother?" the LORD says. "Yet I have loved Jacob, 3but Esau I have hated, and I have turned his mountains into a wasteland and left his inheritance to the desert jackals."

4Edom may say, "Though we have been crushed, we will rebuild the ruins."

But this is what the LORD Almighty says: "They may build, but I will demolish. They will be called the Wicked Land, a people always under the wrath of the LORD. 5You will see it with your own eyes and say, 'Great is the LORD—even beyond the borders of Israel!' "

NRSV

2I have loved you, says the LORD. But you say, "How have you loved us?" Is not Esau Jacob's brother? says the LORD. Yet I have loved Jacob 3but I have hated Esau; I have made his hill country a desolation and his heritage a desert for jackals. 4If Edom says, "We are shattered but we will rebuild the ruins," the LORD of hosts says: They may build, but I will tear down, until they are called the wicked country, the people with whom the LORD is angry forever. 5Your own eyes shall see this, and you shall say, "Great is the LORD beyond the borders of Israel!"

COMMENTARY

The opening statement of the book, a word from God, "I have loved you" (v. 1) is not so much a statement about the past as about the present. It could be translated simply "I love you." These words provide the overarching framework for the entire book; whatever will be said—accusation, judgment, promise—will come under this fundamental divine assertion.

On one level, then, this first unit serves as a prolegomenon to the book as a whole, laying out certain major themes and the basic covenantal framework within which Malachi will present his message. In content, vv. 2-5 are distinctive in that there is no element of accusation or charge of wrongdoing against the people. Yet this unit does not really stand apart, since, on formal grounds, it is bound very tightly to the other five units and, in fact, establishes the fundamental pattern (statement, question, and response) that is repeated (with modifications) as the book progresses.

The language of love evokes the rich covenant

tradition of the theology of Deuteronomy, with its attendant themes of election, obligation, and loyalty: "It was not because you were more numerous than any other people that the LORD set his heart on you and chose you. . . . It was because the LORD loved you" (Deut 7:7-8 NRSV; see also Deut 7:12-13; 10:15; 23:5). Earlier prophets had told of God's love for Israel ("When Israel was a child, I loved him" [Hos 11:1 NRSV]), but the dialogical "I-you" formulation gives this articulation a special intimacy (cf. Jer 31:3). In addition to expressing the relationship of covenant partners (see 1 Kgs 5:1, 15; Jer 22:20-23; Hos 8:8-9), the language of love also belongs to and introduces a whole range of human relationships that will find their place later in the book: husband-wife (e.g., Gen 24:67; 1 Sam 1:5; Hos 3:1), parent-child (e.g., Gen 22:2; 25:28; 37:3), even master-slave (Exod 21:5).[12]

12. The Near Eastern background of "love" and "hate" as covenant language is explored in a classic article by W. Moran, "The Ancient Near Eastern Background of the Love of God in Deuteronomy," *CBQ* 25 (1963) 77-87.

The people do not question the theoretical concept of divine love. Their response is more specific: "How/in what way have you loved us?" That is, how is that love made manifest in the present situation? Implied in the question is a perceived disparity between the divine statement of reality and what is in fact experienced. The crisp dialogue pattern does not spell out any specific reasons why the people question that God is still sovereign and their covenantal relationship secure. The loss of political independence and the reality of life under Persian rule, the failure to realize the magnificent promises of Haggai (2:7-9, 21-23) and Zechariah (1:17; 2:4, 9; 6:15; 8:12-13), and harsh economic conditions can be assumed as factors generating the complaint.

The reply is given as a divine word. God does not recite the standard "mighty works of God"— creation, exodus, granting of the land—that had traditionally been cited as signs of divine love and election (Psalms 135; 136). Rather, we are taken back to the patriarchal era and the story of the twin brothers, Esau and Jacob (Genesis 24–28). In fact, the brief retelling here goes considerably beyond the Genesis story when it sets up an absolute dichotomy between the brothers (Genesis 24 talks only of division: one stronger, one serving the other).

God's choice of Jacob as covenant partner and the attendant non-choice of Esau worked itself out in the history of the subsequent kingdoms of Israel (Jacob) and Edom (Esau). Historical sources and archaeological evidence indicate that the kingdom of Edom had been brought to an end, probably by Nabonidus in 552 BCE.[13] Although there is evidence of continuing occupation at sites such as Buseirah (Bozrah) and Tell el-Kheleifeh, Edom never recovered as a political entity, and the Nabataeans infiltrated the area from the fifth century BCE onward.

The description of the destruction of Edom in

13. For the history of the kingdom of Edom, see J. Bartlett, *Edom and the Edomites,* JSOTSup 77 (Sheffield: Sheffield Academic, 1989).

the language of the covenantal curses (v. 3) could not but stir memories of the time, not so long before in the days of Nebuchadnezzar, when Jerusalem and Judah were made a desolation, a home for the jackals (note the same combination in Jer 9:11; 10:22). It is not so much the destruction of Edom that is the key to the argument, but the fact that Edom was not successfully rebuilt. Unfortunately so little is known about Edom in the late sixth and fifth centuries BCE that it is impossible to say whether some concrete incident or attempt at reestablishment lies behind Mal 1:2-5. But the fact that the efforts of the Edomnites came to naught is interpreted as visible proof of God's rejection. In contrast, Israel's continued existence is proof of God's love. In spite of its smallness under Persian rule, in spite of economic hardships and internal discord, the Yehud community does exist. The people have rebuilt—not as before to be sure, but the present life of the community provides evidence that God is still fulfilling the obligations of covenant love.

It is the people (as quoted by God) who have the last word (v. 5), and it is a word of doxology. Similar expressions of praise are heard at various intervals throughout the first part of the book (1:11, 14) in a manner reminiscent of hymnic passages that likewise conclude key oracles in Amos (Amos 4:13; 5:8; 9:5). The people will take up the traditional cultic refrain "Great is the LORD" (Pss 35:27; 40:16; 48:1; 70:4; 96:4; 99:2; 104:1; 145:3) as they acknowledge and make their own the prophetic interpretation of their present reality. Both the NRSV and the NIV understand the last phrase as "beyond the borders of Israel" (מעל לגבול ישראל *mē ʿal ligĕbûl yiśrā ʾēl*), a translation that highlights the universal dimension of divine activity; however, the preposition in Hebrew also can mean "above the borders of Israel" (as it is translated in the Septuagint and the Vulgate). Surely both senses are appropriate; God is great in Edom and among the nations, but first and fundamentally God is great in Israel.

REFLECTIONS

1. Modern sensibility finds particularly problematic the language of God hating Esau/Edom. Clearly the text is talking about something other than simply an emotional or a psychological "feeling." Within the whole covenant framework of the book, the fundamental issue is that of election and non-election: God has chosen Jacob and has not chosen Esau. Yet the fact remains that the retelling in Malachi is much harsher than the Genesis version of the story. Only in Malachi is the language of hating actually applied to God; in Genesis, it is Esau who hates Jacob (Gen 27:41).

We tend to think immediately in terms of moral causality and ask what Esau/Edom did so wrong as to merit this rejection. But this is precisely the connection that Malachi never makes. The rejection of Edom is not linked to any action or sin on its part, and this stands in marked contrast to passages like Joel 3:19 or Obad 10, which see a causal relationship between Edom's destruction and "the slaughter and violence done to your brother Jacob" (Obad 10 NRSV). Romans 9:13 draws upon the Jacob/Esau story (and quotes Mal 1:2-3: "I have loved Jacob but I have hated Esau") precisely as an example of the absolute freedom of divine choice. Esau's rejection has nothing to do with wrongdoings, but is "so that God's purpose of election might continue, not by works but by his call" (Rom 9:11-12 NRSV).

If God's rejection of Esau is rooted in this inscrutable divine freedom, so too, by implication, is the choice of Jacob. The divine choice to love/choose Jacob is as great a mystery as the choice to love/hate Esau. When the passage is read by those who see themselves in some way as the descendants of Jacob, it serves not as a source of pride or "we/them" speculation, but as a cautionary reminder that our status as a beloved child is a free, unmerited, inexplicable gift.

2. The nature of this first question, "How have you loved us?" and, indeed, of all the questions that the people voice throughout the book merits reflection. What kind of question is this? It is not simply a request for information. Nor does it have quite the same tenor as the anguished cry of the innocent sufferer in the psalms of lament or the wisdom tradition. There is an element of skepticism and doubt, a challenge to God. Some commentators have heard "a cynical sneer."[14] Perhaps that is too harsh, and the questioner is more like an insistent pre-adolescent who demands that the parent produce proof and evidence for every accusation. Or maybe the comparison should be with "those students who have enough knowledge to hold up a lecture, but who do not really want to make any progress with the matter which is questioning them!"[15]

What is significant is that in the book of Malachi these difficult questions are not met with silence. Within the literary structure of the book (whether this reflects an actual dialogue or is a second-level restructuring of the material), it is the articulation of such disconcerting questions that elicits the divine response.

In recent biblical, pastoral, and liturgical study, considerable attention has been directed to the way the church deals with the issue of lament that arises out of intense suffering and brokenness. There is much more awareness today of the value and healing power of articulating the questions and doubts, and the need for developing structures, both personal and public, where the voicing of such laments can take place freely. But we have thought much less about what to do with the questions of the skeptic and the disillusioned. Should they receive a hearing? If even some members of the community speak openly of the possibility that God is no longer active, if they push the point and demand a concrete answer—"Well, *how* does God love us?"—this can be profoundly disturbing, not only to the questioner but also to others who hear voiced out aloud what they have perhaps not even dared to articulate. Yet the book of Malachi suggests that the articulation of such questions may be necessary for allowing the dialogue to progress to deeper levels.

Perhaps particularly when faced with questions that arise from skepticism and disillusionment, the answers may not be found in the most familiar stories and foundational themes of biblical tradition. The reviving of the less-central Esau/Jacob story seemed to speak to Malachi's

14. E. Achtemeier, *Nahum–Malachi* (Atlanta: John Knox, 1986) 174.
15. M. E. Andrew, "Post-Exilic Prophets and the Ministry of Creating Community," *ExpTim* 98 (1981–82) 45.

audience in a way that yet another recital of the wonders of the exodus could not. Ours is an age when faith is not self-evident and the simple affirmation of fundamental statements like "God loves you" no longer guarantees assent. But are there elements of the Christian tradition that might strike a cord of resonance even when the "old story" no longer generates a response? Perhaps the recovery of feminine imagery for God, creation-based ecological reflection, and a wisdom christology can serve such a function.

MALACHI 1:6–2:9, ACCUSATION AGAINST THE PRIESTS

NIV

⁶"A son honors his father, and a servant his master. If I am a father, where is the honor due me? If I am a master, where is the respect due me?" says the Lord Almighty. "It is you, O priests, who show contempt for my name.

"But you ask, 'How have we shown contempt for your name?'

⁷"You place defiled food on my altar.

"But you ask, 'How have we defiled you?'

"By saying that the Lord's table is contemptible. ⁸When you bring blind animals for sacrifice, is that not wrong? When you sacrifice crippled or diseased animals, is that not wrong? Try offering them to your governor! Would he be pleased with you? Would he accept you?" says the Lord Almighty.

⁹"Now implore God to be gracious to us. With such offerings from your hands, will he accept you?"—says the Lord Almighty.

¹⁰"Oh, that one of you would shut the temple doors, so that you would not light useless fires on my altar! I am not pleased with you," says the Lord Almighty, "and I will accept no offering from your hands. ¹¹My name will be great among the nations, from the rising to the setting of the sun. In every place incense and pure offerings will be brought to my name, because my name will be great among the nations," says the Lord Almighty.

¹²"But you profane it by saying of the Lord's table, 'It is defiled,' and of its food, 'It is contemptible.' ¹³And you say, 'What a burden!' and you sniff at it contemptuously," says the Lord Almighty.

"When you bring injured, crippled or diseased animals and offer them as sacrifices, should I

NRSV

6A son honors his father, and servants their master. If then I am a father, where is the honor due me? And if I am a master, where is the respect due me? says the Lord of hosts to you, O priests, who despise my name. You say, "How have we despised your name?" ⁷By offering polluted food on my altar. And you say, "How have we polluted it?"ᵃ By thinking that the Lord's table may be despised. ⁸When you offer blind animals in sacrifice, is that not wrong? And when you offer those that are lame or sick, is that not wrong? Try presenting that to your governor; will he be pleased with you or show you favor? says the Lord of hosts. ⁹And now implore the favor of God, that he may be gracious to us. The fault is yours. Will he show favor to any of you? says the Lord of hosts. ¹⁰Oh, that someone among you would shut the templeᵇ doors, so that you would not kindle fire on my altar in vain! I have no pleasure in you, says the Lord of hosts, and I will not accept an offering from your hands. ¹¹For from the rising of the sun to its setting my name is great among the nations, and in every place incense is offered to my name, and a pure offering; for my name is great among the nations, says the Lord of hosts. ¹²But you profane it when you say that the Lord's table is polluted, and the food for itᶜ may be despised. ¹³"What a weariness this is," you say, and you sniff at me,ᵈ says the Lord of hosts. You bring what has been taken by violence or is lame or sick, and this you bring as your offering! Shall I accept that from your hand? says the Lord. ¹⁴Cursed be the cheat who has a male

ᵃ Gk: Heb *you* ᵇ Heb lacks *temple* ᶜ Compare Syr Tg: Heb *its* *fruit, its food* ᵈ Another reading is *at it*

NIV

accept them from your hands?" says the LORD. [14]"Cursed is the cheat who has an acceptable male in his flock and vows to give it, but then sacrifices a blemished animal to the Lord. For I am a great king," says the LORD Almighty, "and my name is to be feared among the nations.

2 "And now this admonition is for you, O priests. [2]If you do not listen, and if you do not set your heart to honor my name," says the LORD Almighty, "I will send a curse upon you, and I will curse your blessings. Yes, I have already cursed them, because you have not set your heart to honor me.

[3]"Because of you I will rebuke[a] your descendants[b]; I will spread on your faces the offal from your festival sacrifices, and you will be carried off with it. [4]And you will know that I have sent you this admonition so that my covenant with Levi may continue," says the LORD Almighty. [5]"My covenant was with him, a covenant of life and peace, and I gave them to him; this called for reverence and he revered me and stood in awe of my name. [6]True instruction was in his mouth and nothing false was found on his lips. He walked with me in peace and uprightness, and turned many from sin.

[7]"For the lips of a priest ought to preserve knowledge, and from his mouth men should seek instruction—because he is the messenger of the LORD Almighty. [8]But you have turned from the way and by your teaching have caused many to stumble; you have violated the covenant with Levi," says the LORD Almighty. [9]"So I have caused you to be despised and humiliated before all the people, because you have not followed my ways but have shown partiality in matters of the law."

[a]3 Or *cut off* (see Septuagint)   [b]3 Or *will blight your grain*

NRSV

in the flock and vows to give it, and yet sacrifices to the Lord what is blemished; for I am a great King, says the LORD of hosts, and my name is reverenced among the nations.

2 And now, O priests, this command is for you. [2]If you will not listen, if you will not lay it to heart to give glory to my name, says the LORD of hosts, then I will send the curse on you and I will curse your blessings; indeed I have already cursed them,[a] because you do not lay it to heart. [3]I will rebuke your offspring, and spread dung on your faces, the dung of your offerings, and I will put you out of my presence.[b]

4Know, then, that I have sent this command to you, that my covenant with Levi may hold, says the LORD of hosts. [5]My covenant with him was a covenant of life and well-being, which I gave him; this called for reverence, and he revered me and stood in awe of my name. [6]True instruction was in his mouth, and no wrong was found on his lips. He walked with me in integrity and uprightness, and he turned many from iniquity. [7]For the lips of a priest should guard knowledge, and people should seek instruction from his mouth, for he is the messenger of the LORD of hosts. [8]But you have turned aside from the way; you have caused many to stumble by your instruction; you have corrupted the covenant of Levi, says the LORD of hosts, [9]and so I make you despised and abased before all the people, inasmuch as you have not kept my ways but have shown partiality in your instruction.

[a] Heb *it*   [b] Cn Compare Gk Syr: Heb *and he shall bear you to it*

COMMENTARY

This longest unit comprises a full third of the total number of verses in Malachi. It can be subdivided into three units, which the prophet ties together with rhetorical patterning and verbal and thematic repetition.

The first subunit, 1:6-11, states the basic accusation: "where is the honor due me?" (1:6). It then identifies specific abuses in the offering of sacrifices. The unit concludes with a doxology that echoes the themes of divine greatness and universality that were already introduced in the brief doxological word at the end of the first unit (1:5).

The next subunit, 1:12-14, takes up once again issues of flagrant disregard for the proper conduct of the cult. While some commentators have judged this to be a secondary expansion, the prophet may have introduced such repetition for a rhetorical purpose: We are in the midst of a discussion going around in a circle with no hope of change! This section concludes with yet another doxological verse (1:14) that combines elements from vv. 5 and 11 so that the interplay of accusation and praise continues.

The third subunit, 2:1-9 might be taken as a fully independent unit, but in fact it continues the address to the priests begun in 1:6. Indeed, the sharpness of the final words of judgment are fully appreciated only when read in close conjunction with the initial accusation: The priests who despise God (1:6) will themselves be despised (2:9). A number of key words bind together both sections, especially "respect" and "reverence" (the Hebrew verbal root ירא [yr']) in 1:6, 14, and 2:5 and "honor" (the root כבד kbd) in 1:6 and 2:2. Thus what seems at first glance a rambling, repetitious tirade is really a carefully structured discourse.

The opening statement in 1:6, which establishes the framework for the entire unit, brings together the language of both familial and covenantal relationships. In contrast to the intensely personal introduction in 1:2 ("I have loved you"), here we have a very general maxim that can presume commonsense assent. This discussion of right relationship between father and son and master and servant is rooted in the specific commandment of the Decalogue (Exod 20:12), standard wisdom reflection (Prov 19:26; 28:24; Sir 3:12-16), and the language of covenant obligation (cf. especially the words of King Ahaz to his Assyrian overlord, Tiglath-pileser: "I am your servant and your son" [2 Kgs 16:7 NRSV]).

The distinctive style of the book is especially evident in 1:6-14, in the series of short, staccato exchanges between God and the priests. In no other biblical text are so many questions and responses hurled back and forth in such short order. Occasionally the voice of the prophet is heard—for example, with the ironic appeal of 1:9a: "Now implore God to be gracious to us." Verse 14 deftly extends the curse to the laity who bring a blemished sacrifice. But 2:1-9 marks a dramatic shift: Suddenly no questions or comments are allowed to interrupt what is the most extended word from the Lord in the whole book.

The accusations against both priests and laity in these first two subunits (1:6-8, 12-14) all involve failure in the performance of their ritual duties as functionaries in the sacrificial system of the Temple. The Deuteronomic and Priestly laws (see Lev 1:3; 22:17-25; Deut 15:19-23), which require that animals be free of defect and blemish, are assumed or even expanded (e.g., to include sick animals, something not specified in any of the legal codes). In the third subunit, a second distinct accusation is introduced in 2:8-9: "caused many to stumble by your instruction." This presentation of the accusation in two stages is a pattern found also in the next major unit of the book (one accusation in 2:10-12 followed by 2:13: "And this you do as well . . . ").

Scholars have long debated whether Malachi's intent in 1:6–2:9 is to set up a fundamental distinction between the Aaronite priests—who are accused, judged, and condemned (1:6-13; 2:1-3, 8-9)—and the Levites, who are praised as being faithful to their task (2:4-7).[16] This issue is related to the equally disputed question of whether Malachi is working from the specialized perspective of the priestly code, with its fundamental distinction between priests and Levites, or whether he considers all Levites as priests, as is the case in Deuteronomy (Deut 17:9; 18:1-8). Some have tried to fit Malachi within the broader framework of a comprehensive struggle between rival priestly groups—an Aaronite priesthood that established its power with Persian support in the early years of the restoration versus the Levites as a subordinate group, disenfranchised and deprived of status.[17] Yet these issues simply do not seem to be the predominant concern of the book. Moreover, the terminology used in conjunction with both priesthood and sacrifice is surprisingly nontechnical and flexible. We are reading a passionate prophetic outcry against blatant abuses, not a sociological survey or a handbook for priests.

The prophet did see very real abuses in the

---

16. For an extensive treatment of these questions, see Julia M. O'Brien, *Priest and Levite in Malachi*, SBLDS 121 (Atlanta: Scholars Press, 1990).
17. P. D. Hanson, in particular, fits the book of Malachi into this reconstruction of the whole post-exilic period. See Hanson's *The People Called: The Growth of Community in the Bible* (San Francisco: Harper & Row, 1986) 277-90.

priesthood and the sacrificial system, but it is difficult to penetrate the highly charged accusatory rhetoric. Did economic, political, or religious factors also contribute to the situation that the prophet judged so harshly? Was it that the priests or the people did not have the financial resources to bring the required sacrifices (cf. 3:10-11), or did the substitution of what was cheaper or damaged mask a fundamental crisis of belief in the efficiency of temple sacrifice: "What a weariness this is!" (1:13)? The ironic challenge, "Try presenting that to your governor" (1:8), may suggest that offerings to the Temple and dues to the foreign rulers were somehow implicitly put on a par, particularly at a time when the Temple was becoming an important economic and political institution in the Yehud community.[18]

While modern sensibilities might predispose us to look for economic and social causes behind the language of cultic abuses (even if we cannot define these causes very precisely), such was not the prophet's focus. For Malachi, failures in the sacrificial realm somehow touch upon the very core of the divine. It is not just the Lord's table, but the very name and essence of God that are despised. It is not just that the people are offering defiled food (1:7); rather, they have defiled *"you"* (as the NIV reads, following the Hebrew [גאלנוך *gē'alnûkā*] exactly; the NRSV follows the Greek [ἠλισγήσαμεν αὐτούς *ēlisgēsamen autous*], which is probably a softening of the strange expression about defiling/polluting God to "we polluted *it"*). In an expression that was considered so blasphemous that the ancient scribes dared to change it, the accusation is made that "you sniff at me" (1:13; the NRSV reading here maintains the uncorrected Hebrew [הפחתם אותו *hippaḥtem 'ôtô*]; the NIV follows the softened text: "you sniff at it").

The accusations end in a word of judgment (1:10), which equates the rejection of sacrifice ("I will not accept an offering from your hands") with the rejection of the people ("I have no pleasure in you"). There has been much discussion and little agreement about how 1:11 fits into this context.[19] By implication, the unacceptable worship offered in Jerusalem (1:6-10) is contrasted with acceptable "incense . . . and pure offering" in every place. Is this worship offered by pagans? Or does the text refer to worship offered by Jews who are not involved in the Jerusalem Temple worship—Jews in the diaspora who worship at other temples, such as at Elephantine in Egypt, or in synagogues and houses of prayer? The NRSV understands this alternate worship as a present reality, while the NIV looks to an eschatological future. To try to find "anonymous Yahwists"[20] who worship the God of Israel without knowing it or to find a startling new revelation of universalism is to read more than these verses can bear. The language is doxological rather than didactic. The words that the people are to proclaim in the future, "great is the LORD" (1:5), are already recast here as a divine self-proclamation: "My name is great" (1:11). Although the abuses in the Temple may touch the very core of the sacred, God's sovereignty and greatness do not depend on what happens in the Temple.

The standard prophetic expression "And now" (2:1) marks the transition from accusation to pronouncement of the words of judgment. The most distinctive aspect of 2:1-9 is that the judgment of the priests, although described in terms of the traditional blessings and curses of the Sinaitic covenant (Deuteronomy 27–28), is rooted in the concept of a special covenant with Levi, the son of Jacob, from whom all priests are descended. Such a concept is not unique to Malachi. Jeremiah 33:21 refers to "my covenant with my ministers the Levites" (NRSV), and Neh 13:29 speaks of "the covenant of the priests and the Levites" (NRSV). But Malachi puts special emphasis on the figure of Levi per se (2:5 NIV captures this nuance of the Hebrew well: "My covenant was *with him,* a covenant of life and peace" [italics added]). Yet nowhere does Genesis say specifically that God entered into a covenant relationship with Levi. Malachi appears to draw upon the blessing of Levi in Deut 33:8-11, with its special emphasis on the instructional role of the Levites ("They teach Jacob your ordinances,/ and Israel your law" [Deut 33:10 NRSV]). This perspective is combined with the description of the covenant made with Phinehas, a descendant of Levi through the line of

18. For changing understandings of the Temple, see S. Japhet, "The Temple in the Restoration Period: Reality and Ideology," *USQR* 44 (1991) 195-251.

19. For a concise survey of the various ways this verse has been interpreted, see P. A. Verhoef, *The Books of Haggai and Malachi,* NICOT (Grand Rapids: Eerdmans, 1987) 222-32.

20. To paraphrase Karl Rahner's "anonymous Christians." See Rahner, *Theological Investigations,* vol. 5 (Baltimore: Helicon, 1966) 115-34.

Aaron (Num 25:10-13); in particular, the phrase "a covenant of peace" (2:5; NRSV, "well-being" [שלום *haššālôm*]) comes from the Phinehas tradition. Just as God's election of the people is traced back—to a very early stage, to the choice of Jacob—so also Malachi goes back beyond the particular line of Zadok or even of Aaron to concentrate on the choice of Levi as founder of the priestly line.[21]

In presenting his distinctive and idealized portrait of the priest, Malachi draws upon a number of expressions that are unique in the OT, or at least not usually associated with the priestly realm (e.g., the particular form of the verb נחת [*nāḥēt*] in 2:5: "stood in awe"). The specific words of praise, "he walked with me" (2:6) associate Levi with the primeval figures of Enoch and Noah (Gen 5:22; 6:9), the two biblical figures who "walked with" God. And, in describing the priest as "the messenger," Malachi links him not only with the figure of the prophet but also with the angelic

messengers of the heavenly court. Like Joshua (see Zech 3:1-7), the priest has the right of access with the other heavenly messengers who stand before God.

The contrast between the ideal of priesthood and the present reality leads to a final reiteration of accusation and judgment (2:8-9). As M. Fishbane has pointed out, in this climactic verse, as in many verses throughout 1:6–2:9, the words of judgment are to be read against the background of the solemn priestly blessing of Num 6:24-26. Throughout this entire passage, the prophet has "taken the contents of that Priestly Blessing, with its emphasis on blessing, the sanctity of the divine Name, and such benefactions as protection, gracious/favorable countenance, and peace—and negated them!"[22] Thus those who "have not kept [שמר *šāmar*] my ways" (2:9) and have been derelict in their task to "guard [*šāmar*] knowledge" (2:7) can no longer be permitted to invoke the solemn priestly words: "The LORD bless you and keep [*šāmar*] you" (Num 6:24 NIV). Those persons who "despise my name" (1:6) will themselves be despised (2:9) and rejected.

---

21. There was great interest in Levi throughout the Second Temple period, and Mal 2:5-7 became a key passage in this development. Texts such as *Jubilees* 30–32, *The Testament of Levi*, and the Aramaic Levi Document describe how Levi ascended to the heavens, received divine instruction from an angel, and was elevated to the priesthood. For further exploration of this rich tradition, see J. Kugel, "Levi's Elevation to the Priesthood in the Second Temple Writings," *HTR* 86 (1993) 1-64.

22. M. Fishbane, "Form and Reformulation of the Biblical Priestly Blessing," *JAOS* 103 (1983) 115-21.

REFLECTIONS

1. Passages like 1:6–2:9 make a prophet like Malachi seem so different from, even inferior to, the so-called classic prophets of the pre-exilic era. The prophet seems concerned only about the minutiae of legal regulations concerning animals fit for sacrifice and judgments rendered by priests about what is acceptable and unacceptable in the sacrificial cult. What has happened to justice rolling down like waters and righteousness like an ever-flowing stream (Amos 5:24)? Modern understanding of prophecy has tended to be much more sympathetic to the voice of Amos, and finds it very difficult to incorporate Malachi into a "working definition" of prophecy.

But this is precisely where the book of Malachi can offer a salutary note of caution against the temptation to dichotomize and divide—between religion as worship and religion as action; between obligations to God and obligations to neighbor; between service and praise. These fundamental conflicts manifest themselves and are played out in very different ways in the concrete life of a community. The facile solution always is to separate, to let the "smells and bells" people do their thing and the social activists do theirs. But Malachi offers a glimpse of another path. Totally at home in the prophetic tradition, he speaks from the center of that tradition "against those who oppress the hired workers in their wages, the widow and the orphan" (3:5 NRSV). Yet the world of the priest and the Temple and meticulous observance of cultic norms are treated with equal gravity. Perhaps most important is that the two poles of social justice and cult are brought together, not just by an intellectual exposition of their complementarity, but also in the lived experience of the prophet.

2. There is something very down-to-earth about the discussion of the physical condition of the animal brought for sacrifice in this passage—to the point that God ends up looking rather mercenary and petty, as if saying, "What you have offered is just not good enough for me." Of course, we recognize that this is not the whole picture, and immediately we want to move to a discussion of the requisite inward spiritual attitude of both priest and offerer. But this passage insists that the inward reality and concrete physical regalia of worship cannot be totally separated. Christian communities are not concerned with blemished animals. But what would Malachi say about the quality of music, books, physical surroundings, bread and wine, and art that are brought forward for use in worship today?

3. Passages that are directed to a particular group within the community always pose a particular challenge. When Malachi addresses the priests (1:6; 2:1), he seems to be speaking only to one segment of the community. For the majority of Christians reading this passage, this is a text about the "other," not me but "them." Although the understanding of the "priesthood of all believers" may be prominent in some churches, few laypeople, on hearing "O priests, who despise my name" will immediately think of themselves. In fact, what may well come to mind is the latest scandal about some pastor, priest, or televangelist. In Christian lectionaries that make use of some selection of verses from this part of Malachi, this impression is reinforced because the passage is paired with Matthew's harsh critique of the leaders of the community who impose heavy burdens and love the places of honor (Matt 23:1-12).[23]

It is relatively easy to apply this passage to the priests and other leaders of the Christian community. But how do the laity hear a Scripture passage that is basically directed to someone else—without its becoming simply an occasion to gloat over that person's failures? One hint may come in 1:14, where the prophet makes a sudden, and on one level seemingly out-of-place, shift to utter a harsh curse against "the cheat," the layperson who brings a blemished animal for sacrifice. The insertion of this indictment of the sins of the laity right in the middle of a word directed to the priests does not allow the laity to stand on the sidelines in righteous self-justification; they, too, are brought under judgment. The sins of the priests are paralleled by, indeed may even be implicitly supported by, the wider lay community. The passage invites reflection on the interdependence of priests and laity in our communities. When are abuses and corruption on the part of priests and leaders in some way a reflection of fundamental problems in the community as a whole? The exposure of the sins of the leaders calls the total community to self-examination and mutual accountability.

4. Malachi emphasizes the role of the priest as teacher (2:5-7), as both the repository and the hander-on of the traditions of the community. The priest speaks, not on the basis of charismatic inspiration, as does the prophet, but from the knowledge of accumulated tradition and professional learning. Priests in the OT and throughout the ancient Near East were not innovators and revealers of new knowledge, but were "faithful custodians" who transmitted the accumulated lore and rules of behavior. In this way, the priesthood functioned as a "conservative force" in Israel's life.[24]

In our age, which values highly creativity and innovation, we are often instinctively fearful of the power of tradition and assume that anyone or anything that speaks out of the past is imposing a memory that will be restrictive and suffocating. Malachi's praise of the priesthood of Levi is rooted in a different understanding of the role of tradition. A fundamental openness to the past and its accumulated wisdom is the prerequisite for allowing a community to reflect carefully and discriminatingly on what knowledge from the past deserves to be preserved and

23. The Roman Catholic lectionary for the 31st Sunday, Year A, reads Mal 1:14-2:2, 8-10 (a most unusual combination of verses from three separate units). The Lutheran *Book of Worship* selects Mal 2:1-2, 4-10.

24. For a thoughtful reflection on this aspect of the OT priesthood, see the section "Faithful Custodians" by R. D. Nelson, *Raising Up a Faithful Priest: Community and Priesthood in Biblical Theology* (Louisville: Westminster/John Knox, 1993) 88-93.

handed on. But such transmission does not take place automatically, or even by individual effort. In praising not so much the individual priest but the institution of the priesthood of Levi, this passage in Malachi invites us to look anew at the institutions in our church and our society that can function as the carriers of "true instruction."

MALACHI 2:10-16, ACCUSATION OF UNFAITHFULNESS

NIV

[10]Have we not all one Father[a]? Did not one God create us? Why do we profane the covenant of our fathers by breaking faith with one another?

[11]Judah has broken faith. A detestable thing has been committed in Israel and in Jerusalem: Judah has desecrated the sanctuary the LORD loves, by marrying the daughter of a foreign god. [12]As for the man who does this, whoever he may be, may the LORD cut him off from the tents of Jacob[b]—even though he brings offerings to the LORD Almighty.

[13]Another thing you do: You flood the LORD's altar with tears. You weep and wail because he no longer pays attention to your offerings or accepts them with pleasure from your hands. [14]You ask, "Why?" It is because the LORD is acting as the witness between you and the wife of your youth, because you have broken faith with her, though she is your partner, the wife of your marriage covenant.

[15]Has not the LORD made them one? In flesh and spirit they are his. And why one? Because he was seeking godly offspring.[c] So guard yourself in your spirit, and do not break faith with the wife of your youth.

[16]"I hate divorce," says the LORD God of Israel, "and I hate a man's covering himself[d] with violence as well as with his garment," says the LORD Almighty.

So guard yourself in your spirit, and do not break faith.

a10 Or father   b12 Or 12May the LORD cut off from the tents of Jacob anyone who gives testimony in behalf of the man who does this   c15 Or 15But the one who is our father, did not do this, not as long as life remained in him. And what was he seeking? An offspring from God   d16 Or his wife

NRSV

10Have we not all one father? Has not one God created us? Why then are we faithless to one another, profaning the covenant of our ancestors? [11]Judah has been faithless, and abomination has been committed in Israel and in Jerusalem; for Judah has profaned the sanctuary of the LORD, which he loves, and has married the daughter of a foreign god. [12]May the LORD cut off from the tents of Jacob anyone who does this—any to witness[a] or answer, or to bring an offering to the LORD of hosts.

13And this you do as well: You cover the LORD's altar with tears, with weeping and groaning because he no longer regards the offering or accepts it with favor at your hand. [14]You ask, "Why does he not?" Because the LORD was a witness between you and the wife of your youth, to whom you have been faithless, though she is your companion and your wife by covenant. [15]Did not one God make her?[b] Both flesh and spirit are his.[c] And what does the one God[d] desire? Godly offspring. So look to yourselves, and do not let anyone be faithless to the wife of his youth. [16]For I hate[e] divorce, says the LORD, the God of Israel, and covering one's garment with violence, says the LORD of hosts. So take heed to yourselves and do not be faithless.

a Cn Compare Gk: Heb arouse   b Or Has he not made one?
c Cn: Heb and a remnant of spirit was his   d Heb he
e Cn: Heb he hates

COMMENTARY

These verses are certainly the most problematic in Malachi. Even a cursory examination of the divergencies in translation in the NRSV and the NIV gives some indication of the problems, particularly since both attempt to translate the Masoretic Text as literally as possible. (It is well worth looking at other Scripture versions just to get a sense of still other alternatives.) Of particular note is the phrase that "has always been a riddle"[25] in v. 12: ער וענה (*'ēr wĕ'ōneh*). The NRSV emends the first word slightly and reads "any to witness or to answer." The NIV understands it as an all-inclusive idiomatic expression: "whoever he may be." In v. 15, the individual words are straightforward, but the passage is so elliptical that most of the context has to be supplied, and this can be been done in quite different ways.

The difficulties of this section, however, go far beyond the translation of specific words and phrases. Scholars have not been able to agree about the fundamental nature of the accusation. One line of interpretation understands the passage as being concerned with specific abuses in marital practices—marriage with foreign women, marital infidelity, and divorce.[26] Whether these are separate issues or somehow related is far from clear. Nor is it clear whether the prophet is reacting to the specific situation of marriage with foreign women, which Ezra and Nehemiah describe (Ezra 9–10; Neh 13:23-29), so that it is justifiable or even helpful to read Malachi specifically in the light of the Ezra–Nehemiah account.

The other major line of interpretation, in keeping with a well-established prophetic tradition (Hosea; Jeremiah), understands this language of husband/wife, unfaithfulness, and divorce as figurative language, so that the issue at stake is really idolatry. That is, Israel (the husband) has been unfaithful to the Lord, "the wife of your youth," and has married "the daughter of a foreign god" (v. 11)—pagan deities, who are worshiped along with Israel's own God (vv. 12-13) in syncretistic fashion.[27] According to this interpretation, the prophet focuses here, as in 1:6–2:9, upon improper worship. Although this commentary will work within the framework that the prophet is speaking of actual marriages, it should still be noted that he chooses to introduce, within a passage on marriage, language that applies basically to idolatry (particularly in v. 11, with the strong term "abomination" [תועבה *tô'ēbâ*]; cf. Deut 7:25-26; 13:14; 17:4; 18:9; 20:18; 32:16; Isa 44:19).

Although vv. 10-16 possess certain distinctive features, the unit is by no means separate, either in form or in content, from the rest of the book. Like 1:6–2:9 and 2:17–3:5, 2:10-16 names a specific cluster of abuses and pronounces a word of judgment. As in the preceding unit, what is at stake is a violation of covenant: The priests "corrupted the covenant of Levi" (2:8), and the people profaned "the covenant of our ancestors" (2:10; a term inclusive of both the Sinai covenant and the covenant with Abraham). The effect is experienced in both instances in the cultic realm: God will not accept offerings (2:10, 13). As elsewhere in the book, the judicious repetition of key words holds this unit together; the fivefold repetition of the verb "to be unfaithful" (בגד *bāgad*; 2:10, 11, 14, 15, 16) and the fourfold repetition of "one" (אחד *'eḥād*; twice in 1:10 and twice in 1:15). Although the manifold questions and the petulant demand "Why?" (2:14) typify the book as a whole, the questions in vv. 10-16 are unusual. This is the only place in Malachi where the self-evident proposal that serves as the foundational starting point for the whole unit is expressed as a rhetorical question: "Have we not all one father? Has not one God created us?" (v. 10). The second question, "Why then are we faithless. . . ?" (v. 10), introduces an unusual communal

---

25. Beth Glazier-McDonald, *Malachi: The Divine Messenger*, SBLDS 98 (Atlanta: Scholars Press, 1987) 94. MacDonald proposes that both words carry a sexual connotation and translates them as "the aroused one and the lover." David Petersen's translation also involves a sexual connotation, "involving nakedness and improper cohabitation" (Petersen, *Zechariah 9–14 and Malachi*, OTL [Louisville: Westminster John Knox, 1995] 194-95).

26. For a recent presentation of this approach, with a particular focus on the phrase "wife of your covenant," see G. P. Hugenberger, *Marriage as Covenant: A Study of Biblical Law and Ethics Governing Marriage, Developed from the Perspective of Malachi*, VTSup 52 (Leiden: E. J. Brill, 1994).

27. For an example of the metaphorical reading, see Petersen, *Zechariah 9–14 and Malachi*, 193-206. In 2:11, Petersen emends a word in the Hebrew text (אשר *'ašer*) to restore a specific reference to the goddess Asherah (אשרה *'ăšērâ*).

self-accusation. The questions in v. 15, although so difficult to interpret, obviously advance the content of the discussion rather than querying a point already made. The refrains in v. 16—"says the LORD of hosts" and "says the LORD, the God of Israel" (a variation attested only here)—do not appear until the very last verse, and even there one cannot be certain that there is a first-person statement of the Lord (see discussion of v. 16). Most of this unit exists as dialogue between the prophet and the people, with both parties referring to God. The prophet, who was almost invisible up to this point, adopts a much more active role. He is the invoker of the curse: "May the LORD cut off" (v. 12). He is the accuser: "You cover the LORD's altar with tears" (v. 13). And he is the exhorter: "So look to yourselves. . . . So take heed to yourselves and do not be faithless (vv. 15-16).

One of the most distinctive features of the passage is the way that Malachi develops his ideas about relationships. In contrast to the divine-human, "I-you," framework for 1:2-5, here the prevailing relational framework is "we," the mutual relationship among members of the community based upon a common father and creator. By capitalizing "Father," the NIV interprets rather than translates the text. The nuances of the fatherhood of Abraham (Isa 51:2) and especially Jacob as father of all Israel (cf. Mal 3:6) should not be erased. This father is the creator of a people (Deut 32:6; Isa 43:1, 15). Malachi condemns marriage with foreign women precisely because such an exogamous (outside the family) relationship goes beyond these boundaries. The foreign woman does not share the same father/creator, and so Malachi coins the unusual phrase "daughter of a foreign god" (בת־אל נכר bat-'ēl nēkār), instead of using the regular term for foreign women, נשים נכריות (nāšîm nokriyyôt; see 1 Kgs 11:1, 8; Ezra 10:2; Neh 13:26). This reference to a breakdown in mutuality among members of the community continues throughout the passage. Such fractured relations may provide the impetus for a number of other unusual expressions. For instance, the prophet alludes to judgment as expulsion from the "tents of Jacob" (v. 12; this expression is used only here and in Jer 30:18). The phrase "the wife of your youth" (אשת נעוריך 'ēšet nĕ'ûrêkā, v. 14; cf. Prov 5:18; Isa 54:6) and the unique terms "your companion" (חברתך

ḥăbertēkā) and "your wife by covenant" (אשת בריתך 'ēšet bĕrîtekā, v. 14) are also relational; the latter emphasizes the shared covenant relationship as members of the same covenant people, rather than the husband-wife relationship per se as a covenant. The passage ends with an exhortation that refocuses attention on the community and mutual obligation: "Take heed to yourselves and do not be faithless" (v. 16).

Verses 13-16 present a distinct but related ("and this you do as well") accusation: Men are unfaithful to their wives. Divorce is mentioned specifically in the context of condemnation (v. 16), but the precise nuance of the text is difficult to recover (see below). It is often assumed that this charge of unfaithfulness and divorce is related to the previous issue of marriage with foreign women—i.e., men abandon the wives of their youth in order to marry foreign women for economic benefit or for elevation in social status. But that understanding depends on a linkage that Malachi neither makes explicitly nor by the order in which he presents the charges.

Verse 15 is very difficult, and it is doubtful that we will ever be certain of its original sense.[28] The individual words are all simple and clear; the problem is to fill in the context, since the questions/answers are so laconic. The NRSV translation, with its repeated "one God," emphasizes the link with the one father and creator in v. 10. The NIV understands the verse as deriving exegetically from the Genesis creation account (Gen 2:24: "and they become one flesh" [NRSV]). The concern with "godly offspring" may derive from the Gen 1:28 injunction to be fruitful and multiply.

Verse 16 introduces the explicit language of divorce, but again the Hebrew (כי־שנא שלח kî-śānē' šallaḥ) is much more uncertain than the straightforward English translation "I hate divorce" would indicate. There is no first-person pronoun in the Hebrew, and a third-person translation "if/for he hates" or a more neutral "divorce is hateful" is possible.[29] In favor of reading a first-person God statement is the prophetic refrain "says the LORD, the God of Israel," which appears

---

28. In the Dead Sea Scroll manuscript 4QXII[a], only three words survive, but they are exactly the same as in the standard Hebrew text ("the one/seeks/seed") and so provide little help.

29. The latter is the translation proposed by Petersen, *Zechariah 9–14 and Malachi*, 194.

for the first time in this unit. In legal papyri from the Jewish colony in Elephantine during the Persian period, "hate" was a legal term for repudiation by divorce, and this technical sense may have influenced the expression found here.[30] Similarly, the phrase "cover one's garments with violence" may also be a legal idiom, but its precise connotation is unknown. If v. 16 is read as an absolute prohibition of divorce, it is difficult to reconcile with the legislation of Deut 24:1-4, which, while circumscribing specific cases, assumes the practice of divorce.[31] In addition, Ezra calls for the "putting away" of foreign wives (Ezra 10:3, 18), although the precise language of divorce is not used.

Scholars are only beginning to explore the economic and social dynamics of marriage and intermarriage in the Persian Empire, and there is still considerable dispute about whether official Persian policy was one of ethnic separation of diverse peoples or of encouraging intermarriage as a means of integration. For the Jewish community, regulation of marriages was essential for maintaining genealogical integrity and community boundaries. Certainly the right of women to inherit property, as attested both in the laws of the priestly code (Num 27:7-8; 36:6-9) and in documents from Elephantine, would provide economic incentives for discouraging both intermarriage and divorce. In the books of Ezra and Nehemiah, we glimpse how these questions were dealt with in the legal and political realms at a certain specific moment. In Malachi, in contrast, we see how a prophet approached the same issues. For the prophet, marriage with foreign women, infidelity, and divorce were, above all else, violations of the fundamental covenantal bonds of the community.

30. The New English Bible treats "hate" in this way and translates 2:16: "If a man divorces or puts away his spouse. . . . "

31. The Hebrew text in 4QXII[a] has a second person, "but if you (the husband) hate (her), divorce," which is basically the understanding of the text found in the Targum and the Vulgate and one manuscript tradition of the Septuagint. This is probably a secondary reading, reflecting an attempt to clarify and resolve the contradiction. See the discussion by Russell Fuller, "Text-Critical Problems in Malachi 2:10-16," *JBL* 110 (1991) 54-56.

REFLECTIONS

1. Although many of the details of this passage are obscure, the commentary emphasizes how consistently Malachi roots his discussion of marriage within the framework of a community that shares a fundamental relationship based on a common father and creator. Thus marriage has a communal dimension; it is not solely, nor even primarily, an individual act and choice. The larger community has a stake in an individual's choice of a marriage partner, the maintenance of fidelity to the marriage bond, and in what happens when that bond is sundered in divorce. The Letter to the Ephesians (5:22-33) presumes a similar communal dimension when it situates marriage within the broad framework of the relationship between Christ and the church.

So much in North American society works on the assumption that marriage and divorce and fidelity within marriage are private matters of the persons concerned. We are rightly concerned with the emotions and needs, the freedom and value of the individual. But in honoring these values, we barely know how then to speak of a sense of responsibility to a larger community. Particularly today one rarely discussed aspect of fidelity in marriage is the service it gives to the whole community of faith and to society in general as a living embodiment of the ideals of fidelity, commitment, and steadfastness. Likewise, infidelity, the failure of a marriage, and divorce are particularly concrete and visible expressions of a breakdown in these ideals. At some level, these realities make it more difficult for all of society to live out the values it recognizes and esteems. It is precisely this sense of interrelatedness that can lead the community as a whole to seek concrete ways to affirm, to strengthen, and to support persons in their efforts to live in faithfulness.

2. How are we to approach a biblical text on divorce, like Mal 2:16, in which the basic understanding of the key verse is so problematic? "I hate divorce" is sometimes put forth in Christian circles as "proof" that already in the OT God absolutely condemns divorce. The commentary has pointed out the manifold problems in understanding the meaning of this verse and the quite divergent ways the text itself was handled in the early tradition (as reflected in Qumran copies of the verse, in the Septuagint, in the Targum, and in the Vulgate). Furthermore, when divorce was prohibited or strictly limited, whether in the early Christian community (Matt 5:31-32; 19:3-9; Mark 10:2-12; Luke 16:18) or in the Jewish communities that produced the *Damascus Document*[32] or the *Temple Scroll,*[33] the scriptural texts that are adduced in support of the prohibition are always Gen 1:27; 2:24; or 7:9. Certainly this reflects the standard practice of quoting from the Torah rather than from the Prophets when establishing an OT precedent. But it does mean that we do not have early examples of this Malachi verse introduced as a prooftext in discussions of divorce. It should be noted, too, that none of the contemporary Christian lectionaries use Mal 2:10-16 for a Sunday reading.

There are times when we simply need to admit that we do not fully understand a biblical text. Particularly when dealing with matters so central and sensitive to people's lives, honesty and truth demand the exercise of a healthy caution. Sometimes the greatest service we can render as biblical interpreters is to refuse to claim to know more than we actually know.

32. CD 4:20–5:2.
33. 11Q Temple 57:16-19.

MALACHI 2:17–3:5, THE GOD OF JUSTICE

NIV

[17]You have wearied the LORD with your words. "How have we wearied him?" you ask.

By saying, "All who do evil are good in the eyes of the LORD, and he is pleased with them" or "Where is the God of justice?"

3 "See, I will send my messenger, who will prepare the way before me. Then suddenly the Lord you are seeking will come to his temple; the messenger of the covenant, whom you desire, will come," says the LORD Almighty.

[2]But who can endure the day of his coming? Who can stand when he appears? For he will be like a refiner's fire or a launderer's soap. [3]He will sit as a refiner and purifier of silver; he will purify the Levites and refine them like gold and silver. Then the LORD will have men who will bring offerings in righteousness, [4]and the offerings of Judah and Jerusalem will be acceptable to the LORD, as in days gone by, as in former years.

[5]"So I will come near to you for judgment. I will be quick to testify against sorcerers, adulterers and perjurers, against those who defraud laborers of their wages, who oppress the widows and the fatherless, and deprive aliens of justice, but do not fear me," says the LORD Almighty.

NRSV

[17]You have wearied the LORD with your words. Yet you say, "How have we wearied him?" By saying, "All who do evil are good in the sight of the LORD, and he delights in them." Or by asking, "Where is the God of justice?"

3 See, I am sending my messenger to prepare the way before me, and the Lord whom you seek will suddenly come to his temple. The messenger of the covenant in whom you delight—indeed, he is coming, says the LORD of hosts. [2]But who can endure the day of his coming, and who can stand when he appears?

For he is like a refiner's fire and like fullers' soap; [3]he will sit as a refiner and purifier of silver, and he will purify the descendants of Levi and refine them like gold and silver, until they present offerings to the LORD in righteousness.[a] [4]Then the offering of Judah and Jerusalem will be pleasing to the LORD as in the days of old and as in former years.

[5]Then I will draw near to you for judgment; I will be swift to bear witness against the sorcerers, against the adulterers, against those who swear falsely, against those who oppress the hired workers in their wages, the widow and the orphan, against those who thrust aside the alien, and do not fear me, says the LORD of hosts.

[a] Or *right offerings to the LORD*

COMMENTARY

As we move into the latter part of the book (2:17–4:3), distinct units are not as sharp and clear cut as in the first part. The same format (statement-question-response) is still discernible and enables us to distinguish three units (2:17–3:5; 3:6-12; 3:13–4:3). But the fact that some commentators consider 3:6 as the end of the first unit, while others put it at the beginning of the second, indicates how the boundaries between the units are fluid. Common themes and vocabulary span the whole section. The fundamental question of justice for both the righteous and the wicked is introduced in the first unit and is not resolved until the third. The solution offered by the divine response in the first and the third units is more eschatological, while the second response is tied more specifically to present reality. Most commentators consider that there is secondary material in at least the first and the third units; indeed, sometimes the whole of 3:16–4:3 has been taken as an independent addition.[34] As we work through each unit, the Commentary will emphasize the complex web of interrelationships in this final section of the book, and the Reflections will follow 3:13–4:3.

Malachi 2:17–3:5 begins with a statement of accusation directed to the people by the prophet (the only unit to begin in this way). The charge is nebulous: "You have wearied the LORD with your words" (a reformulation of Isa 43:24: "You have wearied me with your iniquities" [NRSV]). The people do not deny the charge but demand that it be specified, and so their own words are quoted back to them.

The people readily admit that God is just, and they take up a traditional phrase from Isa 30:18: "For the LORD is a God of justice" (NRSV). The issue is not a denial of divine justice as an attribute, but rather a complaint that this justice is not being experienced. Similarly, the people had complained in the first unit (1:2), not that God was not a God of love, but that they could not perceive this love in their present reality. There is, of course, a long biblical tradition of questioning the prosperity of the wicked (see Job 21:7-25; Psalm

73; Jer 12:1) and God's apparent silence and inactivity before evildoers (Hab 1:13). But the complaints here are particularly audacious; it is not only that the wicked prosper, but that they are considered good (cf. Isa 5:20). God even seems to delight in them! Such a claim challenges the basic presuppositions of a covenantal framework; when the wicked enjoy the blessings and prosperity of the righteous, the very categories of good and evil lose all meaning.

Although the people talk vaguely of "all who do evil," the corresponding judgments in 3:3, 5 are more specific. In the final form of the text (assuming 3:1b-4 is an added section; see below), the two groups singled out for purification and judgment are the sons of Levi (3:3) and those persons who disregard the fundamental commands of the Decalogue (adulterers, false swearers) and exploit the weak, the widow, the orphan, the alien, and the paid laborer (3:5). The nations, even the dominating Persian Empire, do not seem to be included in "all who do evil"; likewise, in the judgment pericope (4:1-3), Malachi is curiously uninterested in the fate of the nations.

In accordance with the format that appears throughout the book, the questions in 2:17 receive a response in 3:1-5. In the first unit of the book, the response (1:2-5) appealed to the ancient Esau/Jacob story and offered a new interpretation of the contemporary historical collapse of Edom. Now the answer looks neither to the past nor to the present, but is entirely eschatological. Justice will be restored only through a future divine intervention. Only on that day, "the day of his coming" for judgment (מִשְׁפָּט *mišpāṭ*), will the "God of justice" (*mišpāṭ*) be recognized.

Most commentators have suggested that 3:1-5 underwent considerable development and secondary expansion. In the present form of the text, the first-person voice (3:1a, 5) alternates with the third person (1b-4), and there is a confusing multiplicity of figures: my messenger, the Lord, the messenger of the covenant. The identity of these various figures remains vague and does not seem to be the main focus of the passage. If we take 3:1a, 5 as the original unit, then these verses

---

34. See Paul Redditt, *Haggai, Zechariah, Malachi,* NCB (Grand Rapids: Eerdmans, 1995) 155, 182-84.

announce the coming of a "great king" (1:14) for whom a messenger is needed to prepare the royal processional way (Isa 40:3). In contrast to Deutero-Isaiah, this king "draws near," not for comfort, but for judgment. Certainly there is an echo, too, of the promise in Exod 23:20: "I am going to send an angel [מלאך *malʾāk*, "messenger"] in front of you." The independent unit in 3:1*b*-4 puts the focus on the Temple as the place of theophany, and on purification of the priests and the restoration of blessing through cultic offering. Both visions of the future emphasize the suddenness of the coming and the dramatic reversal of present reality.

Since the identity of the messenger in 3:1 is not specified, some commentators have raised the possibility that he is, in fact, the prophet of the book (Malachi, "my messenger"). But this is unlikely, since it would eliminate the whole eschatological thrust of the passage. By the time the prophetic corpus was brought together and the verses in Mal 4:5-6 added as an epilogue, at least one stream of Jewish tradition had already identified the messenger with the prophet Elijah and his promised return. In the New Testament, the synoptic Gospels identify explicitly the unnamed messenger of Mal 3:1 with John the Baptist (Matt 11:10//Luke 7:27; Mark 1:2, Luke 1:76).

MALACHI 3:6-12, ACCUSATION CONCERNING TITHES

NIV

6"I the LORD do not change. So you, O descendants of Jacob, are not destroyed. 7Ever since the time of your forefathers you have turned away from my decrees and have not kept them. Return to me, and I will return to you," says the LORD Almighty.

"But you ask, 'How are we to return?'

8"Will a man rob God? Yet you rob me.

"But you ask, 'How do we rob you?'

"In tithes and offerings. 9You are under a curse—the whole nation of you—because you are robbing me. 10Bring the whole tithe into the storehouse, that there may be food in my house. Test me in this," says the LORD Almighty, "and see if I will not throw open the floodgates of heaven and pour out so much blessing that you will not have room enough for it. 11I will prevent pests from devouring your crops, and the vines in your fields will not cast their fruit," says the LORD Almighty. 12"Then all the nations will call you blessed, for yours will be a delightful land," says the LORD Almighty.

NRSV

6For I the LORD do not change; therefore you, O children of Jacob, have not perished. 7Ever since the days of your ancestors you have turned aside from my statutes and have not kept them. Return to me, and I will return to you, says the LORD of hosts. But you say, "How shall we return?"

8Will anyone rob God? Yet you are robbing me! But you say, "How are we robbing you?" In your tithes and offerings! 9You are cursed with a curse, for you are robbing me—the whole nation of you! 10Bring the full tithe into the storehouse, so that there may be food in my house, and thus put me to the test, says the LORD of hosts; see if I will not open the windows of heaven for you and pour down for you an overflowing blessing. 11I will rebuke the locust[a] for you, so that it will not destroy the produce of your soil; and your vine in the field shall not be barren, says the LORD of hosts. 12Then all nations will count you happy, for you will be a land of delight, says the LORD of hosts.

[a] Heb *devourer*

COMMENTARY

The divine word in v. 6 serves to make the transition from the anticipated future divine intervention to present reality. The NRSV follows the Hebrew exactly in beginning with the conjunction "For" (כִּי *kî*), thus recognizing that this unit is not entirely independent. The first-person "I" statement about God's unchangeable nature and the designation "children of Jacob" tie this verse very closely to 1:2-5. The God who does not change is the God who loves Jacob and his descendants, and because of this election, they continue to exist. But it has been an existence of sin "ever since your ancestors." In a play on two similar Hebrew roots, the descendants of Jacob "the supplanter" (יַעֲקֹב *y'qb*) "rob" (קָבַע *qb'*) the very God who had chosen them.[35]

As in the accusation against the priests (1:6-10), a general accusation ("you have turned aside from my statutes," v. 7) is followed by a very specific charge. This whole unit is concerned specifically with failure in the payment of tithes (i.e., one-tenth of agricultural produce, from both livestock and produce); the "offering" in v. 8 is a technical term for the one-tenth of the tithe given to the Levites that was in turn given to God (Num 18:25-32). Both the Deuteronomic (Deut 14:22-29; 26:12-15) and the Priestly (Lev 27:30-33; Num 18:21-32) codes had developed extensive legislation governing the exact tithes to be paid, where they were to be taken, and the rights and privileges of both Levites and Aaronite priests to receive set portions for their support.[36] A series of passages in Nehemiah (10:37-39; 12:44; 13:5, 10-13) attests to the economic and social ramifications of the tithing system with special importance for priestly status and maintenance of the Temple during the Persian period.

Although Nehemiah characterizes the failure to pay tithes as neglect of the Temple (Neh 10:40; 13:11), Malachi personalizes the charge (cf. Mal 1:6-14). This is a direct offense against God: "You are robbing me!" (v. 8). This section does not conclude simply with an oracle of judgment, "You are cursed with a curse" (v. 9). Rather, vv. 10-12 go on to develop an unexpected and effusive portrayal of the salvation promised upon payment of the full tithe. The description of fertility and prosperity in the realm of nature and acknowledgment by the nations draws upon the language of the blessings promised to those who keep the covenant (Deut 28:8-12). But a more mythic, cosmic dimension is added with expressions like "the windows of heaven" (Gen 7:11; 8:2) and "the devourer" (בָאֹכֵל *bā'ōkēl*), which is perhaps a better rendering of the Hebrew word translated as "locusts" in the NRSV and "pests" in the NIV (v. 11). When we consider this unit as an intrinsic part of the whole section of 2:17–4:3, the overarching question becomes: Where is the God of justice? In 2:17–3:5, the response was eschatological. Here a this-worldly, temporal response is offered. In the prosperity that is promised based upon the payment of tithes, divine justice will be visible and the good will be recognized as good. The people will no longer be able to claim that God delights in the wicked (2:17), for it will be clear that they, the righteous, are the "land of delight" (v. 12). (See Reflections at 3:13–4:3.)

---

35. See Gen 25:20 and 27:36 for the play on Jacob's name from the root עָקַב ('*qb*), meaning "to grasp," "to supplant." The word קָבַע (*qb'*) is used only here and in Prov 22:23, obviously chosen because of the similar root letters.

36. For more detailed discussion of OT tithes, see H. Jagersma, "The Tithes in the Old Testament," *OTS* 21 (1981) 116-28.

MALACHI 3:13–4:3, THE RIGHTEOUS AND THE WICKED

NIV

13"You have said harsh things against me," says the LORD.

"Yet you ask, 'What have we said against you?'

14"You have said, 'It is futile to serve God. What did we gain by carrying out his requirements and going about like mourners before the LORD Almighty? 15But now we call the arrogant blessed. Certainly the evildoers prosper, and even those who challenge God escape.'"

16Then those who feared the LORD talked with each other, and the LORD listened and heard. A scroll of remembrance was written in his presence concerning those who feared the LORD and honored his name.

17"They will be mine," says the LORD Almighty, "in the day when I make up my treasured possession.ᵃ I will spare them, just as in compassion a man spares his son who serves him. 18And you will again see the distinction between the righteous and the wicked, between those who serve God and those who do not.

4 "Surely the day is coming; it will burn like a furnace. All the arrogant and every evildoer will be stubble, and that day that is coming will set them on fire," says the LORD Almighty. "Not a root or a branch will be left to them. 2But for you who revere my name, the sun of righteousness will rise with healing in its wings. And you will go out and leap like calves released from the stall. 3Then you will trample down the wicked; they will be ashes under the soles of your feet on the day when I do these things," says the LORD Almighty.

ᵃ17 Or Almighty, "my treasured possession, in the day when I act

NRSV

13You have spoken harsh words against me, says the LORD. Yet you say, "How have we spoken against you?" 14You have said, "It is vain to serve God. What do we profit by keeping his command or by going about as mourners before the LORD of hosts? 15Now we count the arrogant happy; evildoers not only prosper, but when they put God to the test they escape."

16Then those who revered the LORD spoke with one another. The LORD took note and listened, and a book of remembrance was written before him of those who revered the LORD and thought on his name. 17They shall be mine, says the LORD of hosts, my special possession on the day when I act, and I will spare them as parents spare their children who serve them. 18Then once more you shall see the difference between the righteous and the wicked, between one who serves God and one who does not serve him.

4ᵃ See, the day is coming, burning like an oven, when all the arrogant and all evildoers will be stubble; the day that comes shall burn them up, says the LORD of hosts, so that it will leave them neither root nor branch. 2But for you who revere my name the sun of righteousness shall rise, with healing in its wings. You shall go out leaping like calves from the stall. 3And you shall tread down the wicked, for they will be ashes under the soles of your feet, on the day when I act, says the LORD of hosts.

ᵃ Ch 4.1-6 are Ch 3.19-24 in Heb

COMMENTARY

Although the Hebrew text is one continuous unit, both the NRSV and the NIV follow the Greek in introducing a new chapter at v. 19. Thus 4:1-3 corresponds to 3:19-21 in Hebrew.

This final section begins with a brief divine word of accusation that intensifies the charge of 2:17. The complaints that "wearied me" now are "strong against me" (to give a very literal rendition of the phrase חזקו עלי דבריכם [ḥāzĕqû 'ālay dibrêkem, 3:13], translated as "harsh words" in the NRSV and the NIV). Perhaps the very generality of the accusation is meant to bring all the previous words of complaint and skepticism into this final confrontation. The people are given their lengthiest, but final, chance to speak (3:14-15). All the words in the book from here on are either from God or constitute third-person comment.

The basic substance of the complaint had already been articulated in 2:17. This time the people talk more directly of their experience in personal terms: "What do we profit?" (3:14); "Now we count . . . " (3:15); and only then move on to describe the more abstract "evildoers." Their self-description, "going about as mourners," is unclear; it may be technical terminology (cf. the mourners in Isa 57:18; 61:2; 66:10). The fact that different Hebrew terms are used in Isaiah and Malachi mitigate against understanding this as a formal designation of a sociological group. The contrast between "us" and "them" is highlighted by the use of specific phrases from earlier in the book. Although there will come a time when the nations will count them happy (3:12), now they count the arrogant happy (3:15); the people are challenged to put God to the test (3:10), but the wicked test God and escape (3:15). The image of the evildoers who are "built up" (the literal translation of "prosper" [בנה bānâ, 3:15]) is particularly poignant in the light of 1:2-5, where the proof of God's love was that wicked Edom could not rebuild. What is to be concluded when the wicked within the community are built up with impunity?

The response in 3:16–4:3 is fundamentally eschatological (as it was in the earlier unit, 3:1-5). Justice will prevail, but it will occur in the future, on the day when God will act. There is no promise of immediate change or rectification of the present social order. Yet there will be a fundamental correspondence between present and future; while serving God may now seem to have no effect (3:14), ultimately the division of righteous/wicked will depend precisely on the basis of "one who serves God and one who does not" (3:18).

Malachi 3:16 is a very unusual sentence, really a mini-narrative. There has been much discussion about whether "those who revered the LORD" are the same people, or at least a subgroup of the "you" who have just been complaining against

God. Some scholars propose that this is a separate, pure group, reflecting a distinct sectarian minority, a group identified with either the prophet or a later redactor.[37] However, it seems better to consider those who revered God as part of the "you" of the book as a whole, that segment of the people who will know ultimate vindication. Unique to Malachi (though drawing on older motifs from Exod 32:32; Pss 69:28; 87:6; Isa 4:3; cf. Rev 20:12) is the people's assurance that their names have been written in the "book of remembrance." The distinction between the righteous and the wicked is already set forth in written form, in black and white as it were, "before the LORD," though this will be revealed only "on the day when I act." In spite of the very familiar language of 3:17, a major reinterpretation of Deuteronomic theology operates here, one in line with later apocalyptic developments. On the day that is coming, the ancient covenantal terms of election—"they will be mine," "my special possession" (cf. Exod 19:5; Deut 7:6; 14:2; 26:18; Ps 135:4)—will be applied, not to all Israel, but only to the righteous segment.

The book concludes with an announcement of the coming day (4:1-3). The description is much less detailed than in some other post-exilic prophetic texts (cf. Zechariah 12–14; Joel 2–3). Particularly noticeable is the total absence of any interest in the fate of the pagan nations. Although other prophets described "a day of darkness and gloom" (Zeph 1:15 NRSV), the images here are all of light and brightness: the destructive fire that burns up the wicked; the rising sun; the righteous leaping like calves set free from their indoor stalls to gambol in the sunshine; and, in contrast, the cold ashes of the wicked trampled underfoot. The theophany of God is described in terms of the image of a winged sun disk, an image widely attested throughout the ancient Near East. This solar imagery for Israel's God is found in graphic presentation on jar handles from pre-monarchic Judah and more indirectly in texts like Num 6:26; Pss 4:6; 31:16; 34:5; 84:11.[38] Thus the question,

37. For a recent reconstruction of various groups and their identification, see J. L. Berquist, "The Social Setting of Malachi," *BTB* 19 (1989) 121-26.

38. For graphic depictions, see O. Keel, *The Symbolism of the Biblical World: Ancient Near Eastern Iconography and the Book of Psalms* (New York: Seabury, 1978) 27-30; J. Glen Taylor, *Yahweh and the Sun: Biblical and Archaeological Evidence for Sun Worship in Ancient Israel,* JSOTSup 111 (Sheffield: JSOT, 1993) 211-16.

"Where is the God of justice?" is finally resolved in 4:1-3 by the assurance of a day to come when "the sun of righteousness shall rise, with healing in its wings" (4:2).

REFLECTIONS

One way of reflecting on this final and difficult section of Malachi is to look at what parts the Christian tradition has chosen to hear on a regular basis in lectionary readings and in what context. In fact, relatively little—only the two brief passages 3:1-4 and 4:1-2*a*—appear in the lectionary.

1. Malachi 3:1-4 is a reading for Advent in some lectionaries (e.g., an alternate text for the Second Sunday of Advent, Year C, in the Revised Common Lectionary). This continues, of course, the tradition of the Gospel writers of identifying the unnamed messenger of Mal 3:1 with John the Baptist (Matt 11:10//Luke 7:27; Mark 1:2; Luke 1:76). In this interpretative move, the whole of Mal 3:1-4 becomes re-read in the light of the figure of John the Baptist and his preaching. Thus, for instance, the purifying fire directed against the descendants of Levi in Mal 3:2-3 is fused with the baptism of fire that will come to all the people (Luke 3:16), as well as the "unquenchable fire" that will destroy the wicked on the day of eschatological judgment (3:17). But Mal 3:1-4 has also been the traditional reading for the Feast of the Presentation of Jesus in the Temple (February 2 in most church calendars). The coming of the Lord into the Temple (Mal 3:1) is thus identified with Mary and Joseph bringing Jesus to present him according to the law of Moses (Luke 2:22-40). Instead of a coming in power, a baby is carried into the Temple. But his coming will still bring turmoil and fear; the question of who can endure the day of his coming is answered in Luke in terms of the fall and rise of many. It is not only that the Levites will be purified, but that a sword will pierce his own mother's heart. Furthermore, the lectionary highlights the priestly dimension of the messenger figure (cf. the designation of the priests in 2:7 as "messengers of the LORD of hosts") by combining this selection from Malachi with Heb 2:10-18, which presents Jesus as "a merciful and faithful high priest" (Heb 2:17 NRSV).

Thus Christian tradition gives not one, but two answers to the question of who is the messenger of Mal 3:1: He is John the Baptist, but he is also the baby Jesus. As already mentioned, another interpretative tradition identified the messenger with Elijah to come (see Introduction), and there is no scarcity of still other proposals in modern commentaries on this passage (the messenger as the prophet himself, as an angel, as God). That such a multiplicity of figures has been claimed as this messenger is seen by some as a failure, a lack of clarity and precision in the words of the text. More positively, it points to the fact that this prophetic text, like so many, fails dismally if it is read only as a source of concrete factual information. Its very ambiguity enables us to ask, in our day, Who are the messengers of the covenant? And it alerts us that we may not all find the same answers. Our attention turns from the single question of who to a host of other questions that might easily be missed: What? (A task of preparation.) When? (Suddenly.) For whom? (The Lord of hosts.) Where? (To the Temple.)

2. Malachi 4:1-2*a* is an alternative reading for Proper 28, Year C, in the Revised Common Lectionary and the set reading for the corresponding Proper 33 in the Roman Catholic Lectionary. In keeping with a longstanding liturgical tradition of not ending a reading with a verse that sounds harsh or vindictive, 4:3 is not included; but it seems a shame that the lectionary also omits 4:2*b*, with its playful image of the frolicking calves leaping about in freedom.

The choice of this reading is governed by the longstanding church tradition of turning attention to "the end of time" as the church year draws to a close (the corresponding Gospel reading is the apocalyptic discourse of Luke 21:5-19). Indeed, one of the advantages for communities that use the lectionary on a regular basis is that it is impossible to avoid hearing and preaching upon texts, such as this, that might otherwise be avoided entirely. While some churches make texts about the "end times" the core and center of their preaching, in other churches such themes are seldom, if ever, heard. Certainly, in much recent systematic study of theology, there has been a renewed interest in eschatology in its broadest sense of "last things"—not only heaven, hell, and judgment, but also reflection on the goal and purpose of history. Eschatology has moved from being a "harmless little chapter at the end of dogmatic theology" (to use Barth's famous description) to the center of theological reflection.

But on a more popular level, concern for the "coming day" is usually viewed with a certain suspicion, as an escape to a "pie-in-the-sky" religion. Malachi 4:1-2 can seem totally removed from present reality, simply a fantasy of the future, when the wicked are burned up and the just receive righteousness and healing. The problem is accentuated when only 4:1-2a are read on a given Sunday, so that the dichotomy between evildoers and righteous persons is completely separated from its context within the whole framework of the prophetic disputes and the complaints about justice. The promise of healing and joy for the righteous and fire and destruction for the wicked is meant to speak to the experience of the hired worker, of the widow, of the orphan, and of the alien (3:5). Indeed, the specific contribution of this text is that it situates the eschatological promises within the framework of the question that haunts us throughout the book: "Where is the God of justice?" (2:17 NRSV).

EPILOGUE

NIV

4"Remember the law of my servant Moses, the decrees and laws I gave him at Horeb for all Israel.

5"See, I will send you the prophet Elijah before that great and dreadful day of the LORD comes. 6He will turn the hearts of the fathers to their children, and the hearts of the children to their fathers; or else I will come and strike the land with a curse."

NRSV

4Remember the teaching of my servant Moses, the statutes and ordinances that I commanded him at Horeb for all Israel.

5Lo, I will send you the prophet Elijah before the great and terrible day of the LORD comes. 6He will turn the hearts of parents to their children and the hearts of children to their parents, so that I will not come and strike the land with a curse.[a]

a Or a ban of utter destruction

COMMENTARY

After the awesome description of the great day to come, with punishment for the wicked and salvation for the righteous, these final verses (numbered 3:22-24 in the Hebrew text) sound a very different, even anticlimactic note. It is not impossible that they are the words of the prophet, transmitted independently of the longer units of discourse, and thus collected together at the end of the book.[39] However, the language is distinctive enough to suggest that these verses come from another source (perhaps even two sources, if v. 4 and vv. 5 and 6 were originally separate). Many of the phrases belong to the standard repertoire of the deuteronomic tradition (e.g., "my servant Moses," "the decrees and laws," "Horeb," "all Israel"). Most striking is the absence of Malachi's distinctive terminology ("the day when I act" and "the day when I come") in favor of the phraseology of Joel 2:31: "the great and terrible day of the LORD" (cf. Joel 2:11).

Such an epilogue may have been appended considerably later than the time of Malachi as a conclusion, not just to Malachi, but to the entire Book of the Twelve, or even to the whole pro-

phetic corpus.[40] There is no comparable ending in any of the other prophetic books (Hos 14:10, which might be adduced as a parallel, is clearly a scribal addendum and not presented as a word from the Lord). Certainly the description of Elijah (vv. 5-6) was known already at the beginning of the second century BCE, since Jesus ben Sirach draws on Malachi in his praise of Elijah (esp. Sir 48:10). Indeed, these final words of promise may have helped to shape Sirach's understanding of the Twelve Prophets as those who "comforted the people of Jacob/ and delivered them with confident hope" (Sir 49:10 NRSV).

Although we cannot be certain of the precise date and source of these verses, the fact that they now stand at the end of the book of Malachi subtly refocuses our reading of the book as a whole. The still-future day of God's final coming is linked with the day of divine manifestation in thunder and fire and smoke long ago on Mount Horeb (Exod 19:16-25). The God who will come in judgment is not an unknown God, but the God who has already come as revealer of statutes and ordinances. The radical dichotomy between the righteous and the wicked on the day to come is set against the day when "all Israel" stood to-

---

39. For a recent presentation of the case for these verses as the word of the prophet Malachi, see B. Glazier-McDonald, *Malachi: The Divine Messenger*, SBLDS 98 (Atlanta: Scholars Press, 1987) 243-70.

40. The verses are part of the Septuagint and also are found in the 4QXII[a] manuscript from about 150 BCE.

gether at Mount Horeb. The final imperative is "Remember," but it is the "teaching of my servant Moses" (v. 4)—that is Torah—that provides the framework within which the prophetic message is to endure.

Although v. 4 is a divine admonition, vv. 5-6 promise a final act of divine intervention. The opening words of v. 5, "Lo, I will send you . . . " clearly depend upon the enigmatic phrase in 3:1: "See, I am sending . . . " (NRSV). The undefined messenger of 3:1 is now identified: the prophet Elijah. This is one of the earliest attestations of what developed into a rich and diffuse "return of Elijah" tradition.[41] The fact that Elijah did not die but was taken up alive to heaven (2 Kgs 2:11-12) may have played a role in the expectation that he, of all the prophets of the past, would be the one to return. But in the context of v. 4 we are certainly invited to think as well of Elijah's zeal for obedience to the law (1 Kings 18) and his own experience of divine manifestation at Mount Horeb (1 Kings 19). In a wonderfully ironic reversal, the prophet who was known as the "troubler of Israel" (1 Kgs 18:17 NRSV) will have the task of peacemaking when he returns. The fundamental breakdown of covenantal and familial relationships, which has surfaced repeatedly throughout the book (1:2-6; 2:10-16), and the threat of the curse (2:2, 12; 3:9) will ultimately be resolved only by this final act of divine intervention.

One of the distinctive features of the eschatological scenario as it is presented in these verses is that Elijah will come and then there will be "the great and terrible day of the LORD." There is no mention of a stage with a messiah or a messianic age in this scenario. Yet in the synoptic Gospels, John the Baptist is identified with Elijah, and he functions as the precursor of the Messiah (Mark 6:14-15; 9:11-13; Matt 11:13-14; 17:9-13; Luke 1:17).[42] There is an ongoing discussion among scholars about whether a tradition had already developed in Judaism by New Testament times that Elijah would come before the Messiah, or whether the linkage of Elijah and the Messiah was a distinctive Christian reworking of the tradition to clarify the relationship between John the Baptist and Jesus.[43]

The precise order of these verses at the end of the book of Malachi is not firmly fixed. There has been a hesitancy to end the book and, indeed, the whole prophetic corpus, with such a terrible and negative word as "curse" (חרם ḥērem), total and absolute destruction. Many Septuagint manuscripts solved the problem by reversing the order of v. 4 and vv. 5-6. When the passage is read in the synagogue, the reader is instructed to repeat v. 4 rather than to end with v. 6. But there is something very powerful about the order in the Hebrew manuscripts. The book of Malachi began with the divine word "I love you" (1:2). In the very last phrase of the book, we are left with the promise that ultimately, "on the great and terrible day of the LORD," this love will prevail "so that I will not come and strike the land with a curse."

41. For a concise survey of such traditions, see the entry "Elijah" in the *Encyclopedia Judaica*, vol. 6, 632-42.

42. In John's Gospel, in contrast, John the Baptist specifically denies that he is to be identified with Elijah (John 1:19-21).

43. A fragmentary section from one of the Dead Sea Scroll texts (4Q521 2.iii.1-2) quotes Mal 4:4 in a passage about the Messiah, which suggests that this sequence of Elijah-Messiah-end time developed in Jewish circles.

REFLECTIONS

1. With its summons to remember the teaching of Moses and its legal language of statutes and ordinances, v. 4 is neither the obvious conclusion of a prophetic book nor the most logical epilogue to the entire prophetic corpus. We might have expected some praise of prophecy and some emphatic statement about the power of the Word of God as delivered through these individuals chosen over the centuries. Instead, we are directed back to Moses and the revelation on Mount Sinai.

This juxtaposition of law and prophecy seems strange to us precisely because both in the church and in much modern biblical scholarship the tendency has been to separate the two, to view law and prophecy as competing, if not opposing, forces. The ending to Malachi is much closer to the traditional Jewish approach that understood the prophet as custodian rather than as innovator, as transmitter rather than as recipient of new revelation. It is this understanding of prophecy that received classic expression in the opening lines of *Pirke Avot:* "Moses received Torah from Sinai and delivered it to Joshua; then Joshua delivered it to the elders, the elders to the prophets, and the prophets delivered it to the men of the Great Assembly."[44]

The final casting of the prophetic corpus under the mantle of the laws and statutes does not provide ready answers to the very practical questions that can arise about how the demands of the two are to be reconciled. But what is clear is that they cannot be separated. As in the transfiguration scene in the Gospels (Matt 17:1-8; Mark 9:2-8; Luke 9:28-36) and with the witnesses of Rev 11:3-6, Moses and Elijah, law and prophecy are to stand together.

2. Elijah's task is one of reconciliation. In Malachi, he is to bring together parents and children. This reconciling task was not understood as limited in scope. Already in the Septuagint translation of v. 6, the sphere of Elijah's activity was extended beyond the family to the restoration of relationships among neighbors; in Sir 48:10 he is "to restore the tribes of Jacob" (NRSV); in Mark 9:12 and Matt 17:11, it is expected that Elijah "will restore all things"; in the Mishnah,[45] he will be involved even in the resurrection of the dead.

The task given to Elijah "to turn the hearts of parents to their children and children to their parents" is particularly poignant in today's society, when so many families are torn apart by discord and dissent. Final redemption will not take place without reconciliation on the most basic level of the family. But, with a stark realism, the tradition recognizes that something more is required than just an appeal to the goodwill and communication skills of the parties involved. Only the prophet who was able to turn the hearts of the people from the gods of the Canaanites (1 Kings 18) is equal to this work of reconciliation within the family. And reconciliation within families is the first, indispensable, step in the reconciliation of all things.

44. See R. Travers Herford, *The Ethics of the Talmud: Sayings of the Fathers* (New York: Schocken, 1962).
45. *m. Sota* 10:15.

Transliteration Schema

HEBREW AND ARAMAIC TRANSLITERATION

Consonants:

א	=	ʾ	ט	=	ṭ	פ or ף	=	p
ב	=	b	י	=	y	צ or ץ	=	ṣ
ג	=	g	כ or ך	=	k	ק	=	q
ד	=	d	ל	=	l	ר	=	r
ה	=	h	מ or ם	=	m	שׂ	=	ś
ו	=	w	נ or ן	=	n	שׁ	=	š
ז	=	z	ס	=	s	ת	=	t
ח	=	ḥ	ע	=	ʿ			

Masoretic Pointing:

Pure-long			Tone-long			Short			Composite *shewa*		
הָ	=	â	ָ	=	ā	ַ	=	a		=	ă
י or ֵ	=	ê	ֵ	=	ē	ֶ	=	e	or	=	ĕ
or ִי	=	î				ִ	=	i			
or וֹ	=	ô	ֹ	=	ō	ָ	=	o		=	ŏ
or וּ	=	û				ֻ	=	u			

GREEK TRANSLITERATION

α	=	a	ι	=	i	ρ	=	r
β	=	b	κ	=	k	σ or ς	=	s
γ	=	g	λ	=	l	τ	=	t
δ	=	d	μ	=	m	υ	=	y
ε	=	e	ν	=	n	φ	=	ph
ζ	=	z	ξ	=	x	χ	=	ch
η	=	ē	ο	=	o	ψ	=	ps
θ	=	th	π	=	p	ω	=	ō

Index of Maps, Charts, and Illustrations

Index of Excursuses

ABBREVIATIONS

General

BCE	Before the Common Era
CE	Common Era
c.	circa
cf.	compare
chap(s).	chapter(s)
esp.	especially
fem.	feminine
lit.	literally
LXX	Septuagint
masc.	masculiine
MS(S)	manuscript(s)
MT	Masoretic Text
OL	Old Latin
n.(n.)	note(s)
NT	New Testament
OL	Old Latin
OT	Old Testament
pl(s).	plate(s)
v(v).	verse(s)
Vg	Vulgate

Names of Biblical Books (with the Apocrypha)

Gen	Nah	1–4 Kgdms	John
Exod	Hab	Add Esth	Acts
Lev	Zeph	Bar	Rom
Num	Hag	Bel	1–2 Cor
Deut	Zech	1–2 Esdr	Gal
Josh	Mal	4 Ezra	Eph
Judg	Ps (Pss)	Jdt	Phil
1–2 Sam	Job	Ep Jer	Col
1–2 Kgs	Prov	1–4 Macc	1–2 Thess
Isa	Ruth	Pr Azar	1–2 Tim
Jer	Cant	Pr Man	Titus
Ezek	Eccl	Sir	Phlm
Hos	Lam	Sus	Heb
Joel	Esth	Tob	Jas
Amos	Dan	Wis	1–2 Pet
Obad	Ezra	Matt	1–3 John
Jonah	Neh	Mark	Jude
Mic	1–2 Chr	Luke	Rev

Names of Pseudepigraphical and Early Patristic Books

1, 2, 3 Enoch	Ethiopic, Slavonic, Hebrew *Enoch*
T. Levi	*Testament of Levi*
T. Naph.	*Testament of Naphtali*

Names of Dead Sea Scrolls and Related Texts

CD	Cairo (Genizah text of the) *Damascus (Document)*
1QM	*Milḥā mā h* (*War Scroll*)
4QFlor	*Florilegium* (or *Eschatological Midrashim*) from Qumran Cave 4
4QPrNab	*Prayer of Nabonidus* from Qumran Cave 4

4QpsDan	Pseudo-Daniel from Qumran Cave 4
4Q246	Text 246 from Qumran Cave 4

Orders and Tractates in Mishnaic and Related Literature

'Abot	'Abot
B. Meṣ.	Baba Meṣi' a
m. Sota	Sota
Ta' an.	Ta' anit

Commonly Used Periodicals, Reference Works, and Serials

AB	Anchor Bible
ABD	Anchor Bible Dictionary
AJT	American Journal of Theology
ANEP	J. B. Pritchard (ed.), Ancient Near East in Pictures
ANET	J. B. Pritchard (ed.), Ancient Near Eastern Texts
ATD	Das Alte Testament Deutsch
ATDan	Acta theologica danica
BASOR	Bulletin of the American Schools of Oriental Research
Bib	Biblica
BibOr	Biblica et orientalia
BJRL	Bulletin of the John Rylands University Library of Manchester
BK	Bibel und Kirche
BLS	Bible and Literature Series
BR	Biblical Research
BSO(A)S	Bulletin of the School of Oriental (and African) Studies
BT	Bible Translator
BTB	Biblical Theology Bulletin
BZ	Biblische Zeitschrift
BZAW	Beihefte zur ZAW
CAD	The Assyrian Dictionary of the Oriental Institute of the University of Chicago
CBC	Cambridge Bible Commentary
CBQ	Catholic Biblical Quarterly
CBOTS	Coniectanea Biblica: Old Testament Series
CBQMS	Catholic Biblical Quarterly—Monograph Series
ConBOT	Coniectanea biblica, New Testament
ETL	Ephemerides theologicae lovanienses
EvT	Evangelische Theologie
ExpTim	Expository Times
FOTL	Forms of Old Testament Literature
FRLANT	Forschungen zur Literatur des Alten und Neuen Testaments
GBS.OTS	Guides to Biblical Scholarship. Old Testament Series
GKC	Gesenius' Hebrew Grammar, ed. E. Kautzsch, trans. A. E. Cowley
GNB	Good News Bible
HAR	Hebrew Annual Review
HAT	Handbuch zum Alten Testament
HBT	Horizons in Biblical Theology
HSM	Harvard Semitic Monographs
HSS	Harvard Semitic Studies
HTR	Harvard Theological Review
HUCA	Hebrew Union College Annual
ICC	International Critical Commentary
IDB	Interpreter's Dictionary of the Bible
IDBSup	Supplementary volume to IDB
ITC	International Theological Commentary
JAOS	Journal of the American Oriental Society
JBL	Journal of Biblical Literature
JETS	Journal of the Evangelical Theological Society
JNES	Journal of Near Eastern Studies
JNSL	Journal of Northwest Semitic Languages
JQR	Jewish Quarterly Review
JSOT	Journal for the Study of the Old Testament
JSS	Journal of Semitic Studies
JSOTSup	Journal for the Study of the Old Testament—Supplement Series
KAT	Kommentar zum Alten Testament
KJV	King James (or Authorized) Version
LCL	Loeb Classical Library

NCB	New Century Bible
NEB	New English Bible
NIB	*New Interpreter's Bible*
NICOT	New International Commentary on the Old Testament
NIV	New International Bible
NJB	New Jerusalem Bible
NJBC	R. E. Brown et al. (eds.), *The New Jerome Biblical Commentary*
NRSV	New Revised Standard Version
NTS	*New Testament Studies*
Or	Orientalia (Rome)
OTL	Old Testament Library
OTS	*Oudtestamentische Studiën*
PEQ	*Palestine Exploration Quarterly*
PTMS	Pittsburgh (Princeton) Theological MOnograph Series
QD	Quaestiones disputatae
RB	*Revue biblique*
REB	Revised English Bible
RevExp	*Review and Expositor*
RSV	Revised Standard Version of the Bible
SBLDS	SBL Dissertation Series
SOTSMS	Society for Old Testament Study Monograph Series
SSN	Studia semitica neerlandica
TDOT	G. Kittel and G. Friedrich (eds.), *Theological Dictionary of the New Testament*
TNK	Tanakh
TQ	*Theologische Quartalschrift*
TSSI	J. C. L. Gibson, *Textbook of Syrian Semitic Inscriptions*
UBS	United Bible Societies
UF	*Ugarit-Forschungen*
USQR	*Union Seminary Quarterly Review*
UUÅ	Uppsala universitetsårsskrift
VT	*Vetus Testamentum*
VTSup	Vetus Testamentum, Supplements
WBC	*Word Biblical Commentary*
ZAW	*Zeitschrift für die alttestamentliche Wissenschaft*
ZDMG	*Zeitschrift der deutschen morgenländischen Gesellschaft*